THE
ENGAGEMENT

THE
ENGAGEMENT

America's Quarter-Century Struggle
Over Same-Sex Marriage

Sasha Issenberg

Pantheon Books, New York

Library of Congress Cataloging-in-Publication Data
Name: Issenberg, Sasha, author.
Title: The engagement: America's quarter-century struggle over
same-sex marriage / Sasha Issenberg.
Description: New York: Pantheon Books, 2020.
Includes bibliographical references and index.
Identifiers: LCCN 2019051707 (print). LCCN 2019051708 (ebook).
ISBN 9781524748739 (hardcover). ISBN 9781524748746 (ebook).
Subjects: LCSH: Same-sex marriage—Law and legislation—
United States—History.
Classification: LCC KF539 .I87 2020 (print) | LCC KF539 (ebook) |
DDC 346.7301/68—dc23
LC record available at lccn.loc.gov/2019051707
LC ebook record available at lccn.loc.gov/2019051708

www.pantheonbooks.com

Jacket design by Kelly Blair

Printed in the United States of America

First Edition

1 3 5 7 9 8 6 4 2

To Amy Levin,

whose love, support, companionship,
and dental coverage have shown me
why marriage is worth fighting for

Contents

....

PART THREE: INSIDE GAMES (1996)

PART FOUR: THE SECOND FRONT (1997–2003)

PART FIVE: "OUR TEAM IS NOT WINNING" (2003–2004)

PART NINE: ENDGAME (2009–2015)

THE
ENGAGEMENT

Introduction

A President Decides

On April 8, 1996, White House counsel Jack Quinn prepared what was known to presidential staffers as a "decision memo" and sent it to the Oval Office. *The Advocate,* the leading newsmagazine for gay America, was planning to report that the Justice Department had begun to explore changes to immigration and tax laws that would place gay couples on the same footing as straight ones. The magazine "would like to include a statement of your position" on gay marriage, Quinn explained to the president. The communications staff was unsure how to answer.

Others were asking similar questions. Marsha Scott, whom Bill Clinton had appointed the previous June as the first-ever full-time presidential liaison to the gay community, had been pressed for her views on "same-gender marriage" while meeting with gay activists in Boston two weeks earlier. She had stumbled through a noncommittal response, saying it was important to "ensure that those of you in these loving, long-term and committed relationships can enjoy all the same benefits" as opposite-sex couples, but "whether marriage is the vehicle to make those changes is something we are looking at." Earlier that winter, a different writer from *The Advocate,* visiting the White House as part of a feature on Clinton's troubled relationship with his gay base over the course of his first term in office, asked Scott how the marriage issue could figure in the reelection campaign. "We must not allow the far right to use this as a wedge between friends," Scott cautioned. "We must keep focused on our final goal."

Scott had been forced to dissemble in part because Clinton's position wasn't entirely clear to anyone who spoke on his behalf. The president's longest documented public comment on the subject was a single sentence, in October 1992, when the Democratic presidential nominee was asked as part of a written interview with *Reader's Digest* whether he agreed that "homosexual couples should have the right to get married." "I've taken a very strong stand against any discrimination against gays and lesbians," the then governor of Arkansas responded, "but I don't favor a law to legalize marriages."

Even when Clinton offered that answer, it seemed to evade the essence of the issue. No state lawmaker, let alone a member of Congress, had ever proposed drafting a law to legalize same-sex marriage. A citizen's right to one was far more likely to be asserted by a court's interpretation of existing law than by a legislature's passage of a new statute. In 1992, the narrowness of Clinton's answer hadn't mattered; the *Reader's Digest* interview passed with barely any notice by other media or interest groups. But Quinn, now the president's lawyer, recognized the ways in which the answer was insufficient to the current moment, and he knew he couldn't afford to have government officials improvising every time they were asked for his client's position on such a potentially contentious topic.

When the *Advocate* request made its way to him, Quinn decided that the issue merited its own set of "talking points," a summary of the White House's perspective that could serve as a point of internal reference within the administration. His solution was for Clinton to say he does "not personally support same-sex marriages" but also that he believed the matter was best left to "state and local governments, as well as the private sector, to consider issues like these involving community values and matters of conscience." With Scott's help, Quinn attempted to frame that ambivalence in terms that reflected a Clintonian theory of politics. "The challenge in addressing these issues is how to remain sensitive to the traditional values of our communities while preserving the fundamental right to live free from unjustified discrimination," he wrote.

Quinn assembled his three curt paragraphs into a one-page memo and sent it to the Oval Office for a decision. The president was given three options: *Agree, Disagree,* or *Discuss.*

In 1973, as Clinton was preparing for his first campaign for office in Arkansas, the prosecuting attorney for the state's sixth judicial district was unexpectedly asked by the clerk of Pulaski County, which includes Little Rock, whether same-sex couples were entitled to marriage licenses. "Please be advised that the law on this question is still evolving, and there is no settled rule," Lee Munson responded. "We feel the Arkansas Supreme

Court would hold against the proposition, but the United States Supreme Court may hold for it."

Same-sex marriage landed in American politics without a natural ideological template. To the extent that politicians ever spoke about the topic, it was as reductio ad absurdum. "Homosexual marriage licenses" featured prominently in the apocalyptic warnings of Phyllis Schlafly, the conservative activist who beginning in the early 1970s marshaled opposition to the Equal Rights Amendment then moving toward ratification. Schlafly argued that forbidding lawmakers to acknowledge distinctions between the sexes would abolish a range of gender-specific roles, including husband and wife. "Militant homosexuals from all over America have made the ERA issue a hot priority. Why?" asked Schlafly's Eagle Forum in a newspaper ad. "To be able finally to get homosexual marriage licenses, to adopt children and raise them to emulate their homosexual 'parents,' and to obtain pension and medical benefits for odd-couple 'spouses.'"

In a 1980 congressional subcommittee hearing, a Republican staff lawyer made a similar charge about a bill that would have made it illegal to consider sexual orientation in hiring and firing decisions. Could bill supporter Art Agnos, counsel Jim Stephens pressed, "make a distinction between prohibiting discrimination in the workplace, on the one hand, and continuing, on the other hand, the historic prohibition against homosexual marriage"?

The few politicians who invoked the menace of gay marriage conceded that the scenario was so farfetched that they had to do so sheepishly. "The idea that this law would legalize sexual activities between persons of the same sex or the marriage of persons of the same sex did not originate with me," Sam J. Ervin Jr., the ERA's most vocal Senate opponent, said in 1972. Twelve years later, another chairman of the Senate's Constitution Subcommittee convened a hearing to probe that very notion, and shared Ervin's self-consciousness about the conjecture. "Proponents of the ERA have made great fun of critics who have stated that the ERA would render unconstitutional State laws against homosexual marriages," Utah senator Orrin Hatch acknowledged before the subcommittee.

"Asking whether the ERA mandates recognition of same-sex marriages is indeed the wrong question," Raymond Marcin of Catholic University School of Law reassured Hatch as he opened his testimony in that 1984 hearing. But, Marcin went on, "it is sometimes necessary to think through the wrong question in order to arrive at the right question."

Even as, in the early 1990s, legal recognition of gay families penetrated the realm of the legally plausible, conservatives rarely found themselves debating the thing itself. For them, gay marriage was a benchmark, a measure of how far the culture might slide down a slippery slope toward moral relativism.

"I'm not sure what you mean by gay rights," Vice President Dan Quayle told a reporter from the *New York Times* aboard his campaign plane while seeking reelection in 1992. "If you're saying we're going to give moral equivalence to a heterosexual marriage between a man and woman and a gay marriage where you have a marriage between those of the same sex, yes, we do not recognize the moral equivalence. And I'm sure the gay rights activists will not allow Bill Clinton to say that there isn't moral equivalence."

President George H. W. Bush had been asked about same-sex marriage for the first time as president a few months earlier, by evangelical leaders intending to test his conservative mettle. Bush's response was tentative and tellingly unrehearsed: "I think I would be opposed to that."

When he announced his challenge to Bush, Clinton's own views on gay rights were largely a mystery. The head of the Arkansas Gay and Lesbian Task Force told national journalists who inquired about his governor's record that "in this state, he has never said the words 'gay' or 'lesbian,' and every time we have approached the Governor's Office, we have been rebuffed." Clinton was more solicitous to their opponents. His wife, Hillary Rodham Clinton, wrote to a retired Navy veteran in North Little Rock in October 1990 that "both Bill and I agree with you that public schools should not promote homosexuality as a life-style and I assure you that no such thing is being or will be done in Arkansas."

A year later, both Clintons would arrive at the Beverly Hills home of Scott Hitt, a prominent AIDS doctor, for their first sustained interrogation on the national gay-rights agenda. A circle of Hitt's peers in Los Angeles had formed Access Now for Gay and Lesbian Equality, effectively designating themselves gatekeepers to the region's gay political money. To them, the Arkansan was a cipher, particularly when compared to the United States senators and California governor also seeking the presidency. "You have no public record to speak of and I can't ask friends in the community to support you without their knowing where you stand," one of the organizers, David Mixner, warned Clinton beforehand.

Before sitting down to lunch, attendees gathered around a fireplace and implored Clinton to take seriously the priorities of the gay community. Several attendees talked about their personal experiences with HIV and

AIDS, others about standing restrictions on federal jobs available to gays and lesbians. Clinton charmed many with his unexpected ease around them and his empathy in a conversation that veered from politics to death and back again.

Throughout the multihour session, Clinton was never asked about his position on gay marriage, according to several attendees. The following spring, as Clinton was moving toward his party's nomination, a number of those who had participated in the ANGLE interview helped organize what would become the largest fundraising event ever for a presidential candidate seeking gay money, at Hollywood's Palace Theatre. The legal status of gay couples was not mentioned there, either.

"It would have been quite amazing had it come up," says Roberta Bennett, a lawyer who served as cochair of the Hollywood fundraiser. "No one was talking about marriage then—it was long before the issue even became an issue."

They were not alone being either disinterested in, or willfully oblivious to, the idea that gay people might want to wed. The only national organization that had formally attached itself to the cause, the American Civil Liberties Union, had done so almost by accident. A vote of its national board, in October 1986, in favor of a resolution endorsing "recognition of gay and lesbian marriage" as "imperative for the complete legal equality of lesbians and gay men" passed with little notice and without impact on the ACLU's activities. It would be nearly two decades before the otherwise litigious organization would see through a lawsuit demanding marriage rights for same-sex couples. In the meantime, its state affiliates and national gay-rights projects turned away, or simply ignored, would-be plaintiffs seeking its help.

Clinton became the first presidential candidate ever endorsed by the Human Rights Campaign Fund, then emerging as the country's dominant gay political action committee. The voter guide that the group distributed to its members during that primary season (titled "1992 Presidential Candidates: Where do they stand on our issues?") tracked policy positions on eight different policy questions, none of which touched on the recognition of same-sex couples or families.

Historians have located evidence of same-sex couples cohabitating in mutually dependent relationships for millennia, across every known society, in a bewildering array of configurations. In nineteenth-century

New England, platonic female friends quietly paired off in what were called "Boston marriages"; in 1920s Harlem, same-sex couples participated in sprawling ceremonies that mimicked straight weddings, even masculinizing or feminizing one of the participants' names in the hopes of passing muster with government clerks. Acknowledgments of long-term same-sex relationships appear across the published words of Cicero, Walt Whitman, and William Wordsworth, the last of whom described two friends as

Sisters in love, a love allowed to climb
Ev'n on this earth above the reach of time.

Yet even as many gay couples formed lasting bonds, few ever defined the gesture in political terms. Even those who preferred assimilation to liberation in other areas cast marriage as ridiculous. "Who would like to hear about some 'gay' marriage that has broken up and all the problems of some 'queen,'" future San Francisco politician Harvey Milk wrote to a friend in 1961, shortly after ending a five-year relationship.

Indeed, through much of the twentieth century's second half, discussions of same-sex marriages served only to plumb the limits of the gay-rights fantasy. "Imagine that the year were 2053 and homosexuality were accepted to the point of being of no importance," the self-described "homophilic" magazine *ONE* conjectured just after its August 1953 launch. "Now, is the deviate allowed to continue his pursuit of physical happiness without restraint as he attempts to do today? Or is he, in this Utopia, subject to marriage laws?"

Beyond gay culture, too, gay marriage existed primarily as a part of intellectual exercise. In the 1972 documentary film *Future Shock,* based on Alvin Toffler's book of that name, a gay wedding is staged purely for dystopian purposes. The ceremony—two men in white tuxedos exchanging rings at a minister's instruction—is presented between images of communal living (including group marriages) and an end to university education, a procession of the possible consequences of rapid technological change. "Our children, will we save them from future shock? Or are they destined to suffer the same illness that rocks today's society?" the film's cigar-smoking narrator, Orson Welles, intones between images. "The choices we make will determine the nature of their world—there is still time."

On the rare occasions when gays and lesbians embraced that nuptial iconography, marriage was a kind of performance. The day before the second National March on Washington for Lesbian and Gay Rights in 1987—

the movement's largest gathering to date—two thousand couples massed outside the Internal Revenue Service to participate in an event called the Wedding. Yet during her remarks, Dina Bachelor, a new-age minister and self-described "transpersonal counselor and hypnotherapist" who led the service, never mentioned the words *marriage, bride, groom, husband, wife,* or *spouse.* When pushed, an organizer insisted that the nonsectarian ceremony should not be in any way considered a demand for recognition of same-sex unions. "It's going to be a political demonstration of equal rights," explained Carey Junkin of Couples, Inc. "The wedding is just a media handle."

At that time, to the extent that any American confronted "gay marriage" as an existing institution—or those words near each other in a mainstream newspaper headline—it characterized relationships that were decaying rather than being enshrined. "They had been married 10 years when Al told Jane he was a homosexual," the *Milwaukee Journal* began a 1984 series, "Gays and Marriage." "Now, seven years later, the two cling to a marriage they both admit is a shambles." When *The Advocate* put the words "Choosing to Marry" in a 1981 headline, it described the dilemma of closeted homosexuals trapped in heterosexual couplings. "This secret double life comprises the major, unwritten chunk of gay history," the magazine concluded. The *Men and Wife* newsletter, which served the world of what *The Advocate* called "mixed-orientation marriages," even ran a story titled "Marriage Made Me Gay."

Among gays and lesbians in the 1970s, marriage was an issue for mavericks. In the 1980s, it became one for theorists. Only in the 1990s did it become one for activists committed to plotting social and political change. Even then, they found little money or backing from the increasingly organized gay establishment. Not a single major gay-rights group formally embraced marriage rights for its core constituency until a state supreme court had given its unexpected blessing to the cause. If anyone in the United States had been forced to articulate a coherent argument against same-sex marriage, it was the small circle of lawyers and legal academics who participated in the confidential meetings of the Lesbian and Gay Litigators' Roundtable starting in the mid-1980s. Even before the questions about strategy and timing, they faced a more paralyzing disagreement: Would winning marriage rights for gays and lesbians push their movement forward or set it back?

Movement organizations found agreement on priorities farther down a hierarchy of needs: making sure it would be legal for gay people to have sex with one another, and illegal for others to deny them jobs or leases based upon that activity. When gay activists won the attention of city or state lawmakers, they usually worked first to pass provisions that named sexual orientation among the identity categories—alongside race, religion, age, and gender—consecrated in nondiscrimination statutes. Such explicit protection opened up new channels for litigation, by forcing those accused of discrimination to justify the exclusion.

Fractured as it was by ideological disputes and divisions along lines of class, gender, and race and ethnicity, the gay-rights movement was united in viewing marriage as a low priority. "One would think that in a move-ment demanding acceptance for this group, legalized marriage would be one of its primary issues," *ONE* wrote in its August 1953 cover story, the first serious consideration of the issue in the nascent gay press. "What a logical and convincing means of assuring society that they are sincere in wanting respect and dignity!"

Yet that logic failed to take hold. Instead, those who broached the ques-tion were often told that winning the right for gays to marry—exalting an ideal of mainstream domesticity at the expense of all other types of intimate relations—would undermine the generation-long struggle for gay liberation. "Why didn't you guys fight for the right to get married instead of the right to legitimize promiscuity?" playwright Larry Kramer pushed back at fellow AIDS activists, via an onstage alter ego in his 1985 play *The Normal Heart.* (The character, writer and activist Ned Weeks, exchanges wedding vows with a lover as he loses him to AIDS.) Merely fighting for it would jeopardize more accessible civil-rights gains in other areas, around which gay activists and their political allies had found consensus. Those who persisted in prioritizing marriage rights were seen as at once both political radicals and ideological reactionaries.

Marriage simply was not a matter of public debate. (Media coverage and criticism of *The Normal Heart*'s stage debut did not even register the deathbed wedding as a political provocation.) Those pursuing gay mar-riage approached the issue on two separate tracks: the fitful efforts by individuals fighting for their own interests—and usually running, all too quickly, up against local authorities and the absence of a legal strategy for getting past them—and legal thinkers whose arguments never graduated beyond the threshold of abstraction.

·   ·   ·

That changed in Hawaii. A crucial legal process set in motion there in December 1990—ultimately leading two and a half years later to the first-ever court decision to validate a claim for same-sex marriage—began to align individual aspirations with tools of civil-rights law.

That action happened to coincide with the start of an unexpectedly placid decade in American political life. The Cold War was about to end, and conflict with Islamist terrorism had yet to replace it as the overarching obsession of the American worldview. Agreement on the core tenets of neoliberal economics was taking hold, layered with conservative doubts about the boldest ambitions of the welfare state. The grandest civil-rights projects—around race, gender, and disability—had been settled, at least as a matter of principle and major legislative action. The result was a decade of relative peace and prosperity, and a lull in high-stakes political conflict.

Ideological détente turned out to be good for social-movement entrepreneurs. Into the breach surged two ascendant movements of the 1980s—one for gay equality and one for traditionalist Christianity—that had spent much of that decade working to win the respect of their putative ideological allies on left and right, respectively. With the biggest questions of economic and national-security policy at least temporarily settled, both parties were increasingly in thrall to their logic of identity politics. Marriage was the issue that would set the gay-equality and traditional-Christianity movements on trajectories to collide. Not until opponents feared the threat of gay marriage, and took steps to forestall its potential, did most gay-rights leaders find it worth fighting for. "Because they say we can't do it, it makes us want to do it all the more," said National Gay and Lesbian Task Force director Virginia Apuzzo.

Across the void of the issue-less 1990s, the centrifugal force of cultural conflict pulled gay marriage from the nebulous margins of American life to its red-hot center.

On May 7, 1996, one month after Quinn sent his memo, Clinton was faced with a decision on gay marriage that he could not ignore. A handful of House Republicans were introducing a bill they called the Defense of Marriage Act; Senate colleagues would follow with their own, identical version the next day. The bill was brief, but it exposed the inadequacy of Clinton's nearly four-year-old response to *Reader's Digest*. If it passed Congress, the president would encounter not a bill to legalize gay marriages, but one that would limit them with every power that legislators believed was at their disposal. Deftly balancing paeans to the traditional family with respect for gay rights, as Quinn had proposed in his talking points, was no longer an option.

Clinton should oppose the Defense of Marriage Act, argued Marsha Scott and her deputy, Richard Socarides. The president could continue to insist that he, too, opposed same-sex marriages on principle, but needed to recognize that singling them out for special legal treatment was "fundamentally unfair," they wrote in a May 10 memo to presidential adviser Harold Ickes. "Our support for the bill would be taken by many in the gay communities as an expression by the President of deep ceded [*sic*] bias against gay people," Scott and Socarides wrote, "and as caving in to Republican scapegoating as gays."

Among those responsible for Clinton's campaign that November, the political calculus around the Defense of Marriage Act was self-evident. While gay activists were an important source of money and energy for Democratic candidates, they didn't control many votes. Gay voters tended to be clustered in states that Clinton would win easily already—and besides, would gay voters ever abandon him en masse for a Republican? The few pollsters who had ever thought to ask about same-sex marriages had found lopsided national majorities opposed. Taking the other side would be a direct route for Clinton out of the American mainstream. By the time the president convened a strategy session to plot his response, his advisers understood that he saw two bad options before him. He could either sign on to a position he thought his opponents had demagogically manufactured to vex him in an election year—or nobly attach himself to an unpopular cause advanced by a marginal interest group.

"Get on record as favoring the principle," strategist Dick Morris told Clinton. A frequent consultant to Republicans as well as Democrats, Morris championed what he called Clinton's "values agenda," a series of ornamental initiatives designed to dominate election-year policymaking. Nearly all of Morris's recommendations added up to a basic theory of centrist politics: deny your opponents the ability to caricature you as a liberal, while dismissing them as the ideological outliers. "Now the Republicans have a bill we can sign," Morris counseled the president. "But if we wait to back it, they'll probably tack all sorts of anti-gay amendments onto it that you'll find difficult to sign."

Adviser George Stephanopoulos urged patience, as rushing to embrace the Defense of Marriage Act would unnecessarily antagonize Clinton's liberal supporters. Avoid committing to a position right away, he told the president, and wait to see how both the legal and political dynamics play out on Capitol Hill. "I think we can work it out," Stephanopoulos said, "but we need some time to smooth it out."

"Well, I get a vote, don't I? I mean I'm the president, so I get a vote, don't I? Don't I?" Clinton exclaimed, according to Morris's recollection. "Well, my vote says I'm going to sign that bill, and I want to announce it right away so there's no confusion about my position."

Clinton's circle had seen an issue materialize, seemingly from nowhere. Perhaps if they refused to engage opponents on their terms, it could just as easily wither from neglect. "They thought it would head off the bill, it would fizzle if the president says he'll sign it," says Socarides. "The strategy was to say: *no problem here, keep moving, nothing to look at here.*"

There wasn't anything to look at, and then there was, and then it was hard to look at anything else. Over the course of a few months in 1996, gay marriage transmogrified from a thought experiment on which few Americans had ever had reason to formulate a position into a subject that no one in political life could escape.

As is often the case in American politics, each side imputed more strategy to the opposition than either was capable of. Those on the right assumed gay-rights advocates had intentionally conceived a multiyear lawsuit in Hawaii as a back door to the mainland, using the Constitution's full-faith-and-credit clause to compel the nation as a whole to adopt a local court's liberal reinterpretation of marriage. The same gay-rights advocates who laughed at such a claim nonetheless believed that the Defense of Marriage Act had been concocted by Republican Party officials as, in the words of Human Rights Campaign executive director Elizabeth Birch, "a ploy by the floundering Dole for President campaign to drive a wedge between the gay community and President Clinton."

It was not until the following decade that either side developed anything that could properly be considered a national strategy, or worthy of the specific paranoias of their opponents. Once Vermont created civil unions in 2000, bestowing upon same-sex couples every equity except the word *marriage,* both sides realized a battle would be inevitable and ongoing. Only at that point did the infrastructure of the perpetual campaign— single-issue groups, multiyear plans, purpose-built tactics—emerge to scaffold the intense debate.

The first efforts to professionalize the politics around gay marriage, starting in the mid-1990s, were secretly cultivated in dueling power centers of the Mountain West. Within the gay community, a galaxy of covert donors orbiting around Denver software millionaire Tim Gill remade the gay-rights movement in their own image, ideologically conservative and strategically radical. Five hundred miles away, in Salt Lake City, they found their match in a yet-more-clandestine cadre of officials at the Church of Latter-day Saints, whose well-funded political operations were—at least in the context of its own traditionalist movement—strategically conservative and ideologically radical.

Before 1996, gay marriage's rise to prominence was driven by smaller-scale factors: principle, hubris, rivalry, opportunism, individual initiative, and institutional incentive. It was not only the major historical shifts of the 1990s that created opportunity for outsider movements and lone political entrepreneurs, but minor serendipities, many of them recognizable only in retrospect. In fact, without a series of coincident actuarial quirks one-fifth of the way around the globe from Washington—including an unexpected death and the arrival of a seventieth birthday—no president might have had to contend with the thorny question of same-sex marriage for decades more.

The notion of an issue thrust on the power centers of American government from its periphery via shortsighted machinations and fortuitous timing was so foreign to the political class that its members lacked a language to describe it. Clinton's first public statement—"This has always been my position on gay marriage," he would eventually say at a May press conference two weeks after the bill was unveiled—gave a misleading impression that it had been a perennial concern throughout his career. Bill Clinton hadn't always had a position on gay marriage any more than he had always had positions on bailing out the Mexican peso or going to war in Bosnia.

The Engagement is the story of the birth and life of an issue. It is the tale of those on both sides who conspired to invent, elevate, and war over a change in policy, and the country transformed along with that debate. In a quarter century, gay marriage went from being a test of the moral and political imagination to settled policy in fifty states and a simple, even banal, fact of everyday life. Many younger Americans today have difficulty understanding what the conflict was all about.

Pollsters regularly observe that they have never seen public opinion on a single issue move as dramatically and swiftly as it has on same-sex marriage. At the time Bill Clinton pondered the politics of the Defense of

Marriage Act, barely one-quarter of Americans said they supported the rights of gays and lesbians to marry. Over the next fifteen years the number of those who embraced what the gay-rights movement has successfully branded "marriage equality" would nearly double—an unimaginable shift in attitudes thought to be set deeply in the everlasting values of religion, family, and tradition.

The speed with which Americans became invested in the issue is a prime example of what the political scientist E. E. Schattschneider called "the tremendous contagiousness of conflict." What had begun as a jostle for primacy among Honolulu activists for control of a single event-planning committee expanded—through both strategy and happenstance—to ensnare interest groups, state governments, religious denominations, national political parties, and even the presidency. "So great is the change in the nature of any conflict likely to be as a consequence of the widening involvement of people in it that the original participants are apt to lose control of the conflict altogether," Schattschneider observed in his 1960 work *The Semisovereign People.* "A host of new considerations and complications are introduced, and a multitude of new resources for a resolution of conflict becomes available; solutions inconceivable at a lower level may be worked out at a higher level."

Barack Obama's announcement in the spring of 2012 that he was among those who had undergone an "evolution" ensured that his would be the third consecutive White House to have its bid for a second term molded by its handling of gay marriage. In 1996, Bill Clinton had the Defense of Marriage Act shoved at him and embraced it apologetically, aware there was only one place where a mainstream politician could afford to land on the issue. Midway through the presidency of his successor, George W. Bush, Massachusetts became the first state to authorize same-sex marriages. Bush found political advantage by recasting the matter as a three-sided issue, championing a Federal Marriage Amendment to the constitution, which he knew his Democratic opponent couldn't possibly support. (The amendment would have precluded states from recognizing a right under their own constitutions for gay couples to marry.)

Eight years later, Obama swung fully in the opposite direction, first by ordering his Justice Department to treat the Defense of Marriage Act as unconstitutional and cease defending the law in court. Then he went further, saying that he believed states should be free to marry gay couples, a position no serious candidate for president had ever before been willing to espouse. (As a senator seeking the presidency, Obama backed civil unions for gay couples but not marriage.) By then, the physics of the issue had been so upended that critics accused him of having adopted the stance to win votes.

Like his two predecessors, Obama's machinations were shaped by both personal principle and political expediency. The explanation for his shift acknowledged how otherwise nimble politicians struggled to catch up with a country that had changed around them in ways they couldn't fully understand or explain. "What you're seeing is, I think, states working through this issue—in fits and starts, all across the country. Different communities are arriving at different conclusions, at different times," Obama explained in May 2012. "And I continue to believe that this is an issue that is gonna be worked out at the local level, because historically, this has not been a federal issue, what's recognized as a marriage."

Stunningly, it would be only another three years until Obama put the weight of the United States government behind the proposition that the rights of gays to marry should be a state issue no longer. In the four cases bundled together as *Obergefell v. Hodges,* the Supreme Court accepted the solicitor general's argument that the country could not sustain a range of conflicting opinions reflected in local law.

That decision arrived just ten days after Donald Trump announced his candidacy for president in 2015. Yet over a seventeen-month campaign—a revanchist enterprise that preyed on nearly every identity-based grievance except those involving sexual orientation—Trump barely acknowledged the momentous ruling and, after the election, declared the same-sex marriage debate moot. "It's irrelevant because it was already settled. It's law. It was settled in the Supreme Court. I mean it's done," Trump told Lesley Stahl of CBS's *60 Minutes* in his first interview as president-elect. "And I'm fine with that." One of the most formidable challengers to emerge against Trump's reelection in 2020 was an upstart politician whose marriage to another man was almost entirely incidental to his political identity.

The timeline to that tidy resolution was beyond the wildest hopes of gay-rights activists just years before. When, in 2005, a group of political operatives and litigators convened at the urging of Tim Gill's donor circle to draft an aspirational long-range strategy—a confidential document that would guide much of their activity—they outlined a path toward a Supreme Court affirming what they called the "freedom to marry." They set a goal of 2025.

Once this end was in sight, participants in and observers of the battles to defend, define, and expand marriage in America worked to shoehorn the narrative into familiar paradigms, in which civil-rights movements slowly build an intellectual and political critical mass to power the legal tactics and political reforms necessary for change. Activists stuck in such deliberate, plodding work often find solace in Martin Luther King Jr.'s observation that "the arc of the moral universe is long, but it bends toward justice."

Against that backdrop, the American debate over marriage will appear infinitesimally short, a meteor that gathered the stray matter and floating detritus of a country's messy politics and grew so fiery that it singed bodies in its path before abruptly burning out for good. But in its day it seemed capable of illuminating the entire moral universe.

Part One

THE LOVE THAT ATE AN ISLAND

(1990–1996)

Seeking License

Genora Dancel never thought she would get married. She had first suspected there was something different about her around the age of five,
when she realized that she preferred holding hands with girls rather than
boys. In the schoolyard demography of 1965 she saw herself from a young
age as an outlier: the boys concerned themselves with trucks and blocks,
the girls played kitchen. Genora was drawn toward the domestic scene,
but she resisted the expectations of femininity that accompanied it. *I'll
go play with the girls,* she thought, *but I want to be the one who brings home the
bacon.* As that inchoate instinct took shape as romantic, and then sexual,
self-awareness, Genora envisioned a future that would defy norms, even if
it was the only thing that to her felt normal. "I was going to have girlfriends
instead of boyfriends," she recalls. "I always thought that was going to be
something I had to deal with. I even thought, *I'm going to have to get surgery,*
but I thought, *I'm just a kid, why am I worrying or thinking about stuff like this?*
I always thought I was going to work it out."

Her family of Filipino immigrants did little to impose their will on
Genora and her two siblings. When Genora turned seven, her mother
threw a birthday party and invited all the kids from their Honolulu neighborhood, half of whom she did not know. A march of unfamiliar faces
to her front door not only failed to cheer the birthday girl, but actually
unsettled her. Afterward, her mother asked Genora if she had had a good
time. "I guess so, but I don't want a birthday party again," she said. "I just
didn't like having all these strangers in my house."

A few years later, the family moved out of the city to Ewa Beach, closer
to the Navy base where Genora's father worked as a munitions specialist. On the weekends, while her sister puttered in the kitchen and her
brother was out practicing martial arts, Genora would help her father. She

learned how to replace a carburetor, fix the family television, and short-wave radio. She took an interest in mechanics. On Mondays, she would return to school and, when exchanging weekend recaps, match classmates' "I went to the beach" with "I fixed my dad's car." "That's not interesting to a lot of girls," she recalls.

As she entered adolescence, Genora found it easy to delay the inevitable reckoning with her sexual identity. The family was Catholic and, although the Dancels did not regularly attend church, they sent their children to catechism class. Yet as Genora grew up there wasn't much of a sense of sexual morality imparted to her, and—despite the image of carefree bodies frolicking on beaches—the archipelago seemed to embody a conflicted view of libertinage. The significant influence of Asian cultures tamped down public demonstrations of intimacy, all while a live-and-let-live island mentality promoted a quiet tolerance of what on the mainland had come to be described as "alternative lifestyles." When Elton John came out as bisexual, a teenaged Genora was jarred by the nationwide backlash among his teenage fans. "Let him be who he wants to be," she told friends.

In high school, Genora grasped at any possible framework for understanding herself. She would turn down men who asked her out, happy to bluntly inform them that "I'm not that interested in you." She did not attend her prom, telling friends she did not care to spend the money. At one point, she thought she might be asexual. None of this seemed to worry her parents. In fact, a teenaged daughter who didn't seem at all distracted by boys meant one fully devoted to her studies.

After college, Genora dated women. She moved in with one girlfriend for nearly two years; after Genora left, the girlfriend eventually settled down with a man, satisfying her parents' expectation of grandchildren. It became a familiar pattern among Genora's exes. "I knew that these women were seeing what they wanted to do. They would try it out, but they weren't really serious about it," she says. "I knew in the back of my mind that these women wanted to be married to a man and have kids." The cautious Genora made a quiet resolution of her own, to avoid any "serious relationship in my twenties because I'm still developing."

Genora was already deeply committed to a career as a broadcast engineer. When she was about seven years old, she had attended the taping of the children's television program *Checkers and Pogo* at a local CBS station and was immediately distracted by the group of men cracking jokes off to the side of the soundstage. Throughout the taping, her eyes remained locked on to the crew, who operated heavy machinery in an air-conditioned room and had fun doing it. Genora had attended a two-year technical school in Washington State, and upon graduating she took the test for a Federal Communications Commission broadcast license. She abandoned the goal of teaching after her first job interview, at a California community college, where she was asked to explain luminescence and after doing so was told: "That's pretty good for a female." Instead, Genora applied for jobs with television stations and became the first woman to integrate the control rooms at a sequence of Honolulu affiliates. She committed to as much work as she could find, and for six years she held two full-time jobs at different stations, a series of eight-hour shifts starting at midnight.

The busy schedule helped ensure that Genora didn't date much. When she did, however, Genora kept quiet about it, because in Honolulu and Hawaii—like all but a handful of very progressive jurisdictions—it was still legal to fire someone because he or she was gay. Even so, the studios' macho environments meant that Genora spent more time fending off approaches from male colleagues than feeling obliged to address her sexual identity around them. "She was just this hot gorgeous girl with this incredible smile, and was very pleasant to everyone," says C.J. Baehr, who helped launch an educational-programming unit housed at the PBS station, "so of course the men were hitting on her."

One day in the summer of 1990, Baehr was getting out of her daughter Ninia's car in the station's parking lot when Genora appeared before them. "Oh, that beautiful woman Genora is my friend and I think she's a lesbian," C.J. told Ninia as she exited the vehicle. "And I think I'd be happy if she were your friend, too." Ninia, who had just returned that month to Hawaii after years on the mainland, was eager to meet people in the place she would again consider home. She had been out of the closet her whole adult life, and was not at all bashful about approaching women who interested her. The next time Ninia returned to the station she announced herself at the front desk. The receptionist paged Genora over the loudspeaker: "Genora Dancel, C.J. Baehr's daughter wants to meet you." *Everybody knows C.J. Baehr has a daughter who is a lesbian,* Ninia thought.

Genora was among them. A year earlier, she had played board games with C.J. during an office bridal shower, and the two talked at length for the first time about their families. In the parking lot, spotting a woman her own age with fair skin—a telltale sign of a recent arrival from the mainland—in the driver's seat of the car transporting her coworker, Genora made the connection. Now, sitting in a control room with a colleague, she was startled to hear her name announced on the public-address system, summoned by the woman who had caught her eye earlier. *Wow, she's beautiful,* Genora had thought. *Why would she want to meet me? She could have anyone.*

She exited the control room, tentatively. Upon making eye contact with the woman, who had long straight hair and wore a burnt-orange dress with thin shoulder straps, Genora nervously stumbled in reverse, backing into a wall. "I'm C.J.'s daughter, and I just wanted to meet you," Ninia said. The two exchanged a few words as others in the office surveilled the awkward scene. Ninia handed a phone number to Genora, who said she'd call. That night the two spoke for hours, concluding with plans for lunch on Saturday.

They headed to a TGI Friday's and realized quickly that they had been born only four days apart at hospitals not far from each other in Honolulu. But from there, their lives had diverged significantly, and each found herself taken by the unfamiliarity of the other's biography. Genora, who had barely left Hawaii, was impressed as Ninia recounted her cosmopolitan upbringing: the daughter of lefty academics, she had grown up in Tennessee, Colorado, and Pennsylvania, and overseas in Norway and American Samoa. She had lived most recently on Manhattan's Lower East Side, working at both a rape crisis center and the women's-erotica store Eve's Garden, for which she traveled throughout the summer selling its sex toys at women's-music festivals. She had returned to Hawaii with a plan to return to school, and hopes of settling down. "I'd see like 8,000 naked lesbians in a weekend and talk to them about their vagina size, and I would think to myself, *Wow, I've met thousands and thousands of lesbians and there isn't one for me,*" Ninia recalled. "I was just so lonely, thinking I was going to be alone for the rest of my life."

Genora knew solitude, too, yet as soon as she started recounting her life story Ninia realized how different their two notions of loneliness were. Ninia appreciated that her lunch companion was someone who rarely had the opportunity to open up around other gay people and was discovering an alien comfort. "I felt I could tell her anything," says Genora. "You can be friends with someone who's straight, but it's more interesting to talk to someone who has the same understanding as you about living the gay life, or how life has been for you."

After lunch, Genora drove Ninia up an extinct volcano to the ridge locals call Tantalus, which in one direction looks out upon the dominant monument on Oahu's natural landscape—the massive volcanic cone known as Diamond Head—and in the other over the skyline of downtown Honolulu, with its emblems of Pacific modernity. Surrounded by tourists whose eyes remained fixed on their cameras' viewfinders, Genora took little interest in the panorama. Instead she was excited to show off her silver Porsche 928, explaining how she had fixed up the used vehicle herself and opening the hood to reveal its engine. She could tell Ninia had little interest in cars, but thought she was being a good sport, and the two retreated afterward to Kailua, near Ninia's mother's house, where they bought a pizza to share on the beach. Their lunch date ended up lasting nine hours.

Baehr and Dancel started scheduling dates to meet with their motorcycles. They would circle the island counterclockwise, a trip that took two and a half hours, unless there was a surfing event on the North Shore, when traffic would back up next to the shrimp trucks, and without accounting for a brunch stop at the Turtle Bay Resort. Dancel was proud that she rode only a BMW, a heavier, shift-driven bike that guaranteed a smoother ride; she looked disapprovingly on Baehr's preference for a smaller Kawasaki, which allowed the rider to rest both feet on the ground. It didn't much matter, though: Baehr seemed more comfortable straddling behind Dancel on her bike as they went for a ride. "I think she wanted to be the passenger more than a rider," Dancel said.

When it came to politics, those roles were reversed. Genora had always kept her distance from advocacy, out of both lack of interest and a shyness that predisposed her against putting herself in the center of attention. When they first started dating, Genora attended one of Ninia's talks and sat in the front row with her eyes fixated on a Nintendo Game Boy device on which she played Tetris. "She hunkered down, almost disappeared, because she was afraid she'd have to say something public," recalls Ninia's mother.

Ninia and Genora amounted to a striking couple. Genora stuck to collared shirts and had a boxy visage, demarcated by a strong, orthogonal jaw. Ninia preferred sinuous floral-print dresses and kept her hair in a bob rounded along the contours of her teardrop-shaped face, a set of aesthetic choices that happened to match their communication styles. Ninia was an expansive speaker who used flowing sentences; Genora was often hesitant and halting in conversation. But they felt completely at ease with each other. Pretty soon, Ninia, who was still living with her mother, began staying regularly at Genora's home in Waipahu, on the other side of Honolulu. During her overnight shifts at the Fox affiliate, Genora would sometimes sneak away from the control room for an hour when her station went off the air and drive to Kailua to see Ninia. When Ninia took a job as codirector of the University of Hawaii's women's center, Genora would often walk up the hill from the television station at midday to bring her girlfriend lunch. Within their first two weeks of dating, Ninia told her mother she had "this feeling I'm going to be with this woman for the rest of our lives."

That fall, less than three months later, Genora reached the same conclusion. She had traveled to Washington, DC, for a two-week course at George Washington University on satellite broadcasting. Afterward, she would fly to San Jose for a one-week training in Sony Betacam technology. It was the first time the pair had found themselves apart since meeting, and as Genora wandered alone through a shopping mall one afternoon, a ruby ring caught her attention. Ninia had mentioned her fondness for rubies, and Genora entered the store and had one sized to fit her lover's ring finger. Days later, Genora sat in her hotel room, clasping the ring in one hand and a phone in the other, as she proposed to Ninia. There wasn't a language for what she was asking or offering. "I just wanted to have a life with her," Genora says. "I thought our love could prevail over anything."

Ninia said yes, but the word carried little weight beyond the phone call. There was only one place in the world where government recognized vows between people of the same sex. In May 1989, following a forty-year campaign by activists, the Danish parliament had approved "registered partnerships." The designation afforded gay and lesbian couples many of the legal entitlements and responsibilities of marriage—with the notable exception of the right to adopt—while pointedly omitting the word *marriage*. When Genora returned to Hawaii and handed Ninia the ring, the two thought they had entered into little more than an "emotional agreement" with each other, as the latter put it, and didn't even tell their friends or family about the commitment they had made.

Three months later, events gave shape to that commitment. One day, Genora returned home from work to find Ninia moaning in pain. She had been suffering from an earache, but her university health coverage had yet to take effect, so she endured it without seeking medical attention. When Genora saw her partner's glassy eyes, she insisted that Ninia could hold out no longer and needed to see a doctor. Genora drove to a local hospital, where Ninia had the infection promptly treated, and was given a bill. Genora actually had two insurance packages, one through each of her employers, but there was nothing for her to do besides ensure that Ninia had enough cash to pay for the treatment. "I wanted to take care of her—and I couldn't," Genora recalls. She felt helpless.

The previous year, in 1989, when Ninia was living in New York, Mayor Ed Koch issued an executive order extending bereavement leave to gay and lesbian partners of city employees. Afterward, Ninia had attended friends' signing parties, as couples tried to elevate the bureaucratic formality of completing the requisite paperwork into an ersatz wedding ceremony. Such domestic-partnership arrangements, as they were known, represented the frontier of governmental recognition of unmarried couples. West Hollywood, California, was the first city in the country to adopt one, in 1985, extending not only insurance for companions of city employees but hospital and jail visitation rights to any pair who registered. By 1990 there were fewer than ten cities—representing a predictable assortment of coastal metropolises and inland college towns—that had established similar legal frameworks. Each offered slightly different combinations of benefits and privileges.

Once she had recovered from her ear infection, Ninia looked up the number for the Gay and Lesbian Community Center and called to ask whether Honolulu offered any legal measures that would allow her to apply for medical coverage under her companion's plan. The man who answered the phone introduced himself as Bill Woods, the center's executive director. He informed Ninia that Honolulu had no domestic-partnership statute, and that Hawaii had taken no action to formally recognize same-sex relationships. But he had been looking closely at the Hawaii constitution, Woods said, and thought it might not explicitly restrict marriage rights to heterosexuals. In fact, Woods went on, in a few days he would lead a group of committed gay and lesbian pairs to the board of health to request marriage licenses. He already had two couples ready to go. Would Ninia and Genora like to be the third?

Ninia was taken by the idea. Woods did not seem to know with confidence exactly how things would go, but it seemed to Ninia that there were two possible outcomes. She and Genora could be awarded licenses, allowing them to begin the process of sharing health insurance and the other material benefits afforded to married couples. Otherwise their application could be denied, positioning them to challenge a set of policies Ninia thought discriminatory, excluding an entire class of people from a civil institution based solely on the gender of the people they loved.

Ninia was a feminist advocate by profession, and something of a scholar of the movement as well. She had just published a pamphlet, *Abortion Without Apology,* that served in part to excavate what Ninia saw as the submerged stories of heroism from a forgotten generation of advocates for women's reproductive rights. She was instinctively drawn to the place where the personal and the political entwined naturally. In her pamphlet, she had written about the abortions she had had, a recurring subject of her occasional public talks.

But Ninia knew marriage would have to be Genora's decision. She was still in the closet to many of her friends and coworkers, and rightfully worried about the workplace consequences once it became known she was gay. Ninia gave Genora's phone number to Woods and told him to make the case to her.

That weekend, Genora was working an unusual Sunday shift at the Fox affiliate when Woods called. She sat alone in a darkened control room as he laid out what he had told Ninia days earlier, only with a new urgency. He had already lined up media coverage for a march to the marriage-license bureau the following morning, and he gave Genora a blunt deadline: she had twenty minutes to let him know whether she and Ninia wanted to take part, because he needed to prepare a press release.

Genora said yes. Her time with Ninia had made her happier than she had ever been, and the timing was right. (Both women had celebrated their thirtieth birthdays that summer.) By validating their casual compact in the eyes of the state, Genora believed she could solemnize the duties along with the joys. "I realized what relationships really were—the responsibilities of it and the whole aspect of building a life together and actually falling in love with somebody you actually wanted to marry," says Genora. She called Ninia and said she was ready to get married, or at least to try.

The next morning, the pair drove together to the Fort Street Mall, a busy, pedestrian-only thoroughfare carved out of Honolulu's downtown. Genora carried glasses, a halfhearted protection against easy recognition. They had been instructed to wait outside the old Blaisdell Hotel, where they would meet the other four people who had joined Woods's appeal to make history on December 17, 1990. None of them seemed to have made more than a token gesture toward dressing up for the occasion.

If Ninia and Genora felt like they had embarked on a shotgun wedding, impulsive with the buzz of both romance and revolutionary purpose, the other couples' stories testified not only to the durability of gay relationships, but to their eventual banality. For nearly a decade, Antoinette Pregil and Tammy Rodrigues had lived together on Oahu's rural western coast more than an hour away, eventually raising ten foster children together. Yet the law refused to see Toni and Tammy, as they were known to friends, as equal parents to any of them.

Another couple, Joe Melillo and Patrick Lagon, had been together even longer, and each looked as though he had grown into the other's company, with complementarily ursine frames and tufts of facial hair that appeared to have been applied with the same brush. Joe had been born Joseph in New Jersey, but had assumed the Hawaiian given name Kealapua when he arrived at the University of Hawaii in 1966 to study food sciences. After teaching home economics and culinary arts at the university, he became a chef at Washington Place, the onetime imperial palace converted into Hawaii's governor's mansion. He moonlighted as a dance teacher. He met Pat one day when another instructor invited the twenty-one-year-old to teach disco after him on the floor of a local club. "I was busy with the students," Melillo recalled. "Then I turned and looked at him, and he looked at me. We instantly fell in love." Patrick had grown up in a Hawaii family of ten children, and his parents treated Joe like another son. "When you're born Catholic, it's bred into you that you will meet someone, fall in love, and get married," said Pat. "And that's the way we wanted it to be." But with time the two men also learned the transactional value of a marriage certificate. When Joe and Pat opened a screenprinting workshop, they imagined it as a mom-and-pop operation. Disqualification from marriage, however, compromised their ability to share benefits the heterosexual proprietors of a family business could.

Standing around the bench, Woods explained to the six what it took to get married in Hawaii. State law detailed a two-step process, plainly separating the bureaucratic element from the romantic pageant and solemn spirituality of a wedding day. First, one had to apply for a marriage license in person before a designated license agent. The one-page application form asked couples to inscribe their full names, dates of birth, places of residence, names of parents, and a description of when, where, and how the most recent of their prior marriages ended. Any two people in Hawaii, either resident or visitor, were eligible to apply together. As long as they were unmarried, unrelated, over the age of sixteen (or, with a family judge's waiver, fifteen), entering into the arrangement consensually, and not "afflicted with any loathsome disease concealed from, and unknown to, the other party," they were entitled to a marriage license. There was a reference in state marriage regulations to "the husband" and "the wife," but no specific indication that there had to be only one of each or requirement that together they be capable of reproduction. In fact, in 1984, the state legislature had removed a clause excluding those "impotent or physically incapable of entering into the marriage state." Couples who qualified would be immediately given a license and could head to a ceremony to solemnize their vows before an authorized officiant. They had thirty days to leverage the license into a marriage certificate before it expired.

There were registered license agents scattered across Hawaii, including government officials and even employees of large resort hotels that catered to wedding parties. (The agents received a portion of the $25 application fee.) But Woods selected the most highly trafficked of the available locations: the one attached to the health department's administrative headquarters in Honolulu's downtown. The choice had symbolic power (it was across the street from the state's striking Bauhaus-style concrete capitol) and practical value (it wasn't far from local television stations and the city's two daily newspapers). But Woods also understood the state bureaucracy well enough to know that going to the department's main office meant that the state's top health officials would be just a short walk away. Woods explained the office's designs and protocols to the three couples, as though preparing a team of robbers for a heist, and then led his new coconspirators down Beretania Street toward their target.

A cluster of journalists who had been summoned by a Woods press release had massed beneath an oleander canopy that shaded the health department's entryway. Genora, wearing her glasses, left Ninia's side in the hopes of denying news cameras the chance to catch them in the same frame. When journalists approached Genora, she asked to be described only as "a woman employed in television engineering." "My mother has pretty much accepted it, but I'm not so sure about my father," the anonymous Genora explained to a reporter from the *Honolulu Advertiser*. "I want to protect my father."

The pack entered the lobby. There a high table used for completing forms was dwarfed by a large sand and cinder mural depicting the history of public health in Hawaii, centuries of smallpox outbreaks and mass immunizations sketched in drab clumps of greens, grays, and taupes. With Woods looking on, each of the three couples took an application and completed it. In sequence, they entered through a door marked MAR-RIAGE LICENSE, greeted by a woman at a desk to whom they presented their completed forms and $25 fee. The clerk calmly said that given the unprecedented nature of their request she could not summarily approve the applications the way she would if heterosexual couples had submitted them. She directed the six applicants and their chaperone toward the back of the office, to speak with her boss.

To this point, Woods had staged everything, but he still did not know what the outcome would be. The seven visitors crowded into the small office belonging to Robert Worth, the state's acting chief health status monitor, who despite his sympathy for the couples' ambitions said he couldn't act on them without further legal guidance. "We will hold your applications until such time as the attorney general gives us a ruling about these specific applications," Worth told them.

Woods exited and declared to reporters that they had not been granted licenses but intended to push on. Then he led his charges back down Beretania to the Hawaii headquarters of the American Civil Liberties Union, where upon arrival each was handed a two-page "Application for Legal Assistance." With a blue ballpoint pen, Ninia checked five of the nearly fifty categories of injustice listed on the form, including both gender and sexual-orientation discrimination and infringement of her reproductive freedom. The Department of Health, Ninia wrote beneath, "will not grant us a marriage license because we are both women."

No one knew what would happen next. "It was all over by lunchtime, and we all went our separate ways," recalls Genora. Joe and Pat headed to work, Tammy and Toni to their home. Ninia and Genora retreated to the TGI Friday's where they had begun their first, epic date just six months before. The two ordered cheeseburgers and reflected on the dizzying sequence of events. "What was that?" Genora asked Ninia, whom she had just committed to marry, pending the looming bureaucratic decision, potential legal battle, and unimaginable political conflict that would end up triggering a quarter century of social upheaval. "What did we just do?"

2

Only One Man Marching

The history of gay activism in Oahu, Hawaii's most populous island, was largely the story of William Everett Woods's coming-out. Woods first saw Hawaii while accompanying a friend and her husband on vacation, and the next year transferred from his small Illinois Presbyterian college to the University of Hawaii, studying psychology as an undergraduate before seeking a master's in public health. Island life offered a new start, and from the moment he touched down he decided, for the first time in his life, to be open about his sexuality.

Soon Woods's public profile was inextricably linked with his status as a gay man. In 1973, he founded a gay social-service organization he called the Sexual Identity Center because he didn't think the prominent, straight psychologists and lawyers whose involvement he sought would flock to serve on a board with a name bearing an explicit reference to homosexuality. (Woods would eventually change it to the Gay Community Center and later include the word *Lesbian,* as well, but he continued to send its newsletter in unmarked envelopes.) Woods used the position to place himself at the forefront of everything within Hawaii's emergent gay community. In 1974, when Oahu held its first gay-pride parade, a curiosity to onlookers along a Waikiki sidewalk, Woods was there. Years later, he became the first openly gay person to testify before the Hawaii legislature, then the first to address a state Democratic Party convention. But Woods proved more skilled at creating new institutions in his own image than building durable coalitions with others. "To be an organizer in the gay community you had to have an incredibly big ego, because you had to take the abuse people were going to give you. If you didn't have a big ego, you wouldn't have gotten anything done in the eighties," says his friend Terry Gregson.

"The problem with Bill was that people liked him more than he thought they liked him. He was always ready to fight people."

That self-confidence propelled Woods to take up arms in the culture wars. When conservative televangelist Jerry Falwell traveled to Hawaii in May 1981 to "save the fiftieth state" by opening a chapter of his Moral Majority, Inc.—anyone who stood in his way must be "a Nazi, a communist, or a homosexual," he warned—Woods led a group that beat him to register the name with state authorities. Their "Moral Majority of Hawaii," as newspaper ads announced, would defend "family planning, civil rights for all people, pro-choice in abortion, child care programs, freedom of speech and religion, and the separation of church and state." When Falwell held an "I Love America" rally outside the State Capitol in Honolulu, more than three-quarters of the estimated 3,500 people in attendance appeared to be protesting his arrival. Onstage, Falwell was confronted by a sheriff who presented him with a summons: the Moral Majority of Hawaii was suing his Moral Majority, Inc. for using its name. Concerned they could get ensnared in the litigation, other venues that had agreed to host stops on Falwell's Hawaii tour canceled. He retreated back to Virginia. Woods claimed victory. "The Moral Majority of Hawaii is using this name to demonstrate that the words 'moral' and 'majority' cannot be monopolized by any one group," he said. "In fact, the variety of lifestyles in Hawaii demonstrates that we are probably the most legitimate entity in using the term 'Moral Majority.'" Before leaving Hawaii, a disconsolate Falwell gave a farewell speech that mentioned only two names: Jesus Christ and Bill Woods.

Woods was driven by an idealistic sense of purpose—he signed off both phone calls and correspondence with "Do Good"—but a skein of entrepreneurial ambition shot through all his advocacy. He edited and published the *Gay Community News,* banishing the racy ads that often sustained gay publications in the hopes that his would find its way into schools and libraries. He organized Hawaii's first Alcoholics Anonymous meeting exclusively for gays and lesbians, often convened under a patch of palms on Waikiki beach. Not far away, at the Hotel Honolulu, Woods hosted a weekly support group for gay men. "He was the gay-rights movement at that time, almost single-handedly," says Jo-Ann Adams, who became involved in gay activism after moving to Honolulu in the late 1980s. "It was his name you saw in the paper; he was always up to something." In 1989, declaring his ambition to become "the gay Larry King," Woods bought a two-hour slot on a local radio station for a weekly talk show he called *Lambda Line,* selling his own ads and splitting the revenue with the station. That year, when Governor John Waihee declared Hawaii's first state-approved Gay and Lesbian Pride Week, it was Woods he singled out for his work "proclaiming our state's commitment to human rights." Only the activist's accountant could have fully understood where one Woods-led project ended and another began.

By 1989, fifteen years had passed since Oahu's first and only gay-pride parade, and Woods thought it was time to try again. The 1974 event had yielded mixed results. An estimated two hundred people turned out for the parade, but it was of questionable public-relations value to the cause of gay pride. In advance, local radio DJs tweaked rivals by accusing one another of serving as the grand marshal. On parade day, many of the stations followed up by positioning staffers at phone booths along Kalakaua Avenue to report mockingly on the spectacle. "The only picture that appeared in *The Honolulu Advertiser*," Woods lamented afterward, "was that of a guy wearing women's clothing, which happened to be the only one in the parade."

There was little motivation for a sequel. Throughout the 1970s, queer culture in Oahu bumped up against mainstream culture in a way it rarely did on the mainland. Families went together to the Glade Show Lounge, a downtown drag club famous for its "Boys Will Be Girls" productions. The hospitality sector welcomed gay tourists to Waikiki, particularly when, like Woolworth heir Jimmy Donahue, they did so on a chartered Boeing 707 filled with young men who would claim the Moana Hotel as their own for stretches at a time. "People always felt, why have a gay-pride parade when we don't have anything to be un-proud about?" says Jack Law, owner of Hula's Bar & Lei Stand, Honolulu's preeminent gay bar.

Local law reflected that lack of stigma. In 1972, Hawaii had become the fifth state in the country to legalize gay sex between consenting adults. When, the following year, the minister of a young gay church congregation sought to develop a social-service program to support gay prisoners, he was confronted with an unexpected problem. "There's not much of a problem with gays in prison because there are so few gay-related arrests," conceded Rev. Tim Earhart of the Metropolitan Community Church. Legal protections induced gays to come out of the closet; their Hawaiian neighbors received them with little fuss. "Policemen who smile at two women dressed in jeans, one of whom looks fairly butch . . . Families who don't reject gay children," lesbian activist and journalist Sasha Gregory wrote in 1972, after moving from San Francisco with her partner. "Here I am a human being. On the mainland, I was a 'dyke.' Do we really need gay lib in Hawaii?"

Gay life in Honolulu unfolded so blissfully unaware of the tensions constraining it in other cities that Law didn't learn about the antipolice riots outside Greenwich Village's Stonewall Inn until he traveled to New York six years after they happened. He was less shocked that gay men had found the courage to assert themselves than he was to learn they had been forced to do so in the first place. "I didn't realize there was that kind of discrimination going on in New York. In all of Hula's time, we didn't have any problems," says Law. "It wasn't like something you heard about—that they're blazing trails for us. It was, 'Why is New York so backwards?'"

Other seminal moments in the maturation of the national gay political consciousness similarly passed Hawaii by. In 1977, Miami-area voters overturned a nondiscrimination ordinance that had been initially drafted by an upstart gay-rights lobbying organization and enacted by the Dade County Metro Commission. It was only the second time gay rights had been abridged by popular vote. "Out of the bars and into the streets," went the chants at impromptu gatherings around the country, and the sense of purpose persisted: membership in the National Gay Task Force would double over the next four months. Yet it was as if the news had never even reached Hawaii. "From New York to San Francisco male gays and lesbians demonstrated against the Florida 'backlash' vote," the *Honolulu Advertiser* editorial page observed. "Here in Hawaii, all was quiet. There was no evidence of unusual activity at Queen's Surf Beach, gay bars or other such gathering places."

After Hawaii's first positive test for AIDS was recorded in the early 1980s, gay life there maintained its innocence. The issue did not become politicized the way it did in mainland cities, where the gay community was torn between its need for self-preservation and a persistent desire for sexual self-determination that almost immediately pitted it against local health authorities. Alerts for AIDS activism never displaced notices for the gay bowling league and gay hiking group in the Honolulu press. "There is an AIDS awareness here, but it is rarely thought about and never mentioned—by the locals anyway," the *New York Native* reported in a 1985 travel story. "Because of the relaxed AIDS awareness, the atmosphere in the bars is one of festivity. You remember festivity."

Even as the threat of epidemic grew, Hawaii did not succumb to panic. The elite private Punahou School introduced an AIDS education program in 1984, followed thereafter by similar initiatives in Hawaii's public schools. It was the first state to approve a legal needle exchange, and Honolulu's two active bathhouses carried on without much debate. Instead of trying to negotiate their closure, government officials and gay community leaders persuaded the facilities' owners to allow them to send in counselors at certain times and distribute materials alerting patrons to the risks of transmission and need for testing. "We decided to turn it into an educational opportunity," says David McEwan, a doctor who headed the Life Foundation, Hawaii's leading anti-AIDS organization.

By 1989, Hawaii was spending the most money per capita on AIDS of any state in the country. The Centers for Disease Control promoted its needle-exchange program as a national model, which could be credited with helping slow the disease's spread on the islands. Still, even in Hawaii, gay life after the end of what was often called "the plague" would never be quite the same as before. And so, by 1989, "it was just time to have fun," says Law. "We had such a long period of being under the pall of AIDS that finally, like everywhere else, we said, 'Fuck it, let's have fun for a change.'"

Without a parade locally, Bill Woods had been traveling to San Francisco for its pride-week festivities since 1974. It was there that he handed supervisor Harvey Milk the flowered lei that the politician draped over his white T-shirt in what emerged as an iconic image after Milk's assassination. Woods became a lifelong parade enthusiast. "Even if there are only two people marching, it is needed," he would say. That August, Woods attended a planning meeting of the Official Gay and Lesbian Pride Week Association of Oahu, to propose that it was time to bring back the parade.

The Gay and Lesbian Pride Week Association existed largely for the purpose of hosting a rally following the concluding picnic of the Imperial Court drag-queen pageant. Its board included Cheryl Embry, who earlier in the year had launched "a gay rag" with a more expansive editorial vision than Woods's four-page photocopied newsletter, *Gay Community News*. The only discouraging word Embry received as she prepared to launch *Island Lifestyle Magazine* was Woods's admonition that he had seen "two hundred publications come and go." Embry had received Woods's advice in his capacity as director of the gay community center, but she came to conclude she had heard the response of a rival publisher looking to deflate a potential competitor. Embry and her other board members were primed to look unfavorably on Woods, and when he described the parade he envisioned—with three thousand people marching—they scoffed at his impertinence. They barely had enough volunteers to organize the rally as it existed. The biggest upgrade they were considering was for a candlelight ceremony the board hoped to add the following year.

But like most efforts to discourage Woods, Embry's failed. He set to work, calling organizers of mainland pride parades and local officials to assess the work necessary to stage such an event in Honolulu. Three months later, Woods incorporated the findings in a report he shared with the pride-week board. ("I have offered to take on the Parade Coordinator's position," Woods wrote, describing a new position he envisioned, "but only with a clear understanding that with the responsibility there must be complete authority to carry it out in a reasonable and prudent manner whereby no other is second guessing or trying to dictate day-to-day operations.") Once committee assignments were distributed, Woods objected that his desired task went unmentioned. "I only wanted to do one thing," he said, "and that was to be a Parade and Rally coordinator." Woods pushed, and the board relented, allowing him to create what they imagined would be a toothless committee to further explore its possibility.

When the board members of the Official Gay and Lesbian Pride Week Association of Oahu opened the December 1989 issue of the local *Gay Community News,* they were shocked by an announcement from its editor. "A separate organization has been established to conduct the planning and promotion of a parade and rally to become a major part of future Gay and Lesbian Pride Weeks in Hawaii," Woods had written. The association's cochairs drafted an outraged response. "At no time was the authority delegated to you to plan a rally," Ashan Nelson and Jovanne Sartre wrote to Woods. "Please work within this organization's framework and abide by its majority findings and decisions."

Woods, naturally, did not oblige. He formed his own nonprofit corporation, the Pride Parade and Rally Council, and relied on friends for help. Sharyle Lyndon, a onetime drag-show producer and brothel manager whom Woods referred to as "Leather," began negotiating with officials from the United States Army for use of the park attached to Fort DeRussy, a former coastal defense converted largely to green space. ("I wore full leather every day," says Lyndon. "In Hawaii that stands out.") Joe Melillo, a chef with catering experience, agreed to oversee the parade's concessions, while Jack Law offered to host fundraising parties at his bar Hula's. When it came time to apply for event permits, Woods picked one day prior to the Sunday when the pride-week association planned to hold its rally and new candlelight ceremony. He scrambled for ways to have his event (draft slogan: "The 50th state is the first state in the Gay Nineties") upstage the established festivities. Woods asked the governor to be his grand marshal, and the Royal Hawaiian Band to perform. An International Cuisine Festival would serve chicken fajitas, kalua pig, German sausage, and shave ice. And there would be a wedding.

Woods wasn't interested in getting married himself. "Bill wasn't a great romantic—he would have a boyfriend and another on the side—and not a big believer in monogamous relationships," says Gregson. The durable fixtures in Woods's domestic life were an assortment of Buddha likenesses hung from walls and a menagerie of pets, including cats, dogs, macaws, parrots, a chameleon, and a chicken named Henrietta. (Each item's provenance attested less to Woods's spiritual life than to a long-lost enterprise he couldn't quite abandon. "I don't think it was an affinity for Buddhism. He had ten of them made, because he thought he might make some money," says Tom Riddle, who first befriended Woods in 1976. "He saw someone had a parrot, so he went out and got ten parrots. He said, 'I'm going to start a business: Birds by Wild Bill.'")

Woods was cloaking a personal desire for attention in a wedding gown—and he was not the first. He had been on the National Mall in 1987 when a March on Washington for Gay and Lesbian Rights was nearly overwhelmed by a ceremony called "The Wedding" staged on its sidelines. The large-scale symbolic vows had been conceived by Los Angeles–based Couples, Inc., the self-described National Organization for the Advancement of Gay and Lesbian Couples, which was incorporated with little political or legal strategy but with the desire to market itself as a support resource for those in committed same-sex relationships. Some movement leaders initially feared that a gathering of formally attired brides and grooms would be a distraction from the weekend's larger goal of projecting political power—many dismissively likened it to the mass-wedding antics of Sun Myung Moon's Unification Church—but the ceremony ended up drawing five thousand of the two hundred thousand who reportedly participated in the following day's march. "Take the power of your freedom and your love to your home, to your careers, to your places of worship, to your family, and friends," the officiant, a self-described metaphysician named Dina Bachelor, told couples before they were doused in rice and flowers. "Let the truth of your relationship radiate so brilliantly that all may know your love is so powerful, so perfect, so right, that there is no fear, no law, no person—indeed, nothing between heaven that can separate you."

Gay couples had been participating in such symbolic displays in Hawaii since the early 1970s, when the Metropolitan Community Church opened its first island outpost in Oahu. The California-based church was the creation of Troy Perry, who had been licensed as a Southern Baptist preacher at the age of fifteen but was defrocked by his Pentecostal denomination after officials discovered he was gay. In 1968, Perry began welcoming a dozen gays and lesbians who felt alienated from organized Christianity into his suburban Los Angeles living room to pray with him. As their ranks expanded, Perry moved the flock into a borrowed Hollywood movie theater for services. The Metropolitan Community Church was a mainline Protestant congregation of no particular sect but with an occasionally revivalist vibe. Soon Perry's "church for homosexuals," as his mother called it, spawned congregations around the country. When Honolulu got its own minister, he led morning worship at a gay bar called the Tomato and evening services at First Unitarian on Pali Highway, where choir members draped aloha-style capes over their black robes. As Perry had done in Los Angeles, the congregation offered gay couples the chance to exchange "holy union" vows, with a minister presiding. To qualify, the couple had to have been together at least six months ("to be sure they're not joining a potential Zsa Zsa or Mickey Rooney," *The Advocate* observed) and attend mandatory counseling sessions.

Woods was not moved by the sentimental force of these arrangements. Instead he saw everything they failed to deliver, from Social Security benefits to airline-ticket rules, which necessitated not only religious acceptance of vows but civil recognition of them. And even if one church sanctified a pair's love, Woods knew, another had the standing to limit its resonance: Catholic Social Services, a state subcontractor that administered Hawaii's largest adoption agency, refused to place children into households whose heads were not legally married. If gay couples wanted to be recognized as families, Woods believed, the state would have to sanction their unions.

Most of those radicalized in the wake of Stonewall were less concerned with joining the established order. "We expose the institution of marriage as one of the most insidious and basic sustainers of the system," said a leader of the Gay Liberation Front, which formed in the weeks after Stonewall and lasted just nine months, collapsing after a debate over whether to ally with the Black Panthers. "The family is the microcosm of oppression." The National Coalition of Gay Organizations' 1972 platform of legal reforms envisioned marriage without monogamous commitment, through "repeal of all legislative provisions that restrict the sex or number of persons entering into a marriage unit and extension of legal benefits of marriage to all persons who cohabit regardless of sex or numbers."

Woods, by contrast, was a traditionalist. On his weekly radio show, after his "Strong, Proud and United" theme song had concluded, he invited callers to set the agenda. Woods would engage any subject they raised—soothing the anxieties of the closeted, rejecting homophobic hecklers, and assessing topical questions, like the exclusion of gays from military service and the Catholic Church's attitude toward homosexuality—but the thirty-nine-year old Woods worked to steer away from frank sex talk and toward a more staid discussion that emphasized commitment. "There's only so many ways that a human body can get together with another human body and expose themselves to love, lust, sex, whatever you might want to call it," Woods said a week after the show's launch. "I'm really most concerned about relationships, and for the straight community to know the truth."

Those values were at the heart of Woods's most audacious plan to draw attention to his parade.

In 1981, two men had applied for a Hawaii marriage license, misleadingly identifying themselves on the application form as husband and wife and using gender-ambiguous names as cover. When the health department asked the state attorney general for a judgment on the validity of the request, lawyers reviewed a handful of instances where similar questions had arrived in other states' courts, and where judges had ruled that governments were under no obligation to recognize same-sex couples. That summer, the attorney general issued a memorandum affirming that only people of opposite sexes could enter into a valid contract under the section of the state code that defines marriage. "We believe that section," the memo read, "is *not* unconstitutional beyond all reasonable doubt and, therefore, must be presumed valid."

But nearly a decade later Woods thought that the time was right to try again. Much had changed in terms of the acceptance of sexual minorities, as his own activism attested: by 1990, Honolulu's mayor had issued an executive order banning employers from discriminating on the basis of sexual orientation. Woods had no legal training, but when he went to the same law books that state attorneys had reviewed in their effort to define marriage, he detected plenty of room for doubt. "In other states, there's a specific definition of a 'couple,'" Woods said, not quite accurately. "Hawaii is the only state that doesn't have a clear definition on the surface."

To sponsor a marriage push of his own, Woods formed the Gay and Lesbian Education Advocacy Association and began looking for allies. He contacted the Honolulu office of the ACLU, which in 1986 had become the first national civil-liberties organization to endorse "the legal recognition of gay and lesbian relationships" to qualify for the "benefits and rights enjoyed by married persons." But when Woods asked for legal help, he did not find the organization eager to follow its declared principles into court. In an April 1990 conversation with program director Bill Wilson, Woods gave the impression he was set in his agenda "to promote legal marriage status to couples of the same sex." Woods had already formed a committee for the purpose, he told Wilson, intent on taking action during Gay Pride Week that June.

Woods's plan was to organize couples who had participated in the Metropolitan Community Church's holy-union ceremonies to seek licenses. (Perry, the church's founder, was invited to officiate, but amid the planning over his travel from Los Angeles to Hawaii he demurred, asserting that "marriage was for heterosexuals and that his church was for holy unions," as Woods recalled.) "Our previous search was for a 'perfect couple,' but the new strategy is to bring together new couples and ones with long-term marriage experience to deal with the reality of responsible relationships," Woods explained to Wilson, formally requesting the ACLU's backing for his initiative, including research and an eventual litigation campaign. But everyone Woods encountered at the state affiliate appeared equally unenthusiastic and noncommittal about picking a fight over same-sex marriage. First he was directed to Carl Varady, an ACLU Hawaii staff attorney, but that didn't seem to bring him any closer to legal action. When Varady asked for more documents to support a potential case, Woods sensed it was merely his way of putting off a response, and the two had a heated phone call. When Woods attempted to bypass Varady by reaching ACLU Hawaii executive director Vanessa Chong and board president Julie Hugo, his calls went unanswered.

In the meantime, the 1990 pride week came and passed. It featured, as Woods's friend Sharyle Lyndon would later claim, the country's "first Gay and Lesbian parade to be staged on a military installation." A straight Honolulu city councilman had served as grand marshal, leading a pack down Waikiki's Kalakaua Avenue that included a Boyz of Waianae truck and self-described Condom Queen tossing her wares to onlookers with pamphlets urging the importance of safe sex. They arrived at Kapiolani Park, where from the bandshell stage a drag queen sang from *La Cage aux Folles*. The upbeat brass of the Royal Hawaiian Band lured sunbathers to leave their positions on the Kuhio Beach sand to the park for a look at the unfamiliar commotion. The event generated the sympathetic press coverage Woods wanted, but nowhere did it mention that he had hoped to preside over a wedding as part of the festivities. "We're here to celebrate who we are," Woods told a reporter for the *Honolulu Advertiser*. "And we are helping the straight community understand we are very qualified, professional people."

It did not take long for Woods to learn the cause of the ACLU's delay. Varady, the staff attorney, was busy asking a local Civil Rights/Sexual Orientation Commission whether the ACLU should back the marriage efforts. He didn't name Woods in the letter sent out to the group's members, referring only to "a local activist," but Woods's friends knew enough to carbon-copy him on their replies. "As a Gay person, and more important, an American citizen, I feel that a person who is Gay should have the right to participate in all of the American culture institutions without hindrance," Howard Lee DeLotelle wrote to Varady, before questioning the ACLU's decision to survey others before committing to its own position. "Do I understand that if only one person is denied their rights ACLU will now not support them?"

Woods shared DeLotelle's indignation. He first wrote to the ACLU's leadership to complain about what Varady's own letter described as a "poll" on the marriage question. Woods accused them of choosing "to reduce the support and recognition of civil rights issues to the level of a popularity contest." Then he took the criticism public, reverting to the journalistic third person to cover the scandal in his own publication, the *Gay Community News*. "HAWAII HORROR STORY! Hawaii's ACLU Takes Public Opinion Poll to Determine If They Will Support Gay Civil Rights," its front page screamed. In the story, Woods tried to shame the ACLU by invoking one of its most controversial moves, a 1977 decision to back the rights of the National Socialist Party of America to march in Skokie, Illinois, a choice designed specifically to rile a suburb with a high concentration of Jewish Holocaust survivors. The matter, which eventually reached the Supreme Court, illustrated a willingness to defend unsympathetic clients regardless of disapprobation, a form of courage at the heart of the civil libertarian's mission, Woods argued. "Will the poll respondents from Skokie, Illinois, please stand up," he posited, "so that the rest of the world can see the popular vote that supported the Nazis to walk down their streets?"

The fracas was noticed by *The Advocate*, the country's leading gay newspaper, which in late September reported on the debate over marriage tactics splitting Hawaii's activist community. Varady claimed that Woods's description of his group's internal consultations was "full of lies," and that characterizing his research as a "poll" misleadingly implied that the ACLU had put the matter out for a public vote. "We wanted to ensure that were we to proceed with litigation, it would be part of an overall strategy for securing full equality under the law for lesbians and gays in Hawaii. Those kinds of strategies are often designed as building blocks and are painstakingly developed by local community leaders," Varady and two national ACLU officials wrote in a letter later published in *The Advocate*. "We had no indication as to how the proposed lawsuit would fit into such a strategy, whether this individual was seeking to use the ACLU to further his own view in an ongoing debate, or whether other, perhaps better, plans were underway for challenging anti-gay discrimination."

If Varady had hoped to deter or deflate Woods with such a public rebuke, it had the opposite effect. In September, Woods sent Chong and Hugo a letter declaring that what he now called his Gay Marriage Project had "a number of couples who would like to be married," and that "if we do not hear formally from you within two weeks we will pursue other assistance." In a letter the same day to Varady, Woods was blunter about how wounded he was. "I have re-invented the wheel with you about Gay marriage because you needed to know why Gay people would want to be married. I have waited and waited and have had no formal word from you in months," Woods wrote. "Now what?"

Throughout the year, Woods insisted he had twenty-five couples who were eager to apply for licenses. He would arrive on Tuesday nights at the Hotel Honolulu for his men's support group with unsolicited updates on his search: "I've got another one!" Convinced he had to persuade the ACLU that his marriage campaign would not fall away as a fleeting fascination, Woods contacted a reporter for the *Honolulu Advertiser* to record his intent. SAME-SEX MARRIAGE BAN MAY BE TESTED, a banner headline declared across the front page of the Sunday paper.

The article beneath, however, identified only one couple Woods had ready for the altar. They happened to be his friends Patrick Lagon and Joe Melillo, the executive chef who had been one of the first volunteers Woods had enlisted when he needed help to stage his parade. "We feel we are a couple and we belong together," Joe told the *Advertiser*, days before submitting an Application for Legal Assistance to the ACLU on behalf of himself and Pat. (Woods informed friends that the couples attached to the Metropolitan Community Church lost interest once it was clear he was proceeding without institutional support.) A few days later, Woods was contacted by two women who had seen the newspaper story and wanted to join his quest for marriage rights because of the challenges they faced as lesbian parents to foster children. He instructed them to complete one of the ACLU's request forms as well. Less than two weeks after that, Ninia Baehr called the community center to inquire about health insurance, and Woods invited her, too, to join in.

Woods believed that the three couples stood a strong chance of walking out of the department of public health as legally married couples. He had not thought through how he would respond if their applications for licenses were denied. He had no budget for a prolonged legal or public-relations campaign to make civil-rights history, and he had not bothered to vet his recruits the way one might if plotting a test case. "He didn't ask, 'Are you an axe murderer?'" recalls Baehr. "He didn't do anything to see, *Are you the Rosa Parks we need?*"

A Distinct Civil-Liberties Question

The office to which Bill Woods delivered his six charges following their health-department exploits represented the only national organization in the United States with a stated goal of supporting same-sex marriage rights. It was not, however, notably one whose concern was with the broader political standing of the gay movement. The ACLU largely avoided early requests to defend the specific rights of gays and lesbians, declaring in 1957 that it was "not within the province of the Union to evaluate the social validity of laws" criminalizing their behavior. When it did occasionally represent gay interests, it approached them in a sidelong fashion, challenging police entrapment tactics as a violation of due-process rights and defending Lillian Hellman's lesbian-themed play *The Children's Hour* on free-speech grounds. But as society changed in the 1960s, the group's leadership expanded its purview to include the bedroom. After the Supreme Court affirmed a right to privacy that covered use of contraception in 1965, the ACLU vowed never to withdraw from "attacking repressive laws and practices in the field of sex."

Across much of the country, the ACLU was the only organization that claimed such a mandate, yet still gays and lesbians usually felt that they were on their own, particularly when it came to marriage rights. In the summer of 1968, a twenty-six-year-old Oklahoman named Jack Baker received an envelope in the mail from the Air Force that included a general discharge, recently issued to replace the honorable discharge Baker had received four years earlier. Baker's homosexuality had been an issue at the time—he had made a pass at a straight airman he mistakenly thought had been flirting with him—and had stunted his military career. Blocked from receiving an officer's commission, Baker was allowed to slink away from the service and take advantage of GI Bill benefits by attending graduate school.

He enrolled in an engineering program at the University of Kansas, where he fell in love with a library-science student named Michael McConnell. After receiving his degree, Baker went to a civilian job at Tinker Air Force Base in Oklahoma. He thought the military had lost interest in his sex life, but the belated withdrawal of the honorary discharge he had received upon leaving the service was, as he understood it, a threat to his livelihood. A copy of the new discharge was sent to his supervisor at the base, who gave Baker an ultimatum: quit or be fired.

His congressman and the American Legion showed no interest in offering Baker legal help, but the ACLU did. He traveled to Washington to meet with one of its lawyers, Stuart Land, who represented federal employees when their jobs became imperiled due to their sexuality. In April 1970, Land won the case: an Air Force review board reinstated Baker's honorable discharge. Now in his first year at University of Minnesota Law School, Baker wrote to Land that he looked "forward to the day when I will join you as a member of the Bar defending the rights of others similarly harassed."

After taking a legal-research class in his first semester, Baker discovered that some provisions of Minnesota marriage law allowed any two "persons" to apply for a license without explicitly excluding two of the same gender from doing so. Three years earlier he had pledged "a committed, long-term, loving relationship," as McConnell recalled, but had not contemplated options to formalize it. The two men had been apart for much of the academic year, with McConnell remaining in Oklahoma as he searched for jobs. As soon as he received an offer for one and headed north to begin work as a campus librarian at the University of Minnesota, Baker decided to act on his research. Dreaming of a summertime garden ceremony, the couple headed to the Hennepin County Courthouse. It would all be, the first-year law student advised his boyfriend, "simple as pie."

Clerk of court Gerald Nelson had no idea how to respond to the two men in front of him, and requested a legal opinion from above. In a seven-page opinion, county attorney George Scott told Nelson to deny the license, and that permitting Baker and McConnell to marry "would be to result in an undermining and destruction of the entire legal concept of our family structure in all areas of law."

Instead of bestowing the benefits of marriage, their license application caused them new problems. When university administrators saw media coverage of the courthouse trip, they rescinded McConnell's job offer. With the well-documented visit to the county clerk, the Faculty, Staff and Student Affairs Committee of the Board of Regents asserted, McConnell had "publicly announced" his intention to violate the state's ban on gay sex. "The only thing the Committee knows about my personal life is: 1) I am a member of F.R.E.E. (Fight Repression of Erotic Expression), a University of Minnesota student group," McConnell wrote to Lynn Castner, executive director of the Minnesota Civil Liberties Union. "And 2) I have applied for a marriage license (May 18) in Hennepin County Court House to be married to my lover Jack Baker."

Without a clear ACLU policy about what the Constitution owed gays and lesbians, Castner had broad leeway about whether to take on McConnell and Baker as clients. The ACLU had always operated as a loose confederation of affiliates spread across the fifty states and Puerto Rico. The affiliates function as their own law firms, free to choose cases as long as local attorneys did not do anything that directly countered ACLU policy and deferred to the national office in New York on any matter headed to the United States Supreme Court. Castner agreed to represent McConnell, but only as a matter of employment discrimination. Same-sex marriage "doesn't involve a civil liberties issue," the couple recorded being told. The retainer agreement the MCLU offered McConnell in July 1970 explicitly covered only "the action of the University of Minnesota in refusing to allow me to work," and its lawyers gently nudged Baker aside. "I believe it would be better if we have exclusive control of this matter," Stephen M. Goldfarb, a volunteer attorney working on McConnell's suit, wrote him after Baker began negotiating with an out-of-state law professor who had read coverage of the case in the *New York Times* and offered to draft an amicus brief.

That fall, a federal district judge reviewing the claim ruled that the university had violated the plaintiff's due-process rights in denying him a job. "An homosexual is after all a human being, and a citizen of the United States, despite the fact that he finds his sex gratification in what most consider to be an unconventional manner," Judge Philip Neville wrote, passing off the request for a marriage license as a "rather bizarre occurrence." A federal appeals court, however, saw "the marriage license incident" as central to the story. "This is not a case involving mere homosexual propensities on the part of a prospective employee," concluded the three-judge panel that overturned the lower court's ruling in McConnell's favor. Instead, Judge Roy Stephenson wrote, the issue was the plaintiff's supposed "right to pursue an activist role in implementing his unconventional ideas concerning the societal status to be accorded homosexuals and, thereby, to foist tacit approval of this socially repugnant concept upon his employer."

After McConnell's lower-court victory, Baker had begun to pursue the marriage issue in earnest. The MCLU rebuffed his requests for help with a second case, leaving Baker little choice but to turn to a roommate to represent him and McConnell. Michael Wetherbee was a year ahead of Baker in law school, and so inexperienced that he made a major procedural error on his first filing in the case. (Over a five-year period, Baker and McConnell would file about eight different lawsuits related to their status as a same-sex pair.) Baker, in a brief he drafted largely himself, would go on to argue that, because Minnesota code did not explicitly exclude same-sex couples from marrying, legislators intended to allow them to do so.

Fearing a potential loss, Baker quietly strategized a complex series of clerical maneuvers he hoped might permit the men to marry before the Minnesota Supreme Court explicitly ruled out the prospect. McConnell legally adopted Baker, allowing them to share basic protections—"about ninety percent of the benefits of marriage," as Baker explained it to McConnell. As the part of the process under way in Hennepin County, Baker filed to change his legal identity, assuming the name Pat Lyn McConnell. They moved in briefly with friends in nearby Mankato, long enough to qualify as residents of Blue Earth County and to begin receiving mail there under their new, gender-neutral names. Minnesota requires only one half of an engaged couple to be present when submitting a marriage license application, so McConnell went alone to the county clerk's office, to avoid special scrutiny. They never learned whether the license was in fact filed—years later, county officials would claim not to have a record—but within weeks it had been rendered moot by a ruling of the Minnesota Supreme Court. "There is no irrational or invidious discrimination," the court wrote, in deferring to a conception of marriage "as old as the book of Genesis."

Within a two-week period in early 1972, he and McConnell each appealed a loss—on the marriage question and the employment dispute—to the U.S. Supreme Court, with backing from the Minnesota Civil Liberties Union. It had been slow to join the marriage suit, doing so only once Wetherbee was hired as a MCLU legal counsel, becoming the first openly gay staff attorney in the ACLU network. Once Wetherbee was involved, the MCLU assumed about half of the approximately $6,000 in costs that Baker incurred with his suit. Yet while the ACLU affixed its name to McConnell's petition to the Supreme Court over the employment issue, it refused entreaties from the president of its Minnesota affiliate to do the same on the marriage question. "I personally went to the ACLU executive committee in New York," Matthew Stark later recalled, "and asked them to join. They said no. We went ahead and litigated anyway."

Only Baker's petition on the marriage issue would receive a substantive response. Five years earlier, the U.S. Supreme Court had guaranteed a fundamental right to marriage when it struck down state laws banning miscegenation in *Loving v. Virginia*. Sexual orientation should be treated like race, Baker's appeal argued, subject to the same constitutional protection against categorical discrimination in state law. On October 17, 1972, the court announced it would not take up *Baker v. Nelson*. In a single published sentence, the justices conceded that while same-sex marriage posed a "federal question," it failed to be "substantial" enough to demand their review.

Along the way, Baker and McConnell had received copious national media attention for their efforts. Boosted in part by the publicity surrounding the two parallel lawsuits, in January 1971 Baker announced his candidacy for president of the forty-three-thousand-member student body at his university's Twin Cities campus. When he won, it was believed to be the first time a self-identified gay man or lesbian had been elected to any office in the country, a marvel reported by Walter Cronkite on the *CBS Evening News* and covered in *Time*. But his quest for marriage had been object of the most intense curiosity, leading to a portrait with McConnell in *Life* and a profile of the two in *Look*. Headlined THE HOMOSEXUAL COUPLE, the article captured the lasting influence of Baker and McConnell on their generation: icons of the latent desire for domesticity within a gay community. "Some homosexuals—a minority—live together in stable, often long-lasting relationships, like Baker's and McConnell's," wrote *Look*.

Despite its Minnesota affiliate's late financial contribution to Baker's marriage lawsuit, to the extent the ACLU saw constitutional interests in the gay bedroom, they concerned a freedom to be left alone by the government rather than any right to have relationships validated by it. "As you know in most states young people peaceably living in communes, hippies, homosexuals, prostitutes, marrieds and singles are subjected to selective enforcement of the criminal statutes which ban adultery, fornication, sodomy and other private consensual activities between adults," Marilyn Haft wrote in the summer of 1973, introducing the ACLU's new Sexual Privacy Project, whose establishment in the wake of *Roe v. Wade* was funded by the Playboy Foundation. "It is imperative that they be eradicated."

At its 1975 biennial conference, the ACLU adopted Policy #261, which broadened that concern by declaring "homosexuals are entitled to the same rights, liberties, lack of harassment and protections as are other citizens." The following year, Los Angeles–area activists organized the first local chapter devoted to raising the profile of gay issues within the organization. "The need to educate is the single most important part of any civil rights struggle," Peter Thomas Judge, the founding president of the ACLU of Southern California Gay Rights Chapter, would write. "Unfortunately, the education of the public has been difficult because the burden has fallen on the gay rights organization [*sic*] themselves to cope with a basically uncooperative media." The ACLU did sometimes fight for the rights of gay families, but only in a reactive way. In 1977, as the California legislature became the country's first to amend a state's marriage statute to explicitly exclude same-sex couplings, an ACLU lobbyist testified in vain against the proposal. (The legislation had been drafted at the urging of the County Clerks' Association of California, whose members found the existing statute's language to be unhelpfully ambiguous about gender qualifications.) Rationales privileging procreative families "fail to account for the many, many people today who have no plans for children," he told an assembly committee.

Two years later, when the federal government found itself inadvertently ruling on the issue of marriage, the ACLU stepped in to defend the interest of a gay couple who considered themselves married. Anthony Sullivan and Richard F. Adams found their way to Boulder, Colorado, when they learned in the spring of 1975 that the county clerk, Clela Rorex, would likely hand them a marriage license. "Who is it going to hurt?" assistant district attorney William C. Wise responded after Rorex asked if anything in the law prevented her from granting such requests. She began striking through the words *male* and *female* on her office's forms, replacing each gender-specific word with *person*. "I don't profess to be knowledgeable about homosexuality or even understand it," Rorex explained. "But it's not my business why people get married. No minority should be discriminated against." She married six couples during a stretch in 1975, turning Colorado into "a mini-Nevada for homosexual couples," as the *New York Times* put it, before the state attorney general stopped her.

For the others, the euphoria had been brief and the fallout swift, as state officials voided the licenses and the couples went back to their unmarried lives. In the case of Adams and Sullivan, there was a complication: the two had met while the latter, an Australian national, was traveling to the United States on a limited-duration tourist visa. Sullivan and Adams eventually applied for permanent residence, a privilege afforded to noncitizens if legally married to an American. An Immigration and Naturalization Service district director responded in writing that their application had "failed to establish that a bona fide marital relationship can exist between two faggots." (The INS would later retract the letter that included the word *faggots*, but insisted that "one of the parties to this union may function as a female in other relationships and situations, but cannot function as a wife assuming female duties and obligations inherent in the marital relationship. A union of this sort was never intended by Congress to form a basis of a visa petition.") An ACLU volunteer attorney helped the couple draft a lawsuit claiming that the rejection of their visa petition amounted to a violation of their constitutional rights. "The refusal to extend the benefits of legal marriage to gay people is a major act of anti-gay discrimination," Sullivan and Adams claimed. (They would exhaust their appeals, and Sullivan went on to live quietly in the United States for decades without resolving his immigration status.) "The issue of legal marriage," they argued to a federal court, "must be dealt with by gay and non-gay society if we are to establish complete equality between our two communities."

Nothing, however, was as threatening to the legal status of homosexuals in America at the time as state laws labeling sodomy a crime. Such laws, which existed in every state before 1961, plainly made potential felons out of anyone engaging in gay sex. (Some states applied the laws to cover anal and oral sex among heterosexuals, as well.) Gay activists had a long list of legal inequities that they said conferred second-class status upon gays and lesbians, but decriminalization of their intimate acts seemed like a necessary first step on the way to addressing any of them. After all, laws codifying various combinations of genital contact defined being gay as a matter of conduct, not status. It was, in essence, a legislative translation of the widely held assumption that homosexuality was a social choice rather than a biological fact. This interpretation appeared to ensure that those who called themselves gay would never succeed in convincing federal courts that their sexuality entitled them to constitutional protections.

Abolishing bans on gay sex had become so central to the larger cause that when an informal advisory network of lawyers who worked on gay and lesbian issues first convened in the ACLU's New York offices, its members called themselves the Sodomy Roundtable. In 1982, an ACLU attorney in Georgia had identified Michael Hardwick—whose recent arrest for consensual, private gay sex looked like ideal conditions to interest federal courts in Georgia's law—as a promising test case, and the lawyers of the Sexual Privacy Project helped guide his appeals. As Hardwick waited for the U.S. Supreme Court to take up his case, the Roundtable was formalized as the Ad-Hoc Task Force to Challenge Sodomy Laws, under the quickly expanding umbrella of the Lambda Legal Defense and Education Fund, which was devoted to gay-rights litigation. With its existing network of affiliates in all states, the ACLU was prepared to expand into other areas of legal concern to the gay community. "Previously, the ACLU lacked a dedicated presence on this issue, and the interest in the area dissolved among the many issues ACLU was involved in," executive director Ira Glasser said in a November 1985 meeting. "This task force encouraged the ACLU to get a gay/lesbian rights project started—not a 'reform sodomy laws' project."

That spring, ACLU officials had invited their membership to help determine what its priorities should be. The group's biennial conference presented the one opportunity for its diffuse constituencies—an odd assemblage of idealistic activists and calculating, unsentimental litigators—to formally contribute to the national organization's direction. It was a relatively democratic process. Through a series of topical workshops, ACLU members could develop resolutions, which would be presented at the end of the multiday conference to a floor vote of all delegates. During the 1980s, the most fraught of these debates fell along the deep cleavage between the organization's civil-libertarian instincts and the institutional priorities of its lefty allies, who often partnered with the ACLU on issues concerning the status of minorities. Many of the resolutions presented to the 1985 conference, on the University of Colorado campus in Boulder, felt more like Democratic Party platform planks: opposition to American support for Nicaragua's Contra rebels, a purchasing policy for products with a union label, divestiture from South Africa in protest against apartheid. When such pet issues of the Reagan-era left landed at the ACLU, they usually had the effect of pitting constitutional absolutists against identity-politics liberals.

Within the gay-rights workshop, such philosophical quarrels were still a distant indulgence. When participants, both gay and straight, went around the room, none mentioned marriage in any way. They dwelled instead on concerns they said were more urgent in their communities: access to jobs and housing and the ability to identify publicly and not be stigmatized due to illness. Attendees had arrived at the workshop held in a student-union meeting room with only two resolutions ready to introduce. The first was to include AIDS as one of the diseases, along with polio and cancer, that the ACLU explicitly classified as a "physical disability" worthy of protection against discrimination. (AIDS was still so unfamiliar a civil-liberties issue that participants had to debate the medical terminology they'd use in the official resolution language.) Then participants turned to ACLU Policy #261, which had been passed at the 1975 conference and continued to define the scope of the group's interest in gay issues. The policy was, staff attorney Abby Rubenfeld explained, outdated in the way it seemed to imply sexuality was always a choice. An amendment that replaced its many mentions of "sexual preference" with "sexual orientation" would be a straightforward fix.

As those in the room began contesting the relative nuances of the two words, Rubenfeld ventured another way to bring the policy's diction up to date. "Might also want to make a change and not use the word 'homosexual' as the descriptive term," she said.

"There's more problems than that with Policy #261, while we're on that policy," interrupted David Waxse, a national board member from the Kansas City area assigned to chair the session. "Since that policy was adopted, ACLU—as often happens—got into another issue and adopted a contrary policy on arrest records. We now have one policy, 261, which says they shouldn't be open, and another one that says they should be open, so that's got to be resolved, too."

All of a sudden, by signaling that the vestigial document could be reconsidered in its entirety, Waxse invited an unscheduled surfacing of a decade's worth of concerns and grievances. Only a committee given a mandate for a complete overhaul, a representative of the San Francisco chapter argued, would have the time to rewrite policy in a way that took into account how thoroughly AIDS had insinuated itself into, and at times complicated, the gay-rights agenda. "I'm real antsy about discussing something like this in three minutes," she said.

Nonetheless, the workshop's assigned hour was winding down and its participants were already heading out the door. Waxse pushed the group to quickly commit to principles that could be sent to the conference floor for consideration that weekend. There was consensus via voice votes that the ACLU should refer no longer to "sexual preference" but "sexual orientation," and that it should classify AIDS as a physical disability worthy of constitutional protection. A committee should be given a year to update the overall policy "particularly in light of threats to civil liberties resulting from the response to AIDS." Also, the group agreed, gay families deserved legal respect.

By the time of the floor vote on Sunday, the minor revisions had morphed into a sweeping declaration. "The ACLU supports the legal recognition of gay and lesbian relationships," the proposed resolution read. "Such recognition is imperative for the complete legal equality of lesbians and gay men. To qualify gay and lesbian couples for the benefits and rights enjoyed by married persons, including the right to become foster parents, such legal recognition must include but not be limited to employee fringe benefits, insurance benefits, income tax benefits, visitation rights when one's partner is hospitalized, survivorship and other personal and economic rights."

On the conference floor there was fierce debate over apartheid and capital punishment, but the gay-rights resolutions coasted to passage. All found their way into the hundred-page "Report of the 1985 ACLU Biennial Conference" that would—after review by the ACLU's executive committee—be presented to the entire board. Unless specifically rejected by a vote of the national board, each would become official ACLU policy in eighteen months. That October, four months after the conference, the executive committee recommended the "sexual orientation" resolution for adoption, and—while sympathetic to the need to articulate its concern for AIDS—hesitated over whether the ACLU's policy on physical disabilities was the best place for it.

But the gay-families resolution posed significant problems. After all, as associate director Alan Reitman pointed out, everything in it was already ACLU policy except for the mention of marriage. On that point, it wasn't entirely clear what the policy change would be—the resolution had not even explicitly proposed allowing gays and lesbians to wed—and the amount of detail that followed only confused the objective. "The resolution mixes various subjects such as 'legal recognition' (marriage) with foster parenthood, spousal benefits and economic rights," Reitman wrote. "These need to be carefully delineated."

More than a year remained before the ACLU's national board would be forced to address the unfamiliar questions raised by the resolution, so Reitman recommended shunting the matter off first to the Equality Committee. There members could disentangle the various elements of the resolution and perhaps rewrite it so the board faced a less ambiguous proposal for a yes-or-no vote. Serious legal research would be necessary to understand the extent to which various forms of relationship status were connected to one another, and that would also help buy time as Reitman wrestled with a deeper doubt: whether there was even "a distinct civil liberties question in the right to marry."

4

....

Rolling the Dice

In the fall of 1985, associate director Alan Reitman tasked intern Sharon Soloff with researching the legal prospects for recognizing same-sex couples. With that assignment, the American Civil Liberties Union became the first major organization to seriously explore the question. Gay marriage had been the pursuit of lone plaintiffs, operating on their own initiative without a legal strategy or the institutional and financial backing necessary for what would ultimately require major constitutional litigation. What Soloff found submerged in the recesses of state and federal case law was not so much a living history of a legal idea but a time capsule from an earlier era of movement activism that *The Advocate* in 1970 described as a "gay-marriage boom."

Two months after Jack Baker and Michael McConnell applied for their license in Minnesota that year, a lesbian couple in Kentucky did the same thing, and sued the county clerk who rejected their application. Both circuit and appellate courts backed the clerk, declaring that "female persons are incapable of entering into a marriage as that term is defined according to common usage," as the appeals court summarized. It ruled that the "relationship proposed by them does not authorize issuance of a marriage license because what they proposed is not a marriage."

Not long after, a young Seattle couple living together in a gay commune followed their lead. Encouraged by a sympathetic state legislator who told them that Washington laws now defined marriage in gender-neutral terms as a contract between two people, Paul Barwick and John Singer sued the county auditor for unconstitutional discrimination. Two separate courts ruled otherwise, with the state appeals court justifying the exclusion of same-sex couples "based upon the state's recognition that our society as a whole views marriage as the appropriate and desirable forum for procreation and the rearing of children." Unable to afford to continue their appeals and lacking a broader legal strategy, Barwick and Singer abandoned their case, as Tracy Knight and Marjorie Jones had at the same stage in Kentucky.

Circumstances did not change much over the next decade. The legal rationales that led plaintiffs to demand equal marriage rights retained their constitutional merit, Soloff concluded, but courts relied on all the same justifications for rejecting them. "While many state statutes are silent on the issue, some states' statutes specifically prohibit marriage between persons of the same sex," she summarized in a memo delivered to the Equality Committee in February 1986. "No court has taken the position that the state prohibition of homosexual marriage is unconstitutional."

Did the ACLU really intend to fight for homosexual marriage? Soloff's research revealed that none of the gay groups that usually supported the ACLU had endorsed such a position, and judges scoffed at plaintiffs who suggested it. Even if successful, such a policy would in effect compel gays to marry in order to have their relationships recognized. What if the ACLU could work to secure for gays and lesbians some, if not all, of the most important rights and benefits accorded to straight couples? Would that be good enough?

When the committee met a week later, its members overwhelmingly found themselves in agreement with the spirit of the resolution the convention had passed that summer. But as soon as the ACLU began debating the question of same-sex marriage, there was plenty of ambivalence. Was a marriage license a privilege, distinct from the material and legal benefits that accompanied it, demanding equal access? Shouldn't civil libertarians, another ventured, be more concerned with stripping the state of its ability to confer favored status on couples rather than with reaffirming it? Wasn't the real issue not so much a matter of laws that were unfair to gay couples but to all single people?

This debate missed the point, said Adrienne Asch, a bioethicist who took the lead on disability-discrimination issues largely as a result of her own experience as a blind woman. The fact remained that if heterosexuals were given the choice and homosexuals weren't, it meant that gays were being denied their constitutional right to equal protection—precisely the type of discrimination that the ACLU existed to address.

When the matter came to a vote, twelve of the fourteen committee members present supported rewriting the first sentence of the resolution to make a straightforward declaration: "The ACLU supports the legal recognition of gay and lesbian marriage." As it explained the reasoning to the board, "the Committee thought that a statement clarifying the Biennial Conference resolution to mean gay and lesbian marriages would be a stronger and more preferable policy statement." The resolution still contained what committee members had taken to calling the "laundry list" of specific rights and benefits, which had been so hastily thrown together at the conference workshop. It was "necessarily incomplete" and even—in the cases of adoption and airfares, for instance—inaccurate, so the committee voted to strike the list altogether.

In October 1986, the national board of the ACLU passed the committee's redrawn resolution: "The ACLU supports the legal recognition of gay and lesbian marriage. Such recognition is imperative for the complete legal equality of lesbians and gay men and to qualify gay men and lesbian couples for all of the benefits, rights and responsibilities of married persons." The ACLU had become the first civil-rights organization in the United States to endorse gay-marriage rights as a matter of official policy. The *New York Times* devoted an article to the news, and a White House librarian contacted the ACLU to request a copy of the resolution.

But within the ACLU priorities remained the same. When attorney Bill Rubenstein of the ACLU's Gay and Lesbian Rights Project described "the most important single step forward in American law toward legal recognition of lesbian and gay relationships" in 1989, he was referring to the case he had just argued before a sympathetic New York state appeals court on behalf of Miguel Braschi, who for more than a decade had shared an apartment with his lover Leslie Blanchard, with the latter's name on the lease. After Blanchard died of AIDS, the couple's landlord moved to evict Braschi, who sued under New York City rent-control laws that allow a member of the tenant's immediate family to remain in the apartment. By a 4–2 vote, New York's Court of Appeals accepted Rubenstein's logic, with Judge Vito J. Titone writing that a "realistic, and certainly equally valid, view of a family includes two adult lifetime partners whose relationship is long-term and characterized by an emotional and financial commitment and interdependence."

Despite the momentousness of the decision, it would have little broader impact. Rubenstein had expressly chosen to argue to Titone that Braschi qualified merely as a "family member," without claiming that their relationship was a spousal equivalent. In so doing, Rubenstein had passed on the opportunity to mount a broader constitutional challenge to laws that had a discriminatory impact on gay couples. "People are being evicted from their apartments. This isn't a time to be rolling the dice for a bigger victory," says Rubenstein. "I think there was a consensus that we have a lot going on right now—and it might be counterproductive."

Rubenstein had no plans to push courts for parallel recognition in areas beyond the city's unusual housing laws. In fact, to the extent that Rubenstein could detect any political pressure within the gay community on the issue, it worked against formalizing the status of same-sex couples. Some of the most vexing opposition to a proposed municipal domestic-partnership law had come from gays and lesbians who feared that registering for benefits would allow city authorities to assemble a list of gay couples for a later, nefarious purpose. When Rubenstein, along with fellow ACLU attorney Matt Coles, presented their paper "Rights of Gays and Lesbians" at the 1989 biennial conference, there was no mention of challenging marriage laws. As an addendum, Rubenstein and Coles included a copy of the newly revised (and renumbered) Policy #264, which now declared that "the ACLU supports the legal recognition of gay and lesbian relationships." Yet in asking local affiliates to "look for the following types of cases," they said nothing about marriage. Instead, more modest cases along the lines of *Braschi*—where amorphous definitions like "family" or "spouse" could be contested with regard to specific benefits—were the priority. "The board would pass these policies," Rubenstein explains. "It was rare I would look at what the ACLU policy book said. I pretty much could do whatever I want."

The only thing that could force the ACLU's hand—or shake the consensus that had hardened among its allies—would be the unstudied gesture of a naïf in their midst, one unburdened with the math of trade-offs or the duty of long-term strategizing. "There were these single-shot people who are after publicity, and uniformly focused on one thing," Rubenstein says, with grudging awe. "You need gadflies to keep things alive."

One month before Bill Woods prepared to pull his marriage-office antics, a young male couple in Washington, DC, did something very similar. On November 13, Craig Dean and Robert Gill had requested a marriage license from the clerk of the superior court of the District of Columbia. At first the clerk obliged, marking Gill as the couple's bride, but eventually backtracked and denied their application. Less than two weeks later, the pair sued the district for a marriage license and $1.25 million in damages. Unlike the emerging Hawaii case, which was covered in Honolulu's two newspapers but never noticed elsewhere beyond a few sentences in *USA Today*'s roundup of state news, the Washington case immediately won international attention. On paper, *Dean v. DC* seemed like a well-engineered test case. Dean and Gill were a clean-cut, telegenic young couple, and Washington had one of the most liberal political cultures of any city in the country. Its Human Rights Act prohibited discrimination based on sexual orientation, and Mayor Marion Barry was celebrated nationwide as a gay-rights champion. In addition, recognizing gay marriage in the capital would, in a sense, give any American instant access to the institution: the District had no residency requirement for marriage applicants.

Yet anyone who looked more closely at the case could see how poorly conceived it was. Washington's liberalism rarely rose from street level: the legal system funneled immediately into federal courts, and Congress could rewrite its laws at their whim. In that respect, it was hard to imagine the District as a place that—even if a judge offered a near-term judicial victory—could sustain the win. Critics of the *Dean* case feared it would result in an unfriendly decision in federal court that would be cited elsewhere. "Better to establish a favorable precedent in other jurisdictions and then come back to the District," Lambda Legal executive director Tom Stoddard told the *Washington Post,* declaring "fervent support" for the couple's goals but bluntly dismissing their tactics as "shortsighted" and potentially self-defeating. "What happens to these two men will affect every other gay man and lesbian in the United States. They therefore have a responsibility to confer with their colleagues."

Stoddard's sniping was the most public scolding the plaintiffs received from those they expected would be allies. (Dean accused "people who call themselves activists and leaders" of "acting like a gay mafia to shut us out.") Most responded to *Dean v. DC* with pointed silence, reflecting a consensus among gay-rights activists and their organizations. Bringing a marriage case anywhere in the United States was not only hopeless at the moment, they believed, but would likely undermine other goals within closer reach.

5

....

Gay Mafia

In Hawaii in 1990, the ACLU sat back, apparently hoping that Bill Woods would lose interest in the marriage issue after he got his parade. When he arrived in the office of ACLU state director Vanessa Chong with three couples and a retinue of local media, there seemed to be one objective: to drag the organization into a news story against its will. Woods's actions convinced ACLU officials of his persistence, but also affirmed their impression of him as an impulsive, impatient pest without the discipline to effect meaningful social change. Woods's approach was not the meticulous building of test cases tied to long-term strategies that civil-rights lawyers had come to consider their particular métier. He had been so relentlessly unmethodical that those who theorized civil-liberties law had trouble imagining how it could possibly succeed. "Major constitutional litigation is more than a one-shot effort to knock out a law; when it is done well, it functions as an important public-education process, thus heightening the chances for political change even if the lawsuit fails," Bill Rubenstein and Nan Hunter, director of the ACLU's Gay and Lesbian Project in New York, wrote when Hawaii staff attorney Carl Varady contacted her about the marriage question. "We believe that the best method for securing those rights incorporates coordination with and respect for local community leaders who are involved in the same struggles."

Rubenstein explained to Varady that the question was not an altogether new one; in fact, the group once known as the Sodomy Roundtable, in which ACLU litigators participated, had established a working group on marriage to consider the issues involved in bringing such cases. The group had drafted a memo identifying ten questions that should be asked to judge the promise of a marriage case in a given state. It could also be read as a list of reasons why it would be crazy to bring a marriage case any-where in the United States in 1990. Rubenstein was about to depart for a semester teaching at Harvard Law School, and his response to Varady carried more of the academic's didacticism than the activist's thrill for the crusade. He provided Varady with the packet he would distribute to his Harvard students that included opinions from the Minnesota, Kentucky, and Washington State cases. "You will find, obviously, that none of these cases has an affirmative outcome," Rubenstein wrote.

Still, the decision about whether to take on the marriage issue ulti-mately rested with the Hawaii ACLU, a state affiliate deeply entangled in the local progressive community. Varady had internalized the national ACLU's ambivalence about acting "in a manner inconsistent with the opin-ion of a substantial number of gays and gay rights activists," as he sum-marized Hunter's advice.

Ten days after the three couples applied for marriage licenses, Hawaii attorney general Warren Price advised the health department that it was right not to have issued them. Both he and health director John Lewin said that even as there was no room for the state to recognize same-sex marriages, they would work with legislators to provide other support to gays and lesbians. For Lewin, the issue prompted "a lot of soul searching," as he put it, since "the trend among homosexuals is to form long-lasting relationships, which is better for themselves and society." Nonetheless he appeared happy to have the matter removed from his domain. "It's a legal issue, not a health issue," Lewin told the media upon receiving Price's opinion. "It's out of the department's hands and into the Legislature."

The couples, however, were intent on heading first to the courts. They had all received letters from Carl Varady declaring that he had plans to spend the holidays on the mainland but would like to meet after the new year to discuss the possibility of signing a retainer agreement. When they met, in the first week of 1991, each of the potential clients talked about their relationships—Joe and Pat excitedly related that they were days from their thirteenth anniversary as a couple—and why they wanted to be mar-ried. Yet it was evident that despite Varady's promises of goodwill he still had little enthusiasm for Woods's ideas about challenging the state's mar-riage laws. Varady was not forthcoming with offers of financial or legal sup-port. He repeatedly invoked the "process," informing Woods that because of Rubenstein's busy schedule and the need to formally present a case to the ACLU-Hawaii litigation committee, it would require at least another month until Varady could tell the couples whether the ACLU wanted to be involved in legal action on their behalf. Woods, frustrated by this languid pace, publicly accused the ACLU of "dragging its feet."

As the couples waited impatiently for Varady to follow up, ACLU staff in New York began working furiously to stave off a potential public-relations crisis over the group's standoff with Woods. On January 9, without any mention of the doomed negotiations under way in Hawaii, the ACLU National Headquarters issued a press release announcing a new push to encourage cities and states to enact domestic-partnership statutes. "Government's refusal to recognize the relationships of lesbians and gay men is one of the clearest examples of discrimination," Rubenstein said. "Changing these laws and winning recognition is among our highest priorities." Along with the statement, the group released a fourteen-page report identified as part of its Legislative Briefing Papers. The ACLU, which had never had such a series of publications, apparently invented the term as cover to become instantly active on an issue it had previously shirked. The suggestion that it was time to look to elected officials rather than appointed judges marked a rather provocative departure from the group's long-standing reliance on impact litigation as the primary channel for securing constitutional liberties. "We can no longer be confident of federal court victories," legal director Ira Glasser announced.

The message to Woods and the couples was that the ACLU was plainly uninterested in doing anything to challenge Hawaii's marriage laws. Furthermore, Chong publicly undercut Woods's arguments for the unique qualities of marriage by proposing that he pare back to a "domestic partnerships" compromise, which she suggested could be enacted through the overwhelmingly Democratic legislature. As ACLU officials dismissed their goals, the couples and Woods decided to seek out a lawyer of their own instead.

6

Making the Case

When Bill Woods arrived in Partington & Foley's twenty-fourth-floor
law suite looking for an ally ready to challenge Hawaii's conception
of marriage, he wasn't so much delivering Dan Foley a case as much as six
plaintiffs in search of one. At first glance, Foley's office may as well have
been a shrine to the traditional nuclear family. The walls were covered
with pictures of his wife and two young children. But the bookshelves
attested to Foley's bent for imagining social change. "I had never thought
of marriage as anything other than a man and a woman, just like everybody
else," he later said. "But I felt, well, being married, having children, having
the rights and benefits of marriage, who am I to say no to them?"

A few days after his first meeting with the civil-rights lawyer, Woods
typed up three identical letters of one sentence each: "Ninia Baehr and
Genora Dancel hereby rescind our request for ACLU-Hawaii help in our
seeking legal Gay marriage in Hawaii." On February 1, the two women
signed it. "We got the sense that the ACLU lawyer we met with didn't seem
to think we had a chance," Baehr later explained.

Foley did. He was already becoming known around Honolulu as a lawyer drawn to unpopular, even unimaginable, causes. His path to the law
was itself untraditional. As a young University of San Francisco graduate
with experience in antiwar activism and an interest in cultural anthro-
pology, he had joined the Peace Corps and was assigned to serve as an
agricultural-extension officer in Lesotho. Observing firsthand how a weak
constitution hobbled the young country, Foley gained a new appreciation
for the rule of law. He returned to the Bay Area for law school and, revering the Warren Court and its success using the Constitution as a driver of
social change, joined a Marin County firm led by a partner who had been
active in the civil-rights movement.

His sympathies often turned specifically west across the Pacific. He had first visited Hawaii as a child, when he came to see an aunt who had moved to the islands and married a native Hawaiian man. Foley was struck by how the indigenous population had found itself disempowered upon statehood, their language and culture relegated by an ascendant political class of relocated outsiders. When he learned of an opportunity to head to Micronesia just as the series of islands were securing their sovereignty from the United States, Foley quit his firm—"to help them avoid the Hawaiians' fate," as he later put it There was little of a local legal establishment, and so the young American lawyer became a trusted adviser to the nations' first leaders, helping draft the countries' constitutions. As a result, Foley became perhaps Micronesia's leading expert on parliamentary procedure, island-hopping from one legislature to the next, teaching freedom-fighters to become lawmakers.

After seven years in the western Pacific, Foley moved to Honolulu to become the first staff attorney of the ACLU of Hawaii. The state chapter didn't have a lawyer in its headquarters—or even a single law book on its shelves—and its leadership feared that locating a qualified candidate, or raising enough money for that lawyer's salary, would prove impossible.

Foley, then single and renting, took the post out of a commitment to a pair of old causes: indigenous Hawaiian issues and confronting injustice. He did not aspire to be Clarence Darrow, bent on dramatic courtroom confrontations or public rabble-rousing, but instead left his greatest mark through more discreet influence. He won enough trust from elected officials that often the state legislature and city council used his language directly when making law, including the rules and regulations that eventually launched the Hawaii Civil Rights Commission. "I think many of my best accomplishments have been without litigation, without publicity," Foley said upon his 1987 departure from the ACLU.

By the time Bill Woods set out to hire an attorney to draft the gay-marriage lawsuit he hoped to bring against state authorities, Foley had moved into private practice. He had partnered with Earle Partington, a specialist in military and criminal law, largely out of economic exigency. Now with a mortgage and a wife pregnant with their second child, Foley felt compelled to take on more predictable, lucrative work from criminal defendants and personal-injury plaintiffs. But his passion remained with the types of clients he had served at the ACLU, and Partington & Foley represented just about the entirety of the Hawaii civil-rights bar. He and

Woods had often found themselves allied on cases of interest to the islands' gay community. In the most prominent, Foley successfully defended the Miss Gay Molokai Pageant after a local official, under pressure from religious conservatives, refused to grant a permit to the hula carnival and cited the potential spread of HIV to justify it.

Even as he made his living as a litigator, Foley maintained the affect of the cultural anthropologist. He wore a neatly cropped salt-and-pepper beard and round, thin-frame tortoiseshell glasses, and a high forehead that exposed thick lines when he concentrated. Like many Hawaii lawyers, he usually wore a suit and tie only when he had to appear in court; on days spent in his office, Foley was as likely to be found in an aloha shirt untucked over jeans. Yet for Foley, modesty and humility weren't merely aesthetic preferences. Raised Catholic and educated by Jesuits, he converted to Buddhism upon marriage to a Japanese-Chinese-Hawaiian woman and he saw diversity as central to the island temperament. "There's no dominant group, religion, race or culture," Foley said of Hawaii. "It breeds tolerance. On the mainland, it's clear who's in control."

He became an adherent of the Soka Gakkai, a denomination derived from thirteenth-century Japan whose practice included a daily thirty-minute morning chant that Foley typically performed before dawn. Foley was impressed by the Soka Gakkai because it had been one of the few Buddhist sects to reject Japan's turn to militarism in the 1930s, opposing the war and Hirohito's efforts to co-opt Shintoism in its service. Soka Gakkai lay leaders went to prison for defying the emperor in the name of pacifism. Foley kept Buddhist prayer beads in his desk for moments when he felt overwhelmed, tangible reminders of a faith that brought him both peace and political inspiration. "A major teaching is that we must challenge and surmount those things that might seem to be impossible," he said.

Now it was Hawaii's marriage code that presented Foley his most immediate obstacle. On April 12, 1991, each of the three couples received a formal notice that the health department would not recognize same-sex unions. The letter from state registrar Alvin T. Onaka cited chapter 572 of the Hawaii Revised Statutes, the same part of the code whose ambiguity about questions of gender emboldened Woods in the first place. "In view of the foregoing, we decline to issue a license for your marriage to one another forming a valid marriage contract," Onaka wrote them all in identical letters. "Even if we did issue a marriage license to you, it would not be a valid marriage under Hawaiian law." The couples visited

Foley and committed themselves to a long fight. "We're not happy with the way the state is interpreting the law," Joe Melillo said. "We want to do it legally—the right way."

Already, though, their lives were changing. Despite Genora's best efforts to evade cameras, her parents had seen her on the local news the night she and Ninia had applied for their marriage license, forcing her to explain the relationship and the rarely discussed matter of her sexuality. They did not raise the topic again. The family Genora was hoping to join was more effusive in its acknowledgment of the news. When she arrived at the PBS station for her shift the next day, Ninia's mother was waiting for her in the lobby. "Walk with me," C.J. said. "We're going to meet people." C.J. chaperoned her around her own workplace, reintroducing her to colleagues as Genora, the woman planning to marry her daughter. "If you have anything to say to anybody," C.J. warned them, "you say it right now."

The social taboos that persisted around gay couples resembled the ones that had long justified antimiscegenation laws, and those who had considered strategies to legalize same-sex marriages often found themselves drawn to the example of *Loving v. Virginia*. The unanimous 1967 decision overturned state laws forbidding interracial marriages, on the grounds that such bans served no function other than racial discrimination. "Marriage is one of the 'basic civil rights of man,' fundamental to our very existence and survival," Chief Justice Earl Warren wrote in his opinion. "Under our Constitution, the freedom to marry, or not marry, a person of another race resides with the individual and cannot be infringed by the State."

Foley may have come of age revering Warren's progressive jurisprudence, but he no longer counted the Supreme Court as a welcoming venue for civil-rights litigation. Indeed, after a decade's worth of appointments by Republican presidents, the federal bench bore a newly conservative finish and had proven itself particularly hostile to sexual minorities. In 1986, the Supreme Court upheld an 1816 Georgia statute that effectively forbade nonreproductive sex after Atlanta prosecutors charged two men whom police stumbled upon together in a closed apartment. Five justices ruled in *Bowers v. Hardwick* that the guarantee of privacy—which the court had acknowledged two decades earlier when it struck down bans on the use of contraceptives—did not extend to all consensual intimacy, and that states could judge which acts they considered acceptable. "There is no such thing as a fundamental right to commit homosexual sodomy," Justice Lewis Powell argued in a concurring opinion that approvingly cited "Judeo-Christian moral and ethical standards" and the Roman penal code. "To hold that the act of homosexual sodomy is somehow protected as a fundamental right would be to cast aside millennia of moral teaching."

Just five years after *Bowers v. Hardwick,* Foley reasoned, gay marriage would be an automatic loser if the matter found its way into federal courts. Instead, he schemed to develop a case that would rely solely on interpretation of state law. In that regard, Foley understood what a useful ally Hawaii's constitution would prove to be: the state was one of only five in the country that explicitly defines a right to privacy. Looking to the language that the U.S. Supreme Court used in its decisions on contraception and abortion rights, Hawaii's 1978 Constitutional Convention pledged in its first article that "the right of the people to privacy is recognized and shall not be infringed without the showing of a compelling state interest."

It would become Foley's good fortune to be given clients whose grievance was with Hawaii authorities, and to shape a strategy around their objectives. Both the *Loving v. Virginia* and *Bowers v. Hardwick* cases had made their way to the Supreme Court in large part because the ACLU had chosen to back them in a quest to undermine local laws it considered vulnerable to a challenge. Foley's agenda was not to have federal courts rewrite the laws of all states, but rather to prove merely that the newest of them had failed to live up to the specific promises it had made to its citizens. Hawaii's constitution already guaranteed all couples the right to marry on equal terms, Foley planned to argue, and a state court could compel the health department to adjust its policy as a result. To quantify the damage his clients experienced through denial of those rights, Foley and one of his law students went page by page through Hawaii's legal books to document each of the more than four hundred benefits accorded uniquely to married couples under state law. They evoked nearly the full range of individual interactions with government, from a spousal privilege for confidential communications to a lower fee for hunting licenses.

Before deciding whether to commit to a major case, Foley always participated in a Buddhist chanting ceremony, part of which involved offering a prayer to dead friends and relatives. As he did, he visualized his uncle, who opened a gay bar in Sausalito, California, after police harassment drove him out of San Francisco. His homosexuality was known to family members but pointedly ignored by them. It was "the pain of tortured silence that so sapped my uncle's spirit," Foley finally concluded. "He was brilliant and talented but he wasted a lot of his potential because he was forced to live in the closet. He never was able to overcome the intense prejudice against homosexuals, and he died without fulfilling his promise," he said. "Buddhism asks us to do everything we can to help others reach their highest potential. We did not do that in my family with my uncle, and I felt bad about that. After chanting about the issue, and talking with my wife, I decided to take the case as a memorial to my uncle."

From that point onward, Foley was so committed to the project that he docked $25 from his normal hourly fee for the case. He prepared a proposal for what he called "the Gay Marriage Project," estimating that his bill could reach $20,000 to introduce the case in a state trial court and follow it through a potential outcome in the Hawaii Supreme Court. Foley's goal was to get the matter in front of those state judges who could rule conclusively on the constitutional questions as quickly as possible. Regardless of which side won there, the case could never be appealed to the United States Supreme Court because there was no federal issue at stake, but Foley still knew he was embarking on a case whose ramifications could be felt far beyond the islands.

"Should we prevail on these issues before our State Supreme Court, there is no question our victory would be nationally recognized and be used by gays and other disenfranchise [sic] groups throughout the United States in combatting discrimination," Foley wrote in a memo to Woods. "Needless to say, our case is more than a gay rights case. It is a human rights case."

Baehr v. Lewin

S hortly after courts opened for business on the morning of May 1, a five-
page document arrived at the First Circuit Court in Honolulu. It was a
lawsuit against the state of Hawaii, demanding injunctive and declaratory
relief on behalf of those who had been unfairly denied marriage licenses
"solely on the ground that" they wanted to wed someone "of the same
sex." An ambitious civil-rights case announced itself as a series of personalized slights: *Ninia Baehr, Genora Dancel, Tammy Rodrigues, Antoinette Pregil,
Pat Lagon, Joseph Melillo v. John C. Lewin, in his official capacity as Director of
the Department of Health, State of Hawaii.*

Dan Foley was aware that the case he had just filed would become
known in shorthand as *Baehr v. Lewin*. All the information he had about
his clients' backgrounds had come from small talk at their first meeting,
and he had specifically avoided any reference to their biographies in the
filing so as to avoid making those facts part of the record of the case that
moved up to a higher court. But Foley knew enough to know he wanted
Ninia Baehr to be the face of the suit. In his limited experience dealing
with gay-rights issues, Foley had become convinced that lesbians tended
to get a more sympathetic reception from heterosexuals than gay men did.
The more established of the two female couples was reluctant to get any
more attention than they had already received by merely attaching their
names to the suit; Toni and Tammy had a child, and they did not want to
subject her to public scrutiny.

Even in Foley's first meeting with the couples and Woods, it became
clear that, among the women, Ninia was the only one ready to be a spokesperson for the case. Her history of involvement in feminist causes made
her confident about dealing with the media, and she found the transition to
agitating for marriage a natural one. "A lot of my work has to do with our

ability to control our own bodies, and by extension or own lives," she says. "And that means freedom from child sexual assault and rape, that means reproductive rights, it means being able to sleep with who you want to and not sleep with who you don't want to."

Ninia became by far the most active of the plaintiffs, often consulting alone with Foley about strategy and taking the initiative in paying off the portion of legal costs for which she and Genora were responsible. Ninia had worked within the nonprofit world, so she set out writing grant applications to win financial support. When the money did not come in as briskly as hoped, she and Genora staged fundraisers in local gay bars and at Imperial Court drag shows. The month after the suit was first filed, it was Ninia and Genora who mounted the back of a convertible with C.J. Baehr under a "Mother of the Bride" banner, handing out flowers to spectators lining the gay-pride parade route.

Even the more introverted Genora was growing more comfortable with the burden of becoming a public figure. Not long after the couples had begun their legal process, Woods asked Genora if she could fulfill a request he had received from a local school to have someone discuss gay issues in front of students. Soon she was appearing at local high schools monthly, talking about the case and quest for marriage in addition to broader appeals for acceptance. She would start all her speeches the same way. "Does anyone know anybody who's gay?" Genora would ask, anticipating (usually correctly) that no hands would rise. "If you don't know anyone who's gay," she went on, "I'm the person."

At each other's side, Ninia and Genora were a striking illustration of what it meant to be a lesbian in Hawaii. Genora's hazel skin and strong features, a fiercely cut jaw and obsidian hair, attested to her Pacific roots, while Ninia's delicate features and pale complexion marked her immediately as *haole,* the old Hawaiian term for a Caucasian not native to the islands. Together they represented an archetype encouragingly familiar to those who had worked, often in vain, to mobilize locals to take an interest in political action. "People involved in gay activism tend to be gay people from the mainland who have partners from here," says Jo-Ann Adams, who became active as a citizen lobbyist on state issues.

On September 3, Ninia and Genora watched as Foley stepped into court for the first time to argue for marriage. When *Baehr v. Lewin* had been filed in May, the attorney general had asked the trial court to dismiss it. Foley, however, won a hearing before trial-court judge Robert Klein in his cozy courtroom on the top floor of Ka'ahumanu Hale, the brutalist concrete edifice that housed Oahu's trial courts. "This will be a turning point in Hawaii for gay rights," Foley declared that day. "Regardless of how the judge rules, it will create awareness." He was pretty confident, though, that he knew how Klein would rule, and that it didn't really much matter. After all, Foley expected the loser to appeal regardless of how things turned out. For that reason, he had from the outset delivered an intentionally thin brief for such a potentially weighty matter, specifically avoiding any discussion of the facts of the case. Foley had a simple objective: to build a trial record a higher court could rely on when adjudicating an appeal that would fully engage the questions of Hawaiian constitutional interpretation on which the suit rested.

Foley's brief worked many angles. It argued that the state's assurance of a right to privacy should keep it out of his clients' intimate affairs, and that his clients had seen their rights abridged without due process. Furthermore, as members of a persecuted minority they had been denied the equal-protection guarantees found in a provision of Hawaii's Constitution written to echo what the U.S. Constitution's Fourteenth Amendment said states owed their citizens. These were standard arrows in the quiver of anyone setting aim at a civil-rights target, but they had never before hit their mark on behalf of same-sex relationships. In his quest for citations, Foley could not quote opinions of the court that became made law but looked instead to the sparse body of work he thought gave gay citizens their due. He plucked from Justice Harry Blackmun's dissenting opinion in the *Bowers v. Hardwick* case, a bit of reasoning Foley believed might resonate with Hawaii's justices since the state had set in stark type the guarantee of privacy where the Supreme Court had acknowledged only its shadow.

Foley also mined a more recent concurring opinion by federal appeals court judge William Norris in *Watkins v. United States Army,* the first instance of a soldier successfully challenging the military ban on gay service. The case had been decided by the Ninth Circuit in Perry J. Watkins's favor on process grounds, because the Army had effectively reneged on its promises to its former soldier. While Norris agreed with that ruling, he issued a separate opinion alongside to argue that Watkins was entitled to a more sweeping judgment. Norris argued that homosexuals should be included among the so-called enumerated classes, such as blacks, Catholics, and Chinese Americans, whose equal-protection claims are most vigorously policed by courts. By applying such "strict scrutiny" to public policies with an uneven impact, judges force the government to justify the reason for its discrimination, thereby advantaging plaintiffs like Watkins. When, in

1990, the Supreme Court let the appeals court's decision stand, it accepted the process rationale and ignored the equal-protection logic of Norris's concurrence. It joined Blackmun's dissent in a lean corpus of legal writings that had earned Foley's admiration but not the weight of law, a valiant rhetoric of lost causes that he brought into court on behalf of the couples.

Foley's antagonist would be Sonia Faust, a deputy in the trial division. In Hawaii, unlike many states, the attorney general is appointed by the governor rather than being an independently elected post. Although the office typically operated autonomously when it came to trial strategy and tactics, that structure could also leave it unusually sensitive to external politics. Faust's boss, Attorney General Warren Price, had been appointed by Governor John Waihee, a relatively liberal Democrat who had been friendly to the gay community, including providing aggressive support for programs fighting AIDS. In March 1991, Waihee had signed Act 2, which made Hawaii only the third state to explicitly ban antigay discrimination in employment. Reporters for the two Honolulu newspapers were in the courtroom, and as soon as the judge gaveled the proceedings to order, just past 10:30 a.m., Faust addressed the bench but appeared to be speaking to the world outside. "Nothing we will say in this case is intended in any way to minimalize plaintiffs or their rights or the relationships they are in or hoping to form," she said. Nestled within the apparent debate over the rapport between government and social tradition and sexuality, Faust claimed, was little more than a matter of bite-size jurisprudence. "This case really asks just one question," she said, "and that question is whether the constitution of Hawaii requires the state to issue licenses of gay marriages."

Judge Klein murmured his understanding, and Faust accepted it as an invitation to work her way through each of Foley's arguments. The inclusion of privacy in Hawaii's constitution, she asserted, described a right to be left alone but did not mandate that government validate equally all private behavior. "There is a very real difference between state interference with protected activity and state encouragement of an activity," Faust said. The equal-protection claim was specious, she said, because marriage by its essential nature required a man and a woman to be present. "The question is," Faust posited, "is the definition of marriage itself a denial of due—of equal protection?" She stepped back to explain why, even if Foley managed to convince the judge that gays were worthy of equal constitutional protections, the state would still have an interest in maintaining a marriage statute that excluded them. "Marriage is unique and has a special place in our society," Faust said. Rewriting the laws around it was a job for the legislature, she intimated, not the obligation of a judge. "The issue is whether this very moment the constitution of Hawaii requires the judicial rewriting of the definition of marriage to include homosexual relationships," Faust said. "State submits that it—the constitution doesn't contain that requirement, Your Honor."

Klein drew Faust back to a point that she had dodged in her presentation. Why, he asked, should gays and lesbians not be defined as a "suspect class" worthy of special protection under the constitution? Faust explained that there was federal precedent that specifically protected individuals against discrimination on the basis of their race, sex, and national origin, but that the U.S. Supreme Court had never said anything about sexual orientation.

But, Klein persisted, Foley's brief had cited *Watkins v. United States Army,* the federal case that reviewed the government's ban on military service by gays and lesbians. In his concurrence in that case, Norris had tried effectively to reverse engineer a formula for coverage as a suspect class, distilling the underlying attributes that courts had accepted: that the members of the class shared a history of oppression, that they were now politically powerless, and that the discrimination they faced was a matter of "gross unfairness," an ambiguous concept that usually became self-evident when people were victimized because of an immutable characteristic. Norris's suggestion was that gays and lesbians qualified under that test, even if his colleagues—and the justices of the U.S. Supreme Court—had never directly engaged with the question. But Foley had included it as a framework for a judge to work through these issues, and now Klein had showed himself at least open to considering it.

Faust fixated on two of the areas where she thought gays were most likely to flunk the *Watkins* standard: the attributes of immutability and political power. The science, she argued, was by no means unanimous in either direction on the question of whether homosexuality is something that people are inescapably born into or a behavior that can be learned and unlearned. On the matter of political power, Faust argued, there was strong evidence that gays should not be seen as an impotent minority. The very passage and enactment earlier that year of Act 2, by large margins in the Hawaii legislature, demonstrated that gays and lesbians were not shut out from the ability to rewrite laws in their favor. "Maybe more needs to be done in the area of homosexual rights," Faust conceded, "but I'm feeling very confident that there is political power, their new people have been working very hard at it and they will succeed."

When Foley approached the bench, Klein pressed him on the same points. Could he prove that homosexuality was a biologically immutable trait, and that the people who had it were so politically powerless that courts were obliged to step in and rewrite laws on their behalf? Foley had specifically dodged these details in his narrowly drawn brief; if Klein was serious about investigating them, it would mean the judge had effectively accepted the plaintiffs' premise that they had presented him with a civil-rights case. The judge, then, would be forced to deny the motion to dismiss and delve more deeply into its claims. "If there's a factual question," Foley told Klein, "and if there is a dispute on that, if it's something the court needs to explore, then the defendant's motion should be denied and that matter can be explored at a future hearing."

After the lawyer had answered all his questions, Klein offered a quick assessment of the case Foley had presented him, with its varied theories for why Hawaii should be obliged to extend the same marital rights and privileges to his clients that it had for decades to opposite-sex couples. He made it clear that he did not think much of the notions Foley had presented that his clients had been victims of sex discrimination or denied their constitutional right to privacy. "I think the far better argument," Klein explained, "would be the argument under the equal protection argument. And that—that obviously, to me, centers around whether or not homo-sexual constitutes a suspect class and whether it's a compelling interest for this law to stand as it is.

"And I must admit to you I'm not ready to rule on that at the present time because there is a lot more room for . . ." Klein went on, stammering momentarily, "for thought. And I'm going to think about it."

A week later, Klein released his judgment, dismissing both the equal-protection and privacy arguments that Foley had put forward in court, and justified the existing opposite-sex marriage statute as "clearly a rational, legislative effort to advance the general welfare of the community." Klein methodically itemized reasons that gays did not qualify as a protected class: they were not a politically powerless minority, Hawaii's "history of tolerance for all people and their cultures" ensured they were not victims of systematic discrimination, and their sexuality was not an "immutable characteristic," like race or gender. "Citizens cannot expect government's policies to support their lifestyle or personal choices," Klein wrote.

But none of the material Klein cited to support one of those central assertions about gays—that they could choose not to be—had been raised in the courtroom the week prior. His claim rested largely on one study published by the Thomas Aquinas Psychological Clinic that asserted biology and heredity "do not seem to play a determining role in homosexuality." Its inclusion did not suggest wide-ranging research on Klein's part; that same study had been mentioned in a syndicated column that had run just days earlier in the *Honolulu Star-Bulletin,* to support the contention that nothing prevents gays from modifying their "ways of thinking and behavior," as conservative commentator Cal Thomas wrote. "He's faulting us for not proving that homosexuals are immutable when he never gave us a hearing," Foley complained. Still, though, Foley had never expected to prevail in Klein's courtroom and now had been given another angle of attack to pursue on appeal. In addition to the constitutional challenge on the grounds that excluding gays from marriage was discriminatory, he could mount a technical quarrel with the way the judge had reached his opinion in apparent violation of civil procedure.

Foley had one month to file a notice of appeal. He had barely been paid for any of his work on the case thus far, but had growing confidence that he was not likely to end up entirely on his own in the matter. After Foley was quoted in the *Honolulu Advertiser* announcing his intent to sue on behalf of three gay and lesbian couples demanding marriage licenses, he was contacted by David McEwan, a family-practice doctor who had detected the islands' first case of AIDS when it was still a mysterious epidemic. McEwan had first met Foley through his activism on behalf of HIV sufferers denied admission to nursing homes because of their condition, and now he volunteered to convene a small group of other gays and lesbians active in Oahu life so that they could hear about the marriage lawsuit directly from him. Already, McEwan was a believer in gay marriage. The previous year, McEwan had lost his boyfriend, Tom, to AIDS, and he responded by looking above and demanding of God the right to marry. "I always thought that marriage brought better health to people," says McEwan. "I thought it might have saved his life had we been married." Foley was known to local gay leaders, through cases he had handled both at the ACLU and in his private practice. If he really had launched a legal process that could spiral into a major constitutional contest, McEwan thought, Foley deserved support from the gay community; perhaps they should even launch a political action committee to back the suit's public objectives.

In late May, three weeks after Foley first filed the suit, McEwan summoned him to the home of Tom Humphreys, a University of Hawaii molecular scientist who had become wealthy by launching a private biotech firm that permitted him to be a benefactor of local progressive causes.

But McEwan's enthusiasm was not shared by others in attendance. Those who articulated unease about Foley's push for marriage were hesitant about the case because of the man who had put the matter in front of them. Robert Morris, one meeting organizer, specifically warned other participants beforehand not to spend their time personalizing grievances against Woods, yet few could help themselves. Most of those in attendance had clashed with him at some point. Those planning the meeting tried to keep Woods out of it: McEwan had made clear to Foley that he didn't want the activist present.

Even the man who had offered to host the meeting did not seem ready to back the cause. Humphreys was a member of the ACLU-Hawaii board and the group's most prominent liaison to the gay community, as the organization responded so warily to Woods's requests for legal assistance. "People are very reluctant to come forward with a case because cases have all been lost in the past," Humphreys had said, "and it's a long and tedious battle."

For most of 1991, the improvised coalition that had brought the case to that point was barely holding together. Woods's gadfly persistence, which had willed the legal process into existence, had begun to grate on his allies. Woods's highly personalized political entrepreneurship—"of the Bill, by the Bill, for the Bill," jokes McEwan—didn't stop when he set the marriage case rolling. He continued looking for new issues and projects, and retained his knack for drawing media coverage as he fought on other fronts: agitating for a boycott of the Boy Scouts for its ban on gay participants, and of the local United Way for its ties to the Scouts. Unlike Foley and McEwan, Woods had started the marriage project with plenty of enemies. His perpetual provocations succeeded only in creating new ones, both within the gay community and among those more naturally opposed to gay-rights initiatives, whose attention was being drawn to the litigation in large part because Woods had so visibly attached himself to it. A month after that first court appearance, Ninia and Genora resigned from the steering committee of Woods's Gay Marriage Project. "We prefer to speak for ourselves rather than have Bill Woods speak for us," Ninia wrote Foley.

With time, Woods's affiliation became a more serious liability. Just after Christmas, he stepped down as treasurer of the Hawaii AIDS Task Force, as the group undertook an audit of Woods's handling of its funds for personal use. It was a story broken by Woods's rival Cheryl Embry, the publisher of *Island Lifestyle*, who claimed that a confidential source had given her three checks that Woods had used to pay for carpentry work in his home. Because some of the money included government grants administered by the state health department, the scandal meant that Woods now found himself under investigation by Jack Lewin, the defendant in the marriage case.

The allegations appeared to validate concerns that the couples had about Woods's business practices. They saw Woods aggressively raising money around the marriage litigation, through his Gay and Lesbian Education Association, but those involved in the case noticed that it never seemed to go to pay off the bills that Foley & Partington tallied each month and sent to its clients. Foley's letters to Woods about the legal process were increasingly antsy about the matter of being paid. "The scandal just made it so we couldn't raise money and have him in any way attached to it," says Tom Ramsey, secretary-treasurer of the Hawaii Equal Rights Marriage Project. "And the couples realized that."

Woods denied the embezzlement charges and set out to fight them in court, but when his onetime collaborators insisted that he keep his distance, he reluctantly obliged. "I wish you and all the litigants well," Woods wrote Foley as he formally severed their ties. "See you at the Supreme Court."

A Chickenskin Moment

On October 13, 1992, Dan Foley awoke at four a.m. and began the morning with a Buddhist chanting ritual. Afterward Foley put on a white shirt, dark blue pinstriped suit, and a burgundy Christian Dior tie. Around 5:30, after resetting the alarm for his wife, Foley left the house, carrying the suit jacket and a briefcase, and traversed the dark, quiet Pali Highway toward downtown.

From the moment he met Ninia and Genora, Toni and Tammy, and Joe and Pat, Foley had anticipated the morning when he would end up pleading their case before the Supreme Court of Hawaii. Foley had appeared just a handful of times before the court, both as a lawyer for the ACLU and arguing his own cases challenging the state's pornography laws and asserting the right of community groups to put zoning issues on the ballot.

That summer he had marked September 25 in his agenda. But it was a much different court than Foley had seen when he had last appeared before it. A freakish series of actuarial events that summer—mandatory retirements, promotions, a death, and a recusal—had turned over a majority of the five seats, some more than once. Now only two normal sitting members remained, with a combined three years of high-court experience between them. Foley didn't know what that would mean for the case he was looking to make. He had little sense of the interplay between the justices, and no ability to project how the delicate backroom negotiations would play out as one side tried to win the requisite three votes to its camp.

As he considered how to present *Baehr v. Lewin* to an unfamiliar court, Foley decided to aim at the justice he knew best. Facing Steven Levinson was as close as Foley would ever come in a Hawaii appeals court to arguing a case before himself. Levinson had moved to Hawaii after law school to clerk for his uncle, Bernard Levinson, a well-regarded liberal former Hawaii Supreme Court judge, and afterward had joined an established firm whose clients were often corporate interests embroiled in civil matters. He and Foley had faced off years before in a trial over a controversial zoning issue at Sandy Beach, with Levinson representing the developer and Foley the aggrieved residents. When Foley's cocounsel tweaked the opposing attorney with an abrasive style, Foley pulled Levinson aside and said, reassuringly, "Don't talk to him, talk to me."

Now they would meet again in another courtroom, as two bearded forty-six-year-old children of the 1960s, both proud card-carrying members of the ACLU. (Levinson discreetly kept his membership active even while on the bench, in violation of ethics guidelines.) When, in September, Foley began scribbling notes for an opening statement on a yellow legal pad, he had Levinson in mind as his audience. He knew that if he was unable to persuade Levinson, he would be unlikely to win over any other justice. If he could get Levinson, then it would become the justice's job to bring over two of his colleagues to form a majority.

Now in an empty dark twenty-fourth-floor office, with the scattered lights from the Honolulu skyline behind him, Foley read the opening argument aloud, timing himself. After completing it twice, in each instance under twenty minutes, Foley sorted his papers in a stack, scooped up his beads, and turned his chair so that it was facing a back wall in the direction of his Kailua home. After closing his office door, Foley began another Buddhist chant and for an hour and a half thought only of the opening argument, focusing his will on the goal of carrying himself well and communicating clearly to the justices. At 8:15 a.m., he opened the door and found his office had begun to rattle with life. Foley believed he was ready but started to fidget and pace anxiously, before gathering his law partner, secretary, and the executive-search consultant who was the office's other tenant and setting off on the four-block walk to Aliiolani Hale, the nineteenth-century building that is home to the highest rungs of the Hawaiian judiciary.

A little before 8:45, Foley arrived at the courthouse's wooden front door and climbed two sets of steps to the floor belonging to the supreme court. On his way inside, Foley navigated a cluster of media massed in the hallway outside the chambers, larger than any he had seen before. Inside he spotted four of his clients, all but Toni and Tammy, along with Bill Woods, who had claimed a spot in the front row and appeared eager to make himself very visible. Foley's wife, mother, and mother-in-law had come to attend the hearing, and before moving to his place at the front of the courtroom Foley made sure they were all situated.

Foley assumed one of two seats at a table to the right of the podium facing the chief justice and set down the three briefs that had been filed in the case, his handwritten oral argument, and a yellow legal pad to take notes. On the opposite table were two deputy attorneys-general, Judy So and Sonia Faust, who were familiar foils to Foley in his suits against the state.

As the appellant, it was Foley's responsibility to go first. His first words at the podium were scripted to reorient the case to what Foley considered its natural scale. "This is not just a case about whether or not homosexual couples should be allowed to marry," he began. "This is a case about homosexuals, and their rights to privacy, equal protection, and due process under the Hawaii Constitution." Foley explained that his case asserted no federal claim, and that the justices would not once hear him invoke rights guaranteed by the United States Constitution. "Appellants concede that in a federal court of law," he went on, "they could not prevail."

The implication was clear. This was a civil-rights case whose consequences for an aggrieved minority group went well beyond the clause in the Hawaii statute that identified the qualifications for marriage. Foley's acknowledgment of weakness before federal courts was in fact its own solicitude to the vanities of the five men before him. No appeal of theirs could take *Baehr v. Lewin* into federal courts, and no judge would have to worry about the eventual indignity of seeing the Supreme Court reject his reasoning. Any three men on the bench were on the precipice of making law, of expanding rights for Hawaiians that could not be easily taken away. Foley was inviting his contemporaries on the bench to do something bold.

Foley had placed his handwritten script on the podium, but he had read through it aloud enough times that he was capable of delivering nearly all of it from memory. It didn't much matter, as Foley had barely finished his privacy-right argument and was moving into his equal-protection claim when he was interrupted by the man sitting directly in front of him. It was Chief Justice Ronald Moon, with questions about the lesser, procedural issue that was part of Foley's appeal: whether trial-court judge Robert Klein had overstepped his bounds by basing his opinion on assumptions about the science of homosexuality on evidence that had never been produced, or contested, in court.

Moon was so insistent on this line of inquiry that Foley intuited the acting chief justice might be seeking a politically palatable way of guiding his makeshift court of temps and fill-ins out of a difficult case. After all, if he could find three votes to rule just on the procedural questions, Moon could possibly send the case back to the lower court while ignoring the delicate issue of whether constitutional protections were relevant to gay relationships. Foley told Moon that there was no way a court could rule on whether suspect-class determination extended to gays and lesbians without an evidentiary hearing to explore the issues involved. "Also, I think, the most controversial area, whether or not sexual orientation is an immutable trait—there seems to be very little agreement on this. Whether or not it has a biological basis, a genetic basis, whether or not sexual orientation is the product of early environment and socialization," Foley said. "These things could not, as a matter of law, be decided. These are factual determinations."

When Justice Walter M. Heen assumed the role of Foley's antagonist, challenging the lawyer about whether the lower court's decision had truly encroached on any fundamental liberty—"the right to practice any sexual orientation"—Levinson politely interrupted and guided the conversation elsewhere. As Foley had hoped, Levinson seemed to be on his side, quietly ushering the lawyer onto a desired path with limited interference or delay. With Levinson's help, Foley steered his answers to cover most of the points he had drafted for his statement. When he finally found a lull in the questioning, Foley stopped and asked to reserve the rest of his time for rebuttal, turning back toward his seat as Faust rose from hers and approached the podium.

"I'd like to focus upon something that's very special about this case in my judgment," she said. "And that is the fact that the appellants are asserting that the Constitution of the State of Hawaii requires the State of Hawaii to issue them marriage licenses. There is no precedent for that kind of conclusion and you really can't get there terribly easily from *State v. Kam* to the requirement that the state issue a marriage license. If we look at . . ."

Faust was barely a minute into her oral argument when the justice sitting to her far left spoke for the first time that day. "Put it another way," James S. Burns said to her. "They want you not to discriminate against *them*."

"Our position is that we are not discriminating against them," she responded.

"Okay," Burns followed up. "A male and a female walk in and they're not married and they want a license; you give it to them. A male and a male walk in and want a license; you won't give it to them. You are discriminating against them."

"Our position," said Faust, "is that that is permissible discrimination."

"Well," Burns replied, "let's talk about that then."

"I'd like to," Faust accepted.

"That's precisely the point," Burns challenged her. "How is it permissible discrimination? You tell me; is it a fundamental right or a suspect class, or neither?"

"I believe it is neither," Faust said.

"Okay," Burns replied. "Is that a question of fact, or a question"—he pulled back a moment and reconsidered his words—"matter of law?"

"I believe it is a question of law," she responded.

"As a matter of law, we don't need to know any facts?" he pushed her. "We don't need to *know* any facts?"

Burns continued in this vein for another four minutes, relentlessly badgering Faust and at times sounding incredulous about the state's logic as he did so. "I read the brief," he said at one point. "I still don't understand what you're saying." Foley was taking notes, but looked up from his yellow legal pad to enjoy the sight of Faust wilting, as he put it, under pressure from both Burns and then Levinson, who returned to the procedural issues with the trial-court decision.

But for Foley, the important part of the exchange was Burns's first set of questions. As soon as the justice said "you are discriminating against them," Foley felt his skin shiver and harden—he was experiencing what Hawaiians refer to as a *chickenskin moment*. Foley had always assumed that the appeal would likely be decided on the procedural grounds where Moon had begun his questioning, with the supreme court reversing Klein's ruling without ever having to contend with the question of whether gays and lesbians were being denied a fundamental right. But to Foley's surprise, Burns seemed to have accepted that constitutional premise right away, and forcefully so. "This was the first time since I filed the complaint," the lawyer reflected later, "that I felt that my clients would be able to prevail on the merits."

As soon as Moon gaveled an end to the hearing and the court into recess, Foley heard a voice behind him: "Let me be the first to congratulate you." He turned to face Carl Varady, staff attorney of the ACLU. The group had filed an amicus brief to the supreme court on behalf of Foley's appeal in *Baehr v. Lewin,* and a week before the oral arguments had offered a token check for $1,000 to support it. Foley's gratitude was tempered by the memory of the point at which Varady's organization had refused entreaties to back his clients' case. The previous hour had given Foley confidence that gay and lesbian legal causes had a much more promising future than anyone, on any side of the issue, had been able to previously conceive. "I believe the '90s will be the decade of gay rights," Foley would say not long after. "What's going to happen is, if we prevail, other states will use our case to have similar victories . . . in their own high courts."

Shoals of Time

The five justices of the Supreme Court of Hawaii stepped down from their wooden rostrum and through a white door, taking their seats in the chief justice's conference room. Lawyers and spectators were still clearing out of the courtroom as the justices began to weigh in on what they had just heard. Moon went around and, as the justices said, counted noses—an early poll to sense where their instincts pointed them. If there were firm positions and clearly defined factions, revealing the contours of a majority and minority, the chief justice could assign colleagues the tasks of writing each opinion. If attitudes were more fluid, the poll would reveal where there was an opportunity for internal politicking to assemble a winning coalition—or guidance on how an opinion might have to be loosened or tightened to get there.

This was all the standard routine immediately after an oral argument, but the justices long knew *Baehr v. Lewin* was not merely one more appeal to the state's court of last resort. It had first appeared on the Hawaii Supreme Court's docket on August 6, when justices were handed their monthly calendar memo outlining the cases that would come before them. Justices never explained their reasons for taking a case, but *Baehr v. Lewin*'s path directly to the supreme court—where it was granted oral arguments instead of a decision based on written briefs alone—testified to the fact that they understood the magnitude of the issue they would be facing and the matters of law at stake.

As the justices retreated into their inner sanctum, the courtroom disgorged its crowd into the plaza in front of Aliiolani Hale. The building, its name Hawaiian for "House of the Heavenly King," had sheltered Hawaii's leaders when the islands were first a kingdom and then a republic. One of them, King Kamehameha V, had it constructed as part of a mid-nineteenth-century lawmaking binge, a working Renaissance Revival monument to the king's constitutional reforms. Since statehood, Aliiolani Hale had been home to Hawaii's judiciary, with a gold-plated statue of Kamehameha standing sentinel outside its doors, as though protecting his enduring legacy with an upright spear.

As *Baehr v. Lewin* arrived, the aura of permanence that surrounded Aliiolani Hale felt particularly at odds with the jarring, even destabilizing churn that was taking place within. Only one of the justices who heard *Baehr v. Lewin* had been part of the court when, in early 1991, Dan Foley had begun plotting a case that would inevitably rise to win its attention— and at that point Ronald Moon was still in his first year as an associate justice. The transformation had happened gradually, a run of procedural incidents that revealed themselves to the public in a series of one-page announcements. At the end of the 1992 term, two justices retired, with one deciding not to seek another ten-year term and the other effectively forced to step down after learning he was unlikely to be renominated. To replace them, the legislature approved the promotion of two younger trial-court justices, Robert Klein and Steven H. Levinson. On July 24, the chief justice, Herman Lum, recused himself from hearing the case, for reasons many around the court speculated were tied to the fact that he would retire within the year. When *Baehr v. Lewin* first appeared on the court's docket, Klein recused himself from hearing the appeal, since he had been the judge who ruled on the original trial-court decision. At the end of the month, Lum issued two assignments to substitute justices elsewhere in the state appeals-court system. He asked intermediate appeals-court judge Walter Heen, who had been a Honolulu city council chairman and state legislator before entering the judiciary, to fill Klein's seat, and Jimmy Burns, the chief judge of the same court and son of Hawaii's first governor, to replace Lum. Associate justice James H. Wakatsuki would serve as acting chief justice for *Baehr v. Lewin*. Then, on September 22, just days before the original hearing date, Wakatsuki died of liver failure. The court pushed *Baehr v. Lewin* onto its October docket, and Moon—who by now had served barely two years on the court—stepped up to serve as acting chief justice. He summoned back Yoshimi Hayashi, one of the two justices who had retired earlier in the year, to fill out the remaining months of Wakatsuki's term.

Only two normal sitting members remained, with a combined three years of high-court experience between them, but they had a long history together. It was in the first week Levinson was admitted to practice, in 1972, that he met Moon, and they had remained close since. When Levinson joined Moon at Aliiolani Hale, their friendship began to shape the internal politics of the court. Unlike the United States Supreme Court, where justices pass all their notes on opinions through written memos, Hawaii's judges would wander down the hall and discuss cases aloud. Moon and Levinson often found themselves in the other's office, puzzling through the details of a case or trying to navigate its logic.

That rapid turnover had also left something of a leadership void on the court, and Levinson—emboldened by his close relationship with the new chief—was eager to start filling it. (When Hayashi returned temporarily, he found that his old chambers had been filled by the rookie justice.) It was apparent to his colleagues that Levinson enjoyed writing majority opinions—his were, plainly, longer than what the court's justices typically produced—and from the moment *Baehr* arrived he had his eye on it.

Levinson had never given much thought to the constitutional issues surrounding gay rights. In fact, at his confirmation hearings before the state senate, Levinson had been asked by the chair of the judiciary committee: *What is your opinion of the equal protection of the laws for gay and lesbian people?* Levinson hadn't prepared for the question, which was not part of the typical battery of constitutional queries put to a nominee, and was taken aback to face it for the first time. As he considered it, the recognition of same-sex couples didn't enter his mind, but when months later the *Baehr* case came before the court, Levinson recalled the response he had blurted out before the committee: *I believe in the equal protection of the law to all people including gays and lesbians.*

Yet the *Baehr* case did not have to be about that. The state had argued that gays and lesbians were not entitled to marriage rights because they had never been recognized as an enumerated class in Hawaii courts. Levinson saw the civil-rights issues involved differently: the slight that counted did not concern sexuality, but rather gender. That approach put the plaintiffs' claim on stronger constitutional footing—since its founding, Hawaii had specifically prohibited sex discrimination in its equal-protection clause—and more directly matched the facts of the case, Levinson believed. The marriage-license applications the plaintiffs had completed, after all, never inquired about the sexual orientation of those hoping to wed each other. "They could have been theoretically heterosexual," he says. "That wasn't about sexual orientation."

This was the point that had been illustrated so orientation in oral arguments by the "a male and a male walk in and want a license" thought experiment that had flustered Sonia Faust, the deputy attorney general. What had surprised Levinson was the justice who had introduced the theme: Jimmy Burns, a Catholic from an old family of the Hawaii political establishment, did not have a radical's pedigree. When Burns cornered Faust on that point and then pursued it so vigorously—helping unwind her entire presentation—the outlines of a majority began to reveal themselves to Levinson. "That's when I knew we had Burns," he reflected after.

The other justices remained stone-faced during oral arguments, leaving Levinson little clue where they stood on the case. When the justices gathered in private afterward, Moon went around the table, asking each justice to pick a side. Burns confirmed Levinson's hunch: he supported the couples' appeal. Moon moved to Heen, who repeated the rationale that judges had used throughout the 1970s to preempt any serious consideration of gay marriage. *Where is the discrimination?* Heen asked. *Marriage is between a man and a woman.* Then Moon turned toward Hayashi, who had been quietest during oral arguments. "I'm a traditional kind of guy," he said, before gesturing at Heen. "I'm with him." To no one's surprise, Levinson announced he joined Burns in standing behind the plaintiffs.

As chief justice, Moon offered up his own view last. When he said he agreed that the plaintiffs had been unfairly denied marriage licenses, he became the third vote in their favor. The demographic divide around the table was clear: it was the three youngest justices—the acting chief justice was only fifty-two, Burns just a few years older—who were taking the side of the gay couples. All had come of age as lawyers amid the women's-liberation movements of the 1960s, and exhibited more imagination than their older colleagues on the broad application of civil-rights law related to gender. (Age was not the only attribute that made the court unusual: it was free of WASPs.) Without that unlikely series of summertime personnel moves, Levinson realized, it was incomprehensible that three such judges would be in the unlikely position to make constitutional law together. "I firmly believe that, if *Baehr* had come up for oral arguments one month before, it would have gone the other way," he says.

Despite his rank, Moon was far from an imperious figure as chief justice. He did not hoard the best opinions for himself, as was his right, and Levinson had not been bashful about expressing his desire to write this one. The justices would often wait as long as eight months to get around to actually drafting their opinions—putting off the most complicated ones for the longest time, to permit the inevitable haggling over footnotes—but Levinson sat down to work right away on *Baehr*. "It was pretty clear it was the most significant appeal I was going to be involved with," he says, "and I think everyone else saw its significance, too."

As Heen took command of the dissent, Burns volunteered to write his own concurring opinion. He agreed with Levinson and Moon that the circuit-court decision should be overturned because the state had discriminated on the basis of sex. But that led to a question that none of the other justices found relevant to the civil-rights issues: What did Hawaii's constitution really mean by *sex*? If it applied to all aspects that were biologically fated, Burns thought, didn't courts have to reckon with how exactly people became homosexual?

The science of sexual attraction was sparse and murky. As Burns was writing his opinion, National Cancer Institute researcher Dean Hamer announced that a study of patterns within and outside family groups was underway to gauge the role genetics played in determining an individual's sexual orientation. A little over a year earlier, Salk Institute neuroscientist Simon LeVay had made his own contribution to the limited body of evidence that homosexuality had a physiological basis. Autopsying the brains of forty-one cadavers, approximately half of them gay men and half heterosexual, LeVay observed a considerable difference in the structure of the hypothalamus. In each case, media coverage quickly placed the lab discoveries in a social and political context. "The issue of whether people become homosexuals because of 'nature or nurture' is one of the most controversial subjects scientists have confronted in recent years," Cox News asserted in a March 1993 article about Hamer's finding. Burns thought this debate deserved its day in court, as well. Before Hawaii could issue marriage licenses to gay couples, Burns argued in his concurrence, a judge should have to tackle the nature-versus-nurture dispute as a question of fact to be explored and assessed by a trial court.

Levinson considered Burns's commitment to collecting newspaper articles about these scientific discoveries to be an unnecessary diversion from the relevant civil-rights issues but did not much mind it. Burns's concurrence could not constrain the plaintiffs' victory, and because his was the only signature on the opinion it wouldn't bear any weight as precedent. Levinson's opinion was the one that would carry the day, and in a sense his take on the issue was the narrowest of the three judges voting with the majority. "Sometimes you have to suck it up and write the best rationale you can to keep your shaky coalition together," Levinson says.

None of the three believed that the supreme court was ready to declare, as Levinson wrote, "that a right to same-sex marriage is implicit in the concept of ordered liberty, and that neither liberty nor justice would exist if it were sacrificed." But they did agree that the circuit court had overstepped its bounds in dismissing the plaintiffs' complaint, particularly without inviting them to introduce facts that could demonstrate the existence of relevant discrimination. "We conclude that the circuit court's order runs aground on the shoals of the Hawaii Constitution's equal protection clause," Levinson wrote in the most vivid phrase of his opinion, plucked to evoke a topographical image made familiar to many Hawaii citizens by a history of their islands, *Shoal of Time.* "Accordingly, we vacate the circuit court's order and judgment and remand this matter to the circuit court for further proceedings consistent with this opinion."

When the opinion went public, it would mark the first time that any court on earth had acknowledged that a fundamental right to marriage could extend to gay couples. Under the strict-scrutiny standard that the state's courts applied to sex discrimination, if Hawaii authorities wanted to continue denying gays and lesbians marriage licenses, their lawyers would have to prove a "compelling state interest" behind the exclusion at a trial. "It would be pretty tough to meet," says Levinson. "At that point, I knew this wasn't the end."

All of a sudden, the tables had turned. In Hawaii, at least, the arguments for same-sex marriage—which had riven the gay community, its political strategists, and its legal theorists—were no longer of much interest to the court. The burden had shifted to the government to come up with a reason why gay marriage shouldn't exist.

Part Two

INVENTING A CONSTITUTIONAL CRISIS

(1996)

10

Wardle's Run

It would take three and a half years after the release of the Hawaii Supreme Court's opinion in *Baehr v. Lewin* on May 5, 1993, for the questions it raised about marriage to be addressed by a Honolulu trial court. During that period, the state's politicians wrestled spasmodically with what role, if any, they would have in shaping the menu of possible legal outcomes. The first out-of-state institution to recognize that those far-off deliberations had national implications was the Church of Jesus Christ of Latter-day Saints, thanks in large part to one legal scholar whose curiosities proved at times a leading indicator of his church's political priorities and at others a lagging indicator of its preoccupations.

On clear afternoons when the running paths were free of snow, Lynn Wardle would often lace up his sneakers and invite his boss to join him for a jog along the western ridge of the Wasatch Range. In only two miles, Wardle and dean Reese Hansen could get from their offices at Brigham Young University's law school to the ridge of Rock Canyon. It was just far enough to distance themselves from the intellectual seat of Mormonism and allow their concerns to recede as matters of faith and law and to reconstitute as personal worries.

On one run, Wardle mentioned to Hansen something he had read in a recent issue of *Family Law Quarterly:* the Supreme Court of Hawaii had ruled in favor of gay and lesbian couples who wanted to get married. Wardle's legal career had been devoted in large part to analyzing and challenging the way that liberal judges systematically undermined the institution of marriage, from allowing no-fault divorce to relaxing age restrictions. (Until the 1970s, when a widespread abolition of limits on minors' rights took hold, most states required individuals to be twenty-one to acquire a marriage license without parental consent.) Ending the heterosexual monopoly on marriage was notable for its novelty, but the rationale didn't shock Wardle; Hawaii's justices were just the latest to abuse the language of rights and freedoms to loosen standards that had for millennia safeguarded the traditional family. Wardle knew, faintly, the prehistory of gay-marriage litigation—the silly lawsuits and desultory appeals of the 1970s—but now something had changed. After twenty years, he explained to Hansen, gay activists might have found a court that was sympathetic to their farfetched claims.

"Why don't you write about that?" Hansen asked.

Wardle knew his dean's motives. Wardle's research interests had once been wide-ranging as he explored the "gap between law and moral order," a gap large enough to contain debates over assisted suicide and cable-television pornography. As abortion laws became the dominant preoccupation of social conservatives in the early 1980s, though, Wardle's writings on the subject—and his willingness to be useful to legislators and litigators—had pulled him into activism. After writing and speaking in defense of a constitutional amendment to supersede *Roe v. Wade,* Wardle was invited in 1982 to join the board of directors of the National Right to Life Committee. When Missouri legislators wanted to defend one of their laws restricting abortion rights, Wardle agreed to write the committee's amicus brief before the U.S. Supreme Court. (In its 1989 case *Webster v. Reproductive Health Services,* the court upheld the state law, the first constraint it had placed on the right to abortion proclaimed in *Roe.*) Abortion had, in many respects, made Wardle—barely forty at the time— one of the school's stars despite the fact that he had chosen to develop his expertise in family law, typically not among legal academia's most glamorous specialties. But it met the demands of the policymaking marketplace. While Wardle thrilled at the political influence that came with seeing his work used in legislative hearings and courtrooms, Hansen agonized over the cost associated with such a profile, especially when attached to such a contentious subject. "Don't get stuck on one issue," he would counsel Wardle. "He kind of thought I was doing too much on abortion," Wardle recalls. "Get out of that politically controversial area, be more scholarly, talk about arcane, obscure things rather than things that have direct political relevance."

When Wardle offhandedly mentioned the ruling that had piqued his interest, his fellow jogger suggested it would make a good subject for the professor's next law-review article. The matter in question was sufficiently obscure, presenting a nimble thinker the type of hypothetical scenario that lent itself to compelling legal scholarship but was unlikely to lure an author into activism. "At that time it wasn't even really a politically viable issue," Wardle recalls.

Indeed, for all Wardle spent his days mapping the assaults that homosexuals and friendly liberal judges planned to wage upon the American family, gay weddings had been beyond his capacity for legal or political inventiveness. Where in Lynn Wardle's understanding of gay culture, obsessing over aestheticized libertinage and trying to bend Western civilization in the direction of permissiveness, would the voluntary pursuit of monogamous commitment possibly fit in? Indeed, if only he had come up with it first, the notion of compelling gays into marriage—the sole structure that converts promiscuity from a moral offense into a legal one—sounded like something that would have made for a good Wardle law-review article.

Wardle believed in the power of law-review articles to argue the heretofore unarguable. In fact, he blamed one of the Supreme Court's worst decisions on the fact that justices had been forced to contend with a novel issue in an intellectual void. When the Supreme Court had heard arguments in 1971 on behalf of a constitutional right to abortion, there was little relevant scholarly literature to consult; in the years after the 1965 contraception case *Griswold v. Connecticut,* few legal academics had explored how that opinion's "right to privacy" might extend to other forms of birth control. "Thus, in *Roe v. Wade,* the Supreme Court unleashed a monstrous new principle without the benefit of mature scholarship seasoned by thorough discussion," Wardle wrote. Even as he welcomed criticism on the reasoning of the *Roe* decision, with time Wardle came to focus on what he considered the overwhelming productivity of those who accepted the ruling's legitimacy. It was that perilous inequity in the scholarly research being generated around abortion that inspired Wardle to throw himself so completely into the topic upon joining the BYU faculty in 1980.

Writings from his peers on the legal status of gay couples up until then were sparse. During the 1970s and 1980s, the limited legal scholarship on gay topics came from outsiders to legal academia: professors of political science, religion, and educational administration and, in one case, an Air Force captain. Same-sex marriage got little attention; before 1986, few articles appeared in prestigious law reviews. The most prominent among them to dignify the subject, the *Yale Law Journal,* had in 1980 ventured that the "zone of privacy" demarcated in *Griswold*'s majority opinion could extend to cover same-sex relationships. To the extent that the motley authors writing about same-sex marriage had anything in common, Wardle realized, it was not their job descriptions but their worldviews. Almost all the law-review articles he consulted seemed to be written by liberals.

As the volume of scholarship on the subject spiked in the 1990s, that disparity became even more pronounced. Wardle collected more than seventy-five articles, comments, and notes on same-sex marriage in law reviews since 1990, and only one of them was written by a skeptic of the idea. Wardle didn't blame gay lawyers for being first to the subject: they were the ones who stood to benefit most from a reinterpretation of existing laws. If he were gay and had a partner, he thought, he too probably would have rushed to publish an article in support of gay marriage. "The only people that are paying attention to the issue are the people it matters to," Wardle told himself. "Everyone else thought *that's bizarre* and didn't think it was realistic."

Wardle could not ascribe this imbalance, as he had in the case of the abortion literature, merely to a perpetual leftward tilt in legal academia. Conservative activists had tried to address such a bias during the 1980s by developing their own institutions, law schools, and think tanks that wouldn't reject religion but instead use it as the basis for research and arguments that could prevail in secular courtrooms. Wardle's dive into the work they produced on gay couples left him "not only unimpressed but angry." The traditionalist legal establishment was failing the movement, allowing pro-gay scholarship to carry the day not only in quantity but quality. The one anti-same-sex-marriage citation he did locate, a 1994 article in which Herbert Titus of Oral Roberts University Law School assessed whether the practice "violates any legal or moral order imposed on mankind by God or nature," particularly enraged Wardle. "It was essentially a scriptural tirade—just quoting Scriptures and 'this is evil,'" he says. "I thought, this isn't a law-review article. This isn't gonna persuade anyone who's not already a supporter of those values."

But even if same-sex marriages still seemed a preposterous notion, Hawaii showed how readily a court could accept the arguments that liberal lawyers presented for them. It had taken only three judges to leave Hawaii on the precipice of legalizing such relationships. The case had been remanded to a trial court, and to win there opponents of the Hawaii Supreme Court decision would need stronger material than the attorney general seemed to have presented on the appeal. And if his side lost in Hawaii, as Wardle realized was probably likely, other states would have to deal with the consequences. What would happen to same-sex couples who had been told by Hawaii authorities that they were married when they started traveling elsewhere?

That presaged a whole series of legal battles, some in states with judges just as secular and liberal as Hawaii's. If guardians of traditional marriage were going to win them, Wardle believed, they needed to devote the same intellectual rigor to challenging same-sex couplings as their opponents brought to the debate.

Wardle decided that his contribution would be a survey of the claims made for and against gay marriage, as a way of unmasking the weaknesses of those in favor. He would demonstrate why constitutional protections of privacy, due process, or equal protection did not compel courts to validate homosexual families in parallel to heterosexual ones. If the right really wanted to protect the traditional family, it couldn't accept that judges would arrive at these reasonable conclusions on their own. It had to take the prospect of same-sex marriage seriously—or at least respect the arguments made in its favor—enough to lodge serious objections. His article would map out those objections, complete with citations. State governments should be able to photocopy it for their attorneys and send them into court with everything necessary to persuade judges that they were within their rights to stick to marriage as it was traditionally understood.

But first Wardle would have to persuade the law students in his midst. Instead of sending the article to one of the more prestigious journals in which he aspired to be published, Wardle delivered it to the *Brigham Young University Law Review*. He did so out of a responsibility to the institution where he had built his career but did not feel that fellowship reciprocated. When he received his article back, Wardle found that the student editors had "just demolished it," cutting it by one-third. The nature of the cuts made it apparent to him that those changes had been made with a political agenda. "They decided that they should make it more toned down, or moderate," he says. "They wanted it to take a different position." The editors, Wardle was convinced, were a familiar archetype: Mormons aggressively bent on "trying to disassociate themselves, and the church, and institutions like BYU, from what they perceive as sort of a stereotypical Mormon—i.e., conservative, you know, wears a tie." Wardle refused to let them. He spent the weekend putting back everything the editors had removed and returned it to them with an ultimatum: "You either publish it this way or I'm pulling the article."

The professor ultimately prevailed over the students, but he resented the struggle it had taken to get his article in print. Wardle even entertained regrets about not offering it first to a journal unaffiliated with a religious institution, where it could be expected to land with more of an immediate impact. Ultimately there was only one thing he wanted to accomplish with "A Critical Analysis of Constitutional Claims for Same-Sex Marriage." Before he could try to persuade liberal judges, Wardle needed to shake right-thinking people out of their complacency, and he wanted to do so before the Hawaii case went back before a judge.

Dominos at the Barn Door

When the marriage question did return to a Hawaii courtroom, it would take the form of a full trial, in which the attorney general would have to persuade a judge that excluding gays and lesbians should pass muster under the state constitution as what one of his deputies had described as "permissible discrimination," a fairly difficult standard to meet. The likeliest outcome of the proceedings, Lynn Wardle had concluded from his vantage point in Utah, was that the state would fail to meet the high standard set by the Hawaii Supreme Court. If the plaintiffs prevailed at trial, the department of health would presumably be forced to immediately grant them marriage licenses. "It would be a huge victory—and the gays were plainly presenting it in that light. I remember reading one article that said if Hawaii legalizes same-sex marriage, one of the islands is likely to sink below the waves because of the number of gay couples that are gonna come here to get married," says Wardle. "My concern was that this is sort of opening the barn door. And you're gonna have a domino effect."

Wardle decided to take his own initiative to insulate his home state from becoming the next domino to fall. He contacted his state representative and suggested a small bit of noncontroversial legislation. Three sentences amending the state code was all it would take to ensure that Hawaii's same-sex marriages—or those of any other state audacious enough to redefine it as anything other than one man and one woman—held no currency in Utah. When asked by a local newspaper whether he had drafted the legislation at the behest of LDS leadership, Wardle insisted he had not. "This is Lynn Wardle the Lone Ranger acting here," he said. "I've talked to no one in the church about this—period."

Wardle understood there was no reason for the church to "spend its political coin," as he later explained it, on winning an easy vote in a state where 80 percent of legislators were Mormon and would share his skepticism about gay rights. In Hawaii, however, the church had few if any allies in positions of power. As a result, the dynamics were inverted. There, Mormons would have to spend heavily to influence the political process and would have little credibility as a messenger.

During the first two years the *Baehr* case moved through Hawaii courts, it had been the job of the plaintiffs to argue that the existing law was unconstitutional; bureaucrats defending the state's interpretation of its marriage statutes hadn't needed much of a legal strategy. But the supreme court's ruling had immediately shifted the burden to the attorney general's office, and as early as December 1993, its lawyers began listing the claims it might make at trial to satisfy the supreme court's requirement that defendants assert a "compelling state interest" in restricting marriage to opposite-sex couples. In pretrial statements, a smattering of them were posited: that Hawaii authorities had a stake in ensuring its legal relationships were recognized in other jurisdictions, that the state had an interest in furthering procreation within marriage, that heterosexual marriages were better for children, that the islands' tourist economy could suffer if Hawaii became Lake Tahoe for gay and lesbian couples.

Wardle despaired. He didn't expect the state to make all the arguments he considered as he worked on his law-review article, but he noted that it seemed to have picked the weakest ones available. Just as its lawyers had done in the first trial hearing, and then before the supreme court, the attorney general's office avoided any claim that hinted at disapproval of homosexuality. It had never explicitly stated that nature and human history pointed to heterosexual marriage as a superior institution. "From the beginning, it was clear that they were not going to be aggressive, and they were not going to match, in terms of passion or in terms of depth of defense, the kind of case the plaintiffs would be making," says Wardle.

Wardle was not the first conservative who took notice of events in Hawaii. The Rutherford Institute, a Virginia-based legal defense fund named for a seventeenth-century Scottish theologian, had been founded in 1982 to protect individual religious expression in public institutions and soon became known as an "ACLU of the right." It took its first interest in Hawaii in 1991, when the legislature began to consider a law banning employment discrimination against gays. After the bill passed the legislature and was signed by the governor—making Hawaii the third state to enact an equal-protection law covering sexual orientation—the president of the Honolulu-based Rutherford chapter, Jim Hochberg, recruited four local religious leaders, representing various denominations, and prepared a federal lawsuit claiming that a bill compelling them to hire gays and lesbians interfered with a "right to hold and practice their religious beliefs." Others joined the lawsuit under assumed names—to avoid being identified by "militant homosexuals" who might seek retribution, Hochberg explained. The case was eventually dismissed by a judge, who determined that the plaintiffs had filed suit before the law had harmed any of them, but by then the Rutherford Institute had found a more attractive target for its media-friendly legal activism.

Only a few weeks in the spring of 1991 separated the nondiscrimination bill's passage and the initial filing of the *Baehr v. Lewin* suit, and the Rutherford Institute was inevitably drawn to fight what appeared a more ominous public sanction of immoral behavior. When a local PBS talk show wanted to book a conservative guest to face off against Dan Foley and Ninia Baehr in a debate over same-sex marriage, producers asked the Rutherford Institute of Hawaii's litigation director, Bill Lawson. After the state supreme court announced it would hear *Baehr* on appeal, the Rutherford Institute filed an amicus brief on the defendant's behalf. It was evident that the Rutherford Institute was ready to say things—both in court briefs and statements to the media—that the attorney general supposedly representing the state's interest would not. No government lawyer, after all, was willing to commit to the certainty that flowed freely from Hochberg's lips: that "homosexuality is a sinful, immoral, learned behavior which is not an immutable trait."

The fact that it had taken a nonprofit headquartered five thousand miles away to bring such simple truths into a Hawaii courtroom confirmed a persistent worry of Wardle's about the structure of legal authority in the state. Not only were judges appointed by politicians, but in Hawaii the attorney general was, too. The person who held that office was obliged to defend the state's laws, but there was no standard for how exactly one was supposed to go about doing it. Wardle anticipated the worst. "Hawaii is the aloha state, and everyone has got the aloha spirit, and they were taking a sort of aloha approach to the defense," he says. "They were going to take a very lofty approach—sort of wink-wink, nudge-nudge, 'we're all good old guys here.'"

Wardle's fears were justified. The attorney general at the time of the appeal, Robert Marks, served at the pleasure of the governor, who happened to be a liberal Democrat running for reelection that year in the closest thing America had to a one-party state. Gays and lesbians were enough of an organized political force that Democratic politicians could not afford to recklessly antagonize them. Even though Governor John Waihee said he was opposed to gay marriage, all his actions suggested he most wanted to see the issue go away—probably determining he had more to fear from his administration appearing antigay than from looking too permissive. "We were the attorney general's office in a pro-civil-liberties state. If we were going to defend the *Baehr* case, we were going to defend it fully cognizant of the civil-liberties implications of this," says Steven Michaels, the assistant attorney general assigned to handle the appeal. "We did not feel it was appropriate to represent the policy of the state of Hawaii as homophobic."

Wardle's opposition to gay marriage was not about disapproving of private conduct as much as it was about validating it with special status: recognition of certain relationships as socially important was a privilege long conferred by the state. In fact, Wardle's method of argumentation was so coolly rational that his opponents found themselves debating, in newspaper columns and the footnotes of academic papers, whether he could just be dismissed as a homophobe. ("Heterosexist, yes," religion professor John-Charles Duffy concluded. "Homophobic, no.") Wardle savored the opportunity to confound that debate further by publishing the provocatively liberal claim that marriage is one of society's most successful "integrationist" institutions, and that permitting men to exclude women from it would amount to its own form of gender discrimination.

Homophobia wasn't necessary to win a marriage case, but you had to be willing to offend gays. A state that went to court to defend its marriage statute but was afraid to state that, simply, there is something wrong with gay couples was crippling itself—and, in Wardle's mind, putting the rest of the country at risk. Someone had to go into court to make a more forceful case, if only to build up a trial record that showed traditionalists putting their best arguments forward. Even though a precedent wouldn't be binding in any other court, judges elsewhere would certainly look to the reasoning that had prevailed in Hawaii for guidance on how to consider similar cases in their states.

In February 1995, just as the Utah legislature took up Wardle's bill, the LDS Church filed a motion in Hawaii circuit court to intervene as codefendants in the *Baehr* lawsuit. "There are times when certain moral issues became so compelling that that churches have a duty to make their feelings known," Don Hallstrom, the LDS Church's regional representative, said to justify his faith's unusual foray into litigation to which it was not a party. "In rare cases, they may need to pursue their own constitutional rights to resist something they feel poses a serious threat to the moral fabric of society. We have reached such a situation in Hawaii."

The filing affirmed Wardle's status as the church's chief legal strategist on issues surrounding what it had taken to calling "same-gender marriages." Because religious institutions perform weddings, the church's attorneys argued, they had a distinct stake in the rules that surrounded them. If the state lost the case, the motion conjectured, and the church subsequently refused to marry gay couples, it would be the one to suffer. The church could see itself defending lawsuits over accusations it had discriminated against gays and lesbians, or even find its authority to solemnize nuptials jeopardized. "Many people are tolerant of private homosexual behavior but oppose giving such relations preferred legal status," Wardle wrote in an affidavit supporting the motion. Unstated in the entire motion or Wardle's affidavit was the obvious implication that Mormons would put up a better fight against gay-rights lawyers than the government bureaucrats whose job it was to do so.

When the church's motion was denied by a judge, Wardle agreed to aid the state's case as a consultant, though he had little but disdain for the bureaucrats who were limply assembling a plan for trial. He was like a sports fan who learns that his favorite team is about to throw the biggest game of the season: the more he saw, the less he could stand to watch. The lawyer whom the attorney general's office tasked to work on the *Baehr* case had just emerged from six months of litigating a water-rights claim on the state's behalf. "That's not exactly a great background for defending constitutional litigation over equal-protection claims for same-sex marriage," Wardle scoffs.

The only consolation could be read on the calendar. That inevitable courtroom reckoning got pushed back over and over again, first to the fall of 1995 and then even beyond, thanks to unexpected motions and postponed filing deadlines. Church sources in Hawaii suggested that the delays were in fact part of a strategy to ensure gay marriage never came to trial. The legislature had embraced the thorny challenge of rewriting the state's marriage statute, and unelected judges were happy to defer to a democratically accountable branch of government to settle the question. (The attorney general seemed in no hurry to head into court, either.) Wardle was trained as an attorney, a believer in the primacy of the law, but seeing the *Baehr* litigation shanghaied by elected officials was encouraging. The political world offered the best hope to defend marriage, and Wardle knew his church had reason to be confident about its abilities in that realm.

A Message from the Presidency

E ven before committing itself to legal and political action in Hawaii, the Church of Jesus Christ of Latter-day Saints had started to drum up support among the faithful. Toward the end of morning services on February 13, 1994, after prayer and before the sermon, local leaders informed their congregations that they had a message from the First Presidency, the pinnacle of the stratified faith's governance structure. "Marriage between a man and a woman is ordained of God to fulfill the eternal destiny of His children. The union of husband and wife assures perpetuation of the race and provides a divinely ordained setting for the nurturing and teaching of children," a ward bishop or branch president read on the eve of Valentine's Day. Then worshippers were told it was their responsibility to "appeal to legislators, judges and other government officials to preserve the purposes and sanctity of marriage between a man and a woman and to reject all efforts to give legal authorization or other official approval or support to marriages between persons of the same gender."

It was not uncommon for one of the First Presidency's messages to yoke worshippers out of an hour-long escape into a world of biblical admonitions and uplifting hymns and back toward the hard realities of modern life. At times, the church used Utah controversies as a justification to demonstrate its concern for all mankind, as when the Reagan administration proposed the mountain state as a base for the MX missile, which the First Presidency rejected as a "mammoth weapons system potentially capable of destroying much of civilization." On other occasions, the church's interest in state politics was purely provincial, such as its blanket opposition to initiatives to liberalize Utah's exceptionally restrictive alcohol laws (by permitting sales of liquor by the drink) and to legalize pari-mutuel betting on horse races. On many of these occasions, well-informed Utah Mormons likely had their own opinion of the issues. They might not be immediately persuaded to change their views, but they could no longer act as if their faith didn't care where they stood.

The February 1994 message about marriage was unambiguously blunt in its moral imperative—no Mormon could be confused about the faith's views toward homosexuality, which it had long since classified as a sin—but obscure in its political allusions. Very few of the nine million Mormons to whom the message was aimed could be expected to understand what "official approval or support to marriages between persons of the same gender" meant, and the announcement made no effort to educate them. It did not mention Hawaii, or the roiling concern among some in the church's leadership that the outcome of legal and political processes under way there could have an immediate impact on marriage beyond the state itself. LDS spokesman Don LeFevre confirmed to a reporter that it was events in Hawaii that had triggered the declaration of policy. At the same time, he dismissed the notion that the church had made such a dramatic gesture in response to a single state's litigation. "The concern is throughout the world," LeFevre explained.

The newspapers that tracked the church most closely covered the First Presidency message with a sense of puzzlement. "The announcement left many Latter-day Saints scratching their heads wondering which lawmakers were pushing for such a law," the *Salt Lake Tribune* observed. "Utah lawmakers were equally perplexed." But the *Deseret News* went on to note that the announcement prompted "some Utahns to wonder whether there was a local effort to legalize homosexual marriages." Journalists covering the church's machinations recognized that while it often stepped gingerly into the political arena, it rarely did so rashly or stopped at half measures.

When Mormons did throw themselves into politics, everyone understood, they could do so with great force. The church had vast financial resources, sustained by its own business interests and reliable tithing among a people who had grown prosperous. Mormons proved an ideal activist corps, as well. Many adults had emerged from their missionary experience with the requisite hard skills for political outreach—knocking on doors and talking to strangers about tough issues. They had an earned familiarity with the limits of persuasion, having been numbed by experience to the sting of rejection.

These qualities, along with the intimately networked nature of their communities, made Mormons the activist equivalent of "dry kindling," ready to be ignited to attention with a single spark, in the description of political scientists Quin Monson and David Campbell. Church officials understood the combustible power in their hands. In 1975, as Utah's legislature was preparing to consider ratification of the Equal Rights Amendment, the LDS Church declared its opposition. The church explained its view—that the proposed law did not appreciate the natural characteristics that distinguished genders and would "stifle many God-given feminine instincts"—in the "Church News" section of the *Deseret News* and then set to work defeating the ERA. (After winning Congress's approval in 1972, the amendment had a decade to win ratification by three-quarters of the states.) The impact of the newly announced position was felt immediately in Utah, which swiftly rejected the amendment even though 63 percent of residents had declared their support to a pollster the previous year (when the church had taken no position).

Defeating the ERA in Utah was easy, and so church strategists turned their attention to legislatures in neighboring states with large and politically active Mormon populations, like Idaho, Nevada, and Arizona. By 1980, with the deadline for ratification of the ERA only two years away, church officials expanded their sights, imploring "Church members, in the exercise of their constitutional right as citizens, to make their influence felt in opposition to the proposed amendment."

Mormons responded. According to one estimate, 85 percent of the mail that Virginia state legislators received in opposition to the ERA came from Mormons, despite the fact that they represented less than 1 percent of the state's population. Phyllis Schlafly, who led the national Stop ERA campaign, credited Mormons for her side's margin of victory in Virginia, along with similar wins in Florida and Nevada.

Church officials did not take credit for such accomplishments, and often went to great lengths to mask even basic involvement in politics. Such subterfuge was possible due to savvy navigation of campaign-finance laws and tax paperwork, aided by local partners eager to be the face of an anti-ERA organization even if the money and strategy were disproportionately generated in Salt Lake City. The church's political style was more ecumenical than its theology. "Allied with whoever sees things the way we do—Catholic, Baptist . . . ," LDS regional representative Julian Lowe explained—even, in North Carolina, with the far-right John Birch Society.

The American right was in a period of flux, thanks to the growth of evangelical Protestantism and the ascendancy of movement conservatism within the Republican Party, culminating in Ronald Reagan's election in 1980. The LDS Church found itself ideologically in sync with the New Right on most social issues, but the institution was so mercurial and opaque that even its own allies could not anticipate where it would act next. Indeed, Mormon leaders engaged in activism with a set of incentives that set them apart from the normal economics of interest-group politics. They weren't looking to build their membership list or donor rolls through recruitment, or to keep existing supporters engaged. They did not enter fights to present a show of force, to make good on threats or exact revenge, or to intimidate their opponents. They did not tally symbolic victories or value noble defeats. They would play in politics only when they could make a difference, and they knew that in most places they could be most influential when they were invisible.

Apostles

LDS Church president Gordon B. Hinckley's speech to the church's women's organization, the Relief Society, was approaching its end when Hinckley signaled he would no longer be speaking for himself, but for the entire institution he led. "With so much of sophistry that is passed off as truth, with so much of deception concerning standards and values, with so much of allurement and enticement to take on the slow stain of the world," he said, "we have felt to warn and forewarn."

That "we" referred to the Quorum of the Twelve Apostles. There was, in the purest sense, nothing new in "The Family: A Proclamation to the World" when Hinckley presented it to the Relief Society in September 1995. It was a recapitulation of long-standing church doctrine—which included a Heavenly Mother alongside the Heavenly Father—and compilation of existing policies asserting a fundamental division of responsibilities between the sexes and touched upon out-of-wedlock births, inattentive parenting, spousal infidelity, and gay marriages. But unlike First Presidency messages that were read only to Sunday worshippers, the proclamation was addressed "to the church and to the world."

The eighty-five-year-old Hinckley had been in his post barely six months, and—given that Mormon temples are closed to nonbelievers—this would be one of his first major occasions to speak beyond the church. Hinckley was one of Mormonism's most media-savvy leaders, with a church career that had taken him through its public communications department, where he had pioneered its use of audiovisual materials, and a six-year stint as president of the Deseret News Publishing Company. The Relief Society meeting welcomed media coverage, and a church video crew recorded everything for its own dissemination later on. Hinckley knew he would be not only counseling Mormons on how to lead their lives, but laying out a Mormon-friendly vision for society as a whole. "The family is ordained of God. Marriage between man and woman is essential to His eternal plan," Hinckley read from the proclamation, before concluding: "We warn that the disintegration of the family will bring upon individuals, communities, and nations the calamities foretold by ancient and modern prophets."

Hinckley was considered God's living prophet on earth, and did not always resign himself to passively accepting the catastrophic future of his vision. At times, he thought it was possible to bend events to his will, and as he enumerated one contemporary threat to the idea of family—"what they choose to call same-sex marriage"—Hinckley was already developing a plan to do so. The president of the LDS Church might be introduced to crowds as "prophet, seer, and revelator," but he also sat astride one of the grandest political organizations in the American West. The colonnaded Church Administration Building was a uniquely formidable monument when it opened in 1917, its imposing Greek facade carved from the same Little Cottonwood Canyon granite that formed the exotic-revival spirals of the nearby Salt Lake Temple. Over the next half century, the church's membership increased sixfold, much of it overseas, leading the administration to outgrow its home. In the 1970s, the church erected a twenty-eight-story modernist structure abutting Temple Square, where it installed its missionary department and a variety of support functions. If the office tower embodied the professionalization of the frontier faith, the classical cube it dwarfed alongside it still shielded an earthbound concentration of its power. It remained, as ever, home to the Brethren, as Mormons referred to the General Authorities, a senior echelon of officers first organized to preside over the religion upon the 1844 death of its prophet, Joseph Smith.

Salt Lake City was settled, and would become the seat of Utah territory, by Mormons who would be forced into politics through national debates over their own status as would-be citizens. By the time Utah prepared to celebrate the centenary of its statehood, in 1996, the leadership of the LDS Church no longer saw politics as a mechanism for defending their sovereign way of life from an encroaching national majority. Instead, the church was committed to using its resources to ensure that America's laws would reflect its values. A politics that existed decidedly outside the American system had been transformed, largely through force of will, into one that savvily navigated it from within.

Nowhere was the impact of that conversion more strongly felt than on the issue of marriage. At one point, the Latter-day Saints were America's most prominent dissidents against the status quo of marriage for insisting polygamy was essential to their way of life. In 1879, the Supreme Court ruled in *Reynolds v. United States* that religious belief was no justification for Mormons to flout a criminal code drafted to hedge against "the evil consequences that were supposed to flow from plural marriages." The unanimous decision forced Mormon leaders to choose whether they would live outside the law and stay honest to their faith or bend to the federally recognized definition of marriage. In 1890, the LDS Church officially renounced plural marriages, a forced compromise with Congress that ensured Utah's statehood six years later.

But as Salt Lake City became base for an ever more global faith, the church's posture toward political activity changed. In the subsequent century Mormons became ardent defenders of the notion that "traditional" marriage amounted to a single, unalterable goal. "Sexual relations are proper only between husband and wife appropriately expressed within the bonds of marriage," the LDS Church had decreed in a 1991 letter issued by the First Presidency, the primary channel for its policy declarations. "Any other sexual contact, including fornication, adultery, and homosexual and lesbian behavior, is sinful."

Yet when same-sex couples made their first serious efforts to join the institution of marriage, the church's public response was muddled by internal turmoil. About a year after the court released its decision in *Baehr*, church president Ezra Taft Benson died, beginning a yearlong church leadership crisis. The First Presidency message about same-sex marriage was read in worship services in Hawaii in February 1994, and at the time church officials had taken the additional step of distributing a flyer there. (The flyers did not make entirely clear that they were the church's work: they bore the name only of the "Hawaii Public Affairs Council," but those who rang the phone number listed as a contact found it answered by LDS local public-affairs missionaries.) Over the next year and a half, however, the church fell largely silent. Only with the ascension of Hinckley to the First Presidency, in the spring of 1995, did the church have a leader positioned to lead it into a political crisis not of its own making. After settling into his post, Hinckley summoned Dallin Oaks and his fellow elder Neal Maxwell to assess what role the church could play to "head off the legalization of same-gender marriage," as one participant in what became regular meetings described it.

Oaks's career exemplified how a new generation of Mormons had begun to use their access to political and legal institutions to further the church's interests. Oaks was a second great-grand-nephew of Martin Harris, one of three men said to have witnessed the revelation of the Book of Mormon to Joseph Smith upon golden plates. In his first year out of school, Oaks served as a clerk to Chief Justice Earl Warren, whose liberal orientation helped teach the University of Chicago Law School graduate to "separate my respect for the position a person holds from the affection I have (or do not have) for him or her as a person and the support or lack of support I feel for his or her actions or policies." Oaks became president of Brigham Young University and eventually left his post to serve on the Utah Supreme Court; while there, he was both considered for a U.S. Supreme Court appointment and sustained as a member of the Quorum of the Twelve. He was the first Mormon elevated to apostleship while serving in government. "Throughout the remainder of your life will you be a lawyer and judge who has been called to be an Apostle," Oaks said he asked himself, "or will you be an Apostle who used to be a lawyer and judge?" The church never forced Oaks to make such a clean split, but in May 1984 he retired from the judiciary to satisfy a lifetime appointment as an apostle.

Oaks was handed some of the church's most delicate tasks, including an assignment to negotiate the purchase of forty historical documents that cast doubt on the circumstances of Mormonism's founding. (The most controversial of the documents was a letter supposedly written by Harris, Oaks's ancestor.) The materials were exposed as counterfeits when the collector who had sold them to the church, Mark Hofmann, set two pipe bombs to distract from his fraud, each claiming a victim. After Hofmann's fraud, it became Oaks's job to explain how the LDS Church had been suckered by a con man over its own history.

Much of Oaks's public portfolio consisted of speaking for the church on social issues. As such, he became the secretive institution's most public voice on homosexuality, which he considered part of a satanic strategy to mislead human beings and undermine God's plans. "God has given us agency—the power to choose between good (the path of life) and evil," Oaks would write. "Once we have reached the age or condition of accountability, the claim 'I was born that way' does not excuse actions or thoughts that fail to conform to the commandments of God. We need to learn how to live so that a weakness that is mortal will not prevent us from achieving the goal that is eternal."

That fixation on homosexuality drew Oaks to deliver what was likely the church's first criticism of official status for gay couples. In a sign of how distant same-sex marriage seemed in 1987—and the lawyer's instinct to conjure the inconceivable in the service of a logical argument—Oaks cited their absence to argue against homosexual activity. "The Church's position is based on scriptural commandments that men and women should refrain from any sexual relations outside the bonds of marriage," Oaks told CBS journalist Charles Kuralt. Intimacy with the same sex was therefore off-limits, Oaks explained, because "there is no scriptural warrant for homosexual marriages."

The experience left Oaks better prepared than any of his colleagues in the Twelve to take seriously the threat posed by the Hawaii Supreme Court. In the fall of 1995, he circulated to church officials a draft of a manuscript by Brigham Young University professor Lynn Wardle. ("Some Objections to Same-Sex Marriage—Part 1," it was called, both modestly and portentously.) "Wardle's work is absolutely first-rate, and extremely thorough," Oaks explained to his colleagues. "The publication of the article," he went on, "may turn out to be one of the very most important resources we have in our national lobbying efforts."

Oaks accepted Wardle's recommendation that in Hawaii it was time for Mormons to begin looking beyond the courts. They needed to push the legislature, or the public, to amend the constitution to prohibit gays from marrying—or find another legislative fix to justify the continued existence of a marriage statute that the state's highest court labeled discriminatory. But in its delayed acknowledgment of those political realities, the church had watched less sophisticated political actors step in to the breach.

In Hawaii, where evangelical Protestants were small in number and had never established a political foothold, the only local social-conservative opposition to same-sex marriage was forged not in fire and brimstone but on the yoga mat. A former dean of American Samoa Community College, Mike Gabbard had come to Hawaii to open a private school in Wahiawä. He had found religion at seventeen, after nearly dying in a surfing accident, and as he aged he became a peculiar voice for public morality. Gabbard called himself an "enigmatic Catholic," but he was also a minister of bhakti yoga who associated with the Science of Identity Foundation, one of a number of names used by a Maui-based religious sect that had splintered from the Hare Krishna movement. Gabbard believed in spirituality as an all-purpose salve for those fighting the impulses of sexual deviance, but unlike many evangelicals entering politics at the time, he saw organized religions in inclusive, even interchangeable, terms. "Ask God for help," he wrote. "A person, regardless of their faith, can look at all revealed scriptures and see the obvious: homosexual behavior is displeasing to God and should therefore be avoided."

The 1989 publication of a children's book called *Heather Has Two Mommies* turned Gabbard's zeal toward politics. Convinced that the education system was being transformed into an "indoctrination program to accept homosexuality," Gabbard started paying for an hourly radio slot on Saturday evenings to air a show called *Let's Talk Straight, Hawaii.* "I was concerned the homosexual movement was starting to blossom here in Hawaii, and there was no counter-voice from the people," he said.

The month *Baehr v. Lewin* was filed, in 1991, Gabbard launched Stop Promoting Homosexuality Hawaii, although his greater concern at the time was the decision by Honolulu officials to award Bill Woods a permit for a second annual gay-pride parade. On the day of the event, his wife, Carol, stationed by the bandstand with two men outfitted as Grim Reapers holding signs that read "Homosexuality, Lifestyle of Death," Mike Gabbard chaperoned supporters along the parade route distributing flyers expounding upon that message. Two of his companions were heckled, but Gabbard was less fazed by the confrontation than by the fact that when he tuned in to the local news that evening there was no mention of it. "You didn't see the groups of homosexuals swarming and punching the hapless protestors," he complained. "You didn't hear about the lewd songs being belted out over the loudspeakers by a homosexual entertainer at the Bandstand not caring about families who were picnicking in the Park."

When the Hawaii Supreme Court issued its opinion, in May 1993, Gabbard told the *Honolulu Advertiser* his phone had been ringing all day from those who shared his outrage. "The Supreme Court is using the force of law to shove this down people's throats, and I don't think the people of Hawaii are going to accept this." As the state's most vocal antigay activist, Gabbard became a focal point for efforts to wrest control of the marriage debate from the courts.

Gabbard may have had an instinct for seizing attention, but he showed little of the organizer's skill at assembling political coalitions. He seemed to act from impulse rather than strategy. Even though he declared to the *Advertiser* that "this should be fought out in the legislature," Gabbard demonstrated quickly that he lacked the discipline to operate successfully there. Soon his overzealous instinct for conflict had ruined the best shot for a swift political victory against same-sex marriage. As the state senate judiciary committee moved toward consensus on a bill that would satisfy the court's demand for a legislative justification for banning gay couples from marrying, Gabbard sent a letter to the five-member minority who had announced themselves opposed. At the same time, Gabbard's Common Sense Now purchased ads in Honolulu's two daily newspapers encouraging readers to call those members to voice disappointment. After the ad appeared, committee chairman Rey Graulty watched his majority for an antimarriage bill disintegrate. Graulty blamed Gabbard's ad for putting undue pressure on delicate efforts to reconcile competing drafts. "It's an issue of conscience," Graulty said. "They didn't want to be stampeded." Even Gabbard acknowledged afterward that "it appeared the ad backfired."

Hinckley was convinced that only the LDS Church could rescue the cause from hapless extremists like Gabbard. "There were some very shrill, harsh, sort of fists-pounding-on-the-table antigay voices," says Wardle. "The church didn't want to be associated with them, and it didn't want to do nothing."

Hinckley had served as a top adviser to President Spencer Kimball during the most intense phase of the campaign against the Equal Rights Amendment, so he had a deep appreciation for its value as a template for how the church could effectively scheme to get its way on distant, seemingly unfavorable terrain. He assigned Loren Dunn, a member of the Quorum of Seventy, to day-to-day management of a campaign to shape Hawaiian public opinion and lobby the legislature. But Hinckley imposed one condition. Before the church could meddle in the state's politics, it had to find appropriate cover—through a coalition that would minimize, or at least distract from, the Mormon role.

14

....

Hawaii's Future Today

In October 1995, the church's public-affairs department began assembling a campaign-in-waiting, and Loren Dunn traveled to Honolulu to meet its members. As was often the case whenever there was important work for Mormons to do, it was never immediately clear who was there because he or she had volunteered, who was being paid to do so, and who was compelled by contract or by a higher form of suasion. Jack Hoag had been president of an Oahu stake—a subdivision roughly equivalent to a diocese—before retiring from his career at a prominent Honolulu bank to manage the church's considerable island land holdings. Debi Hartmann, who worked at Brigham Young's Hawaii campus, had served for six years as an elected member of the State Board of Education. There were four representatives of McNeil Wilson Communications—which already handled public relations for local LDS entities, including the church-owned Polynesian Cultural Center theme park—and the lobbyist it had enlisted for that work, Linda Rosehill. After meeting with them all, Dunn reported back to the committee on what he had found. "The court wants to hear from the legislature but is not bound" by its views, he wrote. "In the meantime, we need ongoing day-to-day leadership on the ground with all the entities moving together."

Yet the meetings still left many matters unresolved. How much of their work had to be done through mass media—including a campaign of television, radio, and print ads proposed by McNeil Wilson—and how much through a quieter effort to persuade targeted lawmakers? If gay rights ended up as an object of legislative horse-trading, was there anything church leaders were willing to deal away to keep gay marriages at bay? Dunn decided that on his return trip, a few weeks later, he would bring along two new members of his retinue to help him make sense of these strategic challenges.

The men whom Dunn recruited to join him in Hawaii were familiar faces around Salt Lake City's Temple Square. To church leaders, Richard Wirthlin was well-known as a son and brother of General Authorities; to the broader world, he was the pollster who had guided Ronald Reagan's rise and helped create the business of measuring public opinion for corporate clients. Wirthlin continued to keep a hand in politics—his current project was trying to convince retired Army general Colin Powell to seek the presidency—but he increasingly gave his time to serve his church. He was seen by its elders as a future leader. When it came to same-sex marriage, Wirthlin could offer a window onto non-Mormon public opinion for an often insular administration, a task he told Dunn would be facilitated by a $100,000 survey conducted by his firm, Wirthlin Worldwide.

When the public-affairs department decided it needed an "experienced person on the ground" in Hawaii, there was consensus it should be "an Art Anderson type." Dunn approached Arthur Anderson himself, a retired Salt Lake City advertising executive, and asked him to take on the role in the form of a short-term mission. Anderson replied that he had to consult with his wife, who said that if the church provided housing they could go. Dunn called an Oahu church member to make housing available and committed Anderson to spend six months there.

Mormons viewed this kind of religious volunteerism as a divine "calling," and from the moment he had been handed his task, Dunn knew he would be able to rely on the church's white-collar volunteer corps for help. Most young men active in the church (and increasingly its young women, too) serve two years on a mission, often overseas, spreading the faith under typically unforgiving conditions. But like soldiers who leave active duty only to sign up for the reserves, Mormons expect to be "called" by their church to service for the rest of their lives. Most give up to twenty hours a week to church activities, in addition to tithing. As Mormonism developed an elite professional class—much of it groomed at, and credentialed by, Brigham Young University—church officials could call upon lawyers and public-relations men for institutional advice as readily as they would help summon carpenters and masons to build a house for a family in need.

Over several days of strategy sessions in November, Dunn handed out assignments to his expanding circle of advisers. Wirthlin would conduct his poll to identify which Hawaiians the church should be trying to persuade and how best to go about it. Lynn Wardle would monitor legislative proposals so the Quorum of the Twelve could decide how and when they might be ready to endorse a compromise. The church's regional representative, Don Hallstrom, would approach other like-minded traditionalists in the hopes of convincing them to join a Mormon-coordinated coalition. Each man was to do his work inconspicuously, fully aware that any sight of a Mormon political apparatus built to influence local policy would be viewed as the tool of a cynical power meddling from afar. "We were careful to make this an [*sic*] Hawaii based group," Dunn would later reflect. "Hawaiian's [*sic*] worrying about Hawaii."

In December, the results of Wirthlin's poll came back. Twice as many Hawaiians as the national average agreed that "the homosexual life is acceptable" for themselves and others. Unlike 60 percent of Americans who said social policy was their greatest priority, among Hawaiians it was "not a top-of-mind issue." (They said they were more concerned with economics.) Honolulu's elite opinion, however, had coalesced behind a more threatening view. The city's two newspapers were editorializing in favor of gay marriage, and the senate—the more liberal of the two Democratic-controlled chambers—seemed predisposed to enshrine it as law. There was cause for caution. "Because of our late arrival," Dunn averred, "it will be an uphill battle."

Even as he worried that the broad support for the church's marriage position was soft, Wirthlin was heartened to discover that whatever pockets of intensity existed around the issue were on its side. Opponents of same-sex marriage were five times more likely than proponents to feel strongly about the issue, a memo to the public-affairs committee observed, "which indicates to us that there is strong grassroots support for our cause." That insight inspired Dunn to resist McNeil Wilson's initial $500,000 proposal for a mass-media campaign to shift opinions around gay marriage, and work first instead on mobilizing already sympathetic social conservatives. "We can draw on this grassroots support to persuade legislators to hold a firm position on traditional values," Dunn concluded, "to prepare the ground for introducing a constitutional amendment, should we choose that route."

Unfortunately, according to Wirthlin's poll, Mormons were poor messengers for such a family-values campaign. When Hawaiians were asked to assess their warmth for various institutions on a 100-point thermometer, the LDS Church scored an average of just 49. "This information suggests that the Church should maintain a very low visibility in this campaign," Dunn reported back to the public-affairs committee. "It is most advisable to keep a formal distance between the Church and the Coalition involved in fighting the issue."

Dunn assigned Stuart C. Reid, a member of the church's public-affairs staff who had also been recently elected to the Salt Lake City Council, to make quiet overtures to representatives of other denominations known for their social conservatism: the Missouri Synod Lutherans, the Church of the Nazarene, the Rabbinical Council of America, the General Conference of Seventh-Day Adventists, the National Association of Evangelicals. One by one, they expressed interest in signing on to a coalition to protect traditional marriage, but that added up to little in Hawaii.

The islands lacked the type of homegrown right that generated such natural alliances in the largely conservative, rural states where Mormons had found such success galvanizing opposition to the Equal Rights Amendment. Televangelist Pat Robertson's 1988 campaign for the Republican presidential nomination lured many evangelicals into politics for the first time; in the wake of his loss, Robertson founded the Christian Coalition to give them ongoing electoral influence. But Robertson's Hawaii supporters found themselves unable to dislodge the moderates who presided over Republican politics in the state, and quickly retreated. "When the Christians got in the party back then, they didn't understand the fundamentals of politics," Dan Hallman, the Christian Coalition's regional director, observed. "If they didn't get everything they wanted they said, 'I'm going home.'"

The most encouraging response to Reid's outreach came from the U.S. Conference of Catholic Bishops, which had the greatest geographical and ideological reach of all and an impressive track record when it came to interfaith organizing around moral issues. A quarter century earlier the Conference of Bishops had successfully incubated the National Right to Life Committee; it became the hub of the country's antiabortion activism once *Roe v. Wade* was decided. After Oaks traveled to Chicago to meet with Catholic leaders, they established a committee to deal with same-sex marriage. Soon conference officials were indicating that they would be ready to help convene and finance a new multidenominational coalition on the issue. "If the Catholics decide to host this first meeting of the coalition," Reid reported back to a colleague, "it will provide valuable support and coverage for the initiative to organize opposition to the legalization of same-gender marriage."

Catholics were a particularly ideal accomplice for political work in Hawaii. In Wirthlin's poll, the Catholic Church had scored a 57 on the feeling-thermometer question, a rating the public-affairs committee characterized as "much more secure" than the Mormons' 49. For both faiths, an outsize presence in the Hawaii mind could be traced to aggressive nineteenth-century missionary work in the Pacific. The Diocese of Honolulu and the LDS Church came by their influence in modern Hawaii the old-fashioned way, however: each church was a significant landholder and major educator, which helped draw the attention of politicians to church priorities.

On his trips to Hawaii, Dunn began paying a visit to the diocese's chancery offices, and on each successive encounter, he saw Bishop Francis X. DiLorenzo warm to an active role in a Mormon-initiated coalition. To serve as the church's representative, DiLorenzo volunteered the thirty-six-year-old Japanese American priest Marc Alexander. As executive director of the Hawaii Catholic Congress, Alexander was already a regular presence at the capitol lobbying lawmakers in the aftermath of the supreme court's *Baehr* decision. "If someone had told me 10 years ago that I would someday have to defend traditional marriage against same-sex marriage, I would have laughed in their face," Alexander had said in 1994. "Yet here I am, doing just that." Alexander agreed to serve as cochair of a new coalition. Although Alexander was officially there in his capacity as a private citizen, as DiLorenzo made clear in a memo to the priests and deacons of the Honolulu Diocese, "he has my permission to do so."

For demographic balance, Dunn had hoped to recruit "an articulate middle-age mother who is neither Catholic nor LDS," but two who fit the category turned down entreaties to join, fearing it could conflict with nonpolitical affiliations like the YWCA. Eventually Dunn had to settle for Debi Hartmann, a Mormon who liked to explain that her turn chairing the education board convinced her of the extent to which "sensitive issues that strike at society's center are divisive and potentially explosive." With Hartmann a perfect chair in every respect but for her public ties to the LDS Church, Dunn was satisfied that he had followed Hinckley's directive to avoid creating a monolithic political entity. "A coalition is hard to attack, particularly a young mother who was Chair of the State Board of Education (Chairman), a popular Catholic Priest with a Jewish-Buddhist background who is noted for his work with the socially disadvantaged (Vice-Chairman) and a businessman who is a trustee of the University of Hawaii, a University that is known for its diversity," Dunn wrote to elder Neal Maxwell.

Representatives of the two churches signed on to a coalition that would be called Hawaii's Future Today and devoted to "family values." Agreeing on which issues beyond gay marriage belonged under such an umbrella presented the first serious hurdle in Dunn's negotiations with DiLorenzo, but eventually they settled on gambling and prostitution. The LDS Church had succeeded in making Utah one of only two states that outlawed all gambling; the other was Hawaii, and Dunn proposed adding opposition to casino gaming to the coalition's agenda. Unlike Mormon doctrine, which considered all gambling (including state lotteries) to be a sin, Catholics accepted it under certain conditions. DiLorenzo was unwilling to commit to a full prohibition on gambling, so Dunn agreed to let the bishop issue a statement to Catholics explaining that the church wasn't universally disapproving of the behavior. Both faiths were equally resistant to prostitution and agreed it should not be legalized. Even as he and Dunn came to some accord on the issues that would fall under the Hawaii's Future Today purview, DiLorenzo wanted the group's materials to emphasize that it believed economic conditions played a role in perpetuating such moral ills in society. Dunn gamely acceded, even as he wondered whether, through all his bargaining, the group's mandate had gone from being too targeted to too general to too variegated in its specificity. "Family and family values is not specific enough. Same-gender marriage is too narrow to get broad support because of fear of reprisal by homosexual radicals," Dunn explained to the public-affairs committee. "The issues of gambling, prostitution and same-gender marriage taken together may cause our issue to become obscured."

Dunn brought together the new leadership of Hawaii's Future Today and laid out the coalition's agenda for the next few months. Its most urgent task would be discrediting the appointed Hawaii Commission on Sexual Orientation and the Law, which had been chartered by the legislature in an advisory role, for having been unfairly stocked with liberals from the start. At the same time, the coalition would be lurking in the shadows of much of the commission's work. "We have extensively assisted" the two minority members, according to Dunn, supplying Wardle and McNeil Wilson staffers to contribute to an early draft of the forty-nine-page minority report. The minority members expressed their gratitude with leaks on commission deliberations, including the encouraging update that they had "been able to raise enough issues to stop the commission from railroading through and because of this, they could miss their reporting date."

But there was work to be done, quietly, before then. McNeil Wilson would try to get the attention of the *Christian Science Monitor* and *Reader's*

Digest, national outlets whose coverage—unlike that of Honolulu's two newspapers—would likely be sympathetic to the conservative point of view. Wirthlin would continue polling, in part to test support for a possible constitutional amendment, which could ultimately require voter approval. (Rosehill's political sources had suggested to her such a referendum could be the only way to ensure same-sex marriage remained permanently illegal.) Meanwhile, Rosehill would keep the pressure on at the capitol. Having gambling and prostitution listed on the group's agenda would afford her more latitude to meet with a diverse array of members.

The coalition would be unveiled in the new year, just as the 1996 legislative session was starting. "Hawaii's Future Today is a coalition of Hawaii citizens united to preserve the islands we love," read a mission statement drafted by coalition leaders. "We are committed to maintain the delicate balance of Aloha that our parents, children, and visitors from around the world hold dear. Therefore, the coalition will dedicate its collective energy to urge our leaders not to sanction activities that would radically change Hawaii's special quality of life, particularly prostitution, casino gambling, and same-sex marriage."

The first two of those concerns were only barely recognizable as political issues in Hawaii, but their inclusion amounted to a triumph of misdirection. Church officials had taken a single-issue lobbying campaign hatched at Temple Square in Salt Lake City and set out to disguise it in the idiosyncratic garb of a far-off political culture. A few months later—after expending prestige, the time of skilled volunteers, and a little bit of money—they had emerged with a movement the coalition's chair could plausibly describe as "a voice and a political vehicle for the silent majority."

Obscuring the actual origins, goals, and machinations of Hawaii's Future Today wasn't merely a rhetorical feat. Based on advice from a local attorney, the public-affairs committee had decided to incorporate the coalition as a nonprofit, which would permit it to raise money from donors while shielding most of its spending from public view. The coalition eschewed tax-exempt status, which would require approval from state authorities. This didn't much matter to the coalition's fortunes, since it saw fundraising as a public-relations tool as much as a financing mechanism. The priority was local donations of less than $25, which could sustain the illusion of grassroots support. "It is likely most of the contributions can be kept from disclosure," Dunn explained to the church's public-affairs committee. Only Rosehill, as a registered lobbyist, would have to report the retainer she received for her work with the coalition. "The initial work will be with the legislature and this will be done as quietly as possible," Dunn wrote in one of his reports. "The opposition has a low profile and the coalition plans to work quietly with key groups, except in an instance or two when large crowds will be gathered to show the strength of the coalition."

One of those occasions came two months later, on the first week of the legislative session, when the group publicly announced its arrival. "All those who share our concerns about the future of our beautiful state, and who want to make sure our legislators are aware of the depth of feeling on those issues, are invited to take part," Hartmann said in the press release promoting a rally on a Saturday morning at the state capitol. A week after, Hallstrom eagerly clipped an item from the *Honolulu Star-Bulletin*'s political column that described "the group lobbying to preserve what it sees as the state's social fabric" and faxed it approvingly to Dunn. "Excellent coverage television [*sic*]," Dunn reported up to elder Neal Maxwell following the rally. "Coalition is referred to as 'broad-based' and 'grass roots.' No mention of involved churches."

With that cover, Hawaii's Future Today was accepted as a mainstream force in the state's politics. Coalition leaders were personally assured by the attorney general that, despite frustration with Mormon efforts to insert themselves in the litigation, she "would welcome any help on the case," as Dunn relayed to Maxwell. Rosehill, the lobbyist, secured meetings with the house Speaker and senate president, along with key committee chairmen, who helped coalition leaders plot a strategy for navigating the legislature.

They succeeded in fending off proposals to legally recognize gay couples and built support for a constitutional amendment that would preempt any court activity by banning same-sex marriage. Hawaii's Future Today recruited the state's three living former governors, two of them Democrats, to release a statement endorsing the proposal to put the amendment before voters, while Hoag was invited to testify before the Senate Judiciary Committee in its favor. To the surprise of LDS officials, just before the legislature was due to adjourn for the year, the house passed the constitutional amendment with the necessary two-thirds supermajority. Even though the amendment stalled in the state senate, Hawaii Future Today's polling showed that the debate had helped move public opinion even further in its direction, measuring support for its marriage agenda rising to 73 percent. "We are currently in a position only dreamed of a few months ago," Hallstrom wrote to Dunn.

One of the reasons for that progress, Hallstrom explained, was the coalition's "success in convincing legislators that it is a voice of reason, not extremes," which was a way of boasting that at every stage of its work Hawaii's Future Today had succeeded at keeping Mike Gabbard at a distance. Those who assembled the coalition had never enlisted his help, even though he had more experience fighting local gay activists than any of them. But Gabbard proved useful to those who had taken up his old crusade. As Rosehill would later confide, Gabbard represented something no campaign budget could buy: a free agent susceptible to being easily baited into delivering provocations that could be disowned by professional forces as evidence of their reasonable moderation. Gabbard may not have realized that at the time his supposed allies valued him only as a patsy, but it was apparent he had been pushed off a stage he once had to himself. Still, he too saw opportunity in the captivating new issue that came from Hawaii. A bigger stage awaited him on the mainland.

15

Kickoff

"Please welcome the man defending America on the front lines of morality," said the emcee. "A big aloha for Mike Gabbard."

A man in a dark suit, orange shirt, colorful tie, and a lei strode out onstage and offered an *aloha*—"which means love, as you know"—in response before explaining why, as he put it, "Hawaii is not an island unto itself."

"Some of you may be thinking, 'This is ridiculous—what does same-sex marriage have to do with my family here in Iowa or in California or wherever?'" Gabbard suggested to the three thousand people who had packed Des Moines's First Federated Church on a Saturday night. "Those crazy Hawaiians are sitting out there underneath their coconut trees, they're stuck out there in the middle of the ocean. Maybe it's water on the brain that's causing them to consider such an absurdity as legalizing homosexual marriage.

"The fact is, friends, if Hawaii legalizes homosexual marriage it will have an impact on every American," he went on. "Homosexual couples from all over will fly to Hawaii, get married, and return to their home states with marriage licenses in hand and demanding the rights and benefits that heterosexual married couples presently receive. And because of the 'full faith and credit' clause of the Constitution, which says that each of the states must recognize the licenses distributed in each of the other states, homosexual marriage will surely become a reality. Tons of lawsuits of course will be filed and the US Supreme Court will most likely be involved."

Gabbard asked for prayers and returned the microphone to Bill Horn. To the national media in attendance, the emcee's affiliation—Horn was introduced as Midwest regional director of *The Report*—likely brought no recognition. But to Iowa conservatives, Horn was known as the westerner who had decamped to their state the previous year with the primary purpose of defeating a member of the Des Moines school board who had served for twelve years before declaring in early 1995 he was gay. (Horn was successful, and offered the defeated candidate some advice: "If Mr. Wilson wants to be a homosexual activist school board member, he needs to move to San Francisco.") Horn remained in Iowa after his victory, and for someone looking to influence more than local curricula, his timing and choice of location were fortuitous, as the First Federated Church's crowded pews attested.

Now it was just forty-eight hours before the state's nominating caucuses in February 1996, a prime moment to introduce issues—particularly those with potential appeal to evangelical conservatives—and force Republican presidential candidates to engage with them.

"Welcome to a historic event tonight," Horn said to the assembled, "the kickoff for the National Campaign to Protect Marriage." There was not, to that point, much to the National Campaign to Protect Marriage, just a video Horn screened called *The Ultimate Target of the Gay Agenda: Same-Sex Marriage,* an official T-shirt emblazoned MARRIAGE: 1 MAN & 1 WOMAN, and some pamphlets with the text of a "Marriage Protection Resolution" on them. Those who called the phone number listed on the pamphlets were connected to the Cincinnati office of a group called Equal Rights, Not Special Rights, where they were invited to send $15 for their own copy of the video.

The national campaign had been conceived less than a month earlier, in Memphis, during the National Affairs Briefing Convention. The first briefing had been held in 1980, when Religious Roundtable organizer Ed McAteer was credited for helping anoint Ronald Reagan as the preferred candidate of evangelicals. It was the first time that conservative clergy and Republican politics had been formally introduced on such a scale. "I know you can't endorse me," Reagan told thousands of ministers in attendance, "but I want you to know that I endorse you."

In fifteen years, much had changed. The bond between conservative clergy and the American right was strong, so much so that by the summer of 1993 Christian Coalition executive director Ralph Reed began to warn of a "communications dilemma." The "pro-family movement," he contended in the Heritage Foundation's *Policy Review,* "has not yet completely connected its agenda with average voters." After religious conservatives helped Republicans win control of Congress in 1994, the movement had, for the first time, a hand in governing and a stake in creating a durable majority. At the Christian Coalition's September 1995 conference, Reed admonished his invited speakers to avoid what authors Chris Bull and John Gallagher called "ad hominem attacks on homosexuals."

But on the margins of the Memphis meeting was a smaller gathering in a Baptist church basement whose participants were not much concerned with governance or mainstream respectability. They were, in essence, trend-spotters—men with a keen eye for up-and-coming issues, ready to make the jump from niche policy interest to mass concern. They were fluent in the lexicon of moralists, but the language they spoke was marketing. They were united in the insight that homosexuality, as Traditional Values Coalition president Louis Sheldon put it, "galvanizes our public more than right-to-life."

Sheldon had seen the opportunity before anyone else. Since the mid-1970s, California had been the vanguard of gay rights, and one Presbyterian minister from Orange County had anointed himself director of the revanche. "If you destroy the heterosexual ethic," Sheldon would say, "then you are destroying a major pillar of Western civilization." At nearly every opportunity, his loose network of conservative churches aimed to restrain the homosexual menace. Sheldon fought repeal of California's antisodomy laws and helped organize a 1978 "Defend Our Children" ballot referendum that would have banned gays and lesbians from serving as public schoolteachers in the state. (The proposal was seen as so extreme that even Reagan, then eager to court religious conservatives in preparation for a third presidential campaign, publicly opposed it.) Like the Defend Our Children initiative, some Traditional Values Coalition proposals failed, such as the 1990 municipal referendum that a state appeals court knocked from the ballot with the judgment "all that is lacking is a sack of stones for throwing." Others succeeded, like lobbying Governor Pete Wilson to veto a 1991 bill that would have protected gays and lesbians from employment discrimination. Around that time, Sheldon began to look beyond California for influence and developed off-the-shelf templates for legislation or ballot initiatives that could be adopted anywhere. After Bill Clinton's victory in 1992, Sheldon found solace in the fact that the rising profile of gay politics would be good for business. "We now have another front-burner issue in addition to protecting the unborn," he told the *New York Times*. "This may be a blessing in disguise. We will fight harder. We will double in size."

By 1995, Sheldon's network had expanded to include thirty-one thousand churches nationwide from a dozen different denominations, many of them in African American or Hispanic communities. It was a diversity that Sheldon had carefully cultivated by an extended attack on civil-rights rhetoric that analogized discrimination on the basis of race and sexual orientation. "The blacks, who cannot change their skin color, are offended that the gays are seeking protection for behavior they can change," Sheldon explained, summarizing a $19.95 video he sold called *Gay Rights, Special Rights*. (Within months of its 1993 release, Sheldon would claim he took in nearly $1 million from sales of the video.) But the U.S. Supreme Court threatened to roll back one of the antigay movement's greatest victories. In February 1995 the court announced it would take up *Romer v. Evans*, an appeal challenging Colorado's Amendment 2, which overturned statutes that shielded citizens from discrimination based on sexual orientation. The immediate result of Amendment 2 had been to eliminate equal-protection ordinances in Denver, Boulder, and Aspen, but its passage left a more enduring impact in Colorado law. Other municipalities would be denied the power to extend such protections to their residents, making gays the only group so explicitly isolated.

Amendment 2 was celebrated as a model for what grassroots religious activists could accomplish using popular politics to undercut the incremental legislative gains of gay-rights advocates. The seven-point margin in its favor was proof that latent statewide majorities could be mobilized to override the policies of leftist big-city politicians. (The fact that it won on a presidential ballot in which Colorado gave Clinton its electoral votes was evidence of how cross-partisan the electoral coalition that sustained Amendment 2 was.) The Colorado win was a particularly useful case study when contrasted with an Oregon ballot initiative that had failed the same day by thirteen points. Measure 9 had been likely the most all-encompassing antigay bill ever, labeling homosexuality "abnormal, wrong, unnatural and perverse"—a definition it applied equally to bestiality, necrophilia, and pedophilia—and imposing a blanket prohibition on any government policy to "promote" it. (Gay advocates said that the prohibition was so broad that it could justify everything from denying gay bars operating licenses to restricting public-school counselors from honestly advising sexually conflicted teens.) Amendment 2 had been more narrowly written, its rhetoric less scabrously judgmental. The "no special rights" rhetoric that had carried the day in Colorado was even liberal in its sensibility, predicated on the idea that gays were the powerful special-interest lobby crafting local laws to their unique benefit. Only at the ballot box could an innocent majority keep them in check.

Many of those who ended up forming the board of the National Campaign to Protect Marriage after the Memphis meeting had been first linked through the Colorado campaign. Several of them then helped franchise Amendment 2 to Cincinnati, where they succeeded in undoing a city-council "human rights" ordinance the following year by replicating almost exactly the Colorado ballot language. "Anyone who's opposed to the militant homosexual agenda can see this is going to be the issue of the nineties," said Phil Burress, a reformed Cincinnati pornography addict whose Citizens for Community Values quickly pivoted to lead the 1993 campaign, which received 80 percent of its funding from Colorado for Family Values.

While the Cincinnati law would ultimately emerge safe from legal challenges, Colorado's Amendment 2 received a less sympathetic reception from the federal judiciary. (The distinction derived from the fact that Colorado's was a state law drafted explicitly to prevent municipalities from exercising the type of local judgment on display in Cincinnati.) When the Supreme Court heard the Colorado case in October 1995, there seemed to be broad acceptance of the premise put forward by those challenging Amendment 2: that the law served no purpose but to communicate public disapproval of gays, and that such majoritarian "animus" was no basis for denying a category of people their constitutional rights to due process. The most ominous sign during oral arguments came from justices Anthony Kennedy and Sandra Day O'Connor, Republican appointees considered part of the court's center-right majority. O'Connor had even been part of the *Hardwick* coalition that had upheld state antisodomy laws, but now both appeared hostile to the notion that voters were entitled to use democratic means to demonstrate their moral disapproval for specific sexual subcultures.

More than Colorado's municipal codes hung in the balance. For nearly a decade, *Hardwick* had offered federal legal cover for the type of localized antigay politics seeded by Louis Sheldon's Traditional Values Coalition. A decision to strike down Colorado's law would "knock out the last prop that allows a state to hold back from accepting 'same-sex marriage,' the gift that is now being prepared for us by the courts in Hawaii," wrote Hadley Arkes, an Amherst College political philosopher who had helped defend the Cincinnati statute as an expert trial witness. If justices decided that Colorado had gone too far in explicitly excluding gays from qualifying for local civil-rights protections, why wouldn't other liberal judges cite that as a basis for telling states that they couldn't discriminate against same-sex couples?

Arkes had gained influence outside the academy as an informal adviser to the National Right to Life Committee and frequent contributor to conservative magazines and think-tank publications about the ways governments failed to respect "natural law." He argued that universal rights and freedoms could exist only if grounded in nature, and thus reflected a godly design. (Citing nature as justification for policy had become so anathema to modern liberalism that Arkes liked to jokingly call it "the 'N' word.") Gay marriage, Arkes wrote, was a novel idea conceived in defiance of human biology. "In traditional marriage, the understanding of monogamy was originally tied to the 'natural teleology' of the body—to the recognition that only two people, no more and no fewer, can generate children," Arkes had written in 1993. "This is not to deny, of course, that men may truly love men, or commit themselves to a life of steady friendship. But many of us have continued to wonder just why any of these relations would be enhanced in any way by adding to them the ingredients of penetration—or marriage." Just as other conservatives were beginning to understand the stakes in Hawaii, Arkes was trying to turn their attention elsewhere. He had resigned himself to the inevitability that the state's liberal judges would take "our laws into the realm of Shangri-La," which meant the real work to be done was in Washington.

Unlike the situation in Honolulu, where the halting work of the legislature and the commission it had created was delaying a trial, the Supreme Court of the United States had a fixed timeline. Justices would have to announce their opinion in the Colorado case by June, when their annual term ended. "The Supreme Court is moving to the threshold of a decision as portentous nearly as *Roe v. Wade*, and hardly anyone seems to be paying much attention," Arkes cautioned.

Sheldon, a pastor with no legal background, had long relied on Arkes to decode for him the moral consequences of American jurisprudence. Arkes's argument that the Hawaii and Colorado cases should be seen as self-reinforcing threats—two separate legal threads intertwined by circumstance—convinced Sheldon that marriage represented the sphere in which the gay menace had to be confronted in 1996. As early as December 1992, Sheldon had included same-sex marriage in a grab bag of policy concerns—along with "promotion of homosexuality in public schools"—that could be addressed through a California ballot proposition to promote "the heterosexual ethic," as he described it in a fundraising appeal to supporters. As the Hawaii case moved through the courts, Sheldon began to talk more about rewriting laws to explicitly preclude gay marriage. "We're looking at our legal options," Sheldon declared to the *Los Angeles Times* in March 1995. "This is a major issue with all our supporters."

Hawaii's looming scrum had already won the attention of Randall Terry, whose pro-life Operation Rescue had pioneered the tactic of picketing abortion clinics until they were forced to shut down. Terry was drawn to big media events—during the 1992 Democratic convention he had been arrested for thrusting an aborted fetus at Clinton—and he planned to visit Honolulu as soon as the legislature took up the marriage issue. Terry's lawyer was among those whom Horn invited to address his kickoff rally.

In his turn at the pulpit in Des Moines, Jay Sekulow said that Operation Rescue's abortion activism had served as a "training ground, I believe, for this fight"—which would similarly demand "aggressive forms of protest, all non-violent but aggressive nonetheless," said Sekulow, chief counsel to the American Center for Law and Justice. "I'm not saying that there's going to be doors blocked to licensing facilities, but one never knows!"

Then Sekulow lifted a folded yellow sheet that he said included the text of something called the Marriage Protection Resolution, a brief document that would commit candidates to take action on the ascendant issue. "I want this signed by everyone running for president of the United States!" he exclaimed. One by one, three Republicans in attendance did, walking amid flashbulbs across the stage where a poster in a hue of colonial parchment sat on an easel. Another three sent word that they were signing in absentia. (Only one Republican presidential candidate, Indiana senator Richard Lugar, refused to endorse the resolution.) The candidate widely expected to win the Republican nomination for president was among those who communicated his regrets for not being able to attend. But as Senate majority leader, Bob Dole was the only one who stood in a position to make policy. Horn read a letter from the front-runner pledging his fidelity to the cause. The resolution, Dole had written, "does not go far enough."

Don & Bob

The national media treated the Saturday night spectacle at Des Moines's First Federated Church in February as just another stop on Iowa's pre-caucus campaign circuit. As a result, few in Washington noticed that Bob Dole had signed the Marriage Protection Resolution, but Senator Don Nickles's office took heed of it. Four years earlier, the veteran Oklahoma senator had chaired the platform committee during a Republican convention that had turned contentious over one speaker's declaration of a "religious war" on prime-time television. The experience acquainted Nickles with the particular challenges posed by wedge issues during a presidential campaign, and also gave him an eye for the opportunity they might provide. As a top liaison to religious conservatives for Dole's 1996 presidential campaign, Nickles was in a position to put that knowledge to work. He was always hunting for ways Dole could demonstrate that he offered a "totally different vision and direction for our country than President Clinton," as Nickles explained in a personal note to Dole, in particular those issues that would make the point "morally."

Nickles was intimately familiar with the cluster of religious conservatives who had succeeded, in a matter of weeks, at forcing the heretofore-invisible matter of same-sex marriage onto Iowa's pre-caucus agenda. In fact, many of those who had gathered in Memphis that January had helped midwife Nickles's own rise. Shortly after his arrival on Capitol Hill in 1981, Nickles received a letter inviting him to join the board of governors of the Council for National Policy. Despite its stately name, the group was a young one, and it had been conceived from the outset to be something of a cipher. The council refused to disclose its roster of seventy-eight members, but its executive director, Woody Jenkins, assured Nickles that "each one is a major national leader in the field of business, politics or religion.

They have another important trait in common—each one deeply believes in the free enterprise system, human liberty, and the need for a moral rebirth in our country." It amounted to a New Right counterestablishment, holding clandestine quarterly gatherings in grand hotels and luxury resorts. Once he had joined the board, Nickles learned that Jenkins had a less romantic description of the type of "truly outstanding characteristic" that made for a recruitment target: "large financial resources, leadership of a national organization or interest group, influence in the media, great intellectual ability, far-reaching political influence and so on."

At the time, Nickles did not yet have any of those qualities, but it did not require much imagination to project that, at a minimum, far-reaching political influence was in his future. He was a freshman state senator when he won his first U.S. Senate race; at thirty-one, he was the youngest member of his party ever elected to that office. To Washington Republicans, the boyish former businessman had seemed like an apparition from the conservative future materializing over the prairie horizon. His sense of ideological purpose was grounded in a moving origin myth. When Nickles was thirteen, his father died, and the federal government was quick to deliver a second trauma: the family had to sell off some of its machine-tools business just to pay the burdensome estate-tax bill. Oklahoma was on its way to becoming perhaps the most reliably Republican state in the country, a western loop of the Bible Belt where the oil boom had inspired a nearly evangelical belief in the free market and distrust for regulation. "Conservatism pervades almost every major voter group within the state," Nickles's pollster, Arthur Finkelstein, explained in a 1980 campaign memo. When he asked Oklahoma Republicans what they were looking for in a senator, Finkelstein found "religious commitment being cited most often as the quality desired."

In that respect, Nickles was highly qualified. He was able to effortlessly project his devoutness—one year his staff would give him a Bible for Christmas—without ever letting on whether it was tethered to a particular theology. While in Oklahoma City as a state senator, he participated in a nondenominational prayer group; in Washington, he would sign up for three of them, including a Jewish one. "I think most people would be surprised if they knew he was Roman Catholic," a Nickles press secretary, Paul Lee, once said. "If you think of Don Nickles and you're a Baptist, you probably think he's a Baptist. If you're Assembly of God, you probably think, 'That's Don Nickles, too.'"

Nickles eked through a crowded primary by emphasizing his youth and integrity. As he rose in politics, Nickles liked to quote one of his favorite Bible verses, an admonition from Galatians to avoid "selfish ambition, dissensions, discord and factions." In the Senate, Nickles proved expert in all four as necessary, but he did so with a congeniality that persuaded more senior legislators not to view him as a threat. "Don Nickles is a representative of the 'silent majority' of the baby boom generation," an ally later wrote. "He votes like Jesse Helms, but he has the genial manner of a Ronald Reagan."

With Reagan's election, those who had marshaled considerable wealth and influence on the outskirts of the American power structure saw an opportunity to influence policy from within it. "How can we be more vocal in urging elected officials to make laws and decisions based on traditional biblical morality?" asked Tim LaHaye, a San Diego pastor whose worldview was shaped by both the New Testament's apocalyptic prophecy and the John Birch Society's anticommunist paranoia, and who established one of the country's first megachurches, with over one thousand active members. When a referendum to ban gay schoolteachers from California classrooms appeared on the 1978 ballot, LaHaye joined the campaign led by his fellow Southern California pastor Lou Sheldon and expressed concern that the new world order had allowed "homosexuality to spread to millions of victims." That same year, LaHaye published a book, *Unhappy Gays*, which ventured that "Old Testament capital punishment" might be the only suitable response.

LaHaye's project was not so much to undermine his opponents' grand plan but to create his own parallel network that could triumph through sheer force. One by one, LaHaye seeded right-wing groups to mirror the most fearsome ones of the godless left. The Council on National Policy would be a secretive power cabal similar to the Council on Foreign Relations. Concerned Women of America, led by LaHaye's wife, Beverly, would be an antifeminist analog to the National Organization for Women, which had been so successful at launching the Equal Rights Amendment.

Tim LaHaye's early insistence that "the largest army of any minority in this country is the Christian army" inspired his peers to renounce the "shelter-belt" separatism favored by fundamentalist preachers who had worried that meddling in politics could taint their ministry. "He'd done something no conservative minister had ever done before: He'd organized hundreds of churches into a political bloc. At the time, I'd never heard of mixing religion and politics," the Virginia preacher Jerry Falwell said after observing LaHaye's operation on a tour of California. "More than any other person, Tim LaHaye challenged me to begin thinking through my involvement." LaHaye joined the board of Falwell's Moral Majority but stayed away from the increasingly visible pulpit available to a televangelist. "He flew under the radar, very behind-the-scenes, and didn't seek publicity," Falwell said.

The new evangelicals also differed from earlier fundamentalist Protestants in their willingness to see past historical and doctrinal differences with Catholics, like Nickles, to understand how politically useful they could be to one another. In the spring of 1993, when Christian Coalition executive director Ralph Reed offered to broker a meeting between Senator Bob Dole and leaders of other "pro-family organizations," his list of prospective invitees included not only those representing his fellow evangelical Protestants but the U.S. Catholic Conference, the National Conference of Catholic Bishops, and the Knights of Columbus. The seating arrangement at the subsequent breakfast meeting in Dole's minority-leader suite revealed the hierarchy of the religious right, at least as viewed by their Capitol Hill allies. None of the Catholic leaders were placed with Dole. Neither were Lou or Andrea Sheldon, each of them shuffled off to a lesser table with one of Dole's junior colleagues. Dole's table included Reed, Beverly LaHaye, and the Family Research Council's Gary Bauer, with Nickles between them.

Bauer was the most seasoned Washington operator in the meeting. He had no clerical credentials: Bauer had come to his post after serving as Reagan's chief domestic-policy adviser. Upon leaving the White House in 1988, Bauer joined the Family Research Council just as the organization saw its profile boosted through a merger with Focus on the Family. With a $10 million annual budget, Bauer liked to describe the Family Research Council's work as a "hybrid" of think tank and political organization, with "a large number of people who are supposed to be thinking great thoughts, but we also do a lot more grassroots work."

One of the group's most valuable relationships on Capitol Hill was with Nickles, who in 1990 had been elected chairman of the Republican Policy Committee. His rise had paralleled that of Christian conservatives within the party, and thanks in part to relationships developed through the Council for National Policy, Nickles remained one of their favorite senators. "You have many old friends in CNP and now a lot of new ones," executive director Morton Blackwell wrote Nickles after the senator participated in a "New Congress and Grassroots America" panel at a suburban Virginia Ritz-Carlton in June 1995.

By then, midway through his third Senate term, Nickles was better placed than ever to advance the movement's agenda. The Republican Policy Committee had been initially developed to serve as an in-house think tank for the party's Senate caucus, but with Republicans controlling both houses of Congress, it shifted from a redoubt of conservatism within a skeptical minority to architect of the majority's work. In the years since Nickles took over the policy committee, the Family Research Council's staff had grown more than fivefold, and the two institutions frequently ended up in a policymaking symbiosis. In 1995, Nickles and his staff played key roles in killing Clinton's appointment of Henry Foster to be surgeon general, because the doctor acknowledged having performed abortions, and moving the Partial-Birth Abortion Ban Act through Congress with large majorities. (Clinton vetoed the bill.) "It is because of our special friends that the FRC is able to do its very best to defend family, faith and freedom," Bauer wrote to Nickles in December 1995. "During these difficult times, I am thankful that God has raised up strong leaders like you to stand firm with us." Unspoken was that Bauer and his ilk felt truly blessed to have such a figure in the Senate's Republican leadership, a structure that too often appeared stacked by centrists.

To Christian conservatives, the most worrisome exemplar of this tradition may have been Dole, a moderate who over two prior presidential campaigns had never developed any real working relationship with his party's activists. ("I don't know where these people come from, you know," he would say of one prominent antiabortion activist.) Dole was not himself particularly religious, and he had little ease with the public displays of faith increasingly expected of Republican politicians. Before his "Pro-Family Breakfast," in May 1993, an aide had to advise Dole via memo that, "given the group," attendees would expect to say grace before eating their fruit and cereal—and suggested that Dole "may want to ask someone like Nickles" to actually lead the prayer for him. Those invited to the breakfast recognized the gesture of goodwill. It was nearly three years before the first of 1996's presidential primaries would be held, and Dole, already understood to be a likely candidate, took the courtship seriously. Even after adding plans to tape *The Tonight Show* in Los Angeles the night before the scheduled breakfast—which would force him to return on a cross-country flight scheduled to arrive in Washington after midnight—Dole insisted on keeping the 8:30 a.m. appointment. "What's so smart about it was he knew that most of those leaders would support someone else, either privately or publicly," Reed said. "But the key was: 'Let's stay close, let's have our line of communication.'"

Often Nickles's Republican Policy Committee was that channel, and as 1996 began, the Family Research Council started scheming to link Nickles's future even more durably to Dole's. Its political director, former congressional aide Marty Dannenfelser, launched a quiet campaign for Nickles to be nominated for the vice presidency. "To Bob Dole, the conservatives in general and the pro-family movement in particular, must at times seem insatiable, a constantly complaining group of critics," wrote a researcher hired to prepare a memo outlining the case for Nickles as a Dole running mate. "No one he is likely to select would please as many conservatives as one of his own best friends. Rarely does a politician have the chance to please one of his toughest constituencies by elevating a trusted ally."

Over fifteen years serving alongside one another, the two senators had established what the *Weekly Standard* described as "almost a father/son relationship," with Nickles "the closest thing the Senate has to a Dole protégé." As Dole's attention shifted over the winter from the daily workings of the Senate to his presidential campaign, he began to delegate responsibilities to his leadership team—and more tasks seemed to fall on Nickles than anyone else. "I have asked Don Nickles to work with our colleagues in the House in planning our broader communications strategy," Dole told a Senate Republican in October. In January, he instructed Nickles to devise "hearings to be held here in Washington, highlighting *our* priorities. This would include coordinating with the House where possible, and working with the RNC and others in promoting these events." Nickles was eager to see his mentor move on from the Senate. Dole's departure would open up the majority leader's post, and—even though he was just forty-eight years old—Nickles had accumulated the experience and seniority to run for the job. Nickles endorsed Dole early for the presidency and offered his campaign strategic guidance about navigating rightward during the Republican primary season along with personal advice for the candidate himself. "Greet everybody you see (and the cameras) with love in your heart ... Jesus said, 'Love one another as I have loved you' ... it is contagious," Nickles wrote Dole in a memo titled "Just a couple of friendly thoughts and suggestions."

When a newspaper in western Iowa reported that Dole had not only agreed with the Marriage Protection Resolution but had sent a supportive letter, the Republican Policy Committee swung into action. One of Nickles's aides quickly submitted a confidential request to the Congressional Research Service's American Law Division. *What did federal law say about interstate recognition of marriages? And what authority did the legislative branch have to limit the national impact if a state's judges overreached?*

The Family Research Council already had its own idea of what it hoped to see Congress do. Robert H. Knight, a former journalist who served as the council's director of cultural studies and in-house expert on gay rights, was a close reader of the gay press, and as early as late 1993 he took note of the boldness with which activists welcomed Hawaii as merely the first stage in a broader project. One passage written by Michelangelo Signorile in *Out* impressed Knight for its candor. "The most subversive action lesbians and gay men can undertake—and one that would perhaps benefit all of society—is to transform the notion of 'family' entirely," Signorile wrote. "Once same-sex marriage is granted, the crucial step in redefining marriage has been taken."

If gay activists had a strategy for dismantling the institution of marriage, shouldn't those devoted to keeping it intact have a plan for reinforcing the legal and political status quo before it became too late? In February, the Family Research Council devoted its bimonthly *Family Policy* publication—which it distributed to members of Congress—exclusively to what it called "Hawaii's Assault on Matrimony." "If more states strengthen their laws, they would also strengthen the marriage defenders in Hawaii, who can cite the 'compelling state interest' of heading off a constitutional crisis," Knight wrote. "At the federal level, Congress may well consider legislation mandating the one-man, one-woman definition of marriage for all federal purposes."

As the Republican Policy Committee staff began exploring its options, its counsel, Lincoln Oliphant, discovered how farsighted Nickles had been on this issue. In 1993, while the Senate considered the Family and Medical Leave Act, Nickles came to the Senate floor to point out what appeared a minor clerical oversight by those who had drafted it. "The bill," Nickles said, "clearly defines other terms like 'parent' and 'eligible employee' and 'son or daughter,' but it did not define 'spouse.'" Nickles planned to vote against the bill, which required employers to grant unpaid leave to workers dealing with sickness, as an unreasonable imposition on businesses. But the bill, a Clinton administration priority backed by congressional Democrats, was likely to become law, so Nickles persuaded its sponsors to add a definition limiting that spouses be of opposite genders. "Under this amendment," Nickles explained to the Senate, "no employer would be required to grant an eligible employee unpaid leave to care for an unmarried domestic partner."

That debate barely caught wider notice, as the same day Nickles's amendment was accepted the Senate was voting on whether homosexuals could serve in the military. The Family and Medical Leave Act had become perhaps the most significant social reform of Clinton's first term, but as Oliphant recounted to his boss in 1996, "it might have been truly revolutionary if it hadn't contained a Nickles amendment that defines the word 'spouse.'" The rule-making process had concluded only a year earlier, after the Labor Department had found itself unexpectedly barraged by comments arguing that the law should be applied to same-sex relationships recognized as domestic partnerships. Many of those lobbying the Clinton administration to do so were its left-wing allies, but Labor Secretary Robert Reich acknowledged he was constrained by Nickles's language limiting the law to married couples. "As you see, your simple amendment had profound implications," Oliphant told Nickles. "It anticipated an effort to redefine 'spouse' (which is to redefine marriage) and it wisely precluded that possibility."

Now it would be time for Nickles to act again. Even before the Congressional Research Service returned its analysis of the legal issues related to marriage recognition, Republican Policy Committee staffers were strategizing with the Family Research Council's Knight and Dannenfelser about what a Senate bill might say. The draft legislation that Knight sent to Oliphant was as plain as a dictionary entry. "In determining the meaning of any Act of Congress," read Knight's draft language, "marriage means only a legal union between one man and one woman as husband and wife; and a reference to a spouse of an individual (including a reference to a husband, wife, widow, or widower) means a second individual only who is of the opposite sex."

Over two weeks, committee staffers exchanged revisions with Knight and Dannenfelser. The new drafts featured only minor adjustments of language, each edit balancing a desire for moral simplicity against a lawyerly interest in precision. None of the drafts changed the scope of the bill, which Oliphant had taken to calling "the Meaning of Marriage Act," or MOMA. Meanwhile, the Republican Policy Committee staff collected polls that attested to how popular such a proposal was likely to be. One taken the previous June in Michigan, considered a crucial presidential battleground state, showed that only 33 percent of people agreed with the statement "If two people love each other, they should be able to get married even if they are of the same sex"—even though it was perhaps the most sympathetic wording a pollster could generate to test public opinion on gay marriage.

On Monday, March 11, the committee staffers gathered to settle on a final text of the bill they could circulate more widely. Afterward, Oliphant drafted two memos. One, titled "A Bill to Define 'Marriage' and 'Spouse,'" was intended for other legislators and lobbyists with a stake in the debate. Oliphant's second memo was for his boss only. Nickles had spent the weekend chaperoning Dole on a campaign swing through Oklahoma, introducing him at home-state rallies in Oklahoma City and Tulsa before the candidate traveled onward to Mississippi. Given Dole's absence from the Senate while campaigning for president, it was the best opportunity the men had had in a while to enjoy each other's company. Dole was on the cusp of clinching his party's nomination, and Nickles was searching for areas in which Dole could demonstrate to the general electorate that he possessed greater moral conscience than Clinton. "I think character is vitally important," Nickles told reporters traveling on Dole's plane.

In his memo, Oliphant explained to Nickles that the brief marriage bill that the Republican Policy Committee had drafted—a single sentence long—could present such an opportunity. "As you might suppose, the proposal has strong support among the pro-family groups," Oliphant wrote. "They want Congress to act this year, and they count this proposal as among their two or three priorities. They also believe it is an essential vote for Congressional Republicans and for the Republican candidate for President."

"I regard this proposal as modest. It merely restates what everyone has supposed American law meant for about 200 years. Naturally, therefore, it probably will be wildly controversial: Two centuries of precedent means nothing when your modern homosexualists set out to redefine the idea of marriage itself, which is much older than 200 years," Oliphant wrote to Nickles. "The sponsor of this bill will be called a 'homophobe,' a 'sexist,' a 'hater,' an opponent of civil rights, and other things more colorful and profane. The challenge is to take and hold the moral high ground. The sponsor will clearly have the greater number of troops (polls show very strong support for denying marriages to homosexuals), but the opposition appears to have the big guns of the electronic and print media."

Instead of intimidating Nickles, the promise of martyrdom inspired him to urgent action. Dole had just returned to Washington, having secured his party's nomination, which meant that—for the first time in months—his attention had shifted back to Senate business. Throughout the second half of March, Dole held a series of meetings with his Republican leadership team, with an eye to long-range planning. The majority leader would shortly return to the life of a full-time campaigner, and his lieutenants were already strategizing about how to structure the congressional calendar in a way that would boost Dole's prospects instead of hindering them. "Without belaboring the matter, I would like to reiterate that we all stand ready to help you win the presidency, and hope that you will let us do the nitty-gritty battles for you," Larry Craig, an Idaho Republican who chaired the party's Senate Steering Committee, wrote to Dole. "We should have a limited and realistic agenda, concentrating on passing the must-pass bills, and only those additional items which advance a very few themes and messages on which Republicans agree."

Nickles had one ready. In the last week of March, he mentioned to Dole the bill his staff had generated about same-sex marriage. It was a subject to which Dole had never given much thought, but Nickles believed he could convince him that it represented both good policy and the type of political gambit that would serve his presidential campaign well. During the primaries, Dole had engaged with social issues only reactively, often just to keep pace with rivals who had stronger conservative credentials and deny them new areas in which to question his sincerity. As he looked to a general election, however, Dole considered anew topics like partial-birth abortion and gay marriage. On social issues, Dole could wield the wedge himself—using his power as majority leader to set the agenda in a way that would force his Democratic opponent to react defensively. "I suggest we move forward on this," Nickles wrote to Dole on April 2. "President Clinton should be given the opportunity to sign it."

The Law Man

Meanwhile, in the House, a freshman representative was looking for a way to stand out from the crowd. "Hearts and flowers and sugar coating—Bob is not," consultant Fred Davis told his new client, Bob Barr, in a March 1, 1996, memo laying out a media strategy for the congressman's first-ever reelection campaign. The two men had never spent much time together, but reading and watching his way through a record of the Georgia Republican's career led Davis to a mordant summary: "a decent human being, yes, and even more so a doer." This was one of what he called "Strategic Image Objectives"—what he saw in Barr that he hoped, through careful marketing, could be reified as the "precise image voters will have of Bob this November." But unbeknownst to Davis, Barr would also be able to expand that list of accomplishments during the election year, by scavenging undervalued issues with no record of ownership and claiming them as his own. "What happened to the old rule," Davis asked from his Hollywood studio, "that Freshmen simply bided their time 'getting to know the place'?"

Unlike many of the Republicans first elected to Congress in 1994—a freshman class whom one member described as "the purest, most worthy group of leaders elected to this body in my lifetime"—Barr had never practiced a confessional, highly personal politics. He had arrived in Washington in a lawman's mufti, with suspenders and collar stickpins that ensured his tie remained tightly fastened around his neck. His stocky physique suggested a tough guy softened by desk jobs, with an overgrown mustache that draped over his thick upper lip like a pelt, and his résumé confirmed the impression. Barr had spent nearly eight years as an analyst at the Central Intelligence Agency, under director George H. W. Bush, and remained loyal to Bush after leaving the agency for a private career as a defense attorney. He had earned enough chits in local Republican politics to win an appointment by President Ronald Reagan to serve as U.S. attorney in Atlanta, even though he immediately admitted the job was a poor fit. "I enjoy defense more than anything," he informed an *Atlanta Journal-Constitution* reporter who had come to profile Georgia's new federal prosecutor. Barr had a verve for generating media coverage with himself at its focus—a local joke was that he would call a press conference to say "no comment"—that led many to accuse him of acting like a candidate, even before he ran for office.

Upon leaving law enforcement, Barr began running in earnest. In 1992, he sought the Republican nomination for Senate, and escaped a five-person field but lost in a runoff, in part because of charges that he was too moderate, specifically on abortion. (Barr said he thought *Roe v. Wade* should be overturned, but was vague about what exceptions to a full ban he thought were appropriate.) From the start, Barr was a flawed messenger for the family-values rhetoric that had become a default for Republicans running in conservative districts. Barr was on his third wife, each of the previous two marriages ending in messily overlapping ways. "He came in one night and told me he didn't love me anymore and was moving out," Gail Barr told a reporter. "The next week he wanted me to go with him to brunch with Larry Thompson, the outgoing U.S. Attorney, to say he was interested in the job." During his Senate primary, a local newspaper ran an account of Barr "licking whipped cream from the chests of two buxom women" at a Leukemia Society fundraising luncheon. (The gesture raised $200 for the charity.)

Two years later, challenging Democratic congressman Buddy Darden, Barr fixated immediately on two areas where the incumbent had aligned himself with the Clinton White House: voting for both a 1993 budget raising taxes and a 1994 ban on assault weapons. "He forgot, for one brief term in Congress," Barr said of Darden, "that there's one thing you do not raise in West Georgia—taxes—and there's one thing you do not take away from citizens—their guns." That left little need to address social issues, and Barr made clear that battling over abortion in particular was not a priority for him. "There's no sense spending a lot of time on it right now because we're never going to get anywhere with this president," Barr said. Barr's slogan was *Tough Enough to ... Cut Spending First,* and when asked for his priorities he repeatedly volunteered crime, national security, taxes, and the federal budget. When Newt Gingrich, who represented a neighboring district, introduced the "Contract with America," a ten-point agenda to keep Republican sights on noncontroversial fiscal and governmental reforms, Barr saw his instincts validated. "We should not focus solely on one or two issues," he said. "You really run the risk of not developing—you know, getting your broad base of votes out."

It was a good year for Republicans, and when the national wave came, Barr was able to ride it to Washington. Even before Gingrich was to meet with the new members of the House—an unprecedented seventy-three Republicans, many of them new to elected office—Barr wrote to the incoming Speaker to request an assignment to the House Permanent Select Committee on Intelligence. He may have been disappointed when Gingrich placed him instead on the House Judiciary Committee, typically a redoubt for each party's most ideologically strident members. The Speaker saw the assignment as a natural complement to a larger task: he invited Barr to chair a newly created Firearms Legislation Task Force. Gingrich had been christening task forces across the House, a mechanism useful "as a device for finessing some institutional obstacles to decision-making," a spokesman explained. It was clear what obstacles he meant. Many of the Republican committee chairmen were avatars of the old guard, more ideologically moderate and temperamentally pragmatic than the incoming class, and Gingrich was happy to weaken competing power centers as he consolidated power within party leadership.

Command of a task force was an unusual responsibility to extend to a freshman representative, but one that Barr, who had grown accustomed to running his own office as a prosecutor, happily assumed. "This is not a group that is simply going to meet from time to time," Barr said. "We intend to be proactive." Hours after being sworn in, Barr introduced the "Taking Back Our Streets Act," which would replace Clinton crime-prevention programs that Republicans mocked as wasteful social spending with new prison construction and mandatory sentences. In the following days, Barr proposed a repeal of Clinton's assault-weapons ban and toyed publicly with abolishing the Bureau of Alcohol, Tobacco and Firearms. Barr told a reporter that Gingrich had promised him that "no issues that relate to firearms are off the table."

For Barr, that meant throwing himself into conservative gun culture. In the mid-1970s, the National Rifle Association—previously little more than a hunters' organization whose primary activity was offering gun-training classes—dove into partisan politics as a critic of new laws prohibiting gun sales and ownership. The time was right to assert itself, as innovations in direct mail allowed membership-based organizations to build national constituencies around issues of narrow interest. A resulting coalition of convenience, known as the New Right, developed institutions of mutual benefit: think tanks, magazines, and umbrella organizations that would look out for their niche concerns as long as the groups ensured their members joined arms to elect sympathetic Republicans to office.

As Gingrich's designated point person on gun issues, Barr became immediately useful to the movement's leaders. In his first month in office, Barr was invited to be an honored guest at a "conservative support group" dinner. Despite a busy night at the Capitol, Barr shuttled back and forth between votes to dine with the New Right's most experienced strategists (Richard Viguerie, David Keene, Morton Blackwell) and rising Gingrich-era lobbyist-operators (Grover Norquist, Jack Abramoff). Barr cultivated them back: a dutiful and often obsequious letter-writer, he asked a staffer immediately after the dinner to compile a "Conservative Leaders" mailing list so he could correspond with them as a group.

For the first three months of 1995, the Republican leadership kept a vigorous schedule as it tried to pass as much of the Contract with America as it could in its first one hundred days. Six of the ten items, procedural reforms including a Balanced Budget Amendment and limits on tort suits, had moved through the Judiciary Committee. (Much of the contract would flounder in the Senate.) But by summer the House leadership had exhausted its plans with a year and a half still to go in the term. "We lost some momentum," Barr later reflected. "There didn't seem to be a great deal of thought or organization to 'Okay, what do we do now to sustain this effort?'"

With the leadership's tacit accord, House Republicans were left to follow their own interests. Some were eager to investigate scandals related to the Clinton White House. Barr believed that "the whole way this administration and this president approached governing was corrupt," and his task-force chairmanship offered him an entry into the right's booming conspiracy subculture. Helen Chenoweth, a volatile right-wing Idaho congresswoman also in her first term, recommended Barr speak to the prosecutor in her district who was investigating the tragic encounter of federal agents and well-armed separatists at Ruby Ridge, Idaho. Because of its purview, outside influence on Judiciary Committee members was less likely to come from industry lobbyists pragmatically counting votes than either side's true believers, who recognized a venue where they could ease otherwise untouchable issues into national circulation. "It was a touch-point for the conservative Christian right, because we could have a lot of hearings and push stuff through," says Kathryn Lehman, a Republican staff attorney to the Judiciary Committee.

That suited Barr, who had an immense appetite for work and the metabolism for it. While at the CIA, he had received a law degree by taking night classes at Georgetown, and he kept the long hours as a congressman. He proved a diligent lawmaker, with a 98.6 percent attendance rating on House votes, and as midnight approached he would still often find himself directing an aide to drive him to an open Starbucks, where he would order a coffee with two shots of espresso to gird him for another shift of work. At various points in his life, Barr consumed up to fifteen shots of espresso a day. "What has to do with your ability to fall asleep is not caffeine," he would explain. "It's having a clean conscience. I have a clean conscience so I can drink all the caffeine I want."

That fall, a constituent passed Barr a piece of paper that would shape his agenda for the rest of his time in Congress. Barr recognized Nancy Bess Johnston when she approached him at an event near the Coosa Valley Fairgrounds in Rome, Georgia, not far from where she lived with her husband, Eddie, a politically active doctor. The Johnstons had been financial supporters of Barr's congressional campaign, and after his election he had invited them to "the Roundtable," as he called a group of constituents he invited to regularly meet with him to share issues of concern.

This time, Johnston was handing her congressman two pages of a newsletter including the admonition that "it is almost certain that Hawaii will grant marriage licenses to homos." Emblazoned *Messiah's Mandate* and dated that September, it was the newsletter of Steve Schlissel, the pastor of Messiah's Congregation in Brooklyn. The Johnstons had subscribed to Schlissel's newsletter for about five years, ever since Eddie had stumbled into Schlissel's congregation when—stuck in New York City one Sunday while traveling for business—he had asked a friend to recommend a place to worship. Schlissel was a known rabble-rouser within the Christian Reformed movement, which practiced an evangelical Calvinism with its roots in Dutch immigrant communities. Schlissel's threat to lead a breakaway faction in protest of efforts to admit female priests had earned him a charge of "schismatic behavior," propelling him to seek alliances with other traditionalist Christian churches outside his small Protestant denomination. No one had ever organized more of them than the Traditional Values Coalition.

Upon returning to Washington, Barr passed the note to Dan Levinson, an aide who had been looking at what Barr's office called the "Hawaii

Marriage Issue." That summer, Oklahoma congressman Ernest Istook, a convert to Mormonism, had clipped an article from the *New Republic* and sent copies to his congressional peers topped with what was known on Capitol Hill as a "Dear Colleague" letter. The article, by Princeton professor Andrew Koppelman, outlined the looming *Baehr v. Lewin* trial and its potential ramifications for gay rights, a series of developments that Istook wrote had "intrigued" him. "This is significant because other states would be asked to give 'full faith and credit' to a same-sex marriage performed in a sister state," Istook wrote. "As a person concerned with preserving traditional family relationships, I wanted to share this article with you because of the many implications it raises for the future of American families." Barr had received Istook's letter, but his congressional office had filed it away with the dozens of other "Dear Colleague" letters that circulate on Capitol Hill to little notice.

Barr's staff began collecting other materials on the subject, many of them by Hadley Arkes, the Amherst political philosopher who had become a familiar figure on Capitol Hill for having helped draft the Partial-Birth Abortion Ban Act. Barr's election, in particular, heartened Arkes, as a prime example of a new member who despite his previous vacillations had effectively flipped a seat from pro-choice to pro-life by defeating a Democratic incumbent, giving hope to yet more aggressive efforts to curtail abortion through legislation. Citing figures from National Right to Life, Arkes estimated that the Republican landslide in 1994 had produced a "net gain of pro-life members in the Congress" totaling forty House votes and six in the Senate. For the first time since abortion and gay rights had become political issues, Republicans controlled the congressional calendar.

Instead of having to organize in the states to fend off liberal efforts to change the constitution, as they had successfully done in blocking the Equal Rights Amendment, now conservatives could marshal the same federal process on behalf of their platform. Arkes proposed adding a single sentence to the founding document: "There is, in the Constitution, no right of homosexual marriage." (That language had been drafted by another member of Arkes's circle of natural-law academics, Notre Dame law professor Charles Rice.) Arkes acknowledged that ratifying a constitutional amendment would be a long and arduous task, if not an impossible one. But merely introducing such an amendment in Congress before judges in Hawaii and elsewhere ruled "would itself send an important signal to the court: it would indicate someone is watching," he wrote in late November

1995. "Republicans on Capitol Hill are too busy in the battle for the budget to notice this sideshow across the street. But they will look up, sometime in the spring, and discover that six justices have transformed the law on marriage and the family. What is needed, then, right now, is someone in Congress to sound the alarm and introduce the amendment." It was not Barr's style to step aside for anyone, or defer to those with more seniority. He was one of only seventeen congressmen to vote against a budget deal Gingrich personally negotiated with Clinton to end a government shutdown. That vote reportedly placed Barr on a list of those in the Speaker's disfavor, but only further endeared him to the movement's grassroots. In February 1996, at the right's most important annual showcase, he was named the Conservative Political Action Conference's outstanding freshman congressman.

Barr was preparing to announce his reelection campaign the following month, his first formal acknowledgment of a challenge from Democratic state representative Charlie Watts. A six-stop weekend tour would be a display of the hard-won enthusiasm Barr now boasted from conservative interest groups. In addition to local representatives of the National Rifle Association and National Federation of Independent Business, Barr would be flanked at his speeches by leaders of Georgia Right to Life and the Christian Coalition. Barr arrived back in his district just as Watts acquired a legislative trophy that would impress many of those same activists. Governor Zell Miller appeared ready to sign a bill clarifying that Georgia would not recognize same-sex marriages, a version of which Watts had been sponsoring in the statehouse. The bill had encountered little friction moving through the general assembly, with overwhelming support in both chambers. The margin was so lopsided that Georgia's Gay Political Action Committee told twenty-one senators who opposed the bill that there was no reason to martyr themselves over a lost cause. Unanimous passage, gay-rights lobbyist Larry Pellegrini explained to the *Atlanta Journal-Constitution*, would deny the Christian Coalition the ability to make gay marriage an election-year issue. "We kept our votes in the closet," Pellegrini said.

But the bill's enactment—and Watts's ability to claim some credit for it—posed a problem for Barr's reelection. It would make it much harder for him to caricature Watts as a Democrat too liberal for a southern district, as Barr had two years earlier with Darden. At the same time, Barr's media tactics were to be predicated on convincing voters of a gap in accomplishment between the two lawmakers. "Instead of trying to reinvent Bob as warm and fuzzy, we should instead play to his strengths: active, quick, intelligent, blunt, tough—and incredibly accomplished in just two short years," consultant Fred Davis had written in his strategy memo earlier that month. Barr's aides exhumed the *Messiah's Mandate* church newsletter that had been languishing in a file cabinet ever since Johnston had handed it over with the suggestion that he look into it further. Now, Barr concluded, it was time for Congress to act on the "Hawaii Marriage Issue." Watts might have helped clarify Georgia's marriage statute, but only Barr was in a position to swoop in and defend the whole country.

For guidance, Barr's counsel Dan Levinson contacted Andrea Sheldon, who had begun lobbying Congress a few years earlier on behalf of her father's Traditional Values Coalition. She shared Arkes's latest missive with him, a memo he had just written to Lou Sheldon titled "Some Notes on Our Current Crisis." It was intended as a private strategy document, but its arguments unfurled in the voice of an essayist, not the logic of a lawyer or self-awareness of a politician. (At one point, with approval and without evident irony Arkes quotes a bon mot from Oscar Wilde's *The Importance of Being Earnest*—whose 1895 theatre début took place at a time when the playwright was being investigated for criminal homosexuality.) "For the past three years, there has been a curious concert of judges, at all levels in our country—federal, state, local—on the matter of gay rights," wrote Arkes. "There is a disposition to strike down anything in our laws that casts an adverse judgment on homosexuality, or implies that homosexuality stands on a lower plane of legitimacy than the sexuality imprinted in our natures."

A Supreme Court ruling on the constitutionality of Colorado's Amendment 2 was likely two months away. What would follow a loss in *Romer v. Evans,* Arkes predicted, was "the 'nationalization' of gay marriage." "What we propose to do then," he advised Sheldon, "is the equivalent of an Incheon landing: We propose to go around the current decision on *Romer v. Evans,* and reach directly to that point to which the justices are heading. We would seek to foreclose, in the Constitution, the prospect of establishing a constitutional right to 'same sex marriage.' We would not forbid the States from accepting this form of marriage, though we would argue against it as a matter of policy in any of the States. We would be making the simple point, however, that the Constitution itself does not entail, or make necessary, a right to marriage on the part of people of the same sex."

Barr was ready to act, but he did not embrace Arkes's ambitious proposal to introduce a constitutional amendment. It was not clear there were the votes or the time. The necessary supermajorities would allow Democrats the ability to block such a proposal from getting through Congress, and even then the ratification process—dependent on the action of state legislatures—would barely start by the time Hawaii triggered the constitutional crisis the amendment was supposed to forestall. It was the proposal of a romantic who had foreseen a crisis and scripted a dramatic valedictory rather than devising a timely escape mechanism.

Barr and Levinson believed that Congress already had all the legal authority it needed to insulate the country from the Hawaiian menace. They turned to the Constitution, whose Article IV included the lever on which gay activists said they could force other states to accept Hawaiian marriage licenses: "Full Faith and Credit shall be given in each State to the public Acts, Records, and judicial Proceedings of every other State." But the second sentence of that same clause gives power to the legislative branch to set standards circumscribing that responsibility: "And the Congress may by general Laws prescribe the Manner in which such Acts, Records and Proceedings shall be proved, and the Effect thereof." Only twice had Congress used that power—both since 1980, and in each instance to strengthen the clause's authority—by expanding the cooperation among states as they chased parental kidnappers and enforced child-support orders. Now Barr was hoping to harness that same constitutional power for the opposite purpose, to free states from a debt of recognizing one another's families, or at least one peculiar new form they could take.

It was not clear such a move was even necessary. Some states, sixteen of them at last count, followed Utah's legislature in taking action to say they wouldn't recognize another's same-sex marriages. In another seventeen capitals, some other legislative activity was afoot to reach such an outcome, many of them adopting Utah's language, which was intended by its author, the LDS Church legal strategist Lynn Wardle, as "a sort of model for other states." If Hawaii actually began allowing gay couples to wed, it was easy to imagine even more states—quite possibly all forty-nine of them—specifying that they wouldn't recognize the licenses. As the law stood, states appeared comfortably within their rights to do so. In the past, federal courts had recognized a public-policy exception to the full-faith-and-credit clause: if a state could assert that it had a rationale for refusing to recognize another state's legal proceedings, it was entitled to do so. Barr's proposal would only clarify that Congress thought same-sex marriage qualified as a suitable public-policy rationale.

More so than some of his Republican peers, Barr harbored a libertarian's fears of Washington expanding its power at the expense of local government. But as Barr saw it, the legal solution was not an example of federal overreach but its opposite. "States rights are protected," Barr would explain, "in that another state cannot force them to recognize same-sex marriages."

How a Grievance Becomes a Bill

By the end of March 1996, two different pieces of legislation were being drafted on opposite sides of the Capitol, each containing a single provision that would empower the federal government to inoculate the country from whatever toxic miasma drifted leeward from Hawaii's laboratory of judicial innovation.

There was the Senate bill by Don Nickles that would redefine the words *marriage* and *spouse* everywhere they appeared in federal law to apply only to opposite-sex couples, ensuring that no local judge could rashly bend national policy to its will. The federal government uses *marriage* in more than eight hundred different locations scattered across the country's laws. *Spouse* appears more than 3,100 times. States' rights meant Hawaii was well within its power to decide who would get its licenses, but when it came to federal taxes and the pensions of government workers, Social Security survivor and veterans-hospital visitation policies—any place Washington put its imprimatur on a committed relation by awarding benefit to its participants—Congress could turn that paper meaningless.

A House bill nurtured by Bob Barr elucidated that states were just as much within their existing constitutional rights to declare another's same-sex marriages unworthy of recognition. That was the one thing that Nickles knew his bill, which concerned itself only with federal policy, wouldn't do. "There is a significant possibility that Hawaii's revolution will be foisted on the other States against their stated wishes," Lincoln Oliphant of the Republican Policy Committee wrote to Nickles. Oliphant conceded that the bill he had helped draft on the senator's behalf "will not affect the Hawaii situation directly. It does not tell Hawaii what it must do, and it does not insulate the other 49 states from Hawaii's policies."

These two bills had emerged from separate corners of the conservative movement, each laundered into Washington by an organization that served as a distinct conduit for channeling religious fervor into political action. The Traditional Values Coalition had its origins in the 1970s, when evangelical Christians were self-conscious outsiders just discovering they could have an impact by organizing to directly enact policy at the ballot box. As it moved beyond the Sun Belt, the coalition saw power deriving from its reach—a grassroots network of churches whose growth increasingly came, denominationally and demographically, from beyond the right's primary constituency of white evangelicals. The Traditional Values Coalition had nurtured Barr's "full faith and credit" legislation, but it never treated federal lobbying as anything more than a mom-and-pop adjunct to its real work outside Washington.

The Family Research Council read power in Washington terms. It had been launched from a position of strength, as part of the right-wing counterestablishment that had supported Ronald Reagan's rise, and it had hardened into an establishment that would survive his reign. Headed by a former White House aide, the Family Research Council was explicitly designed to sit alongside the lobbying shops that measured their influence in terms of access and think tanks that did so through comprehension of policy minutiae. The "meaning of marriage" provision that council lobbyists placed in Nickles's hands reflected those priorities: instead of marginalizing the federal government, it ensured new relevance for Congress in the making of family policy.

Each legislator stood as a natural champion for the organization whose legislative priorities he promoted. Nickles was a methodical institutionalist, with a policymaking fiefdom he used as a way station en route to becoming Senate majority leader or even vice president. Barr was, by his own proud self-conception, "his own man from the day he was born," as an adviser put it. While Nickles sought out his mentor Bob Dole as a cosponsor, Barr had no interest in taking his new issue to Newt Gingrich. That disregard was standard for members of the House Judiciary Committee. "We were sort of the redheaded stepchild to leadership," says Kathryn Lehman, a Republican lawyer for the committee. "We'd bring something to the floor and the floor staff would be like, 'Oh, it's you again? We're going to talk about these hugely controversial and divisive social issues that no one wants to discuss in polite company and we're going to have to vote on them?'"

The two legislators were linked by Representative Steve Largent, an Oklahoma Republican who had previously set National Football League records as a wide receiver. To the rookie politician, Nickles was an object of admiration—"thanks for being such a good role model," Largent wrote shortly after entering Congress—and Barr a supplicant, begging to have his most famous colleague campaign with him in Georgia. Largent's election, just as he was about to enter his sport's hall of fame, cheered religious conservatives pleased to have a telegenic athlete with a national profile as their champion in Washington. Largent was one of two new congressmen-elect singled out for praise by Family Research Council president Gary Bauer, in a 1994 Christmas message to supporters. Within months, Largent had demonstrated his utility to the movement, introducing a bill to protect parental rights against governmental interference, a longtime priority of religious homeschoolers. He also had never been bashful about his disapproval of homosexuality; in a letter to the *Tulsa World,* written before his election to Congress, he had labeled it an "evil practice."

When Barr sought him out to collaborate on a bill to stop same-sex marriages, Largent's staff feared that Barr had calculated their boss's celebrity and credibility within the conservative movement could be leveraged for his own benefit. "The big joke was that Barr was the last person who should be arguing for DOMA because he had been married three times," says Nick Thimmesch II, Largent's press secretary. Largent's communications office served mostly to parry interview requests from national media, while Barr—who faced the threat of a tough reelection—was constantly scheming for attention.

Neither Barr nor Largent, however, sat on the House Judiciary subcommittee that would likely handle any bill dealing with the full-faith-and-credit issue. (Largent had no legal background at all.) The Subcommittee on the Constitution was the preserve of Charles Canady, a Florida Republican in only his second term in the House. While practicing as a real-estate lawyer, Canady had won election to his state's legislature as a Democrat but switched parties and in 1992 ran for Congress as a Republican. In Washington, Canady—who was single and since childhood had counted reading as his primary diversion—impressed even the committee's Democrats for his seriousness. On a committee that typically attracted, and eventually cultivated, bomb-throwers, Canady was remarkable for the most unremarkable of traits: the Yale Law alum was a fastidious lawyer. Judiciary Committee members knew that their chairman, Henry Hyde, held Canady in high regard, since he had skipped over several of them with greater seniority in granting chairmanship of the Constitution subcommittee to Canady. Hyde's passion was pro-life issues, and he knew the subcommittee would take command of any bills generated by the new Republican majority. Just after assuming its chairmanship, in 1995, Canady introduced a ban on second-trimester abortions, a novel procedure that the National Right to Life Committee had begun to call "partial-birth abortion." Canady shepherded the Partial-Birth Abortion Ban Act through his committee and then to a bipartisan win on the House floor as a different version of the bill moved through the Senate. On March 27, 1996, the House passed the Senate version by an impressive 289–129 margin.

Fresh off that victory, Canady now turned his attention to the same-sex marriage issue. He conceived a more ambitious bill than either Barr or Nickles had, one that would marshal at once all the legal tools that Congress possessed to contain same-sex marriages. Canady persuaded Barr that stitching together the two distinct legislative strands into a single bill offered a political advantage by ensuring that the legislation would have an immediate impact were Hawaii to begin marrying gay couples. "This two-pronged approach would achieve much," Barr and Canady wrote to Hyde, informing him of their collaboration. "It would make a plain statement of the federal government's policy on this matter. It would arm the States with strong policy arguments regarding the common understanding of the term marriage."

By April 9, just as Congress prepared to recess for the Easter holiday, Barr and Canady delivered Hyde a confidential letter, with a report on their work and a copy of Arkes's latest memo to Sheldon warning of a "looming crisis." "We would like to introduce a bill in the very near future, and would hope that the Committee could put it on the fast track," they wrote. "We expect that our Leadership would support our initiative, and we believe that it will be supported by large, bi-partisan majorities in both the House and the Senate."

But they still had to reconcile the different approaches emerging out of the two chambers. With Largent as a go-between, Canady tried to persuade Nickles that his bill would be strengthened by an effective merger with Barr's. "We are confident that the full faith and credit provision we drafted is not only constitutionally permissible; we also believe it makes this bill much more meaningful, and it does so in a manner fully consistent with principles of federalism," Bill McGrath, Canady's counsel on the Constitution subcommittee, wrote to Lincoln Oliphant. "All we are doing is defending the right of each State to determine its own policy on this important issue free from the legal maneuverings of gay rights legal groups."

Eventually, the various camps came to agreement on the structure of a unified bill, but not its timing. Unlike Barr, Largent saw himself as a team player, and he asked for the leadership's blessing to sign on as a sponsor of the bill. By the middle of April, Largent had received a firm admonition: leadership wanted him to wait until the Supreme Court had ruled on Colorado's Amendment 2 before moving forward with the legislation. Nickles, too, was holding back to talk to more of his Senate colleagues about the bill before committing publicly to it, and accepted the House leadership's rationale. After all, waiting until the Supreme Court had overreached would make it easier for congressional Republicans to demonstrate they were responding to an urgent constitutional crisis, rather than prematurely initiating one. "The leadership believes that the bill should be introduced in conjunction with a national story," Doug Badger, the Republican Policy Committee's staff director, reported to Nickles after speaking with two members of Largent's staff. "They believe that this would be an appropriate news hook."

Then came a better one. On April 18, the *Washington Times* ran a story on its front page that declared, CLINTON OFFERS NEW PROMISES TO GAYS: HINTS HE'LL PUSH LEGAL "MARRIAGES." The newspaper had the country's most exhaustive regular coverage of gay-rights politics, mostly documented in a way that responded to the existing anxieties of its right-wing audience. The *Times* was the first media organization outside New England to pick up on comments that Marsha Scott, Bill Clinton's liaison to the gay community, had made on an election-year trip to Boston. According to *Bay Windows*, a Massachusetts weekly, Scott had told local activists in a private meeting: "We [need] to find ways to ensure that those of you in these loving, long-term and committed relationships can enjoy all the same benefits that [heterosexual couples] are entitled to under the law." There was good reason to be doubtful that Scott, who had been quoted by *Bay Windows* specifying that marriage was not the right "vehicle," was making any declaration of White House policy. The *Times* report in fact quoted an anonymous presidential aide saying that same-sex marriage was "not something we intend to espouse" and emphasizing that Clinton was "personally" opposed to it. That was little assurance, however, for social conservatives: they had watched Clinton approach partial-birth abortion with a similar ambivalence, describing how disturbed he was by the procedure while vetoing a bill that would ban it. To those in pursuit of an opening to make same-sex marriage a federal issue, the Clinton White House might have just inadvertently presented them with one. "Interesting story in the *Washington Times* today," Nickles emailed his staff.

"Sounds like an opportunity for us," the senator's legislative director, Bret Bernhardt, wrote back.

As April ended, the various House and Senate staffers who had developed different versions of a marriage bill met to settle on a final text and common strategy. Arrangements were made for Lou Sheldon to participate by phone. Afterward, Oliphant returned to his Republican Policy Committee office to produce a new draft of the bill, this time with three sections. The first section merely clarified the bill's name: the Defense of Marriage Act. The second included Nickles's previous "Definition of 'Marriage' and 'Spouse'" language, with the addition of one further clause clarifying that "spouse" could refer only to a husband or a wife who is "a person of the opposite sex." For the third section, under the rubric "Powers Reserved to the States," Oliphant imported the text of Barr's full-faith-and-credit exemption.

When unveiled at a May 8 press conference, sections two and three had been flipped and Barr's name stood atop the legislation with Largent's following. Canady did not even appear at the event, even though without him it is unclear Barr would have had the guile to translate the notion of federal lawmakers intervening in state marriage policy from an election-year fever dream to legislative reality. "If it weren't for Canady," says Lehman, the subcommittee's chief counsel, "Barr wouldn't have gotten anywhere with it." One day after the two congressmen stood at a press conference to unveil their bill, Nickles formally introduced an identical bill in the Senate, with Dole named as coauthor. Given that Largent had served as the fulcrum between competing interests—the House and Senate, Republican congressional leaders and their defiant members, the right's Beltway institutions and its far-flung grassroots—his staff felt their boss had been denied the credit he was due. "We felt that Barr came in," says Thimmesch, "and was stealing the thunder."

Less than two weeks after the bill was introduced, the Supreme Court released its opinion in *Romer v. Evans*. It was exactly as Hadley Arkes had warned: six votes to overturn Colorado's Amendment 2, with Anthony Kennedy writing in the majority opinion that the law "seems inexplicable by anything but animus toward the class that it affects," he wrote. The *Romer* decision was the greatest victory an American court had ever awarded to sexual minorities, yet gay activists were not as jubilant as one might have expected from Arkes's predictions. They certainly were not acting as though *Romer* was the beginning of their winning streak. Even as White House press secretary Mike McCurry welcomed the Supreme Court's judgment as "appropriate," he confirmed Clinton's "personally stated view that he opposes same-sex marriage." If presented with the current version of the Defense of Marriage Act, McCurry indicated, he would probably sign it. "He believes this is a time when we need to do more things to strengthen the American family, and that's why he's taken this position," McCurry said.

The previous month's *Washington Times* report had clearly overstated Clinton's interest in placating gay supporters over marriage. In fact, the White House seemed intent on denying Republicans the contrast on moral values that Nickles thought would serve a Dole candidacy. Some congressional Republicans began to have second thoughts. They had tried to back their opponents into a corner over gay marriage, and had succeeded. Now congressional Republicans risked the most damage. If Clinton acknowledged he would sign the Defense of Marriage Act, why would House or Senate Democrats bother voting against such a popular bill? In fact, it would be politically foolish for Republicans to present the opportunity, granting opponents a free pass on a vote they could take back to their constituents as evidence of their moderation on social issues.

Despite majority leader Dick Armey's earlier assurances that the bill was on a "fast track," Barr now began to hear rumors that Armey was thinking about pulling back. "Continue on the course we have charted," Barr prodded Gingrich and Armey, along with party whip Tom DeLay and conference chair John Boehner. "This legislation is precisely where we want it. It is poised for victory. For heaven's sake, even the President has pulled the rug out from under the extremists on the other side by indicating he would sign it," Barr explained in a private memo. "Why back off at this point? Why give the homosexual extremists time to continue to pressure those political points and persons who may be susceptible to pressure?"

It was nearly Memorial Day, and Republicans had only a limited legislative calendar available before Congress recessed for the summer and wound down its work for the autumn election season. "Among the most important reasons to press forward is that Clinton is trying to buy time," argued Barr. "He thinks that by telling activists in the homosexual community that Congress is moving slowly and may not get the measure to his desk, and simultaneously trying to convince political opponents that this is not a 'wedge issue' (thus removing some of the reason to move forward immediately) he may succeed in slowing down momentum. Clinton was forced to issue the statement that he opposed same sex marriage because we were driving the issue and holding hearings. We must force him to sign (or reject) the bill by moving on this immediately.

"The Supreme Court decision earlier this week highlights the need to move on this issue, and it also has had the effect of riveting attention on this crucial issue, in a positive way," Barr persisted. "The decision shows how effective homosexual activists have been working through the court system at defeating the will of the majority in our democratic republic."

That Friday morning, House subcommittee counsel McGrath acquired a copy of an email blast sent to something called the Freedom to Marry Coalition. According to the subject line, the group was "Fighting Past Clinton," with instructions for coalition members to lobby members of both parties in both the House and the Senate "to urge them to block, delay, question, amend/amend/amend these bills." "Our enemies want to shut down the marriage discussion," wrote the message's author, Evan Wolfson. "We must not let them think their state-by-state aggression, or this federal assault, will stop us from engaging the non-gay persuadable public."

McGrath forwarded Wolfson's message to Barr's office with a terse cover message: "They're not about to give up on this one."

Part Three

INSIDE GAMES

(1996)

March On, Washington

There was never much reason to doubt that, if presented with the Defense of Marriage Act, Bill Clinton would sign it into law. Nevertheless the response of gay-rights activists and their political allies to the bill's emergence showed how overly optimistic they had grown by the mid-1990s about their ability to navigate Washington.

Long before marriage emerged as an issue, the earliest gay-rights lobbying efforts had been focused on winning federal protection from discrimination in employment, housing, and public accommodations. In 1974, New York congresswoman Bella Abzug introduced the first bill to offer it, by adding sexual orientation to the classes protected under the Civil Rights Act. Abzug's bill won backing from the chamber's most progressive members, primarily from districts in New York and California, and then disappeared from view. Other members inherited the issue from Abzug and reintroduced their own civil-rights legislation, each time accumulating the support of a few additional Democrats. But despite strong Democratic control of the House of Representatives throughout the 1970s and 1980s, neither Abzug's bill nor any of its successors came near a vote.

This routine proved a biennial reminder of the extent to which gays remained outsiders on Capitol Hill. Most legislators were happy to ignore political questions around homosexuality altogether, and even the traditional liberal establishment kept gay lobbying organizations at a wary remove. Perhaps the greatest indignity they suffered was exclusion from the capital's circuit of legalized graft. When the Human Rights Campaign Fund began in 1980, as a political action committee focused on gay rights, its strategy for winning influence was a typical one: buy access to members of Congress by raising money for them as candidates. But even when an increasingly wealthy, organized gay community pooled financial resources, they had trouble giving it away. Politicians were so afraid of any association that they refused contributions from anything affiliated with the gay movement. "There weren't a lot of candidates who wanted to take gay money," says Wayne Smith, a gay House and Senate staffer who later became a lobbyist, "so that was a tough climb." In 1982, both the Human Rights Campaign Fund and the National Gay and Lesbian Task Force were welcomed into the Leadership Conference on Civil Rights, but with a deal that the conference was under no obligation to back any gay civil-rights bill.

But by the early 1990s, it was no longer possible for Democratic leadership to push gay interests aside. The AIDS crisis had forced a reckoning with at least some of the community's concerns, and it gave gay lobbyists a point of entry to members of Congress and their staffs. Early victories on that front, however, had a Pyrrhic quality for gay activists, whose efforts at getting the government to take AIDS seriously succeeded only when the problem was symbolically uncoupled from sex. The Ryan White Comprehensive AIDS Resources Emergency Act, enacted in 1990, was named for an Indiana teenager who had contracted the disease through a blood transfusion, not the thousands of gay men who had contracted it sexually, leading Ronald Reagan's communications director to call AIDS "nature's revenge" on gay men.

The end of the Reagan-Bush era, though, brought reason for optimism. During his campaign, Bill Clinton had embraced the gay community without apology—"I have a vision, you're part of it," he had said at a Hollywood fundraiser—and immediately after his election, movement strategists decided to make a reinvigorated push for an omnibus gay-rights bill. Instead of merely tweaking Abzug's legislative language, they started from scratch to deal with new realities. After a decade of studied indifference to the issue, the Leadership Conference for Civil Rights was finally ready to throw its support behind a version. "It ensured, for the first time in the bill's history, that gay rights lawyers and mainstream civil rights lawyers would come together to develop the content of the bill," reflected Chai Feldblum, a Georgetown law professor contracted by the Human Rights Campaign Fund to help draft the legislation. The goal was to have it ready to unveil in time for the third March on Washington, scheduled for April 25, 1993.

In both 1979 and 1987, a National March on Washington for Lesbian and Gay Rights had served as a show of force designed to offset the reality that gay power was largely invisible in the daily machinations of the capital. In scheduling the third such pilgrimage for local activists from around the country, organizers zeroed in on a spring date when Congress would be in session. (The previous marches had each taken place in October.) When they formalized plans for a 1993 march, a year and a half prior, George H. W. Bush had been heavily favored to win reelection. The gathering, activist Robin Tyler promised, would serve as "the booster shot our movement needs."

But by the time the march took place, the gay-rights movement's leaders were no longer in control of their agenda. One of Clinton's first actions as president-elect, barely a week after his victory, was a vow to follow through on a campaign promise to end the military's ban on homosexuality. The move placed him immediately at odds with both the Pentagon and senior members of Congress, including members of his own party, who argued such integration would be bad for staff cohesion and troop morale. The president-elect didn't entirely choose his timing, which was forced by a court ruling that demanded an administration response. Nonetheless, gay-rights advocates were unprepared for the political controversy that followed. On the day that Clinton made the announcement at a press conference, lawyers handling the issue for the ACLU were still haggling over edits to the introductory briefing books they would present to officials managing Clinton's transition.

The debate dominated Clinton's first weeks in office, pitting the young president against his own military leadership. Clinton responded by clumsily backtracking from his campaign promise, at one point proposing that gays be permitted to serve openly but still held back from certain assignments, promotions, and living arrangements. Activists close to the White House accused it of endorsing a resegregation of the armed forces, this time along lines of sexual orientation. "Clinton's indecision reflects that there is no Clinton transition team member with political responsibility for this issue, or that if there is, he or she is not doing a very good job," Lambda Legal cooperating attorney Marc Wolinsky wrote to members of a working group established to strategize over the military issue.

As April 25 approached, what had been billed as "a Fight for Life and a Celebration of Love" risked collapsing into what Campaign for Military Service executive director Tom Stoddard labeled "an anti-Clinton march." Many gay activists accused the president of outright betrayal, while others conceded that he had merely revealed their naïveté. "On the whole, the road to achieving our goals has been bumpier than we expected," Eric Rosenthal, the Human Rights Campaign Fund's political director, told the *Washington Post* after a tense meeting with White House staff in late March.

The eventual compromise known as "Don't Ask Don't Tell"—in which service members' sexuality would not be subject to investigation or judgment as long as they kept it secret—satisfied few on either side. Clinton had reneged on his boldest campaign promise to gay activists, while still appearing to their opponents as though he had caved to gay interests. "We lost with our friends, we lost with our enemies," says Robert Raben, who that year joined the staff of Barney Frank, one of two openly gay members in the House of Representatives. "We were all scarred by that."

It wasn't the only trauma that gay staffers like Raben would endure in 1993. That October, three Oklahoma representatives told the *Tulsa World* that they would not hire a homosexual for their offices. "I don't think it would work very well," Congressman Ernest Istook said to the newspaper. "They may have attitudes that are totally inconsistent with some of our initiatives." Within days, a staffer for another congressman—James Inhofe, who, echoing the debate over discrimination in the military, had said that a gay employee would be "disruptive in terms of unit cohesion"—anonymously told the *Washington Post* that "if my sexual orientation became known I would probably be asked to leave or told to leave."

When asked about the controversy over Istook's remarks, Democratic House Speaker Tom Foley had surprised Democrats by expressing deference to the right of legislators to make "personal judgments on the individuals that they hire in their personal offices." It was a position from which he later retreated, albeit still leaving unclear his position on such discrimination. "That really echoed on the Hill," says Mark Agrast, a top aide to representative Gerry Studds, like Frank an openly gay Massachusetts Democrat. "We felt threatened as congressional staffers."

By then, a small group of openly gay aides to gay-friendly members were well organized enough, and sufficiently emboldened, that Istook's comments spurred the development of precisely the type of secret gay cabal he may have feared. The experience prompted Agrast and others to launch the Lesbian and Gay Congressional Staff Association to support unelected officials working under adverse circumstances, with a calendar of group dinners and brown-bag lunches where they could speak freely about life and work. Eventually there was the goal of counting those within their ranks, both in and out of the closet, a sort of census of Hill homosexuality. "We wanted these congressmen to know they're working with gay people," Agrast says.

But the association began to serve another, unplanned function: an early-warning system for looming legislative fights. A network of gay staffers working for conservative members—and sometimes straight allies working for moderate, gay-friendly Republicans—would surreptitiously report on the latest antigay maneuvers being plotted on their side of the aisle. Those on the other side could go to their bosses and begin planning their own strategic responses, and prepare Democratic leadership for what were almost always emotionally difficult fights around delicate political fault lines. "People started informing us about what was coming," says Agrast.

To many on Capitol Hill, Foley's comments arrived as an unwelcome distraction from the all-consuming struggle with the White House over Don't Ask Don't Tell, and a reminder of how much even in a phase of complete Democratic control the capital remained enemy territory. Despite a supposedly friendly regime in Washington, gay-rights lobbyists were at a loss about what to do next. There would be the inevitable work of fighting off legislative riders that specifically excluded gays from certain provisions of a bill, or attempts to squelch pro-gay initiatives developed by politicians in the District of Columbia, the only place where Congress had jurisdiction over local policy. But there was no hope for a proactive agenda, certainly not one including anything as bold as an omnibus gay-rights bill. Even sympathetic liberals were talking of "gay fatigue" by the end of 1993. "There was this sense: 'Why do we talk about the gays all the time?'" recalls the fund's public-policy director, Daniel Zingale.

The controversy over congressional workplace discrimination appeared an opportunity to "change the dynamic," as Zingale put it. Throughout the debate over gay military service, the fund's lobbyists repeatedly heard from members of Congress that they personally wouldn't discriminate but thought the national-security establishment was entitled to operate under its own, different rules. Why not, especially after the adverse publicity Istook and Inhofe had received, hold them to their word? "I hope that you will reassure your staff and your constituents as soon as possible that you do not discriminate on the basis of sexual orientation," Zingale wrote in a form letter sent to every member of Congress in October 1993.

The fund staffer assigned to monitor their progress, Julio Abreu, may have had the easiest task a gay-rights lobbyist had ever undertaken on Capitol Hill. By March, majorities in both House and Senate had sent the Human Rights Campaign Fund either a copy of an office policy that specified employees could not be hired or fired for their sexuality, or a new declaration to that effect. After his office was informed that sixteen Republican senators were among them, including Richard Lugar and John

McCain, even the party's minority leader, Bob Dole, signed a one-sentence nondiscrimination statement and sent it to the Human Rights Campaign Fund. In April, the group called a press conference to declare the project a success, its first big breakthrough on Capitol Hill. "It was something to breathe a little more hope into our troops, and our donors," says Zingale. "We were using it to start our engine."

It wasn't a politically risky move for most legislators, as Zingale had reminded them: 78 percent of Americans believed gays and lesbians should have equal job opportunities, according to a recent *New York Times*/CBS poll. Perhaps for the first time, it was those resistant to gay rights who seemed unreasonable. Asking members to take a stand about their own employment practices had presented perhaps the broadest victory ever for gay rights on Capitol Hill, and Zingale argued the experience should inspire gay activists to rethink their legislative aims. Members of Congress in both parties had readily (and painlessly) accepted that discrimination should be impermissible in their own office—why not ask them to extend the principle to the whole country? "If 'gay' was going to enter the conversation, that's where you wanted to have it—where we had the strategic advantage," Zingale says.

So gay political leaders decided to abandon the two-decade-old goal of a comprehensive antidiscrimination bill. Instead they spent the first six months of 1994 shrinking it into a more modest version that would extend equal protection for gays and lesbians only in the workplace. "While obviously we would love to have an omnibus bill, having this bill pass will make an incredible difference in our lives as gay people," Chai Feldblum wrote to Deputy Attorney General Jamie Gorelick that April.

A White House desperate to charm disgruntled gay activists and donors came to stand behind such an initiative. If the gay community could get the bill passed through Congress, Clinton would sign it into law. More discreetly, gay-rights activists began working to insert "sexual orientation" as a nondiscrimination category into the budgets for individual cabinet departments in a piecemeal fashion—first Education and Labor, then Energy and Commerce.

In the summer of 1994, Studds and Frank presented the Employment Non-Discrimination Act to the House while their state's senior senator, Ted Kennedy, did the same in the Senate. All the atmospherics were designed to make the bill appear practical and noncontroversial, much as the Americans with Disabilities Act had been when it had passed Congress and been signed into law in 1990. Even as their bill had the full support of nongay civil-rights groups—Coretta Scott King joined Studds at a press conference to unveil the bill—sponsors kept the words *civil rights* out of its title, with the explicit goal of narrowing its cultural impact. The bill's supporters noted that the press conference was covered by 180 mainstream media outlets, an early sign that unlike past gay-rights bills, this one was not going to be treated as boutique interest-group legislation. "ENDA felt like it changed the conversation," says Zingale. "We had found an Achilles heel of discrimination."

By late September, the bill had survived a committee hearing in the Senate and could claim 134 cosponsors in the House, seven of them Republicans. Gay-rights lobbyists were unexpectedly optimistic that they had stumbled into a winning issue that could reverse the movement's dismal fortunes in Washington. "It's our top priority right now," Tim McFeeley, the Human Rights Campaign Fund's executive director, said in October. "If people are secure that they won't be fired from their jobs, we will see an explosion of coming out and that will help in so many other areas as well."

But that month, Zingale and McFeeley received a one-page memo from David Sobelsohn, the Human Rights Campaign Fund's chief legislative counsel, which turned their attention elsewhere. He had just returned from a meeting in Boston of lawyers representing major gay-rights organizations nationwide. "Those attending the roundtable all believe that, sometime in the next two years, the Hawaii Supreme Court will interpret the Hawaii Constitution to require the state to recognize same-sex marriages," Sobelsohn reported back to his colleagues. "This will raise a host of tricky legal questions, many focusing on the recognition by other states of Hawaiian same-sex marriages."

At the time, Zingale's attention was occupied with the imminent midterm elections. Zingale had assumed that if the Democrats could keep control of both House and Senate, ENDA stood a decent chance of being passed and enacted in the next session of Congress. Now he was cautioned to worry not only about Republican electoral wins, but his own movement's success in a far-off courtroom. The Hawaii case could easily disrupt a well-plotted plan to focus the debate over gay rights on workplace discrimination. "Marriage is the opposite, it made people uncomfortable," says Zingale. "It was sensational, the way gays in the military had been. They would sensationalize it."

Fights of the Roundtable

Everyone in the United States is talking about gay relationships," the ACLU's Bill Rubenstein told the two dozen lawyers who had convened in Boston in October 1994 for a meeting of what had once been known as the Ad Hoc Task Force to Challenge Sodomy Laws. Deliberations were confidential, and public references to the group's existence were rare. Everyone who attended knew the biennial meetings as, simply, "the Roundtable."

A large chunk of the two-day meeting held at the offices of Gay & Lesbian Advocates and Defenders was given over to a discussion of marriage led by Evan Wolfson, one of seven attorneys in attendance from the Lambda Legal Defense and Education Fund. A year earlier, after the Hawaii Supreme Court ruling, he had successfully convinced Lambda to get involved in its first marriage case. As a result, the thirty-six-year-old Wolfson had joined Dan Foley as cocounsel, with particular responsibility for researching and deposing witnesses on the mainland who would be prohibitively difficult for Foley to reach. Wolfson explained to the Roundtable that he and Foley had been "deliberately putting the case on a slow path, but we can't slow it down any further." Wolfson laid out a likely timetable for the case now known as *Baehr v. Miike,* due to a change in the office of state health director: a motion for summary judgment the next month, an evidentiary hearing in April 1995, and regardless of the trial verdict a return on appeal to the Hawaii Supreme Court. That decision would likely arrive by spring 1996, Wolfson projected, and given the justices' disposition they were likely to legalize same-sex marriage for good. Then the responsibility would fall to the gay community nationwide to defend the gains won in Hawaii. "We can create a climate of inevitability about same-sex marriage," Wolfson explained.

At that point, a new staff attorney with the National Center for Lesbian Rights innocently questioned Wolfson's objective. "Why do we really want the right to marry, anyway?" Kate Kendell asked.

Wolfson glared back. "For just a flash of a second, I feared Evan was going to crawl over the table and throttle me," Kendell later recalled. "In a very measured but I could tell sort of furious tone, he explained to me why marriage was important."

Kendell noticed that no one else seemed to be as startled by Wolfson's ferocity as she was. When she looked over at Suzanne Goldberg, who had been attending Roundtable meetings for a few years, Kendell saw bemusement. *Okay, well, now she's done it,* Goldberg's expression seemed to say.

Such ideologically impassioned hazing was especially familiar to those like Goldberg who had spent time at Lambda, the largest of the gay and lesbian community's legal institutions. New to her job, with only a one-year clerkship between her and law school, Goldberg dutifully arrived at one of the biweekly legal-department meetings in early 1992 to report on a conversation she had just had with a Maryland couple expressing an interest in pursuing marriage rights. "That blew up into an argument," says Goldberg. "I didn't know what I was walking into."

The Lambda Legal Defense and Education Fund was founded in 1973 by a consortium of gay attorneys and straight New York City politicians determined to advance gay interests through the courts, using the NAACP Legal Defense Fund as a model. Lambda's mandate was to pursue "impact litigation," as attorneys termed lawsuits that would overturn detrimental laws, help set favorable precedents other judges would have to follow, or exert indirect influence on the legislative process by drawing media or political attention. When it came time to file with the state, Lambda's founder took incorporation papers used by the Puerto Rican Defense Fund and replaced every mention of "Puerto Rican" with "homosexuals." (It turned out not to be so easily done; judges ruled that, unlike the group defending Puerto Rican interests, the gay group couldn't file as a nonprofit because its work was neither "benevolent" nor "charitable.")

The Greek character that gave Lambda Legal its name had been appropriated for the cause by the Gay Activists Alliance, the most prominent new political entity to emerge from New York's post-Stonewall period. Spartan fighters had entered battle with the letter lambda etched into shields; activists said it symbolized their unity in the face of oppression. Organized by veterans of the antiwar and civil-rights movements who wanted to bring their confrontational tactics to the gay-rights project, the alliance pioneered a novel performance known as a "zap," which *Life* described as "part picket line and part sit-in." At one such gathering outside New York city hall, in the spring of 1971, activists held a mock wedding reception and entered the clerk's office to present its employees with coffee and a wedding cake. Once police arrived, the protesters dispersed without confrontation. The icing on the cake they left was festooned with a lambda, along with a heart on which had been inscribed GAY POWER FOR GAY LOVER.

But even though they borrowed the zappers' insignia, Lambda Legal's lawyers kept their distance from the era's "marriage boom" of isolated lawsuits. As Goldberg had discovered, avoidance of the subject had been reduced to a well-perfected routine, in which paralyzing internal debates kept gay-rights groups publicly silent on the topic. Many involved were simply uninterested in the objective, but those who thought most about the legal structure of gay relationships were often actively contemptuous of the notion. The growing field of family law was dominated by women, as both advocates and clients. When agonizing about the cost of the law's disregard for their relationships, they were likely to think of themselves foremost as mothers, contending with the prospect of losing access to one's birth children after coming out of the closet or being judged unfit to adopt solely on the basis of sexuality.

It took Sharon Kowalski's car accident for national attention to focus on the legal limbo in which gay and lesbian couples were forced to live. In 1983, after the twenty-seven-year-old Minnesotan was paralyzed after a collision with a drunk driver, her parents learned that for four years she had been living with a woman named Karen Thompson. Kowalski's father was named Sharon's legal guardian and denied Thompson any ability to visit her, now stuck in a wheelchair with permanent mental disabilities, at a nursing home. Thompson asked courts to appoint her Kowalski's guardian, but even that seemed to dodge the underlying issue: in the eyes of the law, the two women were no more than friends or roommates. "We all knew that was a problem," says Abby Rubenfeld, then Lambda's managing attorney. "But the question was what the remedy should be."

Lambda's narrow interest in the case that became known as *In re guardianship of Sharon Kowalski* was to help Thompson wrest guardianship from the Kowalskis. When it came to imagining a more durable solution, a way for gay and lesbian couples to define their mutual dependence, the woman who had shared her life with Kowalski defaulted to a familiar paradigm. "If I were her normal spouse, I would have been encouraged to take part in her rehabilitation process," Thompson said at the wedding ceremony held alongside the March on Washington in 1987, two years after she had last seen her partner.

But the person at Lambda who aided Thompson with the lawsuit, drafting briefs on her behalf before a Minnesota appeals court, did not look as enviously upon spousehood. "I do not want to be known as 'Mrs. Attached-to-Somebody-Else,'" Paula Ettelbrick would write. "Nor do I want to give the state the power to regulate my primary relationship." Ettelbrick had begun her career as a social worker committed to homelessness and tenants' issues. She then spent two years working at Michigan's largest law firm, in Detroit, while volunteering for a statewide gay-rights group. In 1986, she became Lambda's first staff attorney, and two years later succeeded Rubenfeld as legal director. In the press release announcing that promotion, she seized what amounted to an expanded mandate to pursue this "feminist and progressive vision." As part of "a broader movement for liberation," Ettelbrick declared her goal would be "making room in our society for broader definitions of family." Ettelbrick had been shaped by feminist theory to be skeptical of marriage itself, and the way for millennia its tyranny had been used to relegate women to subservient roles. Why, she asked, should gays undercut the project of their own liberation by aspiring to inclusion in an institution that had excluded them—instead of fighting for laws that respected the sovereignty of sexual minorities to define relationships in their own terms? "I would like us to move to an unhooking of a variety of benefits from the institution of marriage," said Nancy Polikoff, an American University law professor and ally of Ettelbrick's in the marriage debates. "It's a flawed institution and there isn't any way that gay and lesbian couples can remedy that flaw."

Wherever legal academics and lawyers working on gay family issues came together, disagreements over whether marriage was a desirable goal became inevitable. On the Litigators' Roundtable's conference calls and in the annual Lavender Law meetings, the sides broke down squarely along gender lines. While men in the conversations may have found themselves at odds with one another over strategies used to pursue marriage rights, female lawyers working toward recognition of "multiple families" were often more intent on minimizing marriage altogether. "It was a real flashpoint for good reason," says Goldberg, "to the extent that the concern about marriage's antifeminist history was more of a concern to women than men."

Ettelbrick received an invitation by the editors of *Out/Look*, which aspired to be a highbrow journal of ideas for the gay community, to make her case against marriage public. At the same time, the magazine asked one of her colleagues to assume the other side of the debate. Tom Stoddard had become Lambda's executive director around the same time Ettelbrick joined the staff, having departed the New York Civil Liberties Union once convinced that he had been passed over for a promotion because he was gay. Stoddard lived with a man he found "exceedingly dear to me," but he wasn't dreaming of marriage. He had seen too many end prematurely, and had observed that those that remained intact often survived only through stultification, defaulting to a formulaic division of husband and wife roles.

But Stoddard nonetheless believed that marriage should be on Lambda's agenda, and that of other gay groups. His appreciation for the institution could first be measured in material terms. When he had sought a group health plan for Lambda employees, many unmarried but registered in domestic partnerships, he could not identify a single insurer authorized to do business in New York State that would issue a policy covering their companions. Lambda ultimately found a way to provide the insurance, paying for individual plans to cover committed same-sex partners of its employees, and Stoddard acknowledged that couples could unearth their own similar workarounds. "It is usually possible, with enough money and the right advice to replicate some of the benefits conferred by the legal status of marriage through the use of documents like wills and power of attorney forms, but that protection will inevitably, under current circumstances, be incomplete," he wrote. "Those who lack the sophistication or the wherewithal to retain a lawyer are simply stuck in most circumstances. Extending the right to marry to gay couples would assure that those at the bottom of the economic ladder have a chance to secure their relationship rights, too."

Stoddard was an attorney, but he approached the issue in political terms that evaded Ettelbrick. "I am not naive about the likelihood of imminent victory. There is none," Stoddard wrote, arguing that it was nonetheless in the best interests of the gay community to push aggressively for marriage rights through both the courts and state legislatures. "Why devote resources to such a distant goal?" he asked. "Because marriage is, I believe, the political issue that most fully tests the dedication of people who are not gay to full equality for gay people, and also the issue most likely to lead ultimately to a world free from discrimination against lesbians and gay men."

Where Stoddard counted benefits for gays in marriage, Ettelbrick theorized the costs. She was particularly concerned about what recognition for married couples would mean for people who were not wed. Society and science had dramatically broadened the possible composition of a household beyond two parents of opposite sex and their biological offspring. She believed the gay-rights movement's objectives should be the acknowledgment of "multiple families": that all sorts of nontraditional household structures should be treated equally under the law. "From the standpoint of civil rights, certainly lesbians and gay men should have the right to marry," Ettelbrick conceded, yet she argued that attaining it could prove counterproductive for the movement's goals. "Obtaining a right does not always result in justice," she went on. "Justice for gay men and lesbians will be achieved only when we are accepted and supported in this society *despite* our differences from the dominant culture and the choices we make regarding our relationships."

The essays appeared side by side in the September 1989 issue of *Out/ Look,* under the headline GAY MARRIAGE: A MUST OR A BUST? An introduction emphasized that the disagreement was an intramural one and had institutional stakes: "two Lambda staffmembers share some of the arguments that have surfaced as their organization has evaluated what kinds of precedent-setting cases it takes on." Their publication exposed latent, and often parallel, fault lines within the gay-rights movement. Questions around marriage divided not only men and women, but coastal metropolises and smaller communities; theorists inspired by legal academia and those propelled by more urgent and pragmatic—even materialistic—concerns; the political values of the big donors and the priorities of the people their work was supposed to serve.

Stoddard and Ettelbrick accepted invitations from gay community centers to air the arguments together, and jokingly called these well-worn debates their "dog-and-pony show." For Lambda, it turned out that the performance was good for business. The group was in the midst of a massive expansion, more than doubling its budget between 1987 and 1991 and beginning to open regional offices around the country—all aided by a new willingness on the part of gay and straight lawyers and legal academics to attach themselves publicly to gay causes. The Stoddard-Ettelbrick debates helped with Lambda's community outreach. Arguing both sides of a provocative political question, rather than dwelling on the arcane procedural matters that often occupied its lawyers, was perhaps even more galvanizing than it would have been to decisively take an institutional stand on the matter. Where the ACLU's premature commitment to the principle of gay marriage had crippled its decision-making when presented with the option of taking action, official indecision offered Lambda something of a stable equilibrium.

Both Stoddard and Ettelbrick had once been fixtures of the Roundtable, and their debate naturally spilled over into its biennial meetings. Yet there, too, argument had become a permanent substitute for action, until subsequent events in Hawaii moved marriage from an abstract intellectual exercise into one demanding urgent consideration and lawyerly focus.

"This is all exciting and interesting," David Sobelsohn of the Human Rights Campaign Fund responded to a cheerful update about the trajectory of the *Baehr v. Miike* case in October 1994. "But I worry about a likely congressional reaction to the Hawaii decision."

Unlike most of those present, Sobelsohn was not a litigator. Four years earlier, Roundtable participants agreed to expand their ranks by inviting representatives from allied political groups like the National Gay and Lesbian Task Force and Human Rights Campaign Fund. But the political groups were rarely staffed by practicing lawyers. Sobelsohn was hired in February 1994 as the Human Rights Campaign Fund's first-ever chief counsel for legislation and public policy, his view of law having been shaped in the committee room rather than the courtroom. He had been sought out to "lead the effort to get a civil rights bill passed," as Sobelsohn had been told upon his hire. The Boston meeting would be just the second Roundtable session Sobelsohn attended in his new job. At his first, in San Francisco that spring just two months after he had joined HRCF, Sobelsohn was so unfamiliar to the organizers that he arrived to find his name misspelled on the agenda.

Sobelsohn was personally excited by the prospect of seeing gay marriage legalized. But as the only Roundtable attendee who worked on Capitol Hill, he was anxious about the political environment in which a legal victory might arrive. The midterm elections were a month away, and Republicans were favored to take back both chambers of Congress.

"I think we need to start talking about what kind of federal response we're likely to get, what kind of response we can live with, and what kind of law we'd like to challenge in court," Sobelsohn averred. "If, when the Hawaii Supreme Court hands down its decision, Orrin Hatch is chairing the Senate Judiciary Committee, he's going to schedule a hearing so fast it'll make your head swim."

"I think it's dangerous to talk now about the possible congressional reaction," Chai Feldblum, the Georgetown University professor who had led the team drafting the federal nondiscrimination bill, responded. "Let's not play out a lot of scenarios. It's counterproductive politically and we really aren't going to need six months to prepare."

Wolfson assured the group that he already had a "political game plan," all about creating a "climate of receptivity" through law-review articles and "an energizing buzz in our community."

That might not be enough, argued Bill Rubenstein of the ACLU. Both *Hardwick* and the military debates had been missed opportunities—the gay community had responded to political and legal losses with a shrug, letting each issue pass quickly from its attention. "We need this discussion in the community, but also to avoid letting this spin out of control," said Rubenstein. "We need to give people something concrete to do." He proposed forming a subcommittee of the political groups to map out a strategy.

"What is this roundtable for? Are we technocrats or are we leading a movement?" asked Kevin Cathcart, Lambda's executive director. "The buzz in the world is not about ENDA; it's about marriage."

The scheduled discussion was coming to a close. Wolfson was eager not to let the impression settle that his win in Hawaii would jeopardize the tentative gains that the movement's lobbyists had made with a more modest, deliberate approach to a gay-rights bill in Congress. "We can't pit ENDA versus marriage. Marriage is happening," he said. "If we win, it'll be a rising tide that lifts all boats, including ENDA. If people think about marriage they'll think about civil rights, too. We need a can-do attitude."

Sobelsohn wasn't convinced. He returned to Washington and wrote up his notes from the Roundtable. He sent them to the offices of Barney Frank and Gerry Studds, along with a cover memo laying out what he thought was likeliest to transpire in Washington after a victory in Hawaii. "The nightmare scenario," he called it.

Waiting for a Nightmare

H{ow could abortion rights supporters have so miscalculated the impact of *Roe v Wade?*"

It was a question that David Sobelsohn kept asking himself throughout his career and especially in the weeks after the Roundtable met in Boston. In many respects, his entire career at the intersection of politics and the law had unfolded in its penumbra. As a sixteen-year-old applying to colleges in 1969, Sobelsohn had chosen to write his admissions essay about why abortion should be legal. Four years later, the Supreme Court was supposed to have settled the matter, once and for all. *Roe v. Wade* hadn't put an end to the debate over abortion rights; instead it had motivated the losing side while inspiring complacency in the winners. As the Supreme Court's guarantee of legal abortion gradually eroded in the two decades that followed, pockmarked with restrictions and exceptions, Sobelsohn concluded that the left deserved much of the blame. Their mistake, he believed, was never "taking seriously the views of abortion opponents."

"The problem of abortion in America was never just the law," Sobelsohn would write in a book review for the *Journal of Sex Research.* "Overturning criminal abortion laws couldn't solve the problem any more than did the enactment of those laws in the first place—no more than repealing Prohibition ended the Mafia, or the enactment of Prohibition did away with alcoholism. No, the source of the problem always lies elsewhere, in the hearts and minds of human beings. Changing hearts and minds takes more than a decision of the U.S. Supreme Court."

In Michigan, where Sobelsohn had served as counsel for the statehouse's judiciary committee, abortion opponents had focused their lobbying on eliminating public funding of the procedure. Throughout the

1980s, they succeeded in the legislature, although pro-choice governors repeatedly restored the money when signing Medicare funding bills. By 1987, however, Michigan Right-to-Life had developed enough grassroots support to circumvent that line-item veto. After the group successfully compelled the legislature (under the state's initiative process) to address the question head-on, abortion-rights advocates were forced to respond by collecting signatures for an initiative campaign of their own. Soon after, Sobelsohn went to the Ann Arbor Folk Festival with a stack of petitions and was pleased during an intermission to encounter a few members of the ACLU's state board, who he thought could help him with the task. "They turned me down," Sobelsohn recalls, glumly. "They said they were there to enjoy the folk festival! Not to get petitions." But when the pro-choice side lost at the ballot box, the ACLU was ready with a lawsuit.

"I actually have had a longtime irritation with the political innocence of people whose positions on issues I agree with," says Sobelsohn. "On the left generally in this country, we had so many successes in the courts in the latter part of the twentieth century that we found ourselves thinking that logical arguments were all we needed to get what we wanted. And the hard work of political organizing wasn't that important."

Demonstrations of that same naïveté at the October 1994 meeting of the Roundtable, as its members considered what would follow the *Baehr v. Miike* trial, left Sobelsohn gobsmacked. Evan Wolfson, the Lambda Legal attorney who had led the discussion in Boston, had begun with the cheerful announcement that "marriage is happening" and insisted that "we need a can-do attitude." When Sobelsohn proposed that the assembled lawyers might nonetheless benefit from anticipating how conservative politicians and activists would respond to a verdict in Hawaii, he was told by Chai Feldblum that it was "dangerous" to even contemplate the prospect. "I never quite understood how it could be dangerous to take precautions against disaster," says Sobelsohn. "That's why people buy fire insurance, that's why people wear seat belts."

Sobelsohn had hoped that seeing Democrats lose both houses of Congress would force gay-rights advocates to "rethink the relative virtues of political action and legal action." But in the middle of December, he traveled to New York to participate in a four-hour lunchtime meeting on marriage strategy at Lambda Legal's offices and was distressed to learn that little had changed. Wolfson's continued upbeat talk of a "climate of inevitability" sounded almost willfully oblivious to the new realities of Washington. "There's something in the human mind that doesn't like to contemplate disaster, and to prepare for disaster," Sobelsohn says. He wasn't so deluded that he thought gay-rights lobbyists would necessarily be able to defeat the type of antimarriage measure that could emerge from a Republican Congress, since it would likely have public opinion and political convenience on its side. But, he said, "we need to be working on coming up with either a law we can live with or a law that's easy to challenge in court."

Sobelsohn returned to Washington with the hopes that those closer to Capitol Hill might be better positioned to take seriously the prospect of a congressional backlash. Already it was clear that the gay-rights bill he had been hired to help work on was doomed. ("We thought we could pull some people over, until the '94 elections," says Sobelsohn. "After the 1994 election, it was not going to pass in the twentieth century.") He met with key gay-rights staffers to the two openly gay Democrats in Congress, who understood Sobelsohn's urgency even if they had given little thought to the Hawaii case. "The first two years of Clinton's first term we saw Capitol Hill as an opportunity," Sobelsohn says. "After the first two years of Clinton's first term we saw Capitol Hill as a challenge."

Baehr v. Miike, Sobelsohn notified anyone who would listen, was "a train bearing down on America's gay-rights movement" with "our hands being tied to the rails." The only possible control the movement had left, he would explain, was over "the size of the train and the time of the collision." In a December memo to Fred Hochberg, an HRCF board member and major political donor with ties to the White House, Sobelsohn outlined his "nightmare scenario":

(1) The community gets excited about the prospects for legal recognition of same-sex marriage. (2) Advocacy for endorsement of same-sex marriage in various non-gay civil-rights organizations goes nowhere and holds up those organization's [*sic*] endorsement of ENDA. (3) The Hawaii Supreme Court issues a pro-gay-marriage decision in spring 1996. (4) We have prepared neither ourselves nor the community for the storm of reaction from Congress. (5) Congress postures for a couple of months, then in late summer 1996 passes a complete prohibition on same-sex marriage. (6) In September 1996, two months before the election, Bill Clinton must either sign or veto a ban on same-sex marriage. (a) Clinton signs the bill; gays, lesbians, bisexuals, and progressives blame the movement's leadership for not being prepared and Bill Clinton for turning on

us. They sit out the 1996 election (or vote for independent candidate Jesse Jackson). (b) Clinton vetoes the bill and loses the election badly; pundits blame his overwhelming defeat on his support for gays-in-the-military and gay marriage. His defeat and the conventional wisdom chill presidential and congressional support for gay rights for 10 years or more (a similar phenomenon occurred in Michigan, where for 10 years after the overwhelming defeat of the member who had introduced a gay civil-rights bill, not one member of the state legislature was willing even to reintroduce the bill).

It wouldn't take long to be given a reason to take seriously gay-marriage opponents. On February 14, 1995, Utah state representative Norm Nielsen introduced his Recognition of Marriages bill, which Lynn Wardle had drafted to specify that Utah authorities could not recognize a marriage officialized elsewhere "if it would be prohibited and declared void in this state." It was pretty much as Sobelsohn had foretold; two months earlier, in his memo to Hochberg, he anticipated "a state could enact a law declaring same-sex marriages illegal or criminal."

Utah's bill became law, after facing little resistance, but parallel efforts at defense-of-marriage bills in South Dakota and Alaska did not get as far before their legislatures adjourned. Most state governments had already completed their legislative work for the year, yet those who monitored the work of social-conservative groups knew they were so well networked that it was inevitable that politicians in other states would be encouraged to follow Utah's example as soon as the calendar turned. "Backlash already coming," Judith Schaeffer of People for the American Way wrote to an email list of gay-rights activists. "Expect to see more once the state legislatures get back in session."

That may have appeared a useful reprieve, compounded later in 1995 by news that a ruling wouldn't emerge from Hawaii for at least another year. The courts there had already been proceeding at a languid pace in moving the *Baehr* case back to trial, by all accounts to permit the state's newly deputized Commission on Sexual Orientation and the Law to complete its study of the subject. But in June 1995, the circuit court agreed to postpone its trial until the following summer, in the apparent hope that in the interim the political system would relieve the judiciary from having to settle the state's laws over such a contentious issue.

To Sobelsohn, that delay was making the "nightmare scenario" even worse, and he spent 1995 delivering warnings that the national gay-marriage debate would now erupt in the middle of a presidential election year. Members of a new Republican Congress, many of them elected to office on "family values" platforms, would be fighting to hold their seats. Meanwhile, the party's presidential candidates were already in the midst of a wide-open primary campaign in which the religious activist class would set the agenda. "Everyone seems to think Congress will sit on their hands," he posted to an online message board frequented by left-leaning legal academics on August 9, 1995. "'Gay marriage' tops the list of radical-right propaganda against the gay-rights movement (we ask for equal-employment rights; the response is, 'the next thing they want will be gay marriage!'; we ask for freedom from gay-bashing; the response is 'the next thing they want [etc.]'). I doubt one week will pass after the final decision of the Hawaii Supreme Court before congressional hearings are scheduled."

By late July, Barney Frank received word that House Republicans were likely to amend a routine appropriations bill to cut funding for the District of Columbia if local officials didn't move to outlaw adoptions by gay couples. Controlling the capital's affairs was a favorite tool for congressional Republicans to meddle tentatively in social policy. Since its enactment in 1992, they had succeeded in gutting a domestic-partnership bill to cover city employees simply by defunding the partners' registry each time the District's appropriations bill came up for a vote. When a district court ruled in June 1995 that unmarried same-sex and mixed-sex couples were entitled to joint-adoption rights, Frank assumed it would provoke a similar response. "In addition to being opposed to the fact of gay or lesbian people adopting, they are further unhappy that this adoption appears to them to recognized [sic] the validity of a gay couple," he wrote in a July 21 memo to the directors of the major national gay advocacy groups.

Whether the Senate took up the adoption fight that fall—which promised to be something of a dress rehearsal for the epic congressional marriage battle Sobelsohn foresaw in 1996—would rest foremost with Bob Dole. The Senate majority leader remained something of an enigma to gay-rights advocates. A social moderate, he had signed the Human Rights Campaign Fund's office-hiring pledge and regularly stated (in ways other Republican candidates never would) that discriminating against homosexuals was wrong. As his party's leader in the Senate, Dole had backed bills to fund AIDS research and collect statistics on antigay hate crimes. But as a presidential candidate, he had been thrown into a tizzy by the matter of a small contribution by the Log Cabin Republicans, which his campaign had welcomed and then returned, a move that Dole himself later repudiated, albeit only ambivalently.

"I think that interplay sort of exemplifies where Senator Dole is on lesbian and gay issues," the Human Rights Campaign's executive director, Elizabeth Birch, said at a November 20 event where she unveiled a briefing book on the gay-rights records of the 1996 presidential candidates. Throughout her press conference, the reporters questioning Birch pressed her on one question. How much would the likely nominee of a Republican party newly rabid in its concern about homosexuality deal with the issue in his campaign?

"The ball is still in play," she said, three months before Dole put his name to the National Campaign to Protect Marriage's resolution. "He really has been on both sides in many ways. And it's not quite clear where he's landing."

The Rebrander and the Firebrand

On the Monday in November 1995 that Elizabeth Birch had selected to deliver her very cautiously optimistic words about Bob Dole at a Human Rights Campaign press conference, Barney Frank wrote her a letter. Frank and his partner, Herb Moses, had had an unexpectedly pleasant dinner with Birch the previous Friday, largely because the country's most prominent gay official and the head of its most important gay advocacy organization had shied away from discussing political strategy or tactics until late in the meal. Yet Frank departed the dinner feeling he had left something insufficiently said, and after a weekend had passed it was time to scold Birch anew for being too accommodating of Republicans.

"I have to say I do not think it is accurate for you to say that the problem is that you do not know anything about politics, that you should just stay away from politicians, etc. Politics is not an arcane science, and someone who is as highly intelligent as you, and as good with people in general, really has no excuse for not being better at the political side," Frank wrote Birch. "I believe the problem is not that you don't know enough, but that you are making one fundamental error in the intellectual framework that you bring to this and I am hoping I can persuade you to rethink it. I do agree that the problem is in part that you have not professionally or personally dealt with politicians a lot, but I think that is something that you can easily overcome—and that you have to do your job as well as you are capable of doing it."

Birch had been named the Human Rights Campaign Fund's executive director almost exactly a year earlier, just weeks after the midterm landslide. The group's existing leadership had not been recruited for a period of Republican dominance. The prior executive director, Tim McFeeley, came to the job with experience in Democratic politics and had spent the 1994 campaign as partisan cheerleader. "Republicans, as a party, do nothing for the gay community, and the Log Cabin people are kidding themselves and our community if they believe the Republican Party cares about the lesbian and gay community," he told a gay newspaper at one point.

If Democrats were going to "recognize the gains we have made, and prepare to defend them," as HRCF public policy director Daniel Zingale put it in a postelection memo, the fund would need constructive relationships with Republicans. Birch didn't have any experience doing that, but both she and the organization she now headed were eager to present her as a different type of leader for a different era in gay politics. "We are living in a complete sea change," Birch told the *New York Times* early in her tenure. "There is no president who is going to ride in on a white horse, and there is no one party that is going to save us."

The thirty-eight-year-old Birch was as close to the white knight as the gay political scene had known. She had come to the Human Rights Campaign Fund from Apple Computer, where she had overseen the company's litigation worldwide. As an out lesbian atop Apple's human-resources department, Birch had helped lead the company to adopt domestic-partnership benefits for its employees in 1993. When, later that year, commissioners in one Texas county threatened to withhold a tax abatement from an office complex that Apple planned to build in suburban Austin due to the company's domestic-partner policy, Apple threatened to walk away from the $80 million project. The county commissioners relented, and a year later Birch went back to Texas to celebrate "National Coming Out Day," a Human Rights Campaign Fund initiative that in 1994 was devoted to the workplace. "This is happening because when gays and lesbians come out at work, they are no longer an abstract notion to the CEO," Birch said in Dallas. "They are faces he or she sees every day."

One of the first steps those enlightened executives took was basic recognition of gay employees' relationships even if they had no legal status. In September 1991, the software maker Lotus Development told its 3,100 employees that those with long-term same-sex partners were eligible for the same benefits it made available to spouses. A smattering of the usual suspects already had similar policies—Ben & Jerry's, Harvard University, the *Village Voice*, Berkeley city hall—but Lotus became the largest for-profit employer to fully recognize gay employees' relationships. In late 1993, the *Austin American-Statesman* estimated that thirty companies in the United States offered domestic-partner benefits, half of them high-tech firms and most based in the Bay Area. By then, Birch was serving as cochair of the National Gay and Lesbian Task Force's board of directors, and helped bring one hundred CEOs—including representatives of every major Northern California company—to Stanford University for a symposium on corporate domestic-partner benefits. "Where Congress and the military have in essence for now turned their backs on gay and lesbian Americans," she would say, "corporate America has stepped to the fore."

In naming Birch as its head, the Human Rights Campaign Fund signaled that any gains in the near future would have to arrive in the private sector. Gay donors frustrated by how hard it had been to win support for the agenda in Washington were fascinated by how easy it appeared to be in Silicon Valley, where gay rights were typically justified with the rhetoric of meritocracy rather than identity politics. Birch promoted what she called her "kingpin" strategy, identifying a dominant player in each sector whose policy changes would serve as an example to competitors and aspirants. "You persuade them, and then everyone else would fall in line," she says. At the same time, Birch began designing a system to rate companies based on how gay-friendly their business practices were, an accountability mechanism that cynics noted could pressure companies not only to change their policies but to make contributions to the Human Rights Campaign Fund. (The Corporate Equality Index was finally launched in 2002.) These initiatives amounted to a market solution to a civil-rights problem. "There's a whole new breed of activist," she said. "An army of people are coming out of the high-tech industry."

There was still old-style lobbying work for them to do in Washington. They would push proactively for a narrow workplace-discrimination bill, while defending against novel right-wing encroachments. In both cases, making peace with business-friendly conservatives would be crucial. If anyone could make a modest gay-rights bill palatable to a party establishment conditioned to taking cues from the Chamber of Commerce, it was the corporate lawyer whose activism had centered largely on enabling Fortune 500 companies to be virtuous. "I had really thrown my heart and soul into changing policies at companies," she reflects. "So I felt like this is a perfect formula for a Republican Congress."

Few within the old guard of gay activists would have thought the Human Rights Campaign Fund needed to become more conservative or corporate. From the start, there was the name: fund officials freely admitted that they kept it unhelpfully nondescript because it was easier to get contributions if donors didn't have to write the words *gay* or *lesbian* on their checks. The Human Rights Campaign Fund was not the only gay political group with an eye on Capitol Hill. By the time Birch took command of the group, it had an annual budget of $8.5 million, along with a staff of forty-five, and had successfully displaced the older, more established National Gay and Lesbian Task Force. "History suggests the access-driven politics of the HRCF would overwhelm the empowerment-driven politics of NGLTF," the latter's executive director, Urvashi Vaid, would lament. "Who has the money controls the agenda."

A willingness to court a political elite only cautiously receptive to gay concerns explained both the Human Rights Campaign Fund's success and the distrust it generated elsewhere in the gay-rights movement. "When you are that closely associated with the law-making process on Capitol Hill and that's pretty much your primary thing, you get sucked into the vortex of legislative compromise, horse-trading, and sometimes that works to our benefit, and sometimes you can fail to see the forest for the trees," says Lorri Jean, executive director of the LA Gay and Lesbian Community Services Center.

Yet if either group was positioned to thrive during a Congress dominated by conservative Republicans, it would be the one that was accommodationist, and proudly so, when it had to be. The Human Rights Campaign Fund, which more than any other entity in the gay-rights movement had set itself up to be judged by political results, would need to justify its existence to donors. "We were about winning," says Zingale. "We needed an inside game."

To do so, Birch was eager to find new avenues to win favor with congressional Republicans, although she often chose showy gamesmanship over quiet diplomacy. She hired openly gay relatives of prominent Republican officials as spokespeople: Candace Gingrich, the Speaker's semi-estranged half sister, and Chastity Bono, the daughter of Congressman Sonny Bono and the singer and actress Cher. Birch was happy to publicize the fact that she studied the Christian Coalition's organizing manual, and asked to address the group's annual conference in the spirit of outreach. When the request was refused, HRCF rented an adjacent hotel meeting space and invited coalition members to hear Birch speak there.

In June 1995, two weeks after Dole's presidential campaign returned a $1,000 contribution from the Log Cabin Republicans, Birch repeated the provocation. She directed a $5,000 contribution from the Human Rights Campaign to the National Republican Congressional Committee, which had coordinated the party's efforts to retake the House the previous year and would be doing the same for their campaign to defend their majority in 1996. In the process of making the donation, Birch won an invitation to the NRCC's headquarters to meet with its chair, New York congressman Bill Paxon, who agreed to adopt an office employment policy that barred discrimination based on sexual orientation. Much as the Log Cabin donation had, the HRCF check managed to provoke recriminations on the right, with the Family Research Council's Gary Bauer rallying other conservative leaders to condemn Paxon and his committee.

But the deal also antagonized some of those who should have been Birch's closest allies. She and Frank had been having tense conversations throughout the year about the Human Rights Campaign Fund's willingness to back gay-friendly Republicans, with endorsements or contributions, at the cost of Democratic efforts to win back congressional majorities. Yet the NRCC contribution, as a gift not to an individual candidate but to the apparatus of a hostile party, enraged Frank. "Sometimes I am guilty of forgetting in the heat of the moment a point that I try very hard not only to remember but to insist that others remember—that tactical and strategic differences among us are trivial compared to the overwhelming areas of agreement," he conceded in one letter. If the November dinner was a successful gesture toward rapprochement, it was only because Frank had managed to keep in check for part of an evening his natural instinct for pedantic condescension.

"It seems to me that you have adopted implicitly a model of the political world in which one group of people, the Republicans, who for a variety of reasons can be expected to be very much opposed to us, and another group, the Democrats, whose support we should be able to count on. Thus when Republicans show some movement in our direction, they are rewarded, in many cases disproportionately to what they have in fact done for us," Frank wrote Birch three days later, explaining that "any Democrat who is less than perfect" ends up maltreated by the Human Rights Campaign Fund's bipartisan outreach.

Politics was about rewarding friends and punishing enemies, Frank liked to say, quoting the labor leader Samuel Gompers. His fellow liberals had often grown too enamored of their purity to deftly practice politics. "Partly out of necessity, winning has come to be undervalued by some of my friends on the left. 'There are worse things than losing elections,' many of them argue," Frank had written in a 1992 book, *Speaking Frankly: What's Wrong with the Democrats and How to Fix It*. "It is hard to understand how people can profess to be seriously concerned about important public-policy goals when they minimize the importance of winning elections. People who do not win elections do not get to implement their ideas; their moral commitments then serve primarily to make them feel better, but not to advance the cause of those about whom they sincerely care."

When the Democrats lost control of Congress two years later, Frank adjusted to the defeat more quickly than nearly all his colleagues. He flourished as "a counterpuncher, happiest fighting on the defensive," as Frank described himself. Even from an impotent minority, he found a remarkable ability to tweak his opponents; within weeks of becoming House majority leader, Dick Armey publicly referred to his nemesis as "Barney Fag." (Armey dismissed the epithet as an unfortunate verbal slip.) The fact that he considered his opponents' policies "bad for the country and for vulnerable people"—graver words than he'd had for the "hypocritical" Republicans whom he threatened to out in 1989 in retaliation for a "seedy" rumor campaign that Speaker Tom Foley was gay—motivated him to keep pushing. "I feel, 'Boy, this is a moral opportunity—you've got to fight this,'" Frank explained. "Also, I'm used to being in a minority. Hey, I'm a left-handed gay Jew. I've never felt, automatically, a member of any majority. So I started swinging from the opening bell of this Congress. It got to the point where Newt Gingrich was saying, 'Barney Frank hates me.'"

It didn't take Frank's hatred to feel the sharp lash of his tongue. His friends, however, were afforded the grace to receive, and to nurse, their wounds in private. "You've made it quite clear that you think gay men and lesbians should sit quietly in the face of bigotry and not embarrass respectable people," Frank wrote the liberal columnist Mary McGrory in the spring of 1993 after she published a lighthearted column that praised Massachusetts voters as "tolerant" for sending Congress its only openly gay representatives. "But even knowing your general views on the subject I was appalled to see Gerry and myself classed with felons as examples of the tolerance of Massachusetts voters. Do you pat yourself on the back for condescending to 'tolerate' us as well?"

To gay activists, Frank—who had been first elected to the Massachusetts state legislature in 1972 and had been a lawmaker ever since—was an object lesson in the danger of having gay politicians who owed their careers to the political establishment rather than the gay community. He and Gerry Studds had been the first two openly gay members of the House, each having his emergence from the closet in the 1980s clouded by adverse circumstances. In both instances, personal relationships became subjects for official investigation: Studds's with a teenage House page, Frank's with a male prostitute who was, for a time, on his congressional payroll. As a result, neither man had ever been able to fully separate the gay political agenda from the imperative of self-preservation.

In fact, Frank credited his first major legislative success on a gay issue, the 1990 amendment to a law permitting immigration authorities to discriminate against gays, lesbians, and bisexuals seeking entry, to his change in public status. "Before I came out, my colleagues respected my insistence on the repeal of the antigay provision as they would respect any colleague's strong feeling on an issue," Frank would later reflect. "But once I had acknowledged that I was gay, this moved from being simply an issue with which I was concerned to something that was obviously deeply personal. Automatically this meant that those of my colleagues who wished to preserve good working relationships with me understood how important this matter was to me, and their willingness to accommodate me increased accordingly."

Decades in government had convinced him that many liberal causes were weakened by activists who looked to politics as a source of solidarity rather than a sphere for confrontation, as came far more naturally to opponents on the right. "The N.R.A. doesn't have demonstrations. They write letters," Frank marveled. "In fact, direct action, as a political tactic, is second-choice. The first choice is to exercise political power, to scare them into voting the right way. Direct action is what you do when you have no power."

As same-sex marriage emerged as a national issue, debates among gay political leaders about strategy revolved around what to do when one has gained just a bit of political power. That was the heart of the quarrel between Frank and Birch, two savvy pragmatists with very different visions about how to navigate the space between an ascendant right wing and an unreliable Democrat in the White House. Frank believed any progress would come only through the party whose strengthening he had made his life's work. Birch, in the fashion of other Washington lobbyists, wanted to cultivate relationships with anyone in a position of authority.

"You see this now with the Human Rights Campaign Fund. Their political tactic is just dumb and, I think, undignified," Frank volunteered to an interviewer from the *New York Times Magazine* in early 1996. "It's one thing to give money to the individual Republicans who are supportive. But to give money to help Newt Gingrich and Dick Armey—that's stupid."

By then, Birch had grown ready to concede as much, at least where that $5,000 check was concerned. "I can't undo that," she wrote Frank at the beginning of 1996, underlining the entire sentence for emphasis. "By day 200 of the Congress, I made the best choice I could given the Board input, the fact that they were/are in power, the issues presented in this Congress and not knowing how the Republicans were going to go. The 73 new members and Gingrich have proven to be extreme, cruel and out of touch. Obviously, you knew better."

That admission aside, Frank's eagerness to treat the Human Rights Campaign Fund "like a punching bag" especially galled Birch because she had spent much of 1995 trying "to get the organization completely ripped apart and rebuilt and branded and repositioned." Once she began making television appearances on behalf of the group, often pitted in debate against bombastic homophobes, Birch was perpetually conscious that she might validate a stereotype as "shrill" and strained not to shout back. "I felt that we needed to pull the LGBT movement out of the streets and put it in the living room," she explained. "We needed to move into an era where we were talking to the country instead of past it."

Birch also reached into what she called her "Silicon Valley toolkit" to engineer a corporate-style rebranding of the Human Rights Campaign Fund. By that October, the group had dropped the last word from its official name because, as communications director David Smith explained, "we believe we are so much more than just a fund." At the same time, the group abandoned the Liberty torch that it had used on letterhead since 1980. It was replaced by a gold equal sign that Birch hoped would grow as iconic as the silhouetted fruit that represented her last employer. "This is what you write," Birch instructed a reporter for the gay magazine *Out*. "'In the 1990s, there had to be a meeting of the minds between raw activist spirit and the communications and marketing techniques that define a new voice for gay America.'"

That image makeover was completed just in time for a presidential election in which the Human Rights Campaign intended to assert itself as the unrivaled force in gay politics and culture. In the summer of 1995, the group had released its new quarterly magazine, a glossy upgrade over the duotone newsletters most advocacy groups used to communicate with members and a natural venue for features on gay celebrities like Nathan Lane or Ellen DeGeneres. "Every communication that came out around HRC had to pass really two tests," Birch reflects. "One is that it would always shore up the 13-year-old gay kid so if they were hearing the message it would be affirming and uplifting. But it also needed to be heard and understood by, say, the dad in Kentucky or the mom in Iowa."

HRC Quarterly's subsequent issue, released as the Republicans began their primary process, carried evidence that Birch's overhaul went beyond mere aesthetics, and that she was intent on being heard within the Beltway, as well. "While we have faced disappointment from this administration, it is essential to remember President Clinton has done more for lesbian, gay and bisexual Americans than any other leader in the history of this nation. Moreover, the Republican field is increasingly looking like an anti-gay snake pit," Birch wrote in a two-page commentary. "So it is in this context that the Human Rights Campaign has the responsibility to exercise leadership and make an early endorsement of President Bill Clinton. We do so because, frankly, he has earned it." It was a particularly bad time for the country's loudest gay political voice—and one with a particular gift for winning media attention—to be characterizing its lobbying techniques as naïve, let alone "dumb" and "stupid." "I would like HRC to have an open and productive relationship with you and your staff. But we feel pretty punished, seldom rewarded, and as you talk about us around the country, an extremely imbalanced picture is painted," Birch wrote to Frank in January 1996.

A month later, after two more rounds of letters, the two still were not finished with their poison-pen correspondence. "OK, Barney. Let's talk facts," Birch wrote him, outlining the Human Rights Campaign's plans to support Clinton's reelection, along with 150 other candidates for office, that year. "We could use your help," she added. "I suggest you go back to beating up Republicans. I have to believe it is a far better use of your time," Birch wrote on February 20. "Let's call a truce and get on with 1996—shall we?"

Somewhere along the way Birch successfully shamed her nemesis—maybe it was the letter in which she wrote the congressman that "you have conducted yourself like a seismograph jar error"—into publicly correcting some of his past misrepresentations. Frank was already working on a long essay for the *Harvard Gay & Lesbian Review* on the relationship between partisanship and pragmatism for social movements, and he agreed to include a measured assessment of the Human Rights Campaign's performance. The result would be a thoughtful document that Birch and her staff could share with donors and the media if they cited his offhanded putdowns toward HRC elsewhere.

The article, "Why Party Politics Matters," was largely an attack on the Log Cabin Republicans, which Frank concluded was "more notable for preaching Republicanism to gay and lesbian activists" than the inverse. But when the quarterly journal released its spring issue with Frank's cover essay, in late April, the author realized that he had spectacularly failed in his ancillary ambition of finding an election-year peace with Birch's organization. After a pacifying paragraph that observed "the Human Rights Campaign finds itself overwhelmingly supporting Democrats," Frank was unable to help himself. "Giving $5,000 to the entity whose job it is to provide funds for all Republican candidates makes no sense at all," he wrote.

In an unusually contrite letter to Birch, Frank explained that he had intended to replace the critical paragraph from an earlier draft with the more complimentary one, and alternated between blaming the editor and himself for the mistake. "I really can't complain because I am undoubtedly a very aggravating person to edit," he wrote her on April 24. "Obviously this is a problem for HRC, for me and the editor—I am being quoted in part as saying things that are more critical than I mean them to be, I also look as if I have a terrible stutter when I write, since I have essentially repeated similar points but with a very different emphasis in two succeeding paragraphs." Frank enclosed a letter he had written to the editor explaining the mix-up and once more clarifying his views. Frank's declaration was now constrained by so much penitence that it read at points like the activist's version of a hostage-tape confession: "I believe that the Human Rights Campaign does an excellent job of advocacy and I agree with most of what it does."

23
....

Smooth Sailing

L ater on TalkBack, a guest who says he's been free from the homosexual lifestyle for 12 years, and his work is to try to help others to escape from being gay," host Miles O'Brien pivoted between segments as CNN devoted a full hour to the matter of gay marriage on March 26, 1996. "Next, Hawaii may be the first state to legalize gay marriages. Should they or shouldn't they? Get ready to debate next. Stay with us." To the extent gay marriage received media coverage, it was usually in this vein, part of the culture-war freak show that could be contemplated as a hypothetical and debated as a choice between extremes. (Coming up on *TalkBack Live:* "Tomorrow, mad cow disease. Is it all a bunch of bull? Are you afraid to eat beef?")

CNN's guest for the Hawaii segment was Elizabeth Birch, and O'Brien introduced her as someone who "wants to make legal recognition the law of the land." Birch was less interested in presenting that case than impugning the motives of those like her fellow guest, National Campaign to Protect Marriage founder Bill Horn, who were intent on making it the type of issue that fit into a should-they-or-shouldn't-they TV debate. "America has never ever really grappled with the issue of same-sex marriage," Birch said. "We're seeing sort of an eruption during this election year because it is being used as a tool, frankly, by political religious extremists."

The Human Rights Campaign was among those who had never really grappled with marriage. The group had asked presidential candidates whether "same-sex couples should have the right to marry" in the questionnaire it presented presidential candidates in 1992, and elicited a series of responses that weren't so much positions but evidence of politicians thinking through a novel question for the first time. Massachusetts senator Paul Tsongas: "My initial reaction is that couples who make a strong legal commitment to each other ought to be entitled to these rights and benefits, but I would like to consider this issue further." Iowa senator Tom Harkin: "As President, I would work with all these constituencies in the hope of reaching a consensus as the appropriate recognition of these relationships." Only Clinton promptly returned a straightforward answer: "No."

Former California governor Jerry Brown, whose campaign had initially missed the deadline, submitted a more sympathetic response but almost immediately began retreating from it. Campaign officials disowned the volunteer they said had completed the survey without authorization and, in so doing, had also violated a Brown campaign policy that "does not allow first person responses on his behalf." Brown's eventual answer: "He does not support federal legislation recognizing Gay and Lesbian marriages."

Five Democratic candidates had answered the question five different ways, and it wasn't entirely clear whether any had done so in a fashion acceptable to the group that had asked them. (The organization didn't endorse a candidate in the primary, waiting until June to back Clinton.) The Human Rights Campaign Fund, as it was still known, never publicized the candidates' responses or committed to its own position on the matter. The only public statement the group made about same-sex marriage over the course of the election year may have been one that discouraged a presidential candidate from thinking same-sex marriage was a matter that ought to have been taken seriously by anyone. "Nor does this legislation sanction gay marriages. I believe your guests have willfully misled you on this point in an effort to inflame passions and fuel the anti-gay bigotry which enables them to raise funds in their direct mail programs," executive director Tim McFeeley wrote President George H. W. Bush following newspaper reports that he had been personally lobbied by Christian leaders to oppose the District of Columbia Health Care Benefits Expansion Act of 1992. "It does not confer the status of marriage on domestic partners, nor any of the other benefits of matrimony."

The Human Rights Campaign was never against same-sex marriage, but before 1995 it had barely spoken a word in its favor, either. As it had become a matter of national interest, Birch had her staff work quietly to map the fluid politics around it. That May, the group had hired pollster Celinda Lake to conduct a national survey of likely voters, along with focus groups in Chicago and Seattle. "Voters are cool towards the idea of gays marrying—no matter how it is phrased," Lake reported back. Even among the one-third of voters sufficiently sympathetic to gay rights to be considered HRC's base, Lake found lukewarm attitudes. Her research left little room for optimism, either. Once presented with the strongest arguments in favor of gay marriage and against a federal ban on it, voters' opinions barely budged. When Lake presented her research the following February to an election briefing the Democratic National Committee convened for gay activists, she could reach an unequivocal conclusion: "we need to stay away from same gender marriage as this is still too tough for most Americans to handle," as one attendee recorded. It was unclear in what capacity Lake was speaking, but it didn't much matter. On this the Human Rights Campaign and the Democratic National Committee could agree.

A year earlier, a White House memo had warned that "an alarming percentage of lesbians and gay men are giving up on President Clinton," concluding that "unless this trend is turned around, it will be virtually impossible for us to energize the gay community with anywhere near the enthusiasm of the 1992 campaign." At that point, gay support for Democrats was almost automatic, but Clinton was slow to appreciate how its dynamics would shift once he was in the White House.

His flat-footed entry into the debate over military service was an early example of internal disarray for which the Clinton White House would remain notable. It was a quality attributed to a young staff without governing experience, the rise of mutually contemptuous factions among top strategists, and the boss's preference to engage in open-ended policy debates that were often unfavorably likened to a collegiate seminar. On gay-rights issues, these deliberations seemed to be further affected by the absence of a dedicated policy expert by the president's side. "To me, the straight white boys always win at the White House," said Bob Hattoy, an openly gay man with AIDS whom Clinton had appointed as his associate director of personnel.

Within Clinton's inner circle, the only person in any way alert to the gay movement's concerns was his press secretary, George Stephanopoulos. He had been selected for the assignment during the campaign because "he was good-looking, young, seemed like someone who would be hip to LGBT rights," according to Richard Socarides, an openly gay White House liaison to the Labor Department. Stephanopoulos had worked for Democratic leaders on Capitol Hill but had little familiarity with the broader gay political world. "His idea of running a gay and lesbian policy operation was picking up the phone and calling Barney Frank," says Socarides. "And if it was okay with Barney—or he could convince Barney—then it was okay."

After flailing through several months as Clinton's spokesman, Stephanopoulos was shifted in the middle of 1993 to a behind-the-scenes advisory role. Along the way, he inherited what was called the "constituency" portfolio, which was the Democrats' euphemism for managing relations with generally friendly identity-based interest groups. That made him responsible for the White House's end of negotiations over gay military service, an episode with no winners. "The military resented the intrusion, Democrats were furious, the public was confused, and the gay community felt betrayed," Stephanopoulos would write. Afterward he worked to convince gay activists that the policy outcome should be considered "a defeat, not a betrayal," and eventually earned a degree of personal trust. Stephanopoulos became the favored point of contact for gay activists seeking to win the administration's attention on an urgent matter, such as whether to intervene in the constitutional challenges to antigay referenda in Colorado and Cincinnati whose cases were on a trajectory toward the Supreme Court.

By the time Clinton faced his second Court vacancy, in the spring of 1994, Human Rights Campaign counsel Chai Feldblum felt comfortable sending Stephanopoulos casually worded faxes at 11:30 p.m. with unsolicited opinions on the merits of candidates under consideration. "Probably would be o.k. in the long run but he worries me a little," Feldblum, a Georgetown Law professor, wrote of federal appellate judge Stephen Breyer, three days before he was nominated by Clinton. "He is incredibly smart, but perhaps a bit too much. [He sometimes gets caught up in his own 'brilliance.'] He would definitely be more quirky and he would always be sure he was absolutely right. Not necessarily the best given the current dynamics on the Court."

As Clinton's reelection approached, the White House formalized the role of gay and lesbian liaison with dedicated constituency outreach. (Jimmy Carter had a staffer who served as his emissary to gay activists, but their concerns were a small fraction of her work.) In 1995, Clinton selected deputy assistant to the president Marsha Scott, a heterosexual Arkansas friend who had developed relationships within the West Coast gay community while running Clinton's presidential campaign in California, to serve as a full-time liaison. Her first day on the job, June 12, was spent welcoming a delegation of gay elected officials to the White House, yet Scott was already on the defensive. Just days earlier, the administration had disappointed gay activists by announcing it would not submit an amicus brief against Colorado's Amendment 2 as the Supreme Court prepared to rule on the constitutionality of the antigay law. "That was the low," Scott reflected the next year. "From then on, it's been pretty much of a high."

By early 1996, Scott had the former Labor Department liaison Richard Socarides working for her as something of an understudy, being groomed to replace Scott when she left for a role on the reelection team. The "liaison operation," as Scott and Socarides called their office, was responsible for internal and external relationships, convening regular meetings of the administration's more than thirty openly gay appointees, and helping expand the Democratic National Committee's database of key contacts. Nineteen identified gays and lesbians were on the 1994 mailing list to receive Christmas cards from the president; in 1995, there were approximately seven hundred.

That outreach, paired with the unappealing look of Clinton's Republican challengers, led gay groups to be among the earliest elements in the liberal coalition to formally endorse the president for a second term. California's Stonewall Democratic Club had voted to do so the previous August, fifteen months before Election Day; New York's Empire State Pride Agenda had privately assured the White House it would follow in June. Clinton would still have to contend with dissatisfied activists—the National Gay and Lesbian Task Force was planning a protest outside the convention that would renominate him in Chicago that summer—but the movement's institutional machinery had fallen effortlessly into place. "We knew that all the gay rights organizations were for us so nobody was thinking about a strategy," says Socarides. "We thought this would be smooth sailing."

At a staff political retreat at HRC headquarters in November 1995, attendees agreed that when it came to marriage, priorities should be "keeping Clinton out of the debate" and "keeping Congress out of the debate," but they had no tools to ensure it happened. "I thought marriage was just like the most difficult issue I could ever imagine. We wanted it to be a very local, slow-moving issue—the slower the better so that we could get other things done that were more palatable," says Birch. "Clinton was under a rock because of gays in the military, and so I spent a ton of time snaking my way up through the White House to build trust, show polling, show what we could win."

An organization that had long strived to be treated as insiders, with a belief in its ability to destigmatize gay activism by the mere fact of its savvy, the Human Rights Campaign worked to refashion itself as a useful cog in the Democratic electoral machinery. It endorsed Clinton's reelection at the start of 1996, delivering his campaign a $5,000 donation, the maximum permitted from a political-action committee. The group's motives in formally committing to Clinton that early were partly self-serving, acknowledging in an internal campaign plan that it could "utilize the 1996 Presidential campaign to identify and attract new members, to expand our fundraising base." Over the course of the year, HRC had committed to spending $2.5 million, much of it in coordination with labor unions and party committees to mobilize likely Democratic voters in 150 of its targeted races nationwide. It would be the first time that a gay group had been able to participate in a so-called coordinated campaign. On Birch's watch, the Human Rights Campaign had fashioned itself an indispensable if unexceptional part of the party coalition—neither as victims to be protected through policy nor a fundraising reserve to be explored, but a sturdy political base that had the resources to buy its way to the table where tactics were determined.

By the time Birch was summoned to meet Clinton in early April, one of five gay leaders among a group of twelve invited to coffee at the White House as "friends of the administration," she had unquestionably earned that label. Birch liked to congratulate herself for being less awed by the presidency and its trappings than many of her peers, which she attributed to a Canadian upbringing, but nonetheless cleared her Friday schedule for her meeting with the president. When Clinton entered the Map Room, he explained to his guests that they had gathered in the same place where Roosevelt had plotted World War II. Over the course of the ninety-minute session, Clinton talked about priorities he would bring to a second term, particularly his concern for the dislocation triggered by economic change. When he had a moment for a personal interaction, Clinton made sure to let Birch know that he was aware of the Human Rights Campaign's endorsement of him earlier that year. Birch had long been skeptical of Clinton's claims of personal solidarity with gays and lesbians, believing that "his commitment on race I think runs very, very deep but I think his commitment on LGBT issues was fairly superficial." But a brief acknowledgment that her early commitment had been noticed in the West Wing affirmed for Birch that she and Clinton could always communicate in the pragmatist's universal language of mutual dependence.

She responded by pushing him on a few discrete policy concerns: the importance of Medicaid funding, the repeal of a ban on military service of HIV-positive people, and the state of gays in the armed forces, which under Don't Ask Don't Tell had shifted to a worry that service members were being subjected to what gay advocates called witch hunts. Birch implored him, as well, not to "let the extreme right define us."

"Be out there," she told the president.

She heard back a promise Clinton would find much easier to make than to deliver on. Opponents of gay rights, Clinton told her, "must be stood up to."

24

....

Endangered Liaisons

On March 27, White House counsel Jack Quinn was dining in the White House mess with one of his attorneys, Kathy Wallman, when Marsha Scott approached their table. Scott came with a warning: a group of supporters who had been invited to an upcoming coffee with the president would include "a woman who advocates recognition of gay marriage" and might press the issue directly with Clinton. A day before, Elizabeth Birch had been doing just that on CNN's *TalkBack Live,* but the following week's coffee in the Map Room came and went without any mention at all of marriage. The fact that Birch did not raise the issue was a relief to the White House, which—recognizing the growing salience of the issue nationally—had been scrambling to formulate a political and legal response.

In October 1995, George Stephanopoulos addressed the National Lesbian and Gay Journalists Association in Washington and was asked during a wide-ranging question-and-answer session whether a position had "been staked out about where the president will stand on gay and lesbian marriage." Stephanopoulos was greeted with hisses when he said that "the president has had a position on gay and lesbian marriage for quite a long time, and he doesn't support extending a federal guarantee or federal protection." An approving burst of applause followed when he was challenged about whether that amounted to "discrimination," as his audience interlocutor put it. "He does not believe that we should endorse or sanction marriages, that's been his position for a long time, and I can't elaborate on it," Stephanopoulos insisted. Two months later, when *Newsweek* followed up on the exchange in an article about the consequences of a trial verdict in Hawaii, a White House spokeswoman staked out a position not in legal conflict with the one Stephanopoulos articulated but very much at odds with its spirit. "The president doesn't think that same-sex marriages should be outlawed," Ginny Terzano told the magazine.

In December, after Hawaii's Commission on Sexual Orientation and the Law recommended that the state legislature allow same-sex couples to marry, Marsha Scott sent a copy of its report to Marvin Krislov, an associate White House counsel. "This may help as we move closer to the Hawaii decision. We need to be prepared with a response," Scott wrote him. "This is starting to become a *real* conversation out in the communities. We must have a statement of some sort." Krislov passed the report along to Chrysanthe Gussis, a law student working in the counsel's office. After Gussis reviewed the commission report, Krislov asked her to prepare a tentative statement of White House policy on the matter of gay marriage. "Think we should say this matter should be left to the states," he instructed her.

Already states seemed to be working through the issue in their own ways, as Gussis discovered when she began to track a series of unrelated local cases about the legal status of gay relationships. The New York Court of Appeals had recently determined that an unmarried person could legally adopt a partner's child. In Georgia, a three-judge federal panel had ruled in favor of law student Robin Shahar, who claimed her constitutional rights had been violated by a would-be employer—who happened to be the state's attorney general—who withdrew a job offer after he learned Shahar was planning a Jewish "wedding" to a female partner. (The defendant named in *Shahar v. Bowers* was the same Georgia official who had defended his state's antisodomy statute all the way to the Supreme Court ten years earlier.)

For White House lawyers, always on the lookout for legal concerns that could ultimately demand presidential action, the only local controversy that demanded urgent attention was in Virginia. In late January, a Republican governor's conservative appointees to the Virginia Housing Development Authority amended its lending standards to replace the word *household* with *families*, thereby making gay and lesbian couples no longer eligible for federally backed home loans. An official at the Department of Housing and Urban Development alerted White House cabinet secretary Kitty Higgins that the policy change was currently being reviewed by the Federal Reserve, which oversaw rules for loans insured by the Federal Housing Administration. Higgins, however, didn't treat it as a typical agency-level administrative matter. She took news of the Virginia upheaval straight to the president's top political advisers, including chief of staff Leon Panetta, press secretary Mike McCurry, and strategist Harold Ickes.

The same day that she did, on February 1, Gussis sent Krislov a draft statement that stuck to his guidance, declaring that "the Administration believes that the legal status of same-sex unions, and the accompanying rights and benefits, should continue to be determined on the state and local level." But Gussis also included an optional paragraph that went a good deal further in its enthusiasm for proactively embracing policy changes. "The lack of legally recognized alternatives to marriage and the exclusion of gay and lesbian relationships from marriage have left many couples unable to define their relationships as they choose, and often has led to disparate and unfair treatment of similarly situated couples," she wrote. "For these reasons, we believe states should give serious consideration to the issue of same-sex unions and the role of marriage in defining the relationship and rights between parties."

That represented a leap from legal analysis to a political position, and ensured that the matter would win the interest of presidential advisers far beyond the counsel's office. Throughout the White House, there was growing awareness that the previous fall's cross talk between Stephanopoulos and the press office wouldn't stand up to serious interrogation. Scott called a series of meetings with the administration's top openly gay appointees and the gay contacts across Capitol Hill and the Democratic National Committee to brainstorm a position she could present to the president's advisers. How could he formally articulate resistance to gay marriage without antagonizing loyal gay supporters or unnecessarily baiting conservative opposition? Socarides watched with awe as Colorado governor Roy Romer, a moderate Democrat with a profile similar to Clinton's who had chaired the party's 1992 platform committee, vetoed a state-level defense-of-marriage bill and seemed to strike the ideal balance. In his daily news clippings, Socarides flagged a quote from Romer's veto message and passed it approvingly to Scott and associate counsel Steve Neuwirth: "It is one thing to believe, as I do, that marriage is the union of a man and a woman. It is quite another to believe that committed same-sex relationships do not exist and should not be recognized by society."

During the final week of March, lawyers and political advisers volleyed a range of draft positions as Scott's liaison operation hunted for other ways to cushion the political impact of a statement that reaffirmed his opposition to same-sex marriage. After hearing Clinton devote his weekly radio address to describing plans to promote "corporate citizenship," Paul Yandura proposed structuring the initiative to include "praising companies that have domestic partnerships" before the program was officially introduced to the public that spring. "If domestic partnership was include [*sic*] in the laundry list of employee benefits that the President praises it would not stick out and attract attention," Yandura, Scott's assistant, wrote in an email message to her. "If the language regarding g/l marriage is going to include a positive rebut of domestic partnership we can point to the corporate citizenship model."

In early April, the White House's press office received word that the gay newsweekly *The Advocate* was at work on a story about tentative steps being taken by Clinton's advisers to prepare for the emergence of gay relations as a national issue. Press officers had parried other inquiries on the subject by merely noting that Clinton had opposed same-sex marriage during his 1992 campaign. But since he had not expounded on the topic, White House spokespeople could not actually refer journalists to an explanation of why Clinton believed that or how he reconciled that view with other positions on gay and lesbian issues. Quinn worked with Scott and Stephanopoulos to prepare such a statement and, the day before *The Advocate*'s deadline, sent it to Clinton for his approval, in the form of a decision memorandum on which he was asked to mark *Agree, Disagree,* or *Discuss.*

The institutions of traditional marriage and family face tremendous pressures in today's society. We must do everything we can to support and strengthen these institutions. The President has previously said that he does not personally support same-sex marriages.

The President is aware that many communities and institutions are considering whether certain basic benefits can be provided outside the context of traditional marriage. The challenge in addressing these issues is to remain sensitive to the traditional values of our communities while preserving the fundamental right to live free from unjustified discrimination.

In our country's history we have, for good reason, looked first to state and local governments, as well as the private sector to consider issues like these involving community values and matters of conscience. The President believes that these issues continue to be best resolved at this level of civic discourse.

That evening, as he waited to address a Democratic National Committee fundraiser at the Sheraton-Carlton Hotel two blocks from the White

House, Clinton scrawled a backward checkmark next to *Agree*. The next day Quinn spoke to the *Advocate* reporter working on the story and repeated nearly verbatim the talking points Clinton had approved. (When the reporter, Josh Moss, told Quinn that sources had informed him that the counsel's office had already begun probing legal issues faced by same-sex couples, Quinn denied it.) Yet despite the fact that Clinton had privately signed off on talking points, not everyone in the White House was as diligent as the president's lawyer in sticking to them. In mid-April, when the *Washington Times* reported on its front page that Scott had told a gay group in Boston that she wanted "to find ways that those of you in these loving, long-term and committed relationships can assume all the same benefits," the comment raised hackles in the morning meeting of the counsel staff. "Not really our message," Wallman alerted Quinn.

25

Two Weeks in May

The White House's gay-and-lesbian liaison operation was built for managing relationships, not handling crisis, as the Defense of Marriage Act's arrival demonstrated. Marsha Scott and Richard Socarides knew they lacked the standing to influence the president's thinking on any sensitive matter. (When they made a courtesy visit to Barney Frank, Socarides recalls, the congressman "was like, 'Who are these people? I'm talking to George, someone with real power.'") Just to get their views fully aired required first winning over Stephanopoulos. "There were no gays in the room," says Daniel Zingale, the Human Rights Campaign's public-policy director. "It was like Lincoln making decisions about slavery without any African-Americans."

The day after the bill was introduced in the Senate, Scott organized her first thoughts on the subject in a memo for Stephanopoulos. She believed there was room for Clinton to finesse the matter, opposing the Defense of Marriage Act without going as far as two Senate Democrats, Ted Kennedy and Ron Wyden, already had by saying gays and lesbians should have the right to marry. "I believe that our strongest counter is around states rights," Scott wrote to Stephanopoulos on May 9. "It can be said that as a former governor, the President has great respect for the right of individual states to define their issues and this issue falls clearly within their prerogative."

Uncertain in their ability to make a principled case for a veto, Scott and Socarides articulated a more bluntly political rationale for Ickes, the White House staffer responsible for Clinton's reelection. On May 10, they sent him a memo urging Clinton to "oppose this bill as an unwarranted intrusion on what for over 200 years has been the sole prerogative of state legislatures." The heart of the argument to Ickes, gatekeeper for considerations that would affect the campaign, concerned the political ramifications of embracing the Defense of Marriage Act. "Up until now our friends in the gay community have generally given us a pass on the President's stated personal opposition to marriage. Recognizing that this is an issue on which public opinion runs against them, gay leaders—while not happy about the President's opposition—are willing to let the courts be the final arbiter of rights on this issue," Scott and Socarides wrote. "I believe we have been extremely successful in rebuilding our relationships to [*sic*] our friends in the gay communities despite the fiasco of gays in the military, the disjointed handling of the Colorado case and the President's stated personal opposition to gay marriage. However, our support for this bill would be taken by many in the gay communities as an expression by the President of deep ceded [*sic*] bias against gay people (ie. they simply should not be entitled to the same benefits as similarly situated straights—even if they work hard and play by the rules) and as caving in to Republican scapegoating of gays."

At no point would Clinton hear any of the arguments for a veto, or even the value of threatening one. "It was political suicide," Socarides reflects on the advice he and Scott gave. "People said it would cost him the election." But even if they were already certain Clinton would have no choice but to sign the bill, his political advisers were split about whether he needed to say so yet.

The memo that ultimately made its way to the president—under the signatures of Stephanopoulos, Quinn, and Scott—laid out the advantages of a noncommittal approach. "We believe your willingness to sign this legislation should not be announced until it is absolutely necessary to do so. While it is critical that your position be unambiguous and unwavering, there is a risk that too early an announcement of a willingness to sign the bill could cause Republicans to add even more draconian provisions," Stephanopoulos's memo proposed, a scenario that might include limits on adoption by same-sex couples or their rights to act as foster parents. "If and when this approach is no longer viable, the White House would state that you would be prepared to sign this bill if enacted by Congress."

The military experience weighed heavily on Stephanopoulos's thinking. By 1993, Clinton had locked himself in early to a position he couldn't hold once squeezed by pressure from both sides. Now Stephanopoulos urged the president to go slow—he could reiterate his opposition to gay marriage while saying he had to wait and see what happened on Capitol Hill. After all, a lot of bills were proposed by members of Congress, and only a small share passed the House and the Senate and went to the president for a signature. Why lock himself into a position before the bills had even had a hearing, let alone a single vote?

Even as the White House refused to say explicitly whether Clinton would sign the Defense of Marriage Act, its tone grew increasingly hostile to the gay cause. On May 14, Clinton authorized a set of talking points that declared, "He does not believe that the federal government should promote gay marriages," even though the word *promote* never featured in the bill or any of his administration's legal analyses of it. (The claim that gay-rights initiatives would "promote" homosexuality was a favored canard of social conservatives well-known to particularly frustrate gay activists.) Those talking points also preemptively closed down any prospect of the liaison operation's long-hoped-for move to offset the embrace of an anti-marriage bill with any initiative to endorse domestic partnerships.

The daylong corporate citizenship event came and went on May 16 without any acknowledgment that the administration wanted to goad companies into respecting their gay employees' relationships. When the chief of staff convened a meeting in his office to discuss marriage, no one from the Domestic Policy Council, which had taken the lead in considering whether there was a way for Clinton to declare himself "opposed to discrimination on basic issues of fairness like insurance," in council staffer Jeremy Ben-Ami's words, was invited. Anticipating questions about domestic partnerships, Clinton authorized his communications office to dismiss them entirely, insinuating that the values of fiscal restraint should guide White House policy toward sexual minorities. "These decisions are best left to state and local governments and private institutions," read the talking points that Clinton approved. "But since the President does not believe the federal government should recognize gay marriage, he does not believe it is appropriate for scarce federal resources to be devoted to providing spousal benefits to partners in gay and lesbian relationships."

Scott was collecting "legal analysis from our gay/lesbian friends," as she described it on a handwritten cover note she routed to the White House counsel's office in the hopes of raising doubts there about the Defense of Marriage Act. Lambda Legal characterized the bill as a "radical, unconstitutional, discriminatory, and impractical redefinition of marriage and the federal-state balance," in a long article coauthored by the director of its marriage project, Evan Wolfson, and cooperating attorney, Michael F. Melcher. A shorter memo by Chai Feldblum and circulated by the Human Rights Campaign concurred that the bill "has some significant constitutional problems" in its "attempt by Congress to restrict and undermine the basic mandate of the Full Faith and Credit clause of the federal constitution," she wrote. Another analysis, solicited by Kennedy from Harvard Law School professor Laurence Tribe, an experienced Supreme Court litigator, affirmed that Congress lacked the power to free states from specific obligations under the clause.

Administration lawyers never gave any credence to such judgments. The White House counsel had become convinced that the bill's second section, which addressed the rights of states in light of the full-faith-and-credit clause, was constitutionally superfluous. "It is already clear that states which do not wish to do so will not be obligated to give recognition to a same sex marriage even if Hawaii (or some other state) recognizes such marriage," Associate Attorney General John R. Schmidt wrote Quinn on May 10. "On this matter, therefore, the proposed federal statute is unnecessary, although also harmless." (Two deputy assistant attorneys general later concluded that Tribe's analysis had relied on a willful misreading of the bill. "We remain convinced that the courts will uphold the Act against constitutional challenge," Randolph D. Moss and H. Jefferson Powell wrote in an internal memo.)

When faced with a routine request from the House Judiciary Committee for a statement of administration policy on a bill it was about to consider, however, White House lawyers did not share that observation with Congress. Instead they stuck to Stephanopoulos's strategy of offering as little as possible, in the hopes that they might still be able to will the issue of same-sex marriage back into oblivion.

During the editing process, Quinn ensured that the statement grew only more terse, striking a line that declared, "We are informed that if H.R. 3396 were presented to the President, he would sign the measure into law." Another line, which repeated the public declaration that "the President has previously stated his opposition to the legalization of marriage between persons of the same sex," was similarly struck from an early draft. "The reference to the President's views may misleadingly give the impression he favors the federal bill, a matter we need not determine now," wrote the head of the office of legal counsel, Walter Dellinger, who recommended that the letter not be released under his signature but that of Assistant Attorney General Andrew Fois. Ultimately, the three-paragraph letter released on May 14 betrayed little of the administration's thinking beyond the fact that "the Department of Justice believes that H.R. 3396 would be sustained as constitutional." By conceding the bill's constitutionality, no administration official would have to testify at the committee's hearings, a move that Quinn had hoped would allow the White House to keep open its political options.

But when Socarides and Scott went to the Hill to observe the Constitution subcommittee hearing on May 15, the Fois letter was being held up as evidence that Clinton—contrary to the recommendations of the gay legal elite—saw no problem with the bill now making its way through Congress. "What was supposed to be a routine notification that we would not testify, has been interpreted by the Republicans and our gay and lesbian friends as an embrace of the bill and a definite statement of its constitutionality," Scott lamented later that day. She and Socarides earlier had proposed that Clinton justify his silence on the bill by saying "that the Justice Department is studying the serious constitutional issues raised by the legislation," but now the White House was beginning to run out of excuses.

Within the West Wing, Stephanopoulos's strategy was growing increasingly unsustainable. Reporters kept on asking Mike McCurry to comment on the issue, in different ways—about both the Defense of Marriage Act itself and the underlying rationale for Clinton's disapproval of same-sex marriage. "He believes this is a time when we need to do things to strengthen the American family, and that's the reason why he's taken this position," McCurry said at his May 13 briefing. McCurry hadn't really spoken inaccurately; a month earlier, Clinton had privately approved talking points that his White House counsel had drafted using all the same words. "We must do everything we can to support and strengthen . . . the institutions of traditional marriage and family," read the memo that Clinton had signed. But the elision of two separate points, and the implication that recognizing same-sex relationships would weaken the American family, didn't sound as harmless to gay ears. "Mike doesn't know how to speak on gay and AIDS issues," Clinton staffer Bob Hattoy confided to *Washington Blade* reporter Lou Chibbaro Jr. "I don't think Mike's at all homophobic or AIDS-phobic. I feel sometimes White House people are homo-stupid and AIDS-stupid."

In the early evening of May 16, Scott met Al Gore to walk with the vice president from his working office in the West Wing to his ceremonial office in the Old Executive Office Building next door. Since starting her job nearly a year earlier, Scott had made a project out of gathering the administration's openly gay appointed officials for small, informal bull sessions on a regular basis. Now as something of a kickoff for the political season, she had expanded the invitation list to include gay and lesbian staffers from the Democratic National Committee and Clinton-Gore reelection effort, and secured Gore to serve as host. It was the first time such a gathering had taken place on the White House grounds, or that a president or vice president had agreed to preside over one anywhere.

Initially planned as a joyful occasion, a coming-out party thrown by a presidential ticket eager to show its comfort with gay friends, the event with Gore threatened to become a dismal standoff. As they walked to the event, Scott updated Gore on how the administration's halting and at times clumsy response to the Defense of Marriage Act, particularly McCurry's remarks a few days earlier, was being viewed by gay political elites. "You must address this issue with the appointees," Scott instructed him. "Many of them are in long-term, committed relationships and are very conflicted and concerned about what they perceive to be our position. There is no consensus within the gay and lesbian communities over the timing of this national discussion. There is a growing fear among the communities that we are doing a 'Sister Souljah' and distancing ourselves from their support and visibility."

There were about sixty people awaiting Gore's arrival in his ceremonial office, and one attendee in particular attested to Scott's fear that what she had begun as a morale-building exercise had grown fraught with electoral peril. For the first time, Scott was joined at one of her gatherings of gay appointees by a more senior White House political staffer—in this case Ickes, minder of Clinton's campaign interests. "Our experience with the gays in the military issue taught us that the cause of gay civil rights will not be advanced over an issue about which there is no public consensus," Gore told the group. "We at the White House have committed ourselves over the last 24 hours to do a better job of talking about this issue, to make sure we do so in a way that is respectful of gay and lesbian relationships."

Gore spoke only of a change in rhetoric and a need for mutual under-standing, but made no effort to persuade those in attendance that Clinton was even entertaining the possibility of a veto. "Friends sometimes differ and we are not going to agree one hundred percent on the issues," he told them. It was now clear that if the Defense of Marriage Act "reaches his desk, it is the opinion of the Senior Staff that he must sign it," as Scott had briefed Gore. Yet that internally accepted truth still was not acknowledged to outsiders. "Until a bill is marked up in committee and passes both houses of Congress, no one knows how it will be when it reaches the president's, desk," Socarides told a reporter from a gay newspaper after the reception with Gore. "In my view, anyone saying Clinton will sign this is just speculating."

To the extent the White House had been making a strategic calculation, it was a wager that Republicans had already accrued the political benefits from the Defense of Marriage Act and would be unable or unwilling to see it through. After all, they had, at no cost to themselves, managed to invent a choice that alienated Clinton from a core part of his Democratic base and would not easily go away. "This is a rough political year for gay people," a *San Francisco Examiner* editorial observed sympathetically. "Even their supposed friends are muttering non sequiturs on questions of equal rights and trying to avoid the cross-fire between gay activists and their sworn enemies on the religious right." The following day, Scott concluded that the situation had reached a breaking point. Waiting had not succeeded in slowing the Defense of Marriage Act's momentum, yet the White House's public ambivalence implied that Clinton was actually wrestling with the possibility of a veto, unnecessarily raising expectations among gay supporters that would eventually provoke an even greater sense of betrayal. Already Socarides was openly acknowledging that "the recent debate over equal marriage rights has proven to be a difficult one for many of us whose personal views are not the same as the President's," as he told the Gay and Lesbian Lawyers Association of Florida. Clinton was scheduled to sign the Ryan White AIDS bill before noon on May 20, which meant Scott couldn't get through the day without facing the gay press. "I've got to have clear direction," she wrote Janice Enright, Ickes's assistant, begging for him to "call a meeting of the talking heads to discuss the next step on this same sex marriage issue."

When those advisers gathered to discuss the issue directly with the president, they were forced to confront a figure operating at a remove from the White House's official decision-making structure. Dick Morris, an on-and-off consultant to Republicans whom Clinton had initially recruited to secretly advise him under a code name, had served as a perpetual foil to Stephanopoulos and others intent on checking some of Clinton's accommodationist impulses. The self-appointed guardian of the president's "values agenda," Morris had from the moment of the Defense of Marriage Act's arrival urged Clinton to throw himself behind the bill quickly enough that he could claim ownership when it became law. The intervening weeks had not been kind to Stephanopoulos's advice to the contrary. If the White House was trying to make same-sex marriage go away, its noncommittal, wait-and-see position on the only piece of federal legislation regarding the subject had plainly failed.

At 7:30 a.m. on May 22, White House counsel Jack Quinn informed the president's staff that Clinton had decided he would sign the Defense of Marriage Act if presented to him in its current form. The bill was coursing through legislative channels with unusual alacrity—having survived its House subcommittee hearing with little trouble—and would only pick up speed because, as Stephanopoulos explained, its backers were "intent on creating differences even when none exist." Putting Clinton's imprimatur on Republican legislation would, his advisers concluded, remove any possible competitive advantage the opposition party had developed around the issue.

Even heterosexual staffers within the White House concluded that Clinton's response to the Defense of Marriage Act was being guided by a narrow set of political concerns detached from the fact that "many gays and lesbians will be hurt, if not offended, by this approach to the proposed legislation," as Stephanopoulos's memo had predicted.

"I realize it's an election year, but the stupidity around here on some of these issues might be tempered somewhat if Leon and/or POTUS could hear some of the counter-arguments on some of these issues," deputy domestic-policy adviser Ben-Ami wrote to his boss after learning that they had been excluded from a key May 13 meeting in Panetta's office. "I just don't think the President is being well-staffed on some of these issues—gay marriage in particular."

26

....

Dear Friends

As soon as Mike McCurry announced at his May 22 briefing that Bill Clinton planned to sign the Defense of Marriage Act, Marsha Scott and Richard Socarides began calling leaders of major gay groups, including several that already decided to endorse his reelection. (They spoke to three officials at the Human Rights Campaign alone.) Scott herself had learned of Clinton's decision from media coverage, so she understood that some of the anger they heard could be attributed to gay supporters being simply "shocked by the suddenness of the announcement." Just the night before, Al Gore had spoken to a group of fifty-two gay and lesbian supporters in New York, where he said the White House would not have any comment on the Defense of Marriage Act until it came to the president's desk. Empire State Pride Agenda chair Jeff Soref responded by demanding a meeting the next business day so that he and other major gay fundraisers could confront Clinton personally. "Depending on the outcome of the meeting request, the monies being raised will either continue to be given to our campaign or will go to an advertising campaign in the *New York Times, LA Times,* and *Washington Post* criticizing the President's new anti-gay stance," Scott told a colleague. At day's end, Socarides reported back to Clinton's political team on the eighteen calls he and Scott had completed. Expectations had been so low that a relieved Socarides optimistically summarized the reaction as "rather muted."

The phone calls illustrated the extent to which two weeks of lumbering prevarications over Clinton's response had created new problems for the White House. "The issues about marriage are not about his position but are about (1) our timing of the announcement to sign; (2) the language used by Mike in his briefings (3) why we didn't let them know we were going to announce the intent to sign. Their overall issues have to do with how we will work with them in the future," Scott wrote to Janice Enright in the chief of staff's office, as she attempted to schedule a meeting of gay leaders with Clinton. "They want to hear from him where we are now going and what role we want them to play."

On May 23, Clinton himself was asked about the matter while standing alongside German chancellor Helmut Kohl during a press conference at Milwaukee's city hall. "As I understand it, what the bill does is state marriage is an institution between a man and a woman that, among other things, is used to bring children into the world, but the legal effect of the bill—as I understand it, the only legal effect of the bill is to make clear that states can deny recognition of gay marriages that occurred in other states," Clinton said. "And if that's all it does, then I will sign it." He deployed a version of the "as I understand it" hedge four times in his answer, each time appearing to pad a mischaracterization of the bill's scope.

Nonetheless, it was the first time he had ever spoken in public about formal legal recognition of same-sex relationships. "This has always been my position on gay marriage. It was my position in '92. I told everybody who asked me about it, straight or gay, what my position was. I can't change my position on that; I have no intention of it," Clinton said. "But I am going to do everything I can to stop this election from degenerating into an attempt to pit one group of Americans against one another."

The next day, Scott distributed a transcript of Clinton's complete remarks to gay leaders and activists pulled from the same contact list she and Socarides had assembled to send presidential Christmas cards. It was an unusual tactic—an urgent mailing for the express purpose of alerting "Dear Friends," as Scott's cover letter was addressed, that she had just done something to inflame them—but the White House was effectively requesting forgiveness, if not absolution. "I know this has been a tough time for many of you. The political season can make life complicated and some of the rhetoric has been particularly painful," read Scott's letter. "As friends, we will sometimes disagree. We must, however, continue to work together, for we are much stronger as a team."

Meanwhile, hundreds of phone calls came into the Democratic National Committee from gay and lesbian voters taking issue with Clinton's position. "Many calls are from people so angry and shocked they don't want to have anything to do with the President or the Party," Brian Bond, director of the committee's lesbian and gay outreach office, wrote in a memo.

Despite Clinton's commitment to enact the law, Socarides still nursed a scenario under which the president would never have to sully himself with it. "I feel this bill may not come to Clinton at all. If it does, it will be changed," he said in one of his calls the day of McCurry's announcement. "I feel Republicans want Clinton to veto this, so they may add things to it to provoke Clinton to veto it."

At times, Socarides couldn't appear to decide whether the president should bait Republicans into going too far and provoking the veto he had wanted in the first place. He drafted a new set of White House talking points describing Clinton's view of adoption by gay and lesbian parents—even though the White House had yet to be in any way questioned about the issue. "Since the Republicans failed to box the President into a corner on the gay marriage issue, they will probably raise gay adoption next," Thomas A. Shea, a special assistant to the president, predicted in early June. "If this is in fact his position, and we expect the GOP to raise the issue anyway, this might be a good time for him to get his position out on his terms, using his choice of words. This would both help to inoculate him on the issue and mollify the g/l community."

Such efforts weren't helped by the fact that Clinton had significantly misrepresented the contents of the Defense of Marriage Act when throwing his support behind it. In speaking only about the full-faith-and-credit issue, Clinton had chosen to selectively describe the least controversial part of the bill—one that some congressional Democrats believed irrelevant because states were already empowered to deny recognition—and ignoring the more constitutionally questionable clause regarding federal definitions. "There's some discrepancy between what the President said today in Milwaukee, and the statements made by Mike. The President said it was his understanding that the only legal effect of the bill is to make it clear that states can deny recognition of gay marriages that occur in other states and if that's all it does, he'll sign it," Patricia Lewis, a spokeswoman who handled the gay media, wrote to a colleague immediately after learning what Clinton had said at his press conference with Helmut Kohl. "But the bill denies any federal marriage benefits as well. And the statement I got yesterday was that the President supports both parts of the bill. I think we need new talking points pretty soon."

That confusion put exceptional pressure on what was known as a statement of administration policy, which the White House had to deliver to the Office of Management and Budget by June 21 so it could be circulated in advance of the House vote. It was a routine matter, an official pronouncement by the executive branch about a legislative proposal that typically went unnoticed everywhere except by lobbyists and interest groups who tracked them closely for mention of their priorities. But in the case of the Defense of Marriage Act, the statement of administration policy was closely managed by everyone up to the chief of staff. The legislative-affairs team responsible for interacting daily with the legislators who had drafted the bill wanted to send Congress a short document that curtly declared the president would sign the bill without justification or context—"although it makes my liberal blood boil," said one administration lobbyist, Peter Jacoby. Clinton's politically minded advisers pushed for a longer version that began by praising the president's record as a "vocal opponent of discrimination against gay and lesbian individuals," before noting his opposition to same-sex marriage. "The only people who will focus on what we say here are the DC based g/l groups to whom this is important," claimed Socarides.

The task of stewarding the White House's relationship with gay and lesbian political elites would fall entirely on Socarides, who replaced Scott while she formally transferred to a job on the reelection campaign. While Clinton had faced pressure over his approach to military-service and non-discrimination issues, the Defense of Marriage Act's introduction placed new internal and external scrutiny anywhere administration policy dealt with families. At one point Shea cautioned during a conversation about a forthcoming speech that "if it's a family values thing and doesn't include a reference to nontraditional families," Clinton's gay allies "would likely get pretty upset."

"In some ways the damage was already done in mid-May when we said that you were against same-gender marriage because you wanted to take steps 'to strengthen the American Family,'" Socarides explained to Clinton in a private memo. "Many gay and lesbian Americans took this to mean that you believed they were not part of the American family." McCurry had apologized privately for those comments to gay officials and had come around to relishing a newfound freedom to savage an act of Congress as "gay-baiting, pure and simple," while at the same time stating plainly that Clinton would sign it into law. "In a sense, I acknowledge that we do have to have it both ways," he conceded under pressure during his daily briefing.

"Great job on same sex marriage today," Socarides wrote to McCurry after hearing the "gay-baiting" line. "The 'liaison operation' appreciates it."

If Socarides had lost the battle to stop Clinton from signing the Defense of Marriage Act, he continued to insist that at least he could shape the way his White House talked about it. At stake, he believed, could be both Clinton's reelection and the Democratic Party's long-term relationship with a key part of its liberal base newly invested in the conflict over marriage.

An Election-Year Baseball Bat

The Human Rights Campaign's immediate response to Bill Clinton's acceptance of the Defense of Marriage Act was a press release in which Elizabeth Birch called the move "a capitulation to religious extremists." Furthermore, the group revealed that it had canceled an invitation that George Stephanopoulos had already accepted to speak at a Human Rights Campaign event in San Francisco the following month. "This is a time to fortify the community," the press release quoted an event cochairman. "We need voices of strength and hope, and at the moment, George Stephanopoulos is neither."

The nation's leading gay-rights organization was criticizing the White House from a position of weakness. From the beginning, Human Rights Campaign officials had hoped for a veto but knowing its unlikelihood were happy just to see the White House silent about the proposed law. "It is election year politics designed to put the President on the defensive. Don't rush to get on the bandwagon. Hold your fire. See what develops," Hilary Rosen, Birch's girlfriend and a former HRC lobbyist, had written Leon Panetta, George Stephanopoulos, and Jack Quinn two days after the legislation was introduced. "If he signs the Bill, much is at risk in terms of an energized electoral base from gay people and their families. Let's try and work together to avoid this 'Sophie's Choice.'"

Birch privately noted the "difference between being against something and creating bad law," but her public communications rarely advanced that argument. Instead, HRC spokespeople tried to make the issue not marriage, or even the constitutionality of the Defense of Marriage Act, but the motives of the bill's backers for introducing it when they did. The group hastily released a report that its researchers had been assembling throughout the spring. Based on scattered news coverage, "Wedded to

Intolerance" documented how a cadre of conservative activists had fixated on the Hawaii marriage case and used the Republican primary season to elevate it to a national issue. "You can honor the marriage between a man and a woman without resorting to gratuitous gay-bashing," read an HRC memo to members of Congress the day the bill was introduced in the Senate. To the Associated Press, Birch called it "an election year baseball bat to bash gay Americans and score political points."

After McCurry made his remarks about the need to "strengthen the American family," Birch sent him a letter demanding that he "publicly acknowledge that you misspoke," as she wrote. "Let me be clear. We understand that we differ with the President's long-stated position opposing same-sex marriage. But one can oppose same-sex marriage without embracing the rhetoric of those who seek to scapegoat lesbian and gay Americans." Birch's success in eliciting an apology drafted by a gay staffer on McCurry's behalf ("my statements were made in haste and do not reflect the view of President Clinton") merely illustrated how powerless her organization was to be heard on more substantive matters. "This," Birch remarked to journalist Andrew Sullivan as the two waited to testify before Congress, "is hell week."

They were among four critics of the bill who had been summoned by Barney Frank, the Constitution subcommittee's ranking Democrat, to back the arguments he and other members of the minority party were making against it. Even though they would appear unified in their opposition during the hearing, Birch and Frank had very different views about how elected Democratic politicians should respond to the Defense of Marriage Act. From the moment he saw the bill, Frank had resigned himself to a dim outcome and a role for his party as willing if uneager collaborators in the bill's enactment. "There was no way Clinton was going to veto that bill, and there was no way I was going to play into Bob Dole's strategy," Frank says. "I didn't want him falling on that particular sword." He scoffed at the "notion that you wait and let them chew on it for a while," promoted by George Stephanopoulos and encouraged by the Human Rights Campaign. "What's the point—to look like he was forced into it, so they could beat him up over it?" says Frank. "He would have been taking a hit for nothing! He would have elevated it, had to talk about it at every press conference. Have you ever seen any politician in that position successfully evade a tough question and benefit from it?"

The day following her congressional testimony, Birch was personally acknowledged by assistant commerce secretary Bruce Lehman, the executive branch's highest-ranking openly gay official, just before Al Gore addressed the gathering in his vice president's ceremonial office. At Scott's request, the Human Rights Campaign had agreed to sponsor the reception for administration appointees, to ensure that costs for the potentially controversial political event would not fall on taxpayers. But Birch hardly felt like a guest of honor once the evening turned substantive. At one point, she pulled Gore to the side, finding herself on the precipice of tears as she begged him to dissuade Clinton from the inevitable. "Elizabeth, we're just going to have to agree to disagree," Gore told her.

The Human Rights Campaign had accumulated more political capital than any gay entity before it, and in an election year it had made an early decision to trade that leverage for access. Even in the anti-DOMA talking points, the group had to concede as much. "While the White House has handled this matter in a dismal fashion, it does not change our endorsement of President Clinton. . . . It is imperative for all fair-minded Americans that Bob Dole is defeated in November."

At least Birch could be satisfied that her group had almost certainly picked a winner. A *Newsweek* poll showed Clinton leading Dole by seventeen points, with 58 percent of voters opposing same-sex marriage and 45 percent saying they would be less likely to support a presidential candidate who supported gay rights, including marriage. For the polling memo it distributed on Capitol Hill the following week, the Human Rights Campaign was able to summon a neutral take on the same public opinion. There's "no consensus on the Defense of Marriage Act," pollster Mark Mellman wrote on June 4, after finding 34 percent of those he had surveyed on the group's behalf described themselves as undecided. Furthermore, Mellman concluded, most voters thought gay marriage shouldn't be a priority, and that it was unlikely to be a voting issue in any direction. None of that ran counter to Lake's polls and focus groups the year before, which, Birch reminded the cluster of high-level donors that HRC called its Federal Club, "told us. . . . that from a legislative and electoral standpoint, we are years away from achieving the right to marry. This is a novel and very difficult issue for most Americans. This is a sacred battle and one in which we should engage, but we should be clear that it will take a very long time."

Well before the emergence of the Defense of Marriage Act, the Human Rights Campaign had decided to place its three-day OutVote '96 conclave in Chicago, explicitly choosing the city where two weeks later Democrats would renominate Clinton for a second term. If gay activists had hoped that juxtaposition would force the party to address its concerns, they were again disappointed. Even though the Human Rights Campaign followed through on its endorsement, Clinton did not accept an invitation to receive it in person, choosing instead to send a brief video message and George Stephanopoulos in his place. "The November election will decide whether we fall back into a shadowy past, where denial and discrimination were the order of the day, or we continue forward in the quest for full equality," Stephanopoulos told the group. "Imagine a Congress led by Newt Gingrich voting on adoption policies for lesbian and gay families." That was, beyond a vague reference to "setbacks and disappointments," the closest he came to addressing the marriage debate.

There was much the same from the president himself in his convention acceptance speech. "If you believe in the values of the Constitution, the Bill of Rights, the Declaration of Independence, if you're willing to work hard and play by the rules, you are part of our family," Clinton said. "Old or young, healthy as a horse or a person with a disability that hadn't kept you down, man or woman, Native American, native born, immigrant, straight or gay." In 1992, the inclusion of the word *gay* in Clinton's acceptance speech was a late addition (absent from the prepared text distributed beforehand) that pleased unsuspecting supporters who knew no party nominee had ever done so before. By 1996, the nominee's lone use of the word teased those who had once hoped in those four years to graduate to a more substantive reference to gay rights. (Nonetheless, "the focus group numbers went into the tank at the very mention," White House deputy staff secretary Paul Richard recalled being told by Stephanopoulos.)

By then, however, the Human Rights Campaign's leadership was no longer looking upon the day the Senate would vote on the Defense of Marriage Act with unalloyed dread. In fact, it was starting to look as though something very good might come out of it.

When the Deal Goes Down

S taffers of the Human Rights Campaign had imagined the collision of interests over gay marriage long before they could see it coming and, like runaway slaves and country singers, they couldn't help but describe it using locomotive imagery. In 1994, David Sobelsohn had warned that the conservative backlash to a Hawaii court decision was "a train bearing down on America's gay-rights movement" with "our hands being tied to the rails." When a year and a half later he wanted to signal that the fight over the Defense of Marriage Act was lost, HRC communications director David M. Smith turned to the same vehicular metaphor, telling the *New York Times* that the bill was "an out-of-control freight train and will be darn near impossible to stop." The front page of the June 7 issue of the *Washington Blade*, the capital's gay weekly, led with an aphorism that for once looked to the rails and saw something other than weapons of death. "If you can't stop the freight train," wrote the *Blade's* Lisa Keen, "make sure it's hauling something you want delivered."

Keen's story detailed "the strategy of Gay activists toward the anti-Gay marriage bill now fast-tracking through Congress." In both the House and Senate, overwhelming majorities were arrayed in favor of the Defense of Marriage Act. The best chance of shaping, or potentially undermining, the bill had come and gone in late May when the Constitution subcommittee had tackled amendments. Ranking member Barney Frank had developed several that would significantly circumscribe the bill's legal impact. One of Frank's proposals would strip the bill's third section, which clarified the federal definitions of *marriage, husband,* and *spouse,* while leaving in place the one that allowed one state to disregard another's marriage should it choose. Another of Frank's amendments would treat gay marriages differently if legalized by legislators or voters, rather than by judges. Both of those changes, he could plausibly claim, focused the bill toward what its supporters said was their underlying worry—one state's judges imposing values upon another's—while respecting the primacy of states to set marriage policy.

When each amendment failed, along roughly partisan lines, Colorado Democrat Pat Schroeder emerged with one of her own conceived purely in a spirit of provocation. "Let's extend our defense of traditional marriage to something that is a much greater threat to traditional marriage than same-sex marriage is, and that is multiple, or serial, heterosexual marriages that are facilitated by no-fault divorce," Schroeder told the committee in introducing a "throwaway spouse" amendment that would deny federal recognition of heterosexual marriages in which either husband or wife had divorced a previous spouse without cause. "We have all heard of the trophy wife who displaces the original wife who worked to put her husband through graduate school." Schroeder's amendment, too, failed, and the subcommittee approved the bill by a party-line vote, eight to four.

Two weeks later, the bill went for further debate and a vote of the full committee. The debate remained as feisty as the subcommittee's, interrupted by one unexpected moment of tenderness from California Republican Sonny Bono, who supported the bill but wanted to record that he was "not homophobic" and "not a bigot." A former performer who had once composed half of the husband-and-wife duo Sonny & Cher, Bono mentioned that his daughter was a lesbian before turning to the committee's only gay member. "I simply can't handle it yet, Barney. It's nothing else. But at least I want to honestly say that to you and throw aside all the legal rhetoric. I wish I was ready," he said to Frank, who already treated Bono as one of the few Republican freshmen worthy of his personal admiration. "I can't go as far as you deserve, and I'm sorry."

That was the closest that the committee's Democrats would come to turning one of the Republicans in their midst against the bill, with the Judiciary Committee approving the Defense of Marriage Act as it had been written by a vote of twenty to ten. It would likely take another month for the matter to arrive on the House calendar for a vote, but Frank—who as the ranking member of the subcommittee was tasked with managing the debate for his party—had few tools at his disposal. The chamber's most liberal Democrats lined up to request time to condemn the bill, but Frank couldn't expect party leaders to push rank-and-file members to vote his way. "If you could win a vote, that's when you force your member to take a hard vote," says Democratic congressional aide Mark Agrast. "When they asked for a vote it was because there was a chance to turn the tide."

With the outcome in the House all but certain, the Human Rights Campaign's lobbyists shifted their efforts to the Senate. Even if they could not count on as many votes—statewide elections meant fewer members representing safely pro-gay constituencies—a small minority could wield more power in the Senate. Foremost among this was the ability to introduce amendments, including those with no relationship to the topic of the bill under consideration. Facing that opportunity, the Human Rights Campaign's lobbying team considered familiar liberal priorities unpopular enough to serve as a "poison pill"—a legislative provision that makes an otherwise appealing treatment too toxic for its supporters to swallow—if they could be inserted into the Defense of Marriage Act. After pondering policies related to gun control and health care, HRC political director Daniel Zingale proposed the legislative priority that had been effectively sidelined by the new Republican majority and its newfound obsession with gay marriage: "What about offering ENDA as an amendment to DOMA?"

Immediately, the Human Rights Campaign's strategists set a low bar for success. They did not need to guarantee the amendment be adopted, but wanted to be sure of a "respectable showing," in the words of Chai Feldblum. After all, the group was eager for any pivot from the purely defensive approach that had dominated their congressional tactics since the midterm elections. Zingale's proposal was particularly enticing: a way to save face after seeing its appeals unheard by the White House, and to retroactively justify an early endorsement of Clinton, whom many gay activists now considered an object of ridicule. "They would always rather compromise and get a deal," says White House adviser Richard Socarides, summarizing HRC's modus operandi, "and they will compromise until they have a deal."

Zingale took the proposal to the staff of Senator Ted Kennedy, who had coauthored ENDA with Vermont's liberal Republican senator Jim Jeffords. From the moment the Defense of Marriage Act was unveiled, one of Kennedy's aides was scheming with Socarides about ways to use the Senate amendment process to their advantage. At that point, the goal was to replace one of the bill's operative sections with something relatively toothless that nonetheless appeared true to its stated spirit: legislative language that was in defense of marriage, while not granting the federal government new powers to define it. A week after the bill was introduced, the aide unearthed a six-year-old amendment from Utah senator Orrin Hatch declaring that "Federal policy should encourage the well-being, financial security, and health of the American family." Hatch had drafted his brief amendment during the 1990 debate over the Hate Crime Statistics Act as a compromise that could head off one from fellow Republican Jesse Helms far more vehement in its disapproval of gays and lesbians. (That Hatch amendment, which passed without any votes against it, nonetheless concluded with what gay activists had taken to calling a *no promo homo* provision: "Nothing in this act shall be construed, nor shall any funds appropriated to carry out the purposes of the act be used, to promote or encourage homosexuality.") "Not exactly appropriate but something like this might work," Michael Iskowitz, Kennedy's lead staffer on gay issues, wrote to Socarides in mid-May.

They never got the chance. Once Clinton committed his support for the bill in its existing form, Republicans had no reason to voluntarily weaken their own legislation. Zingale's proposal adjusted to those new conditions with a different tactic. While adding the nondiscrimination language as an amendment could lead to a hard choice for the Senate's most relentlessly antigay members, the Human Rights Campaign hoped it might also present an easier decision for its very cautiously pro-gay ones. "Time and again, we've heard proponents of discriminatory measures say things like 'I'm not anti-gay, but the military is different' or 'I'm not anti-gay, but marriage is different,'" communications director David M. Smith wrote in late June. "Fine. Offering ENDA as an amendment to the anti-marriage bill asks these folks to be true to their word. As Barry Goldwater said when he endorsed ENDA in 1994, 'now's their chance to put up or shut up.'"

Workplace equality was certainly more promising terrain for lobbying than anything related to same-sex relationships. A poll taken by *Newsweek* in May found a healthy majority against gay marriage but showed the politics inverted around the Employment Non-Discrimination Act: 84 percent of voters said they were opposed to job discrimination. Years of work on Capitol Hill around the issue meant the bill had thirty Senate cosponsors already. The Human Rights Campaign's strategists concluded that putting it forward as an amendment made sense only once they marshaled more than forty firm pledges of support. After clearing that threshold, they could enlist the broader civil-rights coalition that had backed a gay-rights bill in 1993 for a final lobbying push ahead of a vote. "Is the strategy plausible?" asked Feldblum. "In Congress, any strategy is plausible if you've got the guts and the votes. Is it bold? Yes, you have no idea what might happen. Is this a moment that calls for a bold strategy? Yes, probably."

Events on the House floor confirmed the need for gay activists to do anything possible to alter the legislative dynamics before the Defense of Marriage Act landed on the Senate calendar. The debate was among the fiercest the chamber had seen in years. "As Rome burned, Nero fiddled. The flames of hedonism, the flames of narcissism, the flames of self-centered morality are licking at the very foundations of our society, the family unit," Bob Barr, the bill's original author in the House, thundered from its well. "What more does it take, my colleagues, to wake up and see that this is an issue being shouted at us by extremists bent on forcing a tortured view of morality on the rest of the country?"

Frank, who was managing the floor activity for the Democrats, knew he had little backup from his party's leadership. When the chamber's top two Democrats, minority leader Dick Gephardt and whip David Bonior, who both represented culturally traditional Midwestern districts, made public their support for the bill, Frank did not challenge them. "They couldn't vote for me and they had a responsibility to protect their members," he says. When Sam Gejdenson, who in 1994 had held his Connecticut seat by just a twenty-one-vote margin, revealed he was planning to oppose the bill, Frank encouraged him to change his position. "I said, 'Sam, you gotta vote for this, save yourself,'" Frank recalls, although Gejdenson rebuffed his advice. "I didn't want martyrs on my side. We do not want to encourage a situation where the right wing makes our best friends commit suicide."

The list Frank kept of Democrats who had requested time to speak out against the bill on the House floor filled up with "all the usual suspects" from safe liberal districts. (Only two of the names came as any surprise: Illinois's Luis Gutierrez and California's Xavier Becerra, who both represented majority-Latino districts. "It was not a gimme that Hispanics were going to go that way," Frank reflects.) As the floor manager for a bill in which his leadership had no interest, he controlled his party's microphone against Republicans who were eager in an election year to be seen on film vocally backing a popular bill. Frank had a long-standing belief that "legislating is the most personal of all government business," as he once wrote, and liked to turn abstract debates abruptly specific, and often discomfitingly so. "Does the fact that I love another man threaten you?" Frank asked the bill's backers. "Is the relationships with your spouses of such fragility that the fact that I have a committed, loving relationship with another man jeopardizes them?"

In the July 12 vote, the bill passed by a margin of 342 to 67, with only one Republican voting against it: the openly gay Steve Gunderson, who had already announced he would not seek reelection that fall. (Another Republican, Jim Kolbe of Arizona, announced weeks later that he was gay after being hounded by gay activists and independent media who accused him of hypocrisy by voting in favor of the bill. "All closeted gay and lesbian members of Congress," a full-page ad in the *Washington Blade* had threatened, "end your silence and defend your community.") Frank had been conditioned by over a decade in the House, where those not in the majority's leadership—or without enough votes to force its hand—learn to cut losses in the face of defeat. Frank could take solace only from minor accomplishments, like the fact that his amendment to treat differently marriages that had been sanctioned by voters rather than judges managed to clear a symbolic one-hundred-vote threshold.

With the Senate margin on the Defense of Marriage Act looking even worse, Ted Kennedy welcomed the Human Rights Campaign's proposal to use the marriage bill as a vehicle for an Employment Non-Discrimination Act. On the eve of the House vote, Kennedy and his two ENDA cosponsors laid out their plan to marry the two bills by offering the entirety of the longer bill as an amendment to the shorter one. (Kennedy was the only of the three who was at all sympathetic to same-sex marriage: coauthors Jeffords and Joe Lieberman, a Republican and Democrat respectively who would each later leave his party to become an independent, both went on to vote for the Defense of Marriage Act without apparent reservation.) An initial private count had thirty-four senators committed to voting yes on ENDA and another seven leaning in that direction. If the total were to approach fifty, it might have a destabilizing effect on even the most solid Republican opposition, potentially forcing Republicans to choose between their opposition to the workplace law and their support for the marriage bill. Even though Frank says he supported the deal because it "gave some of the Democrats a chance to show they were supportive of us," at the time he dismissed it—as he did many of the Human Rights Campaign's initiatives—as naïve. "Barney didn't want a vote on ENDA. He was arguing we'd get slaughtered in the Senate," says Zingale. "Ted Kennedy knew the Senate better than he did."

Kennedy had unexpectedly willing negotiating partners. Don Nickles, who had ascended to become the majority whip upon his friend Bob Dole's departure from the Senate, was eager to see the bill he had helped draft come to a vote before Congress disbanded to focus on the fall elections. Through each of their party's leaders, Kennedy negotiated an agreement with Nickles to guarantee a timely vote on the Defense of Marriage Act without Democratic interference, but only after members had had the opportunity to insert amendments. Each side would be able to introduce up to four amendments, but the specifics of the deal made clear what had really been negotiated: seven of them would be allocated forty-five minutes of debate each, while Kennedy's Employment Non-Discrimination Act would get ninety. Either party could void the deal until five p.m. on September 4, the eve of the scheduled vote.

That agreement itself amounted to a victory to gay-rights lobbyists, who would have never been confident of moving a nondiscrimination bill anywhere near a Senate floor under Republican control. Even so, they considered victory unlikely, but a respectable showing of bipartisan support—and the glare of heightened attention reflecting off the shiny gay-marriage debate—would surely advance the cause. "The amendment has provided an excellent opportunity to educate Congress and the American public about the very real problem of job discrimination on the basis of sexual orientation and is exposing the true motivation of those Senators who are pushing for passage of DOMA," Zingale wrote Senator John Kerry.

Those briefing members about the terms of the compromise quickly discovered that they might have changed the dynamics in a more significant way. The uninvited emergence of a new gay-rights issue appeared to have recentered congressional politics around the whole bundle of gay-rights issues, by default mainstreaming others that were not long before easily dismissed as "special rights." Allowing gay people to hold jobs seemed like a very modest concession when juxtaposed with certifying their domestic arrangements. Being able to approach lawmakers on two questions simultaneously—and willing to accept a yes on only one of them—improved the negotiating position held by gay lobbyists.

With the two issues paired, several moderate Democrats generally cautious about associating with pro-gay causes were willing to do so if able to simultaneously put their opposition to same-sex marriage on the record. After Kennedy's maneuver, House Democratic leader Dick Gephardt and Nevada senator Harry Reid both signed on as cosponsors of the Employment Non-Discrimination Act; South Carolina senator Fritz Hollings subsequently pledged his vote for it. All three were Democrats who never wavered in their intention to vote for the Defense of Marriage Act. "Oddly enough, it did help with ENDA," says Agrast. "By the vote, they felt they owed us for it."

While the Human Rights Campaign's lobbyists hunted for votes, each party's caucus faced a struggle over which amendments they would present on September 5. Many reflected individual members' pet initiatives that had piled up throughout the year, on issues as varied as union dues, the District of Columbia's welfare benefits, and hospital stays for newborns and their mothers. A few of the Democratic amendments attempted to advance other gay interests, like the proposal from Dianne Feinstein and Ron Wyden to extend federal hate-crimes laws to cover sexual orientation. For some Democrats who had antagonized gay supporters by supporting DOMA, the amendment process offered welcome penance. Minnesota's Paul Wellstone, the most liberal senator to announce he would vote for the bill, hoped to regain favor with disappointed gay supporters by demanding that the General Accounting Office prepare a study assessing the "disparity between the treatment of committed same-sex couples and married couples." Even if these were initiatives that gay activists would have otherwise been eager to see fast-tracked to the Senate floor, presenting Democrats multiple options to register a pro-gay vote in exchange for supporting DOMA would undermine Kennedy's strategy. "We did not say 'don't do this,'" David Smith of the Human Rights Campaign confided in a reporter. "We said let us get past ENDA now and consider hate crimes afterwards."

By early September, Republicans had also grown wary of the deal that their leaders had struck a month earlier. If Kennedy could muster forty votes for ENDA, he could find himself with enough support to sustain a filibuster of the Defense of Marriage Act—an outcome that was inconceivable if the bill came to a vote in the form it had passed the House. When majority leader Trent Lott decided not to permit amendments, Kennedy countered with a threat: he would work to attach ENDA to one of the appropriations bills that Lott needed to pass that month. Ultimately, both sides had reason to scrap the carefully laid plans to spend September 5 voting on amendments to DOMA. Instead, Lott and Kennedy arrived at a simpler bargain. The Republican leadership would allow the Employment Non-Discrimination Act to reach the floor as a stand-alone bill the following week, immediately after the Senate dispatched the Defense of Marriage Act—both bills arriving free of amendments for an up-or-down vote. (This also ensured that ENDA would not be undermined with amendments, including one Senator John McCain wanted to introduce that would create different rules for gay employees who supervised children under the age of seventeen, such as teachers or scout leaders.)

That arrangement set up as cleanly as possible the trade-off that Kennedy had initially envisioned appealing to moderates of both parties: the opportunity to let their vote against gay marriage—by far the issue with greater cultural salience—cast shade over a vote for an end to job discrimination. Instead of loading up an unwanted train with desirable cargo, gay activists were being invited to charter their own vehicle leaving the station at the same time. "The House is a long shot," Smith told the *New York Times* just before the scheduled September 10 votes, "but we never expected to be in this good a shape in the Senate."

Kennedy began that consequential day with an unusual concession speech. "I oppose the so-called Defense of Marriage Act, and I regret that the Senate is allocating scarce time at the end of this Congress to consider this unconstitutional, unnecessary and divisive legislation," he said on the floor of the chamber. "There is, however, a silver lining to the Republican Leadership's decision to schedule this debate. It gave many of us the opening we needed to raise a serious civil rights concern—the festering problem of unacceptable discrimination against gays and lesbians in the workplace. We debated that issue at length on Friday, and we will vote on it later this afternoon. I am very hopeful that a ban on job discrimination will pass the Senate. If it does, we will have the Defense of Marriage Act to thank for that achievement."

As Kennedy had forecast, the Defense of Marriage Act's sacrifice was dramatic and violent—passing by an even more lopsided margin than it had in the House. The bill received eighty-five votes, representing every one of the Senate's Republicans and a supermajority of its Democrats. Just fourteen Democrats voted no.

The one vote that kept the total shy of one hundred was Arkansas Democrat David Pryor, who was at a Little Rock hospital, where his thirty-three-year-old son Mark had entered surgery the previous day related to an obscure cancer recently found in his leg. Despite representing a socially conservative state, David Pryor was a mentor of Clinton's and months away from his retirement. He had assured Kennedy that he would vote for ENDA and travel to Washington to deliver that vote should it prove essential to the bill's passage. "We had Pryor," says Zingale. "It was very clear he would come back to cast the tie vote if we were at fifty."

Those whipping the bill found that goal moving unexpectedly into sight, as conservative Democrats—perhaps liberated by the ability to balance a vote for gay rights with one against—began indicating they would support the Employment Non-Discrimination Act. At 10:30 a.m., Iskowitz called Socarides at the White House with an urgent request: "Get your ass down here because we're getting votes for this and you guys aren't doing anything." Socarides rushed to an anteroom off the Senate floor, where he joined Coretta Scott King, Dorothy Height, and Justin Dart— the nongay civil-rights leaders who had lent the cause of protecting gays from discrimination early credibility in the Capitol. Iskowitz welcomed Socarides with another command. "Get your guys on the phone," he said, referring to the president and vice president. From a campaign stop in Pennsylvania, Gore called ambivalent Democrats, many of them his former Senate colleagues, letting them know each of their votes was necessary and potentially crucial to the outcome. "You have to vote for this," Gore said to one of North Dakota's two wavering senators. "I'm not asking you, I'm telling you."

Eventually the challenge moved from one of politics to logistics. If Kennedy could get up to fifty votes for the nondiscrimination bill, the vice president would possess the tie-breaking vote in his role as Senate president. Democrats might not have controlled Congress, but they still had the White House and the machinery of the United States government. Within twenty minutes, plans had fallen into place: Air Force Two would be on standby to ferry Gore back to Washington, where a landing pad at the Capitol was being readied to welcome an arriving helicopter. Kennedy's vote count got to forty-nine, and stuck there.

Pryor wasn't yet ready to leave his son's bedside while he recovered from twelve hours of surgery. As long as he stayed in Little Rock, there couldn't be a tie for Gore to break. Iskowitz was in tears, pounding his fist in anger. He asked Kennedy if it would be possible to hold the vote open indefinitely, or to dispatch a military plane that could ferry Pryor back and forth to Washington to let him cast the vote. "We've done all we can," Kennedy tried to reassure his aide. "There will be another day."

Midnight Cowboy

At the hour on September 10, 1996, when the United States Senate passed the Defense of Marriage Act, President Bill Clinton was somewhere between Kansas City, where he had a series of midday events, and St. Louis, where he would speak at an evening rally at a new magnet school campus before heading to a DNC fundraiser at a local Hyatt.

From the moment Clinton had announced three and a half months earlier that he would sign the bill if presented to him by Congress, his White House's gay-and-lesbian liaison operation had agonized about how that moment would play out. Typically it is showpiece legislation whose final passage through Congress awakens the White House's interest in stage-managing its enactment—a unique opportunity to wrangle credit for a change he might not have initiated but that only he can finalize. But even as the Founders delineated all the ways a bill can become law, they never advised on how to play one's assigned role in the constitutional process while projecting an attitude calibrated to fall between indifference and contempt.

As soon as the Defense of Marriage Act passed the House in July, and it became apparent that Republicans were not going to let the matter go away just because they had won Clinton's acquiescence, Marsha Scott worked to negotiate a deal with his political team. All agreed that, in keeping with Clinton's declaration of disdain for the bill's motives, neither the White House nor the reelection campaign would tout the new law.

Even as broader public opinion continued to back Clinton's decision to embrace the Defense of Marriage Act, the private correspondence arriving in the White House mailroom attested to the intensity of disagreement, particularly from those who identified themselves as Clinton supporters. The office of presidential correspondence was receiving between fifty and one hundred letters daily about marriage, many with so angry a tone that the office's director concluded the standard gay-issues form letter was an insufficient response. "I want to get them the best answer they can as soon as possible (not that there is a good answer!)," Kyle Baker, director of presidential correspondence, wrote to Richard Socarides in mid-July. That picked up during the summer, with 4,300 similar anti-DOMA email messages arriving over the first two weeks of August, evidence of an organized Internet campaign that the White House had never before seen. "No same-letter coordinated effort has caught on quite like this one," Steve Horn, the correspondence office's email director, reported to Socarides.

Yet by the time the Defense of Marriage Act passed in midafternoon of September 10, it wasn't even the gay-rights news of the day. In early August, the White House—which had already endorsed the Employment Non-Discrimination Act—had formally decided to throw its support behind the compromise strategy that the Human Rights Campaign had engineered early that summer to partner the two bills. Gay lobbyists had dreaded the day that the Defense of Marriage Act would come for a Senate vote, and yet there was little glumness after. Indeed, September 10 felt like as close to an outright gay political triumph as the movement had yet known in official Washington. Watching the White House coordinate a military helicopter in the service of gay rights was exhilarating. The Employment Non-Discrimination Act, which had been assumed dead for the 104th Congress, had come a single, promised vote short of becoming the first piece of gay civil-rights legislation to pass a house of Congress, and had done so in a Republican-controlled Senate. "We came within a breath of victory today," the Human Rights Campaign's Elizabeth Birch had declared. "We'll hit the ground running in the 105th Congress."

The unexpected turn of events offered Clinton the opportunity to quietly sign the Defense of Marriage Act while the gay community was distracted by its unexpected near triumph. Unlike the Employment Non-Discrimination Act, which promised immediate gains for gays, the marriage bill threatened no immediate damage. Once the bill passed the Senate, that became the source of some consolation. From a practical perspective, the Defense of Marriage Act would become law and absolutely nothing would change. No one would be harmed, for now at least.

Obviously Clinton wouldn't sign the bill in a Rose Garden ceremony, handing out souvenir pens to the bill's Republican sponsors. But he would still have to put pen to paper. Socarides had proposed just letting the bill become law—it would happen automatically if the White House held on to a bill for ten days without any presidential action—but political advisers dismissed that, saying it would make Clinton look weak and wishy-washy. Socarides implored the staff responsible for managing the president's schedule to nonetheless make the experience as swift and painless as possible. "Let's not let it sit around, sign it as soon as we can," he argued, "so it's not news any longer."

Yet a president cannot sign a bill immediately after Congress approves it. The seven lean paragraphs that had passed both House and Senate had to be printed on paper with a coating designed to resemble parchment, formally signed by the Speaker of the House and president pro tempore of the Senate, then delivered to the White House. "Could you be sure to tell me and Richard Socarides the moment the same-sex marriage bill comes in?" deputy counsel Elena Kagan wrote staff secretary Todd Stern. A week after it had passed the Senate, the bill still had not made the short trip down Pennsylvania Avenue. "I think their [sic] holding it so that we have to sign as close to the election as possible," Socarides worried to a colleague.

The waiting opened a new window for Democratic protests, including by people personally close to Clinton and even some within his own White House. The Presidential Advisory Council on HIV/AIDS voted to draft a letter to Clinton encouraging him to "reconsider your stated intention" to sign the bill. "DOMA perpetuates the homophobia that hinders effective HIV prevention . . . individuals who lack basic self-respect because they are victims of homophobia are less likely to heed prevention messages that urge persons to protect themselves and others," read the letter signed by the council's chair, Scott Hitt, the AIDS doctor whose Hollywood Hills home had in 1991 hosted Clinton's first introduction to the West Coast gay political elite. The man who had squired Clinton through that event, his old friend David Mixner, was busy rallying people to participate in a September 16 protest in Los Angeles, in which demonstrators planned to line the sidewalks of a busy West Hollywood intersection with the goal of provoking arrests.

On September 20, seven bills passed by Congress arrived at the White House. Only one of the seven was accompanied by any controversy, and when Stern learned just after two p.m. that the Defense of Marriage Act was in the stack of new documents, he asked Socarides if he wanted to travel by plane to courier the bill to Clinton himself. At that hour, the president and first lady were arriving at the Oregon Museum of Science and Industry in Portland, their final stop on a two-day bus tour through the Pacific Northwest. Air Force One would be making its way back east that evening, and Socarides decided that even if he could meet the president en route, long-distance hand-delivery would only draw more attention to the act of signing and perhaps signal a misleading eagerness. It could wait until Clinton returned to the White House, Socarides told Stern, as long as it was taken care of before Clinton turned in for the night.

But the bill would require more than just a signature. Clinton still had not been forced to update the initial remarks he had made in Milwaukee four months earlier. Throughout the summer, those prevarications weighed heavily on the advisers managing the White House's response to the bill, to the extent that two of them felt compelled to make sure Clinton knew what was in the Defense of Marriage Act before following through on his pledge to enact it. "You have said that 'the only legal effect of the bill is to make it clear that states can deny recognition of gay marriages that occurred in other states. And if that's all it does, then I will sign it.' Actually, that analysis covers only the first substantive provision of the bill, which provides that no state shall be forced to recognize a same sex marriage recognized by any other state," Socarides and George Stephanopoulos wrote Clinton in a September 11 memo. "You should be aware that some may argue that the bill, in fact, does more than you suggested when you announced your intention to sign it."

In part to clarify the historical record about Clinton's rationale for signing, Socarides drafted a "Statement by the President" that for once in Clinton's own voice acknowledged the bill's impact on definitions of *marriage* and *spouse* under federal law. "I also want to make clear to all that the enactment of this legislation should not, despite the fierce and at times divisive rhetoric surrounding it, be understood to provide an excuse for discrimination, violence and intimidation against any person on the basis of sexual orientation," the statement concluded. "Discrimination, violence and intimidation for that reason, as well as others, violate the principle of equal protection under the law and have no place in American society." It circulated within senior staff within the White House and was approved for release by Jack Quinn, Leon Panetta, Al Gore, and Kagan, among others.

The one-page statement was distributed to the White House press corps as they were settling into their work space on a high school's practice field in Brandon, South Dakota. Air Force One had just landed at the airport in nearby Sioux Falls airport, and the Clintons were en route to Brandon to host a rally just before kickoff of the school's homecoming high-school football game. As the president and first lady took pictures with the Brandon Valley High School Lynx and the Huron High School

Tigers, those in the press area were busy decoding what the document they had just been handed said about Clinton's view of gay rights. The signing statement didn't offer anything new about the president's attitude toward the Defense of Marriage Act, but the way it had been released might.

Reporters had the president's official travel schedule, which showed the Clintons due to arrive home at 12:40 a.m., after a two-hour-and-fifteen-minute flight back to Andrews Air Force Base and from there a ten-minute helicopter ride to the White House lawn. The early wire-service stories, written before Clinton had even departed South Dakota, made note of what this meant for the circumstances under which the bill signing would actually take place. "The late-night announcement of Clinton's action—well after the evening news broadcasts—raised questions about the timing of his move," wrote the Associated Press's Terence Hunt. McCurry was happy to answer those questions, articulating Socarides's rationale: "The president believes that the motives of this bill are dubious and he wants to get it over with as soon as possible."

Clinton arrived at the White House still wearing the brown leather jacket, jeans, and cowboy boots into which he had changed between his Oregon and South Dakota events. A packet awaited him, including the official copy of the Defense of Marriage Act and a cover note from Stern. "Mike McCurry has already released a statement from you (copy attached) about the bill and told reporters that you would be signing it when you get back to the White House. Consequently, you should sign this tonight," Stern wrote, putting the final sentence in bold for emphasis. At 12:50 a.m., the president scrawled *William J. Clinton* with his left hand, dashing two lines under his name in a way that could be read as a gesture of either emphasis or pique. "To the President's credit, he was angry at being told when he came back from a trip that he had to sign that bill then," Rahm Emanuel recalled after the election. "He said this is going to look bad."

The Defense of Marriage Act was now the law of the land, but Clinton did not have anything further to say about it. In his weekly radio address, which Clinton had recorded on Friday afternoon in a planetarium class-room at the Portland museum to air nationally on Saturday morning, he praised one of the other pieces of family-oriented legislation to emerge that week from Congress: a bill to double the length of hospital stays that insurance companies would cover for mothers of newborns, to forty-eight hours. "America has a responsibility to protect the health of our families," he said.

Yet by Sunday morning, it was the peculiar circumstances of the Defense of Marriage Act's enactment that continued to make news. The *Washington Post* noted prominently that he had "waited until the dead of night." The *New York Times's* story was headlined GAY RIGHTS GROUPS ATTACK CLINTON ON MIDNIGHT SIGNING. The only person cited in any newspaper story who referred specifically to the logistics of the bill signing was a White House spokeswoman, Mary Ellen Glynn, who told the *Washington Post:* "He did it at midnight because that's when it deserved to be signed." What had been arranged as a gesture of disdain had become interpreted as subterfuge.

The day after the Defense of Marriage Act became law, Socarides transferred off the government payroll to spend the final six weeks of the election working full-time for the campaign. He drafted Clinton's scripted lines on gay issues in preparation for the two debates with Dole, including these on marriage: "A. It's a personal belief based on my collective life experience. This has been my longstanding position. I also believe that some have used this issues to try to divide us as Americans. And I will do everything in my power to try to prevent that. [DON'T go any further. The more you say, the more trouble it will cause. Everything you say will be picked apart. Stay as general as possible and avoid use of the words "traditional" or "traditional family" and don't talk about marriage as the vehicle by which people have children. Gay people also have children.]"

For a few weeks, these efforts at dodging discussion of gay families appeared to be succeeding, in part because Republicans had chosen to focus their campaign messaging on Clinton's personal ethics rather than the nation's morality. On the afternoon of October 14, Socarides received a call at his campaign office from David Smith, and the Human Rights Campaign's communications director was irate: How could Clinton possibly be running ads bragging about his opposition to gay marriage? Socarides was befuddled by the claim; such a thing was simply impossible.

But Smith played him over the phone the faint and fuzzy recording of a sixty-second ad that an HRC supporter had captured off a local radio broadcast. Socarides eventually learned from the campaign's media team that the ad titled "Freedom" was in fact airing on religious radio stations reaching as many as fifteen, mostly southern, states. Its nominal subject was a time "the Justice Department went after a church to get at a parishioner's tithing money"—and Clinton stepped in to protect "religious freedom," according to the script that Socarides acquired. "It's not the only time he's defended our values," it read, then a cascade of items from Dick

Morris's "values agenda," including: "The President supports teaching children abstinence; teen pregnancy is down for the fourth year in a row. The President signed the Defense of Marriage Act. Supports curfews and school uniforms."

It was specifically what the liaison operation had been promised wouldn't happen: the bill that a hangdog president had said he had to grudgingly embrace now conveniently held up as one of his first-term accomplishments. The ad "is a mistake and a serious political miscalculation," Birch said, "designed to pander to a segment of the electorate that isn't going to support the president under any circumstances. It completely contradicts the president's past statements." A Dole campaign spokesman crowed: "This is a President who signed the Defense of Marriage Act in the middle of the night so it wouldn't be news, but now he does paid advertising to promote it."

The origins of the ad—specifically whether its release was a careless mistake or an approved tactic—remained opaque, even to those within Clinton's orbit who set out to identify a responsible party. The ad was produced by Squier Knapp Ochs, Clinton-Gore '96's lead media consultant, its script circulating on the firm's letterhead, but campaign officials would never say who had approved it. Private concessions to gay activists that the ad was a mistake were never matched with such a public acknowledgment. "They didn't want to pull it, because it would look like backtracking, trying to cover it up," says Socarides. After a few days, the campaign replaced the ad with a new version, in which the reference to the Defense of Marriage Act was replaced with an expanded mention of his opposition to late-term abortion. Even Barney Frank, who had supported Clinton's decision to announce early that he would sign the bill, called his sister, then working as Clinton's deputy campaign manager, to complain. "I understand the political necessity of it," Frank recalls thinking, "but don't use this crappy language."

The president, after acknowledging he wanted it both ways, couldn't figure out how to get away with having it. "Wouldn't it have been cheaper," a reporter asked at a White House press briefing, "to sign the bill in the daytime and you wouldn't have had to run an ad?"

Trial at Honolulu

In a few years when we all have some true perspective, gay and lesbian Americans will look back on 1996 as a turning point for our movement for two very critical reasons," Elizabeth Birch reflected at the end of that "year of great hope and progress." It was an unexpectedly cheerful verdict on twelve months that for gay movement advocates had often seemed traumatic.

"First, 1996 was the year gay marriage hit the national consciousness—for better or for worse (although I would argue ultimately for better)," Birch explained. "By plucking the question of gay marriage out of the Hawaiian universe and depositing it in the living rooms of Americans everywhere, religious political extremists have, I believe, helped advance *our* case in the long run. Rather than pouring into the streets to stop the terrifying gay marriage juggernaut, people are pausing to think about the question, most for the first time."

Hawaii was not yet done with the question of gay marriage, however. Even as Washington treated the state's issuance of marriage licenses to same-sex couples as a fait accompli, Hawaiians remained fixated on the process that would get them there. The first day of the *Baehr v. Miike* trial happened to be the same one, in early September, that the Defense of Marriage Act would come for a Senate vote; closing arguments were the same day that Bill Clinton signed it into law. It was those events, rather than the developments in circuit court, that Honolulu's newspapers treated as a far-off sideshow.

The whole notion of taking gay marriage to trial was a novel one. The spate of cases in the 1970s had been resolved through summary judgments, in which judges assess a case's legal merits without a full trial. (In 1971, a

Kentucky county judge ordered a two-hour evidentiary hearing before rejecting a complaint from two women seeking to marry.) Dan Foley had hoped to follow the same procedural path, making a conscious effort in his first brief to avoid any claims that a judge would claim required fact-finding. The nature of the Hawaii Supreme Court's decision, and the order it gave to the court that received the remanded *Baehr* case, meant such factual consideration could not be dodged any longer. From the outset, the state circumscribed its areas of contention to exclude the big debate over the nature of sexual identity, stipulating that its biological underpinnings were irrelevant to the case they would present. "What we were looking for was evidence—some kind of demographic or sociological study—about what's best for kids," says Attorney General Bob Marks, who formulated the state's early strategy for the trial. "Hawaii wasn't going to have a trial about homosexuality."

That did not diminish the sense of drama that attended the trial's opening. In addition to the metal detectors permanently stationed at the building's front doors, a second set was erected outside the hallway approaching Judge Kevin Chang's courtroom. A three-drawer file cabinet in the attorney general's office was filled with unsolicited letters about the case, some of them so startling in their content that Deputy Attorney General Rick Eichor checked his witnesses into a Waikiki hotel under assumed names and had investigators escort them to and from the trial each day. Proceedings were once postponed due to a bomb threat. "I've been an attorney for a long time, and you just get a sense of when you should be afraid and when you shouldn't," says Eichor. "I had a sense you needed to be careful."

After the first day of crowded bleachers, spectators stopped showing up in large numbers. This latter-day *Scopes* trial was more thrilling in concept than in execution—a battle over scientific expertise in an area where the science was still too young to be seriously fought over. Among the parade of experts testifying—four psychologists, two sociologists, one pediatrician, and a child psychiatrist—those doing so on the plaintiffs' behalf had the more impressive credentials and the easier task. They had only to incite doubts about the state's evidence, rather than present any of their own. Neither side was surprised, ten weeks later, when Chang ruled that the state had failed to prove that there was a public interest in denying same-sex couples the right to marry. Eichor was granted a stay so that the attorney general could exhaust the state's options with an appeal, but he nevertheless conceded to Chang that "the likelihood of success is not particularly tremendous in this case."

Even as Foley declared that "I like my odds" on an appeal, politics was rendering gay marriage a long shot. Throughout the year, the cause's legislative allies found themselves facing unexpectedly well-funded challenges from gay-marriage opponents as they sought reelection. One prominent booster, House Judiciary Committee chair Rey Graulty, lost his seat in a Democratic primary; another, Senate president Norman Mizuguchi, barely held on to his. In November's general election, four Democratic lawmakers who supported gay marriage were defeated by Republican neophytes. In several instances, the challengers were proud single-issue candidates whose entry into politics was eased by support from both the Hawaii's Future Today coalition arranged by the Mormon and Catholic churches and Mike Gabbard's Alliance for Traditional Marriage. Those lawmakers who survived got the message. The day after Chang's decision, Mizuguchi told the *Advertiser* that "I believe we can find a ground upon which we can agree with the House so that the issue is laid to rest."

The following month, as they returned to session, legislators revived two types of proposals on which they had failed to act in 1996 but now embraced with renewed urgency. One set of bills would create a legal framework, along the lines of a domestic partnership, that would permit gay and lesbian couples to receive legal protections while specifying that marriage was available only to those of opposite sex. Another set of bills cleared the way for a constitutional amendment that, if approved by voters, would seize from Hawaii's courts their ability to play any role in adjudicating the issue. Both types of proposals found support, conspiring together to silhouette a workable compromise. Hawaii's gays and lesbians would emerge with the most generous set of benefits ever made available to same-sex couples in the Americas, and no hope for ever claiming marriage as a civil right.

On February 2, Birch dispatched national field director Donna Red Wing and senior policy advocate Nancy Buermeyer to Honolulu to assess the prospects for HRC to make a sustained investment in the likely battle over amending the state constitution. "Almost immediately, we found that the community effort around the issue of same-gender marriage was rather limited," Red Wing and Buermeyer reported. "This is due in part to the fact that the issue didn't begin as a typical grassroots movement but as a highly technical court case involving a limited number of players. Thus, there had been no real impetus to do the kind of outreach and education that needs to happen to create a groundswell of support and financial investment."

Many in that community held the Human Rights Campaign itself responsible for their situation. Birch certainly liked to talk about her ties to Hawaii. As a teenager she had run away to the islands from her Saskatchewan home, eventually enrolling at the University of Hawaii and studying the Hawaiian language. Even as she was engaged with events in Washington, Birch prided herself on being particularly alert to developments in the state she once called home. The first recorded remarks she ever made about marriage were prompted by a Hawaii Commission on Sexual Orientation and the Law report recommending the legislature approve full rights for same-sex couples. "Many Americans have never thought about marriage in connection with gay and lesbian people, or even about the reality that same-gender couples form families that need protection and deserve support," Birch said in a December 1995 press release. "The commission did its homework, and looked at equal marriage rights fairly and methodically. We invite the public, judges, and legislators in the rest of the country to do the same."

A close read of those remarks showed that Birch never said that she or HRC supported legalizing same-sex marriage, or were prepared to do anything on its behalf. Hawaii activists, therefore, were taken aback the next year to learn that Birch was telling her mainland contacts that "a top priority" for the Human Rights Campaign was helping island politicians who had taken unpopular pro-marriage positions. "Foley was surprised to learn this, because he knows first hand that HRC's net contribution to local races is $750 while many thousands more are needed to protect key legislators," Tom Ramsey and Tom Humphreys of Hawaii's Alliance for Equal Rights, the group coordinating pro-marriage electoral activity, wrote to Birch in the summer of 1996.

Activists saw that stinginess rooted in a deeper sense of caution. These were by now familiar critiques to Birch: that she had fashioned an organization too timid to fight for marriage and too image-conscious to dirty itself with partisan politics. The Human Rights Campaign had helped promote the Hawaii Equal Rights Marriage Project's 1-900-97-MARRY phone line. (Callers would have a $5 contribution to support the court case automatically added to their phone bills.) The group also mailed a solicitation to its members in Hawaii encouraging them to attend an Alliance for Equal Rights fundraiser. When asked to get more directly involved, however, HRC officials cited the group's status under the federal tax code as a reason to limit involvement in state elections. Activists heard it as an excuse to avoid the trying task of small-scale politicking away from the cameras. "There's the rub: every creative idea we've had for increasing HRC's support of local races appears to meet insurmountable legal obstacles," wrote Ramsey and Humphreys.

When the Human Rights Campaign eventually agreed to send $4,250 to the Alliance for Equal Rights to help print and distribute a "voter education brochure" in targeted districts, the recipients felt the gift was accompanied with a sense of superiority from the movement's political professionals toward its activist class. "How will this pamphlet convince them to vote for the right people in September?" western regional field organizer Becky Dinwoodie wrote Humphreys from Washington. While the Human Rights Campaign boasted of its lobbying skill in Congress, it had nothing to offer as Hawaii legislators emerged from November spooked by colleagues' losses attributed to their pro-marriage positions. Such complacency "snatched defeat from the jaws of almost certain victory," claimed columnist Gabriel Rotello. "After the election, gay groups continued to ignore pleas to mount a major political and cultural battle against the now-looming amendment," he wrote in *The Advocate.*

Birch's "site team," as she called Red Wing and Buermeyer, told her that it would take at least $100,000 just to map out a prospective campaign's media and field plans, including a large-sample poll to guide strategy and tactics. There was enough publicly available polling to know how much it would doom the prospects for same-sex marriage if the question were put to a statewide vote. According to a *Honolulu Star-Bulletin* survey in February, 70 percent of Hawaiians said they disapproved. Earlier complacency had been costly. Over the previous three years, in which it had been the dominant issue in the islands' politics, the share of Hawaiians who favored legalizing same-sex marriages had actually fallen, by more than one-third.

Eager to keep the matter off the ballot, HRC rushed $24,000 to air a television ad during what it considered a crucial week in April 1997, as the legislative session was approaching its end. The ad, "urging citizens to call and write their legislators asking them not to tamper with Hawaii's constitution," appeared to have little impact on negotiations. Legislators were on their way to a novel legal structure they called "reciprocal beneficiaries," an arrangement at once more expansive and more limited than same-sex marriage would be. Any two adults ineligible to be wedded—including, for example, platonic straight roommates or a pair of sisters—would be able to apply for a package of dozens of benefits, including inheritance rights, the ability to sue for a partner's wrongful death, and spousal coverage for insurance and pensions. (The *Star-Bulletin* poll two months earlier showed 55 percent of Hawaiians disapproving of a proposal to "grant gay and lesbian couples some marital benefits through domestic partnerships or a similar arrangement.") When paired with legislative support for an antimarriage amendment, most gay activists viewed the compromise as capitulation they were powerless to halt. "HRC aired a last-minute TV commercial, true, but it was way too little, way too late," *The Advocate*'s Rotello wrote. "In the end, so far as I can tell, not a single phone call was made to a single wavering senator promising a strong, well-financed campaign to defend his position and support his reelection—even as right-wing groups across the nation, proactive as usual, pledged to work overtime to defeat any senator who stood with the queers."

Just before their session expired, legislators approved a statewide ballot question for the next statewide general election. In November 1998, voters would be asked if "the State Constitution should be amended to specify that the Legislature shall have the power to reserve marriage to opposite-sex couples." For the first time since the Hawaii Supreme Court's decision four years earlier, the uneasy coalition of gay-marriage opponents was able to claim momentum on their side. Debi Hartmann, the chair of Hawaii's Future Today, vowed her group would "make the 1998 voter turn out the largest ever to show our support and unity for traditional marriage." Gabbard was less circumspect in his enthusiasm for the coming campaign. "It'll be the World Series in media wars for public opinion," he exulted.

Birch declared the Human Rights Campaign "fully committed to this fight." In July, HRC officials met with Hawaii activists to finalize a plan for a $1.1 million campaign that would become known as Protect Our Constitution. Much of the budget would go to support the work of local organizers. ("We recognize the strong skepticism towards those perceived to be carpetbaggers or mainlanders," Red Wing and Buermeyer had cautioned after their visit.) The benchmark polls commissioned that month affirmed an overwhelming majority opposed to same-sex marriage, although also reticent about cavalierly amending the constitution. "This research showed that if the battle was framed as an up-or-down vote on same-sex marriage, we would lose," HRC's David Smith would write. "We would have a chance if we could reframe the debate around the constitutional process."

The most optimistic conclusion that Foley could muster for a reporter was that he believed the referendum battle was "winnable, if we organize well and run a good campaign." A loss in November 1998 would almost certainly be followed by the legislature acting as soon as it convened in

1999 on its newfound ability to define marriage. The Hawaii Supreme Court would then likely interpret the amendment as permitting the new law to stand.

When that came to pass, the long odyssey of the *Baehr* case through the state's court system would reach its anticlimactic end. The future of marriage rights in Hawaii ultimately had slipped from the control of judges and attorneys; voters and politicians would decide the matter.

"In all our excitement in Hawaii, I forgot to flag this for you. We are going ahead with our 'second front' (a phrase we won't use in public)," Foley's cocounsel, Evan Wolfson, faxed him from New York in mid-July 1997. He had news of another state in which couples were about to sue for their right to marry, this time with the help of a lawyer who had spent years looking for just the right way to do it. "I hope this both takes the pressure off—and puts pressure on—the Hawaii S. Ct. Pressure off, because they're not alone. Pressure on, because they're in a race for first!"

Part Four

....

THE SECOND FRONT

(1997–2003)

Shameless Agitator

From the moment in late 1996 that Bill Clinton signed the Defense of Marriage Act, Mary Bonauto began thinking about how a single lawyer might begin the work of undercutting it. Bonauto was the civil-rights director of Gay & Lesbian Advocates and Defenders, although that was perhaps a misleadingly august title: for most of her time at GLAD, Bonauto had been its only attorney. The Boston public-interest law firm had been founded in July 1978, in the midst of an election year in which gays felt targeted, tarred in newspapers with reports of "child sex rings" and subjected to police stings in the restrooms of the Boston Public Library. In 1980, GLAD attorneys helped persuade the Massachusetts Supreme Judicial Court that a state law against a "lewd, wanton and lascivious person," which had served as the legal justification for such entrapment of gay men, was unconstitutionally vague. Afterward, GLAD was able to shift from merely defending gays from unfairly aggressive law enforcement to proactively winning them new protections. These efforts culminated in the 1989 passage of an omnibus gay-rights bill, a version of which had been first introduced sixteen years earlier by state representative Barney Frank. When Governor Michael Dukakis signed the bill, only the country's second to forbid discrimination in housing and employment statewide, gay-rights lobbyist David LaFontaine boasted that it "shows we can win against almost insurmountable odds by putting pressure on the system."

The Defense of Marriage Act seemed to represent a failure of that type of pressure-group politics. A self-described "shameless agitator," Bonauto found her outrage most strongly directed toward the parts of the gay-rights movement that she felt had failed to properly navigate Washington. "I was really concerned at the time that our side hadn't fought the good fight," she says.

Bonauto had been raised in a devout Roman Catholic family in a depressed industrial town along the Hudson River. As a child, she was drawn to athletics, competing in high-school tennis, although only as a doubles player. She moved to New England for law school at Northeastern University and headed north to Maine after graduating, where she joined a small Portland firm in 1987. There Bonauto learned she was only one of three openly gay attorneys in private practice across the state. Three years later, she joined GLAD, where her self-effacing modesty proved an asset for a public-interest lawyer who would instinctively redirect attention away from herself onto her clients and their challenges. "I don't like to have my personal profile so high," she explained. "I mean, it's okay to be a private person, right? I think there are other people very capable of it and who would probably enjoy it more than I would. It's not something I enjoy as much as I enjoy being a lawyer."

Bonauto had been hired as GLAD's first staff attorney in large part to file discrimination cases under the new gay-rights law. ("People were just so offended at being sued by 'a fag,'" she would recall of that early litigation.) Among the matters awaiting her was a lesbian couple in western Massachusetts looking to get married. She demurred, but not out of distaste for the objective. While other lesbian attorneys had been supercilious toward an assertion of marriage rights, Bonauto had always embraced the goal. "I agreed with the feminist critique as to the institution historically, I just didn't think it applied to the institution today, and I don't think it takes a rocket scientist to realize that being excluded from this massive institution says something about your level of citizenship, degrades your level of citizenship," she says.

Yet she was a realist about what was possible. When the Boston City Council considered its first domestic-partnership bill, Bonauto endorsed it unreservedly, telling the *Boston Globe* in late 1990, "It's a far cry from marriage, but it's as close as we are going to get." (The effort would not succeed until later in the decade.) Over the next few years, she pursued other incremental measures toward recognition of gay and lesbian families in court, including cases around child custody, foster care, and second-parent adoption while shelving the question of marriage. "I just wanted to make sure that if we did it, we would win," says Bonauto.

Among those she discouraged from pursuing marriage rights were her clients Todd and Jonathan Barr-Sawyer, New Hampshire men who in 1990 committed to each other in a Unitarian Universalist Church ceremony before 150 friends and family and jointly assumed a common name after the service. They quickly learned the rest of the world did not take their "holy union" as seriously. Todd, a US Air flight attendant, saw his employer cancel the laminated travel pass he had requested for his spouse, ruining their plans for a West Coast honeymoon. "The company sent telexes to all US Air locations saying Jonathan was blacklisted," Todd complained. A few weeks later, Todd learned that his partner had been disenrolled from his Blue Cross/Blue Shield family insurance plan, even after Jonathan (who was self-employed) had accumulated $12,000 in unpaid bills during a three-week hospitalization. "The Barr-Sawyers are committed to change the laws in this country to protect gay people, allow same-sex marriages, have the right to file a joint tax return, and protect survivorship," read the invitation to a dinner program organized by the Greater Boston Business Council, an organization of gay professionals, at which they appeared with Bonauto. (The organization called spousal rights "one of the most relevant issues of the year.") Bonauto helped win attention for the Barr-Sawyers' predicament—the *Boston Globe* featured their story prominently—but did not encourage them to sue for the right to a marriage license. "I would get nervous about people thinking that they could just unilaterally take things into their own hands and change state law when there is in fact a process for doing so," she says. "We were extremely focused on trying to build up precedents of respect."

At times, that even involved advocating on behalf of heterosexual couples. In June 1992, the Massachusetts Supreme Judicial Court ruled that the state owed unemployment compensation to one of its employees, Kathy Reep, after she moved across the state to stay with her partner, Robert Kurnit. Reep and Kurnit had been together as a couple for thirteen years but remained unmarried, a distinction that the court ruled was irrelevant in determining whether Kurnit's relocation qualified as an "urgent, compelling or necessitous" reason for Reep to have to leave her job. It was not an obvious place to begin an assault on the traditional definition of family; even GLAD's own press release celebrating the decision acknowledged that "at issue in the case was a seemingly innocuous provision in the law." Bonauto had written an amicus brief on behalf of several organizations, including the American Civil Liberties Union, arguing that state authorities should not treat "marriage as the sole marker for determining which families deserve legal protections," as she put it. After drafting the brief, Bonauto had considered not even putting GLAD's name on it, for fear of signaling that *Kathy Reep v. Department of Employment and Training* had implications for gay couples. Yet Bonauto considered the victory an important success in breaking up the heterosexual monopoly on symbolically resonant language. "The idea of calling a same-sex couple a family was not in the vernacular at this point," she says. "We would be able to make the argument that families should be treated alike."

Although much of Bonauto's early work for GLAD had been arguing that the recently enacted gay-rights bill should not be subject to repeal by referendum, years later she would learn that one of the most significant political accomplishments ever by the gay political movement in the United States also foreclosed a path to recognition for gay couples. In 1993, Bonauto agreed to represent Christine Huff, an assistant dean at a suburban Boston boarding school who claimed that "I lost my job because I was forced to choose between the career I love and the woman I love." As head houseparent at the Chapel Hill–Chauncy Hall School, Huff was required to live on campus, but school administrators would not allow her female partner to join her there, citing a policy that prohibited unmarried couples from living together. In October 1994, Huff was informed by the Massachusetts Commission Against Discrimination that she had no legal recourse. The commission's chair, Michael T. Duffy, was an openly gay man who acknowledged that Huff was indeed the victim of bias. But the 1989 bill that forbade discrimination due to sexual orientation, and that Bonauto had spent her early career working to enforce, appeared to justify discrimination on the basis of "marital status." Duffy drew attention to a particular line in the legislation that asserted that "nothing in this act shall be construed so as to legitimize or validate a 'homosexual marriage,' so-called..." The only way to change that policy, Duffy instructed Huff, was to go back to the legislature and have the law changed there. At that point, Bonauto advised Huff not to pursue an appeal to the Supreme Judicial Court. "I felt like the court was not there. Ultimately, the clients agreed not to go forward," Bonauto recalls. "I still angst about it to this day but I think it was the right choice."

In October 1994, GLAD welcomed the nation's top gay and lesbian lawyers to its small downtown Boston office. The meeting was dominated by discussion of the *Baehr* case and what would attend a favorable verdict in the forthcoming trial, including the warning by the Human Rights Campaign's David Sobelsohn of a potential "nightmare scenario" on Capitol Hill. The three GLAD attorneys present were largely quiet as Evan Wolfson, serving as the Hawaii plaintiffs' cocounsel, encouraged movement lawyers to prepare for follow-up litigation when local couples sought to have their Hawaii licenses accepted in other states. In the spring of 1990, Wolfson had come up to introduce himself to Bonauto at her first Roundtable meeting. They were contemporaries, four years apart in age and both relatively new to the world of full-time lawyering that some jokingly called "Gay for Pay." "It was pretty clear that we were allies right away in terms of thinking that marriage was something important and worth fighting for," says Bonauto.

While many Roundtable attendees left Boston resistant to Wolfson's call for them to reorient their priorities, the GLAD lawyers took it seriously. Two months later, they convened representatives of gay groups in the six New England states "to discuss the legal and political ramifications of winning the equal right to marry in Hawaii," as GLAD's executive director Jan Platner explained to her organization's board. Like many non-profits, GLAD struggled with funding, and the rising prominence of marriage made it a particularly appealing cause to take to donors. "GLAD's work in this area would have national implications," read a summary of pitches used to approach major donors. "If we don't do it, it won't happen."

Yet the organization still had to determine where. Since its founding, GLAD had been gradually shifting its attention beyond Boston and into five states neighboring Massachusetts. Lambda typically deferred to GLAD when cases emerged in New England, where in many cases GLAD was viewed by local activists with less suspicion than national groups. In advance of the regional summit, in December 1995, the group's lawyers assembled background on which of the six New England states could be most easily pushed to recognize gay couples married in Hawaii. Rhode Island had the most favorable case law, particularly a 1904 decision in which judges decided to recognize as married a couple who had traveled to another state for the express purposes of securing a marriage license that Rhode Island would not have issued itself. In that case, the issue had nothing to do with sexuality but mental capacity: the groom was a ward marrying without his guardian's written permission, which was prohibited in his home state but permitted in Massachusetts. Bonauto knew she would have to weigh that strong precedent against the perceived unfriendliness of Rhode Island's judiciary. It had often shown itself unresponsive to the concerns of sexual minorities, including as recently as that June, when the state's supreme court upheld a nineteenth-century law criminalizing sodomy. Even though the defendant in that case was a straight man whose charges stemmed from the alleged rape of a woman, GLAD had filed a brief arguing that the law under which he had been charged was used to unfairly criminalize consensual gay sex, a claim the court declared irrelevant to its considerations. (Three years later, Rhode Island's legislature would strike the statute from the state's law books.) Vermont and Massachusetts, on the other hand, had judges with a record of interpreting state laws in ways favorable to gays and lesbians, often at GLAD's prompting. But neither of those states offered case law with such tantalizing precedents.

But before she could try to select the ideal venue for a marriage-recognition suit, Bonauto would have to see the Hawaii case through to its conclusion. To aid the *Baehr* plaintiffs, Bonauto agreed to draft an amicus brief on what lawyers referred to as "the extraterritorial question," rebutting an assertion made by Hawaii's attorney general that the unlikelihood its same-sex marriage licenses would be recognized elsewhere devalued them enough that the state had an interest in refusing to issue any at all. By extending other state governments a de facto veto over Hawaii's civil-rights guarantees, Bonauto wrote, the attorney general "reduces the protections of state constitutions to the lowest common denominator." GLAD recruited several mainland civil-rights groups to join the brief, including the National Organization for Women, People for the American Way, and the Mexican American Legal Defense and Education Fund. In a memo to representatives of those groups, Bonauto cast their undertaking in a civil-rights tradition well beyond the gay movement. "We will also remind the Court that they have been on the side of history before, particularly with respect to honoring interracial marriages long before the decision in *Loving v. Virginia*," she explained. (Hawaii was one of ten states that had never enacted an antimiscegenation law.)

Bonauto's plan to assert "that marriages performed in Hawaii should/ must be recognized elsewhere" did not remain a question solely for state courts for long, as any challenge to the Defense of Marriage Act would require a federal lawsuit. Of the bill's two operative sections, she believed the most logical target was the second, which exempted states from any duty under the Constitution's full-faith-and-credit clause to recognize others' marriages, rather than the third, which controlled definitions under federal law. As long as Hawaii's legal process continued, neither would have a real-world impact, but from a constitutional perspective Bonauto saw a crucial difference in the two provisions' language. Section III was written affirmatively ("only a legal union between one man and one woman"), while Section II singled out same-sex relationships for unique exclusion under state laws. "People couldn't wrap their minds around Section III because we didn't have marriage anywhere," says Bonauto. "Section II was more of a focus because it seemed like you were so clearly changing the law of recognition to one of disrespect . . . for one group of people."

To file a successful suit in federal court against the Defense of Marriage Act, Bonauto would have to wait until a person could claim to have been harmed by the unconstitutionality of one of its provisions. She had anticipated that a DOMA test case would follow a verdict in Hawaii: perhaps a couple from Massachusetts or Rhode Island could travel to the Hawaiian Islands for a wedding and demand that their local government identify each as the other's next of kin. The question of where a federal case originated would matter less than in a recognition case decided according to state law, and Bonauto anticipated that as soon as Hawaii started issuing licenses there would be a surfeit of potential plaintiffs. "People from every state would have gone," Bonauto says. "I don't think we would have had the luxury of saying, 'I think we should go forward in this state and not in that one.'"

But as 1997 wore on, and Hawaii's legislature handed the marriage question to voters in the form of a constitutional amendment, it grew increasingly unlikely that Hawaii would ever actually issue licenses to same-sex couples. That meant Bonauto's next step could not be either a state-level recognition suit or a federal challenge to the Defense of Marriage Act. If she wanted to pursue a marriage case, Bonauto would have a clean slate. Those circumstances would afford her the prerogative of picking a state with an optimal environment and patiently selecting the ideal plaintiffs. She knew enough about the origins of the Hawaii case to know that no one there had had such foresight. In fact, it was pure luck that the state's courts turned out to be receptive to Dan Foley's arguments and that the plaintiffs had done nothing to undermine them. But as the legislature was getting ready to deflect the marriage question onto an electorate unlikely to receive it favorably, Bonauto had before her a cautionary tale of what could happen if the legal process began before political preparations. Choosing a jurisdiction, she knew, would require a read of local conditions beyond existing case law and the sensibility of judges.

Bonauto tried to monitor political developments across New England through subscriptions to alternative and gay newspapers. The newspapers that arrived at GLAD's offices from around the region were a motley bunch, their relative focus determined largely by whether their editorial decisions were made to satisfy activists or advertisers, which were overwhelmingly bars and sex-related businesses. With each month's arrival of the exceedingly serious *Out in the Mountains*—a two-color tabloid subtitled "Vermont's Newspaper for Lesbians, Gay Men, and Bisexuals"—Bonauto saw an ideal jurisdiction come into focus on the far end of the Connecticut River, which bisected the region. Beyond the view of the national press and urban gay elites, Vermonters were doing all the things that Hawaiians had never done. An all-local, handcrafted, organic marriage movement was emerging.

Queer Town Meetings

In June 1993, one month after the Hawaii Supreme Court issued the first-ever court decision in favor of gay couples seeking marriage licenses, the Vermont Supreme Court issued its own landmark ruling declaiming that two people didn't have to wed to secure some of the rights typically reserved for the married. *In re Adoptions of B.L.V.B. & E.L.V.B.* marked the first time that a state appellate court had affirmed a right to so-called second-parent adoption—allowing a person to become a legal parent of a partner's children, even without a biological tie or marriage to link them. "Some people say this is about gay marriage," Bonauto, who was contesting a similar case in Massachusetts at the time, told the *Boston Globe.* "It's not. The relationship between the adults does not change; they still can't file joint tax returns or get joint health coverage. It's the relationship between the two sons and nonbiological parent that has changed. It's not a back-door marriage."

Indeed, the facts of the Vermont case served those who argued that the purpose of gay family law should be to win legal validation for a range of interpersonal relationships. Deborah Lashman and Jane Van Buren had been together since 1986, raising two boys. Van Buren was their biological mother, but Lashman had been about as involved as one could be other-wise, plotting the process of artificial insemination (via an anonymous donor) and present at the birth of each. In the seventh month of her second pregnancy, Van Buren was laid off from her job, leaving her with no way to provide health insurance for either of her children. Lashman, a computer consultant, attempted to add them to her policy, but the insurer rebuffed her, asserting that she was not their mother. A county probate judge agreed, citing a statute that required a spouse to consent to any adoption, and

Lashman took her petition to the Vermont Supreme Court. In June 1993, the Vermont Supreme Court overturned the probate judge, ruling that an existing "step-parent exception" should also cover unmarried same-sex couples. "Not only will this provide uniformity throughout one state, but it may also have a persuasive effect on other states," said Paula Ettelbrick of Lambda Legal, who with Bonauto had submitted the case's sole amicus brief.

That December, Ettelbrick traveled to Vermont Technical College in Randolph, a small town surrounded by sheep farms in the middle of the trapezoidal state, at the invitation of local activists. A year earlier, the state's legislature passed its first law banning antigay discrimination, and afterward about a dozen of those most involved in the lobbying efforts decided to formalize their efforts as the Vermont Coalition for Lesbian and Gay Rights. They started planning an event that would be, outside of Burlington's summertime pride parade, almost certainly the largest gathering ever of Vermont's gay activists. The decision to pick a venue away from Burlington, Vermont's only true city, was an explicit acknowledgment of what some called "Chittenocentrism," defined by *Out in the Mountains* as "the belief that the majority of g/l/b events occur in Chittenden County," home to Burlington in the northwest corner of the state.

Instead of a keynote speech at their daylong conference, coalition organizers decided to stage a version of a "marriage: pros and cons" debate, even though Ettelbrick's familiar sparring partner on the subject, Tom Stoddard, was unavailable due to illness. It had been four years since their dueling essays had appeared in *Out/Look,* and the lunch-hour debate had been scheduled as "almost a throwaway, something to entertain people rather than nothing," according to one organizer. But the enthusiasm for it among the 350 attendees indicated something about Vermont's gay community: isolated, earnest, immune to fashion.

"The groups have always underestimated the interest people in the community have in this issue," Abby Rubenfeld, a former legal director of Lambda Legal, says of the largely metropolitan organizations that worked to set the movement's agenda. "There's always been a big divide between the big gay ghettos on the coast and flyover country. For the gay groups, those pockets in liberal areas are where the money is. The feminists in New York generally took the position that Paula took—that if you were invested in getting the right to marry that somehow you were caving into The Man and the system."

With the Hawaii Supreme Court's decision that May, same-sex marriage rights had become less conjectural, but Ettelbrick's language had barely changed. Winning the right to marry, she argued, would be a "narrow victory" that failed "to recognize the need for a broader definition of family." Stoddard's stand-in, University of Michigan law professor David Chambers, did not put up much of a fight. *Out in the Mountains* concluded that the two "shared an opinion that the [*sic*] obtaining the right to marry should be low on the community's priority list."

The community disagreed. Unlike in many cities where Stoddard and Ettelbrick had put on their self-described "dog-and-pony show" as a useful fundraising event for Lambda and civic good for the local gay community, at least some of those who saw the debate in Randolph didn't treat it as a one-time-only performance. Marriage was on the agenda again at the following year's conference, now named the Queer Town Meeting. The question was growing less abstract: "Gay Marriage: Do We Want It? How Do We Get It?"

It was no longer scheduled as entertainment for a captive lunchtime audience, but the subject of a practically minded afternoon workshop competing for attendees with "Coming Out in the Workplace" (featuring a Huntington "high school teacher who recently came out to both the faculty and her students"), "Single in the Sticks" ("doesn't have to mean the TV is your sole companion"), and "Lesbian Sexuality" ("ever wonder what lesbians do in bed?"). Only fourteen people showed up to the marriage workshop, and even among those who did, many departed still skeptical about whether there was any way to win marriage. "There wasn't one-hundred-percent buy-in," says Joseph Watson, a coalition board member. "There were various reasons people had why they didn't think it was a great idea."

But events the next year heartened them. Prompted in part by the *B.L.V.B.* case, legislators in 1995 set out to pass a bill to standardize state laws around adoption. The bill had a number of provisions unrelated to sexual orientation—including the right of adoptees to trace their biological parents and vice versa—but when it emerged from committee it had one that caught the attention of Vermont's gay community: the measure explicitly restricted the ability to adopt to single or married parents. The exemption of unmarried couples living together galvanized gay and lesbian Vermonters, who initiated an unprecedented campaign to lobby their representatives directly and overwhelm legislative hearings. They ended up forcing the legislature to strip the antigay provision, demonstrating that gays could not only win over judges, but protect their gains through political might. "The victory in the adoption battle was intoxicating, and infectious," says Susan Murray, an attorney who had worked with Ettelbrick on the *B.L.V.B.* amicus brief and then took charge of the legislative effort around the adoption bill. "It think it helped to give us our voice, and helped show us that we could, as a community, fight the marriage fight."

After these advances supporting gays' rights as parents, Murray became convinced marriage rights was the natural next step. "It's sort of like there's a triangle: the two adults and the kid," says Murray. "Now we had connections on these two sides of the triangle, between the two adults and the kid, but we had no connection between the two adults. And that's where marriage came in."

A Massachusetts native, Murray had come to Vermont to clerk for a judge on the state's supreme court. During her clerkship, she noticed that many of the most interesting cases that reached the court's docket originated from Langrock Sperry & Wool in Middlebury. After her clerkship ended, Murray applied for a job there. "That was the sort of firm I wanted to be associated with," she recalled. "It was obvious that my mind was going to be challenged, and I wasn't simply going to do residential real-estate closings for the rest of my life."

Murray ended up coming out to her new colleagues before she did to her parents. Raised in a Catholic family as the oldest of seven children, Murray, upon realizing she was gay, "despaired of ever having a life, and a love like that of her parents," as she later recalled. But in the mid-1980s, she met a woman named Karen Hibbard, a physician assistant who handled walk-in emergencies at their local hospital. Murray enjoyed pointing out their superficial differences—Susan liked hiking and the Red Sox, Karen preferred to swim and paint watercolors—but still the two fell in love. They eventually made a shared project of restoring an aging farmhouse, where they moved in together.

Her work may have been free of deed signings, but divorce filings were an unavoidable part of the culture at Langrock Sperry & Wool. At one point, a partner at the firm enlisted Murray to write a brief in an appeal to the supreme court that ultimately changed the way alimony was awarded in Vermont. Word of the lesbian lawyer who had been involved in the big divorce case traveled quickly to same-sex couples, who sought out Murray to represent them in their own family-law and estate-planning matters. "It's a small state," she explained.

Nonetheless, Vermont's lesbians and gay men occupied largely distinct spheres, with few common spaces for them to mix. "Unlike other locales, Vermont never developed a large commercial infrastructure of bars and bathhouses," the sociologist Mary Bernstein has documented. One of the few venues that fit the bill—the Andrews Inn, a self-described "gay hotel" with a disco and café on the town square in Bellows Falls—primarily served holidaymakers arriving by train from Boston and New York. (The inn closed in 1984 after a raid by police conducting a prostitution investigation.) As in many rural states, uncommonly low prevalences of HIV and AIDS cases kept gay men in Vermont from developing the political and social service organizations that linked them in more urbanized areas. Meanwhile, lesbian women were drawn to political activity through feminist causes, like a failed 1986 campaign to add an equal-rights amendment to the state constitution, and more likely to see their closest allies as heterosexual women than gay men.

Murray was pulled into advocacy only when she realized the needs of her clients required it. Even then, she felt she had to struggle to convince the media and members of the legal community not to characterize her work on their behalf as that of a lesbian activist. "It wasn't about me and my relationship," says Murray, who has the warm, empathic affect of someone used to entering other people's lives only in exigent situations. "It was about me doing a legal job."

In August 1994, a new colleague presented Murray with a wedding announcement that had appeared in the *Burlington Free Press* featuring two women. Earlier that month, Pasha and Penny Rivers-McMahon had managed to get the South Burlington town clerk to issue the couple a marriage license, only to receive a phone call the following day and a subsequent letter asking them to return it. The couple instead sought out a Unitarian Universalist minister willing to sign it, the standard prerequisite before the document could be converted into a marriage certificate. Penny and Pasha told the world that they were getting ready to exchange vows. When their engagement notice reached Murray, there was a sticky note attached: "This is great! I want to work on it!"

The author of that short message, Beth Robinson, was a young lawyer who had recently arrived at the firm with an impressive résumé but few markers of an activist mind-set. She had gone straight from Dartmouth to the University of Chicago Law School and onto a clerkship on the U.S. Court of Appeals for the DC Circuit under David Sentelle, a prominent conservative jurist appointed by Ronald Reagan. Then she worked at a white-collar criminal defense firm in Washington for a few years, before choosing the life of a small-town lawyer not unlike her adolescent hero,

Atticus Finch. She took a two-thirds salary cut to accept a job at the Vermont firm where she had once been a summer law clerk.

Murray and Robinson were born on opposite sides of the baby-boom divide, and had experienced the gay-liberation and feminist movements from different generational vantages. Robinson had been a student throughout the 1980s and was shaped by academic currents at the time. "I say that I was out in law school, but then my law school friends laugh when I say that," she recalls. "So I may not have been as out as I thought I was." One formative experience was a course taught by the feminist legal scholar Catharine MacKinnon, who was then campaigning to restrict or ban pornography on the grounds that it was inherently sexist. "I ran in feminist circles, particularly in law school and its aftermath, and the critique of marriage and the debate about whether the quest for the right to marry was a worthy one swirled around me in those early days," recalls Robinson.

At the same time, Robinson held on to a memory from her Indiana childhood whose innocent joy pushed her thinking about the institution in a different direction. Robinson recalled soaping "Just Married" onto the windows of a car outside the church in which her widowed grandmother, whom Beth called Babbo, married a widower named Dudley. Both Babbo and Dudley were in their seventies, obviously certain not to produce children together—what was beginning to emerge as the leading defense from those who argued same-sex marriages could be treated differently under the law—but no one rose to stop them. Eventually Robinson reconciled the two views, concluding that gays and lesbians shouldn't necessarily want to get married but should not be denied the option. "I really felt strongly that the choice to not marry ought to be ours, not the state's," she says. "That's really what this was about for me."

Winning that right in Vermont, Murray and Robinson learned, would entail a full challenge to the state's interpretation of its existing laws. Negotiations between South Burlington and state officials had surfaced a 1975 opinion, previously unknown to Murray and Robinson, in which Deputy Attorney General Gregory McKenzie had written, "The Legislature contemplated and explicitly recognized only heterosexual marriages." Based on that conclusion, state officials instructed the clerk not to record the license. In early October, three months after she first contacted Murray about her desire to get married, Pasha Rivers-McMahon was informed by the town clerk that it would not happen. At that point, the only remaining option for the Rivers-McMahons was a lawsuit, which Murray successfully discouraged them from pursuing.

But Murray and Robinson decided they would be ready to file such a suit with the proper planning. A few months later, in December 1994, they traveled to Boston to participate in GLAD's meeting for New England lawyers and activists to discuss what the implications of the Hawaii case would be in their states. They had left, said Robinson, with an "understanding that our counterparts in Hawaii were really having to play catch-up and we wanted to try to set this up so that we were driving rather than chasing."

With the passage of time, the lessons of *Baehr* grew even more clear. That case had begun with plaintiffs intent on filing a suit and hoping to keep it contained in the courts. Only after years of drawing attention to the novel issue, and only once a well-funded opposition had mobilized against it in the political sphere, did those who wanted to change Hawaii's marriage laws treat public opinion as a primary concern.

Murray and Robinson set a strategy that would invert that sequence. They would start by building a movement to educate Vermont citizens about same-sex marriage, winning supporters or at least neutralizing skeptics. Then they would work to win over the political leaders whom opponents were likely to see as a backstop if the matter ever won traction in the courts. Once Murray and Robinson decided that the conditions were right to file a lawsuit, plaintiffs would be the last piece to slot in.

Murray began by trying to win over the Vermont Coalition for Lesbian and Gay Rights board. She made the case throughout 1994 that the organization should sign a marriage resolution that Lambda Legal's Marriage Project was circulating for release around Valentine's Day 1995. The board argued over the topic for months, and finally agreed to do so only after editing the text to make its commitment more tentative—a move that defied the entire purpose of becoming signatory to a national resolution. "We also strongly believe that the institution of marriage tends to marginalize people in our society," explained board member Mary Hurlie.

Faced with that ambivalence, Murray and Robinson decided to bypass the state's existing gay political infrastructure and develop their own. They made plans to lead another marriage workshop at the next Queer Town Meeting, to be held in October 1995. The program description would give no indication there was room for any debate on the merits: "A discussion of the current cultural and legal issues involved in the attempt to gain same sex couples the equal right to marry." That summary lured about eighty people, more than the designated classroom at Montpelier High School could hold. Attendees crouched on the floor, sat on desks. "We started off the conversation the same way we did the year before, getting ready for the skepticism and the outright opposition—and there was none of it," recalls Murray. "It disappeared."

The response at the Queer Town Meeting convinced Murray and Robinson that there might be enough grassroots interest in the topic to begin organizing in earnest. They sent a mailer to everyone who had signed in at the workshop, inviting those interested in pursuing marriage rights to meet two months later at an Episcopal church in Montpelier.

Twelve women showed up on a predictably cold and dark December day. In a church basement a short walk from the statehouse, they decided that they were ready to start anew, severing any ties to the Vermont Coalition for Lesbian and Gay Rights. "That was basically the beginning of the end for them," Robinson says of the old coalition. "They didn't recognize that marriage was going to be the next big thing."

Marriage 101

In January 1996, one month after the meeting in Montpelier, Susan Murray and Beth Robinson had welcomed the thirteen volunteers to their firm's Burlington offices in a redbrick Greek Revival office midway up the slope from the east banks of Lake Champlain near the University of Vermont campus. Most of those who showed up that day were otherwise new to the world of gay politics. "These weren't people who had been involved as activists or advocates in the LGBT community at all," says Robinson. "That was like their coming-out."

As a result, few present had any sense of obligation to the existing gay-rights infrastructure in the state, and affirmed at the outset that they did not aspire to serve as any sort of subset or committee of the existing Vermont Coalition for Lesbian and Gay Rights. The group decided it would call itself Vermont Freedom to Marry Task Force, informally splitting off into one branch covering the northern part of the state, including Burlington, and one covering the south. Attendees were given gay-friendly entities—from student associations on college campuses to Vermont Gay Volleyball and the Pink Triangle Bowling League—whom they could approach to sign the marriage resolution that had made the coalition so nervous. The group would also spend the spring developing a speakers bureau that could send out representatives to discuss marriage before civic and religious organizations. The attendees resolved to meet monthly with the goal of going public by June 15, at Burlington's gay-pride parade.

The Vermont Freedom to Marry Task Force was intent on introducing a debate over marriage on its own terms. As part of their training, volunteers were given a thirty-five-page set of "speaking points." Instead of "gay marriage" they were taught to use "civil marriage," and instead of "same-sex marriage" they were told to use "civil marriage of same-gender couples." Task force members worked to get a spokesperson for marriage on the official program, but agreed that they were not seeking exposure at any cost. "We decided *not* to promote a group wedding ceremony this year," minutes from an April meeting summarized. "Although the exercise is a nice way of drawing attention to the issue, the consensus was that we didn't want to blur the distinction between civil and religious marriages and the event would not be our best next step at this point. We won't however, try to oppose such an event if some other group decides to do it."

By May, the statehouse had inadvertently passed a bill that Murray and Robinson might have received as a step toward legalizing gay marriage, but they were put in the unexpected position of trying to quash it. The bill was conceived as a straightforward reform to modernize one of Vermont's unusually localized governmental procedures, an old-fashioned rule requiring a Vermont marriage license to "be issued by the clerk of the town where either the bride or the groom resides." The new bill would have made it possible for a state resident to secure a license from any town's clerk. It appeared an uncontroversial reform, and only once it had passed the house did any legislators note that by stripping that provision they had removed every reference in state code to a "bride" or "groom." In every other instance, the law spoke in gender-neutral terms of a "partner," "party," "applicant," or "person." That change had not been made with same-sex couples in mind; the staffers who drafted the bill had merely followed a recent directive by the Legislative Council to use gender-neutral language wherever possible. Passage of such a bill would have likely eased the way for an eventual legal challenge by gay couples, but the lawyers sensed risk. Vermont was not among the states that had faced a so-called mini-DOMA in response to the Hawaii threat, and Murray and Robinson wanted to keep legislators' attention being drawn to the existing law. Any process that opened up the marriage statute could only leave them worse off than they had been beforehand.

Pride day festivities were a far better venue to make a point about marriage. On June 15, the day of the parade, the front page of the *Burlington Free Press,* the state's largest and most important newspaper, featured the headline GAY COUPLES IN VERMONT FIGHT FOR MARRIAGE RIGHTS; ADVOCATES WANT EQUALITY IN BENEFITS OF CIVIL MARRIAGE. Alongside the article was a portrait of board member Joseph Watson and his partner, Michael Warner, cutting the cake at their commitment ceremony three years earlier. Watson, who designated himself and Warner the task force's "first 'poster couple,'" was busy hunting for others. The morning of the parade, he collected photographs and other mementos from couples whose commitment he intended to chronicle in a video that could be aired on local television and screened for groups. They hoped for diversity, in all the obvious respects and also covering what may have been the most important demographic divide in the state—"transplants from the flatlands as well as third-generation Vermonters," according to coproducer Ellen Hill. By the standard of the group's paltry finances, the video was a costly project. (As the project reached completion, the task force had $450 in its bank account. Production costs for the video would total $400.) But it was also the only means the task force had to control what same-sex couples looked like to Vermonters who might never have come into contact with one.

After Labor Day, task force members gathered at Beth Robinson's house in Ferrisburgh, a spot midway between Burlington and Middlebury from which the Adirondack mountains shimmered on the horizon. They had been encouraged to bring family members and significant others along— they could play croquet or hike local trails while task force members dealt with increasingly urgent business. Anticipating that the fall would bring both the Hawaii trial and final passage of the Defense of Marriage Act, Murray and Robinson decided they needed to intensify their efforts. New attention would come their way, and the gauzy work of public education would likely be met for the first time with blunt political opposition. Although serious organizing experience was sparse within the group, the two lawyers were deliberate about opening up strategic deliberations to their fellow task force members. "Something I really appreciated about Beth and Susan was how inclusive they were when it came to decision-making," says Watson. "They were really strong leaders, but not out in front ideologically."

Even so, there was a lot of confusion about where all the organizing was headed. With such a focus on developing public support throughout the year, many task force members had naturally assumed that they were following an arc like that of adoption reform, working toward votes in the legislature and the signature of a governor. But Murray and Robinson explained that the involvement of politicians would represent not the goal but some version of a worst-case scenario. "Essentially our message was, 'We don't want you to do anything, this is likely to be decided by the courts, that's what the courts' role is,'" says Murray. "'And if we win in the courts, or when we win in the courts, we hope you'll not take the bait on a constitutional amendment,'" adds Robinson. "'You'll say the court has spoken and it's time to move on together as a state.'"

Along with Keith Goslant, the gay community's appointed liaison to the governor, Murray and Robinson had sought out elected officials willing to meet with them. "The purpose of the meetings is," Robinson wrote, "to let them know that we decidedly do not have any desire to make this a campaign issue or a legislative issue next year, even though we might find ourselves in a defensive position because a bad, anti-marriage bill is likely to be proposed."

They had not started with a clear idea of the endpoint for this phase of the task force's work, but as fall wore on they were starting to feel as though they were reaching it. Before Election Day, they and Goslant had managed to meet with the governor, along with nearly every other important state official, a slew of state legislators, and Congressman Bernie Sanders, the former Burlington mayor who had been the only member of Vermont's small congressional delegation to oppose the Defense of Marriage Act.

Watson's seventeen-minute video, a bucolic ramble titled *Freedom to Marry: A Green Mountain View*, was nearly complete—ready to be unveiled at the Queer Town Meeting, which would be held in Brattleboro in November—and stories about same-sex couples seeking marriage rights had begun to seep into local media. Task force members had already engaged with most of the groups in Vermont likely to be immediately open to hearing about gay marriage. Without news events to drive further interest in the subject, it would be tough to expand their reach. "It's hard to get a Rotary Club to come in and have a speaker about some cockamamie issue that's not really in the paper," says Robinson. "We were going to get diminishing returns on organizing." Only a lawsuit would move the public discussion forward.

In late October, Murray and Robinson traveled to New Orleans for Lavender Law, the annual conference of gay and lesbian attorneys, with plans to brief Mary Bonauto on their progress. It was at past Lavender Law conferences that Murray and Robinson had each, separately, first met Bonauto, and then begun the relationship between Langrock Sperry & Wool and GLAD that facilitated the Boston organization's initial foothold in Vermont through collaboration on adoption issues. Bonauto understood the ways in which Vermont could be a promising venue for marriage litigation, as well, and now they were updating her on the work that the task force had done over the course of the year and the subsequent changes to the political environment.

The only question now was what a lawsuit would look like and when it would be filed. Ever since 1975, Vermont's constitution has been protected by a process called "time lock," which ensures that amendments could be proposed in the legislature only on previously determined four-year cycles. Such a cycle had begun in 1995, which meant that the next constitutional amendments could not be introduced until 1999.

Beyond the "time lock" restriction guarding Vermont's constitution, the state's framers had also included a provision designed to prevent the legislature from acting impulsively. Even when lawmakers succeeded in passing a constitutional amendment during the designated quadrennial window, it still had to be approved twice, in consecutive years. Thus, anyone who could get the supreme court to deliver a favorable interpretation of the state's existing jurisprudence had an advantage, in the form of a multiyear buffer, against those who wanted to use the political process to rewrite the underlying legal principles. It seemed the right time to file a lawsuit would be as soon as the legislature closed out its 1997 session, ending its work for the year and ensuring that the earliest it could possibly move an amendment to a statewide ballot would be in the fall of 2000.

"You guys are prepared," Bonauto responded.

She explained that she had been in the midst of conversations within the national Freedom to Marry Coalition coordinated by Lambda Legal. The Hawaii process had been moving so slowly that others were getting antsy, fearful that they might lose the momentum they had gained—especially if a trial victory in late 1996 were followed by another appeal or a return to the legislative wrangling that had delayed the trial in the first place. A consensus developed that there was a need for a "second front" after Hawaii.

"We don't need your permission," Murray told Bonauto, "but we've been thinking about this as well, and we really don't want to be cowboys out there."

Anything But the Slam-Dunk Cases

Even without a paying client in sight, Beth Robinson and Susan Murray never had to work hard to convince anyone at their firm to let them sue Vermont for a change in the state's marriage laws. Langrock Sperry & Wool had been founded in Middlebury, about an hour south of Burlington, where Peter Langrock had started as a sole practitioner in 1960. Throughout his career, Langrock had defied expectations of both the country lawyer and Renaissance man. ("Peter handles matters from traffic cases to arguments before the U.S. Supreme Court," reads his official law-firm biography. "He is also a farmer, an author, a painter, a world traveler, and a chef.") In Langrock's hands, even cases with seemingly small stakes became fraught with purpose. He continued to accept divorce cases because they made him "feel good about empowering women, helping them see where their lives could be once this is over," as he once put it. "If you never take anything but the slam-dunk cases, it's not challenging," Langrock has said. "I have two rules: One is that 25 percent of your time is give-back time; the other is that you never turn down a case that's fun."

Even as Langrock's firm grew into one of Vermont's largest, it retained much of that quaint quirk. Most of the staff in Middlebury would lunch together daily, a pack of besuited attorneys marauding three times a week through the creekfront college town to share a table at one of its small circuit of restaurants. (Since that exhausted the desirable local dining options, twice weekly they would stay in, order sandwiches, and eat together around a conference-room table.) After a 1982 merger, the firm opened a Burlington office, and it eventually grew too quickly to be comfortably seated around a single restaurant table; employees nonetheless kept the custom, traveling en masse to secure takeout and returning to the office to eat as a group. "There are some firms where you go and do your work and you don't necessarily know people's views," says Robinson. "There was definitely a shared set of values at the firm."

Langrock gave Murray and Robinson free rein to pursue a marriage lawsuit, although when Mary Bonauto extended a formal offer of assistance from GLAD, the firm seized it. With Bonauto as cocounsel, GLAD could help fund appellate litigation and serve as a liaison to the world beyond New England. GLAD could function as Vermont's representatives before the Roundtable and Freedom to Marry Coalition, a coordinator of amicus briefs from academics and civil-rights groups and a public-relations clearinghouse to satisfy what Murray and Robinson hoped would eventually be global media interest.

GLAD staff had been involved in the formation of the Vermont Freedom to Marry Task Force from its outset, although they knew not to make a fuss about their role. Nothing would muddy the carefully maintained image of a local grassroots movement around marriage more than the impression that its moves had been hatched in a big-city law office hundreds of miles away. GLAD had always shown deference to its local partners, but especially so in Vermont.

From the outset of its first Vermont appearance, in 1992, in the appellate case about whether same-sex couples could jointly adopt a child, GLAD adopted a policy to actively discourage any publicity for the case. It was remarkable for an organization whose mission was to bring impact litigation in part for public education. As they prepared in early 1997 to launch a marriage suit in Vermont, Bonauto assumed a role of full partnership with Robinson and Murray, but every press statement they prepared for local media—including background documents developed by GLAD's researchers in Boston—went out only on Langrock letterhead. "We are asking non-Vermont people to respond to press inquiries but otherwise keep a low profile so this can look like an indigenous Vermont effort," the monthly update from GLAD's civil-rights department advised the firm's board.

Indeed, the suit that the three lawyers were developing was very much dependent on law indigenous to Vermont. The state had been quick to ratify the federal Equal Rights Amendment, in 1973, but unlike Hawaii had never inserted language about gender equality in its own state constitution. The attorney general was likely to argue in responding to any marriage challenge that if the legislature had disagreed with his office's 1975 reading of the constitution, it had had ample opportunity to address the issue and clarify the law.

The state constitution dated from the days of the Vermont Republic, drafted in 1777 to assert the commonwealth's independence from New York as much as from Great Britain. Adopted at a tavern in Windsor, the Vermont constitution has some New England touches—a reminder to citizens that in choosing their leaders, "moderation, temperance, industry and frugality, are absolutely necessary to preserve the blessings of liberty"—and others that with time would reveal a liberal vision missing from the document's national analogue. The first article of the first chapter forbids any man or woman from being held as a "servant, slave, or apprentice," and later the Vermont constitution makes a less ambiguous assertion of eminent domain than the federal version, noting plainly that "private property ought to be subservient to public uses."

Even once Vermont joined the United States of America, a more specific streak of equality persisted in its constitution than that of the larger country. In 1793, Vermont held a Constitutional Convention to reshape its founding document to fit within a federal system. Officials struck a passage from the preamble declaring that government should operate "without partiality for, or prejudice against, any particular class, sect, or denomination of men whatever," but it retained, in article seven, an echo of that ideal. "That government is, or ought to be, instituted for the common benefit, protection, and security of the people, nation, or community, and not for the particular emolument or advantage of any single person, family, or set of persons." With time, it would become known as the "Common Benefits Clause."

Such passages had become increasingly useful to civil-rights litigators as the U.S. Supreme Court grew less friendly to their calls for recognition of rights explicitly named in the Constitution. In 1988, David Schuman identified more than four hundred instances in which state courts interpreted their constitutions to confer more expansive guarantees than had been located in the federal constitution. "As the states' independent constitutional decisions proliferate, they will demonstrate some theories and methods that deserve to be adopted elsewhere," wrote Schuman, who became an appeals-court judge in Oregon. "Such is the Darwinian dynamic of cross-fertilization and experimentation known as 'horizontal federalism,' or the tendency of one state to look to the decisions of sister states instead of to Washington, D.C."

When it came to civil-rights claims, rights were often broader because the states' equal-protection clauses dramatically predated the federal one. The Fourteenth Amendment of the United States Constitution, ratified in 1868, ensured that no authority could "deny to any person within its jurisdiction the equal protection of the laws" or withhold "life, liberty or property, without due process of law." Courts subsequently interpreted this in the context in which it was written, a post–Civil War effort to dismantle the legal scaffolding of white supremacy and ensure equal rights for a predefined racial minority. Most of the state equal-protection language, including Vermont's, was not drafted with any notion of specific disadvantaged identity groups. Instead, their objective was to eliminate the state-sponsored favoritism of privileged individuals or families embodied in the revolutionary rejection of aristocracy.

In February 1997, the Vermont Supreme Court had forced the state legislature to redraw its entire school-funding formula on the basis that the Common Benefits Clause implied "a right to equal educational opportunities." As was the case in many states, wealthy towns in Vermont had long had better schools than their poorer neighbors because the majority of their budgets were determined by local property-tax revenues. Government typically shrugged at such inequities as a simple consequence of unevenly distributed wealth. A cluster of different entities from "property poor" towns—students, taxpayers who claimed they were compelled to pay disproportionately for local schools, and the school districts themselves— argued that Vermont's constitution promised otherwise. "The conclusion becomes inescapable that the present system has fallen short of providing every school-age child in Vermont an equal educational opportunity," the supreme court's majority opinion in *Brigham v. State* declared. (Among the lawyers representing the large squad of plaintiffs in the case, organized by the ACLU of Vermont, was one from Langrock Sperry & Wool's Middlebury office.)

During the same period in early 1997, Murray and Robinson advised marriage activists on how to set up the legal grounds necessary to sue. As a result, three couples went individually to their local town clerks, as Vermont law required, and requested marriage licenses. There was no effort to win media coverage for the event, with the couples calling ahead to warn a town clerk that they would be coming with an unusual request. Although in every instance the couples were greeted kindly, the clerks had little flexibility when it came to policy. The couples received similar letters, explaining that the attorney general had chosen to stand by his predecessor's 1975 opinion that Vermont's marriage laws applied only to opposite-sex couples.

Now Murray, Robinson, and Bonauto were steering the Common Benefits Clause to attack the attorney general's definition of marriage. Across Vermont law, there were more than 150 specific examples of support or protection for wedded couples that could each be construed as a benefit that the state offered to the particular advantage of one "set of persons": heterosexuals. Pursuing their claim under that clause in the state's constitution, the trio believed, would allow them to bypass the typical arc of equal-protection claims, which in most instances start with haggling over the "standard of review," in which a petitioner first has to win the court's agreement about what degree of legal protection has been earned by the category of people allegedly discriminated against. The attorneys thought such a path would be a diversion from their core claim and potentially a trap, because it put the burden on the plaintiff to justify his or her right to be covered by civil-rights law rather than upon the defendant to explain why the law should be permitted to discriminate. "We really wanted to take the conversation past the standard of review and to the rationales," says Robinson. "Because we wanted to engage the state and say, 'Even under the lowest possible standard, you can't justify this and we want to challenge you to tell us what your reasons are and let us rebut them.'"

On July 22, 1997, Bonauto stood alongside her cocounsels Murray and Robinson at a press conference in Burlington as they announced they were suing the state of Vermont, along with the three towns in Chittenden County—Shelburne, South Burlington, and Milton—whose clerks had refused to issue marriage licenses to the plaintiffs. (Murray and Robinson had selected couples from Chittenden to guarantee that their case started in the county that was home to Burlington and its suburbs, where the case would be easier for the attorneys to oversee.) Bonauto had traveled to Burlington in the morning to join the press conference unveiling *Baker et al. v. State of Vermont*, with plans to return to her Boston office by midafternoon so she could handle the anticipated interest from national media. "We are challenging the notion that a couple in love can't marry each other," Bonauto told reporters, "simply because they made the mistake of falling in love with someone of the 'wrong' gender."

Baker v. State

Before he lent his name to a lawsuit against Vermont, Stannard Baker had given his voice to the video that activists had used to introduce their cause across the state. A California transplant who worked as a therapist at the county's mental-health center, Baker had discovered the Vermont Freedom to Marry Task Force at the 1996 gay-pride parade. He volunteered to help, and found his mellifluous tenor was of special use. The experience of narrating *Freedom to Marry: A Green Mountain View,* Baker would recall, "nudged me to go home to Peter and discuss marriage." Baker had been living with Peter Harrigan for two years, and when Susan Murray and Beth Robinson began approaching couples active in the task force to see if any might be interested in serving as plaintiffs, they were ready to say yes. The two men perfectly embodied a bourgeois ideal; before filing the suit they had an accountant estimate what being married would do to their taxes. (They learned they would pay $1,200 more by filing as a couple.) "Chase Manhattan Bank married us in May of '96," Baker said of the day the two men received a mortgage to buy a home in Shelburne.

Baker and Harrigan represented one identifiable archetype of Vermont couplehood that Murray and Robinson had sought to help sustain sympathetic human-interest media coverage for *Baker v. State of Vermont.* Another, Lois Farnham and Holly Puterbaugh, had been together since a 1972 commitment ceremony. Together they ran the Red Shovel Christmas tree farm and volunteered for the town library and local Girl Scouts. They had stumbled into the awareness that something was missing when Farnham, a substitute school nurse who handled the tree business, learned that she was ineligible for benefits from the pension Puterbaugh had earned over her twenty-seven years teaching math at the University of Vermont.

Farnham and Puterbaugh stood alongside Baker and Harrigan at the press conference announcing their lawsuit, but the third couple Murray and Robinson had convinced to join it weren't there. Nina Beck and Stacy Jolles, who had been together for seven years, had a two-year-old child. Jolles was a biological parent to Noah, and only under Vermont's second-parent adoption case law had Beck been allowed to assume joint custody of her partner's son. (The pair had moved to Vermont from North Carolina, where such second-parent adoption by same-sex couples would remain illegal for decades.) But even though each woman was permitted a legally recognized relationship with Noah, they couldn't have one with each other. "Our son will be better off if his parents can marry and enjoy the legal support and protection that the civil marriage laws provide," Beck, a physical therapist, was quoted as saying in the July press release announcing the suit. "He needs and deserves to know that his parents have a legal connection to one another, as well as to him."

On the day of the press conference, Beck and Jolles were at Dartmouth-Hitchcock Medical Center in New Hampshire with Noah as he was being treated for heart problems. Noah had suffered from circulatory issues throughout his short life, and a week before the lawsuit was announced, his mothers checked him in for what Noah initially described as a "tummy ache" and doctors assessed was a result of hypertrophic cardiomyopathy. Five weeks later, in late August 1997, as he awaited a heart transplant at Boston Children's Hospital, he died. "At least we have each other," Beck said.

The parenting angle had been what made Beck and Jolles uniquely valuable to Murray and Robinson's media strategy, and the lawyers told the grieving parents that they could remove themselves as plaintiffs and the case would proceed without them if they wished. The offer was rebuffed, with the women crediting a shared status as the daughters of Holocaust survivors for their stubborn commitment to fighting for civil rights. "I started this case for Noah," Jolles said, "and none of that has changed because he died." They dedicated a small maple tree to him during a service in a Burlington park, but they treated the case as his true memorial. A reporter from *Out in the Mountains* who asked at the outset of an interview whether they were comfortable talking about his loss was told, "All we want to talk about is Noah." When the magazine *Out* arranged to take a portrait of the couple, they insisted on holding a picture of Noah against the photographer's wishes.

Other than respond to media queries, there was not much for the plaintiffs to do for the remainder of the summer and into the fall. The attorneys laid out all their arguments in a seventy-five-page memo that tried to anticipate the state's moves in a way that would obviate any need for a trial. "We both felt like the longer it languished," says Robinson, the likelier that "Vermont would become a pawn in a bigger battle."

Both sides agreed that they wanted to accelerate the case's trajectory to the state's highest court. But evidence suggested it was unlikely. In early November, just ahead of the deadline by which the state was required to reply to their suit, the *Baker* team read in *Out in the Mountains* Attorney General William Sorrell's expectation that, while it was possible that the Vermont Supreme Court could settle the matter within a year, "it's probably equally likely that three years from now the matter is still going through the courts."

Sorrell had a responsibility to defend the state in constitutional matters, but served in an administration whose leader was noncommittal about his own views toward the legal status of same-sex couples. A Democrat with a friendly record on gay issues, Governor Howard Dean described marriage as "a very difficult issue for many Vermonters." He gave credence to competing concerns for marriage as "a tradition that goes back thousands of years" on the one hand and the fact that "gay couples do not have all the civil rights enjoyed by the majority population" on the other in his responses to citizens who wrote him about the case. "Three gay couples have decided that the courts should determine where to establish the balance between these competing interests and I believe it is appropriate under these circumstances for the courts to do so," he wrote to one constituent.

By summoning a reporter for a gay-community newspaper to his office in Montpelier, Sorrell was eager to demonstrate that—even as his staff worked on their motion to dismiss *Baker v. State*—he did not want to be seen as contemptuous of it. (Sorrell later acknowledged to another local journalist that "if we had taken a poll in the office, there was probably a majority sentiment in favor of granting gay marriage or at least civil unions.") He expressed to *Out in the Mountains* his hope for "a Vermont-style lawsuit where there's not a lot of animosity and not a lot of running out to the media and making this some kind of O.J.-type trial circus." Sorrell could have stepped aside and allowed lawyers for the three towns also named in the suit to defend it, but that risked inviting even more chaos. The case "deserves to be fairly litigated," he explained to *Out in the Mountains,* and "if the court finds a right under the constitution for same-gender marriage, not specifically granted but in a general grant of equal rights under the Vermont constitution, then that's what the role of the court is all about."

Sorrell was making substantive moves to defuse a potentially combustible legal encounter. He quietly struck a secret side deal with Murray and Robinson, with the two parties by mutual agreement swapping concessions on tactical or procedural matters that each side anticipated were, as Murray put it, "really going to piss us off." At Sorrell's urging, Murray and Robinson had agreed that they would not file a request for attorney's fees, an ongoing source of frustration for an official managing a small state's litigation budget. In return, Murray and Robinson asked that the state not present arguments that homosexuality was by its nature immoral, which they felt would "make the gay community and the progressive straight community in Vermont very upset." In deference to Murray and Robinson, the state's brief dispensed with explicit reference to gay immorality but nonetheless declared "an interest in using the law to make normative statements." "We were just as mad at them saying this is a 'normative statement' position as if they'd said the word *morality*," says Murray.

Sorrell's first move was to ask a state court to dismiss *Baker v. State* as it sat on a Chittenden County docket, listing the state's reasons for permitting only opposite-sex couples to marry. In December, Judge Linda Levitt ruled in his favor, but even as she came down against the plaintiffs she prepared them well for an appeal. Levitt wrote that all but one of the "state interests" that the attorney general had asserted in his sixty-five-page response to the complaint failed to meet even the lowest legal standard. (Some of them were plainly tautological, such as "The State has an inherent interest in promoting the institution of marriage in its current form because it unites men and women.") Even the "state interest" that survived Levitt's review, the claim that government "has an interest in promoting child-rearing in a setting which provides both male and female role models," was characterized by Levitt as a "not flawless" rationale.

As they prepared their appeal to the Vermont Supreme Court, Murray, Robinson, and Bonauto worked to demonstrate those flaws. They marshaled social-science research demonstrating there was, at best, little evidence that opposite-sex couples were better parents than same-sex ones. They also revealed enough faulty logic in the supposed "link between procreation and child-rearing" to yield koan-like section headings: "Married Couples Do Not Necessarily Procreate, and Parents Do Not Necessarily Marry."

The plaintiffs' attorneys knew they would face a friendly audience for their argument that the "plain meaning" of marriage was less relevant than its "underlying purpose." The court they were about to face had five years earlier ruled in favor of a lesbian couple seeking joint custody of a child to whom only one was a biological parent. "When social mores change, governing statutes must be interpreted to allow for those changes in a manner that does not frustrate the purposes behind their enactment," Justice Denise Johnson, previously a civil-rights attorney in both public and private practice, wrote in the majority opinion in the *B.L.V.B.* custody case, backed by a unanimous vote of her colleagues.

Three justices who had been present for the *B.L.V.B.* case were still sitting on the Vermont Supreme Court when it was gaveled into session on November 18, 1998, to hear *Baker v. State*. It was a cold morning, but people had been waiting since before dawn for spectators' seats. Anticipating such a turnout, judicial officers had devised a ticketing system to allocate the seats on a first-come-first-serve basis. By 7:45 a.m., nearly three hours before the hearing was scheduled to begin, all the tickets were gone. Those who wanted to follow the arguments in real time were allowed to congregate in the lobby, where officials had made arrangements to relay audio from the small wood-paneled courtroom.

The plaintiffs had front-row seats reserved behind their attorneys' table, but had to hide out in a holding room so as to avoid a confrontation with the media massed in the courthouse lobby. They would conduct a press conference after, but did not want to redirect press attention from the arguments that would be made in court. In an exception to standard practice, justices had permitted a local community-television station to videotape the proceedings for broadcast, allowing many Vermonters their first-ever glimpse at the court in session. The case was poised to yield, as Justice John Dooley would later write, "the most closely watched opinion in this court's history."

The stakes for the rest of the country had increased significantly, too. Unlike when *Baker v. State* had first been filed one and a half years earlier, Vermont was now the only jurisdiction in the United States with an active legal process that could result in legalizing gay marriage. Less than two weeks before, Hawaii and Alaska voters had both passed constitutional amendments erasing any gains from successful litigation and making each state's law less friendly to same-sex marriage than it had been before. However disheartening those outcomes may have been, they affirmed that the early work Murray and Robinson had done with the task force had been prudent. "Because of the Hawaii lesson," Robinson says, "I think we very much bought into the notion that a legal win by itself was not going to be enough."

Robinson faced an encouraging reminder of that political preparation as soon as she stepped up from the dark-green carpet onto a platform that put her at eye level with the five justices. In the center was the man who had called the session to order, the newly appointed chief justice, Jeffrey Amestoy, a former Vermont attorney general whom Murray and Robinson had met when they were making the rounds of local politicians in 1996 with their "Marriage 101" presentation. Developing relationships with officials before deciding how and when to sue them was already yielding rewards.

After setting a hefty three-ring binder on the podium, Robinson began by invoking a fortuitous occasion, the fiftieth anniversary of the California Supreme Court decision in *Perez v. Sharp*. In 1948, that court had confronted an appeal by a Mexican American woman and an African American man who had seen their marriage application rejected by the Los Angeles county clerk and subsequently challenged the state's ban on mixed-race marriages. California became the first state to strike down such a law on constitutional grounds. Within twenty years, the U.S. Supreme Court had decided that all such state bans had to fall. Both *Perez* and the federal case, *Loving v. Virginia*, figured heavily in the plaintiffs' appeal in *Baker*, particularly the latter's determination that marriage was a "basic civil right . . . fundamental to our very existence," as Chief Justice Earl Warren wrote in the unanimous opinion. "The freedom to marry, or not marry, a person of another race resides with the individual and cannot be infringed by the State."

The justices of the Vermont Supreme Court already knew that the two assistant attorneys-general arguing the state's case rejected the plaintiffs' analogy to interracial marriage. Virginia's ban on interracial marriages had been an example of racial discrimination because it only banned whites from marrying anyone of any other race, they pointed out in their brief; the law did not constrain unions among members of different racial minorities. Because the weight of Vermont's marriage statute falls equally on both sexes, the state argued, it could not amount to gender discrimination.

Facing the justices of the Vermont Supreme Court, Robinson now discussed not the legal underpinnings of the *Perez* opinion but the qualities of the individuals who had arrived at it. "It's easy to sit here in 1998 and look back at *Perez* and say that decision was an easy one," Robinson said.

In fact, the California Supreme Court's action was both "controversial" and "courageous," she reminded the judges. Thirty states had such racial restrictions in place, and polls showed 90 percent of Americans disapproved of racially mixed unions. "The notion of a black person and a white person marrying was as antithetical to many people's concept of what a marriage was as the notion of a man marrying a man or a woman marrying a woman appears to be to the state of Vermont today," Robinson said.

In contrast, many of the arguments presented by the state encouraged the court to be deferential to tradition and apparent consensus, noting that not a single country on earth recognized marriage as anything other than one man and one woman. That was, the state asserted, the plain meaning of the word itself, citing entries on *marriage* from both *Black's Law Dictionary* and *Webster's* for support. (A union of two men or two women was possible, the state's briefs appeared to argue, but it would be something other than marriage.) "Vast societal changes should not be wrought at the point of a judicial ruling," the state wrote in its brief.

Amestoy was first to engage with the interracial-marriage analogy during oral arguments. In *Loving v. Virginia,* the U.S. Supreme Court had discounted the state's justifications for its ban as mere cover for white supremacy, an impermissible motivation for a government policy. If, Amestoy asked Robinson, "the State cannot even show that its discrimination is reasonably related to the promotion of a valid public purpose," then what was the real reason the state had been so insistent over decades about excluding gays from marriage?

Robinson contended the state's arguments were a "sham," although she evaded Amestoy's request to characterize an underlying motive that the court could deem as impermissible as white supremacy. "We don't have to show that the legislature hates gay people in order to demonstrate that the state's classification which denies these folks an extremely important right" is unjust, Robinson said. "When you peel away all the justifications that don't make sense, all you're left with is a bare preference" for some Vermonters over others.

As a rule, courts have so little patience for the denial of fundamental rights that they tend to be unsatisfied with half measures. In these cases, judges are usually unwilling to fall back on other branches of government to find solutions. They are not looking for compromises or politically palatable bargains. Judges usually demand immediate relief for those who have successfully convinced them that they are victims of civil-rights violations. When states determined that racial restrictions on marriage were unconstitutional, or bans on sodomy, they simply forbade authorities from enforcing the discredited statutes.

The chief justice was plainly sympathetic to the plaintiffs' claim that they were being maltreated by Vermont's marriage laws, but he did not reflexively see theirs as a civil-rights case. While Robinson beseeched him to apply the common-benefits language as though it was an ancestor of the federal equal-protection clause, Amestoy's questions indicated he saw it otherwise. Instead he considered its origins as a response to the wanton taxation policies of the British crown rather than a precursor to guarantees of identity-based justice. Viewed as such, the marriage laws could amount to a practice of economic unfairness that favored heterosexuals with benefits denied to homosexuals. The Vermont Supreme Court had made a similar determination in 1982, when it invalidated a statute banning Sunday sales that applied only to large retailers; the distinction was deemed impermissible because it had been written for the "special protection of the economic health of small, locally owned, retail stores." If Amestoy wanted to see the *Baker* plaintiffs as a similar kind of victim—closer to a corporation losing sales to small grocers than lovers denied the right to marry because of their race—what would be a just remedy?

The Remedy

Susan Murray and Beth Robinson had to wait more than a year for the Vermont Supreme Court to return with its judgment in *Baker v. State*. Every Friday was a "decision day" for the court, when it released new opinions without any advance notice of which ones would arrive that week. As a result, Murray and Robinson began each Friday morning knowing it could be the day that would hold the fate of the biggest case either attorney was ever likely to handle. When the decision came, the lawyers had plans to head immediately to South Burlington, where they had booked a meeting room at the Ramada Inn for an afternoon press conference with their clients. Afterward they would all make their way to the Unitarian Universalist Society in Burlington, where rainbow flags and multicolored balloons had been stocked for a public event. The lawyers were armed with two press releases: one that would go out in the occasion of a victory, the other for a loss.

Then all those plans fell apart, as every Friday in 1999 came and went without news. In mid-December, the court issued notice that, with the holidays approaching, it might issue rulings on a day other than Friday. Still, Murray and Robinson were not ready for the decision handed down on Monday, December 20, and not only because the two staff assistants who were supposed to aid them with decision-day logistics were both out with the flu. The lawyers had girded themselves for either the ecstasy of victory or despair of defeat but not what Murray described as a "confusing mixture of joy and despondency." Robinson later called it "the most difficult day of my professional life."

At 10:55 a.m. that morning, Robinson received a phone call from Larry Abbott, the clerk of the Vermont Supreme Court. It was a courtesy call, five minutes before the opinion would be posted on the court's website, and he was empowered to share only the court's ruling. "The judgment of the superior court upholding the constitutionality of the Vermont marriage statutes under Chapter I, Article 7 of the Vermont Constitution is reversed," he read to Robinson. She smiled as she heard the court recognize that same-sex couples could not be denied the "common benefits" of marriage.

But Abbott had more to read. "The effect of the Court's decision is suspended, and jurisdiction is retained in this Court," he went on, "to permit the Legislature to consider and enact legislation consistent with the constitutional mandate described herein."

"Larry, what does that mean?" Robinson asked.

She had to wait five minutes. At eleven a.m., the full opinion would be posted on the Internet, and at two p.m. the lawyers and their six clients were supposed to face the media in South Burlington. (Bonauto would fly from Boston to meet them.) Robinson pulled Murray out of a meeting to give her the news. Together they agreed to scrap their plans to meet the plaintiffs in South Burlington, instead summoning them first to the office in Middlebury so they could synchronize their reactions. Neither of their press releases—nor the many hours they had spent anticipating their response on decision day—had accounted for such a scenario.

Throughout the arc of *Baker v. State*, Murray and Robinson had been thoroughly prepared. At their opening press conference, every question a reporter had put to them and the plaintiffs who were present was one they expected. Each parry from a Supreme Court justice during oral arguments was one that Robinson had rehearsed with her cocounsels. (She was taken aback only once: when Justice James L. Morse raised the issue of cloning—in the news after a Scottish scientist announced earlier the cloning of a sheep named Dolly—before one of the assistant attorneys-general arguing the other side.) But the lawyers had not expected that the court could agree that the state went beyond its powers to deny marriage to same-sex couples yet simultaneously decide not to require Vermont to allow it as a form of redress. "It was really the first time in the entire course of this that we hadn't anticipated everything that happened the way it happened," says Robinson. "It was the first surprise of the whole process."

The shape of the unusual majority opinion had revealed itself in the line of questioning Chief Justice Jeffrey Amestoy had pursued during oral arguments. When given the chance to interrogate Robinson, he appeared to be searching for any valve that could allow the court to evade the duty of compelling same-sex marriage in Vermont. (While it was certainly possible the court could remand the case to trial, as the Hawaii Supreme Court had when faced with a similar decision, Murray and Robinson considered the prospect unlikely, since neither they nor the state were arguing that the introduction of further facts would be necessary.)

Amestoy wasn't alone. Justice John Dooley had mused over a new legal arrangement, "What if it gave them all of the bundle of rights but was unwilling to call it marriage? Would that be sufficient in your view?" After Robinson dismissed that as amounting to a "separate-but-equal régime," Morse echoed Amestoy's suggestion that the state could just stop issuing marriage licenses altogether. "If the Legislature just said we are changing the label and calling marriage domestic partnership instead of marriage, but you get all the bundle of rights that marriage has, then it couldn't do that?" Morse asked.

"Probably not," Robinson had responded. "All we need to show is that the constitution requires that the Legislature provide marriage on an equal basis for everyone."

In the moment, it is never easy to discern a judge's motive for a provocative line of questioning. Is she earnestly curious or playing devil's advocate? Is he trying to unmask the vulnerabilities of an argument's weaknesses to discredit it before other judges, or working to excavate one so he can methodically rebuild it on a more logically sound foundation?

Reading his forty-page opinion posted online, Murray and Robinson saw that Amestoy had been completely earnest when he had wrestled with these questions in public. Noting that "the State made every conceivable argument in support of the marriage laws," the chief justice wrote, "it would be pointless to remand this matter for further proceedings in the trial court." He had bought into Robinson's argument that the Common Benefits Clause applied to marriage, but wasn't persuaded that the designation itself amounted to a benefit. Given that uncertainty about the symbolic power of the term *marriage*, Amestoy believed it was beyond the capability of the judiciary to determine a proper remedy for the situation. "Whether this ultimately takes the form of inclusion within the marriage laws themselves or a parallel 'domestic partnership' system or some equivalent statutory alternative, rests with the Legislature," he wrote.

The majority opinion was just part of the bundle that Murray and Robinson could print out for their anxious drive to South Burlington. There were two other opinions that had no bearing on the case's outcome but helped illuminate just how idiosyncratic a consensus the chief justice had been able to assemble. A fifteen-page concurrence from Justice John

Dooley supported the court's holding but argued that arriving at it by means of a more conventional equal-protection logic would better help "the Legislature, the trial courts, or Vermonters in general to predict the outcome of future cases." There was also a thirty-page opinion from Justice Denise Johnson, who concurred with Amestoy's constitutional finding but thought clerks should be compelled to immediately issue marriage licenses to all couples. Johnson called Amestoy's legislative mandate a "novel and truncated remedy, which in my view abdicates this Court's constitutional duty to redress violations of constitutional rights."

Those words captured the attitudes of Robinson and Murray. Their visceral reactions were uneven, as Murray "felt like it was a great day" while Robinson "was devastated." Calibrating their public response would require more than merely drafting a fresh press release to address the new complications. It was becoming apparent that the decision would win international coverage—already the ruling had necessitated the only "FLASH" of news from Vermont to move over the Associated Press wire in decades—but there was still a lot of work to do shaping how the media would interpret what they considered a mixed verdict. Theirs was a remarkable triumph, one Bonauto described to the Associated Press as "a legal and cultural milestone," but they could not claim victory in any way that suggested they were satisfied with their circumstances.

Later that afternoon, the couples gathered at a press conference in South Burlington and then traveled together two miles to a Unitarian Universalist church downtown for an unqualified celebration. Nina Beck and Stacy Jolles brought their second child. "It's clear we won and that they just need to work out the logistics. It's clear that he's going to be better protected," said Jolles, bobbing one-month-old Seth in her arms. "The train has left the station. We may need one stop to get there, but we're going to get there," Stan Baker said at the church that night, where a crowd of one hundred had gathered to celebrate the decision. "There's no stopping us now." An AP reporter who covered the couples' statements seemed to accept their sense of inevitability. The headline on his story that moved across the wire the next day asserted that GAY MARRIAGE ISSUE HEADED FOR LAWMAKERS' FINE-TUNING.

But the lawyers knew they faced far more than tweaks. Robinson told the Vermont Press Bureau that she was "confident that the legislature is going to do the right thing," but privately she was far less sanguine about their prospects. Despite her initial buoyancy, Murray felt consumed with "dread about the fate to which the Court had just consigned us: difficult,

politically-charged debates in the legislature." The two realized immediately that they would be forced to put their law practices on hold. A
loose grassroots network cultivated to fend off a statehouse backlash would
have to be rejiggered into something sturdy enough to support a lobbying
campaign behind a piece of legislation that didn't yet exist. The court,
Robinson concluded, was "sending us to the very political cauldron from
which the Constitution is designed to shield unpopular minorities."

37

Scenes from a Civil Union

Howard Dean had spent years evading questions about gay marriage, and had little respect for the two coequal branches of state government now about to squeeze his governorship like a pincer. During his time in office, Dean had accused Vermont Supreme Court justices of thinking they were God and dismissed the legislature as a zoo. But the inconclusive majority opinion in *Baker v. State* just days before the end of 1999 presented an unexpected opening for the personally forceful if politically cautious governor to assert himself in the debate without having to take a position on the controversial question of marriage. "As soon as the Supreme Court handed down their ruling, I knew where I stood," Dean would later reflect. "This is the right thing to do. I believe in the innate dignity and humanity of all people; therefore, I believe all people ought to be treated respectfully. This is an equal-rights issue."

The first words out of Dean's mouth were somewhat less charitable. When asked at the press conference what he personally thought of gay marriage, he said, "It makes me uncomfortable, the same as anyone else." For the next day's *Burlington Free Press*, he expounded on that point. "Most Vermonters are uncomfortable with the notion of marriage being anything but a union between a heterosexual couple," Dean was quoted saying, while appearing to endorse some sort of compromise benefits package. "This decision is where a large majority of Vermonters can feel very comfortable, and I see no reason the Legislature shouldn't pass such a bill."

In his 1992 State of the State address, his first as governor, Dean had come out in favor of a gay civil-rights bill "so that no group of Vermonters suffers from bigotry and intolerance." But Dean was also a calculating political figure who was alert to the risk of being portrayed as a leftist.

When, in 1994, his administration's Department of Personnel struck a deal with its public employees' union to extend insurance benefits to members' domestic partners, Dean supported the action, as long as unmarried heterosexuals would be eligible for the same coverage. During his 1996 campaign for reelection, the platform of the state Democratic Party whose ticket he headed opposed the federal Defense of Marriage Act and encouraged extending full faith and credit to other states' recognized domestic partners but avoided taking any position on the legality of same-sex marriage itself. By the end of the decade, Dean was contemplating his future in national politics, meeting in secret weeks after his 1998 reelection with former senator Bill Bradley as each man pondered whether to challenge Vice President Al Gore for the Democratic presidential nomination two years later. Even as his lieutenant governor, Doug Racine, declared in the midst of the *Baker* appeal that he supported gay marriage, Dean consistently rebuffed efforts by journalists to share his opinion on what he described as "a very difficult issue for many Vermonters."

Dean's dodge had been repeatedly that the issue was one for courts to assess. He may have been uncomfortable with same-sex marriage as a binary proposition, but the court's decision freed him to be the first politician to assert ownership of the emergent face of a newly three-sided issue. Dean was eminently comfortable declaring himself champion of the notion that gays and lesbians were due every entitlement of marriage except the word itself. "It's in the best interests of all Vermonters, gay and straight, to go forward with the domestic partnership act and not the gay marriage act," Dean said at a statehouse press conference less than an hour after the opinions were released on December 20, 1999. When asked that day if he would veto a bill to enact gay marriage, Dean refused to state his preference. "It's not something the legislature will do," he told the Vermont Press Bureau. "It's just not going to happen."

At his State of the State address two weeks later, Dean reiterated the need for a bill recognizing gay couples, although when he did not specify that he preferred domestic partnerships some gay activists optimistically thought he might be signaling openness to a marriage bill instead. "This year we must make every effort to comply with the new Supreme Court ruling, which confirms that all Vermonters—including gay and lesbian Vermonters—are to have equal benefits under the law," Dean told legislators on January 5, 2000. "We were the first state to outlaw slavery in 1777, and we will remain in the forefront of the struggle for equal justice under the law."

Other politicians were less assertive than Dean. A decision designed to give deference to the legislature was greeted by many as an unwelcome burden. State representative John Edwards, a member of the Vermont House Judiciary Committee, said his first reaction was "Oh, shit." Those who felt strongly in favor of gay rights thought the court had abdicated its responsibility, while those opposed felt it had gone too far. Those ambivalent about the question—or wary of letting the question of how to recognize same-sex couples define their political careers—resented having the matter thrust upon them under such intense, urgent circumstances. As "a legislator who was interested in self-preservation I wanted to find a way to delay having the Judiciary Committee take up the issue," Edwards later conceded. Some ventured creating a commission to study the court's mandate and review policy options, if only as a means of pushing any eventual vote until after the 2000 elections.

But the Vermont House Judiciary Committee's chair was not so ready to relinquish the responsibility thrust upon him. Thomas Little was a moderate Republican who had ended up in a powerful committee post only by dint of a power-sharing arrangement with the Democrats, who controlled both houses of the legislature. In early January, Little privately informed members of his committee that they would take sole responsibility for generating the legislative fix that had been demanded by the court. "I was committed to a full and complete examination of the facts and law, and to whatever solution or legislative response was best," he reflected later.

Little embraced the idea that only one bill come for a vote in the House before being taken up by the Senate. He wanted the legislation to be a group project, one over which his committee could take common ownership after input from a wide range of sources including experts, activists, and the public. (The committee itself was balanced with five Democrats, five Republicans, and one progressive; its Democratic vice chair, Bill Lippert, was the legislature's only openly gay member.) "In view of the intense feelings and concerns that will be raised by and in our work on *Baker v. State*," Little wrote to committee members, "my goal is not only to keep the Committee's 'eye' on the Constitutional principles, but also to build consensus and avoid divisiveness."

Other legislators were not planning to wait for Little to realize his idea of consensus. The House and Senate clerks were overwhelmed by new bills articulating nearly every possible response to the court's decision. One proposed bill would legalize marriage for same-sex couples, while two separate ones offered equal benefits in a nonmarriage arrangement as part of what some supporters described as a "civil-rights act for gay and lesbian families." From the other side, there was a Defense of Marriage Act–style bill that would forbid Vermont from recognizing other states' same-sex marriages and a proposed amendment to the Vermont constitution to explicitly define marriage as between only a man and a woman. (Because of the constitution's time-lock provision, though, the amendment would have to pass in consecutive legislative sessions and could not appear on a referendum ballot for ratification before November 2005.)

On the day of Dean's State of the State address, Little set out a timeline for his committee. During its first two weeks of work, the committee would summon legal scholars to analyze the three opinions issued by the court in the context of Vermont's existing marriage laws to weigh whether they should be rewritten to include gays and lesbians or supplemented with an altogether new institution for same-sex couples. At that point, Little told members, he hoped the committee would be "in a position to make an informed decision about which basic option, or model, it will proceed with." That would leave the committee a little less than a month to have a bill ready by February 23, the informal deadline Little had set for delivery to the House floor.

Susan Murray and Beth Robinson were called to testify on the first day of hearings, the beginning of a complicated dance between the lawyers and legislature. As soon as Little signaled that he intended to have his committee quickly draft a bill from scratch, it became clear that the attorneys could make themselves indispensable partners to its work, since over the previous five years they had become expert in all the "common benefits" that the state associates with marriage. "At that point there was nobody who knew more about how it would need to be drafted if it was going to be an effective parallel structure," says Robinson.

But they also were now lobbying the legislature themselves for a different outcome, one that would presumably require less legislative lawyering than pure political influence. Murray and Robinson still had relationships with a number of statehouse figures from their work on the adoption bill and their circuit of "Marriage 101" briefings before filing *Baker v. State.* In the wake of the supreme court decision, they had also hired two outside firms, one with connections to the gay community and the other with experience around state government in Montpelier. When Kevin Ellis called on the day of the decision and pitched his firm to be the Freedom to Marry Task Force's lobbyists before the legislature, Murray had to sheepishly inform him that the group's political arm had only $250 in the bank. (She and Robinson had contributed $125 each to meet the minimum deposit necessary to open a new account.) Ellis agreed to begin working, effectively, on a pro bono basis. "You're about to move from an arena that is very defined, structured and clear in the courts to an arena that is undefined, unclear and a little like the circus," Ellis warned Murray.

By the count of lobbyists at his firm, Kimbell Sherman Ellis, nine out of the eleven members of the House Judiciary Committee should be considered potential targets to support a marriage bill. One of them was Little himself, and the lobbyists settled on a strategy that began with winning him over. Little was known in Montpelier as a pragmatist and appeared genuinely open-minded about marriage. If the moderate Republican could be persuaded to push a marriage bill out of his committee, Democratic leadership might feel they were politically safe in backing it. Dean might not have been enthusiastic about legalizing gay marriage, but he had pointedly refused to say he would veto it. If the legislature passed a bill doing so at the court's instruction, how could he?

In early February, after weeks of testimony about the variety of domestic-partnership arrangements available to gay and straight couples around the world, Robinson and Murray were called back before Little's committee. They discussed the *Loving* precedent, with the insistence that the only proper legislative response was full equality in marriage rights. They also brought the moral language of that era with them, too, reading a passage from "Letter from a Birmingham Jail," in which Martin Luther King Jr. described a "white moderate who is more devoted to 'order' than to justice" as the greatest obstacle for the civil-rights movement. "Shallow understanding from people of good will is more frustrating than absolute misunderstanding from people of ill will," Robinson read from King's words. "Lukewarm acceptance is much more bewildering than outright rejection."

A few days later, Little took a straw poll of raised hands around the U-shaped committee table to see which path members favored. There had been consensus from the outset that the legislature should do something in line with the court's ruling in *Baker* and not push a constitutional amendment to supersede it, but the committee split into three camps. Three committee members wanted to rewrite the marriage laws in a gender-neutral way, and three others wanted to leave straight couples on the same footing as gay ones by abolishing civil marriage altogether. Five favored some new institution that included the benefits of marriage under a different legal rubric. Little threw his own support behind the last option, declaiming that a "legal benefits act is the right thing for the people of the State of Vermont now, and not an expansion of the marriage laws."

Newspaper headlines used the same term Dean had in December to describe the marriage-lite path—PANEL BACKS DOMESTIC PARTNERSHIP, the next day's *Rutland Herald* proclaimed—but legislators who supported the option were looking for new words to describe what they expected would be an altogether original approach to recognizing couples. That day several of the members who voted for the compromise option called it a "civil rights package," although Little preferred a "legal benefits" act and Republican Cathy Voyer "a civil union package."

At that point, the Freedom to Marry Task Force was forced to consider how much it wanted to collaborate with such moderate allies. Murray and Robinson had faced a similar crisis in the frenzied hours between the court's release of its opinion and the press conference scheduled to respond to it. They had already heard Dean outline his preference for some sort of domestic-partnership structure, and had to decide how much they wanted to facilitate it. In theory, they could have tried to block anything from being enacted that was short of a bill to fully legalize same-sex marriage, and—perhaps once the four-month legislative session had passed—gone back to the supreme court to argue that the politicians had not done their part, leaving it incumbent upon the court to act unilaterally. But after a brief deliberation they decided that they couldn't abandon the field to their opponents. "We had to play," says Robinson.

Now six weeks later they saw the contours of an actual compromise, and the choice presented itself anew. The task force and its lobbyists could have decided to lean on friendly legislators to vote against whatever came out of the committee. "We could've easily killed that bill," says Murray. The three cocounsels set odds for what they thought might happen if they did so and subsequently asked the court to impose the relief that the legislature had failed to deliver. Robinson predicted a two-in-three chance that under those circumstances they could win marriage by court order. Bonauto was more pessimistic, putting the likelihood at one in three. Murray fell in between the two.

On one Saturday in February, they gathered the task force's regional coordinators, along with the three couples who had filed the lawsuit, at Kimbell Sherman Ellis's Montpelier office to take their own straw poll. The lawyers described the options, by then well-known to everyone present. They were completely deadlocked, with three plaintiffs in favor of backing the "civil rights package" likely to emerge from the committee, and three opposed to a compromise. Murray and Robinson, too, were split.

For about a week or so they withdrew from the efforts to draft a new bill, and the negotiations proceeded without them. Everyone understood that the court required gay couples to be treated equally in the tax code, probate proceedings, and criminal investigations. But there were well-established protocols for entering and exiting a marriage, some of them, like divorce law, shaped by over a century of court precedent. How could a new domestic-partnership structure mimic that? Furthermore, marriage laws had been adjusted with the understanding that separate entities—private employers, banks and insurers, other governments—relied on the designation to guide their own policies. Should a new law take that into account?

Vermont's was a part-time legislature, where rank-and-file members were citizen-legislators with no dedicated staff. Members were thus unusually reliant on outside experts working in tandem with the nonpartisan committee lawyers who actually drafted most bills. The absence of Murray and Robinson during a week of urgent yet delicate negotiations was noticed, especially by allies in the legislature who had little idea what they should want to see in a new-style domestic-partnership package. "Where the hell are you guys?" Lippert, the Democratic vice chair, demanded. "You need to be at the table."

On March 2, 2000, the House Judiciary Committee delivered its bill for its first reading before the entire chamber. The legislation was relatively brief, relying on blanket language to cover every corner of Vermont law that addressed benefits extended to married couples rather than itemizing them individually. Perhaps most challengingly for the bill's drafters, it appeared to fulfill the objective to mimic the most dramatic parts of a marriage—"the exact same way to get in and get out," as Murray put it. Couples would have to secure licenses from the same town clerks required to issue marriage licenses and certificates signed by the same religious or secular figures who were authorized to perform weddings. Instead of divorce, civil unions would be ended with a dissolution, but the same standard applied. Both parties had to be residents of Vermont for a year after, an artifact of nineteenth-century laws to keep states from being destinations for quickie divorces. Cathy Voyer's three-week-old neologism for this novel but familiar legal institution—"marriage by another name," in Robinson's words—stuck. H.847 was known as "A Bill for Civil Unions."

Murray and Robinson convened another conference call with the plaintiffs and task force leadership for a final decision on strategy. Many of those on the call who had been contemptuous of a moderate compromise just weeks earlier had grown protective of it. Now that the civil-unions bill, offering some of the most expansive protections on earth for gay families, was headed to the full house, there was a clear consensus that it was time to rally the community to call legislators on its behalf.

Opponents weren't looking to kill the bill, either. (Sending the legislature home empty-handed risked having a gay-friendly court impose same-sex marriage on the state.) Take It to the People, a group that had been agitating for years for a statewide referendum on a constitutional ban on same-sex marriage, instead pushed legislators to introduce a variety of amendments, punting the decision into the public hands, from an advisory referendum to a full-fledged Constitutional Convention. As the civil-unions bill moved toward the floor, the popular movement against it found strength. March 9, 2000, was Town Meeting Day, and in as many as fifty communities across the state—primarily those where opponents saw benefit in pushing for a vote—the gatherings had included nonbinding referenda in which Vermonters showed a strong preference for the pre-*Baker* status quo.

Vermont fetishized its commitment to such devolved democracy, and throughout the winter the legislative process had been uncommonly open. The House Judiciary Committee opened up hearings to public testimony for two three-hour sessions, broadcast to statewide audiences on public radio and television. Those who brought any vitriol to the debate were quickly dismissed by media and political leaders as unworthy of the state's civil society. "The people of Vermont are in this together," wrote David Moats, the editorial-page editor for the *Rutland Herald,* who would go on to receive a Pulitzer Prize for his patient, evenhanded commentary over the course of the year. "Opponents and supporters of the Supreme Court's ruling are part of the same community, and as the discussion moves forward it is important to cultivate a charitable view of those on the other side."

It was as much drama as Vermont politics could handle, but there was little suspense about the outcome. What started as a three-sided issue shifted quickly into two. Nearly everyone who saw marriage as the ideal result grew invested in defending civil unions and protecting the politicians who felt they were brave to back them. "At some point I knew that the right thing to do was to fully support the *Baker* decision through appropriate legislation. I also knew that it most likely would mean the end of my legislative career," John Edwards, who had been a state trooper before running for the statehouse, reflected. "From the time the *Baker* decision was published, my life was full of anxiety. I really knew what the right thing to do was, but I had to screw up the courage to do it."

On March 15, 2000, the civil-unions bill passed its first vote in the Vermont House, with all the most destructive amendments failing in floor votes. The senate passed the bill a month later, without any significant changes, and on April 25 the two chambers synthesized the versions into a single bill. The following day, Dean signed An Act for Civil Unions into law, choosing to do so with only members of his staff present, out of what he described as an effort to minimize histrionics around the contentious event.

Things had ended up exactly where Dean had guided them. Dean's first remarks, barely an hour after the court issued its opinion in *Baker v. State*, in favor of "the domestic partnership act and not the gay marriage act"—even before any bill had been offered—set the terms of the debate. The chief justice of the Vermont Supreme Court had instructed legislators to devise "a parallel 'domestic partnership' system or some equivalent statutory alternative," and they had responded by devising exactly what he proposed, only rebranded to maintain the illusion of novelty. Dean had latched onto this prescription of a third way through the debate with such confidence that those who stuck to their previous views about the merits of same-sex marriage could be marginalized by politicians as stubborn outliers. "It was dead from that moment forward," Robinson says. "We had to pretend like it was alive and go through the exercise knowing that the best we were going to get was what we got."

38

Down from the Mountains

On September 27, 2000, Mary Bonauto typed out her latest "Vermont Ruling: A Status Update." Throughout the year she had issued a series of memos to allies around the country as a mechanism for keeping them invested in the Vermont fight while discouraging outsiders from meddling unproductively in the state's insular politics. During the summer, she had some good news to report. The July 1 implementation date for civil unions passed with little incident, as a handful of mutinous town clerks backed away from threats to ignore the law. Instead, the Fourth of July weekend had featured joyous celebrations within the gay community across the state, often with couples who had been together for decades exchanging vows for the first time. "With the civil union law, we turn a corner in the United States and arrive in a new era," Bonauto exulted in a guest column for the Human Rights Campaign's quarterly magazine. "The existence of civil unions will highlight that what counts as a 'family' is a defining civil rights issue."

But the events that autumn suggested that the old era had not fully passed. On September 12, in Vermont's first vote after the establishment of civil unions, five of the Republican legislators who backed the bill failed to win renomination amid a summertime blossoming of TAKE BACK VERMONT lawn signs and concurrent spike in registration by new voters. "I knew there were strong feelings, but I didn't realize they were quite that strong," Representative Marion Milne, one of the defeated, told the *Los Angeles Times* for a story headlined VOTERS OUST 5 WHO BACKED VT. CIVIL UNION LAW.

Such national media attention, Bonauto knew, could contribute to a backlash beyond Vermont. She had observed from afar what had happened in 1996 to the Hawaiian lawmakers targeted for their views on marriage, and had tried to learn from the experience when advising the Vermont Freedom to Marry Task Force on strategy. While Beth Robinson and Susan Murray were still agonizing over whether to cooperate with a compromise or help one die, Bonauto called Dan Foley in Honolulu for insight. "Delay is not our friend," Bonauto wrote to Foley afterward, summarizing his advice. "If we do not get a bill passed this session, you are concerned that our enemies will smell blood in the water."

This time, the legislature had worked quickly, and blood was nonetheless in the water. In her memo, Bonauto attempted to minimize what had happened in Vermont. "Republican primaries are not a time when we should expect civil union supporters to shine," she wrote, noting a few legislators—including Cathy Voyer, the representative who inadvertently devised the "civil union" formulation—were able to retain their seats amid the assault. Even the good news wasn't particularly encouraging, though; Representative Tom Little, the judiciary committee chairman who became the face of the legislative compromise, won only 60 percent of the vote against an unknown challenger after facing no opposition whatsoever over the previous three election cycles.

Those results presaged an even greater chill that fall. Every politician in Vermont who had been compelled by the court to play a role in the law's creation—each legislator who voted for it and the governor who signed it—would be on the ballot in November. One consequence of the primary was to guarantee that the general election, too, would be engulfed by the debate over the status of gay couples. Because of threats, Governor Howard Dean had begun wearing a bulletproof vest as he campaigned for reelection. Even those who hadn't been directly involved in legislating civil unions saw the matter define their campaigns. If not for civil unions, state auditor Ed Flanagan, the first openly gay candidate ever nominated for the U.S. Senate by a major party in the United States, lamented to *Newsweek* during his campaign, "My sexual orientation would be a distinctly second issue, if an issue at all."

Dean was unlikely to lose the governorship—he was in a rematch with a poorly funded candidate he had beaten by fourteen points two years earlier—but less-established legislators were certainly vulnerable to challenges. With losses there, the civil-unions law itself might be in jeopardy. Take It to the People had failed to get a constitutional amendment out of the legislature that spring, but if Republicans claimed control of either chamber they could begin the process anew. Enough legislators losing their seats over civil unions might scare those who returned to agree at least to put the question to a referendum, which is all Take It to the People was demanding. "This is probably something that's going to take a generation to resolve," Little had told the *Los Angeles Times*.

Either way, Bonauto conceded in her "status update" memo, the way the vitriol around the civil-unions debate so quickly poisoned the state's political environment "makes people sick of the whole issue, and of the gay people who brought it to the fore." She was afraid that this mentality might spread. "This affects *you*, in *your* state, because lawmakers in your state may well view the election results in Vermont as a measure of how safe it is for them to introduce civil union and marriage legislation," Bonauto explained. "It is entirely possible that a few people will lose their seats. While that should not surprise anyone, it can be used as an excuse for not going forward with equality measures in other states."

It would be a "chilling message" if losses in November led to a roll-back or wholesale repeal of the civil-unions bill, she wrote. "Regardless of the outcome of the elections, we believe lawmakers should file marriage legislation, and, in some cases, also file comprehensive civil union legislation," Bonauto averred. "It may not pass right away, but the only way to get what you want is to ask for it. And of course, advocates should continue to explore well-planned and well-placed litigation."

Like many in the state's gay and lesbian community, including her two cocounsels there, Bonauto had mixed feelings about the outcome in Vermont. She celebrated what had been gained through civil unions while lamenting loss in pursuit of marriage rights. The experience did little to change her future strategy. Civil unions represented a significant new legal edifice, but it wasn't worth much as a building block. For years, Bonauto's assumed course of action for the next round of litigation had been predicated on winning marriage in one state and using it to maneuver her way into another state's courts by having married couples file for recognition at home.

Even though three states had supreme courts rule in favor of gay-marriage appellants, none of them had ever issued licenses. In December 1999, the Hawaii Supreme Court dismissed *Baehr v. Anderson,* as the case that had begun as *Baehr v. Lewin* was now named. A few months earlier, Alaska's had done the same with *Brause v. Bureau of Vital Statistics,* filed by two Anchorage gay activists. In both Hawaii and Alaska, courts had been given no option after voters the previous year changed state constitutions by referendum to rule out same-sex marriage.

Since Vermont's legislature had created a legal classification that existed in no other jurisdiction in the world, there was little basis on which to demand that other states recognize a civil-union license. Bonauto was also still itching to mount a challenge to the Defense of Marriage Act in federal court, but—again because Vermont had pointedly decided to give gay couples everything other than the legal designation of "married"—none of them could claim to have been harmed by Congress's decision to single them out for unfair exclusion under law.

She would have to start from scratch, and on the surface Massachusetts appeared an odd place to do so. Its highest appellate court, the Supreme Judicial Court, had in 1999 invalidated Boston's year-old domestic-partnership benefits for city workers. The program had been imposed by Mayor Tom Menino via executive order, and was popular among Boston politicians and public-employees unions, whose members were now eligible to register members of their household for health benefits even if no one was married. The Catholic Action League of Massachusetts challenged Menino's order under a narrow matter of state law codified in 1955. The court's reasoning had little to do with gay rights, but those who had initiated the *Connors v. Boston* lawsuit (which was litigated by lawyers from the American Center for Law and Justice founded by Pat Robertson) boasted about it on those merits all the same. "It's a victory for the traditional family and a triumph for the taxpayers over special-interest politics," the Catholic Action League's executive director, C. J. Doyle, told the *Boston Herald.*

Much as it had in Boston, the Catholic Action League hunted for local taxpayers to serve as plaintiffs for a parallel suit in Cambridge, which already had its own domestic-partnership ordinance on the books. GLAD had served as a defendant alongside the city of Boston, on behalf of a lesbian employee about to lose benefits for her domestic partner, and ghost-wrote an amicus brief signed by several labor unions. After the loss in Boston, the firm offered help to other municipalities likely to face similar lawsuits—first Cambridge, but with Springfield, Northampton, Brookline, and Provincetown inevitably not far behind—although the assumption within GLAD was that they would end up in the same position Boston had. "I don't know what Cambridge can come up with for an argument, but maybe they can come up with something that no one has come up with before," Bonauto, herself a Cambridge resident, mused to a reporter. "All we can do is hope."

The legislature could have easily amended the 1955 law, but such an effort was unlikely to be treated by politicians as a simple legal adjustment to modernize an outdated statute. When a bill that would have done so came up in 1998, House Speaker Thomas Finneran, who represented a Boston district, declared his opposition. Domestic-partnership programs, he said, discriminated against single heterosexuals while extending "an exalted status to some people because of sexual orientation." As a result, the bill to allow municipalities to go further than the state in extending benefits to their employees lingered in the legislature, with a standing threat of a veto by Governor Paul Cellucci.

In March 1999, the Catholic Action League filed its anticipated suit against Cambridge. A week later, a coalition of city officials, pro-gay activists, and labor unions stormed the Massachusetts statehouse for a "DP Lobby Day," trying with newfound urgency to convince legislative leaders to move the bill out of committee. But the leadership remained resistant, effectively killing any impetus for an incrementalist strategy in which same-sex couples in Massachusetts would win their rights piecemeal at the local level with passive cooperation from state officials. MASS. ACTIVISTS HAVE DISCOVERED THAT BEACON HILL IS STACKED AGAINST THEM IN WAYS NOT SEEN IN DECADES, a headline in the gay community newspaper *Bay Windows* observed.

The elected officials blocking the necessary legislative fix now appeared to be a greater impediment than the courts that had invalidated those same local laws in the first place. The Supreme Judicial Court had been unnecessarily gracious to the same-sex couples who stood to be most affected by its decision in *Connors v. Boston*, even apologetic for judicial helplessness in the face of unambiguous law. "We recognize that the category of covered dependents of city employees, as defined by the Legislature in 1955 and 1960, no longer fully reflects all household members for whom city employees are likely to have continuing obligations to provide support," Chief Justice Margaret Marshall had written in her opinion. "A 'family' may no longer be constituted simply of a wage-earning father, his dependent wife and the couple's children."

Gay leaders may have been disappointed by the results—GLAD highlighted approximately two hundred Bostonians who lost their health insurance as a result of the decision, and forty-six Cantabridgians facing a similar fate—but they were heartened by the content and tone of Marshall's opinion. "The court is not homophobic," said Jarrett Barrios, an openly gay state representative whose district included Cambridge. "In fact, in this case, they have actually been quite friendly. Their reasoning was fair-minded, and now it is my job, and the job of other legislators, to move on this."

Throughout the decade, the Supreme Judicial Court had made other rulings sympathetic to nontraditional families, including a recent 1999 decision that permitted visitation rights for people not biologically or adoptively related to their children. But among all those "precedents of respect for gay and lesbian people," as Bonauto called them, the one that seemed most instructive might have come in the high-profile case where the court unanimously ruled against them. "There were tea leaves that this is what the court felt it had to do legally, but nobody felt good about denying people insurance that their employer wanted to provide them simply because the legislature refused to amend the laws and allow the cities to do this," says Bonauto.

Bonauto, who had been casting about for a venue to mount her first post-Vermont challenge to state marriage laws, grew certain that the time was right to start in the Massachusetts courts. The legislative fix languishing in committee would at best cover only public employees in the state's most progressive cities and towns; the only way to affect all families in one swoop was to permit same-sex couples to marry. The court appeared to be going out of its way in *Connors v. Boston* to signal an interest in rewriting family law where the constitution would allow it. Why not give it the chance to go all the way?

The Next Town Over

On October 19, 2000, Susan Murray and Beth Robinson made the four-hour drive from Vermont for a very public meeting with Mary Bonauto. At a large banquet dinner at Boston's Park Plaza Hotel, the three attorneys who had successfully litigated the *Baker v. State* case were presented with the Roger Baldwin Award from the ACLU, named for the founder of the group Bonauto described as "an incredible ally in our fights." The trio were introduced by Matt Coles, director of the ACLU's Lesbian and Gay Rights Project and a forceful presence at meetings of the Roundtable, which helped determine legal strategies and priorities across the movement. Coles told the four hundred attendees that "Massachusetts folks are extraordinarily lucky to have one of the best civil-rights organizations in the country."

But when Bonauto privately informed him offstage that GLAD's next move was likely to be a lawsuit challenging marriage law in Massachusetts, Coles lost his sense of cheer. "I don't think you've laid the political groundwork yet," he told her. Election Day was three weeks away, and Massachusetts legislators were likely to become only more fearful of any action on marriage after they saw what had become of peers in Vermont who had accepted civil unions. In her remarks at the ACLU dinner, Murray reported on "an extraordinary amount of meanness and mean-spiritedness" that had been unleashed by the *Baker* decision, describing "graffiti about 'killing fags' in some towns." She said she and Robinson were raising money for newspaper ads and lawn signs to try to protect candidates who had voted for civil unions from the backlash. "But let's not fool ourselves," Murray said. "We need as much help as we can get."

Bonauto had a different view of Coles's resistance. "There were a lot of people who really liked the Vermont resolution. And that was something different from marriage," Bonauto says of Coles. "That's where he was. And I think he also just believed that marriage was going to bring more venom, and the civil-union approach was a way of moving forward."

Bonauto had been hearing similar doubts from others closer to home. In August, she had convened a group of gay activists at GLAD's office to say she thought the time was right to begin preparing a lawsuit that would force the Massachusetts Supreme Judicial Court to rule on the constitutionality of restricting marriage to opposite-sex couples. About two dozen people squeezed into a conference room as Bonauto laid out her reasoning. Many of them had watched in recent weeks as Massachusetts couples traveled to neighboring Vermont to secure civil-unions licenses that were worthless at home, and were enthusiastic about the idea of pushing to change their own state's laws. But those who had spent the spring discouraged by the resistance of politicians to a far more modest acknowledgment of gay families were stunned by Bonauto's lack of caution. Arline Isaacson, who as the state's most influential gay-rights lobbyist had helped organize the "DP Lobby Day" for domestic-partnership legislation, knew any public talk of marriage would solidify the forces against them and prompt a wider backlash. "Shouldn't we wait a few years?" asked Isaacson, cochair of the Massachusetts Gay and Lesbian Political Caucus.

Having seen what had transpired over the course of the year in Vermont had soured Bonauto on her side's decision to compromise before the legislature there, or to embrace incrementalism as a model for Massachusetts. "Although I accepted the decision to proceed with the civil-union approach, I believe the day will come when it is seen as an unequal and lesser status than marriage, and as a stepping stone to marriage," Bonauto reflected shortly thereafter. "I believe that a number of legislators voted for civil union thinking that something less than marriage would blunt the vehement attacks by our opponents, but of course it did not." (Seventeen Vermont legislators who voted in favor of the civil-unions bill lost their seats on November 2.)

Regardless of Bonauto's decisions about the timing of litigation, conflict over same-sex unions in Massachusetts seemed to be inevitable. As the statehouse came into session the next January, a bipartisan team of senior legislators prepared to introduce a bill specifying that only opposite-sex couples could be recognized as married under state law. Massachusetts was among the sixteen states that had never enacted a defense-of-marriage bill, with the most recent effort to pass one floundering in committee in the summer of 1999, but after Vermont the proposal was reborn. When a fresh version of the bill emerged in January 2001, it had been augmented with a new clause: "Any other relationship shall not be recognized as a marriage, or its legal equivalent, or receive the benefits exclusive to marriage." That seemed to foreclose a Vermont-style civil-unions package, and possibly even interfere with any sort of domestic-partnership benefits offered by private employers. Its potential impact would be so much more sweeping than earlier versions that drafters dubbed it a "super DOMA."

Bonauto came to believe that the bill justified moving ahead quickly with a marriage case so that the state's gay activists could, as she put it, "engage affirmatively and with the voices of real couples and families, not defensively." As cocounsel in *Baker v. State*, Mary Bonauto had been a full partner to Susan Murray and Beth Robinson in the development of legal strategy and the writing of briefs. In Massachusetts, Bonauto would have control of every aspect of the litigation from the outset. As much as *Baker v. State* had been plotted to evade the political trap that had doomed the Hawaii case, Bonauto's lawsuit in Massachusetts would correct for the shortcomings in the Vermont strategy.

Bonauto had grown convinced that her side in Vermont had not done enough to humanize the stories of why plaintiffs wanted to marry, which helped the court accept a bloodless, technocratic solution like civil unions. All three couples who ended up with their names on the *Baker v. State* suit lived in the Burlington area, to ensure that the matter would first appear before a Chittenden County judge. "I had really wished we'd had plaintiffs from other places, because there's nothing like when it's one of your neighbors or it's the next town over to sharpen the issues a little bit for people," Bonauto says.

Unlike in Vermont, where the task force was pulling from a small and insular world of activists, GLAD had plenty of prospective plaintiffs identified through years of legal work on behalf of gays and lesbians in Massachusetts. (The recent lobbying to save municipal domestic-partnership ordinances had helped in particular to surface same-sex couples interested in asserting their rights.) Throughout the second half of 2000, Bonauto traveled across the state, often visiting couples in their homes to assess how well suited they would be to serve as spokespeople for a case.

She wanted couples where both parties would pass criminal background checks and had the "fortitude to endure the scrutiny"; also, as Bonauto had learned from her experience in Vermont, they required schedules flexible enough to allow participation in midday press conferences on short notice. Across the group, there would need to be diversity in terms of age, gender, class, family structure, life experience, and geography. The last was especially true in Massachusetts, a larger landmass with greater regional distinctions than Vermont and more diverse local media. One of the things that had kept Bonauto from suing that fall, when she had begun alerting lawyers in the national gay-rights movement that she planned to challenge the state's marriage law, was her search for one last, perfect couple. "There was one geographic area in the state where I couldn't find a plaintiff, and I was not moving forward without that area being represented," she says.

Massachusetts may have been among the country's most politically liberal states, but it also had a strong streak of white-ethnic social conservatism informed by the outsize historical role of the Catholic Church and a larger African American population (with its own politically influential clergy) than Hawaii, Alaska, or Vermont. To shape how it would communicate with the public about the case, GLAD commissioned three focus groups. One would include only members of the gay community who had "no firm opinion" on marriage. Two would focus on what had been identified through polls as a crucial swing constituency: Democratic or independent women, aged 28–47, either divorced, widowed, or separated. Based on the findings from those groups, Bonauto and her cocounsel Jennifer Levi minimized any aspect of marriage that could possibly be delivered via another sanctioned vehicle.

By the end of March 2001, Bonauto had her plaintiffs in place and a publicist on retainer to stage-manage their introduction to the public. There were fourteen of them, seven couples who had over the previous fortnight requested marriage licenses from five different town clerks' offices around the state. They were geographically diverse, not only from the Boston area but also Northampton and Worcester, and ranged in age from thirty-five to sixty. Two were African American. Four were parents of young children and one a grandfather to four.

Much of the thirty-page complaint that Bonauto prepared was filled with accounts of the couplings, including the otherwise mundane facts of their domestic lives: family reunions and Cape Cod vacations, karate and violin classes for first-graders, hip-replacement surgeries, auto-insurance policies, and potentially fraught interactions with former spouses. It would, Bonauto hoped, keep "the focus on real people rather than allow an abstract debate."

The lawsuit bore the name of Hilary and Julie Goodridge, a white-collar Jamaica Plain couple who had been together for thirteen years and had adopted a common surname ever since exchanging vows in a backyard commitment ceremony. In interviews, the Goodridges liked to trace their commitment to litigation to a moment the previous winter when their daughter Annie told them, "If you loved each other you'd get married." Annie was Julie's biological child, but Hilary later adopted her as a coparent, which the Massachusetts Supreme Judicial Court had determined could be in the best interests of the child even if the parents were strangers to each other under the law. "It ultimately hurts Annie more than anyone for Julie and I not to have a legal relationship to one another," Goodridge would tell the *Boston Globe.* "It puts me at risk financially, and ultimately puts Annie at risk."

On April 11, 2001, Bonauto stood behind a podium in a hotel ballroom at the Omni Parker House, a strand of pearls visible through the open collar of her shirt, to announce that the Goodridges and twelve others had just sued the state of Massachusetts. It was the first of three conferences that day in different cities, scheduled to generate unique local coverage in each of the state's media markets.

When asked what impact the Vermont events would have on the Massachusetts suit, Bonauto said that it would be only "helpful in a generic, cultural fashion." A focus on the specific entitlements that accrued to married couples had made for a strong case under Vermont's Common Benefits Clause, and permitted some judges to avoid having to wrestle with whether gays and lesbians were entitled to full civil-rights protections. At the same time, however, that approach invited the court to decouple those benefits from the institution of marriage and assume they could be equitably issued under a different name.

In *Goodridge v. Department of Public Health,* Bonauto made clear, both her briefs and public statements would never fail to emphasize the unique cultural salience of the institution her clients were now petitioning to join. "Marriage," she explained, "is a legal relationship and a social status understood everywhere."

40

....

Goodridge

A few weeks after Mary Bonauto filed *Goodridge v. Department of Public Health*, a group calling itself Massachusetts Citizens for Marriage started circulating petitions to begin the process of amending Massachusetts's constitution to take the matter away from the state courts. The Protection of Marriage Amendment largely adopted the language of the super-DOMA bill that had failed to progress in the legislature and repurposed it for what Massachusetts Family Institute president Ronald Crews hailed as "the ultimate legal remedy."

If the amendment's sponsors did succeed in collecting the necessary 57,100 signatures for a so-called citizen initiative, they would trigger a series of Constitutional Conventions. There the amendment would need to secure the votes of one-quarter of state legislators in consecutive years. Only then would the question make the November 2004 ballot, ensuring what the *Berkshire Eagle*'s liberal editorial page speculated would be "a three-year campaign from intolerant busybodies and social engineers." By aiming to amend the constitution rather than statutes, gay-marriage opponents would shift from the hard lobbying work of navigating the Democratic-controlled statehouse toward the much more straightforward (if also more costly) task of assembling a majority coalition of voters. Rather than hoarding resources for a statewide ballot campaign, gay activists worked to interfere with the signature-gathering process, including reportedly trailing out-of-town contractors hired by the Massachusetts Citizens for Marriage from their hotels to the supermarkets and churches they used as canvass sites. It was a choice made of desperation. "We were going to get massacred," reflected Arline Isaacson, who as cochair of the Massachusetts Gay and Lesbian Political Caucus encouraged a "Decline to Sign" pressure campaign. "It was unequivocally clear that there was no chance of winning at the polls whatsoever."

By year's end, the amendment's backers had collected enough signatures to bring the question to the Constitutional Convention, and Isaacson reoriented her lobbying toward legislators who would face the measure there. She tried to avoid what she called "the 'm-word'" and instead emphasized the way the ban would permanently forbid any sort of domestic-partner benefits from state or local governments. "Our opponents could have gone just for marriage. But they were greedy, God bless them, and they went for marriage and benefits," said Isaacson. "That was the best gift they could have given us."

Senate president Tom Birmingham, a liberal then looking for an edge in a Democratic primary for governor, was persuaded to embrace an audacious if underhanded procedural maneuver against a measure he considered "wrong-hearted, mean-spirited, discriminatory and unfair." As soon as he gaveled in the Constitutional Convention, Birmingham recognized a motion to adjourn, ending the session in a few minutes and denying supporters even the chance to introduce the amendment. Cries of "We want a vote!" rained down on Birmingham from spectators who had crowded the gallery. His gambit did not rule out that possibility, but he had succeeded in postponing it for a full election cycle.

Bonauto welcomed the delay, as it would create a useful buffer between the eventual resolution of all legal appeals and the settling of political accounts. "If we won the case and the amendment proceeded to the ballot, voters would know what it looked like when same-sex couples married before casting their vote," she calculated. "Likewise, if we lost the case, we would minimize any perceived 'need' to amend the constitution, thus keeping the door open for a legislative change to the marriage laws."

At the first hearing over summary-judgment motions, in March 2002, Assistant Attorney General Judith Yogman asserted in Suffolk Superior Court that the marriage statute reflected a reasonable civic interest in encouraging procreation and child-rearing by opposite-sex couples. Two months later, a judge agreed with Yogman, observing that the legislature had had ample opportunity in recent years to rewrite the laws to accommodate gays and lesbians and had chosen not to. "While this court understands the reasons for the plaintiffs' request to reverse the Commonwealth's centuries-old legal tradition of restricting marriage to opposite-sex couples, their request should be directed to the Legislature, not the courts," Judge Thomas Connolly wrote.

That exchange had gone as Bonauto anticipated, but she had had to observe it from a distance. She was pregnant with twins due in late 2001, and GLAD's employment policy extended her a maternity leave for a few months afterward. It was unclear whether even in case of ultimate victory she would be able to get married in Massachusetts, as she and Jenny Wriggins, her partner of nearly fifteen years, were no longer residents; the pair was in the process of moving from Boston back to Portland, Maine, closer to Wriggins's work as a professor at the University of Maine Law School. But even among those contesting Bonauto's claims that such families should be worthy of equal treatment under the law, news of her pregnancy—and the idea of scheduling high-stakes litigation around it—were treated as matter-of-factly as it would have been had a married heterosexual lawyer decided to conceive. ("The plaintiffs' lead attorney will be taking a parental leave that both sides agree to accommodate," Governor Jane Swift was informed in a memo from her chief legal counsel.)

The Massachusetts Supreme Judicial Court set a date in early 2003 to hear Bonauto's appeal of her lower-court defeat. The brief she drafted hinged on the promises made by Article I of the state's Declaration of Rights, which begins by proclaiming that "all people are born free and equal and have certain natural, essential and unalienable rights; among which may be reckoned the right of enjoying and defending their lives and liberties." The language was a vestige of the Massachusetts constitution authored by John Adams in 1780, which influenced the federal constitution that followed seven years later. Throughout Massachusetts history, the state's judiciary has read into the state's constitution a particularly progressive view of individual freedoms, forbidding the death penalty and ensuring public funding for abortions at times when federal courts would not.

The court's recently elevated chief justice, Margaret Marshall, proudly embraced that tradition. She had been raised in South Africa, and was drawn during her teenage years to protest the country's apartheid system. As president of the National Union of South African Students, Marshall fell under police surveillance, her phones tapped. In 1968, she won a scholarship to study art history at Harvard and—partly out of a concern for her safety—fellow activists helped send her to the United States. While she was at Harvard, the political situation for antiapartheid activists grew even more dire, and Marshall never returned to her homeland. In 1973, she both enrolled at Yale Law School and met Anthony Lewis, the *New York Times* columnist and former Supreme Court correspondent, whom she would later marry. The two settled in Boston, where Marshall worked as a corporate litigator and Harvard's counsel before being named by a Republican governor to the Supreme Judicial Court. Learning the law in the United States, of which she became a citizen in 1978, gave "expression to some of the longings and the leanings and the values that I had come to respect in South Africa," Marshall explained.

Once seated on the Massachusetts Supreme Judicial Court, Marshall particularly liked to recount the example of Quock Walker, a slave who came before the body in 1781 to demand his liberty. The year-old constitution made no mention of slavery, but Walker's attorneys persuaded the court that its born-free-and-equal language should ban the "perpetual servitude of a rational creature," as Chief Justice William Cushing wrote in his opinion ensuring Walker's freedom. Even though Massachusetts would never amend its constitution or statutes to expressly prohibit slavery, the court's judgment effectively killed off the practice in the state; by 1790 census takers did not record the presence of a single slave in Massachusetts. As Emily Bazelon noted in *Legal Affairs*, the Walker story "celebrates a court that led the public to a watershed conclusion that it should have, but hadn't, reached on its own."

Marshall sent specific signals that her court could usher in a similar watershed on civil-rights protections for gays and lesbians. In 1999, the year she was elevated to chief justice, Marshall delivered the keynote address at the annual dinner of the Massachusetts Lesbian and Gay Bar Association. There Marshall expressed pride that her homeland had become the first nation on earth to explicitly mention sexual orientation and identity in its constitution.

On the morning of March 4, 2003, Bonauto finally stood before Marshall—recognizable with a mane of white hair, thin red-framed glasses, and faraway accent—to present her appeal in *Goodridge v. Department of Public Health*. The attorney was so eager to make her case that she began to speak before the timer had begun to count down the fourteen minutes she was allotted. "Wait until your green light goes on," one of the justices advised her.

Bonauto began by introducing her clients, noting that Gloria Bailey and Linda Davies were about to celebrate their thirty-second anniversary as a couple. "Everyone is aging, everyone is getting older, but some are also facing illness and the pressures of retirement, but because they cannot marry, they have added burdens," Bonauto said. Her brief had outlined the various legal measures the plaintiffs had taken to solidify their relationships—joint adoption, powers of attorney, shared ownership of property—but to the judges Bonauto emphasized the inadequacy of every arrangement short of marriage itself. "They are locked out of a precious right," she said, "one of the most important decisions any person can make in life, one that transforms an individual's legal status from an individual into a family with reciprocal obligations and extensive protections for that family."

Unlike in Hawaii and Vermont, Massachusetts lawmakers had taken proactive measures to restrict same-sex couples from marrying. The 1989 gay-rights bill that had generated Bonauto's first cases at GLAD had included, as a noncontroversial penultimate clause, "Nothing in this act shall be construed so as to legitimize or validate a 'homosexual marriage.'" When in 1993 the court ruled in favor of coparent adoption rights, observing that state statutes lack "any prohibition on adoption by two unmarried individuals," it noted that lesbian plaintiffs acknowledged "the laws of the Commonwealth do not permit them to enter into a legally cognizable marriage."

Indeed, lawyers at GLAD had previously taken pains when representing gay families in such matters not to provoke the court to express an opinion about marriage itself. "We needed to be extremely cautious about litigating marriage discrimination through the side door," wrote Bonauto. That was her rationale for discouraging the Chapel Hill Chauncy Hall School's Christine Huff from appealing the Massachusetts Commission on Discrimination's decision denying her the ability to live with her female companion "out of concern about muddying the waters for a possible marriage case some day."

Now Bonauto was finally in a position to argue not only that the state constitution compelled recognition of gay couples but, perhaps even more strenuously, that "the Vermont approach is not the best approach for this Court to take," as she put it. "When it comes to marriage, there really is no such thing as separating the word 'marriage' from the protections it provides. The reason for that is that one of the most important protections of marriage is the word, because the word is what conveys the status that everyone understands as the ultimate expression of love and commitment." In fact, asserted Bonauto, the Vermont outcome was not just a half measure that failed to go far enough—civil unions actually left gays and lesbians worse off than they had been before. "Creating a separate system, just for gay people," she said, "simply perpetuates the stigma of exclusion that we now face because it would essentially be branding gay people and our relationships as unworthy of this civil institution of marriage."

John Greaney, the only justice nominated by a Democratic governor, told Bonauto plainly that he was "certain" her side would prevail. "In an ideal world, perhaps, we should be able to get the people of Massachusetts to vote on this," he went on. Greaney then asked what would happen if Massachusetts voters were to be given the chance to amend the state's constitution at the next available opportunity, in November 2006. "I think by the end of those three years nothing has been taken away from their marriages," Bonauto responded. "But these other families who are now allowed to marry have been strengthened and that's good for the community as a whole."

Assistant Attorney General Yogman's speaking was monopolized by aggressive interrogation from Greaney and Marshall, who questioned the logic of the state's declared interest in strengthening the link between marriage, procreation, and child-rearing. "How do you reconcile what to me is a paradox, that the state acknowledges that same sex couples with children, who are permitted obviously to adopt children," Greaney asked Yogman, "don't constitute a family for purposes of being married?"

The entire oral argument lasted barely a half hour, and most of the seven justices did not betray an indication of how they were likely to vote once they reconvened in private. One early question to Bonauto from the bench indicated that the judges were not wrestling with the law as much as their possible place in history. "Why should we do something," asked Justice Judith Cowin, "no other state has done?"

Part Five

"OUR TEAM IS NOT WINNING"

(2003–2004)

We're the Marriage People

Barely one month had passed since oral arguments at Massachusetts's highest court left that state on the cusp of doing what both Hawaii and Vermont had not, fully recognizing same-sex unions without pause or compromise. But the secret deliberations under way in the justices' chambers in Boston, and the matter of same-sex marriage altogether, were far from David Blankenhorn's mind as he set out from his New York home for a five-hour southbound drive. When he reached the eastern shore of the Chesapeake Bay, he would reunite two dozen like-minded people from different walks of life, and Blankenhorn's thoughts were occupied with the fate of the cause to which they had devoted much of their lives. Was there anything in what they called the marriage movement left to fight for?

Blankenhorn was the child of Presbyterian deacons at a church that had been the first in its region of Mississippi to welcome black parishioners. As a fifteen-year-old, he started the Mississippi Community Service Corps, which brought together teenagers of both races to jointly tutor elementary-school students. When his family relocated to southwestern Virginia in the middle of high school, Blankenhorn canvassed church youth groups to start a new service corps there. His conscience shaped by the civil-rights movement, Blankenhorn went to work as a VISTA volunteer and then became an itinerant community organizer. In between, he earned a graduate degree from the University of Warwick, in England, with a distinction in comparative labor history. (His dissertation concerned a nineteenth-century British cabinetmakers' union.) Blankenhorn had little doubt about where those experiences and influences placed him on an ideological spectrum. "I considered myself politically left of center," he said.

As he spent time in disadvantaged communities, however, he grew bothered that political leaders who claimed to share his orientation rarely mentioned the number of children being raised by unmarried parents, or the absence of fathers altogether. Liberals treated family structure as a series of personal choices that should be free of judgment, and instead of looking within households saved their scorn for the outside forces that made life difficult for the inhabitants. They raged at landlords who ripped off tenants, utilities that capriciously raised rates, city governments that failed to deliver city services equitably across neighborhoods. "All of which were important and legitimate grievances," says Blankenhorn, "but they weren't fundamentally as important to why these communities were suffering as the decay of the basic family system."

In the middle of the Reagan years, this was emerging as a core divide in Washington. Republicans were espousing "family values," but Blankenhorn saw it as a shallow commitment, rhetorical cover for a moralizing politics free of any underlying interest in the social welfare of the disadvantaged. Meanwhile, Democratic leaders resisted the subject altogether, fearful of scolding what had become a core constituency or discounting the role of economic policy. "I thought what I was doing at the time was thinking about some important issues that the left had not really been dealing with," Blankenhorn says. "The left can and should do work on making families stronger."

By 1985, Blankenhorn had moved to New York City to be with the woman who would become his wife, and was trying to find work as a writer while driving a taxi to support himself. He was thirty years old. "As grandiose as only a young person can be," he says, "I decided to start a think tank to kind of rethink liberalism." To defy the existing polarization of the issue, he picked as conservative-sounding a name as he could come up with: the Institute for American Values. An editor placed atop a *New York Times* op-ed he wrote in 1986 a headline that Blankenhorn thought perfectly captured the spirit of his project: FAMILY VALUES, WITHOUT SUGARY PIETIES.

He described the institute's interests in broad terms—there was a lot of talk about "strengthening the family as an institution"—but he dismissed the goal of effecting policy change as "downstream" from its activity of shaping elite opinion. Blankenhorn worried that it had become out of vogue for academics to study the family in any way that could appear moralistic, and so a lot of what he wanted to do was merely support and incentivize that kind of research. He aspired to be "promiscuously interdisciplinary," as interested in what theologians had to say about the state of family as economists. In 1993, Blankenhorn helped cofound the National Father-hood Initiative, which could be involved in more direct advocacy than the think tank. Blankenhorn became chairman of the board; the group's founding president was Wade Horn, a clinical psychologist with a far more conventional orientation as a social conservative. "The argument must be made," Horn wrote in a 1999 collection he coedited with Blankenhorn, "frequently and with great passion—that society needs a critical mass of married two-parent families, both to raise their own children well and to serve as models for children growing up in alternative family structures."

These views were not without controversy. The emphasis on paternal obligation was intended to correct what Blankenhorn called the "excesses of feminism" and its demand for complete parity in matters such as "diaper changes or bottle feedings." In his book *Fatherless America*, Blankenhorn called for a restoration of traditional gender roles. "Historically, the good father protects his family, provides for its material needs, devotes himself to the education of his children, and represents his family's interests in the larger world. This work is necessarily rooted in a repertoire of inherited male values," he wrote. "The old father, with some updating in the nurtur-ing department, will do just fine."

The marriage movement inspired unusual coalition-building amid the fractious social politics of the 1990s. George H. W. Bush named Blanken-horn to his National Commission on America's Urban Families, and Bill Clinton hired a domestic-policy adviser, Bill Galston, from the Institute for American Values board. Vice President Al Gore summoned Blanken-horn to meet with him at the White House. Upon release of the insti-tute's 2000 manifesto, *The Marriage Movement: A Statement of Principles*, both parties' presidential nominees issued near-simultaneous messages of congratulation.

That document, which included 113 signatories, was remarkably plural-istic in its influences. There was still the language of the left that would have come naturally to a young Blankenhorn: "Marriage, a rich generator of social and human capital, must not become the private hoard of the upper-middle class, creating a new, disturbing marital divide between the haves and have-nots in America." But many of the specific policy initiatives it championed grew out of the religious right, like "covenant marriage" laws, recently enacted in two states, which allowed couples about to wed the opportunity to preemptively foreclose the option of no-fault divorce. The marriage movement was quite unambiguously a fan of intrusive big-government solutions to America's family crisis, citing with approval a policy enacted in 1999 by Texas governor George W. Bush to raise the state's marriage licensing fee by five dollars. The new funds were earmarked to create a "premarital education manual for distribution to all marrying couples" and require county clerks to keep a register of educators that would be provided to potential spouses.

Bush thought the marriage movement was the perfect embodiment of the "compassionate conservatism" on which he had run for the office, yet it was free of obvious political opponents. Bush could signal kinship to religious conservatives without alienating moderates, all while introducing policies that would most directly benefit the minority voters whom Bush adviser Karl Rove was eager to bring into the Republican coalition. Bush introduced a Healthy Marriage Initiative, which would offer federal support for local projects, targeted especially at low-income communities, such as counseling programs for couples before they wed. Bush named Horn, Blankenhorn's longtime collaborator, to a position at the Department of Health and Human Services from which it was understood he could nudge government resources and policy in family-friendly directions, some as simple as encouraging what Horn called "good casework" in welfare programs or Head Start. "I don't want to play Cupid," Horn told the *Weekly Standard*. "This isn't about telling anybody who should marry who. But when you have a couple who say, we're interested in getting married, or who are already married, it's about helping them develop the skills and knowledge necessary to form and sustain healthy marriages."

"Now everyone from the government to intellectuals are pushing marriage," the journalist Alex Kotlowitz reported in a PBS *Frontline* documentary on the "burgeoning marriage movement." For the first time since founding the Institute for American Values in 1987, Blankenhorn was dumbfounded about what to do next. In the summer of 2001, his institute released a report titled *Hooking Up, Hanging Out and Hoping for Mr. Right: College Women on Dating and Mating Today*. (Blankenhorn had always had an eye toward less grave manifestations of societal decline; at one point he wrote a short essay titled "I Do?" complaining about the trend of couples drafting their own wedding vows.)

In a pushback to the complacency bred by consensus, Blankenhorn made plans to host a conference in April 2003 labeled "The Future of the Marriage Movement." A New York summit in January 2000 had generated *The Marriage Movement: A Statement of Principles*, with its public commitment to "reduce divorce and unmarried childbearing," through a combination of policy interventions and cultural influence. Those whom Blankenhorn invited to meet him on a tributary of the Chesapeake Bay in Royal Oak, Maryland, would review what had happened in the three years since and update the earlier paper for publication the following year. "Are we making good on that pledge?" a document laying out the meeting's purpose asked. "What have we achieved? What are our main challenges for the rest of this decade? What are our goals for the immediate future?"

The venue that Blankenhorn selected, the Osprey Point Leadership Center, was an oversized colonial-style country house with a wraparound veranda. A few years earlier, a Christian nonprofit had acquired the waterfront compound and set out to renovate in the style of a luxurious monastery. (Its amenities included both tennis court and chapel.) Not long after Blankenhorn sent out invitations, the *Washington Times* would describe the compound as "a meeting place for leaders to reflect on meaningful issues."

Shortly after the twenty-seven attendees settled at the waterfront estate for their weekend-long session, one brought up something that Blankenhorn's coordinating team seemed to have overlooked in its meticulous planning of the conference. Massachusetts judges then deliberating over *Goodridge v. Department of Public Health* might not deliver their opinion until much later in 2003, but the friendly reception they had given Mary Bonauto during oral arguments appeared to prefigure a ruling in favor of the seven same-sex couples seeking to marry. In various corners of the American right, political and legal strategists were already plotting whether to amend the U.S. Constitution—for the first time in a generation—to preempt Massachusetts and other states from deviating from the historical definition of what constituted a marriage.

Certainly a statement about the condition of marriage in America would have to contend with these developments. When the attendee raised the Massachusetts lawsuit, Blankenhorn attempted to steer the conversation away from it. At its first meeting, in 1987, the Institute of American Values' board came to agreement that there were two matters the organization would not address in any form—abortion and homosexuality—"because those were issues that would make any broad based coalition on anything else impossible," according to Blankenhorn. In 2002, he had presided over a marriage conference in Washington and had proudly avoided any mention of gay unions—an act of avoidance so conspicuous that a reporter for the *Washington Post* wrote about how the marriage controversy of the day had gone unaddressed at a marriage conference. Blankenhorn had been hoping to repeat that feat. Gay marriage wasn't on the agenda, he insisted.

A pale woman with a bowl cut raised her hand. She was head of the Institute for American Values' Marriage Program, contributor to its Family Scholars blog, and a regular participant in these conferences. She was also, by dint of a syndicated newspaper column that regularly appeared in the *New York Post* and *Washington Times*, and an earlier book *Enemies of Eros*, one of the few people in the room whose name might be recognized by laypeople.

"We're the marriage movement," protested Maggie Gallagher. She insisted on a discussion about the merits of same-sex marriage. "It's not theoretical, it's coming. I don't even know what you think about this. I don't know what anyone here thinks about this!"

Gallagher nevertheless understood Blankenhorn's hesitation. One of the reasons the marriage movement "thought we had won the intellectual debate," as she put it, was that it had avoided the most immediately vituperative quarrels over sexual politics. Never typecast as an offshoot of the religious right, the marriage movement had instead found consensus by picking around the edges of the "family values" debate for priorities much harder to polarize. "After ten years I could walk into any room and say that ideally it's better for children to be born to married couples, provided that that marriage is not high-conflict or violent, and almost nobody wanted to disagree," she says.

For someone who wrote almost exclusively about marriage, Gallagher had been conspicuously understated about whether or how gay people should be granted access to it. In 1995, she had contributed to the Council on Families in America's *Marriage in America: A Report to the Nation*, where she wryly proposed the policy objective of having "more marriages that succeed than fail." A book she wrote the following year, *The Abolition of Marriage*, was far more concerned with the advent of no-fault divorces than recognition of same-sex relationships. In fact, during the summer of 1996 when Congress was consumed by an emotionally intense debate over the Defense of Marriage Act, Gallagher shunned it. Instead, in the month that the bill came to the House floor, she devoted one of her newspaper columns to assessing the tax-credit provisions in a Democratic "Family First Agenda."

Gay marriage was easy to ignore because it seemed like an issue generated by the media and stoked by activists. When in 1989 she saw the *New Republic*'s cover story titled "The Case for Gay Marriage," Gallagher laughed—not because she was immediately contemptuous of its argument but because she found the idea simply implausible. She followed lefty thought closely enough to realize that the gay community was far from unified behind marriage as an objective, and that pro-gay politicians were never going to champion it. "I thought it was kind of a red herring, so I didn't write about it, I didn't think a lot about it," says Gallagher. "I wasn't very concerned about it."

But it was no longer possible to laugh it off. Coverage of the oral arguments in Massachusetts suggested that it was very likely that gay-rights activists could prevail there, and certainly after Vermont that did not seem implausible at all. Gallagher's insistence that the subject was worth at least a discussion carried the day. Acknowledging Blankenhorn's protests that it was not on his agenda, the attendees agreed to adjourn the meeting and start a new conversation about marriage in an adjacent room.

The meeting reassembled there. William Doherty, a University of Minnesota professor of family social sciences who was part of the Institute for American Values, coordinating team for the conference, took charge to get the conversation started. Doherty proposed what counselors called a "fishbowl technique," in which he would interview five people as a way of starting a broader conversation. Doherty requested volunteers, and Gallagher offered herself as one of the five. He began by asking her what she thought about homosexuality.

"Bill," she said, "that's really not what's weighing on my heart."

In her newspaper columns, Gallagher had touched on the issue of same-sex marriage, intuitively resistant to change in that direction but never having fully thought out why. Two years earlier, she and a sociologist named Linda J. Waite had collaborated on a book titled *The Case for Marriage: Why Married People Are Happier, Healthier, and Better Off Financially*. Unable to dodge the question of gay relationships altogether, they included this almost legalistically cautious note before tepidly exploring the subject: "As private citizens, the authors have reached different conclusions, with Linda Waite tending to favor and Maggie Gallagher tending to oppose extending marriage to same-sex couples." Gallagher considered herself foremost a writer, not a political figure, with no obligation to maintain a firmly held, unequivocal position on every issue of the day.

It was under Doherty's questioning that Gallagher felt for the first time truly forced to formulate a rationale for "tending to oppose extending marriage to same-sex couples." She began by reiterating the movement's gospel, that marriage existed to raise children, who needed both a mother and father to thrive. Marriage was the one social institution that claimed that objective as its sole priority. If those who believed in marriage weakened their insistence that it was about a mother and a father together, what other concessions would they be expected to make? How could she possibly go to Massachusetts and argue that "marriage really matters because children need a mom and a dad" if the law said otherwise?

Gallagher looked around the room and noted, with unexpected satisfaction, that what she said seemed to be resonating with the other attendees, but despite their agreement they were nonetheless taken aback by what she had said. "It startled them because no one had heard this," she says.

Not long thereafter, Gallagher approached Blankenhorn and told him, "I have to do something about this." As she saw it, if there was to be a national debate over gay marriage, it should not be left only to those who reflexively fought any move toward gay rights. "You know, we're the marriage people," she insisted. "Everyone wants to talk about it as being about homosexuality. We have to explain what's at stake for marriage."

In the preamble to *The Marriage Movement: A Statement of Principles*, Blankenhorn had asserted that "whether an individual ever personally marries or not, a healthy marriage culture benefits every citizen in the United States: rich or poor, churched or unchurched, gay or straight," although he had never elucidated that last point. When sought out for his opinion on recognizing gay couples, Blankenhorn seemed to be less disturbed by the relationships themselves than by the reputational damage that would be done to marriage by generating contractual facsimiles. Domestic partnerships, he told *Time* in 1989, "just misses the whole point of why we confer privileges on family relationships." When the city of Philadelphia the next year considered granting benefits to municipal workers' unmarried partners, Blankenhorn cautioned that "there is a difference between what we permit and what we promote." He told the *Philadelphia Inquirer* that "I'm glad we do not outlaw alternative living arrangements. But where I part company is where that's not enough, where we promote them as the moral and social equal of any other type of relationship."

Pushed by Gallagher to recognize the urgency of addressing same-sex marriage, Blankenhorn was just as uncertain of his position on it. It was a potentially existential misalignment, not over the substance of the issue but how readily it could be avoided. Blankenhorn told her the issue was a "tar baby." He would not let himself get stuck to it, or defined by it. After the Osprey Point meeting, Blankenhorn offered Gallagher a deal. He would grant her permission to begin raising money to develop a program at the Institute for American Values to focus on gay marriage, but it could not be used to promote only one perspective on the issue. When the *New York Times*'s religion columnist called in June, Blankenhorn had a well-constructed quip at the ready—"People who haven't had much positive to say about marriage are suddenly enthusiastic, as long as you put the words 'same sex' in front of it"—but nothing substantive to say about the policy itself. "David had a vision of entering the marriage debate as a debate," says Gallagher, "gathering people on both sides as long as they had a sincere commitment to marriage as a social institution."

She found a donor willing to contribute $15,000 to get her new program started, and began to design a website that would be a hub for the institute's work. At the same time, Gallagher sought out Jonathan Rauch, a gay journalist who had been among the most industrious proponents of same-sex marriage but always within a traditionalist vernacular that the Institute for American Values crowd shared. (As early as 1994, on the *Wall Street Journal* op-ed page, Rauch had proposed a truce with Christian conservatives under the rubric of "A Pro-Gay, Pro-Family Policy," dismissing benefits for unmarried couples in terms similar to Blankenhorn's.) With Rauch committed to serving as her principal sparring partner, Gallagher made plans to launch MarriageDebate.com to coincide with the arrival of the *Goodridge* decision from Massachusetts.

In late June 2003, a number of those who had been present at Osprey Point met again in Reno. The Smart Marriages conference was a sector-wide event for those involved in the ongoing work of making marriages work, with copious continuing-education credits on offer for therapists and counselors. The gathering was suffused with the triumphalist spirit that comes with seeing what were once pet initiatives and one-off experiments now being sponsored by the president of the United States. Doherty, who had helped moderate the splinter session at Osprey Point, remarked in a keynote speech that at that point only two things could divide the marriage movement: disputes over who gets funding and the issue already riving the Institute for American Values. "If we do not deliberate about gay marriage," Doherty said, "we are at risk of splitting apart over it."

42

A Sense of Where the Culture Is Headed

Many of the social-conservative leaders who had been loudest in agitating for a nationwide response to the situation in Hawaii went largely quiet about same-sex unions after the passage of the Defense of Marriage Act. In their view, the law had successfully insulated the rest of the country from one state's activist judges, as other states would have no responsibility to acknowledge its marriages and federal benefits would become off-limits to gay couples. National attention moved away from the cause, onto other culture-war conflicts. But some who shunned the limelight continued strategizing in the shadows. They adjudged that their work was, in fact, far from over, and that only a far more drastic series of political actions, in both Washington and the states, could truly keep same-sex marriage at bay.

In early 1996, just as it was kicking off its Hawaii's Future Today campaign and months before the issue was taken up on Capitol Hill, the Church of Jesus Christ of Latter-day Saints formed the Interfaith Discussion Group on the Legislation of Same-Sex Marriage to expand upon its ad hoc Honolulu coalition and enlist leaders of other religious denominations to coordinate efforts on the mainland. The Marriage Law Project was founded later that year, in collaboration with Mormon and Catholic leaders, to generate scholarly research, but it was often deployed as a research arm for church officials working to stymie gay-marriage efforts in the states. "Direct funding by the Church of a scholarly conference, however, may provoke criticism and raise questions that could divert attention from the purpose of the conference and even detract from the credibility of the conference," Brigham Young University law professor Lynn Wardle wrote to Elder Marlin K. Jensen in May 1997. "One way would be to make the funds transfer directly to and for the Marriage Law Project, not to or explicitly for the conference."

The Marriage Law Project's director, David Orgon Coolidge, claimed his official home at the Ethics and Public Policy Center, a conservative Washington think tank, but throughout the late 1990s he was often wherever a state appeared to be on the cusp of making gay marriage a reality. "It's the great American game: Sue until you win," Coolidge would joke. He hopscotched from one playing field to the next, blurring the roles of academic researcher, freelance legal strategist, lobbyist, and journalist. In Honolulu, he had secured a press credential to cover the *Baehr* trial for the *Hawaii Catholic Herald,* but also plotted with state legislators about the best language for a reciprocal-beneficiaries bill and offered strategic advice to local Catholic officials, as he did with the dioceses of Anchorage and Burlington. He was most useful as a source of human intelligence about the relative strength of local players. This kept church leaders ahead of official reports in newspapers and court dockets. While denominational officials were content with their eventual successes blocking the legalization of gay marriage, Coolidge was already anticipating the next phase. "What do we do if we lose somewhere?" he asked.

In the fall of 1998, Coolidge had posed that question to lawyers who had gathered in Scottsdale, Arizona. The aim of the meeting was to plot a common strategy for their efforts to beat back gay marriage. Scottsdale was home of the Alliance Defense Fund, which had been established in 1993 by some of the country's most influential religious conservatives, including James Dobson and Gary Bauer, to support "the legal defense and advocacy of religious freedom, the sanctity of human life and family values." Various legal organizations had popped up around the country with similar ends, each invariably claiming it intended to be the right's answer to the ACLU. The Alliance Defense Fund wanted to become a central funding source for all: small, public-interest firms would no longer rely entirely on their own fundraising, and in exchange political leaders would be able to exert some control over their movement's legal priorities. Several of those groups were represented at the Scottsdale meeting, along with a number of law professors on whom their attorneys often relied. They listened as activists from each of the states with active marriage litigation—at that point Hawaii, Alaska, and Vermont—reported on local conditions, followed by one from California, where a Mormon-led group had begun supporting efforts to place an initiative to ban gay marriage on the state's ballot.

When it was Coolidge's turn, he wondered what would happen when gay activists won a court case in a state where there was no option of taking the matter directly to the people via referendum. Coolidge was ushering the group to an unavoidable conclusion. Only by amending the Constitution could they safely abolish same-sex marriage for all time in the United States. The most active voices in the discussion were enthusiastic about the idea. Wardle, attending the meeting as an emissary of the Latter-day Saints, was the most vocal dissenter.

"While a proposal for a constitutional amendment may help to show how serious the situation is and might even be considered a last-resort measure, I think it would be divisive, cloud the issue, divert attention and would be at best premature as the first-response," Wardle reported back to church elders in Salt Lake City, including Apostle Dallin Oaks. "Advocates of radical proposals like same-sex marriage must now convince 50 courts or legal systems (one in each state) to legalize same-sex marriage; if the issue is constitutionalized, they will have to convince only one court system. I suggested that the best way to respond to any state legalizing same-sex marriage is on a state-by-state rejection basis. That requires a lot of work, 50 diverse state efforts rather than just one national effort, but the process of working state-by-state will be educational for the citizenry, strengthen local family values, and I believe that family policy should reflect local mores."

Wardle's caution was not well received among the other attendees at the Scottsdale session, most of whom represented organizations national in scope or with ambition to become so. Only one attendee, a legislative aide from Sacramento, voiced agreement with Wardle. Supporters of a constitutional amendment thought it could get through Congress in nine months, before going out to the states for ratification. Regardless, it was agreed, only until after a state had changed its marriage laws did it make sense to begin the effort in earnest.

In 1999, Coolidge observed events in Massachusetts that persuaded him there might be someone capable of taking the issue of a constitutional amendment to the American public even in the absence of a major precipitating event. Late the previous year, a Democratic state representative in Massachusetts had introduced a bill to limit marriage to opposite-sex couples, effectively a state-level Defense of Marriage Act even if its supporters shied away from that description. By that point, nearly three dozen states had enacted such laws, but what was notable about the (ultimately unsuccessful) effort in Massachusetts was the May 1999 press conference to announce it. Standing together were an Orthodox rabbi, the imam of the Islamic Center of New England, the pastor of the region's largest Asian evangelical church, and leaders of the Black Ministerial Alliance, which had endorsed the bill. "You might say a rainbow coalition had turned out to stand up for marriage," Coolidge marveled in the *Weekly Standard* the following month. "This development was no happenstance, but the fruit of long efforts by the Massachusetts Family Institute to build a coalition as ecumenical as marriage itself. Over three years, director Matt Daniels had forged the relationships that made this day possible."

Coolidge was not the first observer to be taken by both the accomplishments and potential of Daniels, who was only thirty-five but already had the bearing of a politician. "With his well-spoken manner, his Ivy League education, and his business card reading 'President, Massachusetts Family Institute,' Mr. Daniels is the picture of youthful American success," a reporter for the *Christian Science Monitor* had written at the top of a profile.

The Massachusetts Family Institute was part of Focus on the Family's network of state affiliates and undertook a combination of lobbying on moral issues and practical work like sending volunteer doctors into schools to teach abstinence. But after becoming its president in 1996, shortly after receiving his law degree and while pursuing doctoral studies at Brandeis, Daniels converted the group into something that looked more like a local clone of the Institute for American Values. He began releasing an annual report on fatherlessness and family decline, timed for media coverage just ahead of Father's Day. The first report, issued in 1997, estimated that over 27 percent of Massachusetts families were fatherless, enough to qualify as an "emergency," as Daniels said. "We've had anti-drug, anti-drunken driving campaigns here in Massachusetts. We'd like to see that kind of attention brought to fatherlessness," he told the Associated Press. He had a raft of policy proposals designed to address the problem: more aggressive child-support collection, tougher penalties for statutory rape, welfare reforms that encouraged marriage, incentives for couples who adopted children, and divorce reform that would include mandatory counseling and a waiting period before couples could split. "Kids do best with a mom and a dad," Daniels explained. "That's not a statement of animosity toward anyone. It's an affirmation of a social norm."

The conflict with gay activists over the marriage ban pushed Daniels to expand his political ambitions. "Our side tends often to think in terms of election cycles. It's very myopic. But the culture is bigger than that. The gay leaders think culturally and they think long-term. They were a socially marginalized group in this society as recently as the 1950s and early 1960s, and they've maneuvered their way into the central culture until they are part of the establishment in Massachusetts and other havens of liberalism," Daniels said in the summer of 1999. "What's going on in Massachusetts is a bit of a foretaste of what will be going on in the American mainstream in 15 or 20 years."

Under those conditions, Daniels concluded, defenders of traditional marriage should be striving to enshrine their views in the U.S. Constitution while still operating from a position of cultural strength. After the birth of his first child, Daniels moved to Washington to plot such a campaign, even if he couched it in the largely noncontroversial language that David Blankenhorn and his marriage-movement allies had routed into the American mainstream. "What is needed now is a broad-based, national movement that unites Americans from all cultural, ethnic, and religious backgrounds to reaffirm and promote marriage in America," the group's mission statement asserted. It was easy to read the entire document, and other materials Daniels produced for public consumption at the time, oblivious that same-sex relations were anywhere on his mind. The draft text Daniels wrote for the group's first brochure went no further than three references to "the union of a man and a woman." None specified that the most urgent threat to that union was the prospect of two women seeking to wed and not, for example, a woman splitting up with a man or his abandoning the child they had together. "Marriage is being taken for granted and has even come under attack. They say it holds back some and oppresses others," Daniels wrote in the most direct reference to the efforts of gay activists. "They wish to tarnish the luster of marriage. And that hurts us all."

The story Daniels told of how he came to the marriage cause had nothing to do with homosexuality. He had been born in Spanish Harlem to an Irish mother and father. His father, a poet who had translated the works of Andrei Sakharov, left the family when Matt was three. Growing up in the 1970s, Daniels was repeatedly mugged in his neighborhood. One day, returning home from her job as a secretary, his mother was beaten by four men, an incident that left her with a bad back, incapable of working, and dependent on welfare and addicted to alcohol. Daniels described his childhood as "miserable" and credits only his mother's "moral compass" for motivating him to escape—first to Dartmouth on a scholarship, and then the University of Pennsylvania for law school. He often recalled the impact of hearing, on his first day of family-law class, a professor assert that she "would challenge anyone to show how the absence of men from families has any adverse effect on children."

Proving that professor wrong may have been his primary cause in Massachusetts, but he made clear by the time he landed in Washington that any talk of divorce or fatherlessness was cover for his true mission. "In addition to general language affirming the importance of marriage for children and society, the committee will also discuss positive proposals completely unrelated to homosexual marriage—touching on areas such as education, business, and government policy—that our alliance should consider endorsing," Daniels wrote to Susan Gibbs of the Roman Catholic Archdiocese of Washington prior to the launch of the Alliance for Marriage.

Gibbs shared the alliance's materials with participants in the Interfaith Discussion Group during its December 1999 meeting, held at the General Conference of Seventh-Day Adventists World Headquarters in Silver Spring, Maryland. Attendees, representing six different denominations, all of which considered themselves Christian, were wary of Daniels— unsure of his motives, his potential funders' motives, afraid of potential turf battles that might ensue—but they did see his use. Given that religious organizations were constrained by the tax code from certain types of direct political activity, a pure advocacy group devoted to fighting gay marriage was legally capable of doing things the churches couldn't. Daniels "may provide a means of responding if Vermont fails," Coolidge advised. "I don't plan to lend my name publicly at this point, but maybe he'll do something good."

Daniels had always struck those who encountered him as a young man in a hurry, but he had been particularly rushed in trying to launch his group for what he described as two reasons: "1) The threat of a pending court action; and 2) The need for materials to help me in my fundraising efforts." He incorporated the Alliance for Marriage just before the end of 1999, but when it became clear early the next year that the Vermont case would end with a resolution other than marriage, Daniels was able to slow down again.

In April 2000, Daniels went to Capitol Hill to test congressional support for a possible constitutional amendment. He had few legislative contacts of his own, but the support of some venerable institutions— notably the Southern Baptist Convention, the country's largest Protestant denomination—validated his efforts. "It is hoped that this meeting will be the start of a quiet campaign to line up support for a federal marriage amendment in advance of a judicially created national crisis on this issue," Daniels wrote to Richard Land, the Southern Baptist Convention's top political official. Daniels presented the draft language to sixteen congressional staffers, including advisers to the House leadership and prominent members of the Senate's Republican majority, and emerged with conditional support for pursuing an amendment. "He's a guy who sees around corners," says Bill Wichterman, who attended the meeting as an aide to Pennsylvania Republican Joe Pitts. "He's got a sense of where the culture is headed."

Coolidge had already begun convening a group at the Ethics and Public Policy Center to determine how to write a definition of marriage into the U.S. Constitution. It would not be unprecedented: Marriage Law Project research uncovered forty-three countries whose national constitutions included some statement about marriage or family. Even if it was understood that the goal was to use the federal constitution to ensure that no state's judges could change the definition of marriage, it was not self-evident what legal mechanisms one would use to do so. The few states that had banned gay marriage by constitutional amendment had found it did not require more than a sentence. (The one passed by Alaska voters had declared, "To be valid or recognized in this State, a marriage may exist only between one man and one woman.")

Two of the scholars Daniels recruited, Hadley Arkes and Robert George, had a common interest in natural law and shared outrage about what a *First Things* symposium in which they both had participated called "the judicial usurpation of politics." (A third legal scholar who joined them, Harvard Law School professor Mary Ann Glendon, was known for her close ties to the Catholic Church hierarchy.) All three had previously worked on drafting and promoting antiabortion laws, an experience that left them familiar with the unsatisfying balancing act between moral principle and the practical consideration necessary to ensure their amendment would be politically viable. "People involved in those early discussions thought same-sex marriage in the courts was going to happen," said George, who taught at Princeton. "But we had a lot of trouble convincing other people to take it seriously. It seemed too distant and unlikely. And politicians weren't going to cross that bridge until they'd come to it."

Partly to help win credibility from lawmakers, the Alliance for Marriage enlisted former federal appeals-court judge Robert Bork to join the group. After he was named to the Supreme Court by Ronald Reagan but was rejected by a Senate that found him at once too candid and too extreme, Bork became a martyr to conservatives. In 1996, while a fellow at the American Enterprise Institute, Bork reached the best-seller list with his jeremiad *Slouching Towards Gomorrah,* in which he declared the United States "on the road to cultural disaster." Often he turned blame for this toward those still on the bench, where he claimed judges were twisting constitutional interpretation toward socially liberal ends they desired. "Because the court misused the state constitution rather than the federal one to achieve its result, review by the U.S. Supreme Court is unavailable," Bork wrote in the *Wall Street Journal* two days after the Vermont Supreme Court's ruling in *Baker v. State.* "The truth is that these are not constitutional rulings but moral edicts, and the morality enforced is a minority morality, one directly contrary to the morality a majority of Americans want to have enforced by statute. What, then, gives what these courts are doing any claim to legitimacy? The answer is, nothing."

After a year of negotiations on the language of the amendment, at a cost of $40,000 to the Alliance Defense Fund, the Alliance for Marriage emerged with two sentences that it called the Federal Marriage Amendment: "Marriage in the United States shall consist only of the union of a man and a woman. Neither this constitution or the constitution of any state, nor state or federal law, shall be construed to require the marital status or the legal incidents thereof be conferred upon unmarried couples or groups."

When he launched the campaign to pass the Federal Marriage Amendment, in July 2001, Daniels was careful to present it as something other than an outright national ban on same-sex marriage. "Let's challenge the homosexual movement to play fair on the playing field of democracy," he told the Associated Press. "If they want the benefits of marriage allocated to a wider circle of groups, they need to convince the majority of people that it's the right thing." He said the bill would be introduced in Congress that fall; for now he was giving the impression that the idea of amending the constitution had bubbled up from the community. "We believe this is more important than partisan politics," he explained. "So we'll announce it with no politicians at the microphone."

43

Enemy of the Good

When he was trying to explain his strategy for passing the Federal Marriage Amendment, Matt Daniels would often cite the example of a mentor, Philadelphia conservative activist Bill Devlin, and his successful campaign to beat back city hall's plan to place casinos near residential areas. "We assembled a multiethnic, interracial coalition with black clergy, Asian clergy, Hispanic clergy, and we said to the politicians, 'We already have enough human wreckage to deal with in our neighborhoods,'" Daniels recalled. "Typically, for lack of sophistication or understanding about how the system works, the Christian community will not be proactive but will wait until a known social evil has been exported into their community before taking action. . . . With a little sophistication, you can go upstream and keep it from coming down in the first place."

As he had in Massachusetts, Daniels had spent much of his time in Washington working to "reach out extensively to groups who will make our alliance more than just a white, conservative, Republican affair," as he explained his objective. At a National Press Club news conference, the results of that approach became evident: Daniels unveiled a forty-five-member advisory board for the Alliance for Marriage, filled primarily with religious leaders, although not a single one given a prominent role was a white Protestant. Instead news coverage identified representatives of the Chinese Community Church of Washington, the Union of Orthodox Jewish Congregations, the African Methodist Episcopal Church, and the Alianza Ministerial Evangélica Nacional.

Daniels credited the black church with his own spiritual awakening—it was volunteering at a Harlem soup kitchen that he said led him to be born again—and in politics he saw African American clergy as a way to preemptively rebut any claim gay activists thought they had to the legacy of the civil-rights movement. In Massachusetts, he had recruited one of Martin Luther King Jr.'s nieces to endorse his anti-gay-marriage bill. Now for the Federal Marriage Amendment, he did even better. Standing beside him at the National Press Club was Reverend Walter Fauntroy, who had helped organize King's March on Washington in 1963 and had been by his side at the White House when the Civil Rights Act was signed the following year. "It is outrageous to claim that any of these people are motivated by hatred or bigotry in standing up because they believe that there is something uniquely beneficial for children and society when the two halves of the human race come together to parent," Daniels said.

The Human Rights Campaign and ACLU followed Daniels's press conference with one of their own, at which an attorney for the latter called the amendment a "legal equivalent of a nuclear bomb." Daniels took solace in the hyperbole. "Perhaps the greatest confirmation of the fact that the modern homosexual movement is threatened by our amendment strategy is the rhetoric that they have used to attack us," Daniels wrote to supporters. "No doubt this is because the ACLU, and homosexual activist groups, understand that the combination of AFM's diverse coalition, reasonable and centrist message, and politically viable marriage amendment text, is profoundly threatening to their goal."

Much of that success had been achieved through intentionally minimizing the contributions of more predictable allies. The Federal Marriage Amendment had active support from some stalwarts of religious conservative politics, including the Traditional Values Coalition, Home School Legal Defense Association, Focus on the Family, and many of its state "family policy council" affiliates. Daniels, however, was conscious not to draw attention to them. "We have confounded many of our critics with our reasonable and centrist message of advocating for both marriage and democracy," Daniels crowed to one evangelical leader.

But a patient, deliberate approach to coalition-building had denied Daniels the opportunity to make his strongest impression on the political culture. He had not, contrary to the plotting from Scottsdale onward, waited until a court shocked the country by actually legalizing gay marriage. When he had announced his campaign to pass a Federal Marriage Amendment, in July 2001, it seemed to come out of nowhere. The *Goodridge* suit had been filed three months earlier, but as the parties were still preparing preliminary motions the case had received scant notice outside Massachusetts.

The closest thing to urgency came from the Netherlands, which that April rewrote its marriage laws to treat same-sex couples no differently than opposite-sex ones. The Defense of Marriage Act's authors had specifically addressed only the full-faith-and-credit issues that would be triggered by a state's change in marriage laws, not a foreign country's. (No one involved in drafting the 1996 bill had speculated about what would happen if, for example, an American citizen wed a Dutchman in Amsterdam and then returned home and asked his home state to treat them as married.) But Americans paid little attention to the news from the Netherlands, and a constitutional amendment continued to seem like a farfetched political prospect irrelevant to the news of the day. The press conference to unveil the Federal Marriage Amendment went unmentioned in the *Washington Post, New York Times,* and *Boston Globe.*

When news organizations eventually did begin to report on the amendment, they usually went back to the same established figures they sought out for a Christian-conservative opinion on any issue related to sexuality. "Few television outlets even know of the existence of Matt Daniels or the Alliance for Marriage. When covering the Federal Marriage Amendment, TV news shows tend to interview spokesmen for the Family Research Counsel [*sic*]," lamented *National Review*'s Stanley Kurtz. "It is simply bad journalism to treat the Family Research Council as the chief spokesman for the Federal Marriage Amendment, while failing to interview Matt Daniels, whose organization actually drafted the amendment and is shepherding it through Congress. So through a kind of ripple effect, the major papers' poor coverage of this issue is already muddling our national debate."

It was an ironic elision, one particularly cruel for Daniels, since the Family Research Council had emerged as his most venomous critic. The day after Daniels's press conference, Family Research Council president Ken Connor accused him of "great confusion where there should be moral clarity." Even Daniels's seemingly innocuous dare of "the homosexual movement to play fair on the playing field of democracy" provoked Connor's ire. "We emphatically disagree with this definition of democracy," he wrote to council supporters.

The Family Research Council had not always been resistant to the idea of using a constitutional amendment to prevent gay marriage. In fact, the group had been active in the early stages of the Alliance for Marriage's work on the subject. In the midst of the drafting process, the Family Research Council—along with Concerned Women for America—walked away from the negotiating table over a very specific disagreement. "The amendment as drafted would protect the word 'marriage,' but not the institution. While it strips the courts of the authority to impose same-sex unions on unwilling states, advocates admit that the amendment would permit state legislatures to enact such unions or extend all legal benefits and incidents of marriage to other novel arrangements, thereby emptying the institution of any meaningful substance," Connor explained. The Federal Marriage Amendment would not have stopped Vermont's civil unions from being enacted, he argued.

In a nine-page memo titled "Why the Family Research Council Cannot Endorse the Proposed Federal Marriage Amendment," the group followed up with a mixture of legal reasoning, social observation, and political calculation. Beyond Vermont, the memo cited the California Family Protection Act of 2001, which proposed creating civil unions for partners of any sex to qualify for all the rights and benefits "currently afforded only to different-sex couples by California's civil marriage laws." It failed to pass the state assembly in 2002, but the FRC memo reasoned that Daniels's amendment would have been helpless to block the bill, which reflected a legislative initiative undertaken free of judicial pressure. "Counterfeit 'marriage' masquerading as a 'civil union' must be resisted as strongly as permitting same-sex individuals to marry," it insisted. At the end of the nine-page memo, the Family Research Council offered up the language of an alternate amendment—inelegant by comparison, a bit longer and far less ambiguous than the Alliance for Marriage's.

Yet the Family Research Council was not quite endorsing its own proposed marriage amendment either. The legislative text it included in the memo had been tethered to a blurry condition: "if a constitutional amendment is introduced, we would suggest the following language be used." Around the same time, Connor told the evangelical magazine *World* that the very idea of an amendment was itself concession of weakness. "The Constitution is not the problem. That's implied when you seek an amendment," said Connor. "The problem is activist judges who don't respect its language. We shouldn't kid ourselves that these judges won't be willing to misconstrue future language."

Connor would later explain that all his skepticism about an amendment campaign had originated from his experience joining Daniels for meetings with congressional Republicans. There, Connor saw that "the political types didn't care about it other than its utility for the upcoming election," as he later explained to a journalist. "I was concerned they'd manipulate us."

The bluntness of the Family Research Council's assault on the Federal Marriage Amendment's credibility rankled some of the group's natural allies. Quite a few in the council's evangelical cohort had lined up with the Alliance for Marriage, some of them particularly impressed with Daniels's ability to launder one of their priorities through a coalition fronted by leaders of other, more demographically diverse and less overtly ideological religious movements. Daniels may have been a parvenu to Washington and the world of conservative lobbying there, but so too was his emergent nemesis. Connor was a Florida attorney and failed political candidate who had been named to the national post only in 2000.

Connor's nominal sponsor was James Dobson, the California therapist who had risen to prominence through books, a newsletter, and a radio show that he consolidated as Focus on the Family. Dobson had spun off the Family Research Council in the late 1980s as a combination of think tank and advocacy organization. Throughout the following decade it had been the most reliable presence lobbying Congress on moral issues. (It was during this period that the council staffers developed the close relationship with Senator Don Nickles that led directly to his work developing the Defense of Marriage Act.) Dobson arranged to support the council's work financially, although the two entities he created operated at a mutually beneficial distance that permitted Focus on the Family's Colorado Springs campus to maintain its tax-exempt status as a ministry while its sister organization spent freely to effect more worldly outcomes. "Focus saw FRC as its Washington embassy," according to Dobson biographer Dan Gilgoff. "To FRC meanwhile, its ties to Dobson, Focus, and their vast constituency were what distinguished it from the Christian Right paper tigers that inhabited Washington."

Fearing that the Family Research Council's attacks could irreparably harm the Federal Marriage Amendment's prospects in Congress, the Southern Baptist Convention's Richard Land sought out Dobson to intercede. The two men agreed on much, but they had begun on opposite sides of the last amendment fight to divide evangelical leaders, one that split the movement for several years in the 1990s. The judicial and legislative branches were in a tug-of-war throughout the decade over how far government could go to ensure a right to religious expression without running afoul of the Constitution's clause separating church and state. Since the 1960s, the Supreme Court had often found itself secularizing the public square, first by ending organized prayer in schools. In 1990, it went even further, upholding the right of Oregon officials to deny unemployment benefits to members of a Native American church who had been fired after testing positive for drugs, even though they claimed it was from peyote ingested as part of a religious ritual. Congress responded by passing the Religious Freedom Restoration Act, which heightened the burden of proof necessary for a government to justify curtailing an individual's free exercise of religion. The Supreme Court in 1997 gutted the act, claiming its standard was overly broad. At that point, congressional Republicans responded with a constitutional amendment that would, as written, "secure the people's right to acknowledge God according to the dictates of conscience."

The Religious Freedom Amendment introduced in 1997 by Congressman Ernest Istook was enthusiastically supported by many of the country's most prominent Christian activist groups, including Dobson's Focus on the Family and Family Research Council. The Southern Baptist Convention and the National Association of Evangelicals opposed it. Land, who had a doctorate in religious history from Oxford University, became the amendment's most erudite critic on the right, arguing that it went too far toward state sponsorship of a religion. While Dobson and others like the American Family Association and Concerned Women for America were eager to deploy the newfound political power of evangelicals to Christianize as much of American life as possible, Land labeled the movement toward "neo-establishment majoritarianism" contrary to the faith shared by many of those groups' members and leaders. He repeatedly cited the Southern Baptist Convention's 1963 confessional statement, Baptist Faith and Message, which declared that "the church should not resort to the civil power to carry on its work."

Within the culture wars that had split Southern Baptists in the 1980s, Land was a conservative. When faced with the binary choices of Capitol Hill his stubborn adherence to what seemed a premodern vision of Baptist retreat from the broader culture occasionally left him allied with church-state separationists like the ACLU. After backing a 1995 Southern Baptist Convention resolution that encouraged lawmakers to draft an amendment that would ensure religious liberty—and personally participating in negotiations with them about specific language—Land concluded that the most viable version of the religious-freedom proposal to emerge was "awful and appalling" and "denies everything we believe as Baptists." As he explained, "Istook's amendment would replace one form of government discrimination (ie; preference for the secular or nonreligious) with another (ie; preference for the religious views of the majority)." Land entreated congressional leaders not to allow the amendment to come to the floor and ultimately asked representatives to vote against it. "One of the oldest axioms in public life is that policies which unite your opponents and divide your friends are a bad idea," Land wrote to House majority leader Dick Armey in 1996. "The Istook amendment proposal embodies precisely that kind of policy. It brings maximum unity to our opponents and maximum division to our friends."

Years later, facing the prospect of another split among religious conservatives over a marriage amendment whose broad goals they all shared, Land pushed Dobson to crack down on the rogue lobbying operation he had chartered. "It is not my habit to appeal to the boards of other organizations; however I believe the threat is so great that I must," Land wrote Dobson. "I share your desire to return our nation to a biblical view of the sanctity of marriage. However, we cannot let the perfect be the enemy of the good."

That uneasy equilibrium within Dobson's empire was broken in 2002 when Princeton professor Robert George was elected to the Family Research Council's board of directors. George was the first Catholic to hold such a post, but given the internal politics at the time it was more notable that he had been on the team of legal scholars whom Daniels had enlisted to draft his Federal Marriage Amendment. George was a believer in the amendment's language, adamant that its provision about the "incidents of marriage" would require a federal court to strike down any civil-union law or other same-sex proxy for marriage. In search of some unity with Dobson and Focus on the Family, the Family Research Council's Ken Connor agreed that he would not promote the alternative amendment language that he had generated.

Connor fell ill in early 2003, bedridden for months with a near-fatal case of pancreatitis. With his absence, the Alliance for Marriage had lost not only its most persistent critic but the one who most baffled Daniels's natural mode of argumentation, which was to confront those to his left explicitly but those to his right only by implicit contrast. Yet Daniels's respite from the Family Research Council barrage turned out to be temporary. When the group's former president would set out to establish what he called a "war cabinet" to prepare for the battle over gay marriage, some of its members clearly thought the first enemy combatant it should identify was the Alliance for Marriage. In what amounted to an epitaph for Daniels's vision for an amendment propelled by a broad-based ecumenical movement, the new president of Concerned Women for America, Sandy Rios, would say, "Matt has done everything he can do, taken it as far as he can take it."

Marriage Movements

From the first time she heard Matt Daniels, Maggie Gallagher considered him something of a kindred spirit, a fellow champion of the traditional family more likely to arm himself with social-science research than biblical certainties. When she introduced him to readers of her newspaper column, in the summer of 2000, Gallagher described his background with a painful familiarity. Recounting his youth in Spanish Harlem, she wrote, Daniels "was just the sort of kid certain sorts of liberals think they are defending when they instruct us to name family breakdown 'family diversity,' as if a fancy new name could fill the void left in a boy's heart when Dad disappears."

Gallagher never spoke publicly of it, but that emptiness was one she knew well. Just months before she was due to graduate from Yale in 1982, she discovered she was pregnant; the father was a boyfriend whom Gallagher had met through her conservative debate society. They dated exclusively for a year but never discussed marriage. Gallagher was intent on giving birth to a son, and backed off her early plans to put him up for adoption. The father never said goodbye at the end of her final semester at Yale; within years, he was out of her life and their child's. "He called me and told me it was too depressing and he didn't want to have anything to do with either of us," she says. Gallagher began life as an Ivy League graduate as a single mom in Oregon, and a few years later moved to New York City. "I became a writer because I had a baby and had to make money," she explained. The experience ultimately drew her deeper into Catholicism and gave her the overarching subject of her career.

"Since I was a girl, in the middle of a sexual revolution, I was repeatedly taught that we had separated sex from reproduction. . . . Under the influence of this teaching, whole generations of formerly young women of my age grew up shocked, shocked to discover they are pregnant, and the men who impregnate them feel minimal responsibility. They had consented to sex, not to babies, and what did sex have to do with babies?" Gallagher would write. "Same-sex marriage is the end point, the ultimate institutionalization of this view of sex, gender and marriage, and it is false. Sex between men and women is freighted with the reality that this is the act that creates new human life, even if in any particular instance, new life never takes place."

Daniels acted upon this worldview in a way Gallagher had seen few others do. She described the Alliance for Marriage as a "new effort to find ways that civil society and public policy can work together to promote and strengthen marriage as an institution," without any mention of its interest in gay issues. In the summer of 2001, Gallagher cheered Daniels's "carefully drawn, measured, centrist amendment" and the way it could undermine gay activists' claims that "those of us who oppose unisex marriage (the majority of Americans) are hate-mongers and bigots, like segregationists in the old South." She subsequently shared concern over reports that Walter Fauntroy, the longtime Washington civil-rights figure who emerged as the Alliance for Marriage's most prominent spokesman, had become an object of harassment over his involvement in the project. (A vice president of the Gay and Lesbian Activist Alliance had shared Fauntroy's home phone number online, along with encouragement to "register your objection to his alliance with anti-gay bigots.") "The quiet, back-door demonization and harassment of Fauntroy is consistent with the ongoing attempt by certain gay organizations to shut down debate over this dangerous transformation that the courts are wreaking on our marriage laws," Gallagher wrote. "Increasingly, gay activists are the self-righteous zealots, stigmatizing any disagreement with their point of view, no matter how reasoned and civil, as bigotry, hate speech and discrimination."

Nearly two years later, after David Blankenhorn granted her permission to formalize her involvement in the debate, Gallagher hardly wrote about anything else. If her writings were thematically repetitive—basically everything Gallagher wrote during the period was about threats to the "shared public norm" of marriage as understood worldwide—she managed to repeatedly find novel ways to make her point about the crisis. In one column, Gallagher began by recounting the tabloid saga of basketball player Kenny Anderson, who while married kept girlfriend Jeanette DiLone and her daughter in a luxury apartment with financial support and promises to one day marry her and buy her a house. When Anderson and DiLone broke up, she sued him for the equivalent of alimony even though they had never married: her lawyer was now arguing he should have to maintain the standard of living to which she had grown comfortable. Gallagher detailed the Anderson-DiLone story with wit and bemused outrage, and a few paragraphs later had effortlessly linked it to the Massachusetts Supreme Judicial Court's looming decision in *Goodridge v. Department of Public Health.* "If the most powerful trends in family law, driven by advocates for family diversity, have their way, the law of marriage will be utterly transfigured, eliminating distinctions between married, adulterous, same-sex and domestic partners," Gallagher wrote.

But throughout those early writings on what she dubbed unisex marriage, Gallagher also wrestled with a conflict closer to home. She launched MarriageDebate.com in late July, fulfilling David Blankenhorn's promise that the Institute for American Values would "move from a silence on this issue, from appearing to be tongue-tied, to participating in and improving the national debate." But in her writings Gallagher appeared to be perpetually rehearsing her conversations with her boss about her own job, about whether it was responsible—or even possible—to have a civil debate about this controversial new concept on which people of good intentions can respectfully disagree. "The debate over same-sex marriage, then, is not some sideline discussion. It is the marriage debate. Either we win—or we lose the central meaning of marriage," Gallagher wrote in July for the *Weekly Standard.* "The great threat unisex marriage poses to marriage as a social institution is not some distant or nearby slippery slope, it is an abyss at our feet. If we cannot explain why unisex marriage is, in itself, a disaster, we have already lost the marriage ideal."

Just a few weeks after she had started MarriageDebate.com, it was written about in *USA Today.* Then Gallagher got a call on a Sunday night from Blankenhorn seeking to adjust her role. He wanted to fold the gay-marriage work into the think tank's broader fundraising operations. Instead of raising money earmarked exclusively for her project, Gallagher would solicit for the institute's general budget, some of which would be directed her way.

Gallagher was taken aback by the proposal. She had been a consultant for the Institute for American Values, paid to contribute to projects as a writer and editor. Raising money had never come easily to her; she had agreed to do so initially only because Blankenhorn had made it a condition of her being able to pursue the work she wanted to do around gay marriage. Now it seemed he was trying to make fundraising a central part of her job at the institute. "When I thought about doing it that way, it just made me so tired," she says. The next day, in Blankenhorn's office, the two had a tearful conversation in which they decided to part ways. She insisted that she be able to keep the $15,000 she had raised thus far; after deducting the costs of developing the MarriageDebate website, Blankenhorn sent her off with a $10,000 check.

Within weeks, Gallagher started her own organization, the Institute for Marriage and Public Policy, and inherited the MarriageDebate web presence. The new organization's motto was "Strengthening Marriage for a New Generation," but there was little time for it to focus on anything other than the threat of legalized gay unions. She assembled a retinue of law professors and journalists to populate a group blog, and reveled in the argumentation that ensued, simultaneously playing the roles of debate-team captain, coach, and competition judge. After viewing gay writer Andrew Sullivan in a PBS *NewsHour* segment about same-sex marriage, Gallagher wrote a post solely "to brag a little" about how Sullivan had failed to engage on what she considered her strongest points. "Andrew wants the debate to be about anything except whether or not children need mothers and fathers, whether societies need babies, and what, if anything, marriage has to do with meeting those needs," she observed on the group blog. When Jonathan Rauch earnestly countered her online advice that gay men "pick a girl, love her, make a family," Gallagher scolded him for even having responded to it. "Oh, Jonathan I knew that would be a lightening [*sic*] rod. I also know that it is not remotely persuasive to anyone and that a more disciplined debater would just avoid the whole subject entirely, then and now," she wrote in a post called "Maggie's Stupid Digression."

In September, Gallagher was invited to testify before a Senate Judiciary subcommittee that had scheduled a hearing on "What is needed to defend the bipartisan Defense of Marriage Act of 1996?" in anticipation of the fallout from the upcoming Massachusetts decision. "Through her writings, Ms. Gallagher has emerged as one of the most influential younger women's voices on marriage, family, and social policy," the subcommittee chairman, Texas Republican John Cornyn, said while introducing her.

Gallagher was stuck in the transitional period between being a provocative voice and a committed activist. In a July post on *National Review Online*, echoing a point made by one of the magazine's writers that it was a sign of rhetorical weakness to rely on the slippery-slope argument that gay marriage would lead to polygamy, Gallagher naturally managed to go further. "Polygamy is not worse than gay marriage, it is better," she wrote. "At least polygamy, for all its ugly flaws, is an attempt to secure stable mother-father families for children."

That observation was not out of place among the daily provocations of the right-wing blogosphere, but its sensibility did not naturally translate to Capitol Hill hearing rooms. At the end of her subcommittee testimony, Senator Russ Feingold read that portion of Gallagher's essay and challenged her about whether she was really endorsing polygamy. "I think that among the really, really, really, really bad ideas, polygamy is at least a cross-cultural marriage option," she responded. "But I am really against polygamy, as well as same-sex marriage. I would just like to make that clear. I think it is clear from the context of the column."

It may have been the last moment when Gallagher could consider herself primarily a commentator. In the fall of 2003, she received an email from Don Wildmon, the head of the American Family Association, inviting her to be part of something called the Arlington Group. The reasons for the name were not immediately apparent to Gallagher: Wildmon's message said that the next meeting, in mid-November, would be held not in the Virginia suburb but at the Family Research Council's headquarters in downtown Washington. The meeting would cover two days, stretching from Tuesday afternoon to midday on Wednesday, scheduled to allow those traveling from outside Washington to require only one night in a hotel. She was asked to RSVP so the hosts would know how many sandwiches to provide for dinner on Tuesday night.

Gallagher had not recognized many names on the list of attendees that Wildmon had circulated before the meeting, or known much about the organizations those people represented. The Arlington Group was informal enough not to have an office, staff, or leadership structure, and secretive enough not to have a website or—at the point Gallagher was first contacted by Wildmon—to have ever had its name mentioned in print. All she really knew about it was that it was a group of people who had come together out of a common interest in pushing Congress to pass a constitutional amendment banning same-sex marriage. Gallagher did not think it was surprising that someone there had thought she would be a valuable part of the group. She had been a frequent presence discussing gay marriage on television, had already testified before the Senate, and that month would be described by the *Washington Post* as "one of the movement's intellectual flag-bearers."

But she had no idea who had invited her. In fact, as she looked around at the other attendees that Tuesday afternoon, hardly anyone was familiar to her. She had clearly passed from one marriage movement into another. "It's not the Institute for American Values crowd," she says. "It's the world of evangelical activists."

Wise as Serpents

Maggie Gallagher may have been mystified by the new sphere she had entered, but religious conservative leaders were accustomed to getting email messages from Don Wildmon beseeching them to action. The founding myth of the American Family Association placed him at home in Mississippi one night unable to find a single television program suitable to watch with his family. His primary tool for shaping mass culture was the corporate boycott, which began by targeting media companies, their advertisers, and sponsors, and expanded to punish any entity whose business practices embraced the immoral or indecent. Usually Wildmon's communications carried a very pointed request. In 1995, he called for others to join him in boycotting Disney's animated G-rated *Toy Story*, because the title figurines are "owned by a child in a single-parent household in which the father is noticeably absent" and the names of characters Woody and Buzz carried sex-and-drugs innuendo. In 1998, Wildmon rallied religious leaders to confront American Airlines executives in their Fort Worth headquarters over the company's decision to extend spousal privileges for its airport lounges to domestic partners of Admirals Club members. Wildmon's email message of May 12, 2003, was directed to many of those who had supported those crusades—the heads of Washington's most influential social-conservative organizations, alongside a few preachers with national followings—but it lacked his usual precision. He was writing his peers to suggest, simply, that they assemble to begin work on something big together, even if he was not quite sure what it ought to be. "I feel the leaders need to get together, set our priorities and then adopt a plan to achieve those priorities," Wildmon wrote.

A week earlier, Wildmon had led a delegation of eleven like-minded religious conservatives to the Republican National Committee's headquarters to confront its chairman, former Montana governor Marc Racicot, over his decision earlier that spring to meet with representatives from the Human Rights Campaign. When Racicot said that "I meet with anyone and everyone," Wildmon countered by inquiring whether he would meet with the North American Man Boy Love Association. Former presidential candidate Gary Bauer wondered the same about the Ku Klux Klan.

Republicans had taken back control of the Senate in 2002, giving them Congress, the White House, and a Supreme Court dominated by their president's nominees. It represented the strongest hold on government a single party had had in years, the culmination of the generation-long return of activist Christians to political life in the United States. Yet instead of expressing gratitude to the people who powered many of their campaigns, Republicans in Washington seemed to be ashamed by the connection to religious conservatives. When Pennsylvania senator Rick Santorum, a devout Catholic beloved by evangelicals, invoked "man on child, man on dog" alongside "homosexual acts" in an interview with an Associated Press reporter that April, many conservatives thought President George W. Bush and the Republican National Committee had failed to sufficiently defend him from the liberal attacks that followed. Seeing the party's chairman act like a supplicant before gay activists was merely the latest affront from an establishment that assumed the loyalty of its base while chasing moderate swing voters. "If Republicans continue to drift in that direction, we will walk," Wildmon said.

Already, he insisted, religious conservatives could observe they were losing the culture war they had helped initiate. "Look at our entertainment programs, listen to the music, listen to the statistics about babies born out of wedlock," said Wildmon. "Our team is not winning, not by any stretch of the imagination."

Wildmon had initiated the frustrating encounter with Racicot and felt it was his responsibility to make something constructive out of it. So the following week, he wrote to a group more than twice as large. It covered nearly everyone who had participated in the Racicot meeting along with some grandees of the movement who had not: Jerry Falwell, James Dobson, Tim LaHaye, and Phyllis Schlafly. When Sandy Rios, the president of Concerned Women for America, saw that Wildmon had been struggling to reserve a meeting space for the group at a Crowne Plaza near National

Airport in Arlington, Virginia, Rios offered a shared conference room a ten-minute walk away, at the Pentagon City apartment complex where she owned a condo.

Those who agreed to gather there on the evening of July 1 may not have been a diverse bunch, but they did reflect a range of institutional interests. Wildmon was insistent that no one would be expected to contribute money, and that no group's carefully guarded turf would be threatened by the collaboration. (The two concerns were linked: many relied on small-dollar direct-mail fundraising operations that pitted them in effective competition with each other.) "Some groups are rivals of each other. Others never had worked with anyone," observed longtime conservative activist and lobbyist Paul Weyrich. "On the right there is a streak of individualism which causes leaders of groups not to want to cooperate with other leaders."

Wildmon set no specific agenda, other than a hope that movement leaders would proactively define what they wanted to accomplish together rather than lurch from one crisis to the next. "There are certainly enough issues that demand our attention," he wrote to invitees a week before the first meeting. "Please give this matter thoughtful attention and come prepared with suggestions."

There were plenty of issues that could emerge. Some invitees wanted to renew their push in Congress for a ban on partial-birth abortion. Others were still angry with Bush for his compromise on stem-cell research, permitting study of existing cell lines but not the harvesting of new ones. Rumors of imminent judicial vacancies were constant. Weyrich had just published a column listing the "top five social priorities for conservatives," among them defeating all hate-crimes legislation and blocking federal funds to universities with speech codes.

But the latest news from the Supreme Court overshadowed all of them. In the last week of June, the court by a six-to-three vote reversed *Bowers v. Hardwick,* the 1986 decision that had upheld Georgia's sodomy ban on the grounds that states were free to use their laws to express "moral disapproval" of gay sex. That determination, Justice Anthony Kennedy wrote in overturning it, "demeans the lives of homosexual persons."

The outcome itself did not surprise religious conservatives as much as the large margin by which the *Lawrence v. Texas* case was decided, and Kennedy's insistence that "the liberty protected by the Constitution allows homosexual persons the right to choose to enter upon relationships in the confines of their homes." (The appeal had been filed by two Houston men arrested by police who entered a private home while investigating a false report of "weapons disturbance" and ended up fining the men $200 each under Texas law for having "engaged in deviate sexual intercourse.") Kennedy was not arguing merely that the government lacked a right to criminalize private sexual behavior, but that it had a duty to treat that behavior with "dignity" and "respect." In his dissent, Justice Antonin Scalia drew particular attention to Kennedy's timely disclaimer that the *Lawrence* decision " 'does not involve whether the government must give formal recognition to any relationship that homosexual persons seek to enter.' Do not believe it," Scalia advised.

Those invited to gather in Arlington certainly did not. According to Robert Destro, a Catholic University professor who would prepare a report for the group through the Marriage Law Project, parallel logic had led the Ontario Court of Appeal to rule in early June that residents of that Canadian province were entitled to marry regardless of gender. "This case is ultimately about the recognition and protection of human dignity and equality in the context of the social structures available to conjugal couples in Canada," the court had written in *Halpern v. The Attorney General of Canada.* It was, Destro explained, "precisely the same reasoning" that sustained Kennedy's analysis in *Lawrence v. Texas.* Following it through, Scalia had asked in his dissent, "What justification could there possibly be for denying the benefits of marriage to homosexual couples?"

Several who came to Arlington had played crucial roles in the passage of the Defense of Marriage Act, including Phil Burress, the Cincinnati antipornography activist who started the National Campaign to Protect Marriage, and Andrea Sheldon Lafferty, who had been the chief lobbyist for her father Lou's Traditional Values Coalition. (In 1999 she had married Jim Lafferty, who was invited to the Arlington meeting in his capacity as head of the Christian Seniors Association, which Lou Sheldon had founded to be "the religious conservative alternative to the ultraliberal AARP.") Like many conservatives, they had been content in 1996 with the assumption that they had done all that was possible to contain whatever damage a single state's judges could do through a ruling in favor of gay marriage. Once the threat from Hawaii had subsided, few had given much thought to what practically the Defense of Marriage Act would do, and what it wouldn't. But starting in March 2003, when the Massachusetts high court heard oral arguments in the *Goodridge* case, the day when gay couples could legally marry again appeared close at hand.

Federal law could no longer be trusted as a sturdy backstop for any effort to constrain state-level marriage policy by statute. The same Supreme Court that had produced *Lawrence* would be the one charged with interpreting the Defense of Marriage Act if it ever came up for a challenge. Why wouldn't five justices who had voted to overturn a state's democratically enacted ban on sodomy move just as easily to gut a federal law they thought failed to offer gay relationships their due respect and dignity? As Rios told *Newsweek* after the *Lawrence* ruling, "We're opening up a complete Pandora's box."

As the host of the gathering, Rios opened with a prayer just after seven p.m. Wildmon said that the first order of business had to be dealing with gay marriage. "We need a marriage amendment in light of the *Lawrence* decision," Weyrich said.

Everyone there knew about the Federal Marriage Amendment that Matt Daniels's Alliance for Marriage had unveiled two years earlier and that was currently languishing in the House of Representatives. The Southern Baptist Convention's Richard Land had been involved throughout the drafting process, and Wildmon and Dallas radio entrepreneur Marlin Maddoux were founders of the Alliance Defense Fund that had underwritten the costs of the project. But despite a well-planned public-relations effort, Daniels's work had made little impression on the broader world.

It was dismissed by most elected officials and the media as an activist hobbyhorse, and by political analysts as impossible to imagine actually viable. Even if an amendment secured congressional supermajorities, ratification would require a long march through thirty-eight statehouses. Just one amendment had become law since 1971, and it affected the timing of congressional pay raises—an uncontroversial measure that could be addressed only by rewriting the Constitution with few obvious stakeholders on either side. In this case, however, advocates would be effectively asking state officials to relinquish authority over the type of social regulation the founders had quite clearly entrusted them to handle. When the Federal Marriage Amendment was introduced, in May 2002, it never escaped the House Judiciary Committee.

Now the idea had been given new life by the Supreme Court's action. Scalia's caustic dissent could be read as a clear set of instructions from a constitutional scholar to lawmakers: if you want to make sure no one who sits here in the future contorts this precedent to justify gay marriage, rewrite the Constitution to explicitly forbid it. Certainly the media who had shrugged off the amendment when it was proposed in the House a year earlier now found it reasonable to ask politicians whether they thought it was worth pursuing.

"I absolutely do, of course I do," Senate majority leader Bill Frist had said on ABC's *This Week* when he was asked that question the weekend after the *Lawrence* decision. He was the first member of the congressional leadership to embrace an amendment—explaining that he believed "marriage is a sacrament, and that sacrament should extend and can extend to that legal entity of a union"—which led reporters to ask the White House whether President George W. Bush agreed with him. After being pressed on the subject in his daily briefing, White House press secretary Ari Fleischer said that "the president believes that marriage is an institution between a man and a woman" but that the matter of a constitutional amendment was "a question in the legal realm."

That evening, Land reassured those in Arlington that Bush, who had been instrumental in Frist's swift ascendance to the Senate's top post earlier that year, was not far behind them. "Frist wouldn't have said what he did," Land remarked of his home-state senator, "if he thought the White House would cut his legs off."

The next morning, they got the perspective of someone who knew what the world looked like from within the White House. Gary Bauer had been a domestic-policy adviser to Ronald Reagan and, after leaving the White House, had helped establish Focus on the Family's presence in the capital through the Family Research Council. He had left the organization to seek the Republican presidential nomination, one of several candidates who attempted to win over conservative primary voters with doubts about whether George W. Bush was truly one of them.

Few questioned the sincerity with which Bush spoke about his personal faith, as a born-again Christian who credited religion with correcting a wayward adulthood. "His father was raised Episcopal in Connecticut, where it is just not considered good form to talk about one's faith in public," Land, like Bush, a native Texan, would explain. "The very warp and woof of the life in the society in which George W. was raised is a very different one. It's an evangelical one. It is one in which faith is something you talk about a good deal. You're encouraged to talk about it, and people talk about it with each other. He knows the lingo, he knows the style, and he has the substance."

But there was still a question about how hard Bush would push on social issues. He had shown little zeal for cultural conflict as governor of

Texas, and was explicit about his intent to run for president by softening his party's Gingrich-era callousness. He found that in "compassionate conservatism," as he dubbed it, whose most inspired proposals involved changing federal policies so the government could collaborate with religious organizations to deliver social services in their communities. Promising to unleash these "armies of compassion" allowed Bush to speak the language of the faithful—and even vow to direct public funds to church-run charities—without having to engage on sexual questions like abortion that risked immediately alienating suburban moderates.

The partial failure of that scheme was central to the Bush White House cosmology. Even before the polls had closed on Election Day in 2000—before the thirty-six-day saga in Florida and federal courts that awarded the election to Bush—strategist Karl Rove had panicked over what looked like depressed turnout from conservative diehards. Exit polls eventually showed that Bush had received an even smaller share of his votes from self-described evangelicals than Bob Dole had in 1996. Rove concluded that four million of them had stayed home, insufficiently motivated by Bush's campaign to cast ballots on his behalf and potentially at risk of retreating from politics altogether. "If this process of withdrawal continues," Rove said in late 2001, "it's bad for conservatives, bad for Republicans but also bad for the country."

Rove was obsessed with making one of the major political projects of Bush's first term winning the confidence of those often called "values voters." He placed Bauer's campaign spokesman, Tim Goeglein, in a job Rove described to him as "the middle man, the point man, for the conservatives and the faith-based groups." Goeglein hosted a weekly Monday afternoon call with a few dozen religious conservatives, including Wildmon and Land. (On Thursday mornings, Goeglein would lead a separate call with Catholic leaders, and in between attended the "Wednesday Strategy Lunch" that Weyrich's Free Congress Foundation hosted each week when Congress was in session.) "In the Reagan administration, they would usually return our phone calls. In the Bush 41 administration, they often would return our phone calls, but not quite as quickly, and sometimes not quite as receptively. In the Clinton administration, they quit accepting our phone calls after a while," Land explained. "In this administration, they call us, and they say, 'What is your take on this? How does your group feel about this?'"

Despite the exposure and access to his staff, Bush remained an enigma to many Christian leaders who did not, like Land, have a long-standing personal familiarity with him. (The two had known each other since 1988, when Bush sought out Land to handle religious outreach for his father's presidential campaign, an offer Land declined.) For all their complaints, most recently voiced to the man Bush had appointed to lead his Republican Party, no one had disputed Land's assessment that Bush's was "the most receptive administration" social conservatives had ever encountered. It showed "less hostility and more receptivity" than any previous White House had—"at least a healthy regard for us," Weyrich told the group that Wildmon had gathered.

Evangelical leaders nonetheless felt that Bush was too eager to appear inclusive toward gays and lesbians. "I don't think that Bush has rolled back any gain that homosexuals gained from Clinton," Wildmon complained. While Bush's Democratic predecessor had refused to issue an official declaration in honor of Gay Pride Week, Wildmon noted, "this year they went ahead."

There had been few real opportunities for the White House to demonstrate its commitment, in either direction, on gay issues of real consequence. At the start of his administration, Bush selected several openly gay figures for prominent positions, including foreign-service officer Michael Guest as ambassador to Romania. The Family Research Council's Ken Connor said that with the appointment Bush was "imparting legitimacy to the homosexual political cause," but its timing—Guest, who over his career had worked closely on NATO issues, was sworn in exactly one week after the September 11 attacks—ensured that no politicians made the nomination a cause of their own. (Just two years earlier, Senate Republicans had blocked Bill Clinton's efforts to name gay philanthropist James Hormel as his ambassador to Luxembourg, forcing Clinton to rely on recess appointments.) Republicans treaded so cautiously around anything related to the administration's antiterrorism policies that there was little fuss when Bush signed the Mychal Judge Act, which expanded the category of beneficiaries eligible for the federal death benefit awarded to firefighters and police officers who die in the line of duty to include same-sex partners. (The legislation was named for an openly gay New York City Fire Department chaplain who died at the World Trade Center.) Bush signed the bill in private and never used the word *gay* in connection with it, a point made by the *New York Times* when it explored the mystery of the gay-rights bill that had become law without fanfare or controversy.

"This is a Washington story of intrigue, and nobody knows why anybody did anything," Log Cabin Republicans executive director Richard Tafel told the paper.

On the first night Wildmon's cadre met, as participants agonized over the Supreme Court and gay rights, conversations about strategy repeatedly deviated into an exchange of theories about why the White House might prove itself similarly squishy if asked to stand up to same-sex marriage. "The people around the President are either gay or ignorant," Rios offered. Mary Matalin "is bad news on this issue," Land said of the political adviser to Vice President Dick Cheney, who had a lesbian daughter and acknowledged that his attitude toward gay rights differed from Bush's. "And there are others," added Land.

But ultimately everything came back to Rove, whose influence within the administration would only expand as reelection concerns predominated. The Family Research Council's Connie Mackey likened Bush to the Wizard of Oz, with Rove the man behind the curtain. "The president won't meet without Karl," she said. But she acknowledged that it was still important to aim for an Oval Office meeting. There won't be a Senate vote unless Bush wants it, Bauer said, and Rove would be inclined to put it off and never have the president take a stand.

Personalities aside, the group faced what amounted to a perpetual legislative conundrum, all the more problematic when it involved a constitutional amendment that required congressional supermajorities to pass and the full support of a national party for any chance of ratification. It was hard to imagine that the congressional Republicans would push ahead if they didn't think the full force of the White House would be behind them, both publicly and privately. But it was also difficult to see the president committing himself to a particular proposal until it was assuredly viable in Congress, or at least until a clear strategy emerged for it there. (Later that day, when asked to respond to Frist's call for an amendment, Bush said, "I don't know if it is necessary yet. Let's let the lawyers look at the full ramifications of the recent Supreme Court hearing. What I do support is the notion that marriage is between a man and a woman.") Staff contacts could share little insight about where Bush would end up. "We did not want to get ahead of the president on the issue," Goeglein would explain.

Even as participants agreed to make their priority passage of a constitutional amendment, the preferred strategy seemed unavailable. An inside game would be focused on privately persuading White House personnel and congressional leaders to pursue an amendment in tandem, but the permanent coalition that had helped elect them—the web of mutually beneficial partnerships between economic and social conservatives—was unlikely to offer support. "Corporate leaders won't stick their neck out on this," said Burress, noting that even Walmart had recently decided to extend benefits to employees' same-sex partners.

What was left was an outside game, at the risk of antagonizing those they had helped put in power and sacrificing their ability to make progress on parallel concerns like abortion. "Our constituencies are going to demand that we fight this issue," Land had warned. "Go back to our constituency and mobilize them." If done correctly, Republicans would realize that by objecting to a marriage amendment, they would risk being just another godless party. Even if Rove's heart would never be in a battle over same-sex marriage, Weyrich suggested, he already knew he could not afford to alienate social conservatives while preparing for Bush's reelection. They had until the end of the year to make an impact on the White House, Weyrich advised. "Starting in January they will be in full political mode," he said.

Bauer proposed "a war cabinet, meeting periodically." Before convening again, participants would get to work, dividing responsibilities including hiring a pollster and developing radio ads that could run on religious networks. Land volunteered the Southern Baptist Convention video unit, part of LifeWay Christian Resources, to work on it, but cautioned that given the complexity of church decision-making, it would likely take at least six months. Florida televangelist D. James Kennedy could probably do it more quickly through his Coral Ridge Ministries, Land suggested. "In terms of being effective, we need to be wise as serpents," said Ron Shuping, vice president for programming at the Inspirational Networks, a Christian satellite-television channel. "We need to engage the culture."

Before disbanding late that morning, the members of the self-appointed war cabinet settled on a few basic rules for conflict. They agreed to keep their ranks secret and avoid any public attention for their work. "Most Americans won't be involved in a debate over the Federal Marriage Amendment," Bauer advised. "The battle will be won on the basis of two groups energizing their base. We'll water down our message by appealing to Middle America." They agreed to henceforth refer to themselves as the Arlington Group. As they planned to force their agenda onto the country's political officials, the suburban designation was a spatial reminder of their animating grievance: that religious conservatives had been exiled from the Washington they helped build.

Dueling Amendments

The Arlington Group meeting on October 1 included two new but very familiar faces. Through a range of levers, Focus on the Family's James Dobson and Jerry Falwell, the founder of the Moral Majority and chancellor of his own Liberty University, had already made their influence felt in the coterie's deliberations. Having developed fiefdoms bridging ministry, media, and advocacy based in Colorado Springs and Lynchburg, respectively, enabled Dobson and Falwell when desirable to feign indifference to the tawdry workings of Washington. The personal presence of the religious right's most successful builders of empire acknowledged what many of the apparatchiks who had established the Arlington Group already believed to be true: that theirs was already the most successful effort ever to transcend the movement's localized interests and factional alliances. After months of plotting in secret, the Arlington Group was about to make its first gambit for attention. At a press conference the next day, Falwell and Dobson would join Don Wildmon, Richard Land, and Sandy Rios to announce they were designating October 12–18 as Marriage Protection Week. That same day, President George W. Bush would issue a supportive proclamation that "Marriage Protection Week provides an opportunity to focus our efforts on preserving the sanctity of marriage," which Arlington Group members hoped would encourage a discussion in Congress about the looming threat of same-sex marriage. "We can move it to the front burner where the politicians will not be able to avoid it," Wildmon had argued in August, when the idea was first proposed.

A decision still had yet to arrive from the Massachusetts high court, but to members of the Arlington Group it felt as though the broader culture had already returned a verdict on the minimal regard it had for the unique nature of traditional marriage. In late July, Wildmon had with alarm distributed a report from the *New York Times* on the decision by *Brides* magazine, the venerable monthly published by Condé Nast, to feature a full-page article about trends in same-sex unions. "This is the first time that any of the five top-selling bridal magazines has published such a feature," reported the *Times,* which itself had the previous August changed the policy for the "Weddings" page in its Sunday Styles section so it could offer parity to same-sex commitment ceremonies under the new rubric "Weddings/Celebrations." One day after the *Brides* article, the *Times* had another story headlined GAY-THEMED TV GAINING A WIDER AUDIENCE. Inspired by the success of the sitcom *Will & Grace,* the paper reported, television executives were rushing to develop shows with gay characters and topics, including a pair of new reality shows on the network Bravo, *Boy Meets Boy* and *Queer Eye for the Straight Guy.* It was a season of similarly alarming shifts toward the destigmatization of homosexuality, in which the Episcopal Church elected its first openly gay bishop, and at the MTV Video Music Awards Madonna anointed the bridal-gown-clad duo of Britney Spears and Christina Aguilera with openmouthed kisses.

The speakers at the press conference described a parallel world in which the values of traditional heterosexual families would be celebrated to the exclusion of gay couples. The Salem Radio Network syndicated religious programs and conservative talk shows to 1,600 stations nationwide, while INSP TV, as the Inspiration Network was known, showed family-friendly entertainment on the bandwidth that televangelists Jim and Tammy Faye Bakker had once used for their PTL Satellite Network. The Southern Baptist Convention would distribute an insert that seventy thousand church congregations could place inside their weekly bulletins, with a resolution expressing concern about the "legal status of the biblical model of marriage." Organizations would engage their own activist constituencies directly: Focus on the Family had an old-fashioned mailing list of about sixty-five thousand names, while D. James Kennedy's Coral Ridge Ministries was said to have collected a half-million email addresses and the American Family Association over three times that. Americans who heard the call of Marriage Protection Week through one medium or another were asked to speak up about the subject, contact their elected officials, write letters to the editor, and encourage friends, family, and coworkers to do the same. "This will be a rolling crescendo," Land prophesied. "Politicians who don't know the radioactive nature of this issue now will by November 2004."

The press conference received less media attention than those scripting it had initially expected. The Arlington Group had been identified publicly by name for the first time the previous week in a *Boston Globe* article so revealing that after reading it Sandy Rios tried to cancel the press conference, only to learn that the payment had already gone through on the room rental. ("The story has been told, circulated, the press conference completely scooped and sabotaged," Rios had written the group. "If we have any real media attendance, it will be a miracle.") "Using pulpits, petitions, and political action committees, conservative activists are mobilizing a grass-roots political movement against gay marriage that they say is more intense and urgent than their campaigns against abortion," the *Globe*'s Mary Leonard had written.

What coverage there was of the plans for Marriage Protection Week, primarily in conservative media, described a united front. But a close read of what exactly those activists were telling their constituencies revealed nontrivial distinctions, far beyond the usual tonal variance that separated preachers from lobbyists and talk-radio hosts. The Southern Baptist Convention was imploring its millions of members to call their senators and representatives and "ask them to support the Federal Marriage Amendment." A press release from Concerned Women for America vowed to "work together to pass a federal marriage amendment." In a column that week, Paul Weyrich wrote that "a Constitutional Marriage Amendment is needed." The Family Research Council was asking every state and federal lawmaker to sign a "Marriage Protection Pledge," which bound them to "protect the inviolable definition of marriage" without any specific legislative action.

In the twenty-four hours before the press conference, the united front began to fissure. Several members of the group had gone the afternoon prior to meet with House Speaker Dennis Hastert and Senate majority leader Bill Frist. Matt Daniels had begun his legislative campaign in the House, which unlike the Senate was under Republican control throughout 2001, but took pains to ensure it had a bipartisan cast. He had asked a Democrat, Mississippian Ronnie Shows, to introduce the amendment on the floor, a partisan complement to the diverse collection of religious leaders he had put before the media months earlier. "He understood that if you want to pass a constitutional amendment you can't do it with a subculture," Frist aide Bill Wichterman says of Daniels's approach. "It's not the way it works: there has to be a broad consensus."

Shows lost his seat the following year, and when the same amendment was introduced in the spring of 2003 its sponsor was Marilyn Musgrave, a Republican newly elected from a Colorado district with strong support from religious activists. Musgrave was not quite new to the topic: as a state legislator, she had been summoned in 1996 to testify before the House Judiciary Committee's hearings over the Defense of Marriage Act because she was in the midst of a battle with her state's Democratic governor over gay marriage. Musgrave had more success than Shows in recruiting cosponsors, aided in part by the sense of urgency that came from the Supreme Court's decision in *Lawrence v. Texas* and anticipation about what would come in Massachusetts. By the time Arlington Group members met with the House Speaker, Musgrave's amendment had ninety-two cosponsors, of which eighty-four were Republicans, and more lawmakers joined the list each day. One of those who had yet to sign on, Indiana Republican John Hostettler, was working on his own bill, which he intended to formally introduce during Marriage Protection Week, that would attempt via a "limitation on jurisdiction" to ensure that no federal court, including the Supreme Court, should be able to hear any appeal related to the interpretation of the Defense of Marriage Act. (Hostettler believed that, under his Marriage Protection Act, even if courts did rule on marriage cases, U.S. marshals would be prevented from using federal funds to enforce their decisions.) But House Judiciary Committee chairman James Sensenbrenner did not plan to move on any marriage legislation until the Massachusetts court returned an unfavorable decision in *Goodridge.*

Things were moving even more slowly in the Senate, where a few weeks earlier the Constitution subcommittee had a hearing to explore, as its chairman John Cornyn had explained, "what steps, if any, are needed to safeguard the institution of marriage, which has been protected under Federal law since the passage of the Defense of Marriage Act in 1996." Days later, while speaking to Weyrich's Wednesday lunch group, Frist insisted he knew the answer, and that the Federal Marriage Amendment was a "crystal-clear issue" for him. He, too, was waiting only for a state court to rule in such a way that allowed senators to claim they had no alternative but to take some drastic action.

That evening, a larger group met at the Family Research Council's office. The meeting began at four p.m., but anticipating it was likely to go on for a while, Wildmon ensured that the hosts had an "evening snack" at the ready. (Without a budget of its own, the Arlington Group never feasted on anything more luxurious than sandwiches and chips, or donuts for breakfast.) The group had already held two long summits over the summer, each time swelling in number until it had outgrown anything Rios's apartment complex could offer. Around thirty people were present on the afternoon of October 1, seated at conference tables arrayed in a square so they could all see one another.

Throughout the early meetings, there had been consensus on seeking a marriage amendment, but participants had expressed different opinions on what exactly it should say or how that substance ought to shape political strategy around it. Both the Family Research Council and Concerned Women for America had broken with Matt Daniels's Alliance for Marriage before the Federal Marriage Amendment was unveiled in 2001, out of concern that as written it would permit states to enact civil unions or other forms of what the council had taken to calling "counterfeit marriage." At the first Arlington Group meeting, Rios had claimed "there's better language available," but Weyrich counseled that the group had little chance of success if it were to let rival amendments emerge. "If you don't get your act together, the White House won't commit," he said. Everyone left Arlington thinking they were on their way to getting what they wanted, or at least that for the time being it was more important to rally to their common purpose in preparing for Marriage Protection Week.

Within the Family Research Council, however, the effect of Dobson's dominion was being felt in the way the Federal Marriage Act surged to the top of its agenda. The council official who attended the first Arlington Group meeting in the place of the ailing Ken Connor, its vice president Connie Mackey, was the only attendee to hold out from the consensus that the group's priority ought to be a marriage amendment. But Connor was replaced as FRC's president by Tony Perkins, a former Louisiana state representative who had made his name as a legislator by working on marriage issues. The change in leadership was understood as a move by Dobson—who would shortly declare, "This effort to save the family is our D-Day. Our Gettysburg. Our Stalingrad"—to ensure his organizations were all fully aligned behind the softer Musgrave amendment. "Hopefully, within the next few weeks we'll all have language or agree to go with the existing language," Perkins told *Human Events* on September 8.

When the Arlington Group met at the council's offices on October 1, the early phase of work plotting Marriage Protection Week activities was done, and those who had never been happy with the Federal Marriage Amendment itself wanted to revisit it. With a more acquiescent leadership in place at the Family Research Council, Rios—a bombastic former radio host who had never before run a political organization—was the most vocal critic. At the Arlington Group's first meeting, she had effectively conceded that the amendment was going to lose either way, asking, "Why do you think we would get two-thirds—sixty-seven votes in the Senate?" Since none of the language was likely to ever become law, she argued, the "major benefit of an amendment is making the issue in the public."

The experience of rallying a coalition made her newly optimistic. Rios had come to believe that activists had all the leverage. Seeing evangelicals come together to form a cohesive group far more monolithically conservative than Daniels's ecumenical, self-consciously nonpartisan alliance, Rios was convinced they could do better than the Musgrave amendment. Given the inclusion of political action committees like Bauer's Campaign for Working Families, the Arlington Group could credibly threaten to challenge Republicans in primaries if they didn't go along with a more restrictive version. Rios pounded the table with fury. "The grassroots will get motivated and members will have to vote for it," she said. "We will take out squishy Republicans."

She was backed up by Bill Bennett, a former cabinet secretary who had become the country's leading communicator about what he called "virtues." Wildmon had not invited him to the first meeting, but as the group expanded, Bennett and Seth Leibsohn, vice president for policy at the Bennett-led group Empower America, joined in August. Unlike Rios, Bennett did not offer a strategy that would afford stronger language any real chance of becoming law. Instead, he said only that he did "not see how we can use the amendment as an education process if it allows fully for civil unions and domestic partnership arrangements—just what will we be teaching?" as Leibsohn put it. "We might as well say what we really want," Bennett told the group on October 1. "We don't want homosexual marriage—but we also don't want faux marriage."

The perils of splitting into two factions, pursuing amendments parallel in intent but distinct in construction, were familiar to conservatives. Within days after the *Roe v. Wade* decision in 1973, members of Congress were plotting to use the Constitution to retroactively restrain the Supreme Court's overreach. (In conservative memory, *Roe v. Wade* marked two distinct shocks. There was the moral outrage of Harry Blackmun's majority opinion determining that a pregnant woman's constitutional rights could smother any protections owed to the fetus inside her. Then there was a simultaneous affront to federalist values, articulated in Justice Byron White's dissent, in the court's decision to overturn five articles of the Texas

Penal Code that had passed the state's legislature and been signed by its governor.) In an effort to undo *Roe v. Wade* and its companion case *Doe v. Bolton*, conservative groups had banded together to draft a Human Life Amendment.

But they quickly ended up in two camps, one led for many years by Utah senator Orrin Hatch to put the question back in the hands of individual states by declaring that "a right to abortion is not secured by this constitution." Another style of amendment, championed most prominently by North Carolina senator Jesse Helms, would have implemented a national ban on abortion by guaranteeing a right to life for every human being "including unborn offspring at every stage of their biological development." (Overturning *Roe* would have the consequences of returning the matter to the states; presumably some would respond by maintaining legal access to abortion while others moved to forbid it.) Over the next thirty years, hundreds of Human Life Amendments were introduced, none of them even getting out of the committees in part because—despite efforts by Weyrich in the early 1980s to broker a compromise—pro-life activists could never agree to rally around a single approach.

When forced to choose between two types of marriage amendments, the Arlington Group voted to take the hardest line possible. It decided to back off its previously understood support for the Federal Marriage Amendment and throw itself behind one that would incontrovertibly block state legislatures from creating civil unions. "If we can't win the whole thing," Falwell applauded, "we ought to just forget it. Let's batten down the hatches and wait for the bell to sound for our society." The group resolved to send word to its congressional allies that it had withdrawn support from the Musgrave amendment, and to start work drafting a new version that reflected newly uncompromising consensus. "I don't know if we could have had as much 'high drama' if it had been scripted," Wildmon remarked after.

Lori Waters of the Eagle Forum called Musgrave's congressional office to relay the group's decision. "They are not ready to move on," Waters reported back to the Arlington Group. "They would like to revisit the decision because they feel that they have not been heard." From the beginning, those familiar with Capitol Hill dynamics had warned that the Federal Marriage Amendment could lose half its support in the House if replaced by stronger language, turning away both moderate Democrats and Republicans who felt the restrictions on state legislatures were an affront to federalism. (At the first Arlington Group meeting, Weyrich said he had already counted votes in the Senate—and there would be twenty fewer of them for an amendment with "harder language.") A Musgrave aide tried to arrange a meeting for the congresswoman and Representative Joe Pitts, who headed the House's conservative Values Action Team, to express their concerns to Arlington Group officials. But before Waters could schedule that meeting, the coalition behind the more militant approach began to collapse. "Some leaders are reverting back to support of the original FMA language, despite the vote that was taken last week," Waters wrote to Arlington Group members on October 9. "If you feel strongly about the language (current vs. stronger), please make arrangements to be at the meeting." Pitts ended up out of the country on the date they had selected, forcing another postponement.

Instead of going to Capitol Hill, Arlington Group members met among themselves at the scheduled time to renegotiate a common position. The designated mediator was Charles Colson, a Nixon White House staffer and convicted felon who emerged as "perhaps the most unifying figure among social conservatives today," according to *National Review*. The Colson-directed compromise added a third sentence to the Musgrave amendment declaring that "neither the federal government nor any state shall predicate benefits, privileges, rights, or immunities on the existence, recognition, or presumption of sexual conduct or relationships." Without specifying that its target was same-sex couples, the new sentence would have the likely effect of making it harder for governments to tailor civil unions specifically to gays and lesbians. Twenty organizations that were part of the Arlington Group coalition endorsed the compromise. The same cadre that two weeks earlier had resolved to take a hard line on "faux marriage" was now committed to fully democratizing it, so that any novel institution a state established to cover gay couples would also have to be made available to heterosexuals, presumably including not only chaste roommates but a pair of relatives.

Two weeks later, Waters rallied a small delegation consisting of Bauer, Wildmon, Perkins, and Weyrich to present their newest proposed amendment to Musgrave. The former state legislator made clear that she had no interest in restricting the ability of legislatures to establish civil unions if they chose; she just wanted to make sure courts did not force them to do so. That, along with permanently blocking any route for a federal court to assert a right for gays to marry, were her only objectives for the Federal Marriage Amendment. She said she was willing to "massage" the language to make its intent more clear, but neither she nor the Republican leadership thought anything stronger stood to pass the House. "In spite of us making it clear that the coalition strongly favored the bolder approach there was no 'give' in the position of our Hill friends," Bauer reported back to the Arlington Group. "If they do say 'no' and since we all agree two different amendments would be a disaster, what portion of our coalition is prepared, reluctantly or otherwise, to support what almost all of us view is a flawed amendment?"

This was the question that consumed the Arlington Group when Maggie Gallagher arrived to participate in her first meeting on November 11. She was a peculiar presence among the thirty-eight other people there, because she arrived with little institutional clout. At that point Gallagher's Institute for Marriage and Public Policy was little more than an embryonic website and a researcher she had inherited from the Marriage Law Project. (The project's founder, David Orgon Coolidge, died of a brain tumor in March 2002, at age forty-six.) Furthermore, while in her writing Gallagher was no friend to gays, she was rarely direct in disparaging them. "Like many Americans, I find the idea of criminalizing private sexual conduct troubling," she wrote in a column in the spring of 2003, anticipating a decision in *Lawrence v. Texas*. "At the same time, I know I do not want to see sex elevated to a constitutional right. Decisions about how to regulate sexuality should be governed by the normal democratic process, not by the weird values of people who go to law school."

This discussion she encountered reminded Gallagher of how different her orientation was. She came to the question of same-sex unions through the secular marriage movement, while religious activists saw it as the latest episode in an ongoing struggle with gays and lesbians for cultural primacy. "I think civil unions are a blow to the body politic, one further degradation of our culture. But gay marriage is a death blow. I don't believe that a civilization can survive that does not sustain the basic marriage idea," Gallagher wrote to members of the Arlington Group in mid-November. "I don't believe there is anything noble about going down to defeat on the marriage question, in order to try to win on civil unions too."

The Arlington Group was still divided among three different approaches—the original Musgrave amendment to ban gay marriage only, the hardline alternative that would also cover civil unions, and the Colson compromise proposal—when the long-dreaded news came the following week that the Massachusetts Supreme Judicial Court ruled in favor of the plaintiffs in *Goodridge v. Department of Public Health*. "Barring an individual from the protections, benefits, and obligations of civil marriage solely because that person would marry a person of the same sex violates the Massachusetts Constitution," Chief Justice Margaret H. Marshall wrote in the majority opinion. The court ruled to stay the entry of judgment for 180 days "to permit the Legislature to take such action as it may deem appropriate in light of this opinion."

A Republican-led government mobilized in response. From London that evening, the White House issued a statement in which Bush condemned the decision and said, "I will work with congressional leaders and others to do what is legally necessary to defend the sanctity of gay marriage." Shortly thereafter, a version of the Federal Marriage Amendment was formally introduced in the Senate, identical to the one Musgrave had sponsored in the House. The new chairman of the Republican National Committee, Ed Gillespie, said he expected the platform approved at the party's convention the following summer would endorse the amendment.

In Massachusetts, however, the 180-day stay included in the Supreme Judicial Court's order opened up a new debate over strategy among marriage opponents. Some, including Governor Mitt Romney, read the stay as an invitation for lawmakers to craft what he called a "civil-union-type provision." Legislative leaders began developing such a bill, and the senate would file a request for the court to respond with an advisory opinion on whether it would fulfill the mandate in *Goodridge*. Others, unwilling to concede even a civil-unions compromise in the face of the loss, began organizing to rewrite the state's constitution to ban any recognition of same-sex couples—even though there was no way voters could ratify such an amendment in a timely fashion.

Gallagher was exasperated by the folly of such a dead-end strategy. "The people whose minds must be changed are not natural allies of the Christian Right. They are moderately liberal and centrist Democrats and independents. Most can be persuaded to move from supporting gay marriage to opposing gay marriage and supporting civil unions. Do we want to push these Americans away from our coalition or bring them in?" Gallagher wrote in the *Weekly Standard*. "At this writing, it is 179 days and counting until gay marriage comes to America."

Lawlessness

On December 16, George W. Bush showed the first signs of succumbing to the pressure he had been receiving from social-conservative activists throughout the second half of 2003. In an interview with ABC News, Bush again expressed disappointment in the Massachusetts ruling that had come down nearly one month earlier, explaining that he thought the court had "overreached" in doing work better left to the legislature. Even as the media and other Republicans took an interest in the looming threat of same-sex unions, Bush had recoiled from the topic. But in his interview with ABC, Bush appeared intent on making news. "If necessary, I will support a constitutional amendment which would honor marriage between a man and a woman, codify that," he told Diane Sawyer. In apparent acquiescence to civil unions, Bush said, "the position of this administration is that whatever legal arrangements people want to make, they're allowed to make, so long as it's embraced by the state or at the state level."

It was an accurate encapsulation of what the Federal Marriage Amendment, which had now been introduced in both the House and Senate, would do. But some conservatives, including those active in the Arlington Group who had never been enthused by the Alliance for Marriage's text, read Bush's voluntary acceptance of civil unions as an early capitulation.

They still believed there was an opportunity to block any sort of recognition for gay couples in Massachusetts. While Governor Mitt Romney and some legislative leaders were preparing to offer the court civil unions as a compromise gesture, other activists—led by the Massachusetts Family Institute, the Focus on the Family state affiliate once headed by Matt Daniels—were looking ahead to a Constitutional Convention in February. Like Vermont, Massachusetts had by design a slow and convoluted system, meaning the amendment could not reach voters for ratification until November 2006.

Starting the process that February, some conservatives speculated, might be able to provoke even pro-marriage justices to back off for fear of launching the state into a multiyear constitutional crisis. "If there's a vote on the amendment, that should send the signal to the SJC that they should hold off on implementing anything, because the constitution could well be amended," Evelyn Reilly, the Massachusetts Family Institute's public-policy director, told the online publication *CitizenLink*. "For them to allow same-sex couples to have marriage licenses in May would create social chaos. Those people would be doing so at their own risk, because those licenses could be invalidated in 2006."

The White House appeared to be waiting, as well, for a neater resolution to the situation in Massachusetts before taking more decisive action. In his State of the Union address in January 2004, Bush devoted two paragraphs to what any viewer fluent in the priorities of religious conservatives would understand as an endorsement of the Federal Marriage Amendment, although "Bush never used the words 'gay,' 'homosexual,' 'same-sex' or 'amendment,'" the *New York Times* noted. The speech's vague policy declaration—"If judges insist on forcing their arbitrary will upon the people, the only alternative left to the people would be the constitutional process"—left those seeking guidance from Bush uncertain about his intentions. Some saw an unequivocal endorsement of the amendment before Congress, while the *Houston Chronicle*, based on postspeech interviews with lawmakers, concluded that "Bush's comments put ban on gay marriage on hold." Within the Arlington Group, reaction was similarly confused. The typically truculent Sandy Rios proclaimed herself reassured by Bush's attention to their cause, but Richard Land was disappointed by the passive voice and lack of specific instruction to Congress. "He made the case for the necessity of an amendment, and I am puzzled as to why he did not, having diagnosed the problem, prescribe the only remedy, a federal marriage amendment," Land told the *Baptist Press*. "I know that millions of social conservatives join me in praying that he does in the very near future."

The Arlington Group did not rely on faith alone. When they met at the Family Research Council on the evening of February 3, Karl Rove was on the line, and members huddled around a speakerphone as Land tried to force him to commit to a plan of action. Throughout the fall, members of the Arlington Group had been hearing that Bush's hesitation in endorsing an amendment derived from the fact that the White House was developing its own language, even softer than Musgrave's, an outcome that Gary Bauer declared "would be a disaster for our cause." Bush's delay seemed to make that unlikely; if he came forward now with his own proposal, he would unnecessarily alienate Republican legislators and interest groups who had made the case to their constituencies for the Musgrave approach above all others.

Paul Weyrich challenged Rove on Bush's coy treatment of marriage during the State of the Union, which sounded like the cautious patter of a candidate more afraid of turning off moderates than communicating his zeal to fellow conservatives (or, for that matter, persuading his audience to amend the constitution). Rove attempted to reassure them, although many in Republican politics understood that Rove believed Bush could win on the marriage issue simply because the Democrats would nominate someone whose extremism on the issue would define a straightforward choice. Throughout the fall, Rove had expected that would be former Vermont governor Howard Dean, the field's most vigorous critic of Bush and its front-runner for much of 2003. Dean was the only governor in the country to have presided over a regime of full legal recognition for gay couples, and even though it had been forced upon him by the courts, Dean claimed the success as his own.

Into January, Rove was betting hamburgers that Dean would win the nomination, and was confident he knew how to run against him: as a radical unable to understand life beyond secular New England. (At Rove's behest, campaign manager Ken Mehlman circulated opposition research to Christian leaders that quoted Dean venturing that the definition of marriage mattered only to those who are "pretty religious.") Even after Dean finished third in the Iowa caucuses, Rove persisted in believing the onetime front-runner could mount a comeback. A loss in the New Hampshire primary, in late January, ended Rove's dream of a Bush-Dean matchup.

Arlington Group members rarely failed to note that their rank-and-file supporters were more engaged on the issue of marriage than they had ever been on any other issue, including abortion. Bush had already alienated fiscal conservatives the previous fall by signing into law a new $400 billion prescription-drug benefit under Medicare, which the Heritage Foundation called a "disaster." Could Bush afford to disappoint social conservatives, too? Surely he had to give religious Christians a reason to turn out in November.

Land pressed Rove for a commitment. Would the president support the

Federal Marriage Amendment publicly? And could they trust him to do it with the zeal that he brought to efforts to pass his Medicare bill? Bush would take the next step, Rove assured, "sooner rather than later."

Even if the political calculations were evident to Rove, who was fixated from the start of the presidency on a goal of mobilizing evangelical voters, others close to Bush were guiding him in different directions. His vice president, Dick Cheney, was uncommonly influential on the matters of foreign policy and national security that dominated most of Bush's first term, but remained conspicuously silent as deliberations about how to proceed on the marriage amendment intensified in February. When under consideration to be nominated as his running mate, Cheney told Bush that he had a lesbian daughter in case that fact would give Bush pause. It did not, and the daughter, Mary, went to work on the campaign; Cheney felt free enough during the vice-presidential debate that year to articulate his own libertarian attitude toward gay marriage. Meanwhile, Bush's wife, Laura, pressured him not to make same-sex marriage a focal point of his reelection. "We have, I reminded him, a number of close friends who are gay or whose children are gay," she later recalled.

A few days later, Bush was given another reason to declare that if "activist judges insist on redefining marriage by court order, the only alternative will be the constitutional process." On February 4, 2004, the Supreme Judicial Court of Massachusetts determined—by the same four-to-three margin that it had initially ruled in *Goodridge*—that it would not accept a civil-unions compromise, concluding that "separate is seldom, if ever, equal." Yet Bush did not announce any change in his position, sticking to the same formulation he had used in his State of the Union speech.

The next week in Boston, the Constitutional Convention began, the first of several days to be scattered over six weeks in which a joint session of the legislature would entertain new amendments. The state's most prominent supporter of one that would ban gay marriage, Romney, also opposed the establishment of civil unions but understood that for any amendment to emerge from the convention it would have to at least leave open that possibility. The governor was afforded no formal role in the convention process, but he was quietly trying to guide Republican lawmakers toward such a compromise. Throughout, his advisers were in regular contact with White House staff, who had little to say about their desired outcome. "George Bush was a governor," says Beth Myers, Romney's chief of staff. "Karl was very respectful of the role of governors. He said, 'You've got to govern your state.'"

While the situation in Massachusetts unfolded in an orderly, if contentious, way, other local officials were not as patient. On February 10, Mayor Gavin Newsom asked the San Francisco county clerk to take whatever steps would be necessary to "provide marriage licenses on a non-discriminatory basis, without regard to gender or sexual orientation." Newsom, who had been in office for barely a month, would trace his motivation to make the move to his experience sitting in the House chamber during Bush's State of the Union speech, which he attended as a guest of House minority leader Nancy Pelosi. That evening he called his chief of staff and said he wanted "to do something," and two weeks later they agreed on what it would be. Late in the afternoon of February 10, Newsom sent his letter to the county clerk, citing little more than his own interpretation of the California constitution's equal-protection clause as justification for resetting the qualifications for marriage in his city. The only preparations necessary to execute Newsom's order were typesetting changes to forms and documents that used the words *bride* and *groom* and *unmarried man* and *unmarried woman*. Two days later, the city assessor signed one of the rewritten licenses for a lesbian couple she married during an improvised ceremony in her office. Twenty people were present and intentionally kept the development secret. Newsom's staff had timed the event with the hope that if they could keep word of the legally dubious enterprise from leaking before Friday, no one would be able to come before a judge to stop it until after the Presidents' Day holiday weekend. That would mean at least three days of marriages without judicial interference—including that Saturday, which happened to be Valentine's Day, and when city hall would stay open for the newly special occasion.

Sixteen hundred couples were married in San Francisco over the course of the weekend, with international television cameras capturing the festive spirit that engulfed city hall there. To the surprise of officials inside who had choreographed little beyond their opening steps, no legal authority emerged over the next week to stop or delay them. Two conservative groups had failed in their motions to do so. Eventually—more than a week after the marriages had started—the state's attorney general, an elected liberal Democrat who acknowledged that his personal preference was for some recognition of gay couples, shut down the enterprise. At that point, San Francisco's city attorney countersued, naming the state and the conservative groups as defendants, declaring he was "going on the offensive today in protecting the mayor's actions." (The city's suit was designed to ensure that the courts had to contend with the substantive claims about marriage rights and not merely overrule the mayor's authority on narrower procedural grounds.) The California Supreme Court did not, however, rule immediately, determining there would be no "irreparable harm" in taking its time.

Members of the Arlington Group were shocked, first by Newsom's action and then by the way it sprawled from a brief public-relations stunt into a rolling, multiweek extravaganza. Several of the group's most visible leaders had been in Massachusetts for the Constitutional Convention, where they saw the Marriage Affirmation and Protection Amendment preferred by Focus on the Family shoved aside in favor of proposals that included language related to civil unions. Media coverage preferred the events on the West Coast, a spectacle wardrobed in gown and tuxedo, to the joint legislative session out east where the drama could be understood only by those with a grasp of *Robert's Rules of Order*. But as much as Arlington Group leaders were aghast at what they saw taking place in San Francisco, it reaffirmed their argument that existing laws could not stop those desperate to force gay marriage upon the country. Since Hawaii, they had complained about activist judges; now there were renegade municipal officers acting beyond their rights.

The entire episode made a mockery of the president's patience. (While Newsom gave advance notice of his move to prominent Democrats in California and Washington, he did not alert the White House.) "I have watched carefully what's happening in San Francisco, where licenses were being issued, even though the law states otherwise," Bush said on February 18. "I have consistently stated that I'll support law to protect marriage between a man and a woman. Obviously these events are influencing my decision."

There would be only more of what the Family Research Council's Tony Perkins called "lawlessness." On February 19, the clerk of Sandoval County, New Mexico, followed Newsom's lead. After determining that nothing in the gender-neutral state code expressly forbid gay marriage— the legislature had not acted on defense-of-marriage bills—clerk Victoria Dunlap offered licenses to same-sex couples. A court order from New Mexico's attorney general successfully halted Dunlap after she had issued more than sixty licenses. California state officials had little such immediate recourse. The attorney general, Bill Lockyer, had filed the state's own motion to stop Newsom, but the court gave the mayor's government until March 29 to answer with a legal justification for his actions. For another month, couples from around the world could come to San Francisco to get married. "We cannot have mayors all of a sudden go hand out licenses for various things," California governor Arnold Schwarzenegger complained in an interview on *Meet the Press* after a second week of vows in San Francisco. "In the next city, it'll be handing out licenses for assault weapons. In the next, it'll be someone handing them out to sell drugs." Schwarzenegger's claim that "we see riots, we see protests, we see people clashing"— although there had been little beyond one incident of demonstrators being arrested at city hall after minimal contact—appeared to raise the stakes on federal inaction.

On February 24, Bush gave a speech at the White House in which he finally laid out what steps he thought federal officials should take to deal with same-sex marriage. Bush promised that his administration would "vigorously defend" the Defense of Marriage Act passed by Congress, although he contended that in the context of the new post-*Lawrence* consensus, the law could be nonetheless doomed. "There is no assurance that the Defense of Marriage Act will not itself be struck down by activist courts. In that event, every state would be forced to recognize any relationship that judges in Boston or officials in San Francisco choose to call a marriage," Bush said. "Furthermore, even if the Defense of Marriage Act is upheld, the law does not protect marriage within any state or city. For this reason, the defense of marriage requires a constitutional amendment."

He did not specify that he was endorsing Musgrave's Federal Marriage Amendment, but that matched Bush's description of the ideal vehicle. "The amendment should fully protect marriage, while leaving the state legislatures free to make their own choices in defining legal arrangements other than marriage," Bush said. The Arlington Group was ready with a letter, signed by its members, that would appear as a full-page ad in *USA Today* thanking Bush. The letter, drafted by Chuck Colson and Robert George, likened the president's "courage" in resisting the work of "runaway courts" to Abraham Lincoln's defiance of the Supreme Court's decision in *Dred Scott*. "We pledge to you that we will do everything in our power to inform and educate our constituents" about the amendment, the letter concluded.

The need to buck up a sitting president reflected the growing skepticism within the Republican political class about embarking on such a culturally divisive legislative project in a presidential election year. Even though Musgrave had introduced her amendment nine months earlier, it still had yet to receive a hearing from the House Judiciary Committee. When asked about it, House majority leader Tom DeLay repeatedly expressed the hesitation that—despite the fact that he would eventually offer his support—"as a basic philosophical point, he doesn't like amending the Constitution," according to an aide. In the Senate, Frist had no such reservations, but he puzzled conservative observers when he tapped Wayne Allard, a mild-mannered former veterinarian midway through an unremarkable Senate career, to be the bill's chief spokesman, rather than more aggressive colleagues like Kansas's Sam Brownback, Pennsylvania's Rick Santorum, Alabama's Jeff Sessions, or Arizona's Jon Kyl. Allard had little profile in the national media, and as a senator had always evinced more interest in issues of federalism than questions of morality. "And it's just traditional marriage that I'm talking about. I'll leave it up to states to deal with civil unions and benefits associated with them," Allard, a former state legislator, said a few days after introducing the bill.

The amendment was scheduled for its first hearing, before the Senate Judiciary subcommittee on the Constitution, on March 23. The day before, Allard and Musgrave announced they had rewritten the amendment to guarantee that states would remain free to engineer civil unions through the legislative process. Musgrave had always insisted that was her intent, although she was undermined by public quarreling among the most prominent members of the drafting team, Robert Bork and Robert George, about whether courts would actually interpret it that way. The initial phrasing had been so "sloppy," Georgetown University law professor Peter J. Rubin told the *Washington Post,* that his first impression was that the Musgrave amendment "couldn't possibly have been the work of a lawyer."

The new version left its first sentence, declaring that marriage "shall consist only of the union of a man and a woman," unchanged. The second sentence was rewritten, stripped of a reference to "state or federal law" that George, among others, had claimed would yank from legislatures their right to extend any of the "legal incidents" of marriage to unmarried couples. Those edits appeared to demonstrate the influence of White House lawyers eager to ensure that an amendment with the president's backing matched his declared interest in preserving some rights for states. "We want to make it clear, without any ambiguity, that states do have a role as far as dealing with civil unions and benefits related to marriage," Allard said. The revision also had the consequence of bringing the Federal Marriage Amendment in line with Matt Daniels's original vision.

That was the final indignity for Arlington Group hard-liners who had never been fond of the amendment language that Musgrave had introduced in Congress. After she parried their supposed compromise text in November, however, "reality set in" for most of the group's members, according to the American Family Association's Don Wildmon. Resigned to the fact that their only legislative option was to push for whatever amendment they could get, they began lobbying the White House to back Musgrave's and developed a new entity, the Marriage Amendment Project, to coordinate political efforts advocating for its passage. But the turn in early 2004, from lamenting that the only passable amendment was one that would permit civil unions to trumpeting that as its virtue, was too much to bear for some in the alliance. Several of those who had been active in the Arlington Group from the beginning recused themselves from the Marriage Amendment Project, afraid its work would serve to legitimize civil unions. "I actually believe we would be in worse shape if the currently proposed Musgrave Federal Marriage Amendment were ratified," wrote Michael Farris, the founder of Patrick Henry College and president of the Home School Legal Defense Association. "If we urge citizens to save marriage, we need to be pushing a plan that saves marriage, not merely redefines it. No one will ever trust us again if we fail to get this one right."

By then, it was apparent that nothing could stop gay couples from being married in Massachusetts that spring. On March 29, its fourth day of debate spread over six weeks, the Constitutional Convention passed an amendment that would ban gay marriage but establish civil unions for same-sex couples. (The amendment passed, by a margin of 105 to 92, with opposition coming from both pro-gay-rights liberals and conservatives unwilling to support civil unions.) A week earlier, State Senate president Robert Travaglini had averred that "no matter what legislative action we take, we cannot affect the issuance of licenses come the 17th of May." As soon as the amendment passed, Romney asked Attorney General Tom Reilly to request another stay from the Supreme Judicial Court to allow for the constitutional process to conclude. Reilly, an elected Democrat, refused to do so, insisting that the majority of judges had "made up their mind" in its two previous decisions about marriage rights.

Romney had warned of "legal limbo" if couples married with the outcome of the amendment process unsettled, but also insisted that "it is of no interest, and I have certainly no intent, to do anything other than to follow the law." In that respect, there was actually little for the governor to do. Under Massachusetts law, responsibilities for issuing marriage licenses fell to individual town and city clerks, which placed a limited burden on state officials to participate in the implementation of the court's mandate. Gubernatorial advisers realized that lack of direct responsibility could allow Romney an opportunity to be a more radical voice in the debate for a constitutional amendment, but he never took it. After March 29, when Reilly refused to mount another challenge on the state's behalf, Romney accepted that marriages would have to proceed as the judges had ordered. He would continue to push to ratify the constitutional amendment, which required another vote of the legislature in 2005 before it could go to voters. But for now, Romney said, he would "abide by the law as it exists on May 17."

City hall in Cambridge opened at midnight that morning to handle the large demand from couples seeking to be among the country's first to legally wed. Police were forced to shut down a sizable stretch of Massachusetts Avenue, which was filled with members of newly enlarged families milling about amid thrown rice. One reveler's sign presciently noted the ways in which the burden of proof in the marriage case had shifted irrevocably onto those predicting societal decay: SEE CHICKEN LITTLE, THE SKY IS NOT FALLING.

Mary Bonauto was present to monitor for potential legal complications. There were none, just as there were not later that morning when Boston city hall opened for business, despite the police detail that surrounded Bonauto and the sharpshooters who tracked her movements from the roof. The lack of crisis resigned the attorney to the role of carefree celebrant as the seven couples named in the lawsuit all wed that day. The mother of one groom had to supply Bonauto with tissues at one church service, her tears yielding to relief upon hearing the words "By the power vested in me by the commonwealth of Massachusetts I now pronounce you legally married." At the wedding of Julie and Hillary Goodridge, Bonauto caught the bouquet. In the days that followed, she said, "I went to as many weddings as I could."

That joy could not be immediately exported. A week earlier, Romney had forewarned that his administration would aggressively enforce a law largely ignored since its 1913 passage that prohibited out-of-state couples whose marriages would be "void if contracted" in their home jurisdiction from being granted licenses in Massachusetts. Clerks would be expected to demand proof of residency from couples; a wayward official found to be violating the statute could be fined between $100 and $500, sentenced to up to one year in prison, or both. This "evasion statute" dated from an era when states had wildly disparate marriage laws, particularly around interracial relationships, and was a way for Massachusetts to avoid becoming "the Las Vegas of same-sex marriage," in Romney's words. Eventually forty-nine states would have to reckon with what to make of these Massachusetts marriages, especially the twelve that had never enacted defense-of-marriage laws specifying a policy on the full-faith-and-credit question. "The rest of the country had to figure it out on their own," says Myers, Romney's chief of staff. "We weren't going to solve the rest of the country's problem."

Issue One

In his retelling, Phil Burress would trace the origins of Ohio's Issue 1 to a meeting in his office in suburban Sharonville on May 18, a day after Massachusetts began permitting same-sex couples to wed.

Throughout the winter the head of Citizens for Community Values had seen gays and lesbians clasping freshly awarded marriage licenses. First there was the rolling circus in San Francisco, then the brief insurrection at the courthouse in Bernalillo, New Mexico, the seat of rural Sandoval County. Over the next few weeks there was more. In the upstate New York college town of New Paltz, the recently elected mayor—a twenty-six-year-old who made his living as a housepainter with a sideline as a puppeteer—signed twenty-five licenses in one day. At a county building in Portland, Oregon, the commissioners of Multnomah County issued nearly three thousand licenses, which they claimed they were required to do under the state's constitution. The deputy mayor of Asbury Park, New Jersey, presided over a gay marriage just because, as he explained, "laws are made to be broken at times to find out if they are really legit or not."

In each case, the paroxysms of joy among celebrants were leavened by the understanding that the marriages they commemorated were almost certainly not going to be credible for long in the eyes of the law. In each case, higher-ranking authorities eventually reined in the dissident officials. (The New Paltz mayor, Jason West, was charged by the local district attorney with nineteen counts of performing a marriage without a license.) But in Massachusetts, town halls were acting with the full sanction of the state judiciary; in fact, it was town clerks refusing to marry gay couples who were told to relinquish their justice-of-the-peace duties.

On May 18, as Burress recalled it, he summoned the staff of his Citizens for Community Values and the group's outside lawyers. They determined that they must do whatever they could to make sure that never happened in Ohio. Until the day before, Burress claimed, he had been "in denial"—unable to conceive that the order the Massachusetts Supreme Judicial Court had issued six months earlier would ever actually be fulfilled. "We were devastated," said Burress. "We had no idea that this was really going to happen."

That naïveté obscured Burress's long record of farsightedness about what gay activists could accomplish. Fresh off his success passing Cincinnati's Issue 3, he had been invited to Colorado Springs in early 1994 for what the one journalist invited to attend called the "first national meeting of its kind" to plot anti-gay-rights strategy. There he met Mike Gabbard, and from that point onward Burress closely watched the situation in Hawaii when few others on the mainland did. He convened conservative leaders in Memphis to launch the National Campaign to Protect Marriage; its kickoff event in Iowa just weeks later secured a commitment from Bob Dole, who went on to co-sponsor the Defense of Marriage Act in the Senate. Concern about marriage from well-established national organizations, like the Family Research Council, followed. We "have to go on the offensive," Burress would say, since movements "never scored a point on defense."

Burress's proactive campaigns against gay rights and pornography in Ohio had given him outsize stature for the leader of an organization whose real focus was on a mere handful of counties in metropolitan Cincinnati. When in 1998 a number of national Christian groups combined to purchase a series of newspaper and television ads under the banner "Truth in Love"—encouraging reparative therapy "toward hope and healing for homosexuals"—Burress's was one of just three state organizations allowed to sign on. The other two were Gabbard's Alliance for Traditional Marriage and Colorado for Family Values.

A few years later, when Don Wildmon invited two dozen conservative leaders to Arlington, Burress was the only state-level official included. From the first Arlington Group meeting, Burress did not hide disdain for his Washington-based peers and their dubious motives. As the conversation turned to the possibility of demanding that the White House receive a delegation that could make the case for a marriage amendment, Burress was the first to question the value of prioritizing such a session. "The success of the meeting depends on which pro-family leaders will be there," Burress said. "Some would be more concerned with access than taking action."

From the outset, while others battled over which amendment language the Arlington Group should embrace, Burress was committed to a different objective. Sandy Rios of the Concerned Women for America, the most vocal of the group's hard-liners, had talked about the need to pursue "two prongs"—to push for a federal constitutional amendment but simultaneously "work state by state on super DOMA." Starting in Utah in February 1995, states had responded to the potential full-faith-and-credit crisis that Hawaii would trigger by passing bills that would—by contrast with the federal Defense of Marriage Act—come to be called "mini-DOMAs." In each case, the bills sought to explicitly define marriage in a way that would permit state officials to assert that an established public policy justified not recognizing other states' gay marriages.

Of course, nothing could stop an appellate court from concluding that such a marriage statute violated a state's constitution. After seeing in 1998 how referenda in Hawaii and Alaska reined in judges, most legislators elsewhere in the country began drafting their bills in the form of constitutional amendments that would make marriage laws immune from judicial interference. Following the cautionary example of Vermont, Nebraska in the fall of 2000 became the first state to amend its constitution to ban same-sex civil unions along with marriages. These became known as "super-DOMAs," immune to any recourse short of a federal court decision that determined that the provision put a state's constitution at odds with the country's.

Especially for those who had lost faith in a federal amendment—either because they thought one would never be ratified or because only the softest possible version could be—the second prong was imperative. "It's all going to go back to the states," Burress warned. Under pressure from Burress and Rios, Paul Weyrich said the Arlington Group "will agree privately with DOMAs as second objective" even as its media efforts were devoted to pursuing a federal amendment. When Wildmon expanded the group's invitation list that fall, to include leaders of American Family Association affiliates in Michigan and Pennsylvania and Focus on the Family's state policy council in Arizona, he did it "because I think we will need their help on down the line."

Even though he had kick-started the process that generated the federal Defense of Marriage Act, Burress was unable to get any sort of marriage ban enacted in Ohio. Bills drifted through three separate sessions of the legislature, under two different governors, with little success. In 2003 that began to change, aided by events elsewhere. Three weeks after the

Goodridge decision, the Ohio House passed its own Defense of Marriage Act, and a month later the Senate did so as well. On February 6, 2004, citing the situation in Massachusetts, Governor Bob Taft signed the bill into law, making Ohio the thirty-eighth state to define same-sex marriages in its statute as "against the strong public policy of the state."

That month, Cincinnati mayor Charlie Luken had announced that he wanted to begin amending the city charter to remove Article XII, which made Cincinnati the only municipality in the country that preemptively forbid elected officials from passing any laws to protect gay citizens from bias. "It singles out one category of citizens for unfair and possibly discriminatory treatment," Luken said in his State of the City address, "and it should be repealed in 2004."

Article XII was the crowning achievement of Burress's political career. Inspired by the constitutional amendment passed in Colorado in 1992, he worked to enact a similar measure in the city where his Citizens for Community Values had been fighting for years against pornography and indecent art. In 1993, nearly two-thirds of Cincinnati voters backed Burress's Issue 3. After the Colorado provision was struck down three years later, the Supreme Court refused to entertain a challenge to Cincinnati's, which was narrower in the limits it placed on pro-gay political activity. In 1998, with all possible court challenges exhausted, Issue 3 became Article XII of the city's charter. By then, Burress's electoral successes had earned him the notice of social conservatives far beyond the Ohio River Valley.

Luken's push for repeal reflected the priorities of the Chamber of Commerce, whose officials blamed the antigay provision for the loss of convention business and an ongoing difficulty local companies encountered as they tried to attract new employees. "Nothing has changed, except that the business community has decided that the amendment needs to be repealed," Burress said. His allies Focus on the Family and the American Family Association responded by calling for a national boycott of Crest and Tide to protest Procter & Gamble's role funding a pro-repeal committee. Burress, meanwhile, prepared to fight again at the ballot box, resurrecting the Equal Rights Not Special Rights Committee that had passed Issue 3 a decade earlier.

With a campaign infrastructure already in place, Burress put it to work trying to effectively upgrade the state's Defense of Marriage Act as an amendment to Ohio's constitution, which would require majority support from voters in a statewide referendum. In mid-April, Burress's Ohio Campaign to Protect Marriage delivered a sample petition to the attorney general, the first step necessary to formally present a state constitutional amendment to the electorate that fall.

Burress's story of a post-Massachusetts epiphany offered some cover for him to claim that the bill the governor had just signed was insufficient to restrain activist judges. "I do consider amending the constitution extreme, but we are forced to do that by a judicial branch that has gone completely haywire," said David R. Langdon, the attorney Burress retained to draft the amendment. "Amending the constitution would keep it in the hands of the people, where it belongs."

He and Burress could be assured the public was on their side. A *Columbus Dispatch* poll taken in March showed 78 percent of Ohio voters opposed recognition of gay marriage, across demographic groups. Winning at the polls was likely to be easier than qualifying for the ballot. Burress had until early August to collect 322,899 signatures, including a critical mass (at least 5 percent of registered voters) from half of the state's eighty-eight counties.

Confident that a majority of voters would support an amendment to protect traditional marriage, Langdon drafted the most expansive version possible. Its first sentence ("Only a union between one man and a woman may be a marriage valid") was fairly standard. The second sentence, however, went well beyond even the state's Defense of Marriage Act's language, which had precluded recognition of civil unions: "This state and its political subdivisions shall not create or recognize a legal status for relationships of unmarried individuals that intends to approximate the design, qualities, significance or effect of marriage."

Thirteen constitutional amendments forbidding gay marriage ended up on state ballots in 2004, and in just fifty-five words Ohio's language went further than most of them. "You really haven't accomplished much if you say marriage is between a man and a woman and then you go down the road of giving to some other combination of individuals all of the rights that accrue to marriage, like filing a joint state tax return," Burress explained. "All you've done then is play a word game with the electorate."

Fear of those far-reaching consequences helped rally an opposition far broader than those that massed to beat back anti-gay-marriage laws in other states. Opponents included many beyond the usual civil-rights coalitions, from business leaders who anticipated further damage to the state's reputation to the American Association of Retired Persons and the president of Ohio State University. It was among four public colleges that offered domestic-partner benefits to its employees, along with the city of Cleveland Heights, all likely to be rendered unconstitutional by the new amendment. Taft, the governor who had signed the Defense of Marriage Act, and the state's two Republican senators all said they would vote against Issue 1. All three were opposed to gay marriage but said that the amendment went too far in curbing what public institutions or local governments could voluntarily provide to their employees.

Similar dynamics were visible in neighboring Michigan, one of two states with a comparably expansive ban on its ballot that year. Over the course of the campaign, opponents of Proposal 2 came close to winning support from the United Auto Workers and corporate executives at the three major car companies. The language proposed by the so-called Michigan Marriage Initiative, they felt, could possibly destabilize collective-bargaining agreements already agreed to by unions and employers and complicate future negotiations.

State-level activity proved to be paramount in 2004. According to news reports at the time, Senate majority leader Bill Frist pushed back a vote on the Federal Marriage Amendment from May to June, and then to July, without moving any closer to the supermajority necessary for passage. Members of the Arlington Group saw value in insisting that a vote be taken that summer, even though it was unlikely to even be close. They knew Democrats from all but the most liberal states would prefer not to be put on record at all on same-sex marriage, and the amendment was the only obvious way to force federal lawmakers to vote on what was typically a state issue.

"No response from Democrats as we filled the morning and part of the afternoon," Frist crowed to Republican senators in an email message after the first of four days of floor activity on the amendment in mid-July. (The two members of the Democrats' presidential ticket, John Kerry and John Edwards, skipped both the debate and vote entirely.) But by then, Frist knew it was doomed to a spectacular failure. "I am proud the senate has initiated the debate for the country," he typed by BlackBerry to Wayne Allard, in the most generous congratulation he could muster for the amendment's sponsor.

Yet with the at least temporary failure of the Federal Marriage Amendment, the full attention of Arlington Group members turned to the thirteen amendments that would be on state ballots that year. Their first test was in Missouri, where in early August an amendment passed with over 70 percent of the vote, even though gay-rights groups spent over one-quarter more than their opponents. "We were out-organized by the competition, which was able to do a lot of organizing with very little resources," Human Rights Campaign national field director Seth Kilbourn told the *Washington Post.* "They activated the churches in a way that was very successful." That result—and another, six weeks later, in which Louisianans passed an amendment by an even larger margin—affirmed a conventional wisdom throughout the political world that marriage amendments in all ten states were likely to pass safely, with the possible exception of liberal Oregon.

Ohio's amendment received the most media attention of them all, because of the state's size and the fact that both presidential campaigns considered it likely to be pivotal in the electoral college. The strong relationships that Burress had with national organizations ensured a major investment, despite the fact that the outcome was never really in doubt. The Ohio Campaign to Protect Marriage was sued in forty-two different counties, and was represented throughout by the Alliance Defense Fund. Focus on the Family collected petition signatures from seventy-eight thousand Ohio members, the American Family Association shared the email addresses of sixty-five thousand of their own, and the Southern Baptist Convention facilitated the placement of 2.5 million pamphlets in church bulletins the Sunday before the election.

On Election Day, Burress saw his beloved Article XII repealed by Cincinnati voters, but he succeeded in changing the Ohio constitution to forbid any recognition of gay couples. While Bush carried the state by only 120,000 votes—close enough to prompt some Democrats to demand a recount—Issue 1 won by a margin of 1.3 million. Everywhere they were on the ballot except Utah, the amendments received a larger share of the vote than Bush; in Michigan and Oregon, battleground states the president lost, Bush ran ten points behind. (In Oregon, where the gay-marriage vote was closest, 57 percent backed Measure 36.) Those figures, along with exit polls that showed "moral values" to be the issue most important to voters, began to assign the issue of marriage a central role in the mythology of the 2004 election.

The data pointing to this conclusion was spurious, but in coming years it would appear frequently in media coverage and was cited approvingly on both the left and the right: Bush had been reelected only because opposition to same-sex marriage had mobilized the voters he needed to win. Those who wanted more direct evidence for this claim ended up in Ohio, which had given Bush his national margin of victory. Organizers on the amendment campaign claimed that they registered fifty-four thousand new voters along the way, including thirty-nine thousand Amish who typically recused themselves from political activity but were supposedly so moved by the marriage crisis that they felt compelled to act. Exit polls showed Bush doing abnormally well among the state's African Americans, who had been targeted through a network of black preachers recruited by Citizens for Community Values.

Beyond Ohio and Oregon, nine states amended their constitutions via referendum that November to exclude same-sex couples. Georgia, Mississippi, Montana, and Oklahoma amended their constitutions to block marriages, while Kentucky, Louisiana, Michigan, North Dakota, and Utah approved more expansive bans that applied to civil unions and possibly domestic partnerships, as well.

The Federal Marriage Amendment had proven to be a disaster, failing dramatically in both houses of Congress even in its softest incarnation. (In September, two months after the Senate vote, the House considered the rewritten Musgrave amendment; it received a majority of votes but fell far short of the two-thirds necessary to pass a constitutional amendment.) But the results from the thirteen state referenda convinced members of the Arlington Group that they would have a stronger hand when they made a new legislative push for a federal amendment in 2005. They would have leverage over members of Congress, who would have new reasons to fear ending up crosswise with constituents on such a high-profile issue, and a president who would surely be in awe of the political power of Christian conservatives and grateful for their help winning a second term. In that respect, the state amendments had helped accomplish precisely what the Arlington Group had been formed to do. They invigorated a drifting religious right with a sense of purpose and earned back the respect of Republican elected officials who had come to take them for granted. "What this has done is brought the people of faith to the table like I have never seen before," Burress said. "This is what the Democrats' biggest fear was—that something would energize the people of faith. And it has."

Part Six

TWENTY TEN TEN TEN

(2003–2007)

When You're Living Through It

A few weeks before Election Day in 2004, Evan Wolfson traveled to Minneapolis to deliver the keynote address at the nation's largest conference for gay and lesbian lawyers. For years, even before he became the founder and executive director of Freedom to Marry, Wolfson had been coming to gatherings such as Lavender Law with a version of the same peppy stump speech about the ineluctability of same-sex marriage. The repetitive nature of these declarations had led Wolfson, as early as 1994, to dub himself the "little Paul Revere of marriage." His message had shifted slightly over time, from a pronouncement that same-sex marriage would be a factor in American political life to the yet bolder claim that a consensus in its favor wasn't far off.

"Thirty years from now—when gay people have won the freedom to marry and our society looks back and wonders what the big deal was—our children, grandchildren, nieces, and nephews will want to know where we stood and what we did at a pivotal moment," Wolfson wrote in his book-length manifesto, *Why Marriage Matters.*

By late 2004, however, those who had bought into Wolfson's vision were likely to feel misled by his optimism. Polls showed that thirteen states were about to amend their constitutions to handcuff judges from determining gay and lesbian citizens had a right to marry. Others would inevitably follow in subsequent years, as conservative activists navigated the often convoluted rules for enacting constitutional change. On Capitol Hill, Republicans had failed to pass a Federal Marriage Amendment out of either chamber, but were likely to feel only more emboldened on their quest, especially as conventional wisdom had begun to set in that the issue helped mobilize religious voters on behalf of George W. Bush's reelection.

An objective review of the situation could lead even gay-marriage backers to determine the quest had not proven worthwhile. While Massachusetts now granted marriage licenses to same-sex couples, only one other state had said it might recognize the relationships solemnized there. Public opinion on same-sex marriage had actually moved backward since 2001, with the Pew Research Center recording support at only 31 percent in 2004. No more than a handful of national political figures were willing to speak favorably about the cause, and a new generation of politicians had been conditioned to view all gay priorities as toxic. Over the past year, one might conclude, champions of same-sex marriage had won a state but lost a country.

Ahead of his arrival in Minnesota, Wolfson decided to discard his standard speech, which he could now deliver by rote, and draft one specifically for an hour of impending crisis without at all conceding defeat. "I knew we were headed to a likely set of losses and that people would freak out and that was going to be a challenge," says Wolfson. "I really wanted to be on record as stating what this meant, where we were in the struggle, where we were going, and what the lessons were going to be."

Wolfson was a compact and fierce former prosecutor, with cherubic features obscured by a goatee and glasses. From the dais at the Radisson Plaza Hotel, he talked about the "moment of peril" back to what he called "the scary, empowering, noble, and transformative work of winning." Wolfson delighted in aphoristic speech, and offered up a pair of catchphrases that he hoped would instill a sense of momentum amid the despair. "Wins trump losses," he said, encouraging his audience to look past defeats, as he argued that in short-term failure the increased public attention and long-range shifts in support meant that the cause of marriage was "losing forward."

Then Wolfson said gay-marriage champions like himself ought to be honest about why they were on such a losing streak against their political opponents. "They have more of a head start, more money, and more infrastructure through their megachurches and right-wing partners—and fearmongering at a time of anxiety is easy to do. And, of course, historically, it is difficult to win civil-rights votes at the early stage of a struggle," he said.

That acknowledgment itself was a departure from the peppy predictions of largely frictionless victory that had led even those who shared his aims to argue he was too cavalier about the hurdles they faced. Wolfson did not abandon his certainty that gay marriage would be universally accepted, but rather reframed it in generational terms. "Remember," he said, "we have a secret weapon—death."

Until younger Americans replaced their more conservative elders in the population, it was not surprising that the movement would lurch between landmark advances and seemingly catastrophic setbacks. "During such patchwork periods, we see some states move towards equality faster, while others resist and even regress, stampeded by pressure groups and pandering politicians into adding additional layers of discrimination before— eventually—buyer's remorse sets in and a national resolution comes," he said. "This patchwork period—and especially the next few weeks and months—will be difficult, painful, even ugly, and we will take hits."

But the movement would rebound, Wolfson assured the crowd. The next stage would require assembling the resources, machinery, and long-term mind-set to match their opponents. "If we see every state, every methodology, every battle, every victory, and even every defeat as part of a campaign," he said, "we will win."

If at that apparent nadir for this project, Wolfson was brimming with confidence, it was because the forty-seven-year-old had spent much of his adult life seeking to expand "the human-rights battlefield of marriage" from coast to coast. That situation had arrived, albeit now in a way rued by gay activists. Even as *Time* said legalized same-sex marriage "would not have come as soon as it did without him"—as part of his entry on the magazine's 2004 list of the world's 100 most influential people—the dominos had not always fallen the way he promised they would.

When writing his Minneapolis speech, Wolfson had drawn inspiration from *Reporting Civil Rights,* a journalism anthology he had received upon signing up for a Library of America book club. Wolfson began toting it on his travels. "To read it is to capture the exhilaration, the empowerment, the being appalled, and the just plain being scared," he shared with the audience. "That is what a civil rights moment feels like when you are living through it—when it is uncertain and not yet wrapped in mythology or triumphant inevitability."

For a decade, Wolfson had been his own cause's most vocal cheerleader and eloquent narrator. Now an unprecedented mixture of crisis and opportunity had created an opening for Wolfson to become its first true strategist. Even those who were never convinced marriage rights were not worth winning grew persuaded it was not a fight worth losing, either. Wolfson's vision for a permanent, national marriage campaign would be accepted by many in the gay-rights movement, including some of its largest donors, few of whom were invested in the issue prior to the convulsions of 2004. All of it was informed by Wolfson's own history as a frustrated witness to events he was unable to shape.

50

Paul Revere Rides In

Evan Wolfson had been analyzing marriage since childhood. When barely the age of eleven, he had told his mother that he did not expect to ever have a spouse. He didn't yet know himself to be gay, but he understood that "the images of marriage in society didn't include me," as he would recall. He didn't acknowledge his sexuality until he was beyond college, serving in Togo as part of the Peace Corps. Over the course of two years teaching English and philosophy, sex education and cattle plowing, in a village school, Wolfson resolved to live his life out of the closet. When he returned home, he enrolled in law school and "learned how to be gay in the United States."

At Harvard Law School, Wolfson began thinking about what a legal foundation for same-sex marriage rights might look like. In his third-year thesis, he extended little deference to critiques of marriage itself, including those about its intrinsically patriarchal character; Wolfson casually minimized feminism as merely the pursuit of equal rights for both genders. "For gay women and men, who also love, samesex [*sic*] marriage is a human aspiration, and a human right. The Constitution and real morality demand its recognition," Wolfson wrote in his paper. "The interests of gay lovers in getting married are the same as any others seeking marriage: an occasion to express their sense of self and their commitment to another human; a chance to establish and plan a life together, partaking of the security, benefits and reinforcement society provides; and an opportunity to deepen themselves and touch immortality through sexuality, transcendence, and love."

Wolfson's paper surveyed the history of cases from the 1970s, which he said were taken up in the "tradition of the great movements against racism, sexism, and bigotry." But in his review of the arguments that had been presented to challenge state restrictions on gay marriage and the reasons used by judges to reject them, Wolfson concluded that plaintiffs had underestimated the "prejudice and unresponsiveness of the courts" that would greet them. Judges unable to look beyond their personal judgments about homosexuality, Wolfson claimed, had failed to objectively weigh the underlying constitutional questions. Once judges were capable of doing so, he argued, "abolishing sexualist discrimination and permitting full and equal self-expression on the part of all lovers for all beloveds, in keeping with the Constitution's human rights spirit, we will create a society more safely and richly founded on our individual freedom and equality."

It was time, the law student ventured, for a new strategy to win what he called "the right to marry." That right, he argued, was grounded in the constitutional claim to privacy affirmed by the Supreme Court when it considered restrictions on other intimate family matters in the 1960s. By failing to appreciate the scope of that privacy guarantee, he wrote, "courts and commentators treating samesex marriage have failed to give adequate weight to the protected human rights values at stake." Instead of trying to win recognition for gays as a protected minority class, Wolfson proposed challenges to existing marriage laws as a form of government-sponsored discrimination based on gender, which courts already defined as worthy of special scrutiny. "It would seem clear that if you could choose to love a particular male if you were female, but may not as a male, you are a victim of gender-based discrimination," Wolfson wrote. He earned a B+ on the paper.

Wolfson set off on a career typical of an ambitious Harvard Law graduate. In quick succession he joined the Brooklyn district attorney's office as a prosecutor, left it for a big New York law firm, and then committed to a stint on the independent counsel's team investigating the Iran-Contra scandal. But gay rights were always his avocation. He volunteered as a pro bono cooperating attorney for Lambda, and was asked to write the group's amicus brief before the Supreme Court in the *Hardwick* case. In 1989, Wolfson was hired as a Lambda staff attorney, picking up as many as twenty clients at a time. When Wolfson contacted the National Gay and Lesbian Law Association the following year to offer himself up as a speaker for its second Lavender Law conference, he pronounced himself qualified to speak on nearly every topic on which there could possibly be a panel. He conveyed to a conference organizer that he would be interested in discussing the "possibility of reclaiming gay history by connecting it with other civil rights." Even though he was young, Wolfson explained, he had read a lot about the topic.

Marriage, however, was not merely an intellectual exercise for Wolfson but something of a professional calling, stemming—as he never hesitated to tell anyone who asked about the origins of his interest—from the law-school thesis he had written. He was far from the first student to write about gay marriage—at least a half dozen had articles published in law reviews, some before Wolfson had graduated high school—but while most of the others moved on, Wolfson allowed his academic curiosity to gestate into a personal and professional passion. As he grew older, he cited with approval a verse from the 1966 musical *Cabaret*'s "Married": "How the world can change, / It can change like that, / Due to one little word: / 'Married.'"

Same-sex marriage was on the cusp of becoming the country's most explosive social issue, and Wolfson fully embodied the paradox at its core. To the nongay world, and even within the less politically conscious corners of the gay and lesbian community, reaching for what the *New York Times* would describe as "the gold ring of marriage"—especially as states remained within their power to outlaw gay sex between consenting adults—seemed so audacious as to mark any proponent as a radical. To peers, however, Wolfson looked a patriarchal fogey, his crusade for marriage rights insufficiently progressive. "I think it's quite a conservative, family-oriented tactic," sniffed Paula Ettelbrick, who as Lambda's legal director hired Wolfson.

When Wolfson arrived there, in 1989, Lambda Legal seemed to be the locus of a rollicking debate about gay marriage. Ettelbrick and Tom Stod-dard, the executive director, were about to publish their dueling essays on the subject and take their colloquy on tour. It amounted to an unusually public celebration of dissension among the leaders of an organization that typically weighed legal options and strategies in private.

Yet the organization's leadership, Wolfson discovered, wasn't quite as divided as it put on. When the question was posed abstractly, Stoddard may have embraced the logic of pursuing equal marriage rights, but he shared Ettelbrick's conclusions about the benefits of inaction. The man who in April 1989 published a *New York Times* op-ed titled "Gay Marriages: Make Them Legal" prevented his staff attorneys from taking on any work that might hasten that outcome. Wolfson tracked Lambda's incoming requests for help and press coverage from around the country in search of any mentions of same-sex marriage, vacillating between hope and fear that someone would make a case of it. "It was very frustrating for me because we weren't really doing anything and they were presenting this debate in this sort of abstract way," he recalls. "It was a diversion from the fight we were having internally. Tom was 'theoretically' on my side and could of course have pushed to do it. But he acquiesced, and Paula at that point did not want to do it. Thus we weren't doing it."

Wolfson assumed his place in the marriage debates with such pugnacity that it became impossible for those around him to remain neutral about the subject. "He started pushing it, pushing it, pushing it—to the point of annoying people," says former Lambda legal director Abby Rubenfeld, who passed over Wolfson when he first applied for a staff job there. (He was hired by Lambda only when Ettelbrick replaced Rubenfeld.) "He had a lot of women he pissed off. It was his style, and some of us tend to be a little too sensitive."

By late 1991, interpersonal tensions within Lambda—which weren't triggered by disagreements over marriage but occasionally intersected with them—led Stoddard to fire Wolfson. Shortly thereafter, Stoddard went on vacation to Paris, and staffers exploited the void he created by turning against his leadership. Wolfson was a beneficiary of the rebellion, with his erstwhile colleagues threatening a strike if he was not immediately reinstated. This caused a panic amid Lambda's board, which demanded that Ettelbrick, the acting executive in Stoddard's absence, resolve the situation. Ettelbrick was not necessarily more fond of Wolfson than Stoddard was—he managed to antagonize both of his bosses more or less equally—but was eager to quell the insurrection, which was dramatic enough to be noticed by the New York gay press. While Stoddard was still on vacation, she reversed his personnel move. "Tom came back, found out that Evan had been rehired, and basically walked," says Kevin Cathcart, who replaced Stoddard as Lambda's executive director.

In the interim, however, Wolfson had been looking for work elsewhere, and used his brief unemployment to give a job talk at the University of Hawaii, where he had applied for a post as a law professor. (Wolfson's brief foray exploring the prospect of an academic career was vexed when he told those interviewing him for another university job that he considered himself an activist and was uninterested in writing for scholarly publication.) One evening while in Honolulu, Wolfson found himself invited to a fundraising event at a private home near the university campus, where local activists were raising money for the marriage suit's appeal to the state supreme court. He and Ninia Baehr had previously met incidentally during the years when she was living in New York, through a mutual friend whose parties were filled with members of the city's gay legal world. Baehr never expected she would run into him in Manoa, and upon encountering Wolfson again they decided to memorialize the unlikely meeting for another mutual friend who worked at Lambda. They scrawled *Hi Jacquie* on a piece of paper and posed for a picture. It was the only interaction he had had with one of the principals in the case bearing Baehr's name, but upon reading the trial-court opinion Wolfson recognized an alter ego at work—the arguments about privacy and gender discrimination, the narrow appeal to constitutional arguments to avoid being entangled in debates about the propriety of homosexuality. Wolfson called Dan Foley, introduced himself, and asked, "What do you need?"

Wolfson would draft an amicus brief in a case even when he thought its initial filing was misguided, as he did in a 1991 lawsuit that attorney William Eskridge had filed against the District of Columbia on behalf of a male couple seeking to marry there. (There were a number of reasons to consider DC an especially poor jurisdiction for such a suit: its legal system funneled into federal courts and Congress could rewrite local laws at whim.) *Baehr v. Lewin* was, however, a much more promising vehicle for securing marriage rights, already on its way to the state supreme court. Wolfson explained to his colleagues that this was the strongest challenge they had yet seen, mounted with circumstances probably as good as they could expect, but he could not convince Ettelbrick to change Lambda's de facto policy against marriage cases. However, Wolfson was again given permission to draft an amicus brief. Foley was limited to thirty-five pages in his brief, so he outsourced a chunk of the argument—summarizing the expert evidence on sexual orientation that the lower court had failed to consider—to Wolfson as the focus of Lambda's brief supporting the plaintiffs. After submitting it, in February 1992, Wolfson returned to other causes closer to home, including a lawsuit filed on behalf of a nineteen-year-old New Jersey scoutmaster against the Boy Scouts for expelling him upon learning he was gay. But as the *Baehr* appeal moved toward its day before Hawaii's Supreme Court, Wolfson often found Foley at the other end of a phone or fax line, looking to discuss matters of law or courtroom strategy.

Late on the night of May 5, 1993, the phone in Wolfson's Brooklyn apartment jangled with news from Honolulu. The Hawaii Supreme Court had just released its opinion in *Baehr v. Lewin,* and—as soon as he made sense of what it meant—Foley recognized he would be overwhelmed with attention from Hawaii media and offered Wolfson a deal. If Lambda wanted to put out a press release announcing the victory, the group could handle any inquiries from the national media. For the first time, the case won the attention of mainstream journalists on the mainland, including coverage in the *Washington Post* and *New York Times*. No one outside Hawaii had noticed when Lambda had filed an amicus brief in the *Baehr* case, but now the group—which was fighting not only against gay-rights opponents but for turf against supposed allies—had for the first time attached itself publicly to the cause of marriage. "It's an enormous step to getting the government out of the business of telling people who they can marry," Wolfson told the *Los Angeles Times*.

Wolfson pushed for Lambda to take on a more aggressive role as *Baehr* returned to trial, and was no longer stymied by his superiors. By early 1993, both Stoddard and Ettelbrick were leading other gay-rights organizations: the Campaign for Military Service and Empire State Pride Agenda, respectively. Wolfson was cheered by the change in leadership, as Stoddard was replaced by Cathcart, whom he had sized up as an ally within the Roundtable's marriage debates. When Wolfson proposed a closer relationship to the Hawaii plaintiffs by investing in their case, he faced little of the prior internal resistance. "Whatever you thought before, wherever you were with all these other divisions, the world had just turned," Wolfson said. "This was a whole new era; it would never be the same again." The following month, Lambda formally offered to be Foley's cocounsel, assuming a major share of trial costs in exchange for an active role in managing the litigation. "As more and more people started to see this is happening, and started to see a good case we could win in Hawaii, there was a thought maybe we could reevaluate this a little. Well, the game's kind of on here, and the choice is to try to support this or not," says Jon Davidson, who joined Lambda in 1995 and later became its legal director. "Even for people who thought this was a good thing, there was not a great understanding of how strong a reaction there would be. We were a little naïve about the repercussions."

Under the new regime, Wolfson was given permission to work full-time on marriage issues. The new role required a split professional identity. In Hawaii, Wolfson would be a full-fledged member of the plaintiffs' legal team whose prosecutorial experience would prove useful handling witnesses. On the mainland, he would have to learn to work as a political strategist and organizer, trying to assemble the fractious gay-rights movement into a force unified enough to take on outside enemies—and formidable enough to draw new, supportive allies. "He was very frustrated with academics who wanted to talk theoretically," says Barbara Cox, a California Western School of Law professor who collaborated with Wolfson on a study of marriage laws in all fifty states. "He was saying we need academics who will address the issues that the other side is raising and help us prepare to do the litigation and the legislative work and the initiative battles."

At its outset, Lambda's Marriage Project was little more than a new email signature identifying Wolfson as the unit's director, with a dedicated assistant and a pool of interns at his disposal. This would be the first sustained national public-relations campaign around marriage, and Wolfson was set on unveiling it on Valentine's Day 1995—an attempt to restore the issue to its romantic context and shrink a ballooning ideological abstraction down to human scale. "Nongay Americans haven't had to deal with the fact that we have serious, loving, committed relationships," Wolfson wrote. "Now they will have to."

His primary tool for rallying a political coalition would be a resolution that Wolfson drew up in the hopes of giving shape to the project's goals:

Because marriage is a fundamental civil right under our Constitution, and because the Constitution guarantees equal protection of the law,
RESOLVED, the State should permit gay and lesbian couples to marry and share fully and equally in the rights and responsibilities of marriage.

Wolfson's plan was to release the resolution, complete with a handful of high-profile signatories, and use it to seek out the official support of other groups. Advocates of same-sex marriage had never before had a formal presence even within gay-rights institutions, and would finally be able to assert their presence with a common language and begin the work of building a coalition that could protect their likely gains in Hawaii.

But that Valentine's Day proved notable for another development, taking place in Salt Lake City. On February 14, state representative Norm Nielsen introduced his Recognition of Marriages bill, which would amend the state's code to specify that Utah authorities could not recognize a marriage "if it would be prohibited and declared void in this state." Wolfson had anticipated that such a move was possible, noting a month earlier the "tendency of some in politics and the judiciary to create a 'gay exception' to even the clearest principle of constitutional law or fairness." But the Utah bill—which had been announced by news reports days before its formal introduction, with Lynn Wardle taking credit—had arrived more quickly than Wolfson had foreseen.

As soon as he looked closely at the Utah situation, Wolfson learned that the strategies favored by gay activists there had been unable to derail the bill's path to becoming law. Rhetoric about equality and civil rights did little to sway the state's Republican legislature or governor. Even though the LDS Church remained officially neutral toward the bill, Wardle's public claims of ownership were a signal to the state's Mormon politicians. "You had all these Utah conservatives in the legislature who went along because they assumed he was talking for the church," says Frank Pignanelli, the state's House minority leader. A five-year-old political action committee, the Gay and Lesbian Utah Democrats, collected anti-Mormon materials disseminated by some of the same Christian activists promoting the marriage bill, but failed to draw outrage that would fracture the antigay coalition. Then they invited outside pressure from the business community by claiming a visible display of antigay politics could harm the state's tourism business and pledged a challenge to Salt Lake City's bid for the 2002 Winter Olympics. Meanwhile, the state chapter of the ACLU, claiming it was "adamantly and resolutely" opposed to a bill it found unconstitutional, implied it would file a lawsuit if passed.

None of these approaches deterred the legislation's supporters. As February wore on, those fighting it nonetheless had reason for optimism. The bill had yet to come to the floor for a vote and the legislature's forty-five-day term would expire at the end of March 1, likely leaving the matter dead for another year. But as the deadline approached, the Recognition of Marriages bill materialized and—without any floor debate—was put to a vote in the senate. "We had it bottled up, but the governor wants it," House majority leader Christine Fox told a colleague who questioned the sudden change in agenda. The bill passed the senate, with just a single Democrat voting against, in a vote recorded a little more than three minutes past midnight. While the bill was on its way to the governor for a signature, Wolfson worked in vain to raise doubts about the legality of its late-night passage. "I reserve for now my concerns with regard to the measure's substantive unconstitutionality and mean-spiritedness," Wolfson wrote the state attorney general, "and focus here solely on the procedure by which

it was railroaded through the legislature in violation of the clear requirements of the Utah Constitution."

Wolfson had shrugged off David Sobelsohn's prophetic warnings, as
early as the fall of 1994, that the Republican Congress would get itself involved, too. If Wolfson had had any impact shaping that debate, it was by
ushering in a backlash that might not have in fact been inevitable but for
his repeated, public pronouncements that a decision in Hawaii would
force the other forty-nine states to respond. "The great majority of those
who travel to Hawaii to marry will return to their homes in the rest of the
country expecting full legal recognition of their unions. Despite a powerful
cluster of expectations, logistics, rights, constitutional obligations, and federalist imperatives, these questions are likely to arise: Will these people's
validly-contracted marriages be recognized by their home states and the
federal government, and will the benefits and responsibilities that marriage
entails be available and enforceable in other jurisdictions?" Wolfson wrote
in a memo he distributed in late 1994 and early 1995. "We at Lambda
believe that the correct answer to these questions is 'Yes.'"

That conclusion was far more controversial than it looked at first
glance, and many of those who disagreed with Wolfson's interpretation of
the full-faith-and-credit clause assumed he was willfully misreading the
law as part of a political strategy. "That was bad constitutional law and
it was politically very damaging," charges Barney Frank, whom Wolfson
visited on Capitol Hill in early 1995 to get the country's most prominent
openly gay politician to sign his marriage pledge. "I asked him not to do
it. At the start, our best hope is state by state. Let's get same-sex marriage
in a couple of jurisdictions, and then we can argue, 'Leave Hawaii alone,
that's up to Hawaii.' I didn't want to nationalize the issue, I wanted to fight
it state by state."

For Wolfson, a seemingly blithe optimism about provoking a fight he
had no possible way to win was both worldview and strategic posture. He
was committed to the idée fixe that marriage should be his generation's primary gay-rights struggle, that other gains would follow, and that the only
way to possibly get marriage was to demand it. Given the internal frac-
tures over whether marriage was even a prize worth having, he needed the
outside pressure to encourage the gay community to act. He had learned,
from the experience within Lambda Legal, that gay activists wouldn't fight
for marriage until their hand was forced to do so—and that the only way
to get there was to hasten the conflict. On that point, he liked to quote the
French suffragist Hubertine Auclert, who while arguing for women's rights

in the late nineteenth century had written, "When one wishes to assert one's claim, one must, after all, have the courage to proclaim it."

Indeed, Wolfson often couldn't summon a whole lot beyond courage to justify a scenario that many legal scholars on his side considered wishful thinking. "Common sense and people's general intuitions both back us up and are there for us to tap into," he wrote in a widely circulated memo that elsewhere carried citations to case law. Even if many of Wolfson's allies doubted that as constitutional analysis, his opponents accepted it unskeptically and acted upon it. His memo, titled "Winning and Keeping Equal Marriage Rights: What Will Follow Victory in *Baehr v. Lewin*," would be quoted in an issue briefing prepared by the House Republican Conference (then chaired by Ohio congressman John Boehner) and even entered into the official record by Congressman Jim Sensenbrenner, who read aloud from Wolfson's memo at a subcommittee hearing. "I think he foolishly overstated this one-state idea—that if we win we get everything—and that led to a backlash," says journalist Andrew Sullivan, who at Wolfson's recommendation appeared as a witness at that hearing. "It gave them something to panic over."

Wolfson was sanguine about such criticism, including from Sullivan and others close to him. In January 1996, he spoke at a "town hall meeting" at the West Hollywood Park Auditorium outside Los Angeles, one of the largest gatherings ever devoted to the issue that so animated him. Wolfson laid out the scenario he had described so many times before, in a cheerful tone and softened with well-timed bits of humor. "The vision that I constantly think of—of lesbians and gay men all across this country, on day one, picking up the phone, calling their travel agent, and doing what non-gay people do all the time: fulfilling the lifelong dream of going to Hawaii and marrying the person they love," Wolfson said. Those couples would return "with their leis, their photo albums, and with a marriage certificate, and at that point those couples—those happy couples—will be married. They will be as married as any people on the planet." They would "do what non-gay married people do all the time," Wolfson went on: asking their employers to enroll spouses on insurance plans, filing joint tax returns, seeking family discounts on their gym memberships. "They will do everything that married people do, and at some point we have to expect that in some state somewhere some employer, some recalcitrant gym attendant, some state tax official, some bureaucrat will say no."

This would prompt a legal and possibly political battle in another state, a version of what was already under way in Hawaii. But, Wolfson went on, gays and lesbians would not be afforded the luxury of waiting for such a confrontation. "The backlash has already begun even before we have lashed," Wolfson said, pausing to enjoy the locution, "even before we have won this basic freedom to marry." This was supposedly the bad-news part of the speech, but Wolfson couldn't suppress his smile. He had the gay-rights movement right where he wanted it.

51

Speaking for the Silent Majority

In 1972, a travel book called *The Gay Insider* had identified West Hollywood as "the very epi-center of gay activity," and by the time in early 1996 that Evan Wolfson laid out his optimistic vision there of how same-sex marriage would come to the mainland, the small California municipality was also as close to a sovereign gay city-state as existed in the Americas. First built in the nineteenth century on a railyard between downtown Los Angeles and the Pacific Ocean, the development of Sherman spent decades fending off absorption by the growing metropolis, remaining an unincorporated part of Los Angeles County. After opportunistically changing its name in 1925, West Hollywood succeeded in capturing some reflected glamour from adjacent Hollywood and Beverly Hills, but never their economic activity, thanks in part to the disruptive freight line that continued to bisect Santa Monica Boulevard. West Hollywood was a 1.9-square-mile cluster dense with immigrants, seniors, and those who kept alive the night-life strip known as Boystown. In the hopes of preserving consumer-friendly rent-control laws, neighborhood activists managed in 1984 to incorporate West Hollywood as their own city. By some measures, 40 percent of the new city's electorate—which voted for independent status—was gay and lesbian. When the five-person city council it elected convened for the first time on the stage of the auditorium of Fiesta Hall in Plummer Park, gay people represented a majority.

That council had within months passed a nondiscrimination statute applying to employment and housing, and another that forbid bars from denying service to customers who wore open-toed shoes. (Many in West Hollywood specified such footwear in their dress codes as a way of keeping lesbians out of bars catering to gay men or of banishing transvestites altogether.) But even before they took effect, the council enacted a domestic-partnership law open to any pair of single, unrelated citizens who declare themselves "responsible for each other's welfare." The law applied to hospital and jail-visitation rights, and when the government couldn't find an insurance company willing to recognize same-sex relationships for its public employees, the city decided to self-insure.

The region's most important gay institution—which eventually claimed to be the world's largest provider of services to gays and lesbians—was the Los Angeles Gay and Lesbian Community Services Center. Established in the same year as the Stonewall riot, it became the first gay institution in the United States to receive a government grant of any kind, from Los Angeles County. Federal money followed, helping fund a robust offering of medical services, including treatment of HIV/AIDS and testing for other sexually transmitted diseases. It also offered other programs for addicts, and homeless queer teens and runaways. Unlike New York's Gay Men's Health Crisis or San Francisco's Harvey Milk Democratic Club, the Los Angeles center kept a low profile outside the gay community, but the federally funded programs established a large, invested constituency within it. "Uncle Sam was paying for the first forty hours of the week," says Lorri Jean, a former deputy regional administrator for the Federal Emergency Management Agency hired in 1992 as the center's executive director, "then for the next forty they could be activists and move the political needle."

Jean joined the center just as the Hawaii case was beginning to be noticed by rank-and-file gays and lesbians on the West Coast, and she was surprised to see that no other organizations were doing much to prepare them for the fallout from a favorable trial verdict. Jean had served on the board of Lambda during its debates over marriage and was sympathetic to Paula Ettelbrick's feminist critique. "I had all those same feelings about the institution of marriage," she says. "That there were other things that we'd rather work on, and it seemed like it would be impossible, and the institution itself was not one that had been particularly good to women, and maybe we should work on disentangling benefits from marriage."

But in Los Angeles she was rarely being confronted with intense ideological skepticism or strategic resistance. In part because so much of the community infrastructure revolved around the center—and West Hollywood could serve as a laboratory for policy reforms—gay politics in Los Angeles always seemed a bit more practical and less fraught than in New York or San Francisco. The lesbians and gay men Jean met through her work were plainly curious, and ultimately excited, about what the ability to get married in Hawaii could mean for their lives in California. "Somebody had to be a representative of the voice of the nonactivists," says Jean. "And the center has involvement with more of those people than any other organization in our movement."

In early 1995, Jean helped establish the Los Angeles Freedom to Marry Coalition. It was the first activist group on the mainland to organize around marriage rights, predicated on the awareness that California—which had an equal-rights amendment in its constitution and a law specifying that it would recognize marriage licenses from other states regardless of whether California would have issued them—would likely be "one of the primary testing grounds for the Hawaii case," as Jean put it. In fact, she thought there was a strategic benefit in promoting marriage, if only as a way of pushing more states and municipalities to consider domestic-partnership arrangements like those recognized in West Hollywood, she explains, "because we've set the bar at a different place."

That approach made Jean a more pragmatic advocate for marriage than an absolutist like Evan Wolfson, whom she had known ever since she served on Lambda's board. "Evan is so brilliant, but he also is not often diplomatic," she says. "He would say things that just came out in such a way that they would offend people and rub people the wrong way. He can be a little brusque. But I have felt for a long time that he is one of the most articulate spokespeople for our movement. And has thought strategically about how we should characterize and talk about things in a way that few people do." But those powers of persuasion, she worried, might fail him when faced with more radical activists, particularly lesbians driven by feminist values. "I think Evan was a sexist. I mean, most men, particularly then, had those parts of them," says Jean. "And he was new to the movement."

Worried that Wolfson would be unable to rally its fractious elements on his own, Jean helped convene a June 1995 "steering committee" meeting at the National Gay and Lesbian Task Force's office in Washington. "I was the one who organized the first meeting of national leaders about marriage," Jean says. "Because Evan couldn't have done that on his own." An agreement to coordinate future efforts around marriage marked the first time all the country's national gay and lesbian groups had banded together on a specific policy project. They had a far-flung roster of attendees, including the Log Cabin Republicans and Parents and Friends of Lesbians and Gays, and a few nongay civil-rights groups, including the National Organization for Women and the Japanese American Citizens League. When they unveiled a national Freedom to Marry Coalition that autumn, Jean's organization handed over her group's name (the phrase "freedom to marry" was most famously used in the *Loving v. Virginia* case striking down bans on interracial marriage) and a logo it had developed featuring two interlocking wedding rings.

Back home, the Los Angeles center began planning a panel discussion for January 23, 1996, to galvanize the local community. Though organizers of the panel were very attentive to diversity in demographic terms, the same did not apply to ideology: they didn't invite a single critic of the idea that marriage was worth fighting for. Nor did they feature on flyers promoting a "Same-Gender Marriage: Crossing the Threshold" town-hall meeting the biracial Jewish woman, African American man, or lesbian rabbi who had been recruited to participate. The only people named were two white men: Dan Foley and Andrew Sullivan. When they took their seats at a long table on the stage that was home to meetings of the West Hollywood city council, sitting alongside them was Wolfson—a figure unfamiliar to the largely male, standing-room-only audience, but a crucial link between the night's two stars.

The diorama illustrated the extent to which Wolfson's success pushing marriage to the top of the gay-rights movement's agenda represented a triumph for its conservatives. Marriage would contribute to "our sense of security, our stability as human beings," Sullivan said, in an English accent that seemed to further emphasize the traditionalism of his views. "We don't want to destroy the heterosexual family. We are, to begin with, the heterosexual family. All of us, almost all of us are born into such a family. We love that family. Why would we want to destroy it?"

Sullivan had never planned to become a mouthpiece for gay marriage. In fact, he had never given the topic much thought in political terms before 1989, when he found himself at an editorial meeting of the *New Republic* as a debate broke out over the merits of New York City's program to recognize domestic partnerships. "Why don't we just get it over with and have marriage?" asked Sullivan, an editor who at the time was the only openly gay member of the magazine's staff. (Even if others were taken aback by the suggestion, only one person present vocally opposed Sullivan's position, as he recalls: Fred Barnes, the token doctrinaire conservative among the magazine's writers.) By that point, the reflexively contrarian posture of the *New Republic* was well established, in large part due to editor Michael Kinsley's skill at prodding his writers to tease argument out of such banter. A Tory who had completed his undergraduate studies at Oxford, Sullivan did not in any way belong to the American gay-rights movement, and he was as eager to antagonize self-described "gay liberationists" as much as he was homophobes. He returned to Boston, where he was completing a doctorate in political science at Harvard, and began to read about some of the recent legal decisions bearing on recognition of gay families.

When he started advocating for the courts to go even further, Sullivan coded his proposal as a conservative one, designed to further assimilate gays and lesbians into mainstream society. Yet unlike the authors of many of the *New Republic*'s provocations, Sullivan believed what he wrote. Its logic was defiantly reactionary, and the prose was unusually earnest and at times even tender. "A need to rebel has quietly ceded to a desire to belong," he wrote. "Certainly since AIDS, to be gay and to be responsible has become a necessity." Sullivan was surprised when Kinsley decided to put the article, which he headlined HERE COMES THE GROOM, on a magazine cover that August, illustrated with an image of a wedding cake topped by a pair of tuxedoed male figurines. "It never occurred to me that this would actually lead to something real," he says. "It seemed at the time utterly unimaginable."

But Wolfson had imagined it, even feverishly, and where others may have glanced at the coverline "The Case for Gay Marriage" and seen the latest installment of the *New Republic*'s routine impudence, Wolfson discerned its sincerity. When he spoke for the first time with Sullivan, each learned that the other had been shaped by their readings of John Boswell's *Christianity, Social Tolerance, and Homosexuality*, a revisionist account of the Catholic Church's relationship with gays. Boswell's conclusion was that the Church's homophobia was a relatively new development in Western history, supported by his later findings that prior to the Middle Ages clerics permitted and at times even encouraged same-sex relationships. For Sullivan, a devout Roman Catholic who said that he first came out as gay to God, that history affirmed a noble patrimony for those who identified as both homosexual and Christian. Wolfson was still wrestling with how to navigate his sexual identity when he encountered Boswell's book—he had slipped on a different cover as he read it on a Florida beach while visiting his grandparents—and as a Jew, nothing he found inside disturbed his personal theology. But Boswell's narrative informed what became a core tenet of his civic faith: "If it had once been different, it could be different again." Only a mistaken understanding of history, Wolfson came to believe, had come to sustain the prejudices that modern institutions used to justify opposite-sex relationships as the only ones worthy of marriage.

Wolfson had his first opportunity to meet Boswell when, just out of school and practicing law in New York, he decided to participate in his first gay-pride parade and ended up marching down Fifth Avenue along-side him. (Both were part of a contingent from Yale University, where Boswell taught history and Wolfson had received his bachelor's degree.) After the two participated on a 1990 panel about same-sex relationships, Wolfson worked assiduously to cultivate a new friend and potential col-laborator. (Wolfson imagined that Boswell could eventually contribute his-torical perspective to one of his briefs in a marriage case.) "Watching you autograph your book while I was fielding questions," Wolfson wrote him following their panel together, "I remembered yet again how influential you have been on me, and how proud I am to have been on the panel with you, and to be on the path to becoming your friend."

Boswell died of AIDS in late 1994, and Wolfson and Sullivan bonded over the transformative role his work had played in allowing them to envi-sion potential for a category of same-sex relationships that many of their peers had reflexively discounted as at odds with gay culture. As they grew closer, the two would joke about the irony of their collaboration. "Both of us at the time never had a serious relationship—and it seemed very strange we were both fighting for this right of which neither of us was ever going to take advantage," says Sullivan.

Onstage in West Hollywood, the two men were a portrait in contrasts: Wolfson in jacket and tie, Sullivan in a stonewashed denim oxford with a white undershirt showing at the collar and sleeves rolled up the forearm. It proved a mutually beneficial relationship. Wolfson gained an unlikely, eloquent accomplice whose looks and charisma had won him a sideline as model in a Gap ad campaign shot by Annie Leibovitz. Sullivan, still not an American citizen, found a point of entry into policy debates that essay-ists usually inform from afar. When Barney Frank's staff had to plan a sub-committee hearing—they had less than a week to secure witnesses and arrange for them to be in Washington with helpful testimony—Wolfson recommended his friend. Sullivan, who had just announced plans to leave his post as editor of the *New Republic* as he contended with a diagnosis as HIV-positive, accepted. "I think Evan grasped that if we co-opt or neutral-ize conservatives and libertarians—present a bipartisan front—it would be a better mode of carrying this beyond, for want of a better word, the ghetto," says Sullivan. "I wasn't preaching to the choir."

Sullivan's conservative arguments for marriage were well received in West Hollywood, but not always beyond what Jean called the "silent majority of LGBT people." Members of the self-described direct-action group Lesbian Avengers protested outside bookstores where Sullivan was promoting his book *Virtually Normal,* in which he continued his advocacy for marriage rights. They toted signs that showed the author's face behind crosshairs. Around the same time, Jean and Wolfson staged a town-hall meeting in San Francisco, along with California-based officials from Lambda and the National Center for Lesbian Rights, and faced similar hostility. Pro-marriage speakers were dismissed as "you white people," despite the fact that the panel featured an Asian man and a biracial woman. "There was an accusation," Jean recalls, "that this was not an issue that people of color care about." A joke that her organization would charter planes to Hawaii as soon as that state legalized gay marriages earned Jean another rebuke from the raucous crowd. "This woman, who was originally from Hawaii, just ripped me a new one about 'Don't I think about the environment in Hawaii?' and 'Planes are killing whales,'" she recalls.

Jean may not have intended to pick sides in an ideological battle by throwing the Los Angeles center wholeheartedly behind marriage advocacy, but she had done so. "What assimilationist gays are really asking is that the heterosexuals share some of their privilege with queers who want to be like them," Kate Raphael and Deeg Gold, two San Francisco lesbian activists in the group LAGAI-Queer Insurrection, wrote in 1996. (The group's name was initially an abbreviation of Lesbians and Gays Against Intervention.) That year, the two women organized a First Ever Mass Gay Divorce on Castro Street, a campy stunt featuring a dish-breaking booth and Go Your Separate Ways Travel Agency.

"What a wonderful variety of relationships we have—from anonymous or casual sex in baths, bathrooms and beaches, to long-term monogamy and everything (and everyone) in between. We say, 'the state can't tell us who, or how, to love.' We say, 'Get your laws off my body.' So how exactly does that become a plea to the state to marry us? Will having state-defined relationships make us better lovers?" read a flyer promoting the divorce ceremony. "There is a basic conflict here, between those who see the gay movement as a way to gain acceptance in a straight society, and lesbians and gay men who are fighting to create a society in our own image. A decent and humane society where we can be free. We do not want the crumbs from this society's table, and we are not fighting for a place at it. We want to overturn the fucking table."

But such a view, which had been widely if more delicately articulated years earlier by some leading gay political and legal advocates, was no longer spoken in the institutions that determined movement priorities. Wolfson had in fact succeeded in baiting his opponents into elevating his pet cause into a national issue, and managed to unite his own fractious side along the way. He no longer had to fight with members of his own move- ment on principle, as new strategic imperatives prompted almost instant unanimity about the urgency of protecting unanticipated gains against opponents. "We were immediately launched into a battle that made it very odd for people like myself because, obviously, in no way was I ever going to defend the attacks on the Hawaii decision as they started playing out in legislatures around the country," reflected Paula Ettelbrick, Wolfson's greatest nemesis within Lambda. "At that point, who knew how it was going to turn out?" she asked. "It looked like the whole world was going up in flames over our relationships."

52

Clear It with Evan

When Evan Wolfson and Andrew Sullivan appeared on that stage in West Hollywood, it was clear that it would eventually be time for a second case. As early as the summer of 1993, Wolfson had been working to develop one that would be all his. With *Baehr*, Wolfson had been forced to angle for Dan Foley's trust and—only after the high-pressure appellate arguments were complete—slide in as his sidekick. Once he had, Wolfson had started trying to rewrite the history of the case for mainland consumption. The role played by Bill Woods—the impulsive, self-promoting noodge who had sparked a landmark legal decision without any sort of legal strategy—was inconvenient to Wolfson as he tried to get the movement's institutions, and their funders, to take seriously the work of developing strong marriage cases and discourage other gadflies from launching weak ones.

For the second case, Wolfson would be able to select both the context and the facts. He chose a jurisdiction, New Jersey, where Lambda had experience before appellate courts and that was convenient to its New York City base. There he would be able to choose the facts—he would winnow the plaintiffs and the terms under which they would show they were harmed by the state's marriage laws—and the timing and trajectory of his challenge. Wolfson was aided by a handful of lawyers at the prestigious Los Angeles–based firm Gibson, Dunn & Crutcher.

That lawsuit did not materialize, as there was never the opportunity to demand that another state recognize a Hawaiian marriage license. But Wolfson didn't stop insisting victory was near. That premature triumphalism had helped lead his opponents into the fray and had forced the old ideological quarrels within his own movement to subside. Yet a new source of friction about marriage within the gay community emerged, as gay activists, lawyers, and individual couples who had never before given much thought to marriage as a personal or political goal started acting upon the enthusiasm stoked by the Hawaii case.

While he was publicly claiming that his issue's time had come and cultivating interest among activists and donors with his happy talk, Wolfson was quietly and desperately trying to deflate those newly emboldened to mount cases of their own. Advocates for recognition of other gay-friendly family types foresaw a post-Hawaii environment where they would finally be in a position to propose such policies—like some version of the domestic-partnership arrangements then recognized by some municipal governments—as a compromise. "Now we're at a real tug-of-war stage" over gay rights, asserted Thomas Coleman, a Los Angeles attorney whose Spectrum Institute's Family Diversity Project championed domestic-partnership laws. "This same-sex marriage thing is throwing gasoline into the fire and it's likely to explode."

Coleman emerged as Wolfson's leading foil within the legal community. They were of the same generation, but where Wolfson maintained his youthful idealism about marriage, Coleman was proudly incrementalist. "You don't build the penthouse until you've constructed the first 19 floors," he would say. Coleman's cause had tallied more successes than Wolfson's—he had advised a handful of Southern California cities on their municipal domestic-partnership ordinances—and was more palatable to members of the political class. In the summer of 1996 Clinton adviser George Stephanopoulos was looking for policy options that might permit support for some recognition of same-sex couples. An assistant of his contacted Coleman to request a copy of an article titled "Democrats for Domestic Partnership," which Coleman had written before the Defense of Marriage Act crisis put the White House on defensive. "I am not alone in my views," Coleman advised Stephanopoulos, "that pushing gay marriage as an 'all or nothing' choice is not in the best interests of the gay community." When Hawaiian officials recognized that they would likely have to do something to respond to a court decision that demanded recognition of gay relationships, Coleman saw his opening to affect state policy. Domestic partnerships, he argued, could present those couples the legal benefits of marriage without triggering the same political resistance.

Wolfson and Coleman had both participated in Roundtable meetings together as early as 1985, but when their trajectories came into conflict a decade later, in the midst of a growing movement, they warred through an email listserv. (The new technology offered an indispensable outlet for gay activists, lawyers, and legal academics on the mainland looking to receive updates about events unfolding in Hawaii.) "This list is for those who wish to learn about, and fight for, our freedom to marry, and not for the endless and umpteenth argument about whether we should be doing that," Wolfson wrote after Coleman circulated versions of a model domestic-partnership ordinance to the marriage listserv. "We have work to do, and ferocious enemies trying—unsuccessfully so far—to shut down the national discussion just as we have begun to engage the American people in a powerful way that we must sustain." Out of public view, Wolfson was even more direct in trying to staunch such dissent. "There is a message to me from Evan expressing 'disappointment' that I would post my views without phoning him first," New Jersey civil libertarian Arthur C. Warner wrote to Coleman, with whom he had seventeen years earlier partnered on a case to fight lewd-conduct laws in California. "Now I have to 'clear it with Evan'?"

When Coleman managed to testify before the Hawaii and Vermont legislatures, Wolfson tried to blunt his influence. "We may leave the room not getting everything we want, but don't go in bargaining against yourself," he would warn allies tempted by such a pragmatic posture. Privately Wolfson characterized Coleman as plainly reckless. "I find several things truly shameful," Wolfson wrote to Foley about one of Coleman's articles, citing (among other defects) "his distraction of potential activists" from urgent work and "his virtual invitation to California legislators to attempt to thwart recognition by legislative amendment."

While visiting Hawaii in February 1996 to appear before the legislature, Coleman ran into Bill Woods, whom Wolfson also attempted to marginalize in the small online community where they dueled for primacy as front men for the Hawaii suit. (Again, when speaking to friends in confidence, Wolfson was even more cutting. "Here's the latest from loony land," Wolfson wrote to Foley on a fax cover sheet accompanying an announcement that Woods would be embarking on a mainland speaking tour. "This one's supposed to be your headache; why are you 'letting' him come over here? :) Sigh.") On the beach, Coleman and Woods bonded over their new status as two men who believed that Wolfson was trying to write them out of history. "I thanked him for his kind words and silently wished that some of the pro-marriage advocates were not so insulting and harsh in their personal attacks on those who favor an alternative approach," Coleman reflected shortly after his encounter with Woods. "Who knows, maybe someday the leadership of the movement for gay and lesbian rights will respect the diversity of opinions and approaches that emerge from within our multi-faceted community."

Wolfson's greatest successes in his new leadership role may have been the cases that never happened. Throughout the mid-to-late 1990s, Wolfson embarked on a national game of whack-a-mole, monitoring local news coverage and chasing reports from state advocacy groups to beat down potential plaintiffs before they popped up in court. Lambda "strongly recommended that people not file lawsuits at this time," Wolfson told the *Washington Blade* in August 1995, describing the consensus among gay political and legal groups that one case was enough (if not too much) already. "Just because there is room for that, and that works at this phase doesn't necessarily mean that you should now just replicate it willy-nilly at every single turn," Wolfson says. "Once we had this promising vehicle of Hawaii, the cost-benefit ratio of other potential lawsuits becomes different. You don't need a galvanizing effect. We had galvanized a national, and indeed it turned out to be an ongoing global, conversation."

Wolfson outlined what some characterized as a "Hawaii First" strategy, asking couples to hold off until the *Baehr* process had concluded. They need not abandon their ambitions to lodge marriage suits in their states, he counseled, but might find easier cases emerge once they had Hawaiian licenses in hand and were asking local authorities to recognize them, rather than issue new ones. "I totally, personally, and deeply understand the frustration and impatience gay and lesbian couples have who are in love and want to be married. That's what we're fighting for," Wolfson said. "But filing the wrong suit in the wrong place at the wrong time is not going to help and what any one couple does affects what all of us are doing."

For those not immediately persuaded by that logic, Wolfson's simple insistence that plaintiffs would be on their own when it came to securing and paying lawyers was enough to discourage them from pushing ahead with suits. One year after Shawna Underwood and Denia Davis sued the state of Florida in 1993, represented in court by a regional ACLU affiliate, a judge threw out their suit. Days later, citing meetings with Lambda Legal and national ACLU officials, Underwood and Davis announced they would drop the case. Similarly, Arizona plaintiffs who lost a 1994 ruling in state superior court decided not to appeal. After seeing their initial petition against the state denied, two Los Angeles–area men who had first requested a license in early 1993 let appeals slide indefinitely, too. Their lawyer, who had developed the suit to be the first test case challenging

California law, carried no grudge toward the man who had pushed them from a distance to put the movement's national priorities ahead of local interests. "It was an unalloyed pleasure finally to meet," Paul Marchand wrote a few years later to Wolfson when he came to West Hollywood for a community forum about marriage, and praised him "for blazing the trail."

But not every would-be plaintiff acquiesced so easily to Wolfson's influence. In both New York and Alaska, couples resisted his efforts, possibly growing even more incalcitrant as they developed their own, mostly symbolic, alliance as dissidents against a gay legal establishment they saw taking cues from Lambda's Marriage Project to shut them out. "I made it clear we're working with you and want to work with you—win or lose," Jay Brause of Anchorage wrote to Phillip and Toshav Storrs of Ithaca, whom he had never met but knew as the other couple very openly defying Wolfson's endeavor to keep new marriage cases off court dockets.

In May 1995, Toshav Greene and Phillip G. Storrs had moved to Ithaca, New York, from nearby Elmira and went to city hall to request a marriage license. In the liberal college town they discovered a friendly city government with an activist mayor eager to champion their rights. "If they really want to go ahead with it, my position is that they should be granted a license," Mayor Benjamin Nichols said. When the city attorney said they lacked the legal foundation for doing so, Nichols declared in a statement that "I regret that the city cannot issue a marriage license to a same-sex couple at this time." It was effectively an invitation for Greene and Storrs to take the matter to court, and the couple filed a petition citing both state and federal constitutions to claim the denial was unconstitutional. The move sent Wolfson into a frenzy, and inspired the rare occasion when he used the press to describe anything other than the rosiest scenario imaginable. "If you go to a court that is uneducated or that is going to rule in a climate that's unreceptive," he told the *New York Times*, "you're almost certainly going to get a decision you didn't really want."

The persistence of the Storrses, who had since decided to share a last name despite not being legally married, was enough of a crisis to prompt Wolfson to team up with an old rival. He and Paula Ettelbrick, then legislative counsel to the Empire State Pride Agenda, headed together to Ithaca, and over the five-hour drive from Manhattan, the two former colleagues found themselves for the first time in years at ease enough with each other to joke freely. The marriage battles that had divided Lambda were over, and even as Ettelbrick confessed that she had a "totally divided heart," the two saw eye to eye about the need to stop what they agreed was a poorly conceived challenge from advancing in court. "Part of me very much wants to say, 'Go for it. The question has been called,'" she said. "But what would be gained if we won the right today and lost it tomorrow because we had not done the grass-roots lobbying that we needed to do?"

In Ithaca, Wolfson and Ettelbrick met with sympathetic local officials and lawyers involved in the case. But the Storrses were not as responsive, arguing that they had specifically crafted their petition so that it would not apply to anything beyond their particular license request. Wolfson and Ettelbrick challenged that claim, arguing that their petition was not written quite so narrowly, and besides, plaintiffs would not be able to fully control subsequent appeals and the breadth of judges' decisions on them. A dinner among the four was so contentious that the Storrses walked out of the restaurant, outraged at the brazenness shown by representatives of two large organizations supposedly charged with promoting gay rights. "I'm disappointed that these groups are thinking about timetables," Toshav Storrs told the *New York Times*. "What rings in my head is the letter from the Birmingham jail in which Martin Luther King says it's always the right time to do right." (An unrelated investigation by *The Daily Oklahoman* newspaper later revealed that Greene—who in 1990 had changed his first name from Tony to Toshav upon conversion to Judaism—had accumulated a variety of criminal convictions for grand larceny, forgery, and fraud offenses in two states.)

In Alaska, Jay Brause and Gene Dugan had begun exploring the prospect of a lawsuit in 1986 and spent three years trying to win the support of national gay organizations to do so. Much as Woods had been around the same time, they were parried and rejected. Unlike Woods, they gave up. Days after the Hawaii Supreme Court ruled in the *Baehr* case—the one Wolfson began immediately celebrating in print as "by far the most important positive ruling ever when it comes to gay rights"—another couple went ahead and applied for a marriage license from the state's Vital Statistics office in Anchorage. A judge who reviewed the request ordered the office to deny it, concluding that "marriage between two persons of the same sex is not contemplated by our statutory scheme." The following year, Brause and Dugan tried themselves, retaining a lawyer and rallying the state's very small gay-rights community as they prepared to file a constitutional claim. "We fully support Jay and Gene's action and are behind them 100%," Alaska Civil Liberties Union executive director Rachel King said, even as her organization chose not to pay their legal fees. "Jay and

Gene are taking a courageous first step to securing the right to marry for gay and lesbian couples."

Wolfson did not share that enthusiasm. Unlike some of the other states where he had worked to discourage lawsuits, Alaska had friendly laws: like Hawaii, its state constitution explicitly defined a right to privacy and barred discrimination by sex. Lambda's own analysis showed it was one of the "most favorable" states in which to mount a marriage case, but Wolfson insisted on sticking to the "Hawaii First" strategy. "Bringing a lawsuit is the easiest thing to do of all the important things that we need to do," he says. "They just wanted to do the case." In August 1995, over Wolfson's objections, Brause and Dugan moved ahead, represented by an Anchorage attorney working pro bono on their behalf. "Here it is, Evan," Brause wrote, along with a copy of their lawsuit against the state of Alaska a few days before it was filed. "Let's wish the best for us all."

When they read of a similar suit filed in Vermont, Brause and Dugan were shocked to learn that Wolfson had been encouraging it along—and lining up the institutional support on its behalf—even as he disparaged their case that had a nearly three-year head start in Alaska. "You now have a growing field of casework and all of us lack financial resources," Brause complained to Wolfson. "This is where you may have thought we would be without a unified front to [do] this work and, in fact, this is where we are." Brause and Dugan would end up winning their argument before the Anchorage Superior Court, and they didn't stop fuming about what they saw as Wolfson's manipulations to deny them support. "This whole matter reminds me of something I learned in politics long ago: stay close to your opposition, but stay closer to your friends," Brause, a former president of the ACLU affiliate in Alaska, wrote to Wolfson.

None of these conflicts stopped Wolfson from continuing to publicly proclaim the cause of marriage ascendant, boasting to members of his National Freedom to Marry Coalition in September 1997 that "we are on the brink of a whole new phase of this struggle." By then, it was apparent that a constitutional referendum was headed to the ballot in Hawaii that would preempt any court victory, and Wolfson knew that polling showed his side losing two-to-one with no viable strategy for closing the gap. (A similar chain of events would follow in Alaska.) But that didn't stop him from telling even his own allies that "the change will be enormous, and it is going to happen within months." For three years, Wolfson had been effectively the country's only full-time spokesman for same-sex marriage rights. By most measures the movement was worse off than it was before he had started: still no state sanctioned gay marriages, but many states—empowered by the federal government—had taken steps to actively foreclose the prospect of ever recognizing them. National polls showed that they had lost public support during the debate over the Defense of Marriage Act. If Wolfson didn't pronounce repeatedly that victory was near, no one would ever believe it was possible.

53

Organization Man

In 2000, the *National Law Journal* named Evan Wolfson one of the "100 most influential lawyers in America" despite the fact that the onetime prosecutor and litigator hardly ever visited a courthouse in a role beyond spectator. Ever since he had been granted permission to launch Lambda's Marriage Project, Wolfson had actively shrugged off new clients as he angled to have marriage advocacy consume the time he had once devoted to more conventional legal work. When Hawaii officials stayed the granting of licenses in the state, pending another round of appeals, he lost the opportunity to bring a suit on behalf of the potential plaintiffs he had cultivated to sue for recognition of their Hawaiian marriage at home. Vermont, not New Jersey, would be the second front. After Hawaii voters passed Amendment 2 in the fall of 1998—effectively ensuring that there would be no further appeals in *Baehr*—it was clear there would never be a need for Wolfson to appear in a Hawaii courtroom again. Success the following year before the Vermont Supreme Court left him superseded by Mary Bonauto, who was emerging as the gay movement's leading marriage litigator.

By decade's end, the only open case left on Wolfson's docket was *Boy Scouts of America v. Dale,* as the 1992 lawsuit he had launched on behalf of the gay scoutmaster James Dale had become known on its latest appeal. In 1999, the New Jersey Supreme Court had awarded Wolfson and his client a victory, ruling that the organization had violated state laws ensuring equal access to public accommodations by discriminating against Dale because of his sexuality. The Boy Scouts asked the Supreme Court to reverse that opinion, on the basis that laws limiting its ability to choose its own members limited freedom of association. On April 26, 2000, Wolfson headed to the Supreme Court.

Wolfson had bittersweet memories of visiting the Supreme Court for the most significant gay-rights case of his lifetime. He had attended oral arguments in *Bowers v. Hardwick* as a junior lawyer who had helped draft Lambda's amicus brief against antisodomy laws. Wolfson had spent the day flirting with the handsome plaintiff, Michael Hardwick, whom he met for the first time in court that morning; that afternoon, the two strolled hand in hand through Washington and shared a kiss in front of the White House. After the justices ruled that Georgia was within its rights to have prosecuted Hardwick years earlier, Wolfson bought two lapel pins shaped as pink triangles. He gave one of them to the man whose name would be permanently attached to the gay-rights movement's greatest-ever legal defeat. "I swore I would not stop wearing that pin until we had overturned that hideous decision," Wolfson said. He brought it with him when he returned to argue Dale's case, but as the court forbade those before them to wear insignia, Wolfson selected a green tie with an inconspicuous pattern of small pink triangles and stashed the pin in the pocket of his black suit.

The morning's argument had nothing to do with marriage, the object of so much of Wolfson's professional passion, but in his mind they were related projects, both about "claiming a vocabulary of full participation in an iconic American institution." This was the logic of a political strategist rather than a litigator. Asserting constitutional claims was mere cover to introduce what Wolfson considered basic facts into that American vocabulary: that there were gay kids, or that same-sex relationships aspired to lifelong monogamy.

He left the courtroom that day with reason for greater pessimism about the fate of Dale's case than Hardwick's team had after their 1986 session. Even one of the court's most liberal justices, Ruth Bader Ginsburg, appeared exasperated by Wolfson, at one point asking him wearily: "Is the best that you could come up with that the Boy Scouts have an expressive policy against . . . I don't know what?" (One of his more awkwardly contentious exchanges came with Justice Anthony Kennedy, who appeared to accuse Wolfson of unreasonably introducing the concept of "intimate association"—which Kennedy himself would invoke fifteen years later when striking down gay-marriage bans—in a case about the right of expression.) But the day had just begun. At 3 p.m., Wolfson learned that, at the statehouse in Montpelier, Vermont governor Howard Dean had just signed the civil-unions bill. The state planned to begin recognizing relationships between gays and lesbians right around the same time that summer that the Supreme Court would announce whether the Boy Scouts could reject them as members.

That resolution to the Vermont process meant that marriage strategists should begin preparing a case in another state, even as they had to tend to the political aftermath they left behind in Montpelier. Conservative forces joined under the campaign Take Back Vermont were already threatening to punish officials who supported the compromise, including legislators and the governor, in the fall elections. If enough of them were unseated for their votes, not only would opponents reopen the question of civil unions during the next legislative session but losses would spook politicians elsewhere whenever the issue arrived in their states. To Wolfson, the day's events represented "two major pieces of my work coming to this exciting culmination point," as he put it at the time.

A couple of months later, the Supreme Court ruled five-to-four against James Dale. Wolfson gamely minimized the outcome as some kind of success. "By fighting, by engaging, you force discussion. Discussion is what we need to move forward," Wolfson said shortly after the Dale case was decided. "The only way to really lose is to give up."

But in one sense, Wolfson was giving up: he decided for himself that the end of the Dale appeals would mark the conclusion of his career as a practicing attorney. "I really felt then that a chapter had closed and it was time to open the next chapter," he explained when he formally announced his departure from Lambda in early 2001. Wolfson would continue to fantasize about the day that a lawyer from one of the country's major gay-rights organizations might stand before the Supreme Court and argue that the "freedom to marry" implied by the U.S. Constitution applied to same-sex couples, but he knew he wouldn't be the one to do so. "I've always really been very deeply impressed by Martin Luther King's observation that there are many methodologies for social change and we really need them all pulled together in partnership and working to make the whole greater than the sum of the parts," he said. "So to my mind the litigation is actually where we're strongest and where I can afford to leave that to my colleagues."

Throughout the late 1990s, Wolfson had seen his side perpetually out-strategized and outspent. Even where gay-marriage advocates had initiated a legal process themselves—effectively setting the time and place and terms of the conflict—they proved politically impotent. In Hawaii, this manifested itself as a series of intersecting defeats: politicians who had voted to protect the possibility of legalizing same-sex marriage lost their seats, lobbyists failed to stop a backlash in the legislature, and over the course of an eighteen-month election season campaigners couldn't change minds on a ballot initiative. Victory in an Alaska court was even more short-lived, as the state's voters would undo that progress months later through a referendum of their own on the same Election Day that Hawaii passed Amendment 2. (Despite the fact that the Hawaii campaign ultimately received nearly $1.5 million in support from national gay interests and the Alaska one hardly any at all, they both ended up losing by a similar two-to-one margin.) Vermont was a version of the same story, with gay activists incapable of getting anything better out of the state legislature than civil unions, aware from the outset that full marriage rights were beyond their grasp.

Social conservatives identified that weakness and adjusted their strategies accordingly. The wave of mini-DOMAs enacted in 1996 had all gone through legislatures and were then signed into law by governors. After the Hawaii and Alaska referenda, antigay activists in other states with accessible ballot-initiative processes saw promise in bypassing the capitals altogether. In 1997, California state senator Pete Knight, who had the prior year passed out of the assembly a bill forbidding recognition of gay marriages only to see it flounder in the senate, decided to go instead to the voters with his proposal to rewrite the California Family Code. Knight's one-sentence Proposition 22 qualified for the same ballot as the state's presidential primary in March 2000. The state's Democratic establishment was almost uniformly opposed to the so-called Knight Initiative—as well as presidential candidates Bill Bradley and Al Gore, then vice president, as they campaigned in the state—but it nonetheless won 61 percent of the vote. The Nebraska Family Council began collecting signatures for a ballot initiative of its own, this time to forbid state government from validating or recognizing any "civil union, domestic partnership, and similar same-sex relationship"—the first of the bans to be so expansive. In November 2000, it passed with 70 percent of the vote.

The disconnect between the legal victories and political defeats that later undermined them amounted to a tragic illustration of the fact that "the law doesn't operate in a vacuum," an observation that had molded Wolfson's view of his profession from his student years onward. As an undergraduate, he participated in the abstract but intense debates hosted by the Yale Political Union, where he was the Liberal Party's floor leader and served as a campus coordinator of the Students for Carter campaign. There he took responsibility for leading a nominally nonpartisan, door-to-door voter-registration drive through dormitories in 1976 and "what was probably the largest leaflet distribution ever at Yale," as he bragged to the student newspaper upon a campus visit by vice-presidential candidate Walter Mondale. As a graduate student teaching political philosophy while studying at Harvard Law School, Wolfson had worked on Carter's reelection campaign and Michael Dukakis's for governor of Massachusetts. When he took a job not long thereafter and joined the group formally known as the Lambda Legal Defense and Education Fund, he thought he stood out for his "non-lawyerishness" and the fact that he retained some of the same energies that had drawn him into political activism. "I brought to it just a very strong commitment to that second half of the equation—that education and organizing side—more so than many of my Lambda colleagues," he says.

On April 30, 2001, Wolfson formally departed Lambda to focus on that organizing work. When pushed on his plans, however, Wolfson would say only that he had a foundation grant to research new strategies to advance the cause of gay marriage. "I think anyone who knows me," he cautioned, "knows that I'm not just going to be sitting around writing a book report."

....

54

Mining the Foundations

As he left Lambda, Evan Wolfson told one journalist, he felt "liberated to bring people together in a new way from a new angle with a new platform, new resources." He was armed with a planning grant from the Evelyn and Walter Haas, Jr. Fund to "explore the next steps for how our movement is going to win the freedom to marry." The grant supported Wolfson as he prepared to return to the San Francisco philanthropy—a family foundation sustained by the wealth of an heir to the Levi Strauss denim fortune—with both a strategy and a structure that would not have left marriage advocates as powerless as they had been in Hawaii and Vermont, California and Nebraska.

"Inconceivable as it may seem to some people, I wish I had been even more of a nag in getting people to focus on some of the threats we were facing at various points in the marriage work," Wolfson said. "I am specifically thinking of some of the right-wing assaults on Hawaii. Had I been better at getting some of the key groups to come in earlier to do the work, we perhaps could have warded off that attack earlier."

The real problem, Wolfson knew, was not that he was an insufficiently hectoring presence within the gay-rights movement but that its "key groups" had to contend with other nags of their own. Ideological divides around marriage may have disappeared by the mid-1990s, but the Human Rights Campaign, the National Gay and Lesbian Task Force, and the desultory state activist coalitions still had other priorities they cared about more. Many of these were concerns that long predated the day "the earth moved," as Wolfson had taken to describing the 1993 Hawaii Supreme Court decision. Other groups had spent years doing research, cultivating supporters, developing strategies, assembling delicately poised coalitions in areas where they thought they could make headway, all of which stood to be upended by conflict over marriage. In many cases, gay leaders were fully aware of the risks they would take by following Wolfson into battle. If fighting the Defense of Marriage Act meant jeopardizing a nondiscrimination bill, or if punishing legislators who opposed gay marriage would lose moderate votes necessary to pass a hate-crimes ban, most gay groups already knew what mattered most to them.

If Wolfson was liberated by leaving Lambda, it was because he was no longer constrained by institutions that refused to accept his argument for the primacy of marriage as a cause above all others. "Marriage is about more than tying the knot," he said in the summer of 2003. "It is about our full inclusion in society and is the platform for discussion by nongay people of who we are." As he spent down his planning grant, Wolfson fixated on that question: What would an organization look like if it was constructed in the image of his own newly liberated life, and didn't have to worry about anything beyond one issue at a time?

There was something of a model in the otherwise forgettable disaster of the gay-rights movement's efforts to hold the White House accountable for Bill Clinton's campaign promises to change Pentagon policies around sexual orientation. The Campaign for Military Service had also been conceived by a former Lambda attorney to focus on a single problem that no one established group had all the tools to address. The group's name was telling: it existed only to manage one campaign with a discrete goal—permanently ending the military's ban on gays and lesbians. When the campaign was launched in early 1993, the White House had already initiated the policy process; everything was to be sorted out, one way or another, within months. The organization hired a range of consultants, including a legislative attorney, lobbyists, and Democratic media and polling firms, at times negotiating open-ended weekly and monthly contracts. The team could claim some small accomplishments, such as a nationwide "Tour of Duty" bus tour (featuring those who had served while in the closet) that succeeded in generating media coverage in outlets that would cover national policy matters only when presented with a local angle. Yet their work, the *Los Angeles Times* reported with a focus on the cluster of local activists and Hollywood donors behind the project, "stirred up turf battles and grumbling about a 'California invasion' of the national gay-rights organizations in Washington."

The Campaign for Military Service was far from self-sufficient. For most of its projects, it had to rely on other organizations—both gay groups and allies like the ACLU and People for the American Way. It even had to turn for support at crucial moments to the people it was trying to lobby. When the coalition wanted to exert pressure on congressional Democrats, it had to beg the Democratic National Committee to share voter files before a grassroots phone or postcard campaign could be launched, and it asked the White House to convene meetings that members of the House and Senate were otherwise happy to ignore. Even when the campaign engaged directly with elected officials, it lacked leverage: it controlled little in terms of votes or money and wouldn't be around long enough to deliver on any promises or threats it made. Among observers of gay politics, the episode was so remembered for its failures that few reflected much on the value of the campaign model of activism.

A campaign around marriage would be much harder to conceptualize. Wolfson was able to define a singular goal: the ability for same-sex couples to marry across the United States of America. But that seemed certain to take decades, without any agreement as to what the scenario would actually entail or what a path to it might look like. "It seemed to me that even at that point, the likelihood of marriage nationwide was not even on the horizon," says Barbara Cox, a California Western School of Law dean who had worked with Wolfson on marriage issues since the mid-1990s. "It was maybe we can get it in one or two states, and how will it impact everybody else."

In practice, Wolfson had defined more than fifty distinct policy objectives—if one considered the District of Columbia, Puerto Rico, Guam, and other territories, not to mention Indian reservations that set their own marriage rules. Constitutional amendments were setting the cause back in some states even as progress was made in others. Any marriage campaign would have to be slogged out across them, simultaneously in courts, legislatures, and at the ballot box. "Unlike the gays-in-the-military fiasco, which caught our national groups off-guard—and whose perilous straits the ill-equipped Campaign for Military Service proved unable to navigate—the battle over gay marriage is essentially local," Marvin Liebman, a longtime Republican operative who came out late in life, wrote in a 1995 op-ed.

There was little existing political infrastructure that Wolfson could commandeer to push for marriage rights. Large swaths of the country went without a statewide gay-rights activist organization, full-time lawyer, or devoted lobbyist. The National Gay and Lesbian Task Force had little footprint in the states, and the Human Rights Campaign insisted that campaign-finance laws complicated the ability of its political action committee to be active in local politics. (When the Human Rights Campaign eventually made a contribution to the political action committee working to protect pro-marriage legislators in Hawaii, it was seen as a token gift that did little to match the money being spent by religious opponents.) Even in states that did have their own professionalized organizations—like New York's Empire State Pride Agenda and Massachusetts's Gay & Lesbian Advocates and Defenders—Wolfson was competing with local agendas.

At Lambda's Marriage Project, he had struggled to secure enough resources to shape the priorities of other organizations. The conventional fundraising targets, broad-based foundations whose munificence had sustained some of the left's major institutions, had always been reticent to back gay-specific causes. When the American Civil Liberties Union typically launched a new project, it sought commitments from foundations, since they were good for multiyear grants insulated from the faddishness that sometimes distracted individual donors. But as the ACLU set out in the mid-1980s to launch a Lesbian and Gay Rights Project, the likes of the Ford Foundation and the Rockefeller Foundation refused to give. "There was no foundation that was going to touch it," says Nan Hunter, who helped lead the ACLU's fundraising for the project and became its first director. "The only way any of the gay-rights organizations would get funded was through private donors." Ultimately unable to find an established foundation willing to back the project, the ACLU took the unlikely approach of relying on a single large donor, openly gay San Francisco philanthropist James Hormel, to back the project's 1986 launch.

A decade later, when Wolfson started raising money for Lambda's Marriage Project, the pool of available donors remained so small that his efforts immediately set him in conflict with local groups. When Hawaii activists began soliciting donations on the mainland, many of the country's most generous benefactors of gay causes—including Hormel, who had previously given to the Hawaii Equal Rights Marriage Project—demurred, citing recent contributions they had made to Lambda's Marriage Project in response to Wolfson's appeals that the money was necessary to sustain the Hawaii case. "Many people are under the impression that their contribution to Lambda is also a direct contribution to HERMP," fundraising consultant Reno Long complained to Lambda's executive director, Kevin Cathcart, in June 1995. "This is creating confusion among contributors and limiting HERMP's support."

But something had clearly changed when the Haas, Jr. Fund, which was started in 1953 by Levi Strauss heirs to back community projects in

San Francisco, decided in 2001 to fund Wolfson's efforts to "explore the next steps for how our movement is going to win." (The institution was in a period of flux after the death of its benefactor, its leadership interested in expanding its footprint into new issues.) The proposal Wolfson delivered to the foundation sketched a single-issue national organization called Freedom to Marry, based on the campaign model that could support political and legal activity. "You should do something nobody else is doing, something much of the gay leadership doesn't even think about. You should go national," he later recalled telling Haas officials.

When the foundation, to Wolfson's pleasant surprise, accepted his proposal, they presented him a choice. He could either join the foundation and direct its gay-marriage work from a position on its staff, or he could spin off and create the organization and run it. He took the latter option, guarding some independence for the campaign's strategic and tactical decisions, but agreeing to nominate someone to be his handler. Wolfson recalled encountering Tim Sweeney in 1982, when Sweeney came to Harvard with Lambda special project attorney Roz Richter as part of a tour to promote the group's work to law-school students. It was the first time, Wolfson would recall for years later, that he realized it was even possible to find full-time employment as a gay-rights litigator. Now after twelve years in that job, he was effectively putting it aside to define a new role as a full-time gay-rights strategist and organizer. Wolfson recommended that Haas hire Sweeney, who after Lambda had gone to work at the Gay Men's Health Crisis and Empire State Pride Agenda, as its first officer overseeing gay-related grants, including Freedom to Marry. "The challenge to us was, we aren't funding this alone," recalls Sweeney. "They were like, 'You need to raise millions.'"

Fortunately, he knew where to find them.

Outgiving

In early 1996, at the urging of her boss, Katherine Pease invited the wealthiest gay people in the United States, or at least those at once openly gay and openly wealthy, to Colorado. Nearly all of them had come into their money by blood. (It would be more than a decade before a major publicly traded company had an openly gay CEO, and he would resign immediately after being outed by journalists.) James Hormel was an heir to the meat marketers who had invented Spam, Fred Hochberg to the Lillian Vernon mail-order catalog, and Henry van Ameringen to the New York–based chemical company International Flavors and Fragrances. Even those who had developed public identities distinct from ancestral affluence would probably not have been there without it. Ellen Malcolm became an influential political operative as founder of the EMILY's List network for pro-choice Democratic female candidates, but was backed by the fortune generated when her great-grandfather's time clock company was absorbed into another to become IBM.

The role of heredity in their wealth illustrated how the seemingly random appearance of sexual and gender minorities served a redistributive, and ultimately politically progressive, purpose. A country with few black multimillionaires would never generate a cohort of philanthropists with a self-interest in African American causes, a predicament that challenged the civil-rights movement of the 1950s and 1960s. The very system of economic dislocation it was fighting left African Americans unable to fund their own activism; at crucial moments, Martin Luther King Jr. had to turn to northern white benefactors like Nelson Rockefeller and the Ford Foundation for financial support. Yet a generation of ascendant gay and lesbian activists included those who had the means to shape public policy even before they had a strategy for doing so.

The host in Aspen, a plastic surgeon's son, had what passed in that company for humble roots. The closest thing Tim Gill had had to an inheritance was a $2,000 loan from his parents as he tried to market homemade software from his apartment. His QuarkXPress would become the world's preeminent desktop-publishing software. With degrees from the University of Colorado in both applied mathematics and computer science, Gill still considered himself a techie, and never quite reengineered his tastes to synchronize with his wealth. "I didn't realize that I was rich. I was still thinking of myself as a college student living on Top Ramen and Doritos," he would say. He never grew much impressed with personal manifestations of power and celebrity. After he began donating to political candidates, he opted not to seek the blandishments he was due in return. When the president came to town, Gill—who described himself as a "pathological introvert"—skipped the fundraising event and sent an assistant to get her picture taken with him in his place. "Sometimes when I go out, I'm one of the better-off people and I'm wearing the scruffiest-looking clothes," he said. "I think it's the computer-geek gene fighting with the gay gene."

Gill had been out of the closet since he was a teenager, and active in a student gay organization during college. But to the extent he had a public profile as a businessman, his sexuality had never been part of it. That changed in 1992, when Colorado voters were presented with Amendment 2, to strip local governments of the right to enact laws protecting gays, lesbians, and bisexuals from discrimination. Gill gave around $40,000 to the campaign that rallied to defeat the measure, enough to become the group's largest donor. Like many of its opponents, Gill was surprised to see Amendment 2 pass handily—polls had shown it likely to lose—but he was not oblivious to the support the cause enjoyed. During the campaign Gill had been startled to spot a "Vote 'Yes' on Amendment 2" sign tacked up at an employee's desk. "Everyone has the right to their opinion, of course," he said. "But I was astonished people would vote against the rights of the person signing their paycheck."

Activists around the country responded to the measure's passage by organizing a campaign to boycott Colorado, and Quark—whose software was used largely by media companies and advertising agencies—felt the liberal backlash more quickly than other businesses in the state. At the time, Gill was busy planning the company's regular weeklong user conference, to be held the following month at its Denver headquarters. When he was informed that *Sports Illustrated*, along with two other customers, decided not to send representatives to Colorado, Gill turned to damage control. On the same day New York City mayor David Dinkins endorsed a travel boycott of the state, Gill pledged $1 million to undo the amendment's damage. Yet that still wasn't enough to overcome a boycott gaining momentum nationwide. Gill persuaded customers to travel to Denver under the condition that there would be a vote on the location of subsequent conferences. Quark's users decided, by a margin of 300 to 2, to go elsewhere in the future. "That makes it much harder for me to do business. It's much more expensive. I've got to take people, move somewhere else, rent computers rather than use ours," Gill said. "But on the other hand, my customers' wishes are very important to me."

Shocked to learn that his mid-five-figure check to the anti–Amendment 2 effort had been the largest single donation the campaign had received, Gill dedicated his new pledge to "changing the thinking that led to Amendment 2," as Pease described it. But there were few existing institutions that specialized in such work, and Gill had no philanthropic infrastructure beyond his personal checkbook. Furthermore, Gill lacked a method for even prioritizing his gifts, as he learned when he and his executive assistant had to sift through requests arriving by mail. "All of a sudden he had all this attention from national organizations," says Pease, "and he had all these scrappy local activists knocking on his door."

Pease had been one of them. As a bisexual and graduate of Colorado College, she had volunteered on the anti–Amendment 2 campaign; the next year, she had organized a "Colorado Unity Rally for Equality," an idea that grew partly out of the failure of the anti–Amendment 2 campaigners to work in tandem with Latino activists fighting in parallel against an English-only initiative on the same ballot. "There was no real history of these two movements working together," says Pease. Marching alongside the National Association for the Advancement of Colored People, American Indian Movement, and Jewish Voices for Justice would, Pease pledged at the time, make it "apparent that the collective clout of minority communities is awesome." To stitch the gay community into the fabric of Colorado's civil society on an ongoing basis, Pease launched a new annual fundraiser in Denver. Even though local gay causes struggled for money, Pease insisted that the Cheshire Ball not benefit them. Instead, as a gesture of goodwill, money was raised for children's charities.

Gill had been thinking in similar terms. His million dollars went largely toward the objective of "normalizing LGBT people in the eyes of the public," as he put it. Gill had little personal passion for the arts, but he recognized that as a philanthropic space they offered a chance to build goodwill with nongay elites. Instead of crediting the contribution to Tim Gill, he asked that the donor be identified as the Gay and Lesbian Fund for Colorado. Soon concertgoers were hearing "gay" and "lesbian" before philharmonic performances, seeing the words on gallery walls.

Behind the scenes, Gill imposed another condition on his gifts: they could go only to institutions that had adopted an employment nondiscrimination policy. (At first Gill insisted that it cover only sexual orientation; shortly thereafter, he expanded the requirement to include gender identity, as well.) Some organizations decided to turn away Gill's money due to the prerequisite. Others, like the Boys & Girls Club of Colorado Springs, endured agonizing board negotiations about whether to adopt the employment policy. A lot of them were small charities with few employees, but their boards were packed with executives and investors from other businesses. By forcing the nonprofit boards to deliberate over his offer, Gill had maneuvered a roundabout way to get key figures in Colorado's corporate sector thinking about how employers ought to treat gay employees. "What the Gill Foundation is attempting to do—and they've been quite successful at it—is to buy legitimacy for the homosexual lifestyle," marveled religious activist Will Perkins. "Part of the deal is to neutralize public opinion on homosexual behavior, and it's been working."

Gill's philanthropic ambitions were growing grander. At the start of 1995, he hired Pease to be executive director of a nascent foundation that would manage his gifts. Gill's first had been for $250,000, but he made clear from the outset that he was preparing to give more. The Gay and Lesbian Fund for Colorado would be headquartered in Colorado Springs, by then seen nationwide as the seat of the evangelical right's power, and also the place Pease called home. By early 1996, she had hired a half dozen employees and formulated funding guidelines that suited Gill's expanded interests, with plans to give away $1.7 million that year. "Tim went from being this software entrepreneur who happened to be gay to immediately becoming one of the largest donors in the whole movement," said Pease.

Gill would back organizations advancing a national gay-rights agenda, eventually including the Human Rights Campaign, the National Gay and Lesbian Task Force, and Lambda Legal. But when it came to local gay groups beyond Colorado, he offered grants only to those who did their work outside major urban centers. (That distinction was enforced according to the population size of the metropolitan area.) "We did not want to pay for the New York Gay and Lesbian Center's work, but we were happy to give money to the Tuscaloosa, Alabama, center," says Pease.

It was an insight that drew on Gill's own relative quarantine as a major gay donor in the Mountain West. Most of the others who gave at his level were clustered in big coastal cities and tended to support projects that enhanced gay life where they lived, part of a vicious cycle that left gay interests in other parts of the country perpetually underserved. "What he knew was that when people were from small communities, when they would come out they would leave those communities and go somewhere LGBT-friendly—and take their money with them," says Lila Gracey, who became Gill's director of donor resources.

His decision, in early 1996, to summon other wealthy gays was an effort to battle loneliness. "Tim wanted a network of peers," recalls Pease. The heirs and heiresses who constituted the face of American gay wealth were not Gill's natural peers—nor for that matter were the entertainment and fashion moguls, like David Geffen and Calvin Klein, who represented the other pole of gay economic might. The small meeting in his office at Quark presaged a larger gathering that spring, at the scenic mountain home of the Aspen Institute. The multiday event, which Gill called OutGiving, was open to any gay donor who made at least $10,000 in total charitable gifts per year. "It broke the isolation for LGBT people of wealth who didn't feel they had the community around them they needed," says Pease. By the second OutGiving, in 1997, the number of attendees had nearly doubled, to around one hundred. "They really wanted to get to know each other," Gracey says.

With time, the minimum contribution would increase, along with a requirement that a fraction of the total gifts be devoted to causes specific to gay, lesbian, bisexual, or transgendered people. Gill also began to push those in his growing circle not to limit their imaginations to priorities that were defined by existing organizations, to causes others had identified. "There was an encouragement for donors to be creative," says Gracey. "Do what they love, start something that had never been started."

....

56

Clarity of Coalition

As soon as he launched his foundation, Tim Gill was looking for an opportunity to quit his day job. He began setting targets for himself. First Gill committed to leaving Quark when he had earned $5 million; later he named his fortieth birthday as a deadline. Finally he pushed it toward a seemingly unreachable horizon: he would quit once he was halfway to becoming a billionaire.

In 1999, when he had the chance to sell his stake in the company he founded for a reported $500 million, Gill seized it. That turned out to be an opportune time for Gill to change careers. Quark's market share had already plateaued, and the next spring, the NASDAQ stock exchange crashed, due largely to a bubble surrounding digital and technology companies.

USA Today described Gill as "the nation's leading philanthropist for gay and lesbian causes," but it was far from a vocation. After formally departing Quark in 2000, Gill vowed to take two years off entirely. He spent much of the time snowboarding and mountain biking. Eventually he took up paragliding lessons and talked about returning to school to study theoretical physics. Even though Gill did not intend to be a full-time philanthropist—he spent only forty days annually in the office—he brought his charitable enterprise closer to home. He located the Gill Foundation in a converted warehouse in a gentrifying corner of downtown Denver, where *Philanthropy* magazine would observe that "the mostly young staff of 35 looks as though it was hired off the set of a Gap commercial." He seeded the operation with $250 million, and set bylaws requiring the foundation's assets be liquidated within twenty years of his death—a timeline that he believed would force the board to remain nimble in decisions about where and how to give.

Even as his involvement in the Amendment 2 campaign and its aftermath had thrust him into the ranks of the liberal donor class, Gill had studiously resisted its ideological underpinnings. He confessed to having "terrible libertarian tendencies," and evoked Ayn Rand when he talked about the relationship of government and market. "I tend to believe you should support people in succeeding but you shouldn't take away their ability to fail," he said. "Failure is an integral part of learning to succeed."

Much of Gill's political education can be attributed to his relationship with a corporate lobbyist named Ted Trimpa. The two had first met in 1996, when Trimpa installed himself on a chair outside the men's room in a Denver bar and relied on a bartender to point out the man he had come to stalk. "You're crashing my birthday party," Gill told Trimpa when the twenty-nine-year-old confronted him to solicit a campaign contribution for Democratic Senate candidate Tom Strickland. But the introverted Gill was impressed by the relentlessness of his stalker. "He can get in to any place, he can talk to anybody, he is willing to go out and drink with people," says Gill.

Liberals aware of Trimpa's record were rarely so admiring. He had made his name in Colorado by helping kill a fifty-cent-per-pack tax on cigarettes in a 1994 ballot measure; Denver was one of four different state capitals where Trimpa was simultaneously employed by the Tobacco Institute, a trade organization. "And most people in the LGBT movement would be so disgusted with that they wouldn't talk to him," says Gill. "Ted is willing to do that, and that's a marvelous skill." When Gill invited him to develop a strategy for his political activity, Trimpa had every motivation to say yes. "I wanted to do politics for the rest of my life to balance out my karma for all the nasty things I did," he says.

Trimpa was not involved in Gill's first real introduction to politics beyond Colorado, the 1998 effort in Hawaii to fend off a constitutional ban on same-sex marriage. Gill became the largest donor to Protect Our Constitution—his $300,000 contribution represented about one-quarter of the total budget—and almost single-handedly kept the effort afloat in the race's closing weeks. (When the effort ran short of money in October, after having been forced to accelerate its spending, the Human Rights Campaign's Elizabeth Birch went first to Gill to bail it out.) By his own admission, Gill was not "being overly sophisticated at that time" about his approach. "It just felt like the right thing to do," he says.

Gill resented that he had never been properly thanked by the Human Rights Campaign. But he was even more frustrated by the organization's ill-preparedness to lead local electoral and lobbying operations. "It's really hard to make state-level stuff sexy and make people want to do it," says Trimpa. "The amount of understanding and sophistication is low about how policy actually happens. People think Congress does everything."

Gill remained focused on state-level activity that other national donors ignored. His foundation's OurVote2000 project positioned field organizers in Ohio, Pennsylvania, Illinois, and Minnesota. Limited by the tax-exempt status of its sponsor, OutVote was unable to target voters with the goal of affecting particular electoral outcomes—but did uncover numerous examples of tactical ineptitude among other gay groups. Some ran registration drives without collecting information on the new voters they had signed up, making it impossible to follow up with subsequent contact to mobilize them. Other groups included donor solicitations in their get-out-the-vote mailings, "weakening the voter message as many people saw it as just another fundraising appeal," as Gill communications advisers James Ross and Scott Blaine Swenson observed in an internal report.

Many of these mistakes could be credited to naïveté, but the Ross and Swenson investigation revealed a deeper cultural problem. Institutional prerogatives took precedence over electoral objectives, with groups too controlling of their small turf to coordinate with would-be allies. "In some cases, organizations would not work with us because rival local organizations had been approached first," wrote Ross and Swenson. In other cases, groups that wanted to support the direct-mail program were unwilling to share membership lists with the Gill Foundation, out of apparent fear that others might try to poach from their donor base. "Political infighting among and between GLBT groups is a significant hindrance to effective political operations," the consultancy Ridder/Braden informed the Gill Foundation in its own postelection assessment. "Without cooperation of existing GLBT entities, particularly as regards data/lists, it will remain very difficult for the 'GLBT voting block' to gain the political capital enjoyed by other 'minority' populations."

It was an auspicious time for a well-financed organization to set a goal of modernizing a movement's approach to electioneering. New types of data were becoming available, along with novel tools to manipulate and analyze them. Liberal interest groups were among the first to exploit these innovations; the ability to efficiently target voters for individualized contact was most immediately valuable to mobilize predictably sympathetic citizens who were unreliable voters, like minorities and young whites. Yet profiling gay voters was far more difficult than other minority groups. As opposed to gender, sexual orientation is not indicated on voter-registration forms. Unlike race and ethnicity, it is not tracked by the Census. Only by solving its data problem could the gay-rights movement find a "clarity of coalition" and a "clarity of message," agreed attendees to an April 2001 summit convened by the Gill Foundation to launch what it would call its Democracy Project.

The sheer size of the Gill Foundation's budget—at nearly $20 million annually, it was giving out one-fifth of the country's total donations to gay-rights groups—overwhelmed the movement's existing capacity. In declaring its intent to be active in up to six states ahead of the 2004 election, spending a total of $1.6 million in what representatives were describing as "a NARAL-style campaign," Gill forced existing gay groups to cater to its objectives. "Our job will be to discover where we fit in," Birch wrote to her staff after meeting with Gill officials.

Colorado provided a template. Gill took an interest in its electoral politics only after Trimpa showed him a measure proposed by state representative Shawn Mitchell to require that parents sign a permission slip before schoolchildren could be exposed to any mention of homosexuality. "I wouldn't, for example, be able to go to my alma mater to tell the story of how I got where I am because that includes mentioning my boyfriend," Gill later explained. "That seemed like a totally unreasonable restriction on free speech." Gill believed he could argue that self-evident logic to Mitchell and those inclined to vote his way, and Trimpa arranged for him to attend a legislative hearing where he could meet all the committee members. When Gill realized they were unsusceptible to persuasion, he resignedly asked his adviser what other options were left to him. "The only way to make *it* go away is to make *them* go away," Trimpa informed him.

Up until that point, Gill's political giving had operated in the same spirit as the Gay and Lesbian Fund's approach to philanthropy. He gave money to initially unfriendly organizations and used the kindness to bend them to respect, or merely to coerce a grudging acceptance of homosexuality. When it came to politics, he brought a pragmatist's evenhandedness to his donations, backing friendly candidates of both parties and expecting that any desirable policy outcomes would arrive only with bipartisan support. "Our idea was, let's find the good Republicans and good Democrats and give them money," Gill said. "But after Bush got into power, the number of Republicans willing to accept money of that kind dried up. There are still good Republicans and we still give money to them. But the social conservatives have such a hammerlock on the Republican Party that the whole strategy of making friends with Republicans would no longer work. My philosophy became, if you can't make friends with people in the Republican Party, then you've got to get rid of the worst ones."

There was already an object lesson in the dangers of allowing enemies to assert themselves unchecked. In 1996, as a Colorado legislator in her second term, Marilyn Musgrave had drafted a bill to ban gay marriages in the state and had been invited to testify about it before the U.S. House of Representatives as it considered the Defense of Marriage Act. When she was elected to that body herself in 2002, she immediately sponsored the Federal Marriage Amendment. "Marilyn Musgrave started on the school board," Gill said. "She would have been so much cheaper to nuke when she was on the school board or even when she was in the legislature. We need to be vigilant and find politicians who are bad and stop them when it's cheap."

Gill was invited by Rutt Bridges to do something about it. Like Gill, Bridges was a late convert to politics: a geophysicist who had become rich by developing software and was positioning himself as a candidate for statewide office. If he and Gill had a common mind-set as scientist-entrepreneurs, the two others Bridges recruited to complete what became known as the Gang of Four—Jared Polis and Pat Stryker—shared Gill's interest in sexual politics. Polis, a young Internet entrepreneur whose well-timed sale of his family's online greeting-card business left him a net worth of over $150 million, was openly gay; Stryker's brother, Jon, was one of the major donors Gill had successfully lured to participate in OutGiving. "We don't agree on everything," says Trimpa. "We actually aren't going to have to talk about policy. We're just going to have to talk about winning."

Beginning in 2004, Trimpa represented Gill when the Gang of Four and their political operatives came together. At the same time they spent more than a half-million dollars each to defeat Republican legislators that November, the quartet committed resources to laying a permanent groundwork for the left's future campaigns in Colorado. Over weekly sessions, they plotted a concatenation of progressive institutions, including nonprofit think tanks and nonpartisan voter-registration projects, media outlets, and watchdog groups. To expand their reach, the Gang of Four developed relationships with others who saw value in ending Republican domination of Colorado politics. Environmental, feminist, and Latino organizations with grassroots networks signed on, while labor unions and trial lawyers promised funds. Gay money would boost groups that might not have an explicitly pro-gay agenda, but whose victories would unquestionably advance the gay cause. "No one expected other groups would do the heavy lifting on the equality issue," says Polis, who had already spent $1 million of his fortune winning election to the state education board. "It was never expected to be at the top of their agenda."

When Gill had started making political donations in the early 1990s, the most straightforward way to have an impact was to give directly to party committees and have them route it to preferred candidates. (On a single day in the fall of 1999, Gill gave $245,000 to the Democratic National Committee.) But federal reforms put hard limits on contributions to partisan entities. Rich people could still make their money have an impact in politics, but they would have to create the organizations that would spend it. When members of the Gang of Four wanted to pool money to defeat Musgrave, they created their own stand-alone committee to produce and place television ads attacking her.

The ads were savage, one of them showing an actress who played the congresswoman reaching into a casket to steal the watch off a corpse. The name of the entity behind the ad, Colorado Families First, was cryptically vague. (The ad's narrator described a vote Musgrave had taken in favor of a bill that would allow nursing homes to bill patients "even after they're dead.") At the same time that the Gang of Four had worked to switch control of the legislature, Trimpa had decided to "pick three seats of vulnerable Republicans that we think we can beat and we beat the living shit out of them." They selected targets that had exceptionally adversarial records—one had sponsored a bill to limit gay adoption, another had mocked a transsexual who had testified before his committee—and whose defeats would be attributed to gay opposition, even if the advertising responsible never mentioned gay issues.

Trimpa's vision was that eventually politicians "see you as part of the power structure" and would develop their own instinct to placate gay interests. He aspired to become "Gay Pfizer," as he delighted in putting it. "When we're seen by these elected officials just like they see pharmaceutical companies, then we're somewhere," Trimpa says. "How do we do that? It's money." More importantly, it required that the money that currently splashed around gay causes be more intelligently diversified. Trimpa described adjusting the business-school formulation of three Ps ("people, process, product") for the goal of social change: "an alignment of philanthropic dollars with policy dollars with political dollars."

Many in Washington and Hollywood rejected the term "gay mafia," but Trimpa welcomed it, and very intentionally approached his work with a wiseguy bravado. He selected Gill's three targets with the goal of making an example out of them, but then pursued their political demise with a gleeful vindictiveness. At one point, Trimpa moved an additional $300,000 to defeat Pam Rhodes, a state representative who had sponsored an anti-gay-adoption bill, even though it was not entirely clear the spending was necessary to defeat her. "Every fucking time she walks out the door I want her to feel like she has a thousand nickels dropped on her head," Trimpa recalls telling the consultant hired to work on the race. "I want more mail going to her house than any other house. When we have people do field, I want them to knock twice as much on her door. Every fucking time she turns around I want her to feel like the gay mafia is everywhere. Every time she gets up in the morning I want her to feel a pain right here and that pain is us."

The Gill approach to electoral politics was notable for the way that irrationally vengeful spirit laced through an otherwise scrupulous approach to outside spending. Generally, Gill's mentality toward political investments—"very engineer-oriented, very ROI-oriented," according to Trimpa—turned out to be better suited for perceiving opportunities to secure gains than defending against previously unimaginable losses.

Before his first foray into marriage politics, in Hawaii, Gill had given little strategic thought to how victory on the issue could come about, or even what it would look like. "I was ambivalent whether it was the right time, and whether it was winnable. But you are always that way when something new comes up, and in a sense we didn't really have a choice," says Gill.

That loss did not change the Gill agenda's bracingly unromantic view of marriage. The foundation's 1999 annual report had described "a better world" as one "where two women—or two men—in love are able to marry," but its funding did not treat that as an attainable objective. "In those early years, for our little political team, the rule was," says Trimpa, "'Thou shalt never do anything that prevents us from getting to it but we don't start with it.' Because you can't—it was too soon." An arm of Gill's OutVote 2000 program was extended to Vermont, where it boosted legislators who faced difficult reelection challenges because of their votes for the civil-unions bill, but the foundation largely kept its distance from events in Massachusetts. Gill made grants totaling $200,000 to the Boston-based Freedom to Marry Foundation, which was coordinating efforts there, but concluded that MassEquality, the Massachusetts Gay and Lesbian Political Caucus, and GLAD were well prepared to handle the serious work on their turf. "They know how to raise money, they know how to get things done," says Donna Red Wing, the Gill Foundation's policy director until 2003. "[Freedom to Marry is] the one state organization that is respected by every national organization, and it is probably run better than most."

Even as Gill spent heavily on Colorado politics in 2004, he did not contribute to any of the political campaigns organized to fight marriage amendments across thirteen other states. "It's a waste of money," says Trimpa. "From my perspective, we should be going for things that we can win." Instead, the largest gay-rights grant the Gill Foundation made that year was the $250,000 it gave to launch the Civil Marriage Collaborative, conceived as a way for nonprofit donors to prioritize marriage work in designated "core states." The first meeting was held at the New York headquarters of the Open Society Institute, the charitable arm of liberal investor George Soros's empire, and brought together seven left-leaning philanthropies not all uniquely focused on gay concerns. An annual grant budget of $1.4 million was enough to ensure state groups were responsive to donors' priorities. But when spread across twenty-four organizations—an average grant was just $71,000—the money was too little, and moved too slowly, to have any input on local operations or tactics. "It was just bureaucratic," says Mary Ellen Capek, an Albuquerque-area activist and professional donor adviser who in 2004 successfully applied for a $125,000 grant from the collaborative for the Coalition for Equality in New Mexico. "It was the worst request for proposal I have ever responded to in my life," she says. "Way beyond anything that was necessary to do."

That November brought mixed results for Gill. The millionaires' Colorado plan had gone swimmingly, with both houses of the state legislature flipping toward the Democrats after four decades of Republican dominance. Two of the Republican targets Gill had selected to serve as examples to others lost their seats in 2004, with the third carrying his district only by a narrow margin. "We are finally realizing that how we win is by creating an environment of fear and respect," Trimpa crowed.

Gay activists had not fared so well nationally. Thirteen states that year passed constitutional amendments to ban same-sex marriage. Almost immediately it became part of Democratic folk wisdom that the issue helped galvanize the voters who granted George W. Bush a second term as president. In the wake of the 2004 election, the foundation commissioned polls to make sense of the public opinion behind the dismal results. "Our goal in this work is to further the knowledge of the LGBT community on marriage issues," Gill Foundation executive director Rodger McFarlane wrote to other gay leaders with whom he shared the poll findings. It seemed inevitable that more ballot measures would pop up by 2006, and that there would be a renewed push on Capitol Hill for a Federal Marriage Amendment. The Gill Foundation embarked on a research project to assess readiness for that looming conflict over marriage, an issue in which none of the gay-rights movement's major political groups were deeply invested. "To get marriage equality would be a profound psychological breakthrough," Matt Foreman, the executive director of the National Gay and Lesbian Task Force, told Gill Foundation researchers. "But we may lose every one of the anti-gay measures on state ballots this year and next. How do we define 'victory' so that the movement isn't set back ten years?"

McFarlane summoned a group of leaders across the gay-rights movement to Gill headquarters to "knock their heads together" over that question, as one invitee put it. McFarlane had made the unusual choice to bring in both operatives and donors to plot the movement's next maneuvers on marriage. "One always has to educate funders," says Urvashi Vaid, a long-time activist who sat on Gill's board. "You always have to create situations where funders and activists are coming together."

Their dialogue pivoted quickly to a ventilation of grievances about the Human Rights Campaign, which seemed unavoidable. ("While we did not ask specifically about HRC in our broad-ranging interviews, a surprising number of participants 'blasted' HRC while sharing observations about the movement," reported a strategy project the Gill Foundation had commissioned from researcher Linda Bush.) The Human Rights Campaign was a recurring object of gripes nearly every time those invested in winning marriage rights convened to discuss the subject, stretching back to the Defense of Marriage Act debate in which HRC officials appeared to preemptively concede defeat.

In late 2004, the nation's preeminent gay-rights organization withdrew once again from a fight over marriage. Immediately after the election, executive director Cheryl Jacques—a former Massachusetts legislator whose appointment earlier that year had been read as an investment in the marriage debate—left her post amid internal rancor over how aggressively to invest in the issue, offensively and defensively. ("Jacques was head of the HRC slightly longer than the ten months it took to recruit her," *Gay City*

News acidly observed.) Indicative of their eagerness to move away from contentious issues, board members selected their first heterosexual chairman, who told the *New York Times* after his appointment that "we need to reintroduce ourselves to America with the stories of our lives." Under new leadership, the Human Rights Campaign would pursue "completely new" strategies with "different approaches, different tactics and different conversations," as a fundraising appeal promised. "This election may have shown us that the change agents for gay marriage are looking too much like a noisy red Ferrari speeding down quiet Main Street," Hilary Rosen, who rejoined the organization as its interim director, explained in *The Advocate* in early December. "If we want to make the lives of GLBT people better, the strategy needs to change. Don't bother telling me that I am committing heresy. It's OK."

McFarlane observed the Human Rights Campaign's very visible retreat and fixated on "not allowing them to own the conversation around marriage," as an interlocutor describes the thinking. Gill still considered marriage a priority, but was reliant on activist organizations to do work that he and his foundation could fund. The Human Rights Campaign remained the biggest among them, with an annual budget over $30 million. (It was, *The Advocate* would note, about the same size as the next three combined: the National Gay and Lesbian Task Force, the Gay and Lesbian Alliance Against Defamation, and Lambda Legal. HRC had ten times more individual donors than any of them.) Jonathan Lewis, a major Democratic donor who participated in OutGiving, had given $1 million to the Human Rights Campaign as it was building a new headquarters that would open in October 2003. When he visited the gleaming ivory structure, Lewis thought it a self-indulgent, ostentatious expense for an organization losing the political battles immediately before it, a monument to concern for image over outcomes. As the AIDS activist and playwright Larry Kramer scrawled on a sign he carried while picketing one of the group's Manhattan fundraisers: HRC WHAT THE FUCK ARE YOU DOING WITH ALL THAT MONEY.

Matt Coles, an attorney who had been invited by McFarlane in his capacity as director of the ACLU's National LGBT Project, fretted as the conversation in Denver turned toward trashing the Human Rights Campaign. "This is really a waste of time," Coles complained to Vaid. In 1999, as director of the National Gay and Lesbian Task Force's Policy Institute, Vaid had engineered the Seattle Accord, a negotiated settlement of enduring hostilities with the Human Rights Campaign that had left state groups often feeling they had to align with one of the major powers over the other.

The two national organizations signed a détente with a "family policy network" to facilitate collaboration, yet by the time of the 2004 federal- and state-level battles, there was nothing to show for the brief rapprochement. "We were collegial, but not really collaborative," says Vaid. "There were rivalries and tensions and political disagreements always, and there were real deep political divisions around race, around class and economic values, or around priorities."

Coles believed his fellow movement leaders were "often unduly distrustful of HRC," and the lapse into their petty, childish rehash of long-standing grievances seemed a predictable response to crisis. Such critiques, Coles knew, typically served as a substitute for a more difficult reckoning over how to define success when their objectives were at odds with the public's sincerely held views. Vaid implored him to speak up in front of others. "We need to stop thinking about the next election cycle," Coles said, "and think about how we're going to fix this long-term."

McFarlane was persuaded of the need to develop a true strategy around marriage, and—bypassing others who had attempted to position themselves as champions of the marriage cause—asked Coles to lead the project. "Only if I get to handpick the participants," said Coles, "and nobody has a seat at the table."

57

After the Bloodbath

When the *Goodridge* appeal moved through Massachusetts courts, and Washington rumbled with talk of a constitutional amendment, executive director Anthony Romero was being asked how the ACLU planned to react. While it had been the first established organization of any kind to support a marriage challenge (in Minnesota in 1971) and the first (in 1986) to adopt a policy endorsing same-sex marriage, the ACLU had not made any proactive moves to advance that goal in court. The group had contributed to amicus briefs in marriage cases and dispatched its lobbyists to defeat the Defense of Marriage Act, but none of those reflected an institutional strategy. Unable to advise Romero how to respond, communications director Emily Tynes turned to Matt Coles, who in 1995 had become head of the ACLU's Lesbian and Gay Rights Project. "What's your long-term plan?" she asked him.

The ACLU was famous for taking on unpopular causes, with a hint of self-congratulation for the moral predicaments that invariably followed its blind allegiance to constitutional principles. The year after Nazis tried to march on Skokie, Coles was starting his law career in San Francisco and being drawn into politics as an informal legal adviser to city supervisor Harvey Milk. When Coles came to the ACLU a decade later, he was part of a generation whose experiences with civil-rights movements had convinced them that the organization had to do more than bend rules in its direction through effective lawyering. "You can't make enduring change in a republic, I believe, unless you can get the public to accept the notion that the change that you're seeking is right even if they don't like it," says Coles.

Coles had participated in Roundtable meetings since joining the ACLU, but he sat back as Evan Wolfson and Mary Bonauto became the loudest voices during debates over marriage. "Mary is kind of the rabbi and Evan is the warrior and Matt is the scholar," says Rebecca Rittgers, a onetime program executive at the Atlantic Philanthropies, which funded gay causes. Some of that could be explained by temperament: a former Connecticut newspaper reporter, Coles was often comfortable keeping an observer's remove from events he couldn't fully control. A full-time gay litigator working for a nongay organization—"a group without a constituency," as he described the ACLU—Coles was never stuck with a fundraising strategy tied to particular cases or policy goals. Unlike Wolfson, who rarely deviated from a stock inventory of crisp press-release sentences, Coles boasted for years about the press conference in which he delivered a "paragraph of perfectly unquotable things" so that the media in attendance would be forced to feature the words of the gay plaintiffs the lawsuit was designed to showcase.

While Lambda Legal had asserted custody of the Hawaii case, and GLAD of those in Vermont and Massachusetts, the ACLU had been largely a bystander. It stuck to the formula that had worked in 1989's seminal *Braschi* case, in which a New York court ruled that an AIDS victim's longtime partner was entitled to remain in their rent-controlled apartment. The ACLU, as Coles describes it, preferred "cases that featured same-sex couples but were not about legal recognition of the couples." (His 1996 book, *Try This at Home!: A Do-It-Yourself Guide to Winning Lesbian and Gay Civil Rights Policy,* made no direct appeal for marriage but devoted a long section to domestic partnerships.)

Yet as the discussion moved to Washington, a group whose lawyers often declared that their only client was the Constitution could not sit out a debate on amending it in a direction the union's policies considered orthogonal to the founding document's values. The ACLU immediately announced itself opposed to the Federal Marriage Amendment, but was uncertain about how to approach the legislative politics. Coles had the ACLU's pollster, Belden Russonello & Stewart, conduct ten focus groups nationwide to shape messages that could rally opposition to a constitutional amendment.

The results suggested that opponents could help kill an amendment as long as they assured voters that doing so would not advance gay marriage. Accordingly, the plan Coles drafted at Tynes's urging was almost entirely defensive. One of the primary goals for 2004, it declared, was to "prevent a vote on, or the adoption of, any measure which would make the effort to recognize same-sex relationships more difficult." The document laid out a preliminary agenda for "priority states," in which marriage was likely to become an election-year issue in some form and where the ACLU wanted to stop politicians from wielding it as a wedge. The only immediate positive objective Coles articulated was "to continue to build sentiment in favor of providing recognition." The document made no mention of litigation in the near term.

Coles completed the document on January 30, and it was quickly rendered obsolete. Just two weeks later, an eruption of local officials—led by San Francisco mayor Gavin Newsom—attempting to marry same-sex couples in defiance of state authorities thrust the matter into court. In tandem with its affiliates in Oregon and New York, the ACLU launched lawsuits in the spring of 2004 alleging that both states' laws impermissibly discriminated by allowing only opposite-sex couples to wed. In Oregon, the plaintiffs included gay couples who had been awarded Multnomah County licenses later voided; in New York, they were those who had put their names on a waiting list with the New Paltz mayor's office. "We felt having the executive branch on our side totally changed the calculus in those cases," says Coles. "Now this wasn't the gay community in essence coming into court and asking to overrule the executive branch. It was the gay community going into court and asking to sustain the executive branch."

That informed Coles's feeling that marriage campaigners needed to consider the long term. After articulating that view at the Gill Foundation's postelection meeting, Coles assembled with Wolfson's help a list of representatives from other political and legal groups active on gay issues and informed them that a year earlier he had embarked on a similar initiative to develop a strategy around marriage. "Like all plans, this one started to become outdated the day it was finished," Coles wrote to them. "One year out, it is clear that a few changes in its basic scenarios are necessary."

Coles had identified nine people to work on what he, for lack of a better term, started calling the "Big Plan." He set out specifically to include not the groups' presidents or executive directors, but rather "the smart policy people who really understood the lay of the land," as he puts it. Coles told their bosses that they would have the right to review everything the group drafted before anyone agreed to it, but worked to insulate them from meddling by colleagues. He settled on a location convenient for attendees coming from New York or Washington, but just far enough from their offices that attendees would be unable to dart back for approval. "Everybody kept thinking about the next six months, the next nine months," says

Coles. "What we all knew we needed was a long-term plan, but nobody was willing to just sort of get out of the moment."

He reserved conference space at a Jersey City hotel for a day and a half and recruited a professional moderator to guide the conversation. Even though the stated goal was to draft a strategy for securing the right for same-sex couples to marry anywhere in the United States, Coles quickly learned that several of his attendees resisted the premise. One faction, led by Human Rights Campaign vice president Seth Kilbourn, argued that gay groups should resign themselves to "play defense" on marriage and attempt to seek policy gains elsewhere, on issues like nondiscrimination and hate-crimes laws, where public opinion was more favorable. Others felt that there was the opportunity to secure incremental progress through other types of relationship recognition around which the politics were less fraught. "Most of the folks in these two groups didn't see how marriage could be won in any foreseeable time frame," Coles later reflected.

There was not a whole lot undergirding the debate over a timeline. It was "a fairly unproductive conversation about who had the best crystal ball," in Coles's words, fraught with residual resentments about how invested various entities had been previously. "There were people, like Evan, who thought, 'You know we could have done it yesterday if we had only put the effort that was necessary into it,'" says Coles.

At the same time, Bonauto and Wolfson—who had defined themselves both inside and outside the movement as its most prominent champions of the marriage cause—argued that advocates could not afford to withdraw from it. "I felt a lot of urgency to move forward in light of the blowback at the federal level and the things that were percolating in the various states," says Bonauto. "Based on my experience in Massachusetts, I saw the tenor of everything change dramatically once people were married. In just over a year, I could see what a difference it made."

Pushing for marriage in Vermont had failed but nonetheless yielded civil unions. Regardless, she posited, reverting in 2005 to a purely defensive strategy was unlikely to even sustain the status quo. "I remember thinking you can't just defend Massachusetts and have it be the only marriage state. That's the strategy that our opponents wanted—to confine marriage to Massachusetts and eventually they would get an amendment, state or federal, that would knock us out of the water. Having only a single state made us very vulnerable," Bonauto says. "There were people, including me, who viewed the states as really different from one another. There were some states that, with the right amount of work, should be able to get to marriage. Not to say that it wouldn't be hard."

When he had prepared a long-term strategy document for the ACLU, Coles had articulated a three-phase timeline. At first, Coles had proposed "the focus would be on states where we were most likely to win," using well-placed litigation to secure marriage rights in "six to eight economically important, friendly states." In the subsequent phase, activists would look for places where they could claim victories through the political process, including more moderate states where civil unions may be the best possible outcome. "Slowly but surely, the litigation and legislation would progress until there was at least legal equality (marriage or full civil unions) in at least half, and more likely 60 percent to two-thirds of the states," Coles wrote.

Only then would attorneys invite the federal judiciary to get involved, in a final phase where it would be called upon to smooth out the ungainly patchwork created by misaligned state laws. "Historically, the Supreme Court has been much more willing to impose social norms that have been widely accepted on 'hold out' states than it has been willing to force norms not generally accepted on most of the nation," Coles wrote. "More important, even if we were to get a good decision from the Supreme Court in the near term, we would likely be unable to sustain it. The argument that states can and (at this stage) should work this issue out for themselves has been critical to holding off a federal constitutional amendment (which would either preempt the Supreme Court or overrule it)."

In Jersey City there was easy consensus around that point. Everyone believed judges were more likely to bring gay marriage to the United States than politicians, much as the Supreme Court had done when it struck down restrictions on private, consensual sex two years earlier. But even so, judges would likely be wary of ushering in dramatic social change nationwide through their actions. The *Lawrence v. Texas* decision in 2003 had been preceded by an earlier loss, when gay-rights activists arrived at the Supreme Court with a challenge to Georgia's sodomy ban—expected to be the apex of a national strategy plotted by the Sodomy Roundtable—well before a majority of justices were ready to declare the statute unconstitutional. *Bowers v. Hardwick* remained the singularly traumatic shock to the gay political and legal elite, and many of those in Jersey City feared the movement was inviting a similar comedown on marriage. They had ended up in a hotel's vast banquet hall, in which eleven people seated around a single dining table could feel isolated, a sense that grew more ominous as they grappled in vain for a common set of expectations about how the Supreme Court might act. During one break midway through the first day, when others were strolling outside on a terrace overlooking the Manhattan skyline, Coles and the moderator, Ellen Carton, shared private worries that they were unlikely to produce any common strategy and be forced to return to Gill empty-handed.

To break the deadlock, Kilbourn asked the group to focus on what they all agreed could be achieved over a twenty-year horizon. He approached an easel and drew up three columns based on what was a plausible expectation for the law in each state by 2025. There was one column for each of the legal regimes that could cover same-sex relationships: full marriage rights, civil unions that were equivalent in all but name, and domestic-partnership benefits extended to gay couples. Many were easy to place: the most culturally liberal states, including New York, California, and New Jersey, joined Massachusetts and Vermont in the marriage column, while all those under civil unions tended to vote Democratic in presidential elections. For other states whose prospects were less self-evident, Coles relied on the expertise of those in the room—many of whom had familiarity with particular states through cases or campaigns there—and moved each one into a category. They found ten states in which marriage equality was attainable, and ten each for civil unions and domestic partnerships. There were twenty left over, from politically moderate states like Virginia and Florida to right-wing strongholds like Mississippi and Oklahoma, where it was impossible to imagine any shift in the legal status of same-sex couples for decades to come.

Some states were harder than others to classify, but the exercise itself broke the impasse. Even those who had dismissed a scenario in which the Supreme Court ruled in 2025 that citizens had a constitutional right to marry regardless of gender could accept that over twenty years a total of thirty states could find their own paths to some recognition of same-sex couples.

Illuminated by bright daylight shining through floor-to-ceiling windows, the number of states scrawled on the easel represented a familiar arithmetic to students of civil-rights litigation. The Supreme Court's 1967 ruling in *Loving v. Virginia* had come only after fifteen years of states gutting their own antimiscegenation laws, through either legislative repeal or court rulings, without any federal interference. (Before California did so in 1948, through the *Perez v. Sharp* decision, it had been sixty years since any change in a state's racial qualifications for marriage.) By the time the Supreme Court had to face two citizens who had been legally married in the District of Columbia but were forbidden from traveling to the neighboring commonwealth as a married couple, the federal government had an obvious stake in their plight. At that point, thirty-four states already accepted the Lovings' marriage—with geographic diversity covering every region beyond the Deep South. This provided confirmation to justices that by acting boldly they did not risk getting too far ahead of the public and their elected officials—precisely the scenario that was giving the more cautious participants in the Jersey City meeting such pause about bringing a marriage case to the Supreme Court.

"Everybody agreed within a few minutes that we can take it all the way home from there," says Coles. "Bingo, there you go."

Over the next six days, Coles locked himself into his apartment to convert the notes that his group had generated into a manifesto titled "Winning Marriage: What We Need to Do." It was maddeningly vague about the overall timeline for the state-level goals—referring, alternately, to "the next 20 years," "15 to 25 years," and "15–20 years," while "marriage nationwide is possible five years later"—but specific about where exactly they should be pursued. After a preamble, the document quickly named the ten states that fell into each of the three categories, and designated the twenty left over as targets for "significant 'climate change' (i.e.; changes in attitudes about LGBT people)." In the short term, activists had to hold fast in Massachusetts and California, preserving marriage in the first and deterring any effort to define it in the California state constitution. By decade's end, they should aim for securing marriage rights in two to three additional states, while fending off any new efforts to define marriage in all moderate states where the matter could find its way to a ballot. "If 30 to 35 states pass constitutional amendments, we will likely have to repeal a significant number of them before we can turn to the federal government to address holdouts," he wrote. With that in mind, Coles continued with bold italics for emphasis, "there is no state in which we should be doing nothing."

Coles circulated a draft for comments, and then the final fifteen-page document for signatures from the organization leaders who had been explicitly excluded from the negotiations themselves. "Even though everybody agreed to follow this, I am not sure that anybody really changed what they were doing," says Kevin Cathcart, the executive director of Lambda Legal. "In some ways I think we could all agree to it because it was the directions we were going in." Yet at the same time, the so-called 10-10-10-20 plan maintained a crucial vagueness—about what specifically would be necessary to move each state, who would be responsible for each task, and thus what the combined fifteen-year project would cost. "A huge number would've scared people away," says Rittgers. "To do that would've been like painting a bull's-eye on your forehead because it would've just been picked apart left, front, and center."

Even though Coles wrote that the document should not be seen as "a fixed set of state-by-state goals or even predictions"—calling the assignment of states across a four-column list purely "illustrative"—it was not always read that way. Wolfson shared the final version with state-based groups who were part of his Freedom to Marry Coalition, none of whom had been asked for input during the process. Many recoiled when they learned that a handful of national operatives meeting in secret strategy sessions had assessed their capability to win marriage and set national expectations for their work. "Either their state was not listed the way they thought it would," recalls Wolfson, "or, 'Who the hell are you to tell us?'"

But the audience for "Winning Marriage: What We Need to Do" ultimately was not the people who would have to weaponize the strategy but those who would finance it. "We were going to have to extend our capacity to carry this out. And if the leading funders weren't pushing for that, we were never going to be able to make it happen," says Coles, who on June 21, 2005, formally delivered the 10-10-10-20 plan to the Gill Foundation with the endorsement of every major national political and legal organization in the gay-rights movement. "We did something that we had never done before, which is we somewhat broke down the firewall between the policy discussions and the money people—and let the money people participate in the policy discussions," he says. "We got people whose financial support we're going to need, bought into the conceptual framework as we created it. And so they were going back and saying, 'You know, this is smart. We can do this.'"

Punish the Wicked

A few weeks after the Jersey City meeting, the Gill Foundation held the tenth installment of its OutGiving conference at Tim Gill's home in Aspen. The conference had grown to about two hundred attendees annually, in part on its reputation for good parties. Gill had met his original objective—he now had a circle of wealthy, philanthropically active peers—but as the movement's needs became more dire, he began to fear that he was doing little more than hosting an annual social mixer for the gay elite. Gill never dialed back the glitz, but over the previous two years, he pushed to make OutGiving more substantive, with serious presentations. Still, throughout the weekend, Gill quietly shared misgivings to some confidants in attendance: participants had become too complacent in their giving. The concluding session of the 2005 OutGiving conference was a brunch at Gill's home, and in the midst of it he mounted an oversize coffee table in his living room to make an unscheduled announcement. One of his well-heeled guests had come to him just beforehand with an idea that would push them all out of their comfort zone, and now Gill was presenting it as a plan. "That's Tim Gill," says Charlie Rounds, who attended OutGiving on behalf of his own Minneapolis-based foundation. "He gets shit done."

Donations to nonprofit organizations had been enough for budding philanthropists to win invitations to OutGiving, but Gill wanted to let those massed before him know that that should no longer be the extent of their largesse. The wealthy had always been drawn to support nonprofit organizations for the tax advantages they could offer, and the purity of their chosen causes. While subsidizing public-education campaigns or think-tank work, gay donors had shirked the serious investments in election spending and lobbying that were necessary for direct policy change. Just years earlier, after all, Gill himself freely acknowledged that he "viewed politics as evil and dirty."

Events in Colorado convinced Gill to overcome his natural aversion to such work. After the Gang of Four helped flip the legislature in 2004, lawmakers passed a nondiscrimination bill and successfully amended a criminal-justice bill to include a hate-crimes provision that covered trans-gendered victims. Ted Trimpa worked with Democratic legislative lead-ers to coordinate the timing so that Governor Bill Owens, a conservative Republican who had been discussed as a potential presidential candidate, could make a show of vetoing the nondiscrimination bill while letting the hate-crimes provision become law. Democratic leaders were also able to approve a domestic-partnership measure for a statewide vote. (It would go to the ballot in November 2006. Voters rejected the measure at the same time they passed an amendment to insert a gay-marriage ban in the state constitution.)

A similar mix of targeted electoral spending, intimidating reprisals, and attentive persuasion of soft Republicans could prove comparably influ-ential everywhere LGBT policies hung in the balance, Trimpa argued to Gill. "Get the right people, and we can get the right policy," Trimpa recalls telling him. "Sometimes you have to play hardball politics to get it, but we can get it done. There's no reason we shouldn't be doing this in other states."

Gill had already made such a case to his peers. In early May, Gill Foundation executive director Rodger McFarlane invited some of the largest donors it had cultivated through OutGiving to a two-day sum-mit in New York City. All those who answered McFarlane's invitation, or sent a representative, were openly gay men; all but one had no profes-sional distractions beyond their philanthropy. James Hormel and Henry van Ameringen, now both well into their seventies, had been part of the first group of gay donors that Gill had invited to Denver in 1996. Jon Stryker, whose Michigan-based Arcus Foundation supported gay causes there and beyond, was the brother of one of Gill's colleagues in the Gang of Four. (The Arcus Foundation also had a focus on saving great apes, by preserving habitats for chimpanzees and orangutans.) The closest thing to a true peer was David Bohnett, who when Gill had launched OutGiving was an executive at GeoCities, a primitive social-networking site he had founded. When the company was sold to Yahoo in 1999 at a valuation of $3.6 billion, Bohnett began giving away his earnings, to gay interests and civic institutions near his Los Angeles home and beyond. Gill called this group—which would expand shortly to a total of seven people, still smaller than the Human Rights Campaign's board—"the Cabinet."

Despite being among the largest individual donors to gay-rights initiatives, they all felt as though they had become instruments of politics rather than agents of it. While lawyers and operatives met in Jersey City to chart a path to the Supreme Court by 2025, at a more prestigious Manhattan address, in a hotel suite ostentatiously decorated with sprays of artificial flowers, Gill and his aides were working to finance whatever that strategy turned out to be. Large donors would have to put up the cash necessary to support the state-by-state strategy.

Some of that would take the form of new institutional sinew to support "the integration of the movement," in the words of Tim Sweeney, who not long thereafter became the Gill Foundation's executive director. Arcus committed $250,000 to launch the Movement Advancement Project, established as a research hub that could assess the effectiveness of existing gay-rights groups and how they fit together, to satisfy large donors. The project came to serve a valuable benchmarking function for the rookie donors being enlisted into the Gill network. Its annual reports, which called out groups whose overhead expenses failed to meet Better Business Bureau standards, were rigorous enough that some took to calling it "the gay I.R.S."

At the same time, the Gill Foundation cultivated Washington organizations where it could fund research projects, including the Center for American Progress, the American Association of Retired Persons, and Third Way. Gill began commissioning research from Third Way after one of its own 2005 surveys showed 57 percent of Americans believed that gays did not share their basic values. Staggered by what they took to calling the "values gap," Gill Foundation officials concluded that the think tank was likely to be more perceptive about the opinions of political moderates than any of the gay-rights groups whose activism it already helped fund. The nascent organization was particularly well connected among Democratic candidates running for office in red and purple states, whom it could effectively lobby on issues under the guise of educating them. "We don't want to do these reports to sit on the shelf," says Sweeney. "We want them to impact the world."

But Gill argued to his peers that they could no longer stick to that kind of nonprofit philanthropy, which offered appealing tax benefits and the freedom to decide which contributions a donor would publicize. Instead they would have to dip into the grubbier side of giving, directly supporting political action committees and party organizations without the institutional buffer of a foundation.

Given his background as a business lobbyist, Trimpa recognized the unique opportunity presented by groups like the Democratic Governors Association, the Democratic Attorneys General Association, and the Democratic Legislative Campaign Committee to activists seeking an audience with state-level decision-makers. "You see telecom, oil, energy, banking, securities lawyers, trial lawyers," says Trimpa. "I'd look around the room and the only social-justice people there would be us."

Beyond the reach of federal or state limits on contributions to candidates or party committees, the associations' regular meetings were one of the few places where it was perfectly legal for a lobbyist to spend unlimited amounts of money for access to elected officials or those who hoped to soon join their ranks. "They kind of liked talking to us because we weren't trying to hit them up for oil-drilling permits and stuff," says Gill. "It gave us a chance to form relationships with them so that when an LGBT-related issue or crisis came up in their state, they would come to us to ask us how to deal with it."

The Cabinet valued secrecy and could afford to be ruthlessly pragmatic. Its members chose to keep their alliance informal: some participants shrugged off the "Cabinet" moniker because it gave their undertaking an undesirable veneer of permanence. (Others called it "the G-7" and, in homage to the tacky surroundings from which it was born, the Silk Flowers Project.) Every few months they would meet, often in a member's hometown, a circuit that covered both Beverly Hills and Kalamazoo, to plot their next round of spending. In between, their advisers—with the exception of van Ameringen, every Cabinet donor had a dedicated political sherpa—participated in weekly conference calls to update strategy. They could pool resources to focus on states where gains were possible and cut losses elsewhere, claiming in the process some of the agenda-setting clout that had rested with the Human Rights Campaign and National Gay and Lesbian Task Force. "There was an energy," says Michael Fleming, who represented Bohnett in the sessions. "Let's go raise some hell, let's go see if we can monkey with the system, maybe we're being too nice to politicians."

The group turned its attention first to Massachusetts, where the initial bonanza of legislative and judicial action that followed the *Goodridge* decision had given way to a need for a more quotidian political apparatus. When MassEquality campaign director Marty Rouse visited Cabinet members shortly after their first meeting in 2005—he could boast that his group had spent more on direct mail during the previous election cycle than the Massachusetts Democratic Party—he laid out the imperative of protecting the statehouse's tenuous pro-marriage coalitions through upcoming Constitutional Conventions. After hearing Rouse's pitch, Cabinet members immediately responded with a total of $805,000, about one-quarter of MassEquality's entire budget the previous year.

While the Cabinet was able to prop up local political organizations, campaign-finance laws denied it the power to directly reward and punish politicians, the maneuvering that so excited Gill. With some of the most restrictive funding limits in the country, at $500 per person, the most Cabinet members could have combined to give any Massachusetts legislator was $3,500, diluting their leverage over any single politician. "The strategic piece of the puzzle we'd been missing—consistent across almost every legislature we examined—is that it's often just a handful of people, two or three, who introduce the most outrageous legislation and force the rest of their colleagues to vote on it," Gill would later explain. "If you could reach these few people or neutralize them by flipping the chamber to leaders who would block bad legislation, you'd have a dramatic effect."

As he mounted his coffee table, Gill explained this vision to OutGiving attendees. If the Cabinet was a triumph of scale, a closely held partnership that multiplied a handful of seven-figure political budgets, new campaign-finance laws required scope for full impact. Caps on individual contributions to candidates demanded a large fleet of those willing to give out of their own pockets, sometimes in installments of just hundreds of dollars, and nimbly in response to the news.

After the conference concluded, Gill made plans to launch another organization that bore his name but would reside in a different part of the tax code than the Denver-based foundation and have an office in Washington, DC. As a so-called issue advocacy organization, the Gill Action Fund would be permitted to spend freely to affect political outcomes through lobbying and issue campaigns around ballot measures. He planned to spin off a second donor gathering, called Political OutGiving, to be held in the alternating years when federal and major state elections took place. (The traditional conference, which continued in odd-numbered years, would become distinguished as "philanthropic" OutGiving.) By the time of the first Political OutGiving, scheduled for March 2006, Gill vowed, he would have developed a process to siphon his own money for political activity nationwide, and would tell attendees what they should be doing with theirs. Unlike Cabinet members, who effectively ran small political clubhouses out of their family offices, the well-to-do gay men and women Gill saw before him at OutGiving lacked any such support. If he wanted to convert them into effective political donors, he would have to provide a common resource that would manage each individual's budget so that it was being doled out for maximum efficiency.

Both of the men he charged with running Gill Action had a background in right-of-center politics. As a small-city mayor and state legislator in Massachusetts in the 1990s, Patrick Guerriero was one of the few openly gay Republican elected officials in the country. After leaving office, he became president of the Log Cabin Republicans as the group faced its biggest-ever crisis: whether to withdraw its support for George W. Bush due to his embrace of the Federal Marriage Amendment. As members deliberated on whether or not to endorse Bush's reelection, Guerriero decided to go public over their differences with the White House and attack the amendment as antithetical to conservative values. (The Log Cabin Republicans decided not to endorse a presidential candidate, choosing instead to back "fair-minded Republican allies to local, state and federal offices" elsewhere on November 2004 ballots.) After raising $1 million to fund a television campaign aimed primarily at elites in Washington, Guerriero turned to one of the few openly gay consultants active in Republican campaigns to develop and place the ads.

Bill Smith was a native Alabamian who had risen in politics through the Montgomery office of Karl Rove & Company, from which the Texas direct-mail vendor had developed a specialty running state judicial races. Smith left Rove's employ around the time Rove became consumed by Bush's presidential ambitions, and eventually joined a Washington media firm for which he began producing ads. Smith was easing his way out of the closet at the time, but his decision to antagonize the White House over gay issues jeopardized other Republican clients. One of them, a campaign in support of a tax-related ballot measure championed by Alabama's conservative governor, told Smith he had to choose between his work for the ballot-measure campaign and the Log Cabin Republicans. Smith refused to quit either, and dared the campaign to fire him if officials were uneasy with his other associations.

Only after the election did Smith learn that the marriage ads had been bankrolled in large part by Tim Gill. Smith had never heard of the Colorado philanthropist, or his interest in developing a national gay campaign operation, and only later learned Gill was the inventor of the software on which his parents had been fully dependent as small-town journalists in

Alabama. (When the two men finally met, Smith began by telling Gill he had "made my beer money in college teaching people how to paginate" in Quark.) Guerriero became the executive director of Gill Action and hired Smith to be national political director. "Gill came along at a terrific time because I was pissed off and I was engaged . . . coming out as gay and realizing you are losing everything," says Smith. "And then there is this person that is strategic, looks at it like a businessman—not afraid to get into the game, play hard to win—and he is like the most compatible political soul mate out there."

When the first Political OutGiving convened in Miami in March 2006, Guerriero rounded out the businessman's critique of gay giving with political detail. To demonstrate how pointless much of it had been, Guerriero reminded attendees of the 2004 campaign of Barack Obama, a previously unknown candidate for the U.S. Senate in Illinois. More than $500,000 of Obama's contributions had come from gay sources, Guerriero recounted from a Gill-sponsored analysis, much of it while Obama was already on course to beat his Republican opponent by nearly fifty points. That sum amounted to a waste for every outcome other than the egos that were satisfied by getting to meet the charismatic young candidate, or a signed thank-you note from a man many assumed would one day be a presidential contender. "For those of us that do this," says Smith, "it was like, 'Are you out of your mind? That's like lighting that money on fire.'"

Instead, Gill was asking donors to send unsolicited checks to candidates they had never heard of and would likely never meet, in states they might never visit. There would be no fundraising banquet or golf outing, maybe never even an expression of gratitude from the politician. "If we have enough people who give five hundred bucks for the candidate for state rep or state senate in Iowa, we all of a sudden become ten percent or twenty percent or thirty percent of someone's campaign funds—versus you get your picture made with somebody," says Smith. "That's the way you ought to be thinking about engaging in politics, not go to a black-tie dinner."

What Smith and Guerriero dismissed as "glamour giving" was prized by many movement leaders as a shining achievement of a generation's activism. At its creation, the Human Rights Campaign Fund had omitted any hint of homosexuality from its name out of a worry that even sympathetic candidates would be afraid of identifying such a group on their campaign-finance disclosure. Gay donors had spent many years so marginalized that they were in the unusual position of feeling grateful that politicians were willing to take their money; in 1988, Massachusetts governor Mike Dukakis had turned away $1 million in potential contributions and refused to appear at a fundraising event organized by gay supporters. Bill Clinton had cultivated gay donors, and over eight years in the White House normalized them. By the time he left office, gay money had come to be seen as an elemental component of the Democratic fundraising base, a parallel niche to trial lawyers, the Jewish community, or the entertainment industry.

Right at the moment when gay political leaders celebrated the fact that prominent Democratic candidates and officeholders (and some Republicans) were aggressively courting them, Gill was telling them it would be a waste to respond too generously to those blandishments. "One of the problems with Tim's strategy is that he's turning people away from national politics at a time when Democrats have just achieved a big victory," said Jeff Soref, a prominent New York gay fundraiser in the Clinton orbit who reported hearing from "Democratic leaders who feel the gay community has not been as supportive" around the 2006 elections.

Gill wanted to train his fellow donors to triage potential recipients of their contributions, dropping both candidates already coasting to victory and those who would nobly champion pro-gay values in the face of certain defeat. "Those are in fact the candidates you shouldn't give to," says Gill. "The ones you want are the ones where your friends' money can make the difference between winning and losing."

Gill Action's initial investments fit the paradigm, Guerriero was able to report to two hundred attendees at the first Political OutGiving. Just ahead of state elections the previous November, the members of the Cabinet funneled $138,000 into local Virginia races, much of it passed through two entities—the statewide group Equality Virginia and a political action committee run by the legislature's only openly gay member—already active there. Democrats ultimately gained only one seat in a Republican-dominated state assembly, but four legislators whom Gill had targeted as antigay were displaced along the way. The legislature had not flipped, but it was getting friendlier.

Smith had been investigating states that the group should prioritize in 2006: where gay issues loomed on the near-term legislative agenda, and where targeted giving could have an outsize impact. Most would not be as easy as Virginia for Gill to "punish the wicked" and reward friends, as he took to describing the strategy. Virginia had some of the country's loosest campaign-finance laws; most other states made it impossible to dump such large sums of money to directly affect local races.

Smith, who served as the group's chief campaign strategist, zeroed in next on Iowa. "They have just left these little time bombs everywhere with these legal cases," he says. In late 2005, attorneys in the Chicago office of Lambda Legal, representing six Des Moines–area same-sex couples, had sued the Polk County recorder who denied them marriage licenses. *Varnum v. Brien* had received little coverage, but the Lambda attorneys told Smith why they were optimistic about the case's prospects on appeal.

Despite its aura of heartland traditionalism and lack of politically visible gay community, Iowa had a long record of state jurisprudence far more progressive than federal courts when it came to matters of civil rights. Already state judges had in 2005 rejected a challenge from a group of Republican politicians who sued to prevent a district judge from dissolving a Vermont-authorized civil union. Some of those legislators later asked the court to permit them to step in as defendants, arguing that Iowa's defense-of-marriage law forbade any legal recognition of same-sex couples. The legislators' next move, inevitably, would be to write a definition of marriage into the state constitution. The only way to stop them and defend a potential victory at the supreme court, Smith realized, would be to ensure that Democrats controlled the state senate—where seats were currently split evenly between the two parties.

Donors committed to a total figure they were willing to give nationally that year, and Gill Action staff prepared personalized spending plans for each. Each donor received what was known as a menu: a list of candidates selected from the Gill slate, with summaries of each race, specific amounts to be given, and instructions for adhering to state law. Then the donor would write individual checks and mail them out directly to the campaigns, without any mention of the Gill connection. As campaigns grew capable of receiving online contributions, Gill Action began sending out links to a customized web page—modeled on an Amazon.com shopping cart—that processed donations directly to candidates while bypassing any middleman.

After the first Political OutGiving, about 140 donors emerged willing to make Gill-directed contributions, with approximately 20 percent of them supplying 80 percent of the total funds. That year, by Trimpa's estimate, the network funneled $600,000 into Iowa alone. At the same time donors sent scattered checks to candidates, Gill Action and the various foundations controlled by Cabinet members were making large gifts to develop a permanent organization in Des Moines. Most important was One Iowa, a group founded in 2005 that served as the face of the gay-rights movement to the state's political class. "Tim was brilliant because he supported local activism. He understood, in Hawaii and around the country, the need for people on the ground to have the resources to fight their own battles," says Donna Red Wing, the onetime Gill Foundation policy director who went on to run One Iowa. "It helped to create a foundation of on-the-ground activists building and sustaining their own piece of the movement."

Following the 2006 elections, national gay leaders could point to one bright spot—Arizona became the only state during that decade to defeat a ballot measure to ban gay marriage—but eight states enacted constitutional amendments via referendum. Even as Democrats benefited from a nationwide partisan wave, for gay rights the 2006 election cycle served as a lackluster sequel to 2004. "A lot of [gay donors] are driven, cycle to cycle, by the notion that there's going to be an epiphany—that one day they'll wake up and accept us," Gill told *The Atlantic*'s Joshua Green that year. "But this group had spent millions of dollars on philanthropy, and yet woken up the morning after the election to see gay-marriage bans enacted all across the country."

A few weeks after the election, one of the candidates who had been targeted by Gill received a dinnertime phone call from Green. Danny Carroll had served six terms in the Iowa House of Representatives, most recently as the chamber's Speaker pro tempore. When he lost his seat in a rematch against the challenger he beat in 2004, the Republican blamed Grinnell College activists for the defeat. As Green later recounted, the journalist's "suggestion that he'd been targeted by a nationwide network of wealthy gay activists was met with polite midwestern skepticism." The two men turned to their computers and logged on simultaneously to the state website that tracks campaign contributions. Green guided Carroll to his opponent's disclosure report, pointing out—among two-figure contributions from local towns—four-figure gifts from California and New York. "I'll be darned," Carroll said. "That doesn't make any sense." He continued scrolling, reading donors' addresses in disbelief. "Denver . . . Dallas . . . Los Angeles . . . Malibu . . . there's New York again . . . San Francisco! I can't—I just cannot believe this," Carroll told Green. "Who is this guy again?"

The decision to cooperate with a long story in *The Atlantic* was the culmination of a gradual shift toward publicizing the donors' efforts. (The Gill Foundation vacillated for years about whether even to launch a website.) When Gill Action launched, its leadership lived in perpetual fear that a journalist would uncover the pattern of out-of-state donors with no obvious connection to the district or candidates they were aiding with the maximum legal contribution. The Gill guidelines encouraged donors to time their gifts so they would arrive too late to be publicly disclosed before the election—an effort to defer media attention so it would not backfire on the candidates Gill wanted to help. But there was an imperative "to grow the network," as Smith puts it, which despite its nodes in Denver and Kalamazoo was still disproportionately rich in New York and San Francisco donors. "Sure, the other side's going to read it," says Sweeney, fully aware his side was abandoning any element of surprise about how and where it would push next for marriage rights. "This was actually convincing our own people that there's a method to the madness."

Let California Ring

The ambitious 10-10-10-20 strategy demanded a motley set of tasks: both political and legal work, offense and defense, aiming for equal rights for gay couples without foreclosing incremental gains that fell short of marriage, beginning in the states but eventually requiring the federal government to play a role, too.

None of the established gay-rights organizations that sent emissaries to Jersey City were built for that work. The largest of them, the Human Rights Campaign, had just backed off its commitment to marriage in the wake of dispiriting losses in 2004, and it seemed unlikely that any group not uniquely devoted to marriage would make a sustained priority of a cause that likely had more heartbreak in its future.

When the ACLU's Matt Coles circulated a draft communiqué that proposed creating a new central organ to centralize implementation of the strategy, the idea was met with dissension. Such a proposal was rejected by state-level organizations, which already had a contentious relationship with the Human Rights Campaign over its sporadic efforts to participate in politics beyond Washington. It was also rebuffed by the Human Rights Campaign itself, which was unwilling to help charter a rival for talent, donations, and influence over how the gay-rights movement practiced politics. "Some thought existing organizations would be unwilling to work with an independent campaign organization, some thought our community would be deeply resistant to anything that highly organized," Coles summarized in a July 2005 email to Jersey City attendees. In it, he explained why the final concept paper reflected a preference for "a staffed, structured, enhanced collaboration between existing state and national groups, gay and non-gay, working on marriage."

That new structure, called the National Collaborative, was chartered in 2007 for a three-year trial period. Upon its creation, the National Collaborative identified seven discrete state-level objectives, prioritizing those where there was a "high potential to advance marriage goals" over the next three years. Participants would be expected to review grant proposals from local organizations and supply staff to coach recipients. The circle of emergent donors cultivated by Tim Gill would drive money to support their work.

California was among those states designated for special attention by the National Collaborative. At the Jersey City summit, it had been among the first to be inscribed on the list of ten states expected to deliver full marriage rights by 2025. But the "Winning Marriage" plan went further in its aims for the country's largest state, identifying it as a short-term priority for the movement, one where gay-marriage advocates stood to notch an imminent win without any help from the courts. "California is a state where marriage through the legislature, or even at the ballot, is a real prospect," the plan declared.

To date, gay-rights strategists in California had stuck to an incrementalist track. The legislature had first established a domestic-partnership registry in 1999, and each year added new benefits until it was so comprehensive that Freedom to Marry's Evan Wolfson described it as "all but marriage." By early 2004, a California domestic partnership was the equal of a Vermont civil union, albeit available to a population over fifty times the size, prompting journalist-activist E. J. Graff to call California's program the "most important same-sex partnership law in the nation." Both Democratic and Republican governors had participated in the expansion, helping boost public support for domestic partnerships over 70 percent. Bills to legalize gay marriage moved through Sacramento with little of the often bilious rhetoric that accompanied consideration of gay unions in Hawaii, Vermont, and Massachusetts. Graff celebrated California's gradualism as an "outstanding political model" for the movement to follow nationally.

But Governor Arnold Schwarzenegger, a self-styled champion of gay rights during the unusual 2003 recall election that marked his entry into politics, refused to cross the threshold to marriage. The Republican signed a spate of gay-rights provisions into law, including those to expand the domestic-partner program. But as a marriage bill moved through the legislature in 2005, Schwarzenegger publicly dithered for months about whether he would let it become law. He ultimately issued a veto, citing the 61 percent of California voters who had voted for Proposition 22, the defense-of-marriage referendum passed in March 2000. "You are holding up history. You are holding up civil rights for an entire state," Molly McKay, a longtime gay-marriage activist serving as field director for Equality California, countered Schwarzenegger. "We're not going to let this issue die."

As its lobbyists waited to push the bill again in the next legislative session, Equality California focused on swaying public opinion. Already views on the matter appeared to have moved significantly in California since the 2000 referendum, with opinions split at 46 percent each in favor of and opposed to full marriage rights, according to a summer 2005 poll from the Public Policy Institute of California. "It seems clear that public exposure to and discussion of our community's issues has increased the comfort level and knowledge level among the general public," the state's dominant gay-rights group wrote in an October 2005 proposal circulated to prospective donors to raise money for what it would come to call the California Equality Project. "The time is ripe to study exactly how and why attitudes have dramatically shifted among Californians, and use that information to support much broader education."

That would require a different type of political organization, and national sponsors saw California as a natural base to prototype one that could be replicated elsewhere. The state already had a sophisticated gay-rights lobby, in the form of Equality California, and its own class of donors. There was a strong foundation of popular support for gay rights, and in the domestic-partnership law a legal basis from which to reach for full equality in marriage. Wolfson, who became chair of its national advisory board, described the California Equality Project as "an ambitious, affirmative public education campaign that will provide templates and lessons for work throughout the country."

National organizations, including the Human Rights Campaign and Gill Foundation, paid $200,000 each to help launch the pilot, buying a stake in the management of a program formally under Equality California's umbrella. This generated a nearly $4 million budget through 2007, with further support arriving in other forms. The Human Rights Campaign shared the results of a costly opinion-research project it had undertaken "to understand the American public's emotional resistance to marriage for same sex couples," as a report later described it. The National Gay and Lesbian Task Force detailed its deputy organizing director, Thalia Zepatos, to oversee the start-up. "Convincing people on the marriage issue takes time," Zepatos would later write. "Our 'new and improved' strategy for California was to initiate a public education campaign that would work to scale, and engage Californians years before a measure was ever placed on the ballot."

Never before had a gay-rights organization attempted to shift public opinion around same-sex unions in the absence of immediate political or legal action. Short-term campaigns had been reasonably aimed solely at turning voters against a constitutional amendment, rather than toward actually supporting something. Other communication efforts, notably in Vermont and Massachusetts, had aimed to discourage legislators from interfering with the work of courts. In no situation had anyone tried, at least not in a sustained fashion with real resources, to explain to citizens why gay people should be permitted to marry. A longtime organizer in various roles around the gay-rights movement, Zepatos was struck upon arriving in Los Angeles to manage the project that, for the first time, "we were playing chess five moves out."

Officials at Let California Ring, as the project was rebranded after its formal launch, freely said their goal was to "spark millions of conversations." Privately, they had more discrete and attainable goals: to increase public support for marriage by at least two percentage points, interacting with 800,000 Californians about the issue, and identifying 400,000 new supporters.

Zepatos designed the program with a publicly unacknowledged agenda: to stitch together a fractured activist coalition in anticipation of a possible statewide campaign. Equality California was viewed as a Bay Area–centric organization with little footprint in Southern California, while gay political leaders had few strong links with racial and ethnic minority communities in a state where they together represented a majority of the population. "We needed a way to get people to start working together," says Zepatos.

The Human Rights Campaign's research helped refine messaging tactics, away from earlier legalistic arguments to more emotionally resonant themes that could be relayed through in-person interactions or packaged with a consumer-marketing sensibility. In response to focus groups showing minority voters saw same-sex relationships as a "white issue," Let California Ring placed full-time staff positions at four nongay civil-rights organizations for the purpose of promoting marriage rights directly to African American, Latino, and Asian communities. Eighty different pieces of specialized advertising on the theme of "Strong Commitments, Strong Families" ran in ethnic newspapers and websites, representing seven languages including Vietnamese and Korean.

The showcase of the project was a sixty-second television ad developed by the Madison Avenue agency DDB Worldwide. In the ad, first aired only in Santa Barbara, a bride encounters a series of impediments en route to the altar: a broken heel, her veil caught in a tree branch, a misplaced cane that causes her to stumble feet away from the groom. "What if you couldn't marry the person you love?" the ad's tagline asked. It had been the most successful of four ads tested, and the only one not to feature a gay couple. "It's putting the people we're trying to talk to, the undecided people, into our shoes," Equality California's Seth Kilbourn explained to the *San Francisco Chronicle.* "We gave them something they can identify with, a wedding. The ad firm really felt that if you're going to try to connect with a certain group of people, you need to talk about them, not yourself."

To assess the impact of its tactics, strategists paired two media markets of comparable size. Santa Barbara received the full force of the Let California Ring pilot program, including four local organizers assigned to stage house parties where supporters could talk to their neighbors about marriage. Monterey, on the other hand, served as a control group that received nothing.

Zepatos didn't need those numbers to know how difficult it was to drive widespread interest in a topic that still seemed remote to many Californians. "We were trying very, very early, to generate conversations," she reflected. "It's sort of hard to engage the public in a conversation if it's totally not even on their radar screen."

That began to change in 2007. Another marriage bill was winding its way through the legislature, accompanied by what the *Los Angeles Times* prominently noted with some surprise was "respectful debate." From the beginning, the bill's sponsor downplayed expectations it would become law. "We're trying to create favorable conditions for a court ruling," said Assemblyman Mark Leno, an openly gay San Francisco Democrat.

One way or another, political conflict over same-sex marriage seemed inevitable, and not far off. When it did, California would be the place the gay-rights movement's new organizational might—the twenty-year plan endorsed by all major institutional players, the newfound willingness of donors to back the national strategy and all its messy local tributaries, and a dedicated experiment in moving public opinion—faced its first major test. By the close of 2008, Wolfson speculated in a Freedom to Marry annual report, California "could well be the Gettysburg of our struggle; not the end, but the turning-point."

Part Seven

THE RIGHT'S LAST STAND

(2007–2008)

It Came from San Diego

When Governor Arnold Schwarzenegger vetoed the second gay-marriage bill to pass California's legislature, in October 2007, he again hid behind a technocratic rationale rather than quarreling with the proposal on its merits. "I maintain my position that the appropriate resolution to this issue is to allow the court to rule," he wrote in a veto message that presaged a titanic political battle. "The people of California should then determine what, if any, statutory changes are needed in response to the court's ruling."

The origins of litigation then before the California Supreme Court could be traced back nearly a decade. After Hawaii and Alaska, California was designated by Mormon and Roman Catholic Church officials as the next terrain for an effort to block gay marriage at the ballot. Their local partner was state senator Pete Knight, who had three times failed to pass his mini-DOMA-style bill and settled on the state's referendum process as a last resort. "He was a little gadflyish," says Sal Russo, a Republican consultant in Sacramento who was involved in the early planning around a marriage ban that ended up qualifying for the February 2000 ballot as Proposition 22. "We thought without the help of the Bishops or LDS he wouldn't get anywhere."

The so-called Knight Initiative was drafted to be as unobjectionable as possible, offering to add to the state family code the declaration that "only marriage between a man and a woman is valid or recognized in California." Upon passage, that one sentence appeared to ensure just that state authorities would not be required to recognize same-sex marriages performed elsewhere. But the fact that it was done through amending a state statute left it vulnerable to a state constitutional challenge. Anticipating one, and worried about how California's liberal judiciary would receive it, Knight in 2001 began raising money for the Proposition 22 Legal Defense and Education Fund.

Over the next few years, social conservatives realized how little those fourteen words were worth, even without legal pressure. A tax-relief bill that moved through the legislature in January 2002 to make couples eligible for a rebate "clearly awards a marriage right to unmarried cohabitants," wrote Campaign for California Families executive director Randy Thomasson. That same month, Democrats pushed a separate bill that allowed unmarried pairs of any gender mix to register their interdependence with the state. It was, Thomasson said upon passage of the 2003 bill that gave California de facto civil unions, "gay marriage by another name."

Those bills showed Proposition 22 to be insufficient for the challenges of a new decade. "We need a full-fledged amendment that does the whole job now, because in 10 to 20 years, more state legislatures will legalize civil unions and domestic partnerships and encourage cohabitation, and it will be too late to pass a better amendment," Thomasson wrote in late 2003 to members of the Arlington Group as they debated the contents of the Federal Marriage Amendment. Once it became evident in 2004 that the federal effort was doomed, local activists began scheming to place on the 2006 ballot an amendment to the state constitution.

Thomasson launched a group called Vote Yes to Marriage, associated with the American Family Association network, that attempted to limit any recognition of nontraditional families. "It is in the child's best interest to have a mother and a father," declared the amendment language, affirming that "marriage between one man and one woman is diminished when government bestows statutory rights or incidents of marriage on unmarried persons." An emergent rival known as the Protect Marriage Coalition simply wanted to take the fourteen words from Proposition 22 and enter them into the state constitution. Protect Marriage claimed to have polls showing its more moderate position—which would let stand the civil-unions program that took effect in early 2005—to be more acceptable among voters.

The divide between a sweeping amendment that could be seen as antigay and a softer alternative focused only on marriage mimicked the one that had split the Arlington Group. (Ironically, Protect Marriage was sponsored by groups that took a hard line on the federal amendment, the Family Research Council and Concerned Women for America.) Recognizing that the two separate amendments were unlikely to coexist, their backers spent much of 2005 discrediting one another. Thomasson claimed that the Protect Marriage proposal amounted to a "counterfeit marriage initiative." He called it "fatally flawed and legally unsound." With social conservatives feeling little urgency, and their leaders divided on language and strategy, neither made much progress toward accumulating the nearly 600,000 signatures necessary to reach voters.

Throughout it all, California's courts were dealing with the fallout from San Francisco mayor Gavin Newsom's decision to have city officials extend marriage licenses to gay and lesbian couples. Within a day of the February 2004 move, both the Campaign for California Families and the Proposition 22 Legal Defense and Education Fund had separately sued to restrain Newsom. The judiciary, however, was slow to oblige. It took nearly a month for a court order to halt the San Francisco marriages. While the California Supreme Court made clear that the mayor had acted beyond his authority, it indicated that it did not consider the underlying question settled, all but inviting a challenge to the constitutionality of California's marriage laws.

By June, there were six such parallel suits in California's courts, which were consolidated as *In re Marriage Cases*. Shortly thereafter, the California Supreme Court invalidated the nearly four thousand marriage licenses that San Francisco had awarded six months earlier. At summer's end, California again had no gay couples legally married within its borders, but its courts were moving quickly toward creating a legal framework in which they would be able to do so freely in the future. In early 2005, a San Francisco–based judge ruled that California's marriage statute could not be justified under the strictest application of equal-protection law. A year later, the ruling was reversed by an intermediate appellate court, which concluded by a two-to-one vote that the lower-court judge had been too liberal in his application of equal-protection analysis. In December 2006, the California Supreme Court agreed to review that decision.

The original controversy over mayoral power that had launched the *In re Marriage Cases* was now moot, as the matter of the disputed San Francisco licenses had been long since settled. But the various entities who had begun the process in 2004 were granted standing to argue the constitutional questions about prohibiting same-sex couples from marrying. The state supreme court certified four petitioners and four respondents, as Newsom's government (the contiguous city and county of San Francisco) led the challenge with support from the ACLU, Lambda Legal, and the National Center for Lesbian Rights. The existing law, informed by the fourteen words approved by voters in 2000, would be defended by

Schwarzenegger and newly elected attorney general Jerry Brown, along with lawyers arguing on behalf of the Campaign for California's Families and the Proposition 22 Legal Defense and Education Fund.

As the court's September 26 filing deadline approached, dozens of other parties scrambled to prepare what was described as an unprecedented number of amicus briefs. Gay legal groups solicited briefs from a long list of supportive organizations, including other civil-rights advocates like the Mexican American Legal Defense and Education Fund, as well as those, like the American Psychoanalytic Association, that brought social-scientific expertise. San Francisco city attorney Dennis J. Herrera volunteered to marshal other municipal and county governments to sign on to a brief that would reflect that cities and counties had an interest in seeing their gay citizens allowed to marry. Los Angeles, Oakland, San Jose, and Long Beach added their names, along with Santa Cruz County and the town of Fairfax. But as the draft versions of Herrera's brief circulated, there was a glaring exception among the state's large metropolitan areas: the most conservative among them, perhaps the most conservative of all the country's big cities.

On September 4, 2007, the question of whether to sign on to the amicus brief came before the San Diego City Council. Debate ended in a four–four tie, with a deal to return for another vote two weeks later. The prospect of a final vote in favor of joining the brief was high. None of the four no votes declared themselves opposed to gay marriage, and one of them indicated she was eager to take the controversial matter to the city as a whole, rather than bury it. "I think we at least need to allow both sides to weigh in on this issue," said councilwoman Donna Frye. "The public has a right to participate, and I do not believe that has occurred."

Little Kingdoms

When he entered the pale-wood-paneled chambers of the San Diego City Council that September 4, 2007, afternoon, Chris Clark knew immediately that he was the only pastor in attendance. Yet he saw many faces he associated with the "Hillcrest business community"—named for San Diego's historically gay neighborhood. "They were there in force," says Clark. "Not that many Christians, because not that many people knew about it."

Clark had learned that the resolution was coming up for a vote only the day before, when he received an email message from an activist he knew named Anne Wigdahl Subia. A layperson, Subia had come to play a key role as conduit among evangelical clergy in the San Diego area, particularly its politically conservative suburbs. Given that the nonhierarchical denominations had to be organized only horizontally—each pastor is "king of their own little kingdom," according to Clark—Subia's database of churches was an essential way for their leaders to find one another.

Clark's East Clairemont Southern Baptist Church was among the smaller congregations on Subia's list, and she knew that Clark was more accessible and often less distracted than his megachurch peers. When Subia's message arrived, alerting him to a matter before the city council, Clark's most significant distraction had been a home-bathroom remodeling project. Clark knew the marriage case was being taken up by the California Supreme Court on appeal, but it had never occurred to him that local politicians would weigh in. The only sign the city council's legislative schedule gave of its likely decision was the recommendation from Toni Atkins, a lesbian councilwoman who had gained citywide stature during a previous stint as interim mayor: *Take the actions.* Subia said she was worried that there would not be anyone there to articulate the opposing view, and

Clark saw little time to recruit another spokesman for the religious community. "Mind you, I'm a pastor, and it's as if God specifically said, 'You're the guy. You're going to go down there,'" recalls Clark. "I didn't want to."

Even though his side had been vastly outnumbered, Clark was heartened by the first, split vote. In the council chambers, he had kept praying for his own councilwoman, Donna Frye, to come around on the issue. *God, you're the one that changes kings' hearts,* Clark had prayed silently. Eventually the light indicating Frye's vote flickered from green to red, deadlocking the tally. The council took a recess and returned with the decision to delay consideration to invite public input. Clark immediately called Subia with the good news. "It's a God thing," he told her. "God did this."

When the city council reconvened two weeks later before a packed chamber, the crowd looked very different: "two-to-one Christians to Hillcrest community," Clark estimated. Not only were other evangelical pastors present, but Clark spotted a man he recognized as the auxiliary bishop of the Roman Catholic Diocese of San Diego. While the two-week delay had granted Christian conservatives time to organize, it did not tip the ultimate outcome; Frye ended up supporting the resolution, sending it to passage by a five-to-three margin.

That put the resolution on the desk of the mayor for his signature. A former police chief whose political base consisted of downtown business elites, Mayor Jerry Sanders had demonstrated an obligatory respect for the city's gay population: when he ran for office in 2005, he marched in a pride parade and expressed support for civil unions. When it came to marriage, he said his personal views were bound by the outcome of Proposition 22. *The people have voted,* Sanders told those who asked. *I'm going to support their vote.* Everyone in city council chambers assumed that Sanders would use his veto power to kill the resolution.

But the arrival of the resolution in the mayor's office that evening prompted Sanders to revise that position. "My opinions on this issue have evolved significantly, as I think the opinions of millions of Americans from all walks of life have," he said at a press conference the next afternoon, for which, in an unusual step, he had positioned his wife by his side. Sanders credited the influence of gay staffers, and his own lesbian daughter Lisa, with his decision to dismiss civil unions as "a separate-but-equal institution." (According to local press coverage, Lisa Sanders's sexuality was well known within San Diego political circles but not at all beyond.) "I decided to lead with my heart," Sanders said, as tears flowed, "which is probably obvious at the moment." He said he had concluded that he could not look members of his staff "in the face and tell them that their relationships . . . were any less meaningful than the marriage I share with my wife."

The entire press conference took less than five minutes. Sanders was among the first prominent Republicans to embrace gay marriage, and the emotional vulnerability he showed when doing so was particularly gripping given his just-the-facts-ma'am bearing. Footage of his remarks would circulate widely on the then-young video site YouTube. "It humanized him and made him seem less the corporate caricature some see," remarked a *San Diego Union-Tribune* blogger. Sanders, preparing to seek reelection in a rematch against a businessman who declared himself content with civil unions, was happy to be defined by the shift. As he formally announced his reelection campaign just one day later, Sanders for once had his daughters at his side.

Practically it did not matter much whether the city of San Diego attached its name to one of dozens of amicus briefs. But to see their Republican mayor abandon a promise to abide by Proposition 22—and then have local media guilelessly celebrate that betrayal as a show of courage—was enraging to San Diego religious leaders. When Clark was invited to a meeting with African American pastors who wanted to hold a press conference attacking Sanders, he signed up for it. "That really woke some folks up," said Clark of Sanders's shift. "We all realized that we had to move on this rapidly, and get people on board quickly."

Several episodes over the previous five years served as test runs for the networking muscle that San Diego's conservative clergy would have to flex now. In 2003, a group of pastors had managed on short notice to organize a four-day mission by Reverend Billy Graham, then suffering from Parkinson's, for what most expected would be his final visit to the region. Even though Graham's earliest large crowds had come in Southern California, the last of his three previous San Diego crusades, in 1976, was nearly disrupted by a fractious relationship among local clergy split along racial and ideological lines. ("During the civil-rights movement the white evangelical church did not sense the pain and the cries and that longing for justice," Bishop George McKinney of St. Stephen's Church of God in Christ, who organized the 1976 crusade, told the *Southern California Christian Times*.) For Graham's 2003 visit, the leaders of more than six hundred congregations, representing dozens of denominations, were involved in bringing their flocks to fill the local football arena, Qualcomm Stadium, for shared prayer. "It cemented this group of pastors that rose together," says Subia.

Five months later, the San Diego suburbs were hit by wildfires that eventually consumed nearly 300,000 acres and 2,000 homes, making them the worst in California's history. Jim Garlow, a part-time radio host who had helped rally his fellow pastors in advance of Graham's visit, invited them to his Skyline Wesleyan Church to plot a collective response to help residents displaced by the catastrophe.

Clark was part of a small group, calling itself the Pastors Rapid Response Team, which continued to meet monthly to discuss policy and political matters. In 2004, they rallied to save the Mount Soledad Cross, an imposing concrete structure standing on federal land outside the city. Courts had deemed public property an inappropriate venue for a religious monument. Hoping to stop the city from being forced to dismantle the cross, the pastors backed a citizens' group collecting signatures so that San Diego voters could decide whether to permit a private buyer to acquire the disputed land beneath it. Proposition K, as the ballot measure was known, lost overwhelmingly.

Team members had never committed themselves as fully to organizing against same-sex marriage, even during the Proposition 22 campaign and the fitful efforts that followed to firm up the law with a constitutional amendment. By the middle of 2007, conservative activists were again, as Clark put it, "stuck in the mud." "There still wasn't enough money. There wasn't a ground game to get enough signatures," he says. "So it was kind of, what do we do?"

The necessary catalyst arrived unexpectedly from San Diego city hall in September of that year. After Sanders's dramatic press conference, Subia set to work activating her network. Other unofficial links among the region's evangelicals also pulsed with the news. The first time Garlow heard it, he was struck by the intensity of the voice on the other end of the line. "What are you going to do about it?" the caller asked.

It took a few beats for Garlow to identify the voice as Jimmy Valentine, a radio producer for Roger Hedgecock, a former San Diego mayor who had become a prominent conservative talk-show host. Valentine was so heated that it took Garlow, whose own religious program appeared on 629 stations, a few more moments to discern what exactly had him worked up.

"About what?" Garlow asked.

"About our mayor's flip-flop on marriage, now coming out in favor of so-called same-sex marriage?" Valentine responded.

Valentine proposed to Garlow that they collaborate on a protest rally, potentially one so big it could fill Qualcomm Stadium with evangelicals again. Garlow dismissed that idea as premature, but he accepted Subia's invitation shortly thereafter to attend the monthly policy-group meeting at Clark's East Clairemont Southern Baptist Church. Garlow took his seat among other pastors in the Sunday-school room, but did not speak over the course of the ninety-minute session. Once it was over, Garlow drew a few of the attendees to a corner table and said, "We have to mobilize pastors across the state, and I'm not leaving here until we have a plan."

God's Way of Bringing People Together

A few weeks after the mayor's about-face, Bishop Salvatore Joseph Cordileone received an invitation from Chris Clark to visit Jim Garlow's Skyline Church. Cordileone accepted and made plans to bring along Charles LiMandri, a lawyer with close church ties who had met Clark and Garlow during the multiyear effort to keep the cross in its place atop Mount Soledad: LiMandri argued the case up to the state supreme court while the pastors mobilized grassroots activists. (The matter was effectively settled in 2006 when Congress passed a bill transferring ownership of the cross to the Defense Department.) The Mount Soledad campaign set a foundation for cooperation between Catholics and evangelical Protestants that both sides were eager to revive in order to get a marriage amendment on the next year's ballot.

Cordileone had an enduring interest in family-values politics, as defined by the Vatican. Despite his standing as auxiliary bishop of the San Diego diocese, just that month he had personally directed a workshop to promote "natural family planning" among parishioners. His critique of same-sex unions rarely touched on homosexuality itself, and despite its theological underpinnings he did not rely solely on scriptural support for his view. Instead Cordileone told a largely secular story about changes in American social policy that placed gay marriage downstream from legalized birth-control pills and abortion on demand. All were part of a "contraceptive mentality," he wrote using a phrase popularized by John Paul II, which "divorces the procreative meaning of the marital embrace from its unitive meaning."

Few other officials in the diocese would have had time for such political diversions. Just weeks earlier, Bishop Robert Brom announced that church lawyers had reached a $198 million settlement with 144 people who had accused its priests of sexual misconduct in incidents reaching as far back as 1938. Brom's public apology for "these crimes and this abuse of power" marked the culmination of a four-year process that had included a failed effort to protect church assets by filing for Chapter 11 bankruptcy. Almost immediately the diocese was forced to sell off scads of property to meet its obligations. Brom committed that no parishes or schools would be closed in the process, but that left nearly everything else vulnerable. Within weeks, the diocese had rolled back publication of the biweekly newspaper that had served the community since 1912.

While much of the diocese's leadership was fixated on the bankruptcy crisis, Cordileone was busy expanding its reach into public policy. Trained in canon law with a degree from Rome's Gregorian University, he had always been oriented toward public debates. Within the pastoral mission, he had followed a lawyer's career trajectory, from judge on San Diego's Diocesan Tribunal and onetime adjutant judicial vicar to a role at the Vatican's highest court, the Apostolic Signatura. In 2002, Brom named Cordileone, who had once been his personal secretary, to serve as an auxiliary bishop in the San Diego diocese. An auxiliary bishop has no power of his own, but Cordileone made clear he wanted to use his position to cultivate an uncommonly high profile in culture-war battles. "To Bishop Brom's credit, although he himself was not, I think, particularly active in these issues, I think he saw the importance of it so that he would not just wait or stop Bishop Cordileone from doing it," says LiMandri. "Some guys wouldn't allow others to do so."

Not long after he assumed that role, Cordileone approached LiMandri with a request to serve with him on a religious-liberty committee organized by the California Conference of Catholic Bishops. Though the men had not been close, their parents had played cards together at a Little Italy fraternal club, and they had attended the University of San Diego at the same time. LiMandri built his law practice on commercial clients, like insurers and the city's tuna-fishing fleet. But in 2003 he attended a legal academy run by the Alliance Defense Fund, the organization established by evangelical leaders including James Dobson and Don Wildmon to fund public-interest litigation of concern to their ministries. After the *Goodridge* decision, LiMandri began briefing Cordileone on the rising specter of gay marriage nationwide, and the two grew closer, shuttling together to Sacramento several times a year to participate in meetings of the bishops' committee.

That summer, shortly after the first gay marriages had become legal in two different Canadian provinces, the Vatican staked out an official position in the policy debate beginning to roil both North America and Europe. "Respect for homosexual persons cannot lead in any way to approval of homosexual behaviour or to legal recognition of homosexual unions," announced the Congregation for the Doctrine of the Faith, a policy body whose prefect was a right-wing German cardinal named Joseph Ratzinger. (*Considerations Regarding Proposals to Give Legal Recognition to Unions Between Homosexual Persons* was released with the imprimatur of Pope John Paul II, but it was signed by the man who would succeed him upon his death two years later.) The pressure the Vatican's move placed on Catholics who held positions of secular authority was notable. "When legislation in favour of the recognition of homosexual unions is proposed for the first time in a legislative assembly, the Catholic law-maker has a moral duty to express his opposition clearly and publicly and to vote against it. To vote in favour of a law so harmful to the common good is gravely immoral," read the ten-point manifesto. "When legislation in favour of the recognition of homosexual unions is already in force, the Catholic politician must oppose it in the ways that are possible for him and make his opposition known; it is his duty to witness to the truth."

As the church's centralized authority made explicit demands on Catholic politicians worldwide, local bishops were given surprising leeway to determine the degree of their own involvement in political matters. When 189 American bishops gathered in the midst of the 2004 general election, they overwhelmingly agreed that individual dioceses were free to show their distaste for Catholic politicians whose views clashed with church teaching. That year, the archbishops of Denver, St. Louis, and Newark all came close to directly endorsing Bush over John Kerry, with some threatening to deny communion to the Democrat, a former altar boy, and his voters. Even so, Bush privately grumbled that the Church was not doing enough to back his support for federal and state amendments to define marriage. "Not all the American bishops are with me," Bush complained to the Vatican secretary of state during a visit to Rome, according to the *National Catholic Reporter*.

A half century earlier, the California Conference of Catholic Bishops had become one of the first religious groups to rush into what would become the great moral-political issue of the generation. In 1962, a liberal legislator proposed changes to the state's hundred-year-old abortion ban—one of the first efforts nationwide to loosen such a law—and the bishops' conference became its leading opponent. They managed to fend off more open abortion laws until 1967, when Governor Ronald Reagan signed a reform bill, but during that period they often struggled to balance the interests of internal constituencies with appeals to the broader population. "Despite its professed interest in an ecumenical pro-life coalition, the Church had insisted on orchestrating the right-to-life movement, and the results had been disastrous," historian Daniel K. Williams has written. "Church officials wanted to entrust the right-to-life cause to Catholic professionals, especially lawyers and doctors who had worked with the Church for years and who, they thought, would have public credibility as legal and medical experts."

It was that political failure, which along with the subsequent rollback of abortion bans in other states set the stage for *Roe v. Wade*, that Cordileone saw inaugurating an era of declension of the American family. "Unfortunately, all of these social forces coalesced right at the moment that the birth-control pill was invented and marketed and presented as if this was something that was going to be liberating and was going to reduce poverty," he said. Then followed no-fault divorce laws ("undermining the understanding of marriage as a permanent commitment"), open marriages ("fidelity wasn't a need to observe"), and those entered into by couples not intending to have children. "We can see what uniquely defines marriage as the good that it is already beginning to erode," Cordileone explained. "What we're facing now in terms of this redefinition of marriage becomes the latest—and perhaps I would suggest the most serious—attack."

With other members of the California Conference of Catholic Bishops more focused on combating the state's latest pro-choice reform, Cordileone and LiMandri argued that a constitutional amendment to define marriage needed to take priority, before it became too late to undo a court's decision. Their agenda reflected a diocese, much like the city itself, far more conservative than those of California's other metropolitan areas. The long-serving archbishop of Los Angeles, Cardinal Roger Mahony, was most vocal on immigrant-related issues and relatively quiet on matters of sexual morality. Shortly after being installed as San Francisco's archbishop in 2006, George Niederauer had chosen to give one of his first interviews in his new post to the gay-issues reporter of the local newspaper. A film buff who had been ordained as a priest while pursuing a doctorate in literature, writing a dissertation on eighteenth-century British satire, Niederauer chose to praise as "very powerful" the gay-cowboy love story *Brokeback Mountain*. One of its lessons, the archbishop said, concerned "the destructiveness of not being honest with yourself and not honest with other people and not being faithful, trying to live a double life."

Even the other members of the bishops' committee who shared Cordileone's perspective dismissed as "alarmist" his insistence that church officials should prepare for the possibility that California judges would act as boldly as those in Massachusetts had. "We kind of anticipated that the marriage thing would become increasingly important," says LiMandri. "The sentiment on the committee was not to move forward on this issue."

Their past forays into state politics had been regulated by the California Conference of Catholic Bishops, but the mayoral apostasy freed Cordileone and LiMandri to take action. Marriage—which had been elevated from a state issue to a national one with the push for a federal marriage amendment—had now in San Diego become a squarely municipal one, and fell under their purview.

Addressing the 150 evangelical pastors Garlow had gathered at his Skyline Church, Cordileone took a dire tone. "The ship is sinking," he said. "That ship is Western civilization. We all have to pull together. We have to bail out water and keep that ship afloat." To Cordileone's surprise, the pastors asked him to pray over them and welcomed the bishop's remarks with cries—foreign to Catholic ears—of "Amen, brother." One of the priests in the bishop's retinue remarked that he had never before set foot in a Protestant church. "I long for the day when we have the luxury of debating our theological differences," Cordileone mused to his hosts.

While Garlow had been successful at convening his fellow pastors, he did not have access to a centralized budget, nor the ability to direct the activities of any other clergy. The Catholics, as a hierarchical church, could "speak with a single voice," says LiMandri. Here was a chance to create the ecumenical coalition that had eluded the Conference of Bishops' efforts to defeat abortion-law liberalization before *Roe v. Wade*. "Both the evangelical pastors I worked closely with and those of us in our Catholic side understood that, yes, this cuts across denominational lines and that really it is an issue that defines civilization. A civilization rises or falls on marriage; we both understood that. We were able to come together in marvelous, very beautiful ways," Cordileone would say. "Marriage is, I believe, God's way of bringing his people together."

Nassau Street

In the fall of 2007, Maggie Gallagher received a call from a woman in Carlsbad, one of San Diego's wealthy northern suburbs, named Michelle O'Reilly. By then, the Institute for Marriage and Public Policy, along with its MarriageDebate website, had been around for four years, and Gallagher had earned a reputation as the most single-mindedly devoted defender of traditional marriage in the national media. O'Reilly began talking about how disgusted she was by what Mayor Jerry Sanders had done, and how she had assembled a group of her fellow Catholics who would be meeting at her home that weekend to figure out what they could do in response. O'Reilly said she was calling for advice on messaging, but Gallagher was not much impressed by her political instincts. *She obviously doesn't know what she's doing,* Gallagher thought, right up until the moment that O'Reilly offhandedly mentioned that among those who would be attending that weekend's meeting was the local auxiliary bishop.

Gallagher interrupted her. "That's kind of interesting," Gallagher remarked, a sly bit of understatement masking her sudden enthusiasm. "Do you want me to come out and talk to your group?"

Gallagher had never heard of Salvatore Cordileone, but news of a fellow Catholic entering the political scrum around marriage—and a diocesan leader, no less—inspired her to book a plane ticket to San Diego. After four years working with evangelical Protestants, Gallagher was finding herself disenchanted. In her view, they attached themselves to grand promises, then rarely lived up to them. Their leaders were not truly committed to the arduous work of cultivating a mass political movement. "The strategy of Christian conservatives generally is to say that the public will rise up if you do this," says Gallagher. "That's nice if it happens, but it's not exactly a plan."

The Christian right might have developed a fearsome reputation during the 1990s, but the closer Gallagher got to the machinery of its power the more she came to believe it had been built on an intellectual foundation unable to sustain its own weight. "Delivering on a restoration of Christianity in the culture is not exactly an attainable goal. So it was hard, I think, for an organization structure like that to end up delivering," says Gallagher. Furthermore, she says, "I think that traditionalists, generally, tend to be less creative thinkers, so that leads to doing the things you know how to do."

The Arlington Group, with its narrow dedication to passing and ratifying a Federal Marriage Amendment, was supposed to be the hub of a new-style evangelical politics. But it had lost sight of that polestar. "In the effort to recruit Moderates and convince current Undecideds," Arlington Group pollster Kellyanne Conway advised in a 2006 presentation, "it is critical to shift the debate over traditional marriage and abortion from a pitched battle of Right vs. Left to a simple question of Right vs. Wrong."

When Democrats reclaimed control of the House and Senate in elections that year, Arlington Group members abandoned any hope of moving along a constitutional amendment and instead shifted their work toward rallying support for George W. Bush's appointments of conservative justices to the Supreme Court. But those projects were episodic, and lacking a long-term goal the organization began to atrophy; when its first staffer, Shannon Royce, departed in 2007 she was never replaced. Attempting to rally around a Republican candidate for the 2008 presidential election, they were paralyzed by the process instead. The only top-tier Republican candidate at the outset of the race to support the amendment, Mitt Romney—who had been critical of the *Goodridge* ruling and led the efforts to avoid the full force of its mandate—gave many Arlington Group members pause due to his Mormon faith. Former Tennessee senator Fred Thompson had the strongest social-conservative credentials, but he opposed any version of the Federal Marriage Amendment on the grounds that it intruded upon states' rights. "We hope to convince all the candidates that on this issue federalism is not as high a value philosophically as making sure marriage has traditional configuration," an anonymous Arlington Group member agonized to *National Review*.

As the Arlington Group disintegrated, its component groups returned to the atomized state in which they had operated before 2003. Most of their activity took place under the umbrella of their ministries, ostensibly apolitical organizations naturally preferred by donors for their tax benefits. "There are many good nonprofits who issue voter guides or get pastors together. There are public-interest law firms galore," says Gallagher. "These are all good things to have—but there is a hole in the center of our movement."

Leaders of that movement recursively fell back on advocacy from the pulpit and the messaging work classified as "public education," too vague to have an impact on electoral or legislative outcomes. "All of the social-conservative movement had defined this as their number one issue, yet when it came to passing a bill through the Massachusetts legislature, there was nobody whose job it was to defeat politicians," says Gallagher. When she had gone to Boston and Worcester during the post-*Goodridge* period to speak in favor of a state amendment, she was surprised to learn that Matt Daniels had been replaced as head of the Massachusetts Family Institute by a former Georgia state legislator named Ron Crews. "So our premier spokesman, locally, who is getting in front of television in Massachusetts, is speaking with a Georgia accent," Gallagher recalls. "And I was like, this is really incompetent."

After a measure to amend the Arizona constitution failed in 2006, the first time traditionalists had lost a statewide referendum over marriage, Gallagher feared it could become a harbinger of future defeats. She drafted a proposal to create the type of unapologetically political and reliably savvy entity missing from the Arlington Group. In July 2007, the National Organization for Marriage held its first board meeting near Princeton University. On the school's faculty sat Catholic natural-law theorist Robert George, one of the few people with whom Gallagher had shared her frustrations about the political naïveté that she was setting out to reverse.

Throughout the nineteenth century, the New Jersey town with which the university shares a name served a crucial function shaping American evangelical Christianity, thanks to the presence of the Presbyterian Church's largest seminary. (The Princeton Theological Seminary was founded in conscious proximity to, but independent of, the university.) As fundamentalist Protestantism waned in national influence following the 1925 *Scopes* trial, which subjected biblical literalism to ridicule at the hands of a secular, modernist elite, so too did Princeton's influence on the politics of American faith. But George's intellectual stature and access to resources restored at least some of that standing as a hub for traditionalist thought. His James Madison Program, which the *Princeton Alumni Weekly* called "a conservative beachhead within the liberal Ivy League," was soon joined by the Witherspoon Institute, which had no ties to the university and could be more overt in its advocacy. In December 2004, the institute sponsored its first conference to unify the disparate strands of gay-marriage opposition across academia: moral philosophers like George and social scientists whose research on marriage could be put before judges and legislators. As George and Gallagher filed papers to formally establish the National Organization for Marriage, they listed Witherspoon Institute director Luis Tellez, who oversaw a regional chapter of the secretive Catholic lay group Opus Dei, as a director and a five-story brick building on Nassau Street, Princeton's main strip, as its headquarters. (Gallagher became president, George chairman of the board.) The inclusion of Brigham Young University political scientist Matthew Holland, who had been a fellow at the James Madison Program, extended the board's reach beyond East Coast Catholics.

Unlike existing institutions on the cultural right, the new organization was devoted solely to resisting changes to the traditional definition of marriage. It was so singular in that focus that when the Connecticut Supreme Court entertained a challenge to the state's 2004 civil-unions law—on the basis that it had created a discriminatory, separate-but-equal alternative to marriage—Gallagher cautioned against engaging on it. Judges, she said, risked turning the question of recognizing same-sex couples into a "black and white, either-or" issue. In fact, Gallagher would not even tell the *New York Times* that she was opposed to civil unions, and appeared to hold up the Connecticut version as something of a model policy about to be undone through litigation. "That is a striking and unfortunate consequence of a compromise," she told the *New York Times*. "That means that every debate will come down to the question of all or nothing; that either you think there is no difference for gay couples or you are a bigot."

Then, when in Hartford in the spring of 2007 to testify against a proposed marriage law, Gallagher discovered the first local organization to impress her in years of dabbling in state-level debates nationwide. The Family Institute of Connecticut's operations exuded competence: a press-conference room filled with local cameras, and several overflow rooms packed with citizen activists all wearing matching "One man, one woman" buttons. When she asked the institute's executive director how he had done it, Brian Brown said, "Assemblies of God creatures: when they tell their people to march, they march."

In conversations, Gallagher learned that Brown shared her vision for what he called "a Club for Growth on marriage," a reference to the Wall Street–funded group that spent heavily in selected Republican primaries to defeat incumbents it found insufficiently conservative on economic issues. Gallagher asked Brown what it would take to hire him, and was able to raise his requested $125,000 salary from the same donor whose initial contribution had launched her think tank. With Brown as its executive director, the group known as NOM set out to, in Gallagher's words, "develop a battle plan and spread it out through the country."

Their initial strategy was shaped by *The Atlantic*'s profile of Tim Gill and its description of how gay donors were surreptitiously targeting vulnerable legislators in key states. Gallagher, who liked to say that "everything I learned about politics I learned from watching the gay rights movement," started to spot traces of Gill's thinking in seemingly isolated local events. The prior month, the New York State Assembly had passed a bill to legalize gay marriage by a daunting 85–61 margin. Yet despite support from the sitting Democratic governor, it was never even introduced in the Republican-controlled senate. "I was like, 'Why are they doing that?'" Gallagher recalls. "It's obvious—they're demonstrating to the politicians that it's safe to vote for gay marriage and they're looking to see what the public reaction is." The National Organization for Marriage had to be just as pragmatic and ruthless on the other side of the marriage debate, willing to raise and spend sufficient cash to make politicians cower. "We wanted to demonstrate that it was a bad idea to vote for gay marriage," says Gallagher.

But New York politicians would not be on the ballot for another year. In fact, there was only one state where gay marriage was an active issue that had legislative elections scheduled in 2007. The previous fall, the New Jersey Supreme Court had ruled its existing marriage laws discriminatory and gave legislators a deadline to develop a regime for recognizing same-sex couples. (By forcing them to pass either a marriage or civil-unions bill, judges had placed lawmakers in a nearly identical position to the one into which Vermont's Supreme Court had forced its legislature almost seven years earlier.) Through a state political action committee, Common Sense America, Gallagher helped direct an estimated $125,000 on radio ads and phone calls attacking Linda Greenstein, the deputy Speaker of the state assembly, as she ran to defend her Trenton seat. The district was one of three participating in a pilot campaign-finance program to limit candidate spending, giving an outside group disproportionate clout. The ads themselves blasted Greenstein's votes in favor of tax increases, but Gallagher was happy for Greenstein to know it was her declared support for gay marriage that had prompted the intense if unsuccessful effort to defeat her. By doing so, Gallagher hoped to intimidate other legislators who might worry they would be next. "Everyone in Washington understands this is where it's coming from," says Gallagher. "I'm not sure it's good for our democracy, but it was an innovation."

After Election Day in November, it wasn't clear where the National Organization for Marriage would go next. The group had purchased a billboard in the district of one of the eleven Massachusetts state representatives who had changed their votes to thwart a marriage ban, accusing him of betrayal. The billboard, which appeared near the Basketball Hall of Fame in Springfield, likened Democrat Angelo Puppolo Jr. to Judas Iscariot and Benedict Arnold. The political battle that could follow a pro-gay-marriage court decision in California presented another situation for NOM to potentially assert itself, and board members discussed a statewide push at a meeting that fall. But cursory research indicated it could cost $2 million to qualify a constitutional amendment for the ballot—an irreconcilably daunting figure for a fledgling group. Then Gallagher got invited to the meeting with Cordileone.

Immediately after Gallagher spoke to the group at O'Reilly's home that weekend, attendees voted to establish themselves as a chapter of her group. Gallagher returned to the East Coast bewildered: the National Organization of Marriage did not have any local chapters, or clear protocols for how they would function. But just before Christmas, Cordileone called Gallagher to formalize the arrangement. She asked Brian Brown, who had been raised in Southern California and had returned to spend the holiday season with relatives, to stay put. Along with his six young children, and the wife who homeschooled them, he would remain on the West Coast and become executive director of the National Organization for Marriage California.

Cordileone and Gallagher set out to introduce the new group to prospective donors. They began hosting sessions together: he would say an opening prayer, and she would make a pitch for the importance of protecting marriage through the political process. The first of these meetings barely raised $10,000, but afterward one attendee took Cordileone aside and vowed to do whatever it took to support their mission. "He pulled out his Rolodex and got all of his San Diego Catholic buddies to attend these meetings," recalls Gallagher.

Over the first six months of 2008, one-third of the money raised statewide to help qualify an amendment for the ballot would come from San Diego. Cordileone would eventually take credit for personally helping to raise $1 million over the course of the year, with many of the largest single donors active Catholics from his diocese. Hotelier and real-estate developer Doug Manchester gave $125,000; the family of Terry Caster, owner of a chain of self-storage facilities, nearly $700,000.

Religious conservatives in California finally had a political movement to match their goals.

To the Ballot

Well before March 4, 2008, the California Supreme Court made clear that the matter which would occupy its attention that morning would be no workaday hearing. Anticipating unusual interest from citizens, court officials opened up an auditorium in a nearby state office building where an overflow crowd could watch the proceedings, which were also broadcast live on a public-affairs television channel statewide. In West Hollywood, Mayor John Duran organized a city hall viewing party.

The day had been long awaited. The court had granted review of *In re Marriage Cases* in December 2006, and the unusually prominent organizing effort around the amicus briefs had only raised anticipation for the oral arguments. The court budgeted an unprecedented three hours for them, only to have the crux of the court's choice distilled in a single question from Justice Carol A. Corrigan: "Is it better for this court to decide or the people of California to decide?"

No matter how the court ruled, the people would have their chance to weigh in. Petitions from groups seeking to place questions before voters were due to the California secretary of state by April 28 that year, and the split that had paralyzed previous efforts to pass a constitutional amendment banning gay marriage in California had not gone away. Randy Thomasson's group called VoteYesMarriage.com was still pushing for a more restrictive version that would gut the domestic-partnership law.

But as the question of marriage became urgent to California conservatives, it was the rival effort—a direct descendant of the political organization that had successfully passed Proposition 22 more than eight years earlier—that gained primacy. Andy Pugno had been a legislative assistant to Pete Knight when the senator worked to place the initiative on the 2000 ballot; once it qualified, Pugno served as the campaign's spokesman and afterward helped launch the Proposition 22 Legal Defense and Education Fund. Knight died in May 2004, just months after the fund filed suit to block San Francisco from marrying gay couples. After his death, his widow, Gail, assumed responsibility for the fund and kept Pugno in charge of the group that became known as ProtectMarriage.com. Pitching both experience and a more moderate tack than Thomasson, Pugno won over Ron Prentice's California Family Council, the state's most significant network of evangelical activists. ProtectMarriage also had an organizational edge over Thomasson's group, quicker to reach beyond California's limited evangelical sphere and develop relationships with conservatives from other denominations. Clearly squeezed out by its rival, VoteYesMarriage eventually abandoned its petition drive, noting in a statement that "funds were insufficient" to "wage a professional multi-million-dollar statewide signature-gathering campaign."

If not for the emergence of the National Organization for Marriage California, Pugno's group would have probably endured the same fate. Over the first three months of 2008, NOM California transferred nearly $700,000 to ProtectMarriage, more than two-thirds of the total amount paid to the consulting firm it hired to circulate its ballot-access petitions. In late April, ProtectMarriage delivered 1,120,801 signatures to the secretary of state's office in Sacramento. While officials there checked for invalid or fraudulent signatures, the measure's sponsors received bad if not entirely shocking news. On May 15, the California Supreme Court handed down its ruling in *In re Marriage Cases*.

By a one-vote margin, the judges labeled unconstitutional the fourteen words that had been made law by Proposition 22. The majority opinion noted that California's judges had been placed in a different position than other states' who had entertained challenges to their marriage laws. Because gay couples were afforded equal rights and protections through domestic partnerships, the decision focused on the symbolic value of the word itself. "Reserving the historic designation of 'marriage' exclusively for opposite-sex couples," the court ruled, "poses at least a serious risk of denying the family relationship of same-sex couples such equal dignity and respect." The language that the court struck down was the exact text of the proposed constitutional amendment that ProtectMarriage had submitted to the secretary of state.

The decision in *In re Marriage Cases* had included instructions for state and local officials to impose the court's mandate. Arguing that the amendment's passage would moot the court's decision, gay-marriage opponents tried to get the court to delay implementation until after the election. Separate petitions for a stay and a rehearing were filed by the Campaign for California Families and the Proposition 22 Legal Defense and Education Fund, respectively, but a majority of judges was unmoved, imposing a June 16 deadline for the ruling to take effect.

As municipal clerks and county registrars prepared for that deadline, state public-health officials redrew official forms to remove the terms *bride* and *groom* from marriage-license applications and replace them with *Party A* and *Party B*. Gays and lesbians would be able to freely wed for more than four months before voters got their chance to override the court, and even then the question of what would happen to those couples' status if California reverted back to its previous definition of marriage was unresolved. "This is a severe constitutional crisis," said the Campaign for California Families' Randy Thomasson, "that can only be solved at the ballot box in November when Californians vote yes to protect marriage licenses for a man and a woman."

More than two dozen state ballot initiatives had been waged over marriage across the country during the previous decade, but never before had there been an evenly matched fight. This time, both sides had had adequate time to prepare, and would have similar war chests to deploy. But supporters of the amendment confronted a unique challenge in California. It would be the first time a successful ban would halt marriages already being performed, placing proponents in the position of asking voters to rescind an ongoing entitlement, rather than take a purely precautionary measure.

On June 2, 2008, the California secretary of state announced that a random check of the 1.1 million signatures from ProtectMarriage revealed no reason to believe that they were incomplete or fraudulent. Seven other initiatives had already been certified for the November ballot: authorizing bonds to pay for a high-speed-rail project and children's hospitals, setting minimum sizes for chicken coops and maximum penalties for nonviolent drug crimes. What had begun as the California Marriage Protection Act—an effort to shore up Proposition 22's statutory ban on gay marriage with a constitutional definition—would now be known officially as Proposition 8.

A few days later, the organizers hired Schubert Flint, a Sacramento firm formed in 2006 through the partnership of consultants Frank Schubert and Jeff Flint. Flint had been a campaign operative for a variety of Republican candidates in Orange County, including one who rose to be Speaker of the state assembly; Schubert was a fixture of the largely nonpartisan (or conspicuously bipartisan) professional class that specialized in California ballot issues. The first major victory of the new firm had come in November 2006, with Schubert and Flint working on behalf of tobacco-industry interests looking to defeat a ballot measure that would have placed a new tax on boxes of cigarettes to fund children's-health initiatives. The men were by no means social conservatives; if their firm had a stable allegiance, it was to the business community against reforms pushed by labor unions, consumer advocates, and trial lawyers.

Unlike many of the issues upon which Californians were expected to weigh in directly, voters had well-formed opinions about gay marriage. A January 2008 study by professors Gregory B. Lewis and Charles W. Gossett analyzing three decades of Field Institute polls found a state electorate growing "strikingly more sympathetic to same-sex marriage." Relocation and demographic patterns played a role in the increase in support from 30 percent in 1985 to 43 percent in 2003. But over half of the growth could be explained by what social scientists call "cohort replacement," with older citizens dying and being supplanted by those just entering adulthood. When asked if their views on homosexuality had changed since turning eighteen, self-described liberals, Democrats, the less religious, and those with gay friends said they had become "more accepting." Only born-again and highly religious Christians reported hardening their resistance in adulthood. "Age is one of the strongest predictors of opposition to same-sex marriage in California, but not because people are becoming more homophobic or sexually more conservative as they age," the study concluded.

ProtectMarriage strategists had initially hoped to place their measure before voters during the primary election in June, which would feature lower turnout and likely an older and more conservative electorate. But the burst of activist energy that had been released by events in San Diego had come too late. Likewise, the supreme court decision took away the option of waiting until 2010, when the midterm electorate would lean more rightward than in a presidential year. Instead Proposition 8 would share a ballot with Democratic nominee Barack Obama, whose candidacy was expected to draw unusually high interest among young whites and African American Democrats.

If earlier polls had measured growing support for gay marriage in principle, new public polls showed voters split on the constitutional amendment before them. Private surveys commissioned by Schubert Flint for the Yes on 8 campaign mapped a solid base of around 40 percent opposed to gay marriage. The persuadable voters necessary for a majority—many of them Democrats or potentially otherwise left-leaning independents—were not instinctively antigay and responded to a "live and let live" message about homosexuality. But focus groups revealed an opening for opponents of same-sex marriage. "There were limits to the degree of tolerance that Californians would afford the gay community," Schubert and Flint wrote. "They would entertain allowing gay marriage, but not if doing so had significant implications for the rest of society."

At 5:01 p.m. on June 16, gay marriage became law across California, with some clerks staying open for the evening to issue licenses. In San Francisco, Del Martin and Phyllis Lyon—the elderly activist couple who had been summoned by Mayor Gavin Newsom as he presided over his first secret ceremony in 2004—were again granted that honor, this time before a bank of cameras with the awareness that their marriage was not likely to be taken away from them again.

Already Massachusetts had been marrying gays and lesbians for four years, and even the most cynical critics of the practice were unable to identify any real social consequences. The lead plaintiffs there, Julie and Hillary Goodridge, whose idealized pairing had been the focal point of the suit's public narrative, were on their way to a divorce. But while a spokesperson's announcement that the two were "amicably living apart" drew national press coverage, their situation was altogether banal—"they are just like any other couple," as the *Boston Globe* observed. Massachusetts's 10,500 legally recognized same-sex unions had produced no transformation or tumult that Yes on 8 campaigners could invoke to scare Californians from risking the same fate.

Typically in initiative campaigns it was the opponents who appealed to voters' fear about the unknown and instinctive resistance to change. In the Proposition 8 debate the burden would be on the proponents to sow fear about leaving the status quo in place. "We made one of the key strategic decisions in the campaign, to apply the principles of running a 'No' campaign—raising doubts and pointing to potential problems—in seeking a 'Yes' vote," wrote Schubert and Flint. "We needed to convince voters that gay marriage was not simply 'live and let live'—that there would be consequences if gay marriage were to be permanently legalized. But how to raise consequences when gay marriage was so recently legalized and not yet taken hold?"

Amen Brothers

Not long after the California Supreme Court issued its *In re Marriage Cases* ruling, Jim Garlow drafted an email message that would ultimately reach thousands of his fellow pastors. "In a few days, the impact of four California Supreme Court judges will be felt throughout our state. Since things will 'feel the same' (no lightning, thunder, earthquakes—likely), the naysayers will say, 'See, we told you, it isn't the end of the world,'" he wrote. "However, there is much more subterranean activity than there is on the surface. Your role—as a Christian pastor in this state—will have changed and it will have changed significantly. We have from now until the November elections."

Garlow laid out an ambitious agenda that would occupy activist pastors during that period. But first he advised them to prepare for the Tuesday morning in mid-June when local clerks' offices were likely to be sardined with gay couples and media inclined to tell a heartwarming story about their long-awaited marriages. Pastors should join the swarm, Garlow instructed, seeking out reporters to whom they should present a business card and volunteer a comment on the record. "This event is an opportunity for Christian pastors to be 'in the mix' and speak out in the media," wrote Garlow. "I cannot emphasize enough the importance of being firm, be loving. If you appear to be scared or angry or portraying 'hate,' then that will be trumpeted by the anti-biblical crowd. It is imperative that we are as loving as Christ, while not flinching under pressure."

Around the same time, Garlow began outlining a manifesto that would guide evangelical activists during the campaign. He called it "The Ten Declarations for Protecting Biblical Marriage: Principles to Unite, Focus and Ground Us During This Precarious Season." Given Garlow's background, the document served a second function, explaining to himself how he had become Proposition 8's most visible evangelical champion. He had been late to the awakening that, as the sixth declaration put it, "winning a defense of marriage vote is of prime importance in the short term." When asked by a *Los Angeles Times* reporter if he had spoken out about marriage during the Proposition 22 campaign, Garlow was unable to recall to what extent he had even mentioned the matter from the pulpit. He was not unusual among evangelical clergy who spoke often about moral issues but resisted pulling their ministries into the scrum of electoral or legislative politics, but now he had thoroughly shaken off that ambivalence. "We refuse the false choice between spiritual and temporal means, since both are used to advance Christ's Kingdom," asserted Garlow's seventh declaration. "We may vote Republican, Democrat or Independent, but ultimately we belong to the 'Jesus Party.' We function within existing political parties for the exclusive reason of having the greatest biblical impact on the culture as possible."

Garlow had been initially drafted to the marriage cause by Anne Wigdahl Subia, but after the first meeting at Chris Clark's church he had taken the burden of organizing upon himself. He had given his team a goal: to "make getting petitions as easy and accessible as getting a coffee at Starbucks," ultimately enlisting three hundred churches willing to serve as staging areas where petition forms could be picked up and dropped off. Encouraged by the success of that operation, Garlow offered to host the June gathering of the Pastors Rapid Response Team, drawing two hundred attendees to his Skyline Wesleyan Church. Among those who attended was Miles McPherson, a retired Chargers cornerback who until then had not been politically active. "When I heard what was happening and what was at stake, I wanted to fight," McPherson told the evangelical *World* magazine. With Clark and McPherson at his side, Garlow set out to motivate other pastors to join their cause. "I'm the clarion-call guy," he said. "Chris is the strategist and Miles is the guy who gets everybody fired up."

On June 25, three weeks after Proposition 8 officially qualified for the ballot, Garlow joined a conference call to greet many of the pastors he had eight days earlier dispatched to local clerks' offices with the goal of winning media coverage. Over one thousand of them were waiting for him. Invitations had been distributed partly through the American Family Association's network, but Subia had continued expanding her database, branching out beyond the San Diego region to include seven thousand churches across California. There was only one county in the state, Alpine near Lake Tahoe, where Subia proved unable to locate a single like-minded pastor. Data collection was essential to the gradual, even tedious, work that reflected the lack of rank among Protestant churches. "The evangelicals are utterly independent. I mean, that's the whole nature of the evangelical," says Frank Schubert, the campaign's chief strategist. "So it was a real challenge to pull them together."

Garlow laid out plans to "create a climate, a culture of fasting and praying for our state" through November 4. The twenty-two-week arc was replete with activities for pastors, their spiritual duties interlaced with election-related demands. They would be counted on to preach to their own congregants, with coordinated themes on designated Sundays, while engaging in high-profile activities designed to win media coverage within their communities. Starting in late September, there would be a forty-day fasting period, culminating in a prayer rally—dubbed "TheCall"—at Qualcomm Stadium the weekend before the election. What had begun with Garlow, Clark, and McPherson—a method of clergy-driven organizing that became known as "the San Diego model"—was being replicated across the state.

If evangelical pastors were happy to become the face of the Proposition 8 campaign, the Catholics who helped fund it were beginning to chafe at public scrutiny of their activity. On July 18, a new group named Californians Against Hate announced its formation in San Diego with a boycott of the Manchester Grand Hyatt Hotel. The group's founder, Fred Karger, had last been in the news earlier that year when he led a protest outside the Los Angeles headquarters of American International Group to help save the Boom Boom Room, a venerable gay bar near his Newport Beach home that was on the verge of being torn down for a new construction project. The media amplified Karger's protest, even if newspapers couldn't easily explain the tenuous financial link between the global insurance behemoth and the small piece of property in question. In the San Diego hotel, Karger had identified a similarly large target: its owner, Doug Manchester, a prominent developer and generous funder of Catholic causes who sat alongside Salvatore Cordileone on the University of San Diego board. Manchester was perhaps the most famous name among large donors to the Proposition 8 campaign, leading even the *New York Times* to cover what Karger called the "March on Manchester."

Karger was known to the experienced political operatives scheming to pass Proposition 8 as one of their own. He had worked for Ronald Reagan, eventually as director of opposition research for the reelection campaign. Now, five years into his retirement, he was keeping his skills sharp. He mined disclosure reports from pro–Proposition 8 committees and listed everyone who gave more than $5,000 on a "Californians Against Hate Dishonor Roll" website, with phone numbers and business addresses. Other activists democratized the practice of shaming, making every individual donor's address searchable via Google Maps. "Individuals and businesses gave a vast amount of money to take away our equality, and we want you to know who they are," Karger wrote on his site.

Karger, his site, and its readers became such a nettlesome presence that ProtectMarriage would later enter federal court with a lawsuit challenging the California campaign-finance system. The existing disclosure rules had chilled First Amendment rights, the group's Ron Prentice claimed, by enabling a "systematic attempt to intimidate, threaten and harass donors to the Proposition 8 campaign." (A Yes on 8 organizer estimated to the *Orange County Register* that over the course of the election season one-third of the twenty-five thousand lawn signs his side distributed were either vandalized, destroyed, or stolen.)

It was a toxic political milieu that would deter the participation of most. But proponents of Proposition 8 were about to take on reinforcements, in the form of a religious faction that historian James L. Clayton, paraphrasing western chronicler Wallace Stegner, described as "indomitable only in the pack and adventurous only on orders." They arrived ready to release an infusion of cash and manpower and enveloped by enduring mystery about their motives and methods. Their role in advancing Proposition 8 would come to overshadow that of Catholics and evangelicals in the minds of their opponents and, eventually, in the public imagination. Mormons, says Republican consultant Sal Russo, "didn't choose the fight, but they weren't willing to lose it."

66

The Mormon Empire Strikes Back

On June 20, 2008, Mormon leaders across California, from ward bishops to stake presidents, received a one-page letter bearing the signatures of the three senior officials who composed their church's First Presidency. The four-paragraph message, titled "Preserving Traditional Marriage and Strengthening Families," explained the political origins of the Proposition 8 campaign and theological underpinnings of the church's devotion to its policy objectives. "We ask that you do all you can to support the proposed constitutional amendment by donating of your means and time," it said.

The message was intended to be read to congregants attending sacrament meetings on June 29. But within days its contents had leaked onto websites and into the press. Since gay marriage had been first legalized in the United States, all indications had been that the Church of Jesus Christ of Latter-day Saints had lost interest in the issue. This First Presidency statement, with its echoes of the one a decade earlier that had explained church involvement in Hawaii, presaged a return to its intense commitment.

Beginning in late 1995, as the *Baehr* case in Honolulu began to elicit interest on the mainland, Mormon officials attempted to assemble their own ecumenical working group on marriage. "Please be assured that we are not seeking the leadership role for this meeting or future meetings which may be scheduled," Elder Marlin K. Jensen of the First Quorum of the Seventy wrote to a Southern Baptist official. "Our interest is to facilitate an initial discussion that will address the consequences of legalizing same-sex marriages."

That interfaith discussion group was driven by Mormon and Catholic strategists who had launched the Marriage Law Project. They won cooperation from Jews, Eastern Orthodox, and Seventh-Day Adventist leaders but never the full involvement of evangelical organizations. By 1998, it became evident that the religions could be separated by more than just doctrinal differences. When Brigham Young University law professor Lynn Wardle and Marriage Law Foundation director William C. Duncan represented church interests that October at a session on gay-marriage opponents' legal strategy in Scottsdale, Arizona, there was largely consensus on how to approach state-level advocacy. But as the conversation veered toward amending the federal constitution as a bulwark against activist courts, Wardle recoiled.

"I told them that I believe that we (pro-family and socially conservative lawyers and groups) would rue the day we passed an amendment that could not help but have the effect of giving the federal government and federal courts greater authority to directly regulate domestic relations.... The last thing we want is for family policy to be dictated for the states from 'inside the beltway,' or by federal judges," Wardle reported back to church elders in Salt Lake City. "The authorian-dictatorial [*sic*] approach may be fine for advocates of radicalism like same-sex marriage, but the sovereign-people-grassroots approach is the one best suited for our position."

While the other religious conservatives stuck with their federal strategies, the LDS Church slinked away from the issue altogether. The Public Affairs Department that had coordinated the church's work on marriage was distracted by the looming Winter Olympics. Salt Lake City had first bid for the Olympics in 1965, when economic-development officials had not expected to win but saw an easy way to promote the region's fledging ski industry. Thirty years later, the city was awarded the 2002 games, and church leaders reveled in the global public-relations potential it would extend to a faith that rarely earned media exposure under purely positive circumstances. Yet the story line soon turned dark. In 1998, a local television station reported that local officials had lavished gifts upon International Olympic Committee members in exchange for supporting the bid. The host committee's president and vice president, both active Mormons who had met through the church, were eventually indicted on bribery charges. (They were acquitted, but not until nearly two years following the games' completion.) "There seemed to be an implied association of the scandal with the standing and character of the state and, further, with the Mormon church," observed Mitt Romney, who was hired to take over the Salt Lake Olympic Committee amid an ongoing FBI investigation.

Within the church, the Public Affairs Department turned to damage control. A five-year media plan emphasized the imperative for coverage around the games was not merely to draw attention to Mormonism but to specifically promote "media stories that help . . . solve problems that affect the reputation of . . . the Church or help the public better understand issues that affect the Church." It seemed to work. A polling project commissioned by the department after the games showed views of the church warming by an average of five percentage points, with a major increase in the number who told survey takers that Mormons believed in Jesus Christ and that they knew "some" or "a great deal" about the faith. "Feelings towards the LDS Church have improved significantly," reported a Public Affairs Department analysis.

Still, when Matt Daniels unveiled his ostentatiously diverse Alliance for Marriage in 2000, Mormons were missing, much as they were from every meeting of the Arlington Group. In July 2004, just before the Senate was to consider the Federal Marriage Amendment, the First Presidency released a statement expressing abstract support without particularly endorsing the bill coming up for a vote. The church-owned *Deseret News* explained that LDS leadership "wanted to express its general support for traditional marriage" and "to avoid the political debate and not get involved in the semantics of specific legislation." Church officials refused to publicly acknowledge Utah's proposed Amendment 3, which prohibited recognition of any "domestic union" other than between a man and a woman, other than to disavow any role in its drafting. That fall, after the federal effort had failed in Congress and amendments had qualified for thirteen state ballots, including Utah's, the church belatedly released a statement declaring it "favors measures that define marriage as the union of a man and a woman and that do not confer legal status on any other sexual relationship." Two years later, as the heavily Mormon states of Idaho and Arizona considered constitutional bans, the church did little beyond reissuing its 2004 statement. (Arizona became the first state to defeat an anti-gay-marriage ballot initiative.) When Wardle contributed to an amicus brief in the *In re Marriage Cases* appeal before the California Supreme Court, he did so in his private capacity, not even mentioning that he served as a legal strategist for the LDS Church.

As the church shirked the marriage debate, its leaders were focused on an even grander political project. In 2005, Romney—a descendant of one of Mormonism's first families who had served as president of the Boston stake before being elected governor—visited the church's president, Gordon Hinckley, to discuss his interest in running for president. When George Romney had sought the presidency in 1968, his religion had not been a subject of much attention. But in the four decades since, evangelical voters had become a crucial bloc in Republican primaries, and the son had begun to plot a path to the nomination that would require winning their votes en masse.

Preparing to leave office at the end of 2006 and launch his candidacy shortly thereafter, Romney worked to win over evangelical leaders with a convert's zeal. That October, Georgia public-relations executive Mark DeMoss invited a delegation of prominent evangelicals to a small lunch meeting at Romney's home in the Boston suburbs. For many of them, it was the first chance to meet Romney and his wife, Ann. "If you believe you would not vote for a Mormon under any circumstances, give serious and prayerful thought to being open-minded about the matter," DeMoss wrote in his invitation. (The sense of ethnographic discovery ran in both directions. "The Romneys were genuinely touched by your love, graciousness, and genuine interest in them," DeMoss told the Southern Baptist Convention's Richard Land after the meeting. "To the extent their impression of evangelicals had been shaped by either bad personal experiences or the way we are often portrayed in the media, it has sufficiently been changed.") While Romney aggressively courted evangelical voters, the LDS Church resolved not to give them any reason to think about Mormonism, minimizing its presence in the political arena altogether.

It was a sensible strategy. A poll conducted by the *Washington Post* and ABC News found 29 percent of respondents would be less likely to vote for a candidate for president because of his or her Mormonism; another from Gallup showed that, even after the Salt Lake City Olympics, more Americans had a negative view of Mormons than a positive one. Around the same time, Mormon pollster Gary Lawrence, who like his former colleague Richard Wirthlin was consulted by church officials, embarked on a major national research project. As individuals, Mormons were seen more positively than the institution that united them, but disturbingly high numbers of Americans maintained "perceptions of the Church as mysterious, secretive, weird, pushy, power hungry, etc." or of its members as "brainwashed, fanatical, naïve, blind followers, narrow-minded, etc.," Lawrence found. "We have taken too lightly the seriousness of our poor public image," he argued. "We know that truth will eventually prevail, and many of us, therefore, have become lackadaisical in doing anything to help it. As a result, the misconceptions, distortions, and untruths being told about us have slowed the growth of the Church."

For much of Romney's campaign the candidate was able to dodge any discussion of his religion, speaking in generic terms of Jesus Christ as "the Savior of mankind" while deflecting any question about doctrinal differences. In early December 2007, Romney gave a speech in Texas about the place of his faith in political life. "Let me assure you that no authorities of my church, or of any other church for that matter, will ever exert influence on presidential decisions," Romney said, in a speech that mentioned the word *Mormon* only once.

But the January 2008 death of Gordon Hinckley, the church's ninety-seven-year-old president, made it impossible for Romney to publicly neglect his faith any longer. He was forced to make a visible detour to Salt Lake City for Hinckley's funeral service at a particularly unwelcome time, pulling off the campaign trail the weekend before crucial Super Tuesday primaries and caucuses. Romney exited the campaign later that week, after a series of victories by Arizona senator John McCain that all but ensured the latter's nomination.

Hinckley's successor, Thomas S. Monson, had barely settled into his new post when church officials received a letter from George Niederauer, the Roman Catholic archbishop of San Francisco. Niederauer was well-known to LDS leaders, having spent more than a decade as bishop of his church's Salt Lake diocese. In that role, he had publicly opposed the 2004 amendment to the Utah constitution to explicitly restrict marriage to opposite-sex couples. (The official diocese position was that the measure was legally unnecessary, and that Catholic voters should follow their own "prudential judgment.") Now, as California hurtled toward a nearly identical amendment, Niederauer encouraged the LDS Church to get involved.

Niederauer was acting on behalf of the Conference of Catholic Bishops, which had asked him to approach his LDS Church contacts with the goal of reviving the Catholic-Mormon alliance that had backed Proposition 22. Niederauer outlined the role that Catholics had played thus far in funding operations to put the amendment on the ballot, and the far more aggressive role that evangelical pastors were playing compared to the 2000 campaign. "California is a huge state, often seen as a bellwether—this was seen as a very, very important test," LDS spokesman Michael R. Otterson later explained.

The Mormon Church's appraisal of Niederauer's invitation was shaped by a long history with California, where church members had been among the earliest Anglo-Americans to settle. Months before his death in 1844, the faith's founder, Joseph Smith, had dispatched a reconnaissance party from his Illinois base west across the plains to site potential Mormon colonies along the Pacific coast. That winter, another group of 238 church members who had deemed themselves ill equipped for the overland crossing gathered in New York harbor and chartered a freighter to make the passage by sea. The *Brooklyn* took six months to travel around Cape Horn, stopping first in Honolulu, then part of the Sandwich Islands, before entering the San Francisco Bay, only weeks after U.S. forces had seized the settlement of Yerba Buena in the Mexican-American War. It had been "perhaps the longest religious sea pilgrimage in recorded history," an LDS Church magazine later ventured, and came a year before Smith's successor, Brigham Young, would reach the Salt Lake and decide to settle there. "That the pioneer groups led westward by Brigham Young did not press forward to California is an evidence of courage, self-sacrifice and devotion to principle. To have pushed their way through to California might in the long run, have been the easier course," former Los Angeles Stake president Leo J. Muir wrote in a 1952 church history. "No doubt they would have come more quickly to economic success."

The vast terrain that Young designated Deseret—and which Wallace Stegner later demarcated as "the Mormon Empire"—stretched across much of the mountainous west, but Young always viewed California with suspicion. In 1851, when he reluctantly permitted a pack of about fifty Mormons to explore a colony in San Bernardino, thirty miles from what would become Los Angeles, he was faced with five hundred who volunteered to make the trip. "I was sick at the sight of so many saints going to California," said a tearful Young, "and was unable to address them." Over the thirty years bridging the two world wars, California's Mormon population grew fiftyfold; by the early twenty-first century California had the second-largest Mormon population of any state, with approximately 750,000 members.

Many were drawn there for work or lifestyle, accepting the state's multiculturalism and internalizing the fact that, unlike in Utah, religion had relatively little impact on public policy. The result was "Mellow Mormonism," as the *Salt Lake Tribune* called it, influenced by public mores set by a far more permissive and culturally diverse majority. "The church has actually been fairly progressive in terms of calling for polite and respectful treatment of gays and lesbians. We don't hear too much gay bashing around here," Russell Frandsen, a Mormon attorney in the Los Angeles suburbs, boasted to the paper. "We are probably much more tolerant of other views and faith than I remember growing up in Utah."

On June 29, Mormons worshipping across California heard Monson's message about the ballot measure. After making clear that the LDS Church was a full participant in the Proposition 8 coalition, the letter was blunt in its instruction that Mormons were expected to do more than just vote for the amendment. "Local Church leaders will provide information about how you may become involved in this important cause," it read. "We ask that you do all you can to support the proposed constitutional amendment by donating of your means and time to assure that marriage in California is legally defined as being between a man and a woman. Our best efforts are required to preserve the sacred institution of marriage."

When journalists attempted to understand what prompted its sudden involvement, the LDS Church—typically secretive about its internal deliberations and willing to let its political machinations speak for themselves—was happy to let it be known that it was Niederauer who invited the collaboration. In his decade in Salt Lake City, the Roman Catholic bishop had developed a reputation as relatively friendly to the gay community. He was unusual among Catholic officials for not dismissing the church's sex scandals as a problem of homosexuality. Notably, when discussing the subject, Niederauer employed the phrase "sexual orientation" where the Vatican described "deep-seated homosexual tendencies." Furthermore, entering late permitted Mormon leaders to portray themselves as reluctant participants in an already broadly ecumenical alliance. "Having Catholics, evangelicals and Jews in a coalition was exactly the right way to do it," Otterson told the *San Francisco Chronicle*. "We knew someone would make this a Mormon-versus-gays battle."

The LDS Church prepared for what the *Salt Lake Tribune* characterized as "its most vigorous and widespread political involvement since the late 1970s." Even though the First Presidency message was distributed on church letterhead and read as part of Sunday worship, church officials were cautious about overstepping legal restrictions on what nonprofit religious groups could do in the political arena. "No work will take place at the church, including no meeting there to hand out precinct walking assignments so as to not even give the appearance of politicking at the church," instructed a training document distributed within a Mormon ward.

As the state's grassroots director, Lawrence overlaid the Mormon map of stakes and wards onto the electoral geography of precincts. An average of twenty-five thousand church members turned out for Saturday canvasses, representing, by strategist Jeff Flint's estimate, more than 80 percent of the campaign's total volunteer corps. They were assigned to varying tasks in a statewide canvass effort: "walkers" would identify voters' preferences, "sellers" would persuade the undecided, and "closers" would mobilize known supporters. "Because of their hierarchal structure, it was much easier for them to really get involved," says campaign manager Frank Schubert.

This was not true of the Catholic Church. Despite the large donations curated by the auxiliary bishop, church leaders did not expect much from their priests. "The Catholic church has a hierarchal structure, but many independent voices," says Schubert. "Bishops don't tell priests what to do, priests are free to do what they want and so, you saw much more diversity in opinion."

As soon as the LDS Church came aboard, Schubert had expected to use Mormon manpower to sustain the Yes on 8 field organization. What he did not anticipate was the extent to which, once their campaign qualified for the ballot, it would also depend on Mormon money to keep pace financially with the No on 8 effort. "In the early stages of the campaign, the summer period, they were disproportionally involved," he says. "The money that they raised was raised early, the organization that they provided deployed early, and others caught up with them." After meeting for two hours in mid-September with the campaign leadership, three church elders emerged surprised to learn how much the Yes on 8 campaign had become reliant on them. "The brethren emphasized that there wasn't much participation from non-LDS people," according to an internal update later released by WikiLeaks. "The work depends on us."

Church officials had already opened a separate post-office box where Mormons could send their donations, so as to track their unique contribution to the cause. Ultimately Mormons would provide approximately half the funds raised by the Yes on 8 campaign. The donations included a $1 million gift from Alan C. Ashton, a grandson of a former LDS Church president, that arrived just days after Schubert called an emergency meeting to sound an alarm: "We're going to lose this campaign if we don't get more money."

67

Proposition 8

In early September, a poll from the Public Policy Institute of California showed Proposition 8 losing by fourteen points. When the No on 8 campaign shortly thereafter released an internal poll indicating its side was actually behind—an inversion of the typical practice—Frank Schubert concluded that his opponents had grown worried about their own complacency, and were desperate to galvanize interest among activists and especially donors who had already taken for granted the measure's defeat.

By the end of September, Proposition 8 backers had raised $25 million for their campaign, compared to just $16 million by opponents. Alongside the influx of funds from Mormon donors was the windfall from an aggressive direct-mail effort soliciting smaller contributions from conservative activists nationwide. When ProtectMarriage filed its campaign-finance report electronically, Schubert noted with satisfaction that the five-thousand-page document crashed the secretary of state's computer system. "Fairly early on, it became apparent that there was going to be a massive amount of money," says Schubert.

The financial advantage enjoyed by Proposition 8 supporters appeared to reflect a broader advantage in both organization and enthusiasm. Yet there was still much work to do persuading an electorate that had been given copious signals that Proposition 8 was beyond the mainstream of California opinion. Most of the state's politicians, including Republican governor Arnold Schwarzenegger and a slew of celebrities—from Barbra Streisand to Fall Out Boy's Pete Wentz—actively opposed the measure. Outside the religious sphere, Arizona senator John McCain was the most prominent public figure to endorse it, although with little ardor. The Republican nominee for president released a terse two-sentence statement in its favor and otherwise attempted to avoid the topic. At the end of September, the Yes on 8 campaign's internal polls showed their side behind by six points.

On the morning of September 29, Schubert and Jeff Flint summoned journalists to the office of their Sacramento lobbying firm to unveil the first television commercial from the Yes on Proposition 8 campaign. The ad featured San Francisco mayor Gavin Newsom at a triumphant rally celebrating the California Supreme Court decision to overturn Proposition 22, declaring with menace that "this door's wide open now. It's going to happen, whether you like it or not." Without a new constitutional amendment, the ad went on to allege, Californians would see churches "lose their tax exemption" and "gay marriage taught in public schools."

If that ad was edited to make voters feel an urgent threat from pro-gay politicians, the next one that Schubert and Flint had queued up would make vivid the consequences of letting that side win. The ad showed a schoolgirl entering her kitchen with a Dutch picture book titled *King & King.* "Mom, guess what I learned in school today?" she asks. "I learned how a prince married a prince and I can marry a princess!" At that point, a Pepperdine University law professor appears on camera to explain that "it's already happened"—citing developments in Massachusetts schools after same-sex marriage was legalized there.

Yet once the "Princes" ad began airing, in a Spanish version on October 6 and in English two days later, Schubert and Flint were bewildered that it took the No on 8 campaign three weeks to muster a response. Indeed, its themes had been part of anti-gay-rights messaging for a long time. An ad very similar to "Princes," showing a boy reading a book titled *Daddy's Wedding,* had run a decade earlier in Hawaii, with the narration "If you don't think homosexual marriage will affect you, how do you think it will affect your children?" The first high-stakes statewide battle over gay rights— California's Proposition 6, the so-called Briggs Initiative, thirty years earlier—was a vote on whether to ban gays and lesbians from employment in public schools. Moreover, the new ad's incendiary message was in keeping with the way Schubert and Flint had positioned their amendment from the beginning. During the summer, in a filing for the official voter's guide that each year presents arguments for and against pending ballot measures, they had emphasized the effect a change in marriage laws would have on children. After opponents sued to challenge the language, the Sacramento County Superior Court ruled that the phrase "will be required to teach young children there is *no difference* between gay marriage and traditional marriage" was permissible as long as the verbal construction was changed to include "may result."

On October 11, Schubert woke to validation for his ad's dire warnings from an unusual source. The *San Francisco Chronicle* was a predictably liberal big-city newspaper whose editorial board had declared "nothing more calming or traditional to American society than giving two people who love each other the opportunity to build a life together." A front-page story that caught Schubert's attention had a similarly celebratory tone. Beneath the headline CLASS SURPRISES LESBIAN TEACHER ON WEDDING DAY, the paper reported that "a group of San Francisco first-graders took an unusual field trip to City Hall on Friday to toss rose petals on their just-married lesbian teacher."

With weeks to go before the vote, the *Chronicle* story told a real-life version of the fictional scenario that the Yes campaign had conjured with its "Princes" ad. Yet for another eleven days, even as polls showed Yes finally surpassing 50 percent support, its opponents still put forward no formal rebuttal. It finally came on October 22, when the No on 8 campaign released an ad featuring state superintendent of public instruction Jack O'Connell, California's top education official. O'Connell called the Yes ads "shameful" and explained that any change in the marriage laws would have no impact on what was taught in schools. In their internal polling, both sides saw the O'Connell ad appear to halve—and even possibly reverse—some of the gains that the "Princes" ad had yielded for the Yes campaign. "This in-your-face response, much delayed but very effective, foretold the final period of the campaign—it would be largely about education," Schubert and Flint wrote.

With a total of $83 million spent, Proposition 8 represented the second-most-expensive election in the country that year, behind only the presidential contest. It cost more than twice Schubert's initial estimates. Over the final week of the campaign, Proposition 8 supporters were unable to match the overwhelming volume of ads from opponents. But Schubert found solace in what he regarded as No on 8's misguided closing message.

"Proposition 8 is not about schools or kids—it's about discrimination," Senator Dianne Feinstein said calmly from what looked like a home study. With five days left, the stately Feinstein ad was pushed off the air for a more vivid illustration of the same argument. Over bleak monochrome footage, actor Samuel L. Jackson recounted the history of internment camps and interracial-marriage bans in California. Both the Feinstein and "Internment" ads were notable for what they omitted: any mention of gays, lesbians, or same-sex relationships. The closest either came was Feinstein's kicker: "No matter how you feel about marriage, vote against discrimination."

Avoiding the gay-marriage question altogether struck Schubert as a concession that the underlying debate had been lost, and the initiative could be defeated only by changing the topic. The turn to alarmist historical analogies to him signaled desperation, especially since one of the ads was particularly aimed at racial minorities—not the type of voters a lefty initiative campaign still wanted to be persuading at such a late date.

With opinion swinging in their direction, Schubert and Flint still had to mobilize those supporters. Mormon volunteers had been at the task since early October, when California opened up its monthlong early-voting period. By working to get backers to return their ballots early, they hoped to free up get-out-the-vote efforts to reach beyond known supporters and into communities where citizens might not be already mobilized by the presidential campaigns. The Pastors Team was sticking to the calendar that Jim Garlow had laid out in early summer, with common activities that would build a sense of statewide community among the rank and file. There were directions for daily prayer for the success of Proposition 8 (at eight a.m. and eight p.m. for eight minutes each, in honor of the measure). The forty-day fast scheduled to end just before Election Day was well under way. ("Individuals may fast portions or all of the 40 days, as they are led, or they may fast in 'relays' as teams," according to instructions from Garlow.) Evangelical clergy also oversaw a "Family Voting Weekend," in which parishioners were encouraged to pray with relatives and complete mail-in ballots together. On his final conference call, on October 22, Garlow had six thousand pastors listening in as he laid out plans for "TheCall," a twelve-hour "solemn assembly" at Qualcomm Stadium in which an estimated thirty-three thousand people gathered to pray for Proposition 8's passage.

On election morning, Yes on 8's final tracking poll had the race even at 48 percent. "We always believed that if we went into Election Day tied, or even a point or two behind, that we would win," Schubert and Flint reflected, citing "the superior nature of our GOTV effort" and a history of polling that had "always understated support for traditional marriage."

Nearly 80 percent of registered voters turned out, the highest rate in California since 1976. But turnout was less than two-thirds in San Francisco and Los Angeles counties, typically troves of votes that boosted Democrats and progressive ballot-initiative campaigns to statewide victory.

In the end, Proposition 8 would pass with more than 52 percent of the vote—a margin of about 600,000 in the high-turnout election. On election night, the Yes on 8 campaign claimed a sweeping victory. They won not only in San Diego, where evangelical pastors and Catholic donors had first partnered to put marriage on the ballot, but in Los Angeles County, where a majority of voters were registered Democrats and one-third of the population nonwhite.

The constitutional amendment was written to take effect the following day. "The people of California stood up for traditional marriage and reclaimed this great institution. We are gratified that voters chose to protect traditional marriage and to enshrine its importance in the state constitution," ProtectMarriage's Ron Prentice declared by press release. "The silent majority is alive and well in California."

Part Eight

THE ROAD FROM JERSEY CITY

(2009–2012)

....

68

Whodunit

If Proposition 8 had failed, and gay couples been allowed to continue marrying in California without hiccup, it is easy to imagine the stage of the main No on 8 election-night party at the Westin St. Francis Hotel on Union Square in San Francisco populated with opportunistic politicians seeking to bask before the triumphant throngs and the risers packed with news cameras from around the state.

The moment that the polls closed in California on November 4, 2008, television networks called the presidential election for Barack Obama. But in the Proposition 8 count, Yes kept a small but steady lead over No. Over the course of the evening, recalled *Frontiers* editor Karen Ocamb, a longtime gay journalist who attended a satellite event at West Hollywood's Music Box Theatre, "a quiet dread crept into the night's festivities." The gap never narrowed, as the constitutional ban triumphed by a margin of nearly five percentage points.

There was no focal point for the emotional cascade that followed. With a faceless question on the ballot, the election-night drama lacked its usual cast of protagonists, antagonists, and foils. Neither side had a figurehead whom the media would seek out to claim victory or to concede defeat. The effort to beat Proposition 8 was a campaign in which a variety of entities had teamed up, and there had never been a single voice of the movement. Instead, attendees heard tearful speeches from community leaders, but they did not concentrate the passion as much as defuse it. "Elation rapidly slid into jaw-dropping shock, depression and anger," wrote Ocamb.

The final numbers delivered confusion rather than clarity. Many of the precincts that helped give Obama his twenty-four-point victory in the state also voted for Proposition 8, with majority opposition contained largely to a skein of northern and coastal counties. Even as Obama won nearly

70 percent in Los Angeles, just over 50 percent of the county's voters cast ballots for Proposition 8. The dismal demographic truth beneath those figures was revealed in CNN's exit polls: 70 percent of African Americans said they voted for the marriage ban. "How did the people that voted for him go against us?" asks Tim Sweeney, the executive director of the Gill Foundation, whose independent political arms had given around $1 million to gay groups fighting Proposition 8. "We lost a whole bunch of people in California we should have won. We just didn't do something quite right."

One of the earliest efforts to make sense of the failure came from Thalia Zepatos, who shortly after the election began work on a memo that would rewrite the history of No on 8's shortcomings before a less contentious mythology could settle in. Zepatos had worked on the campaign to defeat a similar constitutional ban in Oregon in 2004. In the aftermath of that loss, she had moved to Los Angeles to oversee Let California Ring, the innovative collaboration that was supposed to put her side on a stronger footing when the issue came to the ballot. Donations jumped to $11.4 million in 2008, as the prospect of a statewide vote grew more immediate. But once Proposition 8 qualified for the ballot, the No on 8 campaign that rallied against it staffed its leadership ranks with veterans of prior California referendum campaigns rather than those operatives who had been working on Let California Ring. By the time Proposition 8 qualified for the ballot, Zepatos and others like her were shunted aside. "Ultimately the Prop 8 campaign hired a bunch of consultants that had not been part at all of anything that we had been learning on the ground in California," she says.

Nearly every other campaign to defeat a gay-marriage ban had suffered from an imbalance in resources and an unwillingness from members of the political establishment to give legitimacy to the cause. Proposition 8, however, had appeared to present a case study in how gay-marriage advocates could get their way: a friendly elected official pushes the issue, gay litigators win at court, and a well-financed, professionally run campaign defends the victory at the ballot box.

But over the course of a six-month campaign, one of the most expensive of any kind in the country's history, No on 8 strategists had seemed wholly unprepared for what their opponents would do. Their campaign had been at once too defensive and insufficiently reactive. It had failed to depict gay families in its advertising, preferring universal antidiscrimination themes, but also neglected outreach to churchgoing Latinos and African Americans while antagonizing them with analogies to the civil-rights experience. Above all, Zepatos homed in on the lackadaisical response to the arrival of children as an issue in the election with the "Princes" ad. A campaign that employed two pollsters had failed to anticipate the most damning line of attack and had proven, for several crucial weeks, incapable or perhaps unwilling to confront it.

Ultimately, the No on 8 campaign had turned out just as Oregon's No on 36 had, with not only the same outcome but similar failures of strategic thinking. In fact, every one of the three dozen efforts to define marriage at the ballot ended up in largely the same place—with gay-marriage campaigners feeling ill equipped to respond to their opponents' powerful arguments. In the weeks after Election Day, Zepatos's thoughts kept turning back to a 1993 comedy starring Bill Murray that captured her sense of hopeless repetition.

"Many funders and national leaders have come to the conclusion that the only way to stop replaying Groundhog Day is to not engage in future ballot measure campaigns," Zepatos wrote in a finger-pointing memo she first passed along to Matt Coles and Evan Wolfson, architects of the 10-10-10-20 strategy she saw as increasingly imperiled by the failure in California. "The truth is, there are few states left for us to lose. However, at some point we need to go back into the states and repeal some Constitutional Amendments, and we might as well start figuring out how to win."

The months after Election Day were thick with recriminations both public and private, limited only by the fact that the campaign kept secret who was actually in charge of its $43 million budget, including the decision to hire the controversial consultants. "It's easier to locate the names of the Chinese politburo than the names of the ruling body of No on 8," activist and blogger Michael Petrelis lamented. When he managed to secure a roster of its sixteen-member executive committee, two and a half months after Election Day, it revealed a decision-making structure rich in lawyers and community leaders deeply familiar with California gay politics but light on professionals with electoral experience. "Where were the people who sit down and figure out how to win a ballot measure in California?" says Joe Solmonese, who was president of the Human Rights Campaign. "They were enormously well respected, but I was like, 'When was the last time you looked at a poll and figured out how to get to fifty-one?'"

Only after the votes had been counted did the public understand how chaotic No on 8's decision-making had been in its final weeks, due to tensions between the executive committee and the political consultants it had hired to run the campaign. In mid-October, just as opponents' claims that homosexuality would be taught in schools had begun to sway voters, the committee responded to the crisis by sidelining chief strategist Steve Smith, along with Ogilvy Public Relations Worldwide, the outside public-relations firm managing No on 8's communications. "The campaign brought in pretty much who was available in Sacramento to really look at the message, ads—everything—to figure out what was going on," Kassy Perry, whose Perry Communications Group was hired to replace Ogilvy, disclosed to the *Sacramento Bee* in the newspaper's devastating front-page reconstruction of an "opposition campaign that was in disarray."

Many of those who had overseen the campaign were quick to advance competing theories that deflected blame outward. "It is a travesty that the Mormon Church bought this election and used a campaign of lies and deception to manipulate voters in the great state of California," said Lorri Jean, the chief executive of the Los Angeles Gay and Lesbian Center, which organized a protest that would draw one thousand activists to the Mormon temple in Westwood. "Then Jean skipped town for several weeks," the *LA Weekly*'s Patrick Range McDonald alleged, "incredibly quick to divert all attention away from the failures of the 'No on 8' campaign— which were many—and point the finger at the Mormon church."

The campaign's principals did not reconvene again after the election until January 24, 2009. If organizers of Equality Summit '09 had been hoping to discourage gawkers from wanting to attend, indulging media coverage of internal deliberations over whether to let journalists cover their daylong gathering was probably not the best tactic. The fifty-three-member planning committee debated for weeks whether to open some, all, or none of their sessions to the public, as leaks eventually made clear. West Coast community newspapers and nationally prominent blogs were already primed to see the gay-rights establishment that had failed to beat back Proposition 8 as a hapless conspiracy. When a prominent lesbian activist quit the committee over its "secretive" ways, the media were onto what looked like an incompetent cover-up. "LGBT journalists," said Ocamb, "represent the thousands of individuals who contributed to and volunteered for the No on Prop 8 campaign and if people are going to be asked to be engaged again, they have a right to know what happened, who will lead them, and (to have) at least a sense of what's coming next. And at this stage, that can only happen through us."

Organizers eventually acquiesced and invited Ocamb to preside over a plenary session called "Looking Backward and Looking Forward." Initial estimates had expected 150 attendees, which were then revised upward to 250. Four hundred people appeared to be in the downtown convention-center ballroom when Ocamb welcomed them to her session on Saturday morning. They were there for a show trial—a chance to determine who had let gay marriage in California die.

After a few of the No on 8 executive committee members had spoken, along with the campaign's pollster and political director, Ocamb turned back to them to pose a common follow-up question. "I'd like to ask each of the panelists very briefly," she said, "to give one point of what went well, one mistake, and also if you could give one solution to how to heal what appears to be a rift between leadership and grassroots."

To the extent that grassroots was reflected in the room, it was less interested in looking forward than back. The ballroom rumbled with apparent dissatisfaction at the moderator's refusal to yield to the inquisition they had been promised. "I don't understand why we aren't asking them questions," one woman yelled from the floor. Ocamb was briefly frozen by the impudent challenge to her journalistic discretion. "Well," she responded, "did you hear anybody announce that there was a mistake made?"

That skepticism was shared by a short and muscular man in the audience who was just beginning to direct his impish intensity to understanding the fault lines that ran through California gay politics. Dave Fleischer, who had led the National Gay and Lesbian Task Force's organizing department, had stood at a distance from gay-rights work for several years—he spent much of 2008 in Ohio with Saul Alinsky's Industrial Areas Foundation— but after the election had his attention drawn to California. Fleischer called Jean's deputy to express disgust that the state's gay community was responding to electoral disappointment with its spleen rather than its brain or hands. "How many times are you guys going to march on a Mormon temple?" asked Fleischer.

Jean responded by giving Fleischer an assignment rejected by every Californian on whom she had tried to foist it. In 2000, facing an unexpected surplus after the passage of Proposition 22, the manager of the No on Knight campaign spent the excess budget to preserve the paperwork of a defunct institution: staff listings and salaries, opposition research, and a timeline of events. Jean, then a board member at the National Gay and Lesbian Task Force, was assigned the job of coauthoring the accompanying analysis, which was vague in its conclusions and diffuse in anything that could be perceived as blame. The campaign to defeat the gay-marriage ban was "a valiant one," the report argued, sympathetic to the idea "that a victory or even a closing of the vote margin would have been impossible." Fleischer did not think much of that 2000 report, which he characterized as "more a summary" than an "evaluation." "They were more or less putting a time capsule for the day which they felt was far in the future where marriage might be winnable," he says.

Eight years later, more was at stake. Jean asked Fleischer to prepare a similar postmortem of the No on 8 effort, vowing to make available all its personnel—staff, volunteer leadership, and outside consultants—for interviews, along with the entirety of its internal materials. No on 8 had commissioned $1.2 million in opinion research, larger than the entire budgets of initiative campaigns in other states; when combined with public and private polls, along with data on each side's television ad buys, Fleischer believed it would get him closer to answering the questions that few leaders at the Equality Summit were able to approach honestly, or wanted to. Which Californians had supplied the votes to pass Proposition 8? Was the result inevitable or could a better campaign have swung their preferences in the other direction? Why had so much polling failed to predict the final outcome?

He accepted Jean's invitation but refused her funding. He would seek his own support from donors, freeing him to publish whatever he uncovered. "There are so few instances of the LGBT community seriously and publicly evaluating any of our achievements," he says. "I can't remember a conversation with an LGBT group where the predominant tone or agenda was curiosity." He thought of the movement as what on a night out he would call a "bar body"—the physique of someone who spends his gym time bulking up his arms and toning his chest while neglecting everything that would go unnoticed at first look.

An autopsy of the No on 8 cadaver, Fleischer suspected, would reveal not only poor decision-making but the weakness of methods—particularly the irrevocable cycle of focus groups, polls, and television ads—that supported and justified them. "The reason the tools persist is people are familiar with them, and people sell them, and they sell them at a cheap enough price so that a lot of people can afford them. But we ought to be very curious about better ways to do our research," Fleischer says. "How many times do we have to fail with the same set of tools before we get more serious about how we change the lightbulb?"

Meet in the Middle

Nearly as quickly as he began work on his evaluation of the No on 8 campaign, Dave Fleischer realized his initial vision for the project—a twenty-five-page document he could produce in months—had been naïve. The campaign's executive committee had promised access to all the campaign's materials, especially the internal polling, but just weeks after its conclusion, Fleischer was unable to locate much of it. Over one million dollars in data had gone missing.

As he hunted for the opinion research for which No on 8 had paid so dearly, Fleischer began collecting some of his own. He launched an organization under the Los Angeles Gay and Lesbian Center's auspices that he would eventually call the Leadership LAB, a place where he could experiment with new messaging tactics to be deployed through face-to-face canvassing. In early 2009, Fleischer convened a meeting at a United Methodist church, in the hills just south of the Hollywood Bowl. Fleischer asked the approximately ninety people who had turned out at the kickoff meeting what they thought the No on 8 campaign had done wrong. Every idea would be heard, Fleischer said, and they were hollered from the pews. Many were variations on the same theme: that gays and lesbians needed to be more assertive about their identities and lives to make heterosexuals more empathetic to their demands for marriage. "There was a lot of faith that if we tell our story, that will persuade people," says Fleischer.

He was receptive to the idea, as he had considered among the self-evident weaknesses of the No on 8 campaign the near-total absence from its television ads of people who would be affected by the vote, or even the word *gay*. But Fleischer was also a natural skeptic who had spent years at doorsteps, even after he had graduated to leadership posts in movement organizations. The mantra of "tell our story" struck him as too facile a recommendation, inviting a one-sided pantomime by canvassers that he thought unlikely to break down deep-seated prejudice.

Let's go talk to the people who voted against us and ask why, Fleischer told himself. He isolated households in precincts that had gone strongly for the constitutional amendment and dispatched canvassers with unusual instructions to open up a free-flowing conversation with voters there about gay marriage. "In a way," he says, "I feel like a schmuck that it took me over forty years of canvassing before it occurred to me to do that."

California was awash in such pop-up projects to undo the damage of Proposition 8. Almost immediately after the amendment passed, lawyers filed suits in state courts to overturn it. (The most prominent, from celebrity attorney Gloria Allred, challenged Proposition 8 on procedural terms, alleging that it was a "disguised constitutional revision" rather than an amendment.) Meanwhile, California's various gay political groups began preparing for what would be in effect a do-over: another statewide ballot measure to remove the Proposition 8 language from the constitution. They were joined by a variety of newly formed entities—at one point Fleischer counted over forty of them—inspired by the 2008 campaign and riled by the finger-pointing aftermath.

Starting in March, the three-year-old Courage Campaign began placing field organizers across twenty-two counties to lay the groundwork for such a referendum. "We are putting in place everything that we can to mobilize our own members and others," the group's founder, Rick Jacobs, said that summer after more than four-fifths of those members voted to push ahead with qualifying a ballot measure in 2010. Another group, Love Honor Cherish, submitted ballot language to the secretary of state for approval. The state's most established gay-rights organization, Equality California, imported an operative from Massachusetts to develop its field infrastructure; Marc Solomon told the *New York Times* he would be "taking a page from the playbook we used in the Northeast." (Solomon's appointment as marriage director was widely seen as Equality California's effort to install him as campaign-manager-in-waiting for the return to the ballot, even as the organization refused to commit to a desired timetable for it.) "Regardless of what the court does, we have to change hearts and minds," executive director Geoff Kors said.

As a conciliatory gesture, Kors and Jacobs announced that their groups would partner on a statewide survey to assess the state of opinion on marriage. It was an unusually collaborative research project undertaken in public: any organization could buy into the poll for $250, with donors willing to defray the cost for any group that wanted to join. More than forty ended up participating, including national gay groups and outsiders like the AFL-CIO, leading to sprawling conference calls with dozens of people negotiating what questions to ask and how to phrase them. The performative exercise in internal democracy served a practical purpose, forcing groups to work from a common set of evidence as they argued about strategy.

They made plans to unveil the results that summer at a "leadership summit" held alongside a statewide gathering called Meet in the Middle. In attendance were representatives of both the established institutions and those founded since Proposition 8, many of which had flailed around without clear direction about what the movement would do next, and when. (Hosting the event in Fresno, which included a march to the city hall from a nearby town conveniently named Selma, was seen as a way to avoid the regional conflict between Los Angeles and San Francisco.) As part of an effort to restore the confidence of the LGBT public, the Poll 4 Equality sponsors then dispatched pollsters David Binder and Amy Simon to present their results at community meetings across the state. But even as some trumpeted the public meetings as an exercise in transparency, one of the coalition's leaders tried to keep the research in question from becoming public. "It gives $86,000 worth of information to the opposition," Jacobs explained to justify kicking a reporter out of a community meeting where the survey findings were being unveiled.

One figure the poll's sponsors did release publicly showed opinion evenly divided, with 47 percent supporting same-sex marriage and 48 percent opposing. For those contemplating the timing of a return to the ballot, Binder and Simon included a complicating detail: those numbers would shift by as many as three points in favor just by waiting for 2012. (The calculations assumed a continuation of the organic opinion change under way, along with a more left-leaning electorate mobilized to participate in the presidential election.) "You can argue to wait until 2014 to do even better, but it's not a reason to wait when you're a second-class citizen," John Henning, Love Honor Cherish's cofounder, told the blog Unite the Fight. "With an 18 month campaign for 2010, we can change minds."

As Fleischer completed a draft of his report, its analysis would amount to forewarning activists to slow that rush toward another statewide campaign. It was, he intimated, foolhardy to assume that tactical adjustments, along with demographic shifts in the electorate, would produce opposite results. "It is prudent to think hard about whether and how we can put ourselves in a significantly stronger position to win," Fleischer wrote in one of his report's recommendations. "For both practical and ethical reasons, we have a responsibility to the LGBT community in particular and to our progressive allies in general to do the hard preparatory work before we instigate the next vote."

Fleischer deflected blame from many of the most common scapegoats—especially African Americans and Latinos, whom many white liberals had accused of abandoning their fellow minorities—and back toward the No on 8 organization and the movement leaders who controlled it. "Given the difficulty our community has experienced with the same-sex marriage measures, all of us, myself included, are still near the beginning of the learning curve," Fleischer concluded in his meticulous report.

As Thalia Zepatos had in her *Groundhog Day* memo, Fleischer laid much of the responsibility for the campaign's errors on the political consultants who had been hired to run it despite their lack of background in gay issues. "As problems arose that were outside of the consultants' experience, too few people were in a position to help the campaign correct course. By September, when the problems were overwhelming, the only apparent option was a complete change in leadership," he wrote. "This extreme response both improved the situation in vitally important ways and led to the single most costly decision of the campaign: the failure to respond in a timely way to the 'kids in danger' message that we should have seen coming."

Fleischer's account matched Frank Schubert's real-time assessment of the potency of Yes on 8's messaging around children, especially when unanswered by gay-rights advocates for several crucial weeks in October. "In the final six weeks of the campaign, a minimum of 687,000 voters moved towards favoring the ban on same-sex marriage. The voters who most dramatically moved toward the ban were not African-Americans or Republicans," concluded Fleischer after a review of internal polls. "Those who moved were largely part of the pro-LGBT base that got peeled away, particularly parents and voters of parenting age. In the closing weeks, almost three-quarters of the net movement toward the ban—approximately 500,000 voters—were parents with children under eighteen living at home."

The report was damning toward No on 8's lackadaisical handling of the

Princes ad, but Fleischer did not suggest that a different tactical reaction or a more nimble operation would have presaged a superior outcome. "Anti-gay forces know how to exploit and stimulate anti-gay prejudice, and the LGBT community has difficulty facing and responding to the attack," Fleischer wrote. It was not so much that gay-rights advocates were slow to answer the charge that their movement was aiming to turn kids gay, he argued, but that so many people who seemed otherwise sympathetic to gay equality were so ready to believe it. The failures of gay-rights messaging had begun long before the Princes ad hit the air.

In essence, Fleischer had concluded that activists could not count on winning marriage campaigns as they popped up on the ballot. They needed to build a reservoir of sympathy or understanding or self-interest—any sort of emotional connection deep enough that it would not just evaporate on contact with the heat of an inflammatory allegation. To understand what his side was up against, Fleischer sent volunteers out to homes— inhabited by those who data showed were likely to have voted in favor of Proposition 8—carrying digital tablets or phones loaded with video. "Do you remember this ad?" they were instructed to inquire, before pressing play.

Placid conversations frequently turned unpleasant as soon as they showed "Princes," and many canvassers reported that they believed they had lost voters by doing so. Fleischer was animated by this insight. Volunteers were initiating the type of personally meaningful exchanges that rarely materialized in the superficial back-and-forth of campaigns. Uncomfortable conversations became a goal unto themselves: Fleischer began to call it "deep canvassing," a central tactic in a slower, more gradual effort to familiarize voters with gay people and to lessen their doubts about homosexuality. "None of the ads created by the No on 8 campaign rebutted this," Fleischer says of the enduring power of "Princes" to unsettle. "I think it's a significant factor into why we lost, although it's hard to know what kind of antidote could have been created."

Fleischer's work on the No on 8 evaluation ended up taking the entire year, with the final version eventually covering more than five hundred pages. Fleischer wrote two different versions of it, one that identified personnel responsible for the campaign's mistakes and one that largely avoided individual blame, worried that the finger-pointing "would be everybody's takeaway and they would have missed the bigger picture." Fleischer chose to release only the less provocative version, filing away the other in case it would be useful to shape future campaigns' decisions about which staff and consultants to hire.

"For those who fear that this report will enlighten our opposition as to how to run an effective campaign, I have a message," Fleischer's report began. "They already know how to do that."

Gathering Storm

In the spring of 2009, the group responsible for Proposition 8's success launched a $1.5 million ad campaign called "The Gathering Storm," in apparent homage to one of Winston Churchill's memoirs of wartime. With a tempestuous sky breaking in the background, a series of people delivered testimonials of harm endured by encroachment of same-sex marriage on their lives. One introduced himself as "a California doctor who must choose between my faith and my job," another a Massachusetts parent "helplessly watching public schools teach my son that gay marriage is okay."

The ad from the National Organization for Marriage was instantly mocked by its natural antagonists. "An Internet camp classic," proclaimed *New York Times* columnist Frank Rich, "what would happen if you crossed that creepy 1960s horror classic *The Village of the Damned* with the Broadway staple *A Chorus Line*." The campaign's distinctive aesthetics lent themselves to parody videos, including one by television satirist Stephen Colbert, who mused that "it's like watching *The 700 Club* and The Weather Channel at the same time." When audition videos for the ads leaked—presumably by someone at the casting studio looking to undermine the client—it vividly illustrated the irony at their heart: the highly personal testimonials were not even being delivered by the people who had suffered harm.

But those who were too bowled over by hapless actors clumsily trying to deliver lines like "a rainbow coalition of people of every creed and color are coming together in love to protect marriage" missed the point. The imagery behind them may have been apocalyptic, but when the actors in "The Gathering Storm"—young and conspicuous for their racial and ethnic diversity—touched on faith, it was with the civic language of religious freedom rather than the theological certainties of biblical doctrine.

The ad buy had notably prioritized Rhode Island, New York, and New Jersey. Among the few states that had never enacted DOMA-style bans, they risked being the next dominos to fall if a strong case wasn't made for leaving marriage as it was.

The following month, the National Organization for Marriage unveiled a new spokeswoman who again enabled the group to assert itself without having to substantively argue against same-sex relationships. At the Miss USA pageant, Miss California, Carrie Prejean, was asked by a judge, openly gay entertainment blogger Perez Hilton, for her views on states legalizing same-sex marriage. The San Diego Christian College student, who claimed the Rock Church's Miles McPherson as her pastor, responded that she believed "marriage should be between a man and a woman." When she failed to win the crown, many on the right blamed political correctness. ("She really did answer also a very, very tough question very well," the pageant's owner, Donald Trump, said afterward. "It wasn't a bad answer, that was simply her belief.") NOM enlisted Prejean, although in a sixty-second ad it portrayed its new twenty-one-year-old spokeswoman as a naïf—"when asked a question about marriage, a young contestant answers honestly"—who required a society that would "protect freedom of speech."

Those forays, both inadvertent and purposeful, into the sphere of pop culture allowed the National Organization for Marriage to step forward as more than just a behind-the-scenes funder of others' activity. That summer, upon the group's opening of a Washington office, executive director Brian Brown invited the *Washington Post* to interview him at a "nearly empty desk in a nearly empty room" for an admiring profile that compared its ambition to the Human Rights Campaign's. (Its legal headquarters remained in Princeton, where chairman Robert George was based.) "The same thing—large, well-publicized, well-organized campaigns—for different purposes," wrote the paper's Monica Hesse. "In the world of activism, what works for one side can work for the other."

The group privately labeled itself "the national party of marriage, the only single-issue national organization making substantial investments in marriage fights in every state." It was the Proposition 8 fight that elevated the group in ways making possible its new reach: the National Organization for Marriage ended the year with eight thousand donors and fifty thousand activists, and a circumstantial alliance of Catholics and Mormons that had hardened into a durable partnership. When Matthew Holland left the board upon being named president of Utah Valley University, he was replaced by science-fiction author Orson Scott Card. What the men had in common was status within the LDS Church hierarchy: Holland's father, Jeffrey, was a member of the church's Quorum of Twelve, and Card a columnist for *Mormon Times*, the weekly features supplement to the church-owned *Deseret News*. There he had staked out positions on same-sex relationships that sat to the right of the church's. "When government is the enemy of marriage, then the people who are actually creating successful marriages have no choice but to change governments, by whatever means is made possible or necessary," Card had written in the summer of 2008 as Mormons threw themselves behind Proposition 8. When Card replaced Holland, the *Deseret News* described the appointment as a way of keeping the church's interests "represented on the board."

Unlike most socially conservative groups, who were usually most active in the places where their members lived, the National Organization for Marriage waged the culture wars from behind enemy lines. When it was formed in 2007, two-thirds of the states had enacted constitutional language that made them effectively immune to same-sex marriage in the near term. With only a few exceptions, like West Virginia and Indiana, the holdout states were among the country's most liberal.

After California, the group turned its attention to the few state capitals where gay activists did not see their path to marriage fully blocked, and suffered a string of losses. In Montpelier, the legislature overrode a Republican governor's veto despite NOM robocalls encouraging residents to call their representatives. Given the difficulty of bringing an amendment to voters, the organization added Vermont to its list of "rollback" targets, where it would collect stories of local citizens affected by the change in marriage laws and angle for the first opening to undo them. States on the list were prioritized based on the legal difficulty of repeal—Massachusetts and Connecticut were, practically, inviolable in the near term—and also their role in a broader national strategy. "If marriage is going to be preserved as between a man and a woman in the United States, the next president must be a man or woman who expressly articulates a pro-marriage culture, and appoints sympathetic Supreme Court justices," declared a 2009 strategy plan. "New Hampshire and Iowa are the two states that have direct implications for the 2012 presidential elections."

That spring, Maine became the first state to see same-sex marriage enacted with a governor's support. But the law never took effect. A day after the bill's signing, on May 6, opponents began collecting signatures to qualify a repeal measure for that November's ballot. The National Organization for Marriage took charge of bringing repeal opponents into the Stand for Marriage Maine campaign, and assumed responsibility for two-thirds of the expected $3 million budget. Within weeks, the group had hired Schubert Flint to run the "people's veto" campaign.

With Frank Schubert as its manager, Stand for Marriage Maine quickly turned into a small-scale reunion of the Yes on 8 campaign. From San Diego, Reverend Chris Clark led webinars for fellow evangelical pastors. The Catholic Diocese of Portland, which donated over $500,000, encouraged canvassers to collect signatures at its churches. When fundraising from other sources came up short, the National Organization for Marriage delivered an additional $800,000 to help the campaign meet its targets.

The campaign for Amendment 1 unfolded in such a way—with the same campaign team, and a similar message and strategy—that many gay-marriage supporters were convinced they had no hope of defeating their opponents at the ballot box. Under Schubert's direction, Stand for Marriage Maine returned to the child-oriented messaging that had dominated the closing weeks of the Proposition 8 campaign. One Maine ad reprised the story of Massachusetts second-graders taught that it was all right for boys to pair off with each other, even picturing the same Mormon family who had been featured in the Yes on 8 ads. A new one showed a young girl who asked if local priests were "bigots" because of their opposition to gay marriage. It was, the girl told her mother, something she had learned at school.

The National Organization for Marriage counted its other 2009 successes by the times it blocked same-sex unions from getting that far. In New York, public pressure on publicly wavering Republicans kept the party unified—and joined by a selection of socially conservative Democrats—to defeat a bill that had already passed the more liberal state assembly. In New Jersey, during a lame-duck session that offered the last chance to get a bill signed by outgoing governor Jon Corzine, senators pushing to expand the state's civil-unions statute into full-fledged marriage withdrew their proposal when it became clear they wouldn't have the votes. "Here's the bottom line: NOM's model for influencing not only referendums but legislatures by adding sophisticated messaging and political know-how to the efforts of local groups has been tested and found to be an effective use of resources," claimed an internal memo, which noted that the work in New York and New Jersey had cost a total of $1.2 million. "Against every prediction, and all the conventional wisdom, marriage is winning."

At the same time, the organization had an unusual opportunity to make its mark in one of the few federal elections scheduled for 2009. An unusual three-way special election in an upstate New York congressional district presented an opportunity to deploy marriage as a wedge issue within the right. NOM spent aggressively to boost third-party Conservative candidate Doug Hoffman against Dede Scozzafava, a liberal Republican who had backed same-sex marriage while in the state assembly. Eventually Hoffman gained such strength on the right that Scozzafava was squeezed out of the race shortly before Election Day. Gallagher joked that the effort helped coin a new verb. "To 'scozzfava' a politician is to inform GOP primary voters that he or she is pro-gay marriage," she wrote on NOM's blog.

By the end of 2009, flush with a run of victories in different settings and an institution that had grown more robust in the process—donors nearly quadrupled and activists grew tenfold over the year—the National Organization for Marriage's ambitions were becoming even more grandiose. NOM announced the creation of a "victory fund" that would raise $20 million by the November 2010 elections. By then NOM hoped to have fifty thousand donors and two million active supporters. "Marriage will be won or lost in the United States in the next two to three years," a 2009 strategy plan predicted. In 2007, Gallagher had launched the National Organization for Marriage out of a sense of the conservative right's tactical inferiority. Two years later, she had come to believe her side was unstoppable. "With adequate resources," declared the strategy plan, "we can win the battle for hearts and minds on the marriage issue."

Up Against the Wall

In the middle of 2009, the ACLU's Matt Coles decided it was time to reconvene the crew of lawyers and political operatives he had once invited to Jersey City. At that point donors had faced an existential crisis about whether the fight for same-sex marriage justified the costs it imposed on the gay-rights movement. The "Winning Marriage" paper—known, almost instantly, to those aware of its existence as the 10-10-10-20 Plan— had helped convince donors and organizational leaders that there was in fact a strategy at work. But the devastating loss in California and a looming replay in Maine had left some asking the same questions anew.

Discussions had come to center more on what gay-marriage campaigners could not do, rather than what they could. Inquests like the one being led in California by Dave Fleischer began to pinpoint some of those shortcomings, but had yet to present a course to rectify them. Meanwhile the opposition appeared to be getting better at funding and coordinating its political operations. Individual state losses were taking their toll on the strategy as a whole, pushing the 10-10-10-20 benchmarks beyond reach.

"We're going to hit a wall," James Esseks, the ACLU's LGBT litigation director, had told his boss.

By some measures what the paper had identified as the first phase of its strategy to bring victory before the Supreme Court within twenty years was remarkably fruitful. The *Goodridge* mandate in Massachusetts, which had been identified as "a top priority on which all else depends," was secure from political meddling. Activists had managed to win a ballot measure in a moderate state two years ahead of schedule, by defeating an overly broad constitutional amendment in Arizona in 2006, although it was reversed by the state's voters two years later.

Another goal outlined in the 10-10-10-20 Plan had been "achieving marriage rights for same-sex couples in 2-3 more states in 4 to 5 years." By late 2009, five states and the District of Columbia extended such rights, in addition to California and Maine, where they had been won and subjected to recall by voters. Two of the five with marriage, Iowa and New Hampshire, had been classified in the plan as states where activists should expect to secure only civil unions within ten to fifteen years. Even in states that had not gone that far, there were indicators of unanticipated progress. In 2009 alone, a handful—Washington, Nevada, Wisconsin, and Colorado—enacted some form of heightened legal recognition for gay families. Across them all, marriage, civil unions, and domestic partnerships had been granted by legislatures and not just courts, as Coles pointed out, "showing that we can create the political and social predicate we need to win."

Yet those four years had also been dominated by painful setbacks. Opponents were notching victories, too, often through voters directly. Two state constitutional amendments had passed in 2005, another eight in 2006, and three in 2008. The 10-10-10-20 Plan had uniquely prioritized "defeating the expected anti-gay-relationship initiative(s) in California," calculating the specific cost of failure there. "A successful initiative, especially if it rolled back protections we've already won, would delay crucial progress," the paper had warned three years before Proposition 8. Thirty states had imposed constitutional amendments restricting marriage to heterosexual couples, and the majority of those amendments also blocked civil unions, domestic partnerships, or other recognition of same-sex relationships.

Those now loomed as a major impediment to the gradual accumulation of victories across the map that the earlier strategy sessions had foreseen hitting a "tipping point." Among the ten that the 2005 paper had targeted for marriage, California and Oregon had enacted their bans in the form of constitutional amendments, while Washington had a mini-DOMA-style statute. The idealized thirty states with some level of legal recognition for couples appeared out of grasp, especially when some that had been designated a target—like Wisconsin and Alaska—had amended their constitutions to make such a policy change impossible. Meanwhile eleven states had statutory bans on gay marriage that could presumably be overturned by state courts, or by legislative efforts, but among them were conservative strongholds like West Virginia, Indiana, and Wyoming where such judicial enterprise seemed unlikely. "Even an optimist's crystal ball clouds over,"

Coles would write. "The problem is not simply the amendments, but the political reality they reflect."

He had forecast this situation. "If 30 or 35 states pass constitutional amendments, we will likely have to repeal a significant number of them before we can turn to the federal government to address holdouts," the 2005 document had asserted. That was now reality: to reach the goal of ten states each extending marriage, civil union, and domestic-partnership rights, gay activists would have to amend state constitutions just to open space for a court or legislature to act. They had struggled everywhere they had been forced to defend the status quo, and could hardly be expected to fare better when they were the ones who demanded changing a constitution. (It was simply more costly to initiate an amendment measure, since typically the proponent faces the burden of gathering petition signatures.) "It was not like, 'We may have to win a ballot or two,' but 'We are going to have to win *some* ballots,'" says Coles.

While the Jersey City strategists had envisioned such a scenario, they had not considered what that contingency plan would look like. The only serious effort to knock down a state ban through the federal judiciary—the 2005 challenge to Nebraska's unusually restrictive amendment—had been a failure, and mounting another such case was fraught with an unappealing degree of legal risk. Conditions had not changed enough to consider pushing a case toward the Supreme Court, with confidence that plaintiffs could mitigate justices' concern about getting ahead of public opinion. "Those blocks reflect an even grimmer political reality; in over half the states, we still have not done enough to begin changing minds on LGBT people at the most basic level, an essential predicate for winning marriage," Coles wrote. "As we face that reality, we must also face a significant failure in our follow up to the paper: we are still without the organized public education capacity we need above all things to win marriage."

This deficiency had been anticipated back in Jersey City, when participants argued over whether to establish a new organization focused solely on winning marriage nationally. Existing entities were reticent to anoint a competitor, and agreed instead to join a collaborative framework under which they would back projects of mutual interest. The National Collaborative had been chartered as a short-term experiment, and few were arguing after its three years that it had been anything other than a failure. "It just was this endless set of transactions," reflected Wolfson, who served as an outside adviser to the group, "not cohesive and strategic and eyes-on-the-prize affirmative."

Even when gay-marriage advocates were finally able to outspend their opponents, as was the case in California and Maine, they had difficulty balancing conflict on multiple fronts. Having spent the spring of 2009 in Maine executing a legislative campaign—and impressively convincing a Democratic governor to sign a marriage bill into law—activists were not prepared to communicate with a broader public across the state. Once Amendment 1 qualified for the ballot, about eight weeks before Election Day, they "just didn't have enough time to go build the campaign, not enough time to do anything," says Matt McTighe, then a public-education director for Gay and Lesbian Advocates and Defenders based in Maine. "You focused all of your energy on legislators," he says, "and now you've got a universe of voters all over the state instead of a handful of legislators."

In California, Proposition 8's passage had sparked a surge of energy among those seeking to strike the new language from the state constitution, but no one could agree on how best to achieve it. The left-wing Courage Campaign began organizing to push a referendum at the next available opportunity, in 2010, while Equality California wanted to wait for 2012. Others wanted to step back from the electoral calendar altogether and take a more gradual approach to shaping public opinion, and a handful of high-profile lawyers in California had resisted ever handing the matter back to voters. Their challenge to the result on procedural grounds—the suit alleged that the initiative had not been an amendment but rather a revision to the state constitution—was rejected by the California Supreme Court in May 2009. The same week that opinion was issued, another group introduced a far more audacious challenge under federal law, designed explicitly to force the U.S. Supreme Court to address the underlying question of whether same-sex couples had a right to marry. The nation's leading gay-rights lawyers publicly shamed the suit's proponents, arguing it was risky and premature, potentially producing a damaging precedent that would set back efforts in states beyond California.

Though bitterness from Proposition 8 had mobilized a new generation of activists and donors nationwide to feel invested in the cause of marriage rights, gay leaders had no consensus about where to direct them. Federal courts were still considered risky, and there were few states left where political activity was a viable short-term option. Pointing toward the 10-10-10-20 Plan was no longer much use, as many of its particulars had become outdated nearly from the moment that Coles circulated the final version in the summer of 2005. The generalized preference it reflected, to work first through courts and legislatures in states where public opinion would be friendliest, was no longer practicable. "We need people to see that the wall is there," says Coles, "and recognize that the sketch in the original paper is not going to work."

The 10-10-10-20 Plan had foreseen the federal government doing only what Coles called "a clean-up job." It was a distant and hazy vision of the strategy's endgame, in which the feds force laggard and outlier states to adhere to some sort of national framework. Basically, the thinking went, if you make enough of a mess that state laws can no longer be synchronized under a federal system, Washington will finally feel compelled to step in.

But by 2009, there was evidence that the federal government might be ready to do more, or at least to act more quickly. Despite his opposition to gay marriage, Barack Obama had campaigned as an opponent of the Defense of Marriage Act and had promised to work to undo it. To that end, Democrats in Congress had introduced the Respect of Marriage Act, which would have repealed the 1996 bill in its entirety. A Democratic White House and Senate were working to stock the federal judiciary—a circumstance unimaginable from the vantage of early 2005, when Republicans controlled all three branches of government. What had been an unlikely obstacle for a civil-rights movement—a national government more conservative, certainly on gay and lesbian issues, than the public it represented—had begun to slacken.

The moment had arrived for revisiting some of the assumptions that had shaped thinking in Jersey City about strategy. The pilot period for the National Collaborative would end in 2010, which was also shaping up to be the first year since 1994 without an active effort under way to amend a state's constitution to limit marriage. Also at the start of 2010, Coles knew, he would shift out of his position into one at the ACLU with broader responsibilities. Before doing so, he committed to overseeing a wholesale revision of the "Winning Marriage" strategy to account for a more dire long-term outlook in the states, but an unexpectedly hopeful near-term one in Washington. Coles drafted a revision of the "Winning Marriage" plan, with its 10-10-10-20 benchmarks, and invited many of the organizations that had signed on to the original version to each send a representative to Boston to negotiate its details. "At this point, people were feeling heat from all sides," says Coles. "I thought losing the consensus at that point would be really bad."

By the time they met, at the Somerville home of former ACLU attorney Bill Rubenstein, then teaching at Harvard Law School, Coles had concluded that "it's going to be both easier and more difficult than we thought to win marriage," as he wrote. "While it may be difficult to get the level of support we would need to overcome the inherent conservatism of political institutions or to repeal ballot initiatives, we can still create widespread public support for marriage."

Participants reviewed the challenge posed by "the wall" of state-level constitutional amendments that Esseks had identified. They also looked at new opportunities posed by rising support from the public and some elected officials. "We need to find a way to get to marriage without quite getting to the tipping points of 'Winning Marriage,' or we need a strategy that gets us past the political barriers that exist in over half the states," Coles ventured. In Somerville, attendees diagrammed two possible scenarios. In both, activists and litigators would sustain their efforts to win marriage in as many states as possible. At that point, the wall would no longer be conjecture but a structural reality.

The first scenario would seek to catapult over it. Unable to attain any of the 10-10-10-20 benchmarks, strategists would establish the base of a "strong national majority in the American public for marriage." With that foundation, litigators would pivot toward the Supreme Court, earlier than had been envisioned in Jersey City. But instead of demanding a "uniform national rule" bringing order to chaos, they would present a more regimented logic of civil-rights grievances. Cases could be related to couples and their families, or to other areas where gays and lesbians received uneven treatment under the law. Recent history validated such a stepping-stone approach: a rejection of statutes denying political protections to sexual minorities in 1996's *Romer v. Evans* set up *Lawrence v. Texas,* seven years later, to strike down any others targeting their intimate behavior.

The second scenario mapped a long path to wind around the wall's edges. Strategists would push for nondiscrimination and antibullying laws where constitutional amendments precluded expanded recognition of gay families. When state-level policies were the impediment, activists could look to municipal government and private employers to extend domestic-partnership benefits, with the aim of tallying at least one such public program in every state. With the 10-10-10-20 criteria unmet, that geographic breadth could signal to federal judges that gay families were not a parochial concern of the progressive coasts. Such a strategy would mark a return to the incrementalism of family-law organizing before Hawaii made marriage seem like an immediately plausible goal, in at least some states. "We'll need to do that to make future progress on relationships possible if the Courts or Congress don't come to the rescue when we've gone as far as we can in the 'possible' states we have now," the final paper declared. "The more we make the public conversation about our lives, including our relationships, the easier our job will ultimately be."

Each of the paper's two scenarios highlighted a different, but equally glaring, deficiency of the National Collaborative. Its focus on cultivating local organizations and working to refine their state plans left it without any mechanism for mass persuasion. For that matter, no one had taken on specific responsibility for compiling or commissioning the type of national polls that could eventually demonstrate to wary federal judges that same-sex marriage had attained majority support. Similarly, no group devoted uniquely to marriage had ever developed the capacity (or legal status) to lobby Congress or the White House. Even as Washington-based Gill Action raised money to defeat and support lawmakers, it did not have the ability to pressure them once in office. "It was clear by early 2009 that the Collaborative was not going to do it," says Coles. "An organization to run the nonlitigation part of a campaign was necessary."

It was precisely the type of structure that the right had developed on the other side of the issue, and what the $20 million "victory fund" it was trying to assemble would further build out. Activists had only the sketchiest understanding of how groups on the other side operated, pieced together from public announcements, tax returns, and public filings with local lobbying and electoral authorities. But gay activists had seen the way California's No on 8 campaign had rolled into Stand for Marriage Maine—seeming to pull from the same pool of money, talent, research, and strategy.

When Maine's Amendment 1 passed by a comfortable margin, in November 2009, the National Organization for Marriage took credit as the driving force behind it. "No other national organization provided anything like the financial support NOM did," the group reported in an internal memo that fall. After leading the early charge in California, it could claim to have twice succeeded at the most difficult political task possible: mobilizing voters in left-leaning states to undo the excesses of their courts or elected officials.

The gay-rights movement knew it needed its own version of the National Organization for Marriage.

Roadmap

Matt Coles likened the 2010 decision to jettison the National Collaborative to the postindependence shift from the Articles of Confederation to a true federal system under the Constitution. The analogy to colonial-era politics was unintentionally salient for one of those in attendance who had taken an outsize interest in what Coles was putting on paper. After being passed over before the Jersey City meeting to serve as author of what became its 10-10-10-20 Plan, Evan Wolfson had found solace in a song from the musical *1776*. In it, John Adams lobbies others to assume responsibility for drafting the Declaration of Independence. "It was like I was too John Adams," he recalls. "I've called for independence."

No one was happier about the decision to jettison the National Collaborative than Wolfson. In launching Freedom to Marry in 2003, he had believed he was declaring his sovereignty from the Washington gay-rights establishment that he felt had never taken his cause seriously, and state and regional groups he considered unqualified to navigate the complicated politics around it. Even once Wolfson had his own organization, more established entities resisted bowing to his self-generated authority. Gary Buseck of Gay and Lesbian Advocates and Defenders, the group that had brought the Massachusetts suit then on the cusp of a state supreme court victory, told *The Advocate* he was skeptical about "whether or not Freedom to Marry can be a unifying thread."

Wolfson did not always make himself such an appealing collaborator for others with more established institutions to their name. In fact, the libretto of *1776* makes no mention of having "called for independence" as the basis of a founding father's unsuitability to draft the declaration. Instead the refrain in "But, Mr. Adams" is: "He's obnoxious and disliked." In Wolfson's case, he made a regular performance of his own certitude, signaling impatience and disapproval through a semaphore of deep sighs and rolled eyes. (Buseck volunteered to *The Advocate* that Wolfson "is an intense person who causes some people consternation.")

From the time he left Lambda Legal, Wolfson had argued the need for an institution committed to what he called the "four multis"—multiyear, multistate, multipartner, multimethodology. His Freedom to Marry was indeed multifaceted, but it did not have the resources to make much of an impact. Without a membership network or the ability to support candidates, it could do little to get the attention of local politicians; unable to direct campaign activity in the states, Freedom to Marry was little more than an appendage to its multiple partners. Despite its own office and public profile, it didn't even have its own legal status, existing under the patronage of the Astraea Lesbian Foundation. Freedom to Marry maintained an internal target of regranting one-quarter of its funds to state organizations, just enough to offer input but too little to exert real influence with them. Tim Sweeney, who as a Haas Foundation official helped fund the group, said Freedom to Marry was launched to be a "a small ship, the glue that held the movement together, a behind-the-scenes cajoler and convener and re-grantor, an adviser to funders." After a few years of existence, *Gay City News* would characterize it simply as "a strategy shop."

Wolfson's hopes were raised in 2005, around the time of the original Jersey City meeting. For the first time the movement would agree to a common plan for winning marriage, with advance support from its largest funder. Yet instead of finally being elevated to the role he had long sought, as the lead strategist for an endowed marriage campaign, Wolfson found himself marginalized anew. He was not only skipped over, in favor of Coles, to lead the process of writing the paper, but the final version reflected a consensus decision to christen a new collaborative structure instead of blessing Wolfson's extant organization with new authority and budget. "There was a pointed refusal on the part of some key players," says Wolfson, "to give Freedom to Marry the mandate."

In 2007, Freedom to Marry published a *Candidates' Guide on How to Support Marriage Equality and Get Elected*, although it lacked the personnel to aid campaigns struggling to translate it into tactics. (Furthermore, the group's tax status constrained any direct involvement in partisan politics.) Two years later, Freedom to Marry issued a report showing that state legislators who had voted for marriage (in the four states where it had come up for a vote) had all kept their seats the previous fall, but it was Gill Action that had spent the money that helped make it possible. Wolfson was frustrated. "The 'cobbled together' approach pursued so far by the marriage movement is not sufficient for today's opportunities and challenges," he wrote in the fall of 2009. "Efforts to spur creation of a national-campaign capacity through various means have advanced our movement, but fallen short of what is needed."

Crucial to Wolfson's future plans was a successful demonstration of past efforts' futility. With a $6,000 grant, he asked NYU politics professor Patrick Egan to look back on all thirty-three statewide ballot campaigns that had been waged around same-sex marriage to that point, and handed him a question familiar to political scientists: How much did the campaigns move people? An analysis of hundreds of polls led Egan to conclude that "the share of the public saying they intend to vote for or against these measures typically changes very little over the course of these campaigns." His conclusion was not that pro-gay-marriage campaigns had been uniquely underachieving, but that few minds at all had really been up for grabs. "Those favoring and opposing the ballot measures have largely fought to a draw," wrote Egan. "Neither side has been more successful than the other on average at changing voter sentiment between the beginning and the end of a campaign."

There had been only one organization whose efforts at changing opinions Wolfson held in high regard. He had joined Let California Ring as chair of its national advisory board and tried to set himself up to serve its staff as a kind of messaging coach. But the group never managed to accomplish the type of mass persuasion that Wolfson and others had envisioned upon its launch. "For more than two years, leaders of Let California Ring met with major national funders, who nitpicked the plan and invested only enough to keep the program running at a level incapable of reaching a critical mass of Californians," Thalia Zepatos would recall. Cash surged in once Proposition 8 was headed to the ballot, but by then it was too late to do anything novel with it. In Santa Barbara, three of four local organizers—assigned to stage house parties where supporters could talk to their neighbors about marriage—were redirected in February 2008 to work on a "Decline to Sign" drive encouraging voters not to add their names to the ballot petition.

That summer, Freedom to Marry seconded its entire seven-person staff to work full-time in support of Let California Ring, but circumstances had converted it into a more conventional political operation. Lawyers scrapped existing canvassing and house-party scripts because it would be impossible to keep them free of election-specific content controlled by campaign-finance regulations. When a statewide ad buy for the "Garden Wedding" ad was finally placed, in August, it was a year behind schedule and could not include an explicit appeal to vote no. The project of broad and gradual opinion change had been again subsumed by the urgency of defeating an amendment.

By the fall of 2008, Wolfson was resigned to trying to manage the stories that would be told about the vote's outcome, whatever it turned out to be. Let California Ring had spent much of its $15 million budget trying to influence black, Latino, and Asian voters, and a distorted snapshot of their behavior could doom future efforts at coalition-building. Wolfson enlisted three political scientists to prepare an explanation of exit polls' deficiency—they have an especially unreliable record in sampling racial and ethnic subgroups—and issued a "media advisory" warning the press not to overinterpret from them. The advisory went largely unheeded. On election night, exit polls indicated 70 percent of African Americans had backed Proposition 8, shaping an early postelection narrative about its passage: black voters, surging to the polls to support Barack Obama, had given the initiative its margin of victory.

The Let California Ring leadership again turned to the academics to marshal a competing set of evidence. Using precinct-level election returns and Census data, Egan and Hunter College political scientist Kenneth Sherrill delivered the conclusion Wolfson had been looking for: the exit polls had dramatically inflated African American support for Proposition 8. (A simultaneous postelection survey by David Binder, commissioned by Freedom to Marry, showed it was still a healthy majority, at 58 percent.) Race and ethnicity were, Egan and Sherrill found, only the fifth most significant variable in predicting individual-level vote choice on Proposition 8, behind party identification, ideology, religiosity, and age. Wolfson later credited the report, published by the National Gay and Lesbian Task Force Policy Institute, with helping "finally put to rest the misconceptions that had been stirred by one bad piece of data."

Wolfson recalled Let California Ring in halcyon terms, and worked to salvage it from the wreck of Proposition 8 as a usable past. After the amendment passed, Let California Ring's leadership commissioned a largely unskeptical assessment of its work by an outside consultant. The report pointed primarily to election results in Santa Barbara for evidence of Let California Ring's impact: in the only county in Southern California where the amendment failed to get a majority, opinion had shifted a total of twenty-four points since the 2000 vote on Proposition 22. (Support for same-sex marriage among voters under the age of thirty had moved nineteen points when the "Garden Wedding" ad first aired, with no movement in Monterey, a demographically similar county cited as a point of comparison.) The retrospective look at Let California Ring cued an alternate history of how campaigners could go about moving opinion on marriage if not perpetually distracted by the need to contend with emergent crises. "One of the lessons from that effort appears to be the importance of having conversations about marriage *before* the heat of the campaign," explained a report commissioned by the Equality California Institute.

In Somerville, Wolfson's claim that Freedom to Marry could successfully coordinate such work nationwide finally persuaded those who had resisted it for years. The blessing he received, and the extent to which it redirected the movement's big donors, made Wolfson much harder to ignore. "It gave Evan a higher stage to stand on," says Charlie Rounds, who represented the Kevin J. Mossier Foundation in donor meetings. "He was taken more seriously, and had a national organization that could clearly articulate a strategy."

Relaunched to take on this expanded role, Freedom to Marry's budget subsequently quadrupled, to about $12 million annually. It spun off from Astraea and established entities that would permit it greater reach into state and federal politics. (With both 501(c)3 and 501(c)4 divisions, the new organization would have the legal status to lobby officials and communicate with voters about issues.) Staff grew from five to fifteen. The new jobs had titles typically reserved for candidate campaigns or party committees: a field director, a political director, an online organizer. "There is little track record for success on this issue at the ballot box," read a memo drafted by Freedom to Marry's campaign team. "Everyone engaged in these campaigns needs to be committed to constant inquiry, experimentation, and course correction—and to being part of a multi-state community of marriage campaign experts."

Yet even though he had set up Freedom to Marry to be on a permanent campaign footing, Wolfson waved away the first chance he had to rush into one. In August 2009, he stepped into the internal debate within California's gay-rights movement and took the side of Equality California, which was arguing that activists should plan to take an initiative to the ballot in 2012, rather than rushing for a 2010 vote preferred by the Courage Campaign. "Equality California's plan to win is not a call to 'wait,'" Wolfson wrote in an August blog post. "It is a call to action, and the work is at hand now."

Even as the new Freedom to Marry launched, Wolfson plotted its extinction: the group would commit itself to go defunct once same-sex marriage was available to Americans nationwide. "Freedom to Marry is not going to engage in mission-creep," Wolfson said. "We're not going to pretend we're doing things we're not. We're not trying to claim we're everything everyone wants. We're not asking people to give us all the money that needs to go to everything we care about. We have said we are a focused campaign to win the freedom to marry and then go out of business."

In early 2010, Freedom to Marry publicly released its "Roadmap to Victory," a simplification and translation of the national strategy. Alert to the value of producing it in a form that could be easily communicated and shared online, Freedom to Marry rendered it as a schematic map showing three roads that converge on the destination of "Marriage Nationwide."

Winding through the center of the map was a road marked "Win More States." Accompanying text laid out that the strategy was agnostic about whether those victories were ultimately delivered by legal or political authorities, but was clear about a benchmark: the thirty-four states that had ended bans on interracial marriage by the time *Loving v. Virginia* reached the Supreme Court in 1967. Internally, Freedom to Marry would track progress on a single-page "Summary Landscape" whose design was cribbed from activists pursuing a national strategy for abolishing the death penalty. Their movement operated under a comparable logic: move enough states away from the practice such that the Supreme Court could eventually be persuaded that the country was ready for a uniform policy. Freedom to Marry's document featured a five-by-seven grid, the matrix of thirty-five squares representing a combination of local factors that could impact the nature and size of the organization's investment there. The first version identified short-term political interests in thirty states, plus the District of Columbia. There was work to do nearly everywhere, including in states where a win was far off but the conditions were right to commence a public-education campaign.

Another thoroughfare traversing the roadmap was labeled "Advance Federally," with a goal of legislative repeal of the Defense of Marriage Act or its invalidation in court. The final road was "Build a Majority," to be measured in national polls that could be supplied to policymakers, up to Supreme Court justices, who might fear otherwise that they were moving too quickly. "There is a strategy that is affirmative, not reactive," Wolfson told *Gay City News*. "Much of the movement's work historically has been reactive and even opportunistic. People go where they see the options, the opportunities, but aren't necessarily laying the foundation for the win they want."

In October 2010, he found himself in New Haven, back at the site of one of his earliest political victories. In 1976, as a college junior and speaker of the Yale Political Union, Wolfson had led his side to victory in the first debate ever between the union and the Yale Debate Team. Arguing that President Gerald Ford did not deserve reelection, Wolfson and his two partners "verbally abused their opponents in a heated, two-hour debate," the *Yale Daily News* reported at the time. On his return to the Yale Political Union, he would face off against another Yale alum, Maggie Gallagher of the National Organization for Marriage, whose career had unspooled as a foil to Wolfson's. Yet they had interacted only incidentally, and then solely at the instigation of a third party, such as when their dueling essays were packaged back-to-back in the 2004 anthology *Same-Sex Marriage: Pro and Con* or a television booker invited them to appear together. Although shortly after launching Freedom to Marry Wolfson had sought out Gallagher's longtime colleague David Blankenhorn with a lunch invitation, he and Gallagher presented themselves as so intellectually unbending that it was impossible to imagine the two even collegially breaking bread.

It was unusual for the Yale Political Union to have nonstudents speak, but the guests were welcomed like family: Gallagher had chaired its Party of the Right, while Wolfson belonged to the rival Liberal Party. (The two never overlapped at Yale; he graduated just as she was being admitted.) Their debate was framed in the form of a rhetorical proposition: "Resolved: Same-Sex Couples Should be Allowed to Marry." As the two sat at the same end of a table on the stage, a student introduced them and said that Wolfson and Gallagher "have worked against each other in the political sphere for years now."

Over many of those years, that work had amounted to little more than a kind of performative shadowboxing, as only recently had either come into enough real political power to truly challenge the other. Yet at the time Wolfson gained his institutional authority, Gallagher walked away from hers. That spring she had stepped down as president of the group she had founded, vowing to remain active on the board of the National Organization for Marriage as she completed a book about same-sex marriage. "I've never had a desire to run a large political and activist organization," Gallagher told a journalist, explaining her departure. "I don't think it is particularly my gift." Wolfson had just been granted his.

For Better or for Worse

In 1831, as he observed the unique standing the Americans afforded the lawyers within their midst, Alexis de Tocqueville observed that "there is hardly a political question in the United States which does not sooner or later turn into a judicial one." Same-sex marriage had begun as a purely judicial question, and for a time gay-rights activists had rejected most efforts to pull it into the political realm. The Defense of Marriage Act, the Federal Marriage Amendment, the jumble of state bans—each was portrayed as an assault on a cardinal constitutional value: that minority rights should not be subject to majority rule.

The presence of "Build a Majority" among Freedom to Marry's objectives quietly altered that. For a while, marriage advocates had taken for granted that long-term trends worked in their favor—whether driven by organic opinion change or generational turnover—and that their impact would be felt in states that became more hospitable to same-sex marriage. But, already pressed for resources necessary to mount local fights, marriage strategists had never prioritized national opinion change for its own sake. They had been transfixed by the analogy to interracial marriage, when the Supreme Court decided that what had been a purely state issue needed to be reconciled to a federal standard. Around the time when *Loving v. Virginia* came before the Supreme Court, only 20 percent of Americans supported marriage between blacks and whites; 73 percent told Gallup that they disapproved.

While it still represented the view of constitutional attorneys that civil liberties should not be a popularity contest, that high-mindedness was no longer useful as a political tactic for winning marriage. At the Jersey City meeting the value of majority consent was a matter of some dispute, never properly resolved by participants but deemed incidental to the strategy as a whole. "Some of us believe that a majority of Americans will have to support ending the exclusion, and that half the states will have to have already given full legal protections to same-sex couples before we'll successfully be able to get federal help. Others believe either or both of those thresholds may be lower," read a footnote in the "Winning Marriage" paper. "We all agree that some critical mass of public support higher and more engaged now will be necessary."

By then, any path to change the law in two-thirds of the states narrowed, and a show of broad popular support became even more imperative. "The legal profession and judges in particular may be ahead of America on civil rights and sexual orientation. If the Supreme Court believes that despite the somewhat slow pace of political change, the country as a whole is ready for marriage, we may be able to persuade it to act when half the states or a little more still don't allow either marriage or full partnership," Coles wrote in the revised Somerville paper released in early 2010. "Above all, this strategy depends on building something more than a simple majority of Americans in favor of marriage. At a minimum, to act, the Court would have to believe that a strong majority of Americans not only supported marriage, but believed that denying it is deeply wrong."

To reach national support above 50 percent, Freedom to Marry would have to dramatically stretch its map. It would begin aiming to move opinion in places, from Massachusetts to Idaho, where any change in state marriage laws was unlikely. Nowhere in the Old Confederacy did Freedom to Marry see any obvious return to state-level political work, but even a small and gradual increase in acceptance of gay marriage there would be felt in national polls. It would also require new range, pushing into moderate states where the public might be receptive but that had been previously neglected because political leadership appeared unfriendly. "They underestimated New Mexico in part because they underestimated our ability to hold off the legislature," says Mary Ellen Capek, a volunteer lobbyist for Equality New Mexico.

At the same time, Freedom to Marry would have to expand its lexicon to speak about same-sex marriage outside an explicitly political or legal context. "I love lawyers, but their mental framework is not useful in a political environment, particularly when you want something from someone," says Phyllis Watts, a clinical therapist and organizational psychologist who advised the No on 8 campaign. "Most human beings don't think in terms of rights. They think in terms of fairness, which is very different."

When gay groups did conduct polls or focus groups to test whether they could win over the broader public, they often ended up working from language originally aimed at judges and politicians. Finding it unconvincing to voters, campaigns instead articulated reasons to vote no: opposition to the specific terms of a ban, to the idea of amending a constitution, to the fact of political intervention or its circumstances and timing. Not only were gay activists being defeated when marriage appeared on the ballot, but such cautious, circumstantial messaging prevented them from intelligently "losing forward," as Evan Wolfson described it—using political conflict to build up support. "We were just constantly recovering from attacks," says Thalia Zepatos, whom he hired to serve as director of research and messaging for the relaunched Freedom to Marry. "We are raising and spending millions of dollars every couple of years. If we don't use some of that money to start to introduce who gay people are, we are never going to build."

Zepatos had come by her cynicism the hard way. A straight woman with the loose, upbeat charm of a field organizer, Zepatos had been active throughout the 1990s in the near-permanent campaign that Oregon's left had waged to beat back a series of antigay ballot measures at the city, county, and state levels. The constitutional amendment that qualified in 2004, Measure 36, was seen nationwide as the most beatable of the year's state-level marriage bans. Although her side was on the defensive, Zepatos saw in the debate's subject an area favorable to gay rights. "Talking about whether or not a gay person could sit at a desk somewhere near you and in an office was one thing," she says. "Whether the love between two people who are the same gender could actually be as valid and recognized in the society as the love between straight couples seemed to me a much more fundamental question."

But Zepatos never saw those themes reflected in the No on 8 campaign's communications. While observing the campaign's focus groups, Zepatos had tallied every time a participant had mentioned "love" in discussing marriage. Yet when she insisted to pollster Celinda Lake that "love is really an emotion we should be talking about," Lake rebuffed her, arguing that such sentiment was likely to turn off heterosexuals who already felt distant from, even squeamish about, gay relationships. Lake, who had previously advised the coalition formed to defeat Proposition 22, instead cited surveys showing that far higher numbers of Californians oppose amending the constitution on principle than support expanding marriage. "But they have done it like five hundred and twenty-eight times!" Zepatos says, exasperatedly. "I mean, if we polled on whether the price of gas was too high and they agreed, would we go out and print literature that said, 'The price of gas is too high, so vote no on this amendment'?"

The resulting rhetoric from No on 8 reflected that apprehension, only sporadically invoking gay people and never the love between them. ("Leave our constitution alone," began the tagline in one No on 8 ad.) Zepatos saw the culprit in a cycle of uncreative opinion research and message development, a path that led many campaigns to keep harping on those same themes. "If you ask thirty questions on a poll and none of the questions talks about love or commitment, you're never going to get a good-testing message that includes that," says Zepatos. "You've already created a bias by the questions you've included on your polling."

After the vote, Zepatos headed north back to the state that had nurtured her initial interest in marriage advocacy. There she drafted the "Groundhog Day" memo impugning the way the Proposition 8 campaign had been waged, in ways both large and small. She shared a draft with Wolfson, whom she had first met on the Let California Ring project. Wolfson signed on to Zepatos's memo and offered her a job overseeing the relaunched Freedom to Marry's "research and message shop" despite the fact that her experience was in other parts of campaigns. "I came out of field organizing, but no matter how many people you train and deploy to go canvassing, if you can't figure out your message, you are dead in the water," she says.

In her new role, Zepatos immediately began pushing grant money to the group Basic Rights Oregon—just over $100,000 in 2009 alone—to turn Oregon into a "laboratory state" for Freedom to Marry's research agenda. She was especially eager to collaborate with the Analyst Institute, a secretive Washington outfit that worked with progressive campaigners (including, at the time, the Democratic National Committee) to administer field experiments, a then-novel technique that one of its clients dubbed "prescription drug trials for democracy." It could develop protocols to randomize delivery of Basic Rights Oregon's direct mail and canvasser visits, and eventually cable television ads. When paired with placebo treatments, like similar contact with a message about recycling, analysts could use polls to track which voters actually changed their opinions and behavior after seeing it.

Zepatos would likely have two years to show results from all the research, as Freedom to Marry's internal planning documents from 2010 identified no goal more immediate than laying "the groundwork that will result in at least one state repealing its anti-marriage constitutional amendment by 2012." She divided that two-year period into different research tracks. She would dedicate the first full year, 2010, to finessing the positive: What language should gay activists deploy when discussing marriage? If legalistic arguments failed to change minds, how should campaigns pitch marriage equality for same-sex couples? Was it even possible to discuss gay romance without provoking what some called "the ick factor"? The following year, 2011, would be devoted to what stood as the bigger puzzle: how to respond to the opposition's negative messaging, especially as it involved children. "Once we have got an answer to question A," says Zepatos, "then we can figure out the answer to question B."

Her first step, in November 2009, was to commission from Oregon-based pollster Lisa Grove a "deep dive" on all available polling data about attitudes toward marriage. Grove compiled seventy-five different surveys, focus groups, and academic studies that had been conducted for ballot campaigns and legislative efforts. Zepatos hoped the report would assimilate that scattered knowledge into a benchmark of shared assumptions, common conclusions, and outstanding hypotheses.

To test them, Zepatos established the Marriage Research Consortium, bringing together the entities doing some of the most adventurous work on the subject outside of election cycles, to avoid duplication and build intelligently on one another's findings. Among them were nongay organizations like the Washington think tank Third Way, which had been formed during George W. Bush's presidency in part to make centrist Democrats comfortable taking progressive positions on social issues. "Just having somebody outside the movement come in who had very little stake in what had been done before and say, very abruptly, 'That's not working.' That was a shock to the system, also very controversial," says Third Way's Lanae Erickson Hatalsky. "There were plenty of people who were like, 'We've been working on this for our entire lives. What do you know about it? And why should this straight organization have anything to say about it?'"

Third Way had pioneered the use of new tools to plumb for otherwise unspoken hangups that stood in the way of support for gay marriage. In 2006, think-tank officials sought out a Boston firm that specialized in what it called the Zaltman metaphor elicitation technique, in which a psychologist conducts intense one-on-one interviews with subjects for up to two hours each. The process had not been applied to politics before; its greatest success was leading Goodyear to develop ads with a baby sitting in a tire after people said they associated the product with keeping families safe. Attendees were told to come to the interview for Third Way bearing pictures from magazines that represented gay people to them. One brought a photo of sushi because it was "icky." Another had an image of a costumed Dalmatian on the basis that, as one Third Way staffer recalls the rationale, "it's just kind of weird when people put sweaters on their dogs." As they assembled collages, interview subjects repeatedly evoked a journey of some sort—some imagined it ending with rainbows and unicorns, others off a cliff into a lake of fire—but the metaphor was "consistent across people that were more hostile and people that were less," says Erickson. "We're all kind of walking this path together and figuring out where this goes."

Few campaigns had the time, budget, or imagination to undertake such studies, but Zepatos wanted to cultivate them, and enlisted Watts as the consortium's in-house psychologist. Watts had begun working alongside campaign operatives while serving as an organizational consultant to Planned Parenthood's California affiliate, which in 2003 sought her advice on how to beat back a referendum that would require parental notification for teenagers seeking abortion. Watts advocated some basic changes in the lexicon—"end of pregnancy" instead of "abortion"—to minimize the use of what she called "triggering" words that provoked a fight-or-flight response. "Most human beings want to see themselves as a good person. They want to practice the values they have. Even if they're not doing it consciously, they want to do it right by others. It's a very delicate motivation and can be easily overwritten when the amygdala is strongly activated," says Watts. "At that point, the capacity to take in any other messaging is completely obliterated."

The consortium embraced input from such unusual sources and eschewed some of the nationally prominent pollsters whose research had shaped responses to the Defense of Marriage Act, Federal Marriage Amendment, and Proposition 8. "Most people don't vote based on analysis, no matter what they say. They vote on their feelings," says Watts. She proposed that instead of asking, *Why do you think gay couples shouldn't be able to marry?* pollsters should frame their query in a way that summoned a less rational response: *Should gay couples marry? What does that mean to you?*

Zepatos inaugurated the consortium's work by standardizing survey questions, so that voters across states were being offered the same question and set of choices. (Some previously used polls, for example, gave respondents the option of preferring civil unions, while others presented support for marriage as a purely binary question.) To compel adoption of the standards, major donors, including the Civil Marriage Collaborative and members of the Cabinet organized by Tim Gill, decided they would include it as a condition of their new grants, along with the requirement that any research they funded had to be shared through the consortium. "That also gave us some leverage," says Ineke Mushovic of the Movement Advancement Project, which had branched out from merely its auditing function as the "Gay IRS" to produce reports that would shape how activists discussed touchy subjects like marriage. "Part of the reason we got organizational participation in things like our messaging work was because people saw us as a representation of the funders."

The monthly calls that Zepatos hosted from her home in Portland, with consortium members and a rotating cast of pollsters and consultants who regularly worked with gay groups, represented a rolling exploration of what exactly it meant for a person to be persuadable on marriage. In a 2009 project for Third Way, Greenberg Quinlan Rosner drafted a long questionnaire to identify those currently opposed to gay marriage but willing to reveal ambivalence about that position or an openness to rethinking it. The next month, Third Way released a memo that summarized the findings. Thirty percent of the national electorate backed full marriage rights, constituting a "pro-equality base." Twenty percent composed the base on the other side, firmly against any legal status for same-sex couples. In between were those amenable to some recognition short of marriage, and free of obvious antigay attitudes. This group was more likely to be older, female, married, and religious. It leaned slightly to the right ideologically but was split evenly among two parties, and composed 46 percent of the country. (The figure varied surprisingly little by region: a bit higher in the Northeast, only slightly lower in the South.) Two-thirds had a close friend or family member who was gay. Third Way called them the "moveable middle."

The research showed a lot of empathy in those who, at least at the moment, opposed same-sex marriage. "We needed to not demonize people that had been in a bad place before," says Hatalsky, "because they were on a journey." Thirty-eight percent of the "moveable middle" said that their views toward gays and lesbians had grown more accepting over the previous decade. (Less than 10 percent said the opposite.) "Their opposition to certain equality measures is not based on bigotry, hatred, or homophobia, but rather stems from more nuanced and answerable concerns about tradition and change," Erickson and two colleagues wrote in a memo summarizing their research. "Most importantly, they respond to, or are repelled by, different arguments than those that appeal to or repel audiences that are considered the base on either side."

Trying to probe those arguments in artificial settings like focus groups was a particular challenge for a researcher, Grove liked to observe, as structured conversations related to gay issues followed a predictable course. Three things would always happen, she quipped: someone would say "feather boa," another would mention *Will & Grace*, and participants would discuss their hairdressers. "There's psychological distance of not understanding how gay people work, no sense that they were living the same lives, had the same goals and aspirations," says Grove.

She decided to adjust her methods over a series of four Portland-area focus groups for Basic Rights Oregon. Grove invited voters who told callers they supported civil unions or domestic partnerships for gay couples but not marriage, yet when they arrived for the sessions the moderator never mentioned anything related to homosexuality. Instead they asked participants what marriage meant to them. There were jokes again, this time about "the ball and chain," followed by knowing laughter. But then people spoke with sentiment about their own marriages, or those of people close to them. Sitting behind glass with a legal pad, Zepatos made hash marks next to the words that came up often: *love, commitment, responsibility.* She came to think of it as the language of vows: *For richer or poorer, for better or for worse.* "Even people who had been divorced or were unmarried or didn't want to get married, there was this real common idea about what marriage meant," Zepatos reflected. Something about the institution remained "aspirational," as Grove liked to say.

The focus-group exchanges inspired Grove to add a new series of questions to her polls for Basic Rights Oregon. "Why did you and your spouse get married?" her survey takers would ask, or "Why do couples like you get married?" Seventy-two percent of respondents chose the option "to publicly acknowledge their love and commitment to each other." But when those same Oregonians were asked why they thought "same-sex couples would choose to get married," barely one-third agreed that the same aspirations applied. Instead, a plurality of 42 percent chose "for rights and benefits, like tax advantages, hospital visitation, or sharing a spouse's pension." Twenty-two percent said they didn't know why gay couples would want to marry.

The language formulated by lawyers had run its course, Grove argued. Voters saw the core element of marriage to be commitment between two people, before their community, not the combination of discrete benefits and responsibilities that had often been itemized by those demanding equal treatment under the law. At the same time, she found, it was ineffective to speak of equality—nongay Americans just didn't buy that gays and lesbians were "just like you"—but persuadable voters did respond to the notion of fairness. The underlying doctrine that most shaped their views was not a constitutional one, but the "Golden Rule" of reciprocity. Simon called it *Christian Lite*. "Heart first, then head," Grove advised.

Money Talks in New York

That was sad. What's next?

The five-word email he had sent to one of his political aides on December 2, 2009, was quintessential Tim Gill—a quick pivot from emotion to action, with only a brief pause for sober assessment of the options. Gill had been monitoring a roll call of the New York state senate, as it considered a bill to legalize same-sex marriage. For years, he had directed cash to legislators in an effort to build a majority, yet when the issue had finally come for a roll call in the upper chamber, a cascade of late votes seemed to all go the other way. What had succeeded so remarkably in Iowa—deploying a small amount of money to quietly displace problematic politicians and count on friendly Democratic leadership to hold the line—had not worked in New York, and likely never would. "The murky, transactional world of Albany had thrown the national gay funders for a loop," Freedom to Marry's incoming campaign chief, Marc Solomon, would later reflect on the episode.

Yet Gill never considered retreat. For some of his peers, the matter was personal; a few members of his Cabinet of top donors, including Henry von Ameringen, either lived in New York or had substantial interests there. There was a broader interest at play, as well. With matters at least temporarily stalled in California, New York stood out for its unique strategic value as home to "the core of America's power," as Matt Coles noted in the revised "Winning Marriage" paper.

Gill dispatched Bill Smith, the Alabama Republican who had helped establish his political operation, as his point man in Albany. As deputy executive director of the Gill Action Fund, Smith had executed the "punish the wicked" strategy in Iowa in 2006, helping to replace marriage obstructionists in the legislature and make its Democratic leadership indebted to gay donors for their majorities. By the time the Iowa Supreme Court ruled in favor of same-sex couples in early 2009, the state's elected leadership had been already conditioned to acquiesce. The day the decision was issued in *Varnum v. Brien,* Democratic leaders of the statehouse and senate issued a joint statement indicating that they would not allow a constitutional amendment to move through their chambers.

In New York, strategists had to get the legislature to move proactively because, starting in 2004, state judges had rejected every case in which they could have asserted a constitutional right for gay couples to marry. Sympathetic governors and attorneys-general had shepherded the cause as far as they could through their executive powers, ensuring that New Yorkers who married elsewhere would be treated as wed under state law. (By the middle of 2009, the only neighboring jurisdictions where gay and lesbian New Yorkers couldn't secure a marriage license were Pennsylvania and New Jersey.) In 2003, the New York State Democratic Committee endorsed gay marriage with a unanimous voice vote. The party's next nominee, Eliot Spitzer, ran in 2006 on a promise to deliver marriage equality as governor—the first successful gubernatorial candidate anywhere in the country to win with such a platform. The next year the state assembly, where Democrats maintained dominant majorities, voted to let same-sex couples marry, but saw the bill die in the more closely split senate. In 2008, Spitzer was succeeded by David Paterson, a liberal Manhattanite whom gay-rights advocates saw as even more committed to the objective.

Paterson introduced his own marriage bill in early 2009, but the one-time senate minority leader could not get it through his old chamber. That December, the bill failed by a margin of 38–24. Republicans were unanimous in their opposition, joined by eight Democrats, a motley bunch stretching from older white men representing upstate rural districts to religious blacks and Latinos from New York City's outer boroughs. "There had been no fear on the part of the Senate Democratic leadership or individual lawmakers about doing the wrong thing," wrote Solomon. "In fact, there was incentive to keep the donors hanging—and investing—as long as they could before they passed a bill and national gay donors put their attention elsewhere. It was time to engage in bare-knuckle politics, with the single-minded purpose of getting thirty-two senators to vote for the marriage equality bill."

Marriage advocates knew which members they needed to win over, because Empire State Pride Agenda had decided to push ahead with the senate vote even when it was clear the bill stood no chance of success. It was an unusual maneuver, as most lobbyists would refrain from showing opponents the weakness of their position and exposing their own allies to unnecessary humiliation. But the roll-call vote presented a blueprint to dismantling the opposition and building a senate majority. "Nothing matters but the path to thirty-two," Smith told allies. "We'll cut the path through whoever's backyard we've got to go through."

Discreet suasion would not work this time. Smith launched a political action committee with the intentionally pugnacious name Fight Back New York, and began polling in opposite ends of the state in search of vulnerable legislators. In both Buffalo and a Hispanic corner of Queens, voters were asked whether learning that their state senator "was being targeted by wealthy homosexual activists for his vote against gay marriage" would affect their support for him. (The polls showed the source of opposition funding mattered little to voters.) In those districts, Fight Back New York set out to topple sitting Democrats in their 2010 primaries, even though so doing risked handing a tightly divided senate to Republicans. "My objective is to benefit as many people as possible, and so I wanted to do that in whatever way that was the most efficient and legal," says Gill. "The objective is to win. So you win on the issue that works for you."

The group attacked Democrat Bill Stachowski for having cast votes against funding mammograms, and Hiram Monserrate over criminal charges that he had beaten up a girlfriend. In the district of one Queens Republican who had billed taxpayers $3 million for office supplies, Fight Back mailers joked that "Frank Padavan's paper clips must be made of gold." It was no secret who was behind it all. In robocalls, Stachowski's campaign rebutted "the innuendo spread by an out-of-state single-issue organization," while Padavan called his tormentors "insidious" for obscuring their true motive for spending $150,000 to defeat him. "Their primary issue was same-sex marriage," he complained to a reporter. "They never even mentioned it."

Fight Back New York dispensed nearly $800,000 across the three districts, making it the biggest player among independent groups in state politics, and succeeded in retiring an incumbent senator in each. Unlike in Iowa, where Gill and his advisers were ambivalent about publicly taking credit for their victories, they were now hungry for media coverage. "This is the first time we're going to name names and say, 'We're coming to get you because you're against marriage equality,'" Smith told *Politico* that December in an article detailing Fight Back New York's operations. "Well-funded gay rights groups will seek to make support for same-sex marriage as mandatory in blue America as allegiance to the Second Amendment is in red America—and to make opposition just as politically suicidal," the publication predicted.

Those successes won the admiration of another on the ballot that fall. Despite a conservative wave nationwide, Democrat Andrew Cuomo defeated hapless first-time Republican candidate Carl Paladino by nearly thirty points in a race that was never competitive. Like his predecessors, Cuomo entered office as a gay-marriage supporter, although activists did not necessarily count him as committed to the cause in the same way as Paterson or Spitzer. A former official in Bill Clinton's cabinet, Cuomo was viewed as a cautious politician from the centrist school of Democratic politics, where gay marriage remained perhaps too far out an issue on which to define a career. He was also one with known ambitions to seek the presidency. Furthermore, the governor's political reputation had long been tied to acts of alleged gay-baiting during his father Mario's two campaigns against Ed Koch—the subject of anonymous "Vote for Cuomo, Not the Homo" signs and mailers. When Cuomo said in his first State of the State address that "we believe in justice for all, then let's pass marriage equality this year once and for all," activists had reason to be skeptical that it would be a priority.

Yet less than two months later, Cuomo summoned gay leaders to Albany to declare he was ready to move forward on the Marriage Equality Act. The governor was known as a canny and ruthless tactician, and before making a legislative push he required commitments from his would-be collaborators. Cuomo insisted that gay leaders work in tandem with his team and demanded assurances that they would not push for another vote, as they had in 2009, unless they agreed there was the support necessary to win. When it came to lobbying the legislature, Cuomo assured those gathered in the executive chamber on March 9, "I will be personally involved."

Cuomo's guests were particularly impressed when he told them he was placing Steve Cohen, the secretary to the governor known as his "number two," in charge of accomplishing the goal. It was an unprecedented commitment from a political figure who had a lot to lose, even (and perhaps especially) if the bill ended up becoming law and he became associated with the issue nationally. Cohen laid out a strategy in which a lobbying effort run out of the governor's office, along with personal efforts by the Catholic governor to tranquilize New York City's politically influential archbishop, would be paired with an aggressive outside game to mobilize pro-marriage constituents to show their support.

The costly mix of activities lent itself perfectly to the campaign model that the reborn Freedom to Marry had been chartered to manage. While the next two calendar years were almost certain to be free of ballot conflict, Evan Wolfson did not want to let them pass without measurable gains. In 2009, gay couples had begun to legally marry in Iowa, New Hampshire, Vermont, and the District of Columbia, in the final three jurisdictions earning the right through political processes rather than the courts. But even as gay-marriage activists found progress elsewhere in 2010—Argentina, Portugal, Iceland, and parts of Mexico all legalized same-sex unions that year—there was little in the United States. A historic Republican landslide at nearly every level of government that November further restricted the statehouses in which incremental advances toward civil unions or domestic partnerships would be available. As 2011 approached, Freedom to Marry identified securing marriage rights in two new states among its internal goals, an accomplishment seen as essential for keeping donors and activists engaged, and to demonstrate to media and political elites that there was a viable strategy at work. As the year began, the best targets appeared to be Maryland and Rhode Island, left-leaning states where voters had defied a national wave by electing socially liberal governors. Freedom to Marry set out to back full-bore legislative campaigns in Annapolis and Providence, but marriage bills in both capitals petered out. "We hadn't had a state win in more than a year," Solomon lamented afterward.

Waiting until the following November for its next victory would carry a cost. Freedom to Marry had just opened its first Washington office, staffed by a bipartisan retinue of lobbyists, to push Congress to pass a bill repealing the Defense of Marriage Act. Given Republican control of Capitol Hill, any real progress for the bill was unlikely, but Freedom to Marry was hoping to use 2012 to move Democrats fully into its fold. The nearest firm objective was getting the Democratic National Committee to include a same-sex-marriage plank in its platform at the convention that summer—with hopes that the sitting president renominated there couldn't stand aslant his party on such a prominent issue—and markers of political momentum were crucial to convincing party bosses that it was a worthy election-year gamble.

Wolfson leapt at news of a 2011 push in Albany. From the first time it compiled a Landscape Summary grid, in February 2010, Freedom to Marry had classified New York a "Tier One" state—one of six where "win marriage" was the "Next Major Goal." But ever since Freedom to Marry's Roadmap had enshrined "Build the Majority" as an objective unto itself, donor investments had been redirected toward the aim of pushing national opinion even if detached from short-term policy movement. By that measure, even an ongoing fight in the New York legislature could produce benefits that redounded far beyond the state's own borders. It was a venue where local political developments were more likely to gain national attention by dint of New York City's status as the country's media capital, and a point of entry into the national business community.

In the month after Cuomo made his commitment, Freedom to Marry brought the Human Rights Campaign and Empire State Pride Agenda together as equal partners. By mid-April the three groups had signed a memorandum of understanding; each contributed $250,000 to fund New Yorkers United for Marriage, which formally introduced itself on a late April conference call with gay media and progressive bloggers. Throughout it all there was an implied threat from Gill Action—"a critical player but preferred working behind the scenes," according to Solomon—of electoral retribution that would be delivered by gay donors onto any legislator who crossed them.

"The gays worked together, which had never happened before. I will not say that they checked their egos at the door; but they at least acknowledged they had them and that sometimes they get in the way," reflected Assemblyman Danny O'Donnell, an openly gay Manhattan Democrat who had introduced marriage legislation in 2007 and 2009. "That was a major improvement from previous years."

Even so, a united gay community was worth little when facing an obdurate Republican senate majority. For guidance on that front, the Gill Action team sought out Ken Mehlman, the former Republican National Committee chairman and manager of George W. Bush's reelection campaign, who had publicly acknowledged his homosexuality in August 2010, years after beginning a second career in Manhattan as a private-equity executive. ("I can't change the fact that I wasn't in this place personally when I was in politics, and I genuinely regret that," he told *The Atlantic* then, when asked about his silence as the president ran as a booster of the Federal Marriage Amendment.) The next month, Mehlman headlined a large fundraiser for the American Foundation for Equal Rights, which had formed to support a federal challenge to Proposition 8 on constitutional grounds. "As someone who regrets very much not being involved, and not being on the right side of this important effort until recently, let me just say this," declared Mehlman. "This will be my first but not my last event."

Mehlman led Smith and Solomon to Elliott Management, a large hedge fund whose headquarters near Central Park doubled as a new-style political clubhouse. Unbeknownst to Mehlman, Elliott's founder, Paul Singer, was harboring his own secret: one of the nation's largest Republican financiers was also giving copious amounts to gay causes.

He had started supporting them when his twenty-one-year-old son, Andrew, came out on a family trip to attend the 1998 World Cup. Singer first backed charities designed to support and protect gay children and students; when Andrew went to work for the National Gay and Lesbian Task Force, Singer had his foundations send checks there, too. Initially all the contributions were anonymous, out of deference to Andrew's concern that his father's other affiliations would prove an unwelcome distraction. Singer was especially sympathetic to the cause of marriage—even proposing to conservative leaders that they try to outflank Democrats by embracing it as a matter of freedom—but put off by a movement's reliance on the courts. "I think it was a better idea to convince people, or to at least do things democratically—through direct votes or state legislatures—not by imposition," says Singer.

Mehlman's decision to come out helped inspire Singer's willingness to go public with his patronage, just as Andrew's September 2009 nuptials in Massachusetts forced him to reconsider the merits of marriage litigation. "While court edicts are not the best way to effect major social change, you've got to weigh alternatives," he says. Singer agreed to host a fundraiser at his Upper West Side apartment, but the event (which raised $1.2 million) was so quickly oversubscribed that it had to move to a nearby hotel. "Good and honorable men and women who do not hate gay people oppose gay marriage, and it would be foolish of us to pretend such a large social change of such a large and vital institution would not elicit some opposition," Singer told attendees. "We may disagree with it, but our task is to deal with skeptics with patient persuasion."

Months later, New Yorkers United for Marriage offered him the chance to do so. Smith and Solomon explained that they had gone as far as possible on Democratic support alone. A marriage bill would likely require four Republican senators, and Gill Action's lobbyist had a list of those considered gettable. But even before that, the senate leadership would have to decide to let it reach the floor. To that challenge, Cuomo brought little sway, and might even find that his association with the issue proved counterproductive: the legislative opposition might be reticent to grant the new governor such a big early win. New York City mayor Mike Bloomberg had already offered his support, but—as a former Democrat who had abandoned the Republican Party to run for his third term as an independent—he had little credibility as a partisan. Singer, however, could not only help finance a strategy to win over legislators but could speak to them as one of their own. Singer committed $425,000 and pledged to help raise the rest of a $1.2 million budget that would be devoted to securing Republican cooperation.

In early May, Singer welcomed senate majority leader Dean G. Skelos and his deputy Tom Libous to the same conference room where just one week earlier he had strategized with Cuomo's advisers. At Singer's side were a pair of other well-known investors, Daniel Loeb and Cliff Asness, and a representative for a third, Steven A. Cohen, the head of SAC. Invitations had gone out to thirty-two Wall Street figures to join Paul Singer's project to win over Republicans on marriage. The three who accepted and made six-figure contributions to New Yorkers United for Marriage, one Singer adviser acknowledged, were "Paul's friends." (A fourth, David Tepper, signed on shortly after.) Singer had arrayed them in his conference room for their unique persuasive power to Republican legislative leaders, who he knew were more likely to welcome arguments from gay-rights activists if they came as heterosexual business leaders with otherwise right-of-center beliefs.

Singer presented Skelos a "pitch book" that his own staff of Republican operatives had assembled with help from Mehlman. Singer's team would go to commission district-by-district polling from Skelos's own preferred pollster, John McLaughlin, showing that none of the swing members would jeopardize reelection by voting for a marriage bill. Other polls showed a majority of New Yorkers supported gay marriage, and demographic change amounted to an inexorable trend. The longer Republicans waited, Singer argued to his guests, the more painful it would be to stand on the wrong side of the issue. The law prohibited a quid pro quo, and so Singer sketched a scenario of "risk mitigation." If Skelos let a marriage bill reach the floor that summer, without pressuring members how to vote, he and his fellow donors were committed to offering them cover. Because they were Republican donors who had established a long-term interest in the party's control of the legislature, Singer argued to the two senate leaders, they could be trusted to do what it took to make sure that they didn't lose their majority. "It had to be a Republican strategy," says Singer aide Margaret Hoover, "to help the Republicans who wanted to get to yes."

On May 11, O'Donnell introduced a version of the 2009 bill that had failed so spectacularly. Over the next month, New Yorkers United spent

$2 million on a combination of mass media and grassroots organizing in targeted districts, and on June 13 Cohen told an Albany radio station that "the votes are there on both sides." It was a bluff—Cohen had counted enough senators who had gotten to maybe but not yet to yes—designed to shift pressure back to Skelos. "The question is not just whether the Republicans will allow it to go to the floor, but whether senators will be allowed to vote their conscience."

The senate was due to head into recess, but Republicans began a week of meetings about how to proceed. As they did, on June 15 three Democrats from New York City's outer boroughs who had voted against the 2009 bill announced in tandem that they now backed the Marriage Equality Act. At a press conference with Cuomo, two expressly cited the results of communication from constituents, much of which had been coordinated by New Yorkers United for Marriage. One, Joseph Addabbo Jr., explained that in his Queens district nearly three-quarters of those who had contacted his office in 2009 had expressed disapproval of same-sex marriage. This time, 4,839 of 6,015 were in favor. "In the end, that is my vote," Addabbo said. The same day, James Alesi—a Republican from Rochester who had publicly agonized over his vote against the 2009 bill—came to Cuomo's office and confided that he was ready to vote yes. Two days later, another Republican followed Alesi's lead, leaving the bill's supporters with thirty-one of the senate's sixty-two members on their side.

Now any member who contemplated being next would bear the weight of knowing he or she would be characterized in perpetuity as the person whose decisive vote brought gay marriage to New York. As such, the few remaining Republicans who had signaled openness to it could no longer imagine hiding in the crowd from possible recriminations, but also found themselves with exceptional leverage in negotiations with Cuomo's office. "There was an extreme national push to put a religious exemption into the bill," said Katherine Grainger, an assistant counsel to the governor, who feared that codifying a religious exemption could undermine other existing antidiscrimination laws. "We have a very strong state constitution and we were trying to add to that by passing the Marriage Equality bill. We were trying to build on New York's civil rights protections, not undo them."

Amid negotiations with wavering Republicans, Cuomo agreed to include a provision to clarify that religious institutions and clergy could suffer no civil or criminal sanction by refusing to participate in same-sex marriages. It was unusually structured as a "reverse-severability clause," specifying that if a court deemed any part of the religious-liberty measure unconstitutional the entirety of the marriage law would be automatically invalidated. To gay-marriage supporters, it felt like a political concession to opponents on the cusp of defeat and threatened to leave a hard-won marriage victory exposed to a legal sideswipe. (Theoretically, a court could invalidate the marriage law just by determining the religious exemption to be unnecessary.) "Did I love it? No," O'Donnell reflected months later. "But I knew politically what needed to happen in the senate was that if you were to get people to change their votes, you had to give them a reason, something to hang their hat on."

Still, Cuomo and his outside allies had to convince senate Republicans to even let the matter come up for a vote. Skelos could protect his members from having to take a difficult vote, although with the risk of having the entire party labeled obstructionists by blocking a measure that had majority support from the public and the backing of a popular governor who had run on the issue. At the same time, failing to use every mechanism available to beat back gay marriage could expose moderate Republicans to challenges from within the right. Under New York's idiosyncratic electoral code, being seen as willful collaborators would not mean just conservative primary opponents but general-election trouble, as well. The independent Conservative Party vowed to defeat any Republican who voted for gay marriage, and certainly had the means to make itself a spoiler for the party's candidates statewide.

When Mehlman and Hoover, the Singer aide well-known among conservatives from her work as a Fox News commentator, went to lobby Republicans in Albany, they were surprised to find individual senators uninterested in their high-minded rationales for the bill. Philosophical appeals to the underlying conservatism of marriage, claims that progressive civil-rights laws were essential to maintain New York's economic standing, or conjecture about the issue's utility to the party's long-term competitiveness all fell flat. "You're either there or you aren't, and if you are you're just trying to figure out how you can vote for it and survive," says Hoover. "Ultimately all they wanted to do was survive the vote."

For a week Republicans debated among themselves how to proceed. Skelos brought together his caucus for a nine-hour debate behind closed doors, eventually succumbing to the external pressure to bring the marriage bill to the floor and let his members follow their conscience without pressure from the party. "The days of just bottling up things, and using these as excuses not to have votes—as far as I'm concerned as leader, it's over with," Skelos said afterward.

Ultimately Stephen Saland was the final of four members of Skelos's party to defect, explaining that he had always "defined doing the right thing as treating all persons with equality." There were now four Republicans who would cross over to join the growing majority, giving each just enough cover that no one of them could be pegged as the single deciding vote.

"How do you feel?" Cuomo asked Alesi as he entered the senate chamber just after the Marriage Equality Act passed with thirty-three votes and hours before he would sign it into law, after being shuttled back quickly through the assembly. "Feels good, doesn't it?"

Public opinion was always incidental to the legislative strategy. From the outset of the Fight Back New York campaign, polls showed more than 50 percent of New Yorkers supported gay marriage. They then had to convince politicians who always kept an eye on reelection that it was in their narrow self-interest to follow along. "The funny thing was, two years ago we voted no because we had to—it was a political ploy," Alesi told the *Albany Times Union.* "But two years later we almost had to vote yes. The politics of it are pretty clear. There would have been a significant amount of money."

A Grave Price

At 11:49 p.m. on the night of Friday, June 24, 2011—less than ninety minutes after the New York state senate passed the Marriage Equality Act and six minutes before Governor Andrew Cuomo would sign it into law—Maggie Gallagher responded with a six-paragraph screed loaded with telegrammatic portentousness. "New York Republicans are responsible for passing gay marriage," Gallagher wrote on the *National Review* website. "The party will pay a grave price."

It was a threat that sounded increasingly hollow. The sudden emergence of the Proposition 8 fight—and the unique demands of qualifying for the ballot in the largest state in the country—had forced the National Organization for Marriage, just months old, to rush into action back in 2008. After the California success and the controversy over the Miss USA pageant, fundraising took off, from just under $3 million in 2008 to just over $7 million the next year. But the organization was unprepared for its immediate growth. "This required us to put on hold many plans for NOM's institutional development and infrastructure improvement," the body's leadership reported to its board in 2009.

The $20 million goal it set that year for a "victory fund" proved too ambitious. After seeing sizable increases over the three years after its founding, peaking at $9.5 million in 2010, the group's revenues began to slide, falling off by $2.4 million over the next year. Much of the decline could be attributed to the Knights of Columbus pulling back and routing gifts through the United States Conference of Catholic Bishops, which launched an Ad Hoc Committee on Defense of Marriage. In the summer of 2010, the bishops conference launched a new initiative to convince both clergy and laypeople that marriage was "unique for a reason," but its committee had another that made it appealing to donors: as part of a church it was not required to publicly disclose the sources of its funding.

The financial advantage that had long boosted those fighting same-sex marriage was slipping away. At the same time gay organizations increased their ranks of contributors, the National Organization for Marriage was struggling to sustain even its most reliable sources of money, thanks to a combination of its own poor administration and opponents' success in stigmatizing its work.

Gay activists had succeeded in making it "socially unacceptable to give huge amounts of money to take away the rights of one particular group," as California activist Fred Karger had put it when he launched his California Against Hate "Dishonor Roll." While some of his most prominent boycott targets, like hotelier Doug Manchester, did not back down from their support for Proposition 8, those worried about their reputations with investors or consumers dreaded controversy. When Karger announced a boycott of Bolthouse Farms, whose namesake founder had donated $100,000 to pass Proposition 8, the private-equity firm that owned the Bakersfield company quickly approached him to make the protests vanish. (Karger had already picketed gourmet supermarkets in Los Angeles, New York, and Washington to discourage purchases of Bolthouse's carrot-based smoothies and dressings.) Karger was able to extract from the company a total of $110,000 in gifts to gay causes, including Equality California and the Los Angeles Gay and Lesbian Center, which the investors understood could freely transfer the funds to the No on 8 committee.

After the election, Karger became obsessed with documenting "the Mormon power grab" that many in the gay community blamed for Proposition 8. That February, he went to Salt Lake City to announce a boycott of the Ken Garff Automotive Group, which operated fifty-three car dealerships across six states, from its Utah headquarters. The matriarch of the Garff family had given $100,000 to Protect Marriage the closing weekend of the campaign, but her son was eager to dispel the taint of antigay politics. It took three weeks for Karger to negotiate a settlement that ended his boycott: Garff made $100,000 in contributions to gay and lesbian causes in Utah and agreed to extend partnership benefits to same-sex couples among its employees.

Karger's successful method for draining his opponents' resources stood in contrast to major gay groups, which had never treated the boycott as a favorite tactic. (The Human Rights Campaign preferred to brandish its leverage over the private sector by offering to add companies to its Corporate Equality Index rather than delivering threats.) But as the Supreme Court's *Citizens United* decision opened up new channels for corporations to spend freely on campaigns, Karger's example proved a model to online rabble-rousers who no longer needed national organizations to mediate their activism. In the summer of 2010, lefty activists pushed Target to repudiate a $150,000 donation the Minneapolis-based company had made to MN Forward, an independent group formed to marshal corporate support for Tom Emmer, the Republican candidate for governor. The non-gay group MoveOn.org collected 240,000 signatures on an anti-Target petition, and another forty-four thousand people expressed support for a Facebook page calling for a boycott. Emmer was a fairly conventional Republican politician, but activists latched onto his support for a constitutional amendment to define marriage as grounds to depict him as an ideological outlier. The backlash, and threat of a nationwide boycott, led the big-box retailer's chief executive, Gregg Steinhafel, to deliver an unusual message to employees saying he was "genuinely sorry" for having sanctioned the gift in the first place.

As he launched a "Mormongate" website to map the church's subterfuge in passing Proposition 8, Karger had grown increasingly savvy about using regulatory agencies to aid his work. Upon seeing that the LDS Church had reported spending only $2,078 on its Proposition 8 advocacy, he filed a challenge with California's Fair Political Practices Commission. The church responded by revising its expenditures upward—to $189,903.58, all through noncash, in-kind contributions—but Karger kept pressing his case. Noting the church's well-documented campaign activities targeted voters beyond its own membership (which it was not required to disclose), he alleged that Yes on 8 had amounted to a "money laundering" operation for Mormon leaders. Karger bragged that the state had never before fined a religious group for illegal activity, and his quest to unmask the extent of the church's involvement won Karger national attention. (In the summer of 2010, the LDS Church settled with the commission by paying a fine of just over five thousand dollars. At the time, it disputed Karger's claim that it had misrepresented its spending, conceding only that over the campaign's final two weeks it had "overlooked the daily reporting process.")

The National Organization for Marriage, which Karger—who in 2010 renamed his organization Rights Equal Rights to reflect its interests beyond

California—repeatedly called a "Mormon front group," could measure the cost of such aggressive advocacy. Gallagher labeled Karger's website "part of a broader personal campaign to harass, threaten, and intimidate members of the LDS church who exercise their core civil rights." NOM executive director Brian Brown accused Karger of leading "the charge to take away people's livelihoods and punish them for personally supporting marriage."

It was the same cry of persecution that had animated the "Gathering Storm" ad and Carrie Prejean's utility as a spokeswoman. But while that theme may have appeared likely to drive secular moderates to fear the illiberal effects of gay marriage, it was likely to spook the type of religious-minded donors that the National Organization for Marriage needed to cultivate to grow its fundraising base. "Every dollar you give," assured one NOM fundraising message, "is private, with no risk of harassment from gay marriage protesters." Another appeal attested that "donations to NOM are NOT public information."

A cross-country "Summer for Marriage" bus tour staged by NOM kicked off in the middle of July 2010. It was similarly overshadowed by the opposition. At the second stop, outside the Rhode Island statehouse, gay-rights activists crashed Brown's speech and drew attention to an otherwise lackluster spectacle. NOM personnel documented the fracas online, as evidence of their courage and the unreasonableness of their opponents. (According to the *Providence Journal,* there were 150 rally-goers and 175 counterprotesters.) "I've never seen anything like I saw in Providence," Brown said days later in Madison, Wisconsin. "Those of you that know what marriage is are going to have to take a stand. It's not always going to be easy, there are going to be difficulties in the way. But we can't allow those that disagree with us to make us ashamed or frightened for speaking up for these truths."

But over the course of the twenty-three-stop tour—primarily at state capitals chosen to impress legislators or judges—the ratios of attendees grew increasingly imbalanced. In multiple cities, as few as twenty people showed up for the opportunity to hear Brown and Gallagher speak, in some instances a small fraction of the gay-rights activists who had gathered to challenge them. "With our depressing turnout in Ohio, what else is there to do than to turn the attention to the couple hundred counter protestors who showed up?" Louis J. Marinelli, a NOM employee who drove the tour bus and documented it on social media, later wrote after a dismally attended event at the statehouse in Columbus. "Why couldn't we get a good turnout even in a busy section of downtown? A plurality of the country opposes gay marriage; I see how adamant they are, how deeply they believe in traditional marriage every day on the Internet. Where are these people?"

Once the marriage debate returned to Albany in 2011, the National Organization for Marriage revealed itself to be a depleted force. When the Cuomo administration made its push to pass the Marriage Equality Act, opponents first attempted to mobilize its supporters to block the vote altogether. "There is no reason the Senate should even vote on this bill. Marriage belongs to the people of New York—not just 62 senators under intense pressure from donors, activists and lobbyists," Brian Brown wrote in an email blast with phone numbers for seven Democratic and Republican legislators. "Please call every senator on the list below and urge them to oppose the same-sex marriage bill and instead support a referendum that would give the people of New York the right to vote on marriage."

By the time Gallagher wrote her late-night screed, it had become clear that her organization had been powerless to match Freedom to Marry in the legislative arena. Senators were now more fearful of what they would lose by crossing the Gill donor network than the religious coalition represented by the National Organization for Marriage.

Even before the first same-sex couples could legally marry in New York, Brown laid out a strategy for rollback there. The plan had three phases stretching over four years, ending with passage of a ballot measure in November 2015. To get there, a constitutional amendment had to pass both legislative chambers in consecutive sessions, which meant that NOM would have to "elect pro-marriage majorities" in both the 2012 and 2014 elections. "A 4-year process seems like a long time—and it is—but it's achievable," Brown wrote. "In New Hampshire and Iowa, they've had same-sex marriage for just 2 years, but are already well on the way to reversal."

It was a generous description of the situation in those two states that Brown's group had designated back in 2009 as priorities because of the crucial role they would play in choosing the next Republican presidential nominee. Even though in 2010 Republicans took back the Iowa House of Representatives, with their new majority quickly passing a constitutional amendment that would effectively overturn the court's mandate, they couldn't push the state senate to take it up—and had no obvious mechanism to pressure Democratic legislators in the way that Marriage Equality New York had proven able to do with Republicans.

Without a legislative path, NOM decided to make an example of the Iowa Supreme Court justices whose unanimous decision in *Varnum v. Brien* had mandated same-sex marriage in the first place. Three of them, including chief justice Marsha Ternus, faced a retention election in November 2010, typically a perfunctory exercise. The votes were held every eight years, on a staggered schedule, and past elections had come and gone without Ternus truly realizing her job had been on the ballot. The National Organization for Marriage ultimately spent over $700,000 in Iowa, partnering with the Family Research Council on a bus tour across forty-five counties and television ads attacking the court for judicial activism. (Karger, naturally, filed a complaint with the Iowa ethics commission over what he claimed was the group's insufficient disclosure of its finances.) "It sends a powerful message," Brown told the *New York Times* a month before the vote, "that if justices go outside the bounds of their oaths, if the justices go outside the bounds of the U.S. and state constitutions they're going to be held accountable."

The gay political networks that had been so effective in turning the Iowa legislature largely stood down. After all, when Tim Gill's operatives had talked about rewarding friends, he had been thinking of politicians, not judges. Facing a conservative electorate in which Democrats were likely to lose the governorship and were in jeopardy of seeing the entire legislature flip, Gill's strategists knew their goal had to be holding at least one chamber as a bulwark against a renewed push for repeal. "We put some very symbolic, or small, amount of money into protecting the judges and we put a lot of money into protecting the senate," says Bill Smith, the group's deputy executive director. "There had to be a calculation because we didn't have the resources to do both."

That left the judges exposed. They were backed for retention by the Iowa Bar Association but only halfheartedly campaigned for their own jobs. "They thought, as we did, that it was unseemly, that it would change the judiciary and impressions of the judiciary in Iowa," says Ternus, who delivered only a handful of speeches to civic groups in which she stressed the value of keeping the court immune from political pressures. "The last thing we want is to act like the politicians that they erroneously said we were."

For the National Organization for Marriage, the defeat of Ternus and two colleagues amounted to an act of lavish vengeance, a belated show of supremacy in a one-sided political contest that would have no impact on the legal status of marriage in Iowa and appeared unlikely to have the intended effect of intimidating judges elsewhere. But it did reveal an enduring advantage of the right. When they could take the debate to the people and make it about marriage, they knew how to win.

Campaign in a Box

The ad that appeared for the first time on CNN on Valentine's Day of 2011 could be mistaken for a consumer marketer's opportunistic holiday rebrand—perhaps a life-insurance company aiming to warm its image or a mattress chain trying a more abstract pitch. A sequence of couples, a mix of races and ages and both gay and straight, sat before a black background with a buoyant soundtrack. They riffed on the duration and meaning of their marriages, in the most anodyne terms possible. "I would just say love is love . . . it belongs to everybody," one woman said, before a closing frame with the identity of the sponsor: Why Marriage Matters, with the tagline "Love. Commitment. Family."

For the first year after its relaunch, Freedom to Marry had existed largely behind the scenes, angling to insinuate itself in other institutions and refine the tactics they would one day use to win marriage. So even when it went public with this ad, whose national reach reflected the new strategic goal of "building majority support for marriage," it did so under its new brand. (The campaign was initially to be called "Marriage Matters," but a religious group in the Midwest already used the phrase for its own communications, so the initial adverb was added—to match the title of Evan Wolfson's 2004 book, which he was able to trademark.) The Why Marriage Matters logo included a heart and stylized house, the symbolic embodiment of what Freedom to Marry staff characterized as their shift from "rights-based" to "value-based" messaging.

They had already rejected what might be called a science-based message. Over the course of 2010, Thalia Zepatos and her Marriage Research Consortium had explored the possibility of developing a public-education campaign that would elucidate the biology behind homosexuality. It would have amounted to an empirical case for the proposition that gays and lesbians were, as in the title phrase of the February 2011 single by Lady Gaga, "born this way." The pop ubiquity and anthemic durability that attended the song's release—Gaga would go on to perform it at a Super Bowl half-time show—attested to the resonance of once-obscure ideas about the persistence of genetics. When Gallup first asked, in 1977, about the basis for homosexuality, only 12 percent of Americans said it was "something a person is born with." By 2011, that share was closing in on half the population, tracking upward with education levels. Polls showed a high correlation between that belief and support for same-sex marriage, although the causality was not clear. ("Less tolerant folks may simply be using the idea that being gay is a choice as a justification for prejudice," Lisa Grove ventured in her meta-analysis of research.) Zepatos backed off the idea of a born-this-way message only when research demonstrated the extent to which parents already had anxiety about whether their young children might already be gay, and could be turned off by a political message that suggested their genes were responsible.

With the new focus on "love and commitment," Wolfson bragged that his organization had begun to " 'crack the code' with Middle America," and he made the fruits of that research available to others working on the issue. The group offered up what it called a "campaign in a box," including a variety of prepackaged videos—one of a straight African American couple with a gay son, the other a white lesbian pair dreaming of marriage—that other groups could edit into their own broadcast or digital ads. Freedom to Marry also offered grants to state organizations that agreed to sign a partnership agreement so they could relaunch their websites under the new slogan "Why Marriage Matters." With these small investments, Freedom to Marry was essentially purchasing options on future ballot measures in a range of states, in 2012 or potentially well beyond. If local partners began to believe the moment was right to formally launch a campaign, Freedom to Marry would already have enough of a stake to help shape whether to proceed and the subsequent process and strategy.

The first state to land on Freedom to Marry's 2012 calendar, however, was not one that it had chosen. Strategy documents had identified Minnesota as a second-tier priority, where activists should be "laying the foundation" for results down the line. Despite the state's generally liberal disposition—Minnesota had the longest streak of giving its electoral votes to the Democratic presidential nominee of any in the country—it remained a tricky place for marriage work. Local dockets were haunted by the long shadow of *Baker v. Nelson,* the 1971 lawsuit by a University of Minnesota couple who ultimately followed their case to the U.S. Supreme Court, where judges turned away their appeal with a cryptic one-sentence dismissal.

It became harder to suppress grassroots demand for marriage after the state supreme court in neighboring Iowa changed its laws in early 2009, luring Minnesotans for weddings there even though the commemoration would have little legal impact on their lives. One Twin Cities couple— who had already enshrined their relationship in Vermont, California, and Canada—decided to push ahead with a lawsuit at home, relying on advice from a small circle of friends who had organized themselves as Marry Me Minnesota. Established gay-rights groups kept the couple at a distance, with the same caution used to counsel delay in other states. In this case, that caution was coupled with the *Baker v. Nelson* precedent, which added an additional level of jeopardy. "If they reaffirm that decision, there's a danger that they do it strongly. The danger is huge and the chance of success is small," Amy Johnson, the executive director of OutFront Minnesota, the state's dominant gay-rights group, told Minnesota Public Radio.

When a Hennepin County judge relied almost exclusively on *Baker v. Nelson* in dismissing the suit, it raised the stakes on pursuing an appeal upward to the Minnesota Supreme Court. "There are both legal and political reasons to believe that this lawsuit is a very risky roll of the dice," Dale Carpenter, a gay University of Minnesota constitutional-law professor, warned in the summer of 2010. "To the extent that this lawsuit fuels dissatisfaction with the incumbents and anyone else supportive of gay marriage, it will actually set us back politically."

That November, amid a national right-wing wave, Republicans had retaken both of Minnesota's legislative chambers. It marked the first time the party had control of the state's lawmaking organs since the introduction of partisan elections nearly forty years earlier. Party leaders quickly rolled out an agenda that reflected national priorities for conservative legislators, with one addition given new salience by the lawsuit lingering on an appellate docket. They put forward a pair of constitutional amendments: one that would require voters to present photo identification before casting a ballot, and another to define marriage as between a man and a woman. While legislators had passed a DOMA-style bill in 1997, repeated efforts between 2004 and 2009 to enact a constitutional amendment had failed.

That changed in 2011. The new Republican majorities quickly voted to put the question before voters at the next general election: "Shall the Minnesota Constitution be amended to provide that only a union of one man and one woman shall be valid or recognized as a marriage in Minnesota?"

Governor Mark Dayton held a ceremony to veto the bill. The event had no legal consequence—a constitutional amendment did not require a gubernatorial signature, and the veto message conceded the action was "symbolic"—but it offered an early sign that Minnesota's Democratic officials would run toward the conflict. On June 6, Minnesotans United for All Families formed; the following week, Dayton attended its first public fundraiser. (Marry Me Minnesota pushed ahead with its lawsuit even as the amendment moved toward the ballot, potentially superseding any court ruling.) With the amendment scheduled to appear on the November 2012 ballot, Minnesotans United was in for an especially long, arduous, and costly campaign.

The first polls showed the amendment already on the cusp of passage, with 49 percent of those surveyed in favor and 43 percent opposed, even as amendment backers had yet to take their most striking arguments before the public. "One of our big vulnerabilities in terms of raising the money needed to win was people just writing us off and thinking that we'd lose," says Richard Carlbom, who was hired later that summer as the Minnesotans United campaign manager. "Our arguments to donors and funders was Minnesota is different because we have eighteen months, and every other state had six months."

Carlbom was a thirty-year-old whose formative political experience had been his two terms as mayor of St. Joseph, a small town near St. Cloud. "Serving as an openly gay elected official in greater Minnesota enabled me to gain a first hand knowledge of how LGBT people are viewed by their fellow citizens outside of the metro area," Carlbom wrote in the cover letter he submitted along with his job application. "Further, it proved to me that personal relationships and individual conversations are a powerful force when breaking down homophobic barriers." Afterward, Carlbom became communications director to St. Paul's mayor and a campaign manager for Congressman Tim Walz, an Army veteran who had held on to his seat in a largely rural patch of southern Minnesota during the conservative wave of 2010. "A Democrat who knows how to be in a Republican district," Carpenter, the law professor who served as treasurer of the Minnesotans United executive committee, says of Carlbom. "He just blew us away."

At his presentation to the committee, Carlbom detailed three concentric circles of individual interest. There was concern for the self, for one's friends and family, and beyond that for the community. Past marriage campaigns had suffered because they connected too often with voters in the outermost circle, Carlbom ventured, and even then did so weakly. When trying to reach those who lacked a personal stake in gay families, they used legalistic arguments about protecting the Constitution; by invoking children, opposition messages to those same people landed in the friends-and-family ring. "We need to figure out how to speak to enough voters to make this issue personal even though they are not gay," Carlbom told the committee. "How do we get voters to understand that this is actually about inherently who they are?"

Yet before being hired by Minnesota United, Carlbom had never worked on a gay-rights campaign. After he got the job, Zepatos presented Carlbom the full dossier assembled by the Marriage Research Consortium, the corpus of post–Proposition 8 inquiry that he came to call "the treasure trove." At the same time, he received a list of political operatives whom Freedom to Marry recommended he hire. Carlbom's entire team of consultants and vendors eventually came from that list, and he gave Zepatos a place on the campaign's "core research team," along with a seat on the steering committee. With an ideal collaborator in place, says Zepatos, "there was no choice for us but to defend."

A slow-building eighteen-month campaign would be conducive to Zepatos's research timetable, but her colleagues did not want to wait until late 2012 to tally their next victory. (Advice to state activists considering their timetable nearly always emphasized that it was preferable to have voters consider a marriage question on the same day they picked a president. Quadrennial elections had far wider participation, typically younger and less conservative.) Already committed to backing a Minnesota effort with an initial estimated budget between $9 and $11 million, Freedom to Marry's strategists were skeptical they could afford to take on any other ballot campaigns that year. "Question 1 in Maine cost our side $5 million," asserted a memo by Zepatos and her colleague Marc Solomon about the merits of heading to the ballot in 2012. "Legislative battles in such states of proportionate size would cost significantly less."

Armed with new ideas after victory in New York and unwilling to wait a year and a half for the vote in Minnesota, the two were spoiling for another fight with the National Organization for Marriage. Rather than going on the offensive, to a venue where it could gain marriage rights, Freedom to Marry picked one where it could accomplish nothing greater than shielding them. There were five states, along with the District of Columbia, which strategy documents classified as ready to "Defend, Document, and Showcase." Two were marked in italics as demanding urgent defensive work in 2011. In Iowa, "after a two-year onslaught of unanswered opposition attacks, public education is sorely needed," according to an internal memo, while in New Hampshire, Republicans who had just retaken control of the legislature had begun to float the idea of repealing a two-year-old marriage law.

On May 15, 2011—exactly one month before the Marriage Equality Act would come up for a vote in the New York state assembly—Freedom to Marry and the Human Rights Campaign filed with authorities in Concord to establish a new nonprofit, Standing Up for New Hampshire Families. The plan was to create an outlet in the region into which momentum from the victory in New York could be shifted. National media and donors, especially the pro-gay Republicans recruited by Paul Singer, were already paying close attention to New Hampshire, where the next January their party would begin the process of selecting a challenger to Barack Obama. Once again, Freedom to Marry and the Human Rights Campaign signed a memorandum of understanding to share ownership of the new New Hampshire–based entity, and Solomon set to work hiring a campaign manager and lobbyists to staff it.

The state's gay leaders had endured enough legislative battles that they did not relish another. Volunteers had created the New Hampshire Freedom to Marry Coalition in 2001, after neighboring Vermont had struggled through its marriage debate. (The coalition had adopted the name years before Wolfson willed his national organization into being.) That year it was called into action to fight legislation that would prohibit New Hampshire officials from recognizing couples who had secured civil unions across the border. The group set its sights lower than its name might suggest; the goal was to "pass legislation that grants same gender couples the rights and responsibilities of marriage in NH," as one strategic document put it. As Massachusetts and Connecticut became the primary New England marriage battlegrounds, the New Hampshire activists struggled to raise money in the smallest increments, eventually securing a $5,000 grant from the Gill Foundation in 2001, and another $5,000 the following year from HRC to conduct a statewide poll. In 2005, when it began seeking larger amounts through the Civil Marriage Collaborative, New Hampshire's was unusual among small-state marriage groups in that it had a full-time staff member even though its budget was under $50,000.

Despite its amateur origins, the New Hampshire Freedom to Marry Coalition had helped secure the votes for civil unions in 2007, for marriage two years later, and to get Governor John Lynch to see the 2009 law as one of his major accomplishments. All could be credited to the type of low-key lobbying that tends to thrive in a state with a massively oversize and underprofessionalized legislature. Now, after taking back both chambers of the legislature in 2010 with staggering majorities, Republicans—who had never given up on unwinding Lynch's law—were trying anew. Since the governor would never entertain repeal, lawmakers proposed a constitutional amendment that would have to go to voters to become law.

The coalition posture, both publicly and privately, was one of dismissiveness toward the proposed amendment. Coalition leaders cited a new poll showing 62 percent of New Hampshirites opposed repeal of the marriage law, including 38 percent of Republicans. "Voters overwhelmingly say their number one concern is the economy. Yet lawmakers," said executive director Mo Baxley, naming the amendment's two Republican sponsors, "would rather pursue a fringe agenda that hurts New Hampshire families." Even if Republicans could secure a majority of votes for repeal in both of the legislative chambers they controlled, they were unlikely to land on the supermajority needed to override the governor's certain veto or the three-fifths to place the question on the 2012 ballot. (It would then require two-thirds of voters to ratify the constitutional amendment.)

Unlike in New York, local activists for same-sex marriage did not acquiesce when the national organization arrived, asserting its desire to direct strategy in the state. Freedom to Marry was promising an injection of cash and expertise in exchange for control, but taking the repeal attempt so seriously would amount to a gift of unearned credibility for opponents who thus far lacked a plausible strategy of their own. "This isn't going to happen," says Baxley, herself a former state representative. "Of course you're going to show up at the hearings, of course we're going to call our legislators, but this isn't going to be the million-dollar fight and let us not make it a million-dollar fight and let us not even entertain the thought of constitutional amendment."

Faced with such truculence, Wolfson decided to pull support for the local group, and other members of the Civil Marriage Collaborative followed its lead. After working for five months without salary, Baxley quit her job, blaming Freedom to Marry's desire to generate a false sense of urgency in its pitches to donors. "We were going to do the work," she says, "but don't alarm the community and don't go to California and tell people we're going to have marriage repealed in New Hampshire, which is not true." The amendment never passed either chamber of the legislature.

Freedom to Marry had been more circumspect about the fiefdom it was building in neighboring Maine. Activists there had been among the first to accept the offer to enrobe themselves in the Why Marriage Matters flag, the trauma of 2009 having made explicit the failures of the existing approach to messaging. Shortly after the vote, No on 1/Protect Maine Equality's largest donor, hedge-fund investor Donald Sussman, had bankrolled a research program under the nonprofit auspices of Gay & Lesbian Advocates and Defenders to assess the options before it. "The first question when I got to Maine was like, 'What are we going to do? Are we going through the legislature? Are we going to go to the voters?'" says Matthew McTighe, whom GLAD hired in 2010 to run the Sussman-funded effort. "I determined really quickly don't even fuck around with the legislature. Because even if we did win again, they were going to go to the ballot. So, one way or another this was going to go end with the voters."

There was little agreement, however, that 2012 would be the best year to do so. Many movement leaders were cynical about the ability of Maine's small gay community to support such a quick turnaround, aware of the unique risk involved. A second ballot defeat, in such quick succession, could sour the state's political elite on the appeal of gay rights for years to come. "That was really hard to sell at first because at the time we'd never won," says McTighe, a onetime Republican congressional staffer who had previously served as HRC's political director for the New England region.

McTighe rebranded the public-education campaign that would begin this work as Why Marriage Matters Maine. (The national organization contributed $12,000 to help launch a website for its new state affiliate.) He integrated Freedom to Marry's content and branding into materials that would supply a purposely inefficient petition drive to qualify for the 2012 ballot. Instead of dispatching canvassers to places where liberal voters were densely packed, like college campuses, field director Amy Mello directed them toward areas where residents were likely to have supported the people's veto in 2009. Signatures would be harder to collect, but it offered a pretext to initiate conversations with the type of voters any amendment campaign would have to win over. "We knew that it was going to be a vessel for education and we knew that it was going to be a great media opportunity," says McTighe.

When McTighe decided to go public with his team's work, in late June, he scheduled a press conference in Lewiston; the city was chosen because it was the largest to have rejected gay marriage in the 2009 referendum. McTighe stood off camera as the head of Equality Maine announced plans to begin collecting the 57,277 signatures that would be required to qualify a marriage question on the ballot, although she did not commit to a campaign. "As a pastor whose faith has been the guiding force throughout my adult life, I had a very traditional view of what marriage meant," said Reverend Michael Gray, of the United Methodist church in Old Orchard Beach, who had been given the symbolic task of requesting petition forms from state authorities. "But over time, as I met more gay and lesbian couples, including some who are active in my parish, I came to learn that gay people are no different from me."

On September 20, McTighe joined one of the Marriage Research Consortium's regular calls. Like Carlbom, he had devoured its research and had hired his consultants from among Freedom to Marry's recommendations. Why Marriage Matters Maine had emerged as a model of the type of coaching relationship that Freedom to Marry hoped to establish with state activists. Already consortium findings had done a lot to shape the messaging of the public-education phase, most visibly the unusually prominent profile afforded to Gray, a mild-mannered minister whom McTighe hoped to feature in television ads with his wife, elaborating on their ambivalence about gay marriage.

Zepatos shared her own progress. She was in the midst of a "simulated campaign," volleying fictive ads to 7,500 voters randomly selected for online focus groups to emulate the "give-and-take" of a real election season. Now in the second round of such tests, Zepatos believed she and Grove were close to isolating broadcast themes that could successfully "inoculate" voters against the kids-and-schools ads that were certain to confront any campaign for gay marriage. "By the end of the year," says Zepatos, they expected to be "satisfied that we had messages that were resonating."

McTighe lived under the same deadline. Even once his team collected the necessary signatures required to qualify for the ballot, however, he did not plan to submit them immediately to the secretary of state along with a demand for another referendum about marriage. Turning in the completed petitions would effectively start the clock on a countdown toward the ballot. By holding them back, Why Marriage Matters Maine could continue interacting with voters, piling up signatures that would identify future supporters, while spending freely (without public disclosure) as a charitable entity engaged in public education to recruit volunteers. It could not, though, go on forever; by January, McTighe would force Why Marriage Matters Maine to set the pace of its march forward. "In terms of persuasion, are we changing the hearts and minds in time for 2012," asks McTighe, "or are we talking in '16 or even '20?"

Land Rush to the Ballot

In October 2011, Thalia Zepatos and Marc Solomon summoned representatives from the national groups and funders who had signed on to the revised 10-10-10-20 Plan to join a conference call for a "special strategy session." There were six states where marriage could find its way onto the ballot the following year—on offense in Maine, Maryland, Oregon, and Washington and defense in Minnesota and North Carolina. It was time to decide which of the embryonic campaigns in those states Freedom to Marry wanted to continue to nurture, and which it needed to starve.

The presidential election year would be rife with competing financial priorities for movement donors: there would be Barack Obama's reelection, and the candidacy of Wisconsin congresswoman Tammy Baldwin, who was hoping to become the first-ever openly gay senator, ideally as part of a Democratic capture of the chamber—one that could ensure Obama was able to confirm judges deferential to gay rights. (The Human Rights Campaign had already signaled that these federal priorities would take precedence within its budget.) Furthermore, there remained a smattering of local races—reelecting New York Republicans who had swung yes, guarding a Democratic majority in Iowa—considered crucial to the protection racket Gill Action promised state legislators who took risky pro-gay votes.

Freedom to Marry responded to the crowded marketplace by rationing resources. State affiliates seeking to develop an online presence under the Why Marriage Matters banner could apply for grants, but Freedom to Marry would not pay to drive traffic to the new websites. Communications staff would remain committed to developing media coverage about active-duty military and veterans seeking to wed, but pull back from a proposed "Business Leaders for the Freedom to Marry" coalition. Anyone looking to house an opposition-research effort aimed at discrediting the National Organization for Marriage, despite media interest in identifying its financial backers and their ties to religious institutions, would have to go elsewhere.

These were difficult decisions for Evan Wolfson, who had envisioned his organization being a hub for all the gay-rights movement's activity around marriage. He had always been forced to play a two-faced role in his advocacy on the topic. In public, Wolfson was the nation's loudest cheerleader for the endless potential of the marriage-equality cause; in private, a stern coach of restraint.

As it had in Hawaii years earlier, victory in New York begot grand expectations. Couples were able to marry just hours after the state senate voted to change its marriage laws, and the ensuing pageant of summer-time nuptials—the bill's passage happened to coincide with Pride Month celebrations—drew activists nationwide to see possibilities in the political process. The joy transmitted from New York was a delayed offset for the despair brought on by Proposition 8's passage, and received outsize attention in part due to celebrities able to broadcast their personal involvement on social media. (They extended beyond the Hollywood figures who had been active around Proposition 8, to include masculine archetypes like New York Rangers forward Sean Avery and chefs Mario Batali, David Chang, and Tom Colicchio.) Support from business leaders and the bipartisan vote in Albany held out the promise that the formula was reproducible even in more politically moderate states.

When participants in the strategy session reviewed the states where political activity around marriage was under way, the biggest problem appeared to be the new outbreak of irrational enthusiasm that movement institutions would be unable to satisfy. "People started seeing momentum and projecting momentum that we can win in a whole lot of states," says Zepatos. "It was like an Oklahoma land rush, with people popping up to start campaigns, but we still had donors who were very cautious."

Zepatos had Freedom to Marry's pollsters draft a memo detailing the benchmarks it would consider as part of a "viability assessment" for any prospective ballot initiative. Before supporting a campaign, Freedom to Marry would demand evidence of majority support for the idea of same-sex marriage that stuck even when voters were subjected to the opposition's messages. It also insisted on a plurality of at least 40 percent who continued to prefer expanded marriage rights when pollsters presented a third option of civil unions. The memo set a distinct goal of 40 percent describing their support as "strong," with that figure higher than the number of strong opponents—meaning fewer people who would need to be persuaded or could be susceptible to opposition messages.

By that standard, only Maine appeared to be at a stage where it was clearly prudent to proceed. Two separate polls showed 53 percent of Mainers in favor, a stronger position in terms of public opinion than any other state had seen before entering an election year with marriage on the ballot. Throughout the summer, petition carriers had collected signatures at a faster clip than had been anticipated; they were now likely to reach their goal of eighty thousand ahead of schedule. At that point, Why Marriage Matters Maine would begin airing television ads.

Throughout the summer, pollster Amy Simon tested a variety of ads, all of which depicted what Zepatos called "journey stories" of those who had converted, at times reluctantly, to support for gay marriage. One featured Reverend Michael Gray, the Methodist minister who had been given a starring role at the Lewiston press conference that summer, sitting alongside his wife, who said the issue "weighed heavy on our hearts." Another showed an older straight couple, Jeanette and Paul Rediker, who conceded they "weren't always so 'gay friendly.'" When they discovered that their eldest daughter was a lesbian, Jeanette recalled, she approached a Catholic priest for guidance. "I'll never forget the answer he told me," she said. "'She is the same person that you loved yesterday.'"

When the Analyst Institute assigned canvassers to show the videos at random doorsteps, more than 40 percent of the people who were shown the Grays' ad moved at least somewhat more accepting of same-sex marriage, and over half of those who saw the Redikers' did. (Even if it didn't switch their vote, messaging that softened up opponents was worthwhile, Zepatos surmised: reducing the intensity of their opposition would make them less likely to donate, volunteer, or advocate for the status quo.) The movement validated the concepts of "identification" and "social modeling" that the consortium's resident psychologist had ventured would prompt voters who might not have felt a personal stake in the marriage debate to rethink their position. "We all do model ourselves after others that we identify with—particularly others that we might look up to," says Phyllis Watts. Spokespeople like the Redikers, she explains, "provided an unexpected messenger because no one at that time thought elder people who've been long time married would be supporting that gays and lesbians could marry."

When Simon provided evidence that first responders would be good spokespeople, McTighe went to his local firehouse to ask his colleagues. He had joined the fire department when he first moved to York—the first place he had lived in years too small for a fully professionalized department—and set out to be up front about his sexuality even if it proved awkward in the macho milieu. McTighe's initial anxieties subsided, as the only person there who appeared to be angered by the news was the chief because, as McTighe recalled, "he actually had designs on me, like, marrying his daughter." After he launched the petition drive, McTighe's fellow fire-fighters collected signatures during their annual community field day and several agreed to appear in a television ad. The idea was that four of them, guided by an off-camera interviewer, would talk about how they came to be accepting of homosexuality in their ranks and receptive to same-sex couples marrying. But over the course of the two-hour shoot, standing alongside a ladder truck, one of the volunteer firefighters disclosed that he was gay—a fact already known to some of his crewmates but that McTighe learned as the cameras were rolling. In what became the ad's closing line, one of the others said, "When we clear the call, I get to go home to my wife. The guys I work with should be able to marry the person they love."

That thinking about who should speak for the cause represented a shift from the last round of ballot campaigns. While "voters know we're discuss-ing marriage for gay and lesbian couples, and we've got to meet that chal-lenge head-on," as she put in a memo that fall, Zepatos had also come to believe activists had been misguided in their insistence that such couples were the best mouthpieces. Focus groups may have shown voters far more accepting of lesbians than gay men, but those who appeared persuadable did not much identify with either. Instead, experiments and polls of those middle-of-the-road voters revealed that the most effective spokespeople were religious leaders, those in uniform, and older heterosexual couples. This insight pushed the makers of Why Marriage Matters ads toward an aesthetics of stolid traditionalism, a perpetual casting call for the types of people who might have been painted by Norman Rockwell or Grant Wood. If gay or lesbian people were to appear in the ad, it was often as little more than a point of reference—a relative or friend sitting alongside the main spokesperson, or a fleeting image of them together for context. "What sounds good to the ears of a gay man like me," McTighe explained, "is seldom what is going to sound right or help convince somebody who's really conflicted on this issue, or somebody who's not personally part of this community and doesn't have the same connection to it."

With such expansive coalitions, legalistic themes had often served as a lowest common denominator for "no" campaigns: something everyone could sign off on, however unenthusiastically. In Minnesota, the committee's Republicans, including a pair of state legislators, were intent on seeing a campaign waged against constitutional meddling rather than reconsideration of the American family. But that, campaign manager Richard Carlbom worried, would keep Minnesotans United in the outer community–level circles of voters' concern while the National Organization for Marriage undertook its familiar approach of burrowing into the innermost family-and-friends circles. "We wanted voters to go into the polling booth and not say, 'I'm going to do this on behalf of my gay niece' or 'I'm going to do this to keep it out of the constitution,'" says Carlbom. "We want our voters to go on there and say, 'If I vote yes, what does that say about who I am?'" The ads he had come to believe would work best—based on research attesting to the value of a "love and commitment" theme and the universal resonance of the Golden Rule—were certain to be dismissed as alternately "schoolmarmish and too touchy-feely," in his words.

Carlbom needed Zepatos to make the case that those novel messages would be more effective than the politically palatable alternatives. Zepatos's deepest experience was in Oregon, which shared with Minnesota a highly educated, politically active, overwhelmingly white population, but Carlbom was intent on convincing her how different she would find politics in his state. He relayed a crucial ethnographic insight in the form of an old saw: *In Minnesota, an extrovert is someone who looks at the other person's shoes while talking.* Zepatos acknowledged at the start of her presentation that people everywhere are often instructed that the three subjects one avoids raising in polite company are politics, sex, and religion. "This is the campaign that is going to combine all three," Zepatos said. "We have to get everyone in Minnesota to talk about gay people getting married."

In other states, where the question on the ballot would be an affirmative vote for marriage, there was no way to avoid or finesse it. Instead, the internal debates centered on whether to provoke such conflict at all, especially in 2012. On the Why Marriage Matters Maine executive committee, there were activists and lawyers who had been contesting gay-rights referenda back to 1995, along with representatives of lefty pressure groups, a few politically minded lawyers, and recently arrived professional operatives. "All the other campaigns were always pretty loose-knit, the advocates who've been doing stuff forever. You have Equality Maine and you have the ACLU affiliate, but then you also just had like random seventy-year-old lesbian activists," says McTighe.

When they all gathered on December 20, in a meeting room at the University of Southern Maine, they were joined by Solomon, who as Freedom to Marry's campaign director served as gatekeeper to national money and expertise. He had a long history with some of those in attendance, thanks to years working with GLAD to ensure the *Goodridge* mandate remained safe from political interference. Solomon had been monitoring Maine's work more closely than any of the other five states under consideration, partly out of close links to its leadership. In Massachusetts, he had been boss to both McTighe and his deputy Amy Mello at MassEquality, and then had lured Mello to follow him west during his brief stint at Equality California.

Solomon could not let Freedom to Marry's decisions be shaped by sentiment. Basic Rights Oregon had been the organization's closest local partner, serving as a "laboratory state" for its most novel field research. Support for gay marriage in Oregon had increased more than eight points since the start of public-education efforts in 2009, but polls showed it still fell short of the benchmarks Freedom to Marry had identified. Even though Zepatos called the state home, she lobbied Basic Rights Oregon to abandon its plans to go to the ballot, and the group's leaders made the difficult decision to pull back. "We didn't want to mess around," says executive director Jeana Frazzini.

It was time for a similar reckoning in Maine. If it chose to submit signed petitions, Why Marriage Matters Maine would spin off a committee that could stump overtly for the ballot question rather than just abstractly educate voters about marriage. Large nonprofit funders might back a gradual public-education effort, but strategists believed a sizable base of online donors making repeated, small contributions would be cultivated only by a real campaign. Then it would make the necessary transition to fighting for the specific text that would appear on the ballot, and hiring staff legally free to discuss the matter at hand with voters. McTighe agreed to ensure a decision was made by early in the new year. "It was time to put up or shut up," he says. "Are we going to turn these signatures in, to start the clock of going to the ballot? Or are we going to just say, 'I don't think we're quite there yet'?"

When 2011 opened, Solomon might have feared that Freedom to Marry would be stuck having to cheerlead reluctant locals into hosting another national-level battle only three years after a demoralizing loss, just to keep its strategy alive. Now as the year was about to close, Freedom to

Marry faced a surfeit of options. In two states where constitutional bans had qualified for the ballot, local groups were clamoring for financial and tactical support to beat them back. In four other states, activists were veering toward the ballot, and Solomon could sit back and let them compete to prove their worthiness to outside backers.

Conversation and Inoculation

In the fall of 2011, as her colleagues in the Marriage Research Consortium were bearing down on Maine and Minnesota, Phyllis Watts headed to Mississippi. Pro-life activists had proposed to amend the state constitution so that any fertilized egg would be considered a person, and afforded all the same legal rights. The so-called personhood amendment was a bold tactic to challenge the reach of *Roe v. Wade*, blocking not only abortions in the state but many other forms of birth control as well. (Many expected that, if passed, the language would be challenged up to the U.S. Supreme Court.) Watts made her first trip, two months before the election, to observe focus groups with churchgoing older white women who were undecided on Amendment 26. All had trouble squaring their religious convictions with the fact that the new law made no accommodations for victims of rape and incest, and could ban contragestive pills. "One woman," Watts would recall, "with such a sweet, Southern nature said, 'I really, really want to vote "no," but what happens when I get to heaven and all the babies are waiting for me there?'"

Watts ended up staying in Mississippi for a month, further mining focus groups and long-form voter interviews as she worked to unpack the internal conflict that made voters persuadable. Her client, a committee called Mississippians for Healthy Families, was sponsored by Planned Parenthood and the ACLU, but Watts pushed them toward a message strategy at odds with both groups' core values. All campaign communication ultimately revolved around one objective: to reassure Mississippians that they could vote against Amendment 26 for its far-reaching consequences and still remain pro-life. "You don't change people by trying to make them accept your values and your way of looking at an issue," Watts later reflected. "A good psychologist would never consider trying to change someone's values."

The amendment failed by a sixteen-point margin, and Watts returned to Northern California raving about the time she had spent in Mississippi. She was still relatively new to the world of politics, and enjoyed getting close to the campaigns she was advising. Watts, who became a licensed Zumba instructor at age sixty-one, liked the youthful energy she found in headquarters and field offices. She knew her presence added clinical heft to the den-mothering useful to organizers contending in close quarters with stress, poor diet, and perpetual exhaustion. But when her clients in Maine and Minnesota invited her to observe their focus groups, she refused to join the cluster of staff and consultants who would gather behind one-way glass to monitor their captive research sample. "If anybody says anything, it breaks my concentration," she says.

Instead Watts had the sessions sent to her on video. From inside the mid-century modern Sacramento house she had daubed with purples, Watts studied the Mainers and Minnesotans being forced to discuss their views on gay people marrying. She would rewind, over and over again, to isolate indicators of hesitance or ambivalence: a single hand gesture or stammer, a telling twitch or slouch. The most revealing moments came when Watts could see on an individual's surface the contours of a deeper internal friction, as though the tectonic plates of their belief system had been jolted into irreconcilable tension along the fault line of gay marriage. Where political researchers usually talked about voters as "persuadable" or "moveable," Watts encouraged them to use the term "conflicted." It captured the unease people felt when they were forced to reconcile existing mental "templates," as she called them—about the opposite-sex nature of marriage, or the highly sexualized sensibility of gay culture—with an instinct for fairness, likely humanized by the empathy that came along with personally knowing gays and lesbians. "I see this base of conflict as an opportunity rather than a negative," says pollster Amy Simon, who worked with Watts on the Maine campaign.

In one of the 2009 focus groups she conducted in California, Simon was at a session with women who had supported Proposition 8 or were uncertain of their views on the issue. Their conversation began so overwhelmingly sympathetic to same-sex marriage that Simon wondered whether the agency she used to recruit focus-group participants had made a mistake. Toward the end of the two-hour period, Simon showed them the Princes ad and watched the seeming unanimity spoil. Doubts rose to the surface, submerging the goodwill they had readily expressed before seeing the ad. Simon spent the session's final half hour trying to guide the conversation back to its previous footing. "They literally lost access to the things that they themselves had been saying for ninety minutes," recalls Simon.

Many were stuck on their newfound doubts about same-sex couples, but by the end two women had reclaimed their original views. "They were triggered, but there was something in them that enabled them to manage their feelings, calm them, and get back to their reasoning range and be in touch with that higher-order self that had emotional positive relations with gay people," says Simon. "What's happening inside them?" she asks. "And how do we package that?"

It was these voters, like Schrödinger's cat at once supportive of gay marriage and opposed to it, who were most vulnerable to "the 'kids and schools' message that continues to peel away support," as Thalia Zepatos wrote in an August 2010 memo. Watts had encouraged the other members of the Marriage Research Consortium to address the "Harm Kids Attack" in two stages. Once the negative ads appeared, they would require a forceful rejoinder, but long before that, campaigners should be trying to "inoculate" persuadable voters so as to strengthen their resistance to such appeals. "Fear-based attacks tend to 'paralyze' voters from absorbing new information—therefore, the best opportunity to impact them may be to provide competing information or an alternate analysis before voters ever see the Princes ad," Zepatos would later explain.

Early in 2011, Lisa Grove had traveled to a patch of suburban Portland not far from Mount Hood for the first of two focus groups in the living rooms of Clackamas County voters. It was as close to dropping in on a kaffeeklatsch as an opinion researcher could imagine. Each host was recruited through a multistage process that started with a list of women who had children under the age of eighteen at home and isolated those who statistical models predicted had muddled positions on gay marriage. (Survey phone calls confirmed this projection.) If they agreed to participate, these hosts were then asked to invite friends, coworkers, and family members who were also moms with children at home. She showed attendees the advertisements opponents had aired in California and Maine about the impact a change in marriage laws would have on children. As expected, they struck a nerve with some. But Grove also identified a promising wrinkle: parents most involved or knowledgeable about their children's schooling were less vulnerable to such fears. "Would providing factual information to parents of school-age children make them less 'susceptible' to the Princes ad or related attacks?" Zepatos asked.

The lack of a holistic strategy in their response to the Princes ad and its ilk was one of the two remaining problems Freedom to Marry faced through 2011 as it weighed the next year's political agenda. The other was what Zepatos had called the "conversations challenge." Over several years, polls and focus groups had all discerned a high correlation between a citizen's support for same-sex marriage and having had a conversation about the subject with a gay or lesbian person he or she knew. Yet engineering those interactions remained a challenge. Interviews with gay and lesbian volunteers showed they preferred to have such chats with strangers rather than friends or relatives.

In Minnesota, that "conversations challenge" preoccupied those who spent 2011 gearing up to fight a constitutional amendment banning gay marriage. In her first poll for the campaign, which showed the amendment with a six-point lead, Grove indicated that the most obvious categories of voters who could be persuaded to vote against it would be women, voters between thirty and forty-nine, and those with college degrees. (Two-thirds of those under thirty were already against the amendment.) In a memo, Grove underscored how persuasive personal conversations with loved ones could be. "Among those who know someone gay and have talked with him or her about marriage, the amendment is failing by an astounding 39 points," Grove and her colleague Melissa Chernaik wrote. "However, among those who know someone gay and have *not* had 'the conversation,' the measure is actually *passing* by 13 points."

In many respects, this was not a surprise to Grove, who had noted in her 2009 report for Freedom to Marry that "few findings are more consistent across all modes of research than the positive effect that personal conversations have on heterosexuals' view toward marriage." Postelection surveys by other pollsters both in California and Maine showed that those who had cited interpersonal discussions on the topic had voted overwhelmingly against the anti-gay-marriage amendments. "What makes the difference is gay Americans engaging with non-gay people in their lives in a conversation about why marriage matters to them, personally," Grove had written.

It was, however, a correlation that had been long misinterpreted. Folk wisdom had often treated this as an organic cycle: gays and lesbians growing comfortable with their sexuality, perhaps encouraged by popular culture; their coming out leads friends and family to realize they know a gay person; liberalized attitudes follow. But research was beginning to suggest that theory had the causality precisely backward. The evidence indicated that those who were openly gay were highly selective about when and where to actually address their identity, even with people they knew well. In 2005, Gregory Herek, a University of California, Davis sociologist, found that half of gay men and lesbians had not discussed their experiences with heterosexual acquaintances or coworkers—and there were higher numbers for nonimmediate family. Grove's own polling four years later revealed the large gulf between familiarity and engagement: while 74 percent of Oregonians said they had a gay friend or family member, only 35 percent had actually spoken with that person about marriage. It was all, Grove concluded, "evidence that many gay and lesbian people are not comfortable having" the conversations necessary to actively push opinion in a winning direction.

"We hung an enormous amount of credence on that data, which also made sense in light of the past failures, which hadn't put as much emphasis on conversation," says Dan Cramer, whose Grassroots Solutions was hired to develop a targeting and field plan for Minnesotans United. "I have been part of really robust field programs that had a lot of conversations and did really interesting organizing. But the idea of 'How do you put conversation at the entire center of this campaign?' leads you into a totally different direction."

The steering committee received its first view of conversations in the campaign plan that Carlbom presented in January. He had divided the yearlong run-up to Election Day into five phases. The first, centered on fundraising toward a budget of $10 million, was already complete. "The second phase, base-building and education, will distinguish the campaign from any other in Minnesota history," it went on. "It will ensure the groundwork has been laid for the largest grassroots movement ever built in this state."

Laying that groundwork amounted to a costly gamble. The campaign already had seven full-time paid organizers, and Carlbom detailed a plan to add an additional fifty by the end of March, in offices throughout the state. The final three phases proceeded along a more familiar arc for campaigns: persuasion through large-scale mass media and get-out-the-vote mobilization. But that sequence could be jeopardized, as early spending on fixed investments would come at the cost of later flexibility. If fundraising revenue over the summer months failed to meet goals, Minnesotans United would enter the post–Labor Day season altogether incapable of matching opponents' advertising volume in the fall. If the National Organization for Marriage devised a new, last-minute attack—something to replace or supersede the children-centric appeals used in California and Maine—Carlbom might find himself without the resources to respond.

In February, Carlbom summoned the Minnesotans United staff and consultants for a two-day retreat to begin putting this plan fully into action. On the first day, he outlined the path to victory and the five-phase timetable already under way. The second day was devoted to the characteristics of a "conversation campaign." The core function of the campaign they were building, Carlbom told attendees, would be to catalyze more conversations. If said in another context, that observation could ring as a platitude, the type of thing that political operatives say to lacquer their cynical work with a humanistic sheen. But when spoken to other operatives, that directive echoed for its defiance of political norms.

The modern American campaign aspired to be a command-and-control operation, where words could be perfected and then repeated at scale with Taylorist efficiency. There were new methods for testing and refining messages, techniques for dispatching them with novel precision, and tools to monitor and track that communication. Most campaigners were drawn to platforms for political speech that operated as one-way vectors, like television and direct mail, in which they could maximize their supervision over content and delivery. Often what passed for conversations in electoral politics, such as phone-bank calls or a canvasser's visits, were mere data-collection exercises, a de facto census of the electorate.

"What do we mean by 'conversation campaign' versus actual conversations?" Carlbom asked attendees at the retreat. While there may have been an idea that reserve was endemic to the Minnesota character, the state also had a proud tradition for civic-minded politesse that should lend itself to genteel exchanges even with strangers. There was a well-drilled volunteer culture within the Democratic-Farmer-Labor Party. With some of the nation's highest voter-registration and participation rates, a campaign could focus its interactions on changing the opinions of a known electorate rather than trying to identify and mobilize new voters.

The core of what became known as the Minnesotans Talking to Minnesotans project would be structured but open-ended exchanges between supporters and those citizens already likely to vote. If successful, these interactions would be longer and deeper than the brisk canvass visits or phone calls, which typically last less than a minute so as to maximize the number completed in a given shift. These would be "less about pushing a message, more about moving people with the method of person-to-person conversation," according to the campaign plan. "The conversations the campaign must have with voters are not initially all about the details of the amendment. In reality, these conversations are about marriage (in essence about people's own homophobia) and these types of conversations take much longer than traditional ID or persuasion conversations," it went on. "MN United does not need to move voters to vote for full marriage recognition. The campaign has to inoculate soft-supporters to oppose the marriage ban and persuade swing voters to vote NO through multiple personal conversations."

Days earlier, Carlbom had signed a contract with a firm named ISSI to sift through what he called "the muddled middle" and assign voters to each category. Microtargeting had been a tool in its infancy just four years earlier, and it went unused by the No on 8 campaign. Now, though, algorithms could help pinpoint individual Minnesotans likely to oppose gay marriage but support civil unions, for instance, or those who were undecided on the amendment but willing to say they found a message in favor of gay marriage convincing. The ability to generate such predictions at the individual level—even distinguishing degrees of persuadability among inhabitants of a common household—enabled the shift from a mass strategy to a more tailored one. Microtargeting models could direct calls and handwritten letters produced by the direct-mail consultancy Mission Control. But attempts to translate the efforts online faltered. A so-called Friends and Family program coded to crawl through a supporter's Facebook network to isolate those identified as persuadable was "harder to operationalize," Carlbom wrote.

Doing any of it at scale remained a daunting project. The targeting math detailed in Carlbom's campaign plan counted 174,000 undecided targets and another 249,400 existing marriage supporters believed susceptible to the "kids and schools"–type negative messaging. "We need to talk with these folks and make the same connection that we're making with the undecided crowd," one training document instructed. To erase the six-point deficit visible in Grove's first poll, the campaign estimated it would have to instigate one million total conversations. Where the Maine campaign had decided it would rely on a paid team of field organizers to oversee a face-to-face canvassing effort, Carlbom concluded that it would be infeasible to reach all his targets on foot. Instead, informed by calculations about efficiency, he made the decision to prioritize volunteer-staffed phone banks.

In the weeks that followed, the campaign opened four of them, hosting volunteers six nights per week. Standard campaign practice would be to offer minimal preliminary guidance—a quick read of the script and basic introduction to the phone system—so as to get volunteers actually placing calls as quickly as possible. When coming into a field office for the first time, Minnesotans Talking to Minnesotans volunteers were instead subjected to an hourlong training session. They worked with staff to hone their "stories," the set spiel about their experience with marriage, before rehearsing a series of role-playing exercises. Only then were volunteers considered ready to deploy those stories to induce a stranger's revelation of ambivalence, discomfort, or conflict. "We said to people, 'It took us all this work to find this person, so don't like limit yourself to sixty seconds or ninety seconds. Talk to them and answer their questions and if you feel comfortable, just say, "Ask me any question you want,"'" says Zepatos. "If you get somebody in a real conversation, stay on the phone for thirty minutes."

At the end of a shift, callers and staff organizers would gather to debrief on their experiences. "This is the most important part of the night because what you learn from your conversations will inform everything from future script changes to what our TV ads end up saying," a training document instructed.

Unable to monitor and manage all the interactions in what Carlbom called a "relational strategy," he sketched a let-a-thousand-flowers-bloom approach to them. "Make the entry level lower," retreat attendees concluded. It would be in the campaign's interest to have conversations take place, he argued, even if they couldn't be directed or surveilled from headquarters. Carlbom encouraged his team to brainstorm "how we can get that two-way street feeling in all communication," and assessed electoral efficiency in those terms. "While a thicket of signs in Minneapolis may be a waste of campaign resources, a single sign in front of a house in Willmar, Hibbing or Third River may actually be worth the cost," the plan observed. "So while signs do not vote, they can impact the context of some conversations in some parts of the state." Encouraging truly open-ended exchanges with voters over such a sensitive topic was fraught with risk, even recklessness. What guarantee was there that conversations could push opinions in the right direction, and not alienate the undecided or harden the opposition of skeptics?

Watts traveled to Minnesota for a week to train volunteers in how to engage the types of conflicted voters she had been watching so intently for months. Much as she had in the Mississippi "personhood" campaign, Watts believed her task was to help campaigners understand the difference between empathy for a voter's views and acceptance of them. Volunteers didn't have to persuade voters as much as help them resolve their internal conflict over gay marriage, Cramer said. "And so to do that, we offer to take them on a journey."

79

Four Ballots

Freedom to Marry began 2012 committed to action in two states. Maine and Minnesota amounted to a manageable demand on the organization's limited budget and staff, and money could be doled out in a way that ensured Freedom to Marry played an active role in both campaigns. The legislative effort in New York provided a template for Freedom to Marry to convene a so-called table into which local groups and national organizations like the Human Rights Campaign would have the option to buy into the new campaigns. A memorandum of understanding would enforce the pay-to-play dynamic. Each investor would acquire clearly assigned responsibilities and, as a consequence, effectively marginalize the in-state sachems whose influence seemed to have led past campaigns astray.

When paired, Minnesota and Maine would offer Freedom to Marry the chance to simultaneously realize its two major goals for 2012: winding back a constitutional amendment banning same-sex marriage and showing it could proactively win marriage rights at the ballot. Winning both would represent a major breakthrough for marriage advocacy, exorcising the hauntings of Proposition 8. Furthermore, such victories would affirm the revised 10-10-10-20 strategy, providing evidence that the wall of constitutional bans might not be as impregnable as it appeared.

In late February, Maine's secretary of state announced that gay-rights advocates had collected enough signatures to ensure the November ballot would include Question 1 on marriage. But already the simple linear geography of Freedom to Marry's 2012 map had been broken, thanks to events in two far-flung state capitals.

In Olympia, Washington, where nearly two years earlier legislators had enacted a civil-unions statute, a bill to legalize same-sex marriages had emerged in part to get ahead of a conservative attorney's effort to present voters with a constitutional amendment banning them. "It's time, it's the right thing to do, and I will introduce a bill to do it," said Governor Christine Gregoire. Signing such a bill into law, as Gregoire did on February 13, did little to forestall a statewide referendum over marriage. A petition drive by opponents to suspend the law delayed implementation— legislators had drafted it to take effect ninety days beyond the end of the legislative session—until after the November elections, when the marriage bill would appear on the ballot as Referendum 74.

Less than three weeks later, Maryland governor Martin O'Malley signed a marriage bill of his own. Annapolis had been the site of one of the biggest disappointments of 2011, despite Democratic majorities. O'Malley had struck observers as a reluctant supporter, unwilling to lean strongly enough on ambivalent African American legislators, including those from Baltimore, where he had previously served as mayor. The bill passed the senate and survived three hours of intense floor debate in the House of Delegates before being pulled out of fear there were not enough votes in the Democratic-controlled chamber for it to pass. "This is a distance run, not a sprint," said House Speaker Michael E. Busch. "We'll come back next year and take a strong look at it."

When they did, a new cost-benefit arithmetic had set in for calculating Democrats assessing how strongly to push for marriage. O'Malley was unabashedly assembling a résumé for a future national campaign, and now stood to be outmatched by his contemporary Andrew Cuomo, whose work on the New York marriage bill had made him a hero to the gay political class. Both governors were moderate Catholic men clutching at a progressive credential to jazz up profiles (pro-business, white-ethnic, career-politician) unlikely to match current Democratic Party fads. O'Malley began 2012 by declaring the Civil Marriage Protection Act a priority, and by March 1—not long after another presidential aspirant, New Jersey Republican Chris Christie, vetoed a similar measure in his state—had a version he could sign into law. It delayed enactment until the following January, an accommodation to lawmakers who wanted to let voters weigh in before the bill took effect. Legislative passage, Republican house leader Anthony O'Donnell insisted, was "beginning a process, not ending a process. The citizens of Maryland will have the final say."

By then, Freedom to Marry had long since given up on Maryland, citing the cautionary experience of 2011. Equality Maryland had exhibited less sway than the Catholic Church and black clergy, which augured poorly for its ability to mount a campaign in a state where half of Democratic voters were African American. The Human Rights Campaign, however, had unique institutional equities in Maryland. The group maintained a strong membership base there, and many among its staff and leadership lived in the Washington suburbs and saw self-interest at stake. It kept organizers in the state after the 2011 legislative session ended, and increased its investment after O'Malley declared his newfound enthusiasm for the cause. When it was time to organize a campaign to pass Question 6, as the marriage referendum became known, Freedom to Marry backed off entirely, ceding the terrain to the Human Rights Campaign, which would be the only major outside backer. "We were feeling much more cautious about Maryland," says Thalia Zepatos. "We tried to hold HRC's feet to the fire and say: if you're going to put Maryland to the ballot, you're going to be responsible."

In Washington State, Freedom to Marry's leadership had reasons to be skeptical about the Washington United for Marriage organization, too. State senator Ed Murray, a longtime gay-rights activist who would shortly thereafter announce his candidacy to be mayor of Seattle, had helped execute a masterful legislative strategy, efficiently maneuvering to get a bill before the governor with scant turmoil. With their focus on lawmakers, Murray and his confederates had chosen a different route than Basic Rights Oregon had, undertaking little of the public-education work designed to warm voters up for a contentious vote.

Polls nonetheless showed Referendum 74 well positioned for passage, surpassing all the benchmarks in Freedom to Marry's viability-assessment memo. For all their cultural and topographical similarities, the neighboring states in the Pacific Northwest differed in a crucial respect. Seattle cast a greater thrall over its state's politics than did Portland, shaping demographics and campaign finance. Oregon was, on the whole, older and more rural, and lacked the progressive donor base enriched by Seattle's technology sector. Freedom to Marry paid to deploy Basic Rights Oregon's longtime organizing director, Thomas Wheatley, to oversee Washington United for Marriage's field operations, and Amy Simon joined the campaign as its pollster. With Oregon's marriage ambitions on hold, volunteers began shuttling north across the border to support the referendum. "We were basically the Southwest Washington campaign," says Basic Rights Oregon's Jeana Frazzini.

So now there were four states on the November ballot instead of two. The National Organization for Marriage supplied most of the budget for the efforts to fend off same-sex marriage, allowing it to claim a leader-ship role in the campaign organization. NOM political director Frank Schubert was assigned the unusual role of chief strategist to all four simultaneously—"One Man Guides the Fight Against Gay Marriage," the *New York Times* wrote in the headline of a profile.

To those in the Marriage Research Consortium who had spent years anticipating what the opposition's next messaging move would be, the unified structure suggested it was likely to play out in parallel across four states. The simulated campaigns that Zepatos had waged throughout 2011 were, in many respects, an effort to inhabit the brain of Schubert. Along with his partner Jeff Flint, Schubert had plotted Yes on 8, and the more gay activists studied that campaign, the more it instilled a fear of his ruth-less ingenuity. The next year, in Maine, Schubert demonstrated that the California tactics were reproducible, and—as the lead spokesman for the Stand for Marriage Maine effort—developed a public image to match his reputation as a strategic mastermind. One Human Rights Campaign official praised Schubert to the *New York Times* as "diabolically smart and creative."

Despite the common foe, each presented a distinct messaging challenge to gay-marriage campaigners. Minnesota was the most familiar situation: beating back a constitutional amendment pushed by a coalition of religious conservatives to maintain the status quo. Maine amounted to an effective do-over from three years earlier, a return to a state that had granted a right for gays to marry through a political process and then withdrew it through another political process months later. Maryland marked a proactive effort to deliver marriage rights to a left-leaning state, although one where most Democrats were African American. In Washington, voters would be given the chance to upgrade an "all but marriage" domestic-partnership regime that had been in place for barely two years.

It was laws like the one enacted in Washington in 2009 that posed the greatest challenge to the pursuit of marriage equality three years later—at least in politically moderate states where near-term progress was conceiv-able. Civil unions had been generated almost by accident in Vermont, a circumstantial collaboration between a cautious court and reluctant leg-islators instructed to devise a framework that would bestow gay couples with all the rights and responsibilities of marriage while avoiding the contentiousness of that word. They had done so with a surprising gift for branding, one that specifically signaled to those with a spiritual attachment to "marriage" that no religious rituals were implicated in the new scheme.

Americans had flocked to the new edge in a contest no longer limited to two sides. When exchanges over marriage grew most intense, civil unions became the natural compromise position, a downy refuge from the debate's most emotionally pointed corners. Polls from the Pew Research Center first demonstrated majority support for civil unions in 2005; four years later, they were backed by 57 percent of Americans. Most Democratic politicians supported establishment of civil unions, and used them to deflect criticism from both sides of the marriage debate. In 2011, a Republican for the first time campaigned for president as a civil-unions supporter: as governor of Utah, Jon Huntsman had backed off his earlier blanket rejection of recognizing gay couples to endorse everything short of the word *marriage*. While the shift caused Huntsman trouble with religious conservatives when he first explored running in a Republican primary, he had staked out the safest position for a general election: even as a national majority objected to gay marriage, according to Pew, only 37 percent reported themselves against civil unions.

In the nearly two decades since the issue had become nationalized after the Hawaii Supreme Court decision, Americans had come to understand that their state and federal governments, along with private companies, made important classifications contingent on marital status. They recognized that the classification also meant something to those who had until very recently been excluded from it everywhere. That gays and lesbians yearned for more than sexual sovereignty was no longer open to debate. They, too, sought the familiar architecture of codependent partnerships, the ability to stand as a single economic and legal unit in the eyes of their government and employers.

As a result, the 2012 campaigns were not, like the previous decade's, fundamentally a quest to convince majorities that gay people deserved the equal protection of their states' laws. For strategists trying to win marriage, the appeal of civil unions risked being a painfully Pyrrhic victory. It amounted to an unforeseen cost of incrementalism: not that major change would come slowly but that the public would think minor change had been the objective all along. For tacticians, however, the plain, safe popularity of civil unions was a gift—an easy way to identify the voters who should be the focus of a campaign's marriage advocacy.

In mid-May, ISSI delivered to Minnesotans United the results of its initial modeling project, personalized probability scores for each of the 3,089,988 people on the state voter rolls. To pick out optimal targets for the conversation campaign, advised ISSI analysts Dan Castleman and David

Radloff, Minnesotans United needed to layer the different scores. Within the pool of those predicted to support the amendment, tacticians could isolate those with the greatest likelihood to choose "civil unions" when asked their preferred legal arrangement for gay couples.

Despite their varied paths to the 2012 ballot, the three campaigns coached by Freedom to Marry followed similar trajectories over the course of the year. They shared a brain trust, through an interlocking web of consultants: Simon advised both the Maine and Washington campaigns, and ISSI developed statistical models for Maine and Minnesota.

All stuck to a similar rhythm. Their advertising featured unexpected advocates for same-sex marriage—grandparents, military veterans, Republican legislators—who could credibly articulate rationales that highlighted the unspoken inadequacies of any otherwise appealing compromise. "In further proof that our the values' [sic] messaging is strong for us, our best assertions go to the value of marriage and how it's a violation of the Golden Rule to deny something so unique, important and special," Lisa Grove wrote in an October presentation to Minnesotans United. "Going negative on civil unions is much less effective."

The ISSI models identified individual voters who were likely to find each of the campaign's secondary messaging themes convincing, and could receive more narrowly targeted communication via direct mail. Those living in houses valued at under $330,000 were most inclined to declare themselves open to a libertarian-minded message attacking the amendment as a form of government intrusion. Donors to environmental causes were receptive to the Golden Rule–style invocation to "treat others" fairly, and African Americans responded to it better than they did the government-intrusion appeal. All of it, Zepatos hoped, was successfully inoculating voters to resist the opposition's late efforts to drive them to fear for their children.

Yet as the calendar passed Labor Day, the NOM-affiliated campaigns demonstrated little of the bile that their opponents had anticipated. "We have run a very strategic, disciplined campaign," Schubert insisted to a Minneapolis newspaper. "Our work has not been about Minnesotans United and responding to their antics. We haven't encouraged a lot of public debates. We haven't gone tit for tat with them in the media." While nearly all the ads during the Proposition 8 campaign (and the next year in Maine) touched on school-related issues, fewer than half of those across the four states in 2012 did.

Efforts to instead warn of "a chilling effect on religious liberty and the right of conscience," as Washington State's four Catholic bishops put it in an early September statement advising a "no" vote on Referendum 74, were limited by the fact that the referendum respected "the right of clergy or religious organizations to refuse to perform, recognize, or accommodate any marriage ceremony." Such provisions for religious exemptions were present in all three states where new marriage laws were on the ballot. A less adversarial approach—which portrayed the faithful as at risk of becoming victims without necessarily identifying homosexuals as their aggressors—led some antigay conservatives to agonize that their side had gone soft. The antigay blog Mass Resistance declared itself confused by the "months of relatively low-conflict campaigning."

That same uneasy quietude only intensified fears among NOM opponents about the ferocity of an eventual attack. Perhaps Schubert had a new trick, refined over the three years since marriage was last on the ballot. If so, it made sense he would save it for a late surprise that would leave gay-marriage campaigners flat-footed, as the then-novel "harms kids" attack had in the last month of the Proposition 8 campaign. Anything he might be planning was expected to arrive as a barrage: an opposition-research briefing prepared for Minnesotans United leadership predicted that Schubert's committee, Minnesotans for Marriage, would spend "whatever it takes"—likely around $10 million. In early October, the *New York Times* reported from Annapolis on gay activists "bracing for a rush of Schubert-designed television ads in the four contested states."

In the last week of October, they finally arrived. In all four states where marriage was on the ballot, the NOM-affiliated campaigns began almost simultaneously airing nearly identical ads featuring David and Tonia Parker. The Massachusetts parents had a story to tell: in 2005, their five-year-old son returned home with a "diversity book bag," which along with recipes for ethnic dishes included a book called *Who's in a Family?* that depicted a lesbian couple with children. When David went to the school to challenge officials over it and refused to leave, he was arrested for trespassing. Along with another set of parents, they sued administrators for failing to let parents shield their children from sex-education lessons. (A federal judge ruled that the parents had not seen their First Amendment religious freedoms violated, and that they should seek to change policy through "normal political processes for change in the town and state." In 2008, the U.S. Supreme Court refused to hear the case on appeal.)

David Parker was arguably the first person in the country to claim real personal harm from the legalization of same-sex marriage, and it became a cause célèbre for those trying to ward off gay-rights advances elsewhere. He starred in his first ad in 2005, when the Coalition for Marriage began a failed effort to undo sexual-orientation protections in Maine law. By the time Proposition 8 strategists decided that their dominant message would be about the impact of the new marriage laws upon children, Parker was the go-to cautionary tale of "coerced homosexual education for their kindergartener," as the Protect Marriage website described it. The 2012 ads all carried the same threat: "If gay marriage happens here, schools could teach that boys can marry boys."

The four campaigns had been prepared not only for this argument, but for the specifics. The Parkers' had been the very first case cited in the research dossier the Human Rights Campaign had distributed in anticipation of opposition ads, and the focal point of a July 31 memo that a communications staffer for Minnesotans United produced to offer "internal background" for those he expected to respond to future attacks. "Our goal is to stick to our core, values-based messages about marriage," Stephen Schreiber wrote to his colleagues. "We do not want to get into the weeds on each case cited by the opposition."

It was time to finally deploy the pushback ads. Over the course of 2011, Phyllis Watts had helped isolate a psychological framework that supported all the ambivalences about same-sex marriage that revealed themselves when children were introduced in polls and focus groups. The "harms kids" ads, she hypothesized, had been effective because parents were already anxious about having lost control of their children to outside influences. Parents needed to be reassured that they still set values at home, and that what happened in schools or popular culture or the political realm could not diminish their authority. While it was useful to present credentialed educators who could inform voters about the facts of local policy, ad makers were instructed to find teachers who were also parents and could personalize the guarantee. "Allowing everyone the freedom to marry won't change our kids' values—because they get those values from us," said John and Elizabeth McClure of Edina in a version of the ad filmed for use in Minnesota. Rigorous testing had revealed other insights: ads seemed more convincing when parents discussing marriage, even if addressing the camera, were shown in the presence of their children. "We felt very confident," says Zepatos, "but it still hadn't been proven in the heart of the campaign."

Schubert did not seem to have a response to the pushback ads emphasizing parental authority. All four of his campaigns kept running the same material, although now layered with complaints about the critical newspaper editorials and fact-check columns that tried to undercut their alarmism. Zepatos had spent four years trying to modernize the gay-rights movement's research techniques and war-gaming possible scenarios so that it would be prepared for whatever would be the latest variation on Schubert's leitmotif. Yet through her simulated campaigns, Zepatos appeared to have given far more advance thought to what Schubert might do to update his tactics than he did. Even though four new states, and the District of Columbia, had legalized gay marriage since the Proposition 8 vote, Schubert's side had not uncovered another example of victimhood, or devised a new way to package the Parkers' familiar tale.

For his part, Schubert had been stretched thin, pinballing across four states and often serving as spokesman for all their campaigns. Even though he had developed a reputation well beyond California for his work on Proposition 8 and been granted an expanded budget through NOM, Schubert struggled to get Republican operatives willing to work alongside him. In February 2009, a former Republican National Committee digital strategist named Patrick Ruffini, who the previous fall had managed the Proposition 8 campaign's website, wrote a blog post mocking the right's willingness to disassociate itself from "sentiments everyone feels, like love" through its vitriol over same-sex marriage. Several of the consultants who signed on with Stand for Marriage Maine that year would do so only anonymously. Both the firms that Schubert hired to poll and to produce its video advertisements set up front companies registered to new post-office boxes that would be listed in public disclosure reports. "I'm not going to blow their cover," he said when the *New York Times* probed the background of a consultant he would identify only as an "East Coast pollster."

Two years later, even Schubert's own partner wanted nothing to do with same-sex marriage. In April 2012, Schubert announced he was splitting with Flint, with whom he had three years earlier jointly accepted the American Association of Political Consultants' Campaign Excellence Award for Public Affairs Team of the Year for their No on 8 collaboration. "It was clear this was a deeper thing to Frank, and he was willing to throw the rest of the business on the trash heap to do this," says Rob Stutzman, another Republican consultant in Sacramento. "He became a true believer." In a press release announcing his departure from Schubert Flint, Schubert explained that his new firm, Mission Public Affairs, would allow him to focus on NOM and like-minded clients without subjecting Flint to further reputational damage. "I don't want my work on social issues to continue to overshadow the people who work for me, or the clients we serve," he said.

Internal tensions thinned the National Organization for Marriage's numbers, too. The tables had largely turned since 2004, when social conservatives were defining the playing field and forcing gay-rights activists to respond. With so few places to implement new constitutional bans, NOM was now in the position of almost exclusively attempting to resist their opponents' efforts to accumulate wins in left-leaning states. "So much was happening that we had to pick where we could be useful," says Maggie Gallagher, the group's founder. When there was a chance to pursue their own initiative—like the opportunity in the fall of 2010 to punish Iowa Supreme Court justices seeking retention—NOM operatives leapt at it.

The Iowa justices' defeat may have helped buff lore about NOM's fierce state campaigns, but internally it provoked a dire debate over priorities. One constant of the marriage debate was the extent to which it had avoided polarization, at least when it came to political elites. Most Republicans were eager to be seen as strenuously fighting gay marriage, and most Democrats had no interest in fighting back. That partisan asymmetry amounted to a structural advantage for gay-marriage opponents when it came to federal policy. The fact that neither wanted to be a pro-gay-marriage party kept the Defense of Marriage Act safe from any repeal and gay-rights litigators from viewing the Supreme Court as a friendly venue for marriage claims. States might be moving left on the issue, but Washington, DC, wasn't.

Even though NOM had sublet an office in the capital starting in 2009, not until May 2012 did it establish a political action committee, the classification necessary to give directly to a politician and typically the first step taken to acquire access to those in the executive or legislative branches. "We didn't really end up with an organization that had a very powerful federal focus—like most of these social-conservative organizations," says Gallagher, "and we ended up being focused more on states where action was easier."

The zest with which ambitious Democratic politicians like Andrew Cuomo and Martin O'Malley wanted to associate themselves with gay marriage, however, appeared a leading indicator of a potential party-wide shift. One hundred twenty congressional Democrats were cosponsoring repeal of the Defense of Marriage Act, including several influential committee chairs; some had begun agitating to replace the pro-civil-unions plank in the party platform with one endorsing full marriage rights. Gallagher argued that the coming election season might be the last chance to scare Democratic elites from moving too far left on the issue. "Continuing to focus on states was going to be counterproductive, and we needed to switch to demonstrating in the 2012 elections that supporting gay marriage was a problem for the Democrats," recalls Gallagher.

Gallagher lost that debate and in 2011 departed NOM, depriving the group of not only its most compelling voice but also an established fundraiser, just as it prepared to contest five ballot initiatives mostly against a reformed Freedom to Marry and its network of donors and operatives. "No one organization can do all things," says Gallagher. "But it is a weakness that there still isn't an organization—actually I don't know now who it would be—pushing for it legislatively, whose job it was to elect senators who are friends and to unelect senators who oppose what we support."

The National Organization for Marriage remained a financial force, its $9.3 million in total gifts to the 2012 state campaigns matching what the Freedom to Marry and the Human Rights Campaign together spent on the other side. But the two major religious hierarchies that had helped NOM raise and spend over $40 million in California alone four years earlier were no longer as invested in its goals.

Instead of inspiring the LDS Church to intensify marriage work, victory in California had spooked it. A documentary film, *8: The Mormon Proposition*, that portrayed the church as the driving force behind the repeal of gay marriage debuted at the Sundance Film Festival in 2010. The next year, the LDS Church set out on an ambitious effort to rebrand itself through consumer marketing, including national television ads and a Times Square billboard, with the tagline "I'm a Mormon" next to those who defied the stereotype of clean-cut, starchy all-American white men. The ads had been developed in response to church-sponsored focus groups conducted in the midst of the Proposition 8 campaign, in which respondents regularly informed church researchers that they considered Mormons "pushy," "secretive," "controlling," and "antigay."

As 2012 approached, the LDS Church fell under unusual scrutiny, but this time most of the pop-culture attention was positive or neutral. A *Newsweek* cover story proclaimed THE MORMON MOMENT, as the affectionate musical *The Book of Mormon* swept the 2011 Tony Awards and two Mormon politicians announced their pursuit of the presidency. With one of them, Mitt Romney, likely to win the Republican nomination, the church saw before it an unmatched occasion to force itself into the political mainstream. The "I'm a Mormon" ads appeared to be helping: church research showed that in media markets where the ads were shown, sentiment had warmed to the church, including fewer people describing it as "antigay." That development was, according to the *Boston Globe*, "a mystery to even the Mormons, since none of the ads features someone who is gay or who advocates for gay rights." Engaging in state-level marriage conflicts—especially in places where the church lacked a strong historical presence or local interests—would represent a wholly unappealing step backward. "I think they felt that they had done more than their share in California," says Schubert. "They had been the focus of the backlash."

Though the Catholic Church entertained no such retreat, the more devolved nature of its power made for an uneven presence across the states. St. Paul and Minneapolis archbishop John Nienstedt had actively lobbied legislators in his state to pass a constitutional ban, and established a Minnesota Catholic Conference Marriage Defense Fund to solicit political support from Catholics nationwide. It raised $2.2 million, and the archdiocese contributed another $650,000 to the campaign. Overall Catholic institutions directly contributed around one-quarter of the $13 million that the Minnesota for Marriage campaign raised, exceeding some of its own early estimates.

Baltimore's archbishop, William E. Lori, was similarly encouraging of the campaign to defeat Question 6 in his state, but overt political moves were complicated by his recent appointment to head the Conference of Catholic Bishops' Ad Hoc Committee for Religious Liberty. "They did not want to contribute as a conference, they wanted to help us raise money," says Schubert. "They did, but not to the extent that we needed." Seattle's archbishop, J. Peter Sartain, had been in his post for barely a year when he encouraged parishes to collect signatures to overturn a new marriage law against which he had testified in the legislature. "Totally with us but new," remarks Schubert. "Major donors typically have to have some relationship with somebody."

Maine's Portland diocese had taken a very visible role in the successful 2009 campaign to amend the state constitution, donating $550,000 in cash—part of $1 million from institutional Catholic sources nationwide—and then seconded public-affairs officer Marc Mutty to serve as Stand for Marriage Maine's chair. Yet after returning to his job with the diocese, Mutty repudiated the campaign's tactics in the 2011 documentary *Question One*. "I fear I'll be remembered for the work I did on this campaign," Mutty told the filmmakers, confessing to an often-hyperbolic dishonesty in its advertising content. By 2012, church officials were overcome with what *Portland Press Herald* columnist Bill Nemitz dubbed "winner's remorse." While the Knights of Columbus donated just over $100,000 to oppose the rematch over Question 1, the diocese directly contributed nothing. "We had trouble with Catholics there," says Schubert. "They certainly didn't want to take the lead in the campaign, and they wanted to oppose the idea from a nonpolitical perspective."

Individual donors, too, were harder to recruit. The type of effort that Fred Karger had initiated in the summer of 2008, to mine campaign-finance reports to identify and shame Yes on 8 donors, had taken its toll. The next year in Maine, NOM attempted to shield its donors, even suing the state's ethics commission for violating its First Amendment rights of speech and association. Due to threats of harassment from Karger and others, NOM attorneys alleged, merely disclosing the names of its donors had a "chilling effect" on its ability to raise money. Even in a country where opposition to same-sex marriage remained dominant, political and business elites had come to fear being attached to that majority view. Passive opposition may have been socially acceptable, but active involvement in the cause carried a stigma that both sides were happy to acknowledge. Only five individuals, none of them well-known nationally, contributed over $100,000 to any of the NOM-supported campaigns in 2012. "The impact of donors being scared off was significant," says Schubert. "The first thing they wanted to know is, 'Am I going to be publicly disclosed?'"

On the other side, however, new donors emerged beyond the tight circle of gay philanthropists and benefactors of the ideological left who had supported previous campaigns. The 2012 public-disclosure reports amounted to a roll call of postindustrial American plutocrats for whom gay marriage fit into some sort of civic vision: Michael Bloomberg, Bill Gates, Peter Thiel, Paul Singer. The actor Brad Pitt donated $400,000, split evenly across four states. In Washington, Amazon founder Jeff Bezos and his wife gave $2.5 million, among the largest single contributions in American political history. "You didn't see Jeff Bezos step up with a two-and-half million dollar gift to campaign two, three years before that . . . because he could get a tax deduction," said Thomas Wheatley of Washington United for Marriage. "You saw him step up when it was a campaign, some state on the line, you could win or lose it in the next ninety days."

Overall, more than two-thirds of the money spent on ballot referenda in 2012 went to advance same-sex marriage. Only in Minnesota was there anything approaching parity between the sides. In Washington, proponents of Referendum 74 to legalize same-sex marriage outspent opponents by more than five-to-one.

When the schools ad aired in Minnesota, amendment opponents were already sitting on $1 million of television time reserved for their pushback ads. Due in part to such cash advantage, none of the states experienced the dramatic last-minute turnabout that had marked the closing weeks of the Proposition 8 campaign. Matt McTighe of Mainers United took to thinking of it as a game of rock-paper-scissors, where successive messages had trumped one another. "We used to have scissors, like *rights and benefits*, and then they figured out this rock, *Your kids are going to be gay*," says McTighe. "Finally we have paper: *shared values and moms* are bigger than all of your bullshit, so we're able to win the day with that."

While Freedom to Marry claimed the results would attest to the persuasive power of its messages—evidence that the group's research had in fact managed to "'crack the code' with Middle America," as Evan Wolfson promised—the most obvious dominance was in volume. In that respect, 2012 was never a fair fight. "We're talking about an issue that's decided on the margins. So, if you take two or three percent of our people and turn them to the other side, you just won. That's what happened—especially in an environment that we're not able to combat effectively," says Schubert. "From a messaging standpoint, it doesn't matter how big your message is if you're getting outspent three-to-one or four-to-one."

In Minnesota, Grove's internal polls showed Amendment 1 to ban gay marriage actually losing ground during the last ten days of October, when Schubert's schools ad hit airwaves. Opponents opened up a seven-point lead entering Election Day. Carlbom spent an hour that morning preparing for the speech he would give that night, in between visits to phone banks conducting last-minute get-out-the-vote calls. He headed that evening to the St. Paul RiverCentre with outlines for the speech he would give in each of three scenarios: one in case the amendment passed, one in case it failed, and another if it was too close to call.

An hour after midnight, Carlbom still did not know which set of notes to unscroll. Victory had been called for their side in Maine and Maryland, and the Washington marriage bill was on its way to a seven-point victory. But the prospects for marriage in Minnesota remained hazy, even though Democrats had retaken both houses of the legislature after two years out of power. The city of Minneapolis offered some explanation for the slow count: ballots had been produced with printing errors that made the ink unreadable by optical scanners, and a manual counting for certain precincts would begin the next day. Minnesotans United, however, was up against the plain language of a rental contract. At two a.m., it had to abandon the room it had reserved.

With fifteen minutes left before his team had to disband for the night, Carlbom rose from the detritus of beer bottles to address the exasperated yet tense staff and volunteer leadership from his too-close-to-call outline. "You all should go to bed tonight, feeling incredibly, incredibly proud of the work you have done," Carlbom said. "You sparked a conversation in Minnesota that has already gotten 1.3 million people to vote no." Carlbom was giving instructions for staffers to dial into a conference call the next morning when he was interrupted by communications director Kelly Schwinghammer. "Hey, Richard," she said, right before her words set off cathartic exultations. "The AP just called it."

That night, Carlbom received questions from journalists about whether he now expected action on marriage at the capitol blocks away. The campaign he had won begged the question. After all, in fighting a constitutional ban, Minnesotans United had chosen to go further than it had to with its messaging, making an affirmative case for marriage and depicting civil unions as an inadequate substitute. Carlbom was pleased to acknowledge the mandate, but reluctant to place demands on the new Democratic majorities. "Give the legislators space," Carlbom recalls thinking. "We wanted to say to them, 'Focus on your budget.' We are going to continue this conversation with voters; that hasn't ended, but we're not promising you a marriage bill."

Within weeks, however, Carlbom had already mapped a strategy to pass one. Within a month, he drafted a proposal to the Civil Marriage Collaborative to fund the next iteration of Minnesotans United. Carlbom hoped to keep together his team of consultants and pollsters, microtargeters and psychologists, with a focus on the same tactics. They would aim to generate 200,000 conversations, this time weighted toward the districts of persuadable legislators. "We will again spark conversations was [sic] by motivating the thousands of volunteers already trained on the elements of a deeply relational conversation on the subject of marriage equality," Carlbom wrote. "Historic advances toward marriage equality nationally, including Minnesota, in 2012 along with successful legislative efforts will inform our approach in this public education campaign."

Those advances would be felt beyond the borders of states who saw their laws changed, and even beyond other state capitals in which gay-rights activists immediately revised upward their view of the possible. Ever since 2009, a pair of lawsuits had been moving toward the Supreme Court, and now despite their divergent and potentially conflicting legal strategies, the lawyers behind both of them were wondering how much the judicial and executive branches of the federal government could also be moved by the political momentum generated in the states.

Part Nine

ENDGAME

(2009–2015)

80

Dooming DOMA

On March 3, 2009, Mary Bonauto returned to the Omni Parker House facing Boston Common for a press conference. After three successful state lawsuits for equal marriage rights, she had just filed her first in federal court, and she wanted to describe it with a phalanx of plaintiffs whose stories she wanted to tell. But to properly do that she knew she had to "reintroduce DOMA," as the only piece of federal legislation to address same-sex marriage was acronymically known.

For a while the Defense of Marriage Act was a legislative curio, provoking an intensity wildly disproportionate to its short-term impact, which was nil. The fact that no one was immediately affected was noted by the bill's opponents as a source of consolation, and cited thenceforth by its unenthusiastic backers—like Bill Clinton, who had made a show of signing it ambivalently—as a mitigating factor. (Even its more moderate supporters said upon passage that, without any state yet marrying gay couples, they intended it only as a prophylactic.) Soon enough, the Defense of Marriage Act was superseded by other legislative proposals on the subject, and politicians were asked instead for their positions on various federal constitutional amendments. Bonauto's task in reintroducing DOMA was to let the world know that the thirteen-year-old law had not just been moldering on the books.

When seeking to justify a nonprofit public-interest law firm's decision to rent a conference room at a marquee hotel around the corner from their downtown headquarters, GLAD officials liked to lean upon the Parker House's history: its location on the Freedom Trail, Malcolm X's time working its dining room as a teenage busboy, and the fact that John F. Kennedy had declared his first candidacy for office there. (That Ho Chi Minh had briefly toiled in its bakery would go unmentioned.) More recently, the hotel had become the site of numerous press conferences focused on the *Goodridge* suit. The Parker House had been a stop on the 2001 statewide tour where Bonauto unveiled her new clients, where she had held the triumphant press conference barely two hours after the Supreme Judicial Court's decision in 2003, and again months later to celebrate the court's ruling that civil unions would not be a sufficient substitute for marriage.

Bonauto had been quietly working on the case that would become *Gill v. Office of Personnel Management* ever since the *Goodridge* mandate took effect on May 17, 2004. Once gays and lesbians could legally marry in Massachusetts, many happy couples found their wedded bliss almost immediately tempered by the realization that they could not get passports reissued in their new, married names. "The LGBT community had so much to learn about what was actually being withheld from them," says Bonauto. "In many ways people did not know what they were missing, both with marriage and then even when they had marriage, because of DOMA."

Nancy Gill and Marcelle Letourneau did not require passports for their honeymoon to Cape Cod—together for twenty-four years, they brought along their two children—but were nonetheless confronted with a bureaucratic challenge upon their return. When Gill, a postal clerk in Brockton, returned to work the following Monday she applied to add her wife to her health-insurance plan. To Gill's surprise, the perfunctory request was denied. Since her workplace was governed by the federal code, it was as if Gill had never been married—one of the 1,138 places where Congress had excluded gay couples from recognition under the Defense of Marriage Act. Being forced to keep separate insurance plans, the couple estimated, cost them $800 more per year.

GLAD was powerless to aid those like Gill who were affected by the Defense of Marriage Act, but it tracked all the incoming calls for help. In 2004, GLAD asked MassEquality to dispatch volunteers to town offices across the state to record names of newly married same-sex couples. (Clerks had removed any specific reference to sex on forms, so volunteers were left looking for couples married since May 17 with similarly gendered names.) In 2005, GLAD sent out a survey to every one of the couples inquiring about their interactions with the federal government once married; two years later, GLAD emailed again, looking for examples of DOMA's impact on everyday lives. In some cases, they theorized types of harm but did not have examples of actual people who had suffered it, and set off on a more targeted search. GLAD ran ads in two Boston-area community newspapers seeking one particularly media-friendly archetype:

a military veteran whose desire was to be buried at Arlington National Cemetery alongside a spouse had been foiled because they were both of the same sex.

As they encountered potential candidates, GLAD's small team of lawyers guided them to request whatever the federal government would owe them if they were straight—whether a tax refund or Social Security check or, for public employees, a period of medical leave—even if the request would be greeted with dismissive skepticism by the federal officials who received it. Attorneys directed their prospective plaintiffs to pursue every turn in the byzantine appeal process, no matter the certain dead end that lay beyond. They had to exhaust all the administrative options so that the only concern left to be resolved would be the underlying constitutional question. "The federal government litigators are known for procedural finesse," says Bonauto, "and they consider it a victory when they can void the merits of the case and just talk about procedure."

Out of public view, she retained a Washington firm that specialized in federal administrative law and put it to work before the Merit Systems Protection Board, which rules on appeals under civil-service regulations. Their client, Dean Hara, was the widower of Representative Gerry Studds, who had become the country's first openly gay congressman when he was outed amid scandal in 1983. Hara and Studds exchanged rings in 1991 after dating for nine months; in 1997, they registered as domestic partners. (Provincetown, where the couple lived part-time, did not require applicants to be residents.) On May 24, 2004, one week after same-sex marriage was made legal in Massachusetts, the two joined another gay couple in a dual ceremony with just a few guests. "It became very obvious it was going to happen," says Hara. "I don't want to take the romance out of it, but it was like, 'We should do it'—because we've been together, and if we don't get married what message would that send? It would be the right thing to do."

Studds was likely the first public figure ever to participate in a legal same-sex marriage, although he and Hara did little to publicize their nuptials. The *New York Times* refused to publish their wedding announcement because it was submitted after the small ceremony had taken place; on the couple's one-year anniversary the *Quincy Patriot Ledger* (based in Studds's old congressional district) reported on the marriage as though unearthing an exclusive. Hara and Studds were well aware that the Defense of Marriage Act limited the value of a Massachusetts marriage license, even within the state's own borders. The pair had been living in Washington in 1996, when DOMA was being debated on the House floor, and Studds—

who had already announced his retirement at the year's end—spoke out against the bill as Hara watched the debate from the House gallery. After Studds died in October 2006, having collapsed from a blood clot in his lung, Hara applied for survivor benefits: his husband's pension and the lifetime health insurance due to the widower of a federal employee. When his application was rejected, Bonauto had her first plaintiff.

Not all of Bonauto's clients were government employees or their spouses. Al Toney had married Keith Fitzpatrick not long after Massachusetts gave them the opportunity to do so, and subsequently Fitzpatrick dropped his birth name so that he could share a surname with their college-age daughter. When the State Department had refused to issue Keith Toney a passport in his new name—citing DOMA in its letters explaining the decision not to recognize a marriage already reflected on his Massachusetts driver's license—Bonauto had another plaintiff. "Given heightened security concerns world-wide since September 11, 2001, traveling in a foreign country with an inconsistent and inaccurate passport that does not match Keith's other identification documents or have his correct, legal name has caused them both to feel vulnerable and insecure when they have travelled abroad," Bonauto asserted to establish the "specific and concrete harm" necessary for the Worcester couple to sue.

The fact that Bonauto aimed her suit at the Defense of Marriage Act's third section represented a major strategic turnabout. At the time of the bill's passage, nearly all the debate inside and outside Congress then concerned the second section, titled "Powers Reserved to the States." Evan Wolfson had trumpeted the Constitution's full-faith-and-credit clause as the mechanism by which success in Hawaii could be leveraged elsewhere. In a 1996 memo on the proposed bill's "constitutional defects," Wolfson described Section II's language carving out an exemption to the clause for same-sex marriages as an "unconstitutional or ill-advised intrusion of the federal government into an area left to the states." Wolfson left Section III, concerning federal definitions, effectively unmentioned until page thirteen of the twenty-four-page memo. "Congress indisputably has significant power to legislate within its own spheres of competence," he and coauthor Michael Melcher conceded in a footnote. Bonauto initially shared Wolfson's focus on Section II; an "Is DOMA Doomed?" fact sheet she wrote upon the bill's passage was devoted almost exclusively to the full-faith-and-credit issues.

But with time, the balance of interest in the bill's two sections flipped. Many scholars concluded that Wolfson's constitutional analysis was legally dubious. "The practice of recognizing out-of-state marriages makes this line of thought very difficult to let go of," says Matt Coles of the ACLU. "But there really turned out not to be much there." If the Constitution did require states to accept one another's judgments on the legality of same-sex unions, why wouldn't it compel it in both directions, whereby states that recognized gay couples would also be required to accept court judgments treating such unions as invalid? Even if the Supreme Court did strike down DOMA's second section, all the state bans passed in 2004 and 2006 would still be in force.

By 2008, the gay legal groups—including GLAD, Lambda Legal, and the ACLU—had all backed away from the once widely accepted assumption that the first step into federal court would be over the full-faith-and-credit clause. That summer, the groups issued a joint memo aimed at would-be plaintiffs that publicly repudiated a challenge to Section II as a matter of both legal theory and strategy.

Challenging DOMA's third section also looked like the more politically palatable route, a comparatively modest request of a federal judiciary fearful of unilaterally imposing major social changes. Editing out opposite-sex-only language from the federal code would affect only married people in the two states that had accepted gay marriage. A theoretical challenge to the second section, however, would implicate the other forty-eight and their resistant politicians. Once there were states that had legalized gay marriage, the Defense of Marriage Act looked less like an assertion of their self-determination than an infringement of it. If Massachusetts through its sovereign institutions had decided to let Nancy Gill and Marcelle Letourneau wed, what right did Congress have to convert theirs into a second-class marriage?

Yet even as GLAD collected evidence, Bonauto was not ready to file a suit, cognizant of the fact that the Massachusetts legislature could still scare up a Constitutional Convention to undo the *Goodridge* decision and theoretically invalidate four years' worth of marriages. Instead, GLAD continued to push ahead with the fight for marriage in neighboring states, like Connecticut, where its senior attorney, Ben Klein, argued its appeal before the state supreme court in May 2007. "Having only a single state made us very vulnerable," says Bonauto. "I remember thinking you can't just defend Massachusetts and have it be the only marriage state. That's the strategy that our opponents wanted—to confine marriage to Massachusetts and eventually they would get an amendment, state or federal, that would knock us out of the water."

By that June, when the legislature rejected the most recent effort at a constitutional amendment, success in Massachusetts was safe. Nonetheless, Bonauto remained alert to the electoral calendar. Out of deference to the movement's political interests, she had decided to hold off until after the 2008 election. The Federal Marriage Amendment had slid from relevance—the Republican nominee, John McCain, had been one of his party's most consistent opponents in the Senate—and a lawsuit could return gay marriage to the presidential debate as a matter of national policy. In early 2009, Bonauto visited the new White House domestic-policy adviser, Melody Barnes, and informed her that she was about to sue the federal government.

As with many litigators, Bonauto was intensely competitive and gifted with a prevailing self-confidence. Unlike many of her peers, however, she spoke softly and without bluster, a combination of traits that some observers mistook for modesty or a lack of ego. Bonauto's swagger was better read in the content of her words than in their volume. At the Parker House press conference, she said something no gay-rights lawyer had ever said before about a piece of marriage litigation, and which several of her peers hoped would ultimately prove false about this one. "This is a case," Bonauto declared, "that should go to the Supreme Court, and in all likelihood will go to the Supreme Court."

Dave & Ted's Excellent Adventure

A little over two months after Mary Bonauto filed her first challenge to the Defense of Marriage Act, Rob Reiner and his wife Michele invited the Los Angeles representatives of Lambda Legal and the American Civil Liberties Union over for lunch. Along with the National Center for Lesbian Rights (NCLR), their two groups were responsible for the original *In re Marriage Cases* suit that had triumphed, and now they were back before the California Supreme Court under less promising circumstances. A day after Proposition 8 passed, they banded together once again as the Our Families Coalition to challenge the result. What became known as *Strauss v. Horton* was a collection of last-gasp lawsuits that contended, through a variety of claims, that Proposition 8 had overstepped what could be accomplished through a constitutional amendment. (The case also dealt with the separate matter of whether the approximately eighteen thousand marriages that had been performed during the five-month window leading up to Election Day should be invalidated as a result of the vote.) The case had been argued before the California Supreme Court in March 2009, which meant a decision was expected in late May, and the fact that its lawyers had been invited to lunch in Brentwood days beforehand indicated that no one present was expecting to win.

Jenny Pizer and Jon Davidson, of Lambda, and Ramona Ripston and Mark Rosenbaum, of the ACLU, arrived unsure of what to expect. The Reiners were among the area's most prominent liberals, and eager to immerse themselves in tactical minutiae in a way many entertainment figures wouldn't. They had invited Bruce Cohen, like Rob a film producer active in lefty Hollywood circles, and Chad Griffin and Kristina Schake, partners in a communications firm that had worked with the Reiners on statewide ballot-initiative campaigns to increase funding for early-childhood education. They were joined by Ted Boutrous, a litigator at the law firm Gibson Dunn. Griffin was the group's ringleader, but Boutrous did most of the talking. He laid out the future of marriage litigation in California if, as anticipated, the *Strauss v. Horton* challenge was rejected. The plaintiffs would be without recourse in California, which Boutrous argued meant it was time to turn to federal courts. He and his companions were cagey about what exactly they would do, or when, but one thing was clear enough to put a scare in the civil-rights lawyers: Griffin and his gang had the U.S. Supreme Court in their sights.

Gay-rights litigators had always assumed that the tangle of legal questions around same-sex marriage could be settled only by the U.S. Supreme Court. Yet they had always worked to delay any invitation for the court to consider the matter as long as it seemed likely to rule unfavorably. From the earliest drafting of his lawsuit against the state of Hawaii, Dan Foley had avoided any claim that could require interpretation of the U.S. Constitution. In her Vermont, Massachusetts, and Connecticut suits, Bonauto had adhered to the same principle.

But in early 2003, gay-rights groups that had cautioned others to avoid federal court agreed to represent a Nebraska activist group, Citizens for Equal Protection, when it sought to have a 2000 amendment to the state constitution struck down for violating federal equal-protection guarantees. The amendment had been so broad that the attorney general ruled that it precluded the legislature from even considering any measure to recognize same-sex couples, which plaintiffs argued helped qualify it as a bill of attainder, a law unfairly targeting particular citizens. Lambda Legal and the ACLU signed on to the suit, somewhat reluctantly, but insisted in their brief that it "is not about marriage; it is about a basic right of citizenship—the right to an even playing field in the political arena." The court did not see it that way, ruling in such a fashion that if plaintiffs pursued further appeals they could risk a precedent that could damage future marriage litigation. After losing in the Eighth Circuit, the groups convinced their clients to drop the matter. "That law's unconstitutional and these are righteous claims," recalls the ACLU's James Esseks. "But in a world in which there is precisely one marriage state in the United States, that's not necessarily something you put before the Supreme Court unless you're taking a real flyer."

The Jersey City summit's 10-10-10-20 strategy had set a plausible horizon in 2025. A case could be made four years later that things might be slightly ahead of schedule, but no one was arguing that the conditions were right in 2009 to trigger the endgame. Bonauto justified her decision to move ahead with the *Gill v. Office of Personnel Management* suit on the grounds that it would have no effect on state laws, but that did not dissipate skepticism from other corners of the gay legal establishment that despite its focused trajectory Bonauto was still charging too quickly into federal court. "It is not hard to see how a ruling in a DOMA case is going to affect the ultimate marriage case," says Esseks. "What is the map of the country going to look like when the court gets this issue? It's got to look a whole lot better than it did in 2000 or 2005 in order to have any prayer that we're going to win."

Such ambiguity was not easily communicated to rank-and-file gays and lesbians who did not understand why the next step for those blocked in state courts should not be the federal judiciary. There was no "magic number" of states that would justify that move, the ACLU's Matt Coles told the Associated Press in the spring of 2006. "We think, strategically, bringing a federal claim for marriage now is not a wise idea," Coles said. "The Supreme Court is the country's institutional conscience, and if you lose there, I think that sets you back."

At that point, he was trying to explain why his group, along with Lambda Legal, were refusing to support a lawsuit by Arthur Smelt and Christopher Hammer, a Southern California couple who had exchanged rings in 1997 and then seven years later sued in federal court over what they said was unconstitutional discrimination that prevented them from making it official. (The pair dissolved a 2000 domestic partnership in late 2004, apparently to strengthen the claim that they were being denied the right to formalize their relationship.) The ACLU and Lambda "would have told Dred Scott, 'Don't bring your case,'" Smelt's attorney, Richard Gilbert, said to the Associated Press. In arguing that the resulting 1857 decision—which equated blacks to property—was productive because a "great stain like that on the courts" helped trigger the Civil War, he had oddly held up perhaps the worst civil-rights ruling in the Supreme Court's history to argue the moral imperative of moving forward at any cost.

Days before the California Supreme Court's *In re Marriage Cases* would take effect in July 2008, the country's gay legal groups had bonded together to articulate their shared disapproval of lawsuits that could reach the Supreme Court. There risked being a lot more Richard Gilberts arguing as he did that "when the building is on fire, you don't stand by and let the building burn down and say we'll fight the fire another day," and hundreds of thousands of potential plaintiffs eager to force the hand of the federal judiciary.

The groups drafted their memo advising readers to "Make Change, Not Lawsuits." The six-page document was written in an unusually plain-spoken voice, aimed not at other lawyers but the same-sex couples—both those who lived in California and those from out of state—who litigators feared would brandish their new paperwork and demand employers or government agencies treat them as married. "One thing couples shouldn't do is just sue the federal government," the document instructed. "Pushing the federal government before we have a critical mass of states recognizing samesex [*sic*] relationships or suing in states where the courts aren't ready is likely to get us bad rulings. Bad rulings will make it much more difficult for us to win marriage, and will certainly make it take much longer."

At the Reiners' home, the dedicated gay-rights litigators reiterated the logic of the memo to which they had been signatories and affirmed its intent. Rosenbaum, speaking for the ACLU, asked Griffin to hold off with his plans to sue, and was dismissed. Davidson would recall the hosts showed "a lot of disrespect for the fact that a lot of people who had been working on these issues for a very long time had a different viewpoint." It should have been apparent that demands to reconsider strategy would be futile as soon as Boutrous revealed that he had attended the lunch as a proxy for a partner at his firm, Ted Olson, whose presence would have made everything yet more contentious. A former solicitor general in George W. Bush's administration, Olson had remained a regular at the Supreme Court bar after he returned to private practice, often as a champion of the type of conservative and corporate interests that Boutrous knew would make public-interest lawyers recoil at mention of his name. "Someone is going to bring a federal marriage lawsuit," Boutrous said. "And you won't find a better advocate than Ted Olson."

Griffin wished for acquiescence from his lunchmates, but he had not gathered them seeking authorization to proceed. As a nineteen-year-old Arkansas Bible-college student, he had parlayed an internship on Bill Clinton's campaign into a job in the White House press office and took to describing himself as the youngest West Wing staffer ever. Griffin had not come out as gay for nearly another decade, but as a Los Angeles political consultant he made a professional trait of his overeagerness. A few weeks before the Brentwood meeting, he had set up a new nonprofit organization to fund the suit and offer communications support he considered crucial to realizing its aims. The group's name was the American Foundation for

Equal Rights, and the only iconography in its logo was a stylized flag—which, Griffin would note proudly, was the Stars and Stripes and not a rainbow. ("It has to have the word 'American' in it," he had told Schake as they brainstormed names. "And it shouldn't sound like a gay rights group.") Already Griffin was in the process of raising "millions of dollars" in a one-month period from "less than a dozen" donors, as he would later put it. AFER would refuse to disclose their names—claiming it would wait until the National Organization for Marriage had done so—although many belonged to prominent Hollywood figures happy to be seen at its swank fundraisers.

A massive war chest would be essential, because Griffin knew from the outset that he would not win any cooperation from the gay-rights groups built to mount such cases. Griffin managed to frame this as both a virtue and a provocation: he would later tell the *New Yorker* that he sought "the lawyers Microsoft is going to want, not the lawyers who are going to do it pro bono." Gibson Dunn agreed to comp the first $100,000 of its services, but charged for its work—albeit in the form of flat fees rather than hourly rates—beyond that. (In its first year, AFER would report income of $3.4 million, about three-quarters of which appeared to go directly to legal expenses connected to the case.)

Although it became known over the course of the spring among both gay-rights lawyers and wealthy Los Angeles liberals that Griffin was plotting a lawsuit, its filing was the subject of great secrecy. Once it was "greenlighted," as Griffin liked to describe it, he focused on the elaborate mise-en-scène that would surround its public introduction. To avoid any incidents that could draw undue attention, the papers were delivered by an attorney, rather than a courier, just before the clerk's office closed for the weekend. "We did not want to have a big debate about what we felt was the right strategy," explained Boutrous. "We did not want that debate to break out before we launched our suit."

On May 26, the California Supreme Court released its opinion in *Strauss v. Horton,* upholding Proposition 8 and ending any hope of restoring same-sex marriage to California by any method other than another constitutional amendment. (In the same ruling, the court let the disputed eighteen thousand marriages stand.) Griffin had already rented a ballroom at the Biltmore Hotel in downtown Los Angeles, and had a satellite truck at the ready so that cable networks could broadcast live. The news would not be as much about what was happening as who was doing it.

The stage was soldiered with American flags, before which stood Griffin, two sets of same-sex couples, and the pair of lawyers who would represent them. Olson stood alongside David Boies, the litigator who had defended IBM, CBS, and New York Yankees owner George Steinbrenner in some of the era's most prominent trials, and had represented the Justice Department in its antitrust case against Microsoft. He and Olson had first met in late 2000, when the two faced off in oral arguments over the allocation of Florida's twenty-five electoral votes: Olson handled George W. Bush's appeal of the state supreme court's order of a statewide recount, while Boies represented Democrat Al Gore. The Supreme Court handed the election to Olson's client, but he and Boies emerged as friends. They had collaborated on other cases as a well-matched pair with complementary specialties—Olson was an appellate litigator, Boies a trial lawyer—but Boies's great value on the stage was for political balance. The two made copious mention of their divergent partisan orientations, and the symbolic value of their partnership—a cause beyond politics.

The two cocounsels in the case known as *Perry v. Schwarzenegger* explained their grounds for challenging Proposition 8. Even if the amendment process had adhered to California state law, the result offended a higher power: the United States Constitution. (The suit was named for Kris Perry, first of the four plaintiffs alphabetically, and the executive of the state that had invalidated her 2004 marriage.) By excluding gays and lesbians from joining on the same terms as heterosexuals, Proposition 8—like, presumably, every state law that distinguished couples based on their gender composition—denied citizens a fundamental right for no defensible reason. The lawyers' stated model was *Loving v. Virginia,* the 1967 case that had helped establish a constitutional right to marry. By striking down Virginia's ban on intermarriage, the Supreme Court also voided fifteen other states' antimiscegenation statutes, as well. "There will be many people who will think this is not the time to go to federal," Olson said at the press conference. "Both David and I have studied the court for more years than probably either one of us would like to admit. We think we know what we are doing."

It was, in many respects, the opposite of the way Bonauto had justified her entry into federal court two months earlier. In Los Angeles, the focus was not on the harm suffered by plaintiffs as much as the benevolent wisdom of the lawyers involved. "That thing had stage presence and legs from the first moment," Coles says of the suit. "What it lacked was heart."

In fact, the plaintiffs had been the last piece of the AFER case to fall into place, slotted in only after the group had filed its papers of incorporation and begun raising money. (After months of seeking out three perfect couples through what they called a "major casting call," Griffin and Schake ended up settling for two they identified via personal ties: they had worked with Kris Perry and Sandy Stier through the Reiners' child-advocacy work, and were introduced to Paul Katami and Jeff Zarrillo by a common realtor.) While GLAD published a twenty-three-page "DOMA Stories" booklet with extended portraits of the seventeen plaintiffs in *Gill v. Office of Public Management*—describing how the couples met, the lives they had built together, and the particular impact of lost federal benefits—the part of the AFER press release devoted to its plaintiffs described the two couples in a few sentences each. On the other hand, Boies's professional biography was covered in seven paragraphs and Olson's in eight.

Bonauto emphasized that her case had been drawn as narrowly as possible, so that only residents of the two states could possibly be affected by its resolution. (She made a virtue of the fact that "this is not going to be a case that results in more people getting married if we win," as she put it.) Boies and Olson declared that their case would challenge one state's laws with the objective of implicating every other state in the decision that emerged, along with the federal definition that the Defense of Marriage Act had rewritten. While Bonauto acknowledged her case could eventually end up before the Supreme Court, Boies and Olson were eager to display their impatience. "Reasonable minds can differ, but when you have people being denied civil rights today, I think it is impossible as lawyers and as an American to say, 'No, you have to wait, now is not the right time,'" Boies said. "I think if we had done that in prior civil rights battles, we would not be where we are."

It was very much constitutional litigation as curated by a public-relations man, and it earned the intended response. The *New York Times* headlined its news report BUSH V. GORE FOES JOIN TO FIGHT GAY MARRIAGE BAN and led the story with this apothegm: "The David and Ted show is back in business." Over the following few weeks, the two attorneys kept up an intense schedule of interviews, surfacing on a majority of cable-news networks to discuss the case before they had appeared in court.

As the *Perry v. Schwarzenegger* suit drew national media attention, much of the coverage centered on its *let's put on a show* origin story. The Reiners had invited Griffin to lunch at the Polo Lounge days after Proposition 8's passage, where they ran into a woman who turned out to be Olson's sister-in-law. Amid the commiseration over the amendment's passage, she volunteered an intriguing fact: the most famous Republican litigator in the country was a gay-marriage supporter who shared their disappointment at the result of the vote. A week later, Griffin met with Olson in his Washington office, and the two began plotting what a federal challenge would look like. Griffin was enamored of the against-type casting of Olson as a potential protagonist, but the attorney knew that as a straight conservative Republican his involvement would leave the case permanently suspect.

Even though in the retelling Olson left the impression that it had been his first instinct to enlist Boies as cocounsel, he had actually extended the invitation first to two other attorneys, each with impeccable gay-rights credentials. Only after both turned down Olson's entreaties, in May, did he ask Boies, who readily accepted. The involvement of another straight attorney from a big corporate firm would do nothing to mitigate the impression that the case was a potentially opportunistic and shortsighted annexation of the gay-rights cause by outsiders. Yet their collaboration made it possible for Griffin to push a new narrative of his case, of two commonsense lawyers letting their common humanity rise above the partisanship that had helped define the marriage debate.

Many gay-rights activists remained suspicious of the pair's motives, though few actual lawyers adopted the theory circulating that the entire project amounted to an elaborate conspiracy to sabotage the gay-rights movement by putting a marriage case in front of the Supreme Court before it could possibly triumph. But the Roundtable litigators were as aware as Griffin was of the public power of a bipartisan-buddy narrative, starring altruistic heterosexual establishmentarians swooping in to save a besieged minority unable to fend for itself. Media coverage was unlikely to focus on the crucial distinction between a litigation strategy in state or federal courts—or the difference between a challenge to the Defense of Marriage Act and a state ban—and instead accept the Boies-Olson self-description as men of bold action against civil-rights advocates shell-shocked into undue caution.

Gay-rights groups not only refused to bless the suit, but savaged it with uncharacteristic bravado. They issued an updated version of the "Make Change, Not Lawsuits" memo from nearly a year earlier. It had been drafted to discourage laypeople from rushing into court and now was being put to work to shame some of the country's most famous attorneys—and perhaps stoke their major donors' doubts about continuing to finance the undertaking. (Even when Lambda Legal submitted an amicus brief in favor of an early procedural motion, its attorney Jenny Pizer insisted that AFER withdraw a press release that had characterized her group as "supporting" the suit.) Litigators who had worked on marriage cases chafed in particular at press coverage that depicted the new undertaking as somehow clever or courageous rather than reckless. "Federal court?" Coles observed sarcastically to the *New York Times*. "Wow. Never thought of that."

Unable to derail the suit by either shame or suasion, gay-rights groups attempted to hijack it in court, much as their counterparts on the far right were used to doing. The Our Families Coalition groups petitioned the court to allow them all to join the case as plaintiffs. Despite the historic ambition of their suit, the groups asserted, Olson and Boies focused too narrow a lens on the ways they hoped to shape future law. They spoke about their case as solely a quest for equal marriage rights, but it stood to affect other legal aspects of the gay experience that the case's sponsors had never articulated as an immediate concern. At the same time, the Our Family Coalition enlisted two other community organizations—Lavender Seniors of the East Bay and Parents, Families, and Friends of Lesbians and Gays—to join their petition. The people whose names were on *Perry v. Schwarzenegger,* all white and in their thirties and forties, did not represent "the full range of lesbian and gay individuals and couples," the groups said in their motion. ("Look at the perfect gay people," the website Gawker would quip about the four plaintiffs.) "These groups wish to illustrate for the court the diverse needs of their members and the lesbian, gay, bisexual, and transgender (LGBT) community generally to provide the full factual record," Pizer explained.

Plaintiffs did not challenge the requests by Proposition 8 backers to be involved, insisting they had no interest in wasting the court's time on the "unnecessary dispute," but aggressively resisted the Our Families Coalition's offer of assistance. "Having declined to bring their own federal challenge to Proposition 8, Our Family Coalition and their counsel should not be allowed to usurp plaintiffs' lawsuit," Boies and Olson wrote in a brief arguing that the court should keep the gay groups out.

Out of court, Griffin was blunter in his accusation about the motives of his putative allies. "Given our willingness to collaborate with you, and your efforts to undercut this case, we were surprised and disappointed when we became aware of your desire to intervene. You have unrelentingly and unequivocally acted to undermine this case even before it was filed. In light of this, it is inconceivable that you would zealously and effectively litigate this case if you were successful in intervening," he wrote to the same officials he had met at the Reiners' for lunch six weeks earlier. "Having gone to such great lengths to dissuade us from filing suit and to tar this case in the press, it seems likely that your misgivings about our strategy will be reflected—either subtly or overtly—in your actions in court."

Even if their intentions were pure, Griffin argued, the groups' involvement would unquestionably complicate what his team had engineered to be a streamlined vehicle. "We could be mired in procedurally convoluted pre-trial maneuvering for years," asserted Griffin, complicating what he said was AFER's goal of "an expeditious, efficient, and inexpensive resolution to the district court proceedings."

The last part hinted at the greatest threat to the Olson-Boies strategy. The lawyers were looking for a fast track to the Supreme Court and rejected anything that could delay or reroute them. On July 2, Olson appeared before Judge Walker and said that he and Chuck Cooper, the lawyer representing Proposition 8's proponents, believed they could agree to all the relevant facts so that Walker could jump ahead directly to the question of constitutional interpretation. "We are very close to the same page on this, actually," Cooper told Walker.

If the opposing lawyers thought they were offering the judge an easy way out of a tricky matter, Walker did not welcome it. Indeed, he had become so convinced of the trajectory that Olson and Boies had outlined through the press that he had come to envision his courtroom as a mere way station. "I'm reasonably sure, given the issues involved and given the personnel that are in the courtroom, that this case is only touching down in this court, that it will have a life after this court, and what happens here, in many ways, is only a prelude to what is going to happen later," Walker said. "So I am inclined to think that how we do things here is more important than what we do, that our job in this case, at this point, is to make a record."

Choosing to stage a trial, especially when neither plaintiffs nor defendants had requested one, was unusual. While 20 percent of federal civil cases went to trial in the 1930s, by 2010 only 2 percent did. (Trials were still twice as prevalent in federal courts as state ones.) Walker, however, insisted that where marriage was concerned it would not be enough for two appellate litigators to joust over interpretations of the law. Both sides would be forced to assemble a stable structure of facts before a judge and opposition who could subject the entire intellectual artifice to a stress test. They would have to justify their claims about the nature of homosexuality and the optimal composition of the American family, and whether either was the type of issue over which society would permit reasonable people to disagree and settle their quarrels through politics.

Even so, Cooper exaggerated the novelty of what was about to unfold.

"As far as our research has been able to turn up, we can't find that any of the marriage cases, the dozen or so of them that have proceeded around the country, actually submitted issues of fact to trial, as opposed to having gone off on summary judgment," Cooper told Walker at a pretrial conference. It was an unusual oversight in particular from Cooper, since he had been involved in the Hawaii case that had gone to trial thirteen years earlier. (Cooper was hired by the state to handle its appeal of the verdict of the 1996 trial in the *Baehr v. Miike* case.)

The unpreparedness of both sides offered the Our Families Coalition another opening to leave its mark on the case. If there was going to be a trial, the groups argued to Walker, it would be better positioned than the two straight attorneys who had never litigated a gay-rights case to marshal the experts, social-science research, and historical background necessary to document that Proposition 8 was unfairly discriminatory. Even before the judge had decided whether they would be granted any formal role in it, the Our Families Coalition groups delivered him a "case management statement"—essentially an outline of the trial they would like to put on, including the names of specific professors who could be called as witnesses and what their testimony would cover.

Following one mid-August session, Olson invited the ACLU, Lambda, and NCLR lawyers to a lunch meeting at his firm's office a mile down Mission Street from the federal courthouse. The decision of how closely they would be forced to collaborate rested with Walker, but ultimately—despite their publicly aired differences over legal strategy and case-management tactics—they would end up on the same side. Now that the case was in front of a judge, the Our Families Coalition could not afford to see it lose. At the same time, AFER realized it would only gain from minimizing outside snipes from gay-rights advocates, and might even benefit from their expertise. "At that point we wanted to make peace," says Coles. "We wanted this done right."

Three days later, Walker ruled as Olson and Boies had hoped he would. The Our Families Coalition would be kept out of the case, asserting that their interests were already well represented by the plaintiffs; the groups could file amicus briefs, but nothing more. At the same time, he granted the plaintiffs' begrudging proposal to admit a less outwardly hostile party. While the row over Our Families Coalition's petition received more attention, the city of San Francisco, which in 2004 had initiated the entire cycle of litigation that led to Proposition 8, had concurrently pursued its own. (The city asserted that the case's outcome would affect both its own citizens' legal status and the government's budget.) While Olson opposed both of the motions to intervene, he eventually conceded that if one outside party were to be let in, "it should be the City alone that is permitted to join."

For the gay legal groups, it was a reasonable consolation. Unlike the team Olson had assembled, San Francisco's lawyers had experience litigating gay-rights cases. Perhaps more importantly, they represented a constituency that would outlive AFER, and with a set of community concerns well beyond the small circle of anonymous donors financing the suit. "In an odd sort of a way," says Coles, "the city and the county had a stronger connection than the Olson and Boies team did."

Duty to Defend

Less than four months into his term, Barack Obama was extended his first opportunity to shape the Supreme Court through the retirement of Justice David Souter, who appeared to have waited for a Democratic administration to ensure he would be replaced by a like-minded judge. Souter had been nominated by a Republican, George H. W. Bush, but in two decades on the bench he often lined up with justices who had been appointed by Democrats. He had been part of the six-vote majorities in *Romer v. Evans* and *Lawrence v. Texas,* the two decisions that had righted the most egregious mistreatment gays and lesbians faced before the law.

Obama's replacement was unlikely to dramatically alter that basic math around gay-rights jurisprudence. But his pick, federal appeals judge Sonia Sotomayor, was nonetheless challenged repeatedly for her views around same-sex marriage. The issue had come up only glancingly in confirmation hearings for George W. Bush's two nominees. Chief Justice John Roberts was not interrogated at all about same-sex marriage, and Samuel Alito faced only one question on the matter. (Kansas senator Sam Brownback, who had just concluded a presidential campaign that had focused almost exclusively on winning over Iowa evangelicals, asked Alito if he believed the full-faith-and-credit clause applied to marriage recognition.)

A year and a half later, however, Sotomayor was greeted in the Senate Judiciary Committee with an extended disquisition by Iowa senator Charles Grassley about the court's obscure 1972 one-sentence dismissal of the Minnesota appeal *Baker v. Nelson.* As opposed to other inquiries she parried by declaring she could not weigh in on matters that might come before the court, Sotomayor pled ignorance about the specifics of the case. (*Baker v. Nelson* had not come up in law school, she explained.) When she asked for "the opportunity to come back tomorrow and just address that issue," Grassley happily sent her off with homework and pressed her the next day to expound on whether *Baker v. Nelson* should bind the court from ruling on state marriage laws.

Later, Texas Republican John Cornyn offered some context for his party's rising interest in her perspective, presenting Sotomayor with a hypothetical scenario rendered with a highly specific sense of urgency. "If the Supreme Court in the next few years holds that there is a constitutional right to same-sex marriage," Cornyn asked her, "would that be making the law or would that be interpreting the law?"

Within the White House that had sent Sotomayor's nomination to Capitol Hill, such a scenario seemed unreasonably farfetched. As a candidate, Obama received few signals that marriage rights were a policy priority within the gay community, or liberal activists more broadly. "Personally I did five hundred events—fundraisers, meetings with activist groups," says David Plouffe, the manager of Obama's 2008 campaign. "I can count on one hand the number of times I got asked about gay marriage."

Most of the demands gay activists placed upon Obama amounted to a backlog of unfinished business from 1994, the last time Democrats had unified control of the executive and legislative branches. There were, at long last, good prospects for a hate-crimes bill that specifically protected gays and lesbians, but other items high on the gay-rights agenda were fraught with complexities. Even though the political environment might be right to pass a nondiscrimination bill covering sexual orientation, now gay activists were divided about whether to hold out for a bill that would forbid discrimination against transgendered people, or to push through more modest coverage for only sexual orientation. The greatest political pressure surrounded the remaining prohibitions on military service enacted by Bill Clinton. It was the gay-rights issue that Obama heard raised most frequently as a candidate, and lifting them demanded a process in which the commander in chief, rather than Congress, would have to take the lead. "They consider that to be a wrong that was created under a Democratic president," says senior adviser Valerie Jarrett, who oversaw White House outreach to gay and lesbian activists. "It just hurt them particularly that happened on a Democrat's watch, and so it was important that President Obama right that one."

In his first meeting with the Joint Chiefs of Staff, Obama informed them of his intent to repeal the Don't Ask Don't Tell rule. "At the time, we were feeling very confident about our promises," says deputy chief of staff Jim Messina. Still, a fight over military service had dominated

Bill Clinton's first year in office—producing a brittle compromise that made for poor policy satisfying no one—and Obama was afraid of leaving himself similarly isolated. While some gay-rights activists argued that the president had authority to unilaterally reverse Don't Ask Don't Tell, the White House committed to passing it legislatively. (Such a path ensured Obama's successor could not easily revert to a prior policy.) At the same time, Obama insisted on winning over military leaders before forging ahead with a legislative push. Even those who did not oppose a policy change in principle saw it as an uninvited distraction at a moment when they were also being asked to develop new strategies for managing conflicts in Afghanistan and Iraq. "The President and I feel like we've got a lot on our plates right now, and let's push that one down the road a little bit," Defense Secretary Robert Gates said in late March.

Government attorneys forced to defend the law that the chief executive opposed were able to adjust their legal strategies to match the new timetable. As Obama took office, they had inherited a suit by an Air Force officer who had been discharged four years earlier when authorities uncovered her relationship with another woman. An appeals court ruled in favor of Major Margaret Witt and ordered a trial at which the federal government would have to demonstrate how Witt's expulsion "significantly furthers the government's interest." After requesting an extension, the administration decided not to appeal the decision, which would require it to argue the law's constitutionality. The official White House response was that Obama wanted to see the issue resolved through legislation, although an anonymous administration official offered a slightly different motive to the *Wall Street Journal* in late May: letting the deadline for an appeal pass without action "takes the issue off the front burner."

There was no such option when it came to marriage litigation. The catalyst again came from Arthur Smelt and Christopher Hammer, the Orange County couple whose strategy their lawyer had compared to Dred Scott's. Their first entry into federal court had hit a dead end: in May 2006, an appeals court judge decided not to consider the substance of Smelt's suit due to procedural complications, and that October the U.S. Supreme Court refused to hear the case altogether. For about eighteen months, that suspended the couple's ambitions—both to marry and to push ahead with a suit in federal court. By legalizing same-sex unions for California residents, the *In re Marriage Cases* decision renewed both opportunities, presenting the men with a chance to wed and a fresh claim of discrimination. Even though after Proposition 8 their marriage was allowed to stand,

Smelt and Hammer sued the federal government over "the refusal of all states and jurisdictions" to recognize their new status.

Smelt v. United States was awaiting a reply from the federal government when Obama was sworn in in January. Early in his term, White House counsel Gregory Craig contacted the Department of Justice for a review of the president's options. A onetime constitutional-law professor, Obama had run for national office claiming he would work to repeal the Defense of Marriage Act, which he considered to be unconstitutional. Given that Smelt's lawsuit asked federal courts to reach the same conclusion, it seemed ridiculous for Obama's own lawyers to approach them arguing the opposite.

Craig's query was handed to two attorneys, David Barron and Marty Lederman, serving as political appointees in the Justice Department's Office of Legal Counsel. Often called "the president's law firm," the office existed to deliver the White House legal analysis about bills under consideration by Congress, and to help other departments and agencies navigate legal challenges that arose in the course of governance. That role rarely if ever included ad hoc constitutional opinions about a law that had been in place across two prior presidential administrations and enforced without controversy for five years. The role of the executive branch, Barron and Lederman argued to Principal Associate Deputy Attorney General Kathryn Ruemmler, was to enforce the laws of the land rather than second-guess them.

Ruemmler guided them to write a long memo explaining what it called the "duty to defend." In a system of judicial review laid out in *Marbury v. Madison,* adversarial litigation compelled the government to stand by its own laws when their validity was challenged; its willingness to do so should not change from one day to the next with every electoral shift. "The Department appropriately refuses to defend an act of Congress only in the rare case when the statute either infringes on the constitutional power of the Executive or when prior precedent overwhelmingly indicates that the statute is invalid," new attorney general William French Smith had explained to Congress in 1981. "In my view, the Department has the duty to defend an act of Congress whenever a reasonable argument can be made in its support."

Ruemmler's memo advised that the Obama administration stick with that standard, and Craig accepted the recommendation. (There was, at the time, far more work to do legally detaching the White House from the previous administration's positions on national-security issues, such as detention, torture, and surveillance policies, and the question of whether terrorists would be tried in civilian or military courts.) *Smelt v. United States* had enough procedural weaknesses—suggesting it had been poorly conceived and incompetently drafted—that the government could move to have it dismissed on those grounds. But it also had to explain how it would go about justifying the Defense of Marriage Act on its merits. The career attorneys charged with articulating a rationale were given no guidance on how to go about doing so as a June 11 deadline approached for the government's response in district court.

The lawyer who took charge of the reply brief, a Brigham Young University Law School graduate named W. Scott Simpson, turned to the report the House Judiciary Committee had issued when it approved the Defense of Marriage Act. Simpson dispensed with the most distinctively 1996-vintage rationale—that the bill had been drafted "to express moral disapproval of homosexuality"—which had grown less likely to pass constitutional muster before a Supreme Court that had since struck down sodomy bans enacted on just those grounds. (The House report did not even pretend that this was a secular interest, declaring that the bill's passage would affirm that "heterosexuality better comports with traditional [especially Judeo-Christian] morality.") Simpson otherwise plucked freely from the reasons congressional Republicans had generated for their work, including the objective of "defending and nurturing the institution of traditional, heterosexual marriage" because of the role it plays in "procreation and child-rearing." In the end, Simpson's entire argument for the constitutionality of the Defense of Marriage Act was predicated on a seemingly disingenuous denial of the law's obvious intent: "DOMA does not discriminate against homosexuals in the provision of federal benefits."

That line antagonized gay and lesbian activists, in particular a group of bloggers who were closely watching to see how the administration handled its first encounter in the legal sphere with an issue that Obama had hoped to avoid politically. Even if the administration was compelled to protect the status quo, critics alleged, government lawyers did not have to echo the rationale that opportunistic conservative politicians had offered when pushing the law through Congress thirteen years earlier. "Our president had a choice," wrote John Aravosis of AMERICAblog, "And he chose to throw us under the bus, and then knife us for good measure." Aravosis led an activist pushback, daring gay and lesbian Democrats in Congress to boycott an upcoming fundraiser honoring Vice President Joe Biden. "Any gay person who attends this event, and gives a dime to the Democratic party, is going to find themselves in some serious hot water with the community," he wrote. "I pity the gay organization that is stupid enough to send a representative."

The ferocious response suggested a minority community on edge about the Obama administration's handling of its issues, and a national media that would monitor gay issues—even when they took the form of procedural moves around matters far from final resolution—as a national political concern. The mishandling of the *Smelt* challenge could be in some part blamed on the Obama administration's languid adjustment to the new posture demanded of it: a political ally forced to play the role of a legal adversary. Justice Department officials believe the brief was sent to the White House counsel's office for review, but failed to earn a thorough study from any senior official there alert to the unique sensitivities that surrounded the issue. "That's an example of where people were just doing their jobs and trying to craft the best possible legal argument without thinking about what the consequences would be," says Jarrett. "I think we made it really clear that that was not language that the administration supported. And so they had to go about their jobs, their independent jobs of defending lawsuits, but we stopped using that kind of derogatory language."

The president shared a somewhat different intent with his staff in a meeting that month. With the *Smelt* suit transmogrifying from a perfunctory matter of civil procedure to a source of ongoing and very public agita for the White House, Obama summoned advisers to the Roosevelt Room to develop a plan for handling the marriage litigation. Sitting next to Obama was Biden, who brought along his top aide, Ron Klain. Obama's leading political hands were there, including Jarrett and strategist David Axelrod, along with a quartet of lawyers from the counsel's office and Justice Department. The president made clear to them that he had examined the *Smelt* brief—the only time during his entire presidency they can remember him reading a lower-court filing—and was angry it had gone out in his name. He told those assembled that he would prefer not to have his government at all defending the Defense of Marriage Act in court. But they had to get him onto strong legal footing from which to stop doing so. *Find me a path,* he instructed the lawyers.

The damage-control session led to an omnibus strategy conference about what the administration could quickly deliver in terms of gay rights, and how to manage expectations of respect and inclusion. Already the administration had exhausted the lowest-cost symbolic gestures. In planning Obama's first Easter Egg Roll, the Office of Public Engagement had sought out gay-rights groups so that same-sex families would be well represented on the South Lawn. The same office also prepared the correspondence office to send congratulatory announcements to same-sex couples who requested them, and trained Secret Service to permit access to approved White House visitors even "if this person's license says it's a dude and they look like a woman," as one Obama adviser puts it. A "working group" of lower-level staffers tasked with gay-rights portfolios across the White House agreed to meet weekly to coordinate more administratively complicated projects. Among the first was standardizing all federal forms to "make sure that they don't alienate people who are in nontraditional relationships," in the words of associate White House counsel Ian Bassin.

Obama already had one substantive olive branch ready to extend. On June 17, he signed a memorandum ordering all departments and agencies of the U.S. government to extend benefits to same-sex partners of its employees. "I think we all have to acknowledge this is only one step," Obama said at his desk in the Oval Office, surrounded by legislators pushing a bill that would allow all federal employees to register a domestic partner for benefits regardless of whether the relationship was legally recognized in their home states. "Among the steps we have not yet taken is to repeal the Defense of Marriage Act. I believe it is discriminatory, I believe it interferes with states' rights, and we will work with Congress to overturn it."

The next day, the State Department announced it would issue a new passport to Al Toney, the Worcester man who had worried about traveling internationally on documents that did not reflect his married name. For subsequent applicants, a copy of a marriage license would be sufficient to have a passport reissued—the same standard straight couples face when undergoing a name change. The Toneys' problem solved, Mary Bonauto removed them from the *Gill v. OPM* suit as plaintiffs and refiled an amended complaint in July.

On September 10, 2009, Bonauto joined a group of gay-rights lawyers heading into the Department of Justice headquarters, known among government lawyers as "Main Justice," and to the fifth-floor office of Assistant Attorney General Tony West. Already in late June, in an effort to reset relations with gay-rights litigators, West invited several of them to meet with the administration's top lawyers, including a deputy attorney general, head of the Office of Legal Counsel, and the solicitor general, Elena Kagan. For West it was the first step toward laying out the "frenemy" relationship the department's civil division would have with the gay groups. Even if they had to be opponents in court, the Justice Department wanted to be collegial outside it.

Bonauto was wary of the effort at outreach. She had been offended by the *Smelt* brief, perhaps, but not shocked by it. If anything, she was surprised by the naïveté of peers who had confused the adversarial posture of litigation with the relational nature of political alliances. "We had a sense of propriety that we weren't going to lobby them about our case," says Bonauto. "We had assumed you put that federal government on the other side of the *v.* and they are against you. We didn't feel like it was all consequential whether it was the Bush administration or the Obama administration. There are people in the Department of Justice who review every complaint, inspect every technical argument that could be made."

Face-to-face with some of them, however, Bonauto did muster one request. In nearly every marriage suit, conservative litigators had angled to get themselves accepted by the court as a party to the case so they could advance arguments they considered beyond the government's ken. The department's lawyers, after all, may have been required to defend the existing statute, but were under no obligation to do so in a way that would expand the range of questions at play and lead to a more broadly damaging precedent. Bonauto asked the Justice Department lawyers to fight any intervention by outside groups. "We wanted to litigate with the federal government," says Bonauto, "not the whole right wing."

Facts of the Matter

When Chad Griffin and Kristina Schake had been in recruiting mode for plaintiffs in their Proposition 8 lawsuit, they offered assurances to couples that—while they would receive public attention for their involvement—they would not have to play a role in the legal proceedings. Just seeing her own name atop the court filing, and reduced to a shorthand for the entire case, amounted to more public exposure than Kris Perry had anticipated. When Judge Vaughn Walker forced a trial to take place in January 2010, though, that changed. Ted Olson did go before the judge right away to ask permission for his four clients, who all had full-time jobs, to be excused from attending every single trial session. But on the first day, he would make them useful. The first witnesses called to testify at *Perry v. Schwarzenegger* were the plaintiffs themselves.

One by one they took the stand to tell the story of their families. Whenever it seemed a happily-ever-after narrative was gaining momentum, David Boies or Ted Boutrous detoured from the direct examination to illustrate the often tragicomic reality in which the witnesses now found themselves. Jeffrey Zarrillo talked about the awkward situation of responding to a hotel clerk who asked whether he and Paul Katami really intended to reserve a king-size bed, or explaining to a bank clerk why they wanted a joint account. "I think the timeline for us has always been marriage first, before family," Katami said, so that their offspring "won't have to say, 'My dad and dad are domestic partners.'" Sandy Stier described having to individually edit doctors' forms to describe how she was related to the children in her blended family. "I viewed the domestic-partnership agreement as precisely that, an agreement, a legal agreement, and in some ways memorializes some of our responsibilities to each other," Perry, Stier's would-be spouse, told the court. "But it isn't the same thing as a celebration."

Demonstrating the harm that same-sex couples had experienced as a result of Proposition 8's passage was arguably the most straightforward of the challenges that the plaintiffs' attorneys faced. Since California already had a robust domestic-partnership statute that delivered many of the legal and material benefits of marriage, Olson said he would show that the attitude of "taking away of the right to marriage is okay, no big deal, because you have a right to domestic partnership" to be "a cruel fiction."

Chuck Cooper, the attorney representing activists who had helped qualify Proposition 8 for the ballot, passed up the chance to cross-examine three of the plaintiffs, and only briefly questioned the other on a technical matter. Indeed, Proposition 8's defenders were focused on their own objective, which was to present a basis for singling out one category of couple under the ban.

Acceptable rationales had grown more scarce in the years since 2003, when the Supreme Court struck down antisodomy laws in *Lawrence v. Texas*. As a result of the opinion, those defending discriminatory laws could no longer rely on claims linked to the essential immorality or criminality of homosexuals. When Cooper indicated he would look elsewhere for less overtly derogatory arguments, Rena Lindevaldsen of the evangelical-dominated public-interest law firm Liberty Counsel argued to Judge Walker that he was "willing to concede too much of the Plaintiffs' case," including the proposition that homosexuality was not a medical disorder.

Over the course of several pretrial hearings, Judge Walker revealed the extent to which he was unlikely to be persuaded by the arguments preferred by many politicians. "Nor is it clear, why it is same-sex marriage (and not, for example, infertile marriage) opens the door to require state recognition of polygamy and incest," Walker said to Cooper in mid-October. "Whatever prevents California now from recognizing the marriage of a brother and a sister would likewise stop it from recognizing the marriage of two sisters in the absence of Proposition 8."

Olson could make Cooper's project even more difficult by convincing Judge Walker to review the new amendment under the more demanding standard known as "strict scrutiny." To do so, Walker would have to be persuaded that Proposition 8 either targeted a protected minority group or jeopardized a fundamental right.

Olson's opening argument made clear that he would argue both points. If Walker accepted either argument, strict scrutiny would apply. Under it, a discriminatory law could stand only if the state demonstrated that it served a "compelling" public interest and that the law advanced that goal in as narrowly tailored a fashion as possible. If, on the other hand, Walker imposed a looser "rational basis" standard, the law's proponents would have to demonstrate just that any rational purpose could justify it, including the idea that heterosexuals make better heads of household. The rational purpose asserted in court could be, in effect, imputed retrospectively; defendants did not have to present the one that motivated voters or legislators to enact it.

At a pretrial conference in December, Walker showed Cooper how much more aggressively he would police the logic behind Proposition 8 if he decided that strict scrutiny applied.

"Assume that you have to have established that this is the minimally effective means of imposing this discrimination between same-sex marriages and opposite-sex marriages," Walker said to Cooper. "So what is the harm to the procreative purpose or function of marriage that you outline of permitting same-sex marriages?"

"Your Honor," Cooper responded, "even under a compelling-state-interest standard, I would submit to the Court that the state's interests in channeling procreative activity into enduring relationships would be vital, and would satisfy a compelling-interest standard."

"I'm asking you to tell me how it would harm opposite-sex marriages," Walker said.

"Your Honor," Cooper responded, "my answer is: I don't know."

"Does that mean," Walker continued, "if this is not determined to be subject to rational-basis review, you lose?"

"No," said Cooper. "I don't believe it does."

Walker needled him. "Just haven't figured out how you're going to win on that basis yet?"

By the time he presented his opening statement, Cooper had locked in on arguments that linked gay parenting to the well-being of children. He put forward a vision of the immemorial "pro-child societal institution" that would stand in contrast to what he implied were the self-centered explanations that the plaintiffs had presented for wanting to wed. "The question is, your Honor, is this institution designed for these pro-child reasons or is it to produce companionship and personal fulfillment and expression of love?" Cooper asked. "Are those purposes themselves important enough to run risks to the accomplishment of the pro-child purposes?" The costs to a relaxed definition of marriage would be of the Dickensian sort, Cooper suggested, as the price of "social ills" typically associated with children from broken homes would fall on California's government and taxpayers.

In Walker's court both issues would be contested simultaneously: the law's proponents working to demonstrate its rationale, while its opponents argued for the nature of the discrimination. Olson and Boies put forward a faculty club's worth of academic expert witnesses. They had two Ivy League historians, one who would describe the long record of oppression to which gays and lesbians had been subjected at the hands of authorities and another who would cast doubt on the notion that there was a "traditional" definition of marriage inviolate over time. A trio of economists would tally the material harm faced by individual families and local governments when gays and lesbians are denied the right to marry. Four psychologists would attest to both the stresses they face and their merits as heads of household—the fact that, as Olson put it in his opening statement, "the quality of a parent is not measured by gender, but by the content of the heart."

Olson and Boies had initially insisted there was no need for a trial, and were flat-footed when Walker insisted on one. They still visualized the prospect of a footrace to bring the Supreme Court its first marriage case, and accepted Walker's offer of a January 2010 trial date despite the short period it would leave for discovery. The accelerated timetable, especially when paired with their team's inexperience around the subject matter, left Boies and Olson newly dependent on the movement groups with whom they clashed through 2009.

In their filing that August, while still hoping to get the Our Family Coalition accepted as a plaintiff in the *Perry* suit, ACLU attorneys laid out a plan for how they would conduct a trial, including specific witnesses. There was a stable of social scientists eager to testify either to their research showing the competence of gays and lesbians as parents, and the absence of credible evidence to the contrary. They had regularly been sought out for amicus briefs assembled by gay-rights litigators in prior cases, but their conclusions had not been tested in the way that they would under cross-examination from a skilled trial attorney. "One of the reasons that we were pushing the trial so hard," says the ACLU's James Esseks, "was that we had gotten burned by not having trials in several of the state cases."

That had been felt most acutely in New York, where in 2006 the court of appeals had ruled that the state legislature had identified a valid interest in maintaining a definition of family open only to those couples who could biologically produce children. "Plaintiffs have not persuaded us that this long-accepted restriction is a wholly irrational one, based solely on ignorance and prejudice against homosexuals," Judge Robert S. Smith wrote in the majority opinion.

Elsewhere judges appeared entirely uncurious about what external research might tell them about the matter at hand. The Maryland appeals court dismissed the suggestion of a trial when in 2006 it considered a Baltimore circuit-court ruling that the state's 1973 marriage law—which city and county clerks used as a basis for turning away same-sex couples seeking licenses—was unconstitutionally discriminatory. "The court doesn't have to disparage gay parenting to uphold this law, it doesn't have to assess the merits of an armload of studies and it doesn't have to find that the institution of marriage is threatened," Assistant Attorney General Robert A. Zarnoch argued before the court. Judges appeared to agree, asking few questions during the hourlong argument and nonetheless declaring in a majority opinion that "the factual background, much like challenges to similar state marriage statutes in other jurisdictions, is undisputed."

That had been the long-held consensus among gay-rights litigators. "These are constitutional facts. These are facts that you don't prove with witnesses because they're not facts that are supposed to change depending on whether you do a good job or a bad job. These are supposed to be things that judges can sort of figure out on their own," says Esseks. "While there may well be merit to that as a legal proposition, we had a challenge of getting judges past their own stereotypes and assumptions about gay people and kids. Some of those enduring antigay stereotypes are that we're pedophiles and we're going to screw kids up and that we're going to make them gay. It turns out that it's enormously powerful to have expert witnesses explain what the social science is."

Trials had proven particularly effective for ACLU attorneys in states known for conservative judiciaries that might not be inclined to accept gay families unless forced to weigh the matter as two competing sets of facts. After six days of testimony in 2004, an Arkansas trial-court judge found that "there is no factual basis for making the statement that heterosexual parents might be better able to guide their children through adolescence than gay parents." Citing that point, one of forty-seven findings of fact generated by the lower court, the Arkansas Supreme Court ruled two years later that the state's justification for a ban on foster parenting in gay households "flies in the face of the evidence." In 2008, a Florida circuit court reached a similar conclusion in striking down a ban on gay couples adopting children, the subject of a decade's worth of litigation. "In addition to the volume, the body of research is broad," the court declared. "These reports and studies find that there are no differences in the parenting of homosexuals or the adjustment of their children."

In the trial-management statement they presented to Judge Walker, the Our Family Coalition groups had explicitly cited the Arkansas and Florida trials as models for what it hoped to mount in California. Those lawsuits challenged different state laws, but given Cooper's decision to make Proposition 8 a case about children, both sides were likely to rely on the same bodies of evidence. The Our Families Coalition pointed to a reliable stable of social scientists who had testified on marriage as far back as Hawaii. Indeed, the *Baehr* trial had been a devastatingly lopsided affair, one that ended with Judge Kevin Chang summoning the lawyers to his chambers before he publicly released his opinion, with findings of fact that concluded there was no evidence to justify any of the rationales offered for excluding gay couples from marriage. "He looked at me like, 'Sorry, Rick,'" recalls Deputy Attorney General Rick Eichor, who argued the state's case. "I got the sense he sympathized with me because he was going to rip me."

Even then, when barely one-quarter of Americans supported gay marriage, the attorney general's office struggled to identify experts willing to testify that it might be bad for children. Eichor had been asking for help with what could be considered the most advantageous conditions possible, under the auspices of a state government merely trying to defend the historical status quo. Little seemed to have changed in the interceding thirteen years, and Cooper found it even harder to recruit expert witnesses when it meant allying with religious activists in a high-profile trial designed to leave a paper trail for the Supreme Court. "It became extremely difficult. No reputable social scientist really wanted to," says Maggie Gallagher of the National Organization for Marriage. "Nobody wanted to go and testify."

Gallagher had been asked by someone connected to the trial team if she could recommend any experts who would. She proposed David Blankenhorn, whose Institute for American Values think tank had established itself precisely to be a clearinghouse for scholars who wanted their research to affect family policy. "People would call and ask me to give the top ten list of people who could testify. They'd already been asked, and they all said no," says Blankenhorn. "Why would they want to have this shit rain down on them for the next five years of their life? Who would volunteer for this?"

Although he had let the bipartisan "marriage movement" be pulled headlong into the conflict over gay unions, Blankenhorn had retreated as he felt the political discourse around them became too vitriolic. "I'm interested in the 'married' part, and I wanted to ignore the gay part," he says. (He insisted that, when juxtaposed on stage against the likes of Evan Wolfson, the exchanges be promoted not as "debates" but "conversations.") An attorney on Cooper's team told Blankenhorn that he would merely be asked to reaffirm that he agreed with the content of chapters from his books that would be presented as evidence, and attest to his credentials as an expert on the American family. Blankenhorn agreed reluctantly to testify, only after being reassured that he wouldn't be "arguing a policy position," as he recalls. "And I said, 'Yes, I would,' even though"—he pauses—"one knows how all this is going to work out."

Blankenhorn was one of six people whom Proposition 8's defenders said they intended to summon as witnesses. But on the trial's first day, Cooper indicated they were not all likely to appear, and he found a politically resonant excuse. Throughout the fall, Judge Walker had been advancing a proposal to broadcast the trial on YouTube, as part of a pilot program to permit cameras in Ninth Circuit courtrooms. "There certainly has been a good deal of interest in the case," Walker explained. The plaintiffs' attorneys welcomed the proposal, with AFER's political operatives developing a public-relations plan around it. Cooper appealed Walker's move, citing the past boycotts and online blacklists targeting Proposition 8 defenders. Even as the matter sat before the Supreme Court, Cooper informed Walker that the academic experts on his witness list "were extremely concerned about their personal safety, and did not want to appear with any recording of any sort, whatsoever." By the time the Supreme Court scratched the camera plan, Cooper had already dropped four of his witnesses amid the controversy, which contributed usefully to the confusion over which side was really the victim of political powerlessness. As opposed to the seventeen witnesses for the plaintiffs, Cooper would put forward just two.

Cooper mentioned only one by name during his opening statement: Blankenhorn. By the time he took the stand, on the penultimate day of the twelve-day trial, much of the weight of justifying Proposition 8 rested on the reluctant advocate. Marriage was, Blankenhorn would testify, the only institution "that performed the task of bringing together the three dimensions of parenthood: the biological, the social—that is the caring for the child—and the legal." Changing the long-standing definition of marriage, he postulated, "loses esteem in the society. It loses respect. It loses its sense of being held in high regard. And the institution becomes less and less able to carry out its contributions to the society."

Yet even before he could elucidate this concept of the "deinstitutionalization of marriage," Blankenhorn was subjected to a death march through his CV—a tommy-gun exchange in which a skilled trial lawyer tried to reveal the public intellectual as poseur. Blankenhorn may have established himself as a convener of those with a scholarly interest in family dynamics, but he had few actual credentials of his own. His doctoral work had been in British labor history. For all he had written on the subject of the American family—newspaper op-eds, magazine essays, his own books and introductions to anthologies he edited—Blankenhorn had never produced any empirical research on the subject, or had his work published in a peer-reviewed journal. He had never taught a college course. Under close questioning from Boies, he was left to concede that he had not undertaken "any scientific study of what effects permitting same-sex marriages have been in any jurisdiction where same-sex marriages have been permitted."

When Boies rose with an objection, Judge Walker had already anticipated it. "The objection is that the witness is not qualified to opine on the subject of marriage, fatherhood, and family structure, correct?" he asked. "With respect to Mr. Blankenhorn's qualifications, were this a jury trial, I think the question might be a close one. But this being a court trial, I'm going to permit the witness to testify."

By the time he was invited to discuss the substance of his declared expertise, Blankenhorn was visibly flustered by an assault on his credentials, and perhaps miffed as well by a mispronunciation of his last name so insistent that he had to have suspected it was intentional. Under questioning from Boies, he conceded that children of gay and lesbian households would be better off if their parents could marry, and that he was unaware of any evidence such a change would impact marriage rates among straight couples. Boies concluded by inducing Blankenhorn to reaffirm a sentiment from one of his own writings that undermined the entirety of Cooper's case: "Insofar as we are a nation founded on this principle, we would be more American on the day we permitted same-sex marriage than we were on the day before."

"I'd like to take some time to go over all of this material," Judge Walker said just before laying down his gavel on January 27. A several-month break would permit him an opportunity to closely review the expert testimony and documentary evidence while the attorneys could solicit amicus briefs on issues insufficiently addressed at trial.

In those five months, David Blankenhorn—previously unknown to anyone outside the narrow circle of those who worked on family-policy issues—became an exemplar of the unevenness of the national debate over marriage. Three times that spring, *New York Times* columnist Frank Rich cited Blankenhorn's testimony in the San Francisco courtroom as evidence of the moral and intellectual bankruptcies of anti-gay-rights advocacy. "That the Prop 8 proponents employed him as their star witness suggests that no actual experts could be found (or rented) to match his disparagement of gay parents," Rich wrote.

Blankenhorn fought back, rallying colleagues—including some prominent supporters of gay marriage—to draft letters to the editor defending his honor. He lamented that he was "losing friends, being told I'm on the wrong side of history," but his riposte was focused on rebutting the allegation that his views on marriage made him antigay. Blankenhorn perched unpleasantly on an inflection point in elite opinion. He was a self-described "liberal Democrat" finding it no longer possible to hold the once stable ground of opposing the redefinition of marriage—even as he endorsed adoption rights for gay couples and left himself open to civil unions—without being dismissed as a bigot. Even polite opposition was easily marginalized as intolerance.

Both sides saw in the San Francisco courtroom a harbinger of future marriage battles. The inability of a well-funded legal team to even present witnesses deemed credible by a federal judge served as a cautionary tale to religious conservatives that their extant political advantage on the issue of marriage might not be long sustainable in court. Walker's cynicism about their slippery-slope rhetoric indicated that arguments that may have carried the day in terms of public opinion might not hold up to judicial scrutiny.

Gallagher set out to commission what would become known as the New Family Structures Study, a political project masquerading as freethinking scholarly inquiry. She offered willing academics generous research grants from a pair of conservative nonprofits on which Princeton University professor Robert George sat as a board member. In exchange they would be expected to produce a credible study that validated the superiority of opposite-sex parenting, with enough size and statistical power that it could be published in a well-regarded journal and not subjected to the dismissive mockery that had dragooned her side's trial presentation in San Francisco. "Naturally we would like to move along as expeditiously as possible," NOM treasurer Luis Tellez would later write in an email to Mark Regnerus, a University of Texas sociologist who was selected to head up the study. "It would be great to have this before major decisions of the Supreme Court."

Appealing Stuff

Mary Bonauto filed *Gill v. Office of Personnel Management* nearly three months before Ted Olson and David Boies unveiled *Perry v. Schwarzenegger*. But the willingness of the Ninth Circuit to acquiesce to their impatience meant that the California arrivistes had already completed a complex trial stretching across three weeks—and were subsequently celebrated as members of the *Time* 100 for having "put on an extraordinary case in the federal court system"—before Bonauto faced a judge in *Gill*. Even though she had been plotting her challenge to the Defense of Marriage Act for years longer, Bonauto now had to define her federal suit in relation to the famous one already under way on the other coast. "GLAD's case and *Perry* seek to cure two important but different injustices," she said. "*Gill* is not a right-to-marry case, since we represent couples who are already married."

The seventeen plaintiffs Bonauto guided into the courthouse abutting Boston Harbor that May 2010 day—too many to be seated together anywhere other than the jury box—had already benefited from the sagacity of U.S. district-court judge Joseph Tauro. On May 13, 2004, just four days before Massachusetts couples were scheduled to begin marrying, litigators from Christian conservative organizations had rushed to the newly erected glass-curtained waterfront structure held up as a model of contemporary governmental architecture. Opponents of gay marriage appeared to have exhausted their existing options on Beacon Hill and had petitioned the federal government as last resort. Tauro refused to interfere with the instructions that the state had given to town clerks, and sent the petitioners back to the sturdy Second Empire masonry pile where the *Goodridge* mandate had originated. The Supreme Judicial Court of Massachusetts rather than the federal judiciary, Tauro informed them, possessed "the final word on the state constitution."

Six years later, Tauro was visited by the Commonwealth of Massachusetts itself, in the form of a deputy attorney general arguing that it, too, had suffered harm because of congressional legislation that degraded the value of marriages solemnized by local officials. Bonauto had begun looking upon state government as an ally in 2006, when Mitt Romney was succeeded as governor by Deval Patrick, a liberal Democrat who was one of only a few statewide officeholders in the nation to enthusiastically embrace gay marriage. As she was preparing to file *Gill*, Bonauto convinced Massachusetts attorney general Martha Coakley to back the litigation with a parallel challenge. In *Massachusetts v. HHS*, the plaintiffs alleged the federal government had overstepped its authority by undermining the ability of states to award benefits related to marriage. Coakley's openly lesbian deputy, Maura Healey, told Tauro that the Defense of Marriage Act "forces the state to discriminate against its own citizens." Healey called it an "animus-based national marriage law," embracing the exact language that the Supreme Court had used when it struck down Colorado's Amendment 2.

The federal government did not fold so easily. "This presidential administration disagrees with DOMA as a matter of policy," Justice Department lawyer Scott Simpson told Tauro in May 2010. "But that does not affect its constitutionality." Simpson had been one of three names on the reply brief to *Smelt*, whose perceived antigay language had so antagonized activists the previous spring. That California-based case had been dismissed, but Simpson had inherited the file of other DOMA challenges, including both *Gill v. OPM* and *Massachusetts v. HHS*. Tauro heard both cases over the course of the same month, and on behalf of the United States, Simpson was requesting both suits be summarily dismissed. "It's really a question for them of institutional integrity to continue to defend the constitutionality of statutes," Bonauto told the *New York Times*. "That's what they've done here."

Even so, the nature of the government's response indicated that the Justice Department was not lawyering at full throttle. Government lawyers disavowed all the reasons—related to procreation and child-rearing, fiscal concerns, moral disapproval—that members of Congress had presented while crafting the legislation. In their place, Justice Department lawyers offered up a rationale that avoided judgment on the merits of same-sex unions: Congress had been, in essence, using the Defense of Marriage Act to buy time for states to work out their marriage policies so that a stable national regime could take hold. In a column, Maggie Gallagher called the *Gill v. OPM* hearing a "sham trial" in which "President Obama's Justice Department sabotaged the defense of DOMA."

On July 8, 2010, Tauro issued his rulings in both *Gill v. OPM* and *Massachusetts v. HHS*. All of the "proffered rationales" for the Defense of Marriage Act were, he wrote, "clearly and manifestly implausible," including the novel one put forward by Obama administration lawyers. "This assertion merely begs the more pertinent question: whether the federal government had any proper role to play in formulating such policy in the first instance," wrote Tauro. "Even assuming for the sake of argument that DOMA succeeded in preserving the federal status quo, which this court has concluded that it did not, such assumption does nothing more than describe what DOMA does. It does not provide a justification for doing it."

A month later on the West Coast, Judge Vaughn Walker similarly ruled in favor of the plaintiffs in his marriage case. He produced a 138-page opinion, fifty-four of them devoted to "findings of fact"—a meticulous examination of the scientific and sociological research that had been presented, largely by the expert witnesses testifying on behalf of the plaintiffs. Walker's analysis was loaded with disdain for "the minimal evidentiary presentation" made by Proposition 8's defenders, and especially scornful in its description of David Blankenhorn as an "unreliable" witness. "The trial evidence provides no basis for establishing that California has an interest in refusing to recognize marriage between two people because of their sex," Walker wrote. The plaintiffs had succeeded in demonstrating gays and lesbians were deserving of the highest tier of equal protection, he went on, but it was irrelevant to the case's outcome because defenders of Proposition 8 had failed to justify it under even a lower standard. Walker issued an injunction to stop the law's implementation, but stayed it—and the resumption of same-sex marriages in California—long enough for the measure's proponents to file an appeal.

Gill, too, was headed to the court of appeals. In the meantime, Bonauto went to work on another lawsuit that would raise nearly all the same questions. She had seen the legal options for a challenge to the Defense of Marriage Act expand due to state-level advances across New England. In October 2008, Connecticut's high court ruled, by a four-to-three margin, that the civil unions authorized by the legislature were an insufficient substitute for the marriages to which same-sex couples were entitled. The next year, both Vermont and New Hampshire legalized gay marriage through the political process. Suddenly three more states were producing potential plaintiffs, and two of them—Connecticut and Vermont—sat in a different circuit of the federal judiciary, revealing another route that a case could take to United States Supreme Court.

Bonauto had defied the wishes of many of her peers by pushing ahead into federal court when she did, although the subsequent filing of the more expansive *Perry v. Schwarzenegger* made her seem—if only by contrast—less of a renegade. "I think about it as building blocks, and, brick by brick, building this structure of equality," Bonauto said. "When does the Supreme Court step in? When the discriminatory states are outliers—when they are not the locus of law and opinion in the country. But someone had to be first."

The ACLU had been among the loudest institutional skeptics of any strategy encouraging a dash to the Supreme Court. "Other folks thought the odds were good enough a little earlier than we did," says the ACLU's Matt Coles, who had helped coordinate the very public pushback when Olson and Boies first announced their plans to sue over Proposition 8. "We wanted to stay in the states, and stay in the progressive states as much as possible because we were trying to win and build critical mass," adds James Esseks, who in 2010 succeeded Coles atop the ACLU's LGBT & HIV Project. "Civil unions and domestic partnerships were still good and worth fighting for." There was more to the incrementalism than timidity: a legal logic that, as Coles wrote, "the closer marriage and full partnership come to being identical, the more likely states are to acknowledge the lack of meaningful difference and convert full partnerships to marriage."

This question of how and when to push ahead to the highest court dominated the debate that rumbled over that winter, as Coles worked to finalize the revision of the 10-10-10-20 strategy. All the legal groups that participated in the negotiations had done everything possible to slow *Perry v. Schwarzenegger*. Even if they had been helping Boies and Olson prepare for trial, none of them were ready to sanction the impudence behind the lawsuit, or encourage others like it.

There remained many appealing options for litigation that would constrain the risk of damaging federal precedents. That included, Coles wrote, "putting questions closely related to marriage before the court, questions however, which don't require the Court to say if the federal constitution requires the states to marry same-sex couples." One such path would be what lawyers had taken to calling "recognition cases," which would claim that gays and lesbians were denied their federal equal-protection and due-process rights by state laws that expressly carved out same-sex marriages performed in other states from being recognized where the couple resides. Another path would be to target state amendments on procedural grounds, much as *Romer v. Evans* had against Colorado's Amendment 2, arguing that it would be reasonable for state courts and legislatures to define marriage, but not to use the constitution to exclude only those affecting gay people. Finally, there was a challenge to the one federal law that dealt with the subject, which as Bonauto frequently noted offered the political advantage of not asking a court to impose same-sex marriage anywhere by decree. "These cases are all focused not on a right to get married, but instead on double standards," Coles wrote. "The advantage of strategies like these is that they could get the Courts familiar with the issue without going directly to the ultimate question."

Even so, Coles and others found them premature. "It is quite possible for a court ruling against us in any of these cases, including the Supreme Court, to reach out and rule broadly in a way that would apply to a federal marriage case. So if one of the cases in this potential 'building block' strategy goes wrong, it could bring about a Supreme Court ruling that would preclude a successful marriage case until the Court were ready to overrule itself (not something it does casually)," he wrote. "Even if we succeed in foundational cases, the Court could simply rule against us when it is presented with a federal marriage case."

With such doubts aired, those whom Coles convened in Somerville could not reach consensus about whether to formally endorse any case that would bring a marriage-related question to federal court. That friction made impossible the type of tidy unanimity that was reached in Jersey City. After five years, the groups had reluctantly acceded to a consensus on the necessary structure for political change, but negotiants differed widely on the question of which lawsuits would be helpful and when. Rather than being named as individual signatories, as they had been on the 2005 paper, the 2010 participants were listed alphabetically as "commissioning organizations," along with the large foundations expected to bankroll their activities. Coles would be listed as the sole author, offering any plausible deniability to disown specific elements of the paper if they conflicted with other institutional interests. One year into her *Gill* suit, Bonauto thought the nonendorsement might undermine her work—a signal to potential donors whose support would be necessary to sustain the case that it was misguided. "We were not happy about it," she says, "but Matt controlled the pen."

Because of that history, Bonauto was surprised to receive a phone call that fall from Esseks informing her that the ACLU was close to filing its own challenge to the Defense of Marriage Act's third section. The lead counsel on the case was Roberta Kaplan, an outsider to the world of the Roundtable even though she had served on the board of Lambda Legal. A commercial litigator by trade, she had one major gay-rights case to her name, a marriage suit that made it to the New York Court of Appeals. Bonauto had drafted an amicus brief in that instance, laying out the Massachusetts experience. When Esseks mentioned Kaplan, she was already front of mind: Bonauto had been invited to her New York City firm just that June, to make a presentation about the *Gill* case and her strategy going forward.

Kaplan said nothing then about her own litigation, even though she was more than a year into working with Edie Windsor, an eighty-one-year-old widowed computer programmer battling the federal government over a tax refund. Kaplan and Windsor had lived just two blocks from one another in Greenwich Village for years; as a young closeted lesbian recently graduated from Columbia Law School, Kaplan had sought therapy from Windsor's longtime partner, Thea Spyer. When Spyer died in 2009, after a long struggle with multiple sclerosis, Windsor was hit with a sizable tax bill over the transfer of Spyer's estate. Even though the two women had wed in Canada in 2007 and their home state subsequently recognized them as married, the Defense of Marriage Act required all agencies of the federal government to treat them as strangers. Kaplan guided Windsor as she requested a refund from the Internal Revenue Service for the approximately $350,000 in estate taxes she had been forced to pay, and then through the labyrinth of administrative appeals once she was rejected. Eventually there was only one option left: to sue the federal government for taxes that would never have been levied, as Windsor liked to say, "if Thea was Theo."

Early in the process, Kaplan contacted Esseks with a request. Kaplan was working pro bono but knew she could use outside organizational resources if, as she suspected, the case stood a chance of making it to the U.S. Supreme Court. She also knew a partnership with the ACLU would insulate her from some of the backlash she had observed against the Proposition 8 lawsuit. Kaplan anticipated a similar response—and without celebrity attorneys or political consultants to receive the flak, more of it was likely to fall upon the plaintiff. "She had to be prepared for criticism, not only from antigay forces but from those on our side, too," Kaplan recalled. "As a result, I decided it was best to keep our work with Edie tightly under wraps."

Esseks initially demurred when Kaplan sought the ACLU's involvement, in part because of the superficially unsympathetic background that Windsor brought to her quarrel with the government. "This was an estate-tax case, and there's baggage that comes with that. She was by definition a multimillionaire, little old lady who dresses nicely and lives at Two Fifth Avenue," says Esseks. "Is it going to play as . . . 'Sorry she has to pay that money, but she clearly has plenty'?"

Kaplan presented Windsor's story as what she had heard old-time New York lawyers describe as a "speaking complaint," more expansive than necessary under the rules of civil procedure and richer in narrative. Kaplan wrote the brief in a voice unusually intimate for a filing from a corporate litigator, identifying the plaintiff and her deceased spouse not by the surnames that usually decorate legal proceedings but the familiar Edie and Thea. In Kaplan's hands, Esseks says, theirs had become "a love story for the ages."

By the time Kaplan was ready to file *Windsor v. United States*, in the fall of 2010, Esseks was pining to be involved as cocounsel. The *Perry v. Schwarzenegger* trial verdict ensured it was too late to keep the marriage question out of federal courts, and other organizations had slackened their resistance. Lambda Legal had signed on to a suit in California, representing a court employee who sought to add her spouse to a domestic-partners plan. The suit was likely to become a frontal challenge to the Defense of Marriage Act. "You never know how the litigation is going to fare," Esseks explained. "So we wanted to get into that game as well."

Even though her latest suit raised the same underlying constitutional questions as *Windsor v. United States*, Bonauto could not have approached it more differently. She had cast *Pedersen v. Office of Personnel Management* as a courtroom epic. Like *Gill*, it included a variety of plaintiffs—this time selected from across Connecticut and Vermont—and sent its message about the Defense of Marriage Act through the scope of the harm it wantonly inflicted on people in their everyday lives. It was, Esseks allowed, far closer to what movement litigators had envisioned as the ideal set of facts for a marriage suit than the "rich old lady" featured in his. "Look, we were all looking for salt of the earth people and the plaintiffs that GLAD found both in *Gill* and in *Pedersen* were much more salt-of-the-earth folks—much more, you know, Regular Joes," he says.

Bonauto took umbrage as to what she saw as an unsporting infraction by an erstwhile ally, particularly given that the ACLU had been the source of so much bile for her decision to move ahead with DOMA litigation before it became fashionable. "It was not one hundred percent collegial of them to jump into a matter where we had invested so much in figuring out how to win legally and where we had been doing tons of public education," says Bonauto. "Everyone knew we were moving forward in the Second Circuit."

Due to a peculiarity of precedent in the circuit that covered New York, Vermont, and Connecticut, far more would be at stake there than had been when Bonauto pushed ahead in the First. The effects could be felt by civil-rights lawyers taking up issues far beyond marriage, the consequences so open-ended that the federal government could not just default to notions of duty. Neither Bonauto nor Kaplan was willing to yield to the other, but they had a common view of *Perry v. Schwarzenegger* as a potential rival for the Supreme Court's attention, and agreed to coordinate their efforts. They would wait until after the midterm elections on November 2, 2010, when crucial New York senate seats would be up for a vote. Then they would file their suits on the same morning—Kaplan in New York, Bonauto in Hartford—with concurrent press conferences to advance, as Bonauto would reluctantly concede, "the idea that the two together were stronger."

Inaction Hero

Among the innovations spurred by the fallout over the *Smelt* brief in the summer of 2009 were a new set of Justice Department protocols to screen and monitor future cases that could be hiding similarly explosive material. Lawyers in the federal government's Civil Division were instructed to spot cases of potentially newsworthy interest once they arrived in district court and enter them into a tracking sheet with alerts for key dates, like filing deadlines and court appearances. In essence, it became the administration's internal docket for legal matters of political consequence. "These are the cases that we think are kind of newsworthy," explains Principal Associate Deputy Attorney General Kathryn Ruemmler, "likely to get attention."

Ruemmler had ordered the memo affirming the Justice Department's "duty to defend," and dreaded the day another marriage case would land on the tracking sheet. For many who had followed Barack Obama into government, the *Smelt* suit had felt like a trap laid before they stumbled onto the scene, forcing them to choose between policy principle and procedural principle. *Gill* had been a vise, clasping even more firmly around the government with each effort to wriggle free: the less aggressive the arguments federal lawyers put forward, the likelier they were to lose, each time rising a level through appeal—and drawing ever more public pressure about their approach. Ironically, it took getting sued twice on the same day in November 2010 for the Obama administration to find a legally elegant if politically risky way out of the conundrum posed by the marriage cases.

A defensive crouch had never suited Ruemmler, who as a federal prosecutor had delivered the closing argument at a trial that jailed Enron's top executives. At the start of 2010, she left the Justice Department and was able to look more opportunistically upon the inevitable prospect of the next DOMA lawsuit. As deputy White House counsel, Ruemmler would serve not the federal government but the presidency, and its current occupant had made clear starting in the summer of 2009 his desire to walk away from the Defense of Marriage Act. So as to be ready to pounce at the first opening, Ruemmler formed the three lawyers in her office who had been assigned gay-related issues into what she called "our little SWAT team." They collected a long history of Office of Legal Counsel opinions touching on the questions of when and how the government had to defend laws and examples of instances where the Department of Justice had determined it no longer had to. Assembled into a binder, the contents painted a portrait of the president as chief constitutional officer, capable of making a determination as to whether a law could credibly be justified in court. "We just needed a place to be able to, in a principled manner, say there's not a reasonable argument," says associate counsel Kathleen Hartnett.

They had an unlikely role model in California, where, as White House associate counsel Kate Shaw would later write, "at every juncture, developments in the law of same-sex marriage have involved questions of executive power." Like Obama, Arnold Schwarzenegger had sought a middle path on gay rights, with enthusiastic support for civil unions even as he twice vetoed bills to legalize same-sex marriages, the second time in 2007. "He had Republican advisers who led him to believe he didn't have a choice," says Daniel Zingale, chief of staff to then–first lady Maria Shriver. "The only time I saw Maria cry was when he vetoed it." The governor got a shot at redemption less than two years later, when *Perry v. Schwarzenegger* was filed. Schwarzenegger told the court that he had no interest in defending Proposition 8, while withholding judgment on its constitutionality. Attorney General Jerry Brown—who as governor in 1977 had signed the first state bill to specifically ban same-sex marriages—went further, arguing the 2008 ban could "not be squared with guarantees of the Fourteenth Amendment." That left California without a single statewide constitutional officer willing to serve as a defendant, leaving it in the hands of citizen-activists to protect what was then the law of the land. When Brown ran to succeed the retiring Schwarzenegger in November 2010, both he and ticketmate Kamala Harris—looking to replace Brown as attorney general—made a refusal to defend Proposition 8 a campaign issue, promising to continue state government's policy of noninvolvement.

At the White House, it was not by then just the Defense of Marriage Act subject to such consideration. On September 9, a California-based federal judge ruled it was unconstitutional for the Department of

Defense to expel employees found to be gay. The Ninth Circuit classified the Don't Ask Don't Tell policy as an unfairly discriminatory one, with federal lawyers unable to demonstrate how it "significantly furthers the government's interest." Although the Ninth Circuit might just order the specific plaintiffs reinstated to their military posts, from there it appeared inevitable that the entire policy would fall. Military leaders would chafe at having their personnel policies micromanaged by judges, and it was hard to imagine anyone—other than, perhaps, the gay-rights litigators behind the precipitating lawsuits—who would be happy with that outcome. The ruling was stayed to give the losers time to appeal, and Ruemmler's team considered whether the time had come for Obama to do more than say he was deferring to Congress to repeal a law he wanted to see fall. "There was a definite concern that if we were to not defend in that sphere that we'd be weakening the overall power of the president," says Hartnett. Obama might be able to avoid enduring damage to executive-branch authority by having his lawyers concede the ban was unconstitutional and ordering his generals to stop enforcing it.

Don't Ask Don't Tell and the Defense of Marriage Act had been political siblings, Clinton offspring that a newer generation hoped to force into retirement. In both instances, scenarios had loomed where Obama would face a choice about whether to do so by walking away from the government's defense of the existing laws in court. As a political proposition, however, White House staff accepted it as fact that the chief constitutional officer could probably use a controversial rationale to justify jettisoning only one. "We probably can't not defend both of them," Hartnett recalls thinking. "We should see where the law takes us, but it would be a pretty major step."

Meanwhile, the prospect of a wartime constitutional crisis helped nudge the Senate, a political institution naturally biased toward idleness. During the brief period when members of Congress returned to Washington after the November 2010 midterm elections, the Pentagon completed a massive study of military attitudes that Obama had ordered to defang Pentagon criticism. With just days left before Democrats would relinquish control of the chamber, senators voted by a large, bipartisan margin to lift the ban and begin the process of integrating gay troops, effectively forestalling the same result by court order. "To do anything in the Senate they have to be backed up against the deadline," says Jim Messina, who had been a longtime Senate staffer before going to work for Obama.

Ruemmler intensified her team's deliberations about killing off the

Defense of Marriage Act, as Obama himself coyly acknowledged publicly for the first time the day he signed the bill repealing the military ban. "I'm always looking for a way to get it done, if possible, through our elected representatives. That may not be possible," he told *The Advocate*'s Kerry Eleveld. "I have a whole bunch of really smart lawyers who are looking at a whole range of options."

The junior attorneys who had been exploring these issues for more than a year had avoided summarizing their conclusions, for fear of creating a written document that would prematurely enter the historical record. But Ruemmler's team believed they had alighted upon a way to adhere to the duty to defend existing laws, while setting a standard by which a judge should be led, inevitably, to share the president's view that the matter was unconstitutional. That strategy satisfied what the lawyers had taken to calling the "Sarah Palin Test"—after the worst conceivable Republican they could envision following Obama. Could the decision not to defend the Defense of Marriage Act be explained in terms that would not also justify a successor choosing to abandon laws that Obama had enacted, like the Affordable Care Act already under assault in court?

It amounted to a three-stage process. The Justice Department would stand by an existing statute until it had exhausted all viable constitutional arguments in its favor. As had been shown with both versions of the *Smelt* brief, one could conjure a rational basis for the Defense of Marriage Act, even if the reasoning struck some of the lawyers who developed it as feeble. But if the government was forced to demonstrate a "compelling state interest" that had been articulated during the legislative process, rather than devised retrospectively, its lawyers believed they would come up short. Only then, White House lawyers believed, could they step away from the Defense of Marriage Act without abrogating their duty to defend. When faced with an October 2010 deadline to appeal Judge Joseph Tauro's district-court decision in *Gill v. OPM*, White House attorneys believed the Justice Department had no choice but to press forward with the rational-basis arguments it had mustered thus far. But, says Hartnett, "everyone was on the lookout for some point at which there could be room for a principled pivot."

There were two ways a federal judge could come to assess the law under the higher standard. First, plaintiffs could assert that the law abridged a fundamental right guaranteed under the Constitution. The Supreme Court had repeatedly identified marriage as one—such as when it ruled that Wisconsin could not deny a marriage license to a man just because he had outstanding child-support debts, or that prisoners were entitled to marry from behind bars. But every instance in which marriage was identified as a fundamental right came in a context where it was understood to apply to a pairing of a man and a woman. Even if the Justice Department could convince a judge to interpret that right more broadly, it would prompt a question that Obama was unready to have his government answer: Were all same-sex couples entitled to a fundamental right to marriage?

White House lawyers focused instead on the alternative logic of equal-protection analysis. Nearly all political activity serves the purpose of advantaging one group over another, and courts will let a policy stand as long as it is possible to identify a rational purpose served by it. But they make exceptions for laws that threaten the constitutional guarantee of equal protection, subject to a higher standard of judicial scrutiny. At stake ultimately is the question of which side would benefit from a judge's assumption of constitutionality. Would plaintiffs have the burden of showing that the law singles out a group without serving any rational purpose? Or would the government have to prove that it had been carefully drafted to advance a crucial objective?

This concept of tiered scrutiny for equal-protection analysis had been the foundation for much of the civil-rights jurisprudence of the twentieth century. It amounted to the crucial hurdle for applying the first article of the Constitution's Fourteenth Amendment, which ensures that no state can "deny to any person within its jurisdiction the equal protection of the laws." The amendment had been drafted in the wake of the Civil War, expressly to render moot the *Dred Scott* decision that had denied African Americans citizenship, thereby sustaining the legal foundation for slavery and helping provoke the Civil War. Yet for years the court applied the equal-protection clause only narrowly, determining in 1896 that a local law segregating train cars by race was supported by a reasonable purpose: "the established usages, customs and traditions of the people," as Justice Henry Brown wrote for the majority in *Plessy v. Ferguson*. It would take more than four decades for the court to awaken to the wisdom of the case's lone dissent. "In the eye of the law, there is in this country no superior, dominant, ruling class of citizens," wrote Justice John Marshall Harlan. The Constitution, he went on, "neither knows nor tolerates classes among citizens."

The realization of that guarantee—in the form of a "more searching judicial scrutiny"—is typically traced to 1938, when in the footnote of an opinion about milk regulation the Supreme Court had declared "discrete and insular minorities" deserving of special defense from laws that directly targeted them. It was, as Daniel A. Farber and Philip P. Frickey wrote, "part of the Court's dramatic change of course in the late 1930s, in which it abandoned strict scrutiny of economic regulations and adopted a new role for itself in protecting civil rights and liberties." The most immediate beneficiaries of that new approach were racial and ethnic groups whose minority status was perceptible on sight.

As new cases came up, the Supreme Court expanded the application of suspect-class doctrine to other minorities, like women and illegitimate children, and isolated the criteria necessary for a group to be eligible for such judicial protection. The minority group had to be united by a characteristic that was outwardly observable, like race, or not easily switched off, like a particular religious belief. That characteristic could have no bearing on whether one was capable to function within society—unlike, say, age or physical disability. Furthermore, the group has to have suffered a history of discrimination that left it suffering from a continued political powerlessness.

This four-prong test had been one of the core concepts in the constitutional-law class that Obama had taught at the University of Chicago as a part-time lecturer. "Con Law III" covered equal protection and due process, and the syllabus guided students through the canon of Supreme Court cases contending with discrimination based on race and gender. Just months after the Illinois legislature, which Obama was weeks from joining as a first-term senator, amended the state's code to define marriage and limit recognition of out-of-state gay unions, he pushed his students to consider how the Constitution ought to assess a statute that made distinctions on the basis of sexual orientation. On the final exam he gave students in December 1996, Obama presented his class with a fictive state law that uniquely excluded same-sex couples from receiving insurance coverage for in-vitro fertilization procedures. In asking students to assess the legal options that would confront a lesbian employee named Helen who sought to reproduce under such a law, Obama seemed to be leading them to consider that something stricter than rational-basis review should apply. Skeptical that the state could demonstrate that the law "either strengthens marriage or prevents out-of-wedlock births in any statistically meaningful way," Obama wrote in the answer-key memo he provided afterward, "Helen could argue that the only conceivable purpose of the law is to harass and stigmatize homosexuals."

Earlier that year, the Supreme Court had invoked such a motivation of "animus" as a reason to overturn Colorado's Amendment 2. But even as justices had overturned an explicitly antigay law in *Romer v. Evans,* they had sidestepped the scrutiny question. As a law professor, Obama noted "the remarkable opacity of Justice Kennedy's opinion," which left open the possibility that the court could continue to invoke "tradition" as a reason for keeping in place laws that enforce ideas about sexual morality. "Which spin on *Romer* the Court might adopt is anybody's guess," Obama wrote to his students. "What is safe to say is that the views of particular justices on the desirability of rearing in [*sic*] children in homosexual households would play a big part in the decision."

Fourteen years later, it was Obama whose analysis would be tested with even higher stakes. If he misinterpreted the law, or misread the court's past decisions no matter how opaquely they were written, he could end up in the uniquely humiliating place of instructing his government to drop its defense of a law the Supreme Court later upheld. "I'm not going to put my constitutional lawyer hat on now, partly because I'm president and I've got to be careful about my role in the three branches of government here," Obama told Eleveld in her December 2010 interview. "With respect to the courts and heightened scrutiny, I think that if you look at where Justice Kennedy is moving, the kind of rational review that he applied in the Texas case was one that feels right to me and says that, even if he was calling it 'rational review,' is one that recognizes that certain groups may be vulnerable to stereotypes, certain groups may be subject to discrimination," Obama went on. "I think that the courts historically have played a critical role in making sure that all Americans are protected under the law. And there are certain groups that are in need of that protection; the court needs to make sure it's there for them."

By then, the Supreme Court had made explicit that tradition and moral disapproval would be unlikely to be accepted as rational justifications for antigay laws. By declaring sodomy bans unconstitutional, the Supreme Court's 2003 decision in *Lawrence v. Texas* eliminated one hurdle for demonstrating heightened scrutiny—removing the stigma around gay sex seemed to establish that homosexuality should not be considered to limit one's ability to function in society. Yet Kennedy again drafted a majority opinion so as to be purposefully vague on the scrutiny question. In the absence of clear guidance from the Supreme Court, any appeals judge handed a Defense of Marriage Act case would have a free hand, possibly an obligation, to reckon with it. As gay-rights cases headed into federal courts at a faster velocity, it would be left to the country's twelve regional circuits to set their own rules about what standard of review applied to laws that made distinctions based on sexual orientation. "This was the unavoidable question," says Ruemmler. "How that question was answered was really important to the president of United States."

Even before Mary Bonauto filed *Gill v. OPM*, the court that would hear it had already decided not to subject claims of antigay discrimination to any scrutiny more rigorous than a rational-basis standard. In the summer of 2008, assessing a challenge to the Don't Ask Don't Tell statute, the First Circuit reviewed the two most recent major gay-rights cases before the Supreme Court and determined that "neither *Romer* nor *Lawrence* mandate heightened scrutiny." In the Ninth Circuit, where *Smelt v. United States* had been filed, past decisions had the opposite effect: sexual-orientation claims were to be considered under a more exacting test. Indeed, the *Perry* trial had served as the highest-profile demonstration of the difficulty that defenders of anti-gay-marriage laws faced when forced to conjure any rationales for those laws. "They basically collapsed under examination," says Associate Deputy Attorney General Stuart Delery.

The Second Circuit, where new Supreme Court justice Sonia Sotomayor sat for a decade, had never been forced to make such a determination. Whereas *Smelt* was constrained by the Ninth Circuit's previous rulings, no precedent controlled the two Second Circuit cases. Not only did the government have a free hand to argue about the relevant standard of review, but the Justice Department was likely to be asked by the judge which standard it thought should be applied. "We all knew eventually we were going to have a case in the Second Circuit," says assistant White House counsel Ian Bassin. "Then what are we going to do?"

The arrival of *Windsor* and *Pedersen* in November 2010 set a deadline for the answer. Defendants typically had sixty days to respond, and administration lawyers wrangled an additional thirty days in both cases. By March 11, the Justice Department would have to submit briefs answering plaintiffs' claims of unconstitutionality. Practically, the government needed to commit to a strategy before that, because the Justice Department was required to give Congress advance warning if it planned to stop defending a statute. (It was assumed that the legislative branch might have an interest in protecting its handiwork even, or perhaps especially when, the executive didn't.) "Now they are being asked what they think the law should be, and not merely how to apply the law as it exists," Cornell University law professor Michael Dorf told the *New York Times*. "There is much less room to hide for that decision."

Within the Justice Department—legendary for its "fifty-lawyer meetings, and paper battles," as one White House attorney puts it—that question was pushed out into the open, with several offices invited to weigh in on both the heightened-scrutiny analysis and what it should mean for current and future cases. "These litigation deadlines are driving policymaking discussions," says Delery. "That was the source of a lot of frustration for a lot of people because it's hard to think through things and make decisions on short notice." The Civil Division was the most aggressive, with Assistant Attorney General Tony West arguing that the department should stop defending the Defense of Marriage Act in any venue, including *Gill v. OPM*. On the other side was the Office of the Solicitor General, whose principal purpose was to defend laws before the Supreme Court. Acting Solicitor General Neal Katyal argued that meant always fighting for the most deferent standard of review possible, the one that would give the government the easiest path to victory. Katyal was so emphatic in doing so that some in the department concluded he wanted to record his dissent in case he was ever nominated to serve on the Supreme Court.

On January 10, Justice Department officials met once again with representatives from gay-rights groups to discuss how the government would answer the new DOMA suits in the Second Circuit. All the visitors had ties to organizations that had negotiated the previous year's revision of the 10-10-10-20 paper, when litigators had identified a change in standard of review as a necessary step on an incremental Supreme Court strategy. "The Court typically issues its most important civil rights rulings after it has built the constitutional principles it will ultimately use," Matt Coles wrote then, such as "a ruling making it clear that sexual orientation discrimination presents a serious constitutional issue that gets careful review from the courts." They had not foreseen the possibility that a friendly Justice Department could offer a boost by voluntarily accepting that premise.

Lobbying attorneys general for policy changes had already proven fruitful beyond Washington. Tim Gill's operatives had bought access to state legal officers through the Democratic Attorneys General Association, and helped convert their offices to redoubts of quiet policymaking in states that had yet to see litigation or legislation around marriage. In Rhode Island, Attorney General Patrick Lynch had issued an advisory opinion that confirmed that no state law prohibited Rhode Island couples from traveling to Massachusetts to marry. In New York, Attorney General Eliot Spitzer had enforced an opinion recognizing same-sex couples married in neighboring Massachusetts even though it would have not let them marry in New York. After Governor Martin O'Malley said that he thought Maryland should do the same, Attorney General Douglas Gansler ordered state agencies to recognize out-of-state marriages—just days before they would become legal in the neighboring District of Columbia. Spitzer's opinion was tied up in court challenges for four years, by which time he had already been elected governor and resigned from the office amid a prostitution scandal. Among the early beneficiaries of the change were Manhattanites Edith Windsor and Thea Spyer, who were recognized as married at home even though wed in Canada. In fact, Spitzer's initiative gave Windsor her grounds to sue the United States for the harm the Defense of Marriage Act inflicted upon her tax bill.

Bonauto had benefited from the willingness of Massachusetts's attorney general to back her lawsuit challenges, but looked askance at other litigators who saw their Washington trips as occasions to lobby the Justice Department to back away from conflict over the DOMA cases. "Our hunt is taking it down in the Supreme Court," she says. In fact, GLAD had publicly invited the federal government to appeal in the First Circuit, heralding "the chance to argue in front of a higher court with a broader reach."

A few weeks later, a Justice Department lawyer asked Robbie Kaplan if she would be willing to grant the government a second, one-month delay of its deadline to answer her client Edie Windsor's lawsuit. When Kaplan didn't acquiesce, noting her client's advanced age and frailty, she got a call from West. "Robbie," the assistant attorney general told Kaplan, "I'm asking you for an extension because we are seriously considering what position the government should take on this case."

White House counsel Bob Bauer delivered the Ruemmler memo to Obama with a clear recommendation that sexual orientation ought to be treated as a suspect class. The memo did not specify which tier of scrutiny should apply, but lawyers would eventually decide that they needed to be consistent even in venues, like the First Circuit, where precedent pointed to a lower standard. "If we were going to change our position in the Second Circuit, we were changing our position forever," says Ruemmler.

At the same time, her team recommended that the Obama administration continue to deny married couples federal benefits, in large part to keep alive the harm that gave plaintiffs the right to sue and keep their litigation active. "It's one thing for the administration just to render the statute null and void by not enforcing it, and quite another to have the Supreme Court strike it down," says Ruemmler. "We felt that in the long term—for the country and for the LGBT community—it was better that we get that finality from the Court."

Over the Presidents' Day weekend, Obama informed Attorney General Eric Holder that he had accepted his counsel's analysis, and that the government should treat gays and lesbians as a protected class. As a result, the two men agreed, the Justice Department should change its posture on Defense of Marriage Act cases, and possibly others to come. "That judgment was viewed as binding," says Delery, then a senior counselor to Holder. "People viewed it as significant that, in fact, the president made the decision."

As a matter of protocol, the February 23 letter informing Congress went out under Holder's signature, along with the administration's only press statement to explain it—and for years journalistic accounts would emphasize the Justice Department's role in deliberations at the expense of the White House's. "I think he got comfortable with it not coming from him—it was coming from the Justice Department, which is different," Jarrett says of Obama. "The president didn't see Eric pursuing a legal argument as the same as the president turning it into a political argument."

Leading from Behind

In 2011, Barack Obama told a largely gay audience that "ever since I have a memory," he "believed that discriminating against people was wrong. I had no choice, I was born that way." About to turn fifty, Obama was the first president from a generation in which homosexuality could be taken for granted as a fact of life. Both Obama's high-school drug dealer and favorite college professor were gay men. In the mid-1980s, he wrote to his first serious girlfriend that he saw homosexuality as "an attempt to remove oneself from the present, a refusal perhaps to perpetuate the endless farce of earthly life. You see, I make love to men daily, but in the imagination. My mind is androgynous to a great extent and I hope to make it more so." Biographer David J. Garrow concluded that Obama "ultimately decided that a same-sex relationship would be less challenging and demanding than developing one with the opposite sex."

Raised in Hawaii, Obama had been much closer to the origins of the same-sex marriage issue than any other national politician. Often that proximity was mere coincidence. Obama had been born in Honolulu, fourteen months after Ninia Baehr at the same hospital. The state official who wrote the April 1991 letter formally informing Baehr that she and Genora Dancel were not eligible for marriage licenses under state law, registrar Alvin T. Onaka, later verified Obama's birth certificate amid allegations from political opponents including Donald Trump that it was fraudulent. The first house of worship to pass a resolution endorsing Baehr's lawsuit, the First Unitarian Church of Honolulu, had been Obama's boyhood Sunday school.

Even so, he seems to have made himself willfully oblivious to the early development of marriage as a legal issue. Obama had been in Honolulu in late December 1990, on a Christmas vacation with girlfriend Michelle Robinson, as both of the city's newspapers covered state government's initially uncertain response to Baehr's request for a marriage license on December 17. But there is no evidence that the *Harvard Law Review* president took note of the emergent constitutional question in his midst: the review did not publish any articles related to gay rights during Obama's term, and the concurrent editor of the *Harvard Civil Rights–Civil Liberties Law Review* does not recall ever discussing them with him. Even though he returned to Hawaii regularly throughout the years that gay marriage dominated public debate across the state, Obama was never listed among the Hawaii Equal Rights Marriage Project's supporters and did not appear to have any interaction with its activist leadership.

The issue washed ashore in mainland politics just as Obama mounted his first campaign for public office. Obama committed to his first position on the topic on January 7, 1996, as he navigated a contentious primary challenge to a Democratic incumbent. He completed a questionnaire from IMPACT, a local gay-rights political action committee, which included the sentence-long "Marriage Resolution" that Evan Wolfson had begun to circulate the previous Valentine's Day. The resolution was framed in passive terms—"the state should not interfere with same-gender couples who choose to marry"—that implied an acceptable status quo. (IMPACT had shifted Wolfson's "the State" to a lowercase form, perhaps tailoring the query to the types of issues that could arise in Springfield.) In block type, Obama scrawled beneath the text, "I would support such a resolution."

The next month, Obama was given the opportunity to assert his own views on marriage, rather than responding to another's formulation. He was presented a different questionnaire, this time from the Chicago gay newspaper *Outlines,* with a February deadline. Obama typed up a one-page sheet of answers, including: "I favor legalizing same-sex marriages, and would fight efforts to prohibit such marriages."

It was a sweeping but still quite abstract declaration, six weeks before Illinois legislators would face their first bill to specify that only opposite-sex marriages would stand in the state, and three months before the federal Defense of Marriage Act elevated the question of same-sex unions to one of national concern. There was little obvious political downside in the absolutist stance for a first-time candidate "up against a progressive incumbent in a very progressive district, who needed all the help he could get," according to Chicago historian Timothy Stewart-Winter. (Obama never faced a real competition that year, successfully knocking the incumbent from the ballot for petition irregularities.) When he was running to represent largely black urban areas, Obama's advertising would style him a "civil-rights lawyer"; when he needed to win over white liberals, he characterized himself as a "constitutional-law professor." Yet he was rarely, if ever, proactive on the rights of sexual minorities.

In 1998, already being spoken of as a promising contender for city- or statewide office, Obama declared he was "Undecided" on a new *Outlines* questionnaire that asked if he favored legalizing same-sex marriage. Obama said he would cosponsor a hypothetical "bill establishing a same-sex domestic partnership registry for the State of Illinois," but when questioned if he would work to repeal the 1996 mini-DOMA, he again responded, "Undecided." (Obama similarly developed a habit of voting "present" on controversial bills related to abortion, among other sensitive topics.)

At the same time, Obama cultivated a record as reliable friend to the gay community, cosponsoring the nondiscrimination Illinois Human Rights Act and appearing at a major fundraising banquet for Equality Illinois. But as he backed off his unequivocal position about marriage, Obama avoided situations where he could be put on the record about the issue altogether. In 2000, when he challenged incumbent U.S. representative Bobby Rush, Obama did not respond to an *Outlines* survey. He also chose not to pursue an endorsement from the Human Rights Campaign, the only group that attempted to place all congressional candidates on the record about LGBT issues, even though Rush left himself potentially vulnerable on them by voting for the Defense of Marriage Act.

Obama was chastened by what would be his only electoral defeat. Even as he did well in the largely white parts of the district, he struggled in the black South Side neighborhoods that produced the majority of its primary voters. Obama's opponents had successfully made him out to be an interloper—"Barack is viewed in part to be the white man in blackface in our community," said state senator Donne Trotter—and he responded by becoming more conspicuous about his ties to the black church and assiduous in pronouncing his belief.

The effect on Obama's views toward recognition of gay families surprised his own staff as he looked to fill Illinois's open seat in the U.S. Senate. Obama's path to victory in the 2004 primary depended on stitching together support from both urban blacks and white liberals, and gay marriage was arguably the issue that demanded the most delicate balancing act between the two ends of that coalition. In completing a candidate questionnaire from Illinois NOW, deputy campaign manager Audra Wilson put down a simple "yes" to a question that asked whether the Senate candidate thought that gay and lesbian couples should be entitled to public benefits. When a draft was shared with Obama, however, he struck Wilson's one-word response and replaced it with a position he offered as a compromise. Obama wrote that he supported "laws recognizing domestic partnerships and providing benefits to domestic partners," but hedged about how far he would go in that area, albeit with a coldly secular rationale. "However, given the precarious financial status of the social security system, I would need to evaluate the fiscal impact of a specific social security reform proposal before supporting it," Obama wrote on the document returned to Illinois NOW in September 2003.

News from Massachusetts two months later made it harder to obfuscate the matter. At the Illinois state capitol in Springfield, the glare of the *Goodridge* decision was blamed for helping derail a nondiscrimination bill that Obama had cosponsored by scaring away Democrats. "Ironically, the ruling hurt more than helped because it fueled fears that gay marriage is the ultimate goal of those backing the gay rights bill—or more importantly, fears that it could be a potent campaign issue," wrote the *Chicago Sun-Times*'s Mark Brown. Within the bounds of a competitive primary, however, the substantiation of marriage in another reliably Democratic state had another effect: it pushed the bounds of the debate leftward. By attaching himself to civil unions, Obama matched the position of the alternating front-runners for the U.S. Senate seat, Blair Hull and Dan Hynes, but no further. Among their three other opponents, former Chicago Public Schools president Gery Chico did support full marriage rights, in one debate calling it "the civil rights issue of our era" as he rejected civil unions as a "separate-but-equal" solution.

Yet it was in that delta between material benefits and symbolic weight that Obama found safety. Civil unions had become law in Vermont during the four years since Obama's previous federal campaign, and added an enticing third option to what elected Democrats tended to view as an unappealingly polarized two-sided issue. Most of the party's leading presidential contenders in 2004—namely John Kerry, Dick Gephardt, and Howard Dean—alighted on civil unions as a chance to describe themselves as in favor of something, while signaling their moderation. When George W. Bush said he was open to states choosing to offer civil unions to their citizens, Obama associated himself with a man whom he considered anathema in nearly every other context. "President Bush and I disagree apparently with Mr. Keyes on this," Obama said during a general-election debate against Republican nominee Alan Keyes.

When pressed from the left, Obama throughout 2004 explained his opposition to marriage "primarily just as a strategic issue," as he characterized it in a January interview with *Windy City Times,* the successor to *Outlines.* "What I'm saying is that strategically, I think we can get civil unions passed," he explained. "I think that to the extent that we can get the rights, I'm less concerned about the name. And I think that is my No. 1 priority, in an environment in which the Republicans are going to use a particular language that has all sorts of connotations in the broader culture as a wedge issue, to prevent us moving forward, in securing those rights, then I don't want to play their game."

The following month, Obama insisted that "it's not just the marriage issue, it's also, you know, the moral issue of recognition and acceptance" in a visit to the editorial board of the suburban *Daily Herald.* "What I also tell my gay and lesbian friends is, look, if I was, you know, functioning in the early '60s trying to get the Voting Rights Act passed and the Civil Rights Act passed, then I might not lead politically with, you know, trying to reverse anti-miscegenation laws. . . . I might really focus on getting rights that are concrete and that are going to be important and politically are achievable." Obama took umbrage when accused of being more "politically expedient than principled," as an editor put it. "This is one of those situations where I genuinely think that I can get more done on an issue that I care deeply about, and I wouldn't consider that political expedience. This is not me avoiding the issue," Obama responded. "It is strategic, and I think that that's fair to say."

Even though it went unnoticed at the time, this posture also led Obama to say that he believed the one federal law constraining same-sex marriage should remain in place. "I do not support legislation to repeal the Defense of Marriage Act," Obama wrote on the 2003 questionnaire for Illinois NOW. "I believe changing the federal definition of 'marriage' would unnecessarily detract from efforts to pass a domestic partnership law," he added on a draft, before asking policy adviser Raja Krishnamoorthi whether that answer "sounds too squirrelly."

On most issues, Obama was proud to stake out the strongest "progressive" position, to use a favorite self-description, but on marriage he remained evasive. Even though he appeared (alongside Hillary Clinton) at a June 2004 fundraiser for the Human Rights Campaign in Chicago,

Obama did not seek out the group's endorsement—which would require submitting to an in-person interview—until he was already coasting to a general-election landslide. Even so, Obama chose not to travel to the group's headquarters, instead summoning the director of its political-action committee to meet him at the offices of the Democrats' Senate campaign arm, where he had other meetings scheduled. When he had visited the *Windy City Times* for an interview earlier that year, Obama asked editor Tracy Baim to turn off her tape recorder once the conversation turned to same-sex marriage so that they could have an off-the-record discussion about the topic. "The unrecorded portion of our discussion was about what is practical and attainable vs. what is fair in an ideal world," Baim would recall. "For Obama, it was all about being realistic and pragmatic. He did not say that his position was based on his religious views."

After he won the Democratic primary for the U.S. Senate, Obama's language on the topic of gay families started to shift. Civil unions were no longer a pragmatist's grudging concession to reality, but a policy end unto itself—the most generous concession to be made by someone whose values could not countenance a challenge to the Judeo-Christian conception of marriage. "What I believe, in my faith, is that a man and a woman when they get married are performing something before God, and it's not simply the two persons who are meeting," Obama said in a debate on WTTW, made visibly uncomfortable when the moderator pressed him about the religious basis for those views. "That doesn't mean that that necessarily translates to a position on public policy."

When he launched a campaign for the presidency in 2007, Obama continued to invoke religious ideas about marriage as the justification for policy, albeit with different emphasis depending on his audience. "My view is that we should try to disentangle what has historically been the issue of the word 'marriage,' which has religious connotations to some people, from the civil rights that are given to couples, in terms of hospital visitation, in terms of whether or not they can transfer property or Social Security benefits and so forth," Obama said at a 2007 candidate forum hosted by the Human Rights Campaign. "It is then, as I said, up to religious denominations to make a determination as to whether they want to recognize that as marriage or not."

To undercut rumors that he was a secret Muslim, Obama began to specify his personal faith, even as he realized that religious certitude did not adhere well to his liberal worldview. In his 2006 book *The Audacity of Hope*, Obama recounted a phone call from a lesbian supporter who took issue not with his position on marriage as much as the rationale. She "felt that by bringing religion into the equation, I was suggesting that she, and others like her, were somehow bad people," wrote Obama. "And I was reminded that it is my obligation, not only as an elected official in a pluralistic society but also as a Christian, to remain open to the possibility that my unwillingness to support gay marriage is misguided, just as I cannot claim infallibility in my support of abortion rights."

In private, however, Obama confessed even more doubt. "I'm just not very good at bullshitting," he told media strategist David Axelrod after one exchange in which he explained his opposition to same-sex marriage. When pressed at fundraisers, with no media present, Obama would note that when he had been born, in 1961, his parents' marriage was illegal in twelve states—an analogy that conveyed to many who heard it a fundamental lack of confidence in his stated position. "It was an answer that was sincere enough in talking about his own personal journey of being a biracial American that the community—the people in the room understood," says Rufus Gifford, a gay fundraiser for the campaign based in Los Angeles. Even donors who "wanted him so badly to say what we wanted him to say," adds Gifford, "wanted him to win more, I think."

Lore had set in around George W. Bush's victory in 2004: the White House had cultivated state marriage amendments expressly to galvanize churchgoing blacks to vote over moral concerns, and reaped the whirlwind in Ohio. Evidence for this was sparse and inconclusive, but for Democrats running four years later it had the power of a cautionary tale. (In 2008, only also-rans Congressman Dennis Kucinich and former senator Mike Gravel endorsed full marriage rights.)

The pollster who guided Obama's outreach to southern blacks during the primaries, Cornell Belcher, had four years earlier surveyed African Americans across battleground states at the behest of the Human Rights Campaign. Only 28 percent of them supported gay marriage; a plurality opposed any sort of legal recognition for same-sex partnerships. They were evenly split on the Federal Marriage Amendment. "In both polling and focus group research, African American voters supporting the amendment point to the Bible and their adherence to its teachings as the reason for their support of the amendment," Belcher wrote. There was a hint of risk for Democrats merely in appearing too responsive to activists on the issue: even while 71 percent of African Americans agreed that gays and lesbians were discriminated against, 53 percent also said they had unfavorable views of the "gay-rights movement." They overwhelmingly rejected any comparison to the civil-rights movement that had delivered racial equality under the law.

Obama's most memorable election-year comments about same-sex marriage reflected Belcher's insights. "I believe that marriage is the union between a man and a woman," Obama told Pastor Rick Warren, a prominent backer of Proposition 8, onstage at his Saddleback Church in Southern California. "Now, for me as a Christian—for me—for me as a Christian, it's also a sacred union. God's in the mix." Weeks earlier, Obama's campaign had made an exception to its policy of avoiding state-level policy issues—"there is no good that comes from weighing on anything beneath you," says campaign manager David Plouffe—so that he could express his views on Proposition 8 in a letter to San Francisco's Alice B. Toklas LGBT Democratic Club. But those words seemed less heartfelt than what he offered Warren, whom Obama continued to court with a key role at his inauguration. "It is difficult to comprehend how our president-elect, who has been so spot-on in nearly every political move and gesture, could fail to grasp the symbolism of inviting an anti-gay theologian to deliver his inaugural invocation," Human Rights Campaign president Joe Solmonese wrote in the *Washington Post*.

The more troubling conclusion for activists like Solmonese was that Obama—who in his most famous speech had declared, "We coach little league in the blue states and, yes, we've got some gay friends in the red states"—saw a culture-war rapprochement as its own end, and was willing to sacrifice sectional concerns to settle on common ground. As Obama let his pledge to repeal Don't Ask Don't Tell drift, skeptics saw a natural conciliator acquiescing to military opposition and congressional inertia. Among the quickly disillusioned was Jonathan Lewis, a major Democratic benefactor and one of the founders of the Cabinet, who had "soured considerably" on a number of the organizations he had once funded to advance gay rights. "However, in 2008 I did donate to Barack Obama, believing him to be a different kind of politician," Lewis would reflect. Even if gay-rights groups were getting better at fighting their opponents, Lewis believed, they were unprepared to have a friend like Obama in the White House—one with decent liberal bona fides but a history of caution on gay issues. "For many years, we had tried to get people elected and play nicely within the system, and still nothing was happening," Paul Yandura, a former Clinton White House official who advised Lewis, told *Politico*. "So we undertook to create such a shitstorm that something would have to happen."

For the first time in his career, Obama had to contend with aggressive, adversarial politics from the gay-rights movement. Lewis quietly seeded a new group, GetEQUAL, whose leaders were a pair of Californians radicalized in the aftermath of the Proposition 8 loss. "We found two activists who didn't give a fuck," says Yandura. "We gave them all the money." GetEQUAL specialized in the type of civil disobedience that had fallen out of vogue among gay activists ever since they had, starting in the mid-1990s, been able to get the attention of politicians and media through lawful means. There were Capitol Hill sit-ins, Lafayette Square arrests, interruptions during presidential speeches, all aimed at pressing Obama to exert more executive power to end the military ban. "The impatience was not so much around marriage at the time because he didn't have any control over marriage," says Gifford, who was Obama's principal liaison to donors as finance director of the Democratic National Committee.

Obama took pride in the calm he usually showed at such moments. Even when he did allow himself to get agitated, the confrontation typically affirmed his self-confidence. "What is it about what we are doing that they don't get?" Obama said to an aide in the limousine after a fundraiser befouled by a heckler challenging Don't Ask Don't Tell. "They put a lot of pressure on in 2009 and 2010. I didn't think that was the smartest thing they did because it's not like somehow that accelerated or changed Obama's decisions," says Plouffe. "He just puts outcome above all else, and so he is willing to take the hits."

The only clear commitment Obama had made around marriage as a candidate was to support the repeal of the Defense of Marriage Act. (Obama differed from his most formidable rival, Hillary Clinton, in that she opposed repealing only one of the bill's two operative sections.) Only after the furor over the *Smelt* brief, and the attention it drew to the administration's uncomfortable position in court, made the topic unavoidable did President Obama seriously advocate for it. "I support ensuring that committed gay couples have the same rights and responsibilities afforded to any married couple in this country," he said to applause at a Human Rights Campaign gala in October 2009. "I've called on Congress to repeal the so-called Defense of Marriage Act and to pass the Domestic Partners Benefits and Obligations Act."

But Obama never pushed hard for either. In the fall of 2009, the House Constitution Subcommittee chairman Jerrold Nadler introduced a bill to repeal the Defense of Marriage Act that his committee had generated thirteen years earlier. Upon its introduction, the Respect for Marriage Act had ninety-one initial cosponsors, all like Nadler left-of-center Democrats—

already two dozen more members than had cast votes against the Defense of Marriage Act upon its passage. "While many of us were thrilled with the courts' actions, we had to build the political will to make it happen if the courts didn't act," says Jared Polis, an openly gay Colorado congressman who was one of the bill's coauthors.

Despite Obama's praise for repeal in general terms, he did not formally endorse the Nadler bill, which fell low on the White House's list of legislative priorities. When Valerie Jarrett, who oversaw the administration's gay-rights portfolio, addressed HRC's annual dinner in 2010 in Washington, she spoke almost exclusively about the pressures faced by gay and lesbian youth but never made any reference to marriage. "On the issue of same-sex marriage, the White House was in a bubble, immune to the changing world outside it," noted Kerry Eleveld, the gay press's closest observer of the Obama administration.

While the top levels of Obama's administration were as uniformly heterosexual as his predecessors'—the president did not have any gay men or lesbians in his inner circle, or in Cabinet-level posts—the middle and lower rungs of White House staff reflected the sexual diversity of the Democratic political class. "We were around each other all the time," says Brian Mosteller, who as director of Oval Office operations sat feet from the president's desk and would marry another male White House staffer while both were still working there. "He probably saw me more than anyone else in his life."

Acceptance of same-sex marriage in the District of Columbia, where out-of-state unions were recognized in 2009 and licenses locally awarded a year later, had an immediate impact on workplace life. (One presidential aide who had married shortly before joining the White House in 2011 was contacted by a human-resources officer who informed him that he had miscalculated his payroll withholdings—unaware that, due to DOMA, he had different tax status under federal and state law.) Some worked to shape the boss's frame of reference by ensuring that in his rare interactions with citizens—at airport welcomes on his travels or meet-and-greets before speeches—the president was being introduced to same-sex families, especially those with children present. "Not knowing what was going through his head, the best we could do is equip him with as many anecdotes as possible," says Gautam Raghavan, Obama's liaison to the LGBT community.

In 2007, Obama said that he had not discussed same-sex marriage with his daughters but "my wife has." By the time four years later that he screened *The Kids Are All Right* in the White House cinema, Obama couldn't avoid telling aides that the film, about a lesbian couple raising a pair of biologically unrelated teenagers, reminded him of the situations faced by parents of his daughters' friends. "Those conversations really touched him," says Jarrett. "And he began to appreciate that no, civil union wasn't marriage even though it legally confers the same rights. It didn't have the same symbolism, and that symbolism was important."

In late October, Obama took his advisers by surprise by publicly acknowledging his ambivalence. In a group interview with five left-wing bloggers, he told AMERICAblog's Joe Sudbay that "attitudes evolve, including mine." Sudbay had asked Obama whether his position on marriage had changed since the 2008 campaign, in light of the summer's federal-court decisions and changes in public opinion. "While I'm not prepared to reverse myself here, sitting in the Roosevelt Room at 3:30 in the afternoon," Obama said, "I think it's fair to say that it's something that I think a lot about. That's probably the best you'll do out of me today."

On the day Obama signed an end to the military ban, he was asked if it was "intellectually consistent to say that gay and lesbians should be able to fight and die for this country but they should not be able to marry the people they love," as ABC News's Jake Tapper put it at a year-end news conference. "My feelings about this are constantly evolving," Obama said. "At this point, what I've said is, is that my baseline is a strong civil union that provides them the protections and the legal rights that married couples have," he expounded. "I recognize that from their perspective it is not enough, and I think is something that we're going to continue to debate and I personally am going to continue to wrestle with going forward."

Obama kept an arm's length from the February 2011 announcement that his government had determined the Defense of Marriage Act unconstitutional. But as had been the case two months earlier, when Obama enacted the repeal of Don't Ask Don't Tell to celebratory media coverage, the caution had been misguided. Those who had once invented gay-related crises to alienate Democrats were largely silent. While a few prominent Republicans alleged that Obama's announcement was "clearly based more on politics than the law," according to Iowa senator Chuck Grassley, the party's ranking Republican on the Senate Judiciary Committee, none were encouraged to awaken a debate on federal marriage policy itself.

"We thought it would be this huge thing that would motivate the far right, and it just didn't," says White House communications director Dan Pfeiffer. "It was really muted. There was no public outcry. You prepare for the worst and the worst did not come."

In the Shadow of Lady Liberty

The realization that gay issues had lost their ability to shock came at the nadir of Barack Obama's political power. In November 2010, Democrats had just suffered the biggest loss any party had experienced in a midterm election since 1938. The large Democratic majority in the House of Representatives that had helped enact monumental legislation during Obama's first two years in office was wiped away, and along with it went any chance of further progress on social issues. Passage of Don't Ask Don't Tell repeal through both chambers in mid-December would end up being Obama's last opportunity to deliver on gay rights through the lawmaking process.

Advocates and lobbyists redoubled their push for an executive order that would require government contractors not to discriminate on the basis of sexual orientation and gender identity. Contracts had long been the most easily reached lever for an administration to influence the practices of private-sector employers; past presidents had used the power to shield other minorities from workplace discrimination. Those rules had presaged the Civil Rights and Americans with Disabilities Acts, and Obama advisers had vowed to adopt one they hoped would soften up congressional resistance to an Employment Non-Discrimination Act protecting gays and lesbians. "The contractor executive order was one of the movement's top priorities going into the new administration because it was seen as a prerequisite" for further progress on a nondiscrimination law, says Jeff Krehely of the Center for American Progress, whose LGBT Research and Communications Project worked intensively on the issue. Think tanks developed an intense interest in its fate, and Jonathan Lewis organized other business-minded donors to join a boycott of Obama's reelection unless the order became law. But the arcane process took place entirely outside public view, and would most affect companies—like Raytheon, ExxonMobil, and Booz Allen Hamilton—with little cultural salience in gay America. For rank-and-file activists looking for an issue on which to pressure the White House, says Krehely, "it was easier to criticize them on marriage than it was to criticize on the contractor executive order."

Freedom to Marry, which had just hired its first federal lobbyist, took advantage. In mid-March, it launched a "Say 'I Do,' Mr. President" campaign, based around an open letter to Obama. "With so many Americans talking it through in heartfelt conversations, it is a question that calls for clarity from the President," it read. "We ask you to complete your journey and join us and the majority of Americans who support the freedom to marry." The letter was publicly released with the signatures of actors Ellen DeGeneres and Martin Sheen, and tech entrepreneurs Jack Dorsey and Sean Parker, to predictable media coverage of the celebrities' involvement. Once it was put online, however, 120,000 people signed their names, such a surprising number that Freedom to Marry's digital director Michael Crawford proposed attempting to hand-deliver the signatures to Obama during the White House Easter Egg Roll. The group's president, Evan Wolfson, rejected the idea, as Crawford recalled, because "he felt like that would be too aggressive a posture."

Obama struggled to find the language to describe his views of marriage once the subject of inspection turned from the policies of his administration to his personal comfort. While the 2010 proclamation he had issued in honor of Lesbian, Gay, Bisexual, and Transgender Pride Month had insisted that "we must give committed gay couples the same rights and responsibilities afforded to any married couple," the 2011 iteration did not refer to gay families at all. The decision to stop defending the Defense of Marriage Act was not included in a recounting of Obama's political accomplishments in the May 2011 proclamation.

Domestic politics were supposed to be an afterthought on Obama's June 23 day trip to New York. It had been scheduled to allow the commander in chief to visit Fort Drum the morning after a White House address announcing plans to withdraw troops from Afghanistan. Under the fussy rules of the campaign-finance code, the military photo op provided enough of an official cover that Obama could take Air Force One to New York City for the true purpose of the journey: a long-scheduled series of fundraisers to back the reelection campaign that Obama had started to build out from a Chicago office tower.

Obama had already been fundraising at a ferocious clip, appearing at thirty events since announcing his reelection campaign earlier in the year. There were three scheduled for his evening in New York, including an intimate $35,800-per-plate dinner at the restaurant Daniel and a performance of the Broadway musical *Sister Act* at which Obama would make remarks following the final curtain. In between, Obama would give a speech to a "Gala with the Gay Community" held at a midtown Sheraton. It was one indicator of the times that a president's participation at an event specifically for gay donors—which itself made national news when Bill Clinton attended one as a candidate in Hollywood in 1992—was no longer remarkable. Instead, it was the context of the event that drove headlines like WHAT WILL OBAMA TELL THE GAYS UNDER THE SHADOW OF LADY LIBERTY? as a blog post by Kerry Eleveld put it.

The $1,250-per-person event had been planned for months, but as the day approached it was clear the president was arriving at a historically auspicious moment for the country's largest gay community. The next day in Albany the state senate would vote on a bill to legalize same-sex marriage, with Governor Andrew Cuomo poised to enact it immediately upon passage. Obama described the events from the remove of a distant observer, remarking wanly that "New York is doing exactly what democracies are supposed to do."

The number of Americans able to legally marry where they lived was about to double, and yet Obama was in no position to share in their joy, or that of a cultural left that had begun to celebrate same-sex marriage as the era's dominant civil-rights cause—and one that appeared ascendant as progress on others, like race relations and reproductive rights, stalled. The previous month, Gallup had shown 53 percent of Americans supporting that same-sex marriages be "recognized by the law as valid," including Bill Clinton, who had just endorsed the New York bill. Obama's own pollster, Joel Benenson, had been preparing an analysis that showed that, after an average increase in support of less than one point per year from 1996 to 2009, same-sex marriage had gained five points in each of 2010 and 2011. One-fifth of the country's marriage supporters had adopted that view during Obama's term, placing the president for the first time in a shrinking minority. "The crowd is so happy, but it's not awesome for Obama because he's like the skunk in the garden party," White House communications director Dan Pfeiffer, who accompanied Obama on the New York trip, says of the fundraiser. "It was bothering him a lot. You could tell."

For the first time, Obama described himself as the protagonist of his government's decision to stop defending the Defense of Marriage Act against lawsuits. "It was wrong, it was unfair, and since I taught constitutional law for a while I thought I was in a pretty good position to agree with courts who have ruled that Section III of DOMA violates the Constitution," Obama explained. "And that's why we decided, with my attorney general, that we could no longer defend the constitutionality of DOMA in the courts."

At the Sheraton, he boasted about what he had accomplished for gays and lesbians in office, apologizing for the fact that the same list had been inventoried earlier by actor Neil Patrick Harris, the master of ceremonies. ("President Obama will be coming out soon," Harris had said, pausing to draw out a titter. "*Out on stage!* Calm down, people.") There was a particular emphasis on rights and benefits that his government had succeeded in extending to couples, but even as he itemized them, he did not bother to make the case for civil unions.

"How about marriage?" a voice cried from the floor of the Sheraton ballroom. "How about marriage?"

Then others joined in, an improvised chorus of "Marriage!"

Obama recoiled slightly at the indignity of the interruption. "I heard you guys," he said. "Believe it or not, I anticipated that somebody might..." he confirmed, before trailing off. Such eruptions had become standard punctuation for his speeches before liberal audiences, which had grown more frequent when he returned to the election-season fundraising circuit. Even at his own events he was being forced to address the marriage question as others chose to define it. "He flubbed it," Jeff Soref told the *Los Angeles Times*. "Why can't you say it? You want my money but you're not willing to treat me as equal?"

On the way out of New York, Obama felt neither contemptuous of his hecklers nor strategically superior to them. For a decade he had been a gradualist on marriage, as a matter of both principle and political contrivance, but there was no longer much logic behind either. Obama told his communications director he might have a different answer to a question he had faced before. During the 2007 candidate forum hosted by the Human Rights Campaign, Obama had been asked, "If you were back in the Illinois legislature where you served and the issue of civil marriage came before you, how would you have voted on that?" His answer dodged the question—"It depends on how the bill would've come up," Obama said—a stance that reasonably reflected some of the legal uncertainties at the time. At that point, no state had enacted same-sex marriage through its legislature; only in California's had a straightforward marriage bill even come for a vote unprompted by court action.

If now asked specifically about the New York law, however, no such evasion would be possible. Furthermore it would be implausible to claim the civil-unions route more expeditious when politicians in New York, a state whose politics did not vary wildly from Illinois's, had just voted for marriage. When a journalist or advocate inquired how he would have voted as a New York legislator, Obama informed Pfeiffer, he would now have to say that he was in favor of same-sex marriage. "We should do it at the time and place of our choosing, not just because some reporter asked you a question," Pfeiffer responded. "We've got to prep for this."

They never did. The summer was dominated by fiscal suspense—nervy negotiations over the long-term budget prompted by a deadline to increase the country's borrowing authority—and few outside the movement had reason to press Obama about gay issues. When, that July, Obama announced he was formally endorsing the Respect for Marriage Act, even though the bill had yet to receive a score of its fiscal impact from the Congressional Budget Office, the media barely took notice. "We could now have a discussion about repeal of DOMA in a way that we could control the conversation," says Winnie Stachelberg, who oversaw gay-rights work at the Center for American Progress. "But the courts were going to be the place for marriage equality."

Even if as the country's top legal official he had done everything then possible to advance the cause of marriage in the courts, activists were starting to view Obama less as an unreliable ally than an impediment to their incipient political momentum. What had been an odd preoccupation for some gay bloggers—an expression of the president's personal sentiment about same-sex marriage—had emerged as the dominant concern for many in gay media and activist circles. "Everyone knew that it was something that the community cared about, but it wasn't a policy change," says White House adviser Gautam Raghavan. "If you're asking someone about their personal perspective, you have to let them say what they want to say when they want to say it. You can't force that."

That fall, Obama informed his advisers he was ready to meet the demand. The high command of his campaign had begun to gather for weekly sessions to scheme a reelection that had grown only more imposing. Battling congressional Republicans over the debt and budget had taken its toll; the president's approval rating had fallen to 40 percent for the first time, according to Gallup. "Obama has gone from a modest favorite to win re-election to, probably, a slight underdog," forecaster Nate Silver wrote in the *New York Times Magazine* in early November. Strategists were still weighing how their approach would change depending on which Republican emerged as the party's nominee, but the president himself had other ambitions for his campaign.

"There are things I feel strongly about," Obama told his advisers, "things I'll want to work on in my second term. Some of them may make you guys nervous. But Axe keeps saying I should be 'authentic.' So maybe I should go out there and just let it rip."

"Given our situation, sir, I'm not sure we're in a position to go all *Bulworth* out there," cracked former White House press secretary Robert Gibbs, an outside adviser to the campaign, referring to the 1998 film about a senator reborn as a teller of blunt truths.

Among those "things I'll want to work on in my second term" that Obama had written on a yellow legal pad was same-sex marriage. He had been promising supporters for a year that he was "evolving," and finally felt he was ready to declare himself not just opposed to federal involvement in the issue but actively supportive of states delivering equal marriage rights. "There wasn't anyone in Barack Obama's inner circle that didn't know that's the way he felt," says campaign manager Jim Messina.

By raising the issue in this setting, however, Obama had completed another evolution on same-sex marriage. He was ready to no longer cabin it as a legal question to be viewed through a constitutional prism, a private matter bounded by religious doctrine, or a series of state-level policy considerations. Instead he realized it was inescapably a national political matter, one that he would have to confront as a candidate—either in response to the taunts of his supporters, or of his own initiative, to the possible jeers of others. If he changed position in the midst of an election campaign, Messina told Obama, "this will be a bigger deal than you think it is."

No one who attended the East Wing meetings counseled the president away from his change of heart, but many expressed concern about the effect it would have on his reelection prospects. The most pointed warning came from Vice President Joe Biden. He had been serving as the administration's chief liaison to the U.S. Conference of Catholic Bishops over the church's objections to new requirements that health-insurance plans include contraception coverage. Already Biden sensed the ticket would have trouble balancing its progressive sexual politics with class-based appeals to white-ethnic Catholics. A presidential repudiation of marriage's traditional definition might be one affront too many for older, working-class whites who stuck with the Democratic Party during the financial crisis even if they felt out of sync with it on matters of culture. *Do that after they reelect you,* Biden advised Obama.

The vice president could be caricatured for his fixation on the demographic group from which he hailed, but in his hesitation he was not alone. Obama's closest campaign advisers were all heterosexual white men whose formative experiences with presidential politics had come during an era when issues related to sexual orientation "were these cultural third rails," according to Pfeiffer. Even if repeal of the military ban had prompted little fuss from opponents, it was still hard for a Democrat to think about taking the initiative to make gay marriage an election issue. "They're always cautious," says Jarrett. "In the reelection campaign, their goal was to have as few variables as possible, and this was a variable. It was an unknown."

The campaign Messina had built was weighted far more lopsidedly toward mobilization than Obama's first run for the presidency had been, based on the assumption that never in the race would the loyalties of more than one-tenth of the electorate be up for grabs. By 2011, focus groups showed persuadable voters whose opinions the Democratic National Committee was tracking on Obama's behalf altogether uninvested in the marriage question. "We weren't talking to base Democrats, we were never talking to base Republicans," says David Simas, the campaign's director of opinion research. "When marriage equality would come up it was always in the frame of a libertarian type of acceptance: It doesn't affect me one bit."

Plouffe asked Messina to assemble a presentation on the politics of the decision. Benenson's polling analysis documented a supportive majority from independents and even one-quarter of Republicans for legalizing same-sex marriage. To the extent there were voters in conflict around the margins of his coalition, they were not in Rust Belt battleground states with large Catholic populations, like Ohio, Pennsylvania, and Wisconsin. "The biggest divides were geographic and by age," says Terry Walsh, who oversaw the campaign's direct-mail program. "We wouldn't pay much of a price in a northern state." Instead the biggest risk seemed to be North Carolina, which Obama had carried by only 14,177 votes in 2008 and where his name would sit alongside a marriage ban on the May primary ballot. Even in places public opinion might be pitched against same-sex marriage, the balance of political energy was moving toward it. "The intensity of opinion is changing at a rapid pace," Benenson and his coauthor Jan van Lohuizen had observed in their memo, commissioned by Freedom to Marry. "As of today, supporters of marriage for gay couples feel as strongly about the issue as opponents do, something that was not the case in the recent past."

Moving left on marriage might sacrifice North Carolina, Messina concluded, but it could prove a boon elsewhere and advance broader strategic goals. With so few voters profiled as persuadable, his campaign plan had outlined a heavy infrastructure of manned offices and a paid workforce of thousands to mobilize those who already backed him. Such a strategy would leave Obama even more reliant on the active engagement of his core supporters than he had been in 2008, and intensified worries about disillusionment among liberal activists. Interest groups, including labor unions and environmentalists, thought Obama at times too easily pressured by business lobbies; Latino immigration activists disappointed by the areas of his inaction; the antiwar left betrayed by the extent to which the Democrat accepted Bush-era assumptions about national security.

Gays and lesbians were possibly the only Democratic bloc more excited about Obama in 2012 than in his first campaign. The *Washington Post* estimated that one in six of Obama's top fundraisers was openly gay; a CNN analysis credited them for a greater share of the campaign's revenue than Hollywood. (There was, naturally, some overlap.) "Gay money, in this election, has replaced Wall Street money," observed NBC News correspondent Chuck Todd, a reflection of both the community's gratitude toward Obama and the maturation of its political giving. "The gay-rights movement groups are less organized," says Messina, but "the bloggers counted more and the donors mattered a lot more."

The White House was backing away from the only other prize it could offer them. In October 2011, Obama launched a We Can't Wait agenda, designed to illustrate his commitment to forging ahead even in the face of congressional obstinance. The major policy and legal work on the executive order forbidding discrimination by government contractors had been completed, but political considerations pushed it aside. Obama advisers, fixated on the need to promote employment gains, worried that the new rule could be attacked not as a civil-rights initiative but as another example of what Republicans had taken to calling "job-killing regulations." As 2012 approached, the White House went quiet on the contractor issue. "The idea of doing it in a nonelection year versus doing it in an election year, I think, came into sharp relief for them," says Krehely.

With volunteer sign-ups lagging nationwide, Messina and Plouffe came to believe that a change of presidential heart on same-sex marriage could galvanize the supporter ranks with a new sense of idealistic purpose. They pulled aside the president to lay out this calculus, and the president asked the campaign manager for his recommendation on how to proceed. "I think you already said you're going to do this," Messina said, "so let's go do it."

A quintet of Obama's top advisers began to discuss the specifics. Some argued for an expansive address along the lines of one he had given about race in Philadelphia in 2008, which the *New York Times* called "powerful and frank," grounded in "an honesty seldom heard in public life." There was greater support for a broadcast interview in a venue that would permit the president to be more conversational. "The question was how do you just kind of get on the record and make a statement without causing a big story around it," says paid-media director Larry Grisolano.

Obama's advisers believed they had a complicated case to make over the next year about his stewardship of the country's economy and security—in both instances about gradual if unsatisfying progress—and needed to begin even before Republicans had selected their nominee. Obama spent the late fall touting something called the JOBS Act that advisers hoped could win some bipartisan support, and in early December traveled to Kansas to give a speech attacking the "breathtaking greed" infecting the American economic system. They intended to frame his reelection candidacy around such populist themes. The rest of the month became engulfed by congressional debate over a payroll-tax cut due to expire on December 31, and planning January's State of the Union. The latter might be the last chance for him to set an election-year agenda with the trappings of an officeholder rather than as a candidate. At every point, making news on same-sex marriage would amount to an unhelpful diversion.

Indeed, inducing one of his Republican opponents into a debate over marriage—even if Obama's position was the more popular—would come with an opportunity cost. Already funding for Planned Parenthood and access to contraception were emerging as key topics of conflict with Republicans, and sexual politics threatened to subsume everything else. Media interest in marriage was high, and the story line of a presidential flip-flop back to a position he had taken and then abandoned would be irresistible. The longer Obama waited to make such an announcement, the more likely it would dominate events that his strategists hoped to steer, like the convention. "My biggest fear was he was going to do it during a debate," says Messina.

Consensus had developed within the small planning team in favor of a relaxed broadcast interview as the prime venue for Obama to reveal his change of heart. Messina had Simas quietly collect research that would guide how he spoke of it. In early February, Simas contacted Lisa Grove, an ancillary member of the campaign's polling team responsible for the noncompetitive states of the Pacific Northwest. Simas knew that, through her work for the Marriage Research Consortium and its partner groups, Grove had spent more time thinking about how people ought to talk about same-sex marriage than perhaps anyone else in American politics. She quickly distilled the research she had done over the years into a memo with a few basic prescriptions. Validate the idea that reconsidering one's prior view was a noble "journey," she advised, to the conclusion that same-sex couples marry out of "love" and "commitment" rather than a pursuit of equal rights.

The following week, timed to coincide with Valentine's Day, Freedom to Marry posted an online petition headlined "Democrats: Say I Do." It was conceived as a sequel to the "Mr. President" campaign, another digital petition but this time with a clear policy outcome: an upgrade in the Democratic platform's existing pro-civil-unions plank toward endorsement of the "freedom to marry." The group's strategists had a detailed timeline, in which public pressure would crest as the party platform committee first met in June, three months before the convention's vote on the final version. "We were going to build momentum so that when they got to Charlotte, there would be this groundswell of support, and we would get really solid language in there," said Freedom to Marry lobbyist Jo Deutsch.

Party elites took note even before the online masses. Two days after the petition was posted, House minority leader Nancy Pelosi endorsed the plank. "That was our snowball. Because once Pelosi came out in support," Deutsch explained, "everybody wanted to come out in support." She was followed shortly by a gang of elected officials who had been designated as cochairs of Obama's campaign and of the convention itself. Within two weeks, nearly half of the Senate's Democrats—many of whom had voted for the Defense of Marriage Act—had signed on, too. Reporters had been given a timely reason to quiz Democrats in national office about their personal views on same-sex marriage; *National Journal*'s Reid Wilson labeled it "the New Democratic Litmus Test." When ABC News anchor George Stephanopoulos asked in late March if the president was "going to fight the inclusion of this plank in the Democratic platform," Plouffe was unable to answer.

Obama had for fifteen years attentively positioned himself in the safe mainstream of center-left politics on the issue, but a monthlong cascade was pushing him outside it. The focus on the platform moved up the de facto deadline to early June to stage an announcement, so that he would not be put in the humiliating situation of having either to fight the party organization he controlled or appear squeezed by it.

The next opportunity that Obama would have to appear with the female quintet of *The View*—which advisers had identified as the optimal setting to talk about his views in the context of his daughters—would be in mid-May, on his next planned fundraising trip to New York. He had other news he wanted to make before then, starting with a ceremony to sign the JOBS Act passed by Congress in late March. There would be a pair of long-scheduled foreign trips, to Asia and Latin America, likely to each dominate news coverage for a week, and on May 1 an unannounced visit to Afghanistan. The first week of May he would formally kick off his candidacy for reelection with back-to-back speeches on college campuses in Ohio and Virginia.

To promote the short tour, the campaign booked Biden to appear on *Meet the Press* the day before. He went to NBC's Washington bureau that Friday afternoon to tape the interview. Host David Gregory asked Biden whether his views on marriage had "evolved." Biden indicated that they had. "The good news is that, as more and more Americans come to understand, what this is all about is a simple proposition: Who do you love and will you be loyal to the person you love?" he said. "And that's what people are finding out is what all marriages at their root are about, whether their marriage is of lesbians or gay men or heterosexuals." Pressed by Gregory, Biden said that he personally endorsed that view. While noting that "the president sets the policy," the vice president declared himself "absolutely comfortable with the fact that men marrying men, women marrying women and heterosexual men and women marrying one another are entitled to the same exact rights, all the civil rights, all the civil liberties. And quite frankly I don't see much of a distinction beyond that."

Biden's own communications team sensed that he had said something potentially newsworthy. When the transcript reached campaign headquarters in Chicago, it was read as an explicit subversion—whether conscious or the result of a verbal inattention for which Biden had become known—of a six-month process under way to permit Obama to make an announcement on his terms. At the White House, Obama and Plouffe were maddened to see their cautious planning disrupted, Jarrett infuriated by what she considered a betrayal of her boss: Obama had updated Biden on those plans over lunch just weeks earlier.

The White House tried, initially, to minimize the gulf between the positions expressed by the two halves of the ticket. Under pressure, Biden's office released a statement insisting he had not said anything different than Obama ever had, only "expressing that he too is evolving on the issue." On Monday morning, however, Education secretary Arne Duncan was asked by an interviewer whether, as a member of Obama's cabinet, he believed same-sex couples should be allowed to marry. "Yes, I do," Duncan said. That day, in his briefing, Press Secretary Jay Carney was asked more than fifty different times about Biden's comments and insisted on each occasion that what the vice president had said was "completely consistent" with the president's position. "This bit of straight talk made Obama's position—neither for nor against such unions but in an evolutionary state, not unlike the Galapagos finch—all the more untenable," observed *Washington Post* columnist Dana Milbank.

Attention was not going to slacken soon, as North Carolina voters were about to decide on Amendment 1 banning same-sex marriage. Six weeks earlier, Obama had again made an exception to a hands-off policy toward state ballot issues by condemning the law that would "single out and discriminate against committed gay and lesbian couples," according to a statement released by his campaign. (Shortly thereafter, another went out about the Minnesota amendment.) Yet Obama's campaign, which had already established a significant foothold in the state—and had taken a deep interest in a Charlotte mayoral election the previous year—did little to mitigate the inevitable landslide. In his commitment to fighting the marriage ban, Obama was again upstaged by Bill Clinton, who recorded phone calls arguing against the amendment.

Gay donors saw a unique moment to exert pressure. Tim Gill, who with his husband had already raised $500,000 for the reelection campaign, began to rally his peers with the threat of withholding future support. Obama was about to head to Hollywood for fundraising events, and then to New York for a gay-themed one days later; two others would follow in Los Angeles thereafter. The leverage that Lewis had developed to push through the somewhat arcane matter of an executive order regulating government contractors could now be deployed to a very different end.

On Tuesday, as the North Carolina amendment was passing by a twenty-point margin, Obama decided he could wait no longer. Plouffe quietly advised the campaign's analytics department—which was responsible for tracking daily shifts in the horse race through a predawn summary called the Golden Report—to increase the sample size for its survey calls into North Carolina the following day. Even beyond what Plouffe and Messina had anticipated the previous fall, circumstances now made it likely that the effect of any news on gay marriage would be felt more acutely there than anywhere else. "It's not rocket science: gay-marriage ban passes by twenty points the day before the announcement, and it's on the top of everyone's mind," says David Shor, the department's battleground state elections analyst. "I was freaking out because we had never polled gay marriage."

By Wednesday morning, Obama's advisers set their plan into motion. Pfeiffer called ABC News's Washington bureau chief to ask if *Good Morning America* anchor Robin Roberts would be available to interview the president that afternoon. An African American woman with a longtime girlfriend but not yet publicly identified as a lesbian, Roberts was likely to be a sympathetic interlocutor who would permit Obama to expound on the personal context for his decision without pushing him too aggressively over the legal reasoning behind it. "I've been going through an evolution on this issue," Obama told Roberts that afternoon in the Cabinet Room, revisiting the various rationales he had previously offered—the sufficiency of civil unions, the religious potency of the word *marriage*—before alighting on the factors that forced him to reconsider "over the course of several years.

"As I talk to friends and family and neighbors; when I think about members of my own staff who are incredibly committed, in monogamous relationships, same-sex relationships, who are raising kids together; when I think about those soldiers or airmen or marines or sailors who are out there fighting on my behalf—and yet, feel constrained, even now that Don't Ask, Don't Tell is gone, because they're not able to commit themselves in a marriage," Obama said. "At a certain point, I've just concluded that for me personally, it is important for me to go ahead and affirm that I think same-sex couples should be able to get married."

His remarks had been thoroughly considered by political aides but reviewed only in passing by lawyers. "That was consistent with stuff that he had said before," says Ruemmler. "That was him talking. We felt that it was a really effective interview because it was just him being him."

Even then, he attempted to contain the scope of his endorsement. "Now I have to tell you that part of my hesitation on this has also been I didn't want to nationalize the issue. There's a tendency when I weigh in to think suddenly it becomes political and it becomes polarized," Obama explained to Roberts. "And what you're seeing is, I think, states working through this issue in fits and starts, all across the country. Different communities are arriving at different conclusions, at different times. And I think that's a healthy process and a healthy debate."

His Republican challenger did not rush to respond, and even when asked in interviews he dodged every invitation to criticize Obama directly over his switch. "It's a position I've had for some time, and I don't intend to make any adjustments at this point—or ever, by the way," Mitt Romney informed an Ohio television station. He tepidly repeated his support for a federal constitutional amendment, but called same-sex marriage a "very tender and sensitive topic" that he suggested should be off-limits from election-season debate. "I don't think the matter of marriage is really a fundraising matter either for the president, and certainly is not for me," he told Fox News. Other Republicans followed Romney's lead, less out of principle than shared expediency. "Everyone in the reelect was bracing for the evangelical backlash and it didn't really happen," says Rufus Gifford, Obama for America's finance director.

Even if both candidates argued in different ways that the president's views ought to be irrelevant, many Americans failed to heed those directions. According to an analysis by political scientists Lynn Vavreck and John Sides, the day of the announcement gave Obama his highest volume of press mentions of any day before the September convention, and the greatest imbalance of positive coverage of any except the one in late June when the Supreme Court upheld his health-care bill. At Obama's headquarters, staffers had developed a ritual practice of ringing a bell to mark the arrival of each new $1 million into the campaign's coffers. For much of the year, the bell would sound about once a week, but it clanged several times in the hours that followed the release of the first clips from the ABC interview; *BuzzFeed* reported that the initial million came in over the first ninety minutes. "You could literally hear the gay money pouring in," says Shor. Within hours, Lewis dropped the donor boycott initially inspired by inaction on the contractor order and sent Obama the maximum permitted contribution.

The campaign received its first indication of the impact on broader voter opinion at five a.m. on Thursday, when results came in from the previous night's survey calls into North Carolina. The Golden Report showed Obama's chance of winning the state had dropped just .02 percent upon the announcement, a movement that analysts determined was statistically insignificant. The campaign immediately inserted clips from Obama's interview into the video playlist it screened at focus groups of persuadable voters, and had trouble finding anyone whose view of the election was moved. "Voters don't care," Simas concluded. Same-sex marriage still did not move those up for grabs, and they did not think less of Obama's character for having switched positions. "Part of what we'd learned was voters were like, *So what? People change their minds*," says Simas.

Indeed, the most immediate demonstration of Obama's impact was in a state inconsequential to the presidential contest. In Maryland, Public Policy Polling had been asking about marriage in its regular surveys, because of the ballot question that voters there would face that November. In March, PPP had found 56 percent of African Americans opposed to the new marriage law, with 39 percent supportive. When it polled again, in mid-May, those numbers had flipped, with a strong majority now in favor of same-sex marriage. The only notable development in the interim was a shift in the president's position. "While the media has been focused on what impact President Obama's announcement will have on his own reelection prospects, the more important fallout may be the impact his position is having on public opinion about same-sex marriage itself," PPP's Tom Jensen perceptively noted.

When the platform-drafting committee voted in late July, it passed a marriage-equality plank unanimously. By the time the entire platform came up for passage in Charlotte, marriage was overshadowed by a far more controversial topic: recognition of Jerusalem as Israel's capital. In his convention speech there, Obama neither defended his switch on marriage nor trumpeted it, offering only a swipe at "Washington politicians who want to decide who you can marry."

No significant entity on the political landscape seemed to have an interest in making same-sex marriage a campaign issue. Not a single ad on the topic was aired by any presidential candidate, party, or outside group, according to an analysis by Vavreck and Sides. In four and a half hours of one-on-one debate between Obama and Romney, the subject never came up once. The morning after the election, the *New York Times* and the *Washington Post* did not even cite his switch on marriage in their lead stories on Obama's resounding victory.

That day, Obama visited his campaign headquarters to thank his staff, and the electoral-college tally was not the only thing on his mind. North Carolina had been one of two states that flipped from 2008, with Romney carrying it by a margin of fewer than 100,000 votes. In Maryland, however, analysts had begun to extend Obama indirect credit for the passage of a marriage law on the ballot. With a presidential endorsement featured across the paid communications in its favor, Measure 6 carried Prince Georges County and Baltimore City, both with African American majority populations, on its way to a come-from-behind victory. Obama quickly internalized the idea that he was the full-fledged member of the winning team—not just there, but in Washington, Maine, and Minnesota—and it would be a core part of his political identity as he began a second term. Obama navigated the floor of the headquarters, offering high fives and posing for pictures. When he encountered an openly gay aide who had been working on LGBT outreach, Obama went in for a hug and exulted: "We went four-for-four!"

88

Shotgun Wedding

On December 7, 2012, just over a month after Barack Obama's reelection, the Supreme Court announced that it would hear arguments in two separate cases related to same-sex marriage before the end of its term the following spring.

As five different Defense of Marriage Act cases had moved through the federal judiciary that year, Justice Department lawyers—including assistant attorneys general who very rarely made court appearances—had stood alongside the plaintiffs at each step to represent the interests of an executive branch that had already committed to the proposition that the law was unconstitutional. Each time an appeals-court ruling came down in one of the cases, the government was among those petitioning the Supreme Court to take up the issue. In one instance, the request was lodged before lower-court appeals had been fully adjudicated, an unusual claim that the matter needed to be resolved promptly because people were suffering grievous discrimination. However the Defense of Marriage Act got to the Supreme Court, the United States government would be an active litigant, as a party to the suit. "We couldn't just back out," says Solicitor General Donald B. Verrilli Jr.

On the other side at each stage was Paul Clement, a former solicitor general thrust into service by the legislative branch to protect its interests. Upon chartering the Bipartisan Legal Advisory Group to manage the defense of the bill that Congress had passed in 1996, Speaker John Boehner had threatened to raid the Justice Department's budget to make sure he was able to afford the services of Clement's firm, King & Spalding. Already the most prolific Supreme Court practitioner of the young century, Clement would establish himself as the Obama administration's most prominent legal foil, profiled in *New York* magazine as "the GOP's great hope for this Supreme Court season" during a year when he argued seven cases, including one in which he represented Republican governors and attorneys general defying Barack Obama's health-care law.

The marriage case over which Verrilli and Clement would clash was *Windsor v. United States,* the single-plaintiff estate-tax case that had emerged from New York. Although all five cases raised the same constitutional issues, Verrilli had played favorites, in both public and private. The solicitor general's office kept dynamic "rankings" about which of the five cases it most wanted to see rise, freely sharing updates with the gay-rights litigators behind them. (Lambda Legal, GLAD, and the ACLU each had a stake in a different appeal.) The criteria were plain: the Justice Department wanted the case with the fewest procedural complications on its path to the highest court, and the cleanest shot at ensuring that the case was decided on the administration's preferred terms.

In mid-November, Verrilli wrote that *Windsor* "now provides the most appropriate vehicle" for the court, because it had emerged from a circuit in which litigants had had to argue that gays and lesbians should be treated as a protected class, without any precedent to constrain them. A clean shot at this equal-protection argument, government lawyers believed, would give them the best chance of dismantling the only federal statute that constrained same-sex marriage without opining on any of the state laws that did so.

Yet when the Supreme Court put *United States v. Windsor* on its calendar for late March, it also brought precisely the question of state bans to the fore. The justices had chosen to schedule the case alongside *Hollingsworth v. Perry,* the latest iteration of the California lawsuit that had gone to trial in early 2010. (The ruling that Proposition 8 was unconstitutional under federal law was subsequently affirmed by a three-judge panel.) The case had previously been known as *Perry v. Schwarzenegger* and *Perry v. Brown;* like Obama, the state's top elected officials had decided, separately, not to defend the new amendment. In their place, and with the blessing of the California Supreme Court, a group of Proposition 8's proponents appealed the unfavorable rulings themselves. The named plaintiff before the Supreme Court, Dennis Hollingsworth, was a retired Republican leader of the state senate active in the group ProtectMarriage.com. Those circumstances brought gay marriage to the Supreme Court tagged with an important jurisdictional asterisk: Was it the sole province of elected officials to defend state laws, or did the citizens who introduced and passed a referendum have the standing to take matters into their own hands?

Rejecting Hollingsworth's right to bring the case in federal court would affirm the trial-court ruling, conclusively strike down Proposition 8, and reinstate same-sex marriage in California on procedural grounds. But if justices legitimized Hollingsworth's appeal, they would likely have to assess whether the United States Constitution guaranteed gays and lesbians the right to marry. At that point, what some had taken to describing as a "fifty-state ruling" might be inevitable, either forcing gay marriage on the whole country or permanently enshrining laws that treated gay couples differently as an appropriate use of local power. (There was one possible intermediate conclusion: that Proposition 8's injustice came through unfairly revoking a right already granted to a unique class of citizens, a circumstance that would not apply beyond California.) It was this looming consequence that left Verrilli shocked by a choice to "put this extremely serious question in front of the Court and therefore in front of the American public in a moment when, at least to me, it didn't feel like the Court was ready for it yet." At least four justices had to agree to accept a case, and it would remain a long-standing mystery where—whether an existing ideological faction, on either left or right, or an ad hoc coalition brought together by other interests—the votes to consider *Hollingsworth v. Perry* would have come from.

The ACLU's Matt Coles took to calling *Windsor* and *Hollingsworth* "a shotgun marriage," to be argued in sequence and likely considered by the justices—whether consciously or not—in tandem. The groups backing the two cases partnered on some aspects of their preparation. They hired former Human Rights Campaign president Hilary Rosen to manage a common "war room," a public-relations and digital communications effort aimed primarily at the elite milieu from which the nine justices, their families, and their clerks consumed information. The legal teams made preparations to run common moot-court sessions and coordinate amicus briefs enough to ensure that they did not introduce material that could undercut the other's arguments.

That coupling was an entirely unwelcome development in a White House that knew gay-rights groups would expect to see the administration involved in both cases by filing an amicus brief in the California suit. "*Hollingsworth vs. Perry* raised the stakes in *Windsor* because it wasn't just going to be about DOMA, it was now going to say something potentially about the marriage question," says Verrilli.

With a deadline looming for amicus briefs, Obama adviser Valerie Jarrett brought White House counsel Kathy Ruemmler in to meet with David

Boies, who months earlier had given $1 million to a super PAC supporting Obama's reelection, and Chad Griffin, the political consultant who in 2009 had helped launch the Proposition 8 lawsuit that Boies and Ted Olson had litigated. Ruemmler had been opposed to the idea of filing an amicus brief, skeptical that a president already accused of politicizing the DOMA defense should get involved in another marriage case on whose merits he appeared to have mixed feelings. Boies convinced her that, for precisely that reason, the silence of an administration that had presented itself as a judicious champion of gay rights would be noticed by justices reckoning with the consequences of siding with the *Perry* plaintiffs. "In other words, neutrality is not an option," says Ruemmler. "Staying out is not being neutral. Staying out is actually putting your thumb on the scale."

At the Justice Department, Verrilli had come to the same conclusion independently. (Per tradition, the solicitor general's office met with lawyers from both sides of the suit while considering whether to file an amicus brief.) With the related cases argued back-to-back, he expected to be asked in the *Windsor* oral arguments what the government's views were on *Perry*. "There was no avoiding that," he says. A solicitor general often determines whether and how to file an amicus brief without even consulting the attorney general. Given that this one threatened to conflict with the administration's earlier justification for not defending DOMA—and aware of both Obama's hands-on role in that process and the centrality of same-sex marriage as an issue in the campaign that had just concluded—Verrilli decided he needed to take the unusual step of asking the president directly.

Exactly one week before the February 28 deadline to file, Verrilli arrived at the Oval Office with Ruemmler and Attorney General Eric Holder. It was late in the afternoon, and Obama was in shirtsleeves, his feet atop the Resolute Desk. "Oh, the lawyers are here," he said to his visitors. "What are we here to talk about?"

Verrilli began to explain the choice that lay before him, and the ways in which strategies over the two cases would intersect in potentially problematic ways. He explained that he had come to believe he could craft an amicus brief that would balance Obama's deference to federalism with his insistence that gays and lesbians be treated as a protected class.

Obama interrupted him and began riffing on the ways the substance of a *Hollingsworth* amicus brief could complicate Verrilli's task with the *Windsor* argument. "Justice Scalia is going to ask," Obama prefaced one remark, and then another, before dropping the Scalia character and treating the session as his own private moot-court session where he got to be all nine justices at once. "That went on for quite a while, and he was obviously enjoying himself playing that role," says Verrilli.

Obama had begun by listing tactical reasons not to file an amicus brief, and then put his reluctance in a broader context. *I think this problem is going to take care of itself within a generation,* he said, citing the fact that his daughters and their friends were already more enlightened on the topic than his own peers. *It's obvious to them what the right answers are. Why don't we just let the democratic process take its course?*

Verrilli was not sure whether his boss was engaging in a purely Socratic exercise, but thought that "it's exactly the right question to ask in this circumstance." Verrilli was familiar with Obama's doubts about whether "if, in our reliance on the courts to vindicate not only our rights but also our values, progressives had lost too much faith in democracy," as he had written in his book *The Audacity of Hope.* As a constitutional-law lecturer seeking to explain to students that "the Court is political and needed support," Obama had applied this skepticism to one of the court's most venerated civil-rights rulings. *Brown v. Board of Education* was a "rare case when the Supreme Court gets out ahead of society," he had said, implying that justices should have waited until African American voting rights were secure before forcing desegregation measures on local governments.

Anticipating Obama's frame of reference, Verrilli had been reading materials from that period, when the solicitor general's office had begun using the amicus channel to insinuate itself into civil-rights cases to which the federal government was not even a party. Harry Truman's Justice Department had begun the practice, citing the Fourteenth Amendment to inveigh against racially restrictive covenants on Detroit property deeds and limits on the ability of Japanese immigrants to acquire California fishing licenses. In 1950, the solicitor general even turned against another part of the federal government, taking the side of a lone black passenger who had sued the Interstate Commerce Commission for authorizing separate-but-equal seating on train cars.

When the Supreme Court heard *Brown,* in 1952, the justices specifically invited the attorney general to weigh in on both constitutional questions and practical matters related to potential enforcement. One of Verrilli's predecessors, J. Lee Rankin, made his debut Supreme Court appearance in response to this request, supporting a six-hundred-page government amicus brief in *Brown v. Board of Education.* It was there that Rankin first introduced the term "with all deliberate speed," describing in his oral argument the unspecified timeline on which the federal government proposed that states would be ordered to desegregate schools—a gradualist compromise that pleased neither party to the case. "For the first time the Court was told that it was not necessarily confronted with an all-or-nothing choice," Justice Department lawyer Philip Elman, who wrote the brief, later reflected. "None of this was based on what I thought was right—I had no idea whether it would have been better educationally or politically to do it immediately—I was simply counting votes on the Supreme Court."

Without that nudge, the justices might never have reached a unanimous decision to overturn *Plessy* and mandate desegregation of public schools. Verrilli hypothesized to Obama that the future of marriage was likely to unspool in much the same way as had laws and customs regarding race before federal intervention. Much of the country would come around organically on the timetable Obama had described, but as long as some states refused there would be a system in which gays and lesbians were "second-class citizens" in some number of them—a morally unsustainable condition of half measure. Much as it had asserted in *Brown*, the federal government had a particular interest in the well-being of children, Verrilli said, in this case those growing up gay or lesbian in jurisdictions whose laws subjected them to permanent stigma.

Obama said that idea brought to mind "Letter from Birmingham Jail," Martin Luther King Jr.'s riposte to white moderates questioning his endorsement of civil disobedience as a tactic. "Why we can't wait," the president said, paraphrasing the essay's most famous construction. Verrilli had read it the night before, and still had a copy among his papers. He pulled it out and drew Obama's attention to a paragraph in which King itemized the daily harms that segregation inflicts on people of both races, including the parent who can't take a daughter to a whites-only amusement park and must "see the ominous clouds of inferiority begin to form in her little mental sky."

"It's going to be the same thing," Verrilli told Obama. The federal government, he went on, had an interest in the self-esteem of young gays and lesbians who were growing up in states whose laws sent a message of their inferiority.

That seemed to move Obama, who went on to say, "We can't just file a brief." It would be the chief executive's responsibility to explain the administration's position to the public. "I'm going to have to go out and say something to the press," Obama added, before disbanding the meeting with a promise to reflect on his options. A few days later, Verrilli received a call from the White House counsel's office, which reported that the president had completed his deliberations. *File the brief,* Verrilli was told.

89

And Then There Were Nine

On March 15, Ohio senator Rob Portman invited reporters from the four largest newspapers in his home state to a joint interview in his office, so that he could share what had been until that day a closely held family secret. The well-planned timing of the disclosure was aimed at the colonnaded temple just hundreds of feet away, yet barely visible from the Russell Senate Office Building through a thick canopy of oaks, where eleven days later the question of same-sex marriage would be put to its first definitive test under the United States Constitution. "I thought it was the right time to let folks know where I stand, so there's no confusion, so I would be clear about it," Portman told CNN in a segment that had begun airing that morning.

Portman, who held two Cabinet-level posts under George W. Bush, saved his technocratic passions for budgetary matters. Even if never vocal on them, as a longtime member of the House of Representatives he had been a reliable adversary of gay families' interests: a sponsor of the Defense of Marriage Act who supported Ohio's 2004 constitutional ban and had voted to deny same-sex couples in the capital the ability to adopt. Since then, however, his had become a gay family, Portman explained to the reporters. In 2011, his younger son Will had come out of the closet while a student at Yale, forcing his father to revisit the assumptions that had justified his prior views on the subject. "One way to look at it is that gay couples' desire to marry doesn't amount to a threat but rather a tribute to marriage," Portman wrote in an op-ed in that day's *Columbus Dispatch*.

With his one-day media bonanza, Portman became the only sitting Republican senator to express support for same-sex marriage, and the country's most powerful conservative to do so. (In a search for role models,

Portman had to look across the Atlantic, to British prime minister David Cameron, whom he paraphrased in the *Dispatch* op-ed: "I don't support gay marriage despite being a Conservative. I support gay marriage because I'm a Conservative.") An amicus brief, delivered to the court by former Bush campaign chief Ken Mehlman, had been signed by seventy-five Republicans, but they were largely anonyms pulled from middle rungs of the party's political class: campaign consultants, former officeholders, failed candidates, and retired functionaries known for work on issues other than domestic policy. (Among them was former Justice Department official James B. Comey, who within months would be named to head the Federal Bureau of Investigation.)

Freedom to Marry lobbyists had worked hard for years getting two Republican members of the House to express support for same-sex marriage, but Portman was of an altogether different rank. Dubbed "the perpetual bridesmaid of the GOP vice presidential race" and frequently mentioned as a promising presidential contender in his own right, Portman was known on Capitol Hill as a particularly judicious manager of his own ambition. His willingness to embrace a position heretofore taboo in his circles led *Washington Post* analyst Chris Cillizza to observe that "the political debate on gay marriage is effectively over."

Indeed, the opposition had grown nearly invisible. The National Organization for Marriage saw its revenue drop by three-fifths from 2012 to 2013. For the next three years, struggling for contributions, the organization operated at a loss, and the lack of pressure on conservatives to speak up about same-sex unions showed. A new Marriage Protection Amendment introduced in 2013, a version of the constitutional amendment once enthusiastically backed by President George W. Bush and the entire congressional leadership, won only fifty-eight House cosponsors (largely right-wing backbenchers) and stalled in committee despite Republican control of the chamber.

Portman's conversion pushed elites in a way Barack Obama's had not ten months earlier. National news coverage prompted constituents and local press to badger Portman's Democratic colleagues about whether they were sticking to the position from which he had moved on. "A Democrat can't be outdone by a Republican, and so really as soon as that first Republican comes out," says lobbyist Tyler Deaton, they flipped. One by one, some of the Democratic Party's most conservative-minded senators, representing states like North Dakota and Indiana, caught up with Portman. Within three weeks, all but three of the Senate's Democrats shared his view. In a gesture that was seen as the first firm evidence that she was considering another run for the presidency, former secretary of state Hillary Clinton recorded a six-minute video message for the Human Rights Campaign in which she reflected on the factors that "inspired me to think anew" about her prior opposition to marriage.

Obama may have been a laggard compared to the opinions of his fellow Americans, and certainly those inside his own party, but he proved a trendsetter when it came to the public performance of conversion on the issue. He had not come up with evolution as governing metaphor— Clinton used it to describe her view on gay rights, more broadly, as early as 2006—but he validated that voters would be forgiving of a politician's change on this issue, at least if he or she could tell a good story about how it came to be. "He gave a vocabulary for people to say, 'I've thought about this more and I've changed, and it doesn't mean I was wrong before or that I'm wishy-washy about it,'" says Jon Davidson of Lambda Legal. On the morning of Portman's announcement, Obama's spokesman Josh Earnest heralded it as part of "a pretty significant sociological shift in this country that's happening at a pretty rapid pace."

Elected officials were in a position to shape more than media coverage and voter opinion, as became evident hours later when the Supreme Court released the schedule for its next two weeks of oral arguments. As was standard, justices had granted the solicitor general's request to participate in oral arguments as a friend of the court. Over just short of three hours stretching across two days at the Supreme Court, eight attorneys were allocated speaking time, either on the merits of the two cases or jurisdictional questions associated with them. The fact that both marriage cases had such asterisks attached to them flowed from the same circumstance: that politicians had found themselves crosswise with their own laws, and in their capacity as constitutional officers had refused to defend them.

The only attorney who would be called upon on both days of oral arguments was Don Verrilli, given a total of twenty-five minutes before the justices. As he prepared, Verrilli felt constrained by the political remarks that Obama had made in his capacity as a candidate and officeholder. Through all his peregrinations along the continuum of views regarding same-sex marriage, Obama had never wavered from the idea that states should be free to set whatever policies they saw fit. In his May 2012 exchange with Robin Roberts, from which Hollingsworth's attorneys had already quoted in their petition asking the Supreme Court to accept their appeal, Obama had insisted that "this is an issue that is gonna be worked out at the local level, because historically, this has not been a federal issue, what's recognized as a marriage." Like many Democrats who had argued against the Defense of Marriage Act starting in 1996, Obama performed this as an act of rhetorical jujitsu, turning a federalism rationale against the conservatives who typically wielded it. To Roberts, Obama had said he was against the Defense of Marriage Act in part because it "tried to federalize what has historically been state law."

In his meeting with Obama, Verrilli had proposed a brief that could square the election-year messaging that championed a states'-rights approach to marriage with his administration's legal view that courts should show little deference to state laws that singled out gays and lesbians. Understood through all these decisions was the reality that any ruling that forced gay marriage onto new states would be hard to sell to a majority of justices. Did four of them vote to accept *Hollingsworth v. Perry* because they believed the court was ready to take on the issue or because they believed that backing their colleagues into doing so now could retard the swift progress of gay rights? A decision in either direction would not sit well with Obama's stated preference to avoid seeing the issue prematurely nationalized.

In facing this conundrum, the civil-rights-era history of the solicitor general's office proved again instructive to Verrilli. Harry Truman's Justice Department had been gung-ho in backing antisegregation plaintiffs, but his successor looked more warily on the role that the federal courts should play in state matters like public education. President Dwight Eisenhower entered office with *Brown v. Board of Education* already before the court, and a clear hope that the matter would be resolved without presidential involvement. But the Supreme Court invited the federal government to be heard, an offer that Eisenhower's lawyers told him could not be lightly ignored. A refusal to restate the Truman administration's blunt assessment that *Plessy v. Ferguson* was wrong and should be overturned might be read as an endorsement of segregation. Eisenhower, however, was reluctant to take a position that would lead to an immediate order to desegregate primary schools. The Justice Department's brief, which Eisenhower personally edited, answered the questions the court asked as narrowly as possible. At oral arguments, assistant attorney general J. Lee Rankin presented a constitutional analysis that was consistent with the White House's timid political position without dangerously undercutting the NAACP's case.

There was no federal right to an education, Rankin told the justices, but any state that did operate public schools "must do it equally . . . on the same basis . . . to all citizens."

Once more, Verrilli believed, an American president could play the role of introducing a constitutional compromise informed by the realities of politics. In a debate during his 2004 campaign for the U.S. Senate, Obama had succinctly expressed a core distinction in layperson's language: "I don't think marriage is a civil right, but I think that not being discriminated against is a civil right." With its focus on treating gays and lesbians as a protected class, rather than on the denial of a fundamental right without due process, Attorney General Eric Holder's February 2011 letter had made that government policy. To argue otherwise could have deleterious effects in cases where the government found itself on the more traditional side of defending economic regulations, including the Dodd-Frank financial-reform law. "It was tricky, figuring out how to argue that DOMA was unconstitutional but to do so in a manner that wasn't threatening to the interest of the United States government, generally," says Verrilli. "The tactical risk comes if we filed the brief in *Hollingsworth v. Perry* saying that the theory we're advocating in *Windsor* should lead you to conclude that Prop 8 is unconstitutional."

He sold Obama on what he called the "eight-state solution," which would target those that offered all of marriage's rights and benefits without its prestige. The Constitution did not guarantee gay couples the right to marry, but any state that chose to recognize same-sex unions had to do it on the same basis for all citizens, without the separate-but-equal substitute of civil unions. The federal government would argue that California needed to let gay couples marry because its "marriage-lite" status quo was more demeaning than no recognition at all.

The moral logic of this was perverse, but the political appeal was undeniable. The "eight-state solution" would begin to align the government's legal stance with the "personal" view Obama had articulated in a political context, without unnecessarily undercutting the *Hollingsworth* plaintiffs' claims that a core constitutional freedom was at stake. As with DOMA repeal, the impact of such a mandate would be felt only in states that had already taken the initiative to extend rights to gay and lesbian couples—all of which Obama had carried in his reelection campaign.

For well over a decade, Obama had supported civil unions as right and just. Now his government was about to argue that they, not marriage bans, were the most immediate threat to equal protection of the laws. Such half measures had already dissolved as a viable gateway for politicians. Portman had mapped a new route: express from opposing marriage to supporting it, without local stops for domestic partnership or civil unions. Obama's administration was about to sanction that binary choice as the only constitutional one available to states.

As he prepared for oral arguments before the Supreme Court, Verrilli concluded it was more plausible to see a majority bring marriage rights to California by determining its civil-union statute was unconstitutional than by striking down not only Proposition 8 but the thirty other state laws like it. "That," says Verrilli, "might scare off Justice Kennedy."

Blinding Times

The first in a rainbow of collapsible beach chairs appeared outside the Supreme Court shortly after the arrival of the vernal equinox, but no one can force the spring by willpower alone. Over the next five days, those lining up for admission to the courthouse on March 26, 2013, would require a calendar's worth of protection from the elements: umbrellas to fend off a cold rain, tarps to line the ice-crusted pavement. By the time attorneys registered to the Supreme Court bar arrived to claim their seats the night before oral arguments were to begin, the plaza amounted to an economically diverse commons. Determined spectators, some grasping homemade signs, mingled with vagrants being paid to hold places that would later be claimed by lawyers or others with a professional interest in observing the proceedings firsthand, paying as much as $6,000 per seat.

The Supreme Court had not been the focal point of national attention in such a way since perhaps *Bush v. Gore.* Same-sex marriage, however, had pervaded American life more deeply than that disputed election. Marriage had been a salient domestic political issue at every level and branch of government, an abiding cultural concern unavoidable in conversation nationwide, and a subject of legal consideration at the highest tier. Already the court had received 156 amicus briefs on the two cases, a record number and more than fourteen times the previous year's average per case, representing the views of religious denominations, local governments, scholarly associations, publicly traded corporations, and a pair of professional football players.

When Chief Justice John Roberts did gavel in the proceedings, he permitted Chuck Cooper only thirty-five words from his prepared opening—about the long-standing "accepted truth" about the nature of marriage—before interrupting him. Roberts instructed the attorney for Proposition 8's proponents to alight first on the question of why his clients had the right to defend a state's law when none of its elected officials wanted to do so.

"The question before this Court is whether the Constitution puts a stop to that ongoing democratic debate and answers this question for all fifty states," said Cooper. "And it does so only if the respondents are correct that no rational, thoughtful person of goodwill could possibly disagree with them, in good faith, on this agonizingly difficult issue."

It was, like nearly everything that would be said over two days of oral arguments, pitched at Justice Anthony Kennedy. When Court observers mapped the nine justices on an ideological continuum, Kennedy always occupied the center spot, wedged between solid four-member blocs on the left and right. In the summer of 2012, *Time* had placed a stark portrait of him on its cover as THE DECIDER.

Despite his place in the court's midstream, Kennedy's could be a jurisprudence of intensely principled extremes. Kennedy was a fierce advocate for federalism, having written a 1997 opinion striking down the Religious Freedom Restoration Act because it too aggressively interfered with local government's abilities to administer its own laws. "The federal system rests on what might at first seem a counterintuitive insight, that 'freedom is enhanced by the creation of two governments, not one,'" Kennedy wrote in 2011, quoting another of his opinions, from twelve years earlier.

Kennedy read a broad mandate for sexual liberty in the Constitution's privacy guarantees. He had been appointed by Ronald Reagan a year and a half after *Bowers v. Hardwick*, and with time made a project of drawing gays and lesbians behind the court's shield. (The source of Kennedy's empathy for sexual minorities was unclear, although many observers pointed to the influence of a mentor at the McGeorge School of Law who was not public about his sexuality but believed to be gay.) Two of his most important opinions unmasked the moralistic purposes of laws singling out gays and lesbians for negative treatment as simple homophobia. In the 1996 case *Romer v. Evans*, Kennedy declared Colorado's Amendment 2 unconstitutional because "a bare desire to harm a politically unpopular group cannot constitute a legitimate governmental interest." He concluded his majority opinion in *Lawrence v. Texas*, seven years later, by observing that "times can blind us to certain truths and later generations can see that laws once thought necessary and proper in fact serve only to oppress."

Gay-rights activists, even as they celebrated their new judicial champion, did not quite know how to read Kennedy's opinions, which substituted flowery trellises of prose for the rigid tiered-scrutiny framework that had scaffolded major advances in equal-protection doctrine for other groups. Kennedy often invoked the concept of "dignity," a term that appears in the United Nations Charter and Universal Declaration of Human Rights but not in the United States Constitution. In *Lawrence,* he struck down sodomy bans because "at the heart of liberty is the right to define one's own concept of existence, of meaning, of the universe, and of the mystery of human life."

Kennedy's opponents ridiculed the mawkish imprecision of these rulings. Dissenting in *Romer,* Antonin Scalia alleged that Kennedy had willfully disregarded the ten-year-old *Bowers* precedent without overturning it, with a "heavy reliance upon principles of righteousness rather than judicial holdings." Similarly, in his *Lawrence* dissent, Scalia claimed that state laws criminalizing gay sex relied on the same type of distinction—not forbidding an individual behavior, but limiting it based on the identity of one's partner—that governed bans on gay marriage. Kennedy's opinions, Scalia went on, would be used to justify recognition of same-sex families even if its author insisted it should not be read that way. "This case 'does not involve' the issue of homosexual marriage only if one entertains the belief that principle and logic have nothing to do with the decisions of this Court," Scalia wrote. "What justification could there possibly be for denying the benefits of marriage to homosexual couples exercising '[t]he liberty protected by the Constitution'?"

From the moment they had hatched *Perry v. Schwarzenegger,* Ted Olson and David Boies had been looking to force Scalia's rhetorical question back onto his court. "If you put the *Lawrence* case together with the marriage cases, *Loving* case, and so on and so forth, you cannot take away that right, which is not a right of same-sex persons. It's a right of all citizens and it's a right to be with the person that they love, to have an association that they select, to live a life of privacy," Olson said before the three-judge appeals panel in San Francisco. It was "a self-identification," as Justice Kennedy talked about in both *Romer* and *Lawrence.* "That right cannot be taken away from individuals in this state because of their sexual orientation."

When their case was accepted by the Supreme Court, Boies and Olson approached it as a mimetic exercise. In their brief, the attorneys attacked Proposition 8 because "it denies gay men and lesbians their identity and their dignity." When he stepped in front of Kennedy, Olson was slightly less overt in his pandering, but still articulated the harm inflicted by the amendment in terms expected to resonate with one justice in particular. "It walls off gays and lesbians from marriage, the most important relation in life, according to this Court, thus stigmatizing a class of Californians based upon their status and labeling their most cherished relationships as second-rate, different, unequal, and not okay," he said.

Yet even if he was sympathetic to the harm Olson described, Kennedy evinced hesitation about whether it was premature to act upon it. "We have five years of information to weigh against two thousand years of history or more," he agonized. His colleague Samuel Alito put it more emphatically. "You want us to step in and render a decision based on an assessment of the effects of this institution which is newer than cell phones or the Internet?" he asked.

The only half measure presented to the court that day—the eight-state solution outlined by the solicitor general—did not appeal to anyone. To the conservatives, it would require ruling that gays and lesbians should be treated as a suspect class under equal-protection doctrine. To the liberals, it would correct the least damaging form of marriage discrimination. California would be "penalized" for being "more open to protecting same-sex couples than almost any State in the Union," observed Kennedy. "A state that has made considerable progress has to go all the way," said Justice Ruth Bader Ginsburg. If, however, "the state has done absolutely nothing at all, then it can do as it will."

If the liberal justices could not win over the swing vote, or reason their own ways to the proposed compromise, they risked a ruling that could significantly set back gay rights. Sensing Kennedy's unease about moving too quickly, Justice Sonia Sotomayor suggested postponing the question of whether marriage bans passed constitutional muster. "If the issue is letting the states experiment and letting the society have more time to figure out its direction," she said, "why is taking a case now the answer?"

Kennedy, already conflicted about his choices, recognized the invitation that had been extended to him. He ventured another procedural option always open to the justices, a way of dismissing the case without having to even address the standing question. "I just wonder," Kennedy mused, "if the case was properly granted."

Less than a day later, a different set of attorneys were in front of the court. They, too, were forced to start on a procedural matter, for fifty minutes thinking through the conditions under which a president could have the executive branch not defend a statute, and who then could have standing to do so. "Obviously nobody's suggesting," said Paul Clement, the lawyer chosen by House Speaker John Boehner to defend the law, "that this is a best-practices situation." All parties to the case were in such agreement that the procedural issues should not impede reaching a decision on the constitutionality of the Defense of Marriage Act that the court had to summon a Harvard professor to argue the opposing, and highly technical, side.

Then the lawyers began pitching their arguments at Kennedy, whose first instinct was to see *Windsor* as a case about "whether the federal government has the authority to regulate marriage." By passing a single bill that affected 1,100 different rights and benefits attached to marriage, Congress was, Kennedy posited, "at real risk of running in conflict with what has always been thought to be the essence of the State police power, which is to regulate marriage, divorce, custody."

Regardless of whether he found that claim persuasive, Chief Justice Roberts knew that neither of the two attorneys trying to swing Kennedy to the liberal bloc wanted to endorse it. When Verrilli rose to the podium, Roberts pressed him on whether the Defense of Marriage Act had a "federalism problem." A veteran of the solicitor general's office, Roberts knew that Verrilli's reflex would be to reject any claim that Congress had overstepped, or concede any existing authority to the states. Roberts badgered Verrilli to get the government on the record discounting a logic that should appeal to Kennedy, and then did the same with Windsor's attorney Robbie Kaplan—aware that it would undercut the federal constitutional claims driving *Hollingsworth v. Perry* and any future case like it. Feeling she did not have the same obligation to directly answer the justices that the government's lawyer did, Kaplan evaded each query touching on states' rights. "You're," Roberts scolded her, "following the lead of the solicitor general and returning to the equal protection clause every time I ask a federalism question."

In her focus on the discriminatory impact, Kaplan had attempted to expand the justices' understanding of the harm—beyond simply exclusion of gay couples and their children from welfare-state benefits like the Family and Medical Leave Act—to see a DOMA-shaped loophole in all sorts of good-government policies that rely on family definitions. "These couples are being treated as unmarried for purposes of federal conflict of interest rules, election laws and anti-nepotism and judicial recusal statutes," Kaplan said. It all amounted, as Ginsburg put it, to "two kinds of marriage: the full marriage, and then this sort of skim milk marriage."

Clement insisted that the opposite was true, that the Defense of Marriage Act avoided creating "an additional class of beneficiaries," because without it same-sex couples in only certain states would be eligible. Congress had a long-standing practice of enforcing such distinctions—as it had by imposing bans on polygamy as a condition of statehood—because it had an intrinsic interest in maintaining a single definition of marriage across time and place.

Justice Elena Kagan pointed out that the federal government had previously attained consistency on this question by simply deferring to the rules set by states. "Do we really think that Congress was doing this for uniformity reasons, or do we think that Congress's judgment was infected by dislike, by fear, by animus, and so forth?" Kagan asked Clement. "I guess the question that this statute raises, this statute that does something that's really never been done before, is whether that sends up a pretty good red flag that's what's going on."

"You have to understand that, in 1996, something's happening that is, in a sense, forcing Congress to choose between its historic practice of deferring to the States and its historic practice of preferring uniformity," he replied. "Up until 1996, it essentially has it both ways: Every State has the traditional definition. Congress knows that's the definition that's embedded in every federal law. So that's fine. We can defer.

"Okay, 1996," Clement went on, hoping to discuss the circumstances posed by the then-imminent Hawaii trial before Kagan interrupted him.

"Well, is what happened in 1996—and I'm going to quote from the House Report here—is that 'Congress decided to reflect an honor of collective moral judgment and to express moral disapproval of homosexuality,'" she said. "Is that what happened in 1996?"

When read by Kagan that sentence provoked murmurs in the courtroom, and perhaps some gasps. But that sentence had gone unremarked upon when first entered into the record during the DOMA debate in Congress. (Not a single major newspaper in 1996 had even mentioned the House report.) Just seven weeks before the House Judiciary Committee produced the report from which Kagan now quoted, the Supreme Court had expressly ruled that it would strike down laws passed through "a bare desire to harm" gays and lesbians. The passage Kagan read was a blithely self-defeating inclusion in a bill already sailing to veto-proof majorities with the promise of a presidential signature after.

Roberts attempted to place the "collective moral judgment" in a more forgiving context. It was, after all, one brief phrase uttered by supporters among many justifications that did not reek of homophobia. Roberts pushed Kaplan to say whether she agreed that "84 Senators based their vote on moral disapproval of gay people," and she was wary of doing so—especially since many of them, or their replacements, had since come around to her view of the merits of same-sex marriage.

Kaplan already had an adage at the ready, one she was hoping to return to the court that had put it into the world with the force of law. "I think what is true, Mr. Chief Justice, is that times can blind, and that back in 1996 people did not have the understanding that they have today," she said, "an incorrect understanding that gay couples were fundamentally different than straight couples, an understanding that I don't think exists today. And that's the sense I'm using that times can blind."

When the Dam Breaks

The Supreme Court handed down rulings in both the marriage appeals on the final day of the term, as often happened for high-profile opinions on which the justices hoped to take as much time as possible. When announced from the bench on June 26, 2013, the marriage opinions were presented separately—in between was an unrelated matter of whether legal advice qualified as "transferable property"—but when read together they added up to a coherent picture of a court sticking to the safest middle path before it.

In *Windsor v. United States,* the justices overturned the only federal law restricting same-sex marriage, with an order to the Treasury Department to pay Edith Windsor the $363,053 she had been unfairly taxed, plus interest and costs. At the same time, by ruling that the *Hollingsworth v. Perry* appellants did not have standing to bring a case, the court reserved judgment on whether states could impose their own marriage bans. That decision on procedural grounds restored a lower-court order, killing off Proposition 8 for good and restoring same-sex unions in the largest state. Between the two opinions, supported by distinct five-to-four majorities, the court left no specific guidance to future courts how they should handle cases involving discrimination against gays and lesbians.

The opinions came down on the tenth anniversary of *Lawrence v. Texas.* The majority opinion that Anthony Kennedy presented in *Windsor* had a more workmanlike logic than in its predecessor's, and discovered its force not in poetic flourishes but bluntly prosaic accountability. "DOMA instructs all federal officials, and indeed all persons with whom same-sex couples interact, including their own children, that their marriage is less worthy than the marriages of others," Kennedy read from the bench. "The differentiation demeans the couple, whose moral and sexual choices the Constitution protects, and whose relationship the State has sought to dignify. And it humiliates tens of thousands of children now being raised by same-sex couples."

In the Detroit suburb of Royal Oak, three such kids had been waiting for the opinions. April DeBoer and Jayne Rowse, a pair of emergency-room nurses, had taken them in as foster children. But even though they raised the trio together, the court would allow only one woman to adopt each child. Drawing up a will that assumed equal custody was impossible. When DeBoer and Rowse filed a suit in federal court challenging the state's ban on adoptions by unmarried gays and lesbians, District Judge Bernard Friedman guided them to aim instead at what he said was the "underlying issue": the fact that those couples were denied the right to marry through a constitutional amendment adopted by Michigan voters in 2004. The state's Republican governor, Rick Snyder, moved to dismiss the case, but Friedman was not ready to rule on the motion. In March, he postponed a decision on the motion pending the outcome of the marriage cases before the Supreme Court; *Hollingsworth v. Perry* raised exactly the same constitutional issues as *DeBoer v. Snyder*.

On July 1, days after the Supreme Court dodged *Hollingsworth*'s most difficult question, Friedman nonetheless rejected the Republican governor's motion for dismissal. "Plaintiffs are prepared to claim *Windsor* as their own; their briefs sure to be replete with references to the newly enthroned triumvirate of *Romer v. Evans, Lawrence v. Texas,* and now *Windsor,*" Friedman wrote. "And why shouldn't they? The Supreme Court has just invalidated a federal statute on equal protection grounds because it 'place[d] same-sex couples in an unstable position of being in a second-tier marriage.'"

In a dissent, Antonin Scalia had ridiculed Kennedy's opinion in *Windsor* as "nonspecific hand-waving" and "legalistic argle-bargle" with incoherent reasoning: "maybe on equal-protection grounds, maybe on substantive-due-process grounds, and perhaps with some amorphous federalism component playing a role." But Friedman discerned enough clarity in it to indicate that Michigan's amendment might run afoul of the same principles as the Defense of Marriage Act.

On July 22, a federal district-court judge in neighboring Ohio interpreted *Windsor* the same way. Ohio had passed its own constitutional amendment in 2004 to recognize only opposite-sex unions under state law, which ensured that official records had to depict John Arthur of Cincinnati as having died alone. Arthur, a hospice patient then dying of Lou Gehrig's disease, had chosen to pass his final days quite differently: he and his companion, James Obergefell, had exchanged vows just days earlier on a Maryland tarmac, in a private jet equipped with medical equipment. Upon their return to Ohio, the two men sued to preemptively enjoin whichever registrar ended up handling Arthur's death certificate from processing one that did not list Obergefell as "surviving spouse."

Within days Judge Timothy Black issued a temporary restraining order to that effect, citing the previous month's "historic decision" as reason to see Obergefell and Arthur as victims of an equal-protection violation. "While the holding in *Windsor* is ostensibly limited to a finding that the federal government cannot refuse to recognize state laws authorizing same sex marriage, the issue whether States can refuse to recognize out-of-state same sex marriages is now surely headed to the fore," wrote Black. Since its founding, Ohio had recognized marriages as long as they had been validly commemorated somewhere, even if under another country's laws, the judge noted. Common-law marriages, those between first cousins or involving adolescent minors, were all accepted regardless of whether Ohio would solemnize them. "How then can Ohio, especially given the historical status of Ohio law, single out same sex marriages as ones it will not recognize?" Black asked. "The short answer is that Ohio cannot . . . at least not under the circumstances here."

In October, John Arthur died, and Black determined he would nonetheless continue to consider whether to make the injunction permanent, with new plaintiffs added. One of them, Robert Grunn, was the funeral director who handled Arthur's corpse. A gay man who ran his business from out of a defunct Cincinnati gay bar, Grunn said he was suing, in part, on behalf of future clients.

That same month, in another Sixth Circuit courtroom, Judge Friedman looked skeptically upon the purposes that Michigan's attorney general had put forward for its amendment, related to child-rearing and procreation, to "tradition and morality." Whether any of them could be justified even under the lowest level of scrutiny, the judge determined, was a "triable issue of fact." Facing the unexpected circumstance of a full trial, Dana Nessel, the lesbian family lawyer who represented the plaintiffs in *DeBoer v. Snyder,* had the head of Equality Michigan place a call to the lawyer with perhaps more courtroom experience than any other arguing for same-sex marriage.

Mary Bonauto remained dispirited to see *Windsor,* rather than either of her Defense of Marriage Act cases, taken up by the Supreme Court. Robbie Kaplan's first phone call after learning the court accepted a *Wind-*

sor appeal was to Bonauto, with a request that she coordinate the pro-plaintiff amicus briefs. Still, the New Englander was frustrated that, after a decade of collecting and vetting dozens of plaintiffs across five states with a baroque set of particularized harms, she had been forced to watch what followed from the outside, as the United States government latched onto a case appealing for its simplicity.

Nevertheless, once the Supreme Court ruled the Defense of Marriage Act unconstitutional, Bonauto's expertise became newly valuable. As Obama was phoning Edith Windsor from Air Force One to congratulate her shortly after the decision came down, the White House released a letter under his signature instructing Attorney General Eric Holder to ensure it was "implemented swiftly and smoothly." By lunchtime, the project had been handed off to Stuart Delery, the openly gay head of the Civil Division who had been in the courtroom that morning with his husband. While the Justice Department is frequently in the position of helping executive-branch agencies interpret Supreme Court mandates, few are ever as far-reaching as *Windsor*'s—an effort to undo a form of discrimination that was intentionally written to touch on everything the federal government might ever do. Despite the fact that dozens of Justice Department lawyers had done work that informed the DOMA cases—including Delery, who had made court appearances in both *Gill* and *Windsor* appeals—no one there had prepared for what would need to be done after victory. "There was a real concern about counting chickens," he says.

Delery formed a working group, many volunteering on top of their typical responsibilities, who set out first to identify a liaison at each department and agency. It was a mammoth task, but Delery was pleasantly surprised by how readily the federal bureaucracy accepted it. "There was basically no resistance internally," he says, either from ideological disagreement or purposeful inertia. The biggest obstacle may have been six governors, who in their capacity as commanders of their national guards insisted that on state-run military bases they would follow state law rather than new Pentagon rules.

Delery also began consulting with Bonauto, who had just moved to Washington, where her wife had taken up a temporary academic post during a sabbatical. Because GLAD had spent years vetting plaintiffs harmed by the Defense of Marriage Act in a wide variety of ways, her organization often had a cleaner perspective than the agency liaisons on the ways that married people interacted with federal programs. "We knew a lot about how they worked," says Bonauto.

At the same time, her long project of bringing full marriage equality to New England was finally complete. On August 1, Rhode Island began marrying same-sex couples after the legislature added the words "regardless of gender" to its family code. It was one of three states that enacted marriage during the months that *Windsor* and *Perry* were before the Supreme Court. In Minnesota, the previous fall's campaign to defeat Amendment 1 had created such a positive momentum that the legislature went from passing a constitutional amendment to ban same-sex marriage in one term to passing a bill to legalize it in the next.

Bonauto had been following the Michigan case only at a distance, in part because it was another example of the contentious relationship between national organizations, local activists, and nonmovement lawyers. Lambda, the ACLU, and HRC had all discouraged DeBoer's case, filing an amicus brief that attempted to talk the judge out of treating the adoption and marriage issues as linked. The groups had been waiting to see how the Supreme Court cases were resolved before taking on any new marriage litigation. The nondecision on the merits in that case seemed to leave untouched the mystery of how federal courts would treat claims that the Constitution guaranteed same-sex marriage rights. When it became clear that judges, including those in the conservative Sixth Circuit, would nevertheless interpret *Windsor* expansively, the national groups began to approach Nessel and her clients constructively.

The American Foundation for Equal Rights, searching for a sequel with its Proposition 8 suit ended, proposed what Nessel understood to be a takeover offer. "There was going to be a trial, there was going to be a show," she complained to a reporter from Bloomberg. Nessel was not going to give over the case to outsiders, even if it meant they would be able to cover expenses for which her small firm struggled to raise money. Because GLAD confined its work to New England, it was just about the only one of the gay legal groups not to have gotten crosswise with Nessel or her clients. Despite the fact that she and her law partner were experienced trial lawyers, Nessel had never navigated the ranks of expert witnesses and social-science research that would drive the proceedings. Bonauto had little trial experience, but had helped organize amicus briefs in marriage cases since the 1990s. With a trial scheduled for February, she joined the plaintiff's team without ever having met her clients or cocounsel. "I just jumped in," she says. "I felt like: you've got to help these people."

The organizations began fortnightly conference calls just to track the shifting landscape of litigation. In the wake of *Windsor,* they had split up the map in an attempt to manage the next round—identifying states and circuits where challenges stood the best chance of success—but within months the situation proved impossible for anyone to manage. Kennedy's opinion, and perhaps more usefully Scalia's dissent, offered a roadmap to any confident attorney, even if he or she had no experience with the subject matter. Many of the new cases had been initiated without advance warning to gay-rights groups, which scrambled to cold-call lawyers unknown to them with offers of help and advice.

At one point, the ACLU alone ended up with a role in seventeen different state and federal lawsuits, including one in which Bonauto had also filed a brief. In late summer, some New Mexico county clerks had begun issuing licenses to gay couples in the absence of law to the contrary: theirs remained one of the few states that had neither legalized same-sex marriage nor explicitly banned it. The clerks came together to demand clarity from the New Mexico Supreme Court, which in mid-December ruled that all of them had to adopt the practice immediately. "The dam breaks, with all this pent-up demand, and people start filing all over the place," says James Esseks, director of its LGBT Project. "*Windsor* turns out to be really powerful."

On December 20, 2013, a federal district court in Utah ruled the state's 2004 marriage amendment incompatible with the U.S. Constitution. The ruling by Judge Robert J. Shelby read like an homage to Kennedy's oeuvre, quoting his "times can blind" line from *Lawrence* while asserting that Utah's laws "demean the dignity of these same-sex couples for no rational reason." It was not, however, a purely scholarly exercise. For the first time, a federal court order demanded that the ruling take effect immediately. Over the weekend that followed, Utahans mobbed clerks' offices seeking marriage licenses before the state attorney general could win a delay.

The following Monday, back in Cincinnati, Judge Black made his injunction permanent, although only as applied to Obergefell and the other parties to his lawsuit. Ohio's governor, John Kasich, moved to appeal the ruling, whose mandate was narrow but whose reasoning looked like it could be easily repurposed to strike down the state's constitutional amendment altogether. In most states that saw their bans come under challenge, attorneys general reflexively appealed to protect their laws. Not all did, however. After the New Jersey Supreme Court issued a ruling to legalize gay marriage, Governor Chris Christie withdrew the government's appeal and let the order take effect without conflict. Christie, a civil-unions supporter just weeks away from reelection and like Kasich eyeing a presidential campaign, suffered few political consequences for the action. Other Republican governors, including in Pennsylvania and Nevada, would follow his lead. When Utah governor Gary Herbert did appeal Shelby's ruling, he felt the need to justify what would have once been a routine move. Refusal to defend laws, he said, was "the next step toward anarchy."

In mid-January, Freedom to Marry held a semiyearly retreat, which in previous years it had used to review progress across states and where necessary adjust strategy. The group's goals were tied to November 2016, when its political operatives hoped to replicate, if not exceed, their 2012 success at the ballot. Already Freedom to Marry had started funding public-education campaigns in five states—Ohio, Michigan, Colorado, Nevada, and Arizona—where they hoped to begin collecting signatures to undo existing constitutional bans and legalize same-sex marriage. His operatives from around the country had come to New York with state-by-state polling results and staffing plans, but Evan Wolfson nervously told them that "we have to throw all these out." The era of state-level political activity had abruptly come to an end. From here on it would all be about federal courts.

The public-education campaigns under way in Ohio and Michigan were repurposed away from the electorate and toward elites around the federal courthouse in Cincinnati that would end up hearing the *Obergefell* and *DeBoer* suits on appeal. "We were thinking about what message do we want the judges to have," says Freedom to Marry's Marc Solomon. "Number one was that the country is ready and the region is ready."

DeBoer v. Snyder may not have had "the star power, location, and timing of the trial against California's Proposition 8," as *BuzzFeed* noted, but the proceeding in a Detroit courtroom shared its lopsided imbalance in the quantity of witnesses. Over eight days in March, the plaintiffs presented twice as many expert reports as did Michigan's attorney general, with a noticeable gap in their quality, as well. Concerted efforts by those associated with the National Organization for Marriage to avoid the courtroom humiliations of the *Hollingsworth v. Perry* trial fell flat, too. The New Family Structures Study that had been published in 2012 to much cheerleading from the conservative press—"Scientifically this is huge," Maggie Gallagher had written in *National Review*—had been gradually cut down by other scholars. The journal that had published the study, *Social Science Research*, repudiated it following an internal audit. On the day its author, University of Texas sociologist Mark Regnerus, was scheduled to testify in Detroit, his own department chair issued a public statement undermining his credibility, asserting that "conclusions he draws from his study of gay parenting are fundamentally flawed." Under cross-examination, Regnerus was forced to defend its methods (which critics said did not select and compare same-sex and opposite-sex parents on equal terms) and its financing (in his deposition, Regnerus was forced to acknowledge the role that National Organization for Marriage officials had played in ordering up the research). Regnerus's performance was not as shambolic as David Blankenhorn's, but just as easily dismissed by the judge. "The funder clearly wanted a certain result, and Regnerus obliged," Friedman concluded, calling his "testimony entirely unbelievable and not worthy of serious consideration."

Bonauto did not even attend the trial to view the production she had helped choreograph. She had moved on to the Tenth Circuit, which had agreed to an expedited schedule in taking up Utah's appeal in *Kitchen v. Herbert*. It marked the first time that a state would defend its marriage law before a federal appellate court, and Bonauto agreed to orchestrate amicus briefs.

Freedom to Marry had already begun trying to influence the thinking of the three-judge panel that would hear the case, through more roundabout means. In Utah, Freedom to Marry commissioned a poll showing that even if support for legalized same-sex marriage failed to reach 50 percent, large majorities believed it was coming anyway, and began airing ads with a tagline reinforcing that sense of inevitability: "It's time to end marriage discrimination." The Tenth Circuit was based in Denver, but its jurisdiction stretched from the Ozarks to Yellowstone. "That really was a no-man's-land," says Solomon, but "we knew the appeals-court judges could come from any of those states." In Oklahoma and Wyoming, which both lacked basic employment nondiscrimination laws and where gay-rights activists had never even bothered to seriously make the case for marriage, Freedom to Marry hired staff to cultivate elite opinion.

On June 25, 2014, two of the three judges who heard *Kitchen v. Herbert* agreed with the lower court that Utah's amendment was unconstitutional, setting a precedent that bound all six states in the circuit. (Five of them had laws like Utah's.) It began a concatenation of appellate decisions all pointing in the same direction. Within a month, the Fourth Circuit had issued a similar ruling in a case from Virginia. On September 4, the Seventh Circuit upheld a decision striking down Indiana's and Wisconsin's bans; a month later, the Ninth Circuit did the same to Nevada's and Idaho's. In some jurisdictions, judges had stayed the rulings so that higher courts could review appeals; politicians frequently ended the suspense by declining to pursue them.

In barely fifteen months after *Windsor v. United States,* the country had developed the kind of unruly patchwork that the 10-10-10-20 strategists had anticipated would take twenty years to emerge. An accelerated sequence of federal and state decisions had made same-sex marriage legal in thirty states, growing an average of more than one new state per month, but with little uniformity. Some states were issuing licenses only to victorious plaintiffs, others just upon death or medical emergencies. In Arkansas, hundreds of couples were able to marry after the state supreme court struck down a ban but before imposing a stay that kept out others who wanted to follow them. For a time, Cook County, Illinois, was marrying gay couples under a federal court order, with about fifteen other Illinois counties following its lead while the remainder waited for the Marriage Equality Act signed by its governor to take effect. At another point, Missouri's constitutional ban was struck down, but only within the city limits of St. Louis.

Yet the U.S. Supreme Court appeared wary of reasserting custody of the issue, turning away petitions from five states looking to defend their cases. "So far the federal courts of appeals have answered the question the same way—holding unconstitutional the bans on same-sex marriage. There is a case now pending before the Court of Appeals for the Sixth Circuit," Justice Ruth Bader Ginsburg explained in rare public remarks that fall. "Now if that court should disagree with the others then there will be some urgency in the Court taking the case."

When the Sixth Circuit did release its ruling, on November 6, it let the Ohio and Michigan bans—along with parallel amendments in Tennessee and Kentucky—stand, all while doing little to justify them on their merits. Instead the opinion by Judge Jeffrey Sutton could be read as unlikely homage to Ginsburg's rueful observation that *Roe v. Wade* had unintentionally set back the emergent cause of abortion rights because it arrived before supporters could build popular support. "When the courts do not let the people resolve new social issues like this one, they perpetuate the idea that the heroes in these change events are judges and lawyers," wrote Sutton, a former clerk of Scalia's. "Better, in this instance, we think, to allow change through the customary political processes, in which the people, gay and straight alike, become the heroes of their own stories by meeting each other not as adversaries in a court system but as fellow citizens seeking to resolve a new social issue in a fair-minded way."

The two-judge majority found its grounding in the Supreme Court's one-sentence decision not to hear a 1972 challenge to Minnesota state law because it lacked a "substantial federal question," as the justices put it in turning away an appeal in *Baker v. Nelson*. "This type of summary decision, it is true, does not bind the Supreme Court in later cases. But it does confine lower federal courts in later cases. It matters not whether we think the decision was right in its time, remains right today, or will be followed by the Court in the future. Only the Supreme Court may overrule its own precedents," Sutton asserted. "*Windsor* does not answer today's question. The decision never mentions *Baker*, much less overrules it. And the outcomes of the cases do not clash. *Windsor* invalidated a federal law that refused to respect state laws permitting gay marriage, while *Baker* upheld the right of the people of a State to define marriage as they see it. To respect one decision does not slight the other."

The next day lawyers for all the Sixth Circuit plaintiffs came together and decided that, instead of asking for the case to be heard by a larger circuit panel, they would go right to the Supreme Court. Those who had won in Cincinnati were eager to see their victory appealed there, as well. "The sooner they rule, the better, for Michigan and the country," said that state's attorney general, Bill Schuette.

At their conference on January 16, 2015, the justices finally acquiesced to Ginsburg's prediction that "sooner or later, yes, the question will come to the Court." The Supreme Court had great discretion over what cases they took, and when, but if faced with a so-called circuit split—irreconcilable interpretations of the Constitution by federal courts in different regions of the country—the justices were stuck. They chose the amalgamated suits of the Sixth Circuit, bearing the name of Jim Obergefell as the lead plaintiff, which meant engaging with the matter on Sutton's terms. "This is a case about change—and how best to handle it under the United States Constitution. From the vantage point of 2014, it would now seem, the question is not whether American law will allow gay couples to marry; it is when and how that will happen," the judge had written. "Is this a matter that the National Constitution commits to resolution by the federal courts or leaves to the less expedient, but usually reliable, work of the state democratic processes?"

Once and for All

The last marriage case arrived in court swaddled in much anticipation but little suspense. The Supreme Court's composition had not changed at all since it decided *Windsor v. United States,* and its inactions since pointed to a presumed outcome. The justices had been receiving petitions to hear marriage appeals for much of the previous year. When they refused to accept them, stays across three federal circuits dissolved, and the lower-court rulings allowed to stand, legalizing marriages in the states covered. To uphold Jeffrey Sutton's ruling in the Sixth Circuit, Justice Anthony Kennedy would have to tell the judges responsible for those marriages that they had misread his *Windsor* opinion. Then those states would be given sanction to restore their previous bans and have to wrestle with the status of tens of thousands of couples who had married legally in the interim. Only a court that had prejudged the outcome to its deliberations would permit such a mess to be made in its name.

The ineluctable conclusion was that the five votes that produced the *Windsor* majority opinion would combine again to deliver what some had taken to calling a fifty-state solution. For the four state-based legal teams whose cases had been consolidated on appeal from the Sixth Circuit—a mix of local private practitioners and national advocacy organizations—this confidence about the outcome strangely raised the stakes for the arguments they would put before the justices. "Their relentless preparation has two goals," observed the *New York Times* legal correspondent Adam Liptak. "One is to win. The other is to win big."

The Supreme Court left it to the lawyers to decide among themselves who would speak at oral arguments. The real prize was in arguing the first of the two questions the court had asked litigants to address: whether the United States Constitution guaranteed gays and lesbians the right to marry. The second question, about whether states had to recognize gay marriages validly performed elsewhere, would be rendered moot if the justices answered the first in favor of the plaintiffs. Even if the court ruled otherwise, it would be difficult to argue the recognition question without knowing the rationale by which the court upheld the state bans.

But over weeks of negotiations, none of the four legal teams was willing to relinquish its fractional claim to the biggest spotlight to which an American lawyer could aspire. Each made a claim to the uniqueness of his or her case, but ultimately the conflict was propelled by universal traits like ego and ambition. Even though the state teams had all begrudgingly accepted the assistance of ACLU or Lambda Legal, there was enough enduring friction with the national organizations that none of the local attorneys—many of whom had been working pro bono at reduced fees—would yield to them. On March 17, five weeks before their day in court, the lawyers sent a request to the court's clerk that the time allocated to the two questions each be broken in half, thereby permitting a slot for an oralist from each team. The justices did not accept the offer.

The next weekend, the lawyers all met in Ann Arbor, Michigan. What had been planned as a moot-court practice turned into a bake-off between two finalists, who arrived with different strengths. Jeffrey Fisher was a Stanford law professor and Supreme Court specialist who had been brought in during the appeal stage to work on the challenge to Kentucky's ban. Carole Stanyar was an appellate lawyer who as a partner at Dana Nessel's firm had been involved in the Michigan case from the outset, and as a lesbian she could speak more directly to the gay experience. The two litigators performed before five of their peers playing the role of judges; four of them preferred Fisher. Without a unanimous decision, however, the group remained at an impasse. They considered flipping a coin, or asking the court to make the decision for them, before alighting on perhaps the only litigator with gay-rights experience with the stature to stand above the self-interest and factional differences that had divided them. "I have only one month to prepare," Mary Bonauto despaired to colleagues after accepting the assignment. One told her, "You've been preparing for this your whole life."

Yet it had previously appeared to Bonauto that her era as the driving force on marriage litigation had come to an end. The court's decision to pass over either of her Defense of Marriage Act cases had relegated her to a tertiary role as *Windsor v. United States* came up for consideration. She had participated in moot-court sessions while Robbie Kaplan rehearsed the lines she would use to make a case against the Defense of Marriage Act that Bonauto had been thinking about pretty much since the bill became law. "You'd have to be an inanimate object not to be disappointed," Bonauto told a Maine newspaper.

Over the next two years her marriage work moved offstage. She worked closely with Justice Department lawyers to implement the *Windsor* mandate, all the way up until the day in July 2014 when Attorney General Eric Holder reported back to Congress that the work was done. Only two problems could not be solved through existing channels, both where federal statutes specified that marriage should be defined by the "place of residence" rather than the "place of celebration." Those would need to be changed either through legislative fixes—unlikely in an unproductive Congress soon to be under unified Republican control—or by the Supreme Court leveling the law nationwide so that there were no differences across states' standards. As that seemingly inevitable day grew near, the attention that came to Bonauto pealed as valedictory. She was awarded a MacArthur "Genius Grant" and profiled in the *New York Times* as a forgotten forebearer of Supreme Court victories, a Moses gazing out on the promised land. "Most Americans have never heard of Mary Bonauto," the paper wrote. "But inside the tightknit world of gay legal advocacy, Ms. Bonauto is a quiet celebrity."

By the hour on April 28, 2015, when she was guided to the lounge reserved for those attorneys whose cases were before the court, Bonauto was more widely known. A new round of media profiles frequently quoted since-retired congressman Barney Frank's description of Bonauto as "our Thurgood Marshall." She may not have strategized the entire arc of litigation with the same precision Marshall did in *Brown v. Board of Education*, but indirectly she had catalyzed the chain of events that brought her at long last to the Supreme Court. The four state laws under challenge had all been enacted as part of the stampede from 2004 through 2006 to conjure constitutional amendments to insulate themselves from Bonauto's own victory before Massachusetts's Supreme Judicial Court. The brown pixie cut she had sported then had turned a dusty beige. Bonauto had approached the courthouse alone, in a dark suit and wheeling a black roll-aboard bag behind her, giving off the preoccupied air of someone boarding a commuter jet on a bereavement fare. Then, shortly before entering the marble edifice, she turned—to the massed cameras and an already jubilant band of spectators—and popped a thumb upward.

Bonauto's opposition experienced no such arrival, evidently choosing a back passage and shunning the chance for entry and exit on the court's famous stairs. In the two big post-*Roe* abortion cases, the attorneys general of Missouri and Pennsylvania—both Republicans seeking to run for governor in the next election—claimed for themselves the ability to argue the case, and the major media attention that followed. Yet none of the four attorneys general whose states were defending marriage bans, including future Michigan gubernatorial candidate Bill Schuette, wanted to be so visibly associated with it. Tennessee sent a deputy solicitor general and Michigan a former solicitor general, John J. Bursch, whose firm's management committee forced its partner not to use his firm's affiliation while working on the matter. (It was a more conciliatory resolution than had been found by the last litigator to oppose gay marriage at the Supreme Court: when King & Spalding refused to allow Paul Clement to take on Congress's DOMA defense, the former solicitor general quit for a smaller, far less eminent firm.) After amicus briefs were delivered in *Obergefell*, Liptak observed that no major offices had worked on those in favor of the state bans. "Leading law firms are willing to represent tobacco companies accused of lying about their deadly products, factories that spew pollution, and corporations said to be complicit in torture and murder abroad," he wrote. "But standing up for traditional marriage has turned out to be too much for the elite bar."

Bonauto had spent her career taking on government authority in the service of equal marriage rights, yet she entered the Supreme Court with the full force of the executive branch of the United States of America at her back. Within hours of the court announcing it would hear a marriage case, the Justice Department declared its intent to join the challenge to state bans. Press coverage treated this as an unremarkable initiative from an administration whose chief was determined to realize *Newsweek*'s anointment of "the First Gay President" as prophecy. (The 2012 cover showed Barack Obama with a rainbow halo encircling his head.) In legal terms, claiming that state bans violated equal-protection principles amounted to a gradual shift from the unappealing "eight-state solution" that Solicitor General Don Verrilli had proposed to the justices in 2013. A fifty-state solution, however, marked a complete departure from everything Barack Obama had ever said about the impropriety of nationalizing marriage policy, including in the interview with Robin Roberts in which he emphasized that states legislating at their own pace without interference was a good thing. Circumstances had progressed so much politically that Obama was never pressed to justify the change in his constitutional thinking.

Unlike in *Windsor*, when the government and plaintiffs shared a goal but divergent strategies, both Verrilli and Bonauto sought the same outcome. They wanted state bans struck down because they unfairly singled out a class of people who deserved special protection, and for the court to be clear about the method it used to reach that conclusion. If *Obergefell* were decided as a case about the fundamental right to marry, the state bans would fall but the gains would likely stop there. If the same majority treated *Obergefell* as a gay-rights case, the effects would be felt permanently across American law, and possibly accelerate a legal revolution for transgender people, too.

Once more the locus of these considerations was Justice Anthony Kennedy. The idiosyncratic centrist was not only presumed to be again the decisive fifth vote but—on the basis of his existing oeuvre of gay-rights cases—expected to write for the majority, as well. Bonauto paid tribute to "a foundation of *Romer*, of *Lawrence*, of *Windsor*" on which she said *Obergefell* would build. She also made a gesture toward Kennedy's interest in international law, citing the nineteen foreign countries that had legalized same-sex marriage—all but one of them in the years since she filed *Goodridge*. Bonauto talked about the "stain of unworthiness" that marriage discrimination imposed, tethering it to the Fourteenth Amendment's obligation to "preclude relegating classes of persons to second-tier status." Twice she quoted Kennedy's line that "times can blind," without any attribution necessary.

Verrilli, too, began as though participating in a Kennedy festschrift. "Excluding gay and lesbian couples from marriage demeans the dignity of these couples," he said in his scripted opening. "It demeans their children, and it denies both the couples and their children the stabilizing structure that marriage affords." Kennedy had included a stray remark in his *Windsor* opinion about the court's interest in minors wrapped up in the debate, and Verrilli made the fates of "hundreds of thousands of children raised in samesex households now" central to his presentation. "*Lawrence* was an important catalyst that has brought us to where we are today," he said. "What *Lawrence* did was provide an assurance that gay and lesbian couples could live openly in society as free people and start families and raise families and participate fully in their communities without fear."

Verrilli also tried to expand upon Bonauto's observation that "the effect of waiting is not neutral" in language likely to disturb Kennedy's innate caution. "The decision to leave this to the political process is going to impose enormous costs that this court thought were costs of constitutional stature in *Windsor*," said Verrilli. "Thousands and thousands of people are going to live out their lives and go to their deaths without their states ever recognizing the equal dignity of their relationships," he said.

Having argued the same subject before the same justices two years earlier, Verrilli was able to treat his 2013 experience as something of a moot-court exercise. "It went over like a lead balloon when I tried to argue in a very doctrinal manner," says Verrilli. "I guess I realized that with an issue of this magnitude, something more than the niceties of legal doctrine was at stake."

For his oral argument in *Obergefell,* Verrilli returned to the themes that had surfaced in the conversation he had had with Obama in the Oval Office two years earlier, and the sense of obligation they agreed was placed upon government by parallels to the civil-rights movement. "To the extent that the thought is that this can be left to the political process because this issue will take care of itself over time," Verrilli told the justices, "the outcome that we're going to end up with is something that will approximate the 'nation as a house divided' that we had with de-jure racial segregation." With a handful of likely holdout states, he said, "I don't know why we would want to repeat that history."

Bursch, the former Michigan solicitor general, pushed ahead with the one rationale for an exclusion that had survived legal argumentation, political pressure, peer review, and the cultural consensus that public officials couldn't be seen as mean to gays and lesbians even when trying to curtail their rights. "When you change the definition of marriage to delink the idea that we're binding children with their biological mom and dad, that has consequences," he said. "Men and women would still be getting together and creating children, but they wouldn't be attached to each other in any social institution. Now, the marriage view on the other side here is that marriage is all about love and commitment. And as a society, we can agree that that's important, but the state doesn't have any interest in that."

That concession amounted to the most stunning reversal of all. Gay and lesbian advocates could have once been fairly accused of emphasizing such a coldly transactional view of marriage, in part to avoid discussion about the nature of same-sex relationships before a squeamish public. Cultural progress had encouraged political activists to humanize their appeals, with little obvious backlash. The placards that gay-rights groups had circulated to spectators outside the court bore slogans like LOVE CAN'T WAIT and LOVE FOR ALL. One homemade sign had been inscribed LOVE IS LOVE; the preferred social-media hashtag for Obergefell's case was #LoveWins.

Only a cynic's take remained for the other side. At the decisive moment, the self-identified guardians of traditional marriage were left protecting a shrunken institution that sounded barely worth the defense. It was "not necessarily dignity" that adhered couples in marriage, Bursch argued. "The glue are benefits and burdens."

This was not a framing that would ever resonate with Kennedy, who also skated by consideration of whether gays and lesbians ought to be treated as a demographic class, and the impact of a new constitutional mandate on religious freedoms. Despite reams of amicus briefs assessing the merits of gays and lesbians as parents—and the lengthy trial record from Michigan over exactly this point—the man in the middle proclaimed himself unmoved by expert studies. "It seems to me," said Kennedy, "that we should not consult at all the social science on this, because it's too new." Colleagues trying to pull Kennedy right emphasized the novelty of it all. "The issue, of course, is not whether there should be same-sex marriage, but who should decide the point," Scalia conceded. "You're asking us to decide it for this society when no other society until 2001 ever had it."

Indeed, Kennedy was transfixed with the question of time's passage. "The word that keeps coming back to me in this case is 'millennia,'" he said early in the session. The spirit of the ninety-minute session was in a dispute over how to read time. Should the American debate over same-sex marriage be measured against the arc of civilization or the entire Anthropocene, the quadrennial electoral calendar or duration of a court term?

Verrilli's preferred historical analogy, to the civil-rights movement, found its target. "It's been about the same time between *Brown* and *Loving* as between *Lawrence* and this case. It's about ten years," Kennedy said. "So there's time for the scholars and the commentators and the bar and the public to engage in it. But still, ten years is—I don't even know how to count the decimals when we talk about millennia. This definition has been with us for millennia. And it's very difficult for the Court to say, 'Oh, well, we know better.'"

Bonauto attempted to elongate Kennedy's timeline, pointing to earlier events that had presaged her successes in Massachusetts. Even if only a decade had passed since same-sex marriage had been legalized there, it had been four since the Minnesota Supreme Court considered the matter and two since Hawaii's had done the same, Bonauto said. "The American people have been debating and discussing this," she insisted. "It has been exhaustively aired."

Roberts did not dispute that conclusion. He approvingly cited the switch in Maine, where in three years the majority position of voters flipped from thumping a people's veto on gay unions to approving them. "That sort of quick change has been a characteristic of this debate, but if you prevail here, there will be no more debate," Roberts said. "Closing the debate can close minds, and it will have a consequence on how this new institution is accepted. People feel very differently about something if they have a chance to vote on it than if it's imposed on them by the courts."

Not long thereafter, Roberts laid down his gavel and led eight of his colleagues beyond the vermilion curtain behind them, to end the marriage debate, once and for all.

Coda

....

Back to Hawaii

On the morning of June 26, 2015, Dan Foley rose to a murky quietude. Summertime storms were a common tropical occurrence, and some time overnight, the eastern part of Hawaii's Oahu Island had been struck by one. The little electric clock at Foley's bedside was blank, and he staggered to the bathroom where he stashed his smartphone overnight to check the time. Instead he was greeted by a headline from CNN's website: SUPREME COURT RULES IN FAVOR OF SAME-SEX MARRIAGE NATIONWIDE.

Foley grabbed his glasses, sat down at his dining-room table, and began scrolling through the digital file containing the majority opinion in *Obergefell v. Hodges*. While Justice Anthony Kennedy read his opinion aloud from the bench in Washington, Foley processed it at his own speed. The five–four decision determined that the constitutional amendments enacted by voters in Ohio, Michigan, Tennessee, and Kentucky—and by extension every state law that banned same-sex unions—violated a fundamental liberty guaranteed by the Constitution's Fourteenth Amendment. "It is demeaning to lock same-sex couples out of a central institution of the Nation's society," Kennedy wrote, "for they too may aspire to the transcendent purposes of marriage."

The lights suddenly flickered on, and Foley got up to make a cup of coffee. He then kneeled before the wood altar and scroll he kept in his home and began to chant: *Nam-myoho-renge-kyo*. As he murmured the mantra, its familiar vibration brought Foley back to the morning in October 1992 when he had sat in his twenty-fourth-floor law office and performed the same Buddhist chant two hours before making his most important argument before the Hawaii Supreme Court. To that point no court had ever looked favorably on a claim for gays and lesbians to marry, and victory in any such case seemed almost inconceivable. And yet, in the decades that followed, events had lined up in such a way that Kennedy's momentous decision appeared to be fated.

"There was a sense of relief," says Foley. "It's exactly what we thought it would be."

S hortly after the Hawaii Supreme Court issued its momentous May 1993 ruling in their favor, Genora Dancel and Ninia Baehr—the latter still wearing the promise ring she had received three years earlier—decamped to Baltimore so that Dancel could complete her schooling. As Dancel took premed classes at Johns Hopkins University, both women were soon back in versions of the same jobs they had had when they met. Dancel worked as an engineer in the educational-television department at the University of Maryland, while Baehr wrote grant applications for a housing nonprofit. The two had been together for barely six months before they got ensnared in Bill Woods's exploits, and where the other plaintiff couples had repaired to their former lives at the first opportunity, Baehr and Dancel had forced themselves into leadership roles, as fundraisers and spokespeople for the case in Hawaii. The case had already transformed the women, and the way they saw each other. "I still marvel at Genora's bravery and at the way this quiet, unassuming, local woman has learned to handle media interviews and public speaking engagements reaching increasingly wide audiences. She has often turned out to be the strong one when I feel overwhelmed by the enormity of our case or the demands of public organizing. I am an activist at heart and by profession, but I have a deadly fear of speaking in public, although with Genora's support, I, too, do it more and more often," Baehr wrote then. "At times we have wondered if pursuing this case—and trying to raise the money to pay for it—is really worth it."

Now they savored the prospect of starting over on the mainland, learning to live in tandem without the self-consciousness that suffused every aspect of their existence in Hawaii. "Our private life had always been a very public, political issue," Baehr explained to a Honolulu newspaper. "We thought it would be nice to just have some private time now."

Baltimore was an effort to loosen some of that pressure without backing out of the litigation altogether. But although Baehr and Dancel were relatively anonymous in their largely working-class, African American neighborhood, the stress they experienced did not subside. (The *Baltimore Sun* perceptively characterized their condition as "asylum.") They continued to fundraise to pay legal costs associated with the case as it worked its way through the appellate process, with Baehr using her increased familiarity with the East Coast grant-giving scene to scavenge funds for the Hawaii Equal Rights Marriage Project. In fact, the couple soon learned that their new location made them doubly useful to those trying to raise awareness on the mainland for the cause of marriage. They traveled to Fire Island as the star attractions at a Veuve Clicquot–sponsored poolside luau, and to Chicago, where they addressed a group of gay and lesbian employees at AT&T and appeared on *Oprah*. "We pretty much had to do those together," recalls Dancel. "There were a couple I missed and that she had to do alone, and she wasn't happy about that."

While Baehr and Dancel had to perform as a real-life illustration of the ideal couple atop the wedding cake, in the stately three-story brick row house they were renovating, the imperfections of their relationship became apparent. They fought often, the tensions magnified by the ongoing pressures of their public responsibility. "I'm not going to bottle all this crap or sweep it under the carpet when you're going around making a muck about the case," Dancel would later write to Baehr. "That's right, mess up your own life, and you were very wrong in trying to mess up mine."

On September 10, the morning the trial made necessary by the Hawaii Supreme Court decision began in Honolulu, the front row of Judge Kevin Chang's courtroom featured two of the beaming couples, both eager to talk about wedding plans that had become only more vivid since victory at the Hawaii Supreme Court. Joe Melillo and Pat Lagon had long spoken of plans to wear white tuxedos to a church service, but they registered as Universal Life Church ministers when it occurred to them that they might be able to officiate their own nuptials. Antoinette Pregil imagined a simple Christmas Day wedding, while Tammy Rodrigues thought herself "old-fashioned" enough that she aspired to a more indulgent celebration. "You do it once and one time only," she would explain.

The couples whose names were first on the historic lawsuit, however, stood nearly five thousand miles away, on the steps of the United States Capitol. Inside, the Senate was considering the Defense of Marriage Act, and opponents of the bill had enlisted Baehr and Dancel to headline a press conference on the topic. Shortly after the vote closed, the women called Foley's office to report the dispiriting 85–14 tally and to wish their lawyer well at a trial whose national impact had just been significantly circumscribed. "Good luck," Baehr said. "Thoughts are with you."

After the nine-day trial ended, the two went back to their lives in

Baltimore. On December 3, they received news from Foley. He had just returned from a meeting in the chambers of Judge Kevin Chang, who had invited the lawyers on both sides of the issue to offer advance warning on the ruling he was about to issue in favor of the plaintiffs. Deputy Attorney General Rick Eichor said the state was ready to appeal its loss, and planned to file a request for a stay that afternoon. Foley informed the judge he would be busy picking his sons up from school, but regardless offered a gentleman's assurance that he would not take advantage of the window to create undue chaos. "Don't worry," Foley had assured Eichor. "My couples won't get married this afternoon."

Baehr and Dancel instead rushed to New York to Lambda Legal's headquarters, where the organization had gathered reporters to discuss the verdict and what it foretold. "Our love made it possible for me and Genora to get through this long legal fight," Baehr told the press. "I'm looking forward to our love getting us to a wedding on a mountain slope in Maui."

But privately they knew that day had grown unlikely, regardless of how the Hawaii Supreme Court handled the next round of appeals. Dancel returned to Hawaii days later for a winter vacation with her family, and came to the conclusion that she was going to end her six-and-a-half-year relationship with Baehr. In February, the pair gathered at a Chinese restaurant in Baltimore for what they knew would be their final meal as a couple. They experienced some catharsis in talking about what they had been through together, and at the end of the meal flipped over one of the placemats and wrote a letter to Foley.

They would henceforth describe themselves as "separated," even though in its seven years their partnership had attained no formal status. It was Foley whom they imagined feeling most acutely the pain of what might have been, and not only because they had promised him the role of best man at their wedding. On behalf of the three couples, Baehr and Dancel owed Foley $60,000 in legal fees they knew they were unlikely to ever fully repay. Furthermore, a split limited the women's value to the case as plaintiffs. After all, the remedy Foley had sought on their behalf was the right for the two to acquire the marriage license they had requested in December 1990. "Breaking up wasn't hard for me," says Dancel. "The biggest thing for me—the biggest heartbreak for me—was telling Dan. I kind of felt I was letting Dan down."

A few months later, Foley wrote back. "You haven't let anyone down," he told Baehr. "As we all know, this is about more than three couples or even marriage. It is about ending discrimination."

. . .

Foley knew that any appeal to Chang's verdict would never get a hearing, with the entire matter likely to conclude without any judicial resolution. He had heard almost immediately after the 1996 elections from legislators who survived the vote and felt they could no longer stand by and watch the courts permit gays to marry. Regardless of their attitudes on the merits, they conceded Mike Gabbard's taunting had worked: they could not afford to be depicted as puppets of outside activists bent on changing Hawaii's families from afar. The chief justice who had presided over Foley's victory at the Hawaii Supreme Court—and had voted with the majority—all but invited politicians to step in. In his annual State of the Judiciary address at the start of the 1997 legislative session, Chief Justice Ronald Moon said "if we stray into legislative prerogative, the legislature has the ability to cure the trespass."

The contours of a political response, in the form of a compromise, quickly revealed themselves. The legislature would begin the process of amending the state constitution so that courts could never read into it an existing right for same-sex couples to marry. At the same time, the state would make committed gay and lesbian couples who registered as "reciprocal beneficiaries" eligible for an unprecedented collection of legal rights and benefits. But instead of banning same-sex marriage outright, Foley stealthily negotiated language that declared the "Legislature shall have the power to reserve marriage to opposite-sex couples." The immediate politics did not change—and Foley would still criticize the amendment as discriminatory overreach—but his allies knew not to tout a concession that amounted to something of a Trojan horse, its true value unlikely to be exposed for some time. "He gave us a gift," says Tom Ramsey, president of the Friends of the Hawaii Equal Rights Marriage Project. Despite its overall opposition to the amendment, which would put an indefinite halt to its quest for marriage rights, the group campaigned to secure support for the deal. "We're saying no now," Ramsey recalls being told by House Judiciary Committee chairman Terrance Tom, a semiprofessional pianist whom Ramsey went to lobby between his sets in the cocktail lounge of the Hilton Hawaii Village, "but you're going to get it in ten years."

The program, called Reciprocal Beneficiaries, was enacted in 1997 and turned Hawaii into an international trailblazer in recognition of same-sex couples. But the scale of the following year's landslide in favor of a constitutional amendment appeared a harbinger of a longer-lasting setback for gay politics in the state. "Marriage brought the community together—people were very passionate about it—but it gave way to defeat," says Marriage Project outreach coordinator Val Tavai. "We didn't think there would be momentum after Hawaii. We thought that would be it. We thought it would die."

The process that began as *Baehr v. Lewin* ended as *Baehr v. Anderson* in late 1999, after judges ruled that the new amendment henceforth sidelined them from ruling on marriage. Not long thereafter, Foley gave up his legal practice upon being named to the state's Intermediate Court of Appeals. Governor Ben Cayetano joked that he made the appointment because it was the only way to get Foley to stop suing him.

The year Foley took his seat on the bench, Vermont overtook Hawaii as the state with the most generous rights for same-sex couples. Civil unions there—and similar programs subsequently in California and New Jersey—illustrated the inadequacy of Hawaii's policy, which neglected many of the four hundred places that state law distinguished treatment based on marital status. (Notably, Hawaii's tax laws made minimal accommodation to gay couples.) Yet there was little political will to build upon it. "People were exhausted and wanted to focus on other things," says state representative Chris Lee. "Being able to say they had done something was enough to satisfy most."

It took a decade for a fresh wave of interest to roll in. When he was elected to the legislature in 2008, Lee—who had been too young to vote on the 1998 amendment—viewed himself as figurehead for a generation of Hawaiians whose progressive views on sexuality were untempered by earlier traumas. In 2009, he helped expand support for a civil-unions proposal beyond a small band of liberal legislators. "Once people saw their friends and colleagues were on the bill, they were more comfortable joining the pack," says house majority leader Blake Oshiro, who had interned for Foley while a law student and came out publicly as gay during the civil-unions debate.

A bill was vetoed by the state's Republican governor, but those legislators who had voted for civil unions suffered no apparent electoral repercussions. In 2011, newly elected Democratic governor Neil Abercrombie signed a similar bill into law, permitting Hawaiians to register for civil unions from the same agents who accepted applications for marriage licenses. But even before state authorities were preparing to implement the new regime, they were taken by surprise when a lesbian couple approached the Department of Health to demand that they have the right to wed.

Natasha Jackson and Janin Kleid were greeted with the same bureaucratic resistance as Baehr and Dancel. The women, however, chose a legal path that Foley had always sedulously avoided, suing the state in federal court on the basis that the 1998 amendment specifying that marriage "shall be only between a man and a woman" violated the due-process and equal-protection guarantees of the U.S. Constitution. "I was looking at stuff on Google, because that's what we do in our generation," Jackson, a former radio DJ, told a local TV station. "There are 1,138 rights to marriage, where there aren't as many to civil unions."

This time, the public-health director was eager to uphold the state code, which unlike in 1990 reflected the clear intent of voters in addition to the legislature. But the governor and his appointed attorney general saw it differently, as Arnold Schwarzenegger had, and Barack Obama would just months later, when put in similar situations. "Under current law, a heterosexual couple can choose to enter into a marriage or a civil union. A same-sex couple, however, may only elect a civil union," Abercrombie said. "My obligation as Governor is to support equality under law. This is inequality, and I will not defend it."

The case that remained known as *Jackson v. Abercrombie* lost in district court in August 2012, and the plaintiffs appealed to the Ninth Circuit, where earlier that year California's marriage amendment had been deemed unconstitutional. There was enough of a distinction between the two states' circumstances, judges ruled in rejecting Jackson's claim, because unlike in California no couples had ever legally married in Hawaii and seen their rights withdrawn without due process. Despite the legal setback, the attention the case drew to the inadequacy of civil unions renewed interest in marriage on the islands. Unlike other states that had amended their constitutions over the issue, the language Foley had helped negotiate meant that in Hawaii, the issue never had to go back before voters; lawmakers could legalize same-sex marriage with a simple majority of votes. Bills introduced that January quickly stalled, but supporters hosted a "Marriage Equality Day" at the capitol to pressure legislators to nonetheless take it seriously.

The star speaker was former Hawaii Supreme Court justice Steven Levinson, who upon retiring from the bench in 2008 had become a dedicated advocate for liberal causes in the state. The infrastructure that surrounded him at the capitol demonstrated how much the gay-rights apparatus had matured since Hawaii politicians had been forced to deal with the fallout from Levinson's 1993 opinion in *Baehr v. Lewin*. Equality

Hawaii, which was founded in 2007 as precisely the type of statewide gay-rights group that the state lacked during the 1990s marriage battles, hosted the newly launched Hawaii United for Marriage. The Human Rights Campaign, whose inconsistent and often halfhearted work in their state frustrated Hawaii activists, was an active partner, as was the state affiliate of the ACLU, on whose board Levinson sat.

The opinion in *Windsor v. United States* had a particular impact in Hawaii. The Obama administration's subsequent determination to quickly grant full federal recognition to all married couples almost instantaneously turned Hawaii's civil-unions regime from separate-but-equal to isolated and materially unequal. Gays and lesbians who had registered for civil unions with the guarantee that they would receive the same tax treatment as heterosexuals now saw how disadvantaged they were relative to same-sex couples in states who were permitted the option of marriage and could file a joint federal return. That fall, Abercrombie called the legislature into a special session with instructions to address the issue.

The bill's legislative boosters tried to direct their rhetoric away from the tallying of discrete rights and benefits that drove activity in the court-room. "I think we had used up arguments for legal this and constitutional that," says Lee. Instead Hawaii United for Marriage promoted the so-called values-based messaging developed by Thalia Zepatos's Marriage Research Consortium, although for Hawaii residents it was framed not in the biblical lexicon of the Golden Rule, but in a more indigenous philosophy. "The whole thing was centered around 'aloha.' You can't argue back against that," says Lee.

Many tried. After the senate passed the bill, two house committees agreed to hold a wide-open hearing prior to a vote. Religious activists took it as an invitation to delay what was looking increasingly inevitable, organizing what they dubbed a "Citizens' Filibuster." More than five thousand people signed up to testify, forcing the committee to hold fifty-five hours of hearings stretching across five days. "It was madness," says Lee, "something no one had seen before." The outpouring of civic energy turned out to be unique across the country. The first state to host a political battle over legislating same-sex marriage was also the last.

One of the loudest voices at the outset of the debate had fallen notably silent by its conclusion. Mike Gabbard, the founder of Stop Promoting Homosexuality Hawaii, joined the state senate in 2007. (His wife, Carol, had just completed a term on the Hawaii Board of Education.) Gabbard sat on the Judiciary Committee, which meant that both the Civil Unions

Act and the Marriage Equality Act came before him. Upon enactment of the first, he proclaimed that it was "a sad day for the people of Hawaii," but could muster no such alarmism during the marriage debate two years later. Some suspected that Gabbard, a Democrat highly regarded by organized labor and environmentalists, had the next generation in mind as he tried to temper his involvement in the cultural issues that had drawn him into politics in the first place. One of his children, Tulsi, who had been homeschooled, ran for the legislature at the age of twenty-one as a legatee of her father's politics. (Her political début had come in an Alliance for Traditional Marriage ad aired during the 1998 referendum campaign, when she perched on her father's shoulder as he explained, "I'm not allowed to marry my daughter.") While in the statehouse, Tulsi did not only vote against a civil-unions bill when her chamber took it up, but led citizens protesting in the capitol's hallways. "As Democrats we should be representing the views of the people, not a small number of homosexual extremists," she explained.

She was elected to Congress in 2012, and after settling in Washington grew quickly adored by mainland progressives, eventually launching a presidential campaign. Somewhere along the way, she developed a set of policy positions to match, an implied repudiation of the views that made her father a significant figure in Hawaii politics. On gay rights, as with abortion, Tulsi Gabbard traced her leftward conversion to military service in Iraq and Kuwait, where she developed a distaste for the idea of a religious government "imposing its will" through social policy. "As long as government is involved in the marriage business, it must recognize and treat all Americans as equal," she said when Hawaii lawmakers, including her father, took up the marriage bill in 2013. Those who spoke to Mike Gabbard believed his thinking had come to focus on the escape hatch: *As long as government is involved in the marriage business . . .*

Dancel was present to witness Abercrombie's bill-signing, held before a large, invitation-only audience in a theater at the Hawaii Convention Center. "To me, it made full circle today," she said, her eyes welling with tears.

Bill Woods had not lived to see even civil unions legalized in Hawaii, but he still got his wedding. He married his partner, Democratic activist Lance Bateman, in British Columbia shortly after marriage was legalized there in 2003. "We decided long ago, if it's ever really, truly legal someplace, we'd do it," Bateman told the *Honolulu Advertiser.* "There is an escape now, and that escape is Canada," Woods said. "As in the time of slavery, we can learn from the experience in Canada that the world does not collapse on us when we achieve justice." After returning to Hawaii, they registered for joint membership in the AARP and were offered health insurance as a married couple. Woods experimented with legally changing his surname to Woods-Bateman, but switched back when he found it meant that it often led to him being identified only as Bateman. When running for the state house of representatives in 2006, he did so as William E. Woods. When Woods died two years after that, Bateman was listed in the *Honolulu Advertiser*'s death notice as a "spouse," even though their marriage was never legally recognized where they lived. Woods was buried in the Illinois town where he was raised. The obituary his family placed in the *Decatur Herald and Review* advised readers that "the best memorial to Bill would be become or remain active in serving your community."

Other *Baehr* plaintiffs had inched away from Woods's idealized ambitions. "We weren't looking for the marriage on paper—that's not what we were fighting for—but the benefits that came with it," Pat Lagon explained of being able to register with Joe Melillo as a reciprocal beneficiary. Tammy Rodrigues said something similar on the day the civil-unions bill was signed, as she and Toni Pregil made plans to register as soon as the law took effect. "This is enough," she informed a local television station. "It will give us the same rights. It doesn't have to be marriage. Marriage is just a word."

Dancel, however, had never abandoned her idealized view of the institution that denied her entry. She had been talking about marriage for over a decade with her girlfriend Kathryn Dennis. The two met through an online-dating site in 1998, a year after Dancel broke off her relationship with Baehr. Dennis, an editor ten years her junior, lived in New York, and after traveling every weekend to see each other, Dancel started looking for a job there. She landed at Broadway Video, which was appealing largely because she could play pool during the workday, and then NBC, where she watched the events of September 11, 2001, unfold from atop Rockefeller Center. General Electric, NBC's parent company, was relatively progressive on issues related to sexual orientation, and Dancel was soon permitted to register her domestic partner to share her health insurance. When colleagues learned of her unique background fighting to get same-sex couples recognized, they asked her to address a new group of the company's gay, lesbian, bisexual, and transgender employees. Dancel declined, partly from fear of seeing her life in a new city, with a new mate, defined by political activism attached to a prior relationship. "My whole life I've been private about stuff like that," she says. "I don't make a really big deal of it." In 2006, the couple moved back to Oahu, where Dennis went to work at a federal fisheries center and Dancel as a technician for the city of Honolulu's Wastewater Division.

Dancel waited three weeks after Abercrombie's signing ceremony before returning to the Health Department office where Bill Woods had led them on a lark that Monday morning in December 1990. Still under the delusion that privacy if not anonymity would be possible, Dancel experienced it all from behind dark glasses, with the anxiety brought on by perpetual consciousness of the news crews tracking her. Her memories of that day were scrambled by time and blurred through subsequent retellings. Years later, she recalled of the government office only that it had "looked like a bank," and imagined the short visit to have taken longer than it actually did.

Twenty-three years later, Dancel pulled her car into the Punchbowl Street parking lot, calm enough to remain fully alert to her surroundings. As she entered, Dancel spotted two other same-sex couples completing their paperwork nearby, without drawing particular notice. The once-forbidding sign MARRIAGE LICENSE above the doorway of the office now seemed like a simple invitation. Dancel was delighted to find the woman seated inside was the same clerk who had rejected her first application for a license. Dancel reintroduced herself, and Irene Takeda attempted to explain what had happened on their previous encounter. "I was told not to give you your licenses," she said, before the two women hugged. The only camera with an interest in documenting this occasion sat in Dancel's pocket.

On the application, Dancel wrote that her ceremony would take place on December 17, the twenty-third anniversary of her first visit to the Health Department offices, and be officiated by Dan Foley. As a sitting judge, Foley was statutorily qualified to serve in the role of "marriage performer," but unlike some of his peers Foley shied away from most opportunities to exercise that power. Only when he had a personal connection to one of the celebrants—a former clerk, a neighbor, an author who had taken an interest in his career—did Foley agree to officiate a wedding.

For Dancel's nuptials, Foley secured use of the supreme court chamber where he had argued the first appeal of *Baehr v. Lewin* in the fall of 1992. Four times he had submitted his name to be considered for an open seat on the high court. On each occasion he had made the nonpartisan selection commission's short list of nominees, and each time he had been passed over, by both Democratic and Republican governors. Foley suspected that his experience with the marriage case made him too politically controversial for such an appointment. (Abercrombie, however, told Foley he preferred a younger nominee.) The penultimate time Foley was passed over for the Hawaii Supreme Court was a particularly bittersweet moment for the islands' gay-rights activists: on the day Abercrombie appointed her, circuit-court judge Sabrina McKenna announced she was a lesbian.

Foley, in a black robe, took a position in the well of the chamber, his back to the dais usually occupied by the judges. The two women also dressed in dark colors, with white leis, and exchanged titanium bands. "I declare, by the virtue of the authority vested in me by the laws of the state of Hawaii, that you are now married," Foley said. "You may now kiss your bride."

Local media had been invited to witness the small event, and in interviews afterward Foley was torn between expressing awe of the historical moment and a sense that what had once been an exceptional request had become a routine administrative procedure. "Now it's the law," he told a local television reporter. "So this is just a regular marriage."

Dancel received a call around this time from Montana, where Baehr worked for the state ACLU and was pursuing a doctorate in history. After years of estrangement, the two women had slowly repaired a friendship, and earlier that year, when Baehr traveled back to Hawaii to celebrate her mother's eighty-third birthday, they gathered at the home where Dancel had once idled her Porsche while picking up Baehr for dates. Standing in her kitchen, C.J. Baehr still looked as affectionately upon Dancel as she had when she hoped to see her become a future daughter-in-law. Baehr had plans to wed, too, as soon as it was legal in Montana.

Three days after Dancel and Dennis married, the federal district court in Utah overturned the state's constitutional ban, citing Anthony Kennedy's nearly six-month-old opinion in *Windsor v. United States*. That ruling began the cascade of state-level decisions, in so rapid a sequence that national observers could barely keep up. At that point, for gay activists, Hawaii was just another row on a fifty-state tracking spreadsheet, the last where change would be delivered by politicians rather than judges.

Baehr monitored it all from her post as deputy director of the Montana affiliate of the American Civil Liberties Union, the same group that had turned away Woods and his three couples in December 1990. When she had joined the ACLU of Montana, as its LGBT advocacy coordinator, the state had some of the country's sparsest coverage of legal protections for sexual minorities. In 2004, Montanans voted to amend their constitution to ban same-sex marriage. When the ACLU helped six same-sex couples sue the state for recognition of their relationships, in 2010, the most they could ask for were the legal benefits of marriage rather than inclusion in the institution itself, and nonetheless hit a dead end when their claim was dismissed in December 2012. In a blog post for the ACLU's website guiding Montanans how to initiate conversation about same-sex relationships with family members over the holiday period, Baehr wrote that "it will be easiest for them to do this not because of a general political discussion about 'rights' and 'equality' but by hearing about specific examples of real-life people being harmed by discrimination."

But as it did nearly everywhere, the *Windsor* decision opened up new legal avenues in Montana. Just under a year after the decision, the ACLU affiliate led four Montana couples into federal court to challenge the 2004 amendment as unconstitutional. One of the four couples, Chase Weinhandl and Benjamin Milano, had traveled to Hawaii after Abercrombie had signed the marriage bill into law, and demanded that they had a right for their new status to be recognized at home in Bozeman. "We definitely believe the time for the case is now," ACLU attorney Jim Taylor said in May 2014. After the Ninth Circuit struck down Idaho's and Nevada's bans, Taylor petitioned the court to do the same. That November, a district judge agreed and, ruling that Montana's constitutional ban defied the equal-protection clause of the U.S. Constitution, ordered local officials to marry gay couples immediately.

Baehr wanted her mother present when she exercised the newly granted right. On December 25, 2014, she and Lori Hiris, her partner for a decade, exchanged vows while standing before a Christmas tree in their home. The couple chose not to dress formally, opting instead to get married in their pajamas, and they had to shovel snow from their driveway to welcome guests. Three weeks later, the Supreme Court decided to hear the appeal from the Sixth Circuit, the first to rule after *Windsor* that states should be free to exclude gays and lesbians from marriage.

As district- and circuit-court judges changed state laws like Montana's, the U.S. Supreme Court had looked on with tacit acceptance. Only when it had no choice, after federal circuits had issued conflicting interpretations of the Constitution, did it step in. In February, anticipating the *Obergefell* oral arguments then weeks away, a Montana-based district court agreed to impose a belated stay of its earlier decision, halting the process that had permitted Baehr and Hiris to marry. Even though it meant temporarily rescinding a constitutional right, the ACLU did not contest the idea of a stay, as it appeared that right would soon be assured everywhere.

On the eve of oral argument in *Obergefell v. Hodges,* Baehr and Dancel entered the office of a Washington law and lobbying firm, the petals on their complementary red-and-white leis beginning to wilt after a long stroll from down Pennsylvania Avenue to the steps of the Supreme Court. There was still one remaining lei that Dancel had delicately transported with her by plane from Honolulu, and it had spent the day in the controlled climate of a hotel refrigerator. As soon as they arrived at a Holland & Knight conference room, Dancel removed the lei—struck through with flashes of blue, orange, and yellow—from its plastic case and presented it to Evan Wolfson, who as a junior attorney for Lambda Legal had latched onto the case after victory at the Hawaii Supreme Court.

With all the plaintiffs from the four consolidated *Obergefell* appeals in Washington for the arguments, Freedom to Marry had attempted to track down every American who had ever sued for the right to marry, stretching back to the 1970s. Wolfson was already planning for life after Freedom to Marry: he had vowed to shut down the organization he founded after victory at the Supreme Court, and the cocktail reception had the spirit of a potentially premature victory. "We've made our case, to the country and to the courts, and tonight is for savoring the moment and looking forward in brave hope," Wolfson began. As attendees packed into a conference room for a toast, Wolfson reflected briefly on their scope—over seventy-five plaintiffs, representing thirty states and fifty-five different cases over four decades—and before lifting his glass selected a few of them for special acknowledgment. "When people ask me if I have a favorite case, I always tell them I love all my children," he said, before gesturing toward the lei draped over his suit and tie, "but I would like to give a special aloha to the Hawaii marriage plaintiffs of the 1990s."

Baehr and Dancel had already drifted away from the crowd, toward a glass-walled corner with a clear view of the White House. But Wolfson's remarks, combined with their own leis, marked them as movement elders for the rest of the evening. Other guests, some of whom looked barely old enough to have read a newspaper when the Hawaii case first made headlines, came over to offer tribute, which the pair graciously if at times sheepishly accepted. "The story of what Genora and I lived is part of me," says Baehr. For the first time, she began to see how it was intertwined with history, part of a larger narrative she could never quite comprehend before.

They were approached by Kim McKeand, whose lawsuit had successfully toppled Alabama's constitutional ban, enabling her to marry the partner with whom she was raising a nine-year-old boy. Despite their legal successes, McKeand agonized, she remained $80,000 in debt to her attorney. Dancel and Baehr delivered a bit of a pep talk, telling McKeand about their struggles to raise the money necessary to finance their case. At one point, it became clear that McKeand assumed that Baehr and Dancel were still a couple, and that the rings on their fingers had been exchanged as part of a single ceremony. "We have a lifelong relationship," Baehr explained. "It's just not the one we anticipated when we first applied for a marriage license."

Few momentous decisions have felt as fated toward a single possible outcome as *Obergefell v. Hodges* as it made its way to the nation's highest court.

As the end of the Supreme Court's term approached that spring, Foley woke each morning with an eagerness to see history made. He had not been involved in the marriage debate since 1999, and—citing his status as a judge on a court that could conceivably hear a case related to the matter— refused all but the most prosaic requests to speak publicly about his work on the *Baehr* litigation. But he vigilantly tracked developments related to gay marriage, aided by Google alerts that plucked news from the far corners of the Internet to satisfy his curiosity, and felt a sense of paternal pride over even small gains. Instigating the national debate on marriage was, he had come to realize, the crowning event of his legal career. He had never reached the Supreme Court of Hawaii, and had set a date in late 2016 for his retirement from the appeals court, at the age of seventy. (He would not retire fully from the bench, however. Since 2013, he had served as an associate justice of the Supreme Court of Palau, where he had first worked as a young man fresh out of law school, commuting several times yearly across the Pacific to sit for oral arguments.) Upon a national resolution to the marriage debate, Foley thought about mining his papers to produce a memoir of his work on the *Baehr v. Lewin* case. *Baehr*'s significance, he felt, had been largely unappreciated by recent accounts that treated the relevant history as having begun in Massachusetts in 2003, or with the organizing that followed Proposition 8 in 2008.

That's what led Foley to stop scrolling on his phone and linger contentedly on the eighth page of the *Obergefell* opinion, where Anthony Kennedy had included a citation of the Hawaii Supreme Court's *Baehr v. Lewin* decision. The date that the *Obergefell* opinion finally arrived offered a symbolic indication that its author brought his own sense of personal investment to the historical arc. Kennedy had also chosen June 26 in previous years to release his opinions in the *Lawrence* and *Windsor* cases. Many believed the timing could not possibly be a coincidence. Foley concluded that Kennedy saw himself assembling a canon of acceptance for same-sex relations in American life. "The Constitution promises liberty to all within its reach," the opinion began, "a liberty that includes certain specific rights that allow persons, within a lawful realm, to define and express their identity."

The decision did indeed overrule the Sixth Circuit on the constitutionality of bans enacted by the voters of Ohio, Michigan, Kentucky, and Tennessee, and other laws like them nationwide. "It is now clear that the challenged laws burden the liberty of same-sex couples, and it must be further acknowledged that they abridge central precepts of equality," Kennedy wrote in *Obergefell*'s predominant passage. "Especially against a long history of disapproval of their relationships, this denial to same-sex couples of the right to marry works a grave and continuing harm. The imposition of this disability on gays and lesbians serves to disrespect and subordinate them. And the Equal Protection Clause, like the Due Process Clause, prohibits this unjustified infringement of the fundamental right to marry."

As it went on, Kennedy turned his agonizing about "millennia" on its head, situating same-sex couplings as the extension of a noble tradition rather than a departure from it. "Since the dawn of history, marriage has transformed strangers into relatives, binding families and societies together," he said. Within the courtroom, Kennedy projected a confidence that suggested he knew he might be completing the body of work for which he would be most remembered. One observer noted that the justice had tapped a more "eloquent vein, not the more businesslike tone he took with his announcement in *United States v. Windsor.*"

Foley waited until he arrived at his chambers to read the dissents offered by each of the four conservative judges. Antonin Scalia derided the "mystical aphorisms of the fortune cookie" that passed for Kennedy's analysis. (In what would be one of his final dissents before his death seven months later, Scalia wrote that if he ever joined such a flakily reasoned opinion, he would "hide my head in a bag.") Chief Justice Roberts back-handedly encouraged gays and lesbians to celebrate their victory but not the Constitution because, as he wrote, "it had nothing to do with it."

Roberts's tone was "bitter and harsh," Foley thought, but he had his own caustic take on Kennedy's opinion, even as it was becoming one of the rare pieces of legal writing widely quoted in the media and lauded by laypeople. "Gays love it because the language is lofty, flowery, broad and inspiring, but it's not how judges write opinions," he said. The cost of Kennedy's lack of analytical rigor was immediately apparent to Foley. Once again Kennedy had made a project of skirting the entire framework of tiered scrutiny, ensuring it would be difficult for any future judge to launder the opinion into realms beyond family law—and limit the value of its reasoning to aid other minority groups, as well. "It was consistent with all Kennedy's opinions where there's no standard of review," says Foley. "He's kind of an enigma because he's not a civil-rights judge. He's a gay-rights judge."

Yet on that Friday in late June 2015—a day that broke as brightly blue in Washington as they do so often on the windward side of Oahu—the limitations of the court's marriage opinion remained undetectable. To the extent that the cause of LGBT equality had come to be defined in the public imagination by the quest for marriage rights, the arrival of the ruling—and its immediate mandate across the fifteen states where gays and lesbians still couldn't marry—was received as the culmination of a movement's effort.

Barack Obama, who within hours described the decision as "justice that arrives like a thunderbolt," had the White House lit in the colors of the rainbow flag for the first time. He was about to take off on Air Force One for a Charleston, South Carolina, church where he would deliver a eulogy after a white supremacist shot nine people in a black church. Obama's speech there would be remembered for leading an impromptu sing-along of "Amazing Grace," a vivid (and audible) reminder of what it meant for the federal government to be embodied by its first African American president. A day earlier the Supreme Court had upheld crucial elements of the Affordable Care Act, Obama's signature legislation and the most important new gusset to be stitched into the social safety net since the Great Society. CNN called it "the week that changed the nation." With time, it would become clear those few days in late June 2015 represented a high-water mark for twenty-first-century liberalism in the United States.

Postscript

Massive Desistance

Forty-eight hours after the release of *Obergefell v. Hodges,* the chief justice of the Alabama Supreme Court took to the Sunday pulpit of the Kimberly Church of God and mused about what obligation local officials had to follow a Supreme Court mandate he compared unfavorably to *Dred Scott v. Sandford,* the 1857 decision that reaffirmed a legal basis for slavery. "When they create it as a national right, a fundamental right," Roy Moore asked from the pulpit, "what are we to do?"

For nearly as long as gay-rights activists had been demanding the right to marry, others had been agonizing about the backlash that might follow—especially if the judgment about local policies enacted by popular majorities was delivered by a narrow majority of far-off judges. Moore seemed poised to stand at the vanguard of the revanche: over the previous winter, he had instructed probate judges in his state not to marry same-sex couples, claiming that the state's 2006 constitutional ban kept its force despite a district-court ruling that found it unconstitutional.

After the *Obergefell* decision, probate judges embraced Moore's logic as a basis to stall its implementation, while at least nine Alabama counties decided not to issue licenses to any couple, gay or straight. Moore had trouble justifying his argument—"If the decision contradicts the Constitution, then it is not law," he explained, "and if it is not a law, then you don't have to obey it"—but took solace in Justice Samuel Alito's dissent and the sense of purpose it bestowed upon the case's losers. The majority's ruling "will be used to vilify Americans who are unwilling to assent to the new orthodoxy," Alito wrote, and "to stamp out every vestige of dissent."

That spirit of self-congratulatory martyrdom pulled a pair of Republican presidential candidates to Grayson, Kentucky, that September. They were there to demand the release of Rowan County clerk Kim Davis from a federal detention center where she had been held after refusing to obey a federal court's order to issue marriage licenses equally to all couples. Davis, an elected Democrat who asserted that homosexuality defied the teachings of her Pentecostal faith, insisted that being forced to play any role in same-sex couplings would violate her First Amendment claim to religious freedom. Presidential contenders Ted Cruz and Mike Huckabee heralded her as a political prisoner. "If you have to put someone in jail, let me go," Huckabee, a Baptist preacher and former Arkansas governor, demanded.

The front-runner for the Republican nomination, however, kept his distance from Grayson. Donald Trump had entered the presidential race ten days before the *Obergefell* decision, but had little to say about it. The thrice-married Trump had unconvincingly declared himself in favor of "traditional marriage," but was audibly halfhearted whenever the topic arose. When pressured by journalists to weigh in on Davis's fate, he did so with uncharacteristic equivocation. "It would certainly be nice if she didn't do it," Trump told the hosts of MSNBC's *Morning Joe.* "She can take a pass and let someone else in the office do it, in terms of religious." He had arrived in politics with a trendspotter's eye for identity-based griev- ance, and deployed it by deftly inflaming historical wounds of race, ethnic- ity, religion, gender, and nationality to great, almost immediate electoral effect. He saw no immediate opportunity in treating gay marriage as an open question, or in villainizing the justices who had closed it. "The deci- sion has been made," he said, "and that is the law of the land."

Those who had feared a "massive resistance" along the lines of that which greeted the Supreme Court's desegregation orders through the 1950s and 1960s were surprised to see that Davis was effectively alone in her persistent defiance. There was less a sustained backlash than a brief lashing-out among politicians coming to terms with defeat in a sphere where they had invested dearly. Louisiana governor Bobby Jindal, who had just announced his candidacy for president, proposed abolishing a Supreme Court that he said had "become a public opinion poll instead of a judicial body." In Utah, some state legislators explored an end to civil marriage altogether. "I would personally like to see the state out of the marriage-license business," explained representative Jake Anderegg, "but then I'd like to see the state out of the liquor-distribution business, too."

In 2019, Alabama governor Kay Ivey signed a bill into law that abolished all marriage-license requirements in her state. Yet Alabama struggled to extricate government entirely from the process, requiring couples to file a notarized affidavit with a probate judge registering their marriage contracts on a state-printed certificate. As one newspaper struggled to describe the new procedure when it took effect that summer, the judge would "then record, not issue, the license."

That represented one direction where social conservatives could take the marriage debate after *Obergefell.* Another came from Texas, where two Houston residents challenged the city's policy of providing benefits to married same-sex partners of public employees. Their lawsuit, *Pidgeon v. Turner,* rested on a technical reading of *Obergefell* and the putatively unresolved question of "whether and the extent to which the Constitution requires states or cities to provide tax-funded benefits to same-sex couples." They acknowledged that the state was required to recognize same-sex marriages, but argued that the state was not compelled to give any of the discrete rights and benefits to those couples. Those on the right argued that in guaranteeing the fundamental right to marry, the Constitution was granting citizens no more than a claim on a meaningless honorific.

Over the span of the marriage battles, gays and lesbians had gone from trying to privatize the conflict over the definition of family to successfully socializing it. Not only had those seeking marriage rights won the intramural skirmish with the feminists and liberationists who wanted to keep a distance from the institution, but they had succeeded with unexpected alacrity at assimilating, even remaking, it in their image. ("Research finds that same-sex unions are happier than heterosexual marriages," read the subtitle of a 2013 feature in *The Atlantic.* "What can gay and lesbian couples teach straight ones about living in harmony?") Privatizing the conflict was the only option left for those who had lost any room to further escalate it.

The same activists and lawyers who were on their second generation of strategizing a path back to unwind *Roe v. Wade,* however, immediately accepted the permanence of *Obergefell.* To the extent there was a systematic response to the marriage opinion, it was manifest in efforts to codify the defiant spirit of Alito's minority opinion. The Alliance Defending Freedom, previously the Alliance Defense Fund, which in 1998 had hosted the first strategy session at which what would be known as a Federal Marriage Amendment was discussed, led the charge lobbying for state-level "religious liberty" or "religious freedom" laws to shield dissidents—from pastors to florists—refusing to cater to same-sex couples from penalties under state or local antidiscrimination statutes. The First Amendment Defense Act, introduced in Congress in the summer of 2015, would specifically enshrine in federal law protection from any action taken "in accordance with a religious belief or moral conviction that: (1) marriage is or should be recognized as the union of one man and one woman, or (2) sexual relations are properly reserved to such a marriage."

That bill could be considered an instrument of surrender in the culture wars, one that would afford Christian conservatives some favorable protections in defeat. Their pursuit of "neo-establishment majoritarianism," as Southern Evangelical Seminary president Richard Land described it, amounted to a generation-long experiment to rewrite the country's laws to enshrine a narrow biblical understanding of the family. With that experiment a failure, the time had come for a retreat to the shelter belt. The political repose of the period between the *Scopes* trial and *Roe v. Wade*, when fundamentalists attempted to insulate themselves from the majority rather than claiming they represented one, beckoned anew.

Conservative journalist Rod Dreher called it "the Benedict Option," for a sixth-century priest who fled the disintegrating Roman Empire for a forest, where he established a spiritual redoubt from secular political chaos. "Could it be that the best way to fight the flood is to . . . stop fighting the flood? That is, to quit piling up the sandbags and to build an ark in which to shelter until the water recedes and we can put our feet on dry land again?" Dreher asked. "Rather than wasting energy and resources fighting unwinnable political battles, we should instead work on building communities, institutions, and networks of resistance that can outwit, outlast, and eventually overcome the occupation."

The hero of this march into exile was Jack C. Phillips, a baker in the Denver suburbs. Charlie Craig and David Mullins had been married in Massachusetts in 2012, and then returned to their home in Colorado to celebrate. Joined by Craig's mother, they entered the Masterpiece Cakeshop in Lakewood with a book of ideas for a custom wedding cake they could serve at a local reception. "Sorry, guys," Phillips told his guests. "I don't make cakes for same-sex weddings." Mullins posted an angry message about the encounter on Facebook, and after the incident drew media attention, the couple learned that any "place of public accommodation" refusing to serve customers on the basis of sexual orientation ran afoul of the state's 2008 nondiscrimination ordinance. They filed a complaint with the Colorado Civil Rights Commission, to which Phillips pleaded that the cake order breached his First Amendment freedoms. Both the commission and the Colorado Court of Appeals rejected his argument, concluding that Masterpiece Cakeshop had illegally engaged in antigay discrimination.

In 2017, Phillips's case found its way to the U.S. Supreme Court, in the first post-*Obergefell* case that touched on how the newly established right for gay couples to marry would be harmonized with other assurances made by the Constitution. Phillips considered his custom cakes to be works of art; to be compelled to produce one whose subject ran contrary to biblical teachings would conflict with his freedoms to expression and religious exercise. (The bakery, according to Phillips, would happily sell Craig and Mullins a premade cake.) Phillips's oppression at the hands of a government agency was not an unusual circumstance, his attorneys from the Alliance Defending Freedom argued in *Masterpiece Cakeshop, Ltd. v. Colorado Civil Rights Commission.*

Before the justices, Phillips's lawyers adopted the language of civil-rights jurisprudence, the claim of an aggrieved minority that declared itself entitled to the special shield of laws and courts because public opinion made the political process unresponsive to their needs. In a parallel lawsuit, involving a New Mexico wedding photographer who refused to shoot a same-sex ceremony, an Alliance Defending Freedom attorney had asserted that "citizens advocating to redefine marriage are among the most influential groups in modern politics; they have attained more legislative victories, political power, and popular favor in less time than virtually any other group in American history."

A seven-judge majority ruled in Phillips's favor, albeit on narrow technical terms that left unsettled broader questions. Another case would have to resolve the question of how the court balanced the Constitution's competing commitments to minority groups demanding respect for their civil rights and liberties. The jurist who had shepherded four monumental gay-rights opinions into law would not play any role in making that determination. Three weeks after the *Masterpiece Cakeshop* ruling, Justice Anthony Kennedy announced his retirement from the court.

The narrowness of Kennedy's decision in *Obergefell* meant that within months gay-rights politicians and litigators were back to fighting many of the same issues they might have confronted years, even decades, earlier. One month after the decision came down, congressional Democrats introduced what they called the Equality Act, a return to the omnibus gay-rights bills that expanded well beyond the more modest Employment

Non-Discrimination Act to cover housing and public accommodations. A series of discrimination lawsuits filed well before the Supreme Court took up *Obergefell*—a skydiving instructor fired because he told a customer he was gay, a funeral-home employee after she transitioned from male to female—continued their stride to the Supreme Court, unaffected by the marriage cases.

The local battles that came after were largely indistinguishable from those that came before, even if the political environment showed signs of transformation in many places. North Carolina passed a bill prohibiting municipalities from enacting their own antidiscrimination ordinances, just as Colorado did in 1992, although they seemed to steer clear of the Supreme Court's 1996 mandate in *Romer v. Evans* by not explicitly singling out a "politically unpopular group" by name. Michigan imposed a law that freed adoption agencies to discriminate against same-sex couples. In Starkville, Mississippi, Robbie Kaplan sued the city on behalf of a local grassroots gay group after the Board of Aldermen effectively banned a pride parade by denying it a permit. The Starkville board reversed its decision under legal pressure, and resistance led by companies like Dow, PayPal, and Biogen helped deny North Carolina's Republican governor a second term after enacting the antigay bill in his first.

Transgendered Americans were certainly no better off than they had been. A majority opinion rooted in more traditional civil-rights jurisprudence might have served to undermine state laws that discriminated on the basis of sexual identity as well as orientation. Instead, conservatives accelerated their efforts to police entry into institutions that had always segregated by sex: the military, schools, sports teams, bathrooms. Perhaps the only traditional gendered institution that had never discriminated against transgender people was marriage, an irony that would become apparent on the stage of the next Democratic convention. In 2016, Sarah McBride, national press secretary of the Human Rights Campaign—which had long been accused of neglecting the last letter in its LGBT constituency—became the first-ever transgender person to address a party convention. In her speech, McBride matter-of-factly noted that she married the trans man with whom she lived in the District of Columbia, in 2014, without any legal hurdle.

By the time plans were finalized for the next Democratic convention, a married gay man was vying for a place on the stage as the party's nominee. Pete Buttigieg had come out as gay at the end of his first term as mayor of South Bend, Indiana, following a six-month deployment to Afghanistan as a naval officer during which he said he determined that he could die without ever being in love. He was reelected overwhelmingly, and toward the end of his second term married Chasten Glezman, a Chicago barista and former drama teacher he had noticed on the dating app Hinge. They kissed onstage after Buttigieg announced his longshot campaign for president in the spring of 2019; even before they celebrated their first wedding anniversary, the Buttigiegs appeared on the cover of *Time*, sandwiched together between their home porch and the words FIRST FAMILY. As Buttigieg reached the head of the pack seeking the Democratic nomination, he faced far more questions about his corporate clients as a McKinsey consultant straight out of college than anything related to his domestic life. When he declared victory in the Iowa caucuses, his status as a married gay man was rarely remarked upon, certainly a less salient part of his political profile than being a small-city municipal officer running for the nation's highest post at the earliest moment he was constitutionally eligible. For his part, Buttigieg usually invoked same-sex marriage only as historical metaphor. When he credited the Iowa Supreme Court's 2009 decision for granting "people like me permission to believe that I might one day be able to wear this wedding ring that I have on my hand right now," as he put it at a Sioux City rally, Buttigieg was trying to make a point about the unimaginable moving within reach. To persuade voters that government actions would be felt in their daily lives, he said his marriage was possible only "by the grace of one vote on the Supreme Court."

In the spring of 2019, just as Buttigieg was emerging as a serious presidential contender, the Supreme Court accepted three appeals that together would address whether discrimination "on the basis of sex" as described in the Civil Rights Act of 1964 applied to sexual orientation and sexual identity as well as gender. Trump's Justice Department dispatched its solicitor general to argue federal law offered no civil-rights guarantees for sexual minorities. In fact, as the solicitor general's brief pointed out, Congress had had many opportunities since 1964 to specify otherwise if it chose to. At that moment, the Equality Act was stalled on Capitol Hill, as had been many other nondiscrimination bills before it.

When it came to gay politics in areas beyond marriage, it was as if *Obergefell* had never happened. Federal courts, however, proved friendly to new demands for equality. In June 2020, the Supreme Court issued its ruling in the three employment-discrimination appeals, which became known together as *Bostock v. Clayton County*. To widespread surprise, a six-vote majority that included two conservative justices came together to conclude that "an employer who fires an individual merely for being gay or transgender defies the law," as Justice Neil Gorsuch wrote. (Similar application in other spheres, like housing and finance, was likely to follow.) The only mention of the marriage cases came in a dissent from the court's other Trump appointee, Justice Brett Kavanaugh, who wondered why the Court had not applied Gorsuch's expansive reading of the Civil Rights Act in its consideration of any of the previous gay-rights appeals.

Even if the reasoning of *Obergefell* was far from Gorsuch's mind as he wrote, it was not hard to imagine the calm of the five years since the ruling sat with him. During oral arguments, Gorsuch had mused aloud about whether a judge should "take into consideration the massive social upheaval that would be entailed in such a decision." But his opinion waved away the fallout of "undesirable policy consequences," especially the concern brought before the court that "sex-segregated bathrooms, locker rooms, and dress codes will prove unsustainable" after such a ruling.

Gorsuch anticipated the realm from which the reaction would come. There was, he wrote, room under the Civil Rights Act for employers to argue that the new rules conflicted with their religious beliefs. Gorsuch expressed sympathy for their concerns and all but instructed them to prepare lawsuits that would invite the Court to rule on "how these doctrines protecting religious liberty interact" with the newly expanded civil-rights protections.

With that invitation, the Supreme Court seemed to close the book on one era of gay-rights jurisprudence and open the next. Five rulings since 1996 had combined to ensure that gays and lesbians had the full protection of the state in their political, sexual, and economic lives and recognition of their choices in making a family. Those who lost the struggle to define marriage would set the terms of the next conflict over the place of gays and lesbians in American society.

Acknowledgments

When a book requires seven years to complete, a lot can happen—in the realm you're documenting, in the broader political environment, in the publishing industry, and in one's own life.

I first had the idea for this book on the night that the New York state senate voted to pass its marriage bill in the summer of 2011. The following spring—after Barack Obama announced his change in position, which seemed likely to accelerate the change I wanted to document—I hastily drew up a proposal. Crown's Molly Stern and Zack Wagman believed in the project and set me off on the right course. When Zack moved on, he handed off the book to Domenica Alioto, who guided me through uncertain moments when the Supreme Court was upending our preferred timeline. I regret that we weren't able to see this through together, but appreciate all the attention and encouragement Zack and Domenica offered along the way. I am grateful, as well, to Emma Berry for the time she spent reading the manuscript.

Above all, I must thank my agent, Larry Weissman, and his partner Sascha Alper, who through all the changes always ensured this book ended up in the best possible hands. Edward Kastenmeier, who gave it a new home at Knopf, has been a smart, sensitive editor of many, many words. Caitlin Landuyt was indispensable as his second chair. I appreciate as well the input of their teammates Dan Frank, Jess Purcell, Kelly Blair, Dan Novack, and Emily Wilkerson, and the backing of Reagan Arthur. I am sad I never got the opportunity to thank Sonny Mehta for his support of this book and so many others I have admired over the years.

Along the way, I had the help of some fine researchers who were generous with their time: Cora Engelbrecht, Amanda Wallner, Colin Diersing, Peter Grogan, Thomas Huling, Madison Johnson, Jordan Feri, and Julia Lee. The book was fact-checked by Mellissa Meisels, Meredith Goff, Reagan Schmidt, Faiz Pirani, Caroline Graham, Sam Trilling, Amanda Tust, and Matt Browne.

The entire operation was headed up by Stephanie Vallejo, who remains the best in the business.

This work would not be possible without the time and candor of hundreds of people who made themselves available for interviews, including those whose contributions are obscured due to a preference for anonymity. In my travels, a few went above and beyond in their efforts to provide me with documents and other historical materials, secure access, or make introductions: Lance Bateman, David McEwan, Dan Foley, Robert Raben, Richard Socarides, Rick Ridder, and the office of Senator Don Nickles.

I also owe a huge thanks to librarians and archivists at the following institutions whose collections I consulted during my research. In Hawaii: the Hawaii State Library, UH School of Law Library and the University Archives and Manuscript Collections, Thomas Hale Hamilton Library, both at the University of Hawai'i at Mānoa. In Vermont: University of Vermont Libraries, Vermont State Archives, Middlebury Library, and the Vermont Queer Archives at Pride Center of Vermont. In Massachusetts: the History Project, Boston Public Library, Massachusetts Archives, Special Collections and University Archives at UMass Amherst, Harvard Kennedy School Library and Widener Library at Harvard University. In Connecticut: Sterling Memorial Library at Yale University. In New York: Human Sexuality Collection of Carl A. Kroch Library at Cornell University, LGBT Community Center National History Archive, New York Public Library, Elmer Holmes Bobst Library at New York University, Rare Book & Manuscript Library, Butler Library at Columbia University. In New Jersey: Seeley G. Mudd Manuscript Library at Princeton University. In the District of Columbia: Special Collections Research Center, Gelman Library at George Washington University, and Library of Congress. In Virginia: Special Collections Research Center at George Mason University. In Georgia: Richard B. Russell Library for Political Research and Studies at the University of Georgia, Special Collections, Irvine Sullivan Ingram Library at the University of West Georgia. In Tennessee: Southern Baptist Historical Library & Archive. In Arkansas: Clinton Presidential Library. In Oklahoma: Oklahoma State University Archives. In Kansas: Robert J. Dole Archive & Special Collections at the University of Kansas. In Iowa: Des Moines Public Library. In Ohio: Ohio University Library Annex. In Minnesota: Minnesota State Archives and the University of Minnesota Libraries' Department of Archives and Special Collections. In Colorado: Denver Public Library, Special Collections, Archives, and Preservation department at University of Colorado Boulder Libraries. In Utah: Utah State Archives, Special Collections at the J. Willard Marriott Library at the University of Utah, Harold B. Lee Library at Brigham Young University. And finally, in my adopted home of California: The Bancroft Library at the University of California, Berkeley, California State Archives, Hoover Institution Library & Archives at Stanford University,

Special Collections at the University of San Diego, UCLA Library Special Collections, ONE National Gay & Lesbian Archives at the USC Libraries, Santa Monica Public Library, Los Angeles Public Library, Archives and Manuscript Collections at the San Francisco Public Library. I owe a particular debt to my home librarians at UCLA's Young Research Library and Hugh and Hazel Darling Law Library, and interlibrary-loan librarians on the other side of transactions everywhere.

I was on the receiving end of beneficence from several academic institutions that welcomed me for periods of days, months, or years as I worked on this project. The Dole Institute for Politics at the University of Kansas backed my work in their archives with a travel grant. I was able to spend a semester living just a half mile from the site of the country's first legal same-sex marriages while spending the fall of 2013 as a Resident Fellow at Harvard's Institute of Politics, and am indebted to the IOP's top-notch staff: Eric Andersen, Alysha Tierney, Trey Grayson, Cathy McLaughlin, Esten Perez, Laura Simolaris, Christian Flynn, Carrie Devine, Cathey Park, Amy Howell, Christian Flynn, Terrie Verbic, and Kerri Collins. And to my fellow fellows for such good company: Ana Navarro, Karen Mills, Senator Mo Cowan, Beth Myers, and Ginny Hunt. Afterward, the Luskin School of Public Affairs brought me to UCLA, and the Department of Political Science there welcomed me into their brood. In Westwood, I'm grateful to Bill Parent, Jeff Lewis, Barbara Geddes, Kathy Bawn, Chris Tausanovitch, Michael Chwe, and Cindy Lebow. Much of this book was written on board the *MSC Lausanne, Hanjin Yantian,* and *Hamburg Süd Monte Azul;* the officers and crews of all three vessels offered hospitality, camaraderie, and invaluably steady seas.

For a long stretch, my other professional home was the late and lamented Bloomberg Politics. Thanks to Josh Tyrangiel and John Heilemann for bringing me aboard, and to the entire gang with which I got to cover the most bonkers presidential election of our lifetimes (or so one hopes): Mark Halperin, Mike Nizza, Kelly Bare, Allison Hoffman, Steve Yaccino, Margaret Talev, Jennifer Epstein, Mike Bender, Matt Negrin, Alex Trowbridge, Griffin Hammond, Andre Tartar, Tanya Singer, T. J. Ducklo, Kendall Breitman, Ellie Titus, Dave Weigel, Zach Mider, Will Leitch, Ann Selzer, John Geddes, Megan Murphy, and above all John Homans. At *Monocle,* my home over a decade, a salute to Tyler Brûlé, Andrew Tuck, Steve Bloomfield, Megan Gibson, and Aisha Spiers; at *New York,* David Wallace-Wells, Genevieve Smith, David Haskell, and Adam Moss; at the Recount, Cristian Rosell, Regina Dellea, and Nomi Leidner.

The manuscript improved due to my Ocean's Thirteen of writers, editors, academics, and lawyers who read parts of it throughout and offered indispensable feedback: Jack Bohrer, Benjamin Wallace-Wells, Lynn Vavreck, Juliet Eilperin, Jonathan Martin, Peter Canellos, Lisa Wangsness, Michael Schaffer,

Geoff Gagnon, Timothy Stewart-Winter, Perry Grossman, and my longest-lasting and most reliable professional coconspirator, James Burnett. Particular gratitude is due to April White, who regularly took time away from writing her own book on the history of American divorce to talk me through issues related to mine on marriage. Mary Krause makes sure my writing gets in front of the right audience, and I appreciate all her effort and good cheer over the years. Dave Garrow is in my highest esteem as a historian, but here he deserves my thanks for his work as a copy editor.

Other friends near and far have shown their support in various forms: Tara McGowan, Scott Mulhauser, Betsy Barnett, Josh Green, Parisa Roshan, Brian Weiss, Dan Reilly, Phil Press, Bridget Morris, Elizabeth Hansen, C. J. Jackson, Matt Viser, Maggie Haberman, Alex Burns, Scott Helman, Michael Levenson, Bryan Bender, Christina Bellantoni, Jennifer Moroz, Marcy Stech, Lisa Lerer, Kevin Arnovitz, Nathaniel Parks, David Nott, Peter Hamby, Farah Stockman, Jason Fagone, Ben Wallace, Chris Rowland, Tom Kretchmar, Andrew Putz, Michael McCormick, J.J. Balaban, Dave Garrison, and the late George Barrett. Paul Kane, Rick Klein, and Michael Steel were graciously willing to field random inquiries about legislative arcana, and Jason McGrath about aldermanic geography. All did so with their typical expertise.

Much love is due to my Washington family for hosting me on many reporting trips, and giving me good practice trying to simplify equal-protection doctrine for a pre-tween audience: Keltie Hawkins, Mike, Eva, and my goddaughter Eleanor Schaffer. Ellie is not old enough to have known a time when same-sex families weren't an accepted and largely uncontroversial part of American life; I hope this book helps her one day understand what all the fuss was about.

Nothing would be possible if not for my parents Bella Brodzki and Henry Issenberg, my aunt Gayle Brodzki, and my sister Sarina Issenberg, who selflessly stepped in to help meet a crucial deadline. Over the course of working on this project, I've crossed the threshold into a new family, who have remained remarkably understanding as the mythical book I've been writing for as long as I've known them has taken form. For that patience, and their warmth, I thank Susan Bass Levin, Ben Levin, and the Beaubaires: Lisa, David, Maddie, Will, and Charlie.

Amy Levin, you came into my life at just the right time, for both me and this work. I dedicate it to you, with boundless anticipation to see what the next quarter century or two of marriage will bring.

A Note on Sources

This book is informed by a wide range of published and unpublished sources, including private notes and correspondence shared under a variety of conditions of journalistic confidentiality. In the narrative, present-tense verbs (such as "says" or "explains") indicate material drawn from one of the author's interviews for this book. Past-tense verbs ("said" or "explained") are used for reconstructed dialogue along with quotations derived from all other sources. The notes below cover only published works; a list of archival collections consulted is included in the Acknowledgments.

Notes

....

Introduction: A President Decides

3 had been pressed for her views: Fred Kuhr, "Marsha Scott: On Marriage, the Military and the '96 Campaign," *Bay Windows*, March 28, 1996.

3 "We must not allow": Sara Miles, "Between Little Rock and a Hard Place," *The Advocate*, April 1996.

4 written interview with *Reader's Digest:* "Bush vs. Clinton: The Candidates Debate," *Reader's Digest*, October 1992.

4 first campaign for office in Arkansas: Associated Press, "Area Man May Seek JPH Post," February 7, 1974.

5 including husband and wife: "ERA and Homosexual 'Marriages,'" *Phyllis Schlafly Report*, vol. 8, no. 2, September 1974.

5 "Militant homosexuals from all over America": Jane J. Mansbridge, *Why We Lost the ERA* (Chicago: University of Chicago Press, 1986), 137.

5 In a 1980 congressional subcommittee hearing: Chai R. Feldblum, "The Federal Gay Rights Bill: From Bella to ENDA," in *Creating Change: Sexuality, Public Policy, and Civil Rights* (New York: St. Martin's Press, 2002), 149.

5 "The idea that this law": 118 Congressional Record 4372, daily edition March 21, 1972.

5 "Proponents of the ERA": U.S. Congress, Senate, Judiciary Committee, "The Impact of the Equal Rights Amendment," May 23, 1984.

6 "I'm not sure": Jeffrey Schmalz, "Gay Politics Goes Mainstream," *New York Times Magazine*, October 11, 1992.

6 "I think I would be opposed": Frank J. Murray, "Bush Sending 'Mixed Signals' on Gays, Evangelical Leaders Say," *Washington Times*, April 22, 1992.

6 "he has never said the words": Rex Wockner, "Democrats Address Gay Issues," *Windy City News*, January 1992.

6 "You have no public record": David Mixner, *Stranger Among Friends* (New York: Bantam Books, 1996), 204.

7 country's dominant gay political action committee: Bettina Boxall, "Gays Alter Dynamics of Politics," *Los Angeles Times*, August 15, 1992.

7 Historians have located evidence: William N. Eskridge Jr., "A History of Same-Sex Marriage," Yale Law School Faculty Scholarship Series, January 1993.

8 what were called "Boston marriages": Lilian Faderman, *Odd Girls and Twilight*

Lovers: A History of Lesbian Life in Twentieth-Century America (New York: Columbia University Press, 1991), 15.

8 "Sisters in love": William Wordsworth, "To the Lady E.B. and the Hon. Miss P.," *The Poems of William Wordsworth* (London: Methuen & Co., 1908), 464.

8 those who preferred assimilation: John D'Emilio, *Sexual Politics, Sexual Communities: The Making of a Homosexual Minority in the United States, 1940–1970*, 2nd ed. (Chicago: University of Chicago Press, 1998), 108–28.

8 limits of the gay-rights fantasy: Nancy L. Cott, *Public Vows: A History of Marriage and the Nation* (Cambridge: Harvard University Press, 2000), 216.

8 "Imagine that the year": "Homosexual Marriage?" *ONE*, August 1953.

8 Self-described "homophilic" magazine: Randy Lloyd, "Let's Push Homophile Marriage," *ONE*, June 1963.

8 Alvin Toffler's book: Alvin Toffler, *Future Shock* (New York: Random House, 1970).

8 "Our children": Ken Rosen, *Future Shock*, directed by Alex Grasshoff (New York: Metromedia Producers Corporation; Del Mar, CA: McGraw-Hill Films, 1972).

9 Massed outside the Internal Revenue Service: Linda Wheeler, "2,000 Gay Couples Exchange Vows in Ceremony of Rights," *Washington Post*, October 11, 1987.

9 "It's going to be a political demonstration": Peter Freiberg, "The March on Washington," *The Advocate*, November 11, 1987.

9 "They had been married 10 years": Gary C. Rammler, "Gays and Marriage: Homosexual, Wife Cling to a Marriage in Ruins," *Milwaukee Journal*, March 4, 1984.

9 "This secret double life": P. Gregory Springer, "Choosing to Marry," *The Advocate*, April 30, 1981.

9 priorities farther down a hierarchy: Gary Mucciaroni, *Same Sex, Different Politics: Success and Failure in the Struggles over Gay Rights* (Chicago: University of Chicago Press, 2008).

10 the gay-rights movement was united: Michael J. Klarman, *From the Closet to the Altar: Courts, Backlash, and the Struggle for Same-Sex Marriage* (New York: Oxford University Press, 2013), 21.

10 "One would think that": E. B. Saunders, "Reformer's Choice: Marriage License or Just License?" *ONE*, August 1953.

10 "Why didn't you guys fight": Randy Shilts, *And the Band Played On: Politics, People, and the AIDS Epidemic* (New York: St. Martin's Press, 1987), 557.

10 Media coverage and criticism: Frank Rich, "'Theater: The Normal Heart,' by Larry Kramer," *New York Times*, April 22, 1985.

11 "Because they say we can't": Virginia Apuzzo, interview by Kelly Anderson, June 2–3, 2004, Voices of Feminism Oral History Project, Sophia Smith Collection, Smith College, Northampton, Massachusetts.

11 A handful of House Republicans: Casandra Burrell, "Bill Would Prevent Same-Sex Marriages from Becoming Legal," Associated Press, May 6, 1996.

12 "Get on record as favoring": Dick Morris, *Behind the Oval Office: Getting Reelected Against All Odds* (New York: Random House, 1997), 230.

15 barely one-quarter of Americans: Pew Research Center, "Growing Public Support for Same-Sex Marriage," February 16, 2012, www.pewresearch.org.

15 "So great is the change": E. E. Schattschneider, *The Semisovereign People: A Realist's View of Democracy in America* (Fort Worth, TX: Holt, Rinehart and Winston, Inc., 1960), 2.

15 Barack Obama's announcement: Devin Dwyer, "Obama's 'Evolving' Gay Marriage Stance," ABC News, May 9, 2012.

16 "What you're seeing is": ABC News, "Transcript: Robin Roberts Interview with President Obama," May 9, 2012.

16 That decision arrived: Alexander Burns, "Donald Trump, Pushing Someone Rich, Offers Himself," *New York Times,* June 17, 2015.

16 "It's irrelevant": Aaron Blake, "Trump Says 17-Month-Old Gay Marriage Ruling Is 'Settled' Law—but 43-Year-Old Abortion Ruling Isn't," *Washington Post,* November 14, 2016.

1: Seeking License

22 When Elton John came out: Elizabeth J. Rosenthal, *His Song: The Musical Journey of Elton John* (New York: Billboard Books, 2001), 148–49.

24 "I'd see like 8,000 naked lesbians": Michelangelo Signorile, "Bridal Wave," *Out,* December 1994.

25 Within their first two weeks: Elaine Herscher, "When Marriage Is a Tough Proposal," *San Francisco Examiner,* May 15, 1995.

26 In May 1989, following: Sheila Rule, "Rights for Gay Couples in Denmark," *New York Times,* October 2, 1989.

26 The previous year, in 1989: Celestine Bohlen, "Koch Widens City's Policy on 'Family,'" *New York Times,* July 10, 1989.

27 By 1990 there were: Peter Nicolas and Mike Strong, *The Geography of Love: Same-Sex Marriage & Relationship Recognition in America (The Story in Maps),* 5th ed. (Scotts Valley, CA: CreateSpace Independent Publishing Platform, 2014), 17.

27 representing a predictable assortment: David L. Chambers, "Tales of Two Cities: AIDS and the Legal Recognition of Domestic Partnerships in San Francisco and New York," *Law & Sexuality: A Review of Gay and Lesbian Legal Issues* 2 (1992), 201.

27 She had just published: Ninia Baehr, *Abortion Without Apology: A Radical History for the 1990s* (Boston: South End Press, 1999).

28 They had been instructed: Pavel Stankov, "Eccentric Businesses at the Blaisdell Hotel," *Hawaii Business Magazine,* July 4, 2013.

28 For nearly a decade: Michelangelo Signorile, "Bridal Wave," *Out,* May 1995.

29 He met Pat: John Gallagher, "Marriage, Hawaiian Style," *The Advocate,* February 4, 1997.

29 Patrick had grown up: Walter Wright, "Same-Sex Marriage Ban May Be Tested," *Honolulu Advertiser,* November 25, 1990.

29 "When you're born": Susan Essoyan, "Hawaiian Wedding Bells Ring Alarm Bills," *Los Angeles Times,* September 9, 1996.

30 "My mother has": Walter Wright, "Couples Challenge Ban on Same-Sex Marriage," *Honolulu Advertiser,* December 18, 1990.

31 "What was that?": Dan Nakaso, "Bill Woods, Advocate for Gays, Civil Rights," *Honolulu Advertiser,* October 1, 2008.

2: Only One Man Marching

32 Woods first saw Hawaii: Dan Nakaso, "Bill Woods, Advocate for Gays, Civil Rights," *Honolulu Advertiser,* October 1, 2008.

32 and the next year transferred: "Bill Woods Obituary," *Decatur (IL) Herald & Review,* November 9, 2008.

32 In 1973, he founded: "Bill Woods Obituary."

32 Years later, he became: Nakaso, "Bill Woods, Advocate for Gays, Civil Rights."

33 When conservative televangelist: Michelangelo Signorile, "Bridal Wave," *Out,* December/January 1994.

33 Woods led a group: "Hawaii to Have Two Moral Majorities," Associated Press, May 10, 1981.

33 Their "Moral Majority of Hawaii": June Watanabe and Nadine Scott, "Scuffles Break Out at Falwell's Rally," *Honolulu Star-Bulletin,* May 28, 1981.

33 as newspaper ads announced: Signorile, "Bridal Wave."

33 When Falwell held: June Watanabe & Nadine Scott, "Scuffles Break Out at Falwell's Rally," *Honolulu Star-Bulletin,* May 28, 1981.

33 "The Moral Majority of Hawaii is using": "Hawaii to Have Two Moral Majorities."

33 Before leaving Hawaii: Signorile, "Bridal Wave."

33 Woods hosted a weekly: "Support Group Meetings," *Gay Community News,* March 22, 1994.

33 In 1989, declaring his ambition: Alan Matsuoka, "Radio Talk Show Host Wants to Clear the Air," *Honolulu Star-Bulletin,* July 10, 1989.

34 it was Woods he singled out: "Waihee Praises Gay-Rights Activist," *Big Island Newspaper,* June 12, 1989.

34 By 1989, fifteen years had passed: "Gay Pride Week Hawaii," *Gay Community News,* June 1980.

34 Families went together: Owen Keehnen, "Documentary on Honolulu Trans Club 'The Glade' in Production," *Windy City Times,* April 6, 2013.

34 In 1972, Hawaii had become: "Hawaii Sex Law Passes Legislature," *The Advocate,* April 26, 1972.

34 "There's not much of a problem with gays": "Says Hawaii Not So Cool," *The Advocate,* February 28, 1973.

34 "Policemen who smile": Sasha Gregory, "Being Liberated Takes Getting Used To," *The Advocate,* December 20, 1972.

35 In 1977, Miami-area voters overturned: Dudley Clendinen and Adam Nagourney, *Out for Good: The Struggle to Build a Gay Rights Movement in America* (New York: Simon & Schuster, 1999), 291–311.

35 "From New York to San Francisco": Editorial Board, "Gay Rights in Hawaii," *Honolulu Advertiser,* June 10, 1977.

35 "There is an AIDS awareness here": Bruce Ward, "The Aloha Spirit," *New York Native,* January 28, 1985.

36 By 1989, Hawaii was spending: "States Use Own Funds on AIDS," *USA Today,* August 31, 1989.

36 launched "a gay rag": "Two Years in Print!" *Island Lifestyle Magazine,* March 1, 1991.

37 Sharyle Lyndon, a onetime drag-show producer: Becky Ashizawa, "Gays and Lesbians to Parade in Waikiki June 23," *Honolulu Star-Bulletin,* June 13, 1990.

38 He had been on the National Mall: Linda Wheeler, "2,000 Gay Couples Exchange Vows in Ceremony of Rights," *Washington Post,* October 11, 1987.

38 The large-scale symbolic vows: J. Carey Junkin and Walter Wheeler, "It Is Time for the Wedding," *Bay Area Reporter,* September 10, 1987.

38 Some movement leaders: Candy J. Cooper, "Lesbians, Gays 'Wed' En Masse," *San Francisco Examiner,* October 11, 1987.

38 The two hundred thousand: Lena Williams, "200,000 March in Capital to Seek Gay Rights and Money for AIDS," *New York Times,* October 12, 1987.

39 Hollywood movie theater for services: Edward B. Fiske, "Homosexuals in Los Angeles, Like Many Elsewhere, Want Religion and Establish Their Own Church," *New York Times,* February 15, 1970.

39 The Metropolitan Community Church was a mainline Protestant congregation: Mark Anderson, "Local Gays: The Boys in the Bars," *Hawaii Observer,* August 28, 1977.

39 as his mother called it: "Our History," Founders Metropolitan Community Church, www.mccla.org.

39 As Perry had done: "Two L.A. Girls Attempt First Legal Gay Marriage," *The Advocate,* July 8–21, 1970.

39 "to be sure they're not joining a potential Zsa Zsa": "They've Only Just Begun," *The Advocate,* July 5, 1988.

39 "We expose the institution": William Eskridge, *The Case for Same-Sex Marriage: From Sexual Liberty to Civilized Commitment* (New York: Free Press, 1996), 53.

39 collapsing after a debate: *Out for Good,* 57.

39 "The family is the microcosm of oppression": Eskridge, *The Case for Same-Sex Marriage,* 54.

40 Woods, by contrast: Alan Matsuoka, "Radio Talk Show Host Wants to Clear the Air," *Honolulu Star-Bulletin,* July 10, 1989.

40 On his weekly radio show: Alan Matsuoka, "Host Pulls Gay Talk Show from Air," *Honolulu Star-Bulletin,* October 30, 1989.

40 "There's only so many ways": Matsuoka, "Radio Talk Show Host Wants to Clear the Air."

40 by 1990, Honolulu's mayor: "Executive Order Protects Gay Workers in Hawaii," *San Francisco Sentinel,* April 3, 1981.

40 "In other states": Linda Hosek, "Attorney General Rules Out Same-Sex Marriage," *Honolulu Star-Bulletin,* December 29, 1990.

41 Perry, the church's founder: William E. Woods, "Marriage's Grass Roots: The Activist Who Led the Equal Marriage Movement in Hawaii Recalls the Long Road to Massachusetts," *The Advocate,* May 11, 2004.

41 In the meantime: Becky Ashizawa, "Gays and Lesbians to Parade in Waikiki June 23," *Honolulu Star-Bulletin,* June 13, 1990.

41 It featured, as Woods's friend: Sharyle Lyndon, "Letter to the Editor," *Gay Community News,* August 1990.

41 A straight Honolulu city councilman: Jon Yoshishige, "Gathering in Park Follows the Gay Parade in Waikiki," *Honolulu Advertiser,* June 24, 1990.

42 Then he took the criticism public: "Hawaii Horror Story! Hawaii's ACLU Takes Public Opinion Poll," *Gay Community News,* July 1990.

42 The fracas was noticed: Robert W. Peterson, "Gay Marriage Query Becomes a Sticky Issue for Hawaii ACLU Chapter," *The Advocate,* September 25, 1990.

42 Varady claimed that Woods's description: Nan D. Hunter, William B. Rubenstein and Carl M. Varady, "ACLU Hawaii, Letter to the Editor," *The Advocate,* October 21, 1990.

43 Throughout the year, Woods insisted: Walter Wright, "Same-Sex Marriage Ban May Be Tested," *Honolulu Advertiser,* November 25, 1990.

43 SAME-SEX MARRIAGE BAN: Wright, "Same-Sex Marriage Ban."

3: A Distinct Civil-Liberties Question

45 The office to which Bill Woods: "ACLU Backs Homosexual Marriage," Associated Press, October 28, 1986.

45 The ACLU largely avoided: Samuel Walker, *In Defense of American Liberties: A History of the ACLU* (Carbondale, IL: Southern Illinois University Press, 1999), 312.

45 defending Lillian Hellman's lesbian-themed: Sarah Stiles, *Intermeddlers; The Censorship of Lillian Hellman,* ed. Frank Hentschker (New York: Martin E. Segal Theatre Center Publications, 2016).

45 After the Supreme Court affirmed: Walker, *In Defense of American Liberties: A History of the ACLU,* 312.

46 Now in his first year: Michael McConnell and Jack Baker, *The Wedding Heard 'Round the World: America's First Gay Marriage* (Minneapolis: University of Minnesota Press, 2018), 63.

46 Three years earlier: McConnell and Baker, *The Wedding Heard 'Round the World,* 21.

46 It would all be: McConnell and Baker, *The Wedding Heard 'Round the World,* 65–74.

46 Clerk of court Gerald Nelson: Dick Heweston, *History of the Gay Movement in Minnesota and the Role of the Minnesota Civil Liberties Union* (Minneapolis: Friends of the Bill of Rights Foundation, 2013), 44.

46 With the well-documented visit: "Judge Hears Homosexual's Job Suit Against 'U,'" *Minneapolis Tribune,* August 6, 1970.

47 Castner agreed to represent McConnell: "Homosexual Gets Defender," *St. Paul Dispatch,* July 8, 1970.

47 "doesn't involve a civil liberties issue": Ken Bronson, *A Quest for Full Equality* (Boston, Beacon Press, 2011).

47 "An homosexual": *McConnell v. Anderson,* 316 F. Supp. 809.

47 "This is not a case involving mere": *McConnell v. Anderson,* 316 F. Supp. 809.

48 Over a five-year period: Tim Campbell, "Long Before DOMA," *Lavender,* November 8, 1996.

48 "about ninety percent of the benefits of marriage": McConnell and Baker, *The Wedding Heard 'Round the World,* 115.

48 They moved in briefly: McConnell and Baker, *The Wedding Heard 'Round the World,* 115–21.

48 "There is no irrational": *Baker v. Nelson,* 291 Minn. 310.

48 It had been slow to join: "Minnesota ACLU Chapter Hires Gay as Its Lawyer," *The Advocate,* May 26, 1971.

49 Matthew Stark later recalled: Marcia Coyle, "Here Comes the Brawl; Special Report: The Legal Fight Over Same-Sex Marriage. The First Case, 40 Years On," *National Law Journal* 32, no. 50, August 23, 2010.

49 Five years earlier, the U.S. Supreme Court: *Loving v. Virginia,* 388 U.S. 1 (1967).

49 In a single published sentence: Robert Barnes, "Supreme Court: Was Gay Marriage Settled in 1972 Case?" *Washington Post,* August 17, 2014.

49 a portrait with McConnell in *Life:* Michael Durham, "Homosexuals in Revolt," *Life,* December 31, 1971.

49 a profile of the two in *Look:* Jack Star, "The Homosexual Couple," *Look,* January 26, 1971.

49 "Some homosexuals": Erik Eckholm, "The Same-Sex Couple Who Got a Marriage License in 1971," *New York Times,* May 16, 2015.

50 In 1977, as the California: John Balzar, "A Vote to Ban Gay Marriages," *San Francisco Chronicle,* June 18, 1977.

50 an ACLU lobbyist: "Gay Marriage Ban Gets Approval," *NewsWest,* April 28, 1977.

50 The legislation had been drafted: *In re Marriage Cases,* 43 Cal.4th 757.

50 Anthony Sullivan and Richard F. Adams: Robert Barnes, "40 Years Later, Story of a Same-Sex Marriage in Colo. Remains Remarkable," *Washington Post,* April 18, 2015.

50 "Who is it going to hurt?": Grace Lichtenstein, "Homosexual Weddings Stir Controversy in Colorado," *New York Times,* April 27, 1975.

50 "I don't profess": Lichtenstein, "Homosexual Weddings Stir Controversy."

50 "a mini-Nevada": Lichtenstein, "Homosexual Weddings Stir Controversy."

50 the state attorney general stopped: "Attorney General Rules on Homosexual Marriage," United Press International, April 28, 1975.

50 In the case of Adams: Troy Masters, "United States Government Says L.A. Gay Couple's 1975 Marriage Is Valid," *The Pride,* June 7, 2016.

50 the two had met: Eric Malnic, "Men Without a Country," *Los Angeles Times,* May 11, 1984.

50 An Immigration and Naturalization Service: "Gay Marriages Ruled Invalid," Associated Press, December 18, 1979.

51 The INS would later: Fred Okrund, "Gays Sue to Obtain Recognition of Legal Colorado Same-Sex Marriage," *Open Forum,* April 1979.

51 An ACLU volunteer attorney: Okrund, "Gays Sue to Obtain Recognition."

51 They would exhaust: Barnes, "40 Years Later."

51 "The issue of legal marriage": Okrund, "Gays Sue to Obtain Recognition."

51 Such laws, which existed: William Eskridge, *Dishonorable Passions: Sodomy Laws in America, 1861–2003* (New York: Viking Press, 2008), 126–27.

4: Rolling the Dice

55 earlier era of movement activism: Michael Boucai, "Glorious Precedents: When Gay Marriage Was Radical," *Yale Journal of Law and Humanities* 27 (2015), 1–82.

55 "gay-marriage boom": Bob Cole, "Gay Marriage 'Boom': Suddenly It's News," *The Advocate,* August 5, 1970.

55 a lesbian couple in Kentucky: John Finley, "2 Louisville Women File for Marriage License," *Louisville Courier-Journal,* July 7, 1970.

55 Both circuit and appellate: "Court Says Female Couple Can't Wed," Associated Press, November 10, 1973.

55 Not long after: Sasha Yasinin, "Gay Marriage Test Due in Washington State Courts," *The Advocate,* January 18, 1974.

55 Encouraged by a sympathetic state: *Singer v. Hara,* 11 Wn. App. 247, 522 P.2d 1187 (1974).

55 with the state appeals court: *Singer v. Hara.*

56 Unable to afford: "Marriage Bid Loses Again in Kentucky," *The Advocate,* December 5, 1973.

56 Circumstances did not change much: David L. Chambers and Nancy D. Polikoff, "Family Law and Gay and Lesbian Family Issues in the Twentieth Century," *Family Law Quarterly* 33, no. 3 (Fall 1999), 524–26.

56 This debate missed: Margalit Fox, "Adrienne Asch, Bioethicist and Pioneer in Disability Studies, Dies at 67," *New York Times,* November 23, 2013.

57 The *New York Times* devoted: "Rights Group Backs Homosexual Marriages," *New York Times,* October 28, 1986.

57 When attorney Bill Rubenstein: Philip S. Gutis, "New York Court Defines Family to Include Homosexual Couples," *New York Times,* July 7, 1989.

57 a sympathetic New York state appeals court: Charles-Edward Anderson, "New Nuclear Family: N.Y. Court Says Gays Are Family Under Rent-Control Laws," *American Bar Association Journal* 75, October 1989.

57 had shared an apartment: Carlos A. Ball, *From the Closet to the Courtroom: Five LGBT Rights Lawsuits That Have Changed Our Nation* (Boston: Beacon Press, 2010), 21–25.

57 a "realistic, and certainly equally valid": *Braschi v. Stahl Assocs. Co.,* 543 N.E.2d 49 (N.Y. 1989).

57 Despite the momentousness: William B. Rubenstein, "We Are Family: A Reflection on the Search for Legal Recognition of Lesbian and Gay Relationships," *Journal of Law and Politics* 8 (1991–1992): 89.

57 would have little broader impact: Carlos A. Ball, *From the Closet to the Courtroom: Five LGBT Rights Lawsuits That Have Changed Our Nation* (Boston: Beacon Press, 2010), 53–65.

58 At first the clerk obliged: Elizabeth Kastor, "The Marriage Proposal," *Washington Post,* January 28. 1991.

59 and Mayor Marion Barry was celebrated: Sasha Issenberg, "Barry, Marion: The Mayor for Life Is One of the Few Politicians to 'Devolve' on Gay Rights," *Washington City Paper,* June 6, 2014.

59 "Better to establish": Elizabeth Kastor, "The Marriage Proposal," *Washington Post,* January 28, 1991.

59 Dean accused: Kastor, "The Marriage Proposal."

5. Gay Mafia

60 When he arrived: Walter Wright, "Couples Challenge Ban on Same-Sex Marriage," *Honolulu Advertiser,* December 12, 1990.

60 to drag the organization: Linda Hosek, "ACLU Probes Taboo on Gay Marriages," *Honolulu Star-Bulletin,* December 19, 1990.

60 once known as the Sodomy Roundtable: Kevin M. Cathcart, "The Sodomy Roundtable" in *Love Unites Us: Winning the Freedom to Marry in America,* eds. Kevin M. Cathcart and Leslie Gabriel-Bretty (New York: New Press, 2016), 51–55.

61 For Lewin, the issue prompted: Hosek, "ACLU Probes Taboo on Gay Marriages."

62 Furthermore, Chong publicly undercut: David Waite, "State Won't Allow Same-Sex Couples to Legally Marry," *Honolulu Advertiser,* December 29, 1990.

6: Making the Case

63 "I had never thought of marriage": Janice Otaguro, "Dan Foley: Islander of the Year," *Honolulu Magazine,* January 1995.

64 "to help them avoid": Helen Altonn, "Foley Bids Adieu to ACLU," *Honolulu Star-Bulletin,* November 4, 1987.

64 "I think many of my best": Altonn, "Foley Bids Adieu to ACLU."

65 In the most prominent: Deb Price, "Lawyer in Hawaiian Same-Sex Marriage Case Has a Long History of Doing the Right Thing," *Detroit News,* July 12, 1996.

65 "There's no dominant group": Linda Hosek, "Isles May Be First for Gay Marriages," *Honolulu Star-Bulletin,* April 1991.

65 Foley was impressed by: Andrew Gebert and Monte Joffee, "Value Creation as the Aim of Education: Tsunesaburo Makiguchi and Soka Education," in *Ethical Visions of Education: Philosophies in Practice*, ed. David T. Hansen (New York: Teachers College Press, 2007), 65–82.

65 Soka Gakkai lay leaders: "Daisaku Ikeda: A Biographical Sketch," *Daisaku Ikeda*, www.daisakuikeda.org.

66 "We're not happy with": Linda Hosek, "3 Isle Gay Pairs' Suit to Wed Will Test Law," *Honolulu Star-Bulletin*, May 2, 1991.

66 "Marriage is one of the 'basic civil rights of man'": *Loving v. Virginia*, 388 US 1 (1967).

66 particularly hostile to sexual minorities: Abby R. Rubenfeld, "Lessons Learned: A Reflection upon *Bowers v. Hardwick*," *Nova Law Review* 11, no. 1, (1986).

66 "There is no such thing": *Bowers v. Hardwick*, 478 US 186 (1986).

67 one of only five: Patricia A. Cain, "The Right to Privacy Under the Montana Constitution: Sex and Intimacy," *Montana Law Review* 64, no. 1 (Winter 2003): 99–132.

67 each of the more than four hundred benefits: State of Hawaii, "Report of the Commission on Sexual Orientation and the Law," December 8, 1995, 105–25.

67 "the pain of tortured silence": Walter Williams, "Lawyer Secures Gay Marriage Rights," *World Tribune*, February 28, 1994.

7: Baehr v. Lewin

71 "This will be a turning point": Linda Hosek, "Court Hears Plea for Gay Marriage," *Honolulu Star-Bulletin*, September 4, 1991.

71 The case had been decided: Tamar Lewin, "Homosexual Ban in Army Rejected by Appeals Court," *New York Times*, February 11, 1988.

71 Norris argued that: Arthur S. Leonard, "Watkins v. United States Army and the Employment Rights of Lesbians and Gay Men," *Labor Law Journal* 40 (1989): 438–45.

71 When, in 1990: *Watkins v. United States Army*, 847 F.2d 1329 (9th Cir. 1988), aff'd en banc, 875 F.2d 699 (9th Cir. 1989), cert. denied, 498 US 957 (1990).

72 the Supreme Court let: David J. Garrow, *Liberty & Sexuality: The Right to Privacy and the Making of Roe v. Wade* (Berkeley, CA: University of California Press, 1998).

72 In March 1991: "Hawaii Makes Three . . . ," *Lesbian & Gay Law Notes*, April 1991.

72 Just past 10:30 a.m.: Hawaii First Circuit Court, Civil Motions Calendar (*Baehr v. Lewin*), September 3, 1991.

75 Its inclusion did not suggest: Cal Thomas, "Does Homosexuality Have a Physical Basis?" *Honolulu Star-Bulletin*, September 6, 1991.

75 After Foley was quoted: Linda Hosek, "3 Unwed Gay Couples to Sue State," *Honolulu Advertiser*, February 22, 1991.

76 "People are very reluctant": Walter Wright, "Same-Sex Marriage Ban May Be Tested," *Honolulu Advertiser*, November 25, 1990.

76 agitating for a boycott: "Gay Rights Activist Calls for Boycott of AUW, Boy Scouts," *Honolulu Advertiser*, July 20, 1992.

76 Unlike Foley and McEwan: "Groups Criticize Gay Lifestyle," *Honolulu Advertiser*, June 26, 1991.

76 Just after Christmas: Kevin Dayton, "AIDS Group Treasurer Quits, Admits Federal Funds Misuse," *Honolulu Advertiser*, December 29, 1991.

76 It was a story broken: Dayton, "AIDS Group Treasurer Quits."

8: A Chickenskin Moment

79 He and Foley had faced off: Lee Catterall, "Court Tells Why Sandy Beach Initiative Denied," *Honolulu Star-Bulletin,* June 22, 1989.

79 the nineteenth-century building: "Guide to Government in Hawaii (Fourteenth Edition)," revised by Claire Marumoto, Hawaii Legislative Reference Bureau, September 2013.

79 Foley's wife: Ken Kobayashi, "Gay Marriage Case Gets Hearing," *Honolulu Advertiser,* October 14, 1992.

83 "I believe the '90s": Susan Miller, "To Thee I Wed," *Island Lifestyle,* April 1993.

9: Shoals of Time

85 king's constitutional reforms: Lawrence H. Fuchs, *Hawaii Pono: A Social History,* New York: Harcourt, Brace & World, 1961. 25–26.

85 and at that point: Benjamin Seto, "Despite GOP Ties, Moon a Shoo-In as Chief Justice," *Honolulu Star-Bulletin,* February 19, 1993.

85 Then, on September 22: "James Wakatsuki Dies," *USA Today,* September 23, 1992.

85 with a combined three years: Ken Kobayashi, "'New Generation' Court Makes Waves Nationwide," *Honolulu Advertiser,* May 7, 1993.

87 from an old family of the Hawaii: Dan Boylan and T. Michael Holmes, *John A. Burns: The Man and His Times* (Honolulu: Latitude 20 Books, University of Hawaii Press, 2000).

87 the acting chief justice: Ken Kobayashi, "1993 Ruling Paved Way for Shifting Views on Marriage Equality, Former Justice Says," *Honolulu Star-Advertiser,* April 30, 2013.

88 The science of sexual attraction: David Nimmons, "Sex and the Brain," *Discover,* March 1994.

88 National Cancer Institute researcher: Jim Dawson, "Scientists Look for Genetic Basis of Homosexuality," *Minneapolis Star-Tribune,* February 15, 1993.

88 A little over a year: David Gelman et al., "Born or Bred," *Newsweek,* February 24, 1992.

88 "The issue of whether": Cox News Service, "Being Gay: Nature or Nurture? Scientists Hunt for an Answer," *Honolulu Star-Bulletin,* March 9, 1993.

89 *Shoal of Time:* Gavan Daws, *Shoal of Time: A History of the Hawaiian Islands* (New York: Macmillan Publishing Company, 1968).

10: Wardle's Run

93 something he had read: Linda D. Elrod, "Summary of the Year in Family Law," *Family Law Quarterly* 27, no. 4 (1994): 485–514.

93 Until the 1970s: Lynn Wardle, "Rethinking Marital Age Restrictions," *Journal of Family Law,* 22, no. 1 (1983).

94 Wardle's research interests: Lynn D. Wardle, "The Gap Between Law and Moral Order: An Examination of the Legitimacy of the Supreme Court Abortion Decisions," *Brigham Young University Law Review* 811 (1980).

94 a gap large enough: Lynn D. Wardle, "Sanctioned Assisted Suicide: Separate but Equal Treatment for the New Illegitimates," *Issues in Law and Medicine* 3, no. 3 (1987): 245; Lynn D. Wardle, "Cable Comes of Age: A Constitutional Analysis

of the Regulation of Indecent Cable Television Programming," *Denver University Law Review* 63 (1986): 621.

94 As abortion laws became: Lynn D. Wardle, "Human Life Federalism Amendment—I. Legal Aspects," *Catholic Lawyer* 28 (1983): 121.

94 In its 1989 case: *Webster v. Reproductive Health Services,* 492 US 490.

95 When the Supreme Court had heard: Lynn Wardle, "Rethinking *Roe v. Wade*," *Brigham Young University Law Review* 231 (1985): 257.

95 "Thus, in *Roe v. Wade*": Wardle, "Rethinking *Roe v. Wade*."

95 Even as he welcomed: Lynn D. Wardle, "The Gap Between Law and Moral Order: An Examination of the Legitimacy of the Supreme Court Abortion Decisions," *Brigham Young University Law Review* 811 (1980).

95 During the 1970s: Christopher R. Leslie, "An Introduction to Festschrift in Honor of Jeffrey Sherman," *Chicago-Kent Law Review* 84, no. 2 (2013): 359–62.

95 The most prominent: Kenneth Karst, "The Freedom of Intimate Association," *Yale Law Journal* 89, no. 4 (1980): 624–92.

95 To the extent that: Lynn Wardle, "A Critical Analysis of Constitutional Claims for Same-Sex Marriage," *Brigham Young University Law Review* 1 (1996).

96 Wardle collected: Wardle, "A Critical Analysis of Constitutional Claims."

96 The one anti-same-sex-marriage: Herbert W. Titus, "Defining Marriage and the Family," *William & Mary Bill of Rights Journal* 3, no. 1 (1994).

97 Wardle decided that: Wardle, "A Critical Analysis of Constitutional Claims."

97 responsibility to the institution: Kaimipono David Wenger, "The Divine Institution of Marriage: An Overview of LDS Involvement in the Proposition 8 Campaign," *Journal of Civil Rights and Economic Development* 26, no. 3 (Spring 2012): 718–19.

98 Ultimately there was only: Wardle, "A Critical Analysis of Constitutional Claims."

II: Dominos at the Barn Door

99 "This is Lynn Wardle": Dan Harrie, "Bill Drafted to Bolster Ban on Homosexual Marriages," *Salt Lake Tribune,* February 9, 1995.

99 Wardle understood there was: Harrie, "Bill Drafted to Bolster Ban."

100 had been founded: R. Jonathan Moore, *Suing for America's Soul: John Whitehead, The Rutherford Institute, and Conservative Christians in the Courts* (Grand Rapids, MI: William B. Eerdmans Publishing Company, 2007), 35.

100 It took its first interest: Kevin Dayton, "Bill on Gays' Job Rights Draws Fire," *Honolulu Advertiser,* March 18, 1991.

100 third state to enact: Arthur S. Leonard, "Hawaii Makes Three . . . Connecticut Makes Four!" *Lesbian/Gay Law Notes,* May 1991.

100 the president of the Honolulu-based: Mary A. Wilkowski, Esq., "Rutherford Institute Challenges Fledgling Law—and Loses," *Island Lifestyle,* August 1, 1992.

101 Others joined the lawsuit: Joyce Price, "Gay-Rights Law Besieged; Religious Organizations File Suit in Hawaii," *Washington Times,* December 18, 1991.

101 When a local PBS talk show: "A 'Dialog' on Gay Rights," *Honolulu Advertiser,* May 31, 1991.

101 It was evident: Susan Miller, "Supreme Court to Rule on Same-Sex Marriage Rights," *Island Lifestyle,* October 1, 1992.

101 No government lawyer: "Religious Coalition Sues State," *Honolulu Star-Bulletin*, December 17, 1991.

102 In fact, Wardle's method: "Homophobia: Calling It as It Is," *Pillar of the Gay and Lesbian Community: Utah's True Alternative Newspaper*, May 2000.

102 he could just be dismissed: Michael Quinn, "Prelude to the National 'Defense of Marriage' Campaign: Civil Discrimination Against Feared or Despised Minorities," *Dialogue: A Journal of Mormon Thought* 33, no. 3 (September 2001): 1–52.

102 "Heterosexist, yes": Quinn, "Prelude to the National 'Defense of Marriage' Campaign."

102 In February 1995: Dan Harrie, "Gays, Lesbians Set to Fight Marriage Bill," *Salt Lake Tribune*, February 21, 1995.

102 "There are times": "Church Opposes Same-Sex Marriages," *Church News*, March 4, 1995.

103 The lawyer whom the attorney general's office: David Orgon Coolidge, "Same-Sex Marriage: As Hawaii Goes . . . ," *First Things* (April 1997): 33.

103 That inevitable courtroom: Steven Michaels, "State Enforces Whatever Law Is on Books," *Honolulu Advertiser*, November 26, 1995.

103 The legislature had embraced: Peter Rosegg, "Same-Sex Amendment Gaining," *Honolulu Advertiser*, February 9, 1994.

12: A Message from the Presidency

104 Toward the end of morning: Jennifer Skordas, "LDS Church Decries Attempts to Legalize Same-Sex Marriages," *Salt Lake Tribune*, February 14, 1994.

104 local leaders informed: "LDS First Presidency Opposes Legalization of Gay Marriages," *Deseret News*, February 14, 1994.

104 At times, the church used Utah: David E. Campbell, John C. Green, and J. Quin Monson, *Seeking the Promised Land: Mormons and American Politics* (Cambridge, UK: Cambridge University Press, 2014), 146.

104 which the First Presidency rejected: Kristen Moulton, "Anti-MX Missile Stand Surprised Some Mormons, Too," *Salt Lake Tribune*, May 2, 2011.

104 On other occasions: Gerry Avant, "Speaking Out on Moral Issues," *Church News*, June 6, 1992.

104 and to legalize pari-mutuel: "Father Figure: LDS Church Instructs Members How to Vote," *Utah Chronicle*, June 2, 1992.

105 On many of these occasions: Mike Carter, "Utah's Mix of Church and State: Theocratic or Just Homogenized?" Associated Press, January 18, 1993.

105 LDS spokesman Don LeFevre: "LDS First Presidency Opposes Legalization of Gay Marriages," *Deseret News*, February 14, 1994.

105 "The announcement left many": Jennifer Skordas, "LDS Church Decries Attempts to Legalize Same-Sex Marriages," *Salt Lake Tribune*, February 14, 1994.

105 But the *Deseret News:* LeFevre, "LDS First Presidency Opposes Legalization of Gay Marriages."

105 When Mormons did throw: Campbell, Green, and Monson, *Seeking the Promised Land*.

105 These qualities, along with: David E. Campbell and J. Quin Monson, "Dry Kindling," in *From Pews to Polling Places: Faith and Politics in the American Religious Mosaic*, ed. J. Matthew Wilson (Washington, DC: Georgetown University Press, 2007), 105–30.

106 In 1975, as Utah's legislature: Elizabeth Ellen Gordon and William Gillespie, "The Culture of Obedience and the Politics of Stealth: Mormon Mobilization Against ERA and Same-Sex Marriage," *Politics and Religion* 5 (2012): 343–66.

106 the LDS Church declared: D. Michael Quinn, *The Mormon Hierarchy: Origins of Power* (Salt Lake City, UT: Signature Books, 1994).

106 "stifle many God-given feminine instincts": Martha Sonntag Bradley-Evans, *Pedestals and Podiums: Utah Women, Religious Authority, and Equal Rights* (Salt Lake City: Signature Books, 2005), 79.

106 The impact of the newly: Bradley-Evans, *Pedestals and Podiums,* 97.

106 Defeating the ERA in Utah: Bradley-Evans, *Pedestals and Podiums,* 281–329.

106 By 1980, with the deadline: "The Church and the Proposed Equal Rights Amendment: A Moral Issue," *Ensign,* March 1980.

106 Phyllis Schlafly, who led: Richard A. Viguerie, *The New Right: We're Ready to Lead* (Arlington Heights, IL: Viguerie Company, 1981), 131.

106 even, in North Carolina: Quinn, *The Mormon Hierarchy,* 387–88.

106 The American right: Viguerie, *The New Right,* 129.

13: Apostles

108 "With so much of sophistry": Gordon Hinckley, "Lesson 159: The Family: A Proclamation to the World," *LDS,* September 23, 1995.

108 There was, in the purest: Hinckley, "Lesson 159: The Family."

108 It was a recapitulation: David L. Paulsen and Martin Pulido, "A Mother There: A Survey of Historical Teachings about Mother in Heaven," *Brigham Young University Studies* 50, no. 1 (2011).

108 Hinckley was one of Mormonism's: Angelyn N. Hutchinson, "LDS Appoint Third Counselor for Presidency, New Apostle," *Salt Lake Tribune,* June 20, 1981.

109 laying out a Mormon-friendly vision: Gregory A. Prince, *Gay Rights and the Mormon Church: Intended Actions, Unintended Consequences* (Salt Lake City: University of Utah Press, 2019), 52–53.

109 "The family is ordained": Hinckley, "Lesson 159: The Family."

109 At times, he thought it was possible: Gordon Hinckley, "The Family: A Proclamation to the World," *LDS,* September 9, 1995.

109 The president of the LDS Church: Peggy Fletcher Stack, "LDS Transition Prompts Look Forward, Back," *Salt Lake Tribune,* June 4, 1994.

109 The colonnaded Church: "Church Administration Building," *Ensign,* June 1971.

109 In the 1970s: "The New General Church Office Building," *Ensign,* January 1973.

109 It remained, as ever: Douglas D. Palmer, "LDS Mantle of Leadership Shifts to Twelve," *Deseret News,* November 7, 1985.

109 Salt Lake City was settled: Randall Balmer and Jana Riess, eds., *Mormonism and American Politics (Religion, Culture, and Public Life)* (New York: Columbia University Press, 2015).

109 By the time Utah prepared: J. B. Haws, *Mormon Image in the American Mind: Fifty Years of Public Perception* (Oxford, UK: Oxford University Press, 2013), 169.

110 In 1879, the Supreme Court ruled: *Reynolds v. United States,* 98 US 145.

110 In 1890, the LDS Church: *Dialogue: A Journal of Mormon Thought* 1, no. 2 (1966): 36.

110 "Sexual relations are proper": Dallin H. Oaks, "Same-Gender Attraction," *Liahona Magazine of the LDS Church,* March 1996.

110 About a year after: John Dart, "Ezra Taft Benson, Leader of Mormons, Dies at 94," *Los Angeles Times,* May 31, 1994.

110 church president Ezra Taft Benson: Peter Scarlet, "Benson's Death Triggers Shift in Church Quorums," *Salt Lake Tribune,* June 4, 1996.

110 The flyers did not make: "Same-Sex Marriage: Are LDS Gearing Up for a Holy War?" Associated Press, March 26, 1994.

110 Only with the ascension: Scott Taylor, "Timeline: LDS Church's First Presidency, Quorum of the Twelve from 1984 to 2018," *Deseret News,* March 29, 2018.

111 Oaks was a second: Scott Taylor, "A Look at President Dallin H. Oaks, First Counselor in the First Presidency," *Deseret News,* January 16, 2018.

111 In his first year out: Dallin Oaks, *Life's Lessons Learned* (Salt Lake City: Deseret Book Company, 2011), 36.

111 while there, he was both: Robert Gehrke, "LDS Apostle Was Studied for '81 Court," *Salt Lake Tribune,* August 8, 2018.

111 He was the first Mormon: Oaks, *Life's Lessons Learned,* 96.

111 "Throughout the remainder": Oaks, *Life's Lessons Learned,* 98.

111 The materials were exposed: J. B. Haws, *Mormon Image in the American Mind,* 126.

111 "Once we have reached": Oaks, "Same-Gender Attraction."

112 "The Church's position": "Apostle Reaffirms Church's Position on Homosexuality During CBS TV Interview," *Church News,* 1987.

112 A former dean: Ronna Bolante, "Who Is Mike Gabbard?" *Honolulu Magazine,* August 1, 2004.

112 Gabbard called himself: Bolante, "Who is Mike Gabbard?"

112 who associated with: Christopher Neil, "Gay, Lesbian Parade Brings Waves of Pride," *Honolulu Advertiser,* June 30, 1991.

113 The 1989 publication: Leanne Italie, "Heather Has Two (Legal) Mommies Now," Associated Press, March 16, 2015.

113 Gabbard started paying: "Gay Power in Paradise," *Honolulu Magazine,* April 1992.

113 The month *Baehr v. Lewin* was filed: "Getting It Straight," *Honolulu Advertiser,* July 2, 1991.

113 although his greater concern: "Groups Criticize Gay Lifestyle," *Honolulu Advertiser,* June 26, 1991.

113 On the day of the event: Christopher Neil, "Gay, Lesbian Parade Brings Waves of Pride," *Honolulu Advertiser,* June 30, 1991.

113 When the Hawaii Supreme Court issued: Walter Wright and Kris M. Tanahara, "State Will Fight Gay Marriage Ruling," *Honolulu Advertiser,* May 7, 1993.

113 Even though he declared: Wright and Tanahara, "State Will Fight Gay Marriage Ruling."

114 "It's an issue of conscience": Peter Freiberg, "Right-Wing Ad Backfires on Marriage Ban," *Washington Blade,* April 1, 1994.

14: Hawaii's Future Today

115 As was often the case: Tony Semerad, "A Mormon Crusade in Hawaii: Church Aims to End Gay Union," *Salt Lake Tribune,* June 9, 1996.

115 Jack Hoag had been: Jeff Barrus, "Jack Hoag's New Mission," *Hawaii Business,* April 1995.

116 To church leaders: "Richard Bitner Wirthlin, LDS General Authority and Pollster for Ronald Reagan, Dies at 80," *Deseret News,* March 16, 2011.

116 to the broader world: Adam Clymer, "Richard Wirthlin, Pollster Who Advised Reagan, Dies at 80," *New York Times,* March 18, 2011.

116 He was seen by its elders: "Eleven Called to New Church Posts," Associated Press, April 7, 1996.

116 Most give up to twenty hours: David Van Biema, "The Church and Gay Marriage: Are Mormons Misunderstood?" *Time*, June 22, 2009.

117 The city's two newspapers: "Same-Sex Marriages," *Honolulu Star-Bulletin*, November 24, 1995.

117 were editorializing in favor: "Same-Sex Marriage: Commission's Reasonable Plan," *Honolulu Advertiser*, November 19, 1995.

118 "When the Christians": William Kresnak, "More Seasoned, Christian Coalition in a Comeback," *Honolulu Advertiser*, May 8, 1993.

118 A quarter century earlier: Daniel K. Williams, *Defenders of the Unborn: The Pro-Life Movement Before Roe v. Wade* (Oxford, UK: Oxford University Press, 2016), 94.

119 "If someone had told me": Ray Kerrison, "Nightmare in Paradise," *New York Post*, March 7, 1994.

120 The LDS Church had succeeded: Heather Vacek, "The History of Gambling," Center for Christian Ethics at Baylor University, 2011.

120 which had been chartered by: Linda Hosek, "House Crushes Same-Sex Marriage," *Honolulu Star-Bulletin*, April 26, 1994.

122 They succeeded in fending off: Greg Barrett, "Same-Sex Debate—Same Time Next Year," *Honolulu Advertiser*, March 4, 1996.

122 Hawaii's Future Today recruited: Alan Matsuoka, "Put Marriage Issue on Ballot, Say 3 Ex-Govs," *Honolulu Star-Bulletin*, April 3, 1996.

122 To the surprise of LDS officials: William Kresnak, "House: Same-Sex Ban to Voters," *Honolulu Advertiser*, March 6, 1996.

122 One of the reasons for that progress: Robbie Dingeman, "Same-Sex Marriage Opponents Outspend Supporters 5–1," *Honolulu Advertiser*, March 30, 1996.

123 As Rosehill would later confide: Jonathan Goldberg-Hiller, *The Limits to Union: Same-Sex Marriage and the Politics of Human Rights* (Ann Arbor: University of Michigan Press, 2002), 93.

15: Kickoff

124 Gabbard suggested: Mark Siebert, "3,000 Meet to Protest Gay Proposal for School," *Des Moines Register*, January 3, 1995.

124 To the national media: David W. Dunlap, "Opponents of Gay Topics Press Crusade," *New York Times*, October 11, 1995.

125 But to Iowa conservatives: "Radio Host Solicits Money for Anti-Gay Campaign," *Des Moines Register*, July 8, 1995.

125 Horn was known as the westerner: David Colker, "Anti-Gay Video Highlights Church's Agenda," *Los Angeles Times*, February 22, 1993.

125 who had decamped to their state: Edward Walsh, "Gay Rights Debate Leaves Iowans Angry and Divided; Paid Activist from California Helps Energize Des Moines," *Washington Post*, February 18, 1995.

125 with the primary purpose of defeating: Bob Sipchen, "Mission to Iowa Broadens Fight Over Moral Agenda; Man's Crusade Against Gay Issues in School Vote Has National Effect," *Los Angeles Times*, September 4, 1995.

125 who had served for twelve years: Scott Canon, "Christian Conservatives Wield Clout," *Kansas City Star*, October 24, 1995.

125 "If Mr. Wilson wants to be": Chris Bull and John Gallagher, *Perfect Enemies: The*

Religious Right, the Gay Movement, and the Politics of the 1990s (New York: Crown, 1996), 256.

125 Now it was just forty-eight hours: Scott Canon, "Christian Conservatives Wield Clout," *Kansas City Star,* October 24, 1995.

125 the National Campaign to Protect Marriage: Bob Sipchen, "Same-Sex Marriage Moves to Forefront of Cultural Debate," *Los Angeles Times,* April 10, 1996.

125 in Memphis: David Waters, "Religious Right's Successes Made Rally Redundant," *Memphis Commercial Appeal,* January 18, 1996.

125 "I know you can't endorse me": Margalit Fox, "Edward McAteer, Who Empowered Christian Right, Dies at 78," *New York Times,* October 10, 2004.

125 The bond between conservative: Bull and Gallagher, *Perfect Enemies,* 258.

125 The "pro-family movement": Ralph Reed, "Casting a Wider Net: Religious Conservatives Move Beyond Abortion and Homosexuality," *Policy Review,* July 1993.

126 At the Christian Coalition's: Bull and Gallagher, *Perfect Enemies,* 238.

126 in a Baptist church basement: William N. Eskridge Jr. and Christopher R. Riano, *Marriage Equality: From Outlaws to In-Laws* (New Haven: Yale University Press, 2020), 119.

126 Sheldon had seen the opportunity: Bruce Mirken, "Hell Raiser," *LA Reader,* August 2, 1991.

126 "If you destroy the heterosexual ethic": Elaine Herscher, "Women's Suit at Heart of Debate Over Same-Sex Unions," *San Francisco Chronicle,* May 15, 1995.

126 The proposal was seen: Dudley Clendinen and Adam Nagourney, *Out for Good,* 385–88.

126 Like the Defend Our Children initiative: Elise Harris, "Seizing the Initiative," *Out,* November 1994: 104.

126 "We now have another front-burner": Jeffrey Schmalz, "Gay Areas Are Jubilant Over Clinton," *New York Times,* November 5, 1992.

127 By 1995, Sheldon's network: David W. Dunlap, "Minister Brings Anti-Gay Message to the Spotlight," *New York Times,* December 29, 1994.

127 "The blacks, who cannot change": Bull and Gallagher, *Perfect Enemies,* 172.

127 Within months of its 1993 release: Bull and Gallagher, *Perfect Enemies,* 171.

127 But the U.S. Supreme Court threatened: Thaddeus Herrick, "Colorado's Gay Law Model for Outsiders," *Rocky Mountain News,* April 13, 1993.

127 In February 1995: Linda Keen, "High Court to Hear Colorado Case," *Washington Blade,* February 24, 1995.

127 The immediate result of Amendment 2: Bull and Gallagher, *Perfect Enemies,* 104.

127 Measure 9 had been likely: Sally Chew, "Ding, Dong Mabon Calling," *Out,* February 1993.

127 labeling homosexuality: John Gallagher, "The Right's New Strategy," *The Advocate,* July 30, 1992.

127 The "no special rights" rhetoric: Bull and Gallagher, *Perfect Enemies.*

128 "Anyone who's opposed": Bull and Gallagher, *Perfect Enemies,* 168.

128 a reformed Cincinnati pornography addict: Mark Curnutte, "Moral Crusaders: Anti-Porn Group Widens Focus," *Cincinnati Enquirer,* February 13, 1994.

128 funding from Colorado for Family Values: "Wedded to Intolerance: Extremists Lead Nationwide Assault on the Lives of Lesbian and Gay People," Human Rights Campaign, February 3, 1999.

128 While the Cincinnati law: Linda Vacariello, "That Was Then, This Is Now," *Cincinnati Magazine,* May 2004.

128 Colorado's Amendment 2: Jeffrey Rosen, "Disoriented," *New Republic*, October 23, 1995.

128 The most ominous sign: Hadley Arkes, "Gay Marriage and the Courts: *Roe v. Wade* II?" *Weekly Standard*, November 20, 1995.

128 A decision to strike down: Arkes, "Gay Marriage and the Courts: *Roe v. Wade* II?"

129 as an informal adviser: Hadley Arkes, *Natural Rights and the Right to Choose* (New York: Cambridge University Press, 2004), 97.

129 Citing nature as justification: Hadley Arkes, "A Natural Law Manifesto," James Wilson Institute on Natural Rights and the American Founding, 2011.

129 "In traditional marriage": Hadley Arkes, "The Closet Straight," *National Review*, July 5, 1993.

129 He had resigned himself: Hadley Arkes, "Will Hawaii's Imperial Judges Give Us Gay Marriage in 1996?" *American Enterprise*, May 1995.

129 "The Supreme Court is moving": Arkes, "Gay Marriage and the Courts: *Roe v. Wade* II?"

129 Sheldon, a pastor: Bull and Gallagher, *Perfect Enemies*, 177.

129 Arkes's argument that the Hawaii: Arkes, "Gay Marriage and the Courts: *Roe v. Wade* II?"

129 As early as December 1992: Terri Vermuelen, "Religious Group Targets Homosexuals in Ballot Proposal," Associated Press, December 9, 1992.

130 "We're looking at our legal options": Bettina Boxall, "Hawaii Justices Open Door to Legalizing Gay Marriages; Law: State High Court Calls Ban Unconstitutional and Orders a Trial Ruling. Stirs Debate Across U.S.," *Los Angeles Times*, March 26, 1995.

130 Terry was drawn: Ronald Sullivan, "Four Surrender in Use of Fetus Against Clinton," *New York Times*, July 17, 1992.

130 Then Sekulow lifted: Deb Price, "Presidential Hopefuls Promise to Support Iowa Rally Against SSM," *Detroit News*, February 10, 1996.

130 Horn read a letter: Richard L. Berke, "Fight for Religious Right's Votes Turns Bitter," *New York Times*, February 10, 1996.

16: Don & Bob

131 few in Washington noticed that Bob Dole: C. David Kotok and Joe Brennan, "Resolution Against Gay Marriages Wins Support of 6 Candidates," *Omaha World-Herald*, February 11, 1996.

131 Four years earlier: Adam Nagourney, "'Cultural War' of 1992 Moves in from the Fringe," *New York Times*, August 29, 2012.

131 In fact, many of those: Edward Eugene McAteer, interview by David Stricklin and Larry Braidfoot, October 27, 1988, Institute for Oral History, Baylor University, Waco, Texas.

132 He was a freshman: Chris Casteel, "Nickles Skillfully Keeps Moral High Ground," *Daily Oklahoman*, March 30, 1992.

132 When Nickles was thirteen: Chris Casteel, "Religion Influences Nickles's Personal, Political Life," *Daily Oklahoman*, March 29, 1992.

132 He was able to effortlessly project: Casteel, "Religion Influences Nickles's Personal, Political Life."

133 As he rose in politics: Casteel, "Religion Influences Nickles's Personal, Political Life."

133 "How can we be more vocal": Michael Standaert, *Skipping Towards Armageddon: The Politics and Propaganda of the Left Behind Novels and the LaHaye Empire* (New York: Soft Skull Press, 2006), 44.

133 one of the country's first megachurches: Darren Dochuk, *From Bible Belt to Sunbelt: Plain-Folk Religion, Grassroots Politics and the Rise of Evangelical Conservatism* (New York: W. W. Norton and Company, 2012), 301.

133 When a referendum to ban: Standaert, *Skipping Towards Armageddon,* 44.

133 Tim LaHaye's early insistence: Standaert, *Skipping Towards Armageddon,* 44.

133 inspired his peers to renounce: Joel A. Carpenter, *Revive Us Again: The Reawakening of American Fundamentalism* (Oxford, UK: Oxford University Press, 1997), 86.

133 "At the time, I'd never heard": Robert Dreyfuss, "Reverend Doomsday," *Rolling Stone,* January 28, 2004.

134 "He flew under the radar": Dreyfuss, "Reverend Doomsday."

134 With a $10 million annual budget: Jamie Stiehm, "Family Research Council: Conservative Think Tank Raises the Flag of Family Values," *The Hill,* October 25, 1995.

134 One of the group's most valuable relationships: Casteel, "Nickles Skillfully Keeps Moral High Ground."

134 who in 1990 had been elected chairman: Walter Pincus, "Orchestrating, Delegating, Legislating; Policy Lunches Sustain Dole Senate Leadership," *Washington Post,* September 15, 1995.

134 the Republican Policy Committee: Pincus, "Orchestrating, Delegating, Legislating."

135 In the years since Nickles took over: Stiehm, "Family Research Council: Conservative Think Tank Raises the Flag of Family Values."

135 "I don't know where these people": Richard L. Berke, "Dole, Ignoring His Advisers, Lashes Out at Abortion Foe," *New York Times,* June 12, 1996.

135 "What's so smart about it": Jason DeParle, "A Fundamental Problem," *New York Times,* July 14, 1996.

136 Over fifteen years serving alongside: Matthew Rees, "The Dole Next Time," *Weekly Standard,* May 20, 1996.

136 Nickles endorsed Dole early: Rees, "The Dole Next Time."

136 When a newspaper in western Iowa: C. David Kotok and Joe Brennan, "Resolution Against Gay Marriages Wins Support of 6 Candidates," *Omaha World-Herald,* February 11, 1996.

137 One passage written by Michelangelo Signorile: Robert H. Knight, "How Domestic Partnerships and 'Gay Marriage' Threaten the Family," *Insight on the News,* June 1994.

137 "The most subversive action lesbians": Michelangelo Signorile, "Bridal Wave," *Out,* December 1993/January 1994.

137 In February, the Family Research Council: Robert H. Knight, "Gay 'Marriage': Hawaii's Assault on Matrimony," *Family Policy,* February 1996.

137 "If more states strengthen their laws": Knight, "Gay 'Marriage': Hawaii's Assault on Matrimony."

137 But the bill, a Clinton administration priority: "Clinton Signs Family Leave Act," *Congressional Quarterly Almanac,* 1993.

138 showed that only 33 percent: "Same-Sex 'Marriage,'" *Washington Times,* July 13, 1995.

139 "I think character is vitally important": Gretchen Cook, "Dole-Clinton Elec-

tion Battle Shapes Up over Character, Foreign Policy," *Agence France-Presse*, March 11, 1996.

17: The Law Man

141 He had arrived in Washington: Deborah Kalb, "Government by Task Force: The Gingrich Model," *The Hill*, February 22, 1995.

142 He had earned enough chits: Jim Achmutey, "He's Every Inch the Barrister— U.S. Attorney Barr Enjoys 'Great Job,' " *Atlanta Journal-Constitution*, December 18, 1987.

142 "I enjoy defense": Achmutey, "He's Every Inch the Barrister."

142 In 1992, he sought: Angela Webster, "Barr Says Fowler Vulnerable," *Newnan (GA) Times-Herald*, February 1, 1992.

142 but lost in a runoff: Mark Sherman, "Coverdell and Barr Argue Over Abortion," *Atlanta Journal-Constitution*, July 31, 1992.

142 he was too moderate: "Abortion Opponents Unhappy: Not Thrilled with GOP Senate Runoff Choices," Associated Press, August 3, 1992.

142 in messily overlapping ways: Faye Fiore, "A Former Elephant in the Room," *Los Angeles Times*, July 23, 2008.

142 "He came in one night": Achmutey, "He's Every Inch the Barrister."

142 During his Senate primary: Lloyd Grove, "Rep. Barr's New Quest: Impeachment," *Washington Post*, February 10, 1998.

142 "He forgot, for one brief term": Bob Barr, *The Meaning of Is: The Squandered Impeachment and Wasted Legacy of William Jefferson Clinton* (Macon, GA: Stroud and Hall Publishers, 2004), 217.

143 Gingrich had been christening: Deborah Kalb, "Government by Task Force: The Gingrich Model," *The Hill*, February 22, 1995.

143 "This is not a group": Kalb, "Government by Task Force."

143 Hours after being sworn in: Editorial, "The Barr Approach," *LaGrange (GA) Daily News*, January 13, 1995.

143 In the following days: Nita Lelyveld, "Fights on the Horizon: Abortion, School Prayer, Guns, Affirmative Action," Associated Press, April 10, 1995.

143 In the mid-1970s: Adam Winkler, "The Secret History of Guns," *The Atlantic*, September 2011.

144 For the first three months: Lelyveld, "Fights on the Horizon."

145 While at the CIA: Achmutey, "He's Every Inch the Barrister."

145 He proved a diligent lawmaker: "Barr Gets High Score in Congress," *Cedartown (GA) Standard*, February 22, 1996.

145 and as midnight approached: Barr, *The Meaning of Is*, 154.

145 "What has to do with your ability": Faye Fiore, "A Former Elephant in the Room," *Los Angeles Times*, July 23, 2008.

145 Emblazoned *Messiah's Mandate:* Steve Schlissel, "City Singles," *Urban Mission 3* (September 1985).

145 Schlissel was a known rabble-rouser: Gustav Spohn, "Christian Reformed Schism Looms," Religious News Service, December 28, 1991.

145 Schlissel's threat to lead: Daniel J. Lehmann, "Bible May Split Christian Reformed Church," *Chicago Sun-Times*, January 5, 1992.

145 had earned him: Spohn, "Christian Reformed Schism Looms."

146 That summer, Oklahoma congressman Ernest Istook: Andrew Koppelman, "No Fantasy Island," *New Republic*, August 6, 1995.

146 Barr's election, in particular: Hadley Arkes, *Natural Rights and the Right to Choose* (Cambridge, UK: Cambridge University Press, 2004), 102.

146 Arkes proposed adding: Whitney Galbraith, "Merits of Amendment Prohibiting Gay Marriage Debated," *Colorado Springs Gazette Telegraph,* January 1, 1996.

146 That language had been drafted: Hadley Arkes, "Gay Marriage and the Courts: *Roe v. Wade* II?" *Weekly Standard,* November 20, 1995.

146 But merely introducing: Arkes, "Gay Marriage and the Courts: *Roe v. Wade* II?"

147 He was one of only seventeen: Garet Calhoun, "Bob Barr Emerges from Gingrich's Shadow," *Cobb (GA) Chronicle,* January 12, 1996.

147 In February 1996, at the right's: Patrick Armstrong, "Barr Picked as Outstanding Freshman Rep," *Dade County (GA) Sentinel,* February 24, 1996.

147 A six-stop weekend tour: Carey Cornwell, "Barr Bids for Re-Election in Cobb," *Marietta (GA) Daily Journal,* March 31, 1996.

147 In addition to local representatives: "Barr Says He'll Seek Second Term," *Cartersville (GA) Daily Tribune,* March 31, 1996.

147 Governor Zell Miller appeared ready to sign: Greg Hoffman, "Barr's Bill Praised," *Marietta (GA) Daily Journal,* May 9, 1996.

147 "We kept our votes": Don Melvin, "Capitol Notebook; The Political Odd Couple of the Capitol," *Atlanta Journal-Constitution,* March 18, 1996.

149 In the past, federal courts had recognized: Barbara J. Cox, "Same-Sex Marriage and Choice-of-Law; If We Marry in Hawaii, Are We Still Married When We Return Home?" *Wisconsin Law Review* (1994): 1065.

150 "States rights are protected": Hoffman, "Barr's Bill Praised."

18: How a Grievance Becomes a Bill

153 Within months, Largent had demonstrated: Chris Casteel, "Largent's Convention Speech on 'Family Values' Hits Home," *Daily Oklahoman,* August 14, 1996.

153 He also had never been bashful: Jim Myers, "Largent Says Bill Protects Family," *Tulsa World,* May 9, 1996.

153 The subcommittee on the Constitution: Charles Canady, "AP Candidate Bios," Associated Press, November 1994.

154 Just after assuming its chairmanship: Julie Rovner, "'Partial-Birth Abortion': Separating Fact from Spin," National Public Radio, February 21, 2006.

155 On April 18, the *Washington Times:* Paul Bedard, "Clinton Offers New Promises to Gays; Hints He'll Push Legal 'Marriages,'" *Washington Times,* April 18, 1996.

155 The *Times* was the first media organization: Fred Kuhr, "President's Liaison Stops in Boston," *Bay Windows,* March 28, 1996.

155 According to *Bay Windows:* Fred Kuhr, "Marsha Scott: On Marriage, the Military and the '96 Campaign," *Bay Windows,* March 28, 1996.

155 There was good reason: Fred Kuhr, "Marsha Scott: On Marriage, the Military and the '96 Campaign," *Bay Windows,* March 28, 1996.

155 The *Times* report in fact quoted: Bedard, "Clinton Offers New Promises to Gays."

155 describing how disturbed: Alison Mitchell, "Clinton, in Emotional Terms, Explains His Abortion Veto," *New York Times,* December 12, 1996.

156 Canady did not even appear: Casandra Burrell, "Bill Would Prevent Same-Sex Marriages from Becoming Legal," Associated Press, May 8, 1996.

156 One day after the two congressmen: Burrell, "Bill Would Prevent Same-Sex Marriages from Becoming Legal."

156 Less than two weeks after: Linda Greenhouse: "Gay Rights Laws Can't Be Banned, High Court Rules," *New York Times,* May 21, 1996.

156 "seems inexplicable by anything but animus": *Romer v. Evans,* 517 US 620.

157 Even as White House press secretary: Paul Bedard and Brian Blomquist, "Clinton Won't Fight for Gay 'Marriage'; Back Bill to Make Ties Non-Binding," *Washington Times,* May 15, 1996.

157 "He believes this is a time": Ron Fournier, "WH Reiterates Clinton's Opposition to Same-Sex Marriages," Associated Press, May 13, 1996.

157 The previous month's *Washington Times:* Bedard, "Clinton Offers New Promises to Gays."

19: March On, Washington

161 In 1974, New York congresswoman Bella Abzug: "'I Am a Homosexual': The Gay Drive for Acceptance," *Time,* September 9, 1975.

161 But despite strong Democratic control: Chai Feldblum, "The Federal Gay Rights Bill: From Bella to ENDA," in John D'Emilio, William B. Turner, and Urvashi Vaid, eds., *Creating Change: Sexuality, Public Policy, and Civil Rights* (London: St. Martin's Press, 2000), 176.

162 In 1982, both the Human Rights Campaign Fund: Feldblum, "The Federal Gay Rights Bill," 176.

162 leading Ronald Reagan's communications director: Pat Buchanan, "AIDS Disease: It's Nature Striking Back," *New York Post,* May 24, 1983.

162 "nature's revenge": Richard Cohen, "New Hampshire Voters Smelled a Phony, and Bashed Bush," *Reno Gazette-Journal,* February 20, 1992.

162 "I have a vision": Adam Nagourney, "Clinton Reaches Out to Gay Community: 'I Have a Vision, You're Part of It," *USA Today,* May 20, 1992.

162 "It ensured, for the first time": Feldblum, "The Federal Gay Rights Bill," 176.

162 In both 1979 and 1987: Amin Ghaziani, *The Dividends of Dissent: How Conflict and Culture Work in Lesbian and Gay Marches on Washington* (Chicago, IL: University of Chicago Press, 2008).

163 The gathering, activist Robin Tyler promised: Ghaziani, *The Dividends of Dissent.*

163 One of Clinton's first actions: Schmitt, "Challenging the Military; In Promising to End Ban on Homosexuals, Clinton Is Confronting a Wall of Tradition," *New York Times,* November 12, 1992.

163 On the day that Clinton made: Schmitt, "Challenging the Military.

163 As April 25 approached: David Mixner, *Stranger Among Friends* (New York: Bantam Books, 1997), 307.

163 Eric Rosenthal, the Human Rights Campaign: Gary Lee, "Gays Get Reassurance on Military," *Washington Post,* March 27, 1993.

164 That October, three Oklahoma representatives: "Three Oklahoma Congressmen Say They Would Not Hire Homosexuals," Associated Press, October 4, 1993.

164 James Inhofe, who, echoing the debate: Craig Winneker, "Heard on the Hill," *Roll Call,* October 18, 1993.

164 anonymously told the *Washington Post:* Kevin Merida and Kenneth J. Cooper, "Foley Denounces Gay Bias Remarks, Sort Of," *Washington Post,* October 22, 1993.

164 When asked about the controversy: "Foley Backs Lawmakers on Hiring Preferences," *USA Today,* October 22, 1993.

164 It was a position from which he later retreated: Jim Myers, "Foley Joins Gay Flap," *Tulsa World*, October 22, 1993.

166 78 percent of Americans believed: Jeffrey Schmalz, "Poll Finds an Even Split on Homosexuality's Cause," *New York Times*, March 5, 1993.

166 came to stand: Lisa Keen, "Clinton Announces Support for ENDA," *Washington Blade*, October 20, 1995.

167 "It's our top priority right now": Lisa Keen, "State of the Movement: Adrift," *Washington Blade*, October 7, 1994.

20: Fights of the Roundtable

169 "Why do we really want the right to marry, anyway?": Peter Freiberg, "Wolfson Leaves Lambda for Freedom-to-Marry Work," *Washington Blade*, January 30, 2001.

169 The Lambda Legal Defense and Education Fund: Joe Kennedy, "Fulltime Legal Force Zeroes In," *The Advocate*, April 24, 1974.

169 Lambda's mandate was to pursue: Jim Merrett, "America's Gay Legal Crusaders," *The Advocate*, January 29, 1991.

169 When it came time to file: Linda Hirshman, *Victory: The Triumphant Gay Revolution* (New York: HarperCollins Publishers, 2012), 148–49.

169 The Greek character that gave Lambda Legal: Lillian Faderman, *The Gay Revolution: The Story of the Struggle* (New York: Simon & Schuster, 2016), 214.

170 At one such gathering: "Homosexuals in Revolt: The Year That One Liberation Movement Turned Militant," *Life*, December 31, 1971.

170 The icing on the cake: "Homosexuals in Revolt."

170 But even though they borrowed: Rob Cole, "Gay Marriage 'Boom': Suddenly, It's News," *The Advocate*, August 5, 1970.

170 foremost as mothers: Daniel Winunwe Rivers, *Radical Relations: Lesbian Mothers, Gay Fathers, and Their Children in the United States Since World War II* (Chapel Hill: University of North Carolina Press, 2013).

170 It took Sharon Kowalski's car accident: Casey Charles, *The Sharon Kowalski Case: Lesbian and Gay Rights on Trial* (Lawrence: University Press of Kansas, 2003).

170 In 1983, after the twenty-seven-year-old: Karen Thompson, "Why Can't Sharon Kowalski Come Home?" *Sojourner's: The Women's Forum*, October 31, 1986.

171 "If I were her normal spouse": Candy J. Cooper, "Lesbians, Gays 'Wed' En Masse," *San Francisco Examiner*, October 11, 1987.

171 "I would like us to move to an unhooking": Bettina Boxall, "Hawaii Justices Open Door to Legalizing Gay Marriages," *Los Angeles Times*, March 26, 1995.

172 Ettelbrick received an invitation: Nancy Polikoff, "Paula Ettelbrick Dies After a Life of Service to LGBT Rights; NY Times Obit Emphasizes Her Skepticism About Marriage," *Beyond (Straight and Gay) Marriage* (blog), October 7, 2011, beyondstraightandgaymarriage.blogspot.com.

172 Tom Stoddard had become Lambda's: Dudley Clendinen and Adam Nagourney, *Out for Good: The Struggle to Build a Gay Rights Movement in America* (New York: Simon & Schuster, 2001), 528.

172 "It is usually possible": Paula Ettelbrick and Tom Stoddard, "Gay Marriage: A Must or a Bust?" *Out/Look*, September 1989.

172 "I am not naive": Ettelbrick and Stoddard, "Gay Marriage: A Must or a Bust?"

173 "From the standpoint of civil rights": Ettelbrick and Stoddard, "Gay Marriage: A Must or a Bust?"

173 Stoddard and Ettelbrick accepted invitations: William B. Rubenstein, "Divided We Litigate: Addressing Disputes Among Group Members and Lawyers in Civil Rights Campaigns," *Yale Law Journal* 106, no. 6 (April 1997).

173 and jokingly called these: Gabriel Rotello, E. J. Graff, and Doug Ireland, "To Have and to Hold: The Case for Gay Marriage," *The Nation,* June 24, 1996.

173 The group was in the midst: Lisa Keen, "How the Six Top Gay Rights Organizations Measure Up," *Washington Blade,* March 1, 1993.

21: Waiting for a Nightmare

176 "How could abortion rights supporters": David Sobelsohn, "Human, All Too Human: Abortion Law in America," Review of *Doctors of Conscience,* by Carole Joffe, *Journal of Sex Research* 33, no. 2 (1996): 169.

176 Four years later, the Supreme Court: *Roe v. Wade,* 410 US 113.

176 "taking seriously the views": Sobelsohn, "Human, All Too Human," 168–70.

176 "The problem of abortion in America": Sobelsohn, "Human, All Too Human," 168–70.

177 Wolfson's continued upbeat talk: Lyn Stoesen, "Legal Activist: Gay Marriage is Coming," *Washington Blade,* December 8, 1994.

178 In a December memo: Lisa Keen and Lou Chibbaro Jr., "White House in Raging Debate Over Support in Colorado Case," *Washington Blade,* June 2, 1995.

179 they were so well networked: Donald P. Haider-Markel, "Policy Diffusion as a Geographical Expansion of the Scope of Political Conflict: Same-Sex Marriage Bans in the 1990s," *State Politics & Policy Quarterly* 1, no. 1 (March 2001): 5–26.

179 Utah's bill became law: Deb Price, "States Will Lead the Way on Marital Laws," *Detroit News,* April 21, 1995.

179 That May have appeared a useful reprieve: Steve Michaels, "State Enforces Whatever Law is on Books," *Honolulu Advertiser,* November 26, 1995.

179 But in June 1995: Michaels, "State Enforces Whatever Law Is on Books."

180 Controlling the capital's affairs: Dave Weigel, "Meet Jason Chaffetz," *Washington City Paper,* October 1, 2010.

180 When a district court ruled in June 1995: *In re M.M.D.* 662 A.2d 837.

180 But as a presidential candidate: Alan Bernstein, "Dole's Denial Puts Spotlight on Gay Group," *Houston Chronicle,* September 6, 1995.

22: The Rebrander and the Firebrand

182 The prior executive director, Tim McFeeley: David Shribman, "Gay Activists Clash with Dukakis," *Wall Street Journal,* May 26, 1988.

183 "Republicans, as a party": Michael Duffy, "Into the Woods," *The Advocate,* December 27, 1994.

183 "We are living in a complete sea change": David W. Dunlap, "Gay Leaders Resisting Attacks Against Gains," *New York Times,* February 12, 1995.

183 She had come to the Human Rights Campaign Fund: Michelle Levander, "Getting Apple to Extend Benefits Wasn't Easy, Gays Say; Official Response Was Like Punching a Pillow—No Overt Prejudice, Just a Lack of Response," *Austin American-Statesman,* December 19, 1993.

183 When, later that year: David W. Dunlap, "Apple Lawyer Will Become New Director of Gay Group," *New York Times,* November 21, 1994.

183 "This is happening because when gays": Frank Trejo, "Business Lauded for Role

in Guarding Gay Rights—Apple Officer Speaks at 'Coming Out Day' Event," *Dallas Morning News*, October 12, 1994.

183 In September 1991, the software-maker Lotus Development: Thomas A. Stewart, "Gay in Corporate America," *Fortune*, December 16, 1991.

183 already had similar policies: "Health Benefits for Gay Couples Fall Short," *Harvard Crimson*, March 12, 1998.

183 In late 1993, the *Austin American-Statesman:* Levander, "Getting Apple to Extend Benefits Wasn't Easy."

184 "Where Congress and the military": Trejo, "Business Lauded for Role in Guarding Gay Rights."

184 The Corporate Equality Index: Marc Gunther, "Queer Inc.: How Corporate America Fell in Love with Gays and Lesbians," *Fortune*, December 11, 2006.

184 "There's a whole new breed": Robert Bellinger, "Electronics Firms Lead the Way as Gays Push Workplace Issues: 'Domestic-Partner Benefits' Emerge," *Electronic Engineering Times*, November 8, 1993.

185 By the time Birch took command: Lisa Keen, "State of the Movement: Adrift," *Washington Blade*, October 7, 1994.

185 displaced the older, more established: John D'Emilio, "Organization Tales: Interpreting the NGLTF Story," in *The World Turned: Essays on Gay History, Politics, and Culture* (Durham: Duke University Press, 2002), 99–122.

185 "History suggests the access-driven politics": Urvashi Vaid, *Virtual Equality: The Mainstreaming of Gay & Lesbian Liberation* (New York: Anchor Books, 1995), 93.

185 She hired openly gay relatives: Megan Rosenfeld, "Across the Great Divide; For Elizabeth Birch, the Ruling Against Colorado's Anti-Gay Law Opens New Frontiers," *Washington Post*, May 22, 1996.

185 Candace Gingrich, the Speaker's semi-estranged: Katharine Q. Seelye, "Speaker's Sister Now Speaking Out," *New York Times*, March 6, 1995.

185 Chastity Bono, the daughter of Congressman Sonny Bono: Chastity Bono, "Sonny & Chas," *The Advocate*, June 11, 1996.

185 Birch was happy to publicize: Megan Rosenfeld, "Across the Great Divide; For Elizabeth Birch, the Ruling Against Colorado's Anti-Gay Law Opens New Frontiers," *Washington Post*, May 22, 1996.

185 She directed a $5,000 contribution: Lou Chibbaro Jr., "GOP Committee Denounced for Accepting Money," September 8, 1995.

186 In the process of making the donation: Chibbaro Jr., "GOP Committee Denounced for Accepting Money."

186 Politics was about rewarding friends: Barney Frank, "Why Party Politics Matters," *Harvard Gay & Lesbian Review* 3, no. 2 (1996).

186 "'There are worse things than losing elections'": Barney Frank, *Speaking Frankly: What's Wrong with the Democrats and How to Fix It* (New York: Times Books, 1992).

187 He flourished as "a counterpuncher": Claudia Dreifus, "And Then There Was Frank," *New York Times Magazine*, February 4, 1996.

187 Even from an impotent minority: Frank Rich, "Closet Clout," *New York Times*, February 2, 1995.

187 within weeks of becoming House majority leader: Jeff Epperly, "Frank Sees Some Benefits from 'Barney Fag' Brouhaha," *Bay Windows*, February 2, 1995.

187 The fact that he considered: Dreifus, "And Then There Was Frank."

187 graver words than he'd had: Lou Chibbaro Jr., "Barney Frank Heads Off a Smear Effort Against Foley," *Washington Blade*, June 9, 1989.

187 "I feel, 'Boy, this is a moral opportunity' ": Dreifus, "And Then There Was Frank."

187 after she published a lighthearted column: Mary McGrory, "Boston Baked Washington," *Washington Post*, May 2, 1993.

187 To gay activists, Frank: Jeffrey Toobin, "Barney's Great Adventure," *New Yorker*, January 12, 2009.

187 He and Gerry Studds had been: Fred Contrada, " 'Coming Out' Less Harmful for Gay, Lesbian Politicians," *Springfield (MA) Republican*, July 29, 1990.

188 In fact, Frank credited: Barney Frank, "American Immigration Law: A Case Study in the Effective Use of the Political Process," in *Creating Change: Sexuality, Public Policy, and Civil Rights*, ed. John D'Emilio, William B. Turner, and Urvashi Vaid (New York: St. Martin's Press, 2000), 209.

188 "Before I came out": Barney Frank, "American Immigration Law," 226.

188 "The N.R.A. doesn't have demonstrations": Dreifus, "And Then There Was Frank."

188 "You see this now": Dreifus, "And Then There Was Frank."

189 Birch also reached into: J. Jennings Moss, "Slick Imaging," *The Advocate*, January 21, 1997.

189 "This is what you write": Alexandra Chasin, *Selling Out: The Gay and Lesbian Movement Goes to Market* (London: Palgrave Macmillan, 2001).

190 "Moreover, the Republican field is increasingly": Elizabeth Birch, "Clinton: The Clear Choice," *Human Rights Campaign Quarterly* (February 1996): 2.

190 The article, "Why Party Politics Matters": Frank, "Why Party Politics Matters."

191 "Giving $5,000 to the entity": Frank, "Why Party Politics Matters."

23: Smooth Sailing

192 "Later on TalkBack": Transcript, "Talk Back Live," hosted by Miles O'Brien, CNN, March 27, 1996.

192 CNN's guest for the Hawaii segment: Transcript, "Talk Back Live."

193 The organization didn't endorse a candidate: Deborah Lashman, "Human Rights Campaign Fund Endorses Clinton," *Out in the Mountains*, July 1992.

194 A year earlier, a White House memo: Sara Miles, "Between Little Rock and a Hard Place," *The Advocate*, April 1996.

194 "To me, the straight white boys": J. Jennings Moss, "Wedding Bell Blues," *The Advocate*, May 14, 1996.

195 "The military resented the intrusion": George Stephanopoulos, *All Too Human* (Boston: Back Bay Books, 2000), 128.

195 "Probably would be o.k.": Gwen Ifill, "President Chooses Breyer, an Appeals Judge in Boston, for Blackmun's Court Seat," *New York Times*, May 14, 1995.

195 Jimmy Carter had a staffer: John L. Mitchell, "Midge Costanza: Carter Aide Recalls Life in the Fishbowl," *Los Angeles Times*, January 26, 1985.

195 In 1995, Clinton selected deputy assistant: David W. Dunlap, "Clinton Names First Liaison to Gay and Lesbian Groups," *New York Times*, June 14, 1995.

195 Her first day on the job: Lisa Keen and Lou Chibbaro Jr., "Clinton Admin Wrestlers Over Colo. Input," *Washington Blade*, June 1, 1995.

196 the National Gay and Lesbian Task Force was planning: Denise Cowie, "A Conciliatory Negotiator Who Gets What She Wants," *Philadelphia Inquirer*, May 2, 1996.

197 Over the course of the year: Paul Bedard, "Clinton Offers New Promises to Gays; Hints He'll Push Legal 'Marriages,' " *Washington Times*, April 18, 1996.

197 one of five gay leaders: Lou Chibbaro Jr., "Clinton, Gays Meet," *Washington Blade,* April 5, 1996.

24: Endangered Liaisons

199 A day before, Elizabeth Birch had been doing: Transcript, "Talk Back Live," hosted by Miles O'Brien, CNN, March 27, 1996.

199 Two months later, when *Newsweek* followed up: Anne Underwood and Bruce Shenitz with Karen Springen, "Do You, Tom, Take Harry," *Newsweek,* December 11, 1995.

200 "The president doesn't think": Underwood and Shenitz with Springen, "Do You, Tom, Take Harry."

200 In December, after Hawaii's Commission: Lisa Keen, "Hawaii Panel Recommends Gay Marriage," *Washington Blade,* December 1, 1995.

200 The New York Court of Appeals had recently: Sherrie E. Nachman, "Winning Adoption Rights for Unmarried Couples," *American Lawyer,* January 1996.

200 who withdrew a job offer: Patricia A. Cain, *Rainbow Rights: The Role of Lawyers and Courts in the Lesbian and Gay Civil Rights Movement* (Boulder, CO: Westview Press, 2000), 217.

200 In late January, a Republican: "Trouble Ahead for Some Nontraditional Home Loans; The Limitations are 'Bigoted Nonsense' Says One Critic," *Norfolk Virginian-Pilot,* January 24, 1996.

200 amended its lending standards: Albert Eisenberg, letter to the editor, "Virginia Housing Law Shift Involves Issue of Fairness," *Washington Times,* July 7, 1994.

200 to replace the word *household:* Sue Robinson, "Housing Eligibility Limited; Board Disallows Single Pairs, Gays," *Roanoke Times & World,* January 24, 1996.

200 thereby making gay and lesbian couples: Peter Baker, "Defying Allen, Panel Approves Home Loans to Unrelated Couples," *Washington Post,* June 22, 1994.

203 When the reporter, Josh Moss: J. Jennings Moss, "Wedding Bell Blues," *The Advocate,* May 14, 1996.

203 In mid-April, when the *Washington Times:* Paul Bedard, "Clinton Offers New Promises to Gays; Hints He'll Push Legal 'Marriage,'" *Washington Times,* April 18, 1996.

25: Two Weeks in May

204 She believed there was room: Frank Rich, "A Gay-Rights Victory Muffled," *New York Times,* May 22, 1996.

205 The military experience weighed heavily: George Stephanopoulos, *All Too Human* (Boston: Back Bay Books, 2000), 128.

206 The claim that gay-rights initiatives: Transcript, "Crossfire" CNN, hosted by John Sununu and Michael Kinsley, September 23, 1992.

208 Since starting her job: David W. Dunlap, "Clinton Names First Liaison to Gay and Lesbian Groups," *New York Times,* June 14, 1995.

210 Dick Morris, an on-and-off: Glenn F. Bunting and Alan C. Miller, "Clinton's Trusted Gatekeeper," *Los Angeles Times,* January 24, 1998.

210 The self-appointed guardian: Dick Morris, *Behind the Oval Office: Getting Reelected Against All Odds* (Kent, UK: Renaissance Books, 1998), 231.

211 The bill was coursing through: Adam Nagourney, "Christian Coalition Pushes for Showdown on Same-Sex Marriage," *New York Times,* May 30, 1996.

26. Dear Friends

212 As soon as Mike McCurry announced: Laura Meckler, "Clinton Would Sign Legislation Outlawing Gay Marriages," Associated Press, May 23, 1996.

27. An Election-Year Baseball Bat

217 "This is a time to fortify the community": Warren P. Strobel, "Clinton Signals He'd Support Curb on Same-Sex Marriage; Spokesman Says President Would Sign House Bill," *Washington Times,* May 23, 1996.

218 To the Associated Press, Birch called it: Rob Peecher, "Barr: Bill Doesn't Outlaw Same-Sex Marriage," *(Carrollton) Times-Georgian,* May 9, 1996.

219 A *Newsweek* poll showed: "58% Oppose Legally-Sanctioned Gay Marriages," *Newsweek,* May 24, 1996.

220 In 1992, the inclusion of the word: J. Jennings Moss, "Off Camera: G&L Dems Vocal—But Not Visible—a Convention," *The Advocate,* October 10, 1996.

28. When the Deal Goes Down

221 When a year and a half later: David W. Dunlap, "Some Gay Rights Advocates Question Drive to Defend Same-Sex Marriage," *New York Times,* June 7, 1996.

221 The front page of the June 7: Lisa Keen, "Anti-Gay Train May Carry Pro-Gay Cargo," *Washington Blade,* June 7, 1996.

221 "If you can't stop the freight train": Keen, "Anti-Gay Train May Carry Pro-Gay Cargo."

222 It would likely take another month: Jerry Gray, "House Passes Bar to U.S. Sanction of Gay Marriage," *New York Times,* July 15, 1996.

223 With the outcome in the House: Cheryl Wetzstein, "House Vote Backs Traditional Wedlock; Debate on Gays Ends with 342–67 Tally," *Washington Times,* July 13, 1996.

223 HRC political director Daniel Zingale: Chai Feldblum, "The Federal Gay Rights Bill: From Bella to ENDA," in John D'Emilio, William B. Turner, and Urvashi Vaid, eds., *Creating Change: Sexuality, Public Policy, and Civil Rights* (London, UK: St. Martin's Press, 2000), 148.

223 They did not need to guarantee: Feldblum, "The Federal Gay Rights Bill."

224 A poll taken by *Newsweek* in May: *Newsweek* poll, "Gay Rights & the Supreme Court Decision," Princeton Survey Research Associates, May 24, 1996.

224 "Is the strategy plausible?": Keen, "Anti-Gay Train May Carry Pro-Gay Cargo."

225 When Sam Gejdenson, who in 1994: Kenneth J. Cooper, "Court Declares Democrat Won in Connecticut," *Washington Post,* December 17, 1994.

225 from safe liberal districts: Gregory B. Lewis and Jonathan L. Edelson, "DOMA and ENDA: Congress Votes on Gay Rights," in *The Politics of Gay Rights,* ed. Craig Rimmerman, Kenneth Wald, and Clyde Wilcox (Chicago: University of Chicago Press, 2000), 203–11.

225 Frank had a long-standing belief: Barney Frank, "American Immigration Law: A Case Study in the Effective Use of the Political Process," in *Creating Change: Sexuality, Public Policy, and Civil Rights,* ed. John D'Emilio, William B. Turner, and Urvashi Vaid (New York: St. Martin's Press, 2000), 225.

225 "Does the fact that I love": Cheryl Wetzstein, "DOMA Spurs Partisan Hill Debate," *Washington Times,* July 12, 1996.

225 the openly gay Steve Gunderson: Andrew Holleran, "Coming-Out Party," Review of *House and Home* by Steve Gunderson, *New York Times Book Review*, August 18, 1996.

226 "All closeted gay and lesbian members": David W. Dunlap, "A Republican Congressman Discloses He Is a Homosexual," *New York Times*, August 3, 1996.

226 On the eve of the House vote: Cassandra Burrell, "Sponsors of SSM Bill Don't Want Amendments," Associated Press, July 16, 1996.

226 Don Nickles, who had ascended: Christina Leonard, "Nickles at Dole's Beck, Call," *Tulsa World*, August 7, 1996.

228 If Kennedy could muster: Carolyn Lochhead, "Vote Stalled on Gay Marriages," *San Francisco Chronicle*, September 5, 1996.

228 When majority leader Trent Lott: Eric Schmitt, "Senate Weighs Bill on Gay Rights on the Job," *New York Times*, September 7, 1996.

229 "The House is a long shot": Schmitt, "Senate Weighs Bill on Gay Rights on the Job."

229 The one vote that kept: Melissa Healy, "Senate OKs Bill Against SSM," *Los Angeles Times*, September 10, 1996.

229 who was at a Little Rock hospital: Terry Lemons, "Senate Votes to Bar Same-Sex Marriages," *Arkansas Democrat-Gazette (Little Rock)*, September 10, 1996.

229 where his thirty-three-year-old son Mark: Aaron Sarlo, "Mark Pryor's Long Shadow," *Arkansas Times*, January 24, 2003.

29. Midnight Cowboy

232 "We came within a breath": John E. Yang, "Senate Backs Gay-Marriage Ban," *Chicago Sun-Times*, September 11, 1996.

234 Air Force One had just landed: "Tickets Required for Clinton Rally in Brandon," Associated Press, September 18, 1996.

234 and the Clintons were en route: "Clinton Plans to Attend Brandon Rally Ahead of High School Football Game," Associated Press, September 18, 1996.

234 As the president and first lady: Bob von Sternberg, "South Dakota Town Abuzz as Clinton Pays a Call," *Minneapolis Star-Tribune*, September 21, 1996.

235 those in the press area: Terence Hunt, "Clinton: Gay Marriage Law No Excuse for Anti-Gay Discrimination," Associated Press, September 20, 1996.

235 The signing statement didn't offer: Peter Baker, "Bill Clinton's Decision, and Regret, on Defense of Marriage Act," *New York Times*, March 25, 2013.

235 The early wire-service stories: Hunt, "Clinton: Gay Marriage Law No Excuse."

235 written before Clinton had even: "Clinton to Sign Ban on Same-Sex Marriages," Reuters, September 21, 1996.

235 "The late-night announcement": Hunt, "Clinton: Gay Marriage Law No Excuse."

235 a bill to double the length: Todd S. Purdum, "Gay Rights Groups Attack Clinton on Midnight Signing," *New York Times*, September 22, 1996.

236 The *Washington Post* noted prominently: Peter Baker, "President Quietly Signs Law Aimed at Gay Marriages," *Washington Post*, September 22, 1996.

236 The *New York Times*'s story was headlined: Purdum, "Gay Rights Groups Attack Clinton."

236 a White House spokeswoman, Mary Ellen Glynn: Baker, "President Quietly Signs Law."

237 The ad "is a mistake": Paul Bedard, "For Christian Radio, Clinton Changes Tune on Gays, Abortion," *Washington Times*, October 16, 1996.

237 A Dole campaign spokesman crowed: "Ad Touts Clinton's Opposing Gay Marriage," Associated Press, October 15, 1996.

237 the campaign replaced the ad: Howard Kurtz, "Clinton Ad Touting Defense of Marriage Is Pulled," *Washington Post*, October 17. 1996.

30. Trial at Honolulu

238 "In a few years when we all have": Elizabeth Birch, "1996 Through the Lens of History: A Year of Great Hope and Progress," *OUTlines: The Voice of the Gay and Lesbian Community*, January 1997.

238 "First, 1996 was the year": Birch, "1996 Through the Lens of History."

238 Hawaii was not yet done: Susan Essoyan, "Hawaiian Wedding Bells Ring Alarm Bells," *Los Angeles Times*, September 9, 1996.

238 The first day of the *Baehr v. Miike* trial: Ken Kobayashi, "Trial Tackles Same-Sex Controversy," *Honolulu Advertiser*, September 11, 1996.

238 The spate of cases: Jason Pierceson, *Same-Sex Marriage in the United States: The Road to the Supreme Court* (Lanham, MD: Rowman & Littlefield, 2013), 97.

238 In 1971, a Kentucky county judge: William N. Eskridge Jr. and Christopher R. Riano, *Marriage Equality: From Outlaws to In-Laws* (New Haven: Yale University Press, 2020), 20–21.

239 From the outset: Kobayashi, "State Bases Same-Sex Case on Children."

239 After the first day of crowded bleachers: Ken Kobayashi, "Bleachers Empty at Same-Sex Trial," *Honolulu Advertiser*, September 15, 1996.

239 Among the parade: Linda Hosek and Helen Altonn, "Expert: Untraditional Family Burdens Kids," *Honolulu Star-Bulletin*, September 11, 1996.

239 those doing so on the plaintiffs' behalf: Ken Kobayashi, "State Rests Same-Sex Case," *Honolulu Advertiser*, September 14, 1996.

240 Even as Foley declared: Ken Kobayashi, "State Appeal on Same-Sex a Long Shot," *Honolulu Advertiser*, December 5, 1996.

240 One prominent booster: Mike Yuen, "Gay Marriage Fighters List Endorsements," *Honolulu Star-Bulletin*, October 25, 1996.

240 In November's general election: Robbie Dingeman, "Slom Upsets Ikeda as GOP Gains in House," *Honolulu Advertiser*, November 6, 1996.

240 In several instances, the challengers: Mike Yuen, "Gay Marriage Fighters List Endorsements," *Honolulu Star-Bulletin*, October 25, 1996.

240 The day after Chang's decision: Ken Kobayashi, "Gay Marriages Upheld," *Honolulu Advertiser*, December 4, 1996.

240 The following month, as they returned: Jim Witty, "Senate Erupts as Gay-Marriage Debate Heats Up," *Honolulu Star-Bulletin*, February 5, 1997.

240 Another set of bills cleared the way: Angela Miller, "House OKs Same-Sex Measure," *Honolulu Advertiser*, January 24, 1997.

242 Such complacency "snatched defeat": Gabriel Rotello, "Too Little, Too Late?" *The Advocate*, June 24, 1997.

242 "After the election": Rotello, "Too Little, Too Late?"

242 According to a *Honolulu Star-Bulletin* survey: "Voters Strongly Oppose Gay Unions," *Honolulu Star-Bulletin*, February 24, 1997.

242 The *Star-Bulletin* poll two months earlier: "Voters Strongly Oppose Gay Unions."

243 When paired with legislative support: William Kresnak, "Accord Reached on Same-Sex Bills," *Honolulu Advertiser,* April 18, 1997.

243 "HRC aired a last-minute TV commercial": Rotello, "Too Little, Too Late?"

243 Just before their session expired: Harold Morse, "Time Crucial in Wording of Same-Sex Ballot Item," *Honolulu Star-Bulletin,* April 20, 1997.

243 In November 1998, voters would be asked: Mike Yuen, "New Isle PAC Hopes to Derail Gay Marriages," *Honolulu Star-Bulletin,* November 13, 1997.

243 "It'll be the World Series": Jess Christensen and William Kresnak, "Same-Sex Dispute Isn't Going Away," *Honolulu Advertiser,* April 18, 1997.

243 The most optimistic conclusion: "Gay Groups Preparing to Wage War in Hawaii," *Washington Blade,* June 20, 1997.

31. Shameless Agitator

247 These efforts culminated: Edward T. McHugh, "Senate OKs Gay Rights Bill 17 Years After First Proposed; Differences in Senate and House Versions May Stall Passage," *Worcester (MA) Telegram & Gazette,* October 12, 1989.

247 a version of which: Stuart E. Weisberg, *Barney Frank: The Story of America's Only Left-Handed, Gay, Jewish Congressman* (Amherst: University of Massachusetts Press, 2009).

247 "shows we can win": Chris Bull, "The Inside Story on the Massachusetts Rights Bill," *The Advocate,* December 19, 1989.

247 "shameless agitator": "Lesbians and Gays Honored," *Apex: A Point of Departure* 1, no. 2 (March 1992).

248 Among the matters awaiting her: David J. Garrow, "Toward a More Perfect Union," *New York Times Magazine,* May 9, 2004.

249 "The company sent telexes": Kay Longcope, "Gay Couples Fight for Spousal Rights," *Boston Globe,* March 4, 1991.

249 In June 1992, the Massachusetts Supreme Judicial Court: *Reep v. Commissioner of the Department of Employment & Training,* 412 Mass. 845.

249 Reep and Kurnit had been together: Doris Sue Wong, "Court Rules Live-in Partner May Collect Jobless Benefits," *Boston Globe,* June 12, 1992.

249 "urgent, compelling or necessitous": Mary Bonauto, "*Goodridge* in Context," *Harvard Civil Rights—Civil Liberties Law Review* 40 (2005): 16.

249 After drafting the brief: *IN Newsweekly,* "GLAD Worried Case Involving Unmarried Straight Couple May Hurt Domestic Partners," February 4, 1992.

250 In 1993, Bonauto agreed to represent: Marla R. Van Schuyver, "Waltham Private School Is Target of Lesbian Teacher's MCAD Suit," *Boston Globe,* August 31, 1993.

250 "I lost my job because": "District News Roundup," *Education Week,* September 22, 1993.

250 "nothing in this act shall be construed": Arthur S. Leonard, "Mass. Commission Rejects Lesbian's Claim Against School," *Lesbian/Gay Law Notes,* October 1994.

251 Rhode Island had the most favorable case law: *Chace, Petitioner,* 26 R.I. 351.

251 when the state's supreme court upheld: *State v. Lopes,* 660 A.2d 707.

252 Three years later, Rhode Island's legislature: "Timeline: Gay and Lesbian History in Rhode Island, and Nationally," *Providence Journal,* July 27, 2014.

252 record of interpreting state laws: Mary L. Bonauto, "Equality and the Impossible—State Constitutions and Marriage," *Rutgers University Law Review* 68, no. 4 (Summer 2016): 1499–1504.

32. Queer Town Meetings

255 the Vermont Supreme Court issued its own: *In re B.L.V.B,* 160 Vt. 368 (Vt. 1993).

255 "Some people say this is about": Doris Sue Wong, "Vt. Court Rules Woman May Adopt Children of Her Lesbian Partner," *Boston Globe,* June 19, 1993.

255 Indeed, the facts of the Vermont case: Deborah Lashman, "Second Parent Adoption: A Personal Perspective," *Duke Journal of Gender Law & Policy* 2 (Spring 1995): 227–32.

256 "Not only will this provide uniformity": "2 Gay Adoption Cases Go to Appeals Courts," *New York Times,* April 18, 1993.

256 the case's sole amicus brief: Carol Hinchey, "Supreme Court Approves Second Parent Adoption," *Out in the Mountains,* July–August 1993.

256 That December, Ettelbrick traveled: Carrie Coy, "Creating Crowds; Hundreds Turn Out for Conference," *Out in the Mountains,* January 1994.

256 A year earlier, the state's legislature passed: Deborah Lashman, "Civil Rights Bill Signed," *Out in the Mountains,* June 1992.

256 "Chittenocentrism": Paul Olsen "Creating Crowds II; A Queer Town Meeting," *Out in the Mountains,* January 1995.

257 "shared an opinion that the": Coy, "Creating Crowds."

257 The bill had a number of provisions: David Moats, *Civil Wars: A Battle for Gay Marriage* (Orlando: Harcourt, Inc., 2004), 98.

258 "That was the sort of firm": Scott Barclay and Anna-Maria Marshall, "Supporting a Cause, Developing a Movement, and Consolidating a Practice: Cause Lawyers and Sexual Orientation Litigation in Vermont," in *The Worlds Cause Lawyers Make: Structure and Agency in Legal Practice,* ed. Austin Sarat and Stuart Scheingold (Stanford, CA: Stanford University Press, 2005), 178.

258 "It's a small state": Barclay and Marshall, "Supporting a Cause, Developing a Movement, and Consolidating a Practice," 178.

258 "Unlike other locales, Vermont never developed": Mary Bernstein, "The Contradictions of Gay Ethnicity: Forging Identity in Vermont," in *Social Movements: Identity, Culture, and the State,* ed. David S. Meyer et al. (New York: Oxford University Press, 2002), 91.

259 One of the few venues that fit: Kate Ratcliff, "Andrews Inn in Historical and Cultural Context," Andrews Inn Oral History Project, Out in the Open, date unknown.

259 The inn closed in 1984: Harmony Birch, "Unveiling the History Behind the Andrews Inn," *Brattleboro (VT) Reformer,* June 13, 2017.

259 As in many rural states, uncommonly low prevalences: *HIV/AIDS Surveillance Year-End Report,* January 1991 (Atlanta: U.S. Department of Health and Human Services, Public Health Service Centers for Disease Control), 6.

259 developing the political and social-service organizations: Jami K. Taylor, Donald P. Haider-Markel, and Benjamin Rogers, "Toward a New Measure of State-Level LGBT Interest Group Strength," *State Politics & Policy Quarterly* 19, no. 3 (September 2019): 339.

259 failed 1986 campaign to add: Meg Dennison, "Propositions '86: Vermont ERA Appears to Be Defeated," Associated Press, November 5, 1986.

259 more likely to see their closest: Mary Bernstein, "The Contradictions of Gay Ethnicity: Forging Identity in Vermont," in *Social Movements: Identity, Culture, and the State,* ed. David S. Meyer et al. (New York: Oxford University Press, 2002), 91.

259 wedding announcement that had appeared: "Couples: Rivers-McMahon," *Burlington Free-Press,* August 28, 1994.

259 Earlier that month, Pasha and Penny: "Wife and Wife: One Couple Fights for the Right to Marry," *Out in the Mountains,* May 1995.

259 The couple instead sought out: Molly Walsh, "Woman & Wife," *Burlington Free Press,* January 8, 1995.

259 under David Sentelle: Lisa Keen, "Vermont Argument Wednesday," *Washington Blade,* November 13, 1998.

259 her adolescent hero, Atticus Finch: Anne Galloway, "Gay Marriage Activist Named to Vermont Supreme Court," *VTDigger,* October 18, 2011. www.vtdigger .org.

260 She took a two-thirds salary cut: David Moats, *Civil Wars: A Battle for Gay Marriage* (Orlando: Harcourt, Inc., 2004), 100.

260 One formative experience was a course: Barclay and Marshall, "Supporting a Cause, Developing a Movement, and Consolidating a Practice," 178.

260 campaigning to restrict or ban: Andrea Dworkin and Catharine MacKinnon, *Pornography and Civil Rights: A New Day for Women's Equality* (Minneapolis: Organizing Against Pornography, 1988), 31.

260 Robinson recalled soaping: Beth Robinson, "The Road to Inclusion for Same-Sex Couples: Lessons from Vermont," *Seton Hall Constitutional Law Journal* 11, no. 237 (2001): 246.

260 "The Legislature contemplated": Abbey Duke and Nancy Remsen, "Vermont Court at Center Stage," *Burlington Free Press,* October 10, 1999.

260 Based on that conclusion, state officials: David Cole, *Engines of Liberty: The Power of Citizen Activists to Make Constitutional Law* (New York: Basic Books, 2016), 33.

261 "We also strongly believe that the institution": Bernstein, "The Contradictions of Gay Ethnicity," 102.

33. Marriage 101

264 By May, the statehouse had inadvertently: "Legislature Unexpectedly Confronts Gay Marriage," *Out in the Mountains,* May 1996.

264 In every other instance, the law spoke: Fred Kuhr, "In Vermont, Three Local Couples Sue for Right to Marry," *Bay Windows,* July 31, 1997.

264 On June 15, the day of the parade: Sona Iyengar, "Gay Couples Fight for Marriage Rights," *Burlington Free Press,* June 15, 1996.

265 "transplants from the flatlands": "Marriage Video in Production," *Out in the Mountains,* June 1996.

266 which would be held in Brattleboro: Hugh Coyle, "Coalition Holds 'Our Town Meeting,'" *Out in the Mountains,* December 1996.

34. Anything But the Slam-Dunk Cases

268 "feel good about empowering": West Johnson, "Legal Ease," *Seven Days,* May 19, 2010.

268 After a 1982 merger: Johnson, "Legal Ease."

270 "As the states' independent constitutional": David Schuman, "Right to Equal Privileges and Immunities: A State's Version of Equal Protection, The Symposium on the Revolution in State Constitutional Law," *Vermont Law Review* 13, no. 221 (1988): 1.

271 In February 1997, the Vermont Supreme Court: Diane Derby, "School Funding Unconstitutional; High Court Rules Rich-Poor Town System Is Unfair," *Rutland (VT) Daily Herald,* February 6, 1997.

271 "The conclusion becomes inescapable": *Brigham v. State,* 166 Vt. 246.

271 As a result, three couples went: David Moats, *Civil Wars: A Battle for Gay Marriage* (Orlando: Harcourt, Inc., 2004), 107–108.

272 On July 22, 1997, Bonauto stood: Peter S. Canellos, "Vt. Gays Sue for Right to Marry," *Boston Globe,* July 22, 1997.

272 "We are challenging the notion": Moats, *Civil Wars,* 108.

35. Baker v. State

273 A California transplant who worked: William N. Eskridge Jr., *Equality Practice: Civil Unions and the Future of Gay Rights* (New York: Routledge, 2002), 47.

273 "nudged me to go home": Stannard Baker, "A Civil Right," *Swarthmore College Bulletin,* July 2014.

273 "Chase Manhattan Bank married us": Christopher Moes, "Marriage Battle Moves to Green Mountains," *Out in the Mountains,* September 1997.

273 Another, Lois Farnham and Holly Puterbaugh: Eskridge Jr., *Equality Practice,* 43–44.

274 Nina Beck and Stacy Jolles: *Out in the Mountains,* "State Files Response to Marriage Suit," December 1997.

274 On the day of the press conference: David Moats, *Civil Wars: A Battle for Gay Marriage* (Orlando: Harcourt, Inc., 2004), 109.

274 Noah had suffered from circulatory: Wendy Johnson, "Love Not Law, Made This Family," *Washington Blade,* date unknown.

274 "At least we have": "All Eyes on Vermont," *Frontiers,* December 25, 1998.

274 "I started this case": "State Files Response to Marriage Suit," *Out in the Mountains,* December 1997.

274 They dedicated a small maple: Moats, *Civil Wars,* 109.

274 "All we want to talk about": "State Files Response to Marriage Suit."

275 "it's probably equally likely that three years": Kim Howard, "AG Sorrell Speaks," *Out in the Mountains,* November 1997.

275 By summoning a reporter: Howard, "AG Sorrell Speaks."

275 "if we had taken a poll": Moats, *Civil Wars,* 126.

275 "a Vermont-style lawsuit where": Howard, "AG Sorrell Speaks."

276 In December, Judge Linda Levitt: Fred Kuhr, "Trial Judge Throws Out Vermont's Gay Marriage Case," *Bay Windows,* January 8, 1998.

276 "The State has an inherent interest": Diane Derby, "In Gay Marriage Case, Arguments Become Extreme," Vermont Press Bureau, November 30, 1997.

276 "Married Couples Do Not Necessarily": Mary Bonauto, Susan M. Murray, and Beth Robinson, "The Freedom to Marry for Same-Sex Couples: The Opening Appellate Brief of Plaintiffs Stan Baker Et Al. In *Baker Et Al. V. State of Vermont,*" *Michigan Journal of Gender and Law* 5, no. 409 (1999).

277 "When social mores change": *In re B.L.V.B,* 160 Vt. 368 (Vt. 1993).

277 previously a civil-rights attorney: Moats, *Civil Wars,* 97.

277 Anticipating such a turnout: Ross Sneyd, "Justices Seem to Lean Against Marriage Ban," Associated Press, November 27, 1998.

277 By 7:45 a.m., nearly three hours: Greg Johnson, "Vermont Civil Unions: The New Language of Marriage," *Vermont Law Review* 25, no. 1 (Fall 2000): 32.

277 "the most closely watched opinion": *Baker v. State,* 170 Vt. 194.

277 The stakes for the rest: Lois R. Shea, "Same-Sex Marriage Hopes Go North," *Boston Globe,* November 17, 1998.

277 Unlike when *Baker v. State* had first been filed: Scott A. Giordano, "Will Vermont Be the First to OK Gay Marriage?" *Bay Windows,* November 12, 1998.

277 Less than two weeks before: "Same-Sex Marriages Banned by Voters," Associated Press, November 4, 1998.

278 Robinson faced an encouraging reminder: Lisa Keen, "Tradition Versus Progress," *Washington Blade,* November 20, 1998.

278 In 1948, that court had confronted: *Perez v. Sharp,* 32 Cal.2d 711.

278 "basic civil right . . . fundamental": *Loving v. Virginia,* 388 US 1.

280 "special protection of the economic health": *State v. Ludlow Supermarkets, Inc.,* 141 Vt. 261.

36. The Remedy

281 Every Friday was a "decision day": David Moats, *Civil Wars: A Battle for Gay Marriage* (Orlando: Harcourt, Inc., 2004), 1–2.

281 where rainbow flags and multicolored balloons: Heather Stephenson, "Couples Say, 'There's No Stopping Us Now,'" *Barre Montpelier (VT) Times Argus,* December 21, 1999.

281 Still, Murray and Robinson were not: Moats, *Civil Wars,* 4.

281 "confusing mixture of joy and despondency": Linda Hollingdale, *Creating Civil Unions: Opening Hearts and Minds* (Hinesburg, VT: Common Humanity Press, 2002), 134.

281 "the most difficult day of my professional life": Hollingdale, *Creating Civil Unions,* 6.

281 At 10:55 a.m. that morning: Moats, *Civil Wars,* 3–4.

282 She had to wait: Moats, *Civil Wars,* 4–5.

283 "the State made every conceivable": *Baker v. State,* 170 Vt. 194.

283 There were two other opinions: *Baker v. State.*

284 already the ruling had necessitated: Chris Graff, *Dateline Vermont: Covering and Uncovering the Newsworthy Stories that Shaped a State—and Influenced a Nation* (North Pomfret, VT: Thistle Hill Publications, 2006), 97.

284 "a legal and cultural milestone": Christopher Graff, "Supreme Court Says Gays, Lesbians Entitled to Rights of Marriage," Associated Press, December 20, 1999.

284 "It's clear we won": Stephenson, "Couples Say."

284 The headline on his story: Ross Sneyd, "Gay Marriage Issue Headed for Lawmakers' Fine-Tuning," Associated Press, December 21, 1999.

284 "confident that the legislature is going to do": Diane Derby, "Gays, Lesbians Now Turn Attention to Legislature," *Barre Montpelier (VT) Times Argus,* December 21, 1999.

285 "debates in the legislature": Linda Hollingdale, *Creating Civil Unions: Opening Hearts and Minds* (Hinesburg, VT: Common Humanity Press, 2002), 134.

285 "sending us to the very political cauldron": Hollingdale, *Creating Civil Unions.*

37. Scenes from a Civil Union

286 During his time in office, Dean had: Chris Graff, *Dateline Vermont: Covering and Uncovering the Newsworthy Stories that Shaped a State—and Influenced a Nation* (North Pomfret, VT: Thistle Hill Publications, 2006), 79.

286 "As soon as the Supreme Court handed": Linda Hollingdale, *Creating Civil Unions: Opening Hearts and Minds* (Hinesburg, VT: Common Humanity Press, 2002), 136.

286 "Most Vermonters are uncomfortable": Adam Lisberg and Nancy Remsen, "Legislators Embrace Idea of 'Domestic Partnership,'" *Burlington Free Press,* December 21, 1999.

286 "so that no group of Vermonters": "Governor Dean Supports Gay Rights," *Out in the Mountains,* February 1992.

287 When, in 1994, his administration's Department of Personnel: Kip Roberson, "VT Becomes 1st State to Extend Benefits," *Out in the Mountains,* September 1994.

287 During his 1996 campaign: Paul Olsen, "Vermont Party Platforms Split on Gay Marriage Issue," *Out in the Mountains,* December 1996.

287 Even as his lieutenant governor, Doug Racine, declared: Scott A. Giordano, "Attempts to Influence Vermont Case May Backfire: HI Mailing Seems to Rally Gay Support," *Bay Windows,* May 12, 1999.

287 "It's in the best interests of all": Graff, *Dateline Vermont,* 105.

287 "It's not something the legislature will do": Diane Derby, "Gays, Lesbians Now Turn Attention to Legislature," *Barre Montpelier (VT) Times Argus,* December 21, 1999.

287 "This year we must make": Jack Hoffman, "Dean Stresses Vermont Values," *Barre Montpelier (VT) Times Argus,* January 5, 2000.

288 "Oh, shit": Hollingdale, *Creating Civil Unions,* 22.

288 "a legislator who was interested": Hollingdale, *Creating Civil Unions,* 22.

288 "I was committed to a full": Hollingdale, *Creating Civil Unions,* 101.

288 "In view of the intense feelings": Mary Lou Killian, "Got Marriage? State-Level Policymaking Regarding Marriage Rights for Gays and Lesbians," doctoral dissertation, Temple University, April 19, 2005, 114.

289 Susan Murray and Beth Robinson were called: David Moats, *Civil Wars: A Battle for Gay Marriage* (Orlando: Harcourt, Inc., 2004), 156.

290 "You're about to move from an arena": Virginia Lindauer Simmon, "The Guys in the Hall," *Business People–Vermont,* July 2003.

290 "white moderate who is more devoted": Martin Luther King Jr., "The Negro Is Your Brother, *Atlantic Monthly,* August 1963.

290 A few days later, Little took: Jack Hoffman, "Panel Backs Domestic Partnership," *Rutland (VT) Herald,* February 10, 2000.

290 There had been consensus: Adam Lisberg, "Panel Backs Gay Partnerships," *Burlington Free Press,* February 10, 2000.

291 "legal benefits act is the right thing": William N. Eskridge Jr., *Equality Practice: Civil Unions and the Future of Gay Rights* (New York: Routledge, 2002), 61.

291 That day several of the members: Moats, *Civil Wars,* 198.

291 "civil rights package": Carey Goldberg, "Vermont Panel Shies from Gay Marriage," *New York Times,* February 10, 2000.

291 "legal benefits" act: Jack Hoffman, "Panel Backs Domestic Partnership," *Rutland (VT) Herald,* February 10, 2000.

293 Take It to the People, a group: Carey Goldberg, "Vermont Supreme Court Takes Up Gay Marriage," *New York Times,* January 19, 1998.

293 pushed legislators to introduce: Jack Hoffman, "Gay Marriage Foes Push for Amendment," *Rutland (VT) Daily Herald,* March 31, 2000.

293 As the civil-unions bill moved: Moats, *Civil Wars,* 205–06.

293 March 9, 2000, was Town Meeting Day: Eskridge Jr., *Equality Practice,* 64.

293 two three-hour sessions: Nancy Remsen, "Hundreds Expected at SSM Hearing," *Burlington Free Press,* January 28, 2000.

293 "The people of Vermont are in this": David Moats, "A Charitable View," *Rutland Herald,* February 9, 2000.

293 "At some point I knew": Hollingdale, *Creating Civil Unions,* 24.

294 On March 15, 2000, the civil-unions bill: Carey Goldberg, "Vermont's House Backs Wide Rights for Gay Couples," *New York Times,* March 17, 2000.

294 The following day, Dean signed: Moats, *Civil Wars,* 242.

294 "the domestic partnership act and not": Graff, *Dateline Vermont,* 105.

294 "a parallel 'domestic partnership' system": Christopher Graff, "Supreme Court Says Gays, Lesbians Entitled to Rights of Marriage," Associated Press, December 20, 1999.

38. Down from the Mountains

295 The July 1 implementation date: "Gay Couples Wed Across Vermont After Civil Union Law Takes Effect," Associated Press, July 2, 2000.

295 "With the civil union law, we turn": Mary Bonauto, "Civil Unions: Vermont Leads the Country," *HRC Quarterly* (Washington: Human Rights Campaign), June 2000.

295 "I knew there were strong feelings": Elizabeth Mehren, "Voters Oust 5 Who Backed Vt. Civil Union Law," *Los Angeles Times,* September 14, 2000.

296 Because of threats, Governor Howard Dean had: Tom Marshall, "Howard Dean's Toughest Campaign," *Hartford Courant,* September 21, 2003.

296 "My sexual orientation would be a distinctly second": Debra Rosenberg, "State of the 'Union,'" *Newsweek,* October 23, 2000.

297 "This is probably something that's going": Mehren, "Voters Oust 5 Who Backed Vt. Civil Union Law."

297 A few months earlier, Alaska's had: Kevin G. Clarkson, David Orgon Coolidge, and William C. Duncan, "The Alaska Marriage Amendment: The People's Choice on the Last Frontier," *Alaska Law Review* 16 (1999): 213–68.

298 Its highest appellate court, the Supreme Judicial Court: *Connors v. City of Boston,* 430 Mass. 31.

298 "It's a victory for the traditional family": Steve Marantz, "Court KOs Benefits for Gay Couples," *Boston Herald,* July 9, 1999.

298 "I don't know what Cambridge can come up": Anthony Giampetruzzi, "Cambridge Putting Up a Fight over Partner Benefits," *In Newsweekly,* April 5, 2000.

299 "an exalted status to some people": Frank Phillips, "Finnegan Unmoved, Vows to Block Bill," *Boston Globe,* July 23, 1998.

299 A week later, a coalition of city officials: Carolyn Federoff, "Mark Your Calendars: March 29, Mass. DP Lobby Day," *In Newsweekly,* March 29, 2000.

299 a headline in the gay community newspaper: Scott A. Giordano, "Mass. Activists Have Discovered Beacon Hill Leadership Stacked Against Them in Ways Not Seen in Decades," *Bay Windows,* May 13, 1999.

299 "We recognize that the category of covered": *Connors v. City of Boston,* 430 Mass. 31.

299 forty-six Cantabridgians facing a similar fate: Scott A. Giordano, "Cambridge Prepares to Defend Its DP Law," *Bay Windows,* March 30, 2000.

299 "The court is not homophobic": Anthony Giampetruzzi, "Mass. High Court Kills Boston Partner Benefits," *In Newsweekly,* July 21, 1999.

300 including a recent 1999 decision: *E.N.O. v. L.M.M.,* 429 Mass. 824.

39. The Next Town Over

301 "an incredible ally in our fights": Beth Berlo, "Three Lesbian Attorneys Honored," *Bay Windows,* October 26, 2000.

301 "an extraordinary amount of meanness": Berlo, "Three Lesbian Attorneys Honored."

302 In August, she had convened: Yvonne Abraham, "10 Years' Work Led to Historic Win in Court," *Boston Globe,* November 23, 2003.

302 Arline Isaacson, who as the state's most influential: Scott A. Giordano, "DP Bill Remains Idle on Beacon Hill," *Bay Windows,* April 15, 2000.

302 "Shouldn't we wait a few years?": Abraham, "10 Years' Work."

302 "Although I accepted the decision": Linda Hollingdale, *Creating Civil Unions: Opening Hearts and Minds* (Hinesburg, VT: Common Humanity Press, 2002), 21.

302 Regardless of Bonauto's decisions: Laura Kiritsy, "Activists Set to Battle Marriage Measure," *Bay Windows,* January 18, 2001.

302 As the statehouse came into session: Rick Klein, "Rogers' Bill Would Rule Out Gay Marriage," *Boston Globe,* February 2, 2001.

303 That seemed to foreclose: Yvonne Abraham, "Bill Targets Domestic Partner Benefits," *Boston Globe,* May 17, 2001.

303 "engage affirmatively and with the voices": Mary Bonauto, "The Litigation: First Judicial Victories in Vermont, Massachusetts, and Connecticut," in *Love Unites Us: Winning the Freedom to Marry in America,* ed. Kevin M. Cathcart and Leslie J. Gabel-Brett (New York: The New Press, 2016), 79.

303 Throughout the second half of 2000: Abraham, "10 Years' Work."

304 By the end of March 2001: Bonauto, "The Litigation," 80.

304 a white-collar Jamaica Plain couple: Kathleen Lahey and Kevin Alderson, *Same-Sex Marriage: The Personal and the Political* (Toronto: Insomniac Press, 2004), 353.

305 "If you loved each other": Evan Thomas, T. Trent Gegax, Debra Rosenberg, Pat Wingert, Mark Miller, Martha Brant, Stuart Taylor Jr., Tamara Lipper, John Barry, Rebecca Sinderbrand, Sarah Childress, and Julie Scelfo, "The War over Gay Marriage," *Newsweek,* July 7, 2003.

305 the Massachusetts Supreme Judicial Court had determined: Marc S. Malkin, "Mass. SJC Approves Lesbians as Co-Parents in Adoption Case," *Bay Windows,* September 16, 1993.

305 "It ultimately hurts Annie more than anyone": Kathleen Burge, "Judge Dismisses Same-Sex Marriage Suit; 7 Gay Couples Plan to Appeal," *Boston Globe,* May 9, 2002.

305 On April 11, 2001, Bonauto stood: Laura Kiritsy, "'All People Are Born Free and Equal,'" *Bay Windows,* April 19, 2001.

305 "helpful in a generic, cultural fashion": Yvonne Abraham, "Gays Seek Right to Marry; Mass. Lawsuit Goes Beyond Civil Unions," *Boston Globe,* April 17, 2001.

305 "a legal relationship and a social status": Beth Berlo, "Marriage Lawsuit Filed on Behalf of Seven Couples," *Bay Windows,* April 12, 2001.

40. *Goodridge*

306 a group calling itself Massachusetts Citizens for Marriage: "Marriage Backers Launch Petition Initiative," *The Pilot,* August 3, 2001.

306 "the ultimate legal remedy": Yvonne Abraham, "10 Years' Work Led to Historic Win in Court," *Boston Globe,* November 23, 2003.

306 If the amendment's sponsors did succeed: "8 Ballot Initiatives Rejected," *Boston Globe,* September 6, 2001.

306 "a three-year campaign from intolerant busybodies": "More Ballot Mayhem for Massachusetts," *Berkshire (MA) Eagle,* September 8, 2001.

306 "We were going to get massacred": Daniel R. Pinello, *America's Struggle for Same-Sex Marriage* (New York: Cambridge University Press, 2006), 36.

307 By year's end, the amendment's backers had collected: "Signatures Back Gay Marriage Ban," Associated Press, December 5, 2001.

307 "Our opponents could have gone": Pinello, *America's Struggle for Same-Sex Marriage.*

307 "wrong-hearted, mean-spirited, discriminatory and unfair": Patricia A. Gozemba and Karen Kahn, *Courting Equality: A Documentary History of America's First Legal Same-Sex Marriages* (Boston: Beacon Press, 2007), 59.

307 As soon as he gaveled in: Yvonne Abraham, "Birmingham Blocks a Vote on Marriage," *Boston Globe,* June 20, 2002.

307 "If we won the case": Mary Bonauto, "The Litigation: First Judicial Victories in Vermont, Massachusetts, and Connecticut," in *Love Unites Us: Winning the Freedom to Marry in America,* ed. Kevin M. Cathcart and Leslie J. Gabel-Brett (New York: The New Press, 2016), 79.

307 At the first hearing over summary-judgment motions: Beth Berlo, "Historic Hearing Over Gay Marriage Begins in Boston," *Bay Windows,* March 14, 2002.

307 "While this court understands the reasons": Kathleen Burge, "Judge Dismisses Same-Sex Marriage Suit; 7 Gay Couples Plan to Appeal," *Boston Globe,* May 9, 2002.

308 in the process of moving: Noah Hurowitz, "Portland Lawyer Mary Bonauto Credited as 'Mastermind' Behind Landmark Gay Rights Court Cases," *Bangor Daily News,* March 30, 2013.

308 The brief she drafted hinged: Mary Bonauto, "*Goodridge* in Context," *Harvard Civil Rights—Civil Liberties Law Review* 40 (2005): 25.

308 The language was a vestige: Ronald M. Peters Jr., *The Massachusetts Constitution of 1780: A Social Compact* (Amherst: The University of Massachusetts, 1978).

309 the example of Quock Walker: Robert M. Spector, "The Quock Walker Cases (1781–83): Slavery, Its Abolition, and Negro Citizenship in Early Massachusetts," *Journal of Negro History,* 53, no. 1 (January 1968): 12–32.

309 "celebrates a court that led": Emily Bazelon, "A Bold Stroke," *Legal Affairs,* May 2004.

310 "the laws of the Commonwealth do not permit": Marc S. Malkin, "Mass. SJC Approves Lesbians as Co-Parents in Adoption Case," *Bay Windows,* September 16, 1993.

310 "We needed to be extremely cautious": Bonauto, "*Goodridge* in Context," 22.

41. We're the Marriage People

315 oral arguments at Massachusetts's highest court: Kathleen Burge, "SJC Peppers Lawyers on Same-Sex Marriage," *Boston Globe,* March 5, 2003.

315 His dissertation concerned: David Blankenhorn, "Cabinet Makers in Victorian Britain: A Study of Two Trade Unions," unpublished MA dissertation, University of Warwick, UK, October 1978.

316 a *New York Times* op-ed he wrote: David Blankenhorn, "Family Values, Without Sugary Pieties," *New York Times,* March 23, 1986.

317 "The argument must be made": Wade F. Horn, "Did You Say 'Movement'?" in *The Fatherhood Movement: A Call to Action,* ed. Wade F. Horn, David Blankenhorn, and Mitchell B. Pearlstein (New York: Lexington Books, 1999), 13.

317 "Historically, the good father protects": David Blankenhorn, *Fatherless America: Confronting Our Most Urgent Social Problem* (New York: Basic Books, 1995), 122.

317 the institute's 2000 manifesto: Institute for American Values, *The Marriage Movement: A Statement of Principles* (New York: Institute for American Values, 2000).

317 both parties' presidential nominees: Judith Stacey, "Family Values Forever: In the Marriage Movement, Conservatives and Centrists Find a Home Together," *The Nation,* July 9, 2001.

317 "Marriage, a rich generator": Institute for American Values, *The Marriage Movement,* 4.

317 But many of the specific policy: Institute for American Values, *The Marriage Movement,* 17–18.

318 Bush introduced a Healthy Marriage Initiative: Sharon Lerner, "Marriage on the Mind," *The Nation,* June 17, 2004.

318 "I don't want to play Cupid": Beth Henry, "Mother and Father Know Best; A New Role for Bush's Health and Human Services Department," *Weekly Standard,* March 4, 2002.

318 "Now everyone from the government": Alex Kotlowitz and Ben Loeterman, "Let's Get Married," directed by Ben Loeterman, *PBS Frontline,* November 14, 2002.

318 In the summer of 2001, his institute: Norval Glenn and Elizabeth Marquardt, *Hooking Up, Hanging Out, and Hoping for Mr. Right: College Women on Dating and Mating Today* (New York: Institute for American Values, 2001).

318 Blankenhorn had always had an eye: David Blankenhorn, "I Do?" *First Things,* November 1997.

319 "a meeting place for leaders": Jen Waters, "Thoughtful Choices; Academies Help Students with Christian Worldview," *Washington Times,* April 16, 2003.

319 the friendly reception they had given: Burge, "SJC Peppers Lawyers."

319 an act of avoidance: Philip Kennicott, "Champions of 'Civil Society' Embrace at Arm's Length," *Washington Post,* February 14, 2002.

320 and an earlier book: Maggie Gallagher, *Enemies of Eros: How the Sexual Revolution Is Killing Family, Marriage, and Sex and What We Can Do About It* (Chicago: Bonus Books, 1989).

320 "more marriages that succeed": David Popenoe, Jean Bethke Elshtain, and David Blankenhorn, eds., *Promises to Keep: Decline and Renewal of Marriage in America* (Lanham, MD: Rowman & Littlefield Publishers, 1996), xi.

320 Instead, in the month that the bill came: Maggie Gallagher, "Family First Fantasies," *Washington Times,* June 24, 1996.

320 the *New Republic*'s cover story titled: Andrew Sullivan, "The Case for Gay Marriage," *New Republic*, August 28, 1989.

321 "As private citizens, the authors have": Linda J. Waite and Maggie Gallagher, *The Case for Marriage: Why Married People Are Happier, Healthier, and Better Off Financially* (New York: Doubleday, 2000), 200.

322 "whether an individual ever personally": Institute for American Values, *The Marriage Movement*, 3.

322 "just misses the whole point": Walter Isaacson, "Should Gays Have Marriage Rights?" *Time*, November 20, 1989.

322 "there is a difference between what we permit": Dan Meyers, "City Considers Extending Job Benefits to Gay Couples," *Philadelphia Inquirer*, June 22, 1990.

323 "People who haven't had much positive": Peter Steinfels, "Efforts to Redefine Marriage Stumble over Same-Sex Unions," *New York Times*, June 6, 2003.

323 the most industrious proponents: *The Economist*, "Let Them Wed," January 6, 1996.

323 As early as 1994: Jonathan Rauch, "A Pro-Gay, Pro-Family Policy," *Wall Street Journal*, November 29, 1994.

323 "If we do not deliberate": Karen S. Peterson, "On Gays, 'Marriage Movement' Is on Both Sides of the Aisle; Group Is All for Stronger Relationships, but Debate Could Splinter Its Own," *USA Today*, August 4, 2003.

42. A Sense of Where the Culture Is Headed

325 "It's the great American game": David Orgon Coolidge, "Vermont: The Rest of the Story," *National Review Online*, January 9, 2001.

325 cover the *Baehr* trial: David Orgon Coolidge, "Marriage on Trial," *Hawaii Catholic Herald*, September 20, 1996.

325 Mormon-led group had begun supporting: Gregory A. Prince, *Gay Rights and the Mormon Church: Intended Actions, Unintended Consequences* (Salt Lake City: University of Utah Press, 2019), 72–82.

327 "You might say a rainbow coalition": David Orgon Coolidge, "Marriage in Massachusetts," *Weekly Standard*, June 7, 1999.

327 "With his well-spoken manner": Marilyn Gardner, "A Man Raised by One Parent Advocates for Two," *Christian Science Monitor*, September 25, 1997.

327 sending volunteer doctors into schools: "Abstinence Group Criticizes Health Officials," Associated Press, February 25, 1998.

327 pursuing doctoral studies at Brandeis: Scott Rubush, "Traditional Values Matter Most to Daniels," *Insight*, August 16, 1999.

327 "We've had anti-drug": Glen Johnson, "As Father's Day Nears, Report Highlights Impact of Fatherlessness," Associated Press, June 11, 1997.

327 "Kids do best": Dan Gilgoff, *The Jesus Machine: How James Dobson, Focus on the Family, and Evangelical America Are Winning the Culture War* (New York: St. Martin's Press, 2007), 143.

327 "Our side tends often to think": Rubush, "Traditional Values Matter Most to Daniels."

328 He had been born in Spanish Harlem: Franklin Foer, "Marriage Counselor," *The Atlantic*, March 2004.

328 Daniels described his childhood as "miserable": Gardner, "A Man Raised by One Parent."

329 "would challenge anyone to show": Maggie Gallagher, "Why Murphy Brown Lost," *New York Post,* September 1, 2000.

330 It would not be unprecedented: David Orgon Coolidge and William C. Duncan, "Reaffirming Marriage: A Presidential Priority," *Harvard Journal of Law & Public Policy* 24, no. 2 (Spring 2001): 645.

330 The one passed by Alaska voters: David Orgon Coolidge and William C. Duncan, "Definition or Discrimination? State Marriage Recognition Statutes in the 'Same-Sex Marriage' Debate," *Creighton Law Review* 32 (1998).

330 All three had previously worked: Hadley Arkes, *Natural Rights and the Right to Choose* (Cambridge, UK: Cambridge University Press, 2002), 97.

330 "People involved in those early discussions": Gilgoff, *The Jesus Machine,* 142.

331 "on the road to cultural disaster": Robert H. Bork, *Slouching Towards Gomorrah: Modern Liberalism and American Decline* (New York: HarperCollins, 1996), 11.

331 "Because the court misused": Robert H. Bork, "Activist Judges Strike Again," *Wall Street Journal,* December 22, 1999.

331 "Let's challenge the homosexual movement": David Crary, "Amendment Sought Against Same-Sex Unions," Associated Press, July 11, 2001.

43. Enemy of the Good

332 "We assembled a multiethnic": Scott Rubush, "Traditional Values Matter Most to Daniels," *Insight,* August 16, 1999.

332 Instead news coverage identified: "Coalition Wants Marriage Amendment," Associated Press, July 10, 2001.

332 Daniels credited the black church: Karen S. Peterson, "Man Behind the Marriage Amendment," *USA Today,* April 12, 2004.

333 In Massachusetts, he had recruited: Diego Ribadeneira and Tatsha Robertson, "Battle Lines Form over Same-Sex Marriage Bill," *Boston Globe,* May 17, 1999.

333 Standing beside him: Carolyn Lochhead, "Constitutional Amendment to Bar Same-Sex Marriage," *San Francisco Chronicle,* July 13, 2001.

333 "It is outrageous to claim": Regan Morris, "The Life and Career of Matt Daniels," Law Crossing, undated, www.lawcrossing.com.

333 "legal equivalent of a nuclear bomb": Rhonda Smith, "Constitutional Claws; Coalition Wants Amendment Banning Legal Recognition of Same-Sex Unions," *Washington Blade,* July 13, 2001.

334 The closest thing to urgency: Rex Wockner, "World's First Gay Marriages Take Place on April 1," *Bay Windows,* April 5, 2001.

334 The press conference to unveil: Stanley Kurtz, "Media Blackout," *National Review,* September 8, 2003.

334 "Few television outlets even know": Kurtz, "Media Blackout."

335 "The amendment as drafted": Kenneth Connor, letter to editor, *National Review,* August 20, 2001.

335 "The Constitution is not the problem": Tim Graham, "Prenuptial Disagreement," *World,* June 8, 2002.

336 Connor was a Florida attorney: Family Research Council, "Over 20 Years," November 29, 2006. Accessed via web.archive.org.

336 "Focus saw FRC": Dan Gilgoff, *The Jesus Machine: How James Dobson, Focus on the Family, and Evangelical America Are Winning the Culture War* (New York: St. Martin's Press, 2007), 148.

336 Since the 1960s, the Supreme Court: *Engel v. Vitale,* 370 US 421.

337 ending organized prayer in schools: *Abington School Dist. v. Schempp,* 374 US 203.

337 In 1990, it went even further: *Employment Div. v. Smith,* 494 US 872.

337 The Supreme Court in 1997 gutted: *City of Boerne v. Flores,* 521 US 507.

337 At that point, congressional Republicans responded: Tom Strode, "House Falls Short of Two-Thirds Vote on Religious Freedom Amendment," *Baptist Press,* June 5, 1998.

337 "neo-establishment majoritarianism": Barry Hankins, *Uneasy in Babylon: Southern Baptist Conservatives and American Culture* (Tuscaloosa: University of Alabama Press, 2002), 160.

337 "awful and appalling": Hankins, *Uneasy in Babylon,* 157–60.

338 believer in the amendment's language: Robert P. George, "The 28th Amendment," *National Review,* July 23, 2001.

338 In search of some unity: Gilgoff, *The Jesus Machine,* 149.

338 Connor fell ill: Gilgoff, *The Jesus Machine,* 149.

44. Marriage Movements

340 "was just the sort of kid": Maggie Gallagher, "Why Murphy Brown Lost," *New York Post,* September 1, 2000.

340 "I became a writer": Mark Oppenheimer, "The Making of Gay Marriage's Top Foe," *Salon,* February 8, 2012.

340 "Since I was a girl": John Corvino and Maggie Gallagher, *Debating Same-Sex Marriage* (New York: Oxford University Press, 2012), 223.

341 "new effort to find ways": Gallagher, "Why Murphy Brown Lost."

341 "carefully drawn, measured, centrist amendment": Maggie Gallagher, "Do We Need a Federal Marriage Amendment?" TownHall.com, July 18, 2001.

341 "The quiet, back-door demonization": Maggie Gallagher, "Hate Speech from Gay Marriage Advocates," TownHall.com, August 7, 2001.

341 "shared public norm": Maggie Gallagher, "The Stakes: Why We Need Marriage," *National Review Online,* August 14, 2003.

342 "If the most powerful trends in family law": Maggie Gallagher, "The New Attack on Marriage," TownHall.com, April 21, 2003.

342 what she dubbed unisex marriage: Maggie Gallagher, "A Federal Marriage Amendment?" *New York Post,* August 17, 2001.

342 "move from a silence on this issue": Karen S. Peterson, "On Gays, 'Marriage Movement' Is on Both Sides of the Aisle; Group Is All for Stronger Relationships, but Debate Could Splinter Its Own," *USA Today,* August 4, 2003.

342 "The debate over same-sex marriage, then": Maggie Gallagher, "What Marriage Is For," *Weekly Standard,* August 4, 2003.

343 "to brag a little": Maggie Gallagher, "Andrew Sullivan's Strange Silence," MariageDebate.com, August 2, 2003. Accessed via web.archive.org.

343 When Jonathan Rauch earnestly countered: Jonathan Rauch, "Jonathan vs. Maggie," MariageDebate.com, August 3, 2003. Accessed via web.archive.org.

343 "Oh, Jonathan I knew that": Maggie Gallagher, "Maggie's Stupid Digression," MarriageDebate.com, August 4, 2003. Accessed via web.archive.org.

343 "Through her writings, Ms. Gallagher": U.S. Congress, Senate, Judiciary Committee, Constitution Subcommittee, hearing on "What is needed to defend the bipartisan Defense of Marriage Act of 1996?" September 4, 2003.

343 a point made by one of the magazine's writers: Ramesh Ponnuru, "Coming Out Ahead," *National Review,* July 28, 2003.

344 "Polygamy is not worse": Gallagher, "The Stakes: Why We Need Marriage."

344 "I think that among the really, really, really, really": U.S. Congress, "What is needed to defend the bipartisan Defense of Marriage Act of 1996?"

344 "one of the movement's intellectual flag-bearers": Alan Cooperman, "Opponents of Gay Marriage Divided; At Issue Is Scope of an Amendment," *Washington Post,* November 28, 2003.

45. Wise as Serpents

346 The founding myth of the American Family Association: People for the American Way, "Donald E. Wildmon & the American Family Association," May 25, 1989.

346 His primary tool for shaping: Marla Dickerson, "Christian Group Escalates Boycott Against Disney," *Los Angeles Tismes,* July 2, 1996.

347 A week earlier, Wildmon had led: Paul Weyrich, "A Fatal Flirtation: The GOP and the Homosexual Movement," *CNS News,* May 12, 2003.

347 Former presidential candidate Gary Bauer wondered: Ralph Z. Hallow, "GOP Leaders Warned to Shun Agenda of Gays," *Washington Times,* May 15, 2003.

347 "man on child, man on dog": Associated Press, "Excerpt from Santorum Interview," April 23, 2003.

347 "If Republicans continue": Hallow, "GOP Leaders Warned."

347 "Look at our entertainment programs": David D. Kirkpatrick, "Conservatives Using Issue of Gay Unions as a Rallying Tool," *New York Times,* February 8, 2004.

348 "Some groups are rivals": Paul Weyrich, "The Arlington Group," Renew America, December 3, 2004.

348 Weyrich had just published: Paul Weyrich, "Top 5 Social Priorities for Conservatives," *CNS News,* June 27, 2003.

348 "demeans the lives of homosexual persons": *Lawrence v. Texas,* 539 US 558.

348 "the liberty protected by the Constitution": *Lawrence v. Texas,* 539 US 558.

348 The appeal had been filed: Dale Carpenter, *Flagrant Conduct: The Story of Lawrence v. Texas,* How a Bedroom Arrest Decriminalized (New York: W. W. Norton, 2012), 152.

349 "'does not involve whether'": *Lawrence v. Texas,* 539 US 558.

349 parallel logic had led the Ontario Court: Sylvain Larocque, *Gay Marriage: The Story of a Canadian Social Revolution* (Toronto: James Lorimer & Company, 2006), 109–25.

349 "This case is ultimately about": *Hedy Halpern and Colleen Rogers, Michael Leshner and Michael Stark, Aloysius Pittman and Thomas Allworth, Dawn Onishenko and Julie Erbland, Carolyn Rowe and Carolyn Moffatt, Barbara McDowall and Gail Donnelly, Alison Kemper and Joyce Barnett v. Attorney General of Canada, The Attorney General of Ontario, and Novina Wong, The Clerk of the City of Toronto,* O.J. No. 2268.

349 In 1999, she had married: Hanna Rosin, "A Family Business," *Washington Post,* May 20, 2004.

349 But starting in March 2003: Kathleen Burge, "SJC Peppers Lawyers on Same-Sex Marriage," *Boston Globe,* March 5, 2003.

350 "We're opening up": Evan Thomas, T. Trent Gegax, Debra Rosenberg, Pat

Wingert, Mark Miller, Martha Brant, Stuart Taylor Jr., Tamara Lipper, John Barry, Rebecca Sinderbrand, Sarah Childress, and Julie Scelfo, "The War over Gay Marriage," *Newsweek*, July 7, 2003.

350 When the Federal Marriage Amendment was introduced: U.S. Congress, House, Proposing an amendment to the Constitution of the United States relating to marriage, H.J.Res.93, 107th Cong., introduced in House July 18, 2012.

351 "I absolutely do": Sheryl Gay Stolberg, "White House Avoids Stand on Gay Marriage Measure," *New York Times*, July 2, 2003.

351 "marriage is a sacrament": Bill Sammon, "Bush Cool on Measure to Ban Gay 'Marriage'; Conservatives Hit Wait-and-See Stance," *Washington Times*, July 3, 2003.

351 "the president believes that marriage": Stolberg, "White House Avoids Stand."

351 "His father was raised Episcopal": Raney Aronson, "The Jesus Factor," directed by Raney Aronson, *PBS Frontline*, April 29, 2004.

352 Promising to unleash: Dan Balz, "'Armies of Compassion' in Bush's Plans," *Washington Post*, April 25, 1999.

352 Even before the polls had closed: Sasha Issenberg, *The Victory Lab: The Secret Science of Winning Campaigns* (New York: Crown, 2012), 87.

352 Exit polls eventually showed: Dan Gilgoff, *The Jesus Machine: How James Dobson, Focus on the Family, and Evangelical America Are Winning the Culture War* (New York: St. Martin's Press, 2007), 186.

352 "If this process of withdrawal continues": Jeff Zeleny, "GOP Failed to Draw Religious Right in 2000, Says Bush Aide," *Chicago Tribune*, December 12, 2001.

352 "the middle man": Timothy S. Goeglein, *The Man in the Middle: An Inside Account of Faith and Politics in the George W. Bush Era* (Nashville: B&H Books, 2011), 46.

352 Goeglein hosted a weekly: Peter H. Stone and Bara Vaida, "Christian Soldiers," *National Journal*, December 4, 2004.

352 On Thursday mornings: Joe Feuerherd, "The Real Deal: How a Philosophy Professor with a Checkered Past Became the Most Influential Catholic Layman in George W. Bush's Washington," *National Catholic Reporter*, August 19, 2004.

352 "In the Reagan administration": Raney Aronson, "The Jesus Factor."

353 The two had known each other: Stone and Vaida, "Christian Soldiers."

353 "imparting legitimacy to the homosexual political cause": Lou Chibbaro Jr., "Right-Wing Groups Blast Bush's Picks," *Washington Blade*, October 5, 2001.

353 Just two years earlier, Senate Republicans: Robert Novak, "A Gay Ambassador," *Washington Post*, January 15, 1998.

354 "This is a Washington story of intrigue": Elisabeth Bumiller, "Unlikely Story Behind a Gay Rights Victory," *New York Times*, June 27, 2002.

354 "I don't know if it is necessary": David Freddoso, "Senators Hesitant to Back Frist on Marriage Amendment," *Human Events*, July 11, 2003.

354 "We did not want to get ahead": Goeglein, *The Man in the Middle*, 119.

355 had been exiled from the Washington: Mark O'Keefe, "Religious Right Rethinks Strategy as Agenda Stalls," Newhouse News Service, July 14, 2003.

46. Dueling Amendments

357 "This is the first time that any": Bill Werde, "A First at Bride's Magazine: A Report on Same-Sex Unions," *New York Times*, July 28, 2003.

357 previous August changed: Jan Thompson, "A Sign of the Times," *Gay City News*, August 23, 2002.

357 Inspired by the success of the sitcom: Jim Rutenberg, "Gay-Themed TV Gaining a Wider Audience," *New York Times*, July 29, 2003.

357 It was a season of similarly alarming: Mark O'Keefe, "Traditional Foes Form the Core of Opposition to Gay Marriage," Newhouse News Service, October 7, 2003.

357 the Episcopal Church elected: Laurie Goodstein, "New Hampshire Episcopalians Choose Gay Bishop, and Conflict," *New York Times*, June 8, 2003.

357 at the MTV Video Music Awards: Imogen Tilden, "Madonna Sexes Up MTV Awards," *The Guardian*, August 29, 2003.

357 The Southern Baptist Convention would distribute: "Conservatives Using Issue of Gay Marriage to Spur Voter Drive," Associated Press, October 2, 2003.

357 "This will be a rolling crescendo": Cheryl Wetzstein, "Groups Pledge to Protect Marriage," *Washington Times*, October 3, 2003.

358 "Using pulpits, petitions, and political action committees": Mary Leonard, "Gay Marriage Stirs Conservatives Again," *Boston Globe*, September 28, 2003.

358 "a Constitutional Marriage Amendment is needed": Paul Weyrich, "Marriage Protection Week," *CNS News*, October 7, 2003.

358 He had asked a Democrat: Tim Graham, "Prenuptial Disagreement," *World*, June 8, 2002.

359 not quite new to the topic: Jacob M. Schlesinger, "How Gay Marriage Thrust 2 Outsiders onto Center Stage," *Wall Street Journal*, February 23, 2004.

359 Hostettler believed that: "FRC President: Marriage Amendment Is Top Issue," *Human Events*, September 15, 2003.

359 "what steps, if any, are needed": U.S. Congress, Senate, Judiciary Committee, Constitution Subcommittee, hearing on "What is needed to defend the bipartisan Defense of Marriage Act of 1996?" May 16, 1996.

360 Around thirty people were present: Marc J. Ambinder, "Where the 'Vast Right-Wing Conspiracy' Hangs Its Hat," *Washingtonian*, December 2005.

360 "counterfeit marriage": Mark A. Regan, *Preserving Marriage in an Age of Counterfeits: How "Civil Unions" Devalue the Real Thing* (Washington, DC: Family Research Council, 2001).

360 But Connor was replaced: Judith Stacey, "Family Values Forever: In the Marriage Movement, Conservatives and Centrists Find a Home Together," *The Nation*, July 9, 2001.

360 "Hopefully, within the next few weeks": *Human Events* interview with Tony Perkins, "FRC President: Marriage Amendment Is Top Issue," September 15, 2003.

361 "The grassroots will get motivated": Ramesh Ponnuru, "Marriage Amendment Jitters," *National Review*, November 24, 2003.

361 "We might as well say": Joel Belz, "Something to Scream About," *World*, October 11, 2003.

361 There was the moral outrage: *Roe v. Wade*, 410 US 113.

362 In an effort to undo: Robert N. Karrer, "The Pro-Life Movement and Its First Years under 'Roe,'" *American Catholic Studies* 122, no. 4 (2011): 58.

362 But they quickly ended up in two camps: David J. Garrow, *Liberty and Sexuality: The Right to Privacy and the Making of Roe v. Wade* (New York: Macmillan, 1994), 639.

362 efforts by Weyrich in the early 1980s: Bill Peterson, "Worries for New Right," *Washington Post*, February 16, 1982.

362 "If we can't win": Belz, "Something to Scream About."

363 "perhaps the most unifying figure": Ponnuru, "Marriage Amendment Jitters."

363 Twenty organizations that were part: Ponnuru, "Marriage Amendment Jitters."

363 The same cadre that two weeks earlier: Belz, "Something to Scream About."

364 The project's founder, David Orgon Coolidge: Michael Cromartie, *A Public Faith: Evangelicals and Civic Engagement* (Lanham, MD: Roman & Littlefield Publishers, Inc., 2003), x.

364 "Like many Americans, I find": Maggie Gallagher, "Gays and Catholics: Can We Tolerate Both?" TownHall.com, May 5, 2003.

364 long-dreaded news came: "Court Rules Couples May Wed," *Bay Windows,* November 19, 2003.

364 "Barring an individual from the protections": *Goodridge v. Dept. of Public Health,* 440 Mass. 309.

365 Shortly thereafter, a version: U.S. Congress, Senate, A joint resolution proposing an amendment to the Constitution of the United States relating to marriage, S.J.Res.26, 108th Cong., introduced in House November 25, 2003.

365 The new chairman of the Republican National Committee: Susan Page, "Gay Marriage Looms Large for '04," *USA Today,* November 19, 2003.

365 "civil-union-type provision": Raphael Lewis, "Groups Muster to Fight Gay Marriage in Mass," *Boston Globe,* November 20, 2003.

365 "The people whose minds must": Maggie Gallagher, "Massachusetts vs. Marriage," *Weekly Standard,* December 1, 2003.

47. Lawlessness

366 "I will support a constitutional amendment": Elisabeth Bumiller, "Marriage Amendment Backed," *New York Times,* December 17, 2003.

366 But some conservatives, including those: Alan Cooperman, "Opponents of Gay Marriage Divided; At Issue Is Scope of an Amendment," *Washington Post,* November 28, 2003.

366 looking ahead to a Constitutional Convention: Maurice T. Cunningham, "Catholics and the ConCon: The Church's Response to the Massachusetts Gay Marriage Decision," *Journal of Church and State* 47, no. 1 (2005): 19–42.

367 "If there's a vote": Karla Dial, "Battle Lines Redrawn in Massachusetts," Citizen-Link, February 4, 2004.

367 "Bush never used the words": David D. Kirkpatrick, "Conservative Groups Differ on Bush Words on Marriage," *New York Times,* January 22, 2004.

367 "Bush's comments put ban": Judy Holland, "Bush's Comments Put Ban on Gay Marriage on Hold," Hearst News Service, January 25, 2004.

367 The typically truculent Sandy Rios: Kirkpatrick, "Conservative Groups Differ."

367 "He made the case": Tom Strode, "Leaders Praise Bush Marriage Statement; Say More Is Needed," *Baptist Press,* January 21, 2004.

367 When they met at the Family Research Council: David D. Kirkpatrick, "Conservatives Using Issue of Gay Unions as a Rallying Tool," *New York Times,* February 8, 2004.

368 Paul Weyrich challenged Rove: Mark Francis Cohen, "Hard Right," *Washingtonian,* April 2004.

368 Throughout the fall, Rove had: Sasha Issenberg, *The Victory Lab: The Secret Science of Winning Campaigns* (New York: Crown, 2012), 259.

368 Dean was the only governor: Thomas B. Edsall, "Gay Community Gave Dean Early Boost," *Washington Post,* January 1, 2004.

368 Into January, Rove was betting: Peter Baker, *Days of Fire: Bush & Cheney in the White House* (New York: Doubleday, 2013), 307.

368 Bush had already alienated: John Maggs, "Grover at the Gate," *National Journal*, October 11, 2003.

369 "sooner rather than later": Kirkpatrick, "Conservatives Using Issue of Gay Unions."

369 When under consideration to be nominated: Baker, *Days of Fire*, 57.

369 Cheney felt free enough: Michael Cooper, "Cheney's Marriage Remarks Irk Conservatives," *New York Times*, October 10, 2000.

369 "We have, I reminded him": Baker, *Days of Fire*, 310.

369 "activist judges insist on": Associated Press, "Bush: Gay-Marriage Ruling 'Deeply Troubling,'" February 5, 2004.

369 "separate is seldom, if ever": Raphael Lewis, "SJC Affirms Gay Marriage," *Boston Globe*, February 5, 2004.

369 The next week in Boston: Rick Klein, "House Speaker's Gambit Sparked Anger, Furious Maneuvering," *Boston Globe*, February 12, 2004.

370 On February 10, Mayor Gavin Newsom: Rachel Gordon, "The Battle over Same-Sex Marriage: Bush's Stance Led Newsom to Take Action," *San Francisco Chronicle*, February 15, 2004.

370 Newsom's staff had timed: David Von Drehle and Alan Cooperman, "Same-Sex Marriage Vaulted into Spotlight," *Washington Post*, March 8, 2004.

370 That would mean at least three: Rone Tempest, "A Nice Day for Gay Weddings," *Los Angeles Times*, February 14, 2004.

370 Sixteen hundred couples were married: Rone Tempest, "SF's Hero of the Moment," *Los Angeles Times*, February 16, 2004.

370 shut down the enterprise: Bob Egelko, "Court Halts Gay Vows," *San Francisco Chronicle*, March 12, 2004.

370 "going on the offensive today": Harriet Chang, "S.F. Sues over Legality of Same-Sex Marriages," *San Francisco Chronicle*, February 20, 2004.

371 Several of the group's most visible: "Marriage Rally to Be Held at Statehouse," *Boston Pilot*, January 30, 2004.

371 where they saw: Yvonne Abraham, "National and Local Lobbying Efforts Ratcheted Up," *Boston Globe*, February 11, 2004.

371 Media coverage preferred: Leigh Moscowitz, *The Battle Over Marriage: Gay Rights Activism Through the Media* (Urbana: University of Illinois Press, 2013), 1–3.

371 "I have watched carefully": "President 'Troubled' by San Francisco's Gay Marriages," Associated Press, February 18, 2004.

371 On February 19, the clerk of Sandoval: Susan Montoya Bryan, "Same-Sex Couples Marry in Sandoval County," Associated Press, February 20, 2004.

371 successfully halted Dunlap: Joshua Akers, "N.M. Same-Sex Marriages Off Again," *Albuquerque Journal*, March 24, 2004.

371 The attorney general, Bill Lockyer: Edward Epstein, "Governor Fears Unrest Unless Same-Sex Marriages Are Halted; Schwarzenegger Voices Concern over Potential Civil Clashes in S.F.," *San Francisco Chronicle*, February 23, 2004.

371 "We cannot have mayors": Epstein, "Governor Fears Unrest."

372 On February 24, Bush gave: Elisabeth Bumiller, "Bush Backs Ban in Constitution on Gay Marriage," *New York Times*, February 25, 2004.

373 "as a basic philosophical point": Katherine Q. Seelye, "Conservatives Mobilize Against Ruling on Gay Marriage," *New York Times*, November 20, 2003.

373 "And it's just traditional marriage": David Persons, "Allard Stays Firm Against Same-Sex Marriage," *Fort Collins Coloradoan,* December 3, 2003.

373 Musgrave had always insisted: Alan Cooperman, "Little Consensus on Marriage Amendment; Even Authors Disagree on the Meaning of Its Text," *Washington Post,* February 14, 2004.

373 "couldn't possibly have been": Cooperman, "Little Consensus on Marriage Amendment."

373 "We want to make it clear": Mary Leonard, "Marriage Measure Is Revised."

373 with Matt Daniels's original vision: Jacob M. Schlesinger, "How Gay Marriage Thrust 2 Outsiders Onto Center Stage," *Wall Street Journal,* February 23, 2004.

373 "reality set in": Kirkpatrick, "Conservatives Using Issue of Gay Unions."

374 Resigned to the fact: "Bringing the Fight Home," *Arlington Connection,* March 2, 2004.

374 "I actually believe we would be": Michael Farris, "Point: Against the Amendment," *World,* May 22, 2004.

374 On March 29, its fourth day: Rick Klein, "Vote Ties Civil Unions to Gay-Marriage Ban," *Boston Globe,* March 30, 2004.

374 "no matter what legislative action": "Doubt Voiced on Gay Marriage Strategy," *Boston Globe,* March 23, 2004.

374 As soon as the amendment passed: Klein, "Vote Ties Civil Unions."

374 "made up their mind": Frank Phillips, "Reilly Gives Governor a Hurdle," *Boston Globe,* March 30, 2004.

374 "it is of no interest": Rick Klein, "Romney Warns of 'Legal Limbo,'" *Boston Globe,* February 14, 2004.

375 "abide by the law": Raphael Lewis, "Gays Fear Fallout of San Francisco Rites," *Boston Globe,* February 23, 2004.

375 One reveler's sign: Joanna Weiss and Lisa Kocian, "Cambridge Plays Host to a Giant Celebration," *Boston Globe,* May 17, 2004.

375 despite the police detail: Mary Breslauer, "In Praise of Those Who Led the Way for Same-Sex Marriage," *Vineyard (MA) Gazette,* November 21, 2013.

375 supply Bonauto with tissues: William N. Eskridge Jr. and Christopher R. Riano, *Marriage Equality: From Outlaws to In-Laws* (New Haven: Yale University Press, 2020), 236.

375 At the wedding of Julie and Hillary: Pam Belluck, "Hundreds of Same-Sex Couples Wed in Massachusetts," *New York Times,* May 18, 2004.

375 "I went to as many": Chris Geidner, "How One Lawyer Turned the Idea of Marriage Equality into Reality," *BuzzFeed,* November 17, 2013.

375 A week earlier, Romney had forewarned: Scott S. Greenberger and Yvonne Abraham, "Gay-Marriage Rule Eased; Romney Aide Says Clerks Have Discretion on Residency Proof," *Boston Globe,* May 5, 2004.

375 a law largely ignored: Raphael Lewis, "Clerks Ask Ruling on Marriage Law; 1913, Rule May Affect Nuptials for Visitors," *Boston Globe,* March 7, 2004.

375 Clerks would be expected: Michael Levenson, "Clerks in Tight Spot Politically," *Boston Globe,* May 17, 2004.

376 "the Las Vegas of same-sex marriage": Pam Belluck, "Gays Elsewhere Eye Marriage Massachusetts Style," *New York Times,* May 14, 2004.

376 especially the twelve that had never: "The Defense of Marriage Act," *PBS NewsHour,* April 30, 2004.

48. Issue One

377 signed twenty-five licenses: Nicole Sacks, "As New Paltz Goes... Mayor Jason West Brings Same-Sex Marriage to New York State," *Gay City News*, March 4, 2004.

377 At a county building in Portland: David Austin, Tom Hallman, Jr., and Scott Learn, "The Marriage Brokers," *The Oregonian*, March 7, 2004.

377 "laws are made to be broken": Tatsha Robertson, "Civil Disobedience Adds to Battle over Same-Sex Marriage," *Boston Globe*, March 15, 2004.

377 But in Massachusetts, town halls were: Emily Shorten, "Clerks in Suburbs Ready for May 17; Gay Marriages 'Business as Usual,'" *Boston Globe*, May 13, 2004.

378 "first national meeting of its kind": Valerie Richardson, "Anti-Gay Rights Leaders Talk of Repeating 1993 Success," *Washington Times*, May 19, 1994.

378 "toward hope and healing for homosexuals": John W. Kennedy, "Ad Campaign Ignites Firestorm," *Christianity Today*, September 7, 1998.

380 "It singles out one category": Linda Vacariello, "That Was Then, This Is Now," *Cincinnati Magazine*, May 2004.

380 he worked to enact a similar measure: "Taking the Initiative: Battles over Gay Rights Intensify in Ohio, Florida, Colorado and Oregon," *The Advocate*, October 5, 1993.

380 fighting for years against pornography: Mark Curnutte, "Moral Crusaders: Anti-Porn Group Widens Focus," *Cincinnati Enquirer*, February 13, 1994.

380 In 1998, with all possible court challenges: Julie Irwin, "Law Denying Gay Protection Stands," *Cincinnati Enquirer*, October 14, 1998.

380 Luken's push for repeal: Vacariello, "That Was Then, This Is Now."

380 "Nothing has changed": Lisa Cornwell, "Cincinnati Voters Deciding Fate of Ban on Gay Rights Laws," Associated Press, October 25, 2004.

380 Burress, meanwhile, prepared to fight: Gregory Korte, "Gay Issue Foes' Names Not Listed," *Cincinnati Enquirer*, October 28, 2004.

381 "I do consider amending": Amy McCullough, "Marriage Amendment in Works," *Cincinnati Enquirer*, April 24, 2004.

381 A *Columbus Dispatch* poll taken: "Poll: Ohioans Oppose Gay Marriage by More Than 3-to-1 Margin," Associated Press, April 6, 2004.

381 Burress had until early August: Alan Johnson, "Foes of Same-Sex Marriage Seek Vote," *Columbus Dispatch*, July 19, 2004.

381 from half of the state's eighty-eight counties: Mark Stricherz, "Marriage at the Polls," *Weekly Standard*, August 30, 2004.

381 Ohio's language went further: Daniel R. Pinello, *America's War on Same-Sex Couples and Their Families: And How the Courts Saved Them* (New York: Cambridge University Press, 2017), 36–37.

381 Opponents included many beyond: Sam Howe Verhovek, "Gay Marriage Ban Faces Some Unlikely Foes," *Los Angeles Times*, October 31, 2004.

382 All three were opposed: Alan Johnson, "Gay-Marriage Ban; Issue 1 Wording Makes It Strictest," *Columbus Dispatch*, October 11, 2004.

382 Frist pushed back a vote: David Freddoso, "No Vote Soon to Marriage Amendment," *Human Events*, May 24, 2004.

382 full attention of Arlington Group members: Alan Cooperman and Thomas B.

Edsall, "Evangelicals Say They Led the Charge for the GOP," *Washington Post,* November 8, 2004.

382 "We were out-organized": Alan Cooperman, "Gay Marriage Ban in Mo. May Resonate Nationwide," *Washington Post,* August 5, 2004.

383 was sued in forty-two different: *State ex Rel. Essig v. Blackwell,* 103 Ohio St. 3d 481 (Ohio 2004).

383 petition signatures from seventy-eight thousand: Alan Johnson, "Foes of Same-Sex Marriage Seek Vote," *Columbus Dispatch,* July 19, 2004.

383 shared the email addresses: Frances FitzGerald, *The Evangelicals: The Struggle to Shape America* (New York: Simon & Schuster, 2017), 502.

383 On Election Day, Burress saw his: Lucy May, "Issue 3 Opponent Makes Threat," *Cincinnati Business Courier,* November 4, 2004.

383 The data pointing to this conclusion: Daniel A. Smith, Matthew DeSantis, and Jason Kassel, "Same-Sex Marriage Ballot Measures and the 2004 Presidential Election," *State & Local Government Review* 38, no. 2 (2006): 78–91.

383 Bush had been reelected only: Michael Foust, "Did the Same-Sex 'Marriage' Issue Hand Bush a Victory in Ohio?" *Baptist Press,* November 4, 2004.

383 including thirty-nine thousand Amish: Robert Knight, "Ohio's Faithful Chorus May Call the Tune on Election Day," Townhall.com, November 5, 2012.

384 In September, two months after: Carolyn Lochhead, "GOP Urges a Vote on Same-Sex Marriage Ban—Some See It as Effort to Stress Gay Issues," *San Francisco Chronicle,* September 28, 2004.

384 But the results from the thirteen: James Dao, "After Victory, Crusader Against Same-Sex Marriage Thinks Big," *New York Times,* November 26, 2004.

49. When You're Living Through It

387 "little Paul Revere of marriage": Lyn Stoesen, "Legal Activist: Gay Marriage Is Coming," *Washington Blade,* December 8, 1994.

387 "Thirty years from now": Evan Wolfson, *Why Marriage Matters: America, Equality, and Gay People's Right to Marry* (New York: Simon & Schuster, 2004), 187.

387 conventional wisdom had begun to set in: Carolyn Lochhead, "Gay Marriage: Did Issue Help Re-elect Bush?" *San Francisco Chronicle,* November 4, 2004.

388 Public opinion on same-sex marriage: Pew Research Center, "Growing Public Support for Same-Sex Marriage," February 16, 2012, www.pewresearch.org.

388 "moment of peril": Evan Wolfson, "Marriage Equality and Some Lessons for the Scary Work of Winning," *Law & Sexuality: A Review of Lesbian, Gay, Bisexual and Transgender Legal Issues* 14, no. 135 (2005).

389 "would not have come as soon as it did": John Cloud, "2004 TIME 100: Evan Wolfson," *Time,* April 26, 2004.

389 journalism anthology he had received: *Reporting Civil Rights, Part One: American Journalism, 1941–1963* (New York: Library of America, 2003).

50. Paul Revere Rides In

390 "the images of marriage in society": Nate Schweber, "Vows: Evan Wolfson and Cheng He," *New York Times,* October 21, 2011.

390 acknowledge his sexuality: Carlos A. Ball, *From the Closet to the Courtroom: Five LGBT Rights Lawsuits That Have Changed the Nation* (Boston: Beacon Press, 2010), 158.

390 two years teaching: "From Peace Corps to Marriage Equality Advocate," *Peace Corps Times,* 2013.

390 "For gay women and men": Evan Wolfson, "Samesex Marriage and Morality: The Human Rights Vision of the Constitution," unpublished thesis, Harvard Law School, April 1983.

391 write the group's amicus brief: Ellen Ann Anderson, *Out of the Closets and into the Courts: Legal Opportunity Structure and Gay Rights Litigation* (Ann Arbor: University of Michigan Press, 2005), 44.

391 picking up as many as twenty clients: Jim Merrett, "America's Gay Legal Crusaders," *The Advocate,* January 29, 1991.

392 "the gold ring of marriage": John M. Broder, "Groups Debate Slower Strategy on Gay Rights," *New York Times,* December 9, 2004.

392 "I think it's quite a conservative": Peter Freiberg, "Movement to Legalize Gay Marriage Gathers Steam," *Washington Blade,* November 8, 1991.

392 Lambda legal seemed to be the locus: Nancy D. Polikoff, "For the Sake of All Children: Opponents and Supporters of Same-Sex Marriage Both Miss the Mark," *New York City Law Review,* 8, no. 2 (2005), 594-98.

392 The man who in April 1989: Thomas B. Stoddard, "Gay Marriages: Make Them Legal," *New York Times,* March 4, 1989.

393 staffers exploited the void: Thomas J. Jackson, "The Resignation of Thomas B. Stoddard," *New York Native,* November 18, 1991.

393 job talk at the University of Hawaii: "University of Hawaii School of Law," *Lambda Update,* Lambda Legal Defense and Education Fund, April 1992, 23.

394 lawsuit that attorney William Eskridge had filed: Patricia Gaines-Carter, "Legal Snag Keeps Gays from Tying the Knot," *Washington Post,* December 6, 1990.

394 Stoddard's doubts about attorney: Andrew Miller, "DC Marriage Lawsuit Irks Gay Attorneys," *Outweek,* December 12, 1990.

394 lawsuit filed on behalf of a nineteen-year-old: *Dale v. Boy Scouts of America,* 160 N.J. 562.

395 the case won the attention of mainstream journalists: Joan Biskupic, "Hawaii Court Opens Way to Gay Marriages," *Washington Post,* May 7, 1993.

395 coverage in the *Washington Post* and *New York Times:* Jeffrey Schmalz, "In Hawaii, Step Toward Legalized Gay Marriage," *New York Times,* May 7, 1993.

395 "It's an enormous step": Bettina Boxall, "Hawaii Court Revives Suit on Gay Marriages," *Los Angeles Times,* May 7, 1993.

395 By early 1993, both Stoddard and Ettelbrick: Chris Bull, "Tom Stoddard, Life After Lambda," *The Advocate,* March 10, 1992.

395 "Whatever you thought before": Chris Geidner, "Domestic Disturbance," *Metro Weekly,* May 4, 2011.

396 on a study of marriage laws: Barbara J. Cox, "The Little Project: From Alternative Families to Domestic Partnerships to Same-Sex Marriage," *Wisconsin Women's Law Journal* 15, no. 1 (Spring 2000), 84–85.

396 "Nongay Americans haven't had to deal": Evan Wolfson, "Altared States: Attorney Evan Wolfson Argues the Case for Marriage," *10 Percent,* May 1995.

397 announced by news reports days before: Dan Harrie, "Bill Drafted to Bolster Ban on Homosexual Marriages," *Salt Lake Tribune,* February 9, 1995.

397 The bill passed the senate: "Utah Won't Accept Same-Sex Marriages," *New York Times,* March 3, 1995.

397 doubts about the legality of its late-night passage: Tony Semerad, "Ban on Gay Marriages to Be Annulled?" *Salt Lake Tribune,* May 3, 1995.

398 backlash that might not have: Randy Frame, "Seeking a Right to the Rite," *Christianity Today*, March 4, 1996.

398 far more controversial than it looked: Linda Silberman, letter to the editor, *New York Times*, "Hawaii Decision on Gay Marriages Should Affect Only Hawaii," April 11, 1996.

399 "When one wishes to assert": International Council of Women and National Woman Suffrage Association (U.S.), *Report of the International Council of Women: Assembled by the National Woman Suffrage Association, Washington, D.C., U.S. of America, March 25 to April 1, 1888* (Washington, DC: National Woman Suffrage Association, 1888).

399 quoted in an issue briefing: "Same-Sex Marriage: An Overview of the Issue," House Republican Conference Issue Brief, U.S. House Republican Conference, June 10, 1996.

399 read aloud from Wolfson's memo: U.S. Congress, House, Judiciary Committee, Constitution Subcommittee, hearing on the Defense of Marriage Act, May 16, 1996.

399 "The vision that I constantly think of": Joe Morris, "Freedom to Marry Town Hall Mtg Draws Record Crowds," *San Diego Gay & Lesbian Times*, January 23, 1996.

51. Speaking for the Silent Majority

401 "The very epi-center of gay activity": John Paul Hudson, *The Gay Insider, USA* (New York: Stonewall Publishing, 1972).

401 West Hollywood was a 1.9-square-mile cluster: Tom Tugend, "Russians & Gays & Lesbians, Oh My . . . ," *Jewish Journal of Los Angeles*, March 23, 2000.

401 When the five-person city council it elected: Robert Lindsey, "The Talk of West Hollywood; West Hollywood Acting on Pledges," *New York Times*, March 19, 1985

401 That council had within months: Lindsey, "The Talk of West Hollywood."

402 "responsible for each other's welfare": Rob Gurwitt, " 'Domestic Partners': How Much Recognition?" *Governing*, October 1990.

402 applied to hospital and jail-visitation rights: Douglas NeJaime, "Before Marriage: the Unexplored History of Nonmarital Recognition and Its Relationship to Marriage," *California Law Review* 102, no. 1 (February 2014): 119–21.

402 Established in the same year as the Stonewall: Nancy Wride, "Morris Kight, 83; Gay Rights Pioneer in the Southland," *Los Angeles Times*, January 20, 2003.

403 "one of the primary testing grounds": J. V. McAuley, "Wedding Row: Newly Formed Freedom to Marry Coalition Lobbies," *LA Weekly*, June 30, 1995.

403 An agreement to coordinate future efforts: "Lambda, Other Groups Back 'Right to Marry' Resolution," *Bay Area Reporter*, July 6, 1995.

404 self-described "gay liberationists": Urvashi Vaid, *Virtual Equality: The Mainstreaming of Gay and Lesbian Liberation* (New York: Doubleday, 1995), 196.

405 recent legal decisions bearing on recognition: Philip S. Gutis, "New York Court Defines Family to Include Homosexual Couples," *New York Times*, July 7, 1989.

405 "Certainly since AIDS, to be gay": Andrew Sullivan, "Here Comes the Groom: A (Conservative) Case for Gay Marriage," *New Republic*, August 28, 1989.

405 a revisionist account of the Catholic Church's relationship: John Boswell, *Christianity, Social Tolerance, and Homosexuality: Gay People in Western Europe from the Be-*

ginning of the Christian Era to the Fourteenth Century (Chicago: University of Chicago Press, 1981).

405 Boswell's conclusion was that the church's homophobia: Richard Hall, "John Boswell on Gay Tolerance and the Christian Tradition," *The Advocate*, May 28, 1981.

406 Boswell died of AIDS: David W. Dunlap, "John E. Boswell, 47, Historian of Medieval Gay Culture, Dies," *New York Times*, December 25, 1994.

406 had won him a sideline as model: Walter Kirn, "The Editor as Gap Model," *New York Times Magazine*, March 7, 1993.

406 Members of the self-described direct-action group: Sara Warner, *Acts of Gaiety: LGBT Performance and the Politics of Pleasure* (Ann Arbor: University of Michigan Press, 2012), 94.

407 in which he continued his advocacy: Andrew Sullivan, *Virtually Normal: An Argument About Homosexuality* (New York: Alfred A. Knopf, 1995).

407 two San Francisco lesbian activists in the group: Ryan Conrad, *Against Equality: Queer Critiques of Gay Marriage*, ed. Ryan Conrad (Lewiston, ME: Against Equality Publishing Collective, 2010), 83–84.

407 "What a wonderful variety of relationships": Kate Raphael and Deeg Gold, "Gay Marriage: Civil Right or Civil Wrong?" Lesbians and Gays Against Intervention (LaGAI) website, April 2004. Reproduced as "Marriage Is Still the Opiate of the Queers," *UltraViolet*, April–May 2004.

408 urgency of protected unanticipated gains: Paula L. Ettelbrick, "Wedlock Alert: A Comment on Lesbian and Gay Family Recognition," *Journal of Law and Policy* 5, no. 1 (1996), 109.

408 "We were immediately launched": Chris Geidner, "Domestic Disturbance," *Metro Weekly*, May 4, 2011.

52. Clear It with Evan

409 aided by a handful of lawyers: Thomas M. Keane, "Aloha, Marriage? Constitutional and Choice of Law Arguments for Recognition of Same-Sex Marriages." *Stanford Law Review* 47, no. 3 (1995): 499–532.

410 "Now we're at a real tug-of-war stage": Bettina Boxall, "Hawaii Justices Open Door to Legalizing Gay Marriages," *Los Angeles Times*, March 26, 1995.

410 championed domestic-partnership laws: Douglas NeJaime, "Before Marriage: the Unexplored History of Nonmarital Recognition and Its Relationship to Marriage," *California Law Review* 102, no. 1 (February 2014): 128–29.

410 "You don't build the penthouse": David Link, "Gay Rites," *Reason*, January 1996.

411 case to fight lewd-conduct laws: George E. Haggerty, *Gay Histories and Cultures: An Encyclopedia, Volume 2* (London: Routledge, 1999), 538.

411 "We may leave the room": Peter Freiberg, "Wolfson Leaves Lambda for Freedom-to-Marry Work," *Washington Blade*, January 30, 2001.

412 "strongly recommended that people not file": Lisa Keen, "Alaska Couple Challenges State on Marriage License," *Washington Blade*, August 11, 1995.

412 "I totally, personally, and deeply understand": Lisa Keen, "Gay Couple Files Petition over Marriage License," *Washington Blade*, April 5, 1996.

412 One year after Shawna Underwood: Jean Patteson, "Gay Couples Seek Benefits, Acceptance of Marriage," *Orlando Sentinel*, September 19, 1993.

412 Days later, citing meetings: Debbie Salamone, "Same-Sex Marriage Suit to End;

Two Orange County Women Will Drop Their Legal Action Because of a Similar Suit in Hawaii," *Orlando Sentinel,* September 9, 1994.

412 Similarly, Arizona plaintiffs who lost: *Callender v. Corbett,* No. 296666, at 3 (Ariz. Super. Ct. Apr. 13, 1994).

413 In the liberal college town they discovered: "Gay Couple's Request for Marriage License Turned Down in Ithaca," Associated Press, December 5, 1995.

413 "If they really want to go ahead": David W. Dunlap, "For Better or Worse, a Marital Milestone," *New York Times,* July 27, 1995.

413 used the press to describe: David W. Dunlap, "Ithaca Denies Gay Men a Marriage License," *New York Times,* December 5, 1995.

414 "Part of me very much wants": Dunlap, "For Better or Worse, a Marital Milestone."

414 "I'm disappointed that these groups": David W. Dunlap, "Ithaca Denies Gay Men a Marriage License," *New York Times,* December 5, 1993.

414 An unrelated investigation by *The Daily Oklahoman:* Randy Ellis, "Exchange-Student Problems Bring Shake-Up," *The Daily Oklahoman,* June 10, 2007.

414 "by far the most important positive ruling ever": "Til Death Do Us Part: A Hawaii Court Upholds a Challenge to the Denial of Same-Sex Marriages," *The Advocate,* June 15, 1993.

415 Lambda's own analysis showed: Lisa Keen, "Alaska Couple Challenges State on Marriage License," *Washington Blade,* August 11, 1995.

415 Brause and Dugan moved ahead: *Brause v. State,* 21 P.3d 357.

415 polling showed his side losing: "Voters strongly oppose gay unions," *Honolulu Star-Bulletin,* February 24, 1997.

416 National polls showed that they had lost: "Public Opinion on Gay Marriage: Opponents Consistently Outnumber Supporters," Pew Research Center, August 9, 2009. www.pewresearch.org.

53. Organization Man

417 In 2000, the *National Law Journal* named: "The 100 Most Influential Lawyers in America," *National Law Journal,* June 7, 2000.

417 When Hawaii officials stayed: Ken Kobayashi, "State to Challenge Ruling," *Honolulu Advertiser,* December 4, 1996.

417 The Boy Scouts asked the Supreme Court: *Boy Scouts of America v. Dale,* 530 US 640.

418 Wolfson had spent the day flirting: Joyce Murdoch and Deb Price, *Courting Justice: Gay Men and Lesbians v. the Supreme Court* (New York: Basic Books, 2001), 502.

418 After the justices ruled that Georgia: *Bowers v. Hardwick,* 478 US 186.

418 "I swore I would not": Joyce Murdoch and Deb Price, *Courting Justice: Gay Men and Lesbians v. the Supreme Court* (New York: Basic Books, 2001), 502.

418 "Is the best that you could": *Boy Scouts of America v. Dale,* 530 US 640, transcript of oral argument.

418 The state planned to begin: Carey Goldberg, "Vermont Gives Final Approval to Same-Sex Unions," *New York Times,* April 26, 2000.

419 "two major pieces of my work coming": Laura Kiritsy, "Evan Wolfson, Leader in Same-Sex Marriage Battle, Says He Is Leaving Lambda," *Bay Windows,* March 29, 2001.

419 the Supreme Court ruled five-to-four: *Boy Scouts of America v. Dale,* 530 US 640.

419 "By fighting, by engaging": Murdoch and Price, *Courting Justice,* 516.

419 "I really felt then that": Kiritsy, "Evan Wolfson, Leader in Same-Sex Marriage Battle."

419 Wolfson would continue to fantasize: Evan Wolfson, "...Domestically Attached," *The Advocate,* October 14, 1997.

419 "I've always really been very deeply impressed": Kiritsy, "Evan Wolfson, Leader in Same-Sex Marriage Battle."

420 The wave of mini-DOMAs enacted: Kenneth Jost, "Gay Marriage," *CQ Researcher,* September 5, 2003.

420 In 1997, California state senator Pete Knight: Mark Newton, "States Resisting Same-Sex Marriages," *Cal State Long Beach On-Line Forty-Niner,* March 15, 1999.

420 decided to go instead: Kenneth P. Miller, *Direct Democracy and the Courts* (Cambridge, UK: Cambridge University Press, 2009), 4.

420 Knight's one-sentence Proposition 22 qualified: Judy Mann, "From California, a Proposal on Gay Marriage," *Washington Post,* December 22, 1999.

420 The state's Democratic establishment was almost uniformly: Thomas D. Elias, "Gay 'Marriage' Initiative Splits GOP in California," *Washington Times,* March 6, 2000.

420 The Nebraska Family Council began collecting: Jeremy Quittner, "Taking Initiatives," *The Advocate,* October 10, 2000.

420 served as a campus coordinator: James Lebovitz, "Campus Registration Drive Draws Big Student Turnout," *Yale Daily News,* October 21, 1976.

420 "what was probably the largest leaflet": "Carter Supporters Here Plan Registration Drive," *Yale Daily News,* September 29, 1976.

421 As a graduate student teaching political philosophy: Yale University, *Five Years Out: Class Directory, 1978–1983,* 137.

421 "I think anyone who knows me": Kiritsy, "Evan Wolfson, Leader in Same-Sex Marriage Battle."

54. Mining the Foundations

422 "liberated to bring people together": Laura Kiritsy, "Evan Wolfson, Leader in Same-Sex Marriage Battle, Says He Is Leaving Lambda," *Bay Windows,* March 29, 2001.

422 a family foundation sustained by the wealth: Joe Garofoli, "S.F. Foundation Supported Gay Marriage Long Before It Was Cool," *San Francisco Chronicle,* June 28, 2015.

422 "Inconceivable as it may seem": Jeremy Quittner, "Scouting for Marriage Rights," *The Advocate,* May 22, 2001.

422 "the earth moved": Evan Wolfson, "The Freedom to Marry: Our Struggle for the Map of the Country," *Quinnipiac Law Review* 16, no. 1–2 (Spring & Summer 1996): 209–16.

423 "Marriage is about more": Mubarak Dahir, "Marriage on His Mind," *The Advocate,* June 26, 2003.

423 The Campaign for Military Service had also been conceived: Jeffrey Schmalz, "Gay Groups Regrouping for War on Military Ban," *New York Times,* February 7, 1993.

423 "stirred up turf battles and grumbling": Bettina Boxall, "L.A.'s New Gay Muscle; with Big Bucks and Connections, the Local Gay Community Is Changing Politics Nationwide," *Los Angeles Times,* March 28, 1993.

424 Among observers of gay politics: Jeffrey Schmalz, "Split on Gay Tactics for Military Ban," *New York Times*, May 23, 1993.

424 "Unlike the gays-in-the-military fiasco": Marvin Liebman, "Are We Ready for Our Most Important Battle?" *Bay Windows*, January 1995.

426 "explore the next steps": Kiritsy, "Evan Wolfson, Leader in Same-Sex Marriage Battle."

426 The institution was in a period: Julian Guthrie, "The Haas Legacy: How One Family's Generosity and Commitment to Civic Life Are Transforming the Bay Area," *San Francisco Chronicle*, July 1, 2007.

55. Outgiving

427 It would be more than a decade: James B. Stewart, "Among Gay C.E.O.s, the Pressure to Conform," *New York Times*, June 27, 2014.

427 James Hormel was an heir: C. W. Nevius, "James Hormel to Be Honored as Early Hero of Gay Rights," *San Francisco Chronicle*, March 4, 2016.

427 Fred Hochberg to the Lillian Vernon mail-order: Fred Hochberg, "On the Passing of My Mother, Lillian Vernon," *Huffington Post*, December 22, 2015.

427 Henry van Ameringen to the New York–based chemical: "H. van Ameringen, Philanthropist, 95," *New York Times*, May 6, 1996.

427 Ellen Malcolm became an influential: Amanda Spake, "Women Can Be Power Brokers, Too," *Washington Post*, June 5, 1988.

427 at crucial moments, Martin Luther King Jr.: David J. Garrow, *Bearing the Cross: Martin Luther King, Jr., and the Southern Christian Leadership Conference* (New York: William Morrow & Company, 1986), 197, 219.

428 a plastic surgeon's son: Chris LaMonte, "Tim Gill," *Westword*, January 29, 1998.

428 The closest thing Tim Gill had had to an inheritance: Joshua Green, "America's Gay Corporate Warrior Wants to Bring Full Equality to Red States," *Bloomberg Businessweek*, April 24, 2015.

428 "I didn't realize that I was rich": LaMonte, "Tim Gill."

428 polls had shown it likely to lose: Dirk Johnson, "Colorado Homosexuals Feel Betrayed," *New York Times*, November 8, 1992.

428 "Everyone has the right": Green, "America's Gay Corporate Warrior."

428 whose software was used largely: Roy Ahn, "Evolution of the Gill Foundation," Harvard Kennedy School Case Study, HKS No, 1717.1 (Cambridge, MA: Harvard Kennedy School, 2004).

428 When he was informed that *Sports Illustrated*: Sally Ruth Bourrie, "Quintessentially Quark: Tim Gill," *Colorado Business*, September 1993.

429 On the same day New York City mayor David Dinkins: "New York City Mayor Urges Travel Boycott of Colorado," Associated Press, December 9, 1992.

429 Gill pledged $1 million: "Quark Chairman Gives $1M for Gay Rights Fight," *Newsbytes*, December 11, 1992.

429 "That makes it much harder": Bourrie, "Quintessentially Quark: Tim Gill."

429 His mid-five-figure check to the anti–Amendment 2 effort: Ray Flack, "Gay Rights Group Lists Funds Raised to Fight Amendment 2—Organization Files Late but Pays Fine," *Colorado Springs Gazette Telegraph*, August 7, 1992.

429 Furthermore, Gill lacked a method: Ahn, "Evolution of the Gill Foundation."

429 the next year, she had organized: Rosemary Harris, "Minority Coalition Sets Agenda for Unity Rally," *Colorado Springs Gazette*, September 5, 1993.

430 "What the Gill Foundation is attempting": Valerie Richardson, "Money Can Buy You Love," *Philanthropy Roundtable,* October 2000.

430 "Tim went from being": Ahn, "Evolution of the Gill Foundation."

430 Gill would back organizations: Gill Foundation, *Shift: The Direction of New Philanthropy,* 1999 Annual Report (Denver: Gill Foundation, 1999).

431 open to any gay donor: Doug Ireland, "Rebuilding the Gay Movement," *The Nation,* July 12, 1999.

56. Clarity of Coalition

432 First Gill committed to leaving: Jim Hopkins, "Quark Founder Becomes Philanthropist," *USA Today,* August 15, 2001.

432 In 1999, when he had the chance: Andy Kroll, "How Tim Gill Turned His Fortune into a Powerful Force for LGBTQ Rights," *Rolling Stone,* June 23, 2017.

432 the next spring, the NASDAQ: Ben Geier, "What Did We Learn from the Dotcom Stock Bubble of 2000?" *Time,* March 12, 2015.

432 "the nation's leading philanthropist": Hopkins, "Quark Founder Becomes Philanthropist."

432 "the mostly young staff of 35 looks": Valerie Richardson, "Money Can Buy You Love," *Philanthropy Roundtable,* October 2000.

432 He seeded the operation: Roy Ahn, "Evolution of the Gill Foundation," Harvard Kennedy School Case Study, HKS No, 1717.1 (Cambridge, MA: Harvard Kennedy School, 2004).

433 "terrible libertarian tendencies": Robert Frank, *Richistan: A Journey Through the American Wealth Boom and the Lives of the New Rich* (New York: Crown Business, 2007), 196.

435 Yet profiling gay voters: Sasha Issenberg, *The Victory Lab: The Secret Science of Winning Campaigns* (New York: Crown, 2012), 294.

435 giving out one-fifth of the country's total: Richardson, "Money Can Buy You Love."

435 Gill took an interest in its electoral politics: Colleen O'Connor, "Who Is the Real Tim Gill?" *Denver Post,* December 12, 2004.

435 "I wouldn't, for example, be able": Stuart Steers, "The Gang of Four," *5280,* May 2005.

435 "Our idea was, let's find the good": Frank, *Richistan,* 196.

436 In 1996, as a Colorado legislator: Thomas Frank, "Veto of Same-Sex Marriage Ban Backfires; Romer Alienates Both Sides," *Denver Post,* March 27, 1996.

436 "Marilyn Musgrave started on the school board": Frank, *Richistan,* 196.

436 Gill was invited by Rutt Bridges: Steers, "The Gang of Four."

437 The ads were savage: David Kelly, "Aggressive TV Ads Enrage Colorado GOP," *Los Angeles Times,* October 1, 2004.

437 The name of the entity: Colleen O'Connor, "Who Is the Real Tim Gill?"

438 "a better world": Gill Foundation, *Shift: The Direction of New Philanthropy,* 1999 Annual Report (Denver: Gill Foundation, 1999).

439 The millionaires' Colorado plan had gone: Steers, "The Gang of Four."

439 "We are finally realizing that how we win": Bob Roehr, "The Gill Action Fund: Serious LGBT politics," *Bay Area Reporter,* March 29, 2006.

440 a former Massachusetts legislator whose appointment: Chris Bull, "Taking Over the Hot Seat," *The Advocate,* January 7, 2004.

440 left her post amid internal rancor: Alan Cooperman, "Philosophical Clashes Cited as Chief Quits Gay Rights Group," *Washington Post,* December 1, 2004.

440 how aggressively to invest: Yvonne Abraham, "Gay Rights Activists Split over Taking Softer Course," *Boston Globe,* December 13, 2004.

440 "Jacques was head of the HRC": Stefen Styrsky, "Jacques to Leave Helm of HRC," *Gay City News,* December 2, 2004.

441 "we need to reintroduce ourselves": John M. Broder, "Groups Debate Slower Strategy on Gay Rights," *New York Times,* December 9, 2004.

441 with "different approaches, different tactics": Nathaniel Frank, *Awakening: How Gays and Lesbians Brought Marriage Equality to America* (Cambridge, MA: Belknap Press of Harvard University, 2017), 166.

441 "This election may have shown": Hilary Rosen, "Paving the Middle Road of Civil Unions Is Not Caving In," *The Advocate,* December 7, 2004.

441 The Human Rights Campaign remained the biggest: Sarah Wildman, "Tough Times at HRC," *The Advocate,* March 29, 2005.

441 Jonathan Lewis, a major Democratic donor: Kerry Eleveld, *Don't Tell Me to Wait: How the Fight for Gay Rights Changed America and Transformed Obama's Presidency* (New York: Basic Books, 2015), 38.

441 As the AIDS activist and playwright Larry Kramer: Wildman, "Tough Times at HRC."

57. After the Bloodbath

443 starting his law career: Carlos A. Ball, *From the Closet to the Courtroom: Five LGBT Rights Lawsuits That Have Changed Our Nation* (Boston: Beacon Press, 2010), 106–9.

444 His 1996 book: Matthew A. Coles, *Try This at Home! A Do-It-Yourself Guide to Winning Gay and Lesbian Civil Rights Policy: An ACLU Guidebook* (New York: New Press, 1996).

444 conduct ten focus groups: Nan D. Hunter, "Varieties of Constitutional Experience: Democracy and the Marriage Equality Campaign," *UCLA Law Review* 64, no. 6 (December 2017): 1685–86.

445 In Oregon, the plaintiffs included: Arthur S. Leonard, "Oregon Court Recognizes Gay Marriages," *Gay City News,* April 22, 2004.

445 in New York, they were those who: "Throngs at City Hall Seek Marriage Licenses," *Gay City News,* March 4, 2004.

446 "Most of the folks in these two groups": Matt Coles, "The Plan to Win Marriage," in *Love Unites Us: Winning the Freedom to Marry in America,* ed. Kevin M. Cathcart and Leslie J. Gabel-Brett (New York: The New Press, 2016), 104.

58. Punish the Wicked

452 "viewed politics as evil and dirty": Robert Frank, *Richistan: A Journey Through the American Wealth Boom and the Lives of the New Rich* (New York: Crown Business, 2007), 197.

452 After the Gang of Four helped flip: Stuart Steers, "The Gang of Four," *5280,* May 2005.

452 Ted Trimpa worked with Democratic legislative leaders: Bob Roehr, "The Gill Action Fund: Serious LGBT Politics," *Bay Area Reporter,* March 29, 2006.

452 could make a show of vetoing: Mark P. Couch, "Owens Vetoes Bill for Gays on the Job," *Denver Post,* May 21, 2005.

452 while letting the hate-crimes provision: "Gov. Owens Wields a Busy, Fair Veto Pen," *Denver Post,* June 3, 2005.

452 All those who answered: John Cloud, "The Gay Mafia That's Redefining Liberal Politics," *Time,* October 31, 2008.

453 "the gay I.R.S.": Cloud, "The Gay Mafia."

453 after one of its own 2005 surveys: Proteus Fund, *Hearts & Minds: The Untold Story of How Philanthropy and the Civil Marriage Collaborative Helped America Embrace Marriage Equality* (Amherst, MA: Proteus Fund, 2015), 8.

454 he could boast that his group: E. J. Graff, "Marital Blitz," *American Prospect,* February 20, 2006.

455 "The strategic piece of the puzzle": Joshua Green, "They Won't Know What Hit Them," *The Atlantic,* March 2007.

455 Gill made plans to launch: Eric Gorski, "Benefactor's Group to Fight Effort to Ban Gay Marriage," *Denver Post,* December 6, 2005.

456 group faced its biggest-ever crisis: Michael Sokolove, "Can This Marriage Be Saved?" *New York Times Magazine,* April 11, 2004.

456 Guerriero decided to go public: Rick Klein and Mary Leonard, "Republican Gay Rights Group Hits Bush, Romney Stances," *Boston Globe,* March 11, 2004.

456 "fair-minded Republican allies": Johanna Neuman, "Gay GOP Group Won't Endorse Bush Reelection," *Los Angeles Times,* September 8, 2004.

456 Bill Smith was a native Alabamian: Bill Smith, "Bill Smith on Political Operations in the Fight to Win the Freedom to Marry: The Freedom to Marry Oral History Project" conducted by Martin Meeker in 2015, Oral History Center, The Bancroft Library, University of California, Berkeley, 2017.

457 in 1988, Massachusetts governor Mike Dukakis had turned away: David Mixner, *Stranger Among Friends* (New York: Bantam Books, 1996), 201.

458 Bill Clinton had cultivated gay donors: Peg Byron, "Meet Mixner the Fixer," *Out,* September 1992.

458 gay money had come to be seen: Melanie Mason, Matea Gold, and Joseph Tanfani, "Gay Political Donors Move from Margins to Mainstream," *Los Angeles Times,* May 13, 2012.

458 "One of the problems with Tim's strategy": Green, "They Won't Know What Hit Them."

458 Just ahead of state elections the previous November: Cloud, "The Gay Mafia."

459 had sued the Polk County recorder: Camilla Taylor, " 'Our Liberties We Prize': Winning Marriage in Iowa," in *Love Unites Us: Winning the Freedom to Marry in America,* ed. Kevin M. Cathcart and Leslie J. Gabel-Brett (New York: The New Press, 2016), 131–41.

459 Already state judges had in 2005 rejected: Paul Brennan, "How a Divorce Helped Kick-Start Marriage Equality in Iowa," *Little Village Magazine,* March 4, 2019.

459 prevent a district judge from dissolving: Kathleen Burge, "Iowa Judge Causes Stir in Granting Gay Divorce," *Boston Globe,* December 13, 2003.

459 Some of those legislators: Tom Witosky and Marc Hansen, *Equal Before the Law* (Iowa City: University of Iowa Press, 2015), 95–99.

460 "driven, cycle to cycle": Green, "They Won't Know What Hit Them."

460 A few weeks after the election: Green, "They Won't Know What Hit Them."

59. Let California Ring

463 stuck to an incrementalist track: Scott L. Cummings and Douglas NeJaime, "Lawyering for Marriage Equality," *UCLA Law Review* 57, 1258–60.

463 "all but marriage": Evan Wolfson, "Marriage Equality and Some Lessons for the Scary Work of Winning," *Law & Sexuality: A Review of Lesbian, Gay, Bisexual and Transgender Legal Issues* 14, no. 135 (2005).

463 By early 2004, a California domestic partnership: E. J. Graff, "Marital Blitz," *American Prospect*, February 20, 2006.

463 self-styled champion of gay rights: Joe Mathews, Peter Nicholas, and Nancy Vogel, "Governor Says Law Permitting Gay Marriage Would Be 'Fine,'" *Los Angeles Times*, March 2, 2004.

463 But as a marriage bill moved through: Joe Dignan, "Marriage Bill Teeters in California—Vote on Measure Open until Friday in Gay-Friendly Assembly, but Tally Six Votes Shy," *Gay City News*, June 2, 2005.

463 He ultimately issued a veto: Michael Finnegan and Maura Dolan, "Citing Prop. 22, Gov. Rejects Gay Marriage Bill," *Los Angeles Times*, September 8, 2005.

464 "You are holding up history": Joe Dignan, "Arnold Says No to Gay Marriage—Schwarzenegger Vows to Veto Historic Law Passed by Legislature," *Gay City News*, September 8, 2005.

464 Already views on the matter appeared: Finnegan and Dolan, "Citing Prop. 22, Gov. Rejects Gay Marriage Bill."

464 "an ambitious, affirmative public education campaign": Freedom to Marry, *2006 Annual Report* (New York: Freedom to Marry, 2006), 5.

466 "It's putting the people we're trying to talk to": Jesse Hamlin, "TV Ad Campaign Attempts to Sway the Undecided on Same-Sex Marriage," *San Francisco Chronicle*, October 9, 2007.

466 "respectful debate": Nancy Vogel, "Same-Sex Unions OKd by Assembly," *Los Angeles Times*, June 6, 2007.

466 "We're trying to create favorable conditions": Bill Ainsworth, "New Year, Old Debate over Gay Marriage," *San Diego Union-Tribune*, December 26, 2006.

466 "could well be the Gettysburg": Freedom to Marry, *1996 Annual Report*, 3.

60. It Came from San Diego

469 When Governor Arnold Schwarzenegger vetoed: Steve Lawrence, "Schwarzenegger Vetoes Gay Marriage Bill Again," Associated Press, October 12, 2007.

469 designated by Mormon and Roman Catholic: Gregory A. Prince, *Gay Rights and the Mormon Church: Intended Actions, Unintended Consequences* (Salt Lake City: University of Utah Press, 2019), 72–82.

469 Their local partner: Jennifer Warren, "Initiative Divides a Family," *Los Angeles Times*, November 24, 1999.

469 The so-called Knight Initiative: Jennifer Warren, "Initiative Divides a Family," *Los Angeles Times*, November 24, 1999.

470 It was, Thomasson said upon passage: Bob Egelko, "Davis to OK Rights for Same-Sex Couples," *San Francisco Chronicle*, August 17, 2003.

470 "It is in the child's best interest": Pauline J. Chang, "Californians Get Two Shots at Protecting Marriage," *Christian Post*, August 19, 2005.

470 Project Marriage claimed: Lisa Leff, "Gay Marriage Opponents Shift Focus to November Election or Beyond," Associated Press, December 28, 2005.

470 The divide between a sweeping amendment: Chang, "Californians Get Two Shots at Protecting Marriage."

471 Within a day: Harriet Chang, "S.F. Sues over Legality of Same-Sex Marriages," *San Francisco Chronicle*, February 20, 2004.

471 It took nearly a month: Bob Egelko, "Court Halts Gay Vows," *San Francisco Chronicle*, March 12, 2004.

471 While the California Supreme Court: Egelko, "Court Halts Gay Vows."

471 led the challenge with support: Scott L. Cummings and Douglas NeJaime, "Lawyering for Marriage Equality," *UCLA Law Review* 57, 1281–93.

471 The existing law: *In re Marriage Cases*, 43 Cal.4th 757.

472 As the court's September 26 filing deadline: Matthew S. Bajko, "Political Notebook: SD Council Deadlocks on Marriage Case," *Bay Area Reporter*, September 6, 2007.

472 But as the draft: Michael Smolens, "Column: In once-red San Diego County, Republicans are searching for way to reverse blue wave," *Los Angeles Times*, December 24, 2018.

472 Debate ended in a four–four tie: Jennifer Vigil, "Council Splits on Gay-Marriage Motion," *San Diego Union-Tribune*, September 5, 2007.

472 "I think we at least": "City Council Declines to Sign On to Gay-Marriage Court Brief," *Sign On San Diego*, September 4, 2007.

61. Little Kingdoms

473 Yet he saw many faces: Lynn Vincent, "The Gay Point of View," *World Magazine*, November 4, 2008

474 When the city council reconvened: Jennifer Vigil, "Gay Marriage Backed—Council Oks Measure, Sanders Promises Veto," *San Diego Union-Tribune*, September 19, 2007.

474 While the two-week delay: Vigil, "Gay Marriage Backed."

474 "My opinions on this issue": Jennifer Vigil, "Mayor Reverses on Gay Marriage," *San Diego Union-Tribune*, September 19, 2007.

474 Sanders credited the influence: Allison Hoffman, "Citing Daughter's Sexual Orientation, US Mayor Recants Disdain for Gay Marriage," Associated Press, September 20, 2007.

474 According to local press: Jennifer Vigil, "Sanders Changes Mind on Gay Marriage; Mayor Supports Effort to Overturn State Ban," *San Diego Union-Tribune*, September 20, 2007.

475 Footage of his remarks: Freedom to Marry, *2007 Annual Report* (New York: Freedom to Marry, 2007), 15.

475 "It humanized him": Chris Reed, "Gay Marriage: Jerry Pulls the Old Switcheroo," *San Diego Union-Tribune*, September 19, 2009.

475 As he formally announced: Matthew T. Hall and Jennifer Vigil, "Sanders Makes It Official: He'll Run—Fallout Unclear from Gay-Marriage Switch," *San Diego Union-Tribune*, September 21, 2007.

475 But to see their Republican: Liz Neely, "Sanders Hears It from Republicans; Politicians Say They Were Duped on Gay Marriage," *San Diego Union-Tribune*, September 26, 2007.

475 "That really woke some folks up": Lynn Vincent, "The Power of Three," *World Magazine,* July 26, 2008.

475 In 2003, a group of pastors: Sandi Dolbee, "Mission Will Be His Fourth S.C. Revival, *San Diego Union-Tribune,* January 10, 2003.

475 four-day mission: Erin Curry, "Mission San Diego with Billy Graham Marks 413th Crusade in Half Century," *Baptist Press,* May 8, 2003.

475 final visit to the region: Steve Hymon, "Faithful Are Expected to Flock to Evangelist's San Diego Visit," *Los Angeles Times,* May 3, 2003.

475 "During the civil-rights movement": Daniel E. Kennedy, "Billy Graham Crusade Marked by Historic Show of Unity in San Diego," *Charisma Magazine,* July 31, 2003.

475 For Graham's 2003 visit: William Lobdell, "Old School Religion: 50 Years Later, Graham Is Still Drawing Crowds," *Los Angeles Times,* May 11, 2003.

475 Five months later: Nick Carbone, "Top 10 Devastating Wildfires," *Time,* June 8, 2011.

476 Jim Garlow, a part-time radio host: Vincent, "The Power of Three."

476 In 2004, they rallied: "Court Rules City Owns Mount Soledad Parcel," *Sign On San Diego,* October 12, 2004.

476 The first time Garlow heard it: Jim Garlow, "Reformation of Marriage," in *The Reformer's Pledge,* compiled by Ché Ahn (Shippensburg, PA: Destiny Image Publishers, 2010).

477 Garlow took his seat: Vincent, "The Power of Three."

62. God's Way of Bringing People Together

478 met Clark and Garlow: Caz Taylor, "Attorney Charles LiMandri Practices Law in the Spirit," *Good News, etc.,* December 2007.

478 LiMandri argued the case: Joan Frawley Desmond, "Charles LiMandri: Lawyer on the Front Lines of the Culture Wars," *National Catholic Register,* August 12, 2013.

478 The matter was effectively settled: Alison St. John, "President Bush to Sign Mt. Soledad Cross Legislation," KPBS, August 14, 2006.

478 Despite his standing: "Family Planning: A Priest's Perspective," *Southern Voice,* October 11, 2007.

478 All were part of: Maria L. La Ganga, "In Tolerant San Francisco, Prop. 8 Backer to Head Catholic Church," *Los Angeles Times,* September 22, 2012.

478 Just weeks earlier: Randal C. Archibald, "San Diego Diocese Settles Lawsuit for $200 Million," *New York Times,* September 8, 2007.

478 Bishop Robert Brom announced: Sandi Dolbee and Mark Sauer, "Settled: $198 Million; Victims Tearful, Elated After Deal with Diocese," *San Diego Union-Tribune,* September 8, 2007.

479 Brom's public apology: Tony Perry, "Orange County Auxiliary Bishop Named Catholic Bishop of San Diego," *Los Angeles Times,* January 4, 2012.

479 Almost immediately: Aubrey Hanson and Cyril Jones-Kellett, "Diocese Settles 144 Abuse Lawsuits for $198 Million," *Southern Cross,* September 13, 2007.

479 Within weeks: "The Southern Cross Cuts Issues and Staff, Moves Towards Web," *Southern Cross,* November 21, 2007.

479 Trained in canon law: "Bishop Cordileone: From His Earliest Years," *Catholic Voice,* May 11, 2009.

479 In 2002, Brom named: Alexa Capeloto, "S.D.'S Auxiliary Bishop to Get Post in Oakland," *San Diego Union-Tribune,* March 24, 2009.

479 An auxiliary bishop: "Meet Bishop Cordileone. Why Is He an Example for Catholic Lay Leaders?" *Catholic Business Journal,* August 12, 2009.

480 When 189 American bishops gathered: David D. Kirkpatrick and Laurie Goodstein, "Group of Bishops Using Influence to Oppose Kerry," *New York Times,* October 12, 2004.

480 "Not all the American bishops": John L. Allen Jr., "The Word from Rome," *National Catholic Reporter,* June 11, 2004.

480 In 1962, a liberal: Daniel K. Williams, *Defenders of the Unborn* (Oxford, UK: Oxford University Press, 2005), 47.

481 "Despite its professed interest": Williams, *Defenders of the Unborn,* 84.

481 "Unfortunately, all of these social forces": Thomas J. McKenna, interview with Salvatore Cordileone, *Catholic Action Insight,* March 12, 2012, www.catholicaction .org.

481 "We can see what uniquely defines": McKenna, interview with Salvatore Cordileone.

481 Shortly after being installed: Larry B. Stammer and John M. Glionna, "Pope Names New S.F. Archbishop," *Los Angeles Times,* December 16, 2005.

481 George Niederauer had chosen: Peggy Fletcher Stack, "Big Year for the Archbishop," *Salt Lake Tribune,* March 10, 2007.

481 A film buff: Stack, "Big Year for the Archbishop."

482 Even the other members: La Ganga, "In Tolerant San Francisco."

482 "The ship is sinking": La Ganga, "In Tolerant San Francisco."

482 "Both the evangelical pastors": McKenna, interview with Salvatore Cordileone.

63. Nassau Street

484 Attempting to rally: Emily Goodin, "Downright Secretive," *National Journal,* March 31, 2007.

484 they were paralyzed: Scott Helman, "Coalition Seeks to Reframe GOP Race," *Boston Globe,* March 25, 2007.

484 "We hope to convince": Jim Geraghty, "The Scoop on Fred and the Arlington Group," *National Review,* September 5, 2007.

485 When she had gone: Laura Kiritsy, "Same-Sex Marriage Opponents to Host Rallies Across Mass," *Bay Windows,* January 22, 2004.

485 first-time traditionalists had lost: Amy L. Stone, *Gay Rights at the Ballot Box* (Minneapolis: University of Minnesota Press, 2012), 136–37.

485 On the school's faculty: J. I. Merritt, "Heretic in the Temple," *Princeton Alumni Weekly,* October 8, 2003.

485 Throughout the nineteenth century: Frances FitzGerald, *The Evangelicals: The Struggle to Shape America* (New York: Simon & Schuster, 2017), 73–74.

485 But George's intellectual stature: Max Blumenthal, "Princeton Tilts Right: Robert George, the Conservative Movement's Favorite Professor, Exerts His Influence," *The Nation,* February 23, 2006.

485 His James Madison Program: Deborah Yaffe, "A Conservative Think Tank with Many Princeton Ties: The Low-Profile Witherspoon Institute Has Strong Links to the Madison Program," *Princeton Alumni Weekly,* July 16, 2008.

486 In December 2004: *Marriage and the Public Good: Ten Principles* (Princeton, NJ: The Witherspoon Institute, 2008).

486 As George and Gallagher filed: "Marriage Warriors," *National Journal,* October 20, 2007.

486 Luis Tellez: Deborah Kovach, "Princeton Catholics Divided; Opus Dei Leaves Liberals Worried," *Trenton Times,* October 22, 1989.

486 The inclusion of: Braley Dodson, "Matthew Holland's BYU Colleagues Recall His Hard Work Ethic and Intramural Basketball Prowess," *Daily Herald,* April 29, 2018.

486 It was so singular in that focus: Jennifer Medina, "Gay Marriage Suit Pushes Connecticut into New Terrain," *New York Times,* May 13, 2007.

486 Then, when in Hartford: Daniela Altimari, "Crowds Jam Gay Marriage Hearing," *Hartford Courant,* March 27, 2007.

487 With Brown as its executive director: "Brian Brown Taking on a National Role," *Connecticut Law Tribune,* July 16, 2007.

487 Their initial strategy: Joshua Green, "They Won't Know What Hit Them," *The Atlantic,* March 2007.

487 The prior month: Paul Schindler, "New York State Assembly Approves Gay Marriage Law," *Gay City News,* June 19, 2007.

487 In fact, there was only one: David Crary, "U.S. Gay-Rights Groups Heartened by Political Gains in the States," Associated Press, June 18, 2007.

487 The previous fall: Arthur S. Leonard, "New Jersey Supreme Court Says Same-Sex Couples Are Constitutionally Entitled to Rights of Marriage . . . but Not to Marriage Itself," *Gay City News,* October 25, 2006.

487 gave legislators a deadline: Anthony Faiola, "Civil Union Laws Don't Ensure Benefits; Same-Sex N.J. Couples Find That Employers Can Get Around New Rules," *Washington Post,* June 30, 2007.

487 By forcing them: Arthur S. Leonard, "Do Rights of Marriage Equal Marriage?" *Gay City News,* October 26, 2006.

487 Through a state political action committee: Tom Moran, "A New Kind of Political Poison," *Newark Star-Ledger,* October 18, 2007.

487 The district was one of three: Dan Murphy, "Clean Elections' Waters Roiled by Outsider," *Newark Star-Ledger,* October 24, 2007.

488 The group had purchased a billboard: Dan Ring, "Billboard Attacks Gay Marriage Vote," *Springfield (MA) Republican,* October 6, 2007.

488 The billboard, which appeared: Ring, "Billboard Attacks Gay Marriage Vote."

488 Immediately after Gallagher spoke: Maggie Gallagher, "Prop. 22 Can Save Traditional Marriage in California," *Human Events,* May 29, 2008.

488 Over the first six months: Rebecca Cathcart, "Donation to Same-Sex Marriage Foes Brings Boycott Calls," *New York Times,* July 17, 2008.

488 Cordileone would eventually take credit: Maria L. La Ganga, "In Tolerant San Francisco, Prop. 8 Backer to Head Catholic Church," *Los Angeles Times,* September 22, 2012.

489 Hotelier and real-estate developer: "Meet Bishop Cordileone. Why Is He an Example for Catholic Lay Leaders?" *Catholic Business Journal,* August 12, 2009.

64. To the Ballot

490 In West Hollywood: Maura Dolan, "Same-Sex Marriage Has Skeptics on Court," *Los Angeles Times,* March 5, 2008.

490 The court had granted review: Ronald M. George, *Chief: The Quest for Justice in California* (Berkeley: Berkeley Public Policy Press, 2013), 628–44.

490 "Is it better for this court": Dolan, "Same-Sex Marriage Has Skeptics."

490 Petitions from groups: Lisa Leff, "California Groups Aiming for Gay Marriage Amendment," Associated Press, February 14, 2008.

490 Randy Thomasson's group: "Pastors Network to Save Traditional Marriage Through Calif. State Amendment," Christian Examiner Newspapers, December 13, 2007.

490 Andy Pugno had been: Jennifer Warren, "Initiative Divides a Family," *Los Angeles Times,* November 24, 1999.

490 when the senator worked: Rone Tempest, "State Senator Fumes over Same-Sex Marriages," *Los Angeles Times,* February 24, 2004.

491 Knight died: Richard Fausset, "GOP's Pete Knight, 74; Former Test Pilot Was Foe of Gay Marriage," *Los Angeles Times,* May 9, 2004.

491 the fund filed suit: Harriet Chang, "S.F. Sues over Legality of Same-Sex Marriages," *San Francisco Chronicle,* February 20, 2004.

491 After his death: Harrison Sheppard, "Effort to Ban Gay Marriage Falls Short of Signatures," *Los Angeles Daily News,* December 28, 2005.

491 Pitching both experience: Lisa Leff, "Signature-Gathering Can Begin for Calif. Gay Marriage Ban," Associated Press, July 25, 2005.

491 Clearly squeezed out: "Calif. Amend. Qualifies; Suit Filed In N.Y." *Baptist Press,* June 3, 2008.

491 While officials there checked: "Gay Marriage Ban Makes California Ballot," Associated Press, June 3, 2008.

491 "Reserving the historic designation": *In re Marriage Cases,* 43 Cal.4th 757.

492 state public-health officials: Sandra Gonzales, "Initiative to Ban Gay Marriage Qualifies for California Ballot," *San Jose Mercury-News,* June 3, 2008.

492 A few days later: Frank Schubert and Jeff Flint, "Passing Prop 8," *Politics Magazine,* February 2009.

493 Schubert was a fixture: Dan Smith, "Capitol Alert: Proposition 8 Campaign Architect Leaves Sacramento Firm," *Sacramento Bee,* June 4, 2013.

493 The first major victory: "Anti-Gay Marriage Mastermind Keeps Ties to Pro-gay Companies," *The Advocate,* November 11, 2009.

493 A January 2008 study: Gregory B. Lewis and Charles W. Gusset, "Changing Public Opinion on Same-Sex Marriage: The Case of California," *Politics & Policy* 36, no. 1 (2008): 4–30.

493 "Age is one of": Lewis and Gusset, "Changing Public Opinion on Same-Sex Marriage," 4–30.

493 ProtectMarriage strategists: Schubert and Flint, "Passing Prop 8."

493 Private surveys: Schubert and Flint, "Passing Prop 8."

494 "There were limits": Schubert and Flint, "Passing Prop 8."

494 At 5:01 p.m.: Marisa Lagos, Rachel Gordon, Chris Heredia, and Jill Tucker, "Same-Sex Weddings Start with Union of Elderly San Francisco Couple," *San Francisco Chronicle,* June 17, 2008.

494 In San Francisco: Audrey Bilger and Michelle Kort, "The First Brides: A Conversation with Kate Kendell & Phyllis Lyon," *Here Come the Brides! Reflections on Lesbian Love and Marriage,* ed. Audrey Bilger and Michelle Kort (Berkeley, CA: Seal Press, 2012), 177–91.

494 identify any real social consequences: M. V. Lee Badgett, *When Gay People Get Married: What Happens When Societies Legalize Same-Sex Marriage* (New York: New York University Press, 2009), 64–85.

494 But while a spokesperson's: "Same-Sex Marriage Pioneers Separate," Associated Press, July 20, 2006.

494 "they are just like any other couple": Michael Levenson, "After 2 Years, Same-Sex Marriage Icons Split Up," *Boston Globe*, July 21, 2006.

494 Massachusetts's 10,500: Jesse McKinley, "Hundreds of Same-Sex Couples Wed in California," *New York Times*, June 18, 2008.

494 "We made one": Schubert and Flint, "Passing Prop 8."

65. Amen Brothers

496 Garlow had been initially: Lynn Vincent, "The Power of Three," *World Magazine*, July 26, 2008.

496 He had given his team: "Sign Here State's Marriage Amendment Drive Heads into Final Month; Evangelicals Urged to Step Up Signature Collection," Christian Examiner Newspapers, March 1, 2008.

496 "When I heard": Vincent, "The Power of Three."

496 On June 25: Jim Garlow, "Reformation of Marriage," in *The Reformer's Pledge*, compiled by Ché Ahn (Shippensburg, PA: Destiny Image Publishers, 2010).

497 The twenty-two-week: Garlow, "Reformation of Marriage."

497 On July 18: Rebecca Cathcart, "Donation to Same-Sex Marriage Foes Brings Boycott Calls," *New York Times*, July 17, 2008.

497 The group's founder: Christa Woodall, "Save the Boom Demonstrators Rally Outside AIG Headquarters," *OC Register*, April 1, 2008.

497 The media amplified: Woodall, "Save the Boom Demonstrators Rally."

497 Manchester was perhaps: Cathcart, "Donation to Same-Sex Marriage Foes."

498 A Yes on 8 organizer: Thomas M. Messner, "The Price of Prop 8," Heritage Foundation, October 22, 2009.

498 a religious faction: James L. Clayton, "From Pioneers to Provincials: Mormonism as Seen by Wallace Stegner," *Dialogue: A Journal of Mormon Thought* 1, no. 4 (December 1966).

498 an infusion of cash and manpower: Mark Schoofs, "Mormons Boost Antigay Marriage Effort," *Wall Street Journal*, September 20, 2008.

66. The Mormon Empire Strikes Back

499 received a one-page letter: Gregory A. Prince, *Gay Rights and the Mormon Church: Intended Actions, Unintended Consequences* (Salt Lake City: University of Utah Press, 2019), 151.

500 When Brigham Young University law professor Lynn Wardle: Lynn Wardle and William C. Duncan, "Foreword," *Creighton Law Review*, "A Symposium on the Implications of Lawrence and Goodridge for the Recognition of Same-Sex Marriages and Validity of DOMA," 2005.

500 Salt Lake City had first: John Keahey, "Utah's Long Road to Olympics Started with a Craving for Tourist Dollars . . . ," *Salt Lake Tribune*, June 4, 1995.

500 The host committee's: Jere Longman, "Leaders of Salt Lake Olympic Bid Are Indicted in Bribery Scandal," *New York Times*, July 21, 2000.

500 They were acquitted: Lex Hemphill, "Acquittals End Bid Scandal That Dogged Winter Games," *New York Times*, December 6, 2003.

500 "There seemed to be": Mitt Romney, *Turnaround: Crisis, Leadership, and the Olympic Games* (Washington, DC: Regnery Publishing, 2004), 4.

500   A five-year media plan: J. B. Haws, *The Mormon Image in the American Mind: Fifty Years of Public Perception* (New York: Oxford University Press, 2013), 360.

501   "Feelings towards the LDS": Haws, *The Mormon Image in the American Mind*, 174.

501   In July 2004: Deborah Bulkeley, "LDS Church Supports Gay-Marriage Bans," *Deseret News*, July 8, 2004.

501   The church-owned *Deseret News:* Bulkeley, "LDS Church Supports Gay-Marriage Bans," *Deseret News*, July 8, 2004.

501   refused to publicly acknowledge: Rebecca Walsh, "LDS Church Shuns Political Fight Over Utah's Marriage Amendment," *Salt Lake Tribune*, August 30, 2004.

501   Romney—a descendant: Benjamin Wallace-Wells, "Mitt's Stake," *New York*, September 21, 2012.

501   visited the church's president: Michael Luo, "Romney Attends Mormon Leader's Funeral," *New York Times*, February 2, 2008.

502   Preparing to leave: Jamie Dean, "Elephant in the Room," *World Magazine*, November 3, 2007.

502   A poll conducted: Frank Newport, "Americans' Views of the Mormon Religion," Gallup News Service, March 2, 2007.

502   another from Gallup: Newport, "Americans' Views of the Mormon Religion."

502   "perceptions of the Church as mysterious": Gary C. Lawrence, *How Americans View Mormonism: Seven Steps to Improve Our Image* (Orange, CA: Parameter Foundation, 2008) 35.

503   In early December 2007: Michael Luo, "Romney, Eye on Evangelicals, Defends His Faith," *New York Times*, December 7, 2007.

503   But the January 2008 death: "LDS President Gordon B. Hinckley Dies at Age 97," *Deseret News*, January 28, 2008.

503   He was forced: Michael Luo, "Romney Attends Mormon Leader's Funeral," *New York Times*, February 2, 2008.

503   Romney exited the campaign: Mike Allen and Jonathan Martin, "Romney Ends Bid, Eyeing 2012," *Politico*, February 7, 2008.

503   Hinckley's successor: Peggy Fletcher Stack, "Prop 8: California Gay Marriage Fight Divides LDS Faithful," *Salt Lake Tribune*, October 26, 2008.

503   letter from George Niederauer: George H. Niederauer, "An Open Letter from Archbishop Niederauer," *Catholic San Francisco*, December 5, 2008.

503   Catholic-Mormon alliance: Prince, *Gay Rights and the Mormon Church*, 72–75.

503   "California is a huge state": Jesse McKinley and Kirk Johnson, "Mormons Tipped Scale in Ban on Gay Marriage," *New York Times*, November 15, 2008.

503   The Mormon Church's appraisal: Leo J. Muir, *A Century of Mormon Activities in California: Volume One, Historical* (Salt Lake City: Deseret News Press, 1952), 44.

504   That winter: Joan S. Hamblin, "Voyage of the 'Brooklyn,'" *Ensign*, July 1997.

504   "perhaps the longest religious sea pilgrimage": "Voyage of the 'Brooklyn.'"

504   To have pushed their way: Muir, *A Century of Mormon Activities in California*, 44.

504   Wallace Stegner later demarcated: Peggy Fletcher Stack and Jessica Ravitz, "Redefining the Mormon Empire," *Salt Lake Tribune*, March 30, 2008.

504   In 1851, when he: Muir, *A Century of Mormon Activities in California*, 44.

504   "I was sick": Muir, *A Century of Mormon Activities in California*, 44.

504   Over the thirty years: Stack and Ravitz, "Redefining the Mormon Empire."

504   The result was "Mellow Mormonism": Stack and Ravitz, "Redefining the Mormon Empire."

504 "The church has actually": Stack and Ravitz, "Redefining the Mormon Empire."

505 Notably, when discussing the subject: John-Henry Westen, "New San Francisco Archbishop Thinks Gay Propaganda Film Brokeback Mountain is 'Very Powerful,'" *Life Site News,* February 13, 2006.

505 "Having Catholics, evangelicals and Jews": Matthai Kuruvila, "S.F. Archbishop Defends Role in Prop. 8 Passage," *San Francisco Chronicle,* December 4, 2008.

505 "No work will take place": McKinley and Johnson, "Mormons Tipped Scale."

505 An average of twenty-five thousand: Karl Vick, "Backers of Gay Marriage Trumpet the Mormon Church's Work Against It," *Washington Post,* May 29, 2009.

505 Jeff Flint's estimate: McKinley and Johnson, "Mormons Tipped Scale."

505 They were assigned: McKinley and Johnson, "Mormons Tipped Scale."

506 depend on Mormon money: Mark Schoofs, "Mormons Boost Antigay Marriage Effort," *Wall Street Journal,* September 20, 2008.

506 After meeting for two hours: McKinley and Johnson, "Mormons Tipped Scale."

506 The donations included: McKinley and Johnson, "Mormons Tipped Scale."

67. Proposition 8

507 In early September: Andy Humm, "New Poll: Majority in California Reject Repeal of Marriage Equality," *Gay City News,* September 4, 2008.

507 When the No on 8: Evelyn Larrubia, "$1 Million from Teachers Union to Oppose Prop. 8," *Los Angeles Times,* October 17, 2008.

507 By the end of September: Mike Swift, "Prop. 8: Money Pours in to Oppose Same-Sex Marriage Ban," *San Jose Mercury News,* October 15, 2008.

507 When ProtectMarriage filed: Tim Dickinson, "Same-Sex Setback," *Rolling Stone,* December 11, 2008.

507 a slew of celebrities: Derrik J. Lang, "Hollywood Comes Out in Support of Gay Marriage," Associated Press, October 23, 2008.

507 Fall Out Boy's Pete Wentz: Kerry Eleveld, "Pete Wentz, Fall Out Boy Donate to No on 8," *The Advocate,* October 30, 2008.

507 Outside the religious sphere: Michael Falcone, "McCain and Obama Differ on Same-Sex Marriage Initiative," *New York Times,* July 3, 2008.

508 At the end of September: Frank Schubert and Jeff Flint, "Passing Prop 8," *Politics Magazine,* February 2009.

508 If that ad was edited to: Mike Swift, "Questions Raised over Yes on Prop. 8 Ads," *San Jose Mercury-News,* October 18, 2008.

508 The ad showed a schoolgirl: Rachel La Corte, "Adwatch: Ad Warns Gay Marriage Could Be Taught in Schools If Referendum 74 Passes," Associated Press, October 29, 2012.

508 Yet once the: Schubert and Flint, "Passing Prop 8."

508 Indeed, its themes had been part: Lynda Gorow, "2 Sides Fuel Hawaii Vote on Same-Sex Marriages," *Boston Globe,* November 2, 1998.

508 An ad very similar: John Cloud, "For Better or Worse," *Time,* October 2, 1998.

508 During the summer: Bob Egelko, "Prop. 8 Backers Take Fight to Kindergarten," *San Francisco Chronicle,* July 25, 2008.

508 After opponents sued: Arthur S. Leonard, "Cal's Ballot Changes OK," *Gay City News,* August 14, 2008.

509 The *San Francisco Chronicle* was a predictably liberal: "Preserve Marriage Rights," *San Francisco Chronicle,* October 1, 2008.

509 Beneath the headline: Jill Tucker, "Class Surprises Lesbian Teacher on Wedding Day," *San Francisco Chronicle*, October 11, 2008.

509 With weeks to go: Tucker, "Class Surprises Lesbian Teacher."

509 Yet for another eleven days: Schubert and Flint, "Passing Prop 8."

509 It finally came: Alex Cohen, "If Gay Marriage Is Allowed, Will Schools Promote It?" National Public Radio, October 23, 2008.

509 In their internal polling: David Fleischer, *The Prop 8 Report: What Defeat in California Can Teach Us About Winning Future Ballot Measures on Same-Sex Marriage* (Los Angeles: LGBT Mentoring Project, 2010), 34.

509 "This in-your-face response": Schubert and Flint, "Passing Prop 8."

509 With a total of $83 million: "More Than $83 Million Spent on Prop 8," Associated Press, February 2, 2009.

509 Over the final week: Schubert and Flint, "Passing Prop 8."

510 With opinion swinging: Schubert and Flint, "Passing Prop 8."

510 "Individuals may fast": Jim Garlow, "Reformation of Marriage," in *The Reformer's Pledge*, compiled by Ché Ahn (Shippensburg, PA: Destiny Image Publishers, 2010).

510 On election morning: Schubert and Flint, "Passing Prop 8."

68. Whodunit

515 If Proposition 8 had failed: Jessica Garrison, Cara Mia DiMassa, and Richard C. Paddock, "Nation Watches as State Weighs Ban," *Los Angeles Times*, November 5, 2008.

515 "a quiet dread": Karen Ocamb, "Special Investigation: Prop 8 Postmortem," *Los Angeles*, December 1, 2018.

515 "Elation rapidly slid": Ocamb, "Special Investigation."

515 The final numbers: Chris Cillizza and Sean Sullivan, "How Proposition 8 Passed in California—and Why It Wouldn't Today," The Fix, *Washington Post*, March 26, 2013.

516 "How did the people": Peter Quist, "The Money Behind the 2008 Same-Sex Partnership Ballot Measures," Follow the Money, February 9, 2010, https://www.followthemoney.org/research/institute-reports/the-money-behind-the-2008-same-sex-partnership-ballot-measures.

517 "It's easier to locate": Michael Petrelis, "Names of All 16 Members of No on 8's Executive Committee Made Public," Petrelis Files, January 21, 2009, mpetrelis.blogspot.com.

517 how chaotic No on 8's decision-making had been: Ben Ehrenreich, "Anatomy of a Failed Campaign," *The Advocate*, November 18, 2008.

517 In mid-October, just as: Aurelio Rojas, "No on 8 Campaign Was in Turmoil in Last Weeks," *Sacramento Bee*, November 13, 2008.

518 "The campaign brought in": Rojas, "No on 8 Campaign."

518 "It is a travesty": Jessica Garrison and Joanna Lin, "Prop. 8 Protestors Target Mormon Temple in Westwood," *Los Angeles Times*, November 7.

518 "Then Jean skipped town": Patrick Range McDonald, "Queer Town: 'No on 8' Executive Committee Revealed," *LA Weekly*, January 22, 2009.

518 The campaign's principals: Connor Fitzpatrick, "Proposition 8 Opponents Should Not Live in the Past," *Daily Bruin*, February 3, 2009.

518 If organizers of Equality Summit: Rex Wockner, "Big Prop 8-Related Summit Will Limit Media Access," *Towleroad*, January 5, 2009.

518 The fifty-three-member planning committee: Rex Wockner, "Equality Summit Drops Restrictions on Media," *Towleroad*, January 5, 2009.

518 "LGBT journalists": Wockner, "Big Prop-8 Related Summit."

518 Organizers eventually acquiesced: Japhy Grant, "More Questions Than Answers at Gay Marriage Equality Summit," *Queerty*, January 26, 2009.

519 led the National Gay and Lesbian Task Force's organizing department: Amy L. Stone, "Winning for LGBT Rights Laws, Losing for Same-Sex Marriage: The LGBT Movement and Campaign Tactics," in *The Marrying Kind? Debating Same-Sex Marriage Within the Lesbian and Gay Movement*, Mary Bernstein and Verta Taylor ed. (Minneapolis: University of Minnesota Press, 2013), 148.

69. Meet in the Middle

521 spent years at doorsteps: Dave Fleischer, "An Army of Volunteers," in *Out for Office: Campaigning in the Gay '90s*, Kathleen DeBold ed. (Washington: Gay and Lesbian Victory Fund, 1994), 175–82.

522 The most prominent: Arthur S. Leonard, "Prop 8 Judicial Review Granted," *Gay City News*, November 10, 2008.

522 Meanwhile, California's various: Lisa Leff, "Gay Rights Activists Consider Timing of Ballot Measure," Associated Press, January 26, 2009.

522 "We are putting": Patrick Range McDonald, "Setting the (Gay) Wedding Table," *LA Weekly*, June 3, 2009.

522 "taking a page": Jesse McKinley, "Group Renews Fight for Same-Sex Marriage," *New York Times*, May 8, 2009.

522 "Regardless of what": Susan Ferriss, "Backers at Work on Next Move," *Sacramento Bee*, March 7, 2009.

523 "It gives $86,000": Cynthia Laird, "Press Kicked Out of Summit over Poll," *Bay Area Reporter*, June 4, 2009.

523 One figure the poll's sponsors: "All the Things Homophobes Can Learn from California's Secret Poll," *Queerty*, June 4, 2009.

523 "You can argue to wait": "Leadership Summit Organizations Going Back to Community to Assess Next Steps on Marriage Equality in CA," Unite the Fight, June 2, 2009, unitethefight.blogspot.com.

524 yes on 8's messaging around children: Melissa Murray, "Marriage Rights and Parental Rights: Parents, the State, and Proposition 8," *Stanford Journal of Civil Rights & Civil Liberties* 5, no. 2 (October 2009): 366–90.

525 To understand what his side: Sasha Issenberg, "How Do You Change Someone's Mind About Abortion? Tell Them You Had One," *Bloomberg Politics*, October 6, 2014.

70. Gathering Storm

527 "An Internet camp classic": Frank Rich, "The Bigots' Last Hurrah," *New York Times*, April 19, 2009.

527 "it's like watching": Judy Berman, "Stephen Colbert's 'Gathering Storm,'" *Salon*, April 17, 2009.

528 The ad buy had notably: Andy Humm, "'Gathering Storm' on the Right," *Gay City News*, April 10, 2009.

528 At the Miss USA pageant: David Hasemyer, "Prejean Stands Up for Her Beliefs," *San Diego Union-Tribune*, April 27, 2009.

528 "She really did answer": "Exclusive: Donald Trump Breaks Silence on Miss California's Gay Marriage Comments," FOX News, April 24, 2009.

528 That summer, upon the group's: Monica Hesse, "Opposing Gay Unions with Sanity and a Smile," *Washington Post*, August 28, 2009.

528 Its legal headquarters: Ryan T. Anderson, "Robert P. George on the Struggle Over Marriage," *Public Discourse*, July 3, 2009.

528 "The same thing": Hesse, "Opposing Gay Unions."

528 When Matthew Holland: Lisa Riley Roche, "Guv Draws Scrutiny over Stance on Civil Unions," *Deseret News*, April 21, 2009.

529 What the men: Don L. Searle, "Elder Jeffrey R. Holland of the Quorum of the Twelve Apostles," *Ensign*, December 1994.

529 "When government is": Orson Scott Card, "State Job Is Not to Redefine Marriage," *Mormon Times*, July 24, 2006.

529 "represented on the board": Roche, "Guv Draws Scrutiny."

529 Given the difficulty of bringing: Maggie Gallagher, "The Carrie Effect: Notes from the Frontlines of the Marriage War," *National Review*, August 10, 2009.

529 A day after the bill's signing: Jenna Russell and Eric Moskowitz, "Maine Governor OK's Gay Marriage," *Boston Globe*, May 7, 2009.

530 Within weeks, the group: "Maine Gay Marriage Foes to Use Prop 8 Firm," Associated Press, June 18, 2009.

530 With Frank Schubert: Bob Drogin, "In Maine, It's Like Prop. 8 All Over Again," *Los Angeles Times*, October 20, 2009.

530 A new one showed: Paul Schindler, "Bitterness and Determination," *Gay City News*, November 5, 2009.

530 In New Jersey: Paul Schindler, "Potential Endgames for NY Marriage Equality," *Gay City News*, January 6, 2010.

531 An unusual three-way special election: Marc Ambinder, "What the NY-23 Special Election Is Really About," *The Atlantic*, October 30, 2009.

531 NOM spent aggressively: Ben Smith, "NOM poll: Marriage a Wedge in NY-23," *Politico*, November 3, 2009.

531 Eventually Hoffman gained: Adam Nagourney and Jeremy W. Peters, "Dede Scozzafava, Republican, Quits House Race in Upstate New York," *New York Times*, October 31, 2009.

531 "To 'scozzfava' a politician": Maggie Gallagher, "NOM Announces Brian Brown as New President!" NOMblog, April 19, 2010, www.nomblog.com.

71. Up Against the Wall

532 "a top priority": Pam Belluck, "Bid to Ban Gay Marriage Fails in Massachusetts," *New York Times*, June 4, 2007.

535 In California, Proposition 8's passage: Lisa Leff, "Gay Rights Activists Consider Timing of Ballot Measure," Associated Press, January 26, 2009.

535 The left-wing Courage Campaign: Seth Hemmelgarn, "Ballot Proposal to Repeal Prop 8 in Planning Stage," *Bay Area Reporter*, February 19, 2009; Jesse McKinley, "Group Renews Fight for Same-Sex Marriage in California," *New York Times*, May 8, 2009.

535 Equality California wanted to wait: "In California, Equality Opposes Courage," *Gay City News*, August 20, 2009.

535 Their challenge to the result: *Strauss v. Horton*, 46 Cal.4th 364.

535 The same week that opinion: Jesse McKinley, "Bush v. Gore Foes Join to Fight Gay Marriage Ban," *New York Times,* May 27, 2009.

535 The nation's leading gay-rights lawyers: Lisa Leff, "Gay Rights Groups Question Timing of Federal Suit to Overturn California Same-Sex Marriage Ban," Associated Press, May 27, 2009.

536 Despite his opposition: Andy Humm, "Obama on Gay Marriage," *Gay City News,* March 27, 2008.

536 A Democratic White House: David G. Savage, "Obama Struggles to Nominate, Confirm Federal Judges," *Los Angeles Times,* January 5, 2013.

72. Roadmap

539 "whether or not Freedom to Marry": Mubarak Dahir, "Marriage on His Mind," *The Advocate,* June 26, 2003.

540 "is an intense person": Dahir, "Marriage on His Mind."

540 "a small ship": *Hearts & Minds: The Untold Story of How Philanthropy and the Civil Marriage Collaborative Helped America Embrace Marriage Equality,* Proteus Fund (2015), 10.

540 "a strategy shop": Duncan Osborne, "Marriage Pioneer Wolfson Moves Group Center Stage," *Gay City News,* September 28, 2011.

540 In 2007, Freedom to Marry published: *Freedom to Marry Annual Report 2007* (Freedom to Marry, 2007), 8.

541 Crucial to Wolfson's future plans: *Freedom to Marry Annual Report 2010* (Freedom to Marry, 2010), 11.

541 "the share of the public": Patrick J. Egan, "Findings from a Decade of Polling on Ballot Measures Regarding the Legal Status of SameSex Couples," Freedom to Marry, June 15, 2010.

541 "Those favoring and opposing": Egan, "Findings from a Decade of Polling."

541 He had joined Let California Ring: *Freedom to Marry Annual Report 2007,* 16.

542 Wolfson enlisted three: *Freedom to Marry, Annual Report 2008* (Freedom to Marry, 2008), 14.

542 postelection narrative about its passage: Leigh Moscowitz, *The Battle Over Marriage: Gay Rights Activism Through the Media* (Urbana: University of Illinois Press, 2013), 115–17.

542 Using precinct-level election returns: Patrick J. Egan and Kenneth Sherrill, "California's Proposition 8: What Happened, and What Does the Future Hold?" National Gay and Lesbian Task Force Policy Institute, January 2009.

542 "finally put to rest": *Freedom to Marry Annual Report 2008,* 14.

543 Relaunched to take on: Richard Wolf, "For Freedom to Marry's Founder, a Date with History," *USA Today,* June 17, 2015.

544 "Freedom to Marry is not going to": Karen Ocamb, "Freedom to Marry Accelerates Its Campaign," *FrontiersLA,* July 25, 2013.

544 "There is a strategy": Osborne, "Marriage Pioneer Wolfson."

545 In October 2010, he found: Zoe Gorman, "Gallagher, Wolfson Debate Gay Marriage," *Yale Daily News,* October 7, 2010.

545 "verbally abused their opponents": Daniel Chow, "P.U. Orators Denounce Ford while Trouncing Yale Debaters," *Yale Daily News,* January 10, 1976.

545 It was unusual for: Zoe Gorman, "Gallagher, Wolfson Debate Gay Marriage," *Yale Daily News,* October 7, 2010.

545 "have worked against each other": Gorman, "Gallagher, Wolfson Debate."

545 "I've never had a desire": Peter J. Smith, "Brian Brown Takes Helm of National Organization for Marriage," *LifeSiteNews*, April 19, 2010.

73. For Better or for Worse

546 "there is hardly a political question": Alexis de Tocqueville, *Democracy in America*, ed. J. P. Mayer, trans. George Lawrence (Garden City, NY: Doubleday, 1969), 1:270.

546 when *Loving v. Virginia:* Joseph Carroll, "Most Americans Approve of Interracial Marriages," Gallup News Service, August 16, 2007.

548 "losing forward": Evan Wolfson, "Marriage Equality and Some Lessons for the Scary Work of Winning," *Law & Sexuality* 14 (2005): 141.

548 A straight woman with the loose, upbeat charm: Sura Rubenstein, "Anti-Gay, County Measures Pass: Cornelius Voters OK Home-Grown Ballot Measure," *Portland Oregonian*, May 19, 1993.

549 In her new role, Zepatos: *Freedom to Marry Annual Report 2009* (Freedom to Marry, 2009); Sasha Issenberg, "Nudge the Vote," *New York Times Magazine*, October 29, 2010.

550 Among them were nongay organizations: Michael D. Shear, "Political Groups Compete to Represent the Center," *New York Times*, February 9, 2011.

552 "Gay IRS": John Cloud, "The Gay Mafia That's Redefining Liberal Politics," *Time*, October 31, 2008.

74. Money Talks in New York

555 *That was sad:* Marc Solomon, *Winning Marriage: The Inside Story of How Same-Sex Couples Took On The Politicians and Pundits—and Won* (Lebanon, NH: ForeEdge, 2014), 156.

555 "The murky, transactional world": Solomon, *Winning Marriage*, 157.

555 For some of his peers: John Cloud, "The Gay Mafia That's Redefining Liberal Politics," *Time*, October 31, 2008.

556 The day the decision: Paul Schindler, "Iowa Marriage Ruling Seems Safe Politically," *Gay City News*, April 3, 2009.

556 In New York, strategists: Arthur S. Leonard, "Another New York State Gay Marriage Setback," *Gay City News*, February 16, 2006; Arthur S. Leonard, "NYS Gay Marriage Setback," *Gay City News*, February 23, 2006; Anemona Hartocolis, "N.Y. Court Upholds Gay Marriage Ban," *New York Times*, July 6, 2006.

556 In 2003, the New York State Democratic Committee: "NY Dems Endorse Gay Marriage," *Gay City News*, September 26, 2003.

556 The party's next nominee: Paul Schindler, "Absorbing Gay Pain & Praise, Clinton Says She's Evolved," *Gay City News*, October 26, 2006.

556 In 2008, Spitzer was succeeded: Paul Schindler, "New Governor, Old Friend; Advocates, Mourning Eliot Spitzer, Upbeat on David Paterson," *Gay City News*, March 12, 2008.

556 Paterson introduced his own: Paul Schindler, "Governor Paterson Ups the Ante," *Gay City News*, March 16, 2009.

556 That December, the bill failed: Jeremy W. Peters, "New York Senate Rejects Gay Marriage Bill," *New York Times*, December 2, 2009.

556 "There had been no fear": Solomon, *Winning Marriage*, 157.

557 "Nothing matters but": Solomon, *Winning Marriage,* 157.

557 Smith launched: Jeremy W. Peters, "New Group That Backs Gay Marriage Takes Aim at Monserrate," *New York Times,* February 24, 2010.

557 The group attacked: Ben Smith and Byron Tau, "Gay Rights Take Center Stage in N.Y.," *Politico,* December 14, 2010.

557 "the innuendo spread": Smith and Tau, "Gay Rights Take Center Stage."

557 "Their primary issue": Smith and Tau, "Gay Rights Take Center Stage."

557 Fight Back New York dispensed: Marc Solomon, "How We Will Win," *The Advocate,* March 1, 2011.

557 "This is the first time": Smith and Tau, "Gay Rights Take Center Stage."

557 "Well-funded gay rights groups": Smith and Tau, "Gay Rights Take Center Stage."

558 Furthermore, the governor's political reputation: Jen Chung, "Ed Koch Held Decades-Long Grudge Against Cuomos Over 'Vote for Cuomo, Not the Homo' Posters," *Gothamist,* February 1, 2013.

558 When it came to lobbying: Michael Barbaro, "The Road to Gay Marriage in New York," *New York Times,* June 25, 2011.

558 personal efforts by the Catholic governor: William N. Eskridge Jr. and Christopher R. Riano, *Marriage Equality: From Outlaws to In-Laws* (New Haven: Yale University Press, 2020), 443, 449.

559 In 2009, gay couples: Richard Wolf, "Timeline: Same-Sex Marriage Through the Years," *USA Today,* May 24, 2015.

559 Freedom to Marry set out to: Paul Schindler, "Maryland, for Now, Steps Back from Marriage Equality," *Gay City News,* March 11, 2011; Julie Bolcer, "RI Committee to Hold Civil Unions Hearing," *The Advocate,* May 11, 2011.

559 "We hadn't had a state win": Solomon, *Winning Marriage,* 174.

560 By mid-April the three groups: Paul Schindler, "NY Marriage Equality Advocates Underscore Unity," *Gay City News,* April 22, 2011.

560 "a critical player": Solomon, *Winning Marriage,* 179.

560 "The gays worked together": J. Stephen Clark, "An Oral History of the Marriage Equality Act in New York," *Albany Government Law Review* 5, no. 4 (2012): 663.

560 who had introduced marriage legislation: Schindler, "Paterson Ups the Ante."

560 For guidance on that front: Marc Ambinder, "Bush Campaign Chief and Former RNC Chair Ken Mehlman: I'm Gay," *The Atlantic,* August 25, 2010.

560 "I can't change the fact": Ambinder, "Bush Campaign Chief."

560 The next month, Mehlman headlined: Corey Johnson, "Ken Mehlman, Peter Thiel, and Paul Singer Host Manhattan Fundraiser for Team Challenging Proposition 8," *Towleroad,* September 23, 2010.

560 "As someone who regrets": Johnson, "Ken Mehlman, Peter Thiel, and Paul Singer."

561 Mehlman's decision to come out: Duncan Osborne, "Wealthy Prop 8 Foe Has Gay Son," *Gay City News,* September 8, 2010.

561 "Good and honorable men and women": Johnson, "Ken Mehlman, Peter Thiel, and Paul Singer."

562 Singer committed: Solomon, *Winning Marriage,* 186.

562 In early May, Singer: Solomon, *Winning Marriage,* 190.

562 On May 11, O'Donnell: "Daniel O'Donnell Introduces Marriage Equality Bill in State Assembly," Joe.My.God, May 11, 2011, joemygod.com.

563 "the votes are there": Casey Seller and Jimmy Vielkind, "History Made Behind Scenes," *Albany Times-Union,* June 25, 2012.

563 "The question is not just": Seller and Vielkind, "History Made Behind the Scenes."

563 As they did, on June 15: Nicholas Confessore and Michael Barbaro, "In Reversal, 3 Democratic Senators Will Back Gay Marriage," *New York Times*, June 13, 2011.

563 "In the end, that is my vote": Geraldine Baum, "New York Gay Marriage: State Senate a Vote Away from Approving Bill," *Los Angeles Times*, June 16, 2011.

563 "There was an extreme": Clark, "An Oral History of the Marriage Equality Act in New York," 673.

563 It was unusually structured: Christopher W. Dickson, "Inseverability, Religious Exemptions, and New York's Same-Sex Marriage Law," *Cornell Law Review* 98, no. 1 (November 2012): 181–208.

564 "Did I love it?": Clark, "An Oral History of the Marriage Equality Act in New York," 667.

564 Skelos brought together: Nicholas Confessore and Michael Barbaro, "New York Allows Same-Sex Marriage, Becoming Largest State to Pass Law," *New York Times*, June 24, 2011.

564 "The days of just bottling up things": Confessore and Barbaro, "New York Allows Same-Sex Marriage."

565 "defined doing the right thing": Reid J. Epstein, "N.Y. Legalizes Gay Marriage," *Politico*, June 24, 2011.

565 "How do you feel?": Confessore and Barbaro, "New York Allows Same-Sex Marriage."

565 "The funny thing was": Seller and Vielkind, "History Made Behind Scenes."

75. A Grave Price

566 At 11:49 p.m.: David Badash, "Can Maggie Gallagher, NOM Get the NY Same-Sex Marriage Law Repealed?" New Civil Rights Movement, June 27, 2011, https://www.thenewcivilrightsmovement.com/2014/04/can_maggie_gallagher_nom_get_the_ny_same_sex_marriage_law_repealed.

566 "New York Republicans are responsible": Maggie Gallagher, "The GOP Will Pay a Grave Price," The Corner, *National Review*, June 25, 2011.

566 In the summer of 2010, the bishops conference: "Bishops Urged to Fight War of Words to Defend Traditional Marriage," *Catholic Review*, June 17, 2011.

567 Gay activists had succeeded: Tamara Audi, "Gay Activists Target Businesses," *Wall Street Journal*, August 27, 2008.

567 "socially unacceptable to give": Alison Stateman, "What Happens If You're on Gay Rights' 'Enemies List,'" *Time*, November 15, 2008.

567 Karger was able to: Fred Karger, "Fred Who?" (n.p.: Fred Karger, 2011), 13.

568 The Human Rights Campaign preferred to: Marc Gunther, "Queer Inc.: How Corporate America Fell in Love with Gays and Lesbians," *Fortune*, December 11, 2006.

568 a model to online rabble-rousers: Monica Youn, "Proposition 8 and the Mormon Church: A Case Study in Donor Disclosure," *George Washington Law Review* 81, no. 6 (November 2013): 2108–60.

568 In the summer of 2010, lefty activists: Tom Hamburger and Jennifer Martinez, "Target Stores Negotiate with Gay-Lesbian Group over Political Spending," *Los Angeles Times*, August 13, 2010.

568 The nongay group MoveOn.org: Tim Pugmire, "Advocacy Group Stages Protest at Target HQ over Donations Flap," Minnesota Public Radio, August 8, 2010.

568 The backlash, and threat of: Jackie Crosby, "Target Apologizes for Giving to Group Backing Emmer," *Star-Tribune*, August 6, 2010.

568 As he launched a "Mormongate" website: Stephanie Mencimer, "Game Changer," *Mother Jones*, March/April 2010.

568 The church responded by: Fred Karger, "Mormongate—the Church's Cover-up of Its Prop 8 Funding," *HuffPost*, March 5, 2009.

568 In the summer of 2010, the LDS Church settled with: Scott Taylor, "Mormon Church Agrees to Pay Small Fine for Mistake That Led to Late Report of Contributions in Prop. 8 Campaign," *Deseret News*, June 9, 2010.

568 "overlooked the daily reporting process": Taylor, "Mormon Church Agrees to Pay Small Fine."

569 "Mormon front group": "Prop. 8 Rivals Take Their Fight National," *Capitol Weekly*, April 13, 2009.

569 "part of a broader": Maggie Gallagher, "The Amazing Power of the Culture (Part 6)," The Corner, *National Review*, March 23, 2009.

569 "Every dollar you give": "Profiles on the Right: National Organization for Marriage (NOM)," Political Research Associates, November 11, 2013.

569 "donations to NOM": Brian S. Brown, "NOM Marriage News," NOMblog, July 3, 2009, www.nomblog.com.

569 A cross-country "Summer for Marriage": Maggie Gallagher, "Obama Sabotages Defense of Marriage Act," *Human Events*, July 14, 2010.

569 At the second stop: Barbara Polichetti, "300 Face Off at RI State House over Same-Sex Marriage," *Providence Journal*, July 18, 2010.

569 According to the *Providence Journal*: Polichetti, "300 Face Off."

569 "I've never seen anything like": Louis J. Marinelli, *A Change of Heart: Working for the National Organization for Marriage Led Me to Support Marriage Equality* (n.p.: Xlibris, 2012), 104.

569 "With our depressing turnout": Marinelli, *A Change of Heart*, 79.

570 "There is no reason the Senate": Brian S. Brown, "Emergency Alert: NY Marriage Vote May Come Tomorrow," NOMblog, June 20, 2011, www.nomblog.com.

570 By the time Gallagher wrote: Badash, "Can Maggie Gallagher, NOM Get the NY Same-Sex Marriage Law Repealed?"

570 "A 4-year process seems": Brian S. Brown, "Reversing SSM in New York: The Campaign Begins," NOMblog, June 28, 2011, www.nomblog.com.

570 Even though in 2010 Republicans: Paul Schindler, "Iowa House Endorses Anti-Gay Constitutional Amendment," *Gay City News*, February 2, 2011.

571 Without a legislative path: Arthur S. Leonard, "Sweeping Affirmation of Marriage Equality in Iowa," *Gay City News*, April 3, 2009.

571 typically a perfunctory exercise: Todd E. Pettys, "Letter from Iowa: Same-Sex Marriage and the Ouster of Three Justices," *University of Kansas Law Review* 59, no. 4 (May 2011): 715–16.

571 The National Organization for Marriage ultimately spent: Sofia Resnick, "National Organization for Marriage's 2010 Financial Records Raise Questions," *Washington Independent*, December 12, 2011; Boo Jarchow, "Following Election and Court Case Gay Rights Groups to Demonstrate for Marriage Equality," *Pride*, November 12, 2010, www.pride.com.

571 "It sends a powerful message": A. G. Sulzberger, "Voters Moving to Oust Judges Over Decisions," *New York Times*, September 24, 2010.

571 They were backed for retention: Craig Robinson, "Ternus Campaigns in Cedar Rapids," *Iowa Republican,* October 25, 2010.

571 For the National Organization for Marriage, the defeat of Ternus: A. G. Sulzberger, "Iowa Judges Defeated After Ruling on Same-Sex Marriage," *New York Times,* November 3, 2010.

76. Campaign in a Box

573 So even when it went public: *Moving Marriage Forward: Building Majority Support for Marriage* (Freedom to Marry, 2010).

574 The pop ubiquity: Phillip Picardi, "If You Think Lady Gaga's Super Bowl Performance Wasn't Political, You Missed the Point," *Teen Vogue,* February 6, 2017.

574 When Gallup first asked: George Gallup, "Gallup Polls on Gay Job Rights Issue," *Bay Area Reporter,* October 10, 1977.

575 One Twin Cities couple: Rachel Olson, "Same Sex Couples File Action Against Marriage Law," *Star-Tribune,* May 12, 2010.

575 Established gay-rights groups: *Benson v. Alverson,* A11-811.

575 "If they reaffirm": Elizabeth Dunbar, "Legal Fight to Lift Minnesota's Gay Marriage Ban Faces Tough Odds," *MPR News,* June 3, 2010.

575 When a Hennepin County judge: Abby Simons, "Judge Dismisses Challenge to Gay Marriage Barriers," *Star-Tribune,* March 9, 2011.

575 "There are both legal and political": Dunbar, "Legal Fight to Lift Minnesota's Gay Marriage."

575 While legislators had passed a DOMA-style bill: Rachel E. Stassen-Berger, "Amendment Would Bar Gay Civil Unions," *St. Paul Pioneer-Press,* March 2, 2004; Michael Khoo, "Gay Marriage Ban Stirs Emotions Inside, Outside Capitol," Minnesota Public Radio, April 7, 2005; Rachel Gold, "Legislature Passes DOMA," *FocusPoint,* March 21, 1997.

576 The new Republican majorities: Patrick Condon and Martiga Lohn, "Minn. House Takes Up Constitutional Gay Marriage Ban; Passage Would Send Question to Voters," Associated Press, April 21, 2011.

576 On June 6, Minnesotans United for All Families: "Dayton to Help Fundraise for Group Working to Defeat Marriage Amendment to Minn. Constitution," Associated Press, June 13, 2011.

576 Marry Me Minnesota pushed ahead: Kaitlyn Walsh, "Marry Me Minnesota Lawsuit Breaks Ranks," *Lavender,* November 17, 2011; Simons, "Judge Dismisses Challenge."

578 As Massachusetts and Connecticut: *Gill Foundation 2001 Annual Report* (Gill Foundation, 2001), 17.

579 civil unions in 2007: Beverly Wang, "Backers Rally for Gay Marriage," Associated Press, March 15, 2007.

579 "Voters overwhelmingly say": Doug Ireland, "NH Weighs Same-Sex Marriage Repeal," *Eagle-Tribune,* February 14, 2011.

580 Shortly after the vote: Tyler Evilsizer, "The Money Behind the Maine Marriage Measure," Follow the Money, November 5, 2009, https://www.followthemoney .org/research/institute-reports/the-money-behind-the-maine-marriage -measure.

581 When McTighe decided to go public: David Sharp, "Maine Gay Marriage Advocates Lay Groundwork for Another Referendum on Same-Sex Unions," Associated Press, June 30, 2011.

581 McTighe stood off camera: Judy Harrison, "Secretary of State Says Same-Sex Marriage Will Be on the Ballot," *Bangor (ME) Daily News,* January 23, 2012.

581 "As a pastor whose faith": Sharp, "Maine Gay Marriage Advocates Lay Groundwork."

77. Land Rush to the Ballot

583 The Human Rights Campaign had already signaled: Chris Johnson, "HRC endorses Obama for Election 2012," *Washington Blade,* May 26, 2011.

584 Couples were able to marry: Michael Barbaro, "After Long Wait, Same-Sex Couples Marry in New York," *New York Times,* July 24, 2011; John Leland, "Thousands Cheer Same-Sex Marriage Law in Euphoric Pride Parade," *New York Times,* June 26, 2011.

584 They extended beyond the Hollywood figures: John Branch, "Rangers' Avery Joins Campaign for Gay Rights," *New York Times,* May 7, 2011.

585 Throughout the summer, petition carriers: Paul Schindler, "Maine Marriage Advocates Begin Referendum Signature Push," *Gay City News,* August 18, 2011.

586 "he actually had designs": Matt McTighe, interview by Martin Meeker, 2016, "Matt McTighe on the Marriage Campaigns in Massachusetts and Maine," Oral History Center, The Bancroft Library, University of California, Berkeley, 74.

586 After he launched the petition drive: Deborah McDermott, "York Firefighters Appear in TV Ad Backing Gay Marriage," *Portsmouth (NH) Herald,* September 26, 2012.

586 "When we clear the call": McDermott, "York Firefighters Appear in TV Ad."

586 "What sounds good": McTighe, interview.

587 On the Why Marriage Matters Maine executive committee: Bob Sipchen, "Maine Voters Reject Rights Referendum," *Los Angeles Times,* November 8, 1995.

588 When they all gathered: Marc Solomon, *Winning Marriage: The Inside Story of How Same-Sex Couples Took On the Politicians and Pundits—and Won* (Lebanon, NH: ForeEdge, 2014), 234.

588 He had a long history: Josh Zeitz, "The Making of the Marriage Equality Revolution," *Politico Magazine,* April 28, 2015.

588 safe from political interference: Andrea Estes and Scott Helman, "Legislature Again Blocks Bid to Ban Gay Marriage," *Boston Globe,* November 10, 2006.

78. Conversation and Inoculation

590 The so-called personhood amendment: Kay Steiger, "What Happens If the Mississippi Personhood Amendment Passes?" *The Atlantic,* November 8, 2011.

590 "You don't change people": Robert Pérez and Amy Simon, *Heartwired: Human Behavior, Strategic Opinion Research and the Audacious Pursuit of Social Change* (Strategies for Good and Goodwin Strategic Research, 2017), 48, heartwiredforchange .com.

596 Microtargeting had been: Sasha Issenberg, *The Victory Lab: The Secret Science of Winning Campaigns* (New York: Crown, 2012).

79. Four Ballots

599 In Olympia, Washington, where nearly two years earlier: Pamela M. Prah, "Gay Marriage Question to Appear on 2012 Ballots," *Stateline,* January 12, 2012.

600 "It's time": Prah, "Gay Marriage Question to Appear on 2012 Ballots."

600 The bill passed the senate: Paul Schindler, "Ballot Fight Looms in Maryland,"

Gay City News, February 29, 2012; Sabrina Tavernise, "Short Votes, Md. Democrats Withdraw Same-Sex Marriage Act," *New York Times,* March 11, 2011.

600 "This is a distance run": Tavernise, "Short Votes, Md. Democrats Withdraw."

600 O'Malley began 2012 by declaring: Annie Linskey, "Searching Souls on Gay Marriage," *Baltimore Sun,* February 19, 2012; Lisa Keen, "Maryland House Passes Marriage Bill," Keen News Service, February 17, 2012.

600 "beginning a process": Sabrina Tavernise, "Maryland House Passes Same-Sex Marriage Bill," *New York Times,* February 17, 2012.

601 State senator Ed Murray, a longtime gay-rights activist: Matt Baume, *Defining Marriage: Voices from a Forty-Year Labor of Love* (Createspace Independent Publishing Platform, 2015), 281–84.

601 execute a masterful legislative strategy: Lisa Keen, "Washington Takes Big Leap, but Effort to Repeal Looms," Keen News Service, February 9, 2012.

601 With their focus on lawmakers: Lisa Keen, "Washington, Oregon, Take Different Paths to Marriage," Keen News Service, November 16, 2011.

602 "One Man Guides the Fight": Erik Eckholm, "One Man Guides the Fight Against Gay Marriage," *New York Times,* October 9, 2012.

602 "diabolically smart and creative": Eckholm, "One Man Guides the Fight."

602 collaboration between a cautious court: Anthony Michael Kreis, "Stages of Constitutional Grief: Democratic Constitutionalism and the Marriage Revolution," *University of Pennsylvania Journal of Constitutional Law* 20, no. 4 (March 2018): 912–15.

603 flocked to the new edge: Nathaniel Persily, "Gay Marriage, Public Opinion and the Courts," *Faculty Scholarship at Penn Law* (2006), 40–42.

603 Polls from the Pew Research Center: "Majority Continues To Support Civil Unions," Pew Research Center, October 9, 2009, www.pewforum.org.

603 In 2011, a Republican for the first time: Robert Gehrke, "Huntsman's Civil-Union Stance May Prove Political Liability," *Salt Lake Tribune,* May 12, 2011; Kirk Johnson, "National Debate About G.O.P. Hits Home in Utah," *New York Times,* May 24, 2009.

603 While the shift caused Huntsman trouble: Sarah Crone, "Utah GOP Gov. Jon Huntsman, Supporter of Civil Unions, to Speak in Kalamazoo," *Kalamazoo Gazette,* April 30, 2009.

604 "We have run a very strategic": Baird Helgeson, "Same-Sex Marriage Ban Nears Defeat," *Star-Tribune,* November 7, 2012.

605 "months of relatively": "Mainstream Media in Four 'Gay Marriage' States Attacking Latest Pro-Marriage Ads Featuring David & Tonia Parker," Mass Resistance, November 5, 2012, www.massresistance.org.

605 "bracing for a rush": Eckholm, "One Man Guides the Fight."

605 The Massachusetts parents had a story: James Vaznis, "Lawsuit Invokes Religious Freedom; Parents Say Beliefs Ignored by School," *Boston Globe,* May 4, 2006.

605 Along with another set of parents: Jonathan Saltzman, "Same-Sex Teaching Upheld; Lexington Parents Say They'll Appeal," *Boston Globe,* February 24, 2007.

605 A federal judge ruled that the parents: *Parker v. Hurley,* 514 F.3d 87.

605 In 2008, the U.S. Supreme Court refused: Kathleen Gilbert, "Mandatory Homosexual Indoctrination in Grade School Survives after Supreme Court Turns Down Case," *LifeSiteNews,* October 8, 2008.

607 "sentiments everyone feels": Patrick Ruffini, "The Joe-the-Plumberization of the GOP," The Next Right, February 25, 2009, accessed via archive.org.

607 Several of the consultants: Jesse McKinley, "California Companies Fight Same-Sex Marriage Nationwide," *New York Times,* December 13, 2009.

607 "I'm not going to blow their cover": McKinley, "California Companies Fight Same-Sex Marriage Nationwide."

608 Even though NOM had sublet: Monica Hesse, "Opposing Gay Unions with Sanity and a Smile," *Washington Post,* August 28, 2009."

609 The National Organization for Marriage remained: "2011–2012 Ballot Measure Overview," Follow the Money, March 3, 2014, www.followthemoney.org.

609 A documentary film: Amy Kaufman, "The Roots of '8: The Mormon Proposition,'" *Los Angeles Times,* June 21, 2010; Jen Chaney, "'8: The Mormon Proposition': Audacious Look at Church's Role in Gay-Marriage Ban," *Washington Post,* January 30, 2010.

609 The next year, the LDS Church: Lisa Wangsness, "In Ads, Mormons Introduce Themselves," *Boston Globe,* June 20, 2011.

609 As 2012 approached, the LDS Church: J. B. Haws, *The Mormon Image in the American Mind: Fifty Years of Public Perception* (New York: Oxford University Press, 2013), chap. 10.

610 "a mystery to even the Mormons": Wangsness, "In Ads, Mormons Introduce Themselves."

610 Baltimore's archbishop, William E. Lori: Daniela Altimari, Jean Marbella, and Mary Gail Hare, "Bridgeport Bishop William Lori Named Archbishop of Baltimore," *Hartford Courant,* March 20, 2012; John Wagner, "Archbishop of Baltimore to Headline Event for Same-Sex Marriage Opponents," *Washington Post,* September 24, 2012.

610 Seattle's archbishop, J. Peter Sartain: Janet I. Tu and Jayme Fraser, "Low-Profile Seattle Archbishop Not Afraid of Controversies," *Seattle Times,* August 4, 2012.

610 Maine's Portland diocese had: Tyler Evilsizer, "the Money Behind the Maine Marriage Measure," Follow the Money, November 5, 2009, www.followthemoney.org.

610 "I fear I'll be remembered": Bill Nemitz, "Documentary Clips Show Sad Face of Yes on 1," *Portland Press-Herald,* April 17, 2011.

611 "winner's remorse": Nemitz, "Documentary Clips Show Sad Face of Yes on 1."

611 The next year in Maine, NOM attempted: *Nat'l Org. for Marriage v. Me. Comm'n on Governmental Ethics,* Superior Court Action Docket No. AP-10-12.

611 Only five individuals: "2011–2012 Ballot Measure Overview."

611 The 2012 public-disclosure reports: "2011–2012 Ballot Measure Overview."

611 "You didn't see Jeff Bezos": Thomas Wheatley, interview by Martin Meeker, 2016, "Thomas Wheatley on Field Organizing with Freedom to Marry," Oral History Center, The Bancroft Library, University of California, Berkeley, 23.

611 Overall, more than two-thirds: "2011–2012 Ballot Measure Overview."

612 While Freedom to Marry claimed the results: Lisa Keen, "Beyond the Blue: Why Marriage Won This Time," Keen News Service, November 28, 2012.

613 With fifteen minutes left: Julie Bolcer, "The Moment of Victory in Minnesota," *The Advocate,* November 8, 2012.

80. Dooming DOMA

617 her first in federal court: *Gill v. Office of Personnel Management,* 699 F. Supp. 2d 374.

617 cited thenceforth by its unenthusiastic backers: Bill Clinton, "It's Time to Overturn DOMA," *Washington Post,* March 7, 2013.

617 the Parker House's history: Susan Wilson, *Heaven, by Hotel Standards: The History of the Omni Parker House* (Boston: Omni Parker House, 2014), 10.

618 stop on the 2001 statewide tour: Beth Berlo, "Marriage Lawsuit Filed on Behalf of Seven Couples," *Bay Windows,* April 12, 2001.

618 held the triumphant press conference: Laura Kiritsy, "Court Rules Couples May Wed," *Bay Windows,* November 18, 2003.

618 celebrate the court's ruling: Laura Kiritsy, "SJC: Civil Unions Don't Cut It," *Bay Windows,* February 5, 2004.

618 Being forced to keep: Jonathan Saltzman, "Same-Sex Spouses Challenge US Curbs, Call Marriage Act Discriminatory," *Boston Globe,* May 3, 2009.

618 GLAD ran ads: Jonathan Saltzman, "Massachusetts Group Girding for Fight to Expand Rights of Same-Sex Married Couples," *Boston Globe,* November 5, 2007.

619 Their client, Dean Hara: Jill Lawrence, "Congressional Spouse a Man of the House," *Washingtonian,* July 1996.

619 on the couple's one-year anniversary: Carol Beggy and Mark Shanahan, "Names: Old Married Couple," *Boston Globe,* May 16, 2005.

619 The pair had been living: Philip Shishkin, "The Battle over Benefits for Same-Sex Spouses; Lawsuit Seeks Same Rights Straight Couples Possess; Opponents Fear Campaign to Advance Gay Marriage Nationally," *Boston Globe,* May 21, 2009.

620 After Studds died: Paul Schindler, "Gerry Studds Is Dead at 69," *Gay City News,* October 21, 2006.

620 nearly all the debate: Patrick J. Borchers, "The Essential Irrelevance of the Full Faith and Credit Clause to the Same-Sex Marriage Debate," *Creighton Law Review* 38, no. 2 (2005): 253–54.

620 "Powers Reserved to the States": U.S. Congress, House, Defense of Marriage Act, HR 3396, 104th Cong., introduced in House May 7, 1996.

621 Many scholars concluded: Andrew Koppelman, *Same Sex, Different States: When Same-Sex Marriages Cross State Lines* (New Haven: Yale University Press, 2006), 114–36.

622 when the legislature rejected: Pam Belluck, "Bid to Ban Gay Marriage Fails in Massachusetts," *New York Times,* June 14, 2007.

622 one of his party's most consistent opponents: Mary Leonard, "GOP Divided on Marriage Amendment," *Boston Globe,* March 28, 2004.

622 several of her peers: Nathaniel Frank, *Awakening: How Gays and Lesbians Brought Marriage Equality to America* (Cambridge, MA: The Belknap Press of Harvard University, 2017), 289.

622 "This is a case": Saltzman, "Same-Sex Spouses Challenge."

81. Dave & Ted's Excellent Adventure

623 Rob Reiner and his wife Michele invited: Jo Becker, *Forcing the Spring: Inside the Fight for Marriage Equality* (New York: The Penguin Press, 2014), 29.

623 What became known: *Strauss v. Horton,* 46 Cal.4th 364.

623 through a variety of claims: Arthur S. Leonard, "Cal Supreme Court May Split Decision," *Gay City News,* May 6, 2009.

623 The case had been argued: Aurelio Rojas, "Proposition 8: Supreme Court Showdown; Dueling Attorneys a Study in Opposites," *Sacramento Bee,* May 1, 2009.

623 arrived unsure: Becker, *Forcing the Spring,* 30.

623 worked with the Reiners: Sabin Russell, "Star Power Fuels Push for Prop. 10; 'Rob Reiner Initiative' Has Steep Cigarette Tax," *San Francisco Chronicle,* October 22, 1998.

624 increase funding for early-childhood education: Dan Morain, "Reiner Quits First 5 Panel," *Los Angeles Times,* May 30, 2006.

624 They were joined: Chuleenan Svetvilas, "Challenging Prop. 8: The Hidden Story," *California Lawyer,* January 2010.

624 sought to have a 2000 amendment: *Citizens for Equal Protection v. Bruning,* No. 05-2604.

624 "is not about marriage": *Citizens for Equal Protection v. Bruning,* No. 05-2604, plaintiffs' brief, October 21, 2005.

625 "We think, strategically": David Kravets, "Two Paths Toward One Goal: Same-Sex Marriage," Associated Press, April 2, 2006.

625 lawsuit by Arthur Smelt: *Smelt v. County of Orange,* 374 F. Supp. 2d 861.

625 The pair dissolved: *Smelt v. County of Orange,* 447 F.3d 673.

625 "would have told Dred Scott": Kravets, "Two Paths Toward One Goal."

625 would take effect in July 2008: Rachel Gordon, Chris Heredia, and Jill Tucker, "Same-Sex Weddings Start with Union of Elderly San Francisco Couple," *San Francisco Chronicle,* June 7, 2008.

626 At the Reiners' home: Becker, *Forcing the Spring,* 29.

626 took to describing himself: Ned Martel, "New Head of Human Rights Campaign Aims to Stop Losing Streak for Gay Marriage," *Washington Post,* July 25, 2015.

626 Griffin had not come out: Leslie Newell Peacock, "From Wal-Mart to the White House," *Arkansas Times,* December 10, 2009.

627 "It has to have": Becker, *Forcing the Spring,* 32.

627 claiming it would wait: Chuleenan Svetvilas, "Challenging Prop. 8: The Hidden Story," *California Lawyer,* January 2010.

627 although many belonged to: Ted Johnson, "Hollywood Rallies Against Prop. 8; Rob Reiner, Bruce Cohen on Board of New Org," *Daily Variety,* June 3, 2009.

627 "the lawyers Microsoft is going to want": Margaret Talbot, "A Risky Proposal," *New Yorker,* January 18, 2010.

627 Gibson Dunn agreed: Ross Todd, "Marriage Brokers: Behind the Scenes of the Odd Couple's Groundbreaking Litigation," *American Lawyer,* March 11, 2011.

627 "greenlighted": Becker, *Forcing the Spring,* 31.

627 "We did not want to have": Svetvilas, "Challenging Prop. 8."

627 the California Supreme Court released: *Strauss v. Horton,* 46 Cal.4th 364.

627 In the same ruling: "18,000 Same-Sex Marriages Ruled Lawful; Court Upholds Prop 8 Decision: Opponents of Gay-Wedding Ban Rally, Vow to Launch Repeal Campaign," *Los Angeles Daily News,* May 27, 2009.

628 He and Olson had first met: Talbot, "A Risky Proposal."

628 the 1967 case that had helped: *Loving v. Virginia,* 388 US 1.

628 "There will be many people": Lisa Leff, "Gay Rights Groups Question Timing of Federal Suit to Overturn California Same-Sex Marriage Ban," Associated Press, May 27, 2009.

628 plaintiffs had been the last piece: Becker, *Forcing the Spring,* 36.

629 "major casting call": Becker, *Forcing the Spring,* 35.

629 identified via personal ties: Becker, *Forcing the Spring,* 37.

629 While GLAD published: Gay & Lesbian Advocates & Defenders, *DOMA Stories: How Federal Marriage Discrimination Hurts American Families* (GLAD, 2011).

629 "this is not going to be a case": Talbot, "A Risky Proposal."

629 "Reasonable minds can differ": Leff, "Gay Rights Groups Question Timing."

629 much of the coverage centered: Jo Becker, "The Road to Championing Same-Sex Marriage," *New York Times,* August 18, 2009.

630 actually extended the invitation first: Becker, *Forcing the Spring,* 39.

631 "Federal court?": Jesse McKinley, "Bush v. Gore Foes Join to Fight Gay Marriage Ban," *New York Times,* May 27, 2009.

631 all white and in their thirties: Becker, *Forcing the Spring,* 39.

631 "Look at the perfect gay people": Rich Juzwiak, "Look at the Perfect Gay People: 'The Case Against 8,'" *Gawker,* June 24, 2014.

631 "unnecessary dispute": *Perry v. Schwarzenegger,* NO. C 09-02292 JW, Plaintiffs, Statement of Non-Opposition to Proposed Intervenors' Motion to Intervene, June 11, 2009.

631 "Having declined to bring": Andrew Davis, "Anti-Prop 8 Lawyers Reject Gay Groups," *Windy City Times,* August 26, 2009.

632 "We are very close": *Perry v. Schwarzenegger,* NO. C 09-02292 JW, Pretrial Status Conference Transcript, July 2, 2009.

632 "I'm reasonably sure": "We are very close": *Perry v. Schwarzenegger,* pretrial transcript.

632 Choosing to stage a trial: Kenji Yoshino, *Speak Now: Marriage Equality on Trial* (New York: Crown, 2014), 8.

632 While 20 percent of federal civil cases: John H. Langbein, "The Disappearance of Civil Trial in the United States," *Yale Law School Faculty Scholarship Series,* Paper 4825, 2012.

633 "As far as our research has been able to turn up": *Perry v. Schwarzenegger,* pretrial transcript, 24.

633 Even before the judge had decided: *Perry v. Schwarzenegger,* NO. C 09-02292 JW, ACLU "[Proposed] Case Management Statement," August 17, 2009.

633 The Our Families Coalition would be kept out: *Perry v. Schwarzenegger,* pretrial transcript, August 8, 2009.

633 granted the plaintiffs' begrudging proposal: Dan Levine, "Rights Groups Shut Out of Prop 8; Walker: S.F. Can Join Challenge, but Not Lambda, ACLU," *The Recorder,* August 20, 2009.

633 petition received more attention: Mike McKee, "Infighting Roils Prop 8 Challenge; Gay Groups Want to Intervene, but Boies/Olson Wary," *The Recorder,* July 21, 2009.

633 initiated the entire cycle: Lyle Denniston, "City Says Gays Have Right to Stay Married; Lawyer Argues Couples Deserve Due Process," *Boston Globe,* April 22, 2004.

634 "it should be the City alone": Svetvilas, "Challenging Prop. 8."

82. Duty to Defend

635 retirement of Justice David Souter: Adam Nagourney and Jeff Zeleny, "Washington Prepares for Fight over Any Nominee," *New York Times,* May 1, 2009.

635 nonetheless challenged repeatedly: U.S. Congress, Senate, Judiciary Committee, "Confirmation Hearing on the Nomination of Hon. Sonia Sotomayor, to be an Associate Justice of the Supreme Court of the United States," July 13, 2009.

635 Roberts was not interrogated at all: U.S. Congress, Senate, Judiciary Commit-

tee, "Confirmation Hearing on the Nomination of John G. Roberts, to be Chief Justice of the Supreme Court of the United States," September 12, 2005.

635 asked Alito if he believed: U.S. Congress, Senate, Judiciary Committee, "Confirmation Hearing on the Nomination of Samuel A. Alito, Jr., to be an Associate Justice of the Supreme Court of the United States," January 9, 2008.

635 "opportunity to come back tomorrow": U.S. Congress, Senate, Judiciary Committee, "Confirmation Hearing on the Nomination of Hon. Sonia Sotomayor, to be an Associate Justice of the Supreme Court of the United States," July 13, 2009.

636 "If the Supreme Court": U.S. Congress, Senate, Judiciary Committee, "Confirmation Hearing on the Nomination of Hon. Sonia Sotomayor, to be an Associate Justice of the Supreme Court of the United States," July 13, 2009.

636 gay activists were divided: Paul Schindler, "HRC Shifts, Actively Pushing Barney Frank's ENDA," *Gay City News,* November 6, 2007.

637 Obama was afraid: Nathaniel Frank, "Obama's False 'Don't Ask, Don't Tell' Narrative," *New Republic,* February 19, 2013.

637 "The President and I feel": Fox News, "Transcript: Secretary Gates on 'FNS,'" *Fox News Sunday,* March 29, 2009.

637 An appeals court ruled: *Witt v. Dept. of Air Force,* 548 F.3d 1264.

637 "takes the issue off": Jess Bravin and Laura Meckler, "Obama Avoids Test on Gays in Military," *Wall Street Journal,* May 21, 2009.

637 The catalyst again came: Sam Miller, "No Same-Sex Weddings in O.C. Yet," *Orange County Register,* May 17, 2008.

637 appeals court judge decided not to consider: *Smelt v. County of Orange,* 447 F.3d 673.

637 By legalizing same-sex unions: Arthur S. Leonard, "Battling over 'Revision'; Legal Challenges to Prop 8 Raise Technical and Constitutional Questions," *Gay City News,* November 12, 2008.

638 "the refusal of all states and jurisdictions": *Smelt v. US,* Notice of Removal by USA, PB-CA-0035-0001.

638 awaiting a reply from the federal government: Arthur S. Leonard, "Obama Administration Versus Candidate Obama," *Gay City News,* June 14, 2009.

638 review of the president's options: Daniel J. Meltzer, "Executive Defense of Congressional Acts," *Duke Law Journal* 61, no. 6 (March 2012): 1183–236.

638 Obama had run for national office: Leonard, "Obama Administration Versus Candidate Obama."

638 The role of the executive branch: David Barron, "Constitutionalism in the Shadow of Doctrine: The President's Non-Enforcement Power," *Law and Contemporary Problems* 63, nos. 1–2 (Winter/Spring 2000): 61–106 (January 2008): 689–804.

638 far more work to do: Charlie Savage, *Power Wars: Inside Obama's Post-9/11 Presidency* (New York: Little, Brown and Company, 2015).

639 deadline approached for the government's response: *Smelt v. United States,* SACV-09-00286.

639 report the House Judiciary Committee had issued: House Judiciary Committee report on Defense of Marriage Act, H.R. 3396, July 6, 1996.

639 "DOMA does not discriminate": *Smelt v. United States,* SACV-09-00286, reply brief from Justice Department, June 11, 2009.

639 bloggers who were closely watching: Chris Geidner, "Obama's DOJ Did Not Have to Go This Far," LawDork, June 12, 2009, accessed via archive.org.

639 "Our president had a choice": John Aravosis, "Obama DOJ Lies to Politico in Defending Hate Brief Against Gays," AMERICAblog, June 12, 2009, accessed via archive.org.

639 "Any gay person who attends": John Aravosis, "Are Barney Frank, Tammy Baldwin, Howard Dean and Jared Polis Really Going to Honor Biden at a Gay DNC Fundraiser This Month?" AMERICAblog, June 12, 2009, accessed via archive .org.

640 Obama summoned advisers: Kerry Eleveld, *Don't Tell Me to Wait: How the Fight for Gay Rights Changed America and Transformed Obama's Presidency* (New York: Basic Books, 2015), 87–88.

641 "I think we all have to acknowledge": Duncan Osborne, "Limited Benefits for Fed Workers; With Fanfare, Obama Announces Partner Rights, but No Health Insurance," *Gay City News,* June 18, 2009.

641 have a passport reissued: John R. Ellement, "Same-Sex Couples Allowed to Use Spouses' Surnames on Passports," *Boston Globe,* June 18, 2009.

641 refiled an amended complaint: Hannah Clay Wareham, "GLAD Amends Complaint in DOMA Lawsuit," *Bay Windows,* August 6, 2009.

83. Facts of the Matter

643 The first witnesses called: *Perry v. Schwarzenegger,* NO. C 09-02292 JW trial transcript, January 11, 2010.

643 "I think the timeline for us": *Perry v. Schwarzenegger,* trial transcript, January 11, 2010.

644 "taking away of the right to marriage": *Perry v. Schwarzenegger,* trial transcript, January 11, 2010.

644 struck down antisodomy laws: *Lawrence v. Texas,* 539 US 558.

644 Olson could make Cooper's project: Kenji Yoshino, *Speak Now: Marriage Equality on Trial* (New York: Crown, 2014), 120.

644 Olson's opening argument made: *Perry v. Schwarzenegger,* trial transcript, January 11, 2010, 18.

645 "Assume that you have": *Perry v. Schwarzenegger,* NO. C 09-02292 JW, pretrial conference transcript, October 14, 2009, 22.

645 "is this institution designed": *Perry v. Schwarzenegger,* trial transcript, January 11, 2010, 60.

646 Olson and Boies put forward: *Perry v. Schwarzenegger,* NO. C 09-02292 JW, plaintiffs' and plaintiff intervenor's trial witness list, December 7, 2009.

646 ACLU attorneys laid out a plan: *Perry v. Schwarzenegger,* NO. C 09-02292. JW, ACLU "[Proposed] Case Management Statement," August 17, 2009.

647 "Plaintiffs have not persuaded": *Hernandez v. Robles,* 7 N.Y.3d 338.

647 Maryland appeals court dismissed: Arthur S. Leonard, "Maryland Judges Inscrutable; A Surprisingly Quiet Maryland Court of Appeals Heard Oral Arguments in the Pending Same-Sex Marriage Case on December 4," *Gay City News,* December 7, 2006.

647 "The court doesn't have to disparage": Kelly Brewington, "Gay Marriage Case in Md. Court; State's Highest Court Weighs Right to Wed Judges," *Baltimore Sun,* December 5, 2006.

647 Trials had proven particularly effective: Suzanne B. Goldberg, "Constitutional Tipping Points: Civil Rights, Social Change, and Fact-Based Adjudication," *Columbia Law Review* 106, no. 8 (December 2006): 1955–2022.

647 "there is no factual basis": *Howard v. Arkansas,* CV 1999-9881, Ark. Circuit Ct. Pulaski County, December 29, 2004.

647 "flies in the face of the evidence": *Human Servs. v. Howard,* 367 Ark. 55.

647 Florida circuit court reached: Yolanne Almanzar, "Florida Gay Adoption Ban Is Ruled Unconstitutional," *New York Times,* November 25, 2008.

648 "In addition to the volume": *Florida Dept. v. Adoption of X.X.G.,* District Court of Appeal of Florida, Third District 45 So. 3d 79 (Fla. Dist. Ct. App. 2010).

648 "In the trial-management statement they presented": *Perry v. Schwarzenegger,* NO. C 09-02292 JW, ACLU "[Proposed] Case Management Statement," August 17, 2009.

648 when barely one-quarter of Americans: Pew Research Center, "Growing Public Support for Same-Sex Marriage," February 16, 2012, www.pewresearch.org.

649 promoted not as "debates": *Perry v. Schwarzenegger,* NO. C 09-02292 JW, ACLU, trial transcript, January 26, 2010.

649 "There certainly has been a good deal": Bob Egelko, "Prop. 8 Trial Will Be Shown on YouTube," *San Francisco Chronicle,* January 7, 2010.

649 the Supreme Court scratched the camera plan: *Hollingsworth v. Perry,* per-curiam opinion from U.S. Supreme Court on broadcast question, January 13, 2010.

649 Cooper mentioned only one: *Perry v. Schwarzenegger,* trial transcript, January 26, 2010.

649 By the time he took the stand: *Perry v. Schwarzenegger,* trial transcript, January 26, 2010.

650 His doctoral work had been: David Blankenhorn, "Cabinet Makers in Victorian Britain: A Study of Two Trade Unions," unpublished MA dissertation, University of Warwick, UK, October 1978.

650 "any scientific study of what effects": *Perry v. Schwarzenegger,* trial transcript, January 26, 2010.

650 "The objection is that the witness": *Perry v. Schwarzenegger,* trial transcript, January 26, 2010.

650 "Insofar as we are a nation": David Blankenhorn, *The Future of Marriage* (New York: Encounter Books, 2007), 2.

650 "I'd like to take some time": *Perry v. Schwarzenegger,* trial transcript, January 27, 2010.

651 "That the Prop 8 proponents employed": Frank Rich, "Two Weddings, a Divorce and 'Glee,'" *New York Times,* June 12, 2010.

651 "losing friends, being told I'm": Duncan Osborne, "Pro-Prop 8 Witness Laments Reaction," *Gay City News,* August 4, 2010.

652 "Naturally we would like to move": Sofia Resnick, "Conservative-Backed Study Intended to Sway Court on Gay Marriage," *American Independent,* March 10, 2013.

84. Appealing Stuff

653 subsequently celebrated as members: Joel Klein "2010 Time 100: David Boies and Theodore Olson," *Time,* April 29, 2010.

653 Bonauto faced a judge: Lisa Keen, "Mass. Likens DOMA to Colorado Initiative That Supreme Court Struck Down," Keen News Service, June 27, 2010.

653 too many to be seated together: Jonathan Saltzman, "Case Is Made vs. US Marriage Law; Court Hears Gay Group's Challenge," *Boston Globe*, May 7, 2010.

654 "final word on the state constitution": Shelley Murphy and Jonathan Saltzman, "US Judge Vows Swift Ruling on Injunction," *Boston Globe*, May 13, 2004.

654 back the litigation with a parallel challenge: "Massachusetts Takes On DOMA," *Gay City News*, July 10, 2009.

654 "forces the state to discriminate": Lisa Keen, "Mass. Likens DOMA to Colorado Initiative."

654 "This presidential administration disagrees": Saltzman, "Case Is Made vs. US Marriage Law."

654 "It's really a question for them": Katharine Q. Seelye, "Marriage Law Is Challenged as Equaling Discrimination," *New York Times*, May 7, 2010.

655 "sham trial": Maggie Gallagher, "Obama Sabotages Defense of Marriage Act," *Human Events*, July 14, 2010.

655 "This assertion merely begs": *Commonwealth of Mass. v. U.S. D. of Health Human SVCS*, 698 F. Supp. 2d 234.

655 A month later on the West Coast: Arthur S. Leonard, "With Sweeping Clarity, Prop 8 Struck Down," *Gay City News*, August 4, 2010.

655 "The trial evidence provides no basis": *Perry v. Schwarzenegger*, 704 F. Supp. 2d 921.

655 Connecticut's high court ruled: Arthur S. Leonard, "Rejecting Civil Union Path, Connecticut Supreme Court Orders Full Marriage Equality," *Gay City News*, October 10, 2008.

656 "I think about it as building blocks": Ariel Levy, "The Perfect Wife," *New Yorker*, September 30, 2013.

658 one major gay-rights case to her name: Anemona Hartocolis, "N.Y. Court Upholds Gay Marriage Ban," *New York Times*, July 6, 2006.

658 more than a year into working: Roberta Kaplan with Lisa Dickey, *Then Comes Marriage: United States v. Windsor and the Defeat of DOMA* (New York: W. W. Norton & Co., 2015), 114–18.

658 "if Thea was Theo": Nina Totenberg, "Meet the 83-Year-Old Taking On the U.S. over Same-Sex Marriage," NPR, March 3, 2013.

658 "She had to be prepared": Kaplan with Dickey, *Then Comes Marriage*, 118.

659 heard old-time New York lawyers describe: Robbie Kaplan, "'It's All About Edie, Stupid': Lessons from Litigating *US v. Windsor*," *Columbia Journal of Gender and Law* (May 22, 2014).

659 organizations had slackened their resistance: Arthur S. Leonard, "New Thrusts at DOMA," *Gay City News*, November 24, 2010.

659 Lambda Legal had signed on to: *Golinski v. U.S. Office of Personnel Management*, 781 F. Supp. 2d 967, Defendants' Supplemental Brief in Response to Court Order of October 15, 2010.

659 "You never know how the litigation": James Esseks, "On Legal Strategy, the ACLU, and LGBT Legal Organizations," Freedom to Marry Oral History Project, The Bancroft Library, University of California, Berkeley, 2015.

659 She had cast *Pedersen: Pedersen v. Office of Personnel Mgmt.*, 881 F. Supp. 2d 294.

660 concurrent press conferences to advance: Lisa Keen, "Two More DOMA Court Challenges Filed; Five Cases Now Pending," Keen News Service, November 9, 2010.

85. Inaction Hero

662 "at every juncture, developments in the law of same-sex marriage": Katherine Shaw, "Constitutional Nondefense in the States," *Columbia Law Review* 114, no. 2 (March 2014).

662 second time in 2007: Jill Tucker, "Schwarzenegger Vetoes Same-Sex Marriage Bill Again," *San Francisco Chronicle*, October 12, 2007.

662 Schwarzenegger told the court: *Perry v. Schwarzenegger*, 704 F. Supp. 2d 921, Answer to Complaint for Declaratory, Injunctive, or Other Relief, June 16, 2009.

662 had signed the first state bill: "Gay Marriage Ban Gets Approval," *NewsWest*, April 28, 1977.

662 That left California without: Maura Dolan, "Schwarzenegger Decides Against Defending Prop. 8 in Federal Court," *Los Angeles Times*, June 18, 2009.

662 both he and ticketmate Kamala Harris: Matt Baume, "Kamala Harris Vows to Abandon Prop 8," NBC Bay Area, December 2, 2010.

662 California-based federal judge ruled: John Schwartz, "Judge Rules That Military Policy Violates Rights of Gays," *New York Times*, September 9, 2010.

663 Obama would face a choice: "DOMA, DADT, and the Duty to Defend: A Conversation," The National LGBT Bar Association, October 18, 2010.

663 voted by a large, bipartisan margin: Carl Hulse, "Senate Repeals Ban on Gays Serving Openly in Military," *New York Times*, December 18, 2010.

664 "I'm always looking for a way": Kerry Eleveld, "Obama: 'Prepared to Implement,'" *The Advocate*, December 22, 2010.

664 calling the "Sarah Palin Test": Marc Solomon, *Winning Marriage: The Inside Story of How Same-Sex Couples Took On the Politicians and Pundits—and Won* (Lebanon, NH: ForeEdge, University Press of New England, 2014), 279.

665 "the established usages, customs and traditions": *Plessy v. Ferguson*, 163 US 537.

665 typically traced to 1938: Louis Lusky, "A 'Carolene Products' Reminiscence," *Columbia Law Review* 82, no. 6 (October 1982).

666 "part of the Court's dramatic change": Daniel A. Farber and Philip P. Frickey, "Is *Carolene Products* Dead—Reflections on Affirmative Action and the Dynamics of Civil Rights Legislation," *California Law Review* 79, no. 3 (1991), Symposium: Civil Rights Legislation in the 1990s, May 1991.

666 isolated the criteria necessary: *Frontiero v. Richardson*, 411 U.S. 677, 93 S. Ct. 1764 (1973).

666 taught at the University of Chicago: Jodi Kantor, "Inside Professor Obama's Classroom," The Caucus, *New York Times*, July 30, 2008.

666 "Con Law III" covered equal protection: David J. Garrow, *Rising Star: The Making of Barack Obama* (New York: HarperCollins, 2017), 614.

667 "I'm not going to put my constitutional lawyer hat": Kerry Eleveld, "Obama: 'Prepared to Implement,'" *The Advocate*, December 22, 2010.

668 "neither *Romer* nor *Lawrence* mandate": *Cook v. Gates*, 528 F.3d 42.

668 "Now they are being asked": Charlie Savage, "Lawsuits on Same-Sex Marriage Challenge Obama Administration," *New York Times*, January 28, 2011.

669 Eliot Spitzer had enforced: Pam Belluck, "Gays Elsewhere Eye Marriage Massachusetts Style," *New York Times*, May 14, 2004.

670 redoubts of quiet policymaking: Anthony Michael Kreis, "Stages of Constitutional Grief: Democratic Constitutionalism and the Marriage Revolution," *University of Pennsylvania Journal of Constitutional Law* 20, no. 4 (March 2018): 975.

670 After Governor Martin O'Malley said: John Wagner, "O'Malley Says Md. Should Recognize Rights of Gay Couples Married Elsewhere," *Washington Post,* July 9, 2009.

670 Gansler ordered state agencies: Arthur S. Leonard, "Maryland AG: No Bar to Recognizing Out-of-State Marriages," *Gay City News,* February 24, 2010.

670 recognized as married at home: Chad Bray, "Two New Lawsuits Filed Challenging U.S. Law Defining Marriage," *Wall Street Journal,* November 9, 2010.

670 litigators who saw their Washington trips: James Esseks, "Don't Postpone Joy: Taking Down the Defense of Marriage Act (DOMA)," in *Love Unites Us: Winning the Freedom to Marry in America,* ed. Kevin M. Cathcart and Leslie J. Gabel-Brett (New York: The New Press, 2016), 214.

670 "I'm asking you for an extension": Roberta Kaplan with Lisa Dickey, *Then Comes Marriage: United States v. Windsor and the Defeat of DOMA* (New York: W. W. Norton & Co., 2015), 138.

86. Leading from Behind

672 "ever since I have a memory": Jackie Calmes, "Obama Speech Interrupted by Gay Marriage Supporters," *New York Times,* June 23, 2011.

672 "ultimately decided that a same-sex relationship": David J. Garrow, *Rising Star: The Making of Barack Obama,* paperback ed. (New York: HarperCollins, 2018), 113.

672 The first house of worship to pass: Jon Yoshihige, "Same-Sex Marriages Get Backing," *Honolulu Advertiser,* June 14, 1991.

672 had been Obama's boyhood Sunday school: Pat Gee, "Isle Church Honored by Obama's Visit," *Honolulu Star-Bulletin,* January 6, 2009.

673 Obama mounted his first campaign: Ryan Lizza, "Making It," *New Yorker,* July 21, 2008.

673 Wolfson's "the State": Evan Wolfson, "Altared States: Attorney Evan Wolfson Argues the Case for Marriage," *10 Percent,* May 1995.

673 Illinois legislators would face their first bill: Michael Dizon, "Senate Approves a Ban on Same-Sex Marriages," *Chicago Tribune,* March 29, 1996.

673 "up against a progressive incumbent": Timothy Stewart-Winter, "Putting Obama's Questionnaire in Context," *Windy City Times,* January 14, 2009.

674 Obama's advertising would style him: Garrow, *Rising Star,* 680.

674 already being spoken of as a promising contender: Garrow, *Rising Star,* 520.

674 Obama said he would cosponsor: Tracy Baim, *Obama and the Gays: A Political Marriage* (Chicago: Prairie Avenue Productions, 2010), 12.

674 Obama similarly developed a habit: Raymond Hernandez and Christopher Drew, "It's Not Just 'Ayes' and 'Nays': Obama's Votes in Illinois Echo," *New York Times,* December 20, 2007.

674 Obama cultivated a record: "Making History: Obama's Marriage Views Changed," *Windy City Times,* January 14, 2009.

674 appearing at a major fundraising banquet: Curtis Lawrence, "Gay Activists Savor Success at Fund-Raiser," *Chicago Sun-Times,* January 30, 2000.

674 Obama did not respond: Baim, *Obama and the Gays,* 3.

674 he struggled in the black South Side neighborhoods: Salim Muwakkil, "Ironies Abound in 1st District," *Chicago Tribune,* March 20, 2000.

674 "Barack is viewed in part": Ted Kleine, "Is Bobby Rush in Trouble?" *Chicago Reader,* March 16, 2000.

675 "Ironically, the ruling hurt more": Mark Brown, "Meet Gays' New Enemy in Springfield: Democrats," *Chicago Sun-Times,* November 20, 2003.

675 "the civil rights issue of our era": Eric Krol, "Only One Candidate Backs Gay Marriage," *Arlington Heights (IL) Daily Herald,* February 15, 2004.

676 "President Bush and I disagree": "Obama In 2004: 'I Don't Think Marriage Is A Civil Right,'" *RealClearPolitics,* May 8, 2012.

676 "primarily just as a strategic issue": Baim, *Obama and the Gays,* 24.

676 "it's not just the marriage issue": Eric Krol, "Then and Now: Obama's Views on Gay Rights," *Arlington Heights (IL) Daily Herald,* March 26, 2007.

676 "I believe changing the federal definition": Garrow, *Rising Star,* 846.

676 Even though he appeared: Baim, *Obama and the Gays,* 27.

677 "The unrecorded portion of our discussion": Baim, *Obama and the Gays,* 19.

677 "What I believe, in my faith": "Election Special," WTTW, *Chicago Tonight,* debate moderated by Phil Ponce, October 26, 2004.

677 "My view is that we should try": "Barack Obama on Gay Rights," OnTheIssues, 2008, ontheissues.org.

678 "felt that by bringing religion": Barack Obama, *The Audacity of Hope: Thoughts on Reclaiming the American Dream* (New York: Crown, 2006), 349–50.

678 "I'm just not very good at bullshitting": David Axelrod, *Believer: My Forty Years in Politics* (New York: Penguin Press, 2015), 447.

678 In 2008, only also-rans: Alex Koppelman, "The Democrats' 'Gay Debate' Dance," *Salon,* August 11, 2007.

679 "I believe that marriage": Paul Schindler, "McCain, Obama Define Marriage the Same, Defend It Differently," *Gay City News,* August 21, 2008.

679 "It is difficult to comprehend": Joe Solmonese, "Obama's Inaugural Mistake," *Washington Post,* December 19, 2008.

679 "However, in 2008 I did donate": Jonathan Lewis, "Mr. President: If Not Now, When?" *Huffington Post,* April 27, 2012.

679 "For many years, we had tried": Kenneth P. Vogel, "The Sons (and Daughters) of Donors Also Rise," *Politico,* December 1, 2014.

680 Lewis quietly seeded a new group: Kerry Eleveld, *Don't Tell Me to Wait: How the Fight for Gay Rights Changed America and Transformed Obama's Presidency* (New York: Basic Books, 2015), 126.

680 "What is it about what we are doing": Marc Ambinder, "Outing the Debate," *National Journal,* December 9, 2010.

680 Jerrold Nadler introduced a bill: "DOMA Repeal Bill Introduced," *Gay City News,* September 17, 2009.

681 "On the issue of same-sex marriage": Eleveld, *Don't Tell Me to Wait,* 195.

681 Acceptance of same-sex marriage in the District of Columbia: Keith L. Alexander, "Judge Declines to Delay Enactment of Law Recognizing Gay Marriage," *Washington Post,* July 1, 2009.

681 By the time four years later that he screened: Mark Halperin and John Heilemann, *Double Down: Game Change 2012* (New York: Penguin Press, 2013), 57.

681 Obama couldn't avoid telling aides: Michael Hastings, *Panic 2012: The Sublime and Terrifying Inside Story of Obama's Final Campaign* (New York: Blue Rider Press, 2013).

682 "attitudes evolve, including mine": Joe Sudbay, "Transcript of Q and A with the President about DADT and Same-Sex Marriage," AMERICAblog, October 27, 2010, americablog.com.

682 On the day Obama signed an end: Carl Hulse, "Senate Repeals Ban on Gays Serving Openly in Military," *New York Times*, December 18, 2010.

682 "My feelings about this are constantly evolving": Russell Goldman and Huma Khan, "Obama Mulls Same-Sex Marriage," ABC News, December 22, 2010.

87. In the Shadow of Lady Liberty

683 In November 2010, Democrats had just suffered: Paul Harris and Ewen Mac-Askill, "US Midterm Election Results Herald New Political Era as Republicans Take House," *The Guardian*, November 3, 2010.

684 "he felt like that would be too aggressive": Michael Crawford, "Michael Crawford on the Digital Campaign at Freedom to Marry: The Freedom to Marry Oral History Project," conducted by Martin Meeker in 2016, Oral History Center, The Bancroft Library, University of California, Berkeley, 2017.

685 Obama had already been fundraising: Geoff Earle, "Big-Bucks Bam Ready for B'Way," *New York Post*, June 21, 2011.

685 There were three scheduled: Julie Pace, "Obama Hits Broadway Looking for Campaign Cash," Associated Press, June 24, 2011.

685 as a blog post by Kerry Eleveld put it: Kerry Eleveld, "What Will Obama Tell the Gays Under the Shadow of Lady Liberty?" Equality Matters, June 24, 2011, www.equalitymatters.org.

685 country's largest gay community: David Leonhardt, "New York Still Has More Gay Residents Than Anywhere Else in U.S.," *New York Times*, March 13, 2015.

685 The number of Americans able to legally marry where they lived: "Number of Americans in Same-Sex Marriage States More Than Doubles," CNN, June 25, 2011.

685 Clinton, who had just endorsed the New York bill: Jennifer Epstein, "Bill Clinton Backs Gay Marriage Bill," *Politico*, May 5, 2011.

686 "How about marriage?": Kerry Eleveld, *Don't Tell Me to Wait: How the Fight for Gay Rights Changed America and Transformed Obama's Presidency* (New York: Basic Books, 2015), 223–24.

686 "He flubbed it": Melanie Mason, Matea Gold, and Joseph Tanfani, "Gay Political Donors Move from Margins to Mainstream," *Los Angeles Times*, May 13, 2012.

686 "If you were back in the Illinois legislature": "Barack Obama on Gay Rights," OnTheIssues, 2008, www.ontheissues.org.

687 Obama announced he was formally endorsing: Paul Schindler, "Obama Endorses Feinstein-Nadler DOMA Repeal," *Gay City News*, July 21, 2011.

688 "Obama has gone from a modest favorite": Nate Silver, "Is Obama Toast? Handicapping the 2012 Election," *New York Times Magazine*, November 3, 2011.

688 "There are things I feel strongly about": David Axelrod, *Believer: My Forty Years in Politics* (New York: The Penguin Press, 2015), 445–46.

688 He had been serving as the administration's chief liaison: Steven Ertelt, "Biden: We 'Screwed Up' Conscience Issues in the Mandate," *Life News*, March 2, 2012.

690 The *Washington Post* estimated: Dan Eggen, "The Influence Industry: Same-Sex Marriage Issue Shows Importance of Gay Fundraisers," *Washington Post*, May 6, 2012.

690 a CNN analysis credited them: Jen Christensen, "LGBT Donors Back President Obama, Big Time," CNN, June 6, 2012.

690 "Gay money, in this election, has replaced": "Chuck Todd: Gay Money in This Election Has Replaced Wall Street Money," *RealClearPolitics*, May 7, 2012.

690 In October 2011, Obama launched: Ewen MacAskill, "Obama's 'We Can't Wait' Jobs Campaign Aims to Spur Congress into Action," *The Guardian*, October 24, 2011.

691 "powerful and frank": "Mr. Obama's Profile in Courage," *New York Times*, March 19, 2008.

691 in early December traveled to Kansas: A. G. Sulzberger, "Obama Strikes Populist Chord with Speech in Kansas," *New York Times*, December 6, 2011.

691 a payroll-tax cut due to expire: Alan Silverleib and Tom Cohen, "Obama Signs Payroll Tax Cut Extension," CNN, December 24, 2011.

692 "We were going to build momentum": Jo Deutsch, "Jo Deutsch and the Federal Campaign: The Freedom to Marry Oral History Project," conducted by Martin Meeker in 2015, Oral History Center, The Bancroft Library, University of California, Berkeley, 2017.

692 "That was our snowball": Deutsch, "Jo Deutsch and the Federal Campaign."

692 "the New Democratic Litmus Test": Charles Mahtesian, "Mainstreaming Gay Marriage," *Politico*, May 10, 2012.

692 Stephanopoulos asked in late March: Amanda Terkel, "Top Obama Adviser Punts on Putting Marriage Equality into Dem Platform," *Huffington Post*, March 25, 2012.

693 The first week of May he would formally: Joe Hallett, "Obama to Kick Off Campaign with Ohio State Rally on May 5," *Columbus Dispatch*, April 25, 2012.

693 Host David Gregory asked: Transcript, *Meet the Press*, NBC News, May 6, 2012.

694 "Yes, I do": Peter Wallsten and Dan Eggen, "Biden Comments on Same-Sex Marriage Expose Internal White House Divisions," *Washington Post*, May 7, 2012.

694 That day, in his briefing: Felicia Sonmez, "White House Spokesman Grilled over Biden's Same-Sex Marriage Comments," *Washington Post*, May 7, 2012.

694 "This bit of straight talk made": Dana Milbank, "Vice President Biden's Gay-Marriage Gaffe Is Mess for White House," *Washington Post*, May 7, 2012.

694 "single out and discriminate against": Lisa Keen, "NC Approves Constitutional Ban: 61 to 39," Keen News Service, May 9, 2012.

694 had taken a deep interest in a Charlotte mayoral election: Jim Rutenberg, "Team Obama Gears Up for 2012," *New York Times*, November 26, 2011.

695 advisers set their plan: Gautham Raghavan, "Evolution," in ed. Gautham Raghavan, *West Wingers: Stories from the Dream Chasers, Change Makers, and Hope Creators Inside the Obama White House* (New York: Penguin Books, 2018), 16–17.

695 not yet publicly identified as a lesbian: Kathy Ehrich Dowd, "Robin Roberts Thanks Longtime Girlfriend After Health Battle," *People*, December 29, 2013.

695 "I've been going through an evolution": "Transcript: Robin Roberts Interview with President Obama," ABC News, May 9, 2012.

696 "It's a position I've had": Wallsten and Eggen, "Biden Comments on Same-Sex Marriage."

696 "very tender and sensitive topic": Lisa Keen, "Loud Clash over Same-Sex Marriage: Where Personal and Political Meet," Keen News Service, May 15, 2012.

696 According to an analysis by political scientists: John Sides and Lynn Vavreck, *The Gamble: Choice and Chance in the 2012 Presidential Election* (Princeton, NJ: Princeton University Press, 2013), 118.

696 *BuzzFeed* reported that the initial million: Zeke Miller, "Gay Marriage Reversal Means Cash for Obama," *BuzzFeed*, May 9, 2012.

696 Within hours, Lewis dropped the donor boycott: Greg Sargent, "For Angry Gay Donors, All Is Forgiven," *Washington Post*, May 10, 2012.

697 "While the media has been focused on what impact": "Maryland Polling Memo," Public Policy Polling, May 24, 2012.

697 overshadowed by a far more controversial topic: Mark Landler, "Pushed by Obama, Democrats Alter Platform Over Jerusalem," *New York Times*, September 5, 2012.

697 Not a single ad on the topic: Sides and Vavreck, *The Gamble*, 118.

697 In four and a half hours of one-on-one: Charles Babington, "Big Issues Left Out of Presidential Race," Associated Press, October 25, 2012.

697 The morning after the election, the *New York Times*: Jeff Zeleny and Jim Rutenberg, "Divided U.S. Gives Obama More Time," *New York Times*, November 6, 2012.

697 the *Washington Post* did not even cite: David A. Fahrenthold, "Obama Reelected as President," *Washington Post*, November 7, 2012.

697 analysts had begun to extend Obama indirect credit: Chris Geidner, "How Marriage Equality Supporters Beat the 'Princess' Ad," *BuzzFeed*, November 19, 2012.

697 passage of a marriage law on the ballot: Annie Linskey, "Gay Marriage Supporters Seized Victory After Tough Start," *Baltimore Sun*, November 10, 2012.

88. Shotgun Wedding

699 Supreme Court announced that it would hear: Lisa Keen, "Court Adds Twist to Announcement on Prop 8, DOMA Cases," Keen News Service, December 7, 2012.

699 In one instance, the request was lodged: Scottie Thomaston, "The Department of Justice Presses the Supreme Court to Resolve DOMA Challenges," *Huffington Post*, August 6, 2012.

699 "the GOP's great hope for this Supreme Court season": Jason Zengerle, "The Paul Clement Court," *New York*, March 18, 2012.

700 "now provides the most appropriate vehicle": *United States v. Windsor*, 570 US 744, Department of Justice Reply Brief to Cert Petition.

700 The ruling that Proposition 8 was unconstitutional: Lisa Keen, "Ninth Circuit Refuses Full Court Review; Prop 8 Headed to Supreme Court," Keen News Service, June 5, 2012.

700 a group of Proposition 8's proponents appealed: Rachael G. Samberg, "California's Proposition 8 in Federal Court: Key Briefs & Filings Leading to *Hollingsworth v. Perry*," Robert Crown Law Library, Stanford University, August 10, 2010.

700 retired Republican leader of the state senate: Michael Gardner, "GOP Leader Reflects on His Tenure," *San Diego Union-Tribune*, November 13, 2010.

700 tagged with an important jurisdictional asterisk: Marty Lederman, "Understanding Standing: The Court's Article III Questions in the Same-Sex Marriage Cases (II)," SCOTUSblog, January 18, 2013.

701 There was one possible intermediate conclusion: Marty Lederman, "The Court's Five Options in the California Marriage Case," SCOTUSblog, March 1, 2013.

701 it would remain a long-standing mystery: Adam Liptak, "Who Wanted to Take the Case on Gay Marriage? Ask Scalia," *New York Times*, March 29, 2013.

701 They hired former Human Rights Campaign president: Chris Geidner, "The New Book About the Marriage Equality Movement Gets the Big Things Wrong," *BuzzFeed,* April 21, 2014.

703 "if, in our reliance on the courts to vindicate": Barack Obama, *The Audacity of Hope: Thoughts on Reclaiming the American Dream* (New York: Crown, 2006), 83.

703 insinuate itself into civil-rights cases: Seth P. Waxman, "Twins at Birth: Civil Rights and the Role of the Solicitor General," *Indiana Law Journal* 75, no. 4 (Fall 2000): 1297–316.

703 In 1950, the solicitor general even turned: *Henderson v. United States,* 339 US 816.

703 made his debut Supreme Court appearance: Richard Kluger, *Simple Justice: The History of Brown v. Board of Education and Black America's Struggle for Equality* (New York: Alfred A. Knopf, 1976), 678.

703 supporting a six-hundred-page government amicus brief: Victor H. Kramer, "President Eisenhower's Handwritten Changes in the Brief on Relief in the School Segregation Cases: Minding the Whys and Wherefores," *Constitutional Commentary* 9, no. 2 (Summer 1992): 223–35.

704 "For the first time the Court was told": Philip Elman and Norman Silber, "The Solicitor General's Office, Justice Frankfurter, and Civil Rights Litigation, 1946–1960: An Oral History," *Harvard Law Review* 100, no. 4 (February 1987): 828.

704 "Why we can't wait": Martin Luther King Jr., "The Negro Is Your Brother," *Atlantic Monthly,* August 1963.

89. And Then There Were Nine

706 invited reporters from the four largest newspapers: Jack Torry and Jessica Wehrman, "Portman Reverses His Stance," *Columbus Dispatch,* March 15, 2013.

706 "I thought it was the right time": Torry and Wehrman, "Portman Reverses His Stance."

706 supported Ohio's 2004 constitutional ban: Sabrina Eaton, "Sen. Rob Portman Comes Out in Favor of Gay Marriage After Son Comes Out as Gay," *Cleveland Plain-Dealer,* March 15, 2013.

706 voted to deny same-sex couples: George E. Condon Jr., "Portman Reverses Position on Same-Sex Marriage," *National Journal,* March 15, 2013.

706 "One way to look at it": Rob Portman, "Gay Couples Also Deserve Chance to Get Married," *Columbus Dispatch,* March 15, 2013.

707 "I don't support gay marriage despite": Portman, "Gay Couples Also Deserve."

707 An amicus brief, delivered to the court: Sheryl Gay Stolberg, "Prominent Republicans Sign Brief in Support of Gay Marriage," *New York Times,* February 25, 2013.

707 who within months would be named: Michael S. Schmidt, "Obama to Pick James B. Comey to Lead F.B.I.," *New York Times,* May 29, 2013.

707 getting two Republican members of the House: Sean Sullivan, "Meet the Four Republicans in Congress Who Support Gay Marriage," *Washington Post,* April 2, 2013.

707 "the perpetual bridesmaid of the GOP vice presidential race": Margaret Hartmann, "Senator Rob Portman Reveals He Has a Gay Son, Now Supports Same-Sex Marriage," Intelligencer, *New York,* March 15, 2013.

707 "the political debate on gay marriage": Chris Cillizza, "Rob Portman and the End of the Gay Marriage Debate," The Fix, *Washington Post,* March 15, 2013.

707 A new Marriage Protection Amendment introduced in 2013: U.S. Congress,

House, Marriage Protection Amendment, H.J.Res.51, 113th Cong., introduced in House June 28, 2013.

707 all but three of the Senate's Democrats: Harry J. Enten, "The Final Three: The Democratic Senators Against Gay Marriage," *The Guardian*, April 10, 2013.

708 In a gesture that was seen: Sheryl Gay Stolberg, "Hillary Clinton Endorses Same-Sex Marriage," *New York Times*, March 28, 2013.

708 "a pretty significant sociological shift in this country": Jessica Wehrman and Joe Vardon, "Portman's Shift Mirrors Many Others'," *Columbus Dispatch*, March 16, 2013.

708 Hollingsworth's attorneys had already quoted: *Hollingsworth v. Perry*, 570 US 693, Petition for Writ of Cert.

709 To Roberts, Obama had said: "Transcript: Robin Roberts Interview with President Obama," ABC News, May 9, 2012.

709 President Dwight Eisenhower entered office: David A. Nichols, *A Matter of Justice: Eisenhower and the Beginning of the Civil Rights Revolution* (New York: Simon & Schuster, 2007), 51–70.

710 "must do it equally": Richard Kluger, *Simple Justice: The History of Brown v. Board of Education and Black America's Struggle for Equality* (New York: Alfred A. Knopf, 1976), 678.

710 "I don't think marriage is a civil right": Devin Dwyer, "Obama's 'Evolving' Gay Marriage Stance," ABC News, May 9, 2012.

90. Blinding Times

712 vagrants being paid to hold places: "High Court Gay Marriage Tickets Cost Time, Money," Associated Press, March 25, 2013.

712 Already the court had received 156 amicus briefs: Anthony J. Franze and R. Reeves Anderson, "In Unusual Term, Big Year for Amicus Briefs at the Supreme Court," *National Law Journal*, September 21, 2013.

713 "The question before this Court": *Hollingsworth v. Perry*, 570 US 693, transcript of oral argument.

713 In the summer of 2012, *Time* had: Massimo Calabresi and David Von Drehle, "What Will Justice Kennedy Do?" *Time*, June 18, 2012.

713 having written a 1997 opinion: *City of Boerne v. Flores*, 521 US 507.

713 "The federal system rests on what": *Bond v. U.S.*, 564 US 211.

713 pointed to the influence: William N. Eskridge Jr. and Christopher R. Riano, *Marriage Equality: From Outlaws to In-Laws* (New Haven: Yale University Press, 2020), 129.

713 "a bare desire to harm": *Romer v. Evans*, 517 US 620.

713 "times can blind us": *Lawrence v. Texas*, 539 US 558.

714 "at the heart of liberty is the right": *Lawrence v. Texas*.

714 "heavy reliance on principles of righteousness": *Romer v. Evans*.

714 "This case 'does not involve' the issue": *Lawrence v. Texas*.

714 "If you put the *Lawrence* case together": Theodore B. Olson and David Boies, *Redeeming the Dream: The Case for Marriage Equality* (New York: Viking, 2014), 201.

714 "it denies gay men and lesbians": *Hollingsworth v. Perry*, 570 US 693, Plaintiffs' Brief.

715 "Obviously nobody's suggesting": *United States v. Windsor*, 570 US 744, transcript of oral argument.

717 "a bare desire to harm": *Romer v. Evans*.

91. When the Dam Breaks

719 "DOMA instructs all federal officials": *United States v. Windsor*, 570 US 744.

720 "underlying issue": Christine Ferretti, "Hazel Park Women Challenge Michigan's Marriage Amendment," *Detroit News*, October 7, 2012.

720 In March, he postponed: Dustin Blitchok, "No Immediate Ruling on Michigan's 2004 Gay Marriage Ban," *Oakland Press*, March 7, 2013.

720 "Plaintiffs are prepared to claim": *Deboer v. Snyder*, 772 F.3d 388.

720 "nonspecific hand-waving": *United States v. Windsor*.

720 But Friedman discerned enough clarity: Chris Geidner, "Federal Judge in Michigan Allows Challenge to Marriage Ban to Go Forward," *BuzzFeed*, July 1, 2013.

720 On July 22, a federal district-court judge in neighboring Ohio: *Obergefell v. Kasich*, Case No. 1:13-cv-501.

720 he and his companion, James Obergefell, had exchanged: Debbie Cenziper and Jim Obergefell, *Love Wins: The Lovers & Lawyers Who Fought the Landmark Case for Marriage Equality* (New York: HarperCollins, 2016), 131.

721 "While the holding in *Windsor* is ostensibly limited": *Obergefell v. Kasich*.

721 In October, John Arthur died: "John Arthur, Pro-Gay Marriage Activist, Dies at 48," Associated Press, October 22, 2013.

721 with new plaintiffs added: Amanda Lee Myers, "Ohio Gay Marriage Lawsuit Expanded to Others," Associated Press, September 25, 2013.

721 "triable issue of fact": *Deboer v. Snyder*, 772 F.3d 388.

722 the openly gay head of the civil division: Chris Geidner, "With West's Promotion, Out Gay Lawyer Delery to Take Helm of Justice Department's Civil Division," *Metro Weekly*, February 27, 2012.

722 had been in the courtroom: William N. Eskridge Jr. and Christopher R. Riano, *Marriage Equality: From Outlaws to In-Laws* (New Haven: Yale University Press, 2020), 545.

722 The biggest obstacle may have been: Richard A. Oppel Jr., "Texas and 5 Other States Resist Processing Benefits for Gay Couples," *New York Times*, November 10, 2013.

723 On August 1, Rhode Island began marrying: Max Ehrenfreund, "Same-Sex Marriages Begin in Minnesota, Rhode Island," *Washington Post*, August 1, 2013.

723 In Minnesota, the previous fall's campaign: Sasha Alsatian, "Richard Carlbom: 'Quiet,' 'Brilliant' General Behind Minnesota's Same-Sex Marriage Law," *MPR News*, May 22, 2013.

723 "There was going to be a trial": Steve Friess, "For Lawyers, a Rocky Walk Down the Gay Marriage Aisle," *Bloomberg Politics*, January 28, 2015.

724 New Mexico county clerks had begun issuing: Richard Gonzales, "How a County Clerk Ignited the Gay Marriage Debate in N.M.," NPR, October 22, 2013.

724 "demean the dignity of these same-sex couples": *Kitchen v. Herbert*, Case No. 2:13-cv-217 (D. Utah Dec. 23, 2013).

724 After the New Jersey Supreme Court issued: Salvador Rizzo, "N.J. Legalizes Gay Marriage After Decade-Long Push," *Newark Star-Ledger*, October 23, 2013.

725 Other Republican governors, including in Pennsylvania: Marc Levy, "Pennsylvania Won't Appeal Same-Sex Marriage Case," Associated Press, May 21, 2014.

725 Would follow his lead: Chris Geidner, "Nevada State Officials Stop Defending Same-Sex Marriage Ban in Appeal," *BuzzFeed*, February 10, 2014.

725 "the next step toward anarchy": Robert Gehrke, "Herbert Says States Have a Duty to Defend Gay-Marriage Bans," *Salt Lake Tribune,* May 23, 2014.

725 "the star power, location, and timing": Steve Friess, "The Same-Sex Marriage Trial You Don't Know About Just Came to a Close," *BuzzFeed,* March 7, 2014.

725 had been published in 2012: Mark Regnerus, "How different are the adult children of parents who have same-sex relationships? Findings from the New Family Structures Study," *Social Science Research* 41, no. 4 (July 2012): 752–70.

725 "Scientifically this is huge": Maggie Gallagher, "Do Children with Gay Parents Do Just As Well? The New Social-Science Debate," *National Review,* June 10, 2012.

725 The journal that had published the study: Tom Bartlett, "Controversial Gay-Parenting Study Is Severely Flawed, Journal's Audit Finds," *Chronicle of Higher Education,* July 26, 2012.

725 "conclusions he draws from his study": Erik Eckholm, "In Gay Marriage Suit, a Battle Over Research," *New York Times,* March 8, 2014.

726 "The funder clearly wanted": *Deboer v. Snyder.*

726 two of the three judges who heard: *Kitchen v. Herbert.*

726 Within a month, the Fourth Circuit: *Bostic v. Schaefer,* 760 F.3d 352.

726 decision striking down Indiana's and Wisconsin's bans: *Baskin v. Bogan,* 766 F.3d 648.

726 Ninth Circuit did the same to Nevada's and Idaho's: *Latta v. Otter,* No. 14-35420.

726 politicians frequently ended the suspense: Betsy Z. Russell, "Same-Sex Marriage Begins in Idaho as 9th Circuit Lifts Stay," *Idaho Spokesman-Review,* October 9, 2014.

727 In Arkansas, hundreds of couples were: "Gay Couples Marry in Arkansas, Most Clerks Sit Out," Associated Press, April 13, 2014.

727 state supreme court struck down a ban: Michael Winter, "Arkansas Judge Strikes Down State's Ban on Gay Marriage," *USA Today,* May 19, 2014.

727 For a time, Cook County, Illinois, was marrying: Tony Meverick, "Illinois Officials Addressing Confusion over Status of Marriage Equality Law," *BuzzFeed,* April 13, 2014.

727 Missouri's constitutional ban was struck down: Doug Moore, "Judge Rules That Gay Marriage Ban in Missouri Is Unconstitutional," *St. Louis Post-Dispatch,* November 6, 2014.

727 "So far the federal courts of appeals have answered": Lyle Denniston, "Mixed Signals on Same-Sex Marriage," SCOTUSblog, September 18, 2014.

727 "When the courts do not let the people": *Deboer v. Snyder.*

728 "This type of summary decision, it is true": *Deboer v. Snyder.*

728 "The sooner they rule": David Crary, "Joy, Dismay as Gay Marriage Advocates, Opponents Assess 6th Circuit Ruling," Associated Press, November 7, 2014.

728 if faced with a so-called circuit split: Lyle Denniston, "Sixth Circuit: Now, a Split on Same-Sex Marriage," SCOTUSblog, November 6, 2014.

728 "This is a case about change": *Deboer v. Snyder.*

92. Once and for All

729 tens of thousands of couples who had married: Robin Fisher, Geof Gee, and Adam Looney, "Working Paper 108: Joint Filing by Same-Sex Couples After Windsor: Characteristics of Married Tax Filers in 2013 and 2014," U.S. Treasury Department, August 2016.

729 "Their relentless preparation has two goals": Adam Liptak, "Lawyers Seek Sea Change on Gay Rights at Supreme Court," *New York Times,* April 27, 2015.

730 "I have only one month to prepare": Nathaniel Frank, *Awakening: How Gays and Lesbians Brought Marriage Equality to America* (Cambridge, MA: Belknap Press of Harvard University, 2017), 339–42.

731 "You'd have to be an inanimate object": Noah Hurowitz, "Portland Lawyer Mary Bonauto Credited as 'Mastermind' Behind Landmark Gay Rights Court Cases," *Bangor (ME) Daily News*, March 31, 2013.

731 "Most Americans have never heard": Sheryl Gay Stolberg, "Maine Lawyer Credited in Fight for Gay Marriage," *New York Times*, March 27, 2013.

731 "our Thurgood Marshall": Joan Biskupic, "Prominent Gay Rights Advocate to Argue Landmark U.S. Marriage Case," Reuters, March 31, 2015.

732 Tennessee sent a deputy solicitor general: Ariane de Vogue, "Meet the Lawyers Who Will Argue the Gay Marriage Case," CNN, April 27, 2015.

732 "Leading law firms are willing": Adam Liptak, "The Case Against Gay Marriage: Top Law Firms Won't Touch It," *New York Times*, April 12, 2015.

732 *Newsweek*'s anointment of "the First Gay President": Andrew Sullivan, "The First Gay President," *Newsweek*, May 21, 2012.

733 "a foundation of *Romer*": *Obergefell v. Hodges*, 135 S. Ct. 2584, transcript of oral argument.

733 nineteen foreign countries that had legalized: Niall McCarthy, "The Countries Where Gay Marriage Is Legal," Forbes.com, June 29, 2015.

733 "hundreds of thousands of children raised": *Obergefell v. Hodges*, transcript of oral argument.

735 "not necessarily dignity": *Obergefell v. Hodges*, transcript of oral argument.

Coda: Back to Hawaii

737 headline from CNN's website: Ariane de Vogue and Jeremy Diamond, "Supreme Court Rules States Must Allow Same-Sex Marriage," CNN, June 26, 2015.

737 "It is demeaning": *Obergefell v. Hodges*, 135 S. Ct. 2584.

738 "Our private life": Alan Matsuoka, "Former Isle Couple Put Issue on Historic Course," *Honolulu Star-Bulletin*, May 14, 1996.

738 relatively anonymous: Fern Shen, "A Same-Sex Couple Married to the Cause," *Washington Post*, September 10, 1996.

738 The *Baltimore Sun* perceptively characterized: Richard O'Mara, "Senate Storm Fails to Disturb Couple's Domestic Tranquillity," *Baltimore Sun*, September 22, 1996.

739 They traveled to Fire Island: Peter Traiano, "Couple's Civil Rights Battle Comes to Grove, Pines," *Fire Island News*, July 20, 1995.

739 addressed a group: Matsuoka, "Former Isle Couple."

739 the front row of Judge Kevin Chang's courtroom: Ken Kobayashi, "Trial Tackles Same-Sex Controversy," *Honolulu Advertiser*, September 11, 1996.

739 plans to wear white tuxedos: Linda Hosek, "3 Isle Gay Pairs' Suit to Wed Will Test Law," *Honolulu Star-Bulletin*, May 2, 1991.

739 registered as Universal Life Church ministers: Carey Goldberg, "Hawaii Judge Ends Gay-Marriage Ban," *New York Times*, December 4, 1996.

739 "You do it once": John Gallagher, "Marriage, Hawaiian Style," *The Advocate*, February 4, 1997.

741 "if we stray": Bruce Dunford, "Justice Warns of Exodus," *Hawaii Tribune-Herald*, February 23, 1997.

741 The contours of a political response: William Kresnak and Angela Miller,

"Same-Sex Plan Bars Marriage, Offers Benefits," *Honolulu Advertiser,* January 18, 1997.

741 "Legislature shall have": "Hawaii Legislative Power to Reserve Marriage, Question 2 (1998)," Ballotpedia, http://www.ballotpedia.com.

741 called Reciprocal Beneficiaries: "Hawaii Approves Benefits Package for Gay Couples," *Los Angeles Times,* April 30, 1997.

742 after judges ruled: Debra Barayuga, "Gays' Fight May Turn to Rights and Benefits," *Honolulu Star-Bulletin,* December 10, 1999.

742 Democratic governor Neil Abercrombie signed: B. J. Reyes, "'Today Is an Amazing Day,'" *Honolulu Star-Advertiser,* February 24, 2011.

743 But even before state authorities: Nelson Daranciang, "2 Women Sue State for Right to Wed," *Honolulu Star-Advertiser,* December 9, 2011.

743 The women, however, chose a legal path: *Jackson v. Abercrombie,* 884 F. Supp. 2d 1065.

743 "I was looking at stuff on Google": Tim Sakahara, "Couple Sues State to Get Same Sex Marriage Rights," *Hawaii News Now,* February 11, 2011.

743 "Under current law, a heterosexual couple": Purna Nemani, "Governor Gives Up in Gay Marriage Case," *Courthouse News,* February 23, 2012.

743 There was enough of a distinction: *Jackson v. Abercrombie* order granting motion for summary judgment, Civ. No. 11-00734 ACK-KSC, August 8, 2012.

744 That fall, Abercrombie called: B. J. Reyes, "Governor Summons Legislators to Special Session," *Honolulu Star-Advertiser,* September 10, 2013.

744 Religious activists took it: Alejandro Lazo, "In Hawaii, 'Citizens' Filibuster' Targets Gay-Marriage Bill," *Wall Street Journal,* November 9, 2013.

744 More than five thousand: "House Panels Pass Gay Marriage Bill After 55 Hours of Testimony," *Honolulu Star-Advertiser,* November 5, 2013.

745 "a sad day": Mike Gabbard, "Civil Union Enactment: Sad Day for Hawaii," *Hawaii Reporter,* February 24, 2011.

745 no such alarmism: Mileka Lincoln, "Hawaii Senate Passes Gay Marriage, Sends to House," *Hawaii News Now,* October 30, 2013.

745 legatee of her father's politics: Bonna Bolante, "Who Is Mike Gabbard?" *Honolulu,* August 2004.

745 led citizens protesting: Gordon Y. K. Pang, "Bill to Allow Civil Unions May Be Stalled in House," *Honolulu Advertiser,* February 20, 2004.

745 "As Democrats we should": Adrienne LaFrance, "Tulsi Gabbard's Leftward Journey," *Honolulu Civil Beat,* January 16, 2012.

745 "imposing its will": Sanjena Sathian, "Is Tulsi Gabbard the Next Bernie Sanders?" *OZY,* September 27, 2015.

745 "To me, it made full circle": Derrick DePledge, "Governor Signs Landmark Law," *Honolulu Star-Advertiser,* November 14, 2013.

745 "We decided long ago": Mary Kaye Ritz, "Canadian Wedding Bells Ring for Island Gay Couples," *Honolulu Advertiser,* August 3, 2002.

745 "There is an escape now": Clifford Krauss, "A Wedding in Canada; Gay Couples Follow a Trail North Blazed by Slaves and War Resisters," *New York Times,* November 23, 2003.

746 After returning to Hawaii: Chad Graham, "Life After Gay Marriage," *The Advocate,* March 18, 2004.

746 When running: Chris Haire, "Changing Minds: Bill Woods Talks About the Future of Gay Marriage in Hawaii," *Honolulu Weekly,* June 21, 2006.

746 When Woods died: "Obituaries: William Everett Woods," *Honolulu Advertiser,* September 30, 2008.

746 "the best memorial to Bill": "Obituaries: Woods," *Decatur (IL) Herald & Review,* November 9, 2008.

746 "We weren't looking for the marriage": Debra Barayuga, "Gay Marriage Case Plaintiff Preached Acceptance," *Honolulu Star-Bulletin,* September 28, 2006.

746 "This is enough": Brooks Baehr, "Original Same Sex Applicants Celebrate Civil Union Law," *Hawaii News Now,* February 23, 2011.

746 General Electric, NBC's parent company: Marc Gunther, "Money and Morals at GE," *Fortune,* November 15, 2004.

748 the day Abercrombie appointed her: Ken Kobayashi, "McKenna Is Named to State's High Court," *Honolulu Star-Advertiser,* January 26, 2011.

748 "Now it's the law": Keoki Kerr, "On Key Anniversary, Same-Sex Marriage Pioneer Weds Her Partner," *Hawaii News Now,* December 17, 2013.

748 federal district court in Utah overturned: *Kitchen v. Herbert,* 755 F.3d 1193.

749 When the ACLU helped: *Donaldson v. State,* 292 P.3d 364.

749 "it will be easiest": Ninia Baehr, "Talking About What Really Matters over the Holidays," ACLU of Montana blog, November 19, 2012, www.acluofmontana.org.

749 the ACLU affiliate led: *Rolando v. Fox,* 23 F. Supp. 3d 1227.

749 "We definitely believe the time": Charles S. Johnson, "'The Time for the Case Is Now': 4 Couples Sue over State Ban on Same-Sex Marriage," *Billings (MT) Gazette,* May 21, 2014.

749 the Supreme Court decided to hear: Robert Barnes, "Supreme Court Agrees to Hear Gay Marriage Issue," *Washington Post,* January 16, 2015.

750 Freedom to Marry had attempted: Chris Johnson, "Marriage Plaintiffs Gather to Celebrate on Eve of Arguments," *Washington Blade,* April 28, 2015.

750 Wolfson was already planning: Amanda Terkel, "This Gay Rights Group Wants the Supreme Court to Shut It Down," *Huffington Post,* March 23, 2015.

750 some of whom looked barely old enough: Samantha Masunaga, "From Traffic Ticket to Supreme Court: A Gay Couple's Legal Odyssey," *Los Angeles Times,* January 18, 2015.

751 whose lawsuit had successfully toppled: Kim Chandler, "Couple Behind Ala. Gay Marriage Case Grateful for Ruling," Associated Press, January 25, 2015.

752 "The Constitution promises liberty": *Obergefell v. Hodges.*

752 "eloquent vein, not the more businesslike": Mark Walsh, "A 'View' from the Courtroom: A Marriage Celebration," SCOTUSblog, June 26, 2015.

752 his death seven months later: Adam Liptak, "Antonin Scalia, Justice on the Supreme Court, Dies at 79," *New York Times,* February 14, 2016.

753 skirting the entire framework: Jack M. Balkin, *What Obergefell v. Hodges Should Have Said: The Nation's Top Legal Experts Rewrite America's Same-Sex Marriage Decision* (New Haven: Yale University Press, 2020), 72–81.

753 "justice that arrives": Jordan Fabian, "Obama: Justice Arrives 'Like a Thunderbolt,'" *The Hill,* June 26, 2015.

753 lit in the colors of the rainbow flag: Adam B. Lerner, "White House Set Aglow with Rainbow Pride," *Politico,* June 26, 2015.

753 Obama's speech there would be remembered: Michiko Kakutani, "Obama's Eulogy, Which Found Its Place in History," *New York Times,* July 3, 2015.

753 Supreme Court had upheld: Robert Barnes, "Affordable Care Act Survives Supreme Court Challenge," *Washington Post,* June 25, 2015.

753 "week that changed the nation": Stephen Collinson, "Gay Rights, Obamacare and a Week That Changed the Nation," CNN, June 27, 2015.

Postscript: Massive Desistance

754 "When they create it": "Roy Moore on Gay Marriage Ruling: 'Christians Are Going to Be Persecuted,'" Associated Press, June 28, 2015.

754 he had instructed probate judges: Alan Blinder, "Alabama Judge Defies Gay Marriage Law," *New York Times,* June 8, 2015.

754 "If the decision contradicts": Isaiah Narciso, "Alabama Chief Justice Roy Moore: 'I Hope We Don't Have a War' over Supreme Court Decision Favoring Same-Sex Marriage," *The Gospel Herald,* July 10, 2015.

754 "will be used to vilify": *Obergefell v. Hodges,* 135 S. Ct. 2584.

754 pulled a pair of Republican presidential candidates: David Weigel, Abby Phillip, and Sarah Larimer, "Kim Davis Released from Jail, Ordered Not to Interfere with Same-Sex Marriage Licenses," *Washington Post,* September 8, 2015.

755 where she had been held: Alan Blinder and Tamar Lewin, "Clerk in Kentucky Chooses Jail over Deal on Same-Sex Marriage," *New York Times,* September 3, 2015.

755 defied the teachings of her Pentecostal faith: Alan Blinder and Richard Fausset, "Kim Davis, a Local Fixture, and Now a National Symbol," *New York Times,* September 1, 2015.

755 The thrice-married Trump: Elise Foley, "Donald Trump Pressed on How 'Traditional' His 3 Marriages Are," *Huffington Post,* June 30, 2015.

755 "It would certainly be nice": Joe Scarborough and Mika Brzezinski, interview of Donald Trump, *Morning Joe,* MSNBC, September 4, 2015.

755 Davis was effectively alone: Dominic Holden, "Same-Sex Couples Still Cannot Marry in Small Pockets of the U.S.," *BuzzFeed,* August 14, 2015.

755 "become a public opinion poll": "US Ruling on Gay Marriage: Louisiana Governor Bobby Jindal Criticises Supreme Court," *Economic Times,* June 27, 2015.

755 "I would personally like to see": Robert Gehrke, "Utah Lawmaker: Does Logic Behind Gay-Marriage Ruling Open Door to 'Polygamy, Bestiality'?" *Salt Lake Tribune,* July 5, 2015.

755 abolished all marriage-license requirements: Brian Lyman, "Bill Ending Marriage Licenses Goes to Ivey," *Montgomery Advertiser,* May 25, 2019.

755 "then record, not issue": Brannon Cahela, "New Marriage Law Takes Effect," *Selma Times-Journal,* August 30, 2019.

756 two Houston residents challenged: *Pidgeon v. Turner,* 538 S.W.3d 73.

756 "Research finds that same-sex unions": Liza Mundy, "The Gay Guide to Wedded Bliss," *The Atlantic,* June 2013.

757 "in accordance with a religious belief": U.S. Congress, House, First Amendment Defense Act, HR 2802, 114th Cong., introduced in House June 17, 2015.

757 retreat to the shelter belt: Joel A. Carpenter, *Revive Us Again: The Reawakening of American Fundamentalism* (New York: Oxford University Press, 1997), 86.

757 period between the *Scopes* trial: Frances FitzGerald, *The Evangelicals: The Struggle to Shape America* (New York: Simon & Schuster, 2018), 140.

757 "Could it be that": Rod Dreher, *The Benedict Option: A Strategy for Christians in a Post-Christian Nation* (New York: Sentinel, 2017), 12.

757 married in Massachusetts in 2012: Robert Barnes, "The Spurned Couple, the

Baker and the Long Wait for the Supreme Court," *Washington Post*, August 13, 2017.

758 Phillips's case found its way: *Masterpiece Cakeshop, Ltd. v. Colo. Civil Rights Comm'n*, 138 S. Ct. 1719.

758 adopted the language of civil-rights jurisprudence: Melissa Murray, "Inverting Animus: Masterpiece Cakeshop and the New Minorities," *Supreme Court Review*, Vol. 2018, 257–98.

758 "citizens advocating to redefine": Sarah Posner, "The Christian Legal Army Behind 'Masterpiece Cakeshop,'" *The Nation*, November 28, 2017.

758 A seven-judge majority ruled: *Masterpiece Cakeshop, Ltd. v. Colo. Civil Rights Comm'n*.

758 Justice Anthony Kennedy announced: Michael D. Shear, "Supreme Court Justice Anthony Kennedy Will Retire," *New York Times*, June 27, 2018.

758 congressional Democrats introduced: U.S. Congress, House, Equality Act, HR 3185, 114th Cong., introduced in House July 23, 2015.

759 A series of discrimination lawsuits: Adam Liptak, "Can Someone Be Fired for Being Gay? The Supreme Court Will Decide," *New York Times*, September 23, 2019.

759 seemed to steer clear: Jeff Guo, "The Cunning Trick in North Carolina's Radical New Anti-LGBT Law," *Washington Post*, April 1, 2016.

759 Michigan imposed a law: Niraj Warikoo, "Mixed Reaction Greets Michigan's New Gay Adoption Law," *Detroit Free Press*, June 12, 2015.

759 In Starkville, Mississippi: Logan Kirkland and Ryan Phillips, "Group Files Lawsuit Against Starkville for Denying LGBT Pride Parade," *Starkville (MS) Daily News*, February 26, 2018.

759 resistance led by companies: Motoko Rich, "North Carolina Gay Bias Law Draws a Sharp Backlash," *New York Times*, March 24, 2016.

759 married the trans man: Sarah McBride, "Forever and Ever: Losing My Husband at 24," *Huffington Post*, August 25, 2018.

760 toward the end of his second term: Ellen McCarthy, "Chasten Buttigieg Has Been a Homeless Community College Student and a Starbucks Barista. Now, He Could Be 'First Gentleman,'" *Washington Post*, May 1, 2019.

760 "appeared on the cover of *Time*": Charlotte Alter, "Mayor Pete Buttigieg's Unprecedented Presidential Campaign," *Time*, May 2, 2019.

760 "people like me permission": Sheila Brummer, "Top-Tier Campaigns Visit Sioux City, Supervisor Steps Down and More," Siouxland Public Media, January 30, 2020, www.kwit.org.

760 "by the grace of one vote": Chelsea Janes, "'It Got Real Gay Real Quick': Pete Buttigieg's Rise Electrifies the Gay Community, But He Could Face a Rocky Road," *Washington Post*, April 6, 2019.

760 Supreme Court accepted three appeals: Adam Liptak, "Supreme Court to Decide Whether Landmark Civil Rights Law Applies to Gay and Transgender Workers," *New York Times*, April 22, 2019.

760 solicitor general's brief pointed out: Robert Barnes, "Supreme Court Term to Begin with Blockbuster Question: Is It Legal to Fire Someone for Being Gay or Transgender?" *Washington Post*, October 3, 2019.

760 In June 2020, the Supreme Court issued: *Bostock v. Clayton County*, 140 S. Ct. 1731, 207 L. Ed. 2d 218 (2020).

Index

....

A Note About the Author

Sasha Issenberg is the author of three previous books, including *The Victory Lab: The Secret Science of Winning Campaigns.* He has covered presidential elections as a national political reporter in the Washington bureau of *The Boston Globe,* a columnist for Slate, and a contributor to Bloomberg Politics and *Businessweek.* He is the Washington correspondent at Monocle, and his work has also appeared in *New York, The New York Times Magazine,* and *George,* where he served as a contributing editor. He teaches in the political science department at UCLA.

A Note on the Type

This book was set in Janson, a typeface named for the Dutchman Anton Janson, but is actually the work of Nicholas Kis (1650–1702). The type is an excellent example of the influential and sturdy Dutch types that prevailed in England up to the time William Caslon (1692–1766) developed his own incomparable designs from them.

Typeset by North Market Street Graphics,
Lancaster, Pennsylvania

Printed and bound by LSC/Harrisonburg North,
Harrisonburg, Virginia

Designed by Betty Lew